Siberia
ASIA
Lake Baikal
Ulaanbaatar
MONGOLIA
ltay Mountains
Gobi Desert
Shenyang
Beijing
NORTH KOREA
P'yongyang
Seoul
SOUTH KOREA
Sea of Japan
JAPAN
Sapporo
Tokyo
Kobe
Osaka
Pusan
Fukuoka
Kyushu
Yellow Sea
CHINA
Huang River
Chengdu
Chang River
Shanghai
30°N
East China Sea
Okinawa
Naha
Taipei
TAIWAN
PACIFIC OCEAN
BHUTAN
Brahmaputra R.
Irrawaddy R.
NGLADESH
Dhaka
Calcutta
MYANMAR (BURMA)
Red River
Guangzhou
Hong Kong
Macao
Hanoi
LAOS
Chiang Mai
Vientiane
Mekong River
Udon Thani
Yangon
Bay of Bengal
THAILAND
VIETNAM
South China Sea
Luzon
Philippine Sea
PHILIPPINES
Manila
Bangkok
Tonle Sap
CAMBODIA
Phnom Penh
Ho Chi Minh City
Andaman Islands
Gulf of Thailand
Spratly Islands
Cebu
Mindanao
PALAU
Koror
Nicobar Islands
Songkhla
Strait of Malacca
Bandar Seri Begawan
BRUNEI
MALAYSIA
Medan
Kuala Lumpur
Sarawak
Singapore
SINGAPORE
Sumatra
Kalimantan
Borneo
0°
INDONESIA
Irian Jaya
PAPUA NEW GUINEA
Jakarta
Surabaya
Java
Bali
Dili
EAST TIMOR
Port Moresby
OCEAN
120°E
150°E
90°E
AUSTRALIA

Encyclopedia of Modern Asia

Editorial Board

Encyclopedia of Modern Asia

Volume 2
China-India Relations to Hyogo

A Berkshire Reference Work
David Levinson · Karen Christensen, Editors

New York • Detroit • San Diego • San Francisco • Cleveland • New Haven, Conn. • Waterville, Maine • London • Munich

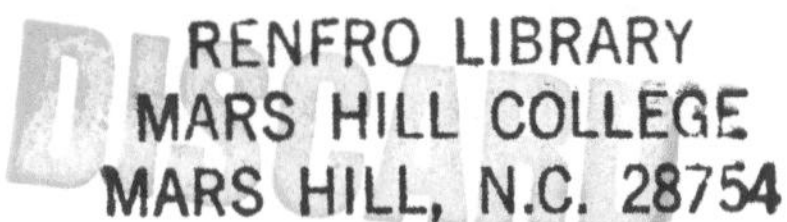

Encyclopedia of Modern Asia

David Levinson and Karen Christensen, Editors

Charles Scribner's Sons
An imprint of The Gale Group
300 Park Avenue South
New York, NY 10010

For more information, contact
The Gale Group, Inc.
27500 Drake Rd.
Farmington Hills, MI 48331–3535
Or you can visit our Internet site at
http://www.gale.com

The paper used in this publication meets the requirements of ANSI/NISO Z39.48-1992 (Permanence of Paper).

LIBRARY OF CONGRESS CATALOGING-IN-PUBLICATION DATA

Levinson, David, 1947-
Encyclopedia of modern Asia : / David Levinson, Karen Christensen,
p. cm.
Includes bibliographical references and index.
ISBN 0-684-80617-7 (set hardcover : alk. paper)
1. Asia—Encyclopedias. I. Christensen, Karen, 1957- II. Title.
DS4 .L48 2002
950'.03—dc21

2002008712

Printed in United States of America
1 3 5 7 9 11 13 15 17 19 20 18 16 14 12 10 8 6 4 2

Contents

List of Maps

Volume 5

Volume 6

Survey of Asia's Regions and Nations

The *Encyclopedia of Modern Asia* covers thirty-three nations in depth and also the Caucasus and Siberia. We have divided Asia into five major subregions and assigned the thirty-three nations to each.

West and Southwest Asia

The West Asian nations covered in detail here are Turkey, Iran, and Iraq. Afghanistan and Pakistan form Southwest Asia, although in some classifications they are placed in Central and South Asia, respectively. Afghanistan, on the crossroads of civilizations for thousands of years, is especially difficult to classify and displays features typical of Central, West, and South Asia.

Despite diversity in language (Persian in Iran, Arabic in Iraq, Turkish in Turkey) form of government (theocracy in Iran, dictatorship in Iraq, and unstable democracy in Turkey) and international ties (Iran to the Islamic world, Iraq to the Arab Middle East, Turkey to the West), there are several sources of unity across West Asia. Perhaps the oldest is geographical location as the site of transportation routes between Europe and Central, East, and South Asia. Since ancient times, people, goods, wealth, and ideas have flowed across the region. In 2002 the flow of oil was most important, from the wells of Iran and Iraq through the pipelines of Turkey. Another source of unity is Sunni Islam, a major feature of life since the seventh century, although Iran is mainly the minority Shi'a tradition and there have long been Zoroastrian, Jewish, Christian, and Baha'i minorities in the region. Diversity is also evident in the fact that Turkey is a "secular" state while Iran is a theocracy, and in the conflict between fundamentalist and mainstream Islam in all the nations.

Another important common thread is the shared historical experience of being part of the Ottoman Empire and having to cope with British and Russian designs on their territory and, more recently, American influence. And, in the twentieth century, all three nations have sought to deal with the Kurdish minority and its demands for a Kurdish state to be established on land taken from all three nations.

Unity across Afghanistan and Pakistan is created by adherence to Sunni Islam (although there is a Shi'ite minority in Afghanistan) and the prominence of the Pashtun ethnic group in each nation. Both nations also experienced British colonialism, although the long-term British influence is more notable in Pakistan, which had been tied to India under British rule. West Asia is the only region in the world never colonized by Britain, although some experts argue that it did experience significant British cultural influence. In all nations resistance to external control—British, Russian, or United States—is another common historical experience.

Across the region (although less so in Afghanistan) is the stark contrast between the traditional culture and the modernity of liberation from imperial rule, still not complete across the region. This contrast is apparent in clothing styles, manners, architecture, recreation, marriage practices, and many elements of daily life.

In 2002 all the nations faced a water crisis of both too little water and water pollution. They all also faced issues of economic and social development, including reducing external debt, controlling inflation, reducing unemployment, improving education and health care, and continually reacting to the ongoing Arab-Israeli conflict, which exacerbates many of these problems. The governments also faced the difficult task of solving these problems while resisting Americanization and also while controlling internal political unrest. Political unrest is often tied to efforts at creating democratic governments and the persistence of elite collaboration with tyrannical governments.

Central Asia

Central Asia is known by many names, including Eurasia, Middle Asia, and Inner Asia. At its core, the region is composed of five states that became independent nations following the collapse of the Soviet Union in 1991: Kazakhstan, Kyrgyzstan, Tajikistan, Turkmenistan, and Uzbekistan. Scholars sometimes include Afghanistan, Mongolia and the Xinjiang province of China within the label Central Asia. For this project, Central Asia is restricted to the five former Soviet countries, while Afghanistan is classified in Southwest Asia, and Mongolia and Xinjiang as part of East Asia. These states have a shared landmass of 1.5 million square miles, about one-half the size of the United States.

The region's unity comes from a shared history and religion. Central Asia saw two cultural and economic traditions blossom and intermix along the famed Silk Road: nomadic and sedentary. Nomadic herdsmen, organized into kinship groupings of clans, lived beside sedentary farmers and oasis city dwellers. Four of the countries share Turkic roots, while the Tajiks are of Indo-European descent, linguistically related to the Iranians. While still recognizable today, this shared heritage has developed into distinct ethnic communities.

The peoples of Central Asia have seen centuries of invasion, notably the legendary Mongol leader Genghis Khan in the thirteenth century, the Russians in the nineteenth and the Soviets in the twentieth century. For better or worse, each invader left behind markers of their presence: the Arabs introduced Islam in the seventh century. Today Islam is the predominant religion in the region, and most Central Asians are Sunni Muslims. The Russians brought the mixed legacy of modernism, including an educated populace, alarming infant mortality rates, strong economic and political participation by women, high agricultural development, and environmental disasters such as the shrinking of the Aral Sea. It was under Russian colonialism that distinct ethno-national boundaries were created to divide the people of the region. These divisions largely shape the contemporary Central Asian landscape.

Today the five Central Asian nations face similar challenges: building robust economies, developing stable, democratic governments, and integrating themselves into the regional and international communities as independent states. They come to these challenges with varied resources: Kazakhstan and Turkmenistan have rich oil reserves; several countries have extensive mineral deposits; and the Fergana Valley is but one example of the region's rich agricultural regions.

Finally, the tragic events of September 11, 2001, cast world attention on Afghanistan's neighbors in Central Asia. The "war on terrorism" forged new alliances and offered a mix of political pressure and economic support for the nations' leaders to suppress their countries' internal fundamentalist Muslim movements.

Southeast Asia

Southeast Asia is conventionally defined as that subregion of Asia consisting of the eleven nation-states of Brunei, Cambodia, East Timor, Indonesia, Laos, Malaysia, Myanmar, Philippines, Singapore, Thailand, and Vietnam. Myanmar is sometimes alternatively classified as part of South Asia and Vietnam as in East Asia. The region may be subdivided into Mainland Southeast Asia (Cambodia, Laos, Myanmar, Thailand, and Vietnam) and Insular Southeast Asia (Brunei, East Timor, Indonesia, Philippines, and Singapore). Malaysia is the one nation in the region that is located both on the mainland and islands, though ethnically it is more linked to the island nations of Indonesia, Brunei, and the Philippines.

Perhaps the key defining features for the region and those that are most widespread are the tropical monsoon climate, rich natural resources, and a way of life in rural areas based on cooperative wet-rice agriculture that goes back several thousand years. In the past unity was also created in various places by major civilizations, including those of Funan, Angkor, Pagan, Sukhothai, Majapahit, Srivijaya, Champa, Ayutthaya, and Melaka. Monarchies continue to be significant in several nation—Brunei, Cambodia, Malaysia, and Thailand—today. Subregional unity has also been created since ancient times by the continued use of written languages, including Vietnamese, Thai, Lao, Khmer and the rich literary traditions associated with those languages.

The region can also be defined as being located between China and India and has been influenced by both, with Indian influence generally broader, deeper, and longer lasting, especially on the mainland, except for Vietnam and Singapore, where influences from China have been more important. Islamic influence is also present in all eleven of the Southeast Asian nations. Culturally, Southeast Asia is notable for the central importance of the family, religion (mainly Buddhism and Islam), and aesthetics in daily life and national consciousness.

In the post–World War II Cold War era, there was a lack of regional unity. Some nations, such as Indonesia under Sukarno, were leaders of the nonaligned nations. Countries such as Thailand and the Philippines joined the U.S. side in the Cold War by being part of the Southeast Asia Treaty Organization (SEATO). A move toward greater unity was achieved with the establishment of the Association of Southeast Asian Nations (ASEAN) in 1967, with the founding members being Indonesia, Malaysia, the Philippines, Singapore, and Thailand. Subsequently other Southeast Asian nations joined ASEAN (Brunei, 1984; Laos, Myanmar, and Vietnam 1997; Cambodia 1999). As of 2002, communism was still the system in Laos and Vietnam and capitalism in Brunei, Cambodia, East Timor, the Philippines Thailand, Indonesia, Malaysia and Singapore. Political, economic, and cultural cooperation is fostered by the Association of Southeast Asian Nations (ASEAN), with headquarters in Jakarta, Indonesia. Economically, all the nations have attempted to move, although at different speeds and with different results, from a reliance on agriculture to an industrial or service-based economy. All nations also suffered in the Asian economic crisis beginning in July 1997.

Alongside these sources of similarity or unity that allow us to speak of Southeast Asia as a region is also considerable diversity. In the past religion, ethnicity, and diverse colonial experience (British, Dutch, French, American) were major sources of diversity. Today, the three major sources of diversity are religion, form of government, and level of economic development. Three nations (Indonesia, Malaysia,

Brunei) are predominately Islamic, five are mainly Buddhist (Vietnam, Laos, Cambodia, Thailand, Myanmar), two are mainly Christian (Philippines and East Timor), and Singapore is religiously heterogeneous. In addition, there is religious diversity within nations, as all these nations have sizeable and visible religious minorities and indigenous religions, in both traditional and syncretic forms, also remain important.

In terms of government, there is considerable variation: communism in Vietnam and Laos; state socialism in Myanmar; absolute monarchy in Brunei; evolving democracy in the Philippines, Thailand, Cambodia, and Indonesia; and authoritarian democracy in Malaysia and Singapore. The economic variation that exists among the nations and also across regions within nations is reflected in different levels of urbanization and economic development, with Singapore and Malaysia at one end of the spectrum and Laos and Cambodia at the other. Myanmar is economically underdeveloped, although it is urbanized, while Brunei is one of the wealthiest nations in the world but not very urbanized.

In 2002, Southeast Asia faced major environmental, political, economic, and health issues. All Southeast Asian nations suffer from serious environmental degradation, including water pollution, soil erosion, air pollution in and around cities, traffic congestion, and species extinctions. To a significant extent all these problems are the result of rapid industrial expansion and overexploitation of natural resources for international trade. The economic crisis has hampered efforts to address these issues and has threatened the economies of some nations, making them more dependent on international loans and assistance from nations such as Japan, Australia, and China. The persisting economic disparities between the rich and the poor are actually exacerbated by rapid economic growth. Related to poverty is the AIDS epidemic, which is especially serious in Cambodia, Myanmar, and Thailand and becoming more serious in Vietnam; in all these nations it associated with the commercial sex industry.

Politically, many Southeast Asian nations faced one or more threats to their stability. Political corruption, lack of transparency, and weak civic institutions are a problem to varying degrees in all the nations but are most severe in Indonesia, which faces threats to its sovereignty. Cambodia and Thailand face problems involving monarch succession, and several nations have had difficulty finding effective leaders. Myanmar's authoritarian rulers face a continual threat from the political opposition and from ethnic and religious separatists.

In addition, several nations faced continuing religious or ethnic-based conflicts that disrupt political stability and economic growth in some provinces. The major conflicts involve Muslim separatists in the southern Philippines, Muslims and Christians in some Indonesian islands and Aceh separatists in northern Sumatra, and Muslims and the Karen and other ethnic groups against the Burman government in Myanmar. Since the economic crisis of 1997, ethnic and religion-based conflict has intensified, as wealthier ethnic or religious minorities have increasingly been attacked by members of the dominant ethnic group. A related issue is the cultural and political future of indigenous peoples, including the so-called hill tribes of the mainland and horticulturalists and former hunter-gatherers of the islands.

In looking to the future, among the region's positive features are the following. First, there is Southeast Asia's strategic location between India and China, between Japan and Europe, and between Europe and Oceania. It stands in close proximity to the world's two most populous countries, China and India. Singapore, the centrally located port in Southeast Asia, is one of two major gateways to the dynamic Pacific Basin (the other is the Panama Canal). Second, there is the region's huge population and related economic market, with a total population approaching that of one half of China's. Indonesia is the world's fourth most populous nation. Third, there is enormous tourist potential in sites and recreational locales such as Angkor Wat, Bali, Borobudur, Phuket, and Ha Long Bay. Fourth, there is the region's notable eclecticism in borrowing from the outside and resiliency in transcending tragedies such as experienced by Cambodia and Vietnam. Fifth, there is the region's significant economic potential: Southeast Asia may well have the world's highest-quality labor force relative to cost. And, sixth, there is the region's openness to new technologies and ideas, an important feature in the modern global community.

South Asia

South Asia is the easiest region to demarcate, as it is bounded by the Hindu Kush and Himalayan ranges to the north and the Bay of Bengal and Arabian Sea to the south. It contains the nation-states of Bangladesh, Bhutan, India, Nepal, and Sri Lanka and the more distant island nations of the Maldives and Mauritius. Myanmar and Pakistan, which are considered part of South Asia in some schemes, are here classified in Southeast Asia and Southwest Asia, respectively.

While the region is diverse economically, culturally, linguistically, and religiously, there is unity that, in some form, has existed for several thousand years. One source of unity is the historical influence of two major civilizations (Indus and Dravidian) and three major religions (Hinduism, Buddhism, and Islam). Regionally, Sikhism and Jainism have been of great importance. There is also considerable economic unity, as the majority of people continue to live by farming, with rice and especially wet-rice the primary crop. In addition, three-quarters of the people continue to live in rural, agricultural villages, although this has now become an important source of diversity, with clear distinctions between urban and rural life. A third source of unity is the caste system, which continues to define life for most people in the three mainland nations. Another source of unity is the nature and structure of society, which was heavily influenced by the several centuries of British rule. A final source of political unity in the twentieth century—although sometimes weakened by ethnic and religious differences—has been nationalism in each nation.

South Asia is diverse linguistically, ethnically, religiously, and economically. This diversity is most obvious in India, but exists in various forms in other nations, except for the isolated Maldives, which is the home of one ethnic group, the Divehi, who are Muslims and who have an economy based largely on tourism and fishing.

The dozens of languages of South Asia fall into four major families: Indo-European, Austroasiatic, Dravidian, and Tibeto-Burman and several cannot be classified at all. Because of its linguistic diversity, India is divided into "linguistic" states with Hindi and English serving as the national languages.

Hinduism is the dominant religion in South Asia, but India is the home also to Buddhism, Jainism, and Sikhism. India also has over 120 million Muslims and the world's largest Zoroastrian population (known in India as Parsis) and Bangladesh is a predominately Muslim nation. India also has about twenty-five million Christians and until recently India had several small but thriving Jewish communities. Nepal is mainly Hindu with a Buddhist minority, and Bhutan the reverse. Sri Lanka is mainly Theravada Buddhist with Hindu, Muslim, and Christian minorities. Mauritius, which has no indigenous population, is about 50 percent Hindu, with a large Christian and smaller Muslim and Buddhist minorities.

Linguistic and religious diversity is more than matched by social diversity. One classification suggests that the sociocultural groups of South Asia can be divided into four general and several subcategories: (1) castes (Hindu and Muslim); (2) modern urban classes (including laborers, non-Hindus, and the Westernized elite); (3) hill tribes of at least six types; and (4) peripatetics.

Economically, there are major distinctions between the rural poor and the urban middle class and elite, and also between the urban poor and urban middle class and elite. There are also significant wealth distinctions based on caste and gender, and a sizeable and wealthy Indian diaspora. There is political diversity as well, with India and Sri Lanka being democracies, Bangladesh shifting back and forth between Islamic democracy and military rule, the Maldives being an Islamic state, and Nepal and Bhutan being constitutional monarchies.

In 2002, South Asia faced several categories of issues. Among the most serious are the ongoing ethnic and religious conflicts between Muslims and Hindus in India, the conflict between the nations of Pakistan and India; the ethnic conflict between the Sinhalese and Sri Lankan Tamils in Sri Lanka; and the conflict between the Nepalese and Bhutanese in both nations. There are also various ethnic separatists movements in the region, as involving some Sikhs in India. The most threatening to order in the region and beyond is the conflict between India and Pakistan over the Kashmir region, as both have nuclear weapons and armies gathered at their respective borders.

A second serious issue is the host of related environmental problems, including pollution; limited water resources; overexploitation of natural resources; destruction and death caused by typhoons, flooding, and earthquakes; famine (less of a problem today), and epidemics of tropical and other diseases. The Maldives faces the unique problem of disappearing into the sea as global warming melts glaciers and raises the sea level. Coastal regions of Bangladesh could also suffer from this.

There are pressing social, economic, and political issues as well. Socially, there are wide and growing gaps between the rich and middle classes and the poor, who are disproportionately women and children and rural. Tribal peoples and untouchables still do not enjoy full civil rights, and women are often discriminated against, although India, Sri Lanka, and Bangladesh have all had women prime ministers. Economically, all the nations continue to wrestle with the issues involved in transforming themselves from mainly rural, agricultural nations to ones with strong industrial and service sectors. Politically, all still also struggle with the task of establishing strong, central governments that can control ethnic, religious, and region variation and provide services to the entire population. Despite these difficulties, there are also positive developments. India continues to benefit from the inflow of wealth earned by Indians outside India and is emerging as a major technological center. And, in Sri Lanka, an early 2002 cease-fire has led to the prospect of a series of peace negotiations in the near future..

East Asia

East Asia is defined here as the nations of Japan, South Korea, North Korea, China, Taiwan, and Mongolia. It should be noted that Taiwan is part of China although the People's Republic of China and the Republic of China (Taiwan) differ over whether it is a province or not. The inclusion of China in East Asia is not entirely geographically and culturally valid, as parts of southern China could be classified as Southeast Asian from a geographical and cultural standpoint, while western China could be classified as Central Asian. However, there is a long tradition of classifying China as part of East Asia, and that is the approach taken here. Likewise, Mongolia is sometimes classified in Central Asia. As noted above, Siberia can be considered as forming North and Northeast Asia.

Economic, political, ideological, and social similarity across China, Korea (North and South), and Japan is the result of several thousand years of Chinese influence (at times strong, at other times weak), which has created considerable similarity on a base of pre-existing Japanese and Korean cultures and civilizations. China's influence was greatest before the modern period and Chinese culture thus in some ways forms the core of East Asian culture and society. At the same time, it must be stressed that Chinese cultural elements merged with existing and new Korean and Japanese ones in ways that produced the unique Japanese and Korean cultures and civilizations, which deserve consideration in their own right.

Among the major cultural elements brought from China were Buddhism and Confucianism, the written language, government bureaucracy, various techniques of rice agriculture, and a patrilineal kinship system based on male dominance and male control of family resources. All of these were shaped over the centuries to fit with existing or developing forms in Korea and Japan. For example, Buddhism coexists with Shinto in Japan. In Korea, it coexists with the indigenous shamanistic religion. In China and Korea traditional folk religion remains strong, while Japan has been the home to dozens of new indigenous religions over the past 150 years.

Diversity in the region has been largely a product of continuing efforts by the Japanese and Koreans to resist Chinese influence and develop and stress Japanese and Korean culture and civilization. In the twentieth century diversity was mainly political and economic. Japanese invasions and conquests of parts of China and all of Korea beginning in the late nineteenth century led to hostile relations that had not been completely overcome in 2002.

In the post–World War II era and after, Taiwan, Japan, and South Korea have been closely allied with the United States and the West; they have all developed powerful industrial and postindustrial economies. During the same period, China became a Communist state; significant ties to the West and economic development did not begin until the late 1980s. North Korea is also a Communist state; it lags behind the other nations in economic development and in recent years has not been able to produce enough food to feed its population. In 2002 China was the emerging economic power in the region, while Taiwan and South Korea hold on and Japan shows signs of serious and long-term economic decline, although it remains the second-largest (after the United States) economy in the world. Mongolia, freed from Soviet rule, is attempting to build its economy following a capitalist model.

Politically, China remains a Communist state despite significant moves toward market capitalism, North Korea is a Communist dictatorship, Japan a democracy, and South Korea and Taiwan in 1990s seem to have become relatively stable democracies following periods of authoritarian rule. Significant contact among the nations is mainly economic, as efforts at forging closer political ties remain stalled over past grievances. For example, in 2001, people in China and South Korea protested publicly about a new Japanese high school history textbook that they believed did not fully describe Japanese atrocities committed toward Chinese and Koreans before and during World War II. Japan has refused to revise the textbook. Similarly, tension remains between Mongolia and China over Mongolian fears about Chinese designs on Mongolian territory. Inner Mongolia is a province of China.

Major issues with regional and broader implications are the reunification of Taiwan and China and North and South Korea, and threat of war should reunification efforts go awry. Other major regional issues include environmental pollution, including air pollution from China that spreads east, and pollution of the Yellow Sea, Taiwan Strait, and South China Sea. A third issue is economic development and stability, and the role of each nation, and the region as a unit, in the growing global economy. A final major issue is the emergence of China as a major world political, economic, and military power at the expense of Taiwan, South Korea, and Japan, and the consequences for regional political relations and stability.

Overview

As the above survey indicates, Asia is a varied and dynamic construct. To some extent the notion of Asia, as well as regions within Asia, are artificial constructs imposed by outside observers to provide some structure to a place and subject matter that might otherwise be incomprehensible. The nations of Asia have rich and deep pasts that continue to inform and shape the present—and that play a significant role in relations with other nations and regions. The nations of Asia also face considerable issues—some unique to the region, others shared by nations around the world—as well as enormous potential for future growth and development. We expect that the next edition of this encyclopedia will portray a very different Asia than does this one, but still an Asia that is in many ways in harmony with its pasts.

David Levinson (with contributions from Virginia Aksan, Edward Beauchamp, Anthony and Rebecca Bichel, Linsun Cheng, Gerald Fry, Bruce Fulton, and Paul Hockings)

Regional Maps

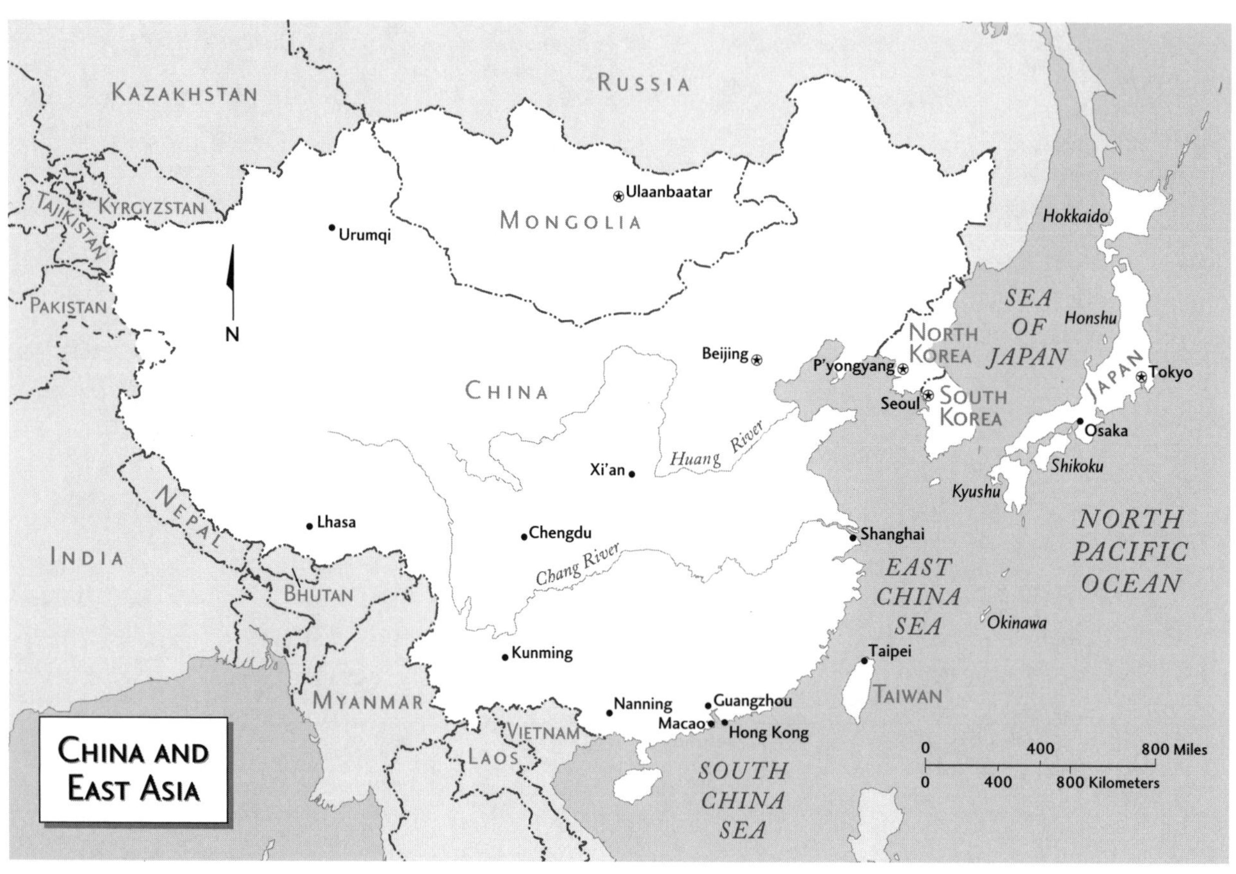
CHINA AND EAST ASIA
KAZAKHSTAN
RUSSIA
KYRGYZSTAN
TAJIKISTAN
PAKISTAN
MONGOLIA
Ulaanbaatar
Urumqi
N
CHINA
Beijing
NORTH KOREA
P'yongyang
Seoul
SOUTH KOREA
SEA OF JAPAN
Hokkaido
Honshu
JAPAN
Tokyo
Osaka
Shikoku
Kyushu
Huang River
Xi'an
NEPAL
Lhasa
Chengdu
Chang River
INDIA
BHUTAN
Shanghai
EAST CHINA SEA
NORTH PACIFIC OCEAN
Okinawa
Taipei
TAIWAN
Kunming
MYANMAR
Nanning
Guangzhou
Macao
Hong Kong
VIETNAM
LAOS
SOUTH CHINA SEA
0 400 800 Miles
0 400 800 Kilometers

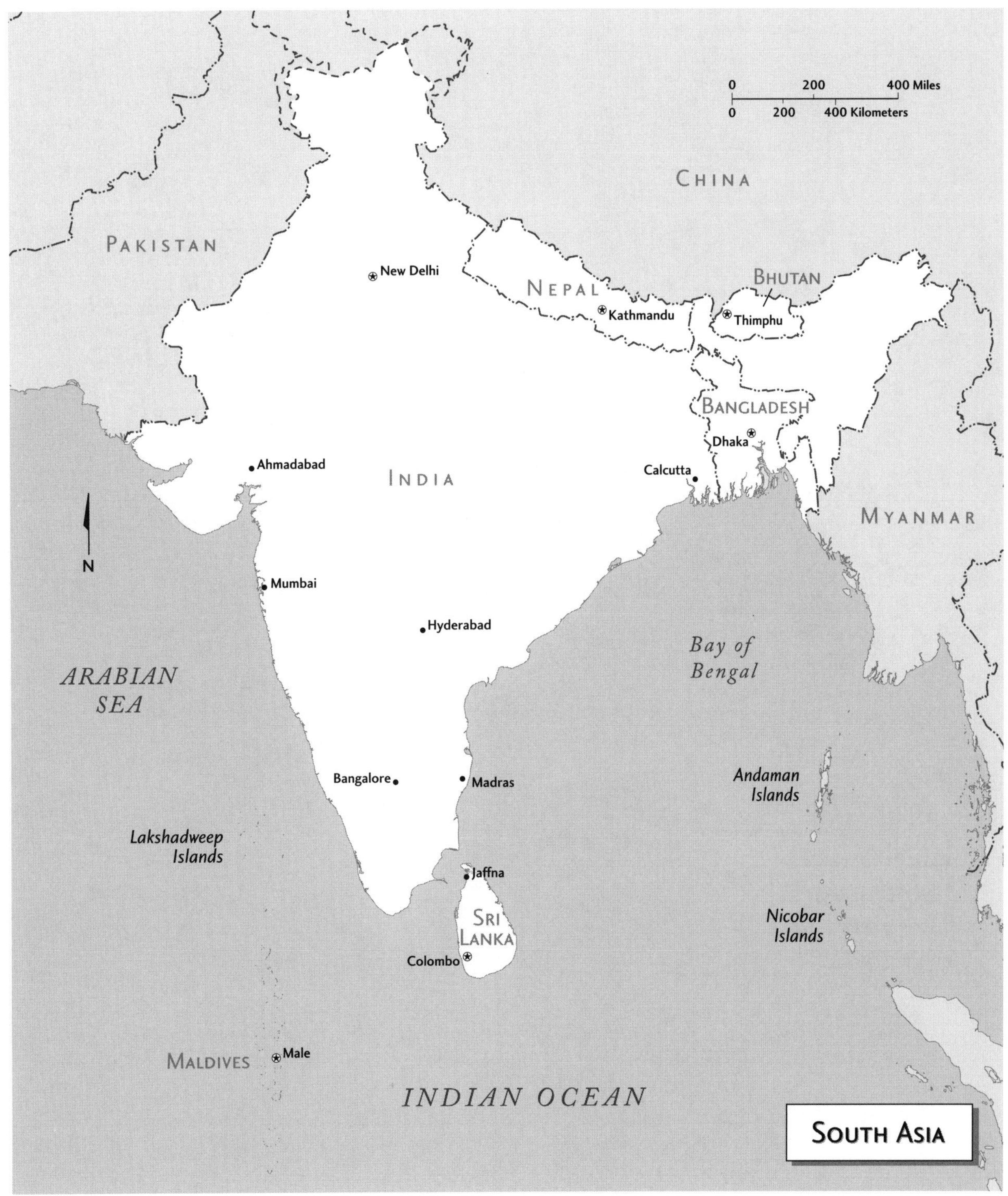
0 200 400 Miles
0 200 400 Kilometers
CHINA
PAKISTAN
New Delhi
NEPAL
Kathmandu
BHUTAN
Thimphu
BANGLADESH
Dhaka
Calcutta
Ahmadabad
INDIA
MYANMAR
N
Mumbai
Hyderabad
Bay of
Bengal
ARABIAN
SEA
Bangalore
Madras
Andaman
Islands
Lakshadweep
Islands
Jaffna
SRI
LANKA
Colombo
Nicobar
Islands
MALDIVES
Male
INDIAN OCEAN
SOUTH ASIA

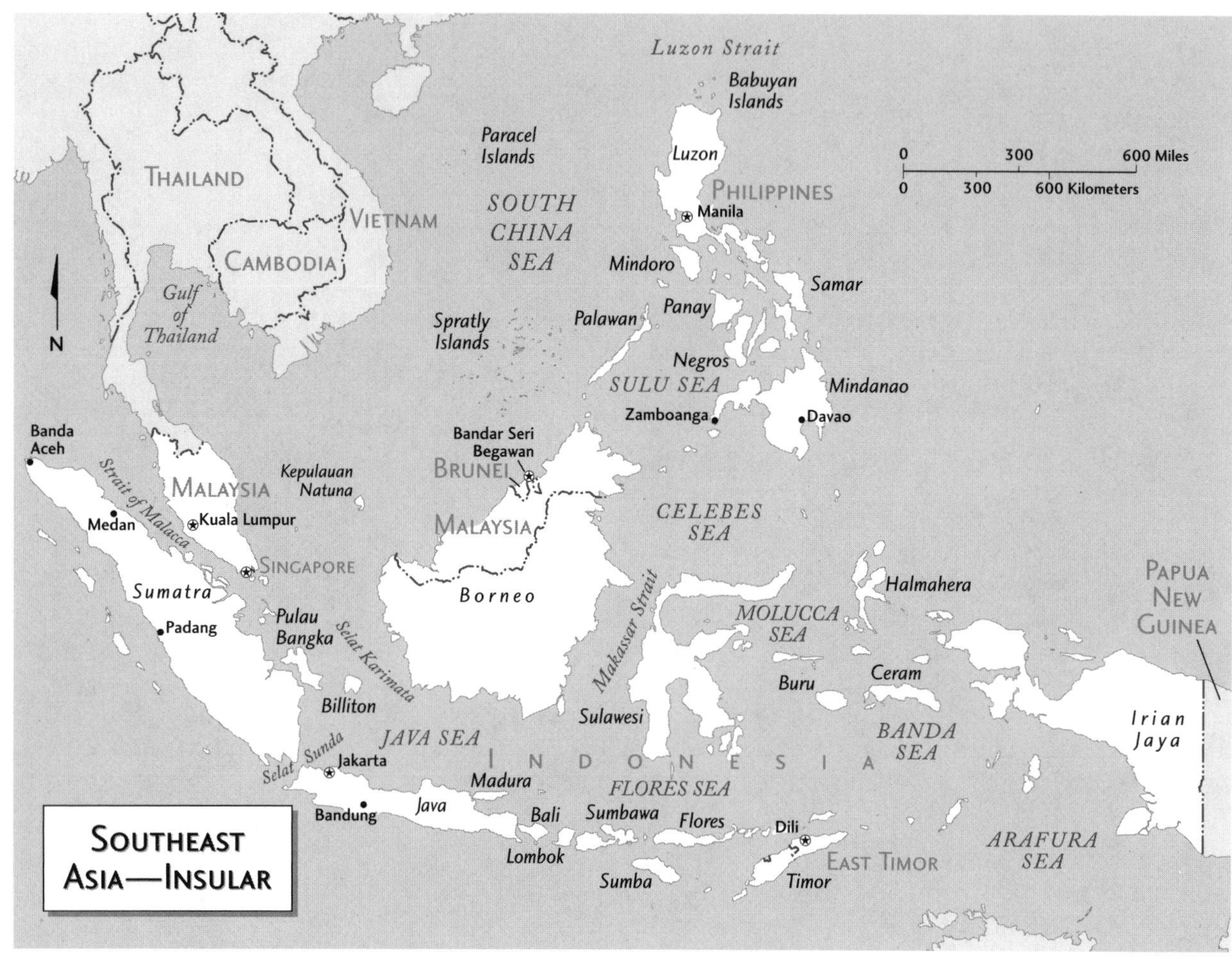
Southeast Asia—Insular
Luzon Strait
Babuyan Islands
Paracel Islands
Luzon
Thailand
Philippines
Manila
Vietnam
South China Sea
Cambodia
Mindoro
Samar
Gulf of Thailand
Panay
Palawan
Spratly Islands
Negros
Sulu Sea
Mindanao
Zamboanga
Davao
Banda Aceh
Bandar Seri Begawan
Brunei
Kepulauan Natuna
Malaysia
Strait of Malacca
Medan
Kuala Lumpur
Malaysia
Celebes Sea
Singapore
Sumatra
Borneo
Halmahera
Papua New Guinea
Padang
Pulau Bangka
Selat Karimata
Makassar Strait
Molucca Sea
Buru
Ceram
Billiton
Sulawesi
Java Sea
Banda Sea
Irian Jaya
Selat Sunda
Jakarta
Indonesia
Madura
Flores Sea
Bandung
Java
Bali
Sumbawa
Flores
Dili
Lombok
East Timor
Arafura Sea
Sumba
Timor
N
0 300 600 Miles
0 300 600 Kilometers

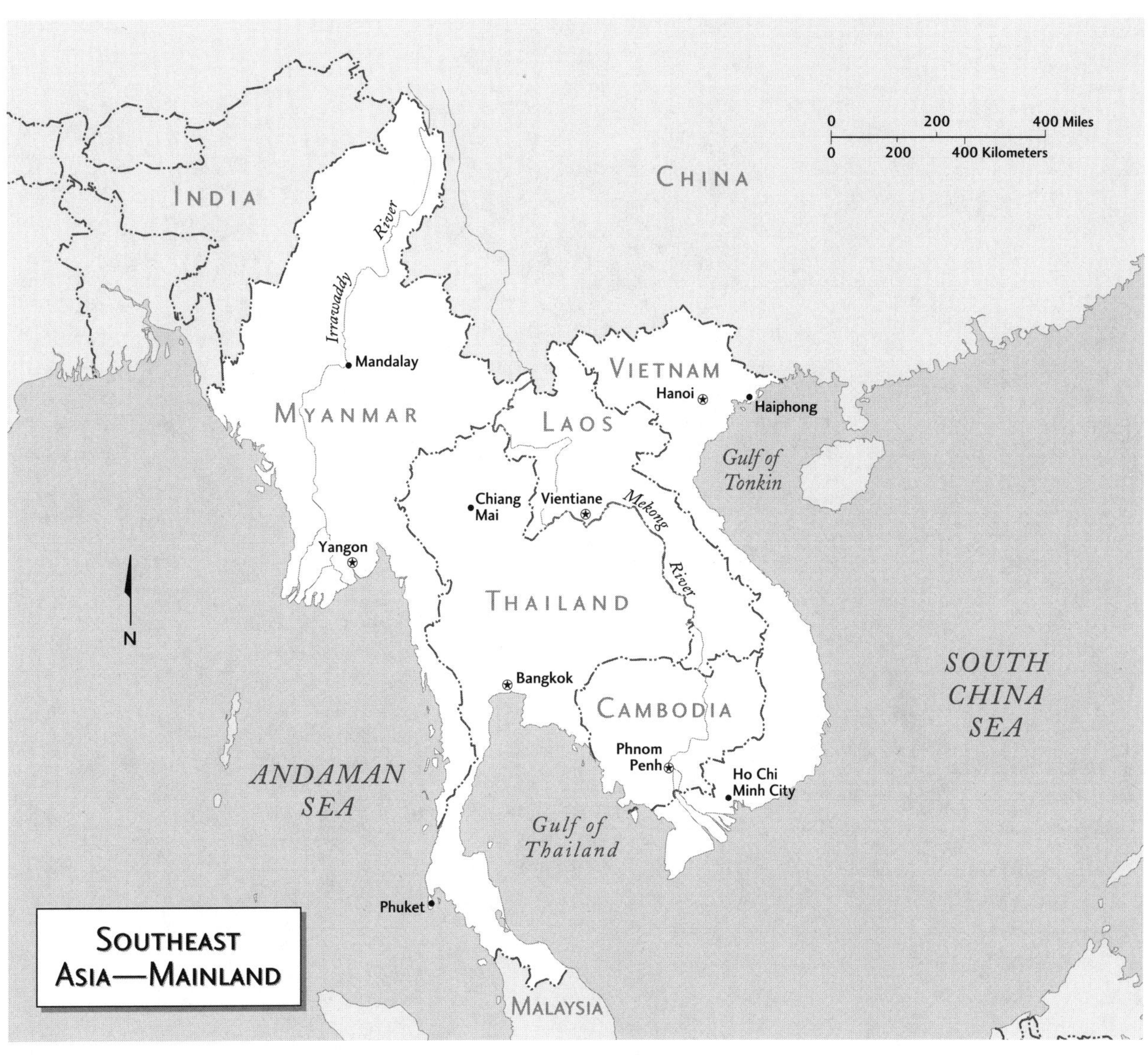

Southeast Asia—Mainland

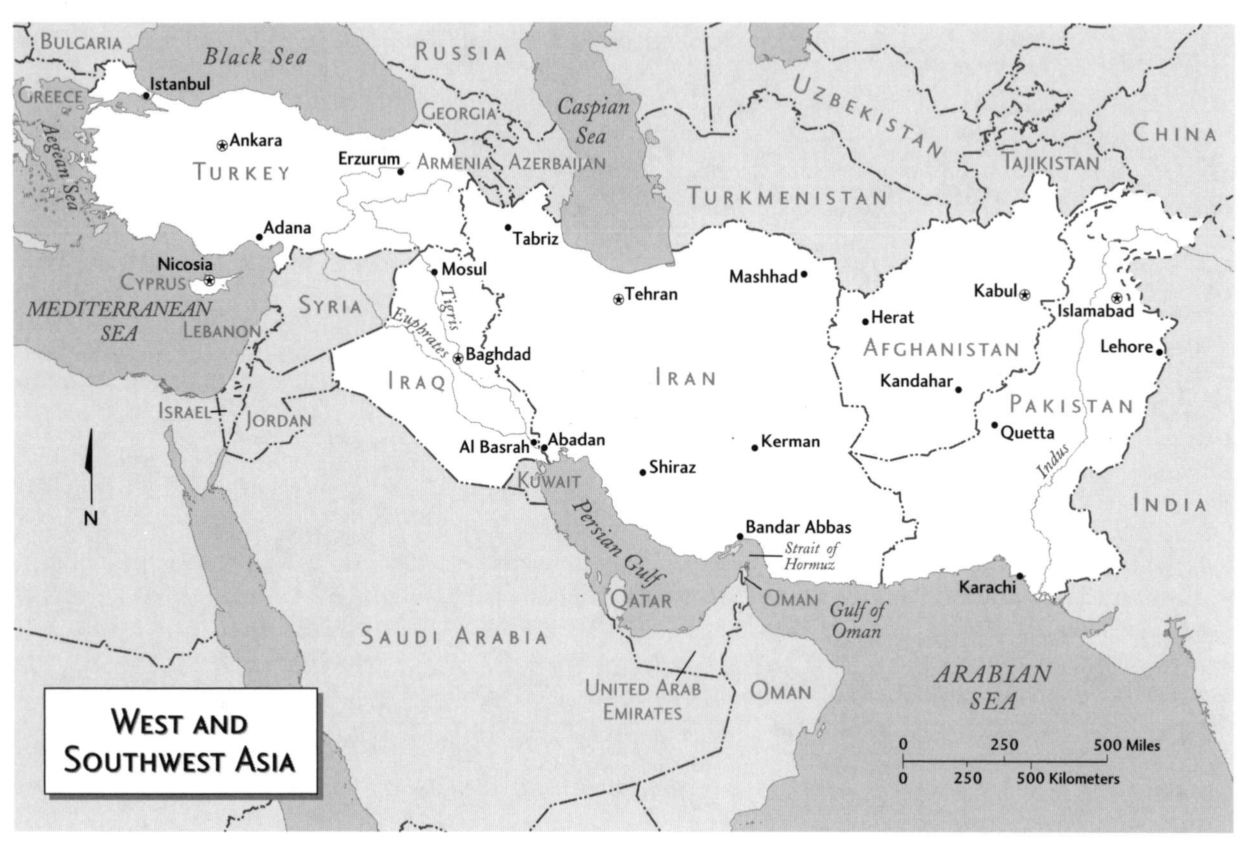
BULGARIA
Black Sea
RUSSIA
GREECE
Istanbul
Aegean Sea
Ankara
TURKEY
Erzurum
GEORGIA
ARMENIA
AZERBAIJAN
Caspian Sea
UZBEKISTAN
CHINA
TAJIKISTAN
TURKMENISTAN
Adana
Tabriz
Nicosia
CYPRUS
MEDITERRANEAN SEA
LEBANON
SYRIA
Mosul
Tigris
Euphrates
Baghdad
Tehran
Mashhad
Kabul
Islamabad
Herat
AFGHANISTAN
Lehore
IRAQ
IRAN
Kandahar
PAKISTAN
Quetta
ISRAEL
JORDAN
Al Basrah
Abadan
Kerman
Shiraz
KUWAIT
Indus
INDIA
N
Persian Gulf
Bandar Abbas
Strait of Hormuz
Karachi
QATAR
OMAN
Gulf of Oman
SAUDI ARABIA
UNITED ARAB EMIRATES
OMAN
ARABIAN SEA
WEST AND SOUTHWEST ASIA
0
250
500 Miles
0
250
500 Kilometers

Reader's Guide

ASIA

Arts, Literature, and Recreation

Asian Games
Board Games
Chinese New Year
Jade
Kabaddi
Kites and Kite Flying
Mountaineering
Olympics
Storytelling

Economics, Commerce, and Transportation

Asian Development Bank
Asian Economic Crisis of 1997
Asia-Pacific Economic Cooperation Forum
Automobile Industry
Bogor Declaration
Drug Trade
Export-Led Development
Golden Crescent
High-Technology Industry
Information Technology Industry
Intellectual Property
Islamic Banking
Manila Action Plan
Measurement Systems
Osaka Action Plan
Shanghai Cooperation Organization
Silk Road
Spice Trade
Sustainability
Tin Industry
Tourism
World Bank in Asia

Geography and the Natural World

Air Pollution
Bamboo
Buffalo, Water
Camel, Bactrian
Caspian Sea
Chicken
Cormorant
Deforestation
Duck and Goose, Domesticated
Earthquakes
Endangered Species
Goat
Mangroves
Monsoons
Opium
Pacific Ocean
Pacific Rim
Pig
Rhinocerous, Asiatic
Rice and Rice Agriculture
Soil Loss
South China Sea
Surkhob River
Tiger
Toxic-Waste Disposal
Typhoons
Volcanoes
Water Issues

Government, Politics, and Law

Corruption

International Relations

Africa-Asia Relations
Australia-Asia Relations

ASIA *(continued)*

International Relations *(continued)*

Europe-Asia Relations
International Monetary Fund
Land Mines
New Zealand-Asia Relations
Nuclear Arms
United Nations
World War I
World War II

Language and Communication

Altaic Languages
Austroasiatic Languages
English in Asia
Hmong-Mien Languages
Indo-European Languages
Language Purification
Media
Self-Censorship
Sinitic Languages
Tibeto-Burman Languages
Turkic Languages
Uralic Languages

Peoples, Cultures, and Society

Fertility
Homosexuality
New Rich
Orientalism

Religion and Philosophy

Asian-Christian Religious Dialogue
Baraka
Muslim Saints
Religious Self-Mortification
Shamanism
Shari'a
Zoroastrianism

Science,Technology, and Health

AIDS
Disease, Tropical
Terrace Irrigation

CENTRAL ASIA

Arts, Literature, and Recreation

Alpamish
Architectural Decoration—Central Asia
Architecture—Central Asia
Buzkashi
Carpets—Central Asia
Chagatay
Cuisine—Central Asia
Dance—Central Asia
Dastan, Turkic
Dombra
Edige
Felting—Central Asia
Fine Arts—Central Asia
Folklore—Central Asia
Gorkut Ata
Koroghli
Literature—Central Asia
Minaret
Music—Central Asia
Nava'i, Mir' Ali Shir
Tile Work—Central Asia
Woodworking—Central Asia

Kazakhstan

Auezov, Mukhtar
Dauylpaz
Dulatov, Mirzhaqyp
Kalmakanov, Bukharzhrau
Kobyz
Kunanbaev, Abai
Mailin, Beiimbet
Makhambet Utemisov
Seifullin, Saduakas
Taimanov, Isatai
Valikhanov, Chokan
Aitmatov, Chingis
Manas Epic

Tajikistan

Bun Bang Fai

Turkmenistan

Kuli, Maktum

Uzbekistan

Abdalrauf Fitrat
Abdullah Quaisi
Mamadali Mahmudov

Economics, Commerce, and Transportation

Agriculture—Central Asia
Caravans
Energy—Central Asia
Oil and Mineral Industries—Central Asia

Kazakhstan

Kazakhstan—Economic System

Kyrgyzstan

Kyrgyzstan—Economic System

Tajikistan

Tajikistan—Economic System

Turkmenistan

Turkmenistan—Economic System

Uzbekistan

Uzbekistan—Economic System

Education

Madrasahs

Kazakhstan

Altynsarin, Ibrahim
Kazakhstan—Education System

Kyrgyzstan
Kyrgyzstan—Education System
Tajikistan
Tajikistan—Education System
Turkmenistan
Turkmenistan—Education System
Uzbekistan
Alisher Navoiy Samarkand State University
Uzbekistan—Education System

Geography and the Natural World

Altay Mountains
Aral Sea
Bactria
Balkhash, Lake
Camel, Arvana Dromedary
Fergana Valley
Horse, Akhal-teke
Horse, Karabair
Horse, Lokai
Kara-Kum Desert
Khwarizm
Leopard, Snow
Murgab River
Pamir Range
Paracel Islands
Radioactive Waste and Contamination—Central Asia
Sheep, Karakul
Sheep, Marco Polo
Syr Dar'ya
Tedzhen River
Tobol River
Trans Alai
Tura Lowland
Turugart Pass
Ustyurt Plateau
Zerafshan River
Kazakhstan
Irtysh River
Ishim River
Kazakh Uplands
Mangyshlak Peninsula
Turgay Plateau
Tajikistan
Kafirnigan River
Sarez Lake
Turkmenistan
Garabil Plateau

Government, Politics, and Law

Basmachi Movement
Communism—Central Asia
Great Game
Russification and Sovietization—Central Asia
Timur
Tribes and Tribal Federations—Central Asia
Urgench
Kazakhstan
Almaty
Astana
Bokeikhanov, Alikhan
Kazakhstan—Political System
Kunaev, Dinmukhamed
Nazarbaev, Nursultan
Oral
Petropavlovsk
Saryshaghan
Semipalatinsk Movement
Seralin, Mukhammedzhan
Suleimenov, Olzhas
Kyrgyzstan
Akaev, Askar
Aksakal
Bishkek
Kurmanjan Datka
Kyrgyzstan—Political System
Osh
Usubaliev, Turdakun Usubalievich
Tajikistan
Dushanbe
Gafurov, Bobojan Gafurovich
Islamic Renaissance Party—Tajikistan
Khorog
Khujand
Kulob
Nabiev, Rakhmon
Qurghonteppa
Rakhmonov, Imomali
Tajikistan—Political System
Tajikistan Civil War
Turkmenistan
Ashgabat
Mary
Niyazov, Saparmurat
Turkmenabat
Turkmenistan—Political System
Uzbekistan
Bukhara
Guliston
Karakalpakstan
Karimov, Islam
Karshi
Mahalla
Nukus
Rashidov, Sharof Rashidovich
Samarqand
Tashkent
Termez
Uzbekistan—Political System

CENTRAL ASIA *(continued)*

History and Profile

Bukhara, Khanate of
Central Asia—Early Medieval Period
Central Asia—Late Medieval and Early Modern
Central Asia—Modern
Khiva, Khanate of
Paleoanthropology—Central Asia
Quqon, Khanate of

Kazakhstan

Kazakhstan—History
Kazakhstan—Profile

Kyrgyzstan

Kyrgyzstan—History
Kyrgyzstan—Profile

Tajikistan

Tajikistan—History
Tajikistan—Profile

Turkmenistan

Turkmenistan—History
Turkmenistan—Profile

Uzbekistan

Uzbekistan—History
Uzbekistan—Profile

International Relations

Central Asia—Human Rights
Central Asia-China Relations
Central Asian Regionalism
Central Asia-Russia Relations

Language and Communication

Central Asian Languages
Farsi-Tajiki
Media—Central Asia

Kazakhstan

Ai Qap
Baitursynov, Akhmet
Kazak
Leninshil Zhas

Peoples, Cultures, and Society

Dungans
Germans in Central Asia
Kalym
Kishlak
Koreans in Central Asia
Marriage and Family—Central Asia
Nomadic Pastoralism—Central Asia
Pamir Peoples
Russians in Central Asia
Westernization—Central Asia
Women in Central Asia
Yurt

Kazakhstan

Kazakhs

Kyrgyzstan

Clothing, Traditional—Kyrgyzstan
Kyrgyz

Tajikistan

Clothing, Traditional—Tajikistan
Tajiks

Turkmenistan

Clothing, Traditional—Turkmenistan
Turkmen

Uzbekistan

Clothing, Traditional—Uzbekistan
Karakalpaks
Uzbeks

Religion and Philosophy

Buddhism—Central Asia
Bukharian Jews
Christianity—Central Asia
Islam—Central Asia
Ismaili Sects—Central Asia
Jadidism
Minaret
Muslim Religious Board of Central Asia
Naqshbandiya

Science,Technology, and Health

Ariq Water System
Ibn Sina
Kara-Kum Canal
Kariz Irrigation System
Medicine, Traditional—Central Asia

EAST ASIA

Arts, Literature, and Recreation

China

Ang Lee
Architecture—China
Architecture, Vernacular—China
Ba Jin
Beijing Opera
Birds and Bird Cages
Calligraphy—China
Cao Xueqin
Chen Kaige
Chuci
Ci
Cinema—China
Cloisonne
Cui Jian
Cuisine—China
Dazu Rock Carvings
Ding Ling
Dragon Boat Festival
Drama—China
Du Fu
Five Classics

Fu Baoshi
Gao Xingjian
Gardening—China
Ginseng
Gong Li
Guo Moruo
Hong lou meng
Hong Shen
Humor in Chinese History
Hungry Ghost Festival
Imperial Palace
International Labor Day—China
Jin ping mei
Lao She
Li Bai
Literature—China
Longmen Grottoes
Lu Xun
Mei Lanfang
Mid-Autumn Festival
Mogao Caves
Music—China
National Day—China
Nu Shooting
Painting—China
Poetry—China
Qi Baishi
Qigong
Qin Tomb
Qingming
Qiu Jin
Quan Tangshi
Shadow Plays and Puppetry
Shen Congwen
Shi
Shijing
Social Realism—China
Sports—China
Spring Festival—China
Summer Palace
Tai Chi
Tea—China
Temple of Heaven
Thirteen Ming Tombs
Tian Han
Tofu
Twelve Muqam
Wang Yiting
Wu Changshi
Wushu
Xiqu
Xu Beihong
Xu Zhimo
Zhang Yimou
Dance, Modern— East Asia
Lacquerware
Masks—East Asia
Porcelain—East Asia

Japan

Aikido
Ando Tadao
Anime
Aoi Matsuri
Arata Isozaki
Architecture—Japan
Architecture—Modern Japan
Baseball—Japan
Basho
Bento
Biwa
Bon Matsuri
Bonsai
Bunjinga
Bunraku
Calligraphy—Japan
Ceramics—Japan
Children's Day—Japan
Chugen
Cinema—Japan
Cinema, Contemporary—Japan
Cuisine—Japan
Dazai Osamu
Drama—Japan
Edogawa Rampo
Emakimono
Enchi Fumiko
Endo Shusaku
Eto Jun
Fugu
Fujieda Shizuo
Fujisawa Takeo
Fujita Tsuguhara
Fukuchi Gen'ichiro
Fukuzawa Yukichi
Funakoshi Gichin
Futabatei, Shimei
Geisha
Gion Matsuri
Haiku
Hakata Matsuri
Hayashi
Hina Matsuri
Hiratsuka Raicho
Iaido
Ito Noe
Judo
Jujutsu
Kabuki

Economic Planning Agency
Economic Stabilization Program
Electronics Industry—Japan
Farmer's Movement
Financial Crisis of 1927
Fishing Industry—Japan
Furukawa Ichibei
Japan—Economic System
Japan—Money
Japanese Firms Abroad
Japanese Foreign Investments
Japanese International Cooperation Agency
Kawasaki
Nikkyoso
Overseas Economic Cooperation Fund
Quality Circles
Ringi System
Settai
Shibusawa Eiichi
Shunto
Whaling—Japan

Koreas

Chaebol
Fishing Industry—Korea
Food Crisis—North Korea
North and South Korean Economic Ventures
North Korea—Economic System
South Korea—Economic System
Steel Industry—Korea

Mongolia

Cashmere Industry
Forest Industry—Mongolia
Mongolia—Economic System
Trans-Mongolian Railway

Education

China

Academia Sinica
China—Education System
Hu Shi
National Taiwan University
Peking University
Taiwan—Education System

Japan

Asiatic Society of Japan
Cram Schools
Daigaku
Ebina Danjo
Gakureki Shakai
Ienaga Saburo
Imperial Rescript on Education
Japan—Education System
Kyoiku Mama
Nitobe Inazo
Shiga Shigetaka

Koreas

Korea Institute of Science and Technology
North Korea—Education System
Seoul National University
South Korea—Education System

Mongolia

Mongolia—Education System

Geography and the Natural World

Siberia
Yellow Sea

China

Bramaputra River
Cathaya Tree
Chang River
East China Sea
Emei, Mount
Famine—China
Greater Xing'an Range
Hengduan Ranges
Huang River
Huang Shan
Huanglongsi
Jiuzhaigou
Kunlun Mountains
Lu, Mount
Panda
Qinling Range
Tai Shan
Taiwan Strait
Taklimakan Desert
Tarim Basin
Tian Shan
Wudang Shan
Wulingyuan
Wuyi, Mount
Yak

Japan

Amami Islands
Chrysanthemum
Chubu
Chugoku
Etorofu Island
Fuji, Mount
Hokkaido
Honshu
Iriomotejima Island
Kansai Region
Kanto Region
Kinki Region
Kunashiro Island
Kyushu
Sado Island
Setouchi Region
Shikoku

EAST ASIA *(continued)*

Geography and the Natural World *(continued)*

Japan (continued)

Tohoku Region
Tokaimura Nuclear Disaster
Tsushima Island
Yakushima Island

Koreas

Amnok River
Han River
Kaema Plateau
Keumkang, Mount
Korea Bay
Korea Strait
Kum River
Naktong River and Delta
Nangnim Range
T'aebaek Mountains
Taedong River
Tumen River

Mongolia

Gobi Desert
Hangai Mountains
Hentii Mountains
Horse, Przewalski's

Government, Politics, and Law

China

Anhui
Beijing
Cadre System—China
Chen Duxiu
Chen Shui-bian
Chen Yun
Chengde
Chengdu
Chiang Kai-shek
Chilung
China—Political System
Chinese Civil War of 1945–1949
Chinese Communist Party
Chongqing
Ci Xi, Empress Dowager
Civil-Service Examination System—China
Communism—China
Corruption—China
Cultural Revolution—China
Deng Xiaoping
Fujian
Gang of Four
Gansu
Great Leap Forward
Guangdong
Guangxi
Guangzhou
Guizhou
Guomindang
Hainan
Hangzhou
Harbin
Hebei
Heilongjiang
Henan
Hong Kong
Hu Jintao
Hu Yaobang
Hubei
Hunan
Hundred Days Reform
Hundred Flowers Campaign
Jiang Zemin
Jiangsu
Jiangxi
Jilin
Kang Youwei
Kao-hsiung
Kong Xiangxi
Lee Teng-hui
Lhasa
Li Hongzhang
Li Peng
Liang Qichao
Liaoning
Lin Biao
Liu Shaoqi
Long March
Macao
Manchuria
Manchurian Incident
Mao Zedong
May Fourth Movement
Nanjing
Nei Monggol
Ningxia
Northern Expedition
People's Liberation Army
Political Participation, Unofficial—China
Qinghai
Quemoy and Matsu
Red Guard Organizations
Republican Revolution of 1911
Self-Strengthening Movement
Shaanxi
Shandong
Shanghai
Shanxi
Sichuan
Socialist Spiritual Civilization—China
Song Ziwen

Sun Yat-sen
Suzhou
Tainan
Taipei
Taiping Rebellion
Taiwan—Political System
Thought Work—China
Three and Five Antis Campaigns
Tiananmen Square
Tianjin
Tibet
Tibetan Uprising
Wang Jingwei
White Terror
Wu Zetian
Xi'an
Xi'an Incident
Xinjiang
Yen, Y.C. James
Yuan Shikai
Yunnan
Zeng Guofan
Zhang Zhidong
Zhao Ziyang
Zhejiang
Zhou Enlai
Zhu De
Zhu Rongji
Zuo Zongtang

Government, Politics, and Law

Japan

Abe Iso
Aichi
Akita
Aomori
Araki Sadao
Aum Shinrikyo Scandal
Baba Tatsui
Buraku Liberation League
Chiba
Citizen's Movement
Constitution, Postwar—Japan
Constitutional Crisis of 1881
Democratic Socialist Party—Japan
Eda Saburo
Ehime
Enomoto Takeaki
Fukuda Hideko
Fukuda Takeo
Fukui
Fukumoto Kazuo
Fukuoka
Fukushima
Gifu
Goto Shinpei
Gumma
Hara Takashi
Hatoyama Ichiro
Higashikuni Naruhiko
Hirohito
Hiroshima
Hyogo
Ibaraki
Ichikawa Fusae
Ikeda Hayato
Ishihara Shintaro
Ishikawa
Iwate
Japan—Political System
Japan Communist Party
Japan Socialist Party
Kagawa
Kagoshima
Kanagawa
Kanno Suga
Kato Takaaki
Kishi Nobusuke
Kochi
Kodama Yoshio
Komeito
Konoe Fumimaro
Kumamoto
Kyoto
Liberal Democratic Party—Japan
Lockheed Scandal
Maruyama Masao
Mie
Minobe Tatsukichi
Miyagi
Miyazaki
Mori Arinori
Nagano
Nagasaki
Nakasone Yasuhiro
Nara
Niigata
Ogasawara
Oita
Okayama
Okinawa
Osaka
Recruit Scandal
Saga
Saionji Kinmochi
Saitama
Sapporo
Sasagawa Ryoichi
Sato Eisaku

EAST ASIA *(continued)*

Government, Politics, and Law *(continued)*

Japan (continued)

Sendai
Shiga
Shimane
Shipbuilding Scandal
Shizuoka
Showa Denko Scandal
Siemens Incident
Tanaka Giichi
Textbook Scandal
Tochigi
Tojo Hideki
Tokushima
Tokyo
Tottori
Toyama
Wakayama
Yamagata
Yamagata Aritomo
Yamaguchi
Yamamoto Isoroku
Yamanashi
Yoshida Shigeru
Yoshida Shoin

Koreas

April 19 Revolution—Korea
Chagang Province
Cheju Province
Ch'ongjin
Chun Doo Hwan
Communism—North Korea
Corruption—Korea
Democratization—South Korea
Haeju
Hamhung
Han Yong-un
Inchon
Juche
Kaesong
Kangwon Province
Kim Dae Jung
Kim Il Sung
Kim Jong Il
Kim Pu-shik
Kim Young-sam
Kim Yu-sin
Kwangju
Kwangju Uprising
Kyonggi Province
March First Independence Movement
Namp'o
North Cholla Province
North Ch'ungch'ong Province
North Hamgyong Province
North Hwanghae Province
North Korea—Political System
North Kyongsang Province
North P'yongan Province
Park Chung Hee
Pusan
Pyongyang
Rhee, Syngman
Roh Tae Woo
Sadaejuui
Sejong, King
Seoul
Sinuiju
South Cholla Province
South Ch'ungch'ong Province
South Hamgyong Province
South Hwanghae Province
South Korea—Political System
South Kyongsang Province
South P'yongan Province
Taegu
Taejon
Three Revolutions Movement
Ulchi Mundok
Wang Kon
Yanggang Province
Yi Ha-ung
Yi Song-gye
Yi T'ae-yong
Yu Kwan Sun
Yushin

Mongolia

Aimag
Batmonkh, Jambyn
Choybalsan, Horloogiyn
Chormaqan, Noyan
Darhan
Erdenet
Genghis Khan
Golden Horde
Gurragchaa, Jugderdemidiyn
Karakorum
Khubilai Khan
Mongolia—Political System
Mongolian Social Democratic Party
Narantsatsralt, Janlavyn
Ochirbat, Punsalmaagiyn
Sukhbaatar, Damdiny
Tsedenbel, Yumjaagiyn
Ulaanbaatar
United Party of Mongolia

History and Profile

East Asia

Paleoanthropology—East Asia

China

China—Profile
Han Dynasty
Hongcun and Xidi
Jurchen Jin Dynasty
Lijiang, Old Town of
Ming Dynasty
Pingyao, Ancient City of
Qin Dynasty
Qing Dynasty
Republican China
Shang Dynasty
Sixteen Kingdoms
Song Dynasty
Sui Dynasty
Taiwan—Profile
Taiwan, Modern
Tang Dynasty
Warring States Period—China
Yuan Dynasty
Zhou Dynasty

Japan

Choshu Expeditions
Heian Period
Heisei Period
Japan—Profile
Jomon Period
Kamakura Period
Meiji Period
Muromachi Period
Nara Period
Showa Period
Taisho Period
Tokugawa Period
Yayoi Period

Koreas

Choson Kingdom
Korea—History
Koryo Kingdom
North Korea—Profile
Parhae Kingdom
South Korea—Profile
Three Kingdoms Period
Unified Shilla Kingdom

Mongolia

Mongol Empire
Mongolia—History
Mongolia—Profile

International Relations

Chinese Influence in East Asia
United Front Strategy

China

Boxer Rebellion
Central Asia-China Relations
China—Human Rights
China-India Relations
China-Japan Peace and Friendship Treaty
China-Japan Relations
China-Korea Relations
China-Russia Relations
China-Taiwan Relations
China-United States Relations
China-Vietnam Relations
Chinese Influence in East Asia
Chinese Influence in Southeast Asia
Hart, Robert
Japan-Taiwan Relations
Mongolia-China-Russia Relations
Nanjing Massacre
Open Door Policy
Opium War
Sino-French War
Spratly Islands Dispute
Taiwan—Human Rights
Taiwan-United States Relations
Tibet—Image in the Modern West

Japan

China-Japan Peace and Friendship Treaty
China-Japan Relations
Comfort Women
Japan—Human Rights
Japan-Africa Relations
Japan-France Relations
Japan-Germany Relations
Japan-Korea Relations
Japan-Latin America Relations
Japan-Pacific Islands Relations
Japan-Philippines Relations
Japan-Russia Relations
Japan-Taiwan Relations
Japan–United Kingdom Relations
Japan–United States Relations
Japanese Expansion
Nixon Shock
Northern Territories
Nuclear Allergy
Plaza Accord
Russo-Japanese War
San Francisco Peace Treaty
Sino-Japanese Conflict, Second
Sino-Japanese War
Status of Forces Agreement
United States Military Bases—Japan
United States-Japan Security Treaty
Yasukuni Shrine Controversy

EAST ASIA *(continued)*

History and Profile *(continued)*

Koreas

China-Korea Relations
Japan-Korea Relations
Korea-Japan Treaty of 1965
Korean War
North Korea—Human Rights
North Korea-South Korea Relations
North Korea-United States Relations
South Korea—Human Rights
South Korea-European Union Relations
South Korea-United States Relations

Mongolia

Mongolia—Human Rights
Mongolia-China-Russia Relations
Mongolia-Soviet Union Relations
Polo, Marco

Language and Communication

China

Chinese, Classical
Dai Qing
Hakka Languages
Mandarin
Media—China
Min
Romanization Systems, Chinese
Sino-Tibetan Languages
Wu
Xiang
Yue

Japan

Feminine Language
Japanese Language
Matsumoto Shigeharu
Media—Japan

Koreas

Hangul Script
Korean Language
Media—South Korea
Romanization Systems, Korean

Mongolia

Khalkha
Mongolian Languages
Tungus Languages

Peoples, Cultures, and Society

Marriage and Family—East Asia
Westernization—East Asia

China

Aboriginal Peoples—Taiwan
China—Internal Migration
China—Population Resettlement
Chinese, Overseas
Clothing, Traditional—China
Clothing, Traditional—Hong Kong
Clothing, Traditional—Taiwan
Clothing, Traditional—Tibet
Courtyards
Foot Binding
Guanxi
Hakka
Han
Hmong
Hui
Manchu
Marriage and Family—China
Miao—China
Moso
Muslim Peoples in China
National Minorities—China
Qingke
Single-Child Phenomenon—China
Social Associations—China
Social Stratification—China
Tibetans
Tujia
Uighurs
Women in China
Yao
Yi
Zhuang

Japan

Aging Population—Japan
Ainu
Burakumin
Chinese in Japan
Clothing, Traditional—Japan
Ijime
Koreans in Japan
Social Relations—Japan
Women in Japan

Koreas

Ch'onmin
Clothing, Traditional—Korea
Koreans
Koreans, Overseas
Kye
Nobi
Women in Korea
Yangban

Mongolia

Clothing, Traditional—Mongolia
Mongols
Russians in Mongolia

Religion and Philosophy

Ancestor Worship—East Asia
Zodiac System—East Asia

China
Analects
Atheism, Official—China
Buddhism—China
Buddhism, Chan
Buddhism—Tibet
Buddhism, Pure Land
Bureau of Religious Affairs
Christianity—China
Confucian Ethics
Confucianism—China
Confucius
Cult of Maitreya
Dalai Lama
Falun Gong
Feng Shui
Five Phases
Four Books
Judaism—China
Laozi
Marxism-Leninism-Mao Zedong Thought
Mencius
Mozi
Neo-Confucianism
Potala Palace
Religion, Folk—China
Ricci, Matteo
Taoism
Xunzi
Zhu Xi
Japan
Atsuta Shrine
Buddhism—Japan
Christianity—Japan
Confucianism—Japan
Hayashi Razan
Honen
Ikkyu
Ise Shrine
Iwashimizu Hachiman Shrine
Izumo Shrine
Kukai
Motoori Norinaga
Nichiren
Nishida Kitaro
Religion, Folk—Japan
Religions, New—Japan
Saicho
Shinran
Shinto
Suzuki Daisetsu Teitaro
Twenty-Six Martyrs
Uchimura Kanzo
Yamato Damashii
Yasukuni Shrine
Koreas
Buddhism—Korea
Ch'ondogyo
Christianity—Korea
Confucianism—Korea
Religions, New—Korea
Seshi Customs
Taejonggyo
Tan'gun Myth
Taoism—Korea
Tonghak
Unification Church
Yi I
Mongolia
Bogdo Khan
Buddhism—Mongolia
Gandan Lamasery
Islam—Mongolia
Shamanism—Mongolia
Science, Technology, and Health
Calendars—East Asia
China
Abacus
Acupuncture
Dujiangyan
Grand Canal
Great Wall
Gunpowder and Rocketry
Junk
Li Shizhen
Magnetism
Massage—China
Medicine, Traditional—China
Moxibustion
Needham, Joseph
Printing and Papermaking
Science, Traditional—China
Sericulture—China
Three Gorges Dam Project
Xu Guangqi
Koreas
Science Towns—Korea

SOUTH ASIA
Arts, Literature, and Recreation
Chitra/Ardhachitra/Chitrabhasha
Conveyance Arts
Cricket
Cuisine—South Asia
Drama—South Asia
Farid, Khwaja Ghulam
Indigo
Islam, Kazi Nazrul

SOUTH ASIA *(continued)*

Arts, Literature, and Recreation *(continued)*

Jatra
Kama Sutra
Kipling, Joseph Rudyard
Literature, Bengali
Literature, Sanskrit
Literature, Tamil
Mahabharata
Manto, Sadaat Hasan
Nur Jehan
Painting—South Asia
Persian Miniature Painting
Raga
Ramayana
Rubab
Sarangi
Sarod
Sculpture—South Asia
Shah, Lalon
Shehnai
Veena

Bangladesh

Dance—Bangladesh
Music—Bangladesh

Bhutan

Textiles—Bhutan

India

Anand, Mulk Raj
Architecture—India
Bachchan, Amitabh
Chatterjee, Bankim Chandra
Chaudhuri, Nirad Chandra
Chughtai, Ismat
Cinema—India
Dance—India
Diwali
Drama—India
Forster, E. M.
Ghalib, Mirza Asadullah Khan
Holi
Kalidasa
Khan, Vilayat
Khusrau, Amir
Kumar, Dilip
Literature—India
Mangeshkar, Lata
Music—India
Music, Devotional—India
Narayan, R.K.
Nataka
Poetry—India
Prakarana
Premchand
Rahman, A.R.
Rao, Raja
Rasa
Ray, Satyajit
Sports—India
Taj Mahal

Sri Lanka

Coomaraswamy, Ananda Kentish
Dance, Kandyan
Literature, Sinhalese

Economics, Commerce, and Transportation

Agriculture—South Asia
British East India Company
French East India Company
Hawkins, William
Nomadic Pastoralism—South Asia
Tea—South Asia

Bangladesh

Bangladesh—Economic System
Grameen Bank

India

Agriculture—South Asia
British East India Company
French East India Company
Hawkins, William
India—Economic System
Nomadic Pastoralism—South Asia
Remittances
Salt Tax
Tea—South Asia

Nepal

Nepal—Economic System

Sri Lanka

Sri Lanka—Economic System

Education

Panini
Sayyid, Ahmad Khan

Bangladesh

Bangladesh—Education System

India

India—Education System

Nepal

Nepal—Education System

Sri Lanka

Sri Lanka—Education System

Geography and the Natural World

Andaman Sea
Bay of Bengal
Bramaputra River
Bustard, Hubara
Chagos Archipelago
Elephant, Asian
Green Revolution—South Asia
Himalaya Range

Indian Ocean
Indian Subcontinent
Indo-Gangetic Plain
Jhelum River
Jute
K2, Mount
Kangchenjunga, Mount
Kaveri River
Kistna River
Mongoose
Punjab
Reunion Island
Sundarbhans
Tarai

India

Abu, Mount
Andaman and Nicobar Islands
Bhopal
Chenab River
Dekkan
Eastern Ghats
Ganges River
Godavari River
Hindu Kush
Jumna River
Lion, Asiatic
Mahanadi River
Narmada Dam Controversy
Narmada River
Rann of Kachchh
Satpura Range
Sutlej River
Thar Desert
Tungabhadra River
Vindhya Mountains
Western Ghats
Zebu

Nepal

Everest, Mount
Kathmandu Valley

Government, Politics, and Law

Bahadur Shah
Birla Family
Colombo Plan
Hastings, Warren
Humayun
Ibn al-Qasim, Muhammad
Jahangir
Marxism—South Asia
Poros
Raziya
Roy, Rammohan
Shah Jahan
Singh, Jai
Tata Family
Tipu Sultan

Bangladesh

Awami League
Bangladesh—Political System
Bangladesh Nationalist Party
Chittagong
Dhaka
Ershad, H.M.
Hasina Wajid, Sheikh
Jatiya Party
Rahman, Mujibur
Rahman, Ziaur
Zia, Khaleda

Bhutan

Thimphu
Wangchuck, King Jigme Singye

India

Afzal Khan
Agartala
Agra
Ahmadabad
Ajanta
Ajodhya
Akbar
Ali Janhar, Mohamed
Allahabad
Ambedkar, B.R.
Amritsar
Andhra Pradesh
Arunachal Pradesh
Asoka
Assam
Aurangabad
Aurangzeb
Awadh
Azad, Abu'l-Kalam
Babur
Bangalore
Bengal, West
Bentinck, William Cavendish
Bhosle, Shivaji
Bhubaneshwar
Bihar
Bodh Gaya
Bose, Subhas Chandra
Calcutta
Calicut
Canning, Charles John
Chandigarh
Chhattisgarh
Coimbatore
Constitution—India

SOUTH ASIA *(continued)*

Government, Politics, and Law *(continued)*

India (continued)

Cranganur
Curzon, George Nathaniel
Dadra and Nagar Haveli Union Territory
Daman and Diu Union Territory
Darjeeling
Dehra Dun
Delhi Union Territory
Devi, Phoolan
Fazl, Abu'l
Gandhi, Indira
Gandhi, Mohandas K.
Gangtok
Goa
Godse, Nathuram Vinayak
Gujarat
Guwahati
Haidar, Ali Khan
Harsa
Haryana
Himachal Pradesh
Hindu Law
Hindu Nationalism
Hyderabad
Imphal
India—Political System
Indore
Jaipur
Jammu and Kashmir
Jharkhand
Jodhpur
Kanpur
Karnataka
Kautilya
Kerala
Khilafat Movement
Kohima
Ladakh
Lakshadweep
Laxmibai
Leh
Lucknow
Macaulay, Thomas B.
Madhya Pradesh
Madras
Madurai
Maharashtra
Mangalore
Manipur
Mathura
Meghalaya
Mizoram
Montagu-Chelmsford Reforms
Morley-Minto Reforms
Mumbai
Muslim League
Mysore
Nagaland
Nehru, Jawaharlal
Nehru, Motilal
Nilgiri District
Ootacamund
Orissa
Patna
Pondicherry
Pune
Puri
Raipur
Rajagopalachari, Chakravarti
Rajasthan
Rajkot
Ramachandran, Marudur Gopalamenon
Sarnath
Satyagraha
Shillong
Sikkim
Simla
Sindhia Family
Srinagar
Tamil Nadu
Thanjavur
Tripura
Trivandrum
Uttar Pradesh
Uttaranchal
Varanasi
Vishakapatnam

Nepal

Kathmandu
Nepal—Political System
Rana

Sri Lanka

Bandaranaike, Sirimavo Ratwatte Dias
Bandaranaike, Solomon West Ridgeway Diaz
Colombo
Jaffna
Kandy
Polonnaruva
Sri Lanka—Political System
Trincomalee

History and Profile

British Indian Empire
Chera
Chola
Dogra Dynasty
Gupta Empire

SOUTH ASIA *(continued)*

Religion and Philosophy *(continued)*

Islam—South Asia
Jones, William
Judaism—South Asia
Khwaja Mu'in al-Din Chishti
Nurbakhshiya
Pilgrimage—South Asia
Sankara
Siddhartha Gautama
Sufism—South Asia
Vivekananda, Swami
Wali Allah, Shah

Bhutan

Bhutan—Religion

India

Blavatsky, Helena Petrovna
Bhakti
Dev, Nanak Guru
Hindu Philosophy
Hindu Values
Hinduism—India
Jainism
Jesuits— India
Lingayat
Nagarjuna
Nizam ad-din Awliya
Possession
Ramakrishna
Ramanuja
Sai Baba, Satya
Sikhism
Tagore, Rabindranath
Teresa, Mother
Upanishads

Science,Technology, and Health

Calendars—South Asia
Climatology—South Asia

India

Medicine, Ayurvedic
Medicine, Unani

SOUTHEAST ASIA

Arts, Literature, and Recreation

Architecture—Southeast Asia
Batik
Cockfighting
Drama—Southeast Asia
Hari Raya Puasa
Kain Batik
Kain Songket
Mendu
Sepak Takraw
Thaipusam

Cambodia

Angkor Wat
Literature, Khmer

Indonesia

Arja
Bali Barong-Rangda
Balinese Sanghyang
Bedaya
Borobudur
Cuisine—Indonesia
Dance—Bali
Gambang Kromong
Gambuh
Gamelan
Hikayat Amir Hamza
Ludruk
Masks, Javanese
Music—Indonesia
Noer, Arifin C.
Pramoedya Ananta Toer
Puisi
Randai
Rendra, W.S.
Riantiarno, Nano
Sandiwara
Wayang Beber
Wayang Golek
Wayang Kulit
Wayang Topeng
Wayang Wong
Wijaya, Putu

Laos

Ikat Dyeing
Luang Prabang
Music, Folk—Laos
Palm-Leaf Manuscripts
Textiles—Laos
That Luang Festival
Wat Xieng Khouan

Malaysia

Bangsawan
Chang Fee Ming
Chuah Thean Teng
Cuisine—Malaysia
Dance—Malaysia
Dikir Barat
Gawai Dayak
Jikey
Jit, Krishen
Labu Sayong
Lim, Shirley
Mak Yong
Maniam, K.S.
Manora

Pesta Menuai
Petronas Towers
Songket
Tarian Asyik
Tarian Portugis
Tay Hooi Keat

Myanmar

Burmese Arts
Literature—Myanmar
Mandalay Palace
Pagodas, Burmese

Philippines

Arnis
Bagonbanta, Fernando
Balisong
Baltazar, Francisco
Bulosan, Carlos
Cuisine—Philippines
Guerrero, Fernando M.
Literature—Philippines
Luna Y Novicio, Juan
Poetry—Philippines

Thailand

Bidyalankarana
Cuisine—Thailand
Damkoeng, Akat
Dokmai Sot
Drama—Thailand
Emerald Buddha
Fish Fighting
Khun Chang, Khun Phaen
Literature—Thailand
Longboat Racing
Muay Thai
Nirat
Phumisak, Chit
Ramakien
Siburapha
Sot Kuramarohit

Vietnam

Ao Dai
Cuisine—Vietnam
Dai Viet Su Ky
Doan Thi Diem
Ho Xuan Huong
Hoang Ngoc Phach
Hoat, Doan Viet
Khai Hung
Linh Nhat
Literature—Vietnam
Nguyen Du
Nguyen Thieu Gia
Opera—Vietnam
Plowing Ritual—Vietnam
Poetry—Vietnam
Puppetry, Water
Tet
Tran Do
Truong Vinh Ky
Tu Luc Van Doan
Wandering Souls

Economics, Commerce, and Transportation

Agriculture—Southeast Asia
Burma-Thailand Railway
Fishing Industry—Southeast Asia
Forest Industry—Southeast Asia
Golden Triangle
Ho Chi Minh Trail
Rubber Industry

Cambodia

Cambodia—Economic System

Indonesia

Indonesia—Economic System
Manufacturing Industry—Indonesia
Repelita

Laos

Chintanakan mai
Laos—Economic System
Mittaphap Bridge

Malaysia

Malaysia—Economic System
Manufacturing Industry—Malaysia
Mineral Industry—Malaysia
New Economic Policy—Malaysia
Rubber Industry—Malaysia
Timber Industry—Malaysia

Myanmar

Burma Road
Myanmar—Economic System

Philippines

Manufacturing Industry—Philippines
Pan-Philippine Highway
Philippines—Economic System
Suki

Singapore

Banking and Finance Industry—Singapore
Singapore—Economic System

Thailand

Thailand—Economic System
Thompson, Jim

Vietnam

Doi Moi
Ho Chi Minh Trail
Mekong Project
New Economic Zones
Vietnam—Economic System

SOUTHEAST ASIA *(continued)*
Education
Brunei
Universiti Brunei Darussalam
Cambodia
Cambodia—Education System
Royal University of Phnom Penh
Indonesia
Bandung Institute of Technology
Gadjah Mada University
Indonesia—Education System
University of Indonesia
Laos
Laos—Education System
Sisavangvong University
Malaysia
Malaysia—Education System
Universiti Sains Malaysia
University of Malaya
Myanmar
Myanmar—Education System
Philippines
Philippines—Education System
Singapore
Nanyang Technological University
National University of Singapore
Singapore—Education System
Thailand
Chulalongkorn University
Thailand—Education System
Vietnam
Vietnam—Education System
Geography and the Natural World
Andaman Sea
Banteng
Borneo
Dangrek Range
Green Revolution—Southeast Asia
Leopard, Clouded
Mongoose
Orangutan
Sun Bear
Cambodia
Cardamon Mountains
Elephant Range
Kompong Som Bay
Tonle Sap
Indonesia
Babirusa
Bali
Banda Sea
Flores Sea
Java Sea
Komodo Dragon
Maluku
Nusa Tenggara
Timor Sea
Laos
Bolovens Plateau
Plain of Jars
Malaysia
Cameron Highlands
Kinabalu, Mount
Strait of Malacca
Myanmar
Arakan Yoma Mountains
Inle Lake Region
Irrawaddy River and Delta
Salween River
Sittang River
Philippines
Agno River
Cagayan River
Caraballo Mountains
Celebes Sea
Cordillera Central
Luzon Group
Maguey
Mindanao
Philippine Sea
Sierra Madre
Sulu Archipelago
Visayan Islands
Zambales Mountains
Thailand
Chao Phraya River and Delta
Doi Inthanon
Gulf of Thailand
Khon Kaen
Nakhon Ratchasima
Peninsular Thailand
Three Pagodas Pass
Vietnam
Cam Ranh Bay
Central Highlands of Vietnam
Con Dao Islands
Ha Long Bay
Ho Dynasty Citadel
Hoan Kiem Lake
Karun River and Shatt al Arab River
Mekong River and Delta
Red River and Delta
Tonkin Gulf
Government, Politics, and Law
Albuquerque, Afonso de
British Military Administration
Doumer, Paul
Dutch East India Company

Romusha
Weld, Frederick

Brunei

Azahari, A.M.
Bandar Seri Begawan
Brooke, James
Hassanal Bolkaih
Parti Rakyat Brunei

Cambodia

Buddhist Liberal Democratic Party—Cambodia
Cambodia—Civil War of 1970-1975
Cambodia—Political System
Cambodian People's Party
Fa Ngoum
FUNCINPEC
Heng Samrin
Hun Sen
Jayavarman II
Jayavarman VII
Khieu Samphan
Khmer Rouge
Killing Fields
Lon Nol
Phnom Penh
Phnom Penh Evacuation
Pol Pot
Ranariddh, Norodom
Sam Rainsy
Sihanouk, Norodom

East Timor

Belo, Bishop Carlos
Dili
Dili Massacre
Fretilin
Gusmao, Xanana
Ramos-Horta, José

Indonesia

Airlangga
Amboina Massacre
Bandung
Batavia
Bosch, Johannes van den
Budi Utomo
Coen, Jan Pieterszoon
Cukong
Daendels, Herman
Darul Islam
Ethnic Colonial Policy—Indonesia
Gajah Mada
Gerindo
Gestapu Affair
Golkar
Habibie, B.J.
Hamengku Buwono IX, Sri Sultan
Hatta, Mohammad
Hizbullah
Indonesia—Political Parties
Indonesia—Political System
Indonesian Democratic Party
Indonesian Revolution
Irian Jaya
Jakarta
Jakarta Riots of May 1998
Java
Kalimantan
Malik, Adam
Medan
Megawati Sukarnoputri
Military, Indonesia
Moerdani, Leonardus Benjamin
New Order
Old Order
Pancasila
Partai Kebangkitan Bangsa
Partai Persatuan Pembangunan
Rais, Muhammad Amien
Sarekat Islam
Solo
Speelman, Cornelius
Suharto
Sukarno
Sulawesi
Sumatra
Surabaya
Taman Siswa
Treaty of Giyanti
Umar, Teuku
Wahid, Abdurrahman
Yogyakarta

Laos

Bokeo
Chao Anou
Civil War of 1956–1975—Laos
Kaysone Phomvihan
Lao People's Revolutionary Party
Laos—Political System
Louangnamtha
Pathet Lao
Setthathirat
Souphanuvong, Prince
Souvanna Phouma, Prince
Vientiane
Xayabury

Malaysia

Abdul Razak
Abu Bakar
Anwar, Ibrahim
Badawi, Abdullah Ahmed

SOUTHEAST ASIA *(continued)*
Government, Politics, and Law *(continued)*
Malaysia (continued)
Bendahara
Birch, James W. W.
Bumiputra
Clifford, Hugh
Federal Territories—Malaysia
Federation of Malaysia
Haji, Raja
Hussein Onn
Iskandar Muda
Johor
Kapitan Cina
Kedah
Kelantan
Kota Kinabalu
Kuala Lumpur
Kuching
Laksamana
Light, Francis
Lim Chong Eu
Mahathir Mohamad
Mahmud Shah
Malay States, Unfederated
Malayan People's Anti-Japanese Army
Malayan Union
Malaysia—Political System
Malaysian Chinese Association
Mansur Shah
Mat Salleh Rebellion
May 13 Ethnic Riots— Malaysia
Melaka
Negeri Sembilan
Ningkan, Stephen Kalong
Onn Bin Jaafar
Pahang
Pangkor Treaty
Penang
Perak
Perlis
Raffles, Thomas Stamford
Resident System
Rukunegara
Sabah
Sarawak
Straits Settlements
Swettenham, Frank
Tan Siew Sin
Temenggong
Templer, Gerald
Trengganu
Wan Ahmad
Yap Ah Loy

Myanmar
All Burma Students Democratic Front
Anawratha
Anti-Fascist People's Freedom League—Myanmar
Aung San
Aung San Suu Kyi
Bassein
Burma Independence Army
Chin State
Communist Party of Burma
Irrawaddy Division
Kachin Independence Organization
Kachin State
Karen National Union
Karen State
Kayah State
Magwe Division
Mandalay
Mandalay Division
Mon State
Mong Tai Army
Moulmein
Myanmar—Political System
National League for Democracy—Myanmar
National Unity Party—Myanmar
Ne Win, U
Nu, U
Palaung State Liberation Party
Pao National Organization
Pegu
Rakhine State
Sagaing Division
Shan State
Shan State Army
State Law and Order Restoration Council—Myanmar
Tenasserim Division
Thakins
Than Shwe
Thant, U
Union Solidarity and Development Association—Mya
United Wa State Party
Yangon
Yangon Division

Philippines
Aquino, Benigno
Aquino, Corazon
Autonomous Region of Muslim Mindanao
Baguio
Cebu
Davao
Estrada, Joseph
Garcia, Carlos P.

Huk Rebellion
Macapagal, Diosdado
MacArthur, Douglas
Magsaysay, Ramon
Manila
Marcos, Ferdinand
Marcos, Imelda
Moro Islamic Liberation Front
Moro National Liberation Front
Nur Misuari
People Power Movement
Philippines—Political System
Ramos, Fidel
Rizal, José
Romulo, Carlos Peña
Urdaneta, Andres de
Zamboanga

Singapore

Barisan Sosialis
Goh Chok Tong
Goh Keng Swee
Jeyaretnam, Joshua Benjamin
Lee Kuan Yew
Lim Chin Siong
Marshall, David
Singapore—Political System
Singapore Democratic Party
Workers' Party—Singapore

Thailand

Anand Panyarachun
Bangkok
Bhumipol Adulyadej
Chart Thai
Chavalit, Yongchaiyudh
Chiang Mai
Chuan Leekpai
Chulalongkorn, King
Ekaphap
Manhattan Incident
Mongkut
National Peacekeeping Council—Thailand
Nation-Religion-Monarch
October 6 Crisis—Thailand
Phalang Dharma Party
Phuket
Phya Taksin
Pibul Songgram
Pridi Banomyong
Rama Khamheng
Rama Tibodi I
Sarit Thanarat
Student Uprising of 1973—Thailand
Sulak Sivaraksa
Thai Revolution of 1932
Thailand—Political Parties
Thailand—Political System
Thaksin Shinawatra
Thanom Kittikachorn
Trailok
Ungphakorn Puey

Vietnam

An Duong Vuong
Anh Dao Duy
Army of the Republic of Vietnam
August Revolution
Ba Trieu
Bac Son Uprising
Bao Dai
Co Loa Thanh
Communism—Vietnam
Da Nang
Dalat
Duong Van Minh
Haiphong
Hanoi
Ho Chi Minh
Ho Chi Minh City
Ho Tung Mau
Hoi An
Hue
Huynh Tan Phat
Iron Triangle
Lac Long Quan
Le Duan
Le Duc Anh
Le Duc Tho
National Front for the Liberation of South Vietnam
Ngo Dinh Diem
Ngo Dinh Nhu
Nguyen Cao Ky
Nguyen Thi Minh Khai
Nguyen Van Thieu
Nhu, Madame Ngo Dinh
People's Army of Vietnam
Phan Boi Chau
Phieu Le Kha
Revolt of the Short Hair
Revolutionary Youth League of Vietnam
Tay Son Rebellion
Tran Van Giau
Trung Sisters
Vietnam—Political System
Vietnam Communist Party
Vo Nguyen Giap
Vo Van Kiet

History and Profile

British in Southeast Asia
Dutch in Southeast Asia

SOUTHEAST ASIA *(continued)*

History and Profile *(continued)*

Paleoanthropology—Southeast Asia
Portuguese in Southeast Asia
Srivijaya

Brunei

Brunei—Political System
Brunei—Profile

Cambodia

Cambodia—History
Cambodia—Profile
Khmer Empire

East Timor

East Timor—Profile

Indonesia

Aceh Rebellion
Amangkurat
British-Dutch Wars
Candi of Java
Indonesia—History
Indonesia—Profile
Java War
Konfrontasi
Majapahit
Mataram
Netherlands East Indies
Padri War
Pakualaman
Sailendra

Laos

Laos—History
Laos—Profile

Malaysia

Anglo-Dutch Treaty
Federated Malay States
Malaysia—History
Malaysia—Profile
Melaka Sultanate
White Rajas

Myanmar

Myanmar—History
Myanmar—Profile
Pagan

Philippines

Philippines—History
Philippines—Profile

Singapore

Singapore—History
Singapore—Profile

Thailand

Ayutthaya, Kingdom of
Ban Chiang
Sukhothai
Thailand—History
Thailand—Profile

Vietnam

Vietnam—History
Vietnam—Profile

International Relations

Association of South-East Asian Nations
Bali Summit
Bandung Conference
Bangkok Declaration
Chinese Influence in Southeast Asia
Five Power Defence Arrangements
India-Southeast Asia Relations
Indochina War of 1940–1941
Piracy—Southeast Asia
Southeast Asia—Human Rights
Southeast Asia Treaty Organization
Treaty of Amity and Co-operation of 1976
ZOPFAN

Cambodia

Cambodia-Laos Relations
Cambodia-Vietnam Relations
United Nations Transitional Authority in Cambodia

East Timor

United Nations in East Timor

Indonesia

Indonesia-Malaysia Relations
Indonesia–United States Relations
Irian Jaya Conquest
Volksraad

Laos

Cambodia-Laos Relations
Laos-Thailand Relations
Laos-Vietnam Relations

Malaysia

Indonesia-Malaysia Relations
Malayan Emergency
Malaysia-Europe Relations
Sabah Dispute

Myanmar

India-Myanmar Relations
Myanmar—Foreign Relations
Myanmar—Human Rights

Philippines

Japan-Philippines Relations
Philippines—Human Rights
Philippines–United States Relations

Thailand

Laos-Thailand Relations

Vietnam

Cambodia-Vietnam Relations
China-Vietnam Relations
Franco-Viet Minh War
Laos-Vietnam Relations
Soviet-Vietnamese TFOC

SOUTHEAST ASIA *(continued)*
Religion and Philosophy *(continued)*
Malaysia
Angkatan Belia Islam Malaysia
Islam—Malaysia
Myanmar
Christianity—Myanmar
Islam—Myanmar
Spirit Cults
Philippines
Catholicism, Roman—Philippines
Iglesia ni Christo
Islam—Philippines
Philippine Independent Church
Ruiz, Saint Lorenzo
Sin, Jaime
Thailand
Buddhadasa, Bhikku
Dhammayut Sect
Hinduism—Thailand
Phra Pathom Chedi
Vietnam
Buddhism—Vietnam
Cao Dai
Catholicism, Roman—Vietnam
Hoa Hao
Thich Nhat Hanh
Science,Technology, and Health
Bedil
Calendars—Southeast Asia
Gunpowder and Rocketry

SOUTHWEST ASIA
Arts, Literature, and Recreation
Alghoza
Bhitai, Shah Abdul Latif
Jami, 'Abdurrahman
Khushal Khan Khatak
Shah, Waris
Afghanistan
Cuisine—Afghanistan
Pakistan
Ali Khan, Bade Ghulam
Bhit Shah
Faiz Ahmed Faiz
Gulgee
Hir Ranjha Story
Iqbal, Muhammad
Makli Hill
Naqsh, Jamil
Nusrat Fateh Ali Khan
Sabri Brothers
Sadequain

Economics, Commerce, and Transportation
Afghanistan
Afghanistan—Economic System
Pakistan
Karakoram Highway
Pakistan—Economic System
Education
Pakistan
Pakistan—Education System
Geography and the Natural World
Badakhshan
Kabul River
Karakoram Mountains
Khyber Pass
Ravi River
Afghanistan
Afghan Hound
Dasht-e Margo
Hunza
Wakhan
Pakistan
Azad Kashmir
Baltistan
Bolan Pass
Indus River
Indus River Dolphin
Khunjerab Pass
Sutlej River
Government, Politics, and Law
Afghani, Jamal ad-din
Baluchistan
Dost Muhammad
Taxila
Afghanistan
Afghanistan—Political System
Amanollah
Bagram
Bamian
Bin Laden, Osama
Daud, Muhammad
Dawai, Abdul Hadi
Din Mohammad, Mushk-e Alam
Ghazna
Herat
Kabul
Mahmud of Ghazna
Mazar-e Sharif
Mujahideen
Omar, Mullah Muhammad
Taliban
Zahir Shah
Pakistan
Abdullah, Muhammad
Anarkali

Ayub Khan
Bhutto, Benazir
Bhutto, Zulfiqar Ali
David, Collin
Hadood
Islamabad
Jama'at-e-Islami
Jinnah, Mohammed Ali
Karachi
Khan, Abdul Ghaffar
Lahore
Mohenjo Daro
Muhajir Qawmi Movement
Multan
Musharraf, Pervez
North-West Frontier Province Sarhad
Pakistan—Political System
Pakistan People's Party
Peshawar
Rahmat Ali, Chauduri
Rohtas Fort
Sehwan
Sind
Zia-ul-Haq, Mohammad

History and Profile

Afghanistan

Afghanistan—History
Afghanistan—Profile
Durrani

Pakistan

Federally Administered Tribal Areas—Pakistan
Pakistan—History
Pakistan—Profile

International Relations

Afghanistan

Afghanistan—Human Rights
Treaty of Gandomak

Pakistan

Bangladesh-Pakistan Relations
India-Pakistan Relations
Pakistan—Human Rights

Language and Communication

Pashto

Afghanistan

Dari

Peoples, Cultures, and Society

Afridi
Baluchi
Brahui
Pashtun
Pashtunwali
Waziri
Clothing, Traditional—Afghanistan
Ethnic Conflict—Afghanistan
Hazara

Pakistan

Sindhi
Siraiki
Women in Pakistan

Religion and Philosophy

Bakhsh, Data Ganj
Islam—Southwest Asia
Shah, Mihr Ali
Shahbaz Qalandar Lal
Sufism—Southwest Asia

Afghanistan

Ansari, Abdullah
Bitab, Sufi

Pakistan

Mawdudi, Abu'l-A'la
Muhajir

WEST ASIA

Arts, Literature, and Recreation

Architecture—West Asia
Architecture, Islamic—West Asia
Cinema—West Asia
Music—West Asia
Rudaki
Shahnameh Epic
Sports—Islamic Asia
Twelver Shi'ism

Iran

Cuisine—Iran
No-ruz
Literature, Persian

Iraq

Cuisine—Iraq
Poetry—Iraq

Turkey

Children's Day—Turkey
Cuisine—Turkey
Guney, Yilmaz
Literature—Turkey
Music—Turkey
Nesin, Aziz
Pamuk, Orhan

Economics, Commerce, and Transportation

Agriculture—West Asia
Industry—West Asia
Oil Industry—West Asia
Organization of Petroleum Exporting Countries

Iran

Iran—Economic System

Iraq

Iraq—Economic System

Turkey

Etatism—Turkey

WEST ASIA *(continued)*

Economics, Commerce, and Transportation *(continued)*

Turkey—Economic System

Education

Iran

Iran—Education System

Iraq

Iraq—Education System

Turkey

Turkey—Education System

Geography and the Natural World

Caucasia
Euphrates River
Sistan
Tigris River

Iran

Abkhazia
Amu Dar'ya
Dagestan
Elburz
Gulf of Oman
Persian Gulf
Zagros Mountains

Turkey

Aegean Sea
Anti-Taurus
Ararat, Mount
Black Sea
Bosporus
Cappadocia
Cilician Gates
Dardanelles
Gaziantep
Izmir
Kizel Irmak River
Marmara, Sea of
Tarsus
Taurus Mountains
Yesilirmak River

Government, Politics, and Law

Aleppo
Karabag
Yerevan

Iran

Abadan
Ardabil
Azerbaijan
Bakhtaran
Bandar Abbas
Bazargan, Mehdi
Constitution, Islamic—Iran
Esfahan
Fars
Hamadan
Iran—Political System
Islamic Revolution—Iran
Kandahar
Kerman
Khomeini, Ayatollah
Khurasan
Khuzestan
Mashhad
Qom
Sana'i
Shariati, Ali
Shiraz
Tabriz
Tehran
Veleyet-e Faqih

Iraq

Al-Najaf
Baghdad
Basra
Hussein, Saddam
Iraq—Political System
Karbala
Kirkuk
Mosul
Sulaymaniya

Turkey

Adalet Partisi
Adana
Afyon
Amasya
Anatolia
Ankara
Antakya
Antalya
Ataturk
Bayar, Mahmut Celal
Bodrum
Bursa
Constitution—Turkey
Demirel, Suleyman
Democrat Party—Turkey
Diyarbakir
Edirne
Erzurum
Halide Edib Adivar
Hikmet, Nazim
Inonu, Mustafa Ismet
Istanbul
Iznik
Kars
Kas
Kemal, Yasar
Konya

Kutahya
Menderes, Adnan
Mersin
North Cyprus, Turkish Republic of
Ozal, Turgut
Pergamon
Refah and Fazilet Parties
Republican People's Party—Turkey
Rize
Samsun
Sardis
Sinop
Sivas
Tanzimat
Trabzon
Turkey—Political System
Urfa
Van
Zonguldak

History and Profile

Iran

Iran—History
Iran—Profile
Pahlavi Dynasty
Qajar Dynasty

Iraq

Iraq—History
Iraq—Profile

Turkey

Archaeology—Turkey
Byzantines
Hittites
Ottoman Empire
Turkey—Profile
Turkey, Republic of

International Relations

Ibn Battutah

Iran

Iran—Human Rights
Iran-Iraq Relations
Iran-Russia Relations
Iran–United States Hostage Crisis
Iran–United States Relations

Iraq

Iran-Iraq Relations
Iraq—Human Rights
Iraq-Turkey Relations
Persian Gulf War

Turkey

European Union and Turkey
Iraq-Turkey Relations
North Atlantic Treaty Organization and Turkey
Turkey—Human Rights
Turkey-Russia Relations
Turkey–United States Relations

Language and Communication

Arabic
Media—West Asia
Persian

Peoples, Cultures, and Society

Arabs
Armenians
Kurds
Marriage and Family—West Asia
Turks—West Asia
Westernization—West Asia
Women in West Asia

Iran

Azerbaijanis
Bakhtiari
Persepolis
Persians

Iraq

Clothing, Traditional—Iraq
Marsh Arabs

Turkey

Albanians
Bulgarians
Circassians
Clothing, Traditional—Turkey
Greeks in Turkey
Miletus
Tatars

Religion and Philosophy

Alevi Muslims
Baha'i
Islam—West Asia
Judaism—West Asia
Muslims, Shi'ite
Muslims, Sunni
Oriental Orthodox Church
Qadiriya
Saint Paul

Iran

Babism

Turkey

Eastern Orthodox Church

Science, Technology, and Health

Calendars—West Asia
Kariz Irrigation System
Medicine, Traditional—West Asia

Encyclopedia of Modern Asia

CHINA–INDIA RELATIONS As ancient civilizations, China and India coexisted in peace and harmony for millennia. However, as postcolonial modern nation-states, with the exception of a very short period of bonhomie in the early 1950s, relations between the two Asian giants have been marked by conflict, containment, mutual suspicion, distrust, and rivalry. Just as the Indian subcontinental plate has a tendency to constantly rub and push against the Eurasian tectonic plate, causing friction and volatility in the entire Himalayan mountain range, India's bilateral relationship with China also remains volatile and friction- and tension-ridden.

Past Perfect: Ancient Civilizations

China and India are two of the world's oldest civilizations, each with the quality of resilience that has enabled it to survive and prosper through the ages and against the odds. During the past three thousand years, every one of the Asian countries—some situated on the continental landmass, others being islands off the Asia mainland—has at some stage been directly influenced by one or both of these two great civilizations.

Both have long, rich strategic traditions: Kautilya's *Arthashastra*—a treatise on war, diplomacy, statecraft and empire—in India and Sunzi's (Sun Tzu's) fourth-century BCE treatise, *Sunzi bingfa* (The Art of War) in China were written over two thousand years ago. The traditional Chinese concept of international relations was based on concentric circles from the imperial capital outward through variously dependent states to the barbarians. It bears remarkable resemblance to the Indian concept of *mandala*, or circles, as outlined in *Arthashastra*, which postulated that a king's neighbor is his natural enemy, while the king beyond his neighbor is his natural ally. The Chinese dynasties followed a similar policy of encircling and attacking nearby neighbors and maintaining friendly relations with more distant kingdoms *(yuan jiao jin gong)*. Much like imperial China, tribute, homage, subservience, and not annexation were the rightful fruits of victory in ancient India.

Political contacts between ancient China and India were few and far between. In the cultural sphere, it was mostly a one-way street—from India to China: Hindu and Buddhist religious and cultural influence spread to China through Central Asia, and Chinese scholars were sent to Indian universities at Nalanda and Taxilla. Though Chinese and Indian civilizations reacted to one another during the first few centuries of the Christian era, the process of religious-cultural interaction on any significant scale ceased after about the tenth century CE. Since then, the two countries lived as if they were oblivious to each other's existence for over a thousand years, until about the advent of the nineteenth century, when both came under the influence of European powers.

Before the age of European colonization, China accounted for about 33 percent of the world's manufactured goods and India for about 25 percent. China under the Song dynasty (960–1267) was the world's superpower. Under the Mughals (1526–1857), India's economic, military, and cultural prowess also was an object of envy. Then in a complete reversal of fortune, the mighty Asian civilizations declined, decayed, and disintegrated and were eventually conquered by European powers.

Present Imperfect: From Civilizations to Nation-States

The gradual westward expansion over the centuries extended China's influence over Tibet and parts of Central Asia (now Xinjiang Province). In contrast, India's boundaries shrank following the 1947 partition that broke up the strategic unity of the subcontinent going back two thousand years to the first Mauryan empire. Then came the Chinese occupation of Tibet in 1950, as a result of which the two nations for the first time came in close physical contact and clashed. India's partition in 1947 and the Chinese occupation of Tibet in 1950 have allowed China to extend its reach and influence into a region where it had, in terms of history and civilization, previously exercised no influence at all.

China–India relations have been tense ever since a border dispute became a full-scale war in 1962. Several rounds of talks since 1981 have failed to resolve the disputed claims. Agreements on maintaining peace and tranquility on the disputed border were signed in 1993 and 1996. However, the prospects of a negotiated settlement of the Sino-Indian border dispute in the near future seem as remote as ever for the simple reason that China cannot brush aside its ally Pakistan's interests in such a settlement. This was not the case with the settlement of China's territorial boundaries with Russia or Vietnam. A resolution of the Sino-Indian border dispute would lead to the deployment of India's mountain divisions and other military assets on the India–Pakistan border, thereby tilting the military balance decisively in India's favor and much to Pakistan's disadvantage. This would deprive Beijing of powerful leverage in its relations with Pakistan and undermine its old strategy of keeping India under strategic pressure on two fronts.

Even if the territorial dispute were resolved, China and India would still retain a competitive relationship in the Asia-Pacific region. Other factors, apart from the territorial dispute, contribute to the fractious and uneasy relationship. These include the nature of China's ties with India's smaller South Asian neighbors (including its arming of them), the legacy of Cold War alignments (Beijing–Islamabad–Washington versus Moscow–New Delhi axis), unrest in Tibet and Kashmir, Chinese encroachments into what India sees as its sphere of influence, Beijing's plans for a naval presence in the Indian Ocean, power asymmetry and a rivalry for the leadership of the developing world, and, more recently, the nuclear and missile proliferation issues.

Since the days of Jawaharlal Nehru (1889–1964), independent India has entertained hopes of a joint Sino-Indian leadership of Asia as a counter to Western influence, but the Chinese have shown no enthusiasm for sharing leadership of Asia with anyone, least of all India. After all, the main objective of China's Asia policy is to prevent the rise of a peer competitor to challenge its status as the Asia-Pacific's sole "Middle Kingdom." As an old Chinese saying goes, "one mountain cannot accommodate two tigers." Checkmated in East Asia by three great powers—Russia, Japan, and the United States—Beijing has long seen South and Southeast Asia as its spheres of influence and India as the main obstacle to achieving its strategic objective of regional supremacy in Asia. Chinese policymakers' preference for a balance of power approach in interstate relations has led them to provide military and political support to those countries that can serve as counterweights to Beijing's perceived enemies and rivals. Recognizing that India has the size, might, numbers, and, above all, the intention to match China, Beijing has long regarded New Delhi as one of its major strategic rivals and has aligned itself with Pakistan to contain the common enemy.

For its part, India has always perceived the Sino-Pakistani nexus as hostile and threatening in nature. As the pivotal power in South Asia, India perceives itself much as China has traditionally perceived itself in relation to East Asia. That the "strategic space" in which India traditionally operated has become increasingly constricted due to Chinese penetration became further evident from Beijing's forays into Myanmar (Burma) and the Bay of Bengal in the 1990s.

India's defense policy has always been based on the principle of "keeping one step ahead of Pakistan and at par with China." Seeing China as the reference point of India's economic, security, and diplomatic policies, India's strategic analysts have long emphasized the need to keep up with China militarily. Initially, India's nuclear capability was aimed solely at deterring China, not Pakistan. It is the adversarial nature of the Sino-Indian relationship that has driven India's and, in turn, Pakistan's nuclear weapons programs. The 1998 Indian nuclear tests were preceded by the Indian defense minister's statements calling China a "bigger potential threat" than Pakistan and describing how his country was being "encircled" by Chinese military activities in Tibet and alliances with Pakistan and Myanmar.

At the heart of Sino-Indian antagonism is the familiar Indian suspicion, which seems to have now matured into a certainty, that China is seeking to deny India its proper stakes in the game of international politics. That China does not want India to emerge as an equal is evident from its opposition to India's membership in the P-5 (UN Security Council), N-5 (Nuclear Club), ASEM (Asia–Europe Summit), APEC (Asia-Pacific Economic Cooperation), and G-8 (Group of Eight). Both remain suspicious of each other's long-term agenda and intentions. Interestingly, both are courting the United States to help balance their relationships with each other until they are strong enough to do so on their own. From New Delhi's perspective, Beijing's gradual but subtle penetration deep into the South Asian region in the second half of the twentieth century was primarily at India's expense.

In terms of history and civilization, India never played a second fiddle to China. Therein lies the root cause of volatile and strained relationship. Both China after a century and India after a millennium of decline are keen to assume the great power roles they believe have been made their right in view of their histories and civilizations. When Chinese and Indian elites speak of restoring their country's rightful place in the world, they give expression to a concept of "preeminence" in Asia and the wider world. This concept reflects their perception that as the foundation of regional cultural patterns, their rightful place is at the apex of world hierarchy. Both want a new international status that is commensurate with their size, strength, and potential. They oppose the economic and political dominance of the United States in world affairs. Both yearn for a truly multipolar world that will provide them the space for growth and freedom of action that befits great powers. Each wants to avoid entangling alliance so as to maximize its options and freedom of action. Both have practiced "tilted nonalignment" while preaching independent, nonaligned foreign policies. China and India have already attained the regional power status.

The similarities between the two countries' outlooks, aspirations, policies, and interests are indeed striking, despite their differing political systems. Both identify the present pattern of international relations with a world order designed to perpetuate the world domination of Western powers. Both oppose the status quo: China in terms of territory, power, and influence; India in terms of status, power, and influence. Furthermore, the Chinese Communist Party's national goal of "rich country, strong military" *(fuguo qiangbing)* bears remarkable resemblance to India's ruling Bharatiya Janata Party's slogan of "prosperous and powerful country." Both are focusing on increasing comprehensive national strength on a solid economic-technological base. Both are major competitors for foreign investment, capital, trade, and markets. Both see themselves as newly rising great Asian powers whose time has finally come. Both have attempted to establish a sort of Monroe Doctrine in their neighborhoods without much success. Both are unable to reassert their traditional suzerainty over their smaller neighbors, as any attempt to do so encounters resistance from regional and extraregional powers.

Both China and India claim that their attitude toward their neighbors is essentially benevolent, while making it clear that those neighbors must not make policies or take actions, or allow other nations to take measures in their countries, that each deems to be against its own interest and security. If they do so, China and India are willing to apply pressure in one fashion or another to bring about desired changes. The two also share remarkable similarity in economic outlooks and policies. Both suffer from a siege mentality borne out of their elites' acute consciousness of the divisive tendencies that make their countries' present political unity so fragile. After all, much of Chinese and Indian history is made up of long periods of internal disunity and turmoil, when centrifugal forces brought down even the most powerful empires.

Future Tense

Obviously, China and India's strategic cultures require both to regain the power and status their leaders consider appropriate to their country's size, population, geographical position, and historical heritage. In the power competition game, while China has surged ahead by acquiring economic and military capabilities underpinned by a clear policy to achieve broader strategic objectives, India has been impeded in its power quest by its incessant political instability and economic weakness. The existing asymmetry in international status and power serves Beijing's interests very well; any attempt by India to challenge or undermine China's power and influence or to achieve strategic parity is going to be strongly resisted through a combination of military and diplomatic means.

The traditional Sino-Indian rivalry is now set to acquire a maritime dimension as China seeks to secure the country's oil supply and trade routes through the Indian Ocean to the Strait of Malacca and the South China Sea and thereby further challenge India's power pretensions in the Indian Ocean in the twenty-first century. Beijing is investing heavily in developing the Bandarabbas base in Iran, the Gwadar deep-sea port in Pakistan, and naval bases in Myanmar. This adds to strains generated by differences over Pakistan, Tibet, and nuclear and missile proliferation. Furthermore, Beijing is now concerned that the logic and pull of geopolitics is pushing India, much like Japan, to a strategic alliance with the United States so as to contain China, even though U.S. relations with China have been much warmer in recent years.

For its part, Beijing is also watching with interest economic developments in India, especially its growing prowess in information technology, as the country could emerge as a potential competitor for foreign investment, technology, and markets. If the twenty-first century's first decade indeed turns out to be India's decade (in terms of a rapid increase in its economic and military might), just as the 1990s belonged to China and the 1980s belonged to Japan, Beijing will have to devise new strategies to keep India in check. Rapid power transitions have always been a major cause of instability and conflict in history, particularly when they are accompanied by arms buildups and sudden changes in regional military balances.

Indications are that bilateral relations are likely to remain adversarial for a long time to come. In the short to medium term, neither New Delhi nor Beijing will do anything that destabilizes their bilateral relationship or arouses the suspicions of their smaller Asian neighbors. Their efforts will be aimed at consolidating their power and position while striving to resolve more pressing domestic problems. However, instability in Tibet, coupled with China's military links with Pakistan and Myanmar, will pose a continuing complication in Sino-Indian relations. At the same time, both will continue to monitor closely each other's activities to expand influence and gain advantage in the wider Asian region and will attempt to fill any perceived power vacuum or block the other from doing so. In other words, China-India relations will be marked more by rivalry and competition than cooperation. However, both sides would want to keep the competition as muted as possible for as long as possible.

In the long term, neither Indian nor Chinese defense planners can rule out the possibility of a renewed confrontation over Tibet, Kashmir, Myanmar, or in the Indian Ocean. A Sino-Indian rivalry in southern Asia and the northern Indian Ocean (especially the Malacca Strait) may well be a dominant feature of future Asian geopolitics of the twenty-first century, which could force their neighbors to choose sides. The nature of the rivalry will be determined by how domestic political and economic developments in these two countries affect their power, their outlook on the region and the world, and their foreign and security policies.

There have been numerous occasions in history when China and India were simultaneously weak; there have been occasional moments of simultaneous cultural blossoming. But for more than half a millennium, Asia has not seen the two giants economically and militarily powerful at the same time. That time now seems to be approaching fast, and it is likely to result in significant new geopolitical realignments in the region. The emergence of China and India as economic giants undoubtedly will throw a huge new weight onto the world's geopolitical balance. New economic prosperity and military strength would reawaken nationalist pride in India, which could bring about a clash with Chinese nationalism.

While they are potential competitors for power and influence in Asia, China and India also share interests in maintaining regional stability (for example, combating the growing Islamic fundamentalist menace), exploiting economic opportunities, maintaining access to energy sources, and enhancing regional cooperation. Cooperation could allow them to balance U.S. influence and increase their negotiating positions with the sole superpower. From only a few hundred million dollars a decade ago, China-India trade has already reached $3 billion and is poised for a quantum jump as both economies further open up. On economic, environmental, and cultural issues, they may have far more reason to cooperate than to collide. It is possible that economically prosperous and militarily confident China and India will come to terms with each other eventually as their mutual containment policies start yielding diminishing returns. There is little doubt that future relations between the world's two most populous nations are critical to Asian—and global—security. A lasting global and regional security structure cannot be built without finding a place for both China and India.

J. Mohan Malik

Further Reading

Garver, John W. (2001) *Protracted Contest: Sino-Indian Rivalry in the Twentieth Century.* Seattle, WA: University of Washington Press.

Hoffmann, Steven A. (1990) *India and the China Crisis.* Berkeley and Los Angeles: University of California Press.

Jian Hua. (2001) "The United States, Japan Want to Rope in India Which Cherishes the Dream of Becoming a Major Power." *Ta Kung Pao* (Hong Kong) (4 June).

Malik, J. Mohan. (1994) "Sino-Indian Rivalry in Myanmar: Implications for Regional Security." *Contemporary Southeast Asia* 16, 2 (September): 137–156.

———. (1999) "India-China Relations in the 21st Century." In *Securing India's Future in the New Millennium*, edited by B. Chellaney. New Delhi: Orient Longman.

———. (1999) "The India-China Divide." *The Hindustan Times* (25 May): 13.

———. (2001) "South Asia in China's Foreign Relations." *Pacifica Review* 13, 1 (February): 73–90.

Pillsbury, Michael. (2000) *China Debates the Future Security Environment.* Washington, DC: National Defense University Press.

Sandeep Shenoy. (2001) "Elephant against the Dragon." *Asia Times Online* (2 August): 1.

Zhang Wenmu. (1998) "Issue of South Asia in Major Power Politics." *Ta Kung Pao* (Hong Kong) (23 September).

CHINA–JAPAN PEACE AND FRIENDSHIP TREATY After forty years of antagonism, China and Japan signed the China-Japan Peace and Friendship Treaty in Beijing on 12 August 1978. This treaty represented the turning point of Sino-Japanese relations and the cornerstone of Chinese foreign policy.

The path to the signing was not smooth. After the signing of the 1972 Sino-Japanese Joint Communique, in which Japan acknowledged the government in Beijing as China's legitimate government and diplomatic relations were reestablished, the path was opened for a treaty reflecting greater rapprochement. In November 1974, negotiations started, but the treaty was not signed until 1978.

Although it is called a peace treaty, it actually deals with political and economic relations. It reflects the principle of the Sino-Japanese Joint Communique and the essential principles of Chinese foreign policy. Article I of the peace treaty contains China's Five Principles of Peaceful Coexistence: mutual respect for sovereignty and territorial integrity, mutual nonaggression, noninterference in each other's internal affairs, equality and mutual benefit, and peaceful coexistence. It does not address the Sino-Japanese territorial dispute over the Diaoyu/Senkaku Islands in the East China Sea. When the China-Japan Peace and Friendship Treaty took effect on 23 October 1978, to celebrate the event, Chinese leader Deng Xiaoping (1904–1997) visited Tokyo and said that the territorial dispute would be left for posterity to settle. It has not been settled.

Unryu Suganuma

Further Reading

Suganuma, Unryu. (2000) *Sovereign Right and Territorial Space in Sino-Japanese Relations.* Honolulu, HI: University of Hawaii Press.

Whiting, Allen S. (1989) *China Eyes Japan.* Berkeley and Los Angeles: University of California Press.

CHINA–JAPAN RELATIONS Geographically, the distance separating Japan from mainland Asia is 144 kilometers from Korea and almost 770 kilometers from China, a distance sometimes referred to poetically as "a narrow strip of water." In prehistoric times, migrants flowed into Japan across that strip of water, particularly from northeastern Asia and the Korean Peninsula. Recurrent flows via Korea explain why Japanese and Korean languages are closely related, whereas neither is related linguistically to Chinese. By the seventh and eighth centuries, when Japan's own written records appear, Korea and China had long been culturally sophisticated, settled, and nonexpansionist. The two nations offered Japan rich materials for borrowing, without risk of invasion or interference—a marvelous advantage for island Japan.

Before 600 CE, local Japanese leaders sought relations with Korea and China for access to raw materials (iron for weapons, copper and tin for bronze) and for other benefits. Then, in 645 CE, a wholly Japanese initiative known as the Taika Reforms, modeled on imperial China, catapulted Japan from a regionally fragmented, often warring, and illiterate society to a rapidly centralizing, nonwarring, and literate society. Determined not to fall behind again, Japan maintained trade and other ties with China for most of its later history.

From this point onward, China-Japan relations fundamentally involved the flow of culture and knowledge to Japan from China, at Japanese initiative. In the late nineteenth and early twentieth centuries, that flow was suddenly reversed—to China and from Japan. This was the result of Japan's successful Meiji-period (1868–1912) transformation to defend against threats from the West. By mutual consent at the turn of the century, Japan served as a model and sympathetic helpmate for China. But rather quickly, Japan became entangled in military actions that, at their height from 1931 to 1945, turned Japan into China's deadly enemy. Japan's defeat in World War II and its postwar economic recovery under its 1947 antiwar constitution, along with China's Communist "liberation" after 1949, set the stage for a more balanced and mutually respectful relationship after diplomatic ties were restored in 1972.

Early Relations to 1200 CE

The only extant written records relating to Japan before 600 CE are Chinese records, because Japan lacked a writing system of its own. The *Shiji* (Records of the Grand Historian) by Sima Qian (145?–86? BCE) alludes to a Taoist mystic reportedly sent by China's first emperor, Qin Shi Huangdi (d. 215 BCE), across the "Eastern Sea" to Japan; brief treatments of Japan appear also in histories of the kingdom of Wei (writing completed c. 297 CE), the latter Han dynasty (completed c. 445 CE), the Liu-Song dynasty (completed c. 513 CE), the Sui dynasty (completed c. 630 CE), and the Tang dynasty (completed in the eleventh century). The first native Japanese accounts of early Japan appeared only in 712 and 720 CE, in the landmark volumes *Kojiki* (Records of Ancient Matters) and

Nihongi (Chronicles of Japan). Thereafter, Japan maintained public records employing China's ideographic writing system, the only writing system in East Asia at the time.

Writing, it could be said, was China's first great gift to Japan. Along with writing came Chinese political, social, and economic thought, public administration, literature and poetry, Buddhism, and much more. In all these arenas, Japan proved an eager and tireless student.

China's histories all report that tribal chieftains or "kings" of Wa ("Wa" was the name used for Japan, written using a Chinese character meaning "dwarf") sought relations with Chinese courts and confirmation of their rulership. Such Japanese efforts quickened in the fifth century as regional rulers sought ascendancy over rivals at home. As China itself neared political reunification under the Sui dynasty (581–618) after nearly four hundred years of political division, the now-dominant Yamato court of Japan in 587 came under the sway of the Soga family of pro-Buddhist and procontinental advocates of reforms. Prince Shotoku (574–622) is credited in 603 with adopting China's twelve-rank court system and, in 604, with promulgating the Seventeen-Article Constitution, a landmark set of principles of government infused with Chinese Confucian ideals. He is also credited with adopting the Chinese calendar, a radical step because it altered native notions of time.

The most encompassing of Japan's borrowings and adaptations from China involved reforms initiated in 645, around the new imperial era known as Taika, meaning "Great Transformation." These brought to full form a Chinese-style centralized state system. Used generically for the larger series of reforms culminating in the Taiho Code of 702, the Taika Reforms concentrated on practical matters of state: land nationalization and redistribution—upon which was based a complex system of taxation (all taken directly from Sui and Tang China)—and division of the nation into Chinese-style provinces, districts, and townships. Underlying this radical restructuring were Chinese political principles and ideals. Chinese-style military conscription was also adopted (but was abolished in 792). The Taiho Code of 702 formalized a fully Chinese-style central governmental structure around the Chinese Tang dynasty system of penal laws and administrative and household guidelines, which served as basic elements of Japanese law until after the Meiji Restoration of 1868, when Western models of governance were embraced.

These self-initiated measures were revolutionary in their consequences in the sense that Japan's public life was radically and permanently restructured. No other large nation in world history has ever so thoroughly transformed itself through voluntary borrowing without the pressure of military threats or actual conquest. On the other hand, it is necessary to point out that elements of China's "core" were rejected by Japan. First, Japan rejected China's worldview of Heaven, Earth, and Man (or human being), a triad interacting to achieve a harmonious whole, in favor of its own primitive founding mythology, which said that the Japanese islands and people were created by sacred spirits, or *kami*. By this claim, Japan privileged itself over its culturally more sophisticated neighbors. Second, Japan rejected China's belief that a Son of Heaven (who acted as intermediary between Heaven, Earth, and Man) earned the Mandate of Heaven, or right to rule (which could be revoked and transferred to a more worthy claimant), through "rule by virtue," or benevolent and morally upright rule. Japan insisted that its imperial line, the Yamato (Sun) line, was divine, eternal, and nontransferable. Third, Japan rejected China's belief in an imperial administration by an "aristocracy of merit," selected increasingly by civil-service examination and open to commoners. Japan held to its idea of a titled and hereditary aristocracy of blood, who alone qualified for appointment to high office. For reasons like these, Japan remained distinctively Japanese despite massive borrowings of Chinese forms.

The intense Japanese interest in China from about 600 to 900 CE is celebrated by Chinese and Japanese alike as a kind of golden age of China–Japan relations. Between 600 and 614, the Japanese court dispatched as many as five diplomatic missions to the Sui court, consisting of scholars, Buddhist monks, and others with orders to report back about Chinese knowledge and institutions. China's short-lived Sui dynasty was followed by the glorious Tang dynasty (618–907). From 630 to 894, the Japanese court sent at least nineteen diplomatic missions to the Tang court.

Courtiers, scholars, and monks featured prominently in the missions, accompanied by physicians, diviners, archers, musicians, craftsmen, and artists. Kibi no Makibi (693–775), a Japanese court official, went to China in 717 as a student, stayed for nineteen years, and brought back texts on Confucianism, Buddhism, astronomy, divination, civil administration, and military organization. During the period 752–754, he went back to China as deputy head of a mission that, on its return, helped the blind Chinese monk Jianzhen (called Ganjin in Japan; 689–763) to reach Japan after having experienced five shipwrecks and other mishaps. Ganjin founded the Japanese Ritsu branch of Buddhism at Nara (imperial capital from 710 to 784) in

754. The Japanese monk Saicho (767–822), of Chinese descent and active at court, was dispatched to China by Emperor Kammu (737–806) in 804 to gain spiritual sanction for a new Buddhist complex on Mount Hiei, near the new imperial capital of Heian (capital from 794 to 1185 and today's Kyoto). In China, Saicho was drawn to Tiantai ("Heaven's Pedestal," called Tendai in Japanese), a syncretic school of Buddhism emphasizing the *Lotus Sutra*, and after returning to Japan in 806 obtained imperial sanction to establish the sect on Mount Hiei, where it flourished.

Fellow monk Kukai (774–835) traveled with Saicho to China in 804 aboard a separate ship. Drawn to the Buddhist master Huiguo (746–805) of the Chinese Zhenyan ("True Words," called Shingon in Japanese) esoteric school of Buddhism, Kukai so impressed Huiguo that Huiguo transmitted his secret teachings to this foreigner rather than to a Chinese disciple. Kukai returned to Japan in 806, held various religious posts, wrote compellingly about Buddhism, and after 823 (as abbot of the great Buddhist temple Toji in the imperial capital of Heian) laid the foundations for Shingon Buddhism, which emerged as the most influential Buddhist school of the Heian period. Partly because of Huiguo's choice of Kukai for his transmission, Zhenyan Buddhism disappeared as a separate sect in China.

The Japanese writing system was an important outcome of this cultural interchange. In China, Kukai had studied Sanskrit, the Indian script in which Buddhist scriptures were sometimes written. Kukai encountered in Sanskrit a syllable-based writing system suitable to the Japanese language, which, like Sanskrit, is multisyllabic with inflected verbs. Chinese, by contrast, is monosyllabic and not inflected. According to tradition, Kukai used the principle of written Sanskrit to invent the Japanese syllabary known as kana, which is still used today.

In 894, the refusal of eminent scholar Sugawara no Michizane (845–903) to lead an embassy to China because of turmoil there brought an end to Japanese diplomatic missions until 1404, more than five hundred years later. The Japanese court continued nonetheless to use Chinese writing for public records; interest remained high in Chinese classical studies, poetry, and the arts; Japanese Buddhist monks traveled to China; and Chinese trading vessels sometimes called at Japanese ports. The truly important story after 900, however, is that Japanese elites used this interlude to digest earlier cultural imports and to find their own path in such areas as women's literature of the court, the warrior tales that followed, and fine arts and crafts, all distinctively Japanese.

Japan's Medieval Period, 1200–1600

The Heian period (794–1185) ended as a result of fighting between factions at court in alliance with provincial military forces. Real power progressively shifted to those military authorities around an emerging system often labeled "feudal." From 1192 to 1868, a series of military governments ruled Japan, sanctioned by the imperial court. Japanese, observing post-Heian developments, looked to Chinese history for precedents and found a comparable Chinese "feudal" system that had existed prior to political unification under the Qin dynasty (221–206 BCE). Japanese proceeded to apply pre-Qin Chinese terminology to post-Heian Japan: The head of the new military government was called shogun (Japanese pronunciation of the Chinese term *"jiangjun,"* meaning "general"); the shogunal government was called *bakufu* (Japanese pronunciation of the Chinese term *"mufu,"* meaning "tent headquarters" or "field headquarters"); and, later, after 1467, when Japan entered into more than a century of civil war, Japanese called the period Warring States, or Sengoku (1457–1568), the Japanese pronunciation of the Chinese period of history known as Zhan'guo (403–221 BCE).

Although China–Japan relations omitted further diplomatic exchanges until after 1404, China was very much alive in Japanese minds. Japan's first military government, the Kamakura *bakufu* (1192–1333), encouraged private trade with China, which made possible the importation of large quantities of Song-dynasty (960–1279) copper coins that fueled Japan's economy and commerce. Kamakura authorities also patronized a school of Buddhism that appealed strongly to Japan's new class of warriors, the samurai or *bushi*. This was Zen Buddhism—"Zen" being the Japanese pronunciation of the Chinese "Chan" (from the Sanskrit *dhyana*, meaning meditation). As in the past, key Buddhist monks went to China and returned with new teachings. The monk Eisai (1141–1215) went to China twice, first in 1168 and again from 1187 to 1191, where his enlightenment within the Linji (in Japanese, Rinzai) school of Zen Buddhism was certified by Linji master Xu'an. Along with Rinzai Buddhism, Eisai brought back Song China's enthusiasm for tea. He successfully urged both Zen and tea upon the new military government at Kamakura, which sought to distinguish itself from Nara and Heian Buddhism and culture. The monk Dogen (1200–1253), who traced his ancestry back to Heian-period emperors and aristocrats, in 1223 went to China, where he visited numerous monasteries and Buddhist masters in search of new teachings, and returned to Japan five years later to introduce Caodong (in Japanese, Soto), the other major branch of Zen Buddhism. Zen flourished and fundamentally enriched all aspects of Japanese culture, including the tea ceremony and Zen gardens, minimalist poetry known as haiku, painting, and martial-arts disciplines. Zen's pervasive influence on Japanese culture far surpassed the influence of Chan Buddhism on Chinese culture.

After Kamakura, Japan established its second *bakufu*, or shogunal government, the Ashikaga shogunate (1338–1573). This period coincided with a vigorous Japanese interest in China under the Mongol Yuan (1279–1368) and the Ming (1368–1644) dynasties and a brief Ming interest in the outside world as expressed through its seven maritime expeditions (1405–1433), some of which reached Arab ports and the east coast of Africa. The third Ashikaga shogun, Yoshimitsu (1358–1408), had interests in China going well beyond trade, and it was he who reinstituted embassies to China in 1404, followed by five more embassies up to 1410. These were received by China under its paternalistic system of foreign relations known as the tribute system. Japan dispatched eleven more embassies to Ming China between 1433 and 1547.

During the momentous sixteenth century, characterized by civil war and the arrival of Westerners and their guns in the 1540s, Japanese adventurers led ruinous pirate raids on the coasts of Korea and China. In 1592 and 1597, military unifier Toyotomi Hideyoshi (1536–1598) led two devastating campaigns against Korea, the first step of an ambitious plan to conquer China. Chinese recall the Japan of this unhappy era as a precursor to the militaristic Japan of the twentieth century.

Japan's Tokugawa Period (1600/1603–1868)

After full political reunification under the new Tokugawa shogunal government (1600/1603–1868), Japanese authorities gave top priority to imposing social and political controls on all of Japan. To this end, the new government borrowed China's open social-class system of scholar-official, peasant, artisan, and merchant and enforced it upon Japanese society as a closed, castelike, and hereditary system, consisting of samurai-official, peasant, artisan, and merchant. Buddhism was also subjected to strict state control. Replacing Buddhism at the heart of Japanese intellectual life was Chinese Confucianism, a secular system devoted to ideals of social harmony and to the training of loyal administrators for the state. Confucianism for the first time formed Japan's true unifying ideological core and served as the content of education for samurai-officials throughout the Tokugawa period.

During Japan's Warring States period, unregulated foreign trade had been a source of danger and disruption to the nation, and it, too, was brought under control by two measures. First, in 1639, the Tokugawa authorities forbade the construction of oceangoing vessels and prohibited Japanese to travel abroad on penalty of death. Simultaneously, the government enforced a national policy of restricted foreign access to Japan, referred to by later historians as *sakoku*, or "closed nation," a form of self-isolation. Foreigners themselves were expelled, with the important exception of those Dutch, Chinese, and Koreans having government authorization. Confined to designated living quarters, these foreigners were allowed entry because they transported precious goods to Japan, like books on Confucianism, medical texts, agricultural manuals, and treatises on astronomy and technology. In this way, China—or at least the China of books and of Japanese imaginings—remained very much on Japanese minds. Japan in Chinese minds, by contrast, became increasingly peripheral, in the absence of pirate raids and military aggression. What shattered this system of regulated and limited contact was Britain's Opium War against China, 1839–1842, which alerted Japan to the rise of an outside enemy that demanded a concerted effort at resistance.

Rapid Transformations after 1840

After the Opium War, four major developments framed and conditioned China–Japan relations: Western imperialism of the nineteenth and early twentieth centuries, China's rapid decline in the nineteenth century, Japan's rapid rise after 1868, and the wars, revolutions, and transformations of the twentieth century. The nineteenth century after 1840 was one of the worst periods of China's history. Faced with serious internal problems, China was diverted from these by relentless imperialist pressures, which led to a series of foreign wars: the Opium War, the Arrow Wars of 1856–1858, the Yili War with Russia of 1871–1872, and the Sino-French War over the Indochinese kingdom of Annam in 1884–1885. Japan watched in growing horror as China, the civilization it had long idealized, lost war after war, all the while proclaiming its own moral and cultural superiority. Alarmed further by instability in Korea, a magnet for Chinese, Russian, and Western intervention, Japan finally went to war with China over Korea. China's defeat in the Sino-Japanese War of 1894–1895 was excruciatingly humiliating for China, robbing even the blindest Chinese of any pretense of superiority. Responsible Chinese became consumed with fears for survival in an imperialist world that, alas, would not go away.

It was to Japan that China then turned for the secrets of wealth and power, cautiously at first but after

EXTRACT FROM THE TREATY OF TIENTSIN

The Treaty of Tientsin was signed by China and Japan on 13 September 1871, a time when China's power was declining and Japan's increasing. It was only 24 years later that Japan would defeat China and establish a dominance that would last into World War II.

> Article I. Relations of amity shall henceforth be maintained in redoubled force between China and Japan, in measure as boundless as the heaven and the earth. In all that regards the territorial possessions of either country the two Governments shall treat each other with proper courtesy, without the slightest infringement or encroachment on either side, to the end that there may be forevermore peace between them undisturbed.
>
> Article II. Friendly intercourse thus existing between the two Governments, it is the duty of each to sympathise with the other, and in the event of any other nation acting unjustly or treating either of the two Powers with contempt, on notice being given [by the one to the other], mutual assistance shall be rendered or mediation offered for the arrangement of the difficulty, in fulfilment of the duty imposed by relations of friendship.
>
> Article III. The system of government and the penal enactments of the two Governments being different from each other, each shall be allowed to act in entire independence. There shall be no interference offered, nor shall requests for innovations be obtruded. Each shall aid the other in enforcement of the laws, nor shall either allow its subjects to entice the people of the other country to commit acts in violation of the laws.
>
> Article IV. It will be competent for either Government to send Plenipotentiary Ministers, with their families and suites, to reside in the capital of the other, either permanently or from time to time. Their traveling expenses as they pass through the country will be defrayed by themselves. In the matter of their hiring ground or buildings to serve as Legations, of the passage of their baggage to and fro, of the conveyance of their correspondence by special couriers, and the like, due assistance shall be rendered on either side.
>
> Article V. Although the functionaries of the two Governments have fixed grades, the nature of the offices conferred are different on either side. Officers of equivalent rank will meet and correspond with each other on a footing of equality. When an officer visits a superior, the intercourse between them will be such as is prescribed by the rites of hospitality. For the transaction of public business, the officials of the two countries will address communications to officers of their own rank, who will report in turn to their respective superiors; they will not address the superior officer directly. In visits, cards with the official title of the visitor shall be sent on either side. All officials sent on the part of either Government to the other shall present for inspection a letter bearing an official stamp, in order to guard against false personation.
>
> Article VI. In official correspondence, China will use the Chinese language, and Japan will either use the Japanese language accompanied by a Chinese version, or a Chinese version alone, as may be found on her side preferable.
>
> Article VII. Friendly intercourse having been established between the two Governments, it will behoove them both to appoint certain ports on the seaboard which their merchants will be authorized to frequent for purposes of trade, and to lay down, separately, Regulations of Trade that their respective mercantile communities may abide by in perpetuity.

Source: Treaties, Conventions, Maritime Customs between China and Foreign State. Vol. II. Shanghai: Imperial Maritime Customs, 1235–36.

1901 in a flood. Japan responded generously, out of a sense of cultural indebtedness to China and of new national pride, but also out of a sense of common threat in the face of Western imperialism. For the first time in its long history, China adopted a policy of sending Chinese students to Japan, to bring back advanced learning. Between 1898 and 1911, 25,000 Chinese students traveled to Japan for all levels of modern

THE TREATY OF SHIMONOSEKI

The Treaty of Peace between China and Japan of 17 April 1895 ended the Sino-Japanese War of 1894–1895. The defeat in the war and the conditions set forth in the treaty extracted below were a humiliation for China and contributed to the long-term mistrust between the two nations.

His Majesty the Emperor of China and His Majesty the Emperor of Japan desiring to restore the blessings of peace to their countries and subjects and to remove all cause for future complications, have named as their Plenipotentiaries for the purpose of concluding a Treaty of peace; that is to say, His Majesty the Emperor of China, Li Hung-chang, Senior Tutor to the Heir Apparent, Senior Grand Secretary of State, Minister Superintendent of Trade for the Northern Ports of China, Viceroy of the Province of Chihli, and Earl of the First Rank, and Li Cing-Long, Ex-Minister to the Diplomatic Service, of the Second Official Rank; and His Majesty the Emperor of Japan, Count Iro Hirobumi, Junii, Grand Cross of the Imperial Order of Paullownia, Minister President of State, and Viscount Mutsu Munemitsu, Junii, First Class of the Imperial Order of the Sacred Treasure, Minister of State for Foreign Affairs; who, after having exchanged their full powers, which were found to be in good and proper form, have agreed to the following Articles:—

Article I. Independence of Korea. China recognizes definitely the full and complete independence and autonomy of Korea, and in consequence the payment of tribute and the performance of ceremonies and formalities by Korea to China, in derogation of such independence and autonomy, shall wholly cease for the future.

Article II. Cession of part of Fengtien Province. China cedes to Japan in perpetuity and full sovereignty the following territories, together with all fortifications, arsenals, and public property thereon:

(a) The southern portion of the province of Fengtien, within the following boundaries:—

The line of demarcation begins at the mouth of the River Yalu and ascends that stream to the mouth of the River An-ping; from thence the line runs to Feng-huang; from thence to Haicheng; from thence to Ying-kow, forming a line which describes the southern portion of the territory. The places above named are included in the ceded territory. When the line reaches the River Liao at Ying-kow, it follows the course of that stream to its mouth where it terminates. The mid-channel of the River Liao shall be taken as the line of demarcation.

This cession also includes all islands appertaining or belonging to the province of Fengtien, situated in the eastern portion of the Bay of Liao-tung and in the northern part of the Yellow Sea.

(b) The island of Formosa, together with all islands appertaining or belonging to said island of Formosa.

(c) The Pescadores Group, that is to say, all islands lying between the 119th and 120th degrees of longitude east of Greenwich and the 23rd and 24th degrees of north latitude.

Article III. Delimitation of ceded territory. The alignments of the Frontiers described in the preceding Article and shown on the annexed map, shall be subject to the verification and demarcation on the spot, by a Joint Commission of Delimitation consisting of two or more Chinese and two or more Japanese Delegates to be appointed immediately after the exchange of the ratifications of this Act. In case the boundaries laid down in this act are found to be defective at any point, either on account of topography or in consideration of good administration, it shall also be the duty of the Delimitation Commission to rectify the same.

The Delimitation Commission will enter upon its duties as soon as possible and will bring its labors to a conclusion within the period of one year after appointment.

The alignments laid down in this Act shall, however, be maintained until the rectifications of the Delimitation Commission, if any are made, shall have received the approval of the Governments of China and Japan.

CONTINUED ON NEXT PAGE

CONTINUED FROM PREVIOUS PAGE

Article IV. War Indemnity to Japan. China agrees to pay to Japan as a war indemnity the sum of 200,000,000 Kuping Taels. The said sum is to be paid in eight installments, The first installment of 50,000,000 Taels to be paid within six months and the second installment of 50,000,000 Taels to be paid within twelve months after the exchange of the ratifications of this Act. The remaining sum to be paid in six equal installments as follows: The first of such equal installments to be paid within two years; the second within three years; the third within four years; the fourth within five years; the fifth within six years; and the sixth within seven years, after the exchange of the ratifications of this Act. Interest at the rate of 5 per centum per annum shall begin to run on all unpaid portions of the said Indemnity from the date the first installment falls due.

Source: John V. A. MacMurray, ed. (1921) *Treaties and Agreements with and Concerning China, 1894-1919*. New York: Oxford University Press, 18–19.

schooling. Some of these students turned against their Manchu-ruled Qing dynasty (1644–1912) and, working with Sun Yat-sen (1866–1925) and other revolutionaries, succeeded in bringing down the dynasty. This brief interlude of good relations was brought to a halt by the Russo-Japanese War of 1904–1905. By this war, Japan acquired vast interests in Manchuria (northeastern China), which shifted Japan's stance from cooperation and support of China to self-serving actions that brought the two into conflict after conflict.

In 1915, Japan presented to the Chinese government of Yuan Shikai (1859–1916) its Twenty-One Demands, which called for the appointment of Japanese advisers to top civilian and military positions. Leaked to the press, these demands triggered an outburst of Chinese nationalist outrage and anti-Japanese sentiment. Under Chinese and international pressure, the most objectionable demands were withdrawn, but Chinese suspicions of Japan persisted.

World War I, which tied down European powers in the West, gave Japan the opportunity to accelerate its trade and involvement in China. China's so-called warlord era of 1917 to 1927 invited even more foreign interference. Growing Japanese militarism at home, accelerated by the world depression of 1929, set Japan on a course of escalating aggression in China: Japanese aggression triggered Chinese resistance, which in turn heightened Japanese demands, which further inflamed Chinese nationalism, until Japan launched its total war against this obstinate nation. More specifically, the Japanese assassination of warlord Zhang Zuolin (1872–1928) of Manchuria in 1928 served as a prelude to the Manchurian Incident of 1931, followed by formation of the puppet state of Manchukuo in 1932; the demilitarization of North China under Japanese pressure in 1933; Japanese-orchestrated efforts to separate the five northern provinces of Hebei, Chahar, Suiyuan, Shanxi, and Shandong from China in 1935; and finally, on 7 July 1937, the Marco Polo Bridge military clash outside Beijing that precipitated seven years of Japanese military rampage in China. Japan's actions in no small way contributed to undermining the Nationalist government of Chiang Kai-shek (1887–1975), which fell in 1949—a parallel to the years after 1550, when Japanese piracy along the China coast and Hideyoshi's invasions of Korea helped to bring down the Ming dynasty in 1644. The intensity and destructiveness of Japanese aggression of the 1930s and 1940s far exceeded that of the earlier period, however, and in Chinese minds brought China-Japan relations to an all-time low.

Japan lost its war against China and its allies. The Allied Occupation (1945–1952) that followed, under U.S. leadership, was the first foreign occupation of Japan in its entire history. Ironically, China accomplished the reverse of foreign occupation less than five years later: In 1949, China "liberated" itself from foreign control and intervention and expelled most foreigners other than its Soviet Russian allies. Relations between China and Japan after 1949 followed the lead of the United States. Japan established diplomatic relations with the Republic of China on Taiwan under Chiang Kai-shek. Then, in 1972, the surprise visit to China of U.S. president Richard Nixon (1913–1994) and Secretary of State Henry Kissinger cleared the way for Japan to restore diplomatic ties with the People's Republic of China (PRC) under Mao Zedong (1893–1976) in September 1972.

China-Japan Relations since 1972

Since 1972, China has made major shifts in policy, bringing itself increasingly in line with international standards and agreements. The death of Mao Zedong in 1976 brought to an end the Cultural Revolution

Soldiers in China's People's Liberation Army carry wreaths at a memorial ceremony for the 300,000 victims of the 1937 Naning massacre by Japanese troops. The ceremony on 14 December 1998 followed a Japanese refusal to provide a written apology for Japanese atrocities. (AFP/CORBIS)

(1966–1976). New policies from 1978 under Deng Xiaoping (1904–1997) emphasized the "four modernizations" in agriculture, industry, science, and defense, accompanied by a commitment to *kaifang*—the policy of opening and reform. In this atmosphere, China-Japan relations have become more balanced and equal than ever before, marked by a resolve to maintain constructive relationships and to work out disagreements.

Providing the framework for relations since 1972 are the Joint Communiqué of the government of Japan and the government of the PRC of 29 September 1972, which affirmed that the government of the PRC is the sole legal government of China, that Taiwan is an inalienable part of China (calling for a peaceful settlement of the Taiwan issue through discussions), and that China–Japan diplomatic relations would be restored as of 29 September 1972, and the Treaty of Peace and Friendship between Japan and the People's Republic of China, signed on 12 August 1978, endorsing economic cooperation and political understanding. On 15 August 1995, Japanese prime minister Murayama Tomiichi (b. 1924) went beyond economics and politics to address officially the touchy subject of Japanese aggression against China, making a personal apology for the actions of Japan during the Sino-Japanese war of the 1930s and 1940s. His 1995 statement has been reaffirmed regularly by subsequent leaders.

Time will tell what effect these repeated apologies have. More notable has been Chinese distrust of Japanese apologies, even as Chinese demand more Japanese bowing and scraping. China plays the "war guilt" card against Japan and has utilized its controlled press to sensationalize outlandish statements by fringe right-wing Japanese elements, while denying any error or shortcoming of its own. Sustained healthy relations are handicapped by such circumstances.

The fact remains that China needs Japan and Japan needs China. Reaffirmation of this truth finds expression in two top-level agreements of 26 November 1998: the Japan–China Joint Declaration on Building a Partnership of Friendship and Cooperation for Peace and Development and the Joint Press Announcement on Strengthening Cooperation between Japan and China toward the Twenty-first Century. Even at low points since 1972, China-Japan relations have been substantial, with Japan usually taking the lead for reasons such as economic gain, security concerns, sense of cultural affinity, curiosity and adventure, war guilt, and feelings of public and international responsibility.

Economic relations have been at the forefront of China-Japan relations since 1949. Before 1978, such relations were surprisingly complex, multilayered, and pluralistic. Trade was relatively substantial and constant as nongovernmental and pro-China trade interests in

Japan found ways to deal directly with China, bypassing official channels constrained by U.S. policies. As a percentage of Japan's world trade, it constituted a modest 2.5 to 3.5 percent, which, however, grew steadily after 1972. By 1985, Japan's exports to China (modern plant and technology, machinery, and petrochemicals) had climbed to about 7 percent of Japan's global export trade, whereas its imports from China (mainly crude oil and coal and, later, textiles) amounted to about 5 percent of Japan's total imports. Japan now ranks as China's largest trading partner, and China as Japan's second-largest, after the United States. To encourage trade liberalization, help manage bilateral economic relations, and resolve trade disputes with China, Japan since 1996 supported China's entry into the World Trade Organization. China achieved full membership in WTO, after fifteen years of negotiations, on 11 December 2001.

Political relations at an official level were meager before the restoration of diplomatic ties in September 1972. Thereafter, Japanese prime ministers (the head of state of Japan) and other high officials have visited China, and Chinese premiers (not the head of state of China, a position held by China's president) and other high officials have visited Japan. In October 1992, no less personages than the emperor and empress of Japan visited China, a first. In early 1993, Jiang Zemin (b. 1926), Chinese president and general secretary of the Communist Party of China, reciprocated in a visit to Japan, also a first for a Chinese head of state. In 1997, when Japanese prime minister Hashimoto Ryutaro (b. 1937) visited China, followed by Chinese premier Li Peng's (b. 1928) visit to Japan, the two nations agreed that every year one of their top leaders should visit the other nation. Annual exchange visits by top leaders of both nations have indeed materialized.

Cultural ties are an arena where attitudes find full expression. Complex sentiments of superiority and inferiority coexist, as assessed by Japanese scholar Ijiri Hidenori:

> The Chinese have a superiority complex deriving from their cultural influence in pre-modern history and hatred stemming from Japanese military aggression against China in the modern period, while having an inferiority complex based upon Japan's co-operation in their modernization, and admiration for Japan's advanced economy. On the other hand, the Japanese have an inferiority complex due to their cultural debt to China and the sense of original sin stemming from their past aggression against China, while having a superiority complex based upon their assistance to China's modernization and contempt for China's backwardness.
>
> *Howe 1996: 60*

These attitudes are part of the cultural baggage of Chinese and Japanese, whose numbers as travelers have exploded. In 1972 only nine thousand Chinese and Japanese traveled between China and Japan; in 1997 that number had risen to well over 1 million—a greater exchange than ever before. Among those were 23,000 Chinese studying in Japan, a figure representing more than 40 percent of all foreign students in Japan. (China began authorizing study and research abroad in 1979.) In the arena of religion, a dynamic Japanese Buddhism is assisting historic centers of Chinese Buddhism, like the home temples of Ganjin and Huiguo, to help Buddhism recover from the hardships, neglect, and attacks of the recent past. Japan is further assisting China at national and local levels to refine modern methods of law and administration and other areas of public life.

Thus, significantly, in matters of trade, diplomacy, study, law and administration, religion, industry, and technology—all areas of importance dating back to Sui and Tang times—relations are very much alive between China and Japan as they enter the new millennium.

Douglas R. Reynolds

Further Reading

de Bary, Wm. Theodore, Donald Keene, George Tanabe, and Paul Varley, eds. (2001) *From Earliest Times to 1600.* Vol 1 of *Sources of Japanese Tradition.* New York: Columbia University Press.

Howe, Christopher, ed. (1996) *China and Japan: History, Trends, and Prospects.* Oxford: Oxford University Press.

Imamura, Keiji, ed. (1996) *Prehistoric Japan: New Perspectives on Insular East Asia.* Honolulu, HI: University of Hawaii Press.

Jansen, Marius B. (1975) *Japan and China: From War to Peace, 1894–1972.* Chicago: Rand McNally.

Reynolds, Douglas R. (1993) *China, 1898–1912: The Xinzheng Revolution and Japan.* Cambridge, MA: Council on East Asian Studies, Harvard University Press.

Soeya, Yoshihide. (1998) *Japan's Economic Diplomacy with China, 1945–1978.* Oxford: Oxford University Press.

Suzuki, Daisetz T. (1959) *Zen and Japanese Culture.* Princeton, NJ: Princeton University Press.

Tsunoda, Ryusaku, and L. Carrington Goodrich. (1951) *Japan in the Chinese Dynastic Histories.* Perkins Asiatic Monograph, no. 2. South Pasadena, CA: P. D. and Ione Perkins.

Whiting, Allen S. (1989) *China Eyes Japan.* Berkeley and Los Angeles: University of California Press.

CHINA–KOREA RELATIONS It is difficult to overstate the comprehensive influence of traditional China on Korea's cultural development and social institutions. That influence remained the single dominating feature of Korean culture until as late as the nineteenth century. Four elements of traditional Korean culture have manifested Chinese influence: political culture, popular and court artistic culture, language, and literature.

The long and continuous history of Chinese influence on Korean culture is said to have began with the Lo-lang Commandery in northwestern Korea (modern P'yongyan province), which was established by the Chinese Han dynasty (206 BCE–220 CE) in 108 BCE. The flourishing commandery led to the sinicization of Korea. Through Lo-lang, the accouterments of the superior Chinese civilization, including advanced techniques in pottery making and iron smelting and an ideographic writing system, were transmitted to the loosely knit Korean tribes. With the Chinese writing system were introduced Chinese notions about statecraft and religion, and with the introduction of iron and bronze tools, the development of agriculture.

Political Culture

It is impossible to understand the traditional cultural affinity between China and Korea without referring to the political culture of Confucianism. The fermentation and development of Confucian ideas and institutions were sustained over the course of Korean dynastic history. Culturally, the Unified Shilla kingdom (668–935) in Korea borrowed extensively from Tang China (618–907) by organizing its central and provincial government administrations, its land and taxation systems, national university, and civil-service examinations along Confucian-Chinese lines.

During the Koryo kingdom (918–1392), Korean social, political, educational, and administrative systems were even more sinicized. The Koryo aristocracy embraced Confucianism for its political precepts and ethical principles and accepted Buddhism for spiritual fulfillment. The later Koryo period saw the decline of Buddhism and the increasing stature of Neo-Confucianism, with a renewed emphasis on the civil-service examination system. Under the Mongol Yuan dynasty (1279–1368) in China, Korea was subject to occasional Mongol political interference but retained its political and cultural identity. Nor did the switch to Manchu Qing vassalage (1644–1912) change the Confucian character of Korean political and civil society. The Manchus themselves relied on the Chinese-run Confucian bureaucracy in China, which they had subjugated politically and militarily but not culturally. Meanwhile, the Choson kingdom (1392–1910) in Korea replaced Buddhism with the Neo-Confucianism of Zhu Xi (Chu Hsi) as the state creed. The essential nature and structure of Sino-Korean cultural relations thus remained intact.

Popular and Court Artistic Culture

From the first major period of Korean art, the Three Kingdoms (c. 57 BCE–668 CE), until the fifteenth century, Buddhism, introduced from China in 372 CE, remained the major source of inspiration in Korean visual art. Architecture, sculpture, and painting of the Koryo dynasty were largely influenced by the style of the Chinese Song dynasty (960–1279). Porcelain making, introduced in the late eleventh century from Zhejiang, China, was transformed by native artisans into a Korean form—kingfisher-colored celadons, which even the Chinese held in high regard.

During the Choson dynasty, Korean arts were influenced by Confucian culture. White porcelain was popular among Koreans for Confucian rites and ancestor worship. In architecture, the Choson court constructed grand buildings in the capital of Seoul, such as the fifteenth-century Kyongbok palace, designed after the Ming dynasty (1368–1644) Chinese prototypes in present-day Beijing. Paintings largely imitated northern Chinese style; professional court artists as well as scholar-gentry painters relied on Chinese themes and conventions. Not until the eighteenth century did distinctively Korean styles emerge.

Chinese music and instruments entered Korea at an early date, and over time Korea developed an extensive repertoire of Chinese-style court music and ritual dance, characterized by slow movements of the shoulders, hands, and neck.

Language

Although Korea has had its own language for several thousand years, its writing system dates only from the mid-fifteenth century; the indigenous Korean script, hangul, was invented in 1443 by King Sejong (1397–1450) during the early Choson dynasty. Most of what is known about the Korean language comes from that period. Information on earlier vocabulary is partly available in vocabularies compiled by the Chinese.

The Korean language borrowed many words from classical Chinese, including most of its technical terms and about 10 percent of its basic nouns, such as *san* (mountain) and *kang* (river). The borrowed words are sometimes written in Chinese characters. It is not known when the Chinese writing system came into widespread use in Korea, but the inscription on a great stele erected to honor the Koguryo king Kwanggaet'o in the early fifth century is the earliest extant historical record written with Chinese characters by Koreans.

Literature

Korean literature was written at first in classical Chinese, then in various transcription (*idu, hyangch'al,* or *kugyol*) systems using Chinese characters, and finally in hangul. Korean scholars were writing poetry in classical Chinese style by at least the fourth century CE. The introduction of Buddhism and of Chinese characters during the Three Kingdoms period enriched Korean literature and changed the Korean worldview. The Unified Shilla court sent many students to study in Tang China (618–907), and a great body of prose narratives written in classical Chinese resulted from these contacts.

From the institutionalization of civil-service examinations in the mid-tenth century until their abolition in 1894, every educated Korean read Confucian classics and Chinese histories and literature. The Korean upper classes (the *yangban*) were bilingual in a special sense: They spoke Korean but wrote in Chinese. Many of their prose works were set in China, while those written by commoners were set in Korea. The most important literary works often belonged to the Confucianist tradition. Extant literary works indicate that despite the transcription systems, before the twentieth century much Korean literature was written in Chinese rather than in Korean even after the invention of hangul. The prestige of Chinese letters was so great that hangul was scorned by most educated people.

China–Korea Relations Today

Although the number of adherents to Confucianism is small in Korea today, most Korean families still follow its principles, including ancestor worship. In North Korea, ideology and philosophy, along with other forms of religion (shamanism, Buddhism, Taoism, and Ch'ondogyo), have been officially repressed since 1945. In South Korea, however, freedom of religion is constitutionally guaranteed. Although there is no national religion in the south, a significant proportion of the population still adheres to Buddhist beliefs.

Because of the predominance of Confucian culture and institutions, the economic aspect of Sino-Korean relations has not traditionally been most important. This is changing, however, as South Korea in particular and post-Mao China have both been striving to achieve higher levels of economic development. As for North Korea, the dissolution of the Soviet Union in 1991 left China as its only major ally. Yet since 1992, China has been cultivating friendly relations with South Korea as well. This is a far cry from the dictates of Communist ideology and from the days of the Korean War (1950–1953), when the People's Republic of China intervened on the side of North Korea. That China now seeks good relations with both North and South Korea augurs well for Sino-Korean relations in the twenty-first century.

Anthony Alexander Loh

Further Reading

Covell, Jon Carter. (1981) *Korea's Cultural Roots*. Seoul: Hollym.

Crane, Paul S. (1978) *Korean Patterns*. 4th rev. ed. Seoul: Published for the Royal Asiatic Society, Korea Branch, by Kwangjin.

Deuchler, Martina. (1992) *The Confucian Transformation of Korea: A Study of Society and Ideology*. Cambridge, MA: Council on East Asian Studies, Harvard University.

Eckert, Carter J., and K. Lee. (1990) *Korea, Old and New*. Seoul: Published for the Korea Institute, Harvard University, by Ilchokak.

Fairbank, John K., and Edwin O. Reischauer. (1960) "Traditional Korea: A Variant of the Chinese Cultural Pattern." In *East Asia: The Great Tradition*. Boston: Houghton Mifflin, 394–449.

Kim Won-Yang. (1986) *Art and Archaeology of Ancient Korea*. Seoul: Tackwang.

———. (1986) *Korean Art Treasures*. Ed. by Roderick Whitfield and Pak Young-sook. Seoul: Yekyong.

Kim Won-Yong, et al. (1983) *Traditional Korean Art*. Arch Cape, OR: Pace International Research.

Nahm, Andrew C. (1988) *Tradition & Transformation: A History of the Korean People*. Elizabeth, NJ: Hollym International.

Palais, James B. ([1975] 1991) *Politics and Policy in Traditional Korea*. Reprint ed.. Cambridge, MA: Council on East Asian Studies, Harvard University.

CHINA–RUSSIA RELATIONS

Political and ideological differences deeply embedded in a long history of conflict and territorial disputes have complicated China–Soviet/Russian relations, long before Communist regimes came to power in either China or Russia. Russian Cossacks pushed into Siberia in the seventeenth century as hunters and trappers. In the later 1600s these settlers moved into the Amur River basin to establish agricultural settlements. This expansion of czarist Russia into regions claimed by China's Qing dynasty (1644–1912) eventually resulted in confrontation along the Far Eastern frontier. The two powers concluded the Treaty of Nerchinsk in August 1689, delimiting the Far Eastern sector of the China-Russia boundary in an effort to avoid further conflict. The 1727 Treaty of Burinsk delimited the middle sector (roughly the current Mongolian–Russian boundary).

During China's decline in the nineteenth century, Russia continued to advance into the Far East. Concluded in 1858, the Treaty of Aigun redrew the boundary between the two countries along the Amur and

ESTABLISHING BOUNDARIES

The Treaty of Nipchu (Nerchinsk) of 27 August 1689 sought to establish and maintain peace on the border between China and Russia.

Article I. The river Gorbitza, which joins the Schilka from its left side near the river Tchernaya, is to form the boundary between the two Empires. The boundary from the source of that river to the sea will run along the top of the mountain chain [in which the river rises]. The jurisdiction of the two Empires will be divided in such a way that [the valleys of] all the rivers or streams flowing from the southern slope of these mountains to join the Amur shall belong to the Empire of China, while [the valleys of] all the rivers flowing down from the other [or northern] side of these mountains shall be similarly under the rule of His Majesty the Czar of the Russian Empire. As to [the valleys of] the other rivers which lie between the Russian river Oud and the aforesaid mountains—running near the Amur and extending to the sea—which are now under Chinese rule, the question of the jurisdiction over them is to remain open. On this point the [Russian] Ambassadors are [at present] without explicit instructions from the Czar. Hereafter, when the Ambassadors on both sides shall have returned [? to their respective countries], the Czar and the Emperor of China will decide the question on terms of amity, either by sending Plenipotentiaries or by written correspondence.

Article II. Similarly, the river Argun, which flows into the Amur, will form the frontier along its whole length. All territory on the left bank is to be under the rule of the Emperor of China; all on the right bank will be included in the Empire of the Czar. All habitations on the south side will be transferred to the other.

Article III. The fortified town of Albazin, built by His Majesty the Czar, is to be completely demolished, and the people residing there, with all military and other stores and equipment, are to be moved into Russian territory. Those moved can take all their property with them, and they are not allowed to suffer loss [by detention of any of it].

Article IV. Fugitives [lit., runaways] from either side who may have settled in the other's country previous to the date of this Treaty may remain. No claims for their rendition will be made on either side. But those who may take refuge in either country after the date of this Treaty of Amity are to be sent without delay to the frontier and at once handed over the to chief local officials.

Article V. It is to be understood by both Governments that from the time when this Treaty of Amity is made, the subjects of either nation, being provided with proper passports, may come and go [across the frontier] on their private business and may carry on commerce [lit., buy and sell].

Article VI. All the differences [lit., quarrels] which may have occurred between the subjects [of each nation] on the frontier up to the date of this Treaty will be forgotten and [claims arising out of them will] not be entertained. But if hereafter any of the subjects [lit., traders or craftsmen] of either nationality pass the frontier [as if] for private [and legitimate] business and [while in the foreign territory] commit crimes of violence to property and life, they are at once to be arrested and sent to the frontier of their own country and handed over to the chief local authority [military], who will inflict on them the death penalty as a punishment of their crimes. Crimes and excesses committed by private people on the frontier must not be made the cause of war and bloodshed by either side. When cases of this kind arise, they are to be reported by [the officers of] the side on which they occur to the Sovereigns of both Powers, for settlement by diplomatic negotiation in an amicable manner.

If the Emperor of China desires to engrave [on stone] the Articles of the above Treaty agreed upon by the Envoys for the determination of the frontier, and to place the same [at certain positions] on the frontier as a record, he is at liberty to do so. Whether this is to be done or not is left entirely to the discretion of His Majesty the Emperor of China.

Source: Treaties, Conventions, etc. between China and Foreign States. (1908) III. Miscellaneous Series, no. 30. China. Shanghai: Imperial Maritime Customs, vol. I: 3–7.

Ussuri Rivers, but left territory east of the rivers in "joint possession" for future negotiations to settle. Two years later Russia prevailed on China to negotiate the Treaty of Peking (Beijing). This treaty granted the territory between the Amur and Ussuri Rivers and the Sea of Japan to Russia.

Russia also advanced into Central Asia, where China claimed control over the area that is today China's autonomous region of Xinjiang. The 1864 Chuguchak Protocol and the 1881 Treaty of Saint Petersburg (Treaty of Ili) defined generally the boundary between Russian Central Asia and Chinese Central Asia. Following the 1881 treaty, many boundary commissions worked to demarcate precisely the China-Russia boundary in Central Asia. This work was completed, except for one sector in the Pamir Mountains that was delineated by the 1884 Protocol on the Sino-Russian Boundary in Kashgaria (modern Chinese Turkestan, in Xinjiang) but was never demarcated. Russian troops occupied the area in the early 1890s, and the Qing court protested by sending Russia a note stating that it retained its claim to the region even if it did not maintain a garrison there.

Following the Japanese defeat of China in the Sino-Japanese War of 1894–1895, Russia prevailed on a weakened China to grant it the right to build a railroad across Manchuria to Vladivostok, with a southern spur running southward through Manchuria to the Chinese port city of Lushun (Port Arthur), which eventually became Russia's principal naval base in East Asia. Just days before the fall of the Qing dynasty, Russia compelled China to sign the 1911 Qiqihar Treaty, which ceded to Russia several hundred square kilometers near the eastern trijunction of Russia, Mongolia, and China. This legacy of Russian encroachment into regions that the Chinese consider their territory continued to plague China-Russia/Soviet relations until the final decade of the twentieth century.

The Sino-Soviet Alliance of the 1950s

Following the establishment of the People's Republic of China in 1949, China and Russia signed a treaty of friendship and alliance. For the next decade, China followed the Soviet development model, adopting a centrally planned economy with state-owned factories emphasizing heavy industry. Thousands of Russian advisers went to China to train Chinese technicians, and Chinese students were sent to the Soviet Union to study. With time, however, China's growing resentment of Soviet domination, ideological differences between the two countries, and boundary disputes left over from the past sowed the seeds of conflict that led to the Sino-Soviet split in 1960, and eventually a border war in 1969.

Territorial Issues in China–Soviet Relations

Following the 1917 October Revolution, the new Soviet government issued the Karakhan Manifestos of 1919 and 1920, which renounced all the treaties concluded by the czarist government with China. However, new boundary treaties were not a high priority in subsequent negotiations, which dealt with the issues of Outer Mongolia and the Chinese Eastern Railway controlled by Russia.

Mao Zedong raised territorial issues in early 1950, while he was in Moscow negotiating the Sino-Soviet alliance. The two nations discussed the status of the Mongolian People's Republic (MPR) during this first Sino-Soviet summit. Mao stated his desire for the eventual reunion of Mongolia with China and raised the boundary issues as well. That the MPR and the Soviet Union were apprehensive about China's ambitions in Mongolia was made clear by Stalin's insistence on a Chinese declaration acknowledging the MPR's independence. Several times during the next ten years China raised the boundary question with the Soviet Union, but in 1960, with the open split in the Sino-Soviet alliance, the boundary dispute became a major source of tension.

As ideological and political tensions escalated between the Soviet Union and China, the Soviets grew concerned that the boundary question had become so salient an issue in Sino-Soviet relations. In May 1963 the Soviet Union proposed holding boundary consultations. At the talks, which began in February 1964, Mao prevented progress toward an agreement when he raised historical issues. He contended that during the czarist period, China had ceded more territory to Russia than to any other imperialist country and that czarist Russia had expanded its borders at the expense of China. Mao stated that the list of "lost" Chinese territory was too long, and the Chinese had not yet "presented their bill" for it. Russia accused China of betraying socialist internationalism, fostering a Maoist personality cult, and adopting radical Maoism. China accused Russia of Soviet imperialism and abandoning Marxism. After this polemical exchange, the two powers made no progress on boundary questions.

During China's Cultural Revolution (1966–1976), the boundary dispute flared up again. In March 1969 a military confrontation at Zhenbao (Damansky) Island in the Ussuri River proved that the boundary dispute could very well be the cause of a larger military conflict. In the wake of the March clashes, tensions

CHINA AND RUSSIA BECOME ALLIES

The Treaty of Friendship, Alliance, and Mutual Assistance between the Union of Soviet Socialist Republics and the People's Republic of China signed on 14 February 1950 formalized cooperative relations between the two nations.

The Presidium of the Supreme Soviet of the Union of Soviet Socialist Republics and the Central People's Government of the People's Republic of China;

Filled with determination jointly to prevent, by the consolidation of friendship and cooperation between the Union of Soviet Socialist Republics and the People's Republic of China, the rebirth of Japanese imperialism and a repetition of aggression on the part of Japan or any other state, which should unite in any form with Japan in acts of aggression;

Imbued with the desire to consolidate lasting peace and universal security in the Far East and throughout the world in conformity with the aims and principles of the United Nations Organization;

Profoundly convinced that the consolidation of good neighborly relations and friendship between the Union of Soviet Socialist Republics and the People's Republic of China meets the fundamental interests of the peoples of the Soviet Union and China;

Resolved for this purpose to conclude the present Treaty and appointed as their plenipotentiary representatives;

The Presidium of the Supreme Soviet of the Union of Soviet Socialist Republics—Andrei Yanuaryevich Vyshinsky, Minister of Foreign Affairs of the Union of Soviet Socialist Republics;

The Central People's Government of the People's Republic of China—Chou En-lai, Prime Minister of the State Administrative Council and Minister of Foreign Affairs of China;

Who, after exchange of their credentials, found in due form and good order, agreed upon the following:

Article I. Both High Contracting Parties undertake jointly to take all the necessary measures at their disposal for the purpose of preventing a repetition of aggression and violation of peace on the part of Japan or any other state which should unite with Japan, directly or indirectly, in acts of aggression. In the event of one of the High Contracting Parties being attacked by Japan or states allied with it, and thus being involved in a state of war, the other High Contracting Party will immediately render military and other assistance with all the means at its disposal.

The High Contracting Parties also declare their readiness in the spirit of sincere cooperation to participate in all international actions aimed at ensuring peace and security throughout the world, and will do all in their power to achieve the speediest implementation of these tasks.

Article II. Both the High Contracting Parties undertake by means of mutual agreement to strive for the earliest conclusion of a peace treaty with Japan, jointly with the other Powers which were allies during the Second World War.

Article III. Both High Contracting Parties undertake not to conclude any alliance directed against the other High Contracting Party, and not to take part in any coalition or in actions or measures directed against the other High Contracting Party.

Article IV. Both High Contracting Parties will consult each other in regard to all important international problems affecting the common interests of the Soviet Union and China, being guided by the interests of the consolidation of peace and universal security.

Article V. Both the High Contracting Parties undertake, in the spirit of friendship and cooperation and in conformity with the principles of equality, mutual interests, and also mutual respect for the state sovereignty and territorial integrity and non-interference in internal affairs of the other High Contracting Party—to develop and consolidate economic and cultural ties between the Soviet Union and

CONTINUED ON NEXT PAGE

CONTINUED FROM PREVIOUS PAGE

China, to render each other every possible economic assistance, and to carry out the necessary economic co-operation.

Article VI. The present Treaty comes into force immediately upon its ratification; the exchange of instruments of ratification will take place in Peking.

The present Treaty will be valid for 30 years. If neither of the High Contracting Parties gives notice one year before the expiration of this term of its desire to denounce the Treaty, it shall remain in force for another five years and will be extended in compliance with this rule.

Done in Moscow on February 14, 1950, in two copies, each in the Russian and Chinese languages, both texts having equal force.

Source: Soviet Monitor. (1950) London: Tass Agency, no. 11 (15 February): 311.

also rose along the border in Xinjiang, and during the summer of 1969 several other military incidents occurred. Moscow became increasingly alarmed and even contemplated a preemptive strike against China's nuclear facilities. Both China and the Soviet Union understood the real possibility of escalation and agreed to renew boundary negotiations.

Boundary Settlement

During the 1970s and early 1980s the two countries made no progress toward a boundary settlement. However, with the rise of Mikhail Gorbachev in the mid-1980s, Chinese-Soviet relations began to improve. A significant breakthrough came when Gorbachev, speaking in July 1986 in Vladivostok, showed a clear willingness to improve China-Soviet relations and publicly stated that Russia was willing to adopt the international standard and draw its eastern boundary with China by using the main channel of the Amur and Ussuri rivers rather than China's shoreline, as it had previously insisted. This significant leadership change, and Russia's new position on a boundary settlement, resulted in renewed negotiations.

Coupled with Gorbachev's Vladivostok initiative was the Soviet Union's growing willingness to withdraw its military from Afghanistan, which it had invaded in 1979, end its support for Vietnam's occupation of Cambodia, and dramatically reduce its troop strength along the Chinese-Russia border and in Mongolia. Progress in satisfying these three Chinese preconditions for normalization of relations resulted in the first Sino-Soviet summit in twenty years in May 1989, when Gorbachev and Deng Xiaoping met in Beijing, formally ending the thirty-year-old Sino-Soviet split.

Mutual interest in improving bilateral relations as both Russia and China pursued economic and political reform led to quick resolution of the boundary dispute. At the outset of new negotiations, both sides agreed to use the old treaties as the basis for determining the border and to delimit the boundary according to internationally accepted principles of international law. Following Gorbachev's May 1989 trip to Beijing, negotiations moved forward rapidly, and in June 1990 China and the Soviet Union agreed to sign a treaty covering areas on which they had reached a compromise. They signed the boundary treaty when the Chinese president Jiang Zemin traveled to Moscow in May 1991. The newly established Supreme Soviet of the Russian Federation ratified the accord on 3 February 1992, and the Standing Committee of the Chinese National Peoples Congress ratified it on 25 February. Russia and China concluded a treaty delimiting the short fifty-three-kilometer boundary to the west of Mongolia in September 1994. The following month China, Mongolia, and Russia jointly drafted a protocol and map of the eastern and western boundary junctures. In April 1999 demarcation of the entire Chinese-Russian boundary was finally completed; the detailed maps and comprehensive documentation weighed more than thirty kilograms.

The only area that remained unsettled was a never-before-demarcated region in the Pamir Mountains of Central Asia. By the late 1980s, Moscow was willing to accept the watershed principle in establishing the boundary; that is, it was willing to draw the boundary along the highest peaks of the mountains. Nevertheless the issues remained complex, and both sides agreed to postpone a final settlement until after negotiations were completed for the eastern sector of the boundary. However, with the breakup of the Soviet Union in 1990, China was faced with negotiating boundary settlements with the newly independent Central Asian states of Kazakstan, Kyrgyzstan, and Tajikistan. China has negotiated boundary settlements with Kazakstan and Kyrgyzstan, but the Pamir Mountain boundary with Tajikistan remains unsettled.

Post–Cold War Relations

With the collapse of the Soviet Union and the end of the Cold War, China–Russia relations entered a new phase. This sudden and fundamental shift in the global balance of power made it imperative for China and Russia to develop closer relations. In the mid-1990s, Chinese and Russian leaders formed a Sino-Russian "strategic partnership" to counterbalance American unilateralism in world affairs. These closer military and strategic relations between China and Russia are due in part to both countries' intensely nationalistic response to American power in the post–Cold War world. China and Russia, both undergoing a difficult transition from Communism to a market economy, have bruised national identities that make them natural allies against America's global cultural, economic, and military influence.

In 1992 President Boris Yeltsin of Russia and President Jiang Zemin of China both began promoting a strategic partnership between China and Russia. This new focus on China–Russia cooperation resulted in several high-level meetings and agreements. The two leaders formally announced the strategic partnership during a summit meeting held in April 1996 in Shanghai. The two countries now have a thriving military relationship, with Russia's cash-strapped military industries supplying China's technologically backward military with sophisticated jet fighters and naval vessels. In 1998 China ranked second, after India, as the major purchaser of Russian military equipment. Besides military hardware, Russia has also sold China production technologies and has helped China develop new weapons systems by sending Russian scientists to work in China's defense industries.

The present China–Russia strategic partnership is unlike the Sino-Soviet alliance of the 1950s. China and Russia are not attempting to establish a formal military alliance. Nevertheless they are cooperating closely to improve military-to-military relations and to develop confidence-building measures. Both nations hope to further reduce tensions over borders, as well as over nuclear weapons, and to make themselves more secure in the face of the threat both countries feel from the United States.

Economic relations have improved more slowly than the military relationship. Trade over the past several years has stagnated at 5 to 6 billion dollars annually, only 2 percent of China's total foreign trade in 1997. However, a robust border trade has developed over the past decade, and several border towns have become "open cities" to facilitate this dynamic local trade. The slow development of economic and trade relations is due largely to the problems both countries are experiencing with the transition from a centrally planned command economy to a market economy.

The greatest potential for cooperation is in developing the energy sector. China's rapid economic development during the past several decades has increased its demand for imported oil and gas. Estimates are that China will import 1.3 million barrels of oil a day in 2000 and 3.6 million by 2010. The Russian Far East has vast undeveloped oil and gas fields. However, Russians living in the Russian Far East are reluctant to develop closer relations with China because of their apprehension about the socioeconomic consequences of a stronger Chinese presence in the region. This apprehension is rooted in the deep historical differences and the history of conflict along the long mutual boundary. The demographic imbalance in the Far Eastern regions of Russia and northeastern China is also a point of concern. The Russian Far East has a population of roughly 8 million, while northeastern China has a population of approximately 100 million; the Russians fear Chinese in-migration will cause them to become a minority in their own country. Regional leaders in the Russian Far East have been more skeptical than leaders in Moscow about developing closer economic relations with China. They would rather develop closer relations with Japan, South Korea, and the United States.

Future Concerns

Although in the post–Cold War world China and Russia share common strategic concerns and some complementary economic interests, they will not easily overcome the deeply rooted historical and geopolitical legacy of conflict. Many inherent tensions are simply due to the fact that China and Russia share a long border. More fundamental causes of friction are the result of China's dynamic economic growth and Russia's precipitous economic decline, resulting in a shift in the balance of power between the two countries over the long term. Russian anxiety, especially in the Russian Far East, over what is perceived as a demographic time bomb just across the border in northeastern China will stymie economic cooperation and integration for the foreseeable future. Nonetheless, if China and Russia effectively manage the inherent tensions in their bilateral relations, closer military and economic cooperation is possible. One factor that will determine the closeness of Russia-China relations is the relationship between the United States and China and between the United States and Russia. Certainly for economic reasons, both countries would value a better relationship with the United States more than a closer relationship with each other. However, concern over American "hegemony" or unilateralism could cause a closer China-Russia strategic relationship that may form the cornerstone of an anti-American coalition seeking to undermine U.S. influence in important regions of the world, including the Middle East and Northeast Asia

Eric Hyer

Further Reading

Burles, Mark. (1999) *Chinese Policy toward Russia and the Central Asian Republics*. Santa Monica: Rand.

Chen, Vincent. (1966) *Sino-Russian Relations in the Seventeenth Century*. The Hague, Netherlands: Martinus Nijhoff.

Clubb, O. Edmund. (1971) *China and Russia: The "Great Game."* New York: Columbia University Press.

Garnett, Sherman W. (2000) *Rapprochement or Rivalry? Russia-China Relations in a Changing Asia*. New York: Carnegie Endowment International Peace.

Garver, John. (1993) *Foreign Relations of the People's Republic of China*. Englewood Cliffs, NJ: Prentice-Hall.

Jacobson, C. G. (1981) *Sino-Soviet Relations since Mao*. New York: Praeger.

Lattimore, Owen. (1962) *China's Inner Asian Frontiers*. Boston: Beacon Press.

Leong, Sow-Theng. (1976) *Sino-Soviet Relations, 1917–1926*. Canberra, Australia: Australian National University Press.

Low, Alfred D. (1976) *The Sino-Soviet Dispute: An Analysis of the Polemics*. Rutherford, NJ: Fairleigh Dickinson University Press.

Nemets, Alexander. (1996) *The Growth of China and Prospects for the Eastern Regions of the Former USSR*. Lewiston, NY: Mellen.

Paine, S. C. M. (1996) *Imperial Rivals: China, Russia, and Their Disputed Frontier*. Armonk, NY: M. E. Sharpe.

Schwartz, Harry. (1964) *Tsars, Mandarins, and the Commissars: A History of Chinese-Russian Relations*. London: Victor Gollancz.

Voskressenski, Alexi D. (1996) *The Difficult Border: Current Russian and Chinese Concepts of Sino-Russian Relations and Frontier Problems*. Commack, NY: Nova Science.

CHINA–TAIWAN RELATIONS

Taiwan's first residents, who make up the island's aboriginal tribes, migrated to the island about six thousand years ago and are related to ethnic groups from southern China, Southeast Asia, and the Philippines. They now constitute just over 1 percent of the total population. Although Taiwan appeared in Chinese historical records before the Han dynasty (206 BCE–220 CE), the colonization of Taiwan by Chinese settlers began only in 610 CE, during the Sui dynasty (581–618 CE). The next large migration of Chinese to Taiwan started in the twelfth century. During the Ming dynasty (1368–1644), many Chinese settlers in Taiwan were ordered to return to the Chinese mainland by imperial edicts. However, Chinese pioneers managed to continue to migrate to Taiwan in spite of the imperial prohibition. Soon Taiwan became a base from which Japanese and Taiwanese pirates attacked shipping in the South China seas.

Europeans also began to arrive on Taiwan. In 1590 Portuguese sailors landed on the main island and named it "ilha Formosa," meaning "beautiful island." Formosa remained the name by which Europeans knew Taiwan for centuries. In 1624 the Dutch invaded and occupied the main island. Two years later, the Spanish landed at Keelung, a northern port; they controlled Taiwan's coastal areas for two years. They were finally driven out by the Dutch in 1641.

In 1661, the Ming-dynasty general Zheng Chenggong (1624–1662), known to the West as Koxinga, took Taiwan from the Dutch and established an exiled Ming government in Anping (Tainan) in southern Taiwan. The Ming dynasty was overthrown by the Manchus on the Chinese mainland, but Zheng's son ruled Taiwan with a large number of Chinese followers until the Manchus finally took Taiwan in 1683. By then, Taiwan's population had exceeded 2.5 million, most of them from China's Fujian and Guangdong provinces.

By the nineteenth century, China was experiencing economic difficulties and political chaos. Western countries controlled territory along the eastern seaboard. At the end of the first Sino-Japanese War in 1895, Taiwan was ceded to Japan. Japan began its colonization of Taiwan and used it as a major military base for fifty years until the end of World War II.

Relations under the Two Chiangs

In 1911, the Manchu empire on the Chinese mainland was overthrown by a nationalist revolution spearheaded by the Guomindang (on Taiwan, Kuomintang) under the leadership of Sun Yat-sen (1866–1925) and Chiang Kai-shek (1887–1975). They established the Republic of China (ROC), which became an ally of the United States during World War II. On 26 November 1943 Chiang met with U.S. president Franklin D. Roosevelt and British prime minister Winston Churchill at Cairo, Egypt. They agreed that at the end of the war, Japan must return Taiwan to China. Taiwan was returned to Chiang's government on 25 October 1945.

A civil war in China erupted in 1945, pitting the Communist forces led by Mao Zedong (1893–1976) against Chiang Kai-shek's ROC government. Chiang was defeated, and Mao established the People's Republic of China (PRC) in Beijing on 1 October 1949. Chiang fled to Taiwan with more than 2 million mainlanders and reestablished his government there on 1 March 1950. It was widely expected within the United States that Mao's forces would soon invade Taiwan.

The outbreak of the Korean War on 25 June 1950 proved to be the saving grace for Taiwan. Fearing the spread of Communism across Asia, U.S. president Harry Truman immediately ordered the U.S. Seventh Fleet to defend Taiwan. Mao's troops on the mainland, virtually without a modern navy and air force, were in no position to challenge the U.S. Seventh Fleet.

In May 1951, the United States established its official Military Assistance Advisory Group in Taiwan to train Chiang's refugee troops. By 1954, Taiwan received a total of $4.2 billion in military aid and $1.7 billion in economic aid from the United States. These assistance programs, plus a 1954 Mutual Defense Treaty with the United States, helped Chiang Kai-shek to build up Taiwan from an impoverished and threatened island into a strong modern state.

During his twenty-five years of authoritarian rule, Chiang Kai-shek focused on preventing the spread of the Chinese Communists' power to Taiwan. He was not in favor of an independent Taiwan but rather considered the island as a base from which to fight Mao's Communism and to recover the mainland by any means at his disposal. He staged commando-style raids on the mainland, often with training and cooperation from the United States. He also forbade all forms of contact with the Communist-controlled mainland, including such seemingly trivial activities as reading mainland newspapers, listening to mainland radio broadcasts, or even receiving mail from friends or relatives still living on the mainland.

After the death of Chiang Kai-shek on 5 April 1975, the real power in Taiwan fell into the hands of his son, Chiang Ching-kuo (1910–1988), who was formally elected to the presidency in May 1978. Like his father, he absolutely opposed any demand for Taiwan's independence. Both Chiangs believed that Taiwan was a base from which the Kuomintang, and thus the ROC, could regain control of the mainland. To the two Chiangs, Taiwan was part of China, period.

However, Chiang Ching-kuo took significant steps to relax tensions with the Communist mainland government. For example, he permitted indirect trade and contacts with the mainland by Taiwan's residents. He was prepared to begin negotiations with the Communist government shortly after lifting the travel ban in October 1987, but before direct negotiations could begin, he died of cardiac and pulmonary failure on 13 January 1988.

Relations under the Native Taiwanese Leaders

The death of Chiang Ching-kuo opened a new era in Taiwanese politics. A native-born Taiwanese, Lee Teng-hui, succeeded him in 1988. Since then Taiwan has become a more democratic and pluralistic society. In addition to the Kuomintang, another major political party, the DPP (Democratic Progressive Party) is gaining considerable support among Taiwanese voters.

At first Lee Teng-hui continued his predecessor's open-door policy toward the Chinese mainland. Lee established the National Unification Council under the auspices of the President's Office (the White House of Taiwan). In February 1991 the council adopted "Guidelines for National Unification," which outlines three phases of unification: short term (exchange and reciprocity), middle term (trust and cooperation), and long term (consultation and unification). However, Lee refused to set a timetable for the implementation of the guidelines.

Lee Teng-hui also authorized the establishment of a semiofficial "Strait Exchange Foundation" (SEF) to make direct contact with the Chinese mainland's counterpart organization, the "Association for Relations across the Taiwan Straits" (ARATS).

The Chinese Communists have always maintained that Taiwan is a Chinese province and must be reunited with the mainland. Their plans to achieve that goal have varied. Before 1978, the official policy was to use military force. In 1978 the third plenum of the Eleventh Chinese Communist Party Congress adopted a new resolution calling for "peaceful reunification" with Taiwan. Beginning in 1983, the late Chinese leader Deng Xiaoping (1904–1997) made a number of concessions to Taiwan, and in early 1984 China offered a proposal that would take into account Taiwan's political and economic concerns: the "one country, two systems" proposal. "One country, two systems" continued to be China's official policy under Jiang Zemin (b. 1926).

Lee Teng-hui visited the United States in 1995 to give a speech at his alma mater, Cornell University. No Taiwanese top official had set foot on U.S. soil since the United States recognized the PRC in 1979. China feared Lee's visit indicated a move toward independence and would lead to recognition of Taiwan as a state by the world community. As a result, China conducted military exercises across the Taiwan Strait involving 400,000 troops. By 1996 four Chinese missiles had been fired within approximately fifty-one kilometers of the island state. During that tense period, the United States dispatched two nuclear-armed aircraft carrier groups into the area. Ultimately, China concluded its military exercises.

Relations between China and Taiwan have become extremely tense again since July 1999. At that time Lee Teng-hui introduced a new element by insisting that negotiations must be based on a "special state-to-state" relationship. As a result, China published a White Paper, "The One-China Principle and the Taiwan Issue" on 21 February 2000, in which it declared that they "cannot allow the resolution of Taiwan issue to be postponed indefinitely."

A political earthquake erupted in Taiwan on 18 March 2000, when Taiwanese voters elected a pro-independence DPP candidate, Chen Shui-bian (1951–), as president of Taiwan with 39 percent of the votes in a three-way race. China immediately demanded that Chen accept the "one-China" principle before any negotiations between China and Taiwan could be resumed. As of 2001, Chen continued to reject the one-China principle.

Future Prospects

If economics is the key to world politics in the twenty-first century, the future of China-Taiwan relations appears bright despite political upsets. Since the opening of trade relations between the two sides in 1979, trade across the Taiwan Strait has become a significant portion of total trade for both China and Taiwan. Taiwan's trade with China via Hong Kong rose from $1.5 billion in 1987 to more than $11 billion in 1997 and continues to rise higher. The Chinese mainland is now Taiwan's fourth-largest trading partner. Taiwan's investment on the mainland from 1979 to 1995, for example, exceeded $11 billion, making Taiwan China's second-largest investor after Hong Kong. Furthermore, Taiwan has enjoyed a handsome trade surplus every year since 1980. Therefore, despite their rocky history, there is hope for better relations to come between China and Taiwan.

Winberg Chai

See also: **Chen Shui-bian; Chiang Kai-shek; Guomindang; Lee Teng-hui; Mao Zedong; Sun Yat-sen; Taiwan—Profile**

Further Reading

Chai, Winberg, ed. (1996) *Chinese Mainland and Taiwan, with Documents.* 2d ed. Dubuque, IA: Kendall/Hunt.

———. (1999) "Relations between China Mainland and Taiwan: Overview and Chronology." *Asian Affairs: An American Review* 26, 2 (Summer).

Chang, Parris H., and Martin L. Lasater. (1993) *If China Crosses the Taiwan Strait.* Lanham, MD: University Press of America.

Cheng, Tun-jen, Chi Huang, and Samuel S. G. Wu. (1995) *Inherited Rivalry.* Boulder, CO: Lynne Rienner.

Chiu, Hungdah, ed. (1979) *China and the Taiwan Issue.* New York: Praeger Publishers.

———. (1973) *China and the Question of Taiwan.* New York: Praeger Publishers.

Clough, Ralph N. (1993) *Reaching across the Taiwan Strait.* Boulder, CO: Westview Press.

Wu, Hsin-Hsiung. (1994) *Bridging the Strait.* New York: Oxford University Press.

Yu, Peter Kien-Hong. (2001) "Misreading Each Other's Minds: Taipei, Beijing, and Washington." *Asian Affairs: An American Review* 28, 2 (Summer).

CHINA–UNITED STATES RELATIONS

Two centuries of relations between China and the United States have included conflict and cooperation in the diplomatic, economic, and social spheres. This relationship has been plagued by cycles of unrealistic expectations on each side of the Pacific, followed by deep disappointment. A common enemy, such as the Japanese during World War II or the Soviets in the latter stages of the Cold War, proved to be the single most important factor in building strong ties.

The Treaty Port Era

Trade formed the basis for the first Sino-U.S. contact. In 1784 the U.S. ship *Empress of China* carried silver and ginseng to the southeast coast of China, then returned to the United States with tea, silk, and porcelain. The *Empress* venture spurred in the United States an interest in goods from East Asia and dreams of prosperity through a limitless China market. The Chinese, then under the Qing dynasty (1644–1912), had little interest in the outside world and saw Americans as no different, albeit weaker, than other "barbarians" such as the British and French. Chinese purchased few Western products, and Americans quickly followed the British lead by selling opium to resolve a persistent trade deficit. Opium smuggling and demands for expanded trade sparked the 1840–1842 Opium War between Great Britain and China. The victorious British forced the Qing to sign the 1842 Treaty of Nanjing, which began a series of unequal treaties that required opening ports to foreign trade ("treaty ports"), limits on tariffs, and extraterritoriality. In 1844 the Qing signed the Treaty of Wangxia with American representatives. This agreement included a provision for most-favored-nation (MFN) status—thus enabling the United States to gain privileges the British enjoyed without firing a shot.

In the mid-1800s, humanitarian interests entered into the relationship, because Americans hoped to change China through Christianity. After France and Great Britain combined to defeat China in the Second Opium War, the resulting unequal treaty expanded trade rights in China, permitted diplomats to reside in the capital, and required that the Qing accept the presence of Christian missionaries. This enabled a growing number of American missionaries, primarily Protestants, to move freely about China.

Each side disappointed the other. Americans discovered that the China market was limited due to poverty and cultural differences, missionaries found the Chinese relatively uninterested in Christianity, and the Qing government showed no inclination to imitate Western political, economic, or social models. The U.S. role in the China trade declined relative to that of the British, Japanese, and Russians after 1900, and by the 1920s, Japan's share of U.S. imports and exports was more than twice that of China's. The most enduring legacy of missionaries was schools, orphanages, and hospitals, not converts. The Chinese became frustrated, because U.S. claims of benevolence did not bring changes to the unequal treaties.

Chinese immigration became another contentious topic. The 1868 Burlingame Treaty encouraged immigration to the United States, though ethnic Chinese had come to the United States earlier to work as miners or railroad workers. Many Chinese were contract laborers whose passage was deducted from their wages in what became known as the "coolie" trade. Growing racial discrimination and violence against the approximately 160,000 Chinese in the United States led to criticism on both sides of the Pacific. In 1882 the U.S. Congress, bowing to union concerns over jobs and cruder racist sentiments, forbade almost all Chinese immigration.

A Special Relationship?

Around the beginning of the twentieth century, U.S. leaders concluded that a unified China was central to long-term U.S. commercial interests and humanitarian endeavors. As the Western powers and Japan appeared poised to divide China into mutually exclusive spheres of interest, in 1899 Secretary of State John Hay issued the first of the Open Door notes, which requested that all nations respect China's territorial integrity. Most recipients were politely noncommittal. During the Boxer Movement (1898–1900), violent antiforeign mobs attacked missionaries and other foreigners in Northeast China, creating a crisis that climaxed with the Qing alliance with the Boxers and declaration of war against the West in 1900. As a multinational expeditionary force prepared to invade China, the United States issued a second note to deter other nations from taking spheres of influence. Following the occupation of Beijing, a coalition of Western powers (including the United States) and Japan forced the Qing to sign the Boxer Protocol, which required a huge indemnity from China. The United States, eager to differentiate itself from other imperialists, devoted its portion of the funds to education in China.

Increasingly, however, nationalistic Chinese rejected the idea of a special relationship, even as it became more deeply entrenched in the minds of U.S. officials and public. The Chinese attacked U.S. treaty privileges. Immigration policies and the treatment of Chinese in the United States spurred a boycott of U.S. goods in the coastal cities of China in 1905. Although the boycott died out after one year, the immigration policies remained unchanged.

Even after the overthrow of the Qing in the Revolution of 1911, many Chinese felt that the United States did not live up to the ideal of a special relationship. The United States supported a former Qing general, Yuan Shikai (1859–1916), rather than the revolutionary nationalists led by Sun Yat-sen (or Sun Zhongshan, 1866–1925). Also, in the Lansing-Ishii Agreement of November 1917, the United States acknowledged Japan's "special interests" in North China and Manchuria, while the Japanese offered lip service to support China's territorial integrity. Nor did American leaders support China's attempt to restore its national sovereignty at the Versailles Peace Conference of 1919.

Treaty revision remained a contentious issue. Western powers, the United States included, used the excuse of instability in China to avoid the issue even after the Nationalists, led by Chiang Kai-shek (or Jiang Jieshi, 1887–1975), unified China through the Northern Expedition of 1926–1928. Chiang carried on Sun's legacy of the Three Principles of the People (nationalism, democracy, and people's livelihood) by emphasizing that the unequal treaties had to be revised. However, Chiang's need for foreign loans and recognition of the Republic of China (ROC) limited his ability to press the issue.

Japanese aggression raised Chinese hopes for closer ties to the United States. In 1931 the Japanese Army plotted an incident as an excuse to occupy Manchuria. Although novels like Pearl Buck's *The Good Earth* built sympathy by portraying China as a nation of poor but hardworking and honest farmers, the United States took few concrete actions to support the republic. Secretary of State Henry Stimson's Nonrecognition Doctrine merely declared the unwillingness of the United States to acknowledge what the Japanese had taken by force. All-out war between the China and Japan in 1937 initially elicited little more than American sympathy.

From Allies to Enemies

In public, the period from Pearl Harbor to Japan's surrender was a golden era in Sino-U.S. relations, because the two peoples faced a common enemy and shared similar dreams of a strong, democratic China in the postwar world. The U.S. government supplied military and financial aid, and the American public, influenced by Chiang's propaganda efforts and the idealization of China offered by publications such as *Time* magazine, almost uniformly supported the Nationalists. Chiang appeared to elevate China to great power status by participating in the Cairo Conference of November 1943, where President Franklin Delano Roosevelt, Prime Minister Winston Churchill, and Chiang discussed the restoration of Chinese territory taken by the Japanese, such as Taiwan. Further, the United States and Britain surrendered extraterritorial privileges.

The reality of Sino-U.S. ties was more complex. The Nationalists often found themselves ignored, because Washington's first priority was defeating Germany, and few Americans perceived any vital interests at stake in China. Americans assumed that Chinese manpower would fight Japan and that aid was a lever to reform Chiang's authoritarian regime. These hopes clashed with the reality of a weak China, led by a regime more concerned with eradicating the Chinese Communist Party (CCP) than confronting the Japanese occupation. The Nationalists expressed dissatisfaction with the volume of U.S. aid and wanted to stockpile war materials in anticipation of a postwar struggle against the CCP. U.S. criticism of Chiang's war effort began within China, with U.S. diplomats and U.S. military adviser General Joseph Stilwell, but it gradually spread to Washington.

Communist leaders, such as Mao Zedong (1893–1976) and Zhou Enlai (1898–1976), wanted closer ties to the United States to balance the Soviets, to weaken the Nationalists, and to obtain military equipment, while Americans hoped that the CCP would serve as a more effective force against the Japanese. Roosevelt accepted the need for contact with the CCP, then based in Yan'an, and in 1944 authorized the Dixie Missions. These missions, conducted over Chiang's objections, led to discussions concerning cooperation against the Japanese. Other than allowing Mao and Zhou an opportunity to portray themselves as moderate agrarian reformers, these delegations accomplished little.

At war's end, the United States continued to support the Nationalists, even as it sought to mediate between Chiang and Mao. Efforts to create a coalition government failed, because the Nationalists assumed they would receive aid regardless of their actions, and the Communists lost faith in the ability of the United States to serve as a neutral arbiter. Civil war began in early 1947, and Chiang's forces, poorly led and overextended into Manchuria, were retreating southward by 1948.

The Nationalists' impending defeat spurred Chiang to request more United States aid, as he attempted to make the civil war part of the global Cold War. President Harry S. Truman, however, sought to distance the United States from its wartime ally. In August 1949, the Department of State released a white paper that signaled the end of support for Chiang, whose corruption and ineptitude were blamed for the Communists' victory. The Nationalists retreated to Taiwan, where they claimed to remain the sole legal government of China.

On 1 October 1949 Mao Zedong proclaimed the establishment of the People's Republic of China (PRC). An uneasy waiting period ensued as Beijing and Washington sought to find a modus vivendi to build a relationship. The PRC's growing ties to the Soviet Union and America's hostility toward Communism made immediate recognition impossible.

Cold War and the Dilemmas of a Divided China

Uncertainty turned to conflict when the Korean War began in 1950. President Truman dispatched the Seventh Fleet to the Taiwan Strait, thus signaling the U.S. determination to protect the Nationalists and contain the Communists. By the end of the year, United States troops and Communist "volunteers" were fighting on the peninsula. The leaders of the People's Republic perceived recognition of Chiang's government as a violation of China's national sovereignty. The mainland gave propaganda, if not material, support to anticolonial and anti-American revolutionary movements around the world, while Washington sought to isolate the PRC through diplomatic, military, and economic means.

To most Americans, Taiwan became China. Chiang offered the United States a staunch Cold War ally and valuable outpost for containing Communist power. U.S. aid and trade proved vital to the initial survival and later "economic miracle" of the ROC. Chiang also received military aid and support in international forums such as the United Nations. The December 1954 Sino-U.S. Mutual Defense Treaty marked the high point of Cold War cooperation between the two. But President Dwight D. Eisen-

FIGHTING A UNITED STATES INVASION

During the Cold War era, the United States was concerned about Chinese expansion while the Chinese were concerned about an American invasion. The following text is Marshall Lin Piao's advice to Chinese generals in 1966 on how to combat an American invasion.

> In order to annihilate the enemy, we must adopt the policy of luring him in deep and abandoning some cities and districts of our own accord in a planned way, so as to let him in. It is only after letting the enemy in that the people can take part in the war in various ways and that the power of a people's war can be fully exerted. It is only after letting the enemy in that he can be compelled to divide up his forces, take on heavy burdens, and commit mistakes. In other words, we must let the enemy become elated, stretch out all his ten fingers and become hopelessly bogged down.
>
> *Source:* Donald S. Zagoria. (1967) *Vietnam Triangle: Moscow/Peking/Hanoi*. New York: Pegasus, 87.

hower emphasized that the treaty obliged the United States to defend the ROC from attack but did not include support for Nationalist raids on the mainland. Nevertheless, the United States did threaten military action against the mainland during military clashes between the PRC and the ROC in 1954–1955 and 1958.

In reality, the United States and the PRC showed restraint, because neither side sought direct military confrontation after the Korean War. Official contact between the two Cold War antagonists was limited. After the 1954 Geneva Conference (devoted to discussions of Korea and Indochina), U.S. and Chinese diplomats held a series of 130 meetings in Geneva, then in Warsaw. These talks accomplished little of substance, but they would offer an avenue for rapprochement in the early 1970s.

Neither President John F. Kennedy nor his successor, Lyndon B. Johnson, showed imagination in their policy toward China, as domestic politics and international alliances made rapprochement seem impossible. In the PRC, the Great Proletarian Cultural Revolution increased the rhetoric attacking the United States and U.S. involvement in Vietnam spurred Chinese support of the Communist Democratic Republic of Vietnam (DRV).

Rapprochement and Beyond

By the late 1960s, Mao Zedong and Zhou Enlai became convinced that the Soviet Union represented a greater threat to China than did the United States. The Soviet invasion of Czechoslovakia in 1968 and border clashes between the PRC and Soviet Union in 1969 heightened fears of an attack from the north. The PRC also sought improved relations with the United States as part of a larger drive to end its international isolation. In the United States, President Richard M. Nixon reasoned that closer ties to the PRC would be a counterweight to the Soviet Union, improve his domestic political standing, and demoralize North Vietnam. This effort began by relaxing restrictions on trade and travel—measures considered but rejected during the final year of the Johnson administration.

At Warsaw talks of January and February 1970, the Chinese offered to arrange a high-level meeting. This opened the door to secret contacts through Pakistan, which, in turn, facilitated National Security Adviser Henry A. Kissinger's trip to Beijing on 9–11 July 1971. Nixon's historic visit to China from 20 to 27 February 1972 marked a huge shift in Sino-U.S. relations. The trip concluded with the Shanghai Communiqué, which made clear that each nation shared concern over Soviet power. One sensitive issue was Taiwan. The United States professed hope that Taiwan's status be resolved peacefully, but acknowledged that both the PRC and ROC claimed Taiwan as part of China (the "one China" policy). Both parties also pledged to work toward normalized relations.

Although each nation opened liaison offices in 1973 in the other's capital, Nixon's domestic political travails delayed progress toward full normalization—much to the chagrin of Mao and Zhou. President Jimmy Carter came into office determined to move ahead. In December 1978 a joint communiqué announced the establishment of diplomatic relations and the termination of official U.S.-ROC ties and the Mutual Defense Treaty.

Normalization with the PRC left a delicate problem—the fate of U.S. ties to the Republic of China on Taiwan. In April 1979 Carter signed the Taiwan Relations Act, which set the rules for unofficial relations through the American Institute on Taiwan (AIT). The U.S. Congress reaffirmed the one China policy but pledged to sell defensive weapons to Taiwan and emphasized its interest in the peaceful settlement of the Taiwan issue. Under pressure from the PRC, in 1982 President Ronald Reagan promised to reduce the level of arms sales to the island. The ROC, however, maintained an effective lobbying effort in the United States, which limited the U.S. government's ability to distance itself from its former ally. PRC leaders such as Deng Xiaoping complained that U.S. arms sales and unofficial ties to Taiwan impeded progress toward reunification. Taiwan's economic success and democratic reform sparked further conflict. In 1987 Chiang Ching-kuo (Chiang Kai-shek's son and successor) lifted martial law on Taiwan, marking an important step toward peaceful democratic change on the island.

After Chiang's death in 1988, Lee Teng-hui, a native Taiwanese, assumed the presidency. His rejection of the one-China formula highlighted the problem of Taiwan's relationship with the mainland, even as his promotion of democracy drew praise in the U.S. media, Congress, and public. Lee's ambivalence over reunification drew threats from the PRC, which, despite U.S. wishes, refused to commit itself to a peaceful solution.

Overall, however, Sino-U.S. relations during the 1980s were strong, because the two nations shared economic interests and antipathy toward the Soviet Union. Under Deng's leadership, the PRC sought contact with the West in order to obtain technology and spur economic development, while the United States saw an opportunity to expand exports and reshape China in the U.S. image of capitalism and democracy. Trade spawned a powerful coalition of business interests in the United States that sought good relations with China. However, the violent suppression of pro-democracy demonstrators in Beijing's Tiananmen Square in June 1989 marked a major turning point. Deng blamed Western influence for the demonstrations, and President George Bush announced sanctions against the Chinese government. U.S. criticism of China's political system and human rights violations became a constant irritant to the PRC. Further, the collapse of the Soviet Union removed a key strategic motivation for rapprochement.

China–U.S. relations became more contentious after the Cold War. Beijing frequently criticized American "hegemony," and objected to the lack of U.S. pressure upon Taiwan to reunify with the mainland, missile defense schemes, the accidental bombing of the Chinese embassy in Yugoslavia, continued intelligence gathering (such as the Hainan island incident of 2001), sympathy for Tibetan dissidents, and U.S. military intervention in the Balkans and the Middle East. Washington complained of Chinese sales of nuclear and missile technology to Iran and Pakistan, trade barriers, human rights violations, and threats against Taiwan. President George W. Bush's public support of a one China policy even as he approved arms sales to Taiwan satisfied neither the PRC nor the ROC. Nevertheless, the United States supported China's integration into the international economic order through institutions such as the World Trade Organization. By the beginning of the twenty-first century, the world's most populous nation and its most powerful nation were increasingly bound together through trade, investment, education exchanges, and immigration.

Steven Phillips

See also: **Boxer Rebellion, China—Profile, Chinese Communist Party, Deng Xiaoping, Mao Zedong, Opium War, Qing Dynasty, Taiwan, Yuan Shikai, Zhou Enlai**

Further Reading

Chang, Gordon. (1990) *Friends and Enemies: The United States, China, and the Soviet Union, 1948–1972.* Stanford, CA: Stanford University Press.

Cohen, Warren I. (1990) *America's Response to China: A History of Sino-American Relations.* 3d ed. New York: Columbia University Press.

Fairbank, John K. (1983) *The United States and China.* 4th ed. Cambridge, MA: Harvard University Press.

Garver, John W. (1997) *Face Off: China, the United States, and Taiwan's Democratization.* Seattle, WA: University of Washington Press.

Harding, Harry. (1992) *A Fragile Relationship: The United States and China since 1972.* Washington, DC: The Brookings Institution.

Harding, Harry, and Yuan Ming, eds. (1989) *Sino-American Relations, 1945–1955: A Joint Reassessment of a Critical Decade.* Wilmington, DE: SR Books.

Hunt, Michael. (1983) *The Making of a Special Relationship: The United States and China to 1914.* New York: Columbia University Press.

Mann, James. (1999) *About Face: A History of America's Curious Relationship with China, from Nixon to Clinton.* New York: Alfred A. Knopf.

Schaller, Michael. (1979) *The U.S. Crusade in China, 1938–1945.* New York: Columbia University Press.

Tucker, Nancy Bernkopf. (1994) *Taiwan, Hong Kong, and the United States, 1945–1992: Uncertain Friendships.* New York: Twayne Publishers.

United States Department of State. (1949) *United States Relations with China, with Special Reference to the Period 1944–1949.* Washington, DC: Department of State.

CHINA–VIETNAM RELATIONS

China and Vietnam share a long history of relations marked by extended periods of collaboration and shorter periods of military conflict. Vietnam was for more then a thousand years a part of the Chinese empire before gaining independence in the tenth century CE. The independent Vietnam remained under Chinese cultural and political influence and a tributary relationship developed. This close relationship was ended by the period of French colonial rule in Vietnam during the second half of the nineteenth century and the first half of the twentieth.

After Vietnam regained independence from France in 1954, relations between China and Vietnam were officially very close up to the end of the War in Vietnam in 1975. Thereafter, relations deteriorated into open hostilities in early 1979, and tension remained high for most of the 1980s. From the late 1980s relations started to improve, leading to full normalization in November 1991. The 1990s have been characterized by two contradictory trends: expanding and improving relations in most fields on the one hand, and recurring periods of tension relating to border disputes on the other. Both countries are making considerable efforts to manage and eventually settle the border disputes.

Background

Relations between the countries were very close in the 1950s, and for two decades China provided the Democratic Republic of Vietnam (DRV) with extensive economic and military assistance. China sent thousands of advisers to assist in various fields. China also provided considerable assistance during the Vietnam War. However, irritants developed during the 1960s and into the first half of the 1970s due to different perceptions of the Soviet Union and divergent views on relations with the United States. After the 1973 Paris agreement, which led to the withdrawal of American troops from Vietnam and established a cease-fire in the Vietnam War, the Vietnamese claimed that Chinese leaders had advised them to diminish the level of the fighting in the south for a few years, advice perceived as aiming at keeping Vietnam divided. China rejected this claim.

Sino-Vietnamese Relations, 1975–1991

Following the end of the war in April 1975 relations between China and Vietnam began to deteriorate over China's uneasiness about Vietnam's relations with the Soviet Union and China's increasing support for Cambodia in the conflict between Vietnam and Cambodia. The Vietnamese military intervention in Cambodia in late December 1978 caused further tension. There were also territorial disputes along the land border, in the Gulf of Tonkin, and in the South China Sea. The clashes that occurred along the border had more significance as an indication of deteriorating relations and of divergence on other issues than as conflicts in their own right. Finally, there was the issue of how the ethnic Chinese in Vietnam were treated by Vietnamese authorities. The mass migration of ethnic Chinese from Vietnam to China in the spring of 1978 led to the open and public deterioration of bilateral relations between the two countries. Vietnam's intervention in Cambodia in December 1978 eventually led to China's attack on Vietnam in February and March 1979.

The normalization process began with low-level contacts in the mid-1980s and expanded to high-level meetings from early 1989. In early September 1990 a secret Vietnamese high-level visit to China took place. Despite this meeting, political normalization did not gain momentum until mid-1991. Increased diplomatic interaction paved the way for a high-level summit on 5–10 November 1991, during which bilateral relations were officially fully normalized.

Relations since 1991

Since full normalization, the relationship between China and Vietnam has been characterized by two contradictory trends: expanding contacts and cooperation in many fields, and continued territorial disputes. The positive trend in bilateral relations can be seen through the expanding political, cultural, economic, and military contacts between the two countries. Official delegations from one country regularly visit the other country to discuss ways of expanding relations in various fields. Increased economic ties since 1991 can be seen through bilateral trade, which grew from $32 million in 1991 to $1 billion in 1996 and was expected to reach $2.8 billion in 2001. China also provides loans and assistance to upgrade Chinese-built factories in northern Vietnam. In the political field the close relationship between the two ruling parties—the Chinese Communist Party (CCP) and the Communist Party of

Vietnam (CPV)—has expanded through a steady stream of exchange visits at various levels. The contacts between the armed forces of the two countries have also expanded through regular exchange visits.

Reverting back to the territorial disputes as a source of tension, it can be noted that since late 1991 sharp differences relating to all the disputes (i.e., overlapping claims to the Paracel and Spratly archipelagos, to water and continental shelf areas in the South China Sea and in the Gulf of Tonkin, and to areas along the land border) were prevalent from May to November 1992. Differences relating to oil exploration in the South China Sea and the signing of contracts with foreign companies for exploration were prevalent during parts of 1994, 1996, and 1997. During 1998 there were shorter periods of tension relating to the disputes. During 1999 the focus was on reaching a settlement of the land border dispute and no significant tension was caused by any of the border disputes. During 2000 the focus was on resolving the Gulf of Tonkin dispute and no significant tension was caused by the remaining border disputes. The major achievements thus far are the signing of the Land Border Treaty on 30 December 1999 and the Agreement on the Demarcation of Waters, Exclusive Economic Zones, and Continental Shelves in the Gulf of Tonkin on 25 December 2000.

The progress in managing the territorial disputes in recent years contributes positively to the prospect of a long-term stability in the Sino-Vietnamese relationship. However, the lack of progress in the talks on the disputes in the South China Sea area remains a potential threat to a stable relationship.

Ramses Amer

Further Reading

Amer, Ramses. (1994) "Sino-Vietnamese Normalization in the Light of the Crisis of the Late 1970s." *Pacific Affairs* 67, 3: 357–383.

———. (1999) "Sino-Vietnamese Relations: Past, Present, and Future." In *Vietnamese Foreign Policy in Transition*, edited by Carlyle A. Thayer and Ramses Amer. Singapore: Institute for Southeast Asian Studies; New York: St. Martin's Press, 68–130.

Thayer, Carlyle A. (1994) "Sino-Vietnamese Relations: The Interplay of Ideology and National Interest." *Asian Survey* 34, 6: 513–528.

Womak, Brantly. (1994) "Sino-Vietnamese Border Trade: The Edge of Normalization." *Asian Survey* 34, 6: 495–512.

CHINESE CIVIL WAR OF 1945–1949

Although the Chinese Nationalist and Communist movements had pledged to unite against Japanese aggression in 1936, conflict between them actually grew during the war against Japan (1937–1945), setting the stage for a civil war. The approaches the Chinese Nationalists and Communists employed during the war against Japan basically determined the outcome of the civil war. From 1941 through 1945 the Nationalist government held back from major offenses against the Japanese while it grew in international stature and acquired a powerful and generous ally in the United States. Nevertheless, the Nationalists suffered from a variety of internal weaknesses, including loss of its economically advanced territories to Japan, serious inflation, and deteriorating popular support. For their part, the Chinese Communists made simple living and self-reliance into a patriotic virtue while winning widespread admiration for their aggressive anti-Japanese nationalism. Most important, they increased their territorial control across North China, where Communist military units, supported by local militias, knitted together popularly based regional governments behind Japanese lines. Operating largely without outside support, the Communists forces grew tremendously and developed a bold confidence in their newfound abilities.

U.S. Attempt at Intervention

The United States, fully aware by early 1945 of the looming Nationalist-Communist conflict, intervened in the hope of creating a single Chinese government as its chief ally in East Asia. When initial efforts by Ambassador Patrick Hurley stumbled, President Harry Truman dispatched General George C. Marshall to China. But Marshall failed to achieve compromises between the two sides during his fourteen-month mission from December 1945 to January 1947.

Full Civil War

As Japan's collapse loomed in early August 1945, both the Communists and the Nationalists set in motion hastily made plans to expand their territorial control. The Nationalists held Sichuan and the southwest as well as some parts of central China, but they needed to reestablish their pre-1937 control over East and South China, especially the rich and fertile coastal provinces of Jiangsu, Zhejiang, Fujian, and Guangdong. Chiang Kai-shek (1887–1975), the leader of the Nationalists, also intended to gain control of huge areas of China where his Nationalist government had never governed before 1937, including North China, Manchuria, Inner Mongolia, the northwest, and the huge but sparsely populated Xinjiang. Yet only two regions, North China under Communist control and Manchuria occupied by the Soviet Union, became the civil war's major battlegrounds.

Chiang rushed his forces to principal cities all around China, typically using U.S. air and naval units to transport his armies while demanding that defeated Japanese units hand over control only to his forces. Consequently, the Nationalists wound up with their armies in important cities throughout China, but their military and political strength was often thinly spread.

Communist strategy called for building on their present strength by surrounding and taking over the cities of North China. In a bold and ultimately decisive move, Communist leader Mao Zedong (1893–1976) dispatched General Lin Biao (1908–1971) with a large army to Manchuria, where he hoped the occupying Soviet forces might aid their fellow Communists.

Lin Biao's forces entering Manchuria received some assistance from the Soviet armies, but primarily in the form of letting Japanese arms fall into their hands. The Soviet Union still recognized Chiang's Nationalist government and so acceded to Nationalist occupation of the region's cities, ports, and railways. Before withdrawing in May 1946, the Soviets concentrated on looting Japanese factory equipment to rebuild their own war-ravaged economy.

On the U.S. side, doubts increased about the long-term prospects of its ally, the Chinese Nationalists. Chiang's problems were compounded in late 1945 as inflation continued, public confidence in the Nationalists did not revive, and relations between Chiang's armies and the recently liberated Chinese in the large coastal cities were uneasy. The Nationalists hoped for massive U.S. intervention on their behalf, but in the United States the postwar atmosphere demanded a return to normalcy. President Truman and General Marshall concluded that the Congress and American people would not be willing to commit the amounts of money, material, and fighting men needed to ensure a Chinese Nationalist victory. Nevertheless, the United States continued to give extensive economic and military support to the Nationalists.

American efforts in 1945 and 1946 to forge a compromise between the Nationalists and the Communists were unsuccessful because Chiang would not enter a coalition with the Communists, while the Communists insisted on maintaining independent control of the territory they administered. As Marshall prepared to return to Washington in mid-1946, he arranged the appointment of an American missionary educator, John Leighton Stuart, as the new U.S. ambassador. Although Stuart knew both the Nationalist and Communist leaderships in China, he was new to diplomacy and lacked Marshall's close connections in Washington, so his appointment indicated the shifting of U.S. attention away from China. After his return from China in January 1947, Marshall became U.S. secretary of state and gave his name to a plan to revive the European economy, signaling that again Europe would be foremost in U.S. foreign policy concerns.

Even during Marshall's mission, Nationalist-Communist armed conflict increased. Overall, Nationalist armies fared well in these battles, and by late 1946 Chiang, certain of victory, reorganized his government with a new constitution followed by national elections. Taking Yan'an, the Communists' wartime capital, in March 1947, buoyed the Chinese Nationalist's military fortunes.

Turning of the Tide against the Nationalists

After July 1947 the Nationalist cause began to sputter. Reconciliation with Chinese who had been under Japanese occupation often proved difficult. The serious wartime inflation deepened, making it difficult to restart the modern sector of the Chinese economy. Fear of Communist influence led the Nationalists into general suppression of freedom of expression.

In the summer and fall of 1947, Communist armies began to win victories in North China. Then from December 1947 to March 1948, Lin Biao's armies won a series of major battles in Manchuria. By early November 1948, Lin had destroyed some of the Nationalist's best armies and taken over Manchuria. In these engagements, the Communist military adopted a new pattern that departed from its preference for guerrilla warfare by moving to regular battlefield formations composed of large infantry armies supported by some tanks, artillery, and aircraft. Nationalist divisions began to surrender to the Communists and then to reappear on the Communist side under new leadership with their modern American equipment.

In North China, Communist commanders used similar tactics with great success. As Manchuria slipped from the Nationalists' grasp, the Communists in October 1948 opened a general offensive in southern Shandong known as the Huaihai campaign. Chiang threw his best remaining divisions into the fray only to lose them by January 1949. As the full enormity of the Nationalist defeat emerged, the Nationalist general in command of the Beijing-Tianjin region surrendered with 200,000 soldiers.

Economic collapse compounded these battlefield disasters. Runaway inflation tore through the Nationalist economy like a great typhoon, leaving ruin everywhere in its wake. Opposition elements within the Nationalist Party forced Chiang to resign in January 1949, and General Li Zongren (1890–1969) became acting president. In April 1949, Communist armies crossed the Chang (Yangtze) River and began the task of mopping up resistance in the huge areas under real or nominal Nationalist control. Chiang directed evacuation of the loyal remnants of his civil and military machines to Taiwan.

Stalemate

In the summer of 1950, with the outbreak of the Korean War, the struggle between the Communists and Nationalists became folded into the Cold War. Small-scale military incidents continued for several years, and then both sides entered a stalemate. By the beginning of the twenty-first century, even though the economies of the People's Republic of China (mainland China) and the Republic of China (Taiwan) have become closely interwoven, the Chinese civil war never has been formally ended.

David D. Buck

Further Reading

Chassin, Lionel M. (1965) *The Communist Conquest of China: A History of the Civil War.* Cambridge, MA: Harvard University Press.

Dreyer, Edward L. (1995) *China at War, 1901–1949.* New York: Longman's.

Eastman, Lloyd E. (1984) *Seeds of Destruction: Nationalist China in War and Revolution.* Stanford, CA: Stanford University Press.

Levine, Steven I. (1984) *The Anvil of Victory: The Communist Victory in Manchuria.* New York: Columbia University Press.

Loh, Pichon P. Y. (1965) *The Kuomintang Debacle of 1949: Conquest or Defeat?* Boston: D. C. Heath.

Pepper, Suzanne. (1978) *The Civil War in China: The Political Struggle, 1945–1949.* Berkeley and Los Angeles: University of California Press.

CHINESE COMMUNIST PARTY

The Chinese Communist Party (CCP) emerged out of the infiltration of Western ideas into China at the end of the nineteenth and beginning of the twentieth century in the environment of the May Fourth Movement (1917–1921), in which Chinese students and intellectuals protested the injustices of the Treaty of Versailles. (The treaty ceded Chinese territory to Japan despite China's having participated in the war on the side of the allies; the actual demonstrations against it took place on 4 May 1919.) The founders of the CCP, Chen Duxiu (1879–1942), and Li Dazhao (1888–1927), were both then at Peking (Beijing) University.

Chen left the university after his arrest for leading street demonstrations. Like many others, he became increasingly radicalized. During this period, Li, the more active Marxist, organized various study groups that included later leaders of the CCP, including Mao Zedong (1893–1976). By this time agents of Comintern, the international Communist organization dominated by the Soviet Union, were actively agitating for the formation of a Chinese Communist Party.

This step was finally taken in July 1921. The first party congress was held in secret at a girls' boarding house in Shanghai. Chen and Li were not among the twelve organizing delegates, but their views dominated. Chen favored revolution based upon urban workers, while Li wished to establish a more popular base for revolution, an idea later taken up by Mao.

The CCP prior to the Long March

The period between 1921 and 1927 was traumatic for the CCP. The Comintern was willing to sacrifice CCP interests to those of Chiang Kai-shek's Nationalist Party (Guomindang), with whom the Comintern compelled the CCP to work. The CCP also found it difficult to foment the urban, workers' revolution desired by Chen in China, as the vast majority of China's population was engaged in agriculture.

In 1927, the Nationalists, who leaned more to the right after the Northern Expedition (a campaign against regional warlords), turned against their CCP allies, more or less destroying its urban base. The CCP had no choice but to regroup in rural areas in south and central China.

Between 1927 and 1934, the CCP fought a losing battle against the well-armed Nationalist army. By 1934, its very survival was at stake, and surviving CCP armies began the trek to the north, then outside direct Nationalist influence, known as the Long March. It was completed in 1936. CCP forces regrouped in a stronghold in Shaanxi. By this time, Mao, by no means dominant before, had emerged as the CCP's leader.

War with Japan, Civil War, and the First Decades of the People's Republic

By 1936 the political situation in China had changed dramatically. Japanese aggression had become overt after the Manchurian Incident of 1931, in which the Japanese created an excuse to attack Chinese troops in Manchuria. Chiang Kai-shek (1887–1975) would have preferred to consolidate his regime and to suppress enemies, including the CCP, but he was propelled into a war with Japan by an outraged public. It was disaster. He lost their capital and most other important Chinese cities, and had to retreat to impotence and isolation in Sichuan.

The CCP, by contrast, safely out of the main line of Japanese advance, could nurture its strength. When the Allied victory in World War II came, the CCP quickly expanded its influence in the chaos following the Japanese surrender. It acquired large stocks of arms through its own efforts and with the help of the Soviets.

The United States wanted the Nationalists to negotiate with their CCP enemies, but the Nationalists trusted in their own power to win any civil war. They proved surprisingly inept militarily, while mismanagement of the economy lost them support. In 1949 they retreated to Taiwan and by 1950 held little else.

The People's Republic of China was proclaimed on 1 October 1949, under Mao's control. The next two decades were a period of national recovery and experimentation. Mao remained true to his populist roots, and radical policy was often the result. The most important of Mao's initiatives were the Great Leap Forward (1958–1960), a failed effort to industrialize China on the village level, and the Cultural Revolution (1966–1976), in which gangs of youth terrorized their elders and those in positions of authority, armed with the words of Mao. Only the behind-the-scenes guidance of Premier Zhou Enlai (1898–1976) prevented a total meltdown. The Great Leap Forward actually set China's industrial production back; it also cause widespread famine. During the same period, China broke with its Soviet ally.

The Era of Reform

In the waning years of the Cultural Revolution, the CCP had to reinvent itself, to become less radical, less isolated internationally, and more approachable to the majority of Chinese. As part of this change, the CCP allowed a normalization of relations with the United States after 1971. That same year, party insiders eliminated Mao's chosen successor, Lin Biao (1908–1971). Although radical leaders of the Cultural Revolution, led by Mao's wife, Jiang Qing (1914–1991), staged a comeback in 1973, the tide turned decisively against them after Mao's death. In 1977, the Gang of Four (as the leaders were known) was ousted and brought to trial. As their influence declined, Deng Xiaoping (1904–1997), previously purged for his perceived capitalist tendencies by Mao's faction, remerged as the dominant force in the party.

After 1977 the CCP decisively rejected radicalism and pushed economic liberalization. This has resulted in rapid growth and the emergence of a new class of wealthy Chinese, whose interests are now intertwined with those of the party. Most important, the party has survived the collapse of Soviet Communism, although at the cost of a frightful massacre of "democratic" elements in 1989. Successions are now orderly rather than through power struggle, and there has been no repetition of the kind of events surrounding the downfall of Lin Biao or the trial of the Gang of Four.

In addition to its success with the economy, the party has achieved a number of foreign-policy successes. They include the 1997 return of Hong Kong to China, followed by that of Macao, and China's assertiveness, against the United States in particular, based upon a rapidly modernizing military.

The CCP in the Twenty-First Century

Nonetheless, the future is clouded. The party remains a geriarchy, staid, conservative, and northern based. That the future may lie elsewhere, with the maritime region of the southwest, and an associated Taiwan and Singapore, and their wider economic community, may not be clear to those in power. Nor is the party actively considering the costs of militarism, perhaps because it is not in the interests of those driving the economy. Although the CCP has changed its spots repeatedly, it may lack the ability to respond to the new world of the twenty-first century. Some old ideas may be too thoroughly engrained within it.

Paul D. Buell

Further Reading

Hsü, Immanuel C. Y. (2000) *The Rise of Modern China*. 6th ed. New York: Oxford University Press.

Nathan, Andrew J., and Perry Link, eds. (2001) *The Tiananmen Papers*. New York: Public Affairs.

Snow, Edgar. (1938) *Red Star Over China*. New York: Grove Press.

CHINESE IN JAPAN

Extending as far back as 219 BCE when alchemist Xu Fu is said to have come to Japan with a shipload of Chinese youth, the presence, through the nineteenth century, of the Chinese in Japan has been characterized by flows from different regions in China. As a result of this diversity, the changing nature of Sino-Japanese relations, labor requirements, and immigration policies, the Chinese in Japan, unlike those in other parts of Asia, have established their own unique history.

Pre-Tokugawa Period

Japanese chronicles make numerous references to migration from the Asian continent from the first century CE. According to the *Shinsen shoji roku* (Newly Compiled Record of Names, 815 CE), 162 naturalized families of Chinese origin lived in the central

A Chinese shrine at the Kiyumiza-Dera Temple in Japan in 1989. (CARL & ANN PURCELL/CORBIS)

provinces during this period. Trade between China and Japan became significant from the late twelfth century and grew steadily until the fifteenth and sixteenth centuries, when it became a large factor in the economic life of Japan. Records indicate the presence of many Chinese enclaves in Satsuma, the fief of the Shimadzu clan in southern Kyushu.

Tokugawa Period (1600/1603–1868)

Although Japan's relations with China were severed as a result of the invasions of Korea (1592, 1597) by the Japanese warlord and statesman Toyotomi Hideyoshi (1536–1596), unofficial trade with China and other countries was encouraged by the first Tokugawa shogun, Ieyasu (1542–1616), and resulted in a flourishing Chinese community in Nagasaki in the seventeenth century. Kyofukuji, Sofukuji, and Fukuzaiji, Chinese temples built in the 1620s, were recognized as Japanese national treasures and attest to the wealth of Chinese merchants of the period. The number of Chinese dropped dramatically after 1688 due to more stringent isolation policies. Many naturalized Chinese took Japanese names, while others used the names of their particular homeland in China.

Meiji Period (1868–1912)

When Japan was opened again in the 1850s, Chinese began to arrive at the various port cities in limited numbers, generally in the service of Western firms and individuals. The Sino-Japanese Commercial Treaty of 1871 granted Chinese port, residence, and trading rights, with residence limited to specified areas in Tokyo, Yokohama, Osaka, Kobe, Nagasaki, and Sakai. In 1899 Chinese and Koreans were granted the same privileges of travel and residence that were extended to Europeans and Americans. During the Meiji period the three pillars of overseas Chinese economy developed: trade with Shanghai, Hong Kong, Southeast Asia, the Americas, and other parts of the British empire; the "three-blades trades" (the cook's knife, the tailor's shears, and the barber's razor); and peddling, which permitted Chinese to travel and reside in areas other than the trade ports. Posts established along peddling routes eventually developed into small communities.

After Japan's victories in the Sino-Japanese War (1895–1896) and the Russo-Japanese War (1904–1905), Chinese students began to flood into Tokyo to learn from Japan's adaptation of Western theories and developments. In 1905 there were as many as eight thousand Chinese students within a mile radius of Tokyo's student quarters. Tokyo also became a haven for many Chinese political refugees and a training ground for political activists. Although most of these students and refugees returned to China, their influence endured in the overseas Chinese community.

The 1930s, World War II, and the Postwar Period

Japan's aggression in China during the 1930s led to dramatic drops in the resident Chinese population in

Japan, a trend that was countered by the importation of approximately forty thousand Chinese for slave labor primarily in Japanese mines. Following Japan's defeat in World War II, Manchurians and Taiwanese, formerly considered subjects of Japan, became Chinese citizens. The American Occupation government reported that there were then 14,941 Chinese of mainland origin and 15,906 Taiwanese in Japan.

When Japan signed a peace treaty with the Republic of China in 1952, many Chinese residents in Japan doubted whether the republic truly represented China and were irritated when the Guomindang tried to exercise authority over all Chinese nationals in Japan. In 1972, with Japan's normalization of relations with the People's Republic of China, there was an increase in the number of Chinese seeking Japanese citizenship.

The Chinese migration to Japan between 1988 and 1998 involved mostly young, unmarried Chinese from the mainland who concentrated in the inner city and subsequently sent for family members and friends to join them. Inner-city ethnic communities began to spill over into adjoining suburbs, leading to increasing diversification in a nation usually thought of as remarkably homogeneous.

Valerie C. Wong

Further Reading

Chang, Aloysius. (1970) "The Chinese Community of Nagasaki in the First Century of Tokugawa Rule." Ph.D. diss. St. John's University.

Chu, Tull. (1967) *Political Attitudes of the Overseas Chinese in Japan*. Hong Kong: Union Research Institute.

Harrell, Paula S. (1970) "The Years of the Young Radicals—The Chinese Students in Japan." Ph.D. diss. Columbia University.

Hirano, Kenichiro, et al. (2000) "Toward a Sociology of Asian Migration and Settlement: Focus on Japan." *Asian and Pacific Migration Journal* 9, 3: 243–254.

Kawakami, K. K. (1924) "Japan's Policy Towards Alien Immigration." *Current History* (June): 472–474.

Komai, Hiroshi. (2000) "Immigrants in Japan." *Asian and Pacific Migration Journal* 9, 3: 311–326.

Newell, William H. (1967) "Some Problems of Integrating Minorities into Japanese Society. *Journal of Asian and African Studies* 2, 3, and 4: 212–229.

Okuda, Michihiro. (2000) "Asian Newcomers in Shinjuku and Ikebukuro Areas, 1988–1998: Reflections on a Decade of Research." *Asian and Pacific Migration Journal* 9, 3: 343–348.

Tajima, Junko. (2000) "A Study of Asian Immigrants in Global City Tokyo." *Asian and Pacific Migration Journal* 9, 3: 349–364.

CHINESE IN MYANMAR

The Chinese in Myanmar (Burma) consist of several communities of different origins. In Upper Myanmar, overland interaction with the province of Yunnan in China has produced Myanmar's oldest Chinese community, drawn from interior China. In Lower Myanmar, immigrants from the Chinese provinces of Fujian, Guangdong, and Hainan, speaking Hokkien, Hakka, Guangdong, and other dialects, have settled in Burma chiefly from the late eighteenth and late nineteenth centuries. Hence the Chinese in Burma are sometimes divided into overland or "mountain" Chinese and overseas or "maritime" Chinese. Other Chinese immigrants included Baba Chinese (Straits-born Chinese) from the British colonial ports of Penang, Melaka, and Singapore in the nineteenth and twentieth centuries, and the remnants of Nationalist Chinese armies cut off from flight to Taiwan during the Chinese Civil War.

Many Chinese in Burma maintained their cultural identity, for example with language schools. During the World War II occupation of Burma by the Japanese, many Chinese fled to China and elsewhere. Between 1945 and the early 1960s, the Chinese in Burma attempted to rebuild their prewar communities and lives. The establishment of military rule in 1962 and actions by the military regime from 1964, however, led to the forcible closure of Chinese language schools, the prohibition of "Chinese" community activities (although Chinese were still allowed to congregate within dialect groups), and the closure of Chinese-language newspapers. As a result, two generations of Chinese have not had formal instruction in Mandarin and rely chiefly upon Burmese or a combination of Burmese and one of several traditional dialects (Hokkien, Guangdong, etc.).

Since the introduction of new citizenship laws in 1982 by the military regime, Chinese have been considered as foreigners and treated as second-class citizens. Carpenters, largely of Guangdong ancestry, for example, are not legally allowed to work without the full citizenship that they are denied, and are thus heavily represented among Chinese emigrants from Myanmar (many to the United States, Australia, and Taiwan). It is partly for this reason that the Chinese population of Burma has dropped from a high of about 350,000 (1.6 percent of Burma's population in 1961) to about 230,000 (0.6 percent of Burma's population in 1983) in the 1980s. Some estimates, however, suggest that the Chinese population in Myanmar in the 1990s is about 400,000 or higher.

Michael W. Charney

Further Reading

Charney, Michael W. (1999) "Problematics and Paradigms in Historicizing the Overseas Chinese in the Nineteenth-

and Twentieth-century Straits and Burma." *Journal of the South Seas Society* 54: 93–106.
Mya Than. (1997) "The Ethnic Chinese in Myanmar and Their Identity." In *Ethnic Chinese as Southeast Asians*, edited by Leo Suryadinata. Singapore: Institute of Southeast Asian Studies, 115–157.

CHINESE IN SOUTHEAST ASIA Since emigration from China began at least a thousand years ago, most migrants have settled in Southeast Asia. At least three-quarters of the world's Chinese outside China reside in the region. However, Southeast Asian Chinese comprise under 5 percent of the region's total population.

Assimilation of Southeast Asian Chinese to indigenous cultures prevents precise measurement of their numbers. Many are more proficient in local languages than Chinese, and most have adopted the citizenship of the countries where they reside. The extent to which Southeast Asian Chinese are considered to belong where they live varies. In Indonesia, for example, a large locally born Chinese community remains distinct from indigenous populations. In Thailand, Chinese descent is a source of pride among the political elite and even in the royal family. In British Malaya, a sizeable Chinese elite became thoroughly Anglicized through business and social interactions with their colonial rulers. In the Philippines, in contrast, an elite group of mixed Chinese-Filipino families become prominent in the anticolonial nationalist movement of the late nineteenth century

Distinctions exist among Southeast Asian Chinese according to ancestral origins within China. Distinct dialects are spoken in the three southeastern coastal regions where most emigrants were born in Guangdong and Fujian Provinces. Dialects and associated occupational differences and loyalties have set Chinese groups apart from each other in Singapore and elsewhere.

Southeast Asian Chinese tend to be urban. They are concentrated in the largest cities of the region, particularly Singapore, where about 70 percent of the population was Chinese in 2000. Because Southeast Asian Chinese are also concentrated in commercial and professional occupations, their economic success has been a sensitive issue. In Indonesia, the Chinese minority, believed to control most of the nation's aggregate wealth, is resented. The apparent dominance of Chinese entrepreneurs in Southeast Asian economies is partly a lasting effect of European colonial policies favoring the employment of Chinese merchants as government revenue agents. Moreover, groups fostering business connections with China and Chinese-owned firms elsewhere in the region have tended to maintain cultural ties as well, strengthening the association of business success with Chinese ethnicity.

A dragon in the Chinese New Year parade in Singapore in February 1987. (TED STRESHINSKY/CORBIS)

The official view of China's imperial government toward emigration linked it to piracy and illicit overseas trade; only in 1893 was an official ban on emigration lifted and protection provided to Chinese nationals sojourning abroad. Although Southeast Asian Chinese strengthened ties to their ancestral homeland in patriotic solidarity during the Sino-Japanese War (1937–1945), during the Cold War most reacted to suspicions of Communist affiliation by emphasizing local loyalties. With economic liberalization of the People's Republic of China (PRC) since the late 1970s, Southeast Asian Chinese investments in the PRC have become significant.

Emily M. Hill

Further Reading

Cushman, Jennifer, and Wang Gungwu. (1988) *The Changing Identities of the Southeast Asian Chinese Since World War II*. Hong Kong: Hong Kong University Press.

Pan, Lynn. (1999) *The Encyclopedia of the Overseas Chinese.* Cambridge, MA: Harvard University Press.

Wang Gungwu. (2000) *The Chinese Overseas: From Earthbound China to the Quest for Autonomy.* Cambridge, MA: Harvard University Press.

CHINESE IN VIETNAM According to the 1989 census, there are 900,185 ethnic Chinese, or "Hoa," in Vietnam. This corresponds to only 1.4 percent of the total Vietnamese population. Nevertheless, as with other Chinese minorities in Southeast Asia, they play a very important role in the economic life of Vietnam. This has been the case since Vietnam gained independence from France in the mid-1950s and was particularly true in the former Republic of Vietnam (RVN) up to 1975. Ethnic Chinese have played a different but still important role in the socialist economy of the Democratic Republic of Vietnam (DRV).

After the end of the Vietnam War and the demise of the RVN, the new Vietnamese authorities opted to pursue economic policies that were characterized by the gradual implementation of socialist transformation and that had a considerable detrimental impact on the economic interests of the ethnic Chinese. Relations between China and Vietnam also gradually deteriorated, and as this occurred, increasingly discriminatory policies were implemented against the ethnic Chinese in Vietnam. These factors caused a large-scale exodus of ethnic Chinese from Vietnam in 1978 and 1979. An estimated 430,000 to 466,000 ethnic Chinese left Vietnam between the end of the war in 1975 and the end of September 1979.

The 1980s and 1990s have been characterized by a slow process of reintegration of ethnic Chinese into Vietnamese society. This has been spearheaded by developments in Ho Chi Minh City, where about half of the ethnic Chinese live. Decrees of the Communist Party of Vietnam and government in 1995 and 1996, respectively, signaled the full reintegration of the ethnic Chinese. Apart from changes in the policies implemented at the local, government, and party levels directed at the ethnic Chinese, the overall policies of *doi moi* ("renovation") and economic liberalization have contributed to reintegration.

Given the overall situation today, the future of the ethnic Chinese in Vietnam looks brighter than at any time since 1978. A pertinent question is whether the process of reintegration will continue or if there are potential pitfalls that could lead to the reemergence of past problems and possibly a new mass migration of Chinese. To a certain degree, the future development will depend on economic policies. As long as the policies of economic renovation and reform are pursued, such a situation will not recur. Another important factor is the impact of China-Vietnam relations. In principle, as long as the bilateral relations are good and there is a willingness to maintain these relations, they will have a positive impact on the ethnic Chinese in Vietnam.

Ramses Amer

See also: **Boat People; China-Vietnam Relations; Ho Chi Minh City; Population Resettlement—Vietnam; Sino-Vietnamese Culture**

Further Reading

Amer, Ramses. (1996) "Vietnam's Policies and the Ethnic Chinese since 1975." *SOJOURN: Journal of Social Issues in Southeast Asia* 11, 1 (April): 76–104.

———. (1998) "Vietnam and Its Chinese Minority: From Socialist Transformation and Exodus to Economic Renovation and Reintegration." *Journal of the South Seas Society* 53 (December): 101–127.

CHINESE INFLUENCE IN EAST ASIA In the seventeenth century, European scholars presented their latest maps to the Chinese court. Although the Chinese were impressed with the cartographers' skills and technological sophistication, the court officials were offended that China was not pictured at the center of the world. Historically, China viewed itself as the Middle Kingdom. Their centrist worldview was based on objective criteria. As late as the Ming dynasty (1368–1644), China continued to be the world's most powerful nation in terms of size, population, commerce, wealth, technology, learning, fine arts, and literature. China's dominance in East Asia (Korea and Japan) for most of this region's recorded history was based on China's supremacy. It was the source rather than the recipient of culture.

Like the waxing and waning of the moon, there were periods when Japan and Korea resembled "little Chinas," because of their conscious imitation of China, while there were other periods of minimal interaction between these states. It is significant that the greatest influence China had on East Asian states occurred during the early centuries of their recorded histories. Consequently, Chinese culture is at the root of East Asian society. As humans are more profoundly influenced by experiences in their early years, Korea and Japan's formative years were marked by their acceptance of the Chinese economic, political, ideological, and social patterns. What Japan and Korea adopted in their early civilizations became the foundation for their more mature states.

Migrants from northern China were among the earliest inhabitants of Korea and Japan. During the first millennium BCE, these migrants developed a hunter-gatherer culture in Japan and Korea. The religion of the area was animistic with an apparent reverence for ancestors and nature. Because Korea was geographically attached to the continent, it was more directly influenced by the political machinations of China. During China's Han dynasty (206 BCE–220 CE), China directly ruled the peninsula. Yet, a recurring theme between China and East Asia is seen early on in that when China faced internal crisis, its political influence in Korea and Japan diminished. Thus, the fall of the Han dynasty coincided with the increased strength of the indigenous Korean kingdoms of Koguryo (37 BCE–668 CE), Paekche (18 BCE–663 CE), and Shilla (57 BCE–935 CE).

Economic stability, brought about by the advent of rice agriculture, shifted the social structure of East Asia from a nomadic existence to a sedentary one with defined geographical boundaries. In battling for supremacy over a particular state, East Asian clans sought legitimacy for their positions by their affiliation with China. The political tug-of-war in the three native states in Korea and the emerging state of Yamato Japan (300–552 CE) produced centralized powers and definite political hierarchies. The rise of dominant states in East Asia coincided with the golden age of China—the period of the Sui (581–618 CE) and Tang (618–907 CE) dynasties. It was during this era that Korea and Japan adopted Chinese patterns in religion, philosophy, political structure, and literature.

Buddhism Spreads

India is the homeland of the Buddha, yet by the Han dynasty this world religion was beginning to flourish in the Middle Kingdom, while its influence waned in India. Buddhism continued to move east. In 372 CE, Buddhism was introduced to the Koguryo court. The religion spread throughout the peninsula as Chinese monks proselytized their faith throughout the Korean states. Concomitantly, Koreans traveled to China to study at influential monasteries. The implications of the Korean states' acceptance of Buddhism as the metaphysical explanation to reality were profound. The ties between Korea and China were now cemented by a common religion. The sacred Buddhist scriptures were written in Chinese characters, and the desire for the Koreans to understand Buddhism solidified the use of Chinese as the mode of written communication throughout Korea. In addition to adopting the Chinese written language, which is a significant gauge of Chinese influence, the Korean states adopted the art and architecture that accompanied Buddhism. Korean dominant art forms mirrored Chinese works—temples and palaces were built according to the popular styles in China.

During the fifth century, elements of Buddhism crossed over from Korea to Japan, but its official introduction did not take place until 552. Chroniclers note that during the first half of the sixth century, the state of Paekche was at war with Shilla and Koguryo and, in an effort to bring Japan into the fray, Paekche offered to introduce a glorious new truth to the islands should Japan offer its assistance. Thus, it was officially through Korea that Buddhism was introduced to the Japanese court. It was adopted by the most powerful families at the court, who were relatively recent emigrants from the peninsula, and, like Korea, Japan's adoption of Buddhism affected language, art, and architecture in Japan. Chinese written language was the means of written communication throughout the islands, and Japanese art was barely distinguishable from the Chinese art of the day.

The influence of Buddhism on East Asia was from the top down. It was the elite families who first embraced it, though it eventually moved into all social classes. The leading states sponsored the propagation of Buddhism by building monasteries and providing economic relief to those tending the temples. Artisans were paid by the state to create Chinese-style Buddhist art pieces and this media filtered down to the general population. It might also be said that Buddhism spread throughout East Asia because indigenous religions were still evolving and they lacked the sophistication of Buddhism. The elaborate rituals, scriptures, mantras, and art that Buddhism offered was accompanied by other cultural influences from China.

Just decades after Buddhism was officially introduced to Japan, China was united under the glorious Tang dynasty. The political and economic splendor of Tang China was copied by the states of East Asia. In the political realm, the Tang concept of the state's supremacy and the emperor's complete authority was adopted in Korea and Japan. In Japan, this firmly established the still-extant imperial throne. Japan and the Korean states also copied the Tang pattern of taxation, which meant that a more sophisticated manner of assessing the land's resources was needed. The rulers of Korea and Japan partitioned their land into provinces, prefectures, and districts, with the assumption that all land belonged to the state, and taxes were required from those who worked the land. In Korea and Japan, as in China, rice was the currency of the day, and a certain percentage of the harvest,

CHINESE INFLUENCE IN EAST ASIA— A TWO-WAY STREET

China influenced Korea and Japan through travels to these nations by Chinese and travels by Koreans and Japanese to China. The following account describes some of the efforts of Korean scholars in bringing Buddhism to Korea.

> Shortly after Buddhism was first introduced into Korea, Koreans began to make pilgrimages to the great temples and teachers of the law in China. A well known Chinese book on Buddhism gives the names of six Koreans who, in the latter part of the seventh century, found their way through China to India. In 583, the son of the King went. In 596, Payak of Kogoryu went to Mt. Tendai in South China and brought back the tenets of the Tendai Sect. In 600, Wunkwang brought back the teachings of the Sinin sect, and, in 634, Myungnang brought more of its rules. Wunkwang also brough copies of the Sungil, Non and the Nirvana Book, the sacred writings most used by this sect. In 617, Wunhyo, and, in 669, Wisang went to the land of Tang in China and brought back many books and relics. These last two were founders of the Pumusa monastery near Fusan, now one of the five largest in the country. Heikwan, in 625, brought back the teachings of the Sam-non Sect from the land of Sul in China. By 625, there were five Buddhists sects in Korea.
>
> *Source:* Charles A. Clark (1932) *Religions of Old Korea.* New York: Fleming H. Revell Company, 30–31.

approximately 40 percent of the crop, was paid to the state. The adoption of the Chinese political and economic patterns increased the political stability in East Asia. The increasingly sinicized states of Japan and Korea continued to look to China for legitimacy, learning, and culture.

The extent of China's influence during this era is exemplified in Japan's so-called seventeen-point constitution that was developed in the seventh century. It began with the Confucian injunction that the goal of the state is to establish harmony above and friendliness below. This was followed by the second point, which asserted that conversion to Buddhism would straighten everything crooked. In Korea, "universities" were established for the exclusive purpose of teaching the Confucian classics, and similar academies were founded in Japan. The Confucian principles of filial piety and rigid rules that govern relationships were propagated through these learning institutions.

Political Institutions Transformed

Political institutions were transformed in Japan and Korea during the Tang dynasty. In Korea, the government adapted the six ministries of the Tang government. In Japan, the ministries of a central secretariat and the imperial household were added to the conventional six of Tang. The most cosmopolitan city of the eighth century was Chang'an, the capital of China. Japan and Korea sent ambassadors to Chang'an. Not only did they borrow the architecture and art of Chang'an, but also they laid out their capitals in the checkerboard fashion that characterized the Tang capital. During the eighth century, Japan established Nara in the fashion of Chang'an. In 794, on the northern end of the Kyoto plain, the city of Heian was founded with dimensions of just over 5 by 5 kilometers, a bit more modest than the Chang'an measurement of approximately 9.5 by 8 kilometers.

Korea and Japan also sought to create a bureaucracy based on merit, as was the case in China. Positions were set up in the government structures with the understanding that they would be filled by men of rank. In 958, the Korean civil-service exam was based on the Confucian classics, and one advanced through knowledge of these Chinese works. Yet, by the tenth century, there was a definite atrophy of Chinese influence in Korea and Japan. This was due to the hard times that faced China following the collapse of the Tang as well as a fundamental shift in China's state revenue system.

While Japan and Korea sought to emulate Tang China, there were aspects of the Chinese world that did not quite fit the Japanese and Korean models. China's neighbors never fully integrated the merit-based bureaucracy system, for example. Aristocratic families dominated the political and economic worlds of Korea and Japan, and an exam to level the playing field did erase the continued dominant role of the elite. The true breakdown of the Chinese system in East Asia, however, was due to the increase of tax-free lands. In Korea and Japan, portions of land were given to monasteries and families to whom the court owed favors. At the outset, these tax-free lands were minimal in size. These small parcels of land, however, grew into enormous tax-free estates. The state could do nothing about its declining tax revenue because the estate owners were either in under the patronage of the elite families or were from the elite families themselves. By the twelfth century, it is estimated that tax-free religious or estate zones accounted for more than 50 percent of the land in Korea and Japan. With the steady diminution of revenue, the states found it difficult to respond to internal crises—particularly in trying to maintain peace in an age in which marauding gangs preyed on farming villages. Estate owners and villagers turned away from the impotent state and to the warrior class for protection. Thus, the pattern of state-control and a scholar-led bureaucracy subtly underwent a change. In Japan, true power moved away from the imperial family to the *bakufu* (tent government), or military government led by the *seii taishogun* (barbarian-suppressing generalissimo, commonly called simply shogun) was headquartered with his retainers and advisors.

Korea and Japan's departure from the Chinese model in the political realm coincided with their adoption of indigenous written languages. Chinese character-based written language was always a difficult fit in the Korean and Japanese polysyllabic and inflected languages. One compromise was to use the Chinese characters to represent sounds rather than words. During the tenth century in Korea, a system called *Idu*—wherein Chinese characters represented sounds—became the mode of written communication. By the fifteenth century, a Korean phonetic system known today as hangul replaced the Chinese character-based written language on the peninsula. In Japan, it was the women in the eleventh-century court that led the way in writing Japanese, while the men continued to use Chinese characters. Moreover, the literature the men produced was inferior to the more adaptable, but new, Japanese written language.

During the Yuan (1279–1368), Ming (1368–1644), and Qing (1644–1912) dynasties, Japan and Korea continued to acknowledge the supremacy of China in East Asia. It is true that Toyotomi Hideyoshi (1537–1598) of Japan had visions of invading China at the end of the sixteenth century, but Hideyoshi's irreverent approach to China was the exception, not the rule. Buddhism, particularly the Chan sect from China (called Son in Korean and Zen in Japanese), profoundly influenced society in art, architecture, and philosophy during the premodern era of Japan and Korea. During Japan's Tokugawa period (1600/1603–1868), the prevailing ideology was Neo-Confucian thought, as this validated the division between the elite, farmers, artisans, and merchants. In Korea, the Choson era (1392–1910) was one of continued deference to China. The "little brother" sent tributary missions to the "elder brother" three times a year. Confucian ideology was more thoroughly integrated into Korean society during this period than it was in China.

China's Weakness Confirmed

It did not go unnoticed by the East Asian nations, however, that during two of its last three dynasties, China was ruled by outsiders, first the Mongols (1279–1368) and then the Manchus (1644–1912). China's vulnerability and weakness were confirmed by humiliating defeats in its wars against the British during the nineteenth century. Concessions were made to foreigners, and China's undisputed leadership of East Asia was soon to be a memory. During the last half of the nineteenth century, both Japan and China sought to strengthen themselves. China wished to stave off the Western imperial countries, while Japan coveted a first-class-nation status. Japan's lack of respect for the once-proud leader in East Asia was demonstrated in the 1984–1895 Sino-Japanese War and subsequent harsh Treaty of Shimonoseki (1895). Korea, the pawn in the game, was forced to recognize Japanese suzerainty.

The first Sino-Japanese conflict was a precursor to a much more bloody affair between these nations. Between 1937 and 1945, Japan and China were locked in mortal combat. The tragedy at Nanjing—often referred to as the Rape of Nanjing, where Japanese soldiers butchered Chinese civilians—demonstrated the animosity Japan felt toward its old tutor. Some speculate that the anger the Japanese had against the Chinese was rooted in the Japanese embarrassment and disgust that the source of their culture had sunk so low. Korea, by contrast, was made part of the Japanese empire (1910–1945), and the Koreans, too, were treated harshly by their new colonial ruler.

Post–World War II East Asia can be understood only in the light of the Cold War. Sino-Japanese relations remained sour because of the memory of the Japanese war brutality and because the United States insisted for decades that Japan should not have relations with Communist China. The Korean peninsula was split in to two countries, with North Korea experiencing warmer relations with China. As China emerged as a free-market state, however, its relations with South Korea improved, while North Korea continued to flounder because of its large military budget and the collapse of its once-powerful ally, the Soviet Union.

Japan and Korea have experienced a sweet-and-sour relationship with China. China's influence in these two countries, however, is beyond estimation, because of the adoption of the Chinese pattern in the early civilizations of East Asian states.

L. Shelton Woods

See also: **China-Japan Relations; China-Korea Relations**

Further Reading

Barnes, Gina Lee. (1993) *China, Korea and Japan: The Rise of Civilization in East Asia*. London: Thames & Hudson.

Fairbank, John King, ed. (1968) *The Chinese World Order: Traditional China's Foreign Relations*. Cambridge, MA: Harvard University Press.

Fogel, Joshua A. (1995) *The Cultural Dimension of Sino-Japanese Relations: Essays on the Nineteenth and Twentieth Centuries*. New York: M. E. Sharpe.

Howe, Christopher, ed. (1996) *China and Japan: History, Trends, and Prospects*. New York: Oxford University Press.

Kim, J. H. (1978) *The Prehistory of Korea*. Honolulu, HI: University of Hawaii Press.

Lardy, Nicholas R. (1987) *China's Entry into the World Economy: Implications for Northeast Asia and the United States*. Lanham, MD: University Press of America.

Lee, Chae-Jin. (1996) *China and Korea: Dynamic Relations*. Stanford, CA: Hoover Institution Press.

Pollack, David. (1986) *The Fracture of Meaning: Japan's Synthesis of China from the Eighth through the Eighteenth Centuries*. Princeton, NJ: Princeton University Press.

Sansom, George. (1958) *A History of Japan to 1334*. Stanford, CA: Stanford University Press.

Tanaka, Stefan. (1993) *Japan's Orient: Rendering Pasts into History*. Berkeley and Los Angeles: University of California Press.

Tsunoda, Ryusaku. (1968) *Japan in the Chinese Dynastic Histories*. Kyoto, Japan: Perkins Oriental Books.

Vasey, Lloyd R. (1993) *China's Growing Military Power and Implications for East Asia*. Honolulu, HI: Pacific Forum/CSIS.

Yu, Ying-shih. (1967) *Trade and Expansion in Han China: A Study in the Structure of Sino-Barbarian Economic Relations*. Berkeley and Los Angeles: University of California Press.

CHINESE INFLUENCE IN SOUTHEAST ASIA

In November 1367, the Chinese, led by its first peasant-emperor, Zhu Yuanzhang (1328–1398), continued to wage war against the retreating Mongols. In calling up fresh troops, the emperor wrote to his subjects that since time immemorial the Chinese emperors ruled everything under heaven and that the outside "barbarians" were privileged to pay homage to China. Indeed, China believed that the world revolved around it, and the Chinese selectively spread their culture to "barbarian" states. Consequently, China's economic, cultural, and political influences in East Asian countries were profound. Moreover, China's prestige extended beyond its immediate neighbors; over the past two millennia its influence on the Southeast Asia has been as varied and complex as the region itself.

China and Vietnam

China's historical relationship with Vietnam did not follow the general principles that governed China's relations with the rest of Southeast Asia. Historically, Vietnam has experienced a deeper and longer-lasting influence from China than any other Southeast Asia country. The Vietnamese state was founded in the third century BCE by a Chinese military governor. Two hundred years later, in 111 BCE, China made much of modern Vietnam into a province in the expanding Han Empire (206 BCE–220 CE). Vietnam remained a part of China for one thousand years. Much like the early inhabitants on the Korean peninsula, urban Vietnamese took on Chinese culture in virtually every sphere of life, including politics, literature, ideology, written language, and religion. It is significant that while Theravada Buddhism came directly from South Asia to Burma, Laos, Cambodia, and Thailand, where it became the established form of Buddhism, Mahayana Buddhism—the form of Buddhism practiced in China—took hold in Vietnam.

It must be noted that despite China's thousand-year-long political domination of Vietnam, the Vietnamese tenaciously held on to some indigenous aspects of culture, including the Vietnamese spoken language and their higher view of women. Scholars note that the more the Vietnamese accepted the culture of the

Chinese, the less likely it was that they would accept China's political suzerainty over their land.

Early Relations Between China and Southeast Asia

Economic opportunities rather than political interests dominated China's early relations with the rest of Southeast Asia. The early state of Funan (c. 50–550 CE) on the Mekong Delta River in modern-day Vietnam was a catalyst for Chinese-Southeast Asian relations. In Funan, Southeast Asians became the intermediaries between Chinese-Indian and Chinese-Middle Eastern traders during the first four centuries CE. By the fifth century, however, Southeast Asian entrepreneurs began substituting indigenous products, such as Sumatra pine resins and sandalwood, for the frankincense and myrrh from further west. With the rise of the Chinese Nan Qi state (479–502), trade between China and Southeast Asia dramatically increased as China was an insatiable market for nutmeg, cloves, and mace from the Moluccas, and for rhinoceros horn—which the Chinese prized as an aphrodisiac—from Borneo.

Between the seventh and thirteenth centuries China's influence in Southeast Asia turned political as more powerful states emerged in the region. Champa in present-day Vietnam, Angkor in present-day Cambodia, Pagan in present-day Myanmar (Burma), and Srivijaya and Majapahit in present-day Indonesia all had some type of political relationship with China though these states were more deeply influenced by India. India's prestige in Southeast Asia was due to the world religions it exported to its eastern neighbors. Buddhism, Hinduism, and Islam took hold of Southeast Asian states, and the missionaries from these religions came mostly from India. It is said that India's influence in Southeast Asia was greater than that of China because India had no political agenda in the region.

The relationship between China and Srivijaya, the dominant state in maritime Southeast Asia between the eighth and fourteenth centuries, showcases China's influence in this region. Located close to the modern city of Palembang in southeastern Sumatra, Srivijaya was able to dominate the area due to its strategic location and its political savvy. The political acumen of its rulers included the decision to pay annual tribute to the greatest power in all of Asia—China. Like most early states in Southeast Asia, Srivijaya sought legitimacy and protection based on its tributary relationship with China. Paying homage to China proved to be a tricky game for Southeast Asian states, however. China promised protection to tributary states, but the bigger fish in Southeast Asia could swallow the smaller ones before China could respond. Again, Srivijaya is a case in point. Majapahit, which was based in Java, gradually increased in wealth, influence, and strength, and was able to defeate Srivijaya before China could come to the latter's rescue. In 1397, twenty years after the fall of Srivijaya, the Chinese emperor wrote a letter to this defunct kingdom castigating it for the breakdown in the tributary relationship, apparently unaware that its client state had fallen.

The Ming-Dynasty Period

Three events led to China's increased economic importance to Southeast Asia during the Ming dynasty (1368–1644). First, China was once again in the hands of the Chinese. The Mongol-dominated Yuan dynasty (1279–1368) had fallen, and under the Ming a series of capable emperors sought to extend their influence over Asia. Second, under the third Ming emperor, Yongle (1360–1424), the Chinese built enormous sailing ships that traveled as far as Mogadishu in western Africa. These impressive ships were more than 130 meters long (by comparison, Columbus's *Santa Maria* was only about 26 meters long that would appear and was built a hundred years later). For three decades these impressive transports traveled throughout Southeast Asia, demanding that each state pay proper tribute to China. Ambassadors from these states were ordered to appear before the Ming emperor and demonstrate the respect due to the Son of Heaven. This gunboat diplomacy not only increased interaction between China and its southern neighbors, it also increased the prestige and political dominance of China throughout East and Southeast Asia.

The third catalyst for China's economic growth in Southeast Asia was the arrival of the Europeans in Asia. The Chinese were able to keep the Western powers on the periphery until the nineteenth century. But when the Portuguese were able to set up a small colony in Macao, just off the major trading port of Guangzhou (Canton) in southern China, China's role in Southeast Asia changed forever. The Portuguese priests and Spanish friars set up a network of trade from Nagasaki to Macao to Melaka and Manila. The key to the entire trading network was the market and materials of China. A case study of the Manila galleon trade demonstrates the power China came to hold in Southeast Asian economics. Silver from Mexico and Peru made its way to China by way of the Philippines; the ship then returned to Acapulco with Chinese goods. Chinese porcelain ware and textiles were coveted in South America and Europe, and the payment for these goods was the silver from across the Pacific Ocean. Manila was where these ships to Acapulco were loaded with Chinese products. This brought a greater number of Chinese into Manila and other parts of Southeast Asia, where global trading was directed by a growing network of colonial powers. Despite the increased presence of Chinese in Southeast Asia during the Ming period, the ethnocentric tendencies of many Chinese prevented their integration into cultures and societies that were unfamiliar to them. Rather, the Chinese in Southeast Asia produced a subculture of exclusive Chinese neighborhoods and schools.

Chinese Migration

The nineteenth century saw unprecedented Chinese migration to Southeast Asia. The internal factors that drove Chinese from their homeland were economic and political. During the first half of the Qing dynasty (1644–1912), China experienced a dramatic increase in its population, so there was not enough land to pass down to the new generations because of the practice of dividing land among all heirs. At the same time, the price of silver—specie used to pay taxes— rose, and farmers weren't able to pay their taxes. Later in the nineteenth century, the Taiping rebellion (1850–1864)—a civil war that was responsible for some 20 million deaths—added to the misery of the Chinese. Revolution was one option to internal crises; migration was another.

Western colonization of Southeast Asia was another stimulus in bringing Chinese south. In the nineteenth-century British Straits Settlements of Singapore, Penang, and Melaka, the English found that the Chinese were willing to do work that the indigenous population found loathsome. In particular, the backbreaking labor in the mines of Malaya was mostly accomplished by Chinese rather than indigenous labor. By the 1860s, Chinese made up more than 50 percent of the population in Singapore, and Chinese businessmen moved to the Malaya Peninsula and helped the British administer the tin mines and rubber plantations. As Malays were reluctant to work for the British or Chinese, an economic opportunity for Chinese opened in the south, and thousands of Chinese, mainly from China's southeastern provinces, flocked to Malaya. Nineteenth-century colonial governments also encouraged Chinese businesspeople to set up shop in Indonesia and the Philippines. These overseas Chinese remained in Southeast Asia. At the beginning of the twenty-first century, the Chinese remain the dominant ethnic group in Singapore, and some 35 percent of Malaysia is ethnically Chinese. Chinese influence is apparent in the region's business communities, and ethnic tension between the Chinese and Southeast Asia's indigenous populations is blamed on the inordinate economic power the Chinese enjoy in the region.

The People's Republic of China

The People's Republic of China (PRC) was formed on 1 October 1949. The PRC, with its Communist ideology, had a pronounced effect on Southeast Asia during the Cold War.Visionaries throughout the region, tired of corrupt governments and the continued presence of imperialist powers, looked to China as an example of a socialist revolution. Vietnam, Indonesia, and the Philippines all looked to China for inspiration.

In the Philippines, landless peasants caught in a cycle of perpetual debt to rich landlords believed that socialism, as expressed in the PRC land reform movement, would bring economic equity to their country. Such Filipino organizations as the New People's Army and the Philippine Communist Party looked to China and its leader, Mao Zedong (1893–1976), for ideological direction. In the 1960s a small minority of disgruntled Indonesians also promoted the PRC ideology as an alternative to the government of President Sukarno (1901–1970). But perhaps the greatest impact of the PRC on these nations is that established leaders used the threat of supposed revolutionary Chinese influence in their countries to impose harsh and authoritarian rule. In Indonesia, thousands of Sino-Indonesians were killed to crush an alleged Chinese Communist coup in 1965. In the Philippines, President Ferdinand Marcos (1917–1989) declared martial law in 1972 in response to the threat of a Communist takeover of the archipelago.

In post–World War II Indochina (Cambodia, Vietnam, and Laos), neutrality between China, the Soviet Union, and the United States proved impossible. The Chinese aided the Communist leaders and movements in each of these countries. During the 1954 Geneva Conference, which ended the conflict between France and its former Indochinese colonies, the enormous prestige China had in the region was demonstrated as China's representative to the conference, Zhou Enlai (1898–1976), helped to bring the various fighting sides into an agreement. While North Vietnam and various Communist elements in Cambodia felt betrayed by the PRC at Geneva, it is instructive to note that they signed the agreement. Chinese advisers continued to make their way into Laos, Vietnam, and Cambodia following the 1954 conference, and war material was sent south to aid North Vietnam.

China's influence in Vietnam declined in the late 1960s, and the U.S. belief that North Vietnam and its leader, Ho Chi Minh (1890–1969), were PRC puppets was false. Indeed, by the early 1970s relations between North Vietnam and China were acrimonious at best. The increasingly strained relationship between North Vietnam and China was due to the growing partnership between North Vietnam and the PRC's enemy, the Soviet Union. The PRC felt North Vietnam's friendship with the USSR was a slap in the face from a nation that had historic and cultural ties with China.

China took its revenge on Vietnam by supporting the Communist Khmer Rouge, who took over in Cambodia in 1975 and whom the Vietnamese opposed. The PRC recognized the Khmer Rouge government and sent high-level personnel to demonstrate its support of the new Communist state. When Vietnam intervened in Cambodia on 25 December 1978, China responded by sending troops into Vietnam to punish its wayward son two months later. Vietnam held its own in the battles with China and for the next decade the two countries sank into a military quagmire as Vietnam continued its military presence in Cambodia while China sent supplies to the Khmer Rouge guerrillas on the Thai border.

Analysts believe that China's influence will continue to grow in Southeast Asia. United, economically vibrant, and accustomed to political primacy, China has increased its hegemony in the potentially oil-rich islands and atolls in the South China Sea. The growing frustration felt in Southeast Asian nations is explained by Indonesia's leading maritime expert, Hashim Djalal who noted that when Southeast Asians try to stem China's increasing presence in the South China Sea, the Chinese respond by talking about dynasties and they bring out old maps. Understanding China's past influence in Southeast Asia may be the key to future relations between these two regions.

L. Shelton Woods

Further Reading

Alexander, Garth. (1974) *Silent Invasion: The Chinese in Southeast Asia.* New York: Macmillan.

Fairbank, John King, ed. (1968) *The Chinese World Order: Traditional China's Foreign Relations.* Cambridge, MA: Harvard University Press.

Grant, Richard L., ed. (1993) *China and Southeast Asia: Into the Twenty-first Century.* Washington, DC: Center for Strategic and International Studies.

Gurtov, Melvin. (1971) *China and Southeast Asia: The Politics of Survival.* Lexington, MA: Heath Lexington Books.

Hill, Ann Maxwell. (1998) *Merchants and Migrants: Ethnicity and Trade Among Yunnanese Chinese in Southeast Asia.* New Haven, CT: Yale University Press.

Hodder, Rupert. (1996) *Merchant Princes of the East: Cultural Delusions, Economic Success, and the Overseas Chinese in Southeast Asia.* New York: John Wiley & Son.

Levathes, Louise. (1994) *When China Ruled the Seas: The Treasure Fleet of the Dragon Throne, 1405–1433.* New York: Simon and Schuster.

Martin, Edwin W. (1977) *Southeast Asia and China: The End of Containment.* Boulder, CO: Westview Press.

Ptak, Roderich. (1999) *China's Seaborne Trade with South and Southeast Asia, 1200–1750.* Brookfield, VT: Ashgate.

Purcell, Victor. (1951) *The Chinese in Southeast Asia.* London: Oxford University Press.

Reid, Anthony, ed. (1996) *Sojourners and Settlers: Histories of Southeast Asia and the Chinese.* St. Leonards, Australia: Allen & Unwin.

Tarling, Nicholas, ed. (1992) *The Cambridge History of Southeast Asia.* 2 vols. Cambridge, UK: Cambridge University Press.

Wong, John. (1984) *The Political Economy of China's Changing Relations with Southeast Asia.* London: Macmillan.

Wu, Yuan-li. (1980) *Economic Development in Southeast Asia: The Chinese Dimension.* Stanford, CA: Hoover Institution Press.

CHINESE NEW YEAR

CHINESE NEW YEAR Chinese New Year *(Chun Jie)* is the most important festival in the Chinese lunar calendar. *Chun Jie* means the "spring festival," and based on the almanac of the emperor Han Wu Di (140–87 BCE), it falls on the first day of the first month, which does not correspond to January first of the Western, Gregorian calendar. It is celebrated for fifteen days and culminates at the first full moon of the new year.

Before the New Year, Chinese families customarily conduct a thorough spring cleaning of their homes. Examples of auspicious Chinese calligraphy, such as *chun* (spring), *fu* (luck or happiness), and *shou* (longevity), as well as red-colored materials, are hung as decorative pieces in the home. In Chinese, the word for "red" sounds the same as the word for "prosperity." Festive delicacies (for example, biscuits and cakes) are prepared and new clothes purchased. On New Year's eve, family members gather for an annual reunion dinner. They offer food to the ancestral tablets, which are believed to embody the spirits of individuals who have produced sons capable of performing ancestral rites. In return for this attention, the ancestors ensure the fertility and prosperity of the lineage. This ritual renews and reaffirms filial ties. After dinner, many people visit local temples to offer prayers.

Throughout the period of the New Year celebrations, relatives and friends visit one another to offer felicitations. Gifts symbolizing tokens of good fortune, such as oranges and *hon poa* or *hong bao* ("red packets") containing money, are exchanged. In multiethnic nations in Southeast Asia, like Malaysia and Singapore, the practice of open houses has sprung up. Friends and acquaintances of other ethnic and religious back-

DEBTS AND NEW YEAR'S

The Chinese New Year celebration is far more than a public festival, as it also marks important social, political, and economic relations among people in the community. The following text points to one important function—the settling of debts.

> But there is another, more serious reason for excitement in this last week of the year; it is the time when one must settle all debts. Western usages spread quickly in China; our business techniques are accepted by the big firms in Tientsin, Shanghai, and Canton, but the small shopkeeper as well as the ordinary citizen still feels obliged to follow this old custom of settling debts three times a year—just before the three great "festivals of living." It is, if one looks for a noneconomical explanation, another of these rites of "cleaning up," of chasing away the bad spirits. Before we enter a new year, everything should be clean—our hearts, our relations with our neighbors. An obligation of the dying year should not be carried over into the new one, just as the old dust in the rooms should not stay there over the New Year.
>
> It is never more difficult to find cash than in these days, and there is no better opportunity for the foreign visitor than now, when someone may be forced to sell an old family piece to get some. Our "January sales" thus take place the week before New Year's in China, with the same "drastic reductions."
>
> *Source:* Wolfram Eberhard (1952) *Chinese Festivals* New York: Henry Schuman, 26–27.

grounds pay visits to Chinese homes as a gesture of goodwill. Localized practices like these may be less in evidence in other parts of Asia.

Seng-Guan Yeoh

Further Reading

Bodde, Derk. (1975) *Festivals in Classical China*. Princeton, NJ: Princeton University Press.

Chinese Customs and Festivals in Singapore. (1989) Singapore: Singapore Federation of Chinese Clan Associations.

Wong, C. S. (1967) *A Cycle of Chinese Festivals*. Singapore: Malaysia Publishing House.

CHINESE, CLASSICAL

Classical Chinese refers to the language of canonical literature and formal documents in China before the twentieth century. In the early twentieth century, language reforms were instituted so that writing was no longer carried out in the classical language, which was understood only by an educated elite, but instead was rendered in an approximation of the modern northern vernacular.

When trying to give a formal definition of classical Chinese, linguists tend to resort to one of two strategies: the first is to treat classical Chinese as all that is not in the vernacular—definition by default; the second is to try to pinpoint the historical period out of which classical Chinese developed and to state that classical Chinese consists of literary traditions that grew out of the speech habits of a particular time and place.

The Classical/Vernacular Divide

When stating that classical Chinese (*wenyanwen*) is the logical complement of vernacular Chinese (*baihuawen*), it is natural to ask where we draw the line and what criteria we are using. Criteria that have traditionally been used to distinguish classical and vernacular Chinese include:

1. Intelligibility: Is it readily understood by the average native speaker? Or is it language that only the educated elite can understand?
2. Spoken versus written mode: Is it more like natural speech or more like stylized writing?
3. Time depth: When we talk about "natural speech" and "average native speaker," are we using contemporary people as a point of reference (modern audience), or are we referring to people at the time the work was written (historical audience)?

Let us first look at the intelligibility criterion. By "intelligible," what is meant is that the language is comprehensible to a general audience; if it cannot be understood by the average native speaker without further training, it is considered "unintelligible." The intelligibility criterion cleverly captures the lay view of the vernacular/classical divide: Vernacular Chinese is Chinese written in language the layperson can understand; everything else is relegated to classical Chinese regardless of the source of the difficulty. This view is often reflected in popular comments about writing styles: certain styles are difficult to understand because they are too *wenyan* (classical/literary), as if classical Chinese stands for all that is obscure or arcane.

There are problems with this approach, however. The first is that intelligibility judgments are necessarily limited to the here and now, for we have no way of determining whether people in ancient times can understand a particular style of writing or not. That is to say, we are tied to the judgments of a modern audience. If we were to do this, we run into a second problem, which is that we would have to exclude from our definition of vernacular Chinese the language of historical popular novels such as *All Men Are Brothers (Shuihu Zhuan)* and *Dream of the Red Chamber (Honglou Meng)*, which are traditionally considered vernacular literature *(baihua xiaoshuo)*, but which in modern times are not readily comprehensible to the uneducated reader.

An alternative to the intelligibility criterion is that of spoken language versus written language. Most of the world's languages maintain a difference between spoken and written varieties: the spoken variety is usually more informal and involved, employing more first and second person pronouns ("I," "you"), conjunctions ("and," "but"), and situation-dependent references ("last night," "over here"), whereas the written variety tends to be more informational, abstract, and explicit, often containing learned or technical vocabulary. Relying on such universal tendencies, we can determine whether the text at hand is closer to typical spoken language or written language. Texts that bear closer resemblance to spoken language are then labeled vernacular Chinese; those with attributes of written language are relegated to classical Chinese.

Note that the intelligible/unintelligible divide is not the same as the spoken/written divide. The reason for this is that most uneducated speakers can understand *some* formal language. It is not the case that uneducated speakers can only understand language in the spoken mode and that they find formal writing totally unintelligible. There is an in-between stage in which language can have characteristics of the written register and is yet comprehensible to the uneducated reader.

Whether we use intelligibility or spoken/written language as criterion, however, an additional variable is the historical period of the intended audience. Writing that is intelligible to or characteristic of the population of one historical period may be unintelligible to or uncharacteristic of the speech of another stage in history. For this reason, it is important to specify the period on which we are to base our definition.

A spoken-language, historical-audience-based definition of classical Chinese was given by the scholar Hu Shi (1891–1962), who was one of the chief proponents of language reform and vernacular writing in early Republican China. In his seminal work, *Baihua wenxue shi* (A History of Vernacular Literature), Hu implied a dichotomy in which vernacular literature is literature written in the spoken language of the day (which may be far removed the spoken language of *today*), and classical literature is that which is excluded from this scope by default. By this definition, what is vernacular and what is classical is not a fixed notion, but rather varies with each historical period. This dichotomy, however, while similar to the European notion of vernacular and mainstream literature, is foreign to the Chinese tradition. Hu's definition is often criticized for framing a definition of vernacular language that is too broad. His definition would necessarily include as vernacular obscure works of oral literature from remote periods, which speakers of modern Chinese have great trouble understanding.

A more widely accepted definition of vernacular and classical Chinese is that of Lü Shuxiang: The vernacular language is written text that corresponds to spoken language from the Tang dynasty (618–907) onward; all else is relegated to classical Chinese. Lü's treatment avoids the shortcomings of both Hu's working definition and the lay notion of the vernacular: It includes as vernacular drama and popular writing from the Ming (1368–1644) and Qing (1644–1912) dynasties while excluding obscure pre-Tang works of oral literature. Lü's definition is sometimes criticized for its arbitrary choice of the Tang dynasty as a divide, but it is worth noting that intermingling of Sinitic and Altaic-speaking populations in cosmopolitan Tang society accounts for the considerable linguistic gap between Middle Chinese (265–1269) and Premodern Chinese (1269–1795). It is also during this period that basic Chinese word order began to shift from Subject-Verb-Object (SVO) to Subject-Object-Verb (SOV)—a change often taken to be an important distinction between classical Chinese and modern Chinese.

Classical Chinese throughout the Ages

Having defined the classical language as writing several degrees removed from the spoken language, it is natural to ask whether this writing style may have been derived from the spoken language of an earlier period. Linguists have found considerable overlap between classical Chinese grammar and the syntax of Old Chinese oracle-bone inscriptions and bronze inscriptions of the Shang (1766–1045 BCE) and Western Zhou (1045–771 BCE) dynasties. The inscriptions are for the most part short sentences describing ceremonies and divinations and are considered a more or less faithful record of the spoken language of the day in the Huang (Yellow) River basin.

With the breakup of the Zhou empire (256 BCE), however, a new culture of pluralism demanded a more stylized form of writing suited to political oratory. This is reflected in the language of works such as Confucius's *Analects (Lunyu)* and *Mencius (Mengzi)*, which is more concise and structured, is richer in rhetorical devices, and shows obvious imitations of earlier classics.

The later Warring States period (402–221 BCE) and the Qin (221–206 BCE) and Han (206 BCE–ce 220) dynasties saw a further move toward allegory and ornamentation, resulting in writing that is stylistically distinct from the vernacular language of the day. It was during this period that classical Chinese forged an identity as a literary language separate from vernacular speech, and it is the conventions of this period that later authors sought to emulate when writing in the "classical style." For this reason, some sinologists reserve the term "classical Chinese" for the writings of the Qin and Han dynasties and refer to the language of later imitations as "literary Chinese."

Following the Han dynasty, worship of form was taken to an extreme at the expense of substance, giving rise to the belletrist "parallel prose" *(pianwen)* of the South dynasties (420–589), in which balance of rhythm, imagery, and tonal patterns reigned supreme. This worship of formal elements created a backlash in the Tang dynasty, in which neoclassicists such as Han Yu (768–824) and Liu Zongyuan (773–819) called for a return to substance and the rhetorical styles of the Qin and the Han. From the Tang onward, different schools of writing offered different takes on the classical language, and literary aesthetics oscillated between form and substance and between arch conservatism and the adoption of new grammar and lexicon.

The dominance of classical Chinese came to an end after the first Opium War (1840–1842) as intellectuals began to see the classical/vernacular gap as a hindrance to greater literacy and called for the replacement of classical Chinese with the modern spoken language in education and media as part and parcel of the modernization of China. In the New Culture Movement of the late 1910s, promotion of Vernacular Chinese gathered momentum through the efforts of noted scholars such as Hu Shi, Chen Duxiu (1879–1942), Qian Xuantong (1887–1939), and Fu Sinian (1896–1950), culminating in the Vernacular Language Movement of 1917–1919. As a result of this movement, vernacular Chinese was adopted as the standard language of textbooks, and influential new works of literature by authors such as Lu Xun (1881–1936) began appearing in the vernacular.

To this day, however, the classical language lives on in government missives and legal documents and in all manner of writing deemed formal. Classical patterns and set expressions appear frequently in vernacular prose—more so in Taiwan than in mainland China. Despite the efforts of early twentieth-century language reformers to make a clean break with *wenyan*, it does look as if it will be some time before the new writing born of the Vernacular Language Movement can forge an identity fully distinct from that of the classical language that has been standard for much of Chinese history.

Chris Wen-Chao Li

Further Reading

Chen Ping. (1999) *Modern Chinese: History and Sociolinguistics*. Cambridge, U.K.: Cambridge University Press.

Hu Shi. (1928) *Baihua wenxue shi* (A History of Vernacular Literature). Shanghai: Xinyue Chubanshe.

Lu Shuxiang. (1992) *Lu Shuxiang wenji* (Collected Works of Lu Shuxiang). Beijing: Shangwu Yinshuguan.

———. (1944) "Wenyan yu baihua" ("Classical and Vernacular Chinese"). *Guowen zazhi* 3, 1: 3–12.

Norman, Jerry. (1988) *Chinese*. Cambridge, U.K.: Cambridge University Press.

Zhang, Zhongxing, ed. 1988. *Wenyan changshi* (Facts about Classical Chinese). Beijing: Renmin Jiaoyu Chubanshe.

CHINESE, OVERSEAS At the end of the twentieth century, an estimated thirty-eight million ethnic Chinese lived outside China in almost every country on the face of the earth, including places as unexpected as Iceland and Panama. This geographic dispersion suggests the difficulties of counting exactly how many Chinese there are outside China. Chinese have moved within and beyond the borders of China for several millennia. Where they have both sojourned and settled among non-Chinese, they have experienced varying degrees of assimilation and acculturation, depending on local reception and opportunities. They have remigrated or returned to China as demanded by necessity and common sense. After multiple generations of life abroad, separate Chinese ethnic communities have become difficult to define, with some fading into local populations in appearance and culture, as in Thailand, and others remaining ethnically distinct but practicing a hybridized culture combining both Chinese and local elements, as in the case of the Babas of Malaya or the Peranakans of Indonesia.

History

People of Chinese origin have been crossing borders since prehistoric times, when the Thai and Burmese languages originated in what is now Chinese territory. Until the late eighteenth century, the small number of Chinese who ventured abroad were mostly

RESTRICTING CHINESE IMMIGRATION TO THE UNITED STATES

Chinese laborers played a major role in opening the western United States to settlement. Nonetheless, when they were no longer needed and thought to be too numerous, the United States enacted laws designed to restrict immigration. This Convention Regulating Chinese Immigration was enacted on 17 March 1894.

> Article I. The High Contracting Parties agree that for a period of ten years, beginning with the date of the exchange of the ratifications of this Convention, the coming, except under the conditions hereinafter specified, of Chinese laborers to the United States shall be absolutely prohibited.
>
> Article III. The provisions of this Convention shall not affect the right at present enjoyed of Chinese subjects, being officials, teachers, students, merchants or travellers for curiosity or pleasure, but not laborers, of coming to the United States and residing therein . . .
>
> Article IV. In pursuance of Article III of the Immigration Treaty between the United States and China, signed at Peking on the 17th day of November, 1880, . . . it is hereby understood and agreed that Chinese laborers or Chinese of any other class, either permanently or temporarily residing in the United States, shall have for the protection of their persons and property all rights that are given by the laws of the United States to citizens of the most favored nation, excepting the right to become naturalized citizens. And the Government of the United States reaffirms its obligation, as stated in said Article III, to exert all its power to secure protection to the persons and property of all Chinese subjects in the United States.

Source: John V. A. MacMurray, ed. (1921) *Treaties and Agreements with and Concerning China, 1894–1919*. New York: Oxford University Press, 9.

merchants, pirates, and government agents. Chinese soldiers arrived on Borneo and Java in the twelfth century as part of an attempted Mongol conquest. Between 1405 and 1433, the Ming eunuch Zheng He (1371?–1435) commanded a flotilla of ships that traversed Southeast Asia, edged around India, and reached the eastern shores of Africa. The pirate Zheng Chenggong (1624–1662), or Koxinga, ruled a naval empire headquartered in Taiwan that stretched from Japan throughout the South China Sea. From this offshore stronghold, Zheng eluded Qing-dynasty (1644–1912) capture for seventeen years while advocating the cause of the fallen Ming dynasty (1368–1644). Fear of such traitors mustering resources to the south led both the Ming and Qing dynasties to forbid emigration, a sporadically enforced ban that did not prevent a steady trickle of enterprising merchants from seeking their fortunes across the ocean for several centuries.

The number and nature of Chinese emigrating changed with European expansion into Asia. Colonial exploitation of land and natural resources provided a wealth of economic opportunity for those willing to work hard and contribute to commercial and industrial growth. Working-class Chinese joined wealthy merchants in the search for prosperity overseas. Growing networks of trade and technological advancements

A street scene in New York City's Chinatown in August 2001. (STEPHEN G. DONALDSON PHOTOGRAPHY)

improved communications, and travel became increasingly accessible through innovations such as credit tickets and steamship lines. To fill the insatiable needs of industry for cheap labor, hundreds of thousands of Chinese ventured overseas both willingly and under duress, as contract workers and as coolies. By 1900 an estimated 3 million Chinese lived abroad, 2.4 million of whom traveled between 1840 and 1900. Economic and political turmoil fueled continued migration throughout the twentieth century, a pattern cut short only by the first thirty years of communist rule. However, migration resumed in the late 1970s. Southeast Asia is still home to the majority of overseas Chinese, about 80 percent, although Australia, Canada, and the United States have become the destinations of choice because of their relatively liberal immigration policies.

Economic Roles

Although widely labeled "the Jews of Asia" for their appearance of disproportionate wealth and economic dominance in countries like Malaysia and Indonesia, overseas Chinese pursue a wide variety of occupations at all levels of society. In the nineteenth and early twentieth centuries, colonial and local modernizing elites nurtured the fortunes of the overseas Chinese by employing Chinese as middlemen—local agents greasing the wheels of economic development who were permitted to become rich even though, as racial outsiders, they had limited access political power. Because a highly visible handful gained wealth through intrinsically unpopular activities such as money lending and tax farming, Chinese in general served as scapegoats during times of economic depression, deflecting public attention from abusive governments. The majority of overseas Chinese, however, lived and continue to live humbly as petty store owners, farmers, miners, artisans, laborers, and service providers. Although they operate on the same business principles as others do, overseas Chinese appear to enjoy higher levels of success because access to a widely dispersed network of fellow Chinese aids their trading activities. Since the late 1970s, Chinese with professional degrees and entrepreneurial skills have become valued cogs in the wheels of global economic markets.

Social Organizations

Like other mobile peoples, Chinese rely heavily on ethnic networks and cooperation for support and survival. Chain migration is commonly practiced, and family remains the primary organizational unit. Continuing the family line through male descendants and advancing family fortunes remain key goals. Family and clan reliably provide future employees, business partners, and capital. In the past, the widely accepted practice of polygyny enabled Chinese men overseas to maintain multiple connections to China and to their places of settlement through the stability and acculturation represented by wives and children in key sites of business contact.

Principles of fictive kinship and native-place loyalty also provide crucial support and resources. The overseas Chinese communities established *huiguan*, or clan and native-place associations, as soon as a critical number of men from a particular place or of a particular surname had arrived. Adapted from migrant practices in Chinese cities, *huiguan* further evolved overseas to include umbrella organizations that combated anti-Chinese discrimination. During the early twentieth century, Chinese organizations emulated Western models in the form of Chinese chambers of commerce and service clubs. Late twentieth-century globalization has produced native-place, kinship, and business associations that are international in scope.

After emigrating, Chinese continued to practice their own religion, worshipping ancestors and a varying pantheon of gods. They established local temples and household altars but also proved fairly syncretic, adapting elements of or converting to local religions, as in the case of Chinese Catholics in the Philippines.

Political Orientation

Until the late nineteenth century, China's rulers usually ignored the overseas Chinese and only intermittently enforced bans on emigration. The status of overseas Chinese improved with imperial recognition of their economic successes, as reported by China's first diplomats during the 1880s. Sun Yat-sen, acknowledged by both the People's Republic of China (PRC) and Taiwan as the "Father of Modern China," enshrined the overseas Chinese in modern conceptions of the Chinese nation by calling them "mother of the Chinese revolution" for their support while he campaigned abroad. During the 1920s and 1930s, Sun's political party, the Guomindang (GMD), courted overseas support through newspapers, schools, and government policies. Facing discrimination abroad and inspired by visions of a modern, strong China, many overseas Chinese responded to GMD appeals by sending money to China and traveling there themselves. And so evolved the concept of *huaqiao*, usually translated as "Overseas Chinese" but meaning Chinese sojourners who remain politically loyal to China despite long-term residence abroad. Although still used by the Chinese government, the term *huaqiao* generated many problems for overseas Chinese, because it carried the implication that Chinese settlers, who in fact were simply interested in economic gain and social stability, maintained loyalty to a foreign government. Fearful of the numerous Chinese in their midst who seemingly were not being assimilated, some host governments imposed harsh restrictions and sanctioned anti-Chinese violence. The rise of the PRC exacerbated fears of overseas Chinese as a colonizing force and led to violence and expulsions from Malaysia and Indonesia during the 1950s and 1960s. Since the 1960s, the term *huaqiao* has been unpopular among most overseas Chinese, who prefer the more neutral *huaren*, or ethnic Chinese. From the late 1970s, in recognition of both the economic potential and the political risks of claiming overseas Chinese, the PRC has promoted business investments and visits in China while encouraging naturalization overseas.

Madeline Y. Hsu

See also: **Chinese in Japan; Chinese in Myanmar; Chinese in Southeast Asia; Chinese in Vietnam**

Further Reading

Chirot, Daniel, and Anthony Reid, eds. (1997) *Essential Outsiders: Chinese and Jews in the Modern Transformation of Southeast Asia and Central Europe*. Seattle, WA: University of Washington Press.

Levathes, Louise. (1994) *When China Ruled the Seas*. New York: Simon and Schuster.

Nee, Victor G., and Brett De Bary. ([1973] 1986) *Longtime Californ': A Documentary Study of an American Chinatown*. Reprint ed. Stanford, CA: Stanford University Press.

Oxfeld, Ellen. (1993) *Blood, Sweat, and Mahjong: Family and Enterprise in an Overseas Chinese Community*. Ithaca, NY: Cornell University Press.

Pan, Lynn, ed. (1999) *The Encyclopedia of Chinese Overseas*. Cambridge, MA: Harvard University Press.

Wang, Ling-chi, and Wang Gungwu, eds. (1998) *The Chinese Diaspora: Selected Essays Vol. I and II*. Singapore: Times Academic Press.

Woon, Yuen-fong. (1998) *The Excluded Wife*. Montreal, Canada: McGill-Queen's University Press.

CHINESE-LANGUAGE NEWSPAPERS—SINGAPORE

Singapore's first Chinese-language daily was *Lat Pau*, which went into circulation in 1881. Modeled on Chinese newspapers in Hong Kong and Shanghai, its coverage aimed to satisfy the interests of the immigrant population by focusing on political and cultural developments in China.

The other two major Chinese newspapers were *Nanyang Siang Pau*, founded by Tan Kah Kee in 1923, and *Sin Chew Jit Poh*, founded by Aw Boon Haw and Aw Boon Par in 1929. *Nanyang Siang Pau* was intended to serve the unorganized Chinese business community and promote Chinese vernacular education. In 1971, the government of Singapore detained its editorial staff for allegedly stirring up communal sentiments. *Sin Chew Jit Poh* was an innovative newspaper and enjoyed high circulation in the 1960s and 1970s.

In 1982 these two papers merged, creating Singapore News and Publications Limited, and *Lianhe Zaobao* and *Lianhe Wanbao* were launched to take their places. Another newspaper, *Shin Min Daily News*, came onto the scene in 1967. The combined circulation of these three Chinese-language newspapers is approximately 500,000.

Khai Leong Ho

Further Reading

Tan, Yew Soon, and Yew Peng Soh. (1994) *The Development of Singapore's Modern Media Industry*. Singapore: Times Academic Press.

CH'ING DYNASTY. See **Qing Dynasty.**

CHINGGIS KHAN. See **Genghis Khan.**

CHINTANAKAN MAI By 1985, the Lao People's Revolutionary Party, which controlled the government of Laos, recognized the need to adjust the nation's transition to socialism, primarily because of a lack of incentives to improve economic productivity. A new policy was introduced at the Fourth Party Congress in 1986 by party leader Kaysone Phomvihane. The new policy was called *chintanakan mai*, which literally means "new imagination" but is commonly translated as "New Economic Mechanism."

This new policy to move away from a state-planned economy to one emphasizing free-market mechanisms paralleled similar trends in Vietnam (introduction of *doi moi*, or renovation) and the former Soviet Union (perestroika, or openness). Among key structural reforms of *chintanakan mai* were deregulating prices; establishing a single floating exchange rate determined by market forces; privatizing state enterprises; opening the financial sector to foreign banks; liberalizing trade; and developing an explicit foreign investment code to facilitate increased international investments in Laos.

The government has implemented these reforms gradually. For example, it has been unwilling to adopt draconian measures to reduce the size of the public sector. Nevertheless, since 1989, Laos has divested itself of a large proportion of its state enterprises. Rather remarkably, even the national telecommunications company is now a foreign joint-venture company. Some privatization has also occurred in the education sector.

At the Fifth Party Congress in 1991, further elaboration of the economic reforms was articulated and specific national goals specified. Among these goals were export expansion, promotion of tourism, and further administrative and legal reforms to enhance the transparency (that is, making the rules of trade more apparent) of the Laotian economic and investment climate. Also in 1991, the hammer and sickle were removed from the state symbol of Laos and replaced by the most revered Laotian Buddhist temple, That Luang.

During the 1990s, Laos also became much more open internationally, with a significant increase in technical and economic assistance from both multilateral (World Bank, Asian Development Bank, and European Union, for example) and bilateral (Japan, Australia, Nordic nations, and Switzerland, for example) donors. Also, in 1997, Laos became the eighth member of the Association of Southeast Asian Nations (ASEAN).

Reflecting the success of the New Economic Mechanism, Laos in the early and mid-1990s had impressive macroeconomic performance with annual economic growth averaging 7 percent, much higher than the 1 percent average of the twenty years before 1985. Initially, it appeared that Laos might not be adversely affected by the Asian economic crisis of 1997, since its currency was not internationally traded and since it did not have a stock market. Unfortunately, in a delayed impact, the Lao economy suffered severely from the crisis, and its currency dropped dramatically, losing 87 percent of its value in only two years, with resulting serious inflation. In the early 2000s, the economy stabilized with real GDP economic growth estimated to be 4 percent in 2000.

In more recent years, some in the international community have expressed concern about the slowing of the reform process because of the political power

AN ECONOMIC MOTTO FOR LAOS

The slogan, "Produce as much as your capacity, consume as much as you desire" reflects the new economic orientation of *Chintanakan mai.*

Source: Vientiane Mai (15 May 1983).

of revolutionary leaders with strong ties to Vietnam and, increasingly, China.

Gerald W. Fry

Further Reading

Bounthavy Sisouphanthong and Christian Taillard (2001) *Atlas of Laos: Spatial Structures of the Economic and Social Development of the Lao People's Democratic Republic.* Copenhagen, Denmark: Nordic Institute of Asian Studies.

Bourdet, Yves (1991). *Laos: Reforming Laos' Economic System.* Stockholm, Sweden: Swedish International Development Authority.

———. (2000). *The Economics of Transition in Laos: From Socialism to ASEAN Integration.* Northampton, MA: Edward Elgar.

Butler-Diaz, Jacqueline, ed. (1998) *New Laos, New Challenges.* Tempe, AZ: Program for Southeast Asian Studies, Arizona State University.

Pham, Chi Do, ed. (1994) *Economic Development in Lao PDR: Horizon 2000.* Vientiane, Laos: IMF Resident Representative Office.

Sunshine, Russell B. (1995) *Managing Foreign Investment: Lessons from Laos.* Honolulu, HI: East-West Center.

CHISHTIYA The Chistis are an important Sufi (Islamic mystic) *silsilah* (order). Each order consists of *murids* (disciples) of a particular sheikh or *pir* (spiritual master). Khwaja Abu Ishaq of Syria (d. 940) started the order in Chist village, Syria. The founder of the order in India, Khwaja Muinuddin Chisti, came from Sajistan in eastern Iran in 1190 CE and set up a *khanqah* (hospice) at Ajmer, India. Known as the Garib Nawaz (Showing Kindness to the Poor), he attracted many followers, and his disciples, such as Qutbuddin Bakhtiar Khaki and Shaikh Fariduddin, further popularized the Chisti order. Sheikh Nizamuddin Auliya (1236–1325) of Delhi, who witnessed the reigns of seven sultans, attracted both Muslims and non-Muslims to the order. The Chistis further expanded to areas of South Asia such as Sind, Punjab, Rajsthan, Bengal, Bihar, and Deccan.

The early Chisti saints were revered because of their religious tolerance, adoption of indigenous traditions, use of local languages, and egalitarianism. The miracles that were attributed to them strongly appealed to the common people. Although there was no digression from the *shari'a* or Islamic holy law, these saints allowed certain deviations. For example, there were *sama* or musical gatherings for personal union with God. A strong dislike for any form of political patronage and a dependence on God for livelihood were hallmarks of the Chisti saints. There was an emphasis on *wahdat al-wujud* (unity of being). The name of God was recited both aloud and in silence *(dhikr jahri, dhikr khafi).*

The proliferation of Chisti branches such as Nagauriya, Sabiriya, Nizamiya, Gaudri Shahi, and Zahuri began in the sixteenth century and continues today. There have been obvious changes in Chisti doctrine, and some of the earlier traditions like noninvolvement in politics and nonpossession of property have been given up. Nizami Chisti Hazarat Inayat Khan (d. 1927) established centers in the United States and Britain to propagate the message of universalism. Sayed Khwaja Habib Ali Shah of Hyderabad, India, inspired the South African branch. The Gaudri Shahi/Zahuri branch, established by Zahurul Hasan Sharib Gudri Shah Baba (1914–1996) of Ajmer and presently headed by Inam Hasan, has centers in Britain and the United States. Websites for the orders feature discussions, online discourses, *qawwalis* (a form of musical chorus, where one singer begins the songs and the followers recite), and so forth. The *urs*, a festival celebrating the anniversary of a saint's death, is held where the saint is buried, and the *dargah* (saint's tomb) attracts both Muslims and non-Muslims in the Indian subcontinent.

Patit Paban Mishra

Further Reading

Earnst, Carl W., and Bruce B. Lawrence. (2001) *Burnt Hearts: The Chishti Sufi Order in South Asia and Beyond.* Richmond, Surrey, U.K.: Curzon Press.

Trimingham, J. Spencer. (1971) *The Sufi Orders of Islam.* Oxford, U.K.: Oxford University Press.

Wilson, Peter Lambon, and Nasrollah Pourjavady. (1987) *Drunken Universe: An Anthology of Persian Sufi Poetry.* Grand Rapids, MI: Phanes Press.

CHITRA/ARDHACHITRA/CHITRABHASHA Standardized aesthetic norms appeared in South Asian art from about the fifth century CE, coinciding with the Gupta hegemony of the subcontinent (c. 320–c. 520 CE). The consequent canonization of art spawned a rich descriptive and normative vocabulary for identifying the scope of Indian artistic representation. The terms *chitra*, *ardhachitra*, and *chitrabhasha* are used in this context to differentiate broadly between sculpture, relief, and painting, respectively.

Distinctions among *Chitra, Ardhachitra,* and *Chitrabhasha*

Although in the earliest theoretical texts on South Asian art, the term *chitra* is used to mean "sculpture" or "painting," in certain texts of the medieval period,

A 2nd century BCE statue of Yakshi, a female earth spirit. The statue is of terracotta and is housed in the National Museum in New Delhi, India. (ANGELO HORNAK/CORBIS)

chitra means "sculpture in the round," and a distinction is made between *chitra* (sculpture), *ardhachitra* (relief), and *chitrabhasha* (painting). Perhaps the most important of these texts is the late sixteenth-century *Shilparatna* attributed to Srikumara of Kerala. The earliest-known text dealing with *chitra* in general is the *Vishnudharmottara*, generally dated as contemporaneous with the flowering of classical South Asian art (fourth–sixth centuries).

Little of ancient South Asian stone sculpture is cut completely in the round. Among the earliest examples of South Asian sculpture in the historic period are the massive *yakshas* and *yakshis* (supernatural elementals) from Mauryan times (third century BCE), chiseled out of sandstone and given the high surface polish characteristic of this period. These figures stand out frontally from the stone base out of which they are carved, giving an impression of sculpture in the round but being, in fact, "flat-backed" stelae (stone slabs). Among the rare examples of true sculpture in the round are animals, such as lions or bulls, standing on Asokan pillar capitals, also from this period. The gates (*toranas*) of the Great Stupa (50 BCE) at Sanchi, near present-day Bhopal in central India, carry what appear to be free-standing sculptures connecting architectural elements, but these, in fact, are slabs of stone rendered on both sides with back-to-back fronts, giving the impression of two reliefs brought together. Later (post–fourth-century) sculpture of India, occurring in temple settings, also features individual stelae, placed in niches or enshrined in a sanctum. A rare example of a popular image sculpted in the round from the early temple period is that of the theriomorphic representation of Varaha, the boar incarnation of Vishnu. Free standing and often colossal in scale, Varaha was evidently meant to be viewed from all sides during circumambulation. After the sixth century, Nandi, the bull-mount of Shiva, situated on an axis with the sanctum to enable a direct view of the shrine-image, is invariably carved in the round. But these are the exception rather than the rule, and it may be safely assumed that the predominant tradition in South Asian sculpture was relief.

The distinction among *chitra*, *ardhachitra*, and *chitrabhasha*, then, should be seen less as a clear separation of distinct modes of expression similar to sculpture, relief, and painting in the Western sense and more as a gradation in solid representation, painting being thought of as a constricted mode of sculpture, with relief occupying an intermediate zone. Several early texts describe painting as a form of illusionary relief, although actually flat. These include fifth-century literary texts, such as *Shakuntala*, where the eyes are said to stumble over the elevations and depressions of the picture surface, the reference being to the representations of landscape backgrounds, the voluptuous female form, or both. However, this illusion of depth is not to be confused with naturalistic illusionism in the Western sense, where the image is objectified through the systematic use of single-point perspective and chiaroscuro based on an external light source. In the South Asian case, the viewer is denied the experience of a privileged spatial inclusion in the three-dimensional reality of the image, an ontology (theory of the nature of being) of universal emergence, subsistence, and disappearance from or into a spaceless, timeless transcendental reality reinforced through the emphatic flatness of the background against which the play of relative depth occurs.

Sculpture

The history of relief sculpture *(ardhachitra)* in South Asia shows an interesting movement, especially when related to painting. Although sculpture in Mauryan times (c. 324–c. 200 BCE) expresses the strongest feeling for plastic volume and, especially in the massive *yaksha* or *yakshini* stelae, comes close to sculpture in the round, relief proper appeared only from the second century BCE, with the establishment of an architectural context for images. Ananda Coomaraswamy pointed out that the early reliefs on the *vedika* (railing enclosure) walls of stupas, as, for example, at Bharhut (second century BCE), south of present-day Allahabad, in central India, approximate painting *(chitrabhasha)* more than solid sculpture *(chitra)*, being closely compressed between the two planes of the wrought surface. On the *torana*s at Sanchi (first century BCE), there is a more heightened relief and a consequent movement in the direction of full sculpture from painting. This tendency continues through the Kushana (first century CE) and later Andhra (second century CE) periods, reaching its fullest expression of realistic emergent figural mass against the flat stone backdrop in the Gupta period and its aftermath (late fourth–sixth centuries). Subsequently, although the quality of the volume represented becomes more fluid and in some respects facile, relief continues to express a fullness of figural depth, the flat expanse of stone wall gradually replaced for its backdrop effect by the massive soaring temple structure, as in the medieval temples (tenth–twelfth centuries) of Khajuraho, Orissa, or the Hoysala kingdom.

In comparison with the shallow beginnings of relief sculpture, South Asian painting, in its earliest phases (i.e., in Caves 9 and 10 at Ajanta, second century BCE), is marked by an emphatic modeling, demonstrating its closeness to sculpture in the round. A similar impression of volume appears in relief much later, although in medieval times (eleventh–fifteenth centuries) a reversal of effect occurs in these two modes of expression. Now temple sculpture persists initially in its maintenance of high relief, whereas painting, particularly in the regions of Gujarat and Rajasthan, survives sculpture but becomes flattened. Coomaraswamy ascribed this flattening to psychological changes at the social level, relating to a shift of focus from a heroic will to a more reflective or contemplative intellect. In an article on *abhasa* (presentation), although Coomaraswamy equated this at first with a slackening of concentration *(shithila samadhi)*, on further exploration, he advised a refusal of comparative judgment, treating the stylistic symptoms of an age phenomenologically in terms of the development of its own aesthetic.

Detail of a stone relief sculpture at the Great Stupa of Sanchi built by Asoka. (ADAM WOOLFITT/CORBIS)

Aesthetics of Sculpture Media used for sculpture included stucco, terra cotta, wood, stone, and metal. Of these the most significant surviving monumental sculpture, occurring invariably in religious contexts, is that made in stone. By the late fourth century (Gupta period), a standardized aesthetic begins to become codified, and sculpture follows an elaborate set of technical and aesthetic guidelines. Figure sculpture predominates from this period, and prescriptional proportions and poetic metaphors, rather than live models, are used for translation into stone. Some of these visual metaphors are as follows: the facial outline should be like a hen's egg *(kukkutandavat)*; the brows should resemble the arc of a bow *(caapaakaaram)*; a variety of analogues could contextually shape the eyes, such as a bow *(caapaakaaram)*, a lotus leaf or bud *(padmapatra)*, the petal of the blue lotus *(nilotpala)*, the eyes of a deer *(mrigaakriti)*, or the belly of a fish *(matyodaram)*. The neck should be shaped after the conch shell *(kambugriva)*; the chin should resemble a mango seed *(aamra-vijam)*; the nose should look like a parrot's beak *(shukanasa)*; the pendant of the arm like an elephant's trunk *(gajatundaakriti)*; the forearm should look like a young plantain tree *(baala kadali kaandam)*; the male waist shaped after a lion's waist *(simhakati)*;

the woman's waist after the middle of an hourglass-shaped drum *(damaru-madhyam);* the kneecap like the contour of a crab *(karkataakriti);* and the calf of the foot after a fish *(matsyaakriti).*

The *Vishnudharmottara* also classifies a set of arrested stances in a rotational scheme of views for figures, ranging from a full frontal view, through a three-quarter view, a one-quarter view, a profile, and several fractional views, until it reaches a complete back view. Foreshortening, related to the preceding stances, is elaborated, as is a classification for feet stances. For each figural type, proportional measures are supplied, as are postures and gestures related to the subject of depiction.

In place of the frontality of Mauryan images, a variety of pleasing figural flexions were prescribed. These included the *samabhanga* or equipoise, with the plumb line passing through the middle of the body; the *abhanga* or gentle flexion, with a single break or bend in the plumb line; the popular *tribhanga* or triple flexion, which gave a sense of relaxed and rhythmic ease to the figure; and the extreme pliancy of *atibhanga*, with its maximum deviation from the plumb line. Similarly, sitting postures were also codified. For deep meditation, the *vajraparyanka* sitting posture was prescribed; for a more relaxed contemplation, the *ardhaparyankasana* was preferred; further relaxation while seated was depicted using the *mahaaraajaalilasana*. An attitude of comfort was designated by the *sukhaasana* posture. A vocabulary of hieratic hand gestures, shared equally by art and dance, was also codified. Popular gestures included the *abhaya mudra*, made usually with the open right hand raised, palm outward, and signifying the gift of fearlessness; the *varada mudra*, made with an open right hand turned downward, palm outward, offering boons; the *dhyana mudra*, signifying meditation; and a number of more specialized gestures corresponding to iconographic context. The powers of gestures *(mudra)* were extolled as devices evoking special states of aesthetic emotion. According to aesthetic texts, where the hand goes, the eye follows; where the eye goes, the mind follows; where the mind goes, the mood follows; where the mood goes, there arises aesthetic mood *(rasa).*

The theory of *rasa*, or aesthetic mood, comes to be fused with the religious consciousness in these sculptural prescriptions. Thus, a classification of the range of emotional states that the sculptor needs to portray effectively is central to this systematization. These emotional states also make their first appearance in the *Vishnudharmottara* and can be enumerated as the erotic *(srngaara)*, the comic *(haasya)*, the pathetic *(karunaa)*, the heroic *(vira)*, the intense *(raudra)*, the terrible *(bhayanaka)*, the grotesque or odious *(bibhatsa)*, the wonderful or mysterious *(adbhuta)*, and the tranquil *(shaanta).*

In the depiction of deities, youth is glorified. Gods are ideally shown to be eternally sixteen years of age and are generally without a beard. A god or goddess may be occasionally shown as a child but never as old or infirm. Emaciated or obese images were avoided because, apart from aesthetic reasons, there were prevailing beliefs that worship of emaciated images would bring famine and that disease would strike on invocation of gross or obese images. Body, life, and mind controlled by spiritual power is the ideal portrayed in images of deities and heroes. Even in the midst of violent action or in erotic scenes, celestials and heroes are shown with an air of detached serenity and self-contained delight. Such an ideal is based on the practice of yoga, leading to a dynamic spiritual union. The features most expressive of this inward power and poise are the eyes, which undergo a development from wide open in the period preceding the fourth century to a half-closed state subsequently, signifying deep meditative concentration. Women, particularly goddesses (*yakshi*s) and heroines (*nayika*s), are shown as voluptuous, with large hips and breasts, signifying creative fecundity, although here, too, tranquillity predominates, and the full maturity of young motherhood is preferred. Corresponding to the postural prescriptions, an elaborate iconography was prescribed for the depiction of supernatural beings. Particularly in Hindu sculpture, this included multiple hands, heads, and eyes to express superhuman omnipresence, omnipotence, and omniscience.

Depiction of Commoners In the depiction of commoners or lesser celestials, various activities with their characteristic postures are expressed. Among the activities most often shown are attendance upon kings and deities and performance of dance and music. The adversarial powers (*asura*s, *rakshasa*s) are shown as powerful and grotesque, although in some cases human likeness is bestowed on them.

Painting

Chitrabhasha literally means the "appearance" or "semblance" of *chitra* and thus prioritizes sculpture as a form of visual expression whose semblance is caught in two dimensions through painting. However, the importance of painting in ancient South Asia is attested to by the fact that the *Kamasutra* lists painting as the fourth of its sixty-four courtly arts and by the references in literary and theoretical texts to the presence of *chitrashala*s, or art galleries, for the pleasure of royalty or urban citizens.

A fresco in Ajanta Cave, Maharashtra, with detail of a yaksha couple. (LINDSAY HEBBERD/CORBIS)

Most texts speak of three surfaces on which painting may be done. These are wall surfaces for murals, wooden board, and cloth. Of these, although a tradition in cloth painting *(pata-chitra)* is alive to this day (for example, in Orissa), only a few surviving murals (as at Ajanta) can be dated to an antiquity contemporary with textual sources such as the *Vishnudharmottara*.

Painting Techniques Several theoretical texts provide glimpses of the techniques in use for painting. Of these, the *Samaraangana Sutradhaara*, a text from the first half of the eleventh century, carries one of the most elaborate and comprehensive accounts of the techniques of painting, codified as the eight limbs *(ashta-angaani)* of painting. These are:

1. *Vartikaa*, or preparation of the "crayon" with which initial outlining of the figures to be painted will be done.
2. *Bhumibandhanam*, or preparation of the ground, enumerated as mentioned into the three surfaces—wall surface, wooden board, and cloth. In the case of murals, where texts imply a use of both tempera and *fresco-secco* (lime medium) techniques, this preparation is usually a mud plaster, sometimes followed by a lime plaster, both reinforced with vegetable fibers.
3. *Lepyakarma*, or priming, where the prepared ground is smoothed and made ready for holding paint.
4. *Rekhakarma*, or the process of making the first line sketch. In discussing this step, most texts emphasize the need for the artist to visualize first the image in detail and with clarity. This act, equated with yogic concentration, is often made the expressive basis for the quality of pictorial realization, a deficient image being attributed to slack meditation. The first outline is drawn with the *vartikaa*, or "crayon"; a second outline is then with a medium-sized brush carrying a pigment derived from ocher.
5. *Karsakarma* (also called *varnakarma)*, or the preparation of colors. There is some variation in texts (sometimes in the same text) on the primary colors to be used. For example, the *Vishnudharmottara* mentions white, yellow, red, black, and blue and, elsewhere, white, red, yellow, black, and green. The *Chitralakshana* section of the *Shilparatna* mentions white, yellow, red, black, and blue. Because, as the *Vishnudharmottara* acknowledges, blue and yellow may be mixed to make green, most scholars take the five primary colors to include blue but not green. The *Vishnudharmottara* mentions the minerals used for paints as gold, silver, copper, mica, lapis lazuli, tin, yellow orpiment, lime, red lake, cinnabar, and indigo. The metal colors are said to be laid on as foil or liquefied. The twelfth-century *Manosollasa* is more explicit about the relationship of color to source. Thus white is derived from conch shell, crimson from cinnabar, red from Asian sumac *(Rhus verniciflua)*, blood red from ocher, yellow from orpiment, and black from lampblack.

6. *Vartanaa*, or modeling. This is among the most important aspects of *chitrabhasha* because it provides the illusion of three-dimensionality that makes the painting a "semblance of sculpture." The effect of depth is obtained through three devices: *patraka*, or cross-hatching, *binduka*, or stippling, and *hairika*, which Sivaramamurti interpreted as a corruption of *raikhika* and which means either fine lines or modulated outline. Mention is made of the use of brighter shades to depict higher grounds and darker shades to depict lower. Indian painting does not use single-point perspective or light and shade to create a consistent naturalistic illusion.

7. *Lekhakarma*, or brushwork. The brush is known as *lekhani* and is differentiated into five types according to thickness. The finest brushes are made from bark fibers and the rest from hair taken from a bull's ear or a mule's mane. Bamboo sticks, attached to the hair with lac resin, are used for handles. In tempera painting, the color is bound by using animal media derived from buffalo hide or elephant hide. In case of *fresco-secco*, lime is used as the binding medium. In the *Vishnudharmottara*, the brushed line is also strongly related to inner concentration. The ideal line is characterized as tranquil *(susnigdha)*, distinct *(vispashta)*, and uncrooked *(ajihma)*.

8. *Dvichakarma (dvi cha karma)*, or retouching. This is the final stage of painting, when highlights are added, particularly for surfaces, ornamentation, expression of depth, or final outlining.

Painting shares with sculpture elaborate classifications for types of figures relating to physiognomy and social differentiation. For each figural type, proportional measures are supplied, as are postures and gestures related to the subject of depiction. A vocabulary of metaphors related to body parts is also developed. All of these classifications and visual similitudes are prescriptive in nature and meant both to standardize figurative expression in a collective context of practice and to guide visualization and execution in a culture that, avoiding live models, turns the artistic gaze within. It is for this reason that these measures are termed *pramanani* (evidentiary standards or guidelines).

Debashish Banerji

Further Reading

Agarwala, Vasudeva Saran, ed. (1966) *Samarangana-Sutradhara*. 2d ed. Baroda, India: Baroda Oriental Institute.

Apte, V. C., ed. (1926) *Kasyapasilpa*. Pune, India: Anandasrama Sanskrit Series 95.

Bhattacharya, Ashok K., ed. (1974) *Chitralakshana of Silparatna (Srikumara): A Treatise on Indian Painting*. Calcutta, India: Saraswati Library.

Biswas, T. K., and Bhogendra Jha. (1985) *Gupta Sculpture*. New Delhi: Munshiram Manoharlal.

Coomaraswamy, Ananda K. ([1927] 1985) *History of Indian and Indonesian Art*. Reprint ed. New York: Dover.

———. (1916) *Rajput Painting: Being an Account of the Hindu Paintings of Rajasthan and the Punjab Himalayas from the Sixteenth to the Nineteenth Century, Described in Their Relation to Contemporary Thought*. London.

———. ([1943] 1956) *The Transformation of Nature in Art*. Reprint ed. New York: Dover.

Sastri, Asoke Chatterjee, ed. and trans. (1987) *Chitralakshana (Nagnajit)* (Exaltation of the Mind). Calcutta, India: Asiatic Society.

Sastri, Devdutta, ed. (1964) *The Kamasutra (Vatsyayana)*. Varanasi, India: Chowkhamba Sanskrit Series Office.

Shrigondekar, G. K., ed. (1925, 1939) *Manasollasa (Someshwaradeva)*, 1 and 2. Baroda, India: Gaekwad's Oriental Series 28, 64.

CHITTAGONG (1991 pop. 1.4 million). Chittagong is the primary port and second largest manufacturing city in Bangladesh. It is located on coast of the Bay of Bengal, 164 miles southeast of Dhaka. Previously a center of Buddhism, Chittagong came under the rule of the Hindu kings of the Sena dynasty in the twelfth century CE. In 1299, it was occupied by Muslim invaders, and by the early fourteenth century it had been incorporated into the Delhi sultanate (1192–1526). It was subsequently controlled by Portuguese pirates and Arakanese conquerors before passing under the Mughal rule in 1666 and British rule a century later. In 1947, after Indian independence, Chittagong became part of the newly created Pakistan. It has been part of Bangladesh since December 1971, when Bangladesh won its liberation struggle against West Pakistan.

Chittagong today has several distinct regions: the Old City, the British City, and the Modern City. The oldest part of the city is the Sadarghat on the banks of the Karnaphuli River. Near the Old City is the British City, now the business center of Chittagaong. The Modern City consists of contemporary buildings, as well as steel mills, an oil refinery, and cigarette factories. Chittagong also has several mosques, the most famous of which is Qadam Mubarak, dating from 1336.

Sanjukta Das Gupta

Further Reading

Murray, Jon. (1991) *Bangladesh: A Travel Survival Kit*. Berkeley, CA: Lonely Planet.

O'Malley, L. S. S. (1908) *Eastern Bengal District Gazetteers: Chittagong*. Calcutta, India: Bengal Secretariat Book Depot.

CH'OE NAMSON (1890–1957), Korean writer, publisher, historian. A leading intellectual of the early twentieth century, Ch'oe Namson introduced modern free-verse poetry, worked to educate Korea's youth and edited numerous classical Korean works, and outlined a nationalistic view on Korean history. Born in Seoul in 1890, he first received a traditional education and later studied history and geography in Japan. Returning to Korea in 1906, he established himself as a publisher and in 1908 published Korea's first popular modern magazine *Sonyon* (Youth, 1908–1911), a monthly magazine that introduced the Western world to Korean youth. The first issues contained his most famous literary piece, the poem "From the Sea to the Young."

Ch'oe Namson drafted the Declaration of Independence on 1 March 1919, for which he was arrested by the Japanese colonial government but later released in 1921. He published several influential articles on Korean culture, among which the most famous are "A Treatise on Tan'gun" (1926) and "A Treatise on Purham Culture" (1927). His reputation as a nationalist was tarnished, however, when he later collaborated with the colonial government and published pro-Japanese articles and speeches. In 1949 he was arrested for his pro-Japanese activities but was soon released due to illness. He continued to edit classical Korean works until his death in 1957 of a cerebral hemorrhage.

Anders Karlsson

Further Reading

Allen, Chizuko T. (1990) "Northeast Asia Centered around Korea: Ch'oe Namson's View of History." *Journal of Asian Studies* 49, 4: 787–806.

Kim, Hung-gyu. (1997) *Understanding Korean Literature*. Armonk, NY: M. E. Sharpe.

Lee, Peter H. (1965) *Korean Literature: Topics and Themes.* Tucson, AZ: University of Arizona Press.

Ryang, Key S. (1976) "Ch'oe Nam-son and His Modern Historiography." *Journal of Korean Affairs* 6, 2: 1–16.

CHOLA Chola (or Cola) was one of three prominent medieval kingdoms in southern India, the others being Chera and Pandya. The realm of the Cholas (Cholamandalam in the Tamil language) centered on the Coromandel coast, the east coast of the modern state of Tamil Nadu, and the lower valley of the Kaveri River. Already in the emperor Asoka's time (c. 265–238 BCE) Chola was mentioned in an inscription as an independent kingdom to which Buddhist missionaries were sent. The earliest historically known king was Karikkal (ruled c. 100 CE), who laid the foundations of the great coastal emporium of Puhar (Kaveripattinam), fought a protracted war with Sri Lanka, and used Ceylonese laborers to build a 160-kilometer embankment along the Kaveri.

When the Chinese traveler Xien Qang visited the area in the seventh century, the dynasty had faded into obscurity, and the kingdom had shrunken. A powerful Chola dynasty reemerged, however, in the reign of Rajaditya I (947–949). Earlier in the tenth century several Chola kings had defeated the Pallava dynasty as well as the combined Pandyan and Sinhalese armies at Vellore. Later Chola rulers incorporated northern Sri Lanka into the kingdom; in 1025 King Rajendra's navy conquered the Andaman and Nicobar Islands. Although toward the end of Kulottunga I's reign (1070–1120) the Hoysalas took some Chola territory, the king maintained trade contacts overseas with Srivijaya, perhaps even with China and the Khmers. The resurgence of the Pandyan dynasty threatened the Cholas, however, and Kulottunga III (reigned 1178–1218) found himself in a complex struggle with the Pandyas, Cheras, and Sri Lankans. At the end of his reign the Pandyas gained a notable victory. In 1279 during the reign of the last Chola ruler, Rajendra IV (reigned 1246–1279), the Pandyas' defeat of both the Cholas and the Hoysalas marked the end of the Chola kingdom. In 1310 Malik Kafur—a eunuch slave who had become the most trusted general of Sultan Ala-ud-din Khalji—overran these former Chola territories, which were absorbed into the Vijayanagar empire.

Paul Hockings

Further Reading

Nilakanta Sastri, K. A. (1955) *The Colas.* 2d rev. ed. Madras, India: University of Madras.

CH'ONDOGYO Ch'ondogyo (Religion of the Heavenly Way) is the oldest organized indigenous religion of Korea. Founded in 1860 by Ch'oe Che-u (1824–1864) as Tonghak (Eastern Learning), it changed its name to Ch'ondogyo in 1905.

The god of Ch'ondogyo is usually referred to as Hanullim, a vernacular Korean term for "Lord of Heaven." Hanullim is not depicted as a deity residing in Heaven above, however. In fact, he is not depicted at all. There are no statues or paintings of God in Ch'ondogyo worship halls. That is because Ch'ondogyo perceives Hanullim as dwelling within the human heart.

The founder is said to have conversed with God and may have conceived of God as a transcendental personality. He emphasized the moral obligation of men and women to serve God. However, Ch'oe Che-u's disciple and successor, Ch'oe Si-hyong (1827–1898), added that just as people should serve God, they should also serve their fellow human beings. Son Pyong-hui (1861–1921), the third man to head the religion, amplified that statement with the phrase "God dwells within each and every human being." This focus on the immanence of God has become a core tenet of Ch'ondogyo doctrine.

Because of this focus on God within, Ch'ondogyo worship services include moments of silent prayer in addition to hymns, sermons, and chants. Silent prayer is the norm because, since God dwells within the human heart, he is best addressed internally.

Ch'ondogyo teachings are summed up in a twenty-one-syllable formula that believers are enjoined to chant daily. That formula reminds men and women that they are filled with the animating presence of the Lord of Heaven and that they should always be mindful of his presence within, a presence that helps them become one not only with God but also with all creation. The doctrines of Ch'ondogyo are expounded upon further in *Ch'ondogyo kyongjon* (Sacred Writings of Ch'ondogyo). It contains the poems, essays, and sermons of the three founding patriarchs of Ch'ondogyo: Ch'oe Che-u, Ch'oe Si-hyong, and Son Pyong-hui.

At the end of the twentieth century, Ch'ondogyo claimed to have over 1 million followers in Korea and close to three hundred worship halls, although a government census found fewer than thirty thousand South Koreans who reported that they were members of Ch'ondogyo.

Don Baker

See also: **Tonghak**

Further Reading

Kim, Yong Choon. (1989) *The Ch'ondogyo Concept of Man: An Essence of Korean Thought.* Seoul: Pan Korea Book Corporation.

Weems, Benjamin B. (1964) *Reform, Rebellion, and the Heavenly Way.* Tucson, AZ: University of Arizona Press.

CH'ONGJIN (2000 est. pop. 1 million). Ch'ongjin is the capital of North Hamgyong Province in North Korea (Democratic People's Republic of Korea). Ch'ongjin is a port city of approximately 275 square kilometers, located on the Sea of Japan (East Sea) about 100 kilometers south of the border between North Korea and Russia. The city became prominent with the establishment of its port in 1908. Ch'ongjin grew in importance with the opening of the Hamgyong rail line connecting Pyongyang and the nearby city of Rajin. Ch'ongjin has been the provincial capital since 1944.

The port of Ch'ongjin accounts for much of the region's commerce. It provides a convenient port for trade between China and Japan. The port is connected by rail to the Musan iron mine, which exports 8 million tons of ore annually. The nearby Rajin-Sonbong Free Trade Zone also benefits from its close proximity to the port.

The region also hosts industries producing metals, machinery, pharmaceuticals, and chemicals. Ch'ongjin and North Hamgyong Province are also noted for their fisheries. Ch'ongjin is home as well to Ch'ongam Mountain, three hot springs, a fortress dating to the fifteenth and sixteenth centuries, and prehistoric artifacts dating to before 3000 BCE.

Jennifer Jung-Kim

Further Reading

Cho, Chung-Kyung, Phyllis Haffner, and Fredric M Kaplan. (1991) *The Korea Guidebook.* 5th ed. Boston: Houghton Mifflin.

Storey, Robert, and Alex English. (2001) *Korea.* 5th ed. Berkeley, CA: Lonely Planet.

CHONGQING (1992 est. pop. 3.8 million). Chongqing, which is the largest city in China's Sichuan Province, is situated where the Jialing River flows into the Chang (Yangtze) River in the southeastern part of Sichuan. The old city, which was the main city in the ancient state of Ba, was originally built on a promontory between the two rivers. Chongqing remained on the fringe of the Chinese empire until the fourteenth century. During the Japanese occupation of eastern China (1937–1945), the Chinese Nationalist Party (Guomindang) moved China's capital to Chongqing, and important industries followed. From the 1950s, Chongqing became a center for trade and transportation, and bridges and railways were built, making the city an important river port for transshipments from railways to the far cheaper transport via the Chang River to the east. Chongqing is also one of the main industrial centers in southwestern China, with such heavy industries as iron works and steel mills, and the city manufactures motorcycles, cars, and heavy machinery. Chemical and electronic industries as well as textile and food processing industries are also located there. In the 1980s Chongqing was chosen as model city for market economics to attract foreign investments, and in 1997 the city became an independent municipality directly under the central government.

Bent Nielsen

Further Reading

Ho, Samuel P. S., and Y. Y. Kueh. (2000) *Chongqing: Sustainable Economic Development in South China.* New York: St. Martin's Press.

CH'ONMIN

Ch'onmin was the lowest social class in Korean society from the seventh to the nineteenth centuries. As with the three other social classes (the *yangban*, or elite; the *nongmin*, or farmers; and the *sangmin*, or freeborn commoners), membership in the *ch'onmin* marked one permanently. The *ch'onmin* class included all people doing dishonorable work; slaves, actors, entertainers, shamans, and butchers were all *ch'onmin*. Class governed the dress, language, and marriage and funeral ceremonies of the people, and relations between the classes were restricted. The people who belonged to the *ch'onmin* class were restricted in where they could live to areas assigned by the government.

Among the *ch'onmin* groups, slaves were treated the worst. They were registered as personal property and were owned entirely by the master, who had the right to trade and inherit them. During the latter years of the Choson dynasty (1392–1910), there were several emancipation movements that resulted in freeing *ch'onmin* to live wherever they pleased. In 1894 the *Kabo* reform policy was launched to prohibit the registration and trading of slaves; this policy finally proclaimed the release of all slaves. Social discrimination against the ex-slaves continued for a long time, but is today no longer an issue.

Seong-Sook Yim

Further Reading

Yoo, Hong-Yeol, ed. (1975) *Kuksa paegkwa sajeon* (Encyclopedia of Korean History). Seoul: DoangA Culture Publishing.

CHORMAQAN, NOYAN

(1200–1240), Mongolian general. Chormaqan Noyan led the armies of the Mongol empire across the Amu Dar'ya River and into the area of present-day Iran in 1230, conquering much of what would later be the Il-Khanate (a Mongol dynasty that ruled in Persia from 1256 to 1353). Genghis Khan (1165–1227) originally delivered the orders for this invasion in 1221 during the war against the Khwarizm empire, which lay on the lower Amu Dar'ya River, but a rebellion delayed the campaign. Chormaqan served in this earlier campaign as a *qorchi* (quiver bearer) for Genghis Khan's bodyguard.

Ogodei (1185–1241), the son and successor of Genghis Khan, renewed the command in 1229. Chormaqan's orders were to expand the Mongol empire and hunt down Jalal al-Din Khwarazmshah (d.1230–1231), the last sultan of the Khwarizm empire. While a subordinate commander, Taimaz, pursued Jalal al-Din, Chormaqan efficiently secured the conquest of Iran through force and diplomacy. By 1232, Iran was firmly under Mongol control.

In 1234, Chormaqan turned his attention to the region of Transcaucasia, the region of modern Georgia, Armenia, Azerbaijan, and parts of Turkey. After a five-year campaign, Chormaqan successfully conquered Transcaucasia. He ruled as the military governor for two years until he died. His wife Altan Khatun (flourished 1220–1245) succeeded him as regent until one of his lieutenants, Baiju (flourished 1230–1260), was named his successor.

Timothy May

Further Reading

Blake, Robert P., and Richard N. Frye (1949) "The History of the Nation of the Archers by Grigor of Akanc." *Harvard Journal of Asiatic Studies* 12: 269–399.

Cleaves, Frances W., trans. and ed. (1982) *The Secret History of the Mongols.* Cambridge, MA: Harvard University Press.

Grousset, René. (1970) *The Empire of the Steppes: A History of Central Asia.* Trans. by Naomi Walford. Rutgers, NJ: Rutgers University Press.

Juvaini, 'Ala-ad-Din Ata-Malik. (1958) *The History of the World-Conqueror.* 2 vols. Trans. by John A. Boyle. Cambridge, MA: Harvard University Press.

May, Timothy. (1996) "Chormaqan Noyan: The First Mongol Military Governor in the Middle East." M.A. thesis, Indiana University.

CHOSHU EXPEDITIONS

Punitive expeditions were launched by the Tokugawa shogunate against the domain of Choshu (located in present-day Yamaguchi Prefecture) in 1864 and 1865. The first was a limited success, the second a bitter failure—and a major factor in the fall of the shogunate in the Meiji Restoration of 1867–1868.

Choshu, a domain long hostile to the Tokugawa government, initially drew the ire of the shogunate in the early 1860s when pro-imperial reformers took control of the domain's capital, Kyoto. In 1863 troops from the domains of Satsuma and Aizu carried out a coup d'état at the court, driving Choshu forces out of the city. Choshu troops marched on Kyoto the following year and were roundly defeated. Spurred to action, the shogunate, by November 1864, had amassed a punitive force of 150,000 samurai from several domains around Choshu's borders. After scattered fighting, Choshu agreed to a limited surrender the following January. Conservative Choshu power holders ordered the execution of three "house elders" and the dissolution of the mixed samurai/peasant rifle troops that had attacked Kyoto. But the radical leaders of the mixed units refused to disband and instead fought the domain government in the Choshu Civil War of 1865. The war brought to power a reformist government committed to the shogunate's overthrow. It was staffed by many lower-ranking samurai who would play prominent roles in national government after 1868, such as Ito Hirobumi and Yamagata Aritomo.

In 1865 Shogun Tokugawa Iemochi led a second expedition to topple the new Choshu government but found circumstances quite different from those of two years earlier. Several domains that had participated in the first expedition refused to contribute troops to the second, and Choshu completed a secret alliance with the powerful Satsuma domain before the shogunate forces arrived to fight. Buoyed by this alliance, as well as the purchase of some 10,000 Western rifles (some from the recently ended American Civil War), the outnumbered Choshu forces easily defeated the shogun's troops. The defeat made it clear that the Tokugawa family's hegemony was over. In 1867–1868 Choshu and Satsuma installed the boy emperor Mutsuhito as the head of a new national government in what is called the Meiji Restoration.

Todd S. Munson

Further Reading

Craig, Albert M. (1961) *Choshu in the Meiji Restoration.* Cambridge, MA: Harvard University Press.

Huber, Thomas M. (1981) *The Revolutionary Origins of Modern Japan.* Stanford, CA: Stanford University Press.

CHOSON KINGDOM

CHOSON KINGDOM Governing the Korean peninsula for over five hundred years (1392–1910), the Choson kingdom was the final stage of dynastic rule in Korea. Also known as the Choson dynasty or Yi dynasty, this era differed from that of its predecessor, the Koryo kingdom (918–1392), in that it formed a highly centralized government under royal authority with the influence of aristocrat-bureaucrats. The Choson kingdom established Confucian rule that continued throughout the entirety of the reign of its twenty-seven kings. During the course of more than five centuries, Choson experienced periods of great development, foreign invasion, factional infighting, and self-isolation from the outside world.

KOREAN KINGDOMS AND DYNASTIES

Koguryo kingdom (37 BCE–668 CE)
Paekche kingdom (18 BCE–663 CE)
Shilla kingdom (57 BCE–935 CE)
Unified Shilla (668–935 CE)
Koryo kingdom (dynasty) (918–1392)
Choson dynasty or Yi dynasty (1392–1910)

Early Choson (1392–1592)

The Choson kingdom began with a Koryo general, Yi Song-gye (1335–1408), seizing military and political power and eventually placing himself on the throne. Neo-Confucian ideology and land reforms, which controlled land accumulation by the *yangban* (office-holding aristocrats) and improved the livelihood of the peasants, were instituted. From the beginning, the *yangban* had the right to intervene in the governmental decision making of the monarchy. Confucian classics were printed with movable metal type to further Confucian learning for the well-being of the newly founded state.

King Sejong the Great (1397–1450), the son of Yi Song-gye and the most renowned of Choson's kings, ruled during a period of marked advancement in numerous fields. He showed great concern for the peasant farmers, providing them with flood and drought relief as well as tax relief. Marked development in science, agriculture, administration, economics, medicine, music, and the humanities also took place. The most noted of his achievements was the creation of the phonetic alphabet for the Korean language, hangul, which enabled the illiterate peasantry to learn to read. Prior to this, all writing was in Chinese characters, which were inaccessible to the uneducated masses. It wasn't until the twentieth century, though, that the popularity of hangul overtook that of Chinese characters.

The century to follow was marked by instability and a decline in prosperity due to power struggles between the monarchy and the *yangban* bureaucrats. To offset *yangban* power gains, royal favor was shown toward Buddhist and Taoist religious orders, and the literati *yangban* were suppressed; as the throne changed hands, however, there was a resurgence of Neo-Confucian rule and *yangban* influence in the royal court and administrative affairs. During this time, the plight of the peasant worsened and the power of the kingdom weakened.

Choson maintained almost no international trade or political ties, but was drawn into international affairs when Japanese warlord Toyotomi Hideyoshi (1536–1598) requested Choson's aid in attacking Ming China to consolidate his power at home. Choson refused and for this was brutally and repeatedly attacked during by Hideyoshi from 1592 through 1598. The Japanese invaders attained initial success in occupying strategic land areas but met stiffer resistance on the seas. Choson's most renowned military leader, Yi Sinsin (1545–1598), devastated the Japanese fleet and its supply lines, eventually forcing a Japanese withdrawal. If it had not been for the ingenious warfare strategies of Commander Yi and his ironclad *kobukson* (turtle ships), Japan would almost assuredly have wrested control of the peninsula from Choson.

The war took a heavy toll on Choson—heavy loss of life, the abduction of artisans and technicians, the devastation of farming land, and the destruction of government records and cultural artifacts. Taking advantage of Choson's weakened state, the Manchus to the north, who had gained control of China, demanded that Choson acknowledge his suzerainty. When Choson refused, the Manchus attacked and overwhelmed Choson in a relatively short war; Chinese suzerainty was acknowledged, as it had been before the Manchu invasions.

Later Choson (1592–1910)

The destruction caused by the wars with the Japanese and the Manchus brought great social and economic upheaval. The cost of reconstruction was high and government financial difficulty led to repeated tax increases and the sale of aristocratic titles. The plight of the peasantry worsened, while the rise of a wealthy merchant class led to a new notion of wealth—mercantile wealth—as well as to the decline of the *yangban* society. All of these factors contributed to the rise of a new generation of scholars critical of the traditional Neo-Confucian order. This reformist school started the Sirhak (Practical Learning) movement in the seventeenth century and advocated the promotion of utilitarian knowledge, as well as political, economic, and educational reforms to promote political integrity, economic stability, and social accord. They had a true concern for the well-being of the common people.

The schism led to fierce factional strife among the *yangban* during the latter half of the seventeenth century. Realizing the seriousness of the situation, King Yongjo (1694–1776) effected a series of reforms. These reforms were intended to end factional feuding, improve the life of the peasants and commoners, and reassert the Confucian monarchy; it enjoyed, however, only limited success. Mercantile activities increased rapidly, with the *yangban* also becoming involved in activities that they once had disdained. The economy and social conditions improved, and, in the early nineteenth century, Western ideas of finance reform were seriously considered, though never implemented due to factional strife.

During first half of the nineteenth century, drought and flood fiercely undermined agricultural productivity, causing widespread famine. Excessive taxes were levied by a chronically debt-ridden government, exploiting the destitute farmers. These intolerable natural and social conditions led to peasant revolts in the northern part of the kingdom in 1812 and in the southern part in 1862. The adverse social conditions also gave rise in the mid-nineteenth century to a new ideology, Tonghak (Eastern Learning), which appealed to the farming class. It sought to rescue the peasantry from poverty and social unrest and to restore political and social stability throughout the kingdom. To succeed in this, it opposed government corruption, the privileged *yangban* class, social injustice, and Sohak (Western Learning), which manifested itself mainly in Catholicism, which had entered Korea in 1593 and had begun to take root among the populace in the late eighteenth century.

Attempts by American and French naval vessels to open Choson to commerce led to the adoption of a policy of isolation in 1871. In 1876, backed by naval force, Japan coerced the signing of a treaty establish-

HWASEONG—WORLD HERITAGE SITE

Hwaseong—an eighteenth-century fort built around Suwon, the capital of Korea's Choson kingdom—was designated a UNESCO World Heritage Site in 1997. Six kilometers of wall, artillery towers, and gates still remain.

ing diplomatic and commercial relations between the two countries. In order to offset the Japanese influence in militarily weak Choson, similar treaties were soon signed with the United States and other Western nations. Choson sent diplomatic missions to Japan and the United States, and an influx of North American Protestant missionaries began.

This newfound knowledge of the outside world led to a progressive movement by young scholars to modernize the government and bring about social reforms. As efforts at modernization were blocked by government officials, the progressives, with Japanese support, resorted in 1884 to a coup, which was put down only with Chinese assistance. Ten years later, the Tonghak rebellion spread throughout the country and brought both Japanese and Chinese troops to Choson.

Japan, China, and Russia were now all vying for influence on the peninsula. Chinese influence was quickly removed by Japan's victory in the Sino-Japanese war (1894–1895). In 1895, the Japanese instigated the assassination of the influential queen consort, Queen Min (1851–1895), the real power behind the throne, to increase their influence. With victory in the Russo-Japanese war (1904–1905), Japan was now unrivaled on the peninsula, and Choson had no choice but to become a Japanese protectorate. Annexation by Japan in 1910 brought an end to the kingdom of Choson and the beginning of thirty-five years of colonial rule.

David E. Shaffer

Further Reading

Eckert, Carter J., et al. (1990) *Korea: Old and New*. Seoul, South Korea: Ilchokak.

Ha, Tae-hung. (1983) *Behind the Scenes of Royal Palaces in Korea (Yi Dynasty)*. Seoul, South Korea: Yonsei University Press.

Han, Woo-keun. (1970) *The History of Korea*. Trans. by Lee Kyung-shik. Seoul, South Korea: Eul-yoo Publishing.

Henthorn, William E. (1971) *A History of Korea*. New York: Free Press.

Joe, Wanne J., and Hongkyu A. Choe. (1997) *Traditional Korea: A Cultural History*. Elizabeth, NJ: Hollym.

Koo, John H., and Andrew C. Nahm, eds. (1997) *An Introduction to Korean Culture*. Elizabeth, NJ: Hollym.

Lee, Ki-baik. (1984) *A New History of Korea*. Trans. by Edward W. Wagner. Seoul, South Korea: Ilchokak.

Lone, Stewart, and Gavan McCormack. (1993) *Korea Since 1850*. New York: St. Martin's Press.

Nahm, Andrew C. (1983) *A Panorama of 5000 Years: Korean History*. Elizabeth, NJ: Hollym.

———. (1988) *Korea: Tradition and Transformation*. Elizabeth, NJ: Hollym.

Osgood, Cornelius. (1954) *The Koreans and Their Culture*. Rutland, VT: Tuttle.

Rutt, Richard. (1983) *History of the Korean People*. 2d ed. Seoul, South Korea: Seoul Computer Press.

CHOU DYNASTY. See **Zhou Dynasty.**

CHOU EN-LAI. See **Zhou Enlai.**

CHOYBALSAN, HORLOOGIYN

(1895–1952), Prime minister of Mongolia. Choybalsan was born in Achit Beysiyn (now the city of Choybalsan) in the Tsetsen Khan aymag (now Dornod province) of Mongolia. After running away from a Buddhist monastery at age seventeen, Choybalsan worked a variety of jobs while attending the Russian School for Translators in Nislel Khuree, as Ulaanbaatar was then called. While attending school in Russia, he became one of the founding members of the Mongolian Peoples Revolutionary Party, which established contact with the Bolsheviks.

After the successful Mongolian Communist revolution in 1921, Choybalsan attended a military academy in Moscow and eventually became the commander in chief of the Mongolian army. He then held several posts in the Mongolian government, ranging from foreign minister to minister of war. In 1939, however, Choybalsan obtained the position of prime minister and held it until his death in 1952.

Choybalsan was a close friend of Josef Stalin and is often referred to as Mongolia's Stalin. Like Stalin, he developed a cult of personality and purged thousands of dissidents. The death toll is still uncertain. In 1962, ten years after Choybalsan's death, the MPRP Central Committee admitted that many innocent people died as a result of his misconduct.

Timothy M. May

Further Reading

Bawden, C. R. (1968) *The Modern History of Mongolia*. New York: Praeger.

Dashpurev, D., and S. K Soni. (1992) *Reign of Terror in Mongolia, 1920–1990*. New Delhi: South Asian Publishers.

Lattimore, Owen. (1962) *Nomads and Commissars*. New York: Oxford University Press.

Rupen, Robert. (1979) *How Mongolia Is Really Ruled*. Stanford, CA: Hoover Institution Press.

Sandag, Shagdariin, and Harry H. Kendall. (1999) *Poisoned Arrows: The Stalin-Choibalsan Mongolian Massacres, 1921–1941*. Boulder, CO: Westview.

CHRISTIANITY. See **Belo, Bishop Carlos; Catholicism, Roman—Philippines; Catholicism,**

Roman—Vietnam; Eastern Orthodox Church—Asia; Endo Shusaku; Jesuits—India; Ricci, Matteo; Oriental Orthodox Church; Protestant Fundamentalism—Southeast Asia; Saint Paul

CHRISTIANITY—CENTRAL ASIA

CHRISTIANITY—CENTRAL ASIA In numbers of adherents, Christianity is Central Asia's second major religion after Islam. Missionaries, merchants, scholars, and diplomatic envoys traveling from Europe to the Far East all contributed to the penetration of Christianity to Central Asia. Over time, Christianity grew and consolidated itself to reach the present state of acceptance and coexistence with Islam. After the fall of the Soviet Union in 1991, the newly independent states of Central Asia guaranteed their populations religious freedom. Nevertheless, recently a new wave of religious regulation has appeared in a number of those states. Some fear that for security reasons new restrictions on religion may be imposed in the fight against Islamic fundamentalism.

The Early Years of Central Asian Christianity

The earliest Christian community in Central Asia emerged in what is now Iran in about 200 CE. Between the fourth and sixth century Christians were also found in China and Mongolia and in the seventh century in the present Central Asian Region. Many of the Turks who in the 1800s served in the army of the Governor of Bukhara (now in Uzbekistan) bore the sign of the cross on their foreheads. Coins and ornaments of the period also bore this cross-like image.

New information has come to light since the 1990s concerning the earlier stages of Christianity in Central Asia, and concerning a Christian community in the city of Merv in Turkmenistan in particular. At the Council of Constantinople (381 CE), the community was the first one granted metropolitan status (that is, it became an episcopal center). This was thanks to Bar Shaba (third century CE), one of the first active promoters of the Eastern Church, which appeared soon after the Roman Empire split in the fourth century. Exiled with his wife from Iran to Merv for his faith, Bar Shaba converted many people to Christianity. He constructed several churches in and near the city, and assigned them preachers, so that they could care for the people and perform religious services.

Churches and monasteries were built and ecclesiastical centers functioned. In Asia, Christians were regarded as excellent doctors, scribes, scholars, diplomats, and theologians, and often included top government officials. The Sogdian period from the sixth to the tenth centuries was the golden age of the Nestorian Christians (Christians who emphasized the independence of Christ's human nature and his divine nature), who left traces of their presence all over Central Asia.

Another important historical site is the Armenian abbey on the shore of lake Issyk-Kul in Kyrgyzstan. According to legend, this is the location of the grave of Saint Matthew. On a hill to the south of Samarqand in Uzbekistan, along with various Christian symbols, a chancel of fire was found. As this is a Zoroastrian symbol, it shows that the two religions mingled.

Roman Catholic Forays into Central Asia and the Rise of Islam

An apostolic nuncio to the Tartars was appointed in April 1245 by Pope Innocent IV and made a long journey through Central Asia. His was probably one of the first Catholic diplomatic missions to the Far East. The Franciscan friar Giovanni da Pian del Carmine, a contemporary and disciple of Saint Francis of Assisi, reached the court of the Great Khan Guyuk in 1246, nearly thirty years before Marco Polo. But Venetians and Genoese merchants were already in Central Asia with their goods and their Catholic faith, and records indicate that Christianity was already current there. During his journey, the friar learned that Prince Michael of Tchernigov, a fervent Christian (later made Saint Michael of Russia) and his assistant Theodore (later Saint Theodore of Russia) had been executed for refusing to recognize the divinity of Genghis Khan. Another Franciscan, the German friar William of Rubruck, visited the area in 1253.

By the thirteenth century, Asia was conquered by the Mongolian Tartars, and Islam started to displace all other religions. But Muslims respected Christians and other "people of the book" and never interfered with their rites; they simply taxed them as foreigners. By the sixteenth century, Christianity in Central Asia came almost to a standstill, and visits by Roman Catholic missionaries became rare.

Eastern Orthodox Christianity in Central Asia

At the end of the seventeenth century, the first Russian settlers appeared in eastern Kazakhstan. In their new land, Russian peasants found an escape from serfdom, and Old Believers (those who refused to accept mid-seventeenth-century reforms to the Russian Orthodox Church) found a break from religious oppression. From the mid-nineteenth century, a new era of Christianity began in Central Asia, arising from the political interest of the Russian Empire in its southern borders. Unusual churches appeared—army garrison churches, mobile vans that serviced the railway builders, and later, the first permanent church—in Kazakhstan, in 1847.

Poor migrants, most of them orthodox Christians, rushed to Asia in the hope of finding free land, jobs, and markets. The officialdom, military officers, and craftspeople included many Germans, Poles, and Lithuanians, who were Catholics and Lutherans. A Mennonite group established three different settlements in today's Kyrgyzstan. In addition, a community of Armenian Christians was engaged in winemaking, silkworm breeding, and trade. The inflow of Christians increased when prisoners and clergymen of World War I—Hungarians, Czechs, Poles, and Austrians—were brought here.

In 1871, the Holy Synod of the Russian Orthodox Church and the State Council of Russia established the Turkestan eparchy with headquarters in Vernyi (now Almaty), and after 1916, in Tashkent. In order to survive, the eparchy—situated in predominantly Islamic territory and uniting a diverse community—had to find its own path. The picture was further confused a few years later by the problems of regulating the different religions' relations with the Soviet authorities. The Orthodox communities, whose numbers decreased sharply, were not allowed to keep their property, which was declared the common property of the people. Soviet authorities disbanded the Catholic and Lutheran communities. Religious celebrations were replaced by revolutionary holidays. A wave of terror was launched against the clergy.

Kazakh women pray during a mass celebrated by Pope John Paul II during his visit to Kazakhstan in September 2001. (AFP/CORBIS)

The Communist attitude toward the Russian Orthodox Church changed somewhat during the World War II, when the Church played a big propaganda role in defending the motherland. But the negative view of any type of religion persisted until the late 1980s and early 1990s, when the collapse of the Soviet system finally removed the trammels of atheism.

Christianity in Central Asia in the Twenty-First Century

Today Christians of different denominations—Russian Orthodox, Roman Catholic, Lutheran, Adventist, Baptist, evangelical, and others—are all actively involved in their pastoral activity and most of them are officially registered in the nations of Central Asia. Islam and Christianity coexist peacefully. Relative stability was achieved at the cost of compromises that the official church had to make with the state during the Soviet period and afterward. Today Christian festivities are celebrated not only by Central Asian Christians but also by people of other faiths.

In autumn 1996, in the presence of the holy patriarch of Moscow and all Russia, Aleksei II, Christians celebrated the 125th anniversary of the Tashkent-Central Asian eparchy. In the same period the Vatican also established a general nunciature (papal diplomatic mission) in Almaty (Kazakhstan), in charge of all Central Asian states and with missions in Kyrgyzstan, Tajikistan, Uzbekistan, and Turkmenistan.

On a darker note, a new wave of religious restrictions has appeared in various Central Asian countries. The secular governments are trying to protect themselves against a wave of Islamic fundamentalism, fearing terrorism and calls for an Islamic state in Central Asia. This new trend is being carefully watched by the democratic institutions in the West and may represent a sad new page in the history of Christianity's development in Central Asia.

Giorgio Fiacconi

Further Reading

Foltz, Richard C. (1999) *Religions of the Silk Road: Overland Trade and Cultural Exchange from Antiquity to the Fifteenth Century*. New York: St. Martin's Press.

Lewis, David C. (2000) *After Atheism: Religion and Ethnicity in Russia and Central Asia*. Richmond, Surrey, U.K.: Curzon.

CHRISTIANITY—CHINA

Christians have been trying to convert the Chinese for over a thousand years. Although Christians make up only a small percentage of the Chinese population, Christianity is an established minority religion in China, and Chinese and foreign Christians have had a great impact on China's modern history.

The Jesuits in China

Christianity first came to China in the Tang dynasty (618–907 CE) when Nestorians established churches in Changan, but the first major attempt at Christianizing China came from the Jesuits. The most important early Jesuit was Matteo Ricci (1552–1610), who arrived in China in 1582. The Jesuits hoped to convert China beginning with the elite, and they managed to establish themselves at court and served the Ming and Qing emperors as astronomers, painters, and weapons makers. The Jesuits won some converts, as did their rivals the Franciscans, who concentrated on the lower classes, but their work was undermined by growing Confucian hostility to Christian philosophy and the long-running Rites Controversy, which ended with a papal decree that Chinese Christians could no longer participate in ancestor worship. In 1724, the emperor declared Catholicism a perverse sect, similar to the White Lotus, a Buddhist sect that was often at odds with the imperial government. The prohibitions against Catholicism were usually not rigorously enforced, but the numbers of Catholics fell. Catholicism remained a viable minority religion in a number of areas, but the greatest significance of the Jesuit interlude was the intellectual exchanges between China and Europe it facilitated.

Nineteenth-Century Missionary Activity in China

The next great attempt at the conversion of China began in the nineteenth century and involved both Catholics and Protestants. The attempts to convert China were only one part of a larger Euro-American drive to evangelize the non-Christian world, and the missionaries were also only part of a larger effort to control and transform China. For at least some of the missionaries the task of making China a modern nation was at least as important as making it a Christian one. Missionaries played a significant role in helping build a new nation, but their connection to foreign imperialism loomed large in the eyes of many Chinese.

In the early nineteenth century, there was a revival of interest in missionary work that led to the creation of bodies like the French Catholic Society for the Propagation of the Faith and the London Missionary Society. Under the Canton system, which restricted where foreign traders could live, foreign missionaries could reside only in Macao and Canton, and until the Treaty of Tienstin (Tianjin) their efforts were mostly confined to translating and publishing Christian works. By 1900, however, there were 886 Catholic priests in China, and in 1905, there were over 3,000 Protestant missionaries, members of 63 missionary societies.

Problems of Acceptance

The presence of missionaries often created trouble at the local level. The gentry resented the political privileges that the treaty system gave the missionaries and saw them as agents of their governments, a charge that was sometimes true. The Christians were also associated in the popular mind with the opium trade and the Taiping Rebellion (1850–1864). Anti-Christian violence was not uncommon. Although missionaries could sometimes reside in China for years without trouble, incidents like the Tianjin Massacre of 1870, which was sparked by rumors that Christian missionaries were using the blood of Chinese infants in their rituals, were also possible. The greatest anti-Christian outbreak was the Boxer Rebellion of 1899–1900, which tied together anti-Christian and anti-Imperialist sentiments.

In addition to problems simply maintaining their presence in China, the missions had far less success in converting the Chinese than had been hoped. Most of the missionaries could count only a handful of converts after years of work, and almost all the financial support for their efforts came from their home countries. At the beginning of the twentieth century there were 700,000 Chinese Catholics and 100,000 Protestants. For most Chinese the foreign religion was simply too foreign, requiring an end to ancestor worship and withdrawal from the religious rituals that defined local communities.

Christians and Education

Like the Jesuits before them, the nineteenth-century missionaries were important cultural conduits between China and the West. In addition to producing religious tracts, they were responsible for translations of many Western books into Chinese, bilingual

RELIGION IN CHINA FROM THE PERSPECTIVE OF A PROTESTANT MISSIONARY

"But whether a Chinaman is a Confucian, Taoist, or a Buddhist, he considers it to be his first duty to sacrifice to his ancestors. This Ancestral Worship, as it is called, is dearer to hearts of Chinese than any other kind of worship. They say that the idols belong to everybody, but their ancestors are their own, therefore they worship them. Of course it is only a dead ancestor who is worshipped; he is in the spirit-world and is supposed to have power over his living relatives, who think that he will cause some evil to fall upon them unless they please him by offering him sacrifices and worship. The relatives also think the departed spirit will in some way be better for these sacrifices. The worship is carried out at the graves and before the ancestral tablets which are put up to the memory of the departed in almost every house.

"In the face of all this the missionaries are bravely advancing, carrying the message of the Gospel into the strongholds of superstition and idolatry. They have made such progress during the last fifty years, that whereas just before the accession of Queen Victoria there were scarcely a dozen Protestant Christians in the land, to-day there are upwards of a hundred thousand."

Source: Mary Isabella Bryson. (1890) *Child Life in China*. London: William Clowes and Sons, Limited, 21–22.

dictionaries, and translation of the Chinese classics into English. James Legge, one of the first to undertake translations of the Chinese classics into English, justified his work on the ground that it was only by understanding the Chinese that missionaries could convert them; he and his compatriots also laid the foundations for the study of China in the West. It was through education and medicine that Christians first began to find a role for themselves in China. Christian-run hospitals were the first to introduce modern medicine to China and Christian schools provided education in Western subjects to a growing number of Chinese. For the many missionaries, especially Protestants, who were influenced by the doctrine of the social gospel, modernizing Chinese culture was as important a mission as evangelism. Missionaries were at the center of early efforts to eliminate opium smoking and improve the position of women.

Revolution

Christian education in China culminated with the founding of universities, perhaps the best-known being St. John's, founded in Shanghai in 1879. The goal of the universities was to create a Chinese Christian elite, and partly because of the universities such an elite came to exist. Like most of the Christian universities, St. John's came to enroll more non-Christian than Christian students. Although the total numbers of Chinese Christians remained small, by the 1920s members of the urban elite were quite likely to have attended a Christian school. Two of China's most famous leaders, Sun Yat-sen (1866–1925) and Chiang Kai-shek (1887–1975), were Christians. Despite this, and in part because of it, there was a considerable amount of anti-Christian feeling among educated Chinese. The May Fourth Movement, which began in 1919, was critical of Confucianism in particular and religion in general and of foreign control of important Chinese institutions, such as universities. This led to a rising tide of criticism of Christianity among the elite in the 1920s.

At the same time members of the elite were attacking the foreign nature of Christianity, more Chinese forms of Christianity were beginning to develop. Making Christianity into an indigenous Chinese religion had been a goal of most missionaries from the beginning, but the mainline missionary organizations made little progress in this direction. In addition to small independent congregations of Chinese Christians, groups like the True Jesus Church and the Little Flock emerged. These movements owed much to the Chinese sectarian tradition and the Pentecostal movement in the West. They were led by charismatic Chinese and often had contentious relationships with foreign-led Christian organizations.

Communism

The Communist victory in 1949 was not good for Chinese Christianity. Many organizations were banned and some individuals arrested. The fact that so many Christians had overseas ties was also a problem. Although official sanctioned churches continued to function, the religion was regarded with great suspicion by the authorities, especially during the Cultural Revolution. Since the death of Mao there has been a great increase of interest in religions of all sorts, and Christianity has grown rapidly. Although the state is not formally opposed to Christianity, it is very much opposed to groups that are not approved by the government.

Alan Baumler

Further Reading

Bays, Daniel, ed. (1996) *Christianity in China: From the Eighteenth Century to the Present.* Stanford, CA: Stanford University Press.

Espey, John. (1994) *Minor Heresies, Major Departures: A China Mission Boyhood.* Berkeley and Los Angeles: University of California Press.

Fairbank, John, ed. (1974) *The Missionary Enterprise in China and America.* Cambridge, MA: Harvard University Press.

CHRISTIANITY—JAPAN

Christianity arrived in Japan with Catholic missionaries in the mid-sixteenth century and flourished for approximately a century before being brutally suppressed. After that, isolated underground communities attempted to maintain Christian teachings without benefit of priests. With the reopening of Japan in the mid-nineteenth century, a new wave of missionaries arrived, and during this period the Japanese people alternated between interest in and rejection of what they saw as foreign to Japanese sensibilities.

First Encounter with Christianity

The history of Christianity in Japan began with the arrival of Portuguese traders, but formal instruction began in 1549 with the arrival of Francis Xavier in Kagoshima, the southernmost city of Kyushu. Xavier and those who followed were generally received amiably by local rulers, partly because the foreigners were obviously educated and partly because they were associated with profitable Portuguese trade. The Jesuits were successful in Kyushu and western Honshu, converting as many as thirty thousand Japanese by 1570, partly as a result of mass conversions under varying degrees of pressure from the local lords. Another factor in their success was an emphasis on conforming as much as possible with Japanese forms and customs and developing a native clergy. By 1614 there were an estimated 300,000 Christians out of a total Japanese population of 20 million.

The early mission activities took place during a nationwide power struggle, in which Oda Nobunaga (1534–1582), the first of the Three Unifiers of Japan, made the first steps toward broad centralized control. Out of hatred for the Buddhist hierarchy and interest in learning about European civilization from men of culture, Nobunaga was friendly toward the Jesuits and tolerant of their activities. Amiable relations continued when Toyotomi Hideyoshi (1536/7–1598), the second Unifier, succeeded to power, culminating in his granting an interview to Vice-Provincial Gaspar Coelho in 1586 at Osaka. The following year, however, saw a radical change. Hideyoshi became incensed at the undue deference paid to the Jesuit fathers by the converted daimyo (regional lords) of Kyushu and at the forcible conversions of people within certain domains. The result was a sudden reversal of the favorable reception of the Jesuits.

Aggravating an already tenuous situation, rivalry between Portuguese and Spaniards and between the Jesuits and the Franciscans, Augustinians, and Dominicans, who arrived in Japan between 1593 and 1602, showed itself as mutual defamation. Things were brought to a head when a Spanish ship, the *San Felipe*, was driven ashore in Shikoku in 1596. The ship was confiscated, and the captain appealed to the representative in charge of negotiations. During the proceedings, the captain showed a map indicating the colonial possessions of the king of Spain, and when asked whether missionaries had played a part in acquiring the colonies, the captain replied that they had. Hideyoshi immediately adopted a policy of complete intolerance toward the missionaries and their Japanese followers.

In 1597 Hideyoshi had foreign and Japanese Franciscans active in the Kyoto area arrested. They were eventually executed by crucifixion as a warning that Christian missionaries and converted Japanese would no longer be tolerated. In 1614 an edict of persecution was issued charging Christians with intent to take charge of the government and the country. Churches were destroyed or closed, missionaries were forbidden to enter the country, and Japanese converts were forced to recant.

THE "ACCEPTANCE" OF CHRISTIANITY IN PREWAR JAPAN

The following description of women's interest in Christianity as depicted by characters in pre–World War II novels by Japanese scholar M. Kawaguchi suggests that Christianity had not taken hold.

> None of the characters in these works has any clear religion. But the women are all "interested in" Christianity. Michiko in *Tsuki yori no Shisha* (Kume) becomes a nurse at the Fujimi Convalescent Home because, she says, "it is only fitting that we should bear all bear the suffering of the cross." Keiko in *San-Katei*, who can no longer bear to live with her unfaithful husband and goes home to her mother, tries to assuage her despair as she waits to bear that husband's child by reading the Bible. Emiko, whose mother is a Christian, sometimes reads the Bible, but in her case it is generally enforced reading as a punishment for coming home late. She reads the Old Testament stories—as literature. But interest in Christianity does not develop into Christian faith. The Christian Madame Isago is said to be "pompous in everything, prejudiced, lacking in understanding and unable to make allowances; her judgment of sin is swift and cunningly ruthless." Christianity is even held to be narrow and oppressive.

Source: R. P. Dore (1967). *City Life in Japan: A Study of a Tokyo Ward.* Berkeley and Los Angeles: University of California Press, 360.

When suppression intensified, there was little choice but to apostatize or go underground. The strength of the conviction of Japanese Christians is witnessed by the estimated forty or fifty thousand who were martyred for their faith. Resistance effectively came to a close with the end of the Shimabara Rebellion (1637–1638). When peasants rose up in rebellion against extortionate taxation, religious persecution, and chronic poverty in Shimabara domain (current Nagasaki prefecture), the government viewed it as inspired by Christians. The rebellion ended with the slaughter of some thirty-seven thousand men, women, and children. The next year the entire country was closed to outside intercourse, with the exception of Dutch trade at Dejima, an island off Nagasaki, and by 1643 Christianity was ostensibly eradicated.

The Second Encounter

When Japan opened to the West in the 1860s, it was discovered that communities of *kakure kirishitan* ("hidden Christians") had survived for two centuries. C. R. Boxer quotes a contemporary estimate that there were some forty thousand Christian believers at the end of the Edo or Tokugawa period (1600/1603–1868). The greatest concentration was in present-day Nagasaki prefecture, primarily in rural areas on islands isolated from the mainland and from each other.

The first Protestant mission to Japan began in 1859, but given Japan's continued hostility toward Christianity, open activity was virtually impossible. In 1873 the proscription against Christianity was lifted and small-scale American and European missions—Catholic, Protestant, and Russian Orthodox—entered Japan. The early years of these missions were taken up with mastering the Japanese language and making the Scriptures available in Japanese translation. The New Testament was published in 1880 and the Old Testament appeared in 1888.

Not every Japanese Christian welcomed the new missionary movement. Among these Christian believers was Uchimura Kanzo (1861–1930), who advocated a return to the simplicity of the gospel and the early church, spurning the divisive denominationalism and stubborn institutionalism of the Christianity that had come in. In response, he sought to make Christian belief more congenial to the Japanese through the *mukyokai* (no-church) movement.

Renewed missionary activity had considerable impact in the field of education. A network of Catholic schools throughout the country led to the establishment of Jochi Daigaku (Sophia University), University of the Sacred Heart, and Nanzan University. The combined Protestant denominations established Doshisha University, Aoyama Gakuin University, Rikkyo University, and, much later, International Christian University. Schools were established also for women and for the physically challenged, both largely ignored by the national government of the day.

With the outbreak of World War II, foreign missionaries were either repatriated or interned, and Japanese Christians once again found themselves forced to keep their beliefs to themselves as nationalism promoted worship of the Shinto deities as an indication of national loyalty.

People pray for victims of the 1945 atomic bombing of Nagasaki in August 2000 at the Uragami Cathedral in Nagasaki. (AFP/CORBIS)

Contemporary Christian Activity

During the Allied Occupation (1945–1952) interest in Christianity was rekindled, but as Japan recovered and society stabilized, its appeal decreased. However, in the postwar period indigenous groups have founded new organizations such as Iesu no Mitama Kyokai ("Spirit of Jesus Church"), founded in 1941 by Murai Jun, and Iesu no Hakobune ("The Ark of Jesus"), formed in 1960. Like Uchimura, these groups share the conviction that their Japanese cultural expressions of Christian faith are truer to the spirit of New Testament Christianity than the distortions of the Western churches.

Today mainstream Christian activity in Japan remains unassuming and the Christian population is estimated at less than 1 percent of the total Japanese population. Primary activities include support of medical, social, and educational organizations.

Summary

When the first Christian missionaries arrived in Japan in the late sixteenth century, there was a spiritual and social openness resulting from a long civil war and increasing dissatisfaction with the political and social conditions that war created. The subsequent rejection of Christianity can be partially attributed to that religion's exclusivist nature. Requiring singular obedience to one religion was at odds with Japanese tolerance of multiple beliefs. Second, the political ramifications of the foreign creed led to a conflict of interests. Loyalty to the deity and its foreign missionaries stood in the way of unchallenged subservience to their lord. For Japan's leaders, the risk of tolerating Christianity was just too great and the religion was suppressed. A similar pattern of acceptance during social instability and rejection as society returned to order followed both the Meiji period (1868–1912) and the years following World War II. It remains to be seen whether Christianity will become more accessible to a broader element of society or remain appealing to only a small segment.

James M. Vardaman, Jr.

Further Reading

Boxer, C. R. (1951) *The Christian Century in Japan 1549–1650.* Berkeley and Los Angeles: University of California Press.

Breen, John, and Mark Williams. (1996) *Japan and Christianity: Impacts and Responses.* New York: St. Martin's Press.

Drummond, Richard H. (1971) *A History of Christianity in Japan.* Grand Rapids, MI: William B. Eerdmans Publishing Company.

Ellison, George. (1973) *Deus Destroyed: The Image of Christianity in Early Modern Japan*. Cambridge, MA: Harvard University Press.

CHRISTIANITY—KOREA Christianity is a major religious force in Korea. Its influence began in the late eighteenth century with small communities of Korean Catholics who had learned the doctrines during encounters with Christians in China. For a century, the highly Confucian Korean royal government viewed Christianity as a dangerous heterodoxy, and there were frequent persecutions. This changed after Korea was "opened" to contact with the West in the 1880s and Korea's Protestant and Catholic Churches began to grow, first under the guidance of foreign missionaries and then under the leadership of Korean clergy. The growth continued under Japanese colonial rule and during the postwar ordeal of national division. By the 1980s in South Korea, where Christianity flourished after the Korean War, fully one-quarter of the population had come to identify itself as Christian.

Development

The success of Christianity in Korea is unique in East Asia, where in most countries the Christian population does not exceed 5 percent of the total. The reasons for this success have to do with Korea's modern history and the things Christianity has represented in the minds of Koreans. Though the traditional ruling elites of Korea disdained it in the beginning, Christianity was associated in the minds of commoners with advancement and better living. The early missionaries started schools that offered education to ordinary people. They promoted the use of the Korean hangul alphabet to boost literacy, which formerly had been reserved for the elite. Under Japanese colonial rule (1910–1945), adopting Western Christianity seemed to be an alternative to adopting the Japanese value system. Churches were among the very few organizational structures not controlled by the Japanese, so Christianity also came to be associated with nationalism.

World War II was a time of persecution for Christians, and their numbers dropped off. After the Allied victory, however, Korea was divided into northern and southern zones. Christianity had actually been stronger in the north than in the south before 1940, but after Korea's division, a Soviet-backed leftist government came to power in the north. Christians opposed the new government's ideology and thus were targeted for new kinds of political persecution. Many of North Korea's Christians moved to South Korea as refugees, starting new churches as centers for mutual support as well as worship. Those who remained in the north were grudgingly tolerated until the Korean War, after which Christianity was officially persecuted as an enemy ideology.

In South Korea, by contrast, Christianity was associated with Western-style prosperity and American power. Koreans looking to the United States for support in their beleaguered situation found Christianity attractive for a combination of reasons. There were those who became Christians as a way of looking modern, of course; but there was also an authentic religious response to the comforts of Christian faith in a country that was undergoing multiple ordeals of reconstruction, urbanization, and revolutionary economic development. Korea's urban churches functioned as networking organizations for people arriving from the countryside, as ready-made communities of supportive cobelievers, and as affirming religious centers that helped maintain human and moral values in a world being turned upside down.

The theological traditions of Korean Christianity, whether Protestant or Catholic, are conservative, emphasizing personal morality, community, and the sovereignty of God. Korea's Christians believe that prayer and piety are keys to winning divine favor and that perseverance in the faith brings blessings in daily life. At times they have seen themselves as a people chosen by God to undergo unique trials that have purified them and empowered them to claim a leading role in society. During the Japanese colonial period especially, they often likened themselves to the children of Israel in the Old Testament. The ideological war between Christianity and communism contributed to this line of thinking, creating a tacit claim that Christians are uniquely suited to be national leaders. While some non-Christians regard this as arrogant, it helps explain the visibility of Christianity as a phenomenon on the contemporary Korean landscape.

South Korea's churches long ago became free of foreign missionary control and have developed into completely "Korean" organizations, being self-financed and self-directed. As a Korean religion, Christianity manifests traditional traits. One such trait is a strong Confucian authority pattern, notably patriarchal despite the fact that a majority of the members of all churches are women. Another is the tendency of Korean pastors to assume charismatic identities that recall Korea's shamanist tradition. The cherished practice of worship in natural settings, long a part of Buddhist practice, is reflected in the penchant for long sessions of prayer and fasting in mountain retreats. The health emphases of traditional Korean religions are reflected in the popularity of healing services, and the expectation of ma-

Worshipers at the Youido Full Gospel Church in Seoul in 1990. (BOHEMIAN NOMAD PICTUREMAKERS/CORBIS)

terial benefit from religious practice is reflected in prayers for blessings. Indeed, some of Korea's fastest-growing churches emphasize the idea that God wants his people to be prosperous. Many churches (and their pastors) are conspicuously wealthy.

South Korea's biggest churches have members numbering in the tens and even hundreds of thousands, making them congregations that are actually denominations in themselves. They often spin off daughter churches and branch churches for immigrant communities overseas. Some of them engage in missionary activity, deploying members to countries in Asia and Africa as doctors, teachers, and evangelistic workers, exercising the same impulse that brought missionaries to Korea a century and more ago.

The first Protestant communities in Korea date from the mid-1880s; a small village church was founded in a house in the 1860s, but the first formal congregation, still extant, was founded in 1885. Protestants far outnumber Catholics in Korea, but the Catholic Church has also grown proportionately since the end of World War II. It was led by foreign priests before that and did not become free of missionary direction until 1962. In the 1960s and 1970s, Catholics were prominent in South Korea's democracy movement, opposing military dictatorship and identifying the Catholic Church with the struggle for political and economic justice. This stance attracted many youth, especially university students. In 1984 Korea's Catholic bicentennial brought Pope John Paul II to celebrate a special mass, attended by many thousands, in which he presided over the canonization of 103 martyrs from the anti-Catholic persecutions of the nineteenth century.

Church and State

The division of Korea has played a major role in shaping the Korean Christian Church. In South Korea, Christian refugees from the north have helped make the Protestant movement strongly anticommunist and therefore inclined to support the South Korean government even during its worst periods of military rule and human-rights abuses. When the Seoul government used the memory of the Korean War and the evil personified in Kim Il Sung and his oligarchy in the north as an excuse to clamp down on dissent and free expression, Korea's conservative Christians tended to go along.

However, the manifest injustices of political life in South Korea under military rule between 1961 and 1992—the suppression of dissent, the use of torture in police interrogations, the low-wage strategy of Korean economic development, the abuse of police power to seek political advantage, and many other obvious violations of human rights—led many Christians in all denominations to demand democratic reforms. As was once the case under colonial rule, Christian leaders found that their institutions constituted platforms from which to speak out against dictatorship. Though they were often blacklisted, arrested, and even tortured, Christians led the human-rights struggle. Prominent among them was Kim Dae Jung (b. 1925), a Catholic, who was once the archenemy of the regime but persevered in politics to be elected president in 1997.

The Future

As South Korea experiences material prosperity for the first time in its history, the church finds itself facing new challenges. Having grown under adversity and having been disciplined by colonialism, war, and political repression, it risks becoming complacent and fractious. Moreover, with national reunification remaining the top item for national discussion and the number-one problem to be solved in the future, Korea's Christians find it oddly difficult to agree on a role in the process. Many rallied to help alleviate the 1990s famine in North Korea, stressing their brotherhood with fellow Koreans in the north. Others, however, have tried to position themselves for an anticipated victory over North Korea. The "Christian reoccupation" of North Korea is unlikely to succeed if it is undertaken as a crusade. For Korea's Christians, reunification may well turn out to be the greatest test of all.

Donald N. Clark

Further Reading

Clark, Donald N. (1986) *Christianity in Modern Korea*. Lanham, MD: University Press of America.

Grayson, James H. (1989) *Korea: A Religious History*. Oxford: Oxford University Press.

Kang, Wi Jo. (1997) *Christ and Caesar in Modern Korea: A History of Christianity and Politics*. Albany, NY: State University of New York Press.

Wells, Kenneth M. (1990) *New God, New Nation: Protestants and Self-Reconstruction in Korea, 1896–1937*. Honolulu, HI: University of Hawaii Press.

CHRISTIANITY—MYANMAR Christians are estimated to constitute only 5 percent of the population of Myanmar (Burma), but the religion is dominant in a number of communities, especially among the ethnic minority Chin, Kachin, Karen, and Karenni peoples. The first Western Christian missionaries were Roman Catholics who arrived with the Portuguese in the sixteenth century. Subsequently, missions were established by Italian and French Catholics. However, it was only during British rule of Burma in the nineteenth century that the spread of Christianity began to accelerate.

The first large-scale conversions were among the Karens in the Tenasserim and Irrawaddy River delta regions of southern Burma. Here, the pioneering Baptist missionary Adoniram Judson arrived in 1813. A key element in the spread of Christianity was the promotion of education among animist or spirit-worshipping communities. Many previously nonliterate languages, such as Karen and Kachin, were transcribed into writing.

The establishment of indigenous churches quickly followed, and in 1881 the Karen National Association was formed by Christian Karens to promote the advancement of the Karen people. Many Christians from ethnic minority communities also joined the government service and armed forces. Although perhaps only one-sixth of modern-day Karens are Christians, such cooperation with the British authorities led Burma's leaders to allege that Christianity was a key element in what they described as the colonial armory of the "Three M's": missionaries, merchants, and military. In response, in 1906 the Young Men's Buddhist Association was formed parallel to the Young Men's Christian Association, signaling the revival of the Burmese nationalist movement.

Further allegations of the divisive role of Christianity were made after the British departure in 1948 when Karen and Karenni leaders, the majority of whom were Christians, took up arms against the central government. In 1961, insurrection also began in Kachin State when Prime Minister U Nu (1907–1995) attempted to make Buddhism the nation's official state religion.

Under General Ne Win's Burma Socialist Program Party (1962–1988), a more secular policy was pursued by the government. All foreign missionaries were expelled from the country during a quarter-century of isolationism. Nevertheless, a diversity of Christian churches survived.

At the end of the twentieth century, the two strongest Christian religious groups were the Baptists (the largest denomination) and Roman Catholics, both of which have more than one-half million members. Other significant groups include Anglicans and Seventh-Day Adventists. Most of these Christian groups continue to work together through two umbrella organizations: the Myanmar Council of Churches, which links Protestant groups, and the Catholic Bishops Conference.

Under the State Law and Order Restoration Council, which assumed control of the country in 1988, church groups became more visibly active again in religion and community development. Although incidents of discrimination against Christians were reported (especially in Chin State), in other areas church leaders acted as intermediaries in peace talks between armed opposition groups and the government, notably in Kachin, Kayah, and Karen States.

Martin Smith

See also: **Kachin Independence Organization; Karen; Karen National Union**

Further Reading

Bigandet, Paul Ambrose. (1887) *An Outline of the History of the Catholic Burmese Mission.* Yangon, Myanmar: Hanthawaddy.

Brumberg, Joan. (1980) *Mission for Life: The Story of the Family of Adoniram Judson.* New York: Free Press.

Maung Shwe Wa. (1963) *Burma Baptist Chronicle.* Yangon, Myanmar: University Press.

Morse, Eugene. (1975) *Exodus to a Hidden Valley.* London: Collins.

Seagrave, Gordon. (1957) *My Hospital in the Hills.* London: Hale.

Smith, Martin. (1999) "Ethnic Conflict and the Challenge of Civil Society in Burma." In *Strengthening Civil Society in Burma: Possibilities and Dilemmas for International NGOs.* Chiang Mai, Thailand: Silkworm Books, 15–53.

Tegenfeldt, Herman. (1974) *A Century of Growth: The Kachin Baptist Church of Burma.* South Pasadena,CA: William Carey Library.

CHRISTIANITY—SOUTH ASIA

Christianity has been an important force in South Asian history. During the period of British rule in India (c. 1757–1947) British Christians were influential in securing social reforms such as the suppression of *sati* (suttee). Protestant and Catholic missionaries established widespread and influential mission school systems, which influenced the attitudes and outlooks those educated there. While some locals welcomed Christian missionary activity, others were hostile and feared conversion. This fear, together with a desire to adopt some teachings of Christianity, encouraged the emergence of Hindu and Buddhist reform and revival movements.

Origin and Character of Precolonial Christian Communities

Christians have been living in the Indian subcontinent since ancient times. A persistent tradition, reflected in the apocryphal Acts of Thomas (probably written in the Syriac language in the fourth century CE) that Saint Thomas preached and died in India, is echoed in Hindu and Christian belief that he founded the community of Saint Thomas Christians on the Kerala coast and was martyred at Mailapur, south of Madras City. The first evidence of Christian communities in Kerala dates from the sixth century. This evidence and subsequent material relating to the period until the arrival of the Portuguese in 1498 show that Saint Thomas Christians maintained close ecclesiastical, commercial, and family links with Syria and the Middle East.

The community's numbers were constantly augmented by settlers from Western Asia. The Christians pledged allegiance to the Syrian Patriarch of the East (whose seat was in present-day Iraq), who was the recognized leader of churches independent of the Church of the Roman Empire. The liturgy was in Syriac and the doctrine influenced by the Nestorians, who taught that Christ had two distinct natures, divine and human. While reflecting Middle Eastern influences, Saint Thomas Christians were also affected by their Hindu environment. Conscious of their high status as warriors and merchants in the caste system, they avoided contact with the lower castes. They enjoyed honored positions as donors or benefactors of Hindu shrines all over Kerala. The management of church affairs, the hereditary nature of the all-male priesthood, the use of torches, umbrellas, and banners in procession, and the performance of some minor Hindu-type rituals, all reflected the Hindu context in which the community developed.

Continuing Spread of Christianity, 1498–2000

In 1503 a West Asian prelate reported some 30,000 Saint Thomas Christian families in Kerala; the census of 1901 estimated the number of individuals in that community at nearly half a million. During the period of Portuguese and British rule the number of Protestant and Catholic Christians (those whose origin is associated with European missions) also steadily grew. In 1991 there were nearly 20 million Christians in India, mostly in the south and northeast, representing 2.34 percent of the total population. Christians represent about 8 percent of the population in Sri Lanka, 2 percent or less in Pakistan, and less than 1 percent in Bangladesh. In 1990 there were an estimated 50,000 Christians in Nepal.

Religious Inquiry and Conversion Movements

Historians place varying emphasis on the political, economic, religious, social, or other factors involved in the rapid expansion of Christianity during colonial rule. Less in dispute is evidence that those who wished to join Christian churches usually acted together rather than as individuals—representatives of caste, family, or other groups approached Christian leaders asking for information or requesting baptism. Some churches welcomed all who came irrespective of motive, hoping

Indian Roman Catholics leave the Sacred Heart Cathedral in New Delhi, India's largest, in September 1998. (AFP/CORBIS)

"inquirers" would grow in faith and practice in the church. Others were more selective, insisting on the application of strict criteria, which varied in different missions and which involved either rejection of the candidate or evidence of changes in belief or behavior before individuals or groups were admitted to full membership.

Issues Still Confronting Christian Communities

Since the development of Christian communities in Kerala and elsewhere, Christians have faced many of the same questions. What ought to be the relationship between Christians and the state or between indigenous Christians and the wider ecclesiastical and Christian movement? What does it mean to express one's faith in and through a South Asian culture as distinct from a Syrian or European culture? How does one preach the Gospel, teach, and heal effectively in the local multireligious environment?

Christians and Politics

One of the most sensitive issues in Christianity is the varying relationship between Christians and political authorities. While Saint Thomas Christians were integrated in the indigenous state system before the arrival of the Portuguese, most Christians in South Asia trace their origins to conversion movements occurring in the context of European missionary activity and colonial rule. European missionary paternalism, which often included a policy of keeping Indian Christians in subordinate positions within the church, created resentment especially among Western-educated Christians. That feeling heightened their awareness of the "evils" of foreign rule and encouraged Christian participation in the early stages of the Indian nationalist movement. However the rise of strident forms of Hindu nationalism soon raised fears among Christians of their eventual fate in a state dominated by the Hindu majority. After a period of considerable anxiety, Protestant and Catholic leaders threw their weight increasingly behind the Gandhian movement and the idea of an independent India as a secular state. Confidence in the new government of India was enhanced by acceptance of a Catholic proposal that minorities' rights be guaranteed in a new constitution.

The Present Pattern of Contrast

While churches operating in postcolonial South Asia continue to face political problems, there are opportunities for growth and participation in nation building. The sense of belonging to a persecuted minority in Pakistan, Bangladesh, and parts of India (where militant anti-Christian forms of Hindu nationalism have been increasing) contrasts with a sense of confidence and optimism associated with the continued rapid expansion of Christianity in northeastern India and Nepal.

The priorities, lifestyles, and forms of worship among Christians also vary. A preoccupation with internal issues such as power, property, and social standing (especially in the Church of South India) contrasts with other church programs of change and reform and increasing involvement in outward-looking welfare projects in rural areas and slums. Traditional forms of Christian worship are maintained alongside experiments in further indigenization and increasingly popular charismatic-type meetings throughout the region. The establishment of interdenominational national Christian councils in most South Asian countries, the formation of the Church of South India (1947), Church of North India, and Church of Pakistan (1970), which bring together Protestant denominations, and increasing Protestant and Catholic collaboration in educational and other programs, reflect both the practical needs of small but growing Christian communities and the new spirit of the global ecumenical movement.

Geoffrey A. Oddie

See also: **Jesuits in India; Syrian Christians of Kerala**

Further Reading

Grafe, Hugald. (1990) *History of Christianity in India: Tamilnadu in the Nineteenth and Twentieth Centuries* 4, 2. Bangalore, India: C.H.A.I.

Mundadan, A. Mathias. (1984) *History of Christianity in India: From the Beginning up to the Middle of the Sixteenth Century* 1. Bangalore, India: C.H.A.I.

Oddie, G. A. (1979) *Social Protest in India: British Protestant Missionaries and Social Reforms*, Delhi: Manohar.

———. (1991) *Religion in South Asia: Religious Conversion and Revival Movements in South Asia in Medieval and Modern Times*. 2d rev. and enlarged ed. Delhi: Manohar.

CHRISTIANITY—SOUTHEAST ASIA With the exception of the Philippines, Christianity in Southeast Asia is statistically a minority religion. Nevertheless, because of its missionary convictions, organizational strength, and transnational connections, institutional Christianity generally has a high profile and exerts an influence far beyond its numbers. But like other religions in the region, it also has to "reinvent" itself in order to compete with powerful secularizing forces, and to maintain its appeal both for its own adherents and for the unevangelized. The Christian intelligentsia in Southeast Asia, as elsewhere in the Third World church, play active roles in theologically delineating the shape and direction of their faith. Christianity in Southeast Asia is not monolithic; it ranges from the hierarchical Roman Catholic, Orthodox, and Anglican churches, through established Protestant denominations—Lutheran, Reformed, Brethren, Methodist, Baptist, Presbyterian, and the Pentecostalist Assembly of God among others—to schismatic churches and fundamentalist, charismatic, and indigenized Christian sects.

History

Christianity in Southeast Asia has a long legacy that predates the arrival of Roman Catholicism in the fifteenth century and Protestant Christianity in the centuries following. Extant archaeological and literary evidence, although sparse, indicates that trading contacts between Persia and countries farther West were already known by the fifth and sixth centuries. Persia itself had been exposed to Nestorian Christianity since the early centuries of the first millennium, when many Aramaic- and Syriac-speaking Jewish and Christian communities fled eastward after the destruction of Jerusalem in 70 CE. Through trading contacts with the region, Nestorian settlements were probably set up in the northwestern part of peninsular Malaysia and in northern Sumatra. As elsewhere, however, their traces have long disappeared because of displacement and persecution.

By the time Roman Catholicism arrived with Portuguese, Spanish, and French adventurers during the European age of exploration, commerce, and conquest in the sixteenth century, the region had long been under the sway of other world religions. At the beginning of the Christian era, Indian kingdoms and their civilizing influences were being established in various parts of Southeast Asia. By the fourteenth century, Theravada Buddhism had assumed dominance in mainland Southeast Asia (except Vietnam), and much of maritime Southeast Asia was Islamicized. Moreover, these religions had been culturally assimilated and translated into local idioms. Conversion to Roman Catholicism, particularly in the Philippines and Vietnam, followed similar processes despite periodic prohibitions and persecutions because of religious rivalry and political intrigue. Protestant Christianity, in comparison, spurred on by evangelical piety, arrived during the high colonial period of the nineteenth century. Adult literacy, modern education, the translation of the Christian Scriptures into the vernacular, and medical services were among the key strategies used to entice "pagans" into the Christian fold. Nevertheless, on the whole the numbers converting to Protestant Christianity are not phenomenal.

In most cases, though colonial governments generally did not openly favor Christianity, indirectly they created conditions that enhanced a degree of openness to the new faith. Christianity and Christian institutions were perceived as the legitimate religion and expressions of colonial power and also as means to escape the constraints of traditional social and economic burdens. In some instances, missionaries adopted a policy of nonintervention with the members of the dominant religion (for example, with Muslim Malays in British Malaya) to stave off political unrest for the sake of lucrative commercial interests. In comparison, post–World War II Southeast Asia and the postindependence milieu have seen the democratic principle of religious liberty enshrined in the constitutions of most countries. By and large, however, the influence of institutional Christianity has been undermined and circumscribed by nationalist forces and the exigencies of

CHRISTIANITY MEETS BUDDHISM

The following conversation between a Buddhist nobleman in Thailand and a Christian missionary in about 1850 makes clear the basic beliefs of each faith and suggests some of the difficulties faced by unsuccessful Christian missionaries in Thailand.

Nobleman. After all, my religion is a better religion than yours.

Missionary. Convince me of that and Your Excellency shall be *my* teacher.

N. This is my religion: To be so little tied to the world that I can leave it without regret; to keep my heart sound; to live doing no injustice to any, but deeds of compassion to all.

M. This is excellent: this accords with my teaching; but will Your Excellency tell me what those must do who have already committed sin?

N. Why should they commit sin?

M. Who has not sinned: We should own we have sinned; we Christians have One who has removed our sins from us, and taken them upon himself; but you—

N. Where have I sinned? I do not acknowledge sin.

M. But it is not enough that men should be honest and kind to one another. They owe allegiance to God, their great Sovereign. To disobey Him, to forget Him, to avoid His presence, to be indifferent to His favor—this is sin.

N. And so you think God is censorious and jealous of His creatures, and wants their services and their praises? No! Let us treat all men justly. God is absorbed, gone into annihilation. We need not be troubled or think about Him.

M. No! He lives above! He is *our* Master. It is not enough that servants should be honest towards their fellows, kind to their wives and children; they owe to *their* Master service and gratitude, and will be punished if they do not render them.

N. Who is to punish? You call sin what is no sin.

M. But does not Your Excellency flog your servants when they disobey? Do you pardon them solely because they have not wronged their fellow servants?

N. *(Much excited).* What service does God want of us? He is not envious and covetous, as you fancy Him to be.

M. Suppose I told Your Excellency's servants that nothing was required of them but to live honestly and pleasantly together; to care nothing about you—neither to seek to please, nor obey, nor serve you, nor be thankful for Your Excellency's kindness: will you allow this? . . .

N. Now I will tell you of your heavy sins.

M. Show it to me and I will confess.

N. Why don't you take a wife?— Why don't you provide successors to teach your religion when you are gone? Christ had thirty disciples, had he not? and his disciples had wives and children; and they multiplied, and have overrun the world; but your religion and your name would perish together if others followed your example.

M. Others will take care of this.

N. No! Each man has a duty for himself.

M. Your Excellency is right. I am beaten here; but your Buddhist priests enjoin celibacy.

N. Battle it then with the Buddhist priests and not with me. . . . Now how long have you American missionaries been here?

M. Nineteen years.

N. Have you made a single convert?

M. Not among the Siamese; and we acknowledge our disappointment but are not discouraged. If a merchant sent out his agents and they failed, he would recall them; but those who sent us would think their sacrifices well repaid if a single soul were saved; for a soul is not extinguished by death, but lives forever; and we know that Siam will become a Christian country.

CONTINUED ON NEXT PAGE

CONTINUED FROM PREVIOUS PAGE

N. But the Siamese are not savages of the woods, having no religion and therefore ready to receive one. We have our religion, in which we have been brought up from our childhood; it will not easily be rooted out. Has it been in any single instance? The work would be difficult.

Source: John Bowring. (1857) *The Kingdom and People of Siam*. London: John W. Parker and Son, vol. I: 378–380.

nation-building, given Christianity's negative association with colonialism. Since the 1980s, aided by modern technology, enterprising Christian fundamentalist groups, particularly from the United States and South Korea, have been successful in appealing to the peripheral and urban populace, as well as in drawing adherents from more well-established Christian denominations.

Brief Survey

Partly because of the longevity of Christianity in the country, the Philippines is the only country in the region where Christians constitute the majority, including some 94 percent of the population in 1999. Roman Catholicism is overwhelmingly dominant and deeply embedded in Filipino everyday life, as well as in religious and political culture.

Vietnam has the largest Catholic population (about 6 million in 1988) after the Philippines, and a long tradition of native clergy and catechists. Traces of Catholic missionary activity as far back as the fourteenth century exist. Having undergone periodic Confucianist persecution in the mid-nineteenth century and having borne restrictive controls imposed by the Communists in the twentieth century, Vietnam is now experiencing a period of religious liberalization and consolidation.

In expansive Indonesia, the Portuguese Roman Catholic mission to the Moluccas in the 1530s was one of the earliest in the region. The arrival of the celebrated Jesuit priest, Francis Xavier (1506–1552), was the highlight of that mission. He laid the foundation for subsequent missionary work by other Catholic orders. Nevertheless, in present-day Indonesia Protestant Christians, belonging to a diverse array of denominations and conciliar groups, exceed Roman Catholics in numbers.

Thailand is the only country in the region that escaped European colonial subjugation, and, despite the efforts of French and Spanish Catholic missionaries since the seventeenth century and Protestant missionaries beginning two centuries later, there are relatively few Christians in the country (totaling less than 1 percent of the population). Myanmar (Burma), like Thailand, is steeped in Theravada Buddhism. Protestant missionary bodies have had more success than their Catholic counterparts in Myanmar. Work among the animist Karen and Kachin hill peoples by the American Baptists, in particular, has yielded one of the well-known missionary success stories of the region.

As elsewhere, Roman Catholicism arrived first in Malaysia with the Portuguese, who captured the important entrepôt of Melaka in 1511. Later, from the nineteenth century onwards, both Protestant and Roman Catholic missions concentrated on the urban non-Malay populations of the British-created Straits Settlements, comprising Melaka (or Malacca), Penang, and Singapore. In East Malaysia (comprising the states of Sabah and Sarawak), conversions among the numerous animist indigenous groups have been notable. Meanwhile, the number of Christian converts in Singapore has increased dramatically in the last decades of the twentieth century. According to a government report, the proportion of Christian adherents jumped from 10 percent in 1980 to 13 percent in 1990 to 15 percent in 1990. Most are young, educated adults with Taoist or Confucianist backgrounds. In March 1992,

A Khmer woman teaches a Thai women the Khmer language for missionary work in Cambodia in 1994. (BOHEMIAN NOMAD PICTUREMAKERS/CORBIS)

Christian demonstrators occupying the grounds of police headquarters in Ambon, Indonesia, in February 2001. They are protesting the killing of Christians by Muslims on the island. (AFP/CORBIS)

the "Maintenance of Religious Harmony" bill was passed by the Singapore government, which, inter alia, allows the authorities to restrain any priest, pastor, imam, or other individual in a position of authority who is believed to have committed or attempted to commit "feelings of enmity, ill-will or hostility between religious groups" or to "promote a political cause under the guise of religious belief.".

Transnational Christianity

Southeast Asian Christianity is anything but monolithic, and long-established doctrinal and ideological positions are further polarized by newer evangelical, ecumenical, charismatic, and fundamentalist nuances. These, in turn, are further shaped by the host cultures and political contexts, giving rise to varieties of indigenous theologies and localized practices.

Transnational Christian institutions in Southeast Asia do not adhere strictly to the boundaries of nation-states or regional blocs; they are linked to wider-based entities in the Asia and Pacific region. Institutionally, Roman Catholics have been organized through their respective parochial bishops. In 1970, a landmark decision was made to form the Federation of Asian Bishops Conference (FABC) as a network of Asian Catholic bishops. Programs and position papers emanating from the FABC bear the hallmarks of the reforming spirit of Vatican II, held in Rome during the early 1960s. Generally, the focus has been to evolve a church imbued with what are seen as the Asian values of harmony, holism, and inclusiveness.

The Christian Conference of Asia (formerly East Asia Christian Conference) is the major regional ecumenical body for Protestant Christians. Although its origins can be traced back to the International Missionary Council meeting held in Tambaram, India, in 1938, it was only officially formed in 1957 at Prapat, Indonesia. Currently, it brings together 119 different churches from 16 Asian countries, and the total membership of these churches exceeds 50 million. Ideologically, the CCA leadership has opted to play an avant-garde role, rethinking traditional Christian doctrines, biblical exegeses, missiology, and ecclesiology in the light of nation-building and contemporary political and economic realities. Particular stress is given to evolving a contextualized theology that addresses the complex realities of unfettered capitalist development, poverty, democracy, and the religious and cultural plurality of the region. Like the FABC, the CCA also gives attention to evolving an Asian ecclesial identity that accords with the ethos of the region.

In the 1980s and 1990s, a number of ecumenical organizations addressing specific regional problems and concerns have also sprung up. They address such issues as human rights, child prostitution, migrant labor, tourism, people's movements, interfaith dialogue and cooperation, and feminism. By comparison, regional evangelical and fundamentalist Christian institutions have shied away from these kinds of Christian activism, contending that while social concerns should be high on the church's agenda, they are not central to the identity and mission of the church.

Future Directions

As Christianity in Southeast Asia develops in the twenty-first century, we can expect to see interchurch understanding and cooperation broaden, deepen, and mature. Additionally, with Southeast Asia's strategic position in the world taking on renewed importance, Christianity in the region is presented with intriguing possibilities as it becomes more localized in a region in which most of the world's major religions thrive.

Yeoh Seng-Guan

Further Reading

Andaya, Barbara, and Yoneo Ishii. (1992) "Religious Development in Southeast Asia, c. 1500–1800." In *The Cambridge History of Southeast Asia, Vol. 1*, edited by Nicholas Tarling. Cambridge, U.K.: Cambridge University Press.

Anderson, Gerald H. (1968) *Christ and Crisis in Southeast Asia*. New York: Friendship Press.

Barrett, David B., ed. (2001) *World Christian Encyclopedia*. 2d ed. Oxford, U.K.: Oxford University Press.

David, M. D., ed. (1988) *Western Colonialism in Asia and Christianity*. Bombay, India: Himalaya Publishing House.

———. (1985) *Asia and Christianity*. Bombay, India: Himalaya Publishing House.

Digan, Parig. (1984) *Churches in Contestation.* Maryknoll, NY: Orbis.

England, John C. (1996) *The Hidden History of Christianity in Asia: The Churches of the East before the Year 1500.* New Delhi, India: ISPCK; Hong Kong: Christian Conference of Asia.

Evers, Hans-Dieter, ed. (1993) *Religious Revivalism in Southeast Asia.* Singapore: Institute of Southeast Asian Studies.

Ileto, Reynaldo. (1992) "Religion and Anti-colonial Movements." In *The Cambridge History of Southeast Asia,* vol. 2, edited by Nicholas Tarling. Cambridge, U.K.: Cambridge University Press.

IMC Publications. (1984, 1987) *For All the Peoples of Asia: The Church in Asia: Asian Bishops' Statements on Mission, Community, and Ministry.* Vol. 1 (1984) and vol. 2 (1987). Manila, the Philippines: IMC Publications.

Keyes, Charles. (1996) "Being Protestant Christians in the Southeast Asian World." *Journal of Southeast Asian Studies.* 27, 2: 280–292.

Latourette, Kenneth. (1971) *A History of the Expansion of Christianity,* vol. 3. Exeter, U.K.: Paternoster Press.

Moffett, Samuel H. (1992) *History of Christianity in Asia,* vol. 1: *Beginnings to 1500.* San Francisco: HarperCollins.

Neil, Stephen. (1966) *Colonialism and Christian Missions.* London: Lutterworth.

Scott, W., ed. (2001) *A Dictionary of Asian Christianity.* Grand Rapids, MI: Eerdmans.

Stange, Paul. (1992) "Religious Change in Southeast Asia." In *The Cambridge History of Southeast Asia,* vol. 2, edited by Nicholas Tarling. Cambridge, U.K.: Cambridge University Press.

Sugirtharajah, R. S., ed. (1993) *Asian Faces of Jesus.* London: SPCK.

Von der Mehden, Fred. (1986) *Religion and Modernization in Southeast Asia.* Syracuse, NY: Syracuse University Press.

Yap, Kim Hao. (1995) *From Prapat to Colombo: History of the Christian Conference of Asia (1957–1995).* Hong Kong: Christian Conference of Asia.

Yates, Timothy. (1994) *Christian Mission in the Twentieth Century.* Cambridge, U.K.: Cambridge University Press.

CHRYSANTHEMUM

The chrysanthemum (Japanese: *kiku*) is a revered flower in Japan, favored for its beauty and fragrance; its cultivation is considered an art form. Reflecting its significance, the Japanese word for chrysanthemum appears in several Japanese names, including *kiku* (chrysanthemum), *kikuko* (chrysanthemum child), and *kikumi* (beautiful chrysanthemum) for women, *kikuo* (chrysanthemum male), *kikuji* (chrysanthemum, second son), and *kikuta* (bold chrysanthemum) for men. The word *kiku* has also been used in place names, such as Kikuchi (chrysanthemum ground) in Kumamoto Prefecture, as well as for businesses. Until 1940, the prominent Kikuya Department Store (chrysanthemum store) operated in the Ikebukuro district of Tokyo, until it was purchased by Seibu Department Store. The Chrysanthemum Festival, held September ninth (the ninth day of the ninth month), is one of five Japanese linked festivals *(gosekku)*, including New Year's Day, involving odd prime numbers in which the number of the month and date coincide. One custom during this festival is drinking *kikuzake*, or sake flavored with bits of chrysanthemum flowers.

Chrysanthemums were used in homemade toiletries since at least the Heian period (794–1185). Cotton was placed over chrysanthemums at night; by morning, it was damp with a dew-like substance extracted from the flowers. These pieces of cotton, rich with the fragrance of chrysanthemums, were then used to wipe one's body, particularly on hot and humid late summer days. Symbolizing purity, chrysanthemums were historically used for funeral and temple displays to ward off negative spirits, while their fragrance helped mask other smells. Chrysanthemums symbolize long life, but are also associated with death because of their funeral usage. The famed *fugu* (globefish), parts of whose internal organs are poisonous, is often presented as *sashimi* slices of raw fish shaped like a chrysanthemum, evoking the deathly possibilities of mistaken preparation.

The chrysanthemum has been the Imperial family's emblem since the Kamakura period (1185–1333). During part of the Meiji period (1868–1912), laws banned its use by anyone outside the Imperial family. Now the chrysanthemum motif is used as a state symbol and appears on Japanese passports.

Japan's Imperial chrysanthemum crest at the Koishikawa Botanical Garden in Tokyo in the 1980s. (MICHAEL S. YAMASHITA/CORBIS)

The chrysanthemum is notably featured in foreign literary depictions and cultural analyses of Japan. Pierre Loti's nineteenth-century novel *Madame Chrysanthemum*, the basis of Puccini's opera *Madame Butterfly*, fascinated the European imagination. Ruth Benedict's classic mid–twentieth century anthropological analysis of Japanese culture *(The Chrysanthemum and the Sword)* highlighted the chrysanthemum as a symbol of Japan. This text was the inspiration for titles of later works on Japanese culture and society. One of these, Mamoru Iga's *The Thorn in the Chrysanthemum*, analyzes the issue of suicide in Japan. Another example is Robert Whiting's *The Chrysanthemum and the Bat*, a tribute to the importance of baseball in contemporary Japanese popular culture.

Millie Creighton

Further Reading

Benedict, Ruth. (1946) *The Chrysanthemum and the Sword: Patterns of Japanese Culture.* Boston: Houghton Mifflin Company.

Creighton, Millie. (1990) "Revisiting Shame and Guilt Cultures: A Forty Year Pilgrimage." *Ethos* 18,3: 279–307.

Iga, Mamoru. (1986) *The Thorn in the Chrysanthemum: Suicide and Economic Success in Modern Japan.* Berkeley and Los Angeles: University of California Press.

Martin, Peter. (1997) *The Chrysanthemum Throne: A History of the Emperor of Japan.* Honolulu, HI: University of Hawaii Press.

Reingold, Edwin. (1992) *Chrysanthemums and Thorns: The Untold Story of Modern Japan.* New York: St. Martin's Press.

Whiting, Robert. (1977) *The Chrysanthemum and the Bat: Baseball Samurai Style.* New York: Dodd, Mead.

CHU HIS. See **Zhu Xi.**

CHU NOM *Chu Nom* or *Nom* is Vietnam's only indigenous writing system. The etymology of the term *Chu Nom* is obscure. *Chu* unambiguously means "character," but *Nom* has been interpreted as "southern," "demotic," or "popular/native speech." Native *Chu Nom* should not be confused with imported *Chu Han* (Chinese characters), though the two scripts look similar to the untrained eye. The latter script was also known as *Chu Nho* (Confucian characters) due to its use in Confucian texts.

Although the precise origins of *Chu Nom* are unknown, it was clearly an offshoot of *Chu Nho*. *Chu Nho* and the Chinese language were imposed upon Vietnam during a millennium of Chinese rule (111 BCE–939 CE). After liberation from China, however, the Vietnamese had no script of their own. The only script they knew was *Chu Nho*, which was specifically designed to write the syllables of Chinese. Hence the Vietnamese modified *Chu Nho* in a number of ways in order to adapt it to their own language. This process probably occurred over several centuries and cannot be attributed to any single person or group.

The resulting *Nom* script that emerged around the twelfth century consisted of three major types of characters: phonetic loans, semanto-phonetic compounds, and semantic compounds. Phonetic loans were *Chu Nho* graphs used as phonetic symbols, that is, the *Chu Nho* graph *da* "many" was used as a phonetic loan for the unrelated but homophonous native words *da* "banyan" and *da* "rice pancake."

Semanto-phonetic compounds each consist of a *Chu Nho* graph or graph element (radical) that hints at the meaning of the word and a *Chu Nho* graph representing the sound of the word. For example, the *Chu Nho* radical *trung* "insect" and the *Chu Nho* graph *de* "emperor" were combined into a semanto-phonetic compound representing the native word *de* "cricket."

Semantic compounds each consist of combinations of two *Chu Nho* graphs that hint at the meaning of the word. For example, the *Chu Nho* graphs *thien* "heaven" and *thuong* "above" were combined to form a semantic compound representing the native word *gioi* "sky." This final class of *Nom* graphs is the rarest.

In spite of the heavily phonetic nature of *Nom*, its thousands of graphs were never standardized and hence were difficult to learn. Nevertheless, *Nom* was in use among educated Vietnamese until the early twentieth century, when it was eclipsed by the *Quoc Ngu* (national language) alphabet devised in the seventeenth century by Catholic missionaries. *Nom* is virtually extinct today.

Marc Hideo Miyake

Further Reading

Nguyen Dinh-Hoa. (1992) "Graphemic Borrowings from Chinese: The Case of Chu Nom—Vietnam's Demotic Script." *Bulletin of the Institute of History and Philology, Academia Sinica* 61, 2: 383–432.

Schneider, Paul. (1992) *Dictionnaire historique des idéogrammes vietnamiens.* Nice, France: Unité de Recherches Interdisciplinaires sur l'Asie du Sud-Est, Madagascar et les Iles de l'Océan Indien (Université de Nice-Sophia Antipolis).

CHU TEH. See **Zhu De.**

CHUAH THEAN TENG (b. 1914), Malaysian painter. Chuah Thean Teng, a Malaysian painter of Chinese descent, achieved an international reputation during the 1950s by developing a new art form that adapted the wax-resist techniques of batik textile production to create a painting medium. Chuah captured traditional Malayan ways of life on canvas in colorful scenes rendered in a semiabstract style.

During the decade following Malaya's establishment as an independent nation in 1957, Chuah was credited with giving artistic expression to a distinctively Malayan visual consciousness. Together with two sons, Chuah Seow Keng and Chuah Siew Tang, who have followed their father as painters in batik, Chuah established the Yahong Gallery in Penang. As well as serving as an exhibition space for the family's work, the gallery has become a well-known emporium for antiques and locally crafted jewelry and curios.

Emily Hill

Further Reading

Sabapathy, T. K., ed. (1994) *Vision and Idea: Relooking Modern Malaysian Art*. Kuala Lumpur, Malaysia: National Art Gallery.

Sullivan, Frank. (1963) "Teng, Master of Batik." *Yahong Gallery Catalogue*. Penang, Malaysia: Phoenix Press.

CHUAN LEEKPAI (b. 1936), **Thai prime minister.** Chuan Leekpai served as Thailand's prime minister twice: in 1992–1995, Thailand's fiftieth government, and again in 1997–2001, Thailand's fifty-third government. He was Thailand's twenty-second prime minister. He served longer as prime minister than any other civilian in the history of Thai politics. He is one of the few Thai prime ministers who had neither top-level military experience nor royal blood. He is of humble background from Trang in Thailand's South.

After a brief legal career, Chuan entered politics in 1969 under the banner of the Democratic Party, Thailand's oldest. At age thirty-three, he became one of the youngest Members of Parliament. In the subsequent twelve national elections, Chuan was elected to Parliament each time. Before serving as prime minister in 1992, he had served in nine different cabinet positions under various governments, handling such portfolios as justice, commerce, public health, education, and agriculture.

In terms of political style, Chuan has a humble, polite demeanor, with impressive interpersonal and public speaking abilities. He is perhaps the smoothest Thai politician since Pibulsongkram and is gifted at crafting complex political compromises. He also has a reputation for being a politician with high personal integrity. He and his party lost the 6 January 2001 national election to the new Thai Rak Thai Party, primarily because of Thailand's persistent economic problems related to the Asian economic crisis. Basically, Chuan was perceived as being honest but weak in dealing with persisting economic problems and issues.

Gerald W. Fry

Further Reading

Leifer, Michael. (2001) "Chuan Leekpai." In *Dictionary of the Modern Politics of Southeast Asia*, edited by Michael Leifer. 3rd ed. London and New York: Routledge, 88–89.

Win, Mark Kyi, and Harold E. Smith. (1995) "Chuan Leekpai." In *Historical Dictionary of Thailand*, edited by Mark Kyi Win and Harold E. Smith. Lanham, MD: Scarecrow Press.

CHUBU (1990 pop. 21 million). Chubu region of Japan is formed of nine prefectures: Niigata, Toyama, Ishikawa, Fukui, Gifu, Nagano, Yamanashi, Shizuoka, and Aichi. It is geographically divided into three areas: the Hokuriku region on the Sea of Japan side, the Central Highlands, and the Tokai region on the Pacific Coast—totaling 67,000 square kilometers. The region is mountainous, dominated by the Japanese Alps, and contains volcanoes such as Mount Fuji (3,800 meters). Some of Japan's longest rivers, the Shinanogawa (367 kilometers), the Kisogawa (227 kilometers), and the Tenryugawa (213 kilometers), flow through the region. The northern part of the region is characterized by heavy snowfalls, two to four meters in the mountain areas. The snow is a major natural resource. The water stored in the form of snow is important for generating electricity, irrigation, and industrial use. The Niigata Plain along the Sea of Japan is one of the major rice growing areas in Japan. Agricultural products include tea and mandarin oranges. Fishing is important all along the coast. The Nobi Plain, densely populated in and around Nagoya on the Pacific Coast, is a highly industrialized area. Chubu region includes three significant industrial areas: Chukyo, Tokai, and Hokuriku. The major industries are textile, ceramics, precision machinery, and automotive.

Nathalie Cavasin

Further Reading

Hiraoka, Akira, and Yuhen Noma, eds. (2000) *Chubu I chizu de yomu hyaku nen: Aichi, Gifu, Shizuoka, Yamagata* (Chubu

I, a Hundred Years in Maps: Aichi, Gifu, Shizuoka, Yamagata). Tokyo: Kokon Shoin.
———. (2000) *Chubu II chizu de yomu hyaku nen: Nagano, Niigata, Toyama, Ishikawa, Fukui* (Chubu II, a Hundred Years in Maps: Nagano, Niigata, Toyama, Ishikawa, Fukui). Tokyo: Kokon Shoin.
Yagasali Noritaka, ed. (1997) *Japan: Geographical Perspectives on an Island Nation.* Tokyo: Teikoku-Shoin.

CHUCHE. See **Juche.**

CHUCI

CHUCI (Verse of the Chu State) is regarded as the ancestor of anthologies in Chinese literature. The earliest known edition of the anthology, in sixteen *juan* ("fascicles" or "volumes"), was recompiled by Liu Xiang (c. 77–6 BCE) from earlier sources; this edition was subsequently augmented to 17 *juan* with commentary by Wang Yi (c. 89–ca. 158). The *Chuci buzhu* (Subcommentary on Chuci) of Hong Xingzu (1019–1155), which incorporates Wang's commentary, is the most important edition.

Most of the *Chuci* poems were written during the Warring States period (475–221 BCE) in the style of folk songs of the southern state of Chu (in modern Hubei and Hunan Provinces). Performed in the Chu dialect and recording Chu culture and history, it presents a distinctive Chu style.

The anthology consists of individual poems and suites. The first and most representative work in the collection is the "Lisao" (Encountering Sorrow). This first-person, politically oriented poem in 187 couplets is one of the greatest, and longest, poems in Chinese literature; the *Chuci* style is often simply named, after this monumental poem, the "Sao" style. The anthology also includes shorter lyrical and narrative poems, dialogues, and hymns to local deities, most of which have traditionally been interpreted as allegories for the poet's frustrations.

The attribution of the Chuci poems is problematic. Qu Yuan (c. 343–290 BCE), a high official of Chu who was later slandered, estranged, and finally exiled, was long considered the author of "Lisao" and of most of the *Chuci*, and these works accordingly were read against the story of his political fortunes. Although this view is not clearly proven by the evidence, it has found sympathy from readers who see in Qu Yuan a patriotic hero, who, thwarted in his efforts to serve his king, ended his life by throwing himself into the Miluo River in northeast part of modern Hunan Province.

Tim W. Chan

Further Reading

Hawkes, David, ed. and trans. (1985) *The Songs of the South: An Ancient Chinese Anthology of Poems by Qu Yuan and Other Poets.* New York: Penguin.
Schneider, Laurence A. (1980) *A Madman of Ch'u: The Chinese Myth of Loyalty and Dissent.* Berkeley and Los Angeles: University of California Press.

CHUGEN

CHUGEN *Chugen* is the traditional period of midsummer gift giving in Japan. Households, businesses, and work associates offer gifts to those they are obligated to, often superiors or customers. The tradition is maintained today in two forms: gifts and bonuses. Gifts, normally costing between 1,000 and 5,000 yen ($8 to $40), are offered, usually from those in subordinate positions to those in higher ones. These gifts are comprised of preserves, cakes, cleaning materials, cooking staples such as oils, and so on. In rural Japan it is still possible to receive homemade *chugen* gifts such as pickles, dried fruit, or tea. Most *chugen* gifts, however, are bought, often as a packed box of several items. Supermarkets, department stores, and mail-order catalogs market a variety of prepackaged items that need only be addressed and delivered.Related to the *chugen* tradition is that of the bonus. Successful firms will normally provide their employees with bonuses of one month's salary. This gift is the formal recognition of the debt the firm owes its employees for their efforts. *O-chugen* (the honorific *o* is normally added) is matched by *o-seibo*, the gift-giving season at the end of December that begins the New Year. *Chugen* is not a religious event, but falls into the category of civil-cultural rituals that are a common part of Japanese heritage.

Michael Ashikenazi

Further Reading

Befu Harumi. (1974) "Gift-Giving in a Modernizing Japan." In *Japanese Culture and Behavior*, edited by T. S. Lebra and W. P. Lebra. Honolulu, HI: University of Hawaii Press.
Hendry, Joy. (1993) *Wrapping Culture: Politeness, Presentation, and Power in Japan and Other Societies.* Oxford: Oxford University Press.

CHUGHTAI, ISMAT

CHUGHTAI, ISMAT (1911–1992), Indian novelist. Chughtai started writing in the fourth decade of the twentieth century when Urdu fiction was still a fledgling enterprise. She and her contemporaries—Saadat Hasan Manto, Rajinder Singh Bedi, and Krishan Chander—freed Urdu fiction from a preoccupation with romance and fantasy and gave it a realistic conviction. Chughtai's contribution lies in her exploration of feminine sensibility and female sexuality. Despite belonging to a movement of progressive writers that had great impact on Urdu literature in the 1940s and 1950s, Chughtai was fiercely independent and crusaded against any orthodoxy, religious or ideological. She wrote about eight novels and novellas—most notably *Terhi Lakeer* (Crooked Line, 1942), an autobiographical novel. Her fame rests chiefly on her short stories, which depict the lives of middle-class Muslims, particularly women, in northern India in the early decades of the twentieth century. Chughtai was a storyteller par excellence; stylistic directness, sparkling dialogue, brilliant turn of phrase, and scintillating humor are hallmarks of her style.

M. Asaduddin

Further Reading

Asaduddin, M. (1999) *Ismat Chughtai.* New Delhi: Sahitya Akademi.

Sukrita, Paul Kumar, and Sadiq, eds.(2000). *Ismat: Her Life, Her Times*. New Delhi: Katha.

CHUGOKU (2000 est. pop. 7.8 million). Chugoku region, with an area of 32,000 square kilometers, encompasses the entire western tip of Honshu and comprises five prefectures: Hiroshima, Okayama, Shimane, Tottori, and Yamaguchi. With the Chugoku Mountains as the dividing lines, the Inland Sea side is called the Sanyo region, and the Sea of Japan side, the Sanin region. It is a mountainous region with many small basins and coastal plains. The natural features of Shimane are characterized by the Oki Kuniga coastline with tall cliffs, as well as Shinji-ko, the sixth-largest lake in Japan. The Tottori Sand Dunes, located in Fukube Village, measure sixteen kilometers from east to west and two kilometers from north to south. Forestry is an important industry with a high quality lumber production. The Okayama Plain and the coastal plains are important areas for the production of rice. Other agricultural products are citrus fruits, melons, and grapes. Industry and commerce characterize the Inland Sea coast. The most heavily populated areas are along the Inland Sea coast, around the cities of Hiroshima, Kurashiki, and Okayama. Coastal waters are among Japan's richest fishing grounds; however, catches of sea bream, prawn, and abalone have been declining due to increasing industrial pollution.

Nathalie Cavasin

Further Reading

Yagasaki Noritaka, ed. (1997) *Japan: Geographical Perspectives on an Island Nation.* Tokyo: Teikoku-Shoin.

CHULALONGKORN, KING (RAMA V) (1853–1910), Siamese monarch. King Chulalongkorn, also known as Rama V, was the fifth king of the Chakri dynasty and ruled from 1868 until his death in 1910. He succeeded his father, King Mongkut, who had begun to modernize Siam in an attempt to stave off European colonial aggression. Educated in part by Anna Leonowens (featured with King Mongkut in the Rodgers and Hammerstein musical *The King and I*), Chulalongkorn was the first Siamese monarch to study abroad and, like his father, he surrounded himself with European advisers. An advocate of Western education, science, and technology, he sent all of his sons abroad to study. At home, Chulalongkorn implemented a Western-style educational system and founded the country's first university (later named Chulalongkorn University) in order to train a modern governmental bureaucracy.

Chulalongkorn implemented sweeping political and economic reforms that radically transformed

CHULALONGKORN'S PHILOSOPHY OF THE KINGSHIP

Chulalongkorn set forth his philosophy of the kingship in letters he wrote to his son Crown Prince Caofa Maha Vajirunhis, who died before he could succeed his father on the throne.

> To live easily, first is to be a priest and second is to be rich. To be a king, there are duties to be performed. You must be restrained in love and conquer hatred, anger, flattery, and laziness. The result of your merit will appear when you die. You will leave a good name as preserver of the family and protector of the people. These are two principles which you must have in mind more than anything else. If you cannot keep them in mind, you cannot rule and take care of the country. . . . It is a blessing that you have everything to make you ready to acquire knowledge, behave well and follow the path of merit.

Source: King Chulalongkorn. (1950) *Letters, Miscellaneous.* Part I: 17. Bangkok, Thailand: n.p.

Siamese society. In 1874 he abolished slavery. Beginning in 1885, he began reforming the government, establishing ministries structured on functional lines. He stripped power from the old nobility, provincial elites, and hereditary court officials. He established a professional military armed with modern weaponry. Chulalongkorn reformed the tax system and established the country's first modern bank, the Siam Commercial Bank. Despite his reforms and attempts to modernize Siam, he resisted establishing a European-style constitutional monarchy, arguing that the people were not ready for it. Chulalongkorn was known for adroit diplomacy that preserved Siam's independence, though he had to accommodate most European demands.

Chulalongkorn died at the age of fifty-seven, having reigned for forty-two years, a period of dramatic change that saw Siam emerge as a modern state. He was succeeded by his eldest son, Vajiravudh (Rama VI), one of his seventy-six children from ninety-two wives.

Zachary Abuza

Further Reading

Chomchai, Prachoom. (1965) *Chulalongkorn the Great.* Tokyo: The Centre for East Asian Cultural Studies.

Wyatt, David K. (1969) *Politics and Reform in Thailand: Education in the Reign of King Chulalongkorn.* New Haven, CT: Yale University Press.

CHULALONGKORN UNIVERSITY Chulalongkorn University was Thailand's first institution of higher learning and remains the nation's most prestigious academic institution. Though founded in March 1917, the school's roots date back to the reign of King Chulalongkorn (1853–1910), who in 1871 established a school that in 1902 became the Royal Pages School. The school's original mission was to train students for the civil service, but other disciplines, including international relations, commerce, agriculture, engineering, medicine, and teacher training, were added to the curriculum. On 1 January 1911, the school was renamed the Civil Service College and on 26 March 1917 was renamed Chulalongkorn University by King Vajiravudh (1881–1925). The original funding for the school came primarily from the royal family, who donated a large parcel of land where the university still resides. The five-hundred-acre campus is in the heart of Bangkok, and the university derives considerable income by renting some of its properties to commercial interests.

The university came under the supervision of the University Affairs Department, Ministry of Education. When it was founded, the university had 380 students taking classes under four faculties: the faculty of medicine located at Siriraj Hospital and the faculties of law and political science, engineering, and arts and sciences. In 1927, the first female students were enrolled. The undergraduate school grew substantially, and, in 1961, the university set up the graduate school. The university currently has over 27,000 students, including 9,000 graduate students, in 351 study programs and 16 specialized institutes and colleges with 19 faculties. It is Thailand's preeminent research institution.

Zachary Abuza

CHUN DOO HWAN (b. 1932). Chun Doo Hwan was the president of South Korea from 1980 until 1987, when his handpicked successor Roh Tae Woo succeeded him. Born in 1932, Chun was raised in North Kyongsang Province, where he was a student at Taegu Middle School. Before he could finish, Chun transferred to the Korean Military Academy, from which he graduated in 1955.

After graduating from the Korean Military Academy, Chun quickly moved up the ranks, holding various army appointments before being named to the Supreme Council for National Reconstruction. Shortly thereafter, Chun was named the chief of the newly formed Korean Central Intelligence Agency before being named Commander of the Capital Garrison. Like his successor, Roh Tae Woo, Chun saw action in Vietnam as a member of the South Korean forces fighting with the Americans.

In 1979, Chun was named the Commander of the Defense Security Command. Following the assassina-

President Chun Doo Hwan and U.S. President Ronald Reagan at the White House on 26 April 1985. (BETTMANN/CORBIS)

tion of President Park Chung Hee (1917–1979) in October 1979, Chun and a group of coconspirators seized control of the military. He was responsible for the brutal suppression of the Kwangju Uprising, a reaction against the military's control of politics in Korea, in May 1980. In August 1980, Chun eased out acting president Ch'oe Kyu-ha and took over the position; he was formally elected president in February 1981.

Chun's term in office can best be characterized by his attempt to open negotiations with North Korea—with little success. Domestically, Chun is best known for his relaxation of the restrictions imposed by the Yushin Constitution.

Keith Leitich

Further Reading

Clark, Donald. N., ed. (1988) *The Kwangju Uprising: Shadows Over the Regime in South Korea.* Boulder, CO: Westview Press.

Kim, Ilpyong J. and Young Whan Kihl, eds. (1988) *Political Change in South Korea.* St. Paul, MN: Paragon House.

CH'USOK The Harvest Moon Festival, known in Korea as *Ch'usok* and sometimes as *Han-gawi*, has been observed for more than two millennia. Along with the Lunar New Year's Day *(Sol)*, it is one of the two most important of Korea's holidays. *Ch'usok* is observed on the fifteenth of the eighth lunar month, which is always a full-moon day. This date is the beginning of the autumn harvest season, in September or early October, and the harvest moon appears as the biggest and brightest of the year's full moons.

Although harvest celebrations by different ethnic groups occurred on or around this date for centuries before, the first nationwide celebrations on this day were held in the Shilla kingdom (57 BCE–935 CE) in the first century CE, originating in the culmination of a month-long hemp-weaving contest among the women of the capital.

As on *Sol*, ancestral rites are the most important events of *Ch'usok*. *Charye*, the early-morning offering of tables of foods, as well as full ceremonial bows, is held in the home of the oldest male of the family, where the extended family has gathered for the occasion. The second rite, *Songmyo*, is held at the tombs of the immediate ancestors. Here, too, foods are prepared as offerings, and ceremonial bows are made.

Because it is harvest time, foods are an important part of the celebration. Boiled rice is made from early-harvested rice from the year's new crop. From this rice is also made the holiday's specialty rice cakes *(song-p'yon)*. These round or half-moon-shaped rice cakes are filled with sesame seeds, boiled chestnuts, red *azuki* beans, or jujubes and are steamed over pine needles to give them a distinctive fragrance. Apples, pears, persimmons, chestnuts, and jujubes are also feasted on throughout the day.

Various games and entertainments are associated with *Ch'usok* festivities. Korean bullfights pitted two bulls against each other. The head butting, ramming, and goring continued until one bull overpowered the other. The tortoise dance *(kobuk-nori)* was among the most eye-catching of entertainments. The tortoise, actually two men covered with a shell-like mat, danced at village houses and then collapsed, feigning hunger until offered food. Food collected in this manner was distributed to the needy. A tug-of-war employing a gigantic, specially woven straw rope was held between teams from neighboring villages. Good fortune was believed to come to the village of the winning team.

The evening was the time for the women to gaze at the rising full moon, good fortune coming to the one who saw it first. While waiting for moonrise, the women would join in the circle dance *(kanggangsullae)*. As the harvest moon rose in the evening sky, supplications were made to the brilliant orb, giving thanks for the harvest and asking for good fortune until the next harvest moon.

David E. Shaffer

Further Reading

Adams, Edward B. (1995) *Korea Guide.* 8th ed. Seoul: Seoul International Publishing House.

Choe, Sang-su. (1983) *Annual Customs of Korea.* Seoul: Seomun-dang Publishing.

Koo, John H., and Andrew C. Nahm, eds. (1997) *An Introduction to Korean Culture.* Elizabeth, NJ: Hollym.

CI *Ci* ("words to be sung") was a type of lyric poetry that originated during the Tang dynasty in China (618–907 CE) and became the most popular style during the Song dynasty (960–1279). Many foreign tunes had made their way into China with foreign travelers, and many of the tunes became popular but needed Chinese words. Although originally associated with singing girls and prostitutes, the new form earned the favor of Emperor Xuanzong (reigned 713–755), who had the court music school add them to its training. Thus *ci* found their way into the repertoire of courtly music. The first anthology of *ci* poetry, *Hua jianji* (Among the Flowers), appeared in the tenth century. When northern China fell in 1127 to the Jin, the court musicians and singers moved south with the rest of the court, taking with them the *ci* form, and its popularity increased.

Ci had lines of uneven length (unlike *shi*, classic Chinese lyric verse, which always had lines of the same length) and were composed to fit with existing popular folk tunes and their rhythmic and rhyme schemes as well as tonal patterns. As *ci* evolved into pure poetry, they eventually became difficult to sing. Thematically, *ci* usually could be divided into two sections, one section focusing on human feelings the other section on the scene. Zhang Yan of the Ming dynasty (1368–1644) broke *ci* poetry into two distinct categories: the first being Wan Yue (graceful and restrained) and the second Hao Fang (heroic and free).

Stacey Fox

Further Reading

Ayling, Alan, and Donald Mackintosh. (1965) *A Collection of Chinese Lyrics*. Nashville, TN: Vanderbilt University Press.

Chang, Kang-i sun. (1980) *The Evolution of Chinese Tz'u Poetry: From Late T'ang to Northern Sung*. Princeton, NJ: Princeton University Press.

Sun, Cecile Chu-chin. (1995) *Pearl from the Dragon's Mouth: Evocation of Scene and Feeling in Chinese Poetry*. Ann Arbor, MI: University of Michigan, Center for Chinese Studies.

Watson, Burton. (1971) *Chinese Lyricism: Shih Poetry from the Second to the Twelfth Century, with Translation*. New York: Columbia University Press.

CI XI, EMPRESS DOWAGER

CI XI, EMPRESS DOWAGER (1835–1908), Dowager empress of China and regent. Nee Yehonala of the Manchu Blue Banner, also known as Ci Xi, held power over China's political life for almost half a century. She was a consort of Emperor Xian Feng (1831–1861, ruled 1850–1861) and bore his successor, Tong Zhi (1856–1875, ruled 1862–1874). After Emperor Xian Feng's death in 1861, Ci Xi seized power by removing eight conservative regents from the court and setting up her own regent over the boy emperor. In 1875, after Emperor Tong Zhi died with no heir, Ci Xi named her three-year-old nephew Guang Xu (1871–1908, ruled 1875–1908) to the throne.

In 1898, Ci Xi resumed the regency as a result of a coup in which she succeeded in crushing the emperor's effort to push through a number of radical proposals designed to renovate and modernize the Chinese government. In 1900, Ci Xi supported officials who encouraged the antiforeign secret society Boxer movement. A coalition of foreign troops soon captured the capital and Ci Xi was forced to flee from Peking to northwestern China, where she accepted the humiliating treaty, the Boxer Protocol, in 1901. Returning to Peking in 1902, she finally began to implement a number of innovations that the reformers had sought in 1898, including the inception of China's constitutional establishment. Ci Xi died on 15 November 1908, one day after the emperor's death.

Shiwei Chen

Further Reading

Der Ling, Princes. (1928) *Old Buddha (Empress Tzu Hsi)*. New York: Dodd, Mead & Company.

Haldane, Charlotte. (1965) *The Last Great Empress of China*. Indianapolis, IN: Bobbs-Merrill.

CILICIAN GATES

CILICIAN GATES The Cilician Gates (Gulek Bogaz) is the key pass leading from the central Anatolian plateau to the Cilician plain and gives access from the cities of Konya and Ankara to Adana and the Mediterranean at Iskenderun and Antakya. Running between the Bolkarlar and Aladag Mountains, the road descends along the course of the Cakir Cay, a tributary of the Seyhan River, to Gulek Bogaz, the narrowest point of the pass, at an altitude of 1,050 meters (3,400 feet). The original passage was cut through rock from gorge to gorge and was so narrow that two caravan camels could barely pass; the cut is now bypassed by the main E90 road. The total length of the narrows, where railway, main road, and river run squeezed together between rock walls, is seventy kilometers from Ulukisla in the north to Gulek in the south.

The pass assumed importance when Asia Minor was a province of the Persian Empire; the Royal Road that supposedly connected Sardis in ancient Lydia with Susa in ancient Persia ran through the gates, and one branch of the Silk Road went from there to Istanbul. It was a key obstacle to the invasion of Persia from the west, and Alexander of Macedon described the desertion of the gates by the Persian defenders (333 BCE) as the most amazing piece of luck in his entire career. The Cilician Gates has remained a major trade route ever since; the Byzantine fortress of Loulon defended approaches from the north, and a chain of ruined Seljuk caravansaries or inns is still visible along the road. The first Crusaders under Baldwin of Boulogne used the pass in 1097, but subsequent Crusaders, aware of the possibilities of ambush, used sea passage or alternative passes. Today the railway is little used, but the multilane highway is continuously and heavily employed by commercial traffic carrying goods from the refineries and steelworks at Iskenderun, the factories at Adana, and the free port at Mersin to the interior.

Kate Clow

Further Reading

Green, Peter. (1974) *Alexander of Macedon.* London: Pelican Books.

Flavius Arrianus (Arrian). (1976) *The Campaigns of Alexander*. Trans. by Aubrey de Selincourt. London: Penguin.

CINEMA—CHINA The history of modern Chinese cinema began on 11 August 1896, when a film by the French production studio Lumière Brothers was shown in Yu Gardens in Shanghai. The first Chinese production, the opera *Dingjun shan* (Dingjun Mountain) was filmed in 1903. In 1916, twenty years after the introduction of Western films into China, the first Chinese-owned film production company was established. From then on, China was able to address topics related to its changing political, economic, social, and international situation through its own lens.

The intended audience of these films, largely Chinese mainlanders, enjoyed the markedly different films made during the various eras of Chinese cinematic history. These included martial arts and romance films in the 1920s, leftist films in the 1930s (the first sound film, *Genu hongmudan* [Singsong Girl Red Peony], was produced in 1931), antiwar films in the 1940s, Soviet-style social realism in the 1950s, a mixture of revolutionary realism and romanticism (spearheaded by Mao Zedong's wife Jiang Qing) in the 1960s, and films of ideological correction and relaxation in the 1970s and early 1980s.

The first generation of Chinese film directors aimed to borrow Western techniques while building a national cinema resistant to Western influences. The second generation of film directors attempted to assist socialist nation-building after the founding of People's Republic of China. The third generation, represented by Xie Jin (*Tianyunshan chuanqi* [The Legend of Tianyun Mountain]), emerged after the Cultural Revolution (1966–1976) and tried to forge Chinese film production with socialist Chinese characteristics. Before Xie chose to reflect the concerns of the majority of the Chinese at the time, film production had been either liable to excessive foreign influences or revolutionary romanticism. The fourth generation, represented by Teng Wenji, pushed Xie Jin's paradigm to its limits. The fifth generation, revolting against the previous schools, aimed at transforming Chinese culture through cinema. The sixth generation is now pushing the fifth generation's approach to its limit in a new historical context.

Censorship and Cinema

Censorship has been omnipresent throughout much of the history of Chinese cinema: against communism by the republican government (1912–1927), and against Soviet revisionism (1958–1978) and "bourgeois liberalization" (1978–present) by the Chinese Communist government. Worthy of special mention is the impact on film production of Mao Zedong's policy of art for the sake of ideology. The policy aimed to maintain political correctness in every film. Mobile film projection teams presented these politically correct films to agricultural production teams and work and military units, helping to disseminate official ideology and policies to the masses in hopes of maintaining its legitimacy and political dominance.

Contemporary Cinema

Dissatisfied with the sterilization and wholesale politicization of the cinema, a younger generation of film directors, trained at the Beijing Film Academy after the Cultural Revolution, forged a new cinematic school characterized by cultural critique and reflection and bold artistic experimentation. These directors include Zhang Yimou *(Red Sorghum, Judou, Raise the Red Lantern, The Story of Qiu Ju)*, Chen Kaige *(Yellow Earth, Farewell My Concubine, The King of Children)*, and Tian Zhuangzhuang *(The Blue Kite, The Horse Thief)*. Their films have not only drawn a large and diverse audience but have also attracted the attention of international film scholars. Many of these films have won international awards despite state censorship and are available in video stores throughout the world. These films have been acclaimed both for their exploration of the Chinese cultural psyche and their artistic innovation. In many ways this generation has renounced Mao's policy of art for the sake of ideology. As Zhang Yimou said: "Chinese filmmaking has to remain an open art, free"(Semel 1987: 140). This not only best sums up the aesthetic vision of the new school of filmmakers, but also applies to China's newest generation of film directors, as they seek to negotiate the forces of localism and globalism in constructing cinematic representations of the deeper flows of Chinese culture.

Wenshan Jia

Further Reading

Berry, Chris, ed. (1991) *Perspectives on Chinese Cinema*. London: BFI Publishing.

Leyda, Jay. (1972) *Dianying: An Account of Films and the Film Audience in China.* Cambridge, MA: The MIT Press.

Lu, Sheldon Hsiao-peng. (1997) *Transnational Chinese Cinemas: Identity, Nationhood, and Gender*. Honolulu, HI: University of Hawaii Press.

Semel, George S., ed. (1987) *Chinese Film: The State of the Art in the People's Republic.* Westport, CT: Praeger.

Semel, George S., Xihe Chen, and Hong Xia, eds. (1993) *Film in Contemporary China: Critical Debates, 1979–1989.* Westport, CT: Praeger.

Tam, Kwok-kan, and Wimal Dissanayake. (1998) *New Chinese Cinema.* Hong Kong: Oxford University Press.

Zhang, Yingjin. (1999) *Cinema and Urban Culture in Shanghai, 1922–1943.* Stanford, CA: Stanford University Press.

CINEMA—INDIA Cinema was introduced in India on 7 July 1896 when the Lumière brothers invited the residents of Mumbai (Bombay) to see their movies brought from France. In the next few years, Indian entrepreneurs flooded India with foreign motion pictures, which were actually of little interest to the Indian masses. It was Dhundhiraj Phalke, a young Brahman student of drawing, painting, and photography, who pawned his wife's ornaments to make the first Indian feature film, *Raja Harishchandra,* a mythological tale with titles in Hindi and English, which opened in Mumbai on 12 April 1913. In the next few years, Phalke made other mythological films, as well as animated films, travelogues, and documentaries. Indian tycoons such as J. F. Madan in Calcutta were responsible for a prodigious output of both social and mythological films in the following years. In spite of the popularity of Indian films, because of higher production values and a superior distribution system, about 85 percent of the movies shown in India by the late 1920s were American, a fact that dismayed both Indian filmmakers and British rulers.

Talking pictures came to India on 14 March 1931 with the showing of Ardeshir Irani's *Alam Ara,* a drama based on a stage play. Another important force in the 1930s was the Prabhat Film Company and its leader, V. Shantaram, who showed a Hindi film, *Amar jyoti* (Eternal Light), about the vengeance of women, at the Venice Film Festival in 1936 and won an award at that festival for his Marathi film *Sant tukaram* (Saint Tukaram) a year later. From the beginning, however, Hindi emerged as the dominant language of Indian cinema, although films in other languages of more limited reach, such as Bengali and Tamil, were also made. Building on the indigenous entertainment of India, every film included a multitude of songs, which rapidly evolved from folk music to a distinctive film song genre with its own emotional identity. The film song gradually became a separate source of entertainment, and the popularity of the songs, which were often released before the movie, determined the success of the movie. Given the importance of the film song and the difficulty of finding actors who were also good singers, by the 1940s the "playback" system had become universal, and the actors mouthing the songs on screen were not the actual singers. The most famous of these playback singers is Lata Mangeshkar, who became the world's most recorded singer in her fifty-year career, which began in 1948.

Indian Cinema since Independence

With the independence of India and the partition of the subcontinent in August 1947, Indian cinema continued its development free of British censorship but subject to the censors and taxation rules of the new Indian government. The 1950s in Mumbai were marked by the filmmaker Raj Kapoor (1924–1988), whose films were mostly scripted by the famous film journalist K. A. Abbas (1914–1987). Kapoor, through his depiction of the lovable vagabond in films, such as *Awara* (Vagabond) and *Shri 420,* became famous not only in India, but also in the Soviet Union and the Middle East. In 1957, ten years after independence, another famous director, Mehboob Khan (1906–1964), made *Mother India,* one of the most popular films ever made in India, in which the Indian woman as mother becomes a symbol for the nation. It was nominated for an Academy Award as best foreign film.

More than half of all the cinema halls in India were in South India, however, and therefore Madras soon became the film capital of India. Most of the films in Madras were made in Tamil, but many were made in Hindi also, such as the 1948 blockbuster, *Chandralekha.* The Tamil cinema also had a strong connection with South Indian politics because the famous Tamil film actor M. G. Ramachandran (1917–1987, known as MGR) became chief minister of the state of Tamil Nadu and was succeeded in that position by the actress Jayalitha.

The New Cinema

Although K. A. Abbas in 1954 made the Hindi film *Munna,* the first Hindi film without any songs or dances, it was in Calcutta that a new kind of Indian cinema arose. There Satyajit Ray (1921–1992), a young advertising man who had been active in the Calcutta Film Society, determined to make a film that would deserve worldwide acclaim. With a small subsidy from the state of Bengal, Ray made a film based on a famous Bengali novel about a boy named Apu who grew up in a small village. The film *Pather panchali* (Song of the Road) was shown at the Museum of Modern Art in New York and became the first Indian film to achieve extensive U.S. distribution. Ray completed the Apu trilogy with *Aparajito* (The Unvanquished) in 1957 and *Apur sansar* (The World of Apu) in 1959. During the centennial of the birth of Rabindranath Tagore, India's only Nobel Prize winner

Large movie billboards such as this one in Madras are a common way of advertising films in India. (HANS GEORG ROTH/ CORBIS)

in literature, Ray made a documentary on Tagore in 1961 and followed that with two films based on Tagore's literary works, *Charulata,* about a lonely wife in nineteenth-century Bengal; and *Two Daughters,* a film based on Tagore's short stories. Another Ray trilogy in the early 1970s dealt with the Calcutta middle class in the turbulent 1960s: *Days and Nights in the Forest* (*Aranyer Din Raatri,* 1969), *The Adversary* (*Pratidwandi,* 1970), and *Company Limited* (*Seemabaddha,* 1971). Ray stayed far away from the Mumbai stereotypes: no songs and dances, careful scripting, strong emphasis on authenticity, shooting on location, and careful selection of actors, who were often inexperienced. But Ray also worked with master actors, whom he had mainly discovered himself. Soumitra Chatterjee, who played the adult Apu in *Apur sansar,* worked with Ray for more than three decades, and Sharmila Tagore, Apu's wife in that film, appeared in Ray films throughout the 1960s. Except for *Shatranj ke khilari* (The Chess Players), which he made in Hindi-Urdu, all of Ray's films were in his native Bengali. Ray's prodigious output continued until his death in 1992, soon after receiving an honorary Academy Award in his Calcutta hospital bed.

The first Hindi movie of the new Indian cinema was made by another famous Bengali director, Mrinal Sen (b. 1923). The film was *Bhuvan Shome* (1969), and its moderate success was a harbinger of a new cinema movement that was vigorous for more than two decades. Actors and directors graduated from the Film Institute in Pune and with the help of state subsidies made some good movies, such as *27 Down* in 1973, which, like *Bhuvan Shome,* had a railroad theme. The most prominent director of the new Indian cinema was probably Shyam Benegal (b. 1934), whose 1973 film *Ankur* (The Seedling), about the cruelty of landlords, was followed by *Mandhan* (The Churning), a film about exploitation of farmers by a dairy owner that was financed by Gujarati farmers.

In the last two decades of the twentieth century, in spite of vigorous production in regional centers like Madras, Mumbai continued its dominance and became universally known as Bollywood, a contraction of Bombay (Mumbai's former name) and Hollywood. After the often violent films starring superheroes such as Amitabh Bachchan, Bollywood in the late 1980s saw the rise of romantic musical films. The trend in musicals culminated with the hugely popular 1994 film *Hum aap ke hain kaun* (Who Are We to You?), which chronicles typical family events instead of including the typical movie plots and subplots. Emigrants from South Asia all over the world—via Indian movie theaters, VCRs, DVDs, and Indian cable channels—have made Indian cinema a world cinema.

Herman H. van Olphen

Further Reading

Barnouw, Erik, and S. Krishnaswamy. (1980) *Indian Film*. New York: Oxford University Press.

Chakravarty, Sumita S. (1993) *National Identity in Indian Popular Cinema 1947–1987*. Austin, TX: University of Texas Press.

Cooper, Darius. (2000) *The Cinema of Satyajit Ray*. New York: Cambridge University Press.

Dwyer, Rachel. (2000) *All You Want Is Money, All You Need Is Love*. London: Cassell.

Garga, B. D. (1996) *So Many Cinemas: The Motion Picture in India*. Mumbai, India: Eminence Designs.

Rajadhyaksha, Ashish, and Paul Willemen. (1995) *Encyclopedia of Indian Cinema*. New Delhi: Oxford University Press.

Vasudevan, Ravi S. (2000) *Making Meaning in Indian Cinema*. New Delhi: Oxford University Press.

CINEMA—JAPAN Developing an art form that had originated in the West, Japanese cinema emerged after Japan's victory in the Sino-Japanese War of 1895. As with the later golden age of Japanese film, film art came into its own in the wake of upheaval. The predominance of ideas, of speculation and introspection, so common in Japanese cinema, began with the *banshi*, the narrator of Japanese silent films. The *banshi* explained, with flourishes, what was happening, with the premise that there was something of moment to communicate beyond what visual images provided.

Japanese cinema of the late 1940s, 1950s, and 1960s owed much to the new drama of Shingeki, the social drama born in the early 1900s and influenced by the works of Henrik Ibsen (1828–1906) and George Bernard Shaw (1856–1950). Film, like theater, would be an arena of social assessment, a means of examining and exploring the fate of society. Kaoru Osanai, a founder of the Shingeki movement, had studied at the Moscow Art Theater, where Sergey Eisenstein (1898–1948) was also a presence. (In this article, Japanese names are presented surname first.) Crucial to the history of Japanese film are Osanai's films and Minoru Murata's landmark *Rojo no Rekion* (Souls on the Road), made in 1921 and based partly on Maxim Gorky's *The Lower Depths*, a work that Akira Kurosawa would adapt as well.

By the late 1920s, the first great Japanese director, Teinosuke Kinugasa, had arrived on the scene. His masterpiece, *Kurutta Ippeiji* (1927; A Crazy Page, also known as A Page of Madness), brought Japanese film a world dimension. Combining German expressionism with Soviet montage (he had studied with Eisenstein), Kinugasa created Japanese film art. The work of Daisuke Ito and Masahiro Makino in the late 1920s prefigured the later golden age of the period film. This work attacked feudal society and, by implication, the current social system. "Tendency" pictures, focusing on social problems and themselves influenced by the Russian Revolution, were a dominant trend when, with Heinosuke Gosho's *Madamu to Nyobo* (The Neighbor's Wife and Mine) in 1931, talking pictures came to Japan.

Just as American cinema distinguished itself in the early years of the twentieth century with the films of D. W. Griffith, and Soviet cinema reached its high point in the 1920s, Japanese cinema truly came into its own at the moment of Japan's defeat in World War II. It is at moments of transition in the social history of a culture that great art flourishes. After Japan's defeat in World War II, the country turned to a political and social reexamination of its national identity. This reexamination was assumed in the arts with the greatest verve and imagination, not by poets and novelists, but by film directors.

Some of the directors, like Ozu Yasujiro (1903–1963), had been making films since silent days. Others, like Kurosawa Akira (1910–1998), came into their own during the war. All explored in their films the theme of what it means to be Japanese. Some of their works, particularly those of Ozu, were set in the present. Other directors, like Kurosawa and Kobayashi Masaki, created their greatest art through period films: stories set as far back as medieval times, but mostly depicting another period of transition—the nineteenth century, which saw the fall of the Tokugawa dynasty and Japan's tentative and then thunderous entrance into modernism.

Kurosawa Akira

Kurosawa's subject, the passing of the samurai class from the stage of history in the sixteenth century, is the theme of the greatest Japanese film ever made, his *Seven Samurai* (1954). In the tragedy of the decline of the samurai, Kurosawa discovered a quality of being Japanese lost in the era in which he himself lived and worked. "Again we've survived—again we're defeated," says Kambei, played by Shimura Takashi, the humane leader of the *ronin*, those disenfranchised samurai who have come to save the peasant village.

The winners are the peasants who will live on in history, not the samurai, whose nobility has been tainted by corruption and upheaval. As Kurosawa revealed, the peasants are able to enlist only six wandering *ronin* to work for them, with no payment but the satisfaction of helping a community survive. Kurosawa depicted the subsequent ascendance of the merchant class in his searing satire *Yojimbo* (1960), a film that despite its historical setting speaks to this director's perception of the corruption of modern-day mercantile Japan: its press, its industry, and its inequitable system of justice.

Ozu's *Tokyo Story*

The very rhythms of Kurosawa's films, from *Rashomon* (1950) to *Red Beard* (1965), trumpeted the inevitability of change, but Kurosawa's later films, from *Dodeskaden* (1970) on, do not share this optimism and belief in the possibility of social and human transformation. Even the Soviet co-production *Dersu Uzala* (1975), which followed *Dodeskaden,* is nostalgic and pictorial rather than full of the dynamic tension and implicit optimism that the world may be transformed, so characteristic of Kurosawa's greatest works.

Ozu's efforts to define being Japanese expressed in the postwar moral chaos a nostalgic appreciation for traditions of graciousness that were being lost as Japan modernized and embraced the values and culture of the West. The most telling moment in all his films may well occur at the climax of *Tokyo Story* (1953). The mother dies at the end of the film, allowing Ozu to offer a dialogue between daughter-in-law and youngest daughter that rises above the plot to speak to Ozu's worldview.

Most of the children have been selfish and mercenary. Appalled by her older sister Shige's selfishness—the materialism that allowed Shige at the moment of the mother's death to demand her best kimono as a "keepsake"—the youngest child, Kyoko, cries out in anger. Her siblings and indeed, for Ozu, people in general were all so selfish, she complains. Her sister-in-law, Noriko, who has lost her husband in the war, demands a more measured response. "At your age I thought so, too," she gently reminds Kyoko. Even Shige "meant no harm."

"Isn't life disappointing!" Kyoko concludes. It is Noriko, however, who speaks for Ozu with the spirit of *mu,* the peace that passeth understanding.

"Yes, it is," she smiles. There is no doubt that Ozu admires Noriko for attempting to retain her Japanese spirit, even as she suffers premature widowhood and is herself uneasy and discontented. "I'm quite selfish," Noriko had admitted to her mother-in-law. "I'm not always thinking of your son."

New Views of Women

Mizoguchi Kenji (1898–1956), following one of the edicts of the Allied Occupation that the efforts of women to assume their independence should be paramount among film subjects, created great works of cinema by depicting women of the past. In *The Life of*

A large billboard advertises a movie in Japan. (EYE UBIQUITOUS/CORBIS)

Oharu (1952) and *A Story from Chikamatsu* (1954), Mizoguchi spoke to the needs of the modern Japanese woman by exploring her subjection to patriarchal domination in the past.

Another director who concentrated on the social restrictions that thwart women was Naruse Mikio, whose greatest film, *A Wandering Life* (1962), depicts the struggle for fulfillment of a woman who became one of Japan's leading writers, Hayashi Fumiko. In 1960, Naruse remarked that people did not write about strong, independent women and that audiences preferred stories about weak women's torment and abuse. In film after film, Naruse transcended that perception. "I shared none of their feelings that untraditional women are unattractive," he confessed to an interviewer for the Japanese film magazine *Kinema Jumpo,* or "that strong-hearted women are despicable and disgusting."

Antiwar Films

Antiwar films flourished in the postwar period under the encouragement of the supreme commander of the Allied powers, General Douglas MacArthur. From the edict that postwar Japanese films reject the values that led to the war came masterpieces of film art revealing the cruelty of the Japanese in China, such as Kobayashi Masaki's three-part epic, *Ningen no Joken* (1959; The Human Condition). Other films depicted how the war brought suffering to the ordinary Japanese who wanted no part of militarism.

The most moving of these films was *Twenty-Four Eyes* (1954), by Kinoshita Keisuke. It is the biography of a teacher on Sado Island in the Inland Sea. Miss Oishi must instruct a child, defying the previously prevailing ideology, that the emperor is not "in the cupboard" and that his portrait is no more than a portrait. The emperor is not omnipotent and omnipresent, but rather a man like any other—a view that was sacrilegious until 1945.

Culture Criticized

That Japanese directors were ready to make films critical of the culture that nurtured the war was revealed in Kurosawa's *No Regrets for Our Youth* (1946), a film about a woman who achieves liberation by marrying an antiwar activist who is murdered by the Japanese secret police. Yukie, played by the greatest actress of her day, Hara Setsuko, goes on to reject traditional Japanese views of femininity in exchange for becoming an assertive citizen of the society that has destroyed her possibility of personal happiness.

The generation of directors who followed Kurosawa, Mizoguchi, Ozu, and Naruse was no less obsessed by the theme of its unique Japanese identity. With passion and urgency, Shinoda Masahiro, Hani Susamu, Oshima Nagisa, and the most talented of them all, Imamura Shohei, explored the turmoil of postwar society. In *Pigs and Battleships* (1961), Imamura created a brilliant protest against the continuing military occupation of Japan; the marauding Americans are the "pigs" of the title, but so are the Japanese gangsters, the *yakuza*, who profit from their presence. Oshima challenged the inability of the older generation to face its responsibility for Japan's moral demise in *Ceremonies* (1971). A groom goes through with his wedding despite the fact that his bride has run away; Japan persists in meaningless traditions that have lost all purpose, even as the nation has lost its moral direction.

Oshima's masterpiece, *In the Realm of the Senses* (1976), located a uniquely Japanese appreciation of sexuality in characters who defy the conventions of the wartime moment, the late 1930s, to devote themselves exclusively to the joy and sensuality that belong to a Japan where sex was not associated with shame. Oshima's Sada and Kichizo invoked the aristocratic culture of tenth-century Japan, when people dedicated themselves to an appreciation of lovemaking, a mood reinvoked for the last time in the flurry of pleasure seeking of late-Tokugawa Japan just prior to the opening of Japan to the West. As did the great generation of filmmakers who preceded him, Oshima used the past as a vehicle into the present.

In that ancient and more beautiful Japan, where sex was divorced from psychopathology and repression, Oshima located the heart of the unique Japanese identity. In that past, women were the equals of men in their mutual abandon. The need to make war was countered by the natural, physical fulfillment of lovemaking, a freedom that came to an end, Oshima suggested, in 1936 with the Officers' Coup that made Japan's participation in World War II inevitable. *In the Realm of the Senses* may indeed itself be seen as the punctuating moment of the great era of Japanese filmmaking. Subsequent directors have been content to revel in satire, outlandish action, and broad humor. Like that of other nations, France and Italy included, the Japanese cinema awaits its next resurgence.

Joan Mellen

See also: **Cinema, Contemporary—Japan**

Further Reading

Anderson, Joseph L., and Donald Richie. (1982) *The Japanese Film: Art and Industry*. Princeton, NJ: Princeton University Press.

Bock, Audie. (1978) *Japanese Film Directors*. Tokyo: Kodansha International.

Burch, Noel. (1979) *To the Distant Observer: Form and Meaning in the Japanese Cinema*. Berkeley and Los Angeles: University of California Press.

Desser, David. (1983) *The Samurai Films of Akira Kurosawa*. Ann Arbor, MI: UMI Research Press.

Kurosawa Akira. (1970) *The Seven Samurai: Modern Film Scripts*. New York: Simon and Schuster.

———. (1982) *Something Like an Autobiography*. New York: Alfred A. Knopf.

Mellen, Joan. (1975) *Voices from the Japanese Cinema*. New York: Liveright.

———. (1976) *The Waves at Genji's Door: Japan through Its Cinema*. New York: Pantheon.

Oshima Nagisa. (1992) *Cinema, Censorship, and the State: The Writings of Nagisa Oshima, 1956–1978*. Cambridge, MA: MIT Press.

Richie, Donald. (1984) *The Films of Akira Kurosawa*. Berkeley and Los Angeles: University of California Press.

———. (1971) *Japanese Cinema*. New York: Anchor Books.

———. (1974) *Ozu: His Life and Films*. Berkeley and Los Angeles: University of California Press.

Sato Tadao. (1982) *Currents in Japanese Cinema*. Tokyo: Kodansha International.

Tucker, Richard N. (1973) *Japan: Film Image*. London: Studio Vista.

"Wide Angle: Japanese Cinema." (1977) *Athens International Film Festival: Ohio University Department of Film* 1, 4.

CINEMA—WEST ASIA Film production in Iraq, Turkey, and Iran has struggled in the face of censorship, lack of government support, and competition from the U.S. film industry. Nevertheless, in the past few decades, Iranian and Turkish films have made their way onto the international scene, where they have garnered awards. Iraqi cinema faces more obstacles than Turkish or Iranian cinema and is rarely seen in the West.

Iraqi Cinema

Documentary films are the most common type of film produced in Iraq because of the prohibitive technical requirements and expenses associated with the production of feature films, and documentary film production is dominated by the state. High costs and lack of state support, combined with a history of domestic unrest, have prevented the emergence of a strong and independent private sector; currently only a limited number of films are privately produced each year. The most successful company is the Babil Corporation, which is partly owned by the government. The primary film producer in Iraq is the state-owned and -operated Cinema and Theatre Administration.

Not surprisingly, most Iraqi films are either complimentary narratives of Iraq's history and development or critical assessments of the impact of United Nations sanctions and military operations against Iraq. Although such films can be seen as mere legitimization exercises by the government, they also represent a viewpoint that is rarely given credence in the West.

Sanctions and Iraq's difficult political and economic situation have meant that few Iraqi films ever reach Western audiences. Furthermore, the future of both public and private sectors has been severely affected by the banning of raw film imports into Iraq under the U.N. sanctions. In light of the nature of Iraq's film industry and the failure of its films to have a presence in the Western market, it is not surprising that Iraqi films have been little studied. Whatever analysis there is has been published exclusively in Arabic.

Turkish Cinema

For many years, Turkish cinema was dominated by cheaply made films produced for a wide audience. Collectively referred to as *Yesilcam* (the Turkish version of Hollywood), such films were Turkey's answer to Hollywood, replete with swooning, blond-tressed falsetto-voiced women and hirsute men with handlebar mustaches. Most were simplistic depictions of life, often based on popular Turkish novels or American films.

However, Turkey's film industry has also been a medium through which the country's various domestic

A billboard advertising an Iranian movie in 1995. (DAVID & PETER TURNLEY/CORBIS)

conflicts are examined. For example, Halit Refig's *Sehirdeki Yavanci* (Stranger in the City, 1963) explored the conflict between Islamic and secular values in Turkey. *Karanlikta Uyananlar* (Those Awaking in Darkness, 1964), directed by Ertem Gorec, dealt with the social consequences of a workers' strike. The conflict over Turkey's ethnic and religious identity has been expressed in various and often differing efforts to develop a national film culture. One example was the Milli Sinema, a national film movement that emerged in the 1970s as a promoter of Turkey's Islamic identity, producing several films with strong religious contents, including *Birlesen Yollar* (Joining Roads, 1970) and *Memleketin* (My Country, 1974).

The long and often bloody history of Turkey's Kurdish minority has also been reflected in the effort to develop a Kurdish film industry. The Kurdish film industry has struggled to survive, severely hampered at various stages by the efforts of Turkey, Iran, Syria, and Iraq to prevent the realization of a Kurdish identity. The technological revolution in the late twentieth century, which saw the introduction of videos and satellite television, has made it easier for Kurdish filmmakers to produce independent films. Perhaps the best-known Kurdish movie is *Yol* (The Road, 1982). It won the Cannes Film Festival's highest award, the Palme d'Or, in 1982 but was not allowed to be seen in Turkey until 1992.

Although films such as *Yol* (The Road, 1982), *Etikiya* (Bandit, 1996), and *Hamman* (Turkish Bath, 1997) have drawn significant international audiences and won rave reviews at European film festivals, the growing international presence of Turkish films has been paralleled by the mounting obstacles that filmmakers face at home. Most filmmakers struggle to make films on limited budgets, with inadequate government support and in the face of the country's often volatile political and economic situation. Turkish films must also compete with American films, which, with the latest filmmaking technology and internationally recognized actors, are very popular in Turkey.

Iranian Cinema

The cinema industry has become one of Iran's best-known exports. During recent decades, Iranian films have won favorable reviews from Western filmgoers and critics alike and have gained numerous awards at international festivals. Two prominent examples are Abbas Kiarostami's *Ta'm-i Gilas* (Taste of Cherry, 1997), which won the Palme d'Or at the Cannes Film Festival in 1997, and Majid Majidi's *Bachchah'ha-yi Aseman* (Children of Heaven, 1997), which received an Oscar nomination in 1998. Aside from their popularity, Iranian films present an alternative view of Iranians, who have traditionally been seen in the West as fanatical and intolerant. However, while displacing one negative image of Iran, the films have to a certain extent been popular because they depict other stereotypical images, of Iran's idealized past or of a sentimental view of children. Consequently, such films have been criticized for seeking popular acceptance by pandering to the Orientalism of the West by exoticizing and patronizing Iranian life.

Iranian filmmakers, however, have emphasized such content because it can easily pass strict government censorship requirements. Under these requirements, there can be no violence, no affection between men and women who are unrelated, no dancing, no female singers or alluring music. The story must not offend the clerical establishment or disagree with Islamic tenets. As a result, Iranian filmmakers have developed ingenious ways to surmount the censorship barriers. Mohsen Makmalbaf overcame the ban on depicting a woman giving birth by donning a skirt and playing the role himself in his 1996 film *Gabbeh* (Gabbeh, 1997). Other directors have cast female and male actors who are related, thereby skirting the rule against characters demonstrating affection. Filmmakers have often resorted to allegory, satire, and symbolism to get their message across—hence the frequent use of small children.

Some filmmakers, however, have willingly dealt frankly with sensitive issues. Ibrahim Hatamikia's *Azhans Shishah'yi* (The Glass Agency, 1998) portrayed the plight of disabled war veterans in the aftermath of the Iran-Iraq war. Davoud Mirbaqeri's *Adambarfi* (The Snowman, 1995) has come under strong criticism from conservative elements in Iran for its depiction of male cross-dressing.

Like the press, television, and universities in Iran, the cinema has become a battleground where a war is waged between opposing ideological views—between those who want to reform Iran's conservative Islamic system and those who campaign for its continuation. Recently reformist politicians, in an effort to liberalize the arts, have encouraged the film industry by attempting to loosen cultural restrictions.

Adrienne Whitby

Further Reading

Dabashi, Hamid. (2001) *Close Up: Iranian Cinema, Past, Present, and Future.* New York: Verso Books.

Kamalipour, Yahya R., and Hamid Mowlana. (1994) *Mass Media in the Middle East: A Comprehensive Handbook.* Westport, CT: Greenwood Press.

Kaplan, Yusuf. (1996) "Turkish Cinema." In *The Oxford History of World Cinema*, edited by Geoffrey Nowell-Smith. Oxford: Oxford University Press.

Shafik, Viola. (1998) *Arab Cinema: History and Cultural Identity*. Cairo, Egypt: American University Press.

Siavoshi, Sussan. (1997) "Cultural Policies and the Islamic Republic: Cinema and Book Publication." *International Journal of Middle East Studies* 29, 4: 509–530.

CINEMA, CONTEMPORARY — JAPAN

Japanese cinema began in 1897 with the importation of motion picture cameras from France. By 1900 the Japanese were manufacturing their own equipment. The earliest Japanese films were actualities along the lines of the Lumiere Brothers in France, brief vignettes of street life or glimpses of landscapes. The Russo-Japanese War, beginning in 1904, was actually a boon to Japanese filmmaking, which catered to a seemingly inexhaustible demand for newsreel footage of the fighting—real or staged. The fiction film came into its own when it was integrated into stage plays to form a unique dramatic presentation known as *rensa-geki* (chain drama). Film sequences shot on location or scenes of dramatic chases became part of live theatrical performances. As the fiction film developed and increased in popularity over the documentary mode, theater, especially kabuki and *shimpa*, became the dominant model for Japanese cinema. Directors like Itami Mansaku (1900–1946), the father of Itami Juzo, and Makino Shozo (1878–1929) pioneered modern cinematic storytelling techniques, often in the *jidai-geki* (period film) mode, paving the way for masters like Mizoguchi Kenji (1898–1956), Yamanaka Sadao (1909–1938), and Ozu Yasujiro (1902–1963) to create a golden age of film in the 1930s. Wartime censorship and the exigencies of war soon put an end to this remarkable period of creativity and commercial success, which would be equaled and perhaps surpassed in the 1950s.

Decline, Fall, and Resurgence

By the 1950s, Japanese cinema was the envy of the world. Filmmakers produced critical favorites at festivals and commercial successes at home year after year. As U.S. cinema went into a decline because of judicially mandated changes in the film industry and increased competition from television, Japan's film industry entered another golden age. The decade came to a close with a record 547 films released in 1960. But this was the beginning of an end. Production levels, attendance, and number of movie screens all went into a gradual decline in Japan, until by 1978 only 350 or so films were released each year, the majority of which were low-budget exploitation films, termed, however unfittingly, *roman-poruno* ("romantic-pornography"). By the end of the 1990s, production of *roman-poruno* declined, as liberalized censorship laws and cheap video production put an end to the genre for all intents and purposes. Production levels fell to around 250 films per year.

That number is deceiving, however, in terms of Japanese cinema as a whole. If one discounts *roman-poruno* from the production numbers of the 1970s, in the 1990s Japanese filmmaking experienced a noticeable increase, not only in quantity but, more important, in quality. While in the minds of many critics Japanese cinema of the 1980s had precious little to offer the serious film fan and even less to offer the national box office, the situation changed in the mid-1990s. With a host of new directors and talented stars, Japanese cinema again found itself the object of critical acclaim and commercial success.

Japanese Cinema in the 1970s and 1980s

One of the structural features of the Japanese cinema that prevented its resurgence amid the decline in the 1970s was the fact that major Japanese production studios were also major distribution outlets for foreign and domestic films, as well as in control of important theater chains. When domestic film production declined, the studios could turn to foreign films for distribution and exhibition. Thus, it is no surprise that the resurgent Hollywood cinema of the 1970s contributed to the declining Japanese cinema of that era. Similarly, the film studios also turned to television production to maintain a steady flow of income. Toei, for instance, reaped the rewards of its animation subsidiary during the *anime* (animation) boom of the 1980s and its live-action offshoots known as *sentai*, or five-hero shows, such as *The Mighty Morphin Power Rangers*. Mostly, however, the major studios kept themselves afloat with big-budget prestige films or middle-budget formula films guaranteed to turn a modest profit through advance ticket sales and block-booking (forcing a theater to book a whole slate of a company's films, often sight unseen, rather than picking and choosing) practices. Toho, for instance, which scored a surprising hit in 1954 with *Gojira (Godzilla)* and then its numerous sequels, had put the venerable monster on hiatus in the mid-1970s. But in the mid-1980s the studio trotted him out again, and during the 1990s he reappeared with startling regularity. And, like Toei, Toho reaped the rewards of its *anime* connection, in particular with the films of Miyazaki Hayao: *Kaze no tani no Naushikaa* (*Nausicaä of the Valley of Wind*, 1984), *Tonari no Totoro* (*My Neighbor Totoro*, 1988) and *Majo no takkyubin* (*Kiki's Delivery Service*,

1989). More impressive was the case of the film studio Shochiku, which had a substantial hit with a light comedy called *Otoko wa tsurai yo (It's Tough Being a Man)* in 1969. From then on, the studio churned out two films per year detailing the romantic misadventures of the lovable Tora-san until the star, Atsumi Kiyoshi, died in 1996.

Serious Japanese cinema was kept alive in the 1980s through independent productions, mostly comedy films which tended to have more critical respect abroad than commercial clout at home. Directors such as Itami Juzo with *Ososhiki* (*The Funeral*, 1985) and *Tampopo* (1986) and Morita Yoshimitsu with *Kazoku Geemu* (*The Family Game*, 1984) appealed to overseas audiences with satire and dark humor by showing the Japanese family system under stress. Meanwhile, younger directors like Kurosawa Kiyoshi and Suo Masayuki were cutting their teeth on comic variations of *roman-poruno* and classical Japanese cinema with films such as Kurosawa's *Do-re-mi-fa-musume no chi wa sawagu* (*The Excitement of the Do-Re-Mi Fa Girl*, 1985) and Suo's *Hentai kazoku: Aniki no yomesan* (*Crazy Family*, 1983). Though often distributed by a major studio, these works owed nothing in style and spirit to the often plodding, formulaic films that passed for mainstream Japanese cinema at the time.

Japanese Cinema in the 1990s

One man deserves much of the credit for returning Japanese cinema to the limelight in the 1990s: Kitano Takeshi, better known as "Beat" Takeshi. A popular television personality, "Beat" Takeshi made his film debut in Oshima Nagisa's *Merry Christmas, Mr. Lawrence* (1983) and continues to act in numerous films, including Oshima's more recent, *Gohatto* (2000). It is, however, the films that he directs that demonstrated the possibility of an original and major voice emerging in Japanese cinema. Violent police or *yakuza* (gangster) films dominate his output (*Sonatine*, 1993; *Hana-bi*, 1997), but he is also capable of dealing sensitively with young people (*Kids Return*, 1996; *Kikujiro*, 1999). If he—along with Imamura Shohei, the 1960s director who has maintained his importance—is a major figure in Japanese cinema today, he is not alone in his impressive output or his interest in violence, loss, and youthful alienation.

A sense of extreme alienation, whether manifested in schizophrenia, murder, or in the death of a young person by disease or suicide, permeates much of the best Japanese cinema of the 1990s and early years of the twenty-first century. This thematic link is also manifested by stylistic similarities primarily revolving around the long take, an uninterrupted, unedited run of the camera, creating single shots. In films as seemingly diverse as *Maborosi* (Koreeda Hirokazu, 1995), *Suzaku* (Kawase Naomi, 1997), *Okaeri* (Shinozaki Makoto, 1996), *Unagi* (*The Eel*, Imamura Shohei, 1997), *Tokyo Yakyoku* (Ichikawa Jun, 1997), *M/Other* (Suwa Nobuhiro, 1999), *Charisma* (Kurosawa Kiyoshi, 1999), and *Eureka* (Aoyoma Shinji, 2000), the canny use of long takes lends emotional depth and stylistic beauty to recent Japanese films dealing with loss, betrayal, and incomprehensible grief.

To counterbalance the long-shot, long-take style, another group of young Japanese directors has appeared with crime films and thrillers in the pulp-fiction mode, creating stylish bullet-ballets that compare with films made by the likes of Quentin Tarantino and John Woo. These directors, including Takashi Miike (*Audition*, 1999; *City of Lost Souls*, 2000), Tsukamoto Shinya (*Tokyo Fist*, 1995; *Bullet Ballet*, 1998), and Tanaka Hiroyuki, working under the pen name of Sabu (*Dangan Runner*, 1996; *Postman Blues*, 1999), have pushed Japanese aesthetics into the MTV-age.

Films with styles somewhere between the austere and the frenetic, such as Suo's *Shall We Dance* (1996), or the veteran director Fukasaku Kinji's controversial *Battle Royale* (2000), have also helped to return Japanese cinema to box office success at home and abroad and to achieve the kind of critical acclaim that films of the 1950s and 1960s received. *Anime* films like *Akira* (1988) and *Mononoke hime* (*Princess Mononoke*, 1997) draw domestic box office numbers unseen in a generation and appeal to worldwide audiences, as well.

In short, the range of subjects, themes, and styles apparent in Japanese cinema of the 1990s and beyond indicates that Japan's cinema continues to reveal the complexity and artistry of Japanese culture as a whole. Youthful alienation and Japan's increasingly multicultural society are likely to remain potent subjects for a newly vibrant Japanese cinema.

David Desser

Further Reading

Anderson, Joseph L., and Donald Richie. (1982) *The Japanese Film: Art and Industry*. Expanded ed. Princeton, NJ: Princeton University Press.

Broderick, Mick, ed. (1996) *Hibakusha Cinema: Hiroshima, Nagasaki, and the Nuclear Image in Japanese Film*. London: Kegan Paul International.

Kinema Club. (1999) "Welcome to Kinema Club." Retrieved 14 November 2001, from: http://pears.lib.ohio-state.edu/Markus/Welcome.html

Napier, Susan J. (2000) *Anime from Akira to Princess Mononoke: Experiencing Contemporary Japanese Animation*. New York: Palgrave.

Nolletti, Arthur, and David Desser, eds. (1992) *Reframing Japanese Cinema: Authorship, Genre, History*. Bloomington, IN: Indiana University Press.

Prince, Stephen. (1999) *The Warrior's Camera: The Cinema of Akira Kurosawa*. Rev. and expanded ed. Princeton, NJ: Princeton University Press.

Schilling, Mark. (1999) *Contemporary Japanese Film*. New York: Weatherhill.

CIRCASSIANS The Circassians (Cerkes in Russian and the Turkic languages or Adygea in the Circassian language) are a people of the northwestern Caucasus and northeastern Black Sea region whose languages belong to the Northwest Caucasian family, a non-Indo-European group. Beginning in the thirteenth century, the Circassians were under the nominal control of the Golden Horde and were a major source of slaves for the armies and households of the Islamic world. This trade was a principal source of wealth for the khanate of the Golden Horde and later for the khanate of the Crimea through the eighteenth century. With the expansion of the Russian empire in the eighteenth century, Circassian independence became more circumscribed; as a defense against Russian expansion, the Circassians fostered closer ties with the Ottoman empire. This move was no more than a temporary impediment to Russian expansion, but the Ottoman association did encourage a major change in Circassian society: the majority of Circassians accepted Islam. With the Treaty of Adrianople in 1829, the Ottomans ceded control of the region to the Russians; resistance to Russian imperial control assumed a more local color and persisted fiercely until about 1864.

Beginning in the 1850s and dramatically increasing after about 1862, many Circassians left the Caucasus for the Ottoman empire. Some one and one-half million Circassians are estimated to have fled to Ottoman territory before 1914. Most originally settled in the Balkans. Eventually, however, they settled mainly in Anatolia and the Ottoman province of Syria.

Today sizable Circassian populations are found in Syria, Jordan, Israel, and Turkey as well as in the republic of Georgia and the Russian Federation. Although the population figures offered here are only rough estimates, more than half of all Circassians presently live outside their homeland. Approximately 500,000 live in Georgia and Russia combined; up to one million live in Turkey, approximately 50,000 in Syria, 30,000 in Jordan, and 2,000 in Israel. These diaspora populations exhibit significant diversity. In Turkey, they largely assimilated into the general population, while the Circassians in Jordan play a notable role in public affairs and commerce and maintain a distinct sense of Circassian identity.

Howard Eissenstat

This illustration shows Circassians migrating to Turkey from Russia to escape persecution in the nineteenth century. (BETTMANN/CORBIS)

Further Reading

Jaimoukha, Amjad. (2001) *The Circassians: A Handbook*. Surrey, U.K.: Curzon Press.

Steny, Shami. (1995) "Disjuncture in Ethnicity: Negotiating Circassian Identity in Jordan, Turkey, and the Caucasus." *New Perspectives in Turkey* 12: 72–95.

CITIZEN'S MOVEMENT

The Japanese citizen's movement (*shimin undo*) was mobilized in the 1950s and early 1960s to oppose nuclear weapons, the United States-Japan security treaty, and the Vietnam War. At this time, citizens' groups joined left-wing students, labor, and socialist organizations to combat the conservative ruling party's decisions on social and political issues. Later in the 1960s, people's concerns turned to the industrial pollution and environmental destruction caused by economic development. Industrial poisoning incidents, such as the Minamata (mid-1950s) and Niigata (1964–1965) mercury poisonings, the Toyama cadmium pollution (1955), and the Yokkaichi asthma outbreaks (1961), led to lawsuits, which in turn forced the government to introduce victims' compensation. Movements organized by ordinary people such as fishermen, farmers, and peasants (*jumin undo*) also dealt with such issues and attempted to prevent the establishment of new polluting industrial plants. In 1964, these actions stopped a planned heavy chemical complex in Mishima and Numazu on the Pacific coast.

Many more such legal actions occurred from 1967 to 1973. By this time, the term *jumin undo* was used interchangeably with *shimin undo* throughout Japan. Citizen-action groups played a decisive role in changing Japan's environmental policy and were responsible for the Basic Law for Pollution Control in 1967, its revision in 1970, and the 1971 establishment of the Environmental Agency. In the 1970s, farmers protested the construction of Narita Airport in Chiba prefecture, and citizens opposed the development of the *shinkansen* (bullet train), because of its environment impact, such as noise and vibration. In the 1980s, housewives demonstrated about consumer issues such as prices and product quality.

The antinuclear movement in Japan had developed rapidly after the end of the U.S. occupation, and it was reinforced in the 1980s by the strong antinuclear and nuclear-freeze protests that spread throughout Europe, the United States, and the South Pacific. Since the 1990s, protests in Japan have concerned such issues as the construction of industrial waste dumpsites, nuclear power plants, and dams and the relocation of U.S. military bases.

Nathalie Cavasin

Further Reading

Broadbent, Jeffrey. (1998) *Environmental Politics in Japan: Networks of Power and Protest*. New York: Cambridge University Press.

Hoye, Timothy. (1998) *Japanese Politics: Fixed and Floating Worlds*. Upper Saddle River, NJ: Prentice Hall.

McKean, Margaret A. (1981) *Environmental Protest and Citizen Politics in Japan*. Berkeley and Los Angeles: University of California Press.

CIVIL-SERVICE EXAMINATION—CHINA

China's examination system started during the Han dynasty (206 BCE–220 CE) and continued until it was abolished by the dowager empress Cixi (1835–1908) in 1905. By the Qing dynasty (1644–1912), the civil-service examination had become the traditional method for recruiting civil servants in China, and this practice was eventually adopted by numerous countries throughout the world.

In traditional China, the concept of a state ruled by people of ability and virtue was an outgrowth of Confucian philosophy, which was concerned with benevolent rulers and rulership. The civil-service examination was an attempt to recruit people on the basis of merit rather than of family or political connections. Since success in the examination system was the basis of people's social status, education became highly regarded as the key to success. The Confucian classics were the texts studied for the examinations.

During the Tang dynasty (618–907), the system was reorganized in an effort to promote efficiency. In the Song dynasty (960–1279), the system again underwent changes, this time to address concerns that the examinations emphasized memorization rather than practical application. Wang Anshi (1021–1086), the prime minister responsible for the reform, stressed the importance of understanding the underlying ideas and being able to apply classical insights to contemporary issues.

Although only a small percentage of those who studied for the examinations could gain office, students spent twenty to thirty years memorizing orthodox commentaries in preparation for a series of as many as eight examinations for the highest degree of civil-service rank.

By the end of the nineteenth century, the examination system had come to be regarded as outdated and inadequate training for officials who faced the task of modernizing China. In addition, students who dropped out often became figures of rebellion in Chinese society. For instance, Hong Xiuquan (1814–1864), who took the examination many times, became a key figure in the disastrous Taiping Rebellion (1850–1864) directed against the Qing government, which Hong hoped to replace with his heavenly kingdom (Taiping); the rebellion failed, and more than 20 million people may have lost their lives in the fighting.

Despite these facts, the examination system has some strong points. Chinese rulers found that the system provided them with an objective and institutionalized method of recruiting loyal government officials. Theoretically, almost all Chinese, regardless of social background, could take the examinations. Today, civil-service examinations in Japan, the United States, and European countries are strongly influenced by the Chinese examination model.

Unryu Suganuma

Further Reading

Elman, Benjamin A. (2000) *A Cultural History of Civil Examinations in Late Imperial China.* Berkeley and Los Angeles: University of California Press.

Miyazaki, Ichisada. (1976) *China's Examination Hell.* Trans. by Conrad Schirokauer. New Haven. CT: Yale University Press.

CIVIL WAR OF 1956–1975—LAOS

Laos's civil war of 1956–1975 was a struggle for power among three factions: the leftist Pathet Lao, the neutralists, and the U.S.-backed right wing. Moderate Souvanna Phouma (1901–1984) was elected premier in the post-independence election of 1956. Souvanna initiated negotiations with the Pathet Lao to reach a peaceful resolution to the conflict. The outcome was the formation of a coalition government installed in 1957. The United States halted its aid to Laos, finding the Communists in the government intolerable. The right retaliated by removing Souvanna from office and arresting Prince Souphanouvong (1909–1995), the leader of the Pathet Lao, and other Pathet Lao members in 1959, dissolving the coalition government. U.S. aid increased, and agencies such as the U.S. Central Intelligence Agency began covert activities in Laos, including the mobilization of the Hmong and other ethnic minorities as a secret army. At the same time, the guerrilla-warfare activities of the Pathet Lao, headquartered in northeastern Laos, grew with the help of North Vietnam.

In 1960, an army captain named Kong Le seized control of the capital, demanding neutrality and returning Souvanna Phouma to power. However, the right quickly overthrew Kong Le, forcing him, Souvanna, and their supporters to flee the capital. The United States backed Prince Boun Oum as the new leader of Laos.

In an attempt to find a peaceful resolution to the war, a second Geneva conference was convened in

A parade in Vientiane in December 1980 marks the fifth anniversary of the end of the civil war and the establishment of the People's Democratic Republic of Laos. (TIM PAGE/CORBIS)

1961. The outcome was the second coalition government of 1962, which had failed by 1964. Souvanna continued as prime minister but held no real power due to U.S. interference. Fighting continued with neither side making any real gains until 1970. The United States began to withdraw its aid, which supported the right wing and thus prolonged the war, in the early 1970s under pressure from U.S. public sentiment.

Both sides began talks to resolve their differences and signed the Agreement on the Restoration of Peace and Reconciliation in Laos, calling for a cease-fire and removal of foreign troops, in 1973. Souvanna remained prime minister in the third coalition government, while Souphanouvong led the National Political Consultative Council. After the Communist takeovers in Saigon and Phnom Penh in 1975, anti-U.S. and anti-rightist demonstrations were held in Vientiane. King Sisa Vatthana abdicated, and Souvanna Phouma resigned. On 2 December 1975, the Pathet Lao gained complete control of the government through the use of military force and established the People's Democratic Republic of Laos. Souphanouvong became president, while the king and the former prime minister served for a time as political advisers to the socialist regime, thus ending the Communist thirty-year struggle.

Linda McIntosh

Further Reading

Hamilton-Merritt, June. (1993) *Tragic Mountains: The Hmong, the Americans, and the Secret Wars of Laos, 1942–1992*. Bloomington, IN: Indiana University Press.

Robbins, Christopher. (1987) *The Ravens: Pilots of the Secret War of Laos*. New York: Crown.

Stuart-Fox, Martin. (1997) *A History of Laos*. Cambridge, U.K.: Cambridge University Press.

CLIFFORD, HUGH (1866–1941), colonial administrator of Malaya. Hugh Charles Clifford, one of the most outstanding colonial administrators of Malaya, had a deep understanding and affection for the Malays. Born in England and educated at Woburn Park, in 1883 he qualified for Sandhurst with a Queen's cadetship, but instead joined the administration of the western peninsular Malay state of Perak.

Clifford became British Agent (1887–1888) and was Resident from 1896 to 1899, and again in 1901. He also held high colonial posts in North Borneo, Trinidad, Ceylon, Ghana, and Nigeria before returning to Malaya as Governor and High Commissioner (1927–1929). But the country was suffering the collapse of rubber and tin prices and the onset of the Great Depression, and Clifford himself was gravely tired. He later suffered a mental breakdown and had to retire in 1930.

Clifford was forthright and impetuous, sympathetic to the peasantry but highly critical of the traditional Malay political structure that he felt victimized the lower classes. He was a prolific writer, and his novel *A Prince of Malaya* (1926) was reprinted in 1989 as *Saleh: A Prince of Malaya*.

Ooi Keat Gin

Further Reading

Aruna, Gopinath. (1991) *Pahang 1880–1933: A Political History*. Kuala Lumpur, Malaysia: Malaysian Branch of the Royal Asiatic Society.

Allen, J. de V. (1964) "Two Imperialists: A Study of Sir Frank Swettenham and Sir Hugh Clifford." *Journal of the Malaysian Branch of the Royal Asiatic Society* 37, 1: 31–73.

Clifford, Hugh. (1897) *In Court and Kampong, Being Tales and Sketches of Native Life in the Malay Peninsula*. London: Grant Richards.

———. ([1926] 1989) *A Prince of Malaya*. New York: Harper. Reprinted as *Saleh: A Prince of Malaya*. Singapore: Oxford University Press.

Gailey, Henry A. (1982) *Clifford: Imperial Proconsul*. London: Collings.

Gullick, J. M. (1992) *Rulers and Residents: Influence and Power in the Malay States, 1870–1920*. Kuala Lumpur, Malaysia: Oxford University Press.

Linehan, W. (1973) *A History of Pahang*. Kuala Lumpur, Malaysia: Malaysian Branch of the Royal Asiatic Society, Reprint No. 2.

Stockwell, A. J. (1976) "Sir Hugh Clifford's Early Career (1866–1903) as Told from His Private Papers." *Journal of the Malaysian Branch of the Royal Asiatic Society* 49, 1: 89–112.

CLIMATOLOGY—SOUTH ASIA In South Asia climate is governed by the tropical monsoon system. The monsoons occur in summer and winter and are variable over space and time.

Monsoons

Because of atmospheric circulation, the monsoon over South Asia alternates seasonally between equatorial westerlies in summer and trade winds (tropical easterlies) in winter, which are mostly deflected to southwesterlies and northeasterlies at ground level. Both flows vary in rain capacity. The southwesterlies are associated with moist and unstable air masses of great rain-carrying capacity; the northeasterlies are comparably dry, stable, continental airflows with little rain-carrying capacity. In most areas the summer monsoon defines the rainy season and the winter monsoon the dry season. The duration of either season varies depending on the region, as do rainfall totals. The summer monsoon is the major agricultural season; winter agriculture depends on irrigation, which is widely used throughout South Asia.

For South Asia the monsoon climate system defines on average four seasons: summer, from June through September; winter, from December through February; and two transition seasons, March through May (premonsoon) and October through November (postmonsoon). The onset of the summer monsoon may vary by several weeks or may even fail, upsetting the agricultural calendar and causing famine. It generally starts between late May in the south to early July in the north, and withdraws between mid-September and early December from north to south, varying in length, therefore, from six to three months. It affects rainfall throughout South Asia. The winter monsoon is a continental flow that establishes a dry season.

Rainfall

The striking seasonal nature of rainfall over South Asia is illustrated by computing the monthly distribution of rainfall through the year for 306 representative stations throughout India for a 120-year recording period (1871–1990). The monthly and seasonal rainfall totals are as follows, given in millimeters:

Dec.	Jan.	Feb.	Mar.	Apr.	May
12	11	13	15	26	52
winter		36	pre-monsoon		93

June	July	Aug.	Sept.	Oct.	Nov.
163	275	243	171	77	31
summer			852	post-monsoon	108

Seventy-eight percent of the annual total of 1,089 millimeters of rain falls during summer, and only 3 percent during winter; the transition seasons have 8.5 percent (premonsoon) and 10 percent (postmonsoon). Hence rainfall other than during the four months of summer is negligible.

In practice, however, rainfall varies to a hazardous degree over South Asia. The world's record rainfall total, at Cherrapunji (located in the Shillong Hills of Assam), averages an annual 10,798 millimeters, with the wettest year being 24,000 millimeters. In extreme contrast, desert conditions occur over most of the Indus plain and Tharr Desert (where in some locations annual rainfall is less than 100 millimeters). The overall distribution of rainfall shows the wettest parts over the western coastal lowlands on the Indian peninsula and its eastern provinces on the Deccan plateau, the Ganges plains, Brahmaputra lowlands, and surrounding parts of northeastern India and the Bengali lowlands. The driest regions are northwestern India and Pakistan. In most parts of South Asia annual rainfalls vary between 750 and 1,500 millimeters, enough to support abundant crop cultivation in the rainy season.

The high interannual variability of rainfall makes monsoon rains unreliable for agriculture. Interannual variability is largest in dry regions, with a coefficient above 30 percent, and lowest in the wettest parts. with less than 15 percent variability.

Rainfall annual totals have changed over the years on a small scale. The maximum annual rainfall increase during the past one hundred years (588 millimeters) occured at Bombay; the maximum decrease (679 millimeters) occurred at Nuwara Eliya, Sri Lanka. In South Asia low rainfall occurs during El Niño years and high rainfall during La Niña years.

Under the prevailing hot and warm conditions large amounts of water are evaporating at all times. Only during the summer monsoon is a rain surplus observed; that is, more water falls as rain than is evaporated. In all other seasons evaporation exceeds rainfall.

Temperatures

Temperatures also vary greatly over South Asia, though tropical temperatures principally prevail. Shown by a cross section from north to south, mean annual temperatures are high. The mean hottest (summer) month shows only slight variation across South Asia, while there is considerable difference in the temperature mean for the coldest (winter) month. The annual temperature range (the difference in temperature between the hottest and coldest month) increases with latitude. Winter and summer are therefore defined only over the northern parts of South Asia, while the southern parts have only slight annual temperature variation. Synchronously, as one moves south, the daily range of temperature also decreases, yet the daily temperature range surpasses the annual temperature range, a characteristic of tropical conditions. Temperature drops with increasing altitude, leading to freezing temperatures in the highlands (above 2,000 meters) of Sri Lanka and South India. The altitudinal decrease of temperature most strikingly affects the Himalayas and Karakoram mountains above 1,500 meters, where precipitation occurs as snow and ice. The affect of global temperature change on South Asia is discussed in the final paragraph.

Rainfall and temperature variabilities over space and time are summarized by climate diagrams in which annual variations in both elements are plotted month to month. Changes in rainfall and temperature in most cases occur synchronously, such that summer is both wet and hot, while winter is dry and cold.

Floods and Cyclones

South Asia suffers from floods and droughts that originate from heavy rainfalls and failure of monsoon rains, respectively. The worst hazards are tropical cyclones, which originate in the Andaman Sea, move in a western direction, and three to five times a year visit the lowlands on the east coasts of India and Bangladesh. Tropical cyclones develop extremely heavy storms moving at over 200 kilometers per hour; they are accompanied by torrential rainfalls and high sea waves, which wreak havoc on the coast and in the hinterlands.

Resulting mostly from the rainfall conditions and to a smaller extent from snow precipitation on the northern fringe of South Asia and the Himalayas, river runoff is subject to extreme variations. The maximum flow is mainly in summer, the minimum in winter. The contrasting discharges of the Himalayan rivers are illustrated by the Brahmaputra at Pandu, with a maximum flood discharge over 70,000 cubic millimeters per second and a minimum at 3,000 cubic millimeters per second. The rivers of peninsular India also show great variation, with the Mahanadi having a maximum of 46,000 cubic millimeters per second and a minimum of only 6 cubic millimeters per second. In summer the rivers regularly inundate the land along their lower stretches, particularly the deltaic regions. Control of river discharge, by dikes and dams, is a major task on all rivers.

Global Temperature Change

Observations during the past one hundred years identify a warming trend over the northern, eastern, central, and southern parts of South Asia, which partly exceeds the global trend (0.55° C per 100 years), whereas a cooling trend prevails over the western and northwestern parts. Both trends show maximum values of 1.2° C. Both temperature increase and decrease are determined by the temperature trend during winter.

Manfred Domrös

Further Reading

Müller, M. J. (1996) *Handbuch ausgewählter Klimastationen der Erde* (Manual of Selected Climate Stations of the Earth). 5th ed. Trier, Germany: Universität Trier, Forschungsstelle Bodenerosion 5.

CLOISONNÉ

Cloisonné is a technique employed in the decorative arts whereby pulverized multicolored glass or enamel is fused onto a metal surface; the enamel is held in wire cells (from the French, *cloisons*). The technique came to China from the West in the fourteenth century (or earlier) and reached its height in the early Ming dynasty (1368–1644) under the rule of the Jingtai emperor (1428–1457). In fact, one of the terms by which cloisonné is known in China is *Jingtai lan*. Other names for cloisonné tell of the technique's foreign origins: a Ming text states that cloisonné came to China from Da Shi (Arabia) and Folang (Byzantium), thus yielding the names *dashi yao*, Arabian ware, and *falan* or *falang*, likely a corruption of the Chinese name for Byzantium.

Cloisonné enameling uses cells formed from slender metal wires to hold the enamel paste. These wires become part of the overall design of the piece and are soldered onto a metal foundation. The enamel paste is added to the cells, and the piece is fired at a temperature high enough to fuse the paste without destroying the metal cells or the foundation. Pieces often need to be fired a second time to correct any flaws in the enamel and to fill up the cells. The piece is then polished with a pumice stone to smooth the surface and increase its luster.

The earliest pieces carrying a reign mark date from the fifteenth-century reign of the Xuande emperor (1399–1435). The usual colors of these early pieces are a distinctive turquoise blue, a lapis lazuli blue, deep brown-red, yellow, green, black, and white. (A true pink was not seen until the famille rose palette was developed for porcelains in the early eighteenth century.) The pieces are strikingly simple in both shape and decoration. One characteristic of Ming cloisonné is the presence in the enamels of the solder used to hold the metal wires to the base. This was remedied in the late seventeenth or early eighteenth century by the use of vegetable glues, which burned away in the heat of the firing.

During the Qing dynasty (1644–1912), production of cloisonné wares increased due to the establishment under the Kangxi emperor (1654–1722) in 1680 of imperial palace workshops. It has been said that the aesthetic quality of pieces during this time suffered in the quest for technical perfection. This was especially true during the reign of the Qianlong emperor (1711–1799), when the wires were gilded, designs were complex and busy, and frequent firings dulled the finish. Despite the technical achievements of the eighteenth century, fifteenth-century pieces remain a high point of the enameler's art.

Catherine Pagani

Further Reading

Brinker, Helmut, and Albert Lutz. (1989) *Chinese Cloisonné: The Pierre Uldry Collection*. New York: The Asia Society Galleries.

Garner, Harry M. (1962) *Chinese and Japanese Cloisonné Enamels*. Rutland, VT: Charles E. Tuttle.

Jenyns, R. Soame. (1980) "Cloisonné and Champlevé Enamels on Copper." In *Chinese Art II*, edited by R. Soame Jenyns and William Watson. New York: Rizzoli, 105–142.

CLOTHING, TRADITIONAL—AFGHANISTAN Traditionally, Afghan dress reflects ethnic diversity and the socio-cultural, historical, and geopolitical dynamics of the region. The country and its people are positioned at the crossroads between the Arab, Persian, Turkish, and Asian empires. Consequently, Afghan dress shows strong aesthetic connections to areas contiguous to its borders: the Arab and Islamic Middle East and Persia, the Turkish Ottoman Empire, and, to a lesser degree, Mughal India.

Since the 1920s, Afghanistan's leaders, in an effort to maintain control of both human and natural resources, have struggled with the definition of women's rights and independence as exemplified in the propriety of dress. Afghan dress also reflects other aspects of identity in a variety of inseparable yet interrelated ways: gendered and generational status; religious affiliation; rural and urban differences; stages of the life cycle; and everyday or special occasions.

Afghan dress first and foremost distinguishes gender. Women customarily wear four items of dress: the pants *(tombaan)*, an overdress *(parahaan)*, a head covering *(chaadar)*, and footwear *(payzaar)*. This ensemble is referred to as *kalaa Afghani*, or Afghan women's dress. Men wear *tombaan*, an overshirt *(payraan)*, a hat or cap *(kullaa)*, and footwear or boots. In addition to this basic ensemble, Afghan men wear a vest *(waaskaat)*, another hat *(pokool)*, and a shawl *(shaal)* during colder seasons.

Women's *tombaan* are made of approximately two yards of cotton or silk-like rayon or acetate fabric. They are usually solid white, gathered drawstring pants with full legs. Frequently the pant cuffs are decorated with white machine- or hand-embroidered patterns. The *parahaan* are typically made from five yards of cotton, silk (or silk-like acetate), and plain or satin woven fabrics in bright colors (for young women) and darker colors (for older women), usually in tone-on-tone or floral patterns. Necklines vary but usually are rounded; occasionally pointed collars are added, as are gathered set-in sleeves with fitted or buttoned cuffs. Dress skirts are full and gathered at the waist and worn mid-calf length. *Chaadars* are made of similar fabrics—usually rectangular pieces of lightweight cotton or silk-like crepe, woven with machine- or hand-embroidered edges. Men's *tombaan* and *payraan* feature fewer decorative details and are typically in natural-colored cotton fabric. *Kulla* exhibit the most variety in shapes, colors, and embroidered patterns.

Dress also differentiates the age and generational status of the wearer. For example, though all females wear pants, overdress, and head and foot coverings, aesthetic characteristics vary according to age throughout women's lives. More costly materials and surface design embellishments are added to women's dowries. The decorative focus is on pants cuffs, dress bodices, and head covering borders as females age and gain more status when they become engaged, marry, and become mothers. These differences are evident to a lesser degree in men's dress as well. Shirtsleeves, bodice shirtfronts, and hats are embroidered in regional and ethnic patterns by either their betrothed or wife.

Two items of dress are worth mentioning since they are the most visible to non-Afghans and are the most politically recognizable dress that Afghans wear. The *pokool* hat worn by Afghan men is a symbol of the Afghan freedom fighters, or the *Mujahideen*. It is a naturally colored wool hat with the characteristic versatile rolled edge. The second distinctive item of dress worn by Afghans is the woman's full body covering known as the *chaadaree*. The *chaadaree*, constructed of nine to ten yards of fabric with an embroidered face piece, conceals the entire women's dress ensemble of pants, overdress, and head covering. The original *chaadaree* is of Persian origins but over time became associated with the urban dress of middle and upper class Afghan women. The *chaadaree* has been incorrectly attributed as Afghan women's traditional dress; it only became mandated women's wear after dress sanctions were imposed by the Taliban in 1996.

Afghan dress also suggests religious affiliation. The majority of Afghans are Muslim, and presumed Islamic prescriptions of propriety and observance govern the manner in which items of dress are worn. For example, Islamic prescriptions govern the fit, transparency, and drape of dress. In general, the everyday dress for both males and females fit loosely so that the contours of the body are less noticeable. Prescriptions also determine the patterns embroidered on men's shirts and hats and women's pants, over dresses, and head coverings. The majority of these embroidered designs are floral, geometric, and abstract shapes, presumably because of Islamic prohibitions on representational art and aesthetics.

Afghan dress is also notable for its embroidery. Embroidery styles tend to be associated with geographic regions and ethnic groups. Whether from

Herat, Kandahar, or Kabul, regional associations are made. Styles generally are distinguishable by the fiber content of the fabric (plain weave cottons, pile woven velvets, or synthetic satin weaves) as well as the kind of thread (cotton, silk or gold metallic threads); a variety of embroidery techniques and the complexity of their execution; the floral and geometric motifs; and the design placement of the embroidery. Three such embroidery styles are the gold stitched embroidery or *chirma dozi*, known for the unique kind of metallic thread and braid used; *tashamaar dozi*, recognizable by the intricate counted stitch technique; and silk stitched flower embroidery or *gul dozi*, distinctive because of the rich use of colored threads.

Afghan dress observed in the context of daily life and during special occasions of secular and religious contexts distinguishes gender and generational, ethnic and regional, and religious identity. Dress serves to unify and maintain a sense of Afghan identity not only among Afghans living in Afghanistan, but also as Afghans differentiate themselves from other Middle Eastern and Central and South Asian populations in the Afghan diaspora.

Catherine Daly

Further Reading

Burhan E. and T. Gouttierre. (1983) *Dari for Foreigners*. Omaha, NE: Center for Afghanistan Studies.

Daly, M. Catherine. (2001) "The Afghan Woman's Chaadaree: An Evocative Religious Expression. In *Undressing Religion: Commitment and Conversion from a Cross Cultural Perspective*, edited by L. Boynton. Oxford: Berg Publishers, 131–145.

Dupaigne, Bernard. (1993) *Afghan Embroidery*. Lahore, Pakistan: Ferozsons Ltd.

Dupree, Louis. (1980) *Afghanistan*. Princeton, NJ: Princeton University Press.

Dupree, Nancy. (1992) "Clothing Afghanistan." In *Encyclopaedia Iranica*, edited by E. Yarshater. Costa Mesa, CA: Mazda Publishers.

CLOTHING, TRADITIONAL—BHUTAN

In 1989 the Tshogdu, or National Assembly, of Bhutan announced that all Bhutanese citizens must wear the appropriate national dress in all public areas. For men in Bhutan, the traditional dress is a robe known as the *go;* women's traditional costume is a wraparound garment called the *kira*. Accounts, both written and pictorial, suggest that until around the seventeenth century the prevalent male dress was different from the current dress. The popularization of the *go* is attributed to Shabdrung Ngawang Namgyal (1594–1651), the creator of a unified Bhutan.

History of the National Costume

In 1616 Shabdrung Ngawang Namgyal fled to Bhutan to escape from conflicts in Tibet and by the time of his death in 1651 had not only set the stage for the creation of a unified Bhutan, but also made sweeping changes in the laws and customs. One such change attributed to him is the *go*, which in most respects resembles the Tibetan dress for males. In time the *go* achieved almost universal usage in Bhutan and even came to be recognized as an important element of Bhutan's distinct identity in the region. In contrast, it is believed that the women's dress, the *kira*, has been in use in Bhutan almost unchanged for centuries.

The national costumes of Bhutan have remained the principal choice of attire in Bhutan. By the end of the twentieth century, with the effects of modernization finally being felt, the national costumes gained even more prominence. For a small country surrounded by giant neighbors, the costumes were seen to be attributes that clearly set Bhutan apart from the rest of the region and gave the inhabitants a Bhutanese identity. Concern that such a symbol would inadvertently be discarded along Bhutan's path toward modernization led to considerable debate in the National Assembly of Bhutan as well as among private citizens in the 1980s and continues today. Thus, according to this pronouncement, the *go* and *kira* were formally declared the national costumes of Bhutan for men and women, respectively. This law ignored the existence of several ethnic minorities, each with a unique dress style, inside Bhutan's borders. Fortunately the seemingly radical move of ordering people to wear national costume was mitigated during its implementation and did not lead to the prosecution of ethnic minorities who wore their own dress in public. The affected minorities were mostly the Westernized Bhutanese youth, who preferred to follow the latest Western trends, and the ethnic Nepalese, who preferred to wear their own traditional costume. Western attire and Nepalese costumes were both considered foreign. The vast majority of Bhutanese were largely unaffected by this law since they already wore the national costumes. Strong calls for continuing the dress code have persisted unabated in the National Assembly.

Women's Dress

Traditional dress for women consists of the *kira*, *kera*, *koma*, *wonju*, *toego*, and petticoat. The *kira* is a large piece of woven cloth that is wrapped around the body in a series of folds. It is worn over a blouse, or *wonju*, and a cotton petticoat. Body-length petticoats are known as *gutsum*, and petticoats from the waist down to the ankle are called *meyo*. Wrapping the *kira* is a complex process: with the *kira* behind the woman, she brings one corner from behind her left shoulder. Wrapping the other end from her right side, she hooks it with the corner by using a *koma*, a two-part brooch with a connecting chain. She then turns the *kira* around until the edges reach her right side, loops it back to her left, and draws it behind to her right shoulder. The two ends are again hooked together with the other end of the *koma*. The resulting pleats are adjusted until they are even, and the dress is fastened at the waist with a belt known as a *kera*. A jacket or *toego* is worn over this. Cuffs are formed by folding the *wonju's* sleeves back over the sleeves of the *toego*. Tying the *kera* creates a pouch in the fabric above it, which is used as an ample pocket to keep anything from money to snacks. Ordinary women and villagers were expected to wear their *kira* ankle length; the nobility and wives of senior officials wore it to the ground, a practice that continues in rural areas.

Men's Dress

For men, the traditional *go* is a robelike dress that extends down to the toes. It is worn over a simple inner shirt known as a *toego* (not to be confused with the women's *toego*). The right half of the *go* is tucked inside the left, and then both ends are raised to around knee level, from where they are folded back to form symmetrical pleats. The garment is fastened by tying the *kera* around the waist. As with the women's dress, folding back the sleeves of the *toego* over the sleeves of the *go* forms the cuffs.

Three aspects of wearing a *go* traditionally reflected the wearer's station in society: the height of the *go*, the length of the cuffs, and the extent of exposure of the *toego* at the collar. Nobility, senior government officials, and members of the religious order generally wore their *go* below the knees. Everyone else wore a *go* that fell above the knee. Similarly, only the elite were permitted to display long cuffs and expose a considerable amount of the *toego* at the collar. By the 1990s however, through social custom, the increasing number of wealthy "commoners" made this distinguishing feature disappear.

Accessories

Most Bhutanese men carry a dagger known as a *dozom* in their *go*. It is a multiutility item whose use ranges from peeling betel nuts, to cooking, to self-defense. Other accessories are used for formal occasions, however. A *kabne* is a long scarf worn when visiting government offices and temples and when meeting senior officials. It is the traditional mark of rank, with the color determining rank. Ordinary people wear a white *kabne;* senior officials wear red, which can be awarded only by the king. Ministers wear an orange *kabne*, and those of the king and the head of the religious body, the Je Khempo, are saffron. People in the military, when wearing the national costume, wear a shoulder sash for the same purpose. Women wear a *rachu*, a woven sash worn on the shoulder, though here there is no distinction of colors to mark rank. On formal occasions, the attire for men requires the traditional boot known as *dalham*, a knee-high boot made of cloth and embroidered with decorations. Senior officials who wear a red scarf and higher must wear the traditional sword known as the *pata* on the right hip.

The textiles with which the *go* and *kira* are made are an important aspect of the national costumes. The different patterns, each with distinctive names, bring the *kira* to life and set the *go* significantly apart from its original form in Tibet. Bhutanese textiles are artistic and cultural assets that are also quickly finding markets outside Bhutan.

Other Ethnic Costumes

In addition to the national dress, other ethnic costumes are worn in Bhutan. The Doya men of southwestern Bhutan wear a dress known as the *pakhi*, a simple wrapped, sleeveless, knee-length garment belted at the waist. Women wear a similar garment that is closer to ankle length. European travelers to Bhutan in the eighteenth century reported that a dress similar to the *pakhi* was in use at the time.

Among the pastoral communities of the northeastern parts of Merak and Sakteng, the men wear thick jackets of yak wool with rawhide jackets over them. The lower garments are leather trousers belted at the waist, over which thick woolen shorts known as *kango* are worn. The women are dressed similarly, except that instead of shorts they wear a sleeveless tunic or *shinkha*, which extends to the knees and is belted at the waist. The pastoralists of Laya wear tunics and garments made of woven yak wool as well, which distinguish them considerably from the rest of the country. Among the Nepali-speaking minorities in the south of Bhutan, the dress is the same as is worn in Nepal. Similarly, the ethnic Tibetans settled in Bhutan wear traditional Tibetan dresses.

Karma L. Dorji

See also: **Textiles—Bhutan**

Further Reading

Collister, Peter. (1987) *Bhutan and the British*. London: Serindia.

Myers, Diana K., and Susan S. Bean, eds. (1994) *From the Land of the Thunder Dragon: Textile Arts of Bhutan.* London, Serindia.

CLOTHING, TRADITIONAL—CAMBODIA The intricately patterned ikat silks (silks that whose threads are tie-dyed before being woven) created by the Khmer and Cham ethnic groups may come to mind when thinking of Cambodian textiles, but the peoples of Cambodia have produced many other cotton and silk textiles. Cambodians traditionally considered both domestic and imported textiles to be markers of identity, prestige, and wealth, and quantity and quality of textiles possessed by an individual or family contributed to their status within society.

Traditional dress in Cambodia is similar to traditional dress in neighboring Laos and Thailand. *Sampot* is the lower garment worn by either sex. The *sampot* for urban lower class and peasant women is a tube-skirt (sarong) approximately one and a half meters in length with both ends sewn together and is worn wrapped around the waist and secured with a cloth belt. Women of the middle and upper classes preferred to wear the *sampot chang kben* on a daily basis until the beginning of the twentieth century. This rectangular piece of cloth is approximately three meters long and one meter wide and is worn by first wrapping the cloth around the waist and stretching the ends away from the body. The outstretched ends are then twisted together and pulled between the legs and toward the back. The ends are tucked into the waist at the back, and the *sampot chang kben* is lastly fastened with a cloth or metal belt. Women of all social strata wear the *sampot chang kben* on special occasions such as religious ceremonies and weddings. Men also wear the *sampot chang kben*, but the traditional textile patterns worn by males differ from those worn by females. Traditionally, neither women nor men wore an upper garment. However, when the French colonial presence grew in Cambodia in the late nineteenth century, both men and women began to wear upper garments.

Even after the French presence in Cambodia from the 1860s onwards, Cambodians continued to wear traditional clothing. The Cambodian royalty and government officials combined the shot silk *sampot chang kben* (in the appropriate color for the day of the week) with a formal jacket. In the beginning of the twentieth century, Cambodians adopted forms of western style clothing such as a blouse or shirt. Men more readily adopted trousers as the lower garment for daily use, and both sexes continue to wear the *sampot chang kben* for formal occasions. Lower class and particularly rural women still wear a tube-skirt, but the material may be printed batik-patterned cloth bought at the market rather than hand-woven silk or cotton.

Silk Textiles

The most important silk textiles of Cambodia are the ikat silks *(hol)*, twill-patterned, weft ikat textiles. The pattern is made by tying vegetable or synthetic fibers on sections of the weft threads before the threads are dyed. This process is repeated for different colored dye baths until the patterns are formed and the cloth is woven. The two types of *hol* textiles have five traditional colors: red, yellow, green, blue, and black. The *sampot hol* is the lower garment mentioned earlier, made from *hol* cloth (*hol* cloth can also be used for *sampot chang kben*). The *pidan hol* is a ceremonial hanging reserved for religious or sacred purposes.

The *pidan hol* is an example of excellent craftsmanship. It may be presented to a Buddhist temple or hung it in homes to create sacred space around the family's personal shrine. In a temple this textile is hung behind, above, or around the base of, a Buddha image. The narrative motifs of a *pidan hol* often depict tales of the previous lives of the Buddha.

Cotton Textiles

The various ethnic groups of Cambodia also produce cotton material for religious clothing and other purposes, such as for bedding and for various household textiles. The royal courts also imported Indian chintz with patterns especially for the Southeast Asian market.

The *kroma* is the all-purpose utility cotton cloth used by either men or women throughout the country as a head or neck scarf, belt, or towel. It is also used as a bag to carry things. This rectangular textile has a checkered pattern, usually blue and white or red and white, with striped ends. Political groups such as the Khmer Rouge have used the *kroma* to symbolize membership.

The Cham, an Austronesian group, are highly skilled silk weavers who produce cotton tube-skirts or sarongs for both men and women. Three or four hundred years ago, the Cham reportedly used to produce batiks (wax resist-dyed fabrics) in cotton similar to that of their kin in insular Southeast Asia. Cham women weave a checked or plaid cotton sarong for men. Natural or white cotton is important in Cham religious activities; it is worn by Cham priests and used as a sacred object during religious ceremonies.

Other Mon-Khmer and Austronesian minorities living in the northeastern region of Cambodia weave cotton cloth on back strap looms for clothing and domestic use. The groups of both of these linguistic families weave similar textiles by attaching the warp beam of the back strap loom to a tree or part of a house in order the achieve the lengths of woven material needed for their loincloths.

The male loincloth is approximately 20 to 25 centimeters wide and 3 to 7 meters long. It is indigo blue or black with large red warp stripes and smaller yellow and white warp stripes. Supplementary patterns also decorate the stripes. The ends of the loincloth are patterned with red bands with supplementary patterns of animal or plant motifs. Red tassels and lead, glass, or plastic beading sometimes decorate the edges and ends of the loincloth. Men of the various Mon-Khmer linguistic groups sometimes wear a blanket over a shoulder during rituals, but otherwise do not wear an upper garment. Occasionally, men wear a simple tunic made from plant fibers such as bark cloth or banana leaves. These plant-fiber tunics are reported to have been more common when the technology to weave cotton was not familiar to these groups. It is now rare to find clothing made from these fibers. Men of the Jarai and Ede Austronesian minorities wear a collarless shirt of indigo or black cotton adorned with red yarn or metal beads on special occasions.

Women of the different ethnic minorities wear tube skirts. The long tube-skirt is worn tucked in around the breasts and is made from two pieces of material sewn together to form a tube. The shorter version is made from one piece of cloth sewn into a tube and is worn tucked in at the waist. The color scheme of the women's tube-skirts is similar to that of the men's loincloth. Women either do not wear an upper garment or wear a simple tunic made from a single piece of cloth with a hole cut in the middle of the textile for the head and the sides sewn together leaving open spaces for the arms. Ede women add sleeves to the tunic and decorate them with red yarn and metal beading.

As with other Khmer and Cham ethnicities, the minority groups of northeast Cambodia presently reserve traditional dress for special occasions. Textile production in Cambodia has experienced disruption because of political conflict, particularly during the Khmer Rouge regime of the late 1970s. Textile production increased in the calmer conditions at the beginning of the twenty-first century, encouraged by renewed local and foreign interest in hand-woven textiles, particularly in mastering the dyeing and weaving of the *pidan hol* produced prior to the twentieth century.

Linda S. McIntosh

Further Reading

Kuan, Chou Ta. (1992) *The Customs of Cambodia.* Trans. by Paul Pelliot. Bangkok, Thailand: White Orchid.

Hope, Jonathan. (1997) "Echoes of a Golden Age: Traditional Cambodian Ikat Cloths." *HALI: The International Magazine of Antique Carpet and Textile Art* 90 (January): 74–85.

Howard, Michael C., and Be Kim Nhung. (2000) "Textiles of the Katuic Speaking Peoples of Central Vietnam." *Arts of Asia* 30, 3 (May/June): 131–138.

Maxwell, Robyn. (1990) *Textiles of Southeast Asia: Tradition, Trade, and Transformation.* Melbourne, Australia: Australian National Gallery of Art.

The Institute for Khmer Traditional Textiles (1999). "Institute for Khmer Traditional Textiles." Retrieved 4 September 2001, from: http://www.geocities.co.JP/SilkRoad-Ocean/4148.

CLOTHING, TRADITIONAL—CHINA

Prehistoric clothing in China was constructed from animal skins, furs, and the natural plant fibers hemp, wisteria, and ramie. Shell, bone, and stone ornaments have been discovered in caves and ancient tombs. Bone needles and awls have also been discovered; the discovery of the awl suggests the use of leather for clothing.

Characteristics of Clothing Before Manchu Rule

By the Shang dynasty (1766–1045 BCE), trade and tribute with neighboring regions were well established. Tribute goods included cloth; weaving and dyeing were common during the Shang. The sericulture industry developed, and Chinese silk fabrics were highly prized trade goods. Simple cut-and-sewn garments such as straight, narrow robes, skirts, and trousers were worn during this period. Robes closed to the right, and sleeves were long and covered the hands to show respect. Hair was braided; hairpins were symbols of distinction and rank. Clothing was used to distinguish the stratified social classes.

Clothing continued to be used to maintain a stratified class system in the Zhou dynasty (1045–256 BCE). The *Zhou li* (Book of the Rites of Zhou) included sumptuary laws regulating the use of dress to show rank; the designation of special robes with special symbols worn by the emperor; and the dictate that all garments must close to the right. The usual clothing worn was the long, slim, narrow-sleeved embroidered robe and trousers or skirt. Hats and shoes were symbols of distinction and rank. As Taoism was incorporated into Chinese life, the symbols for the Taoist immortals were frequently embroidered on clothing. These symbols include the fan (life infused into the dead), the bamboo tube (longevity), the magic saber (magic), the pair of castanets (music), the magic gourd (medicine), the flute (harmony), the basket of flowers (longevity), and the lotus flower (purity).

Minority clothing influenced Chinese dress during the Warring States period (475–221 BCE). The *hu fu*, a short jacket and long trousers, was introduced. The *hu fu* was widely adopted throughout China by men and women, particularly those from rural areas. Robe sleeves began widening near the end of this period.

During the Qin (221–206 BCE) and Han dynasties (206 BCE–220 CE), color symbolism was defined and became an important characteristic of ceremonial and ritual robes. Black denoted darkness, dawn, or evening; green or blue was considered the color of creation or life; red meant burning brightly and was the color of the sun and happiness; white was associated with opening, clearing, and cracked ice; and yellow denoted sparkling light and sunshine. These colors also symbolized the universe and the elements: black signified North or water; green or blue indicated East or wood; red symbolized South or fire; white meant West or metal; yellow indicated center or earth. From the *Yi jing* (or *I ching*), red became associated with the masculine concept *(yang)* and blue became associated with the feminine concept *(yin)*. During this period, the one-piece robe was the most popular garment. It was characterized by a straight cut silhouette and large, wide, curved sleeves. Wealth was displayed by type and amount of embellishment and amount of fabric used in the robe. Hats and ribbons continued to denote rank; the texture, color, and size of the silk ribbons were used to distinguish between social classes.

Buddhism reached China by the end of the Han dynasty, and Buddhist symbols were used as embroidery motifs on clothing; these symbols included the parasol (charity), fish (tenacity), the sacred vase (ceremonial), the lotus (purity and marriage), the seashell (appeal to wisdom), the canopy (spiritual authority), and the Wheel of the Law (infinite changing). Toward the end of the Han dynasty, women began to favor a two-piece ensemble consisting of a long, pleated, wraparound skirt and short jacket.

Sui dynasty (581–618 BCE) clothing featured a narrow silhouette. Women continued to wear the jacket and skirt; red became the most popular skirt color. Sleeves could be narrow or wide. A popular nonceremonial robe style that was worn by men was the "band robe." This robe featured a round neckline and a section of fabric sewn to the lower half of the front and back of the robe in a wide, horizontal band. Colors and fabrics continued to be used to indicate the rank of the wearer.

During the Tang dynasty (618–907 CE) Chinese envoys spread Chinese costume throughout Asia, particularly affecting court dress in Japan and Korea. Tang-dynasty dress became fuller and more elaborate than the dress of previous eras. High-ranking men wore a stiff leather hoop belt with decorative plaques, often of jade, gold, or silver.

In the Song dynasty (960–1267 CE) cotton was introduced from India. It became an important textile crop in China for domestic use and foreign export and started to replace indigenous cellulosic fibers used in Chinese clothing. In particular, cotton became widely used in the clothing of the lower classes. Elements of Song dress included large, full robes, with large, wide sleeves. Robes opened down center front or closed to the right. Hoop belts with decorated plaques were also worn.

The tradition of foot binding, which was practiced in China before the Tang, was well established by the Song dynasty. Foot binding was usually characteristic of Han Chinese women (that is, women of the dominant Chinese ethnic group as opposed to women of ethnic minorities) only. Tiny, intricately embroidered shoes, called "lotus slippers" or "lily slippers" became important dress and cultural items.

Under the Mongol Yuan dynasty (1267–1368 CE), trade with other countries was encouraged. The cotton industries were well established. The Mongols considered the Han Chinese inferior but borrowed many Han Chinese dress traditions, such as color symbolism and items denoting rank. Mongols reduced the width of the robe, and introduced the finial, an ornament worn on the top of hats to designate rank.

The Ming dynasty (1368–1644 BCE) was the last Han Chinese dynasty to rule China. Ming means "brilliant" or "glorious," and red was its dynastic color. Sumptuary laws from the Han, Tang, and Song dynasties were reestablished and clothing regulations for all social classes were strictly codified in such documents as the *Ming Hui Dian*. For the upper classes, Ming dress was characterized by extreme width and very long, wide sleeves.

Changes Brought by the Qing

China's final dynasty was ruled by a conquering group of horsemen from the north, the Manchu (1644–1912 CE). The Manchu dynasty took the Chinese name Qing, which means "pure" or "clear." The Manchu instituted new sumptuary laws, many designed to assimilate the Han Chinese into Manchu culture. All Han Chinese men were forced shave their forehead and wear their hair in a long queue (braid) in the Manchu style; those in government positions had to wear Manchu-style garments, namely, one-piece robes with no pleats, sleeves ending in the distinctive horse-hoof cuffs. Horse-hoof cuffs were distinctive features of Manchu robes and derived their name from their resemblance to the hoof of a horse. They were wide, flaring cuffs that, when turned-down, extended over the hands of the wearer. The cuffs were turned down to protect the back of the hand, to help keep hands warm in cold weather, or to show respect when saluting high-ranking military, civil, or imperial officials. The Qing dynasty was also responsible for many regulations that controlled the use and the possession of the dragon robe as a court and official costume. Robes with dragons as the main design appear to have been in existence since at least the Tang dynasty and were worn by imperial and high-ranking officials of each successive dynasty; there are also records that robes with dragon motifs were also given as gifts to foreign heads of state. However, it was not until the Qing that the dragon robe became part of the Chinese official costume; in 1759, an imperial edict codified the use of dragon robes according to rank.

The styles characteristic of dragon robes worn by the emperor were regulated to set him apart from any other official. Qing imperial dragon robes had nine dragons embroidered on them and only the emperor could have five clawed *long* dragons. The emperor was the only person who could have all Twelve Auspicious symbols embroidered on his robe. These symbols, whose use dates back to the Han dynasty, represented the qualities desirable in an emperor: the sun, moon and stars (or constellations), enlightenment; the mountain as the ability of the emperor to protect his people; the dragon as adaptability; the pheasant as literary refinement; the water weed, purity; two sacrificial cups as filial piety (family devotion and loyalty); a plate of millet as the ability of the emperor to empathize with his people; fire or the flame as the brilliance of the emperor; the axe as the emperor's power to punish; and the *fu* symbol to represent the power of the emperor to discriminate between right and wrong. Groupings and placement of these symbols also had meaning. The sun and moon placed at the shoulder and the starts and mountains at the chest and back represented four important annual sacrifices that only the emperor could make. The *fu* symbol and axe groupings represented the emperor's authority over the natural world. The five elements of the natural world were also represented with a grouping of the mountain (earth), waterweed (water), flame (fire), sacrificial cups (metal), and plate of millet (wood or plant life).

Rank or insignia badges that indicated the rank of military and civil officials were also costume items that were regulated by Qing sumptuary laws. These badges, known as mandarin squares in the West, had been used at least as early as the Ming dynasty to embellish robes; not until the Qing were regulations for their use formally structured. Qing rank badges were square-shaped and were sewn to the upper back and chest areas of robes. Animals were embroidered on badges awarded to military officials; birds were embroidered on badges awarded to civil officials.

ADMIRATION FOR CLOTHING IN THE *BOOK OF SONGS*

The following short poem is from the *Book of Songs*, one of the Five Classics of Chinese literature, compiled about 600 BC.

How well your black coat fits!
Where it is worn I will turn it for you.
Let us go to where you lodge,
And there I will hand your food to you.

How nice your black coat looks!
Where it is worn I shall mend it for you.
Let us go to where you lodge,
And there I will hand your food to you.

How broad your black coat is!
Where it is torn I shall alter it for you.
Let us go to where you lodge,
And there I will hand your food to you.

Source: Arthur Waley, trans. (1937) *The Book of Songs*. Boston and New York: Houghton Mifflin Company, 75.

Three basic types of robes were worn by men in the Qing court. The most formal was the *qao fu*, a one-piece dragon robe with a pleated skirt attached at the waist and horse-hoof cuffs on the sleeves. The heavily embroidered *pi-ling*, or cloud collar, was worn with this robe. The *qi fu* was a semi-formal dragon robe worn for festive occasions. It was in the typical Manchu style, having no pleats, horse-hoof cuffs, and side and center front and back slits (women's robes had only side slits). The *pu fu*, a plain surcoat, was often worn over the *qi fu*. The third robe was the *qang fu*, an ordinary robe worn for informal occasions. This robe was generally not embroidered, and was often worn with the *ma gua* or short jacket.

For women, the rules of dress were more relaxed, particularly for Han Chinese women, and there were distinct visual differences between Han Chinese and Manchu women's dress. Han Chinese women typically had bound feet, wore a two-piece garment (a jacket and long pleated skirt or trousers), maintained regional hairstyles, and continued using embroidered sleeve band cuffs instead of the horse-hoof cuff. Manchu women did not bind their feet, usually wore the one-piece *qi pao*, and wore the distinctive Manchu black cloud headdress or *liang pa tou erh*, the "two handle headdress." This headdress consisted of a wire framework covered with black thread or yarn and with a black-satin-covered T-shaped projection rising from the framework. The black satin was draped over the T-shaped projection for an effect of wings spread out on each side. Hair, either real or false, could be draped over this framework and then decorated with various hair ornaments. Han Chinese women were also allowed to wear their husband's mandarin square on their outer jacket. Han Chinese women did not appear to borrow many Manchu dress traditions; Manchu women, however, frequently borrowed Han Chinese dress elements, such as the embroidered sleeve bands.

Everyday dress worn by the lower classes in the Qing Dynasty was simply cut and decorated. The *shan ku (sam fu)*, a two-piece ensemble, was worn by men, women, and children. The *sham sam)* was a long- or short-sleeved, hip-length jacket that closed to the right, and the *ku (fu)* was a pair of trousers. These were usually made from wool, hemp, or cotton fabrics, and could be lined, quilted, or padded for warmth. These garments were cut to be comfortable, and to allow the wearer to work efficiently. By the end of the Qing, *sham* for men used a center front closure. Men who were wealthier wore a long robe, the cheongsam, with a center-opening hip-length jacket. A variety of sleeveless jackets could also be worn over the cheongsam. After 1912 the cheongsam was usually worn with a short jacket, the *ma gua*.

Western Influence After the Qing

After the overthrow of the Qing dynasty, Western influence became strong, especially in the coastal urban areas. Men who dealt with Westerners on a daily basis, such as bankers or businessmen, were the first to cut their queue and adopt total Western dress. More typical was the incorporation of Western dress with traditional clothing, such as wearing the *qang pao* and cheongsam with Western hats, shoes, and a suit coat. Men in rural areas were less likely to adopt Western clothing.

Urban women in China embraced Western dress quickly, especially hairstyles and shoes, and many totally abandoned traditional clothing. Most urban women wore modernized versions of the jacket and skirt, and also adapted the Manchu *qi pao* to Western design and style lines. Western trousers were not considered acceptable women's attire for social occasions. Peasant or lower-class women in urban and rural areas continued to wear the *shan ku*.

Changes During the Regime of Mao

Under Mao Zedong's regime, many restrictions on apparel were instituted, and people were allowed to own only a small quantity of clothing. The *qi pao* for women was not considered representative of the Communist regime, and after 1949, disappeared from mainland China. Mao favored a jacket and trouser combination for men and women, the *chieh fang i fu* or "liberation dress"; although originally the uniform of the Nationalist army, which opposed the Communists during China's civil war of the 1930s and 1940s, this suit became known as the "Mao suit." Under Mao, this was the only approved apparel and was usually made of blue cotton twill fabric. A uniform look was believed to be in keeping with the Communist precepts of universal comradeship and equality; wealthy Chinese, however, often had hand-tailored Mao suits of luxury wools.

During the last three decades of the twentieth century, clothing restrictions in China gradually relaxed as the result of changes in government policies. The Mao suit continued to be worn, especially by older people and those who lived in rural areas. Western clothing is nevertheless quite prevalent throughout the Chinese mainland. China plays an important role in apparel manufacturing for Western companies, and the high-fashion industry in China is experiencing a period of rapid growth. Historical Chinese costume also plays an important role for Western fashion designers, providing inspiration and new avenues to express creativity.

Laura K. Kidd

Further Reading

Cammann, Schuyler. (1952) *China's Dragon Robes*. New York: The Ronald Press.

Ferrald, Helen. (1946) *Chinese Court Costumes*. Toronto: Royal Ontario Museum of Archaeology.

Garrett, Valery. (1987) *Traditional Chinese Clothing in Hong Kong and South China, 1840–1980*. Hong Kong: Oxford University Press.

Scott, A.E. (1988) *Chinese Costume in Transition*. Singapore: Donald Moore.

Vollmer, John E. (1977) *In the Presence of the Dragon Throne*. Toronto: Royal Ontario Museum.

Wang, Yu-Ching. *The Research and Examination of Chinese Women's Gowns of Successive Dynasties*. Taipei, Taiwan: Chinese Chi Pao Research Association.

Xun, Zhou and Gao Chunming. (1988) *5000 Years of Chinese Costumes*. San Francisco: China Books and Periodicals.

CLOTHING, TRADITIONAL — HONG KONG During the Qing dynasty (1644–1912), the local Hong Kong population wore the same garments, made of silk or cotton, as the rest of the Han Chinese (ethnic Chinese majority) mainlanders. The *changshan*, or long gowns, for men, had a curved front opening on the right side, fastened with buttons and loops, and an upright collar. Silk was often used for summer garments; winter garments were wadded or lined with fur. Women wore the *ao*, a knee-length dress styled like the *changshan*, with a full-length skirt consisting of front and back panels with pleats or godets (cloth inserts) at the sides to allow movement. The portion of the skirt that showed below the *ao* was originally heavily embroidered but later was made in plain black or other dark, undecorated fabric. Originally, loose baggy trousers, or *ku*, were worn under the *ao*, and these continued to be worn by women who performed physical labor. For middle- and upper-class women, accessories included an embroidered headband that concealed the plucked forehead, bound-foot shoes, and ankle covers.

A version of these garments continued to be worn through the latter part of the twentieth century as part of traditional ceremonial dress. *Changshan* for men and *qun gua*, skirts and jackets, for women, and *dajinshan*, blouses with large lapels that fastened with *huaniu* (buttons and loops) to the right, had their origins in everyday dress of previous decades. As heavily embroidered versions of earlier clothing, they were most fashionable between the 1960s and 1970s. Shops sold or rented traditional ceremonial costumes, the *changshan magua* (long gowns and short jackets) for men and *qun gua* (*gua*, a red front-opening jacket; *qun*, a long black skirt) for women. These garments were worn by upper- and middle-class people for birthday banquets or other formal occasions. Later the *qun qua*, made in red and embroidered with *longfeng*, the dragon-and-phoenix motif, became the ceremonial costume for brides. Other embroidered motifs included mandarin ducks, flowers, and plants. Traditionally, two decorative sashes are embroidered at the center of the lapel, *zisundai*, or offspring bands. Today, a version of the Western white wedding dress—theatrically styled with a padded bust, off-the-shoulder straps, tight waist, and hooped shirt—has replaced the red wedding dress, although a red dress may be worn for part of the wedding ceremony.

Styles after the Qing Dynasty

Qipao or *cheung sam*, literally meaning "long dress" or "Manchu gown," and *magua* (horse jacket), a man's short jacket, were worn after the overthrow of the Qing dynasty. The jacket was slimmer-fitting than previously, had side slits, tight-fitting sleeves, and a high collar. Unusual for Asia, the *cheung sam* developed into a tailored garment; the front of the garment was constructed using bias-cut fabric to fit the chest area of the wearer in much the same way that a Western tailored jacket is molded to the body shape of its wearer. Later, the addition of darts allowed for an even closer fit. The fastened edge usually has a contrasting satin binding stiffened by glue. The *cheung sam* is characterized by its right-front fastening, standing collar, and side slits.

Originally worn by urban Chinese as a signifier of modernity in the early decades of the twentieth century, the *cheung sam* was worn with Western hairstyles, makeup, stockings, and high-heeled shoes. The depiction of girls wearing tight-fitting *cheung sam* in advertisements and in the prewar Shanghai film industry associated the *cheung sam* with fashion, overseas Chinese, and Hong Kong, where it became something of a national dress. It was considered a symbol of decadence in China after the Communist Revolution (1949) and was banned on the mainland during the Cultural Revolution (1966–1976). The link with alluring theatrical costume continued as the *cheung sam* became tighter and shorter, reflecting both Western fashion from the 1940s through the 1960s and the uniformity prevalent beyond the Hong Kong border in China during this period. The garment was worn by all of the local female population, and its tightness varied depending on the wearer's position and role in society, conforming to traditional Chinese ideas of modesty by concealing the neck, arms, and legs. Variations included sleeveless *cheung sam*, the use of shoulder pads, and zippers set in the slits at the hem that could be decorously lowered en route to work and raised after work in a club or bar. It was worn as a full-length garment for evening wear, and knee-length—reflecting Western fashion—for everyday use. Fabrics used included silks, rayon brocade, and, for everyday, printed cottons. The tailor was responsible for selecting the *huaniu*—the choice being an indication of his taste. The *cheung sam* continues to exist today as a theatrical dress-up item, worn by actresses, movie stars, and some local people at Chinese New Year. A small number of older women in prominent professional, social, or political positions wear the *cheung sam* on a daily basis, and many elderly women wear it on special occasions. Made of a plain woven cotton, the *cheung sam* is a much disliked school uniform at a number of Protestant girls' schools in Hong Kong.

The buttons and loops used on the *cheung sam* are made from bias-cut strips of glue-stiffened satin reinforced with an iron wire. They were most in demand when fashions for the *qipao* were at their zenith in the late 1950s, early 1960s. In Hong Kong two styles seem to have been used; *luosiniu* for men's and *huaniu* for women's wear. They may include one, two, or three colors matched to the garment and its trimmings. Patterns include flowers, birds, fish, or insects, symbolizing Chinese characters with auspicious meanings. Each *huaniu* is part of a pair; the knotted end, *gong*, is male, and the part with the eye, *na*, is female. *Huaniu* of the same size are used on women's gowns, while men's gowns have a larger *gong* and a smaller *na* stitched nearer the shoulder.

Bound-Foot Shoemaking

Bound-foot shoes were usually made by the women who needed them. In the past, the practice of binding women's feet was common among wealthy families, but women with bound feet are now very rare in Hong Kong. Having learned embroidery, women would start to learn how to make shoes for themselves at the age of eleven or twelve. The cutout parts of the shoe were embroidered before assembly. The sole was made from bamboo culm, washed, straightened, bound with layers of cloth, and stitched together with a thin linen rope. Winter shoes were lined with cotton wool. Heels were made from carved pomegranate or lychee tree wood wrapped in fabric. These were either self-made or purchased from vendors of string and wool. Fake bound-foot shoes, designed at first glance to mistake the heel for the ankle, also existed for women who had not had their feet bound but wished to look as though they had.

Clothing among Minority Peoples

The Hoklo people, of Fujian or Hokkien origin, make and continue to use a number of traditional items of clothing for festive occasions. Their everyday clothing is dark, but festive clothing is brightly colored. Children's garments and accessories, such as baby carriers, are elaborately decorated with beads, bells, decorative trim, and embroidery; small boys' hats are made in the shape of animals to confuse the evil spirits so that the child may grow up safely. Cotton purses are appliquéd with brightly colored thread and worn around the waist. Another minority group, the Tanka, who fish the waters around Hong Kong, also make brightly colored items such as baby carriers.

Hemp weaving was practiced in the early part of the twentieth century by the Hakka women. They wove narrow braids, *huadai*, on looms tied around their waists. These were used as straps to keep their *liangmao*, a flat, circular bamboo brimmed hat with a blue or black cloth fringe, in place. Hemp, handspun onto a bamboo pole, would also be woven by local weavers for use as blouses and dyed—usually dark colors—by boiling yam and dyer's weed in water or in commercial dyehouses in Kowloon.

Contemporary Styles

In Hong Kong today, the *cheung sam* is regularly revived by local fashion designers attempting to capitalize on Hong Kong's fashion past to create new collections, and by local design students attempting to find a new way to wear clothing that is now only associated with old people. Occasionally, international fashion adopts the *cheung sam* as a look, as most recently in 1997, when the fashionably dressed women of Hong Kong wore Christian Dior versions of the *cheung sam*. The most successful use of elements of traditional clothing are seen in the collections of New York designer Vivienne Tam, who references her origins in her collections, which are very popular in Hong Kong. The process of reappropriation via New York appears to be a critical element in her commercial success. Although a simplified phoenix-and-dragon robe is still worn at many weddings, more generally the use of traditional clothing is declining, both among the Cantonese and minority peoples of Hong Kong.

Valerie Wilson Trower

Further Reading

Clark, Hazel. (2000) *The Cheongsam*. Oxford: Oxford University Press.

———. (1999) "The *Cheung Sam:* Issues of Fashion and Cultural Identity." In *China Chic: East Meets West*, edited by Valerie Steele and John S. Major. New Haven, CT: Yale University Press, 155–166.

Garrett, Valery, M. (1994) *Chinese Clothing: An Illustrated Guide*. Oxford: Oxford University Press.

Szeto, Naomi. (1996) *Of Hearts and Hands; Hong Kong's Traditional Trades and Crafts*. Hong Kong: Urban Council of Hong Kong.

CLOTHING, TRADITIONAL—INDIA Archaeological finds four millennia old mark the beginning of information on Indian dress, though sufficient information to develop a costume history is only available from the Mauryan dynasty, beginning 324 BCE. Study of Indian dress is further complicated by the high degree of social stratification, cultural diversity, and climate variation within the subcontinent. Similar garments, too, have different names by region. Moreover, India has always provided textiles and other components of dress to the world through trade, thereby influencing and being influenced by the dress of other societies as its industries negotiated the aesthetic requirements of its world markets. Thus Indian dress has never been a closed, unified, or rigid cultural tradition.

Wrapped Garments

Of all the countries in the world, India is most closely associated with wrapped cloth garments, the ephemeral form of folds, pleats, tucks, rolls, and knots which disappears as soon as the garment is taken off. The woman's sari; wrapped forms of men's dress such as the *dhoti* and *lungi*; and the unisex *veshti* of southwestern India are the primary garments worn by the adult population. They vary slightly in width but generally cover the distance between ankle and waist and range from 2 1/2 to 11 yards in length. They are wrapped to cover the lower torso in styles—from simple to complex—specific to region, caste, religion, or ethnicity. Women wear longer saris that cover both the lower and upper torso. The end of the sari, or the edge of any wrapped garment lying next to the waist, can be used to secure small objects such as money or tobacco. A wrapped garment easily accommodates changes in body size from aging, illness, diet, or pregnancy since fit is redetermined each time the garment is donned. Simple wrapping adjustments further adapt the garment to changes of temperature or activity through the day.

Head coverings, most commonly worn in the north and west, also consist of wrapped or draped cloth. The head wraps of men of specific communities, such as the Sikhs, or of high-ranking men, consist of a 12–22-foot-long cloth arranged in styles determined by sociocultural factors. Manual laborers casually wrap a much shorter cloth around the head. This informal 1 1/2-yard garment can also be used for incidental tasks such as wiping a seat or wrapping a small bundle around the waist.

Many married women in the north use part of the sari to cover their heads. Where the sari is not worn, the head covering consists of a cloth, the *dupatta* or *orhni*, for instance, 2 or 3 yards long, draped from the top of the head. Its ends dangle behind, are tucked into the waistline or neckline of other garments, or are drawn around the body to provide protection from cold or the unwanted gaze of others, according to customs of respect and avoidance.

Wrapped garments are surface designed or woven to size in decorative patterns. Decorations include woven or applied borders or more extensive designs in printing, tie dye, or embroidery. Border designs emphasize the style of wrapping.

Preshaped Garments

Through the ninth century CE, the wrapped garment remained the primary and often sole garment worn by men and women, though soldiers always wore preshaped garments and the many foreigners in residence or traveling through early India wore a variety of stitched garments. Over the next thousand years a variety of stitched and, much later, knit garments were broadly incorporated during the periods of Muslim influence and subsequent rule (beginning with raiding parties in 997 CE) and then European ascendency (beginning with Portuguese capture of Goa in 1510). The history of particular garments that now comprise Indian dress is a complex intertwining of broad regional trends and court fashions. For example, the women's *coli*, a bodice front and sleeves secured by back ties, probably appeared in pre-Muslim Gujarat in the tenth century, yet only became widespread in the north as Muslim power spread. The modern sari developed from the ensembles of *veshti* and *mumdnai*, upper body cloth, and *ghaghra*, a gathered skirt reaching to the lower calf, and *orhni*.

While men's dress has evolved, women largely have adhered to wrapped garments, merely adding stitched accessories. In the twentieth century, a tight blouse, complete with back but baring midriff, became the common accessory to the sari or *veshti*. A petticoat was also incorporated, although some pant-like styles of wrapping the sari precluded it. Primarily stitched ensembles of *salwar* (loose-legged pants that narrow at the ankles) and *qamiz* (a knee-length tunic) with *dupatta*, or *ghaghra* and *coli* with *orhni* are characteristic of women's dress in specific communities in the north and west.

Men adhering to the wrapped *dhoti*, *lungi*, or *veshti* in the early 2000s commonly accessorized it with preshaped tunics including *kurta* and Western-inspired shirts, including cotton knit shirts. Fully stitched male ensembles extended this variety of tunics to include the *achkan*, a knee-length jacket closed with buttons down the front, and paired them with a variety of pant types to create ensembles that marked the social occasion and identity of the wearer. Pajama, *curidar* pajama (pants that are skintight below the knee with extra length gathered at the ankles), trousers, shorts, and *salwar* were popular pants for men.

Gender Differentiation

A woman's marital and reproductive status is marked by elements of her head covering, such as specific items of jewelry, garment colors, body markings, or a veiling garment. Among orthodox Hindu women, the absence of decorative elements in a woman's dress indicates that she is currently menstruating or that her husband is out of town or deceased. Motherhood, especially the birth of sons, is marked in some subgroups by small changes in dress. In veiling practices, characteristic of the north, arrangement of a woman's dress can further communicate that she is in the presence of her husband's senior relatives, before whom she always covers her head. In her natal family village or far from her husband's village she need not do so. Similar information is conveyed by the way a Muslim woman adjusts the several layers of face veils of her *burqa*, a preshaped garment donned over normal dress when outside the home to cover the body from head to toe.

Gender differences are apparent in the use of world dress in India. Men drawn away from the agriculture-based economy incorporate items or don complete ensembles of world dress. Cultural authentication of originally foreign garments makes them Indian; businessmen, for example, wear sandals, trousers, and a front-buttoning shirt with sleeves and European collar, with the straight hem of the shirt worn hanging out over the hips. The specific form and use of such garments follow the dictates of local environmental and non-verbal communication requirements, as well as Indian fashions in cut, fit, color, surface design, and ensemble building. Such localized forms represent Indian participation in the globalization of dress, and would be deemed foreign if worn in business contexts outside India.

Diversity in Dress

Because India contains one-sixth of the world's population and incorporates diverse cultural groups, dress quite distinct from that described above often constitutes the norm within specific groups or regions. The distinctive modes of dress worn by hundreds of millions of people in remote regions or among minority groups is nevertheless sometimes unfamiliar to members of mainstream Indian society. The Bondo, for example, are easily mistaken for residents of other continents. Women crop their hair close to the head, barely cover their hips with a narrow piece of cloth, and let their many necklaces suffice to dress the upper torso. Bondo men grow their hair long and wear a brief loincloth. The dress of some Assamese tribes indicates ancient connections to peoples in highland Southeast Asia. The dress of still other Assamese communities, and some central Indian tribes, mirrors ancient Indian dress, but with the addition of the modern sari blouse.

A 1993 government study of tattoo, jewelry, and headdress revealed that designs communicate the caste, religion, and regional or ethnic identity of much of the population. Such distinctions are also often made in the cut, surface design, color, or wrapping style of garments. Indian dress is thus characteristically diverse. Anonymity regarding caste, religion, and ethnicity are more characteristic of the less than 30 percent of the population residing in cities. There, the *nivi* wrapping style for sari and Indian fashions in tradition-based and world dress garments create relative homogeneity.

Politics and Dress

Politics play a significant role in the design of Indian dress. Throughout history the political elite have enjoyed greater access to foreign dress and traders' wares. Muslim rule of the north, from 1192 to 1857 CE, radically influenced men's dress. Similarly, during European rule, ending in 1947, high-ranking men donned garments or complete ensembles fashioned on European lines. Eventually, various redesigned European garments were broadly culturally authenticated into Indian practice through all social ranks. The redesigned garments, no longer appropriate to European dress, became truly Indian in character. Common examples in the early 2000s included the sari blouse and man's shirt. Simultaneously, colonial rulers participated in the development of Indian dress traditions, such as the codification of Sikh headdress, still worn worldwide by Sikh men.

During the independence struggle, culminating in 1947, industrially produced cloth and overtly European or luxurious forms of dress were rejected. Nationalists donned plainer and tradition-based dress in sympathy with the most exploited members of colonial society. The fervent wore *khadi*, a cloth handwoven from handspun yarn. *Khadi* was woven into saris and sewn into the garments of an ensemble developed by Mahatma Gandhi. His design communicated a unified national identity, in contrast to conventional dress, which revealed the wearer's distinctive social identity. This chiefly male ensemble included pajama, *kurta*, and Gandhian cap. *Khadi* and the cap were also incorporated into other ensembles.

India's postindependence economic planning profoundly influenced dress. The government supported the handloom industry to maintain employment levels, and discouraged imports or the mechanization of weaving. Cotton fiber agriculture was encouraged until population increases demanded conversion of land to food production in the 1980s. Synthetic fiber production and blends with cotton are now encouraged. Thus, handwoven cotton wrapped garments remained a dress staple from ancient times until the mid 1980s. Handwoven synthetic blends have subsequently become popular. In contrast, luxury garments throughout the twentieth century consisted of handwoven silk or industrially loomed synthetics, especially the discouraged imports from Europe and, later, Japan.

Fashion

Traditional forms of dress for the elite have undergone fashion changes well documented through two thousand years of artwork in stone, metal, and paint. Strong documentation for the dress of lower and middle ranks of society exists from the nineteenth century. Until the advent of Muslim influence in the north, fashionability in dress consisted largely in developments in wrapping style, garment dimensions, woven or surface design, color, and border widths. The addition of preshaped garments, with the associated possibilities of design through garment cut, and the covering up of the female upper torso, constitute the major cumulative changes in dress from 1000 CE to the present, though innumerable fashions in wrap or cut of garment have come and gone. Still, topless female dress sporadically occurs in minority communities in central and southern India and among the elder population in parts of the east and south.

The urban elite and youth led twentieth century women's fashion, which involved a movement toward gold jewelry and away from silver, experiments in surface design of fabrics, developments in the cut of commonly worn stitched garments, and increasing abandonment of caste-specific wrapping styles. Participation in broad fashion trends of the West also occurred, as in the rising and falling of *qamiz* and sari *pallav* (end-border design) lengths with Western skirt lengths. Yet women's dress generally maintained traditional silhouettes.

Two current trends mark urban professionals' and young educated women's dress practice. Ethnic Chic, beginning in the 1980s, consists in historic revivals and commodified ethnic traditions in dress spreading across the nation and its worldwide diaspora. Styles include a Gujarati way of wrapping the sari, *ghaghra-coli* ensembles, regional traditions in surface embellishment applied to saris and other garments, and most popularly the *salwar qamiz* ensemble. Ethnic Chic also affects menswear, primarily producing luxurious ensembles for urban elite and diaspora bridegrooms.

Indian forms of world dress are now appearing among urban upper class young women. As promulgated by Indian films serving both diaspora and national audiences, world dress is restyled to an Indian aesthetic in Bombay film industry costume workshops. Male youth, constituting the primary film audience, have long worn world dress, but increasingly young elite women are donning jeans and shirts, too. Indian dress norms require that the shirt hang outside the jeans to obscure definition of a woman's hips and crotch. Despite this trend, the more than 70 percent of the Indian population residing in rural areas will continue to anchor women's dress for some time to come in the tradition of wrapping elegant saris.

Hazel A. Lutz

Further Reading

Boulanger, Chantal. (1997) *Saris: An Illustrated Guide to the Indian Art of Draping*. New York: Shakti Press International.

Castelino, Meher. (1994) *Fashion Kaleidoscope*. Calcutta, India: Rupa and Company.

Chishti, Rta Kapur, ed. (1995) *Saris of India: Bihar & West Bengal*. New Delhi, India: Wiley Eastern Ltd.: National Institute of Fashion Technology & Amr Vastra Kosh.

———, and Amba Sanyal. (1989) *Saris of India: Madhya Pradesh*, New Delhi: Wiley Eastern Ltd. & Amr Vastra Kosh.

Cohn, Bernard. (1989) "Cloth, Clothes, and Colonialism: India in the Nineteenth Century." In *Cloth and Human Experience*, edited by Annette B. Weiner and Jane Schneider. Washington, DC: Smithsonian Institution Press, 303–353.

Dhamija, Jasleen, ed. (1995) *The Woven Silks of India*. Mumbai (Bombay), India: Marg Publications.

Fabri, Charles. (1977) *Indian Dress: A Brief History*. New Delhi, India: Sangam Books (Orient Longman Limited).

Frater, Judy. (1995) *Threads of Identity: Embroidery and Adornment of the Nomadic Rabaris*. Ahmedabad, India: Mapin Publishing Pvt. Ltd.

Ghurye, G. S. (1966) *Indian Costume*. Mumbai (Bombay), India: Popular Prakashan.

Golish, Vitold de. (1954) *Primitive India: Expedition "Tortoise" 1950–1952, Africa, Middle East, India*. London: Harrap.

Kumar, Ritu. (1999) *Costumes and Textiles of Royal India*, edited by Cathy Muscat. London: Christie's Books.

Leslie, Julia. (1992) "The Significance of Dress for the Orthodox Hindu Woman." In *Dress and Gender: Making and Meaning*, edited by Ruth Barnes and Joanne B. Eicher. Oxford: Berg, 198–213.

Sing, K. S. (1993) *The Anthropological Atlas: Ecology and Cultural Traits, Languages and Linguistic Traits, Demographic and Biological Traits*. People of India, no. 11. Delhi, India: Oxford University Press

Tarlo, Emma. (1996) *Clothing Matters: Dress and Identity in India*. Chicago: The University of Chicago Press.

Untracht, Oppi. (1997) *Traditional Jewelry of India*. New York: Harry N. Abrams, Inc.

CLOTHING, TRADITIONAL—INDONESIA

CLOTHING, TRADITIONAL—INDONESIA Indonesia has three hundred ethnic groups, each with their own costume variations. The majority of the population, the Javanese, wear Indonesian national dress. Western dress arrived in Indonesia in the sixteenth century and has been one of many sources of

Performers in traditional costume performing the Batak dance at Lake Toba, Sumatra, Indonesia, in 1996. (STEPHEN G. DONLADSON PHOTOGRAPHY)

tension between indigenous groups and colonizers. Dress is an indicator of cultural change in Indonesia; indeed, history can be divided into three eras categorized by dress terms: sarong (local dress), *jubbah* (Islamic influences), and trousers (Western influences).

The function of dress in Indonesia, with a population that is primarily Muslim, is complex. Although Islam had an impact on Indonesia prior to that of the Europeans, after centuries of Dutch domination, dress in Indonesia has become a way to express attitudes toward foreign, cultural, political, and religious influences. Although Western dress is most commonly worn today, traditional dress continues to be important in Indonesia, where varied forms of traditional dress testify to the wide variety of cultural subgroups in the nation.

Textiles

Indonesia has a long history of fine textile production; this traditional art is still considered important, despite Westernization. Indonesia is particularly noted for its textiles made with complex resist-dyed techniques. Batik is a patterned fabric produced by using wax as a resist agent. Where the wax has been applied, it prevents the dye from penetrating.

Another resist-dyed technique is ikat, in which the dye is applied to the warp yarns prior to weaving. The design is seen in the finished yarn goods, and is a result of the dyed warp yarns being woven with plain weft yarns, a process known as single ikat. When the warp and weft yarns are both resist dyed, an extremely complex form of double ikat results; these *geringsing* cloths are rare and are made only in Tenganan on Bali. These cloths are the most highly prized Indonesian textiles.

Other fine textiles produced in Indonesia include *songket*, a heavy silk handwoven fabric with gold- or silver-wire-wrapped thread used as a supplementary weft to form the pattern. *Pelangi* is a tie-dyed fabric, common in Bali. *Prada* cloth is a fine cotton fabric in vivid colors with floral motifs printed in gold dust or applied with gold foil and is often worn by Balinese dancers.

Traditional Dress

Traditional dress is still commonly seen in rural areas and is especially important throughout Indonesia for national ceremonial occasions. For both men and women, traditional dress in Indonesia includes a wraparound lower-body cover—a *kain* (a rectangular length of fabric, generally in batik) or a sarong (a length of fabric with ends sewn together, more often in ikat). Women in Java and Bali wear sarongs and *kain*, held in place with a *stagen*, a narrow sash. The *kebaya* is a tight, often sheer, long-sleeved blouse worn on the upper body. It is often made of lace, but can also be made of lightweight, sheer, elaborately embroidered cottons. In addition, women generally have a large rectangle of cloth called a *selendang (ikat or batik)* draped over the shoulder (on less formal occasions a large *selendang* is used to carry babies or objects); on Bali the *pelangi* (a sash) is worn over the *kebaya* around the waist when going to temple.

Indonesian men generally wear *kain* or sarongs only in the home or on informal occasions. A black felt cap, or *peci*, is occasionally worn; although it was once associated with Islam, it has acquired a more secular, national meaning since Indonesia's independence. These ensembles have become national dress in Indonesia because the vast majority of the population lives on Java and Bali. *Kebaya* and batik *kain* are considered Indonesia's national dress for women, and *teluk beskap*, a combination of the Javanese jacket and *kain*, are national dress for Indonesian men.

Linda B. Arthur

Further Reading

Acjhadi, Judy. (1976) "Traditional Costumes of Indonesia." *Arts of Asia* 6, 5: 74–79.

Arthur, Linda. (2000) "School Uniforms as Symbolic Metaphor for Competing Ideologies in Indonesia." In *Undressing Religion: Commitment and Conversion from a Cross-cultural Perspective*, edited by L. B. Arthur. Oxford: Berg Publishers, 201–16.

Van Dijk, K. (1997) "Sarong, Jubbah, and Trousers: Appearance as a means of distinction and discrimination." In *Outward Appearances: Dressing, State, and Society in Indonesia*, edited by H. S. Nordholt. Leiden, Netherlands: KITLV (Royal Institute of Linguistics and Anthropology) Press, 39–83.

CLOTHING, TRADITIONAL—IRAQ

Artifacts found in Sumerian tombs suggest that the early inhabitants of Mesopotamia (c. 3500–2500 BCE) wore a wrapped sheepskin skirt, called *kaunakes*, with one end of the garment passed under a wide belt in front and over the left shoulder. After woven cloth was available, the garment was fringed at the hem to simulate the effect of fleece. Cloaks covered the upper body, and royal women wore elaborate gold jewelry. Later Babylonian and Assyrian (c. 1000–600 BCE) costume shifted from draped garments to tunics. Assyrian law codes prescribed veiling for free, married women and prohibited it for prostitutes and slaves. Mesopotamia was the land of wool production and weaving, and wool was the primary fiber for clothes, tapestries, and curtains, although linen, cotton, and even silk are mentioned. The industry was technologically sophisticated enough to produce elaborate woven and embroidered figural motifs. Evidence of weaving guilds and apprenticeships, plus textile trade with other countries, attests to the importance of the textile industry.

The traditional dress of Iraq is a reflection of Iraqi technical skills, aesthetic and political ideals, moral standards, and religious values. Members of Iraqi society are deeply immersed in Islamic fundamentalism; consequently, costume reflects these ideals and values. Traditional dress is less prevalent in urban centers such as Baghdad and Basra than in rural areas. All social classes wear the same clothing, with only subtle differences. Arabs and Kurds exhibit distinct differences in their clothing, though both are predominantly Muslim.

The traditional dress of Arab Iraqi men includes the *dishdasha*, an ankle-length, typically white, loose-fitting, shirtlike garment allowing free air circulation over the body; the *aba*, a long cloak, tan or neutral in color, for cool weather; the *kaffiyeh*, a white or checked square scarf folded into a triangle and sometimes worn over a small white cap with the *agal*, a circular black rope or plaited-cord device to hold the *kaffiyeh* in place; and sandals. Men also wear undershirts and

Iraqi women at Friday prayers in a mosque in Baghdad on 1 January 1999. (AFP/CORBIS)

drawers, loose trousers, and a cotton or wool coat. The *dishdasha* may be hoisted up and secured for greater freedom of movement, and the *aba* may be doubled up over the head. To further protect against the elements, the ends of the headdress may be wrapped loosely around the neck, across the ears and lower face, or around the top of the head.

The Arab Iraqi woman's traditional costume is designed to conceal the woman and achieves this through *hijab,* or veiling, the practice of covering the woman's hair and body for the sake of modesty and adherence to socioreligious requirements. Veiling is believed to prevent men from falling into temptation and to protect women from unwanted sexual advances. The traditional costume includes the *abayah*, a long black cloak worn over a dress and covering the wearer from head to foot; the *asha*, a black head scarf; the *foota*, a black chin scarf; sandals or clogs; and gold or silver jewelry (for example, ankle bracelets, earrings, or pendants, valued not only as ornament but as insurance in case a woman's husband dies, leaves, or divorces her). The dress under the *abayah* is traditionally a black long-sleeved, ankle-length shift or yoke-style, but may be other colors. Younger women may wear the *abayah* and veil only when they leave the house but indoors wear dresses of printed cotton (during the summer) and flannelette (during the winter). In winter women may wear four or five layers of clothing—heavy black sweaters and black imitation caracul jackets—under the *abayah*. The *hashmiya* is a wide-sleeved full net or sheer black ceremonial gown that women wear for certain religious ceremonies.

The traditional costume of Kurdish men includes baggy pantaloons, a shirt, a cummerbund (in which valuables are kept, as well as a dagger or two), peaked leather slippers, a close-fitting cap or turbanlike head wrap, and, in winter, a quilted jacket and long cloak in bright colors. Kurdish women have never practiced veiling and enjoy considerable latitude in community activities. The traditional costume is modest but colorful, and it includes a loose-fitting dress or kirtle, a short collarless jacket, a headscarf or turban, and several pieces of jewelry. At times they wear a bifurcated garment similar to Turkish trousers.

An Islamic man may have up to four wives, and a large family is highly desirable, since the greater the number of children, especially sons, the greater the prestige of the father. Young girls are dressed in brightly colored print dresses, and boys are clothed in candy-striped *dishdashas*, or trousers. Typical footwear is sandals or tennis shoes. Children often wear sweaters, wool scarves, and caps in winter. Boys and girls are traditionally separated at puberty, and girls are excluded from male society outside the family circle. Parents generally arrange marriages, preferably between relatives, and part of preparation for the ceremony includes decorative painting of the bride's hands and feet with henna, a natural red dye.

Westernization of traditional costume is prevalent throughout Iraq, and increasing educational levels and opportunities in the workforce encourage the abandoning of all or parts of traditional dress. Wealthy professionals in urban centers have adopted Western dress to a greater extent than other components of the population. Most men who have visited the city own at least one Western-style business suit, and women may wear highly fashionable Western dresses or suits with or without the *abayah*. Many women who discarded traditional dress after the revolution, however, have reverted to traditional dress as an expression of national pride.

Martha C. Jenkins

Further Reading

Foster, Leila M. (1991) *Iraq: Enchantment of the World.* Chicago: Children's Press.

Harik, Ramsay M., and Elsa Marston. (1996) *Women in the Middle East: Tradition and Change.* New York: Franklin Watts.

Harris, George L. (1958) *Iraq: Its People, Its Society, Its Culture.* New Haven, CT: Hraf Press.

Hitchens, Christopher. (1992) "Struggle of the Kurds." *National Geographic* 182, 2 (August): 32–61.

CLOTHING, TRADITIONAL — JAPAN

The basis of Japanese traditional costume is the kimono, a loose-fitting cloth garment constructed only of various sizes of flat rectangles, wrapped around the body and held in place with strings or sashes. Throughout its historical development, the structure of the kimono has remained basically the same.

Early Period to Premodern Period

Clay figurines and wall paintings found in prehistoric tombs show that the clothing of ancient Japan was similar to that of China and Korea, attesting to its cultural attachment to continental civilization. In 603, Prince Shotoku (574–622) established the first dress code in Japan and, following a Chinese model, fixed twelve court ranks distinguished by the color of their headgear. During the Nara period (710–794), intensive assimilation of continental culture continued. The oldest-surviving Japanese textiles were brought to Japan along the Silk Road through China and Korea from remote areas as far away as the Middle East.

During the Heian period (794–1192), Japanese native styles emerged. Male aristocrats wore *sokutai*, a combination of a cloak with a long tail and wide trousers, at official court ceremonies, and *ikan*, *noshi*, or *kariginu*, round-necked broad-sleeved cloaks, for less formal occasions. The most formal attire for female aristocrats was *karaginu-mo*, the so-called *junihitoe* (twelve-layered gown), which consisted of many layers of undergarments, a long-sleeved jacket *(karaginu)*, a long, pleated divided skirt *(hakama)*, and a long train *(mo)*. When layering garments, the aesthetics of color combinations were particularly important. Color schemes were formulated, and sets of different colors were linked to specific flowers, seasons, or weather conditions.

In the Kamakura period (1192–1333), as the military class came to power, the ruling class adapted a more practical and restrained style of clothing based on warrior garments. *Hitatare*, a tailored suit with a broad-sleeved cloak and *hakama* trousers became the standard for men's clothing. Family crests often appeared as dyed motifs on fabrics. Meanwhile, a narrow-sleeved kimono called a *kosode*, originally an undergarment, became an outer garment. From this period through the Muromachi period (1336–1573), the *kosode* continued evolving and became the common dress for almost all classes of women. As it came to be worn alone without *hakama*, its full-length flat surface provided larger continuous spaces for two-dimensional decoration and encouraged new designs with striking colors and patterns.

The Momoyama period (1573–1603) was generally characterized by its bold extremes of taste initiated by dynamic social changes and economic growth. Costumes of this period displayed flamboyant designs. *Tsujigahana* dyeing, a method of exquisite surface decoration produced by a combination of stitched tie-dyeing, hand painting, and embroidery, was popular. Surviving cloaks *(dofuku)* decorated with *tsujigahana* worn by military leaders exhibit their extravagant taste.

During the Edo period (1603–1868), the urban population exhibited a passion for fresh textile designs. Some of the most celebrated painters of the time were involved in the textile industry, including Ogata Korin (1658–1716), a celebrated Kyoto painter. *Yuzen* dyeing, a technique of rendering detailed images on fabrics by defining outlines with rice-paste resist, was perfected by Miyazaki Yuzensai. Wealthy people sported garments dyed in the *yuzen* style, often combined with other embellishments such as tie-dyeing and embroidery, despite sumptuary laws set by the government. From the late eighteenth century, a more understated style became popular around Edo (present-day Tokyo). This style employed simple patterns such as stripes or tiny repeated patterns in neutral or grayish colors, following the fashions of famous actors or smart customers of the pleasure quarters.

Modern Period

In 1854, Japan fully opened to the outside world after more than two hundred years of relative seclusion, and rapid Westernization began. The government adapted Western clothing styles for the official uniforms of national institutions and formal occasions, and Western costume became a sign of authority. A few decades later, however, intense reaction against rapid Westernization resulted in nationalistic movements aimed at preserving traditional Japanese culture. From then until the end of World War II in 1945, when Western-style clothing finally became the norm in everyday life, Western and Japanese styles coexisted and often were mixed according to individual needs. For example, Western dress tended to be worn more often by men than by women in formal settings, and Japanese dress continued to be worn in domestic settings by older women.

In the late twentieth and early twenty-first centuries, the kimono has survived mainly as a representation of or as a means to communicate Japan's cultural heritage. Many textiles and costumes have been designated as National Treasures or Important Cultural Properties to be exhibited at museums, and skilled textile craftspeople have been appointed as Living National Treasures for the preservation of traditional techniques. At the same time, many people still prefer traditional costumes for formal occasions such as wedding ceremonies, funerals, and coming-of-age celebrations. The kimono also plays an important role in other traditional activities such as performances of music and dance and in the tea ceremony. In addition to luxury kimonos worn at those formal occasions, *yukata*, an informal cotton kimono, is often seen at summer festivals and hot-spring resorts.

Augmenting the efforts to conserve the tradition as it is, a group of Japanese designers started to incorporate kimono designs into contemporary international fashions in the 1970s and 1980s. The kimono, with its delicate surface decorations and its flexible sizing, provided designers with new approaches to the body and clothing. Meanwhile, with the recently revived interest in the kimono, the kimono industry is promoting a new type that can be worn and laundered more easily.

Izumi Taksaki

Further Reading

Gluckman, Dale Carolyn, and Sharon S. Takeda. (1992) *When Art Became Fashion: Kosode in Edo-Period Japan*. New York: Weatherhill.

Kennedy, Alan. (1990) *Japanese Costume: History and Tradition*. Paris: Éditions Adam Biro.

Munsterberg, Hugo. (1996) *The Japanese Kimono*. Oxford, U.K.: Oxford University Press.

Rhode Island School of Design Museum of Art. (1992) *Patterns and Poetry: No Robes from the Lucy Truman Albrich Collection at the Museum of Art, Rhode Island School of Design*. Providence, RI: Rhode Island School of Design.

Stinchecum, A. M. (1984) *Kosode: 16th–19th Century Textiles from the Nomura Collection*. New York: Kodansha International.

CLOTHING, TRADITIONAL — KOREA

Hanbok, the Korean traditional costume, is characterized by a keen appreciation and consciousness of the seasons, a sensitivity to color, symbolic motifs from myth and legend, and individual taste, value, and style. *Hanbok* offers a glimpse of Korea's past, representing hundreds of years of colorful history before modernization. Korean costume also reflects the lifestyles of aristocrats, nobility, and commoners in very distinct ways.

Hanbok consists of a jacket called *juhgori* and trousers called *baji* for men, and *juhgori* and skirts called *chima* for women. For men, a hat is essential for all occasions, as is a sash at the waist and high- or low-cut shoes. These are the basic attributes of dress in cold countries and are especially suitable for farming and hunting. Laces *(daenim)* are tied around the ankles of men's baggy trousers to facilitate movement. Headdresses are important for presenting a refined appearance.

The textiles used for costume include *sambae* (hemp), *mosi* (ramie), *sa* and *ra* (stiffened silk gauze), *myungju* (soft silk pongee), and *dan* (opaque silk). A variety of accessories, such as highly ornamented royal crowns, elaborate earrings, necklaces, bracelets, hairpins, belts, and bronze shoes, adorned dress. Under the influence of Chinese culture, from the seventh century CE onward the sleeves of Korean jackets and robes became larger and trousers wider. Headdresses and robes were similarly modified.

Shilla Period

During the Unified Shilla dynasty (668–935 CE), which maintained close ties with Tang China, China's influence on Korean costume became more evident. Korean figurines unearthed from a mid-eighth century tomb in Kyongju, the capital city of the Shilla kingdom, were depicted in Chinese-style dress. In earlier tomb mural paintings, long jackets with belts at the waist were worn over long, pleated skirts, but the figurines from the Unified Shilla wore skirts over their jackets, a distinctively Tang Chinese style.

Korean girls in traditional dress in 1989. (DAVID & PETER TURNLEY/CORBIS)

Koryo Period

Extravagant style prevailed during the succeeding Koryo period (918–1392), until the Chinese styles of the Yuan dynasty (1267–1368) became popular in the declining years of Koryo. The Yuan Chinese influence dictated tighter sleeves and shorter jackets. (Previously, jackets were long enough to cover the hip line, with a sash tied around the waist.) The wearing of a *dae* (a belt or girdle) of jade, leather, or cloth, which indicated the rank of the wearer, ended with the advent of the Koryo period. Instead of the *dae*, the palace adopted the Chinese clothing and hat system to indicate rank. The *jogdoori* (today's women's wedding crown) and *doturak-daenggi* (doubled-long hair ribbon with embroidery and ornaments) were Yuan Chinese features adopted by Korea and were worn until the Choson dynasty (1392–1910). Commoner women wore white *guhn* (head scarves) and white clothes, but did not cover their face. Noblewomen wore *nuhwool* (a veil) made from a foot or more of black, soft silk or *sa* (stiffened silk) over a small, umbrella-like cover worn on the head. The material and size of a woman's *nuhwool* indicated her social status.

Official court attire was worn with *hwa* (boots). From the time of the Koryo dynasty's King Wu (c. thirteenth century CE), when a new dress system was decided, until the end of the Choson dynasty, black leather *hwa* were worn with official attire. On the other hand, commoners were absolutely prohibited from wearing *hwa*. They generally wore white clothes and straw sandals.

Choson Period

Clothing during the Choson dynasty was influenced by China's Ming dynasty (1368–1644); influences are apparent in the official and unofficial costumes of the royal court, where the Chinese ceremonial robe was adopted. For traditional ceremonies, a specific dress for a particular occasion was stipulated. A dress style intended for a certain ceremonial occasion could never be worn at another time. Under the ceremonial robe, however, women always wore the traditional *chima-juhgori* and men wore the *baji-juhgori*. Costume materials varied with seasonal change; cut and length of the *juhgori* went up and down with fashion and social standing; an individual's rank, class, sex, and age were distinguished by specific colors, lengths, and styles. Muted colors for the everyday wear of commoners persisted, as did the splendid, vibrant colors of the royal household, a statement of their absolute authority.

Twenty-First Century

Traditional *hanbok* are worn by men and women of all ages only as ceremonial dress on special occasions, such as for traditional festivals, wedding ceremonies, and so on. Numerous prohibitions and sumptuary laws were decreed by almost every new king, leading to a gradual simplification of the clothing and the eventual evolution of the *hanbok* of today. The simplified version of *hanbok* remains a very common sight in the busy streets of modern Seoul.

Hyunsook Chung

Further Reading

Lee Hun-jung. (1989) *2000 Years of Korean Costume.* Seoul: Ministry of Culture and Tourism

Yang, Sunny. (1997) *Hanbok: The Art of Korean Clothing.* Elizabeth, NJ: Hollym International.

CLOTHING, TRADITIONAL—KYRGYZSTAN

CLOTHING, TRADITIONAL—KYRGYZSTAN Dress in Kyrgyzstan developed as a part of Central Asian costume, with clothing styles that were adapted to either a sedentary or nomadic lifestyle. In general, the styles and design of Kyrgyz costume were similar to those found in Uzbekistan and Tajikstan and reflect the old traditions of textile manufacture and design that developed along the Silk Road. Political conquests brought in new techniques, such as felting, weaving, and quilting, that were adopted for clothing and textiles in the region. It is difficult to estimate origins of any kind of ethnic dress, but it is safe to say that traditional Kyrgyz dress developed over a few centuries and only began to show significant change in the mid-twentieth century after Westernization began.

As in much of Asia, men in Kyrgyzstan rapidly adopted Western dress and today few wear the traditional costume except for the hat *(kolpok)*. For festivals, men may wear a traditional jacket *(jelek)* made of blue, black, or brown velvet, with a belt at the waist. Men's jackets have very little decoration, but may have trim around the neckline, at the sleeve edges, and down the center front. Pants are velvet and cut like Western pants, but might have decorations at the hem, like the *salwar* of India.

Women's dress is much more complex. Traditional dress is worn more frequently by women and is commonly seen at weddings, rituals, festivals, and other cultural events. There are three categories of female dress, based on age.

Girls' Dress

Girls up to age seventeen wear long dresses *(koinok)*. These dresses are semi-sheer, have high necklines, and have many layers of flounces or frills at the neck, sleeves, and skirt. White, red, yellow, and other bright colors indicating youth are preferred for girls. A sleeveless jacket *(kamzol)* is worn with the dress. These vests come in different lengths, but girls usually wear the shortest vests. The *kamzol* is made from heavy fabrics, usually velvet, and can be many colors; it is decorated with embellishments referred to as *saima*. The decorations are most extensive on the center front corners of the *kamzol*.

Girls' hair is traditionally arranged in about forty braids *(besh kokul)* and is covered by headdresses such as a cone-shaped hat *(tebetei)* that may have feathers and silver or gold coins, precious stones, pearls, threads, and beads.

Young Married Women

For their weddings, brides wear more elaborate versions of the traditional dress; the wedding dress is long and white, and the *kamzol* is richly decorated. The special bridal headdress, or *shokulo*, is very high and cone-shaped, with a veil falling down the back; the veil may be used to cover the bride's face. Once a girl marries, her attire becomes a visible symbol of her married status. Dresses are longer and have fewer frills. For married women, *kamzols* are longer and plainer. In the winter, velvet wrap skirts *(beldemchi)* with appliqué designs decorating the edges and hem can be worn over the *koinok*. They are sometimes lined with fur.

Hair and headdresses also change with marriage, in deference to values of female modesty. Hair must be kept covered after marriage and is worn parted into two plaits (symbolizing the couple). If a woman's husband were to die, she would braid her hair into only one plait, indicating her solitary status.

Older Married Women

As women age, their entire ensembles continually become simpler, plainer, longer, and duller in color. Middle-aged and elderly women wear big white headdresses called *elechek*. Approximately ten meters of fabric are needed to make this turbanlike headdress with a drape under the chin, similar to a wimple from the European Middle Ages. In winter, shawls are worn for warmth, as are jackets (called *chapan*), often made of velvet or fur.

Linda B. Arthur

See also: **Women in Central Asia**

Further Reading

Kennett, Frances, with Caroline MacDonald-Haig. (1995) *Ethnic Dress*. New York: Facts On File.

CLOTHING, TRADITIONAL—LAOS

The geographical distributions of most Lao ethnic groups extend beyond Lao national borders into the surrounding countries of China, Vietnam, Cambodia, Thailand, and Myanmar (Burma). Across national borders as well as within nations, a group's costumes may differ. Additionally, costume components—from yarn, weaving techniques, and cloth to design, decorative elements, and jewelry—manufactured by one group may be used or adopted by another. This results in the complicated interdependence for which mainland Southeast Asia interethnic relations are famous.

Tai-Kadai Linguistic Groups

Tai-Kadai populations (approximately 66 percent of the population) came into Laos from what is now northern Vietnam, probably originating in southern China, during the last millennium and a half. Tai women brought with them the freestanding frame loom, silkworm cultivation and yarn preparation, and a three-part design for women's sarongs or wraparound skirts *(sin)*.

The adoption of Theravada Buddhism by many Tai speakers had a major impact on textile production and meanings. Theravada Buddhist monks may neither weave nor cook. Thus women's work includes not only the preparation of cloth for secular and ritual purposes but also the provision of textiles to members outside the family. Tai women provide white cloth to monks, who cut, sew, and dye it for the robes *(siiwon)* they will wear.

Women's *sin* display traditional designs abstracted from the natural and mythological worlds; men wear sarongs with blocked or checked patterns. The man's sarong is an elegant garment. Woven in plaid two-ply silk heavier than that used in a woman's skirt, or in cotton, it produces a shimmering color. The man's longer wraparound skirt *(yao* or *hang)*, with its ends twisted together in front, pulled between the legs, and fixed into the waist band at the small of the back, is the product of many months of labor, with heavy plied silk forming both warp and weft. Utilitarian textiles, such as blankets and shawls, are usually without design, but can be checkered or have subdued patterns.

During the nineteenth century, European travelers recorded that everyday men's clothing was skimpy at best, and women were often bare breasted, wearing drab skirts. The *biang* (shoulder cloth) was a common woman's garment, draped over the shoulder and often used on ritual occasions. These long, narrow pieces often served to display a woman's aptitude for design as well as her command of weaving technology and dyes. In addition, explorers remarked that the blanket or shawl *(hom)*, made of two or more two-meter warp lengths sewn along the selvage, which could be draped around the shoulders to keep warm during chilly nights and mornings, was a major garment well known even in early colonial Cambodia and Saigon. In the early nineteenth century, large quantities of English textiles began appearing in Lao markets. Royalty was usually clothed, at least for state occasions, in Chinese imported textiles.

Austroasiatic Linguistic Groups

Documentation of Lao Austroasiatic-speaking groups (23 percent of the population) is sparse, particularly regarding costume history. Some have sought better lives by moving to lower elevations and assimilating into other ethnic groups through marriage. In the 1950s and 1960s, Khmu women wore a cotton sarong with simple horizontal stripes or with designs influenced by weavers of the Tai-Lue ethnic group. Their upper garment, a long-sleeved black blouse with a slight flare at the waist, had a center diagonal closure fastened at the side and sometimes decorated with sequins, appliqué, embroidery, or silver coins.

Austroasiatic speakers in southern Laos include a cluster of ethnic groups that historically had close trade relations. Some of these included the Katu, Nha Heun, Ta-Oi, and Alak. The Alak in the Attoupeu and Saravane provinces were known as fine weavers. In addition to weaving for themselves, they traded long lengths of cloth for making loincloths *(katiao)*, sarongs, and blouses. A particular pattern was woven exclusively for the use of one ethnic group.

Men wore loincloths of varying degrees of elaboration according to their status within their village. Some were heavily beaded, the beads being strung on the weft before weaving. Women wore sarongs with horizontal stripes and sleeveless blouses made of two strips of cloth joined by side and center seams. Silver coins sometimes decorated the bottom edges. Brass and silver necklaces, anklets, and bracelets were also common. Most men wore loincloths until the 1960s. By 1970, only a few village elders wore them, and then only for special ceremonies. Because of heavy conscription during the war, many men switched to wearing army fatigues on an almost regular basis. In the 1990s, there seemed to be a revival of beaded weaving among the Katu in Champassak province, possibly stimulated by tourism.

Hmong-Mien and Sino-Tibetan Linguistic Groups

Lao highland groups (11 percent of the population) include the Hmong, Mien, Lahu, Akha, and Lisu, and

Hmong women in Laos in traditional costume. (BOHEMIAN NOMAD PICTUREMAKERS/CORBIS)

their traditional dress is basically the same as in Thailand. During the war in Indochina in the 1960s and 1970s, the lives of many of these groups were disrupted. Many Hmong and Mien were resettled internally in camps at lower elevations, and others eventually fled the country as refugees to camps in Thailand and then to third countries. Ethnic dress was largely exchanged for lowland sarongs, partly due to the hotter climate and partly to disguise identity in a strange environment where their ethnicity might cause problems. Life in the camps brought more free time, commercial marketing of textiles, and exposure to new designs and styles. Hmong and Mien who fled as refugees to other countries such as the United States and France began ordering traditional clothing from refugee camps in Thailand or from relatives in Laos. These costume components ordered from abroad were executed in much finer stitches and with more elaboration of appliqué, silver, and other ornamentation than had previously occurred in Laos.

Current Trends

Copious quantities of beautiful Tai textiles from Laos appeared in world markets in the 1980s and 1990s. These elegant pieces ably demonstrate Tai women's exemplary command of a technology for producing artistic masterpieces.

The Lao People's Revolutionary Party, which has had control of the country since 1975, imposed a standardized women's costume focused on the *sin* and *biang*, displacing more ethnic costume except in tourist contexts. However, commercialization, interest from abroad, and refugees nostalgic for their homeland have brought about a revival of indigenous production.

Today, Lao costume provides myriad meanings for a diverse clientele of ethnic groups and outside observers.

Leedom Lefferts and Jacqueline Butler-Diaz

Further Reading

Cheesman, Patricia. (1982) "The Antique Weavings of Lao Neua." *Arts of Asia* 12, 3: 120–125.

———. (1988) *Lao Textiles: Ancient Symbols, Living Art*. Bangkok, Thailand: White Lotus Press.

Gittinger, Mattiebelle, and Leedom Lefferts. (1992) *Textiles and the Tai Experience in Southeast Asia*. Washington, DC: Textile Museum.

Goldman, Ann Y. (1995) *Lao Mien Embroidery: Migration and Change*. Bangkok, Thailand: White Lotus Press.

Sage, William W. (1998) "Catalog to the William W. Sage Collection of Laotian Ethnographica." Manuscript, Museum of Anthropology, Arizona State University, Tempe.

Van Esterik, Penny. (1999) "Fabricating National Identity: Textiles in Lao PDR." *Museum Anthropology* 23, 1: 47–56.

CLOTHING, TRADITIONAL—MALAYSIA

Malays, the majority population in Malaysia, are a Muslim people indigenous to villages *(kampung)* in Southeast Asia. Village dress is situational and reflects relationships and contexts. Traditional dress for women is the *sarung kebaya*. The *kebaya* (blouse) may be diaphanous to near transparent and is commonly pleated significantly above and below the part of the garment covering the breasts. The *sarung*, a cotton skirt hemmed into a cylindrical shape, is stepped into, folded right to left, and tucked at the waist. It is commonly of a floral pattern. Although normally worn with a blouse or pullover top, it can also be worn alone; this is commonly done when sleeping or bathing. The final piece of traditional women's dress is a head scarf *(selendang)*; although often serving as a veil, it can be worn in a number of ways.

The male shirt *(baju)* and small black hat *(songkok)* are usually reserved for formal occasions, such as Friday prayers or certain feasts. Men often wear *sarung*, differentiated from women's by the fold (left to right, below the navel) and the pattern (plaid, rather than floral).

In the distant past, both men and women used the *sarung* as the primary and often sole garment. However, varieties of dress have risen with increased trade and contact with other cultural groups. Even so, women are careful to conform to public forms of dress in the market, the mosque, and village celebrations. The more accepted contemporary form of public village dress is the *tudung*. Commonly, this consists of a matching long sleeved tunic and floor length skirt *(baju kurung)*, accompanied by a head scarf *(anak tudung)*. It is not uncommon for women to mix and match long skirts and tunics, even substituting short-sleeved blouses or tee-shirts. The *baju kurung* is often made from very colorful cloth, and may also be patterned. In recent times, the *sarung kebaya* has fallen into disrepute as a public garment and been replaced by more modest clothing, usually a variation of the *baju kurung* ensemble. The *sarung* itself, however, continues to be a staple of the *kampung*.

A Malay bride and groom in traditional wedding attire in Singapore. (EARL & NAZIMA KOWALL/CORBIS)

Joseph Stimpfl

Further Reading

Karim, W. J. (1992) *Women and Culture: Between Malay Adat and Islam*. Boulder, CO: Westview Press.

Nagata, J. (1995) "Modern Malay Women and the Message of the Veil." In *"Male" and "Female" in Developing Southeast Asia*, edited by W. J. Karim. Oxford: Berg Publishers, 101–120.

Ong, A. (1995) "State Versus Islam: Malay Families, Women's Bodies, and the Body Politic in Malaysia." In *Bewitching*

Women, Pious Men: Gender and Body Politics in Southeast Asia, edited by A. Ong and M. G. Peletz. Berkeley and Los Angeles, CA: University of California Press, 159–194.

CLOTHING, TRADITIONAL—MONGOLIA

Mongolian costume shares many characteristics with Chinese, Tibetan, and Manchurian costume forms and its manufacture and styling reflect a nomadic lifestyle. Because the climate is often very cold, costume pieces are worn layered and may be padded and quilted. Many of the long robes worn in Mongolia also have side or front and back slits to accommodate horse riding. Garments are cut and sewn with as little waste as possible, and are not closely tailored to the body. They are cut to hang loosely and comfortably on the body. Garments can be folded easily for storage and transport.

Fabrics used for Mongolian garments include imported cotton, silk, and velvet, indigenous wool fabrics, and animal skins and furs. Chinese silk fabrics are prized, especially silver and gold silk brocade fabrics. Cotton is used for the everyday dress of the common people and as a lining for silk garments. Chinese color symbolism is used in Mongolian costume, and yellow and red are considered to be sacred colors. Colors used in Mongolian costume are stronger in value and hue, however, than those used in Chinese costume. The use of animal skins with the fur worn towards the body is common, and is necessary for warmth in the winter season.

Garment details and embellishments vary depending on the tribe, but basic costume forms are similar for men and women throughout Mongolia. The *debel* is a long caftan-type robe, fastened at the throat, right shoulder, and down the right side with a variety of knot-and-loop closures. This basic garment is constructed from silk fabrics, cotton fabrics, wool felt, or animal skins. Often fur-lined, the *debel* has long sleeves that end in horse-hoof cuffs or in wide striped cuffs. (Horse-hoof cuffs resemble the hoof of a horse: they are wide, flaring cuffs that, when turned down, extend over the hands of the wearer.) The *debel* is seldom completely hidden by other garments layered over it.

Garments worn over the *debel* may fasten down center front or to the right. The *uudji* is a long, sleeveless, collarless robe that often has center back slits; those that close to the right have side slits. The *olba* is a sleeved garment that ends just below the waist; it may be collarless or have a stand-up or shawl collar. The sleeveless *khargilchi* is a vest that is collarless or has a stand-up collar.

Omudun are pants worn by men and women and constructed by sewing two leggings together with a crotch gusset. Men and women may also wear *khoshiya*, or wraparound petticoats; when worn by men, these may be hunting and dancing skirts. The *khoshiya* is also part of lama dress. Mongolian footwear includes shoes and boots made from materials such as black cotton, silk, velvet, and black or brown leather; the surfaces of shoes or boots are usually highly decorated with embroidery. Mongolian shoes may be similar to the flat-soled Chinese shoe, or may have a wooden platform sole in the style common in the Manchu court of China's Qing dynasty (1644–1912). Boots, or *grotal*, have flat leather soles that cover the bottom and sides of the foot and that turn up at the toes. Stockings are cloth or felt and may be padded and quilted.

Diverse headwear is worn in Mongolia, not only for protection, but also to designate rank, status, and tribal or regional affiliation. Headwear includes conical hats, broad brimmed and upturned brim hats, bonnets, and hoods made from a variety of materials; headwear is often lined with fur. A popular soft hat has a helmet-like crown, with front and back brims and fur-lined

Mongolian men in traditional dress in Ulan Ude. (WOLFGANG KAEHLER/CORBIS)

earflaps; this hat may be fabricated from velvet, cloth, cotton, or fur and the brims may be turned up.

Although men and women share general costume, there are differences that distinguish the sexes. Women are more likely to wear the *uudji*. Women's *omudun* are never visible. Women may also wear a highly decorated separate neckpiece, the *ningdjala*, which is worn so that only its stand-up collar is visible. Waistsashes or *bous* are worn with *debel* by men and unmarried women; married women wear unbelted *debel*. Other costume is used to signify marital status and varies tribe to tribe. One special costume piece is often called the "elephant ears" or "mountain-goat horn" headdress. Sleeves on a married woman's *debel* have a tall, stiffly padded sleeve cap; married women also wear embroidered boots with felt uppers, and a red dot on each cheek. Married women wear much jewelry, including earrings, bracelets, pendants, necklaces, and hair ornaments; the jewelry is part of the wealth of the family.

Special costumes also exist for lamas, shamans, and wrestlers. Lama costumes are usually red or yellow, and many items are deliberately pieced or patched together. The *orkimdji* is a toga-like garment draped asymmetrically around the body leaving the right shoulder bare. Other lama costumes include a leather *debel*, a *khoshiya* or petticoat, a shawl-collared patchwork jacket, and a *dagham*, a full-length, pleated cloak with a red collar; a helmet with a red or yellow plume is also worn for certain ceremonies. Ritual costumes include the skeleton dress, a two-piece red and white costume representing a stylized skeleton; this is worn with a mask. Other ritual lama robes are similar to Qing court costume and include a dragon robe; many of these robes do not have closures and slip on over the head. Masks are worn for many ritual dances.

Shaman costumes include leather tunics and pants; the tunics have no closures and slip on over the head. They are embellished with a number of materials, including metal objects, shells, beads, animal fur, horn, and stuffed animals. Shaman costumes also include stylized animal masks. Wrestling matches are an important part of Mongolian festivals, and wrestlers accordingly have a costume that is very different from standard male costume. Wrestling costume includes a short-sleeved jacket that exposes the breast, very full trousers; embroidered leggings, a loincloth of embellished silk, and leather boots with upturned toes.

Laura K. Kidd

Further Reading

Hansen, Henny Harald. (1950) *Mongol Costumes*. Copenhagen, Denmark: Gyldendalske Boghandel.

CLOTHING, TRADITIONAL—SOUTHEAST ASIA, TRIBAL Six colorful tribal groups in Thailand are the Karen, Hmong, Mien, Lahu, Akha, and Lisu. All have migrated from southwest and south-central China and have been mountain dwellers for many generations. All but the Karen can still be found in southern China, as well as in bordering countries. These groups have remarkable artistic skills, which the women express in the production of beautiful clothing for themselves and their families, providing their only relief from the rigors of subsistence agriculture. Although these six tribal groups live as neighbors, the techniques and skills they use in producing their clothing are unique for each group.

Karen

Karen girls and unmarried women typically wear simple white shifts with red trim. Married women typically wear red skirts and indigo-dyed blouses. Young boys typically wear red-striped shirts that hang down below their knees. Men wear red hip-length shirts that resemble those of boys', along with loose black pants. The upper garments for men, women, and children are basically of the same style: two strips of material folded lengthwise and stitched together with openings for the head and arms. Various lengths and embellishment indicate age, gender, and marital status.

While little girls' simple shifts have only a minimum of red at the waist, seams, and hemline, teenaged girls, who weave their own clothing, add color and attractive designs to their dresses. When they are betrothed, they weave their married woman's two-piece costume. The upper part of the blouse will be plain, but the lower third will either be beautifully embroidered or have an intricate woven design if the girl is a Sgaw Karen. If the girl is a Pwo Karen, the woven design will be in the upper part.

Karen women reign supreme among the tribes as skilled weavers. Skirts of the oldest style are woven of homespun thread. Some of the thread is tied with jungle grass, and then dyed with a rust-colored vegetable dye. When woven, this results in ikat patterns that are alternated with stripes of rust-colored thread. Some skirts are woven of commercial thread into very intricate colorful designs, with red predominant. Their distinctive embroidery is mainly created using the satin stitch, tastefully embellished with white rice-shaped Job's-tear seeds.

Sgaw women wear many colorful waist-length strands of beads around their necks and silver bangles on their wrist. Pwo Karen women, on the other hand, wear large quantities of beads wrapped layer upon layer around their necks and tiered down to their waists. Their arms, both above and below their elbows, are lined with metal bracelets. Both Sgaw and Pwo women wear cup-shaped earrings with a cylindrical post that is inserted into large holes in their earlobes.

Hmong (Meo)

Unique among Blue Hmong women are their indigo-colored batiked skirts with bright cross-stitched and appliquéd borders. This full, accordion-pleated skirt swings gracefully from the waist. Women's jackets, with bold patterns of red appliqué and embroidery, large showy collars that hang in the back, and batiked and embroidered aprons with magenta tassels, are among the spectacular tribal costumes in Thailand. Although the white pleated skirts of the White Hmong women are not as spectacular as those of the Blue Hmong, the delicate embroidery, appliqué, and reverse appliqué that grace their jackets reveal unexcelled artistry.

The clothing worn by Blue and White Hmong men and children on special occasions is particularly splendid. At the New Year's festival, all the splendor of Hmong costumes can be seen. Family members, including the smallest children, don their finest clothing, enhancing it with the family's silver jewelry and ornamentation. Heavy chains with pendants of various shapes, four or five-tiered neck rings, finger rings, and earrings are worn, with the most elaborate pieces going to young men and women of marriageable age. The New Year's celebration is of utmost importance in each young person's life, since it is the time for courtship.

While everyday garb is less spectacular, most village Hmong people wear their traditional garb all the time. Little children nearly always wear beautiful caps, such as the rooster cap, bird cap, or flower cap, that showcase their mothers' finest skills.

Mien (Yao)

Mien women typically wear solidly embroidered pants and black tunics with red ruffs. While women of all tribes embroider, the Mien are most noted for their embroidery skills. Mien girls are taught to embroider from the age of five or six; by the time a girl enters her teens she can embroider a large assortment of designs, perhaps even inventing new ones. After her betrothal, she will use her finest embroidery skills to make her own wedding garments, as well as embroidered pants for her groom's mother.

Spectacular appliqué work is another skill of Mien women. Elaborate patterns of symmetrical shapes with many lobes and curlicues in red, black, and blue are edged with white braid and appliquéd to women's aprons (also used as baby-carrying cloths), boys' caps, and saddlebags for horseback riders.

Elaborate caps are made for small children. The black or indigo homespun material of girls' caps is covered with beautiful embroidery. A large red, doughnut-shaped pompon circles the top, and ball-shaped pompons are sewn over each ear and in front. Other decorations may include silver buttons or coins, silk tassels, and small black and white beads. These caps are designed to make the little girls look like flowers. Boys' caps may boast bold appliquéd designs on panels of red and black cloth, an embroidered border, red pompons, and silver buttons.

Lahu

The Chinese-style Lahu woman's ankle-length black tunic opens on the sides, which are split to the waist. The edges of the split sides are embellished with neat bands of cut fold-and-stitch geometric piecework in primary colors, with red predominating. Around the neck and crossing the chest to the fastening under the right arm is a band encrusted with small silver buttons and dangles, some of which may be in the form of fish. Red and blue bands add a touch of color on the sleeves. The Lahu woman's sarong-style skirt is made of black homespun cotton or commercial cloth. The modern-style sarong is often brightened with strips of red and other colors appliquéd to the lower part of the skirt in decorative patterns. Each woman devises her own pattern, such as flowers, scallops, and zigzag designs. The short Chinese-style jacket of the Lahu man's black or indigo suit will have lines of red embroidery edging the jacket. Clusters of silver ball-shaped buttons will be inserted into loops to close the jacket. Very wide pant legs have lines of red embroidery on the cuffs.

Both men and women carry shoulder bags of the same appliquéd design that is on the woman's tunic. At New Year's, men carry bags that are decorated with an abundance of wool tufting and pompons to augment the gaiety of New Year's dancing. There are three other subtribes of Lahu in Thailand, but the Lahu Na, described above, are considered to be the group from which the others have branched out, both genealogically and fashion-wise.

Akha

Akha women are distinguished by their short dark skirts and ornate headdresses. Several styles of headdresses are lavishly decorated with silver ornaments, beads, Job's-tear seeds, buttons, feathers, and coins. Their dark jackets and colorful leggings are resplendent with embroidery and intricate appliqué in bright colors and are edged with Job's-tear seeds or white beads. Quantities of glass beads hang around their necks and are slung from one shoulder to the waist on the opposite side. Men's indigo-dyed jackets are of a smart cut and are brightened with colored embroidery and appliqué. Silver medallion buttons or silver balls fasten them. A young man going courting wears a turban at a rakish angle, with silver rings threaded into it; he also wears heavy silver chains with dangles in the forms of fish, butterflies, and wheels. Children wear a miniature version of adult clothing, except for their close-fitting caps that have been embroidered and appliquéd by their mothers and studded with coins, silver ornaments, feathers, and pompons.

Lisu

Young Lisu women are characterized by their colorful blue or green tunics, full black pants, and bright red leggings. Their tunics have a wide yoke that consists of numerous narrow strips of bright-colored cloth. Similar multicolored bands are sewn to the red sleeves at the shoulders. They wear a wide black sash tightly wound around their waists, with two long tassels hanging in the back. These extraordinary tassels consist of a bundle of long strands made of tightly rolled cloth in bright colors with small pompons at the ends.

At New Year's the young women wear neatly wound turbans with red and yellow wool yarn attached at the front to fall over the crown and down to the shoulders in back. They wear velvet vests encrusted with silver buttons and ornaments over their tunics, and rings with a multitude of dangles around their necks. Young men wear velvet jackets studded with silver buttons, blue knee-length pants, and white turbans. They also wear black sashes with tassels like the women, but they wear them in front. Some young men wear "courting bags" over their shoulders. These bags are covered with a network of small beads, and silver dangles hang from the top border.

Most of the tribal people continue to wear their traditional clothing with some modern adaptations, but may wear them only at festive occasions. For convenience sake, many have adopted Thai or Western dress for daily wear, although there are those who still wear their own distinctive dress all the time.

Elaine T. Lewis

Further Reading

Lewis, Paul, and Elaine T. Lewis. (1984) *Peoples of the Golden Triangle*. New York: Thames and Hudson.

CLOTHING, TRADITIONAL—TAIWAN

The clothing worn by indigenous Taiwanese people was traditionally manufactured from locally available materials derived from plants and animals, and was of crude construction when compared with the garments of the mainland Han Chinese. Later, when Taiwan was incorporated into China during the Qing dynasty (1644–1912), Taiwan was subjected to the same dress regulations as the rest of China, and Taiwanese aboriginal groups were largely assimilated into the society of the mainland emigrants. Taiwanese dress began to diverge from mainland dress when Taiwan was occupied by Japan between 1895–1945.

Some traditional dress of the Paiwan and Puyama aboriginal tribes of southwest Taiwan has survived and can be seen at the Musée de l' Homme, Paris. A man's black cotton top made of rectangles of fabric with brightly colored embroidered edges, fastened with frog fastenings and silver buttons, was worn with a narrow, indigo-dyed, double ikat waist tie. Multicolor leg coverings made of strips of red, yellow, and green fabric, with insets of indigo-dyed double ikat around the crotch, were tied tightly with black braids around the knee and calf. The front thigh and calf area of the machine-stitched leg coverings were decorated with lozenges of geometric-patterned embroidery in red, yellow, blue, white, and black. A narrow, braided linen waist tie with embroidered ends and fringing was attached to the top of the leg coverings and tied twice around the waist; a second waist tie held an eighteen-inch-long dagger in place. A rectangular weft-faced linen cape—probably a woman's mourning cape—is also exhibited. Made in three sections, the cape has a cream background with red double stripes and edging, and is embellished with navy blue geometric embroidery. The cape ties with a thin braid around the neck. It is displayed with a padded, geometrically embroidered headband that resembles a simple turban and has an overlap allowing for size adjustment at the back.

Women wore a *zhanpao*, a long robe that fastened on the right and left and was decorated with a line of embroidery on both arms and brass bells. The *zhanpao* was worn with geometrically embroidered hand covers tied with cerise braids. Leg covers, similar to those worn by men, were made of indigo-dyed fabric with a double ikat spot motif. The below-knee length apron/skirt had an ikat spot motif, indigo-dyed edging, vertical bands of royal blue, and a central panel of geometric and stylized plant motif embroidery in black, red, and blue on an un-dyed linen ground. An older band in brown, red, and blue (possibly using natural dies) was set in nearer the waist. Strands of conch shells were worn around the neck but may also have been used to decorate garments.

During the Qing period, Taiwanese men wore the *zhanpao*and a *magua*, an outer jacket, or *gua*, a vest, worn outside the long gown. The horse jacket, shorter than the *gua* and reaching only to the mid-abdomen, was worn with skullcaps called "melon rind." Officials wore long "python gowns" and a short gown over it called *guazi* (longer than the *gua*), which resembled a modern windbreaker jacket. The garments were of plain colors and were worn in contrasting color combinations: dark or light green, blue, gray, white, or red. *Shan*, a shirt, and trousers, together known as *dangshan*, were worn with a bamboo hat by those engaged in manual work. Women wore *tadaoshan*, a tight-fitting, wide-sleeved jacket trimmed with ribbon, with *mamian chun*, a long skirt, for formal wear. *Gu*, trousers made of silk, were worn for formal occasions, and a cotton version was worn for everyday use. These were worn with bound-foot shoes and a headband. Shades of red were popular for women's dress, including carmine, peach, and pink. The upper and lower garments were often in contrasting shades.

Western Influences

When the Japanese took over Taiwan in 1895, they made little effort to introduce changes in dress, apart from banning the practice of foot binding. Residents of Taiwan soon began to combine Western dress with traditional Chinese dress. In the late nineteenth and early twentieth centuries, Han Chinese men in Taiwan wore the *zhangshan* with Western leather shoes and hats. In Japan at this time, Western dress was embraced as a manifestation of a forward-looking ideology. In 1911 men in Taiwan cut their queues, as did those on the mainland, and women adopted Western style leather shoes worn with a traditional jacket and pants. In the 1920s women wore silk stockings and knee-length skirts with traditional style short-sleeved velvet jackets, and carried a parasol and handkerchief. By the 1920s Western dress had largely replaced traditional Taiwanese dress, but differences between Han Chinese women who originated from the Fujian or Guangdong (Hakka) provinces were visible in their dress; Fujian styles were more lavish and intricate, while the Hakka preferred simple, decorative but durable materials.

Chinese and Japanese Influences

Under Chinese rule, imported Chinese cloth was used to make clothes, as there was no sericulture and little cotton or hemp grown. That which was grown was dyed locally, with chemical dyes gradually replacing plant dyes. Pineapple fiber, taro flax, jute, and banana fiber were also used for textiles. Pineapple fiber was the most successful as it did not cling to the body in Taiwan's humid climate. After 1918, Japanese spinning and weaving technology was imported and large-scale production developed using Japanese cotton, which became the fabric of everyday wear, replacing Chinese imports by the middle or end of the Japanese occupation. After two to three decades of occupation, Japanese fabric patterns and the pale "refined" colors favored by the Japanese (pink, baby-blue, lake-green, grayish blue, and beige), became standard, replacing the patterns and bright colors favored during the Qing dynasty and earlier.

Only after Japan declared war on China in 1937 did the Japanese attempt to weaken Taiwanese cultural links with China and discourage adoption of Chinese fashion. While older men continued to wear traditional dress, many young men adopted military uniforms, *muge* (Japanese wooden clogs), and "duck's tongue" hats—a wider version of the cloth cap traditionally worn by working class men in northern British cities. Women adopted the kimono and both genders adopted Japanese-style names.

As on the mainland, children were dressed like small adults: hats and cloaks had decorated hems, tassels, and embroidery for special occasions. Like mainland garments, pants had split seats. Western-style school uniforms were introduced in 1925.

The *qipao*, or cheongsam (as it became more widely known internationally), that is, the asymmetrically fastened dress worn by women, was worn in Taiwan during the twentieth century, peaking in popularity the 1940s, 1950s, and 1960s. The Sun Yat-sen suit went out of fashion after Communist rule was established on the mainland, but continued to be worn by a few older officials of Taiwan's republican government on formal occasions. Tailored in khaki colored woven wool cloth, it featured breast pockets with military style flaps, brass buttons, and a high collar.

In the mid-twentieth century, the *hong gua*, which consisted of a red embroidered jacket and a black embroidered skirt featuring phoenix and dragon motifs, was worn for special occasions with an elaborate headdress. In rural areas, for special occasions, men wore a traditional blue gown with a red sash worn diagonally, and gilt hat sprays on each side of a trilby hat or skullcap. There was a gradual discontinuance of traditional styles during the 1960s and 1970s as fashions from the West were adopted.

Valerie Wilson Trower

Further Reading

Copper, John. (2000) *Historical Dictionary of Taiwan (Republic of China)*. Lanham, MD: Scarecrow Press.

Garrett, Valery M. (1994) *Chinese Clothing: An Illustrated Guide*. 2d ed. Oxford: Oxford University Press.

Lee, Saalih. (1998) *Culture of Clothing among Taiwan Aborigines, Tradition, Meaning, Images*. Taipei, Taiwan: SMC Publishing Inc.

Steele, Valery and John S. Major. (1999) *China Chic; East Meets West*. New Haven, CT: Yale University Press, 13–69.

Hsui-chun, Su. (1997) "Images of Taiwanese Fashion 1860–1960." In *Evolution and Revolution: Chinese Dress 1700s–1900s*, edited by Claire Roberts. Sydney: Powerhouse Museum, 76–86.

Wei, Te-wen. (1995) *Traditional Dress in Taiwan 1860–1945*. Taipei, Taiwan: SMC Publishing Inc.

CLOTHING, TRADITIONAL — TAJIKISTAN

CLOTHING, TRADITIONAL — TAJIKISTAN Traditional Tajik costume developed as a part of Central Asian costume, and had common style and design features with other countries in the region. Until the twentieth century, both men and women wore bulky pants and long tunic shirts with no opening down the center front. The only difference between shirts for males and females was in the neckline shape: men's shirts had horizontal necklines, while women's had vertical necklines, designed for breastfeeding. In some ethnic groups young women's tunic shirts had the horizontal neckline shape until they were married or had their first child. Tunics for men and women had the same cut. The body of the garment, front and back, was made of one rectangular piece folded at the shoulders with underarm panels. The sleeves usually had a rectangular shape as well, or were slightly narrowed to the wrists. This design did not require scissors to cut; often the fabric was torn by hand. The center and side panels were cut with the fabric grain going lengthwise, while the grain in the sleeves went across, creating interesting pattern with the stripes in the men's coat, called *khalat*. The coat had no fastener, but could be tied with a sash or big colorful handkerchief folded diagonally. Money, tobacco, and other personal effects were kept in the folds of the sash.

In common with all Central Asian men, Tajik men had a large variety of headwear. They wore fur hats, turbans, and stiff squared little black caps, called *tubeteika*, with a white stylized pepper or cucumber embroidered on them. Men wore their hair closely cropped.

As in many Asian countries, women wore pants under their tunics, which were made in white or other light colors; to wear only a tunic was considered sinful. Pants were very wide at the waist and hips, tight at the ankle, and had a decorative trim at the bottom. Pants were an important part of the costume—women kept them on, even while sleeping. It was common to make the pants of two fabrics: plain white cotton for the upper part, and a colorful patterned silk or fine calico for the legs, which could be seen from under the dress. This tradition was developed not only to save expensive fabric, but also because they believed in the magical power of the color white, which was supposed to provide a woman with fertility and happiness.

A Tajik woman was not allowed to put her arms into the sleeves of a coat or wear any tops with a center front opening. A well-known proverb of the time explained this rule: "God told men to wear coats, but not women." Although women had a special kind of coat, called a *parandja*, they could wear it only with the a high neckline. In the winter females wore a little padded shirt under the long tunic. In the cities during the nineteenth century, women were required to cover entire their body, including the face. They used a specially designed scarf or net made of horsehair. A big white square scarf made of high-quality cotton or silk was used to cover the head. The typical jewelry was silver earrings, rings, and necklaces of coral or coins. Women braided their hair into thirty or forty tiny long plaits: the number marked the degree of beauty.

When this region of Asia was joined to czarist Russia at the end of the nineteenth century, traditional costume began to respond to Western culture, trade, and fashion. These changes were new for a Muslim country, where traditions and stability in the costume had been strictly protected by religion and prejudices. Mass-produced, inexpensive fabrics from Russian mills began to predominate over domestic home-woven textiles, making clothing cheaper and more affordable for everybody. The greatest transformation in traditional costume, however, occurred after the October Revolution (1917). The transformation continued during the building of the Asian Soviet republics over the following decades.

Modifications in traditional costume started with reforming the basic tunic cut. A more flattering shoulder line and a round armhole and sleeve cap made the garment more comfortable. In the late 1920s women started to wear *tubeteika*, which usually were made of black velvet or wool, embroidered with silver and colored threads, and decorated with hanging silver coins. Later, Tajik women adopted Western style for outerwear: the *parandja* was transformed into a fairly tight-fitting jacket. Some elements of the traditional costume—such as the *tubeteika*—are still widely used in Tajikistan. The men's coat is still tied with a sash, especially by old men or in the villages. Tajiks often wear contemporary fashion but made from textiles with traditional patterns and hues.

Elena E. Karpova

Further Reading

Fairservis, Walter Jr. (1971) *Costumes of the East.* New York: Devin-Adair.

Sukhareva, O. A. (1982) *Istoriya Sredneasiatskogo Costuma* (The History of Central Asian Costume). Trans. by Elena Karpova.

CLOTHING, TRADITIONAL — THAILAND

The numerous ethnic groups of Thailand traditionally have produced a wide array of cotton and silk textiles. Each ethnic group wove textiles in distinctive patterns for clothing, domestic, and ceremonial purposes, thus transforming textiles into markers of identity. The various Thai linguistic groups, as well as the Khmer, Kui, and Malay ethnic minority groups living in the lowland areas of Thailand used cotton and silk fibers to create their textiles. A combination of fiber, color, and technique distinguishes a textile of one group from that of another, but the structure of textiles made throughout Thailand is similar.

Women's Traditional Dress

The *pha sin*, or tube skirt, is the traditional lower garment for women of the various ethnic groups of lowland Thailand. The *pha sin* consists of three sections: *hua sin* (head or top), *tua sin* (body or midsection), and *tin sin* (foot or border). The three sections of the *pha sin* are either woven in one piece of cloth with patterns differentiating the three sections or are made from two or more pieces of cloth sewn together.

The top section is made from plain-woven cotton cloth of various colors. The Tai Lue of northern Thailand and the Lao Song Dam of central Thailand use indigo cotton for the top section, while the Tai Yuan living in the north prefer natural or white cotton, sometimes with a strip of red cotton, for this section. The Tai Lao and Khmer use a single piece of material for all three sections of the *pha sin*; they distinguish the top section by the absence of motifs.

The midsection is the largest section of the tube skirt. Weavers of the various ethnic groups use a variety of techniques to decorate the midsection, including ikat (tye-dying the thread before weaving it), tapestry, and supplementary warp and weft patterning. The Tai Lao, Lao Khrang, Khmer, and Kui weavers favor weft ikat or *mat mii* technique, while the Tai Lue employ tapestry and other techniques to create complex patterns. The Lao Phuan of Sukothai and Uttaradit provinces weave an overall supplementary warp pattern for the midsection and attach a complicated patterned border to their tube skirt.

The skirt border is either plainly woven or very elaborate. The most intricately patterned border is the *tin chok*, a border pattern with decorated *chok*, or discontinuous supplementary weft motifs. The skirt border is highly valued, and many women of various ethnic groups possess a *pha sin tin chok* (a *pha sin*, or tube skirt, decorated with a discontinuous supplementary weft border) for special occasions. The Tai Lue prefer a simple border of plain indigo cotton, while the Phu Tai and Lao Song Dam weave a thicker border, approximately five centimeters wide, decorated with supplementary patterns or stripes. Some women dress in tube skirts or sarongs with an overall pattern. Mature Khmer women of northeast Thailand often wear tube skirts with a checked or plaid pattern. Malay women in the south favor batik or wax-resist-dyed sarongs similar to Malay dress of neighboring countries.

The *chong kraben* wasthe lower garment traditionally worn by women of central Thailand and Cambodia. Central Thai women used a variety of textiles for the *chong kraben* including Indian chintz; they also used different types of silk textiles such as silver and gold brocades on silk made locally or from India; local weft ikat silk; and imported Chinese and Cambodian silk. The use of an upper garment by women varied until the beginning of the twentieth century. Most women did not wear an upper garment, but wrapped a rectangular cloth, *pha sabai*, around the breasts or across a shoulder when attending religious or ceremonial functions. Prior to the twentieth century, women belonging to ethnic groups originating in colder climates (for example, the Tai Lue, Lao Song Dam, and Phu

Costumed lakorn dancers perform at the Lak Muang shrine in Bangkok in 1995. (KEVIN R. MORRIS/CORBIS)

Tai) wore blouses or shirts of indigo or black cotton decorated with silver buttons, embroidery, or appliqué. For special occasions, an elaborately patterned shoulder or breast cloth was added to complete the outfit. The Phu Tai *pha phrae wa* was an outstanding example of a shoulder cloth; this red silk textile is decorated with bands of complex patterns and is approximately three meters long. Women began to wear European-style blouses in the 1900s.

Men's Traditional Dress

Unlike women, men no longer commonly wear traditional clothing. The traditional clothing of men was not as elaborate as women's dress and did not vary much among the different ethnic groups. Men wore a short version of the *chong kraben* as a loincloth, made of plain or plaid patterned cotton. This shortened version of the *chong kraben* exposed the wearer's thighs, which were usually tattooed. Men reserved a silk *chong kraben* for special occasions such as weddings and ordination ceremonies into the Buddhist monkhood. A plaid or checked cotton sarong was another lower garment favored by Malay men in the southern region of Thailand.

Men did not wear an upper garment on a daily basis, and draped a cloth over one or a both shoulders for special events. Men of ethnicities from colder climates dressed in cotton shirts with a shoulder cloth for ceremonies and religious activities. Men also used a plaid cotton cloth or *pha khao ma* as a sash, bag, belt, head cloth, scarf, and towel. Both sexes carried a shoulder bag that could be plainly or elaborately patterned. A young woman might create an intricate bag to give to a man as a token of her affection.

Household Textiles

Women produce an array of textiles used for such purposes as mattresses, blankets and covers, pillows, and mosquito nets. These items are made from cotton, but items reserved for a wedding may be silk or decorated with silk and often contain elaborate motifs. The Tai Lue favor black and red geometric motifs on a natural cotton background. The Lao Song Dam adorn their special household textiles with green, red, orange, and white silk appliqué. The Lao Khrang prefer a natural cotton blanket with elaborate supplementary patterns at the ends, bordered with red cotton.

Religious or Ceremonial Textiles

Women also weave textiles for religious or ceremonial purposes. Laywomen provide dyed cotton cloth for Buddhist monks' robes, as well as household textiles. Family members usually donate these items to monks at ordination ceremonies and at subsequent religious festivals. Ceremonial textiles are also donated to hang inside and outside a temple and to cover palm-leaf manuscripts.

Textiles for the Royalty

Until the beginning of the twentieth century, Thai royalty consumed textiles that were similar in design and structure to villagers' textiles but were of higher quality. Court weavers produced gold and silver supplementary-patterned silks for the royal family and aristocracy. The elite also commissioned highly skilled weavers throughout the kingdom to supply finely woven silk and cotton textiles. The royalty imported specially designed textiles from India, China, and Cambodia; their laws restricted the use of the imported fabrics to the higher strata of society. Thai kings wore the finest materials when their dress mimicked the deities.

The adoption of Western-style clothing among the Thai elite began in the mid-nineteenth century. Western missionaries also introduced and persuaded women to wear blouses with the traditional lower garment in the late 1800s. Men more readily adopted Western clothing (such as trousers) during the first quarter of the twentieth century. The *pha sin* continues to be worn in rural areas on a daily basis by some women, and the elite are returning to modernized versions of traditional dress inspired by Her Majesty Queen Sirikit of Thailand for special events. Local and foreign interests alike currently sustain traditional textile production, and perhaps will continue to do so into the near future.

Linda S. McIntosh

Further Reading

Fraser-Lu, Sylvia. (1988) *Hand-woven Textiles of Southeast Asia*. Singapore: Oxford University Press.

Gittinger, Mattibelle, and H. Leedom Lefferts. (1992) *Textiles and the Tai Experience* Washington DC: Textile Museum of America.

Maxwell, Robyn. (1990) *Textiles of Southeast Asia: Tradition, Trade, and Transformation* Melbourne, Australia: Australian National Gallery of Art.

National Identity Board (NIB). (1996) *Thai Textiles: Threads of a Cultural Heritage* Chiang Mai, Thailand: Chiang Mai University Press.

Songsak Pranwatthanakul, ed. (1993) *Asia's Textile Heritage* Chiang Mai, Thailand: Chiang Mai University Press.

CLOTHING, TRADITIONAL — TIBET

Tibetan costume reflects the environment and nomadic lifestyle of many of Tibet's people. A long his-

TIBET DRESS IN THE 1840s

The dress of the Thibetan women closely resembles that of the men; the main difference is, that over the robe they add a short, many-coloured tunic, and that they divide their hair into two braids, one hanging down each shoulder. The women of the humbler classes wear a small yellow cap, like the cap of liberty that was in fashion in France at the time of our first republic.

Source: Huc Evariste-Regis and Joseph Gabet.([1851] 1987) *Travels in Tartary, Thibet and China, 1844–1846.* New York: Dover Publications, 174.

tory of intermarriage between Chinese and Tibetan nobility, resulting in exchanges of material culture, has also influenced Tibetan dress. Fabrics used for Tibetan clothing include hemp, Chinese cottons and silks, rayon, indigenous animal furs, felted fabric derived from the hair of the yak, and *pulu,* a traditional woolen cloth. Chinese silks are believed to have been brought to Tibet when a Chinese princess married a Tibetan noble during the Tang dynasty (618–907). *Pulu* became a popular tribute item given to China. Other Chinese costume characteristics, such as color symbolism and the right-over-left closure method, are also reflected in Tibetan costume. Tibetan and Mongolian traditional costumes also share characteristics; in particular, lamas of both countries share similar costumes, among them the *zi xia* (crested helmets). Although basic garments worn throughout central and northern Asia may be similar, distinctions exist not only between countries, but also between regions and tribes within each nation.

Tibetan garments are worn layered, and many basic pieces are worn by men and women alike. Most garments close to the right and are fastened with a variety of closures. The *anju* is a full-length, long-sleeved garment made of silk, cotton, or rayon, worn close to the body. Over the *anju* is worn the *anduh,* a full-length, sleeveless garment usually made of black *pulu* and lined with blue fabric. Men and women also wear leggings tied to a waist girdle. The basic Tibetan outer garment is the *giuba,* a long-sleeved, round-collared, loose-fitting robe of *pulu;* it closes to the right and is tied at the waist with a sash or belt. The *giuba* may be as long as seven feet, with the upper part bloused over the waist tie to adjust the length to knee level for men and ankle level for women and priests. Waist ties—leather belts or silk or cotton sashes—keep the *giuba* in place and allow the wearer to pull out his or her arms for cooling. This garment can also be used as a blanket or sleeping bag.

Other robes include the *giuiu,* a sleeveless, broad-shouldered robe made of black *pulu* or animal skins, and the *giubjialo,* a lined *pulu* robe with a floral design on the collar. The *cha* is a fur-lined robe worn by men and is made either from jacquard silk fabric (for special occasions) or plain-colored leather (for everyday wear). Waist-length jackets, both sleeved and sleeveless, may also be worn over the *guiba.* Square-toed *sunpa* (boots) are a popular type of footwear. *Sunpa* have soles of thick yak hide and fabric foot and leg sections. They are secured with cloth ties and often have embroidery at the ankle area.

Headwear is also an important part of Tibetan costume, and the shape and quality of the hat indicate rank, status, and regional and tribal affiliation. The *xi-*

A woman in Lanmdakh wearing a *peyrak,* the traditional headwear for married women in Tibet and northern India. (RIC ERGENBRIGHT/CORBIS)

amou jiasi (golden flower) hat is worn in winter by men, women, and children. The *xianmou jiasi* has a tall crown of fabric, felt, or leather, four fur flaps, and is often trimmed with gold rickrack imported from India or China.

Costume indicates a woman's marriage status. Married women wear the *bangdian*, an apron-like garment made from three widths of hand-woven, horizontally striped fabric in shades of red. Different hairstyles and hair ornaments are also important marital indicators and vary by region and tribe. A basic married woman's hairstyle is a Y-shaped style, or *peyrak*, with the hair curving into two ram-shaped horns that encircle the head. Women's hair is also embellished with many hair ornaments of precious metals and materials.

Accessories are important to Tibetan costume, serving decorative and practical purposes. Silver belt buckles and belts are common for both sexes. Many accessories hang from the waist ties. Males typically hang Buddhist boxes, cartridge clips and belts, and *bagu* (metal wallets) from their waist ties or belts. Women often hang needle cases from their waist ties. Men and women wear jewelry such as earrings, bracelets, and necklaces; men may wear only one large dangling earring. Coral, jade, silver, and gold are highly prized jewelry materials. Women wear more jewelry than men; part of the wealth of the family is kept in women's jewelry. One of the most important accessories worn by women is the *kou*, a square metal box with a diamond shape on it. The *kou* is worn around the neck on a chain so that it rests on the woman's chest and contains a Buddhist religious artifact.

The *kha-btags* or *kata* is an important Tibetan textile material artifact. It is a white scarf symbolizing purity that is offered as a gift when greeting people. The *kha-btags* are also used as offerings when visiting shrines and during other rituals such as wedding and funeral rites. This tradition is believed to have evolved from an ancient custom of clothing statues of deities.

Laura Klosterman Kidd

Further Reading

An Hsu. (1988) *Tsang tsu fu shih i shu* (The Art of Tibetan Costume and Ornaments). Tianjin, China: Nan kai ta hsueh ch'u pan she.

CLOTHING, TRADITIONAL—TURKEY

In Turkish costume, highly ornate ensembles are composed of many layers of textile and nontextile items. Older forms of Turkish traditional dress do not include Western-style dress, which exhibits rapid change and is available through a system of mass production and distribution. Traditional dress was once the everyday dress of people living in the rural areas of Turkey; today it is worn daily only by a few rural women, by others for ceremonial use, and by Turkish folk-dance groups.

The traditional dress of Turkey has changed slowly; this is important historically because it informs us about the people who produced it. Surface decoration and the way costume elements are arranged on the body serve as a means of communication, indicating membership in tribal or village groups, and myriad other anthropological messages.

Turkish traditional dress exhibits tribal and village distinctions while sharing features with Central Asian dress, the dress of the Ottoman Court, and Middle Eastern dress. The common features can be attributed to the cultural contacts of the Turkic peoples over the centuries. The Turkish people are believed to have migrated south and west from the Altai Mountain regions south of Lake Baikal, entering Persia, Iraq, Central Asia and Eastern Europe. By the eleventh century they penetrated the Anatolian plateau, the landmass forming the peninsula in western Asia that comprises the bulk of the modern Republic of Turkey. By the fifteenth and sixteenth centuries Turkic groups formed many villages, some of which remain intact today. This stability of geographic location coupled with relative isolation in inner Anatolia, away from the waterways on the periphery, allowed for stability and slow change in traditions of dress.

Turkic peoples influenced and were influenced by cultural contact with civilizations along their migration routes, by the earlier inhabitants of Anatolia, and by the remains of Anatolia's ancient civilizations. The vast Ottoman empire (fourteenth–nineteenth centuries), which eventually encompassed the Balkan Peninsula, Greece, Transylvania, Moldavia, Wallachia, most of Hungary, Podolia, the entire north coast of the Black Sea, Crete, Cyprus and the Aegean isles, Armenia, most of the Caucasus, the Tigris and Euphrates valleys to the Persian Gulf, the eastern Mediterranean coast, a strip along the Arabian peninsula, Egypt, Tripoli, Tunisia, Algeria, and the Anatolian peninsula, brought the Turks in contact with people from other lands. Those contacts also had an effect on the dress and textiles of Turkey.

Forms of Turkish Traditional Dress

Characteristic features of Turkish traditional dress include the layering of garments, distinctive surface or woven-in decoration on the fabrics, and a geometric

Men in traditional dress at the festival of Edirne in 1954. (STUDIO PATELLANI/CORBIS)

cut. Wool, silk, and cotton, fibers indigenous to Turkey, are commonly used for apparel. Separate garments are layered to accommodate the need for adjustments according to climate; to create storage areas for coins and other small items in fabric folds; and to create a system for holding garments onto the body. Careful cutting exposes portions of garments underneath the top layers. Surface design is achieved by embroidering, dyeing, or weaving.

Common items are the *salvar* (baggy trouser), *gomlek* (chemise), *ucetek* (three-skirted cloak), and elaborate headgear that always includes one or more headscarves for women. Sleeveless vests and waist-length jackets are also common, as are aprons for women. The layers are held together by a girdle or belt, or by a shawl (*sal kusak*) that is folded and wrapped around the waist. With the exception of the face, the body completely covered. Portions of the men's body are left exposed, such as the head, face, and neck, with the exception of a headdress. In the traditional dress of some areas of Turkey, portions of the legs are exposed. Turkish traditional dress was relatively unisex, but certain distinguishing features clearly indicated gender. Primary among these was the style of headdress. In the Ottoman court, male headdress distinguished social and economic positions. Headdresses such as the turban, used throughout the Ottoman empire from before the Turks' capture of Constantinople in 1453 to the early nineteenth century, and the fez, used for about 100 years after the demise of the turban, became symbols of identity for Turkish men during their respective periods of use. Both were outlawed: the turban in 1829 when the fez was adopted, and the fez in 1925—in favor of the Western-style brimmed hat. The headscarf for women remains an important article of dress among segments of the population in modern Turkey.

Recent Changes

Over 60 percent of the inhabitants of modern Turkey live in urban areas. Forces of the global economy have created changes in lifestyles, particularly since 1970. Traditional dress and textile production is disappearing at an astounding rate. Fabrics formerly were produced in villages, but now changing markets and improved infrastructure have made it possible for women to purchase fabrics and trims, produced throughout Turkey and the world, in their local markets. Women in some villages continue to wear all or parts of their traditional dress, especially for ceremonial events such as weddings. Common in most villages is the baggy trouser (*salvar*) worn sometimes with a skirt over the top, a long-sleeved blouse or T-shirt, a sweater-vest, and a headscarf. Turkish folk dance groups have kept some of the elaborate dress ensemble traditions alive. In the urban areas of Turkey, men and women wear typical Western clothing, although some Muslim women cover this dress with a coat and wear a headscarf, or cover themselves completely with a black cloak.

Marlene R. Breu

Further Readings

Breu, Marlene R. (1999) "Traditional Turkish Women's Dress: A Source of Common Understandings for Expected Behaviors." In *Folk Dress in Europe and Anatolia: Beliefs About Protection and Fertility*, edited by Linda Welters. Oxford: Berg, 33–51.

Erden, Attila. (1998) *Anadolu Giysi K lt r* (Anatolian Garment Culture). Ankara, Turkey: Ministry of Culture.

Jirousek, Charlotte A. (1996) "Dress and Social Policy: Change in Women's Dress in a Southwestern Turkish Village." *Dress* 23: 47–62.

Norton, John. (1997) "Faith and Fashion in Turkey." In *Language of Dress in the Middle East*, edited by Nancy Lindisfarne-Tapper and Bruce Ingham. Richmond, U.K.: Curzon.

Scarce, Jennifer. (1987) *Women's Costumes of the Near and Middle East*. London: Unwin Hyman.

CLOTHING, TRADITIONAL — TURKMENISTAN

Dress in Turkmenistan developed as a part of Central Asian costume, and the styles and design of clothing were similar to those in Uzbekistan and Tajikistan. Until the 1880s, traditional clothing had the same basic form—a long, loose, simple tunic style. Styles were similar for all social classes, often differentiated only by the quality of the cloth and accessories, and the quantity of clothing in a wardrobe. The costume, however, was visibly different depending on the individual's age and social status.

The modern Turkmen women's costume includes a colorful, three-quarter-length jacket, or caftan, over a fairly tight-fitting dress with narrow sleeves and a little stand-up collar. The front panel, center front edges, and neckline of the dress are outlined in white embroidery. The jacket's front edge, hem, and bottom of the sleeves are decorated with velvet bands, metal disks, and beads. The cap, or *tubeteika*, in a bright color matching the jacket, is covered with silver jewelry and hanging coins.

The famous Karakul sheep are bred in Turkmenistan, and their gray, black, or brown wool has always been used extensively in clothing. Cotton and heavy silk were used in traditional clothing for the summer season. Women's costume was usually made from plain fabrics. All colors were used, but yellow, red, green, and blue were especially popular. The most popular color was red, in all its shades.

Everyday clothing was simple and consisted of a long tunic shirt and pants. The upper part of pants was wide, gathered with a lace. Pants were worn very low, almost at the hip level, leaving the belly bared. Pants' legs narrowed from knee level down. Women wore scarves and little woolen dome-shaped caps on their heads. Women's flat, soft, leather shoes or boots had pointed, slightly upturned toes.

An important part of the Turkmen women's costume was silver jewelry with semiprecious stones, which were necessary elements of everyday attire. Women wore rings, earrings, necklaces, and special decorations for forehead, temples, overcap and dress. The jewelry was often heavy with hanging coins. Even women from the poorest families had to have some jewelry—at least a ring—because the Turkmen believed that food cooked by a woman with no ring was bad. Children, both girls and boys, began to wear silver decorations at the age of five. Girls from nine to twelve years old, who were ready for marriage, and married women who had not yet had their first baby, had many more decorations than middle-aged women (thirty to thirty-five years of age).

Until the middle of the twentieth century, basic dress for men included a cotton or woolen shirt in dark colors and black or brown pants tucked into leather boots. The shirt had a rounded neckline with an opening on the right side and was worn over the pants and tied with a brightly colored sash; men would keep little necessities and tools in the pleats of the sash. For outerwear, men wore a three-quarter-length cotton robe or long sheepskin coat. The robe had dolman sleeves (wide at the shoulders but coming to a tight cuff), was decorated with a braid on the outer edges, and could be padded. Every Turkmen man carried arms, which was a part of the costume. A high, sheepskin bonnet, or *papakha*, was worn during summer and winter.

Today in Turkmenistan people wear a mixture of modern Western dress and traditional costume. The most complete version of the traditional costume can be seen during national holidays or special occasions, such as wedding ceremonies. However, some elements of the traditional costume, such as the *tubeteika*, and specific textile colors and patterns in the cloth, can be seen every day in the streets of big cities and tiny villages. Women still wear pants under their dresses, and older females always cover their heads with scarves. During the last decade of the twentieth century, after Turkmenistan became independent from the former Soviet Union (1991), the country began to revive its native culture, and interest in the history and style of the traditional costume increased.

Elena E. Karpova

Further Reading

Fairservis, Walter, Jr., (1971) *Costumes of the East*. Riverside, CT: Chatham.

CLOTHING, TRADITIONAL — UZBEKISTAN Traditional Uzbek costume remained unchanged until the end of the nineteenth century. As in all Muslim countries, Islamic values in Uzbekistan were reflected in the style of dress. Men and women alike had limited items in their wardrobe; these included a long tunic shirt, pants, and a coat. The style of a garment was not subject to change and was similar for both sexes and all social classes. For example, the only difference in a tunic shirt for men and women was in the neckline openings—horizontal for men, vertical for women. Wealthy people could be distinguished from the poor by the superior quality of their fabrics, their more expensive jewelry, and the presence of decorative elements in their costume, such as embroidery, studded stones, and beads.

Despite similarities in costume style, each ethnic group created a unique look, artistically combining the elements of design, color palettes, textile patterns, and trims. Within an ethnic group or region, costume differed because each family had to spin, weave, and dye its own fabrics to make clothing. This led to the colorful variety in Uzbek traditional dress.

Men's Clothing

The most important part of Uzbek men's costume was the loose-fitting cotton coat, called the *khalat*. The *khalat* was long-sleeved, knee length or longer, and made from fabric with a variety of colorful stripes. The bottom of the sleeves, center edges, hem, and neckline of the coat were sewn round with a decorative braid, which was believed to protect a person from evil powers. The side seams were slit for ease when walking, riding a horse, or sitting down. Wearing two or more coats at the same time was common in both winter and summer, and gave a man a certain prestige while showing the prosperity of the family. The outer coat could be padded with batting. A white tunic shirt was worn under the coat. The coat or shirt was tied with a big folded handkerchief or a band. This band was an important accessory, and could be made of fine fabrics, decorated with complicated silver embroidery, studded with stones and silver coins, and hung with little bags for tobacco and keys. Pants were loosely cut but narrowed to the bottom and were tucked into soft leather boots with pointed toes. Skullcaps were popular all over Central Asia. The *tubeteika* is an Uzbek cap made of velvet or wool, beautifully embroidered with silk or silver threads. Over the cap men could drape a turban, or *chalma*, in different colors. Fur hats were also worn.

Women's Clothing

Women's traditional dress consisted of a tunic, pants, a scarf, and a coat. The long, loose tunic had wide sleeves reaching to the wrists. Loose-cut pants were often made of the same fabric as the tunic, or out of complementary fabric. The bottom of the pants was gathered and decorated with embroidered braid. Women's coats were similar to men's *khalat*.

For centuries cotton has been used extensively for clothing in Uzbekistan. Home-woven striped and white cotton were the most common fabrics for everyday wear. Textile patterns often included up to six or seven different colors in the typical geometrical or stylized floral design. Fabrics were brightly colored, in shades of red, yellow, blue, green, violet, and orange. The color of the costume was an important signal of a person's age or social status. Red and pink were common for girls and young women; middle-aged women were supposed to wear shades of light blue and gray. White was the most popular color and appropriate for all ages, especially for the elderly. Black, dark blue, and violet were colors of mourning.

It was not appropriate for a woman to be seen bareheaded, even by family members. The scarf was tied round the head, leaving long ends hanging down the back. Similarly, a woman was required to cover herself with a cloak when outside of the house. In different ethnic groups a big scarf or a special kind of stylized coat, or *parandja*, was used. *Parandja* was worn with the neckline resting on the top of the head, partially covering the woman's face and draping around the entire body. In many Muslim countries females are not allowed to show their faces in public, and one common cover in Central Asia was a black net made of horsehair. The length of the net varied, depending on the region, from waist-level to the hip-level, or sometimes longer. Only in large Central Asian cities such as Tashkent, Farghona, and Bukhoro was the veil a necessary part of a woman's wardrobe at the end of the nineteenth century. In villages, women used the hanging ends of the scarf tied round the head to cover their faces when in public.

Women's long, black hair was braided into two or more plaits. In addition to common Central Asian jewelry, it was popular among young Uzbek women to pierce the nose and decorate it with a ring set with stones. Shoes were made of felt or colored leathers and had low heels.

Clothing in the Twentieth Century

Russian influence was seen in the early twentieth century. Shirts and coats became more comfortable and closer fitting with the introduction of shoulder seams, cut armholes, and rounded sleeve caps. The traditional tunic shirt evolved into a dress with a waist seam and, later, a front yoke. Today the dress with a yoke is considered the traditional Uzbek women's costume.

In the 1920s, during the Civil War and the creation of the Asian Soviet Republics, Western clothing began to appear in Central Asian wardrobes. This trend first developed in larger cities. Men added pieces from military uniforms as well as civil Western dress to their everyday attire. Although women were more conservative and slow in reshaping their wardrobe than men were, they started to appear in public with uncovered faces.

The modern version of traditional women's costume consists of the dress, pants, and headwear. Dress length varies from the knee to calf level. Pants, which are still an irreplaceable part of an Uzbek woman's wardrobe, can be very long, draping over shoes, or shortened for young women. A hip-length jacket or a waist-length vest can be worn over the dress. The skullcap, or *tubeteika*, is now extremely common. A tassel is placed on the top of a woman's cap for festive occasions.

At the end of the twentieth century, Western fashion dominated, but fashionable styles are still produced with native design elements and in traditional multicolored textile patterns and hues. Since the disintegration of the Soviet Union and the creation of an independent Uzbekistan in 1991, the culture as well as the economy has been in transition, influencing modern Uzbek appearance.

Elena E. Karpova

Further Reading

Fairservis, Walter, Jr. (1971) *Costumes of the East*. Riverside, CT: Chatham.

CLOTHING, TRADITIONAL — VIETNAM Most Vietnamese men now wear Western clothing but most Vietnamese women wear the *ao dai*, a front opening, knee-length, coat-like garment with a stand collar and splits from hem to waist level at each side. The *ao dai* is tailor-made from plain or printed cotton for summer use, or from silk for special occasions; these fabrics often are mixed with polyester to reduce creasing. The *ao dai*, worn in winter, is made from wool, or a wool/polyester mix. The *ao dai* is always worn over *quan*, zip-fronted pants with two buttons at the waist. *Quan* may be black or white depending on the *ao dai*; women wear matching *ao dai* and *quan* if wealthy or for special occasions. Schoolgirls and students often wear *ao dai* with a white ground with white pants, but blue and lavender are also popular. Elderly women prefer brown and navy blue, worn with black pants. Black is not worn much in the hot southern summers. The *ao dai* may also be embroidered. The length of the *ao dai* varies, depending on fashion and occasion, from a few inches above the ankle (for evening wear) to just below the knee. The collar may also be round necked or V-necked, depending on fashion. Sleeve lengths are long or three-quarter length.

Although it has not been commonly worn since the 1930s, men's traditional dress displayed features similar to women's dress. It comprised a long-sleeved, indigo-dyed tunic with silver button fastenings. As with women's dress, the tunic sometimes had contrast edging on the collar, cuffs, and lower hem, and was worn with either a woven, skirtlike garment to mid-calf, or with simple pants. Tunics were worn loose, tied with a sash, or worn with a tabard. Headdresses varied from plain wrapped fabric to tassel-decorated caps.

Tribal Clothing

As recently as the 1930s and 1940s tribal women wore elaborately decorated, woven traditional dress; this has largely been replaced by a simplified version of dress worn everyday in rural areas. In the north, women wear a loose-fitting shirt with a skirt and headscarf, while women in the south may wear a loose-fitting shirt and pants with a headscarf. Among tribal groups, fabrics are woven on back strap or simple looms, using homegrown cotton, hemp, or ramie, to make striped waistcloths and warp-faced ikat. Embroidery includes motifs of trees, flowers, eight-pointed stars, and sugarcane leaves. Brocade fabric is produced using up to 150 supplementary threads in cotton or silk. Dress is worn with pride as a marker of ethnic identity among hill tribes and subgroups. Each group has local nuances in spoken dialect and in women's clothing.

In the North The Tai people form eight subgroups totaling over three million people in northern Vietnam. Other tribal groups living in northern Vietnam are the Jarai, the Phen, the Lao, the Lu, the Nung, and the Pa Di, while the Hmong, Yao, and Pathern spread from the north to the northwest. Women's garments are distinctive to each group, and permutations of indigo-dyed cotton, embroidery, and silver decoration signify tribe membership, gender, and status.

Many Tai women wear long black tunics, while those worn by the Nung (Ngan) are shorter. The Tai also wear a wrapped, sarong-style waistcloth with bands of decoration. Pants or leggings are worn under the skirt, a waist tie holds the waistcloth in place, and pendants on chains of silver links complete the ensemble. The Jarai decorate loincloths and waistcloths with geometric bands of supplementary weft decoration. The Phen wear brown-colored clothing; the Lao wrap their heads in cone-shaped headdresses; the Pa Di women wear a headdress shaped like a house roof and trimmed with silver balls.

The garments of some groups are similar to those of other groups; for example, Nung and Pa Di women both wear a short black tunic that opens on the right, with a decorated stand collar, and contrasting blue and white cuffs. The fabric seam at the sleeve join is embroidered and the front fastening is decorated and fastened with silver balls. The Lu wear a short black cotton tunic with a peplum (a short overskirt attached at the waist). The tunic is decorated at all seam joins with embroidery, and adorned with silver coins at the front. The waistcloth has a vertically embroidered and appliquéd central panel, and an outer waistcloth with an embroidered panel is worn around the hips. The Hmong batik the central panel of their distinctive circular skirts using bamboo pens and beeswax. Made from hemp, cotton, and silk, and now stitched by ma-

Vietnamese women in *ao dai*s on the street in Hanoi in 1993. (OWEN FRANKEN/CORBIS)

chine, women's circular pleated skirts are indigo dyed, batiked, embroidered, and appliquéd. Additional Yao decoration includes tassels, beading, fringing, and silver lozenges used as fastenings. The linear-patterned batik is applied using different sized pens for eight-pointed stars, spirals, flowers, and gourds. The Yao use larger motifs, and the Pathern, use red as a ground color rather than black. The Lisu, Akha, Hmong and Micu all use Chinese methods in the construction of their garments, especially jackets, trousers, pleated skirts, aprons, and kaftans. Indigo dye on cotton cloth is decorated with colorful bands of appliqué, cross-stitch embroidery, and the inclusion of tufts of wool, seeds, silver bosses, and club-shaped pendants. Motifs are mostly geometric or record the natural environment. Weaving and needlework are prized skills; a prospective bride's work may be examined by future in-laws as a means to determine character. The Muong live in an intermediate area between the mountains and the coastal plains; here they grow cotton used for white, front buttoning, women's tunics and folded headdresses, similar to the caps of Western nurses. These are worn with plain green or patterned waist sashes and long waistcloths.

In Central and Southern Vietnam The Mon-Khmer of Truong Son Cordillera and the Central Highlands are spread throughout the central and southern areas of Vietnam. Other groups in this area include the Bahnar, the Ta Oi, the Cotu, and the Gie-Trieng. The Mon-Khmer has a population of three-quarters of a million people, and includes fifteen subgroups. The Khmer people have rich textile traditions, producing belted aprons, vests, skirts, waist ties, scarves, blankets, bags, and baby carriers. The Bahnar weave cotton on an Indonesian-style loom on which the warp threads are held stretched between beams six feet above the ground and tensioned by a wooden back rest. This kind of loom is used to produce supplementary weft cloth up to a meter wide. Fabric is indigo and may combine pre-dyed threads. The Mon-Khmer use predominantly black, dark red, and ochre colors. The fabric of the Ta Oi, the Cotu, and some Gie-Trieng has glass or lead beads strung on the horizontal weft threads before weaving the decorative motifs.

Outlook for Traditional Clothing

As education and economic opportunities become increasingly available to the tribes of Vietnam, all aspects of women's dress is evolving, including the fabrics and dyes used, types of decoration, and construction (generally moving to simpler construction). The future of Vietnamese dress seems intimately bound up with the country's future economic prosperity: If industrialization continues at its current pace, with increased communications and logistics, the availability and affordability of Western goods will bring a multitude of fashion choices to people of Vietnam, and it is likely that the popularity of traditional Vietnamese women's dress will decline as men's dress has already done. Alternatively, a sense of cultural identity and nationalism—strongly felt in Vietnam—may help retain the use of Vietnamese dress in the same way that the Indonesian sarong has remained part of the Balinese dress.

Valerie Wilson Trower

Further Reading

Fraser-Lu, Sylvia. (1993) "South East Asia." In *5000 Years of Textiles*, edited by Sylvia Fraser-Lu. London: British Museum Press, 153–165.

Hemmet, Christine. (1995) *Montagnards des Pays D'Indochine; dans les collections du Musee de l'Homme*. Ville de Boulogne-Billancourt, France: Editions Sepia.

Nguyen Van Huy. (1998) *Vietnam Museum of Ethnology*. Hanoi, Vietnam: Vietnam Museum of Ethnology.

CO LOA THANH Co Loa Thanh (Co Loa Citadel) is located approximately 20 kilometers north of Hanoi, Vietnam, in the Dong Anh district. The citadel and the city were built around 257 BCE by King An Duong Vuong (Thuc Phan, reigned c. 257–c. 207 BCE) to enhance defense of the area from Chinese invasion. An Duong Vuong made Co Loa Thanh the capital of his Au Lac kingdom.

The shape of the citadel gives it its name, Loa Thanh, which means "snail-shaped citadel." The three principal mud walls of the citadel were constructed in a pattern of concentric circles resembling the shell of a snail. The first, outer wall had a perimeter of 7.6 kilometers; the second, 6 kilometers; and the third, 1.6 kilometers. The walls rose from 4 to 12 meters in height and were from 8 to 30 meters thick.

Following King An Duong Vuong's military defeat and subsequent suicide in 207 BCE, Co Loa Thanh was pillaged and abandoned throughout the period of Chinese rule in Vietnam (111 BCE–939 CE). After Chinese rule ended in 939 CE, Prince Ngo Quyen (897–944) made Co Loa Thanh the capital city of his new Vietnamese administration. It remained the capital city until 944.

Micheline R. Lessard

Further Reading

Taylor, Keith Weller. (1983) *The Birth of Vietnam*. Berkeley and Los Angeles: University of California Press.

COASTAL MALAYS The origins of the modern Deutero-Malay or Coastal Malay people are the subject of much debate. Some believe they came to the coastal regions of the Malay Peninsula from mainland Southeast Asia around 2000 BCE. The Malay settlers who first came to the peninsula kept to the rivers, and earlier races were driven inland to the mountains and swamps. These Malays intermarried with the indigenous peoples but failed to absorb them.

Folklore recorded in the Malay Annals has it that the founder of the Malay dynasties in much of insular Southeast Asia from the Malay Peninsula through the archipelago was a prince named Sang Sapurba. He was the son of Raja Suran, the "Ruler of the East and the West," by his marriage to a mermaid who was the daughter of the Kings of the Sea. This prince was believed to have revealed himself on the hill of Si-guntang, near Mount Mahameru, in the hinterland of Palembang, a port city near the east coast of Sumatra.

The legendary Sang Sapurba was said to have crossed the central range of Sumatra into the mountains of Minangkabau, where he slew the dragon Si-katimuna and became king and founded the line of princes of Minangkabau, the noblest Malay dynasty. His relative, Nila Utama from Palembang, had meanwhile crossed the sea, first reaching the island of Bintan and then the island of Temasik, on which he founded Singapore.

The modern or Deutero-Malay of Southeast Asia are believed to be descended from Proto-Malays who lived in the southern states of the Malay Peninsula, the Riau-Lingga Archipelago, Bangka Island, and certain districts in eastern Sumatra. Anthropologists caution against inferring that every modern Malay is descended from Proto-Malay tribe membes. The modern Malay are a mixed race and differ among themselves considerably. They developed from intermarriage with Chinese (as early as the Chou period), Indians from Bengal and Deccan, Arabs, and Thais.

The earliest immigrants to the Malay Peninsula from the Indonesian archipelago were Minangkabaus from Sumatra. Attracted by the wealth and commerce of Melaka, they moved into what are now the Malaysian states of Negri Sembilan and Melaka. Their legacy of matriarchal social structures remains visible in Malay culture today. In the early eighteenth century, the Bugis of Celebes established themselves in what is now the state of Selangor, later becoming politically dominant in the Riau-Johor empire.

This migration from the archipelago differentiates southern Malays from those in north of the Peninsula in Kedah and Kelantan. These differ from other groups, such as the Patani Malays of northern Perak (another state in modern peninsular Malaysia). These Malays were driven south from Thailand in the mid-nineteenth century and retain aspects of Thai culture.

Southern Malay communities generally spoke Malayan dialects or a language from which Malay has developed. In British Malaya they were known as Biduanda, while in the south and on the islands they were called Orang Laut, or people of the sea. Many of these people were unacquainted with agriculture and lived by fishing. The coastal Malays did well by the sea, as the coasts and rivers of Southeast Asia where they settled were rich in marine life, and the waters yielded more than did the inland jungles. The Orang Laut in their coastal villages had specific indigenous customs, but few of these are left to the Malay.

Coastal Malays appear to have settled along the coasts of Malaya and surrounding areas and intermarried with Chinese and Indians who migrated to and traded in the region, giving rise to the Deutero-Malay. The Malay spoken today is thought to have originated in a language from the archipelago. In the remote past, it is believed that the two great language groups—the language spoken on the archipelago and that spoken by the Indo-Chinese—were connected.

Historians agree that prior to recorded history in the Malay Peninsula and archipelago, there was already a substantial population with a fairly well-developed culture. Early Malays knew how to navigate by the stars on the open ocean and maintained some sort of political and social organization.

Unlike their predecessors, modern Malays are preeminently an agricultural people, and wet rice cultivation and fishing have been traditionally their main occupations wherever they settled. In the Melaka and Kelantan-Trengganu regions, fishing was revived as the main occupation because of better transportation in the eastern coastal region and the substitution of money for barter, which allowed for the division of labor and specialization in fishing by the coastal Malays.

The Malays today number over 200 million people in the Philippines, Indonesia, and Malaysia who share similarities in religion, language, general culture, and even political identity. Islam has proven to be a unifying force whose extranational character links the most remote mountain farmers to the townspeople of other Muslim communities in Southeast Asia.

Kog Yue Choong

Further Reading

Firth, Raymond. (1950) "The Peasantry in South-East Asia." *International Affairs* (October): 511.

Ginsburg, Norton, and Chester F. Roberts, Jr. (1958) *Malaya*. Seattle, WA: University of Washington Press.

Harrison, Brian. (1954) *Southeast Asia: A Short History*. London: Macmillan.

Wilkinson, R. J. (1923) *A History of the Peninsular Malays with Chapters on Perak and Selangor*. Singapore: Kelly and Walsh.

Winstedt, Richard Olof. (1961) *The Malays, a Cultural History*. 6th ed. London: Routledge and Kegan Paul.

COCKFIGHTING

Cockfighting, which pits two male chickens against each other, is a blood sport indigenous to Asia. The chicken, or common fowl, is most likely a native of the Indian subcontinent, where both a red jungle fowl (*Gallus gallus*, 65 centimeters long) and a gray one (*G. sonneratii*, 80 centimeters long) are found. Chickens were domesticated in the forests of mainland Southeast Asia perhaps as long as six thousand years ago. Over the years, a variety of domestic fowl was bred for culinary and ritual purposes, and some were bred for their fighting ability as well. When cockfighting first appeared is unknown, but sculptures found at Angkor Wat in Cambodia indicate cockfighting took place there one thousand years ago. As the chicken spread around the world, cockfighting followed, and it became a worldwide activity.

In Asia, cockfighting remains popular in Indonesia, Malaysia, Thailand, Vietnam, and the Philippines. In all places, the basic elements of the fight are the same. The key players are the cocks, the breeder-owners, and the audience. Betting is a vital component, and various rules and structures are in place that ensure that bets are collected and paid quickly and fairly. Fights take place in cockfighting pits and are attended almost exclusively by men. The goal of the fight might be for one bird to be killed or for one bird to be judged victorious without necessarily killing the other. Cocks may fight with their spurs, with attached blades, or with their spurs covered with padded gloves.

David Levinson

Further Reading

Donlon, J. G. (1990) "Fighting Cocks, Feathered Warriors, and Little Heroes." *Play & Culture* 3, 4: 273–285.

Geertz, Clifford. (1972) "Deep Play: Notes on the Balinese Cockfight." *Daedalus, The Journal of the American Academy* 101 (Winter): 1–37.

COEN, JAN PIETERSZOON

(c. 1586–1629), governor-general of the Dutch East Indies Company in Indonesia. Born to a burgher family in Hoorn, the Netherlands, Jan Pieterszoon Coen learned bookkeeping in Rome before joining the Dutch East Indies Company (VOC, Verenigd Oostindische Compagnie, United East Indies Company) at the age of twenty.

After his first visit to Indonesia in 1607, Coen rose in the ranks of the VOC. In 1614 he wrote an influential analysis of the company's strategic position, arguing for monopolization of the spice trade, the establishment of strong bases in the Indies, and the expulsion of other Europeans and introduction of Dutch settlers. Coen was appointed fourth governor-general in 1617, taking up his post in 1619. He was convinced of the need to establish a central headquarters for the company in Asia, both for military and administrative reasons, and for this headquarters to become the hub of a network of Asian trade routes. In 1618 Coen established a fort at Jayakarta (now Jakarta) in western Java for this purpose, later naming it Batavia.

Coen ruthlessly enforced the VOC's spice monopoly in eastern Indonesia, attacking the nutmeg-producing Banda Islands in 1621 and slaughtering or deporting the entire indigenous population. Coen left for Holland in 1623, but returned for a second term as governor-general in 1627 and died in Batavia during a siege by Javanese forces.

Robert Cribb

Further Reading

Vlekke, Bernard H. M. (1943) *Nusantara: A History of the East Indian Archipelago.* Cambridge, MA: Harvard University Press.

COIMBATORE (2001 est. pop. 923,000). Coimbatore is situated on the banks of the Noyil River on the Coimbatore Plain 425 kilometers southwest of Madras City (now Chennai). It is an industrial city of the northwestern Tamil Nadu state and the headquarters of Coimbatore District. It was an important site along a trade route between the east coast and the west coast even in Roman times; numerous Roman coins have been found in the district. Several medieval kingdoms maintained a fortified stronghold there. Coimbatore was developed as an administrative and industrial center under the British administration, and during the twentieth century, it has had varied industries: hides, glass, photographic goods, coffee, sugar, cotton cloth, electrical goods, tea, fertilizer, and other agricultural products. Coimbatore is the site of the Tamil Nadu Agricultural University, Bharatiar University, and several others institutions of higher learning. It has an airport and a military airfield.

The extensive Coimbatore District (7,469 square kilometers) was under British rule from 1799 until Independence in 1947. Bordered on its northern edge by the Nilgiri and Periyar districts (and the Bavani River, which forms the border of these two districts), the Coimbatore District has rich farmland that is irrigated in several areas. The Bavani Sagar dam is an important part of the irrigation system, but many farmers who are unable to get water from the dam system use wells instead.

Paul Hockings

Further Reading

Baliga, B. S. (1966) *Madras District Gazetteers: Coimbatore.* Madras, India:
Director of Stationery and Printing.

COLOMBO (2001 est. pop. 770,000). The commercial and business center of Sri Lanka, Colombo is a multifunctional and multicultural cosmopolitan city. Colombo city is merely the core of the Greater Colombo agglomeration that sprawls over 60 kilometers in a narrow band along the west coast of Sri Lanka near the Indian Ocean. Greater Colombo, with a total population of approximately 1.5 million, suffers from burgeoning social, traffic, and environmental problems resulting from high population and insufficient urban planning. As one of the major harbors in Asia, Colombo is the overseas port of call for Sri Lanka, and it lies at the crossroads of all domestic road and rail traffic. The international airport of Colombo (the only international airport in Sri Lanka) is located at Katunayake, at the northern edge of the Greater Colombo agglomeration, 38 kilometers from the city center, next to the biggest free-trade zone in Sri Lanka.

Greater Colombo has a decentralized structure, with light industry and working-class quarters at the peripheries, and the city center, called Fort (as a reminder of the old colonial fortification), accommodating the commercial district. The bustling traditional bazaar quarter (Pettah) and the fashionable residential quarter (Cinnamon Gardens) are adjacent to the center. Mount Lavinia (in the south) and Negombo (in the north), also part of greater Colombo, are home to many tourist resorts. Despite its great cultural and religious diversity, Colombo's many ethnic and religious groups enjoy peaceful coexistence. Colombo's religious diversity is evident from its many Buddhist and Hindu temples as well as its churches and mosques. Present-day Colombo proudly preserves the impressive colonial buildings of its colonial past, but it is also well stocked with modern hotels and futuristic shopping centers, suggesting that Colombo is forward-looking. Colombo is still regarded as the capital of Sri Lanka, although in 1982 Sri Jayawardenapura Kotte (located on the western outskirts of Colombo), which houses a modern parliament complex, officially became the nation's capital.

Manfred Domroes

Further Reading

Williams, Harry. (1950) *Ceylon, Pearl of the East.* London: Hale.

COLOMBO PLAN The Colombo Plan for Cooperative Economic Development in South and Southeast Asia was proposed at the Colombo, Sri Lanka, meeting of the foreign ministers of the British Commonwealth nations—Australia, Ceylon, India, New Zealand, Pakistan, and the United Kingdom—in January 1950. Later these nations were joined by Cambodia, Laos, and Vietnam and still later by Myanmar (Burma), Nepal, and Indonesia.

The meeting was intended to discuss international affairs, but the ministers realized that unless there was economic stability in Asia, there would be revolutionary disturbances, most often of the community sort. They understood that progress depended on economic improvement. It was decided that to promote development in Southeast Asia, they would give financial and technical assistance to their Asian counterparts.

The Consultative Committee, representing British Commonwealth governments, met in Sydney at the behest of the Australian government. At the meeting, nations planning development were asked to submit a "reliable" scheme for the next six years to act as a draft on their own future economic progress.

Next came the scheme for technical assistance and expertise necessary to practicalize large development programs. Governments providing aid were to bear the cost of basic salaries of experts they made available, and governments receiving aid were to bear the local costs of the experts. To aid in the preparation of the details of the scheme, a council for technical cooperation was proposed to meet at Colombo to aid in the economic development of Southeast Asia by providing technical assistance. This also required experts to participate directly in the process of development in Asia.

But this did not mean that there was a general Colombo Plan fund, although at the Sydney meeting the British Commonwealth governments had promised to provide 8 million pounds for the ensuing three years.

Every offer of assistance would be subjected to bilateral negotiation between the nations concerned, and the progress reports would be discussed at periodic meetings. This was stipulated as a necessary caveat.

Finally, in September and October 1950, there was a further meeting of ministers in London, during which several development schemes were cleared and the need for "financial support of outside agencies" was approved. The Colombo Plan was originally proposed to run for six years, but at the Singapore meeting in 1956, its tenure was extended to 1961.

Ranjit Roy

Further Reading

Benham, Frederic Chasler. (1956) *The Colombo Plan and Other Essays.* London: Royal Institute of International Affairs.

Bridson, Douglas Geoffrey. (1953) *Progress in Asia: The Colombo Plan in Action.* London: Her Majesty's Stationery Office.

COMFORT WOMEN From 1938 until its surrender at the end of World War II in 1945, Japan forced women from regions captured or otherwise occupied to serve as prostitutes for its military forces. The terms "comfort women" and "comfort stations" (the brothels set up by the Japanese military forces) are euphemisms for these women and the facilities set up for them. The Japanese word for comfort women, *ianfu*, is equivalent to the Korean *chongshindae* and the Tagalog *lola* (grandmother).

Japan's System of Military Prostitution

The establishment of a system of military prostitutes began with use of Japanese professional prostitutes who would be sent to overseas locations. These women were provided to Japanese military forces beginning in the 1920s, but often had high levels of venereal diseases. It was later decided to use foreign women, who, not being prostitutes to start out with, were relatively free of disease. An estimated 200,000 women from Korea, the Philippines, Indonesia, Thailand, China, Taiwan, and to a lesser degree Burma (now Myanmar), Malaya (now part of Malaysia), and Vietnam, as well as some British and Dutch women were used as comfort women. As the war drew to a close, many of these women were abandoned or killed, or claims were made by the Japanese that they had been nurses. Discussion of forced military prostitution was avoided during the American military occupation of Japan because of cultural sensitivities; women who had been forced into sexual slavery were unlikely to admit to the experience in the decades following the

Two elderly Korean women at a rally in Seoul, in May 2001. Both were forced to serve as comfort women to Japanese soldiers during World War II. They are protesting a new Japanese history textbook which Koreans feel downplays Japanese atrocities. (REUTERS NEWMEDIA INC./CORBIS)

war, due in part to the psychological pressures which had resulted from the experience.

The Positions of the Japanese Government

The involvement of the Japanese army was denied by the government of Japan until 1992, when documents implicating the imperial government were discovered by a Japanese historian. Since that time the Japanese government has held that the "comfort women issue" is not one to be resolved through official channels, since war reparations had been agreed upon with its wartime enemies years before.

To be more precise, the government of Japan has adopted a series of official positions that acknowledge varying degrees of complicity, while maintaining that it holds no blame for any wrongdoing that may have occurred. The positions range from absolute denial that comfort women ever existed to an acknowledgment that the current government should accept historical evidence and apologize to the few who are still alive.

The Japanese educational system has also been hesitant to include discussions of comfort women. In 1997, for the first time, middle school social studies texts included references to *ianfu* (without explaining what they were). This drew criticism from politicians who criticized what they characterized as the "masochistic" inclusion of such material. The Japanese Ministry of Education was required to review all proposed school texts before they could be used, and could require publishers to change or delete passages that did not comply with official policy.

Two sets of feelings were apparent by the mid-1990s: members of the wartime generation, who were by that time in their sixties or older, saw themselves as victims and felt little remorse for other, non-Japanese victims. Members of the postwar generation, for their part, have been educated to believe in personal accountability for actions, not collective accountability, and therefore feel no sense of responsibility for acts carried out by the army before they were even born.

The Controversy Surrounding the Asian Women's Fund

To deal with public pressure to acknowledge past wrongdoing while still avoiding a public apology, in 1995 the Asian Peace and Friendship Fund for Women (commonly known as the Asian Women's Fund, or AWF) was established. As first proposed, the AWF was to be a nongovernmental means to make amends to former comfort women. This, it was thought, would settle the issue of reparations without involving formal channels. Payments of approximately $20,000 from the fund (which would be created from private and government contributions) would be accompanied by a letter of apology from the Japanese prime minister. This approach was widely criticized by former comfort women, and led to refusal to accept the payments. Former comfort women from South Korea, the Philippines, Taiwan, and the Netherlands asked Japanese legal and labor organizations to end support for the AWF, saying that the fund ignored the victims, who had declared they would not accept payments from it. Lila-Pilipina, a Philippines-based Filipina support group for former comfort women, announced its members would reject the offer from the AWF since it did not constitute a formal apology. The AWF's ability to make payments was complicated by an unwillingness on the part of those to be compensated to accept payments from an organization perceived as a smokescreen for the Japanese government.

The AWF attempted to defuse the issue by pledging to give 380 million yen over a ten-year period to the Indonesian government for distribution to private social institutions. This backfired when the Indonesian Legal Aid Foundation criticized the government plan to accept the AWF payments without an official apology from the Japanese government. The South Korean government asked Japan to cease payments because the AWF was seen as an attempt to avoid an official admission of responsibility, and interfered with South Korea's own support programs, since payments to former comfort women are made in secret.

The Japanese stance has also been criticized by the United Nations. In 1998, the United Nations Subcommission on Human Rights denounced the AWF for its failure to provide legal compensation to former comfort women. In 1999, the special investigator for the United Nations Commission on Human Rights commented that the AWF would be viewed with suspicion as long as Japan attempted to avoid responsibility.

The comfort women issue will not likely be forgotten. South of Seoul, the Historical Museum of Japanese Military Sexual Slavery depicts the sufferings of those Korean girls who were taken from their homes to be used as *ianfu.*

Thomas P. Dolan

Further Reading

Chang, Iris. (1997) *The Rape of Nanking: The Forgotten Holocaust of World War II.* New York: Basic Books.

Hicks, George. (1995) *The Comfort Women: Japan's Brutal Regime of Enforced Prostitution in the Second World War.* New York: Norton.

Reid, Anthony, and Oki Akira, eds. (1986) *The Japanese Experience in Indonesia: Selected Memoirs of 1942–1945.* Athens OH: Ohio University, Center for International Studies, Center for Southeast Asian Studies.

COMMUNISM—CENTRAL ASIA

The application of Communist ideology to the Central Asian environment was always a difficult undertaking. Throughout much of the Soviet Union's history, efforts were made to revise, adapt, or forcibly introduce Communist thought in the region, with mixed results. As was often the case, local leaders made use of the structure of the Soviet state and the rhetoric of Communism, but maintained their traditional views on power relations and society. Thus, when the Soviet Union collapsed in 1991, it was no surprise that Communism, as an ideological force, dissipated.

The Introduction of Communism to Central Asia

According to Marxist thought, the Socialist-cum-Communist revolution was to take place first in industrialized countries and only then proceed to the feudal (that is, less-developed) states. Imperial Russia was in the process of industrialization when Vladimir Ilyich Lenin (1870–1924) sparked the Bolshevik Revolution. In that empire, the Central Asian region was largely agrarian or pastoral. The small communities of industrial workers that existed were overwhelmingly ethnic Slavs. Thus, one of the more significant problems for the Bolshevik leadership and theoreticians was how to introduce Communism to a region that had recently been under either feudal or precapitalist forms of government and society. (The Bolsheviks sometimes called Czarist Russia "precapitalist," suggesting that the basic elements of capitalism were present in the industrial sector, but that other parts of the economy and the mentality of the population were still lagging behind.)

During the Bolshevik Revolution, the local population in Central Asia generally viewed the new ideology as a foreign import and stayed away from much of the political wrangling that took place in 1917 and 1918. However, the collapse of the Russian empire did prompt members of indigenous elites to call for independence and for new states in Central Asia, and during the Civil War, a myriad of conflicting organizations and groups vied for power.

Many in Central Asia viewed Communism not necessarily as an ideology, but as a political and military force that would ensure continued Russian domination of the region. Some opposition groups of native inhabitants became part of the Basmachi revolt, a movement of Central Asians of all ethnicities who sought to create an independent political entity in the region. The weakness of the Basmachi was the varying views of participants—from Jadidist ("New School") thinkers who wanted to emulate the Young Turk movement in Turkey (Ottoman military officers who sought to reform what they saw as a corrupt political system in the late 1800s and early 1900s) to Islamic fundamentalists who wanted to recreate a caliphate in the region and base the new society on precepts of Islamic law. The divergence of views ensured that the Basmachi would not be able to cooperate successfully, and by 1922, the Bolshevik Red Army controlled much of the region.

In contrast, the reformist elite in Central Asia, particularly those living in the principalities of Bukhara and Khiva, saw the Bolsheviks as potential allies in their efforts to modernize the region. By enlisting the support of the Red Army, it was argued, the reformists could overthrow the repressive and conservative regimes in the respective states (ruled by executive councils modeled somewhat after the Bolshevik leadership structure in Russia) and create new, progressive entities. However, instead of being able to create their own independent states, these leaders found themselves beholden to the Bolshevik victors. By 1924–1925, Central Asia was delimited along ethnic- or national-republic borders—in spite of the fact that Lenin had originally rejected the notion of national republics and had adhered to the classic Marxist belief that ethnic identities would disappear in the new state.

Communism and the Stalinist State

During the 1920s, Joseph Stalin (1879–1953), as the Commissar for Nationalities, developed the policy for minority groups in the Soviet Union. In theory, minorities were to be given rights in the areas of language and cultural policies, but the eventual goal—according to Marxist theory—was for these groups to merge into one Soviet people. Relics *(perezhitki)*, such as religious practices and certain backward aspects of a society, were discouraged, with the thought that they would finally disappear.

This theory required some creative explanation of Marxist thought when it was applied to the Central Asian region. Even Lenin thought that this area would be difficult to incorporate, and he reluctantly tolerated the national Communism exhibited by Central Asians, who followed the example of the Tatar, Mir Said Sultangaliev (1880–1939?). In the 1910s and 1920s, this activist presented to the Muslim peoples of the Soviet Union a form of Communism that underscored how one could blend Communist ideology with nationalist sentiments. He suggested that national differences would continue for some time but that, at some point, different nationalities would start to band together to work for larger, transnational ideals, assisting in the spread of Communism to other countries. The notion of combining national liberation with Communism was expressed in such places as the University of the Toilers of the East, an institution located in Tashkent (in present-day Uzbekistan), which was devoted to educating anticolonial revolutionaries.

Communism became the dominant, and then sole, ideology of the region, as it was an integral part of the Soviet Union's ideology. Leadership changes that took place in the 1920s and 1930s focused on the removal of nationalist and feudal leaders in favor of a young, pro-Communist elite. However, even these fell victim to the Stalinist purges of the 1930s.

In particular, the Communist ideology required that the local elite focus on education, improved social conditions, and women's rights—all sectors in which progress was demonstrated in the Soviet period. The Communists decided on women's liberation as a vehicle through which the basic tenets of Marxism-Leninism could take hold in the region of Central Asia. Families were largely patriarchal, and women were traditionally not afforded educational and career opportunities. In the 1920s, universities, gymnasiums, and primary schools were opened to women and girls in Central Asia.

One of the more dramatic liberation campaigns was the 1926 unveiling *(hujum)* campaign. Women, particularly wives, daughters, and sisters of Communist Party officials, were encouraged not to wear veils and even to remove and burn them in public ceremonies. Reactions to the campaign were mixed, with some fathers murdering daughters who disgraced themselves by unveiling.

Islam became another key target for Communism in Central Asia. By definition, the inherent atheism of Communist thought gave theoretical credence to any effort to curtail religious activity. The state policies on religion dictated in 1918 and 1928 clearly reduced the formal role of religion in Central Asia. Through the 1920s and 1930s, thousands of mosques and *madrasahs* were closed, and religious leaders were persecuted. In the campaign against religion, Communism was an atheist ideology with its own principles, in opposition to all religions. Yet although official mosques and religious institutions were limited, Islam still survived during this period. What was often called parallel Islam began to emerge as a powerful force in Central Asia, particularly the Sufi orders that had existed in the region in centuries past. Studies today note that Muslims were able to adapt to the repressive environment, and Islamic customs were practiced during the entire Soviet period, albeit often in secret.

In 1942, while the outcome of the Great Patriotic War (World War II) was uncertain, the Soviet leadership decided to enlist the support of religious leaders throughout the Soviet Union to boost morale and offer yet other legitimizing reasons for supporting the war effort. In the following year, 1943, the Spiritual Directorate system was introduced, creating a structure through which Islam could be practiced and controlled. Mullahs and other religious figures were limited in their activity, but as long as they were state sanctioned, they could legally carry out their responsibilities.

Postwar Communism in Central Asia

From 1945 to 1991, the force and importance of Communist ideology went through several cycles. As an ideology, it was laying the groundwork for the eventual movement to a pure socialist and then Communist state. As the Central Asian region was considered backward, massive industrialization campaigns took place there in the 1950s and 1960s. In particular, major cities such as Tashkent and Alma-Ata (now Almaty), as well as the belt of cities in northern Kazakhstan, experienced significant developments.

Leadership policies saw a softening during this period. While the Stalinist years were typified by regional leaders who were devout Communists first and then national figures, during the post-Stalinist years leaders thrived who paid proper fealty and loyalty to Moscow while maintaining more traditional forms of power in their respective republics. For example, Dinmukhamed Kunaev (1911–1991) of Kazakhstan and Sharaf Rashidov (1917–1983) of Uzbekistan were first secretaries of their respective republics for almost twenty-five years each. They, as well as their contemporaries in the other Central Asian republics, maintained intricate networks of authority in their republics that resembled the pre-Soviet period rather than the organizations that the regime in Moscow would have preferred. Both Kunaev and Rashidov rose to the ranks of the Politburo of the Communist Party of the Soviet Union (CPSU), although neither was viewed as a top decision maker in that elite body, which was dominated by ethnic Slavs.

Communist thought with respect to national merging was also softened. Indeed, under the administration of Leonid Brezhnev (1906–1982), the official ideology favored the flowering *(rasvet)* of nationalities. It was declared that in the future Soviet state, national and cultural distinctions would remain and would actually compliment each other. For the Central Asians, this cultural relativism meant that they were now encouraged to demonstrate and hone their "national music," "national costume," and "national traditions." Not surprisingly, the Russian culture remained supreme in the country vis-à-vis the Central Asian cultures.

It was still difficult to discuss fully the early nationalists, and, in classic Communist verbiage, most histories of Central Asia continued to focus on the overall forces of social development in the region, led by Russians. In the 1970s and early 1980s, several Central Asian authors, including Chingiz Aitmatov (b. 1928) and Mamadali Makhmudov (b.1943), wrote on nationalist themes, but couched them sufficiently in the language of Socialist Realism (realistic style and content prescribed for Soviet arts) to have them published. These efforts, and the push to increase the study of local languages in schools, were the early forms of national awakening in Central Asia.

However, it should be noted that most Central Asians seemed to like the social and economic benefits derived from being part of the Soviet Union. The Communist social contract, in which the state maintained authority and the population received extensive social-welfare benefits as justified in Communist thought, was maintained throughout much of the later Soviet period. Indeed, Central Asia was often presented as a success story to the developing world, especially to those states in Africa, South and Southeast Asia, and Latin America that were allies to or sympathetic of the Soviet Union.

Communism and the Gorbachev Reforms in Central Asia

During the years of Mikhail Gorbachev (b. 1931), as the Communist Party attempted to reevaluate itself and become more efficient, interest in Communism as an ideology and as a form of political power waned in Central Asia. According to the Gorbachev leadership, Communism, as a belief system, could exist in the Soviet Union, with its diverse societies and cultures. However, it was essential that the old guard, who were continuing to take advantage of the spoils system of Communist Party leadership, be removed. The general populations took such sackings of old party bosses as signs of national crackdowns and actually protested the removal of co-ethnic figures, even if they were corrupt. Gorbachev ousted Kunaev because he felt that this long-time office-holder in Kazakhstan was simply too corrupt and extremely nepotistic. However, when Kunaev was replaced by an ethnic Russian, Gennadi Kolbin, riots erupted in the Kazakh capital of Alma-Ata. This ouster was considered an affront by Central Asians, who saw Gorbachev as more of a Russian chauvinist than a modernizer.

The Central Asian people had a similar reaction to Gorbachev's condemnation of Rashidov regime and the infamous Uzbek cotton scandal. Although the investigation of financial improprieties in Uzbekistan took place during the years of Yuri Andropov (1914–1984), the case became a national issue in the late 1980s. In the so-called scandal, over three hundred top Uzbek officials were arrested and imprisoned for long-term falsification of cotton-harvest records and the resulting overpayment by Moscow of countless millions of rubles to local economic units. The Uzbek Communist Party was decimated as key personnel were implicated in the crime. The culprits were often described in Communist terms as closet capitalists and even feudal warlords, and stories of regional bosses amassing great fortunes appeared in the Soviet press. From the Central Asian perspective, these were not criminal investigations at all, but rather assaults on local cultures and leaders.

At this time, Communism as such was equated with Russia or Russians. In the Central Asian states, the non-Russian peoples began to assert themselves in the areas of political and cultural rights. In Uzbekistan, demonstrations with over twenty thousand participants took place in the late 1980s over the issues of language rights and primacy of the Uzbek language in the republic. Such sentiments were expressed in the other Central Asian states as well, although not at the level of protest seen in the Baltic republics and Ukraine.

Past leaders who had been declared nationalists were reexamined, and a number of victims of the Great Purge (the Stalinist campaign of 1934–1939 to eliminate opponents within the Communist Party apparatus and the Soviet military) were rehabilitated. Communist excesses were highlighted, much to the discredit of the official ideology that was being challenged throughout the Soviet Union. Thus, by the time of the Soviet collapse, the Central Asian view of Communist ideology was already low. However, this discrediting of Communism was not equated with a drive for independence, as the Central Asian peoples still saw the benefits of staying within the union.

The Collapse of Communism in Central Asia

In 1990, requests to join the Communist Party were decreasing as people no longer seemed to believe in the ideology. The politically savvy first secretaries in each of the Central Asian republics followed the examples of their counterparts in other republics of the Soviet Union and focused on their political offices, often being elected president of the respective republics. In a sense, their legitimacy was now derived from constitutional or institutional sources and not from being part of the Communist system.

In the last year of Gorbachev's tenure as General Secretary of the CPSU, the Politburo was reconstructed to include the first secretary of each of the republics of the Soviet Union. In theory, the goal was to diversify the leadership and elevate the position of the marginal republics. The Central Asian leaders appear to have been supportive of this and, in contrast to the other republics, maintained fairly strong support for remaining in the USSR. The Communist system's centrally planned economy, in general, benefited the Central Asian states in that they received more state subsidies than they paid to the central planners, in contrast to, say, the Baltic states, which paid more than they received. While the region was weaker relative to the European republics, conditions in Central Asia had improved considerably over time. Compared to the situation prior to the Russian/Soviet period, levels of education, health care, women's rights, industry, and transportation all improved. There were also costs—loss of sovereignty and many casualties during the collectivization campaign and the Great Purge. But die-hard supporters of the regime equated Communism with social and economic success, contrasting conditions in the Central Asian states with the conditions in war-torn Afghanistan to the south.

The collapse of the Soviet Union was soon followed by the gutting of Communism as a force in Central Asia. Quickly, the ideological veneer of Communism and the hierarchy of the Communist Party structure were replaced by new forms of regionally based nationalism and political authority founded in the presidential apparatuses of the respective countries. Within months, the Communist Parties of each of the Central Asian republics were renamed, and the notion of having a Communist Party was challenged. Tajikistan was an exception in that its Communist Party did not change its name until three years after independence.

Attitudes toward Communism in Central Asia in the Twenty-First Century

All five Central Asian states are in the process of rewriting their histories, attempting to purge them of Communist ideology and Soviet political correctness. Unfortunately, these past portrayals are being replaced by similarly dogmatic nationalist concepts, often using the same techniques of their Communist predecessors. Communism as an ideology never quite took hold in Central Asia but remained a force in opposition to strong local values and belief systems. That Central Asian leaders were able to work within the Communist system and perpetuated their own power relationships underscores this failure.

Roger D. Kangas

Further Reading

Allworth, Edward, ed. (1989) *Central Asia: 120 Years of Russian Rule.* Durham, NC: Duke University Press.

Bennigsen, Alexandre A., and S. Enders Wimbush. (1979) *Muslim National Communism in the Soviet Union: A Revolutionary Strategy for the Colonial World.* Chicago: University of Chicago Press.

Fierman, William, ed. (1991) *Soviet Central Asia: The Failed Transformation.* Boulder, CO: Westview.

Khalid, Adeeb. (1998) *The Politics of Muslim Cultural Reform: Jadidism in Central Asia.* Berkeley and Los Angeles: University of California Press.

Pipes, Richard. (1980) *The Formation of the Soviet Union: Communism and Nationalism, 1917–1923.* New York: Atheneum.

Roi, Yaacov, ed. (1995) *Muslim Eurasia: Conflicting Legacies.* London: Frank Cass.

COMMUNISM—CHINA The decay and fall of the Qing dynasty (1644–1912) produced a China racked by sociopolitical instability and unable to prevent foreign military attacks and political interference, including the imposition of concessions over which foreign powers had control and under which foreigners were not subject to Chinese law (extraterritoriality). These problems caused many Chinese to search widely for explanations; traditional thought systems such as Confucianism offered inadequate answers. The New Culture Movement of 1915 spurred students to investigate competing foreign ideas, including the ideologies of socialism and anarchism, but anarchist and socialist initiatives failed.

Early Days

In early 1920, the Communist International (Comintern) sent the young revolutionary organizer, Gregori Voitinsky (1893–1953), to China to establish a Chinese Communist party. Before he arrived, the Soviet Union issued the Karakhan Declaration renouncing imperial Russia's claims on China. This declaration set the Soviet Union apart from the West, which continued its exploitation, passing Germany's concessions in China to Japan in the 1919 Treaty of Versailles, despite China's having been an ally in World War I. As a consequence, many Chinese lost faith in Western ideals, and Voitinsky found a warm welcome.

Voitinsky helped Chinese intellectuals such as Li Dazhao (1889–1927) and Chen Duxiu (1880–1942) form Marxist study groups in Beijing, Shanghai, Changsha, Guangzhou (Canton), and Jinan. In mid-1921, delegates representing about sixty members became the core of the Chinese Communist Party (CCP), committed to ending exploitation based on private ownership. Yet the CCP was tiny, while the Guomindang (GMD), or Nationalists, led by Sun Yat-sen (1866–1925) was a growing revolutionary anti-imperialist party with an army. To promote revolution, the Comintern pressed the CCP into an alliance with the Nationalists. The aim was for the CCP to help the GMD develop while simultaneously extending Communist influence to eventually make the Nationalist Party a Communist one.

The first period of GMD-CCP cooperation (The First United Front) ended in April 1927, when Chiang Kai-shek (1887–1975), the commander of the GMD forces, turned on the Communists. Communist membership fell from 58,000 to 4,000 active members, now experienced in organization, activism, and military and political affairs. While its urban influence evaporated, the CCP survived in the countryside, where, under Comintern direction, it instigated a series of failed uprisings, established worker-peasant-soldier soviets (councils), and implemented radical agrarian revolution, violently confiscating and redistributing land to the poor.

In October 1934, encirclement and attacks by GMD and local elite forces forced the CCP to flee the Chinese Soviet Republic it had established in Jiangxi, southeastern China, in November 1927. During this retreat, known as the Long March, Mao Zedong (1893–1976) rose to prominence. The threat of war with Japan allowed the Communists to portray themselves as patriots heroically advancing to fight Japan despite GMD resistance.

From the Second United Front to Civil War

In 1937, popular opinion and pressure from the Soviet Union forced the GMD and CCP into their second period of cooperation, this time against Japan. This alliance formed half of the CCP's Second United Front. The other half consisted of winning as many allies as possible among intellectuals, warlords, landlords, and others by making concessions in Communist ideology and practice. Mao justified these concessions by invoking the idea of "New Democracy," a period of transition from the allegedly old "semi-feudal, semi-colonial" society to a socialist one. This transition would entail the long-term coexistence of different classes and forms of property ownership until the forces for the final transition to a classless socialism were strong enough. During this time, all classes allied to the CCP would be represented in the political system. This policy was reflected in moderate policies including rent and interest-rate reductions rather than radical land confiscation and redistribution.

Inside its rural bases, the CCP experimented with policies determined by local class structures and attitudes, GMD responses, rural conditions, attitudes of local elites, and international conditions. There was no overarching revolutionary theme of nationalism or land revolution that would guarantee success for any one policy throughout China, although the CCP made much of its patriotism and worked extremely hard to win support from the poor and landless in particular.

After the end of World War II in 1945, the CCP delayed civil war as long possible, building military and political strength. Meanwhile, the GMD, racked by infighting and corruption, rapidly deteriorated. The GMD lacked a strong political and social base, while the economy suffered hyperinflation, further undermining the GMD's legitimacy. Reviving the anti-CCP civil war cost the Guomindang more support, and its political weakness became increasingly obvious. The GMD was eventually defeated by CCP armies of rural soldiers won over by the promise of land, GMD deserters, disaffected students, and others who were promised a New China. The GMD fled to Taiwan.

The People's Republic of China

On 1 October 1949, Mao declared the founding of the People's Republic of China. The CCP quickly

CHAIRMAN MAO ON COMMUNISM

A well disciplined Party armed with the theory of Marxism-Leninism, using the method of self-criticism and linked with the masses of the people; an army under the leadership of such a people; a united front of all revolutionary classes and all revolutionary groups under the leadership of such a Party—these are the three main weapons with which we have defeated the enemy.

Source: Mao Zedong (1976). *Quotations from Chairman Mao Tsetung*. Beijing, China: Foreign Language Press, 3.

moved to eliminate potential enemies, institute thought reform, confiscate many businesses, and implement land reform. The CCP subjected private businesses to repeated campaigns aimed at delegitimizing them and forcing them into state or cooperative ownership. Soviet-model rapid industrialization using central planning to develop state-owned enterprises was implemented according to five-year plans. Despite the Korean War (1950–1953), in which China was involved, the economy grew quickly. In 1956, Mao declared the transition to socialism complete and ended New Democracy.

Maoism

Despite the apparent success, Mao also saw increasing bureaucratism, dogmatism, and sectarianism in the CCP. Mao's methods for rectifying these problems included allowing intellectuals to criticize government. Mao's 1957 speech, "On the Correct Handling of Contradictions," implied there was no more need for class struggle and reassured many that it was safe to speak up. However, Mao was shocked when his Hundred Flowers Movement, intended to encourage constructive criticism of CCP shortcomings, including criticism from the CCP's united front allies, also elicited severe criticisms of both the party and himself. In response he launched the Anti-Rightist Campaign. This campaign reemphasized class struggle and encouraged anti-intellectualism. Mao promoted the use of big character posters, public meetings, and debates to force criticism and self-criticism, so-called big democracy. These methods often involved public humiliation and even torture of critics. Accusations of rightism could refer to denying the centrality of class struggle, advocating markets in economics, or opposing central planning or party control over politics and culture. Hundreds of thousands were labeled, exiled, imprisoned, demoted, and sidelined. These features of Maoism also marked the Great Leap Forward (1958–1960) and the Cultural Revolution (1966–1976).

The Great Leap Forward was an experiment by Mao to overcome the problems of central planning and to speed up industrialization. These goals were to be achieved by emphasizing mass mobilization, native ingenuity, and correct ideological viewpoint. Moral incentives rather than financial rewards were stressed, and distinctions between politics and technical knowledge were to be eliminated to make individuals both "red and expert." Relying on surpluses from agriculture to fund industrialization, the Great Leap accelerated the socialization and industrialization of agriculture by creating communes of up to five thousand households, where private plots, markets, and sideline businesses such as selling homemade pickled vegetables were eliminated. Decentralization and self-sufficiency were also key goals. The most famous Great Leap initiative was the building of backyard furnaces to raise steel output, but instead created large amounts of unusable pig iron at enormous cost in labor, raw materials, and wasted resources. The CCP mobilized the masses to build rural infrastructure such as dams and irrigation projects. Unfortunately, poor planning, excessive state extraction of grain taxes, shortcomings in communes, and other problems, together with bad weather, resulted in an estimated 20 million deaths from starvation in rural areas.

After 1959, stung by the failure of the Great Leap, Mao retreated from leadership. Pragmatic leaders, including Liu Shaoqi (1898–1969) and Deng Xiaoping (1904–1997), then instituted moderate policies, allowed private plots and sidelines, and rehabilitated some alleged rightists. Mao saw this moderation as revisionism and betrayal of revolutionary ideals. He began building support in China's army (the People's Liberation Army) and in September 1962 asked everyone never to forget the class struggle. In 1964, Mao began to reimpose his will and ultimately created the Cultural Revolution.

Through the Great Proletarian Cultural Revolution, as it was officially named, Mao encouraged the army and students in particular to criticize those like Liu and Deng whom he saw as taking the capitalist road. Mao told students that rebellion is justified and that they should fight selfishness and criticize revisionism. CCP leaders and intellectuals such as teachers became targets of student Red Guards, who had prepared themselves by memorizing *Mao zhuxi yulu*

(Quotations from Chairman Mao Zedong), nicknamed the Little Red Book. Many people, including Liu Shaoqi, were tortured and died as a result. In line with Mao's calls, students also worked to destroy old ideology, culture, customs, and habits (the "four olds"). However, Mao's egalitarianism also spurred the development of basic health care and education and attacked traditional elitism.

China and the CCP since Mao

The CCP now describes the Cultural Revolution as ten years of chaos and waste. After Mao's death in September 1976, there was an interregnum under Chairman Hua Guofeng (b. 1921), during which the so-called Gang of Four (including Mao's wife, Jiang Qing, 1914–1991) and others were arrested and blamed for the Cultural Revolution. In 1978, Zhao Ziyang (b. 1919) replaced Hua as China's premier, but it was Deng Xiaoping who came to wield the most power. The new leaders began rebuilding support among non-"Red" classes, especially intellectuals, former business people, and those with overseas connections. The goals were the four modernizations (agriculture, industry, science and technology, defense) and a dramatic increase in economic growth. Farmers benefited first when the communes were replaced with the Household Responsibility System, under which individual families again had responsibility for many decisions in the management of agriculture and rewards related directly to their success in production. The state increased produce prices and allowed the revival of private markets.

In 1980, Special Economic Zones (SEZs) were established in China's south, where foreigners, overseas Chinese especially, could invest in manufacturing for export. After the SEZs proved successful, efforts to attract foreign investors spread widely. The state also began gradually relaxing controls on private business. Rural industries built by communes for self-reliance assisted rapid rural industrialization, because their products could be sold at the revived rural markets or exported. Township and village enterprises (both village and privately owned) are now a major feature of the Chinese economy. State-owned enterprises have dramatically declined in importance and efficiency, and most are now heavily indebted and a drag on the economy. The CCP's reform and opening-up policy marked a shift from autarky. The intent was not to abandon Communist ideals but to create a socialism with Chinese characteristics, which proved itself by building national strength and raising living standards.

The changes created by reform have created major dilemmas for the CCP and its ideology. China is now a major economic power, but only after abandoning most tenets of its original ideology and retreating from full socialization of ownership to mixed ownership and markets. In 1987, Zhao Ziyang justified the CCP's return to a New Democracy–type economy by declaring that China was in the initial stage of socialism and that full socialism could be achieved only when all the productive forces were fully developed and modernized. This formulation was reinforced by the 1992 promulgation of the concept of the socialist market economy, under which the declining state-owned sector coexists with cooperatives and foreign-owned and joint-venture businesses as well as, increasingly, Chinese privately owned enterprises.

In 1980, Deng Xiaoping had mooted major political reforms after blaming feudal and undemocratic traditions for the overconcentration of power in one person, which resulted in excesses like the Cultural Revolution. Deng advocated a separation of the roles and powers of the CCP and government and called for more people's democracy and debate in the party itself. A party theorist, Liao Gailong (b. 1919), promoted reforms, including direct elections at all levels and a two-house national parliament—one for regions and one representing economic interests—but with the CCP maintaining overall power. Deng's ideas and Liao's corporatist proposal were forgotten after the rise of Poland's Solidarity trade-union movement highlighted the threat of relaxing controls over mass movements by demonstrating how such movements could easily become dangerously politicized and threaten CCP rule.

A similar fate befell Zhao Ziyang's modest late-1980s proposals to build socialist democracy, a broadening of representation and participation in the political system by new groups and experts in particular areas, by developing the national and lower-level People's Congresses and by expanding united-front work and its public face, the Chinese People's Political Consultative Conference. While the congresses are elected and have nominal power to make decisions, conference representatives are appointed. They can only review laws and policies and can only make recommendations to the government, the CCP, and public organizations. The student movement of April–June 1989, during which student demands for better living conditions, jobs, and less corruption, escalated to calls for an undefined democracy; the army violently suppressed the protests on 4 June 1989. Zhao was sacked for his sympathy for the students' demands, and his reforms were dropped.

The current leader, President Jiang Zemin (b. 1926), endorses Deng Xiaoping's four cardinal principles:

upholding the socialist path, proletarian dictatorship, leadership of the CCP, and Marxism-Leninism-Mao Zedong thought. While maintaining CCP dominance, these principles leave little room for democratization. The party repeatedly campaigns against bourgeois liberalization (any calls for Western-style political reforms) and spiritual pollution while promoting construction of an ill-defined socialist spiritual civilization and nationalism as counterweights.

The Future

Since 1987, there have been incremental improvements in village elections, and in 2000 there were indications that this experiment would be extended to towns. There have also been steady improvements in China's legal system, but toward establishing rule-by-law rather than a rule-of-law that would better guarantee the rights of Chinese citizens as written in the Chinese constitution. This development and China's accession to the World Trade Organization will promote rule-based decision making over arbitrary fiat.

Among possible indications of the direction of future change are experiments in Hainan Island and Shenzhen to develop a "small state, big society" in which groups themselves, rather than the state, police their own members. In February 2000, President Jiang Zemin began promoting the CCP as being the representative of advanced forces of production, of the fundamental interests of the broad masses, and of advanced culture. These three forces could all be used to advance radical change, including fundamentally altering the political system and the CCP itself. Only the future will tell whether the CCP can attempt such change and succeed.

Gerry Groot

Further Reading

Brodsgaard, Kjeld Eric, and David Strand. (1998) *Reconstructing Twentieth-Century China: State Control, Civil Society, and National Identity*. Oxford, U.K.: Clarendon.

Brugger, Bill, and Stephen Reglar. (1994) *Politics, Economy, and Society in Contemporary China*. Basingstoke, U.K.: Macmillan.

Feng, Chongyi, and David S. G. Goodman, eds. (2000) *North China at War: The Social Ecology of Revolution*. Lanham, MD: Rowan and Littlefield.

Saich, Tony. (1996) *The Rise to Power of the Chinese Communist Party: Documents and Analysis*. Armonk, NY: M. E. Sharpe.

Saich, Tony, and Hans Van Den Ven, eds. (1994) *New Perspectives on the Chinese Revolution*. Armonk, NY: M. E. Sharpe.

Yang, Dali. (1996) *Calamity and Reform in China: State, Rural Society, and Institutional Change since the Great Leap Famine*. Stanford, CA: Stanford University Press.

COMMUNISM—NORTH KOREA

COMMUNISM—NORTH KOREA The core of the original North Korean communists consisted primarily of Koreans who lived out the Japanese occupation in either the Soviet Far East or in various parts of China. Upon Japan's defeat they returned to Korea and organized into the Korean Workers' Party (KWP); factions grew among KWP members based on their colonial-era locations as refugees. The party served as the nucleus of the communist state since its inception in 1948. Following the Korean War, in 1955 Kim Il Sung (1912–1994) unified the factions through successfully purging his opposition. Throughout the remainder of his life he strengthened his power base through building a near-religious cult, his name appearing on everything from flowers to universities. His "on-the-spot guidance" and that of his son Kim Jong Il (b. 1942), it was reported, helped strengthen North Korea's industrial, educational, and military sectors. He initiated mobilization campaigns, similar to China's Great Leap Forward, to stimulate labor toward increased production. Kim Jong Il officially inherited the elder Kim's titles in 1994 following Kim Il Sung's death; the son (and the North Korean people) had been preparing for this transition from the 1980s.

Bruce Cumings describes this form of communism as "socialist corporatism," a political system built around a social family (Cumings 1998, 398). The glue holding this corporate family together is the ideology of *chuch'e* (or *juch'e*), a term that has most often been translated as "self-reliance" but behaves closer to the idea of "self-determination." This thinking was obvious in the 1960s with the Democratic People's Republic of Korea's (DPRK's) success in playing off the two communist giants, the USSR and China. It is seen in the dynamics of the DPRK in its negotiations with the United States. The KWP remains to this day the central organizing body of North Korean communism.

Mark E. Caprio

Further Reading

Cumings, Bruce. (1998) *Korea's Place in the Sun: A Modern History*. New York: Norton.

Scalapino, Robert A., and Chong-sik Lee. (1972) *Communism in Korea*. 2 vols. Berkeley and Los Angeles: University of California Press.

Suh Dae-sook. (1988) *Kim Il Sung: The North Korean Leader*. New York: Columbia University Press.

COMMUNISM—VIETNAM

COMMUNISM—VIETNAM Communism in Vietnam developed in the context of Vietnam's anticolonial struggle against France, the growing Sino-Soviet ideological and military conflict, and Vietnam's localization of foreign influences.

The political memorial billboard at Reunification Palace in Ho Chi Minh City in 1996. (STEPHEN G. DONALDSON PHOTOGRAPHY)

Communism was adopted in Vietnam as an anticolonial solution. Ho Chi Minh (1890–1969), founder of the Vietnamese Communist Party and father of Vietnam's independence, noted that it was patriotism rather than communism that led him the ideas of Lenin. This approach remained valid into the 1950s during Vietnam's war with France and into the 1960s and 1970s during Vietnam's war with the United States. Although Leninism was often cited in Vietnamese Communist writings, the Communist system that developed in Vietnam was mainly shaped by Stalinism and Maoism. The Vietnamese Communist movement adhered to the Moscow line in the 1930s, adopted the Maoist model of guerrilla warfare in the late 1930s, and executed Stalin's suggestion of, and the Maoist model of, land reform in the 1950s. The government in Hanoi vacillated between Moscow and Beijing in the 1960s, culminating in an internal conflict that is called the "revisionist" incident. Hanoi clashed with Beijing between 1979 and 1991 over Cambodia and moved closer to the Soviet bloc.

Tensions in Vietnamese Communism

Throughout the history of the Communist period, however, there was not only conflict between the Stalinist and Maoist models of socialist development but also between Communism as a foreign ideology and Vietnamese political tradition, three salient elements of which were patriotism, Confucianism, and village culture. This conflict with Vietnamese political tradition can be seen in several examples: (1) Ho Chi Minh's conflict with the Moscow-led Comintern in 1930, when he named the Communist party he founded the Vietnamese Communist Party instead of the Indochinese Communist Party (though the name was later changed); (2) his drafting a political thesis that did not advocate the Moscow line of class struggle; (3) the founding of a united front organization known as the Vietnam Independence League, or Viet Minh, that incorporated every sector of society; (4) the dissolution of the Indochinese Communist Party in 1945 after the revolution; (5) the public apology for the mishandling of land reform in the mid-1950s; and (6) the absence of the use of brutal force as a means to develop socialism or to deal with political opponents.

Confucianism and Communism

Ho Chi Minh relied on Confucian concepts and terms in introducing, recasting, and propagating Communist ideological concepts, making the latter more compatible with Vietnam's Confucian-based tradition. Presented in Confucian terms, Ho's revolutionary ethics consisted of the five principles of *nhan* (humanity), *nghia* (duty), *tri* (knowledge), *dung* (courage), and *liem* (integrity). Selected elements of village culture were incorporated into the new socialist discourse. One aspect of village culture selected was the image of the peasant family as a stable social unit engaged in agricultural activities. Internal family relations were marked by equality, reciprocity, and mutual sacrifice, and family work was characterized by equal distribution of responsibilities. These aspects of family relations were extended to govern relationships among friends and in society at large.

The Development of Vietnamese Communism

The Vietnamese Communist movement was founded in 1930 by Ho, then known as Nguyen Ai Quoc. Since then, the movement has assumed several names: the Vietnamese Communist Party (February–October 1930), the Indochinese Communist Party (1930–1945), the Vietnam Worker Party (1951–1976), and the Communist Party of Vietnam (1976–present). The revolution that broke out in August 1945 can be considered a war for independence. It was not until the years 1949–1950 that the war became a socialist revolution. This development unfolded in the context of intensified military conflict with France in the 1940s and 1950s, the crystallization of the Cold War in the 1940s and 1950s, and the victory of the Communists in China's civil war in 1949. Politically, signs of a socialist revolution were seen through the revival of the Indochinese Communist Party under the name Vietnam Worker Party in 1951 and a rise of absolute party control over the state apparatus. Economically, socialist development can be seen in the land reform of 1954–1956, in the collectivization of agriculture and nationalization of domestic industries beginning in the late 1950s, and in the imposition of central planning in the 1960s. In the intellectual realm, Maoist practices of ideological rectification were imported into Vietnam in 1949–1950, and the period between 1953 and 1956 was one in which peasant-based political and economic ethics penetrated the content of every type of writing. This intellectual trend led to conflicts between the party-state and intellectuals known as the Nhan Van Giai Pham Affairs in the mid-1950s.

Communism in South Vietnam

Until 1975, Communism developed only in Vietnam north of the seventeenth parallel, in the area known as the Democratic Republic of Vietnam, or North Vietnam. Communism was imposed on the South only after reunification in 1975. The Hanoi regime moved to collectivize agriculture, nationalize industries, and control wholesale and retail trade. In the south, agricultural collectivization did not succeed because by the mid-1970s the distribution of land ownership had already become fairly egalitarian; the Hanoi government's agricultural collectivization turned out to be an attack on the interests of the middle-income and rich peasants who had benefited from the land distribution policy of the National Liberation Front for South Vietnam in the 1960s. The government's move to nationalize industries and control retail and wholesale trade disrupted production and supply in the south. Severe economic crises resulted and led to the practice of "fence breaking," whereby production units spontaneously violated rules and regulations. The party-state responded by endorsing policies to reform the socialist system.

The reform process can be divided into two phases. The first phase lasted from 1979 to 1985, when reforms were carried out within the framework of central planning. Measures adopted included the endorsement of the concept of a multisectoral economy in 1979 and subsequent reform policies in the areas of foreign trade, agriculture, industry, and the pricing system in the early 1980s. The second phase lasted from 1986 to 1989. In 1986, the Sixth Party Congress endorsed a policy of reform known as *doi moi* (renewal), calling for abolition of the central planning system. Major policies put forth during this period included the promulgation of a law dealing with foreign investment in 1987, the call for withdrawal of troops from Cambodia in 1987, the decollectivization of agriculture in 1988, and abolition of the two-price system in 1989.

Vietnamese Communism's contribution to the process of national liberation and its localized nature helped legitimize the authority of the Vietnamese Communist Party in the face of the collapse of Communism in the Soviet Union and Eastern Europe and the challenge to Communism in China between 1989 and 1991.

Thaveeporn Vasavakul

Further Reading

Dang Phong and Melanie Beresford. (1998) *Authority Relations and Economic Decision Making in Vietnam*. Copenhagen, Denmark: NIAS.

Duiker, William. (2000) *Ho Chi Minh*. New York: Hyperion.

Fforde, Adam. (1998) *The Agrarian Question in North Vietnam, 1974–1979*. Armonk, NY: M. E. Sharpe.

———, and Stefan de Vylder. (1996) *From Plan to Market: The Economic Transition in Vietnam*. Boulder, CO: Westview Press.

Huynh Kim Khanh. (1982) *Vietnamese Communism, 1925–1945*. Berkeley and Los Angeles: University of California Press.

Vasavakul, Thaveeporn. (1995) "Vietnam: The Changing Model of Legitimation" In *Political Legitimation in Southeast Asia: The Quest for Moral Authority*, edited by Muthiah Alagappa. Stanford, CA: Stanford University Press, 257–271.

COMMUNIST PARTY OF BURMA Despite failing to gain power, the Communist Party of Burma (CPB) was a major influence on political life in Myanmar (Burma) during the twentieth century. Marxist ideology played an important role in the national liberation struggle, leading to the formation of the CPB by a cell meeting of underground leaders in 1939. The most famous of these, Aung San (1915–1947), subsequently left the party over political differences, but CPB membership grew rapidly during resistance to the Japanese occupation (1941–1945). At one stage, the CPB was reputedly the strongest organization within the coalition Anti-Fascist People's Freedom League (AFPFL) that later led the country to independence.

Ideological differences, however, caused the CPB to walk out from the AFPFL in 1946, and, in March 1948, the party began armed insurrection. Inspired by communist victories elsewhere in Asia, CPB militia seized control of vast central areas of the country with the aid of several senior commanders in the Burmese army who deserted with their troops. In the Chin-Arakan borderlands, a smaller "Red Flag" faction, headed by Thakin Soe (1905–1989), gradually dwindled in strength, but the mainstream "White Flag" party, led by Thakin Than Tun (1911–1968), remained a considerable thorn in the government side for many years in central and southern regions of the country. Staging frequent guerrilla raids, it also enjoyed the support of both trade union and student activists in the towns.

In the mid-1960s, an internecine "Cultural Revolution" saw the party take a dogmatic turn towards Maoism, which was modeled on developments in China. This precipitated the deaths of Than Tun and other key leaders in a series of violent incidents. However, following anti-Chinese riots in Yangon (Rangoon), the CPB was able to open a major new front along the Chinese border in 1968 with full-scale military backing from the People's Republic of China. In the following decade, the CPB's Northeast Command built up significant "liberated zones" in the Shan and Kachin States, with its own radio station and 15,000-strong People's Army. The scale of this new front compensated, in part, for the loss of the party's remaining base areas in the Pegu Yoma highlands during the mid-1970s.

The CPB's Northeast Command, however, was never able to break out from its strongholds along the China border. Here the CPB, which was mostly led by ethnic Burmans, clashed as often with ethnic insurgent forces as with government troops. Eventually, it was ethnic dissatisfaction that led to mass mutinies from the CPB's People's Army and the party's virtual collapse in 1989. Thakin Ba Thein Tin (b. 1914) and the party's veteran leaders retired into China, and during the 1990s only a few loyal cadres were occasionally reported to be still active inside Myanmar.

Martin Smith

Further Reading

Becka, Jan. (1983) *The National Liberation Movement in Burma during the Japanese Occupation Period (1941–1945)*. Dissertationes Orientales 42. Prague, Czechoslovakia: Publishing House of the Czechoslovak Academy of Sciences.

Fleischmann, Klaus, ed. (1989) *Documents on Communism in Burma 1945–1977*. Hamburg: Institut fur Asienkunde.

Lintner, Bertil. (1990) *Land of Jade: A Journey through Insurgent Burma*. Edinburgh: Kiscadale.

———. (1990) *The Rise and Fall of the Communist Party of Burma*. Ithaca, NY: Cornell University Southeast Asia Program.

Smith, Martin. (1999) *Burma: Insurgency and the Politics of Ethnicity*. 2d ed. London: Zed Books.

Taylor, Robert. (1984) *Marxism and Resistance in Burma 1942–45: Thein Pe Myint's Wartime Traveler*. Athens, OH: Ohio University Press.

CON DAO ISLANDS The Con Dao Islands consist of fourteen islands located southeast of Vinh Loi off the coast of southern Vietnam. Until the eighteenth century, there were no permanent settlements or inhabitants on the islands. In 1702, Britain's East India Company established a base on Con Son (Poulo Condore), the largest island on the archipelago. The British ultimately left following a rebellion, and France took possession of the islands in 1861. On Poulo Condore, the French found a prison with 119 inmates of Vietnam's Hue government. The French continued to use the island as a prison, which they expanded on over the course of their rule in Vietnam.

A great number of Vietnamese patriots and revolutionaries, such as Phan Chu Trinh, Luong Van Can, and Le Duan, served time on Poulo Condore, earning the prison the reputation of being a "revolutionary training ground." By 1934, there were at least 2,700 Vietnamese prisoners on the island.

Following France's defeat in 1954, Poulo Condore continued to be used as a prison by the government of the Republic of Vietnam. In 1993, Poulo Condore became a national park and the archipelago now boasts a population of about 1,500 residents. There are plans to further develop the area for tourism.

Micheline Lessard

Further Reading

Demariaux, Maurice. (1999) *Poulo-Condore, archipel du Vietnam*. Paris: L'Harmattan.

Hemery, Daniel. (1975) *Revolutionnaires vietnamiens et pouvoir colonial en Indochine*. Paris: Maspero.

CONFUCIAN ETHICS Confucian ethics is best understood as a contextualistic virtue ethics based on self-cultivation. There are three general categories that are used to classify moral systems: absolutism, relativism, and contextualism. Ethical contextualism means that there are no absolute moral rules and that cultural customs or feelings cannot be blindly followed; alleged absolute codes or customs and feelings can serve only as guidelines. Each person must decide what is the best that she or he can do in that particular context to complete in action a higher value such as authenticity, love, or virtue. The philosophies of Aristotle, Confucius, and the existentialists and modern situation ethics are examples of ethical contextualism. Confucian ethics can be summarized as the art of contextualizing the practice of virtue.

Confucian ethics bears some similarity to Aristotelian ethics. Both are virtue-based systems (virtue ethics refers to the moral quality of one's character or personality as opposed to merely obeying moral rules), which acknowledge that there are no fixed and binding rules to govern the moral life. Rather a person must be well trained and habituated to weighing the relative value of actions in specific situations in regard to particular persons.

Confucians and Aristotelians soon part company, however. Aristotle held what has been called the doctrine of the golden mean, namely, that most of the virtues are at the midpoint between the extremes of deficiency and excess. Regrettably, *Zhongyong* ("centrality and commonality") was misleadingly translated as the Doctrine of the Mean, allowing for superficial comparisons. The Confucian concept of "centrality" refers to the condition before feelings of pleasure, anger, sorrow, and joy are expressed; clearly it is not the mean between extremes.

Confucius and Before

Confucian ethics began long before the time of Confucius (551–479 BCE). It was rooted in the clan values of the early Zhou dynasty (1045–256 BCE) aristocracy. Confucius was both a traditional and an innovative thinker; he breathed new life into the traditional aristocratic clan ethics of the Zhou. Confucius's innovation was that he sought to transform aristocratic values and practices into everyday practices and values for common people. Thus, he reinterpreted the label for "prince" (*junzi*, "the son of the ruler") to mean any person who achieves the status of being a noble and moral example for others, that is, a "prince of virtue."

Although Confucius had his gender biases, the content and practice of his moral teachings are similar to those of the feminists who advocate a contextual care ethic. Speaking very generally, Confucius, like the feminists of care, was concerned about interpersonal relationships founded on love and affection; his known writings contain nothing of an ethics based on impersonal duty. In the writings of both Confucius and certain feminists, moral values are learned at home by participating in a morally healthy parent-child relationship. The writings of Confucius emphasized the father-son relationship rather than the feminist mother-child relationship, but both advance the importance of proper child rearing for the cultivation of a moral personality that learns to contextualize values and actions in particular situations in relation with unique persons.

All Confucians agree that moral education begins at home. Only after a child learns filial respect for parents and brotherly love for siblings can he or she be expected to extend respect and love beyond the family. Methodologically, filial piety *(xiao)* is primary; ontologically, person-to-person care (*ren*, usually rendered as "benevolence" or "humanity") is the significant trait of being human. To be a caring person is to be a moral example or moral authority for others to follow. After proper rearing, a person needs instruction from a Confucian teacher to develop his or her practice of caring. This instruction focuses primarily on literary achievement *(wen)*; memorizing the Four Books (four ancient and venerated Confucian texts), large sections of the Five Classics (also important Confucian texts), and other important Confucian works; and learning Confucian rituals and music so as to habituate the student in the practice of being virtuous.

The Confucian virtues are best understood in terms of actual human behavior, rather than intellectual beliefs. Confucians, both past and present-day, are concerned with the practice of taking care of others, not the abstract idea of care. The five constant virtues are person-to-person care *(ren)*, ritual action *(li)*, rightness *(yi)*, trustworthiness *(xin)*, and moral wisdom *(zhi)*. Person-to-person care is defined as "love" in the *Analects*. Confucians do not advocate random acts of love; all of the virtues must be practiced according to the requirements of ritual action. Confucian society is one of ritual order, not legal order.

The art of contextualizing the virtues in practice is clearly expressed in being a person of rightness *(yi)*.

Although the examples of the ancient sages serve as a guide, there are no absolute standards of rightness. Rightness entails doing the right thing to the right people at the right time in the most appropriate manner. Confucius invested a lot in trustworthiness *(xin);* exemplars of the moral must stand by their words. They must practice before they teach others, and they must teach only what they themselves have practiced.

Even moral wisdom *(zhi)* should be understood in terms of practice, or doing the right thing, rather than merely knowing what should be done. It is bolstered by the virtues of literary accomplishment *(wen)* and studiousness *(xue)*. Any virtue may have to be practiced with bravery *(yong)*. The virtues of reverence *(jing)* and sincerity *(cheng)*, only briefly mentioned by Confucius, were developed by later Confucians and were understood to be part of the structure of the universe.

Mencius and Later Philosophers

Where the writings attributed to Confucius were primarily concerned with the practice of moral behavior, those attributed to Mencius (372?–289? BCE) understood the cardinal virtues to constitute the operations of the human heart-mind. While the writings of Mencius and Xunzi (c. 310–213? BCE) disagreed on the natural goodness of humans, with Mencius claiming that people are basically good and Kunzi that they are basically deviant, both emphasized the importance of proper rearing, education, and ritual action for the correct expression of moral virtues. It was not until Zhou Dunyi (1017–1073) and Zhang Zai (1020–1077) revitalized the study of Confucianism that all the Confucian virtues came to take on a cosmological as well as a social moral role. To the extent that Korean, Japanese, Vietnamese, and other Southeast Asian cultures adopted and adapted Confucianism, they also accepted and transformed Confucian ethics to meet their social and moral needs.

James D. Sellmann

See also: **Confucius; Mencius; Xunzi; Zhou Dynasty**

Further Reading

Allan, Sarah. (1997) *The Way of Water and Sprouts of Virtue.* Albany, NY: State University of New York Press.

Ames, Roger T., and Henry Rosemont, Jr., trans. (1998) *The Analects of Confucius: A Philosophical Translation.* New York: Ballantine.

Chan, Wing-tsit. (1963) *A Source Book in Chinese Philosophy.* Princeton, NJ: Princeton University Press.

Ivanhoe, P. J. (1993) *Confucian Moral Self-Cultivation.* New York: Peter Lang.

Tu Wei-ming. (1985) *Confucian Thought: Selfhood as Creative Transformation.* Albany, NY: State University of New York Press.

———. (1979) *Humanity and Self-Cultivation: Essays in Confucian Thought.* Berkeley, CA: Asian Humanities Press.

CONFUCIANISM—CHINA The system of thought known as Confucianism derives its name from the highly esteemed teacher and sage Confucius (551–479 BCE), or Kong Fuzi (Grand Master Kong). Confucianism includes the complete literature, practices, and teachings of the traditions which align themselves with Confucius. It is interesting to note that in the Chinese language there is no equivalent expression for Confucianism. The Chinese refer to specific thinkers or trends; for example, they refer to the *Kongmeng shi xue* (teachings of Confucius and Mencius) or to the Song- and Ming-dynasty study of principle *(Song Ming lixue)*, which is called "Neo-Confucianism" in English. When bibliographers of the Han dynasty (206 BCE–220 CE) codified the books in the imperial library, they classified the works of Confucius and his followers under the heading "Literati."

The basic teachings of Confucianism stress the importance of education for moral development of the individual so that the state can be governed by moral virtue rather than by the use of coercive laws.

Syncretism in Confucianism

It is often said that traditional China was a Confucian society or that Confucianism was the official state religion and philosophy of China before the twentieth century. Such claims are misleading overgeneralizations. First, the syncretic nature of both early and later Confucian thought must be understood. Second, the hybrid syncretic character of later state-sanctioned Confucianism must be explained.

Generally speaking, East Asian cultures, philosophies, and religions are syncretic or composite in nature. Because of their practical orientation, they do not place great store in exclusive ideas or practices, but rather prefer to absorb and integrate whatever proves useful or satisfying. This is especially true of Chinese culture and philosophy, and is in large part the reason why the dynastic system was effective and long lasting.

What made the teachings of Confucius so compelling and attractive to so many thinkers for over 2,500 years is their syncretic amalgamated content and character. Confucius, his disciples, and most of the later followers celebrated and incorporated various forms of literature. They emphasized poetry, history and legend, divination, music, and ritual. They integrated self-cultivation and virtue with the notions of harmony and a political philosophy of rulership. The Confucian curriculum was well rounded and eclectic, consisting of the six arts: ritual, music, archery, charioteering, calligraphy, and mathematics. Confucius also advocated that any serious student, even a commoner, should have some training in military arts. The Confucians assumed that the masses would be vigorously engaged in agriculture and related industry. In this regard, the Confucians incorporated agricultural skills into their social program, though they did not place great emphasis on these because they were far more concerned with moral cultivation.

Given the number of shared values found in the *Analects (Lunyu)* of Confucius (one of the basic texts of Confucianism) and the *Daodejing* (one of the basic texts of Taoism) it is likely that those who later generations labeled as Confucians and Taoists originally shared a common ground. Both stressed the significance of self-cultivation, acknowledging the need for special training that would make one a true and better person. Although the Confucians emphasized the human-to-human relationships and the Taoists underscored the human-to-nature affinity, nevertheless the writers of the *Zhongyong* (Centrality and Commonality, another basic text of Confucianism) reasserted the importance of the relationship between humans and nature in Confucianism. In their emphasis on the mutual complementarity of opposites (such as yin and yang), Confucianism and Taoism have borrowed and absorbed ideas and practices from each other, increasing their respective longevity and profundity.

Borrowing from the statesmen who debated and were concerned about properly naming job titles and evaluating job performance, Confucius and others, especially Mencius (372?–289? BCE) and Xunzi (310–213? BCE), delineated the meaning of the "rectification or attunement of names" *(zhengming)*. This was important because knowing the precise name for one's position in the world (as prince, for instance, or father, or son) let one know one's duties and responsibilities.

Superficially speaking, the Confucians appear to have been most at odds with the Legalists *(fajia)*, who advocated a rigorous notion of the rule of law—as opposed to the Confucian notion of rule by example. Although Confucius, Mencius, and Xunzi advocated ruling the people with virtue by setting a moral example, they certainly recognized the need for law. Tradition has it that when Confucius was the chief of police, even he had to authorize the execution of a criminal. The Confucians, like the Legalists, wanted to standardize a code of human conduct, but the Legalists sought to do so by instituting public law, whereas the Confucians placed greater emphasis on instituting a homogeneous system of ethics to govern human interactions, holding the law in reserve for when egregious behavior occurred.

It is clear, then, that Confucius did not create a pure philosophical system; he borrowed from various approaches. The followers of Confucius likewise absorbed elements from the other schools of philosophy to bolster their interpretation of Confucius.

Mencius and Xunzi

Mencius is noted for advancing Confucius' teachings. Confucius was concerned with the details of proper moral behavior; Mencius advocated a more abstract philosophy, focusing on goodness of human nature *(xing)* and the development of the mind *(xin)*. Although Mencius had syncretic tendencies, he also vehemently attacked other philosophers, including the early Taoist Yang Zhu (c. late fourth century BCE); Mozi (479–438 BCE), the founder of Mohism, a philosophy that stressed universal love; and Xu Xing (c. late fourth century BCE), who argued that a king should labor in the field alongside his subjects. (Mencius answered that the king should concentrate on ruling and leave agriculture to the farmer.)

A century later, Xunzi revitalized Confucian teachings by invigorating them with practical political measures such as economic means to enrich the state and placing greater emphasis on public law. Xunzi is noted for soundly attacking Mencius' idea that human nature is basically good; on the contrary, Xunzi argued that people are basically selfish given limited resources, but that they can be trained to be good through the practice of ritual action and education. Xunzi's approach dominated Confucian thinking from the Han dynasty to the Song dynasty (960–1279). During the Song dynasty, Mencius' philosophy was used to develop Neo-Confucianism.

Syncretism and State-Sponsored Confucianism

The syncretic approach to philosophy and the arts of rulership became especially popular toward the end of the Warring States period (475–221 BCE) and during the first portion of the Han dynasty (the so-called Western Han; 206 BCE–8 CE).

After the short-lived Qin dynasty (221–206 BCE), the Han emperors continued to grapple with the problem of systematizing political philosophy and the arts of rulership. During the reign of Emperor Wu of the Han (156–87 BCE) Dong Zhongshu (c. 179–104 BCE) constructed a composite syncretic form of Confucianism that became the state-sanctioned philosophy. Dong was a Confucian in that he praised Confucius and generally adhered to the Confucian ideas of self-cultivation and rule by virtue, but he effectively integrated aspects of the Five Phases philosophy (a philosophy of the mystical composition of the universe out of five elements), Taoism, and Legalism into Confucianism. Dong established his philosophy on a temporal order, and explained history and dynastic succession in terms reminiscent of the Five Phases, although he delineated only three stages. The authoritarian structure of his sociopolitical philosophy made it attractive to Han rulers. Dong advocated the "three bonds" in which the king rules the people, the father disciplines the son, and the husband provides for the wife.

After the Han dynasty, the intellectual life of Confucianism stagnated, becoming a lifeless dogma for nearly seven hundred years. In the Tang dynasty (618–907), Han Yu (768–824) reawakened Confucianism with his study of the moral way *(daoxue)*, claiming that he had received the correct transmission of the teachings via Mencius; he rejected Xunzi and emphased the goodness of human nature.

Zhou Dunyi, the Cheng Brothers, and Zhu Xi

A Tang-dynasty Taoist alchemical document called the Diagram of the Great Ultimate *(Taijitu)* was transmitted to Zhou Dunyi (1017–1073) in the Song dynasty. Zhou Dunyi wrote a short but profound work on that document, in which he linked the moral nature of human beings with the nature of the universe, putting forward the notion that the goodness of human nature is part and parcel of the moral goodness of the universe. Zhou was also influenced by Buddhism, especially Zen. He also taught the Cheng brothers.

Cheng Hao (1032–1085) and his younger brother Cheng Yi (1033–1107) developed Zhuo's idea of a universal principle *(li)* inherent in all things, making it the cornerstone of their respective philosophies and the main concept of Song-dynasty Neo-Confucianism. They proposed that the proper subjects for study were principle *(li)* and human nature *(xing)* and that ultimately human nature was identical to principle. For them, the investigation of things is crucial for self-cultivation. They asserted that the universe is a process of giving life and that the life-giving principle is goodness. They influenced the Neo-Confucian scholar Zhu Xi (1130–1200).

Zhu Xi systematized the teachings of Zhou Dunyi and the Cheng brothers. Zhu Xi argued that reality consists of two components: principle *(li)* and material force *(qi)*. Principle is the form of all that exists, while material force fills and activates things. Zhu said that human nature is basically good because it is endowed with the principle *(li)* that is goodness. People learn to be bad, and so the purpose of education is to retain the good principle in one's original nature and remove acquired pollutants. Zhu Xi sided with the rationalistic tendencies in Cheng Yi's philosophy, and what is called the Cheng-Zhu school of Neo-Confucianism dominated China for several hundred years. Zhu Xi debated with Lu Xiangshan (1139–1193) who supported the idealistic tendencies in Cheng Hao's philosophy. Lu did not emphasize human nature the way Zhu did. Instead, Lu focused on the human mind, advocating that it is one with principle. For Lu, the investigation of things meant the study of the mind. Lu argued for the unity of the Way *(tao)*, opposing Zhu's distinction between principle and material force.

Confucianism in the Ming and Qing Dynasties

In the Ming dynasty (1368–1644), Wang Yangming (1472–1529) developed the idealism of Lu Xiangshan. The reader should note that in philosophy "idealism" means that reality is in the mind, or in the ideas of the mind; it does not denote a perfect (ideal) world. Wang championed the School of Mind *(xinxue)*, in contradistinction to Zhu's School of Principle *(lixue)*. Wang argued that anyone could become a sage because everyone possesses a mind that contains innate knowledge of the good. This innate goodness extends outward, starting with a natural love for oneself and one's family, extending to one's community, and then outward to all other people, creatures, and things. Wang is also well known for advocating that knowledge and action form a unity. The purposeful character of his philosophy influenced later thinkers such as Tan Sitong (1865–1898) and Sun Yat-sen (1866–1925).

In 1644, the Manchus conquered China, establishing the Qing dynasty (1644–1912). Under foreign occupation, Chinese government officials were marginalized, and many turned to scholarship and the study of Confucian philosophy to avoid criticism or punishment by the Manchus. Dai Zhen (1724–1777) and Kang Youwei (1858–1927) are two important Confucians of the Qing. Dai Zhen dedicated his life to studying the *Mencius* (the text associated with the philosopher of the same name). The rationalism of the Cheng-Zhu school was still popular in his day, but Dai Zhen boldly rejected it. Dai proposed that human morality had its origin in blood-and-material force and the knowing mind. He argued that principle only exists when the feelings are not mistaken. Kang Youwei accepted a basic tenant of the Lu-Wang school that book learning must be complemented with profound action. He was a learned scholar, and he also advocated social and political reform. Kang understood Confucius to be an innovative institutional reformer. He also proposed that Confucius was a divine being or god, and the founder of a great religion. Borrowing an expression from the Mencius, Kang argued that the core of human nature was the mind that cannot bear to see the suffering of others. Kang adapted Dong Zhongshu's idea of the three ages and modified it into a theory of historical evolution, proposing that human history begins with an Age of Disorder, followed by an Age of Small Peace, and culminating in an Age of Great Peace. In the Age of Great Peace, everyone and everything will be treated exactly the same; there will be one humanity, one world order, one great unity *(datong)*.

Confucianism in the Twentieth Century

In the twentieth century, Feng Youlan (1895–1990) revitalized rationalistic Neo-Confucianism. He argued that everything that exists is undergoing a continuous process of realizing principle *(li)* by means of material force *(qi)*. He proposed that humans live in one of four spheres of life: the innocent sphere, the utilitarian or practical sphere, the moral sphere, and the transcendent sphere. Philosophy, he contended, assists people to live in the last two higher spheres of life. Xiong Shili (1883–1968) reconstructed idealistic Neo-Confucianism. Xiong advocates that reality is change, a perpetual process of production and reproduction, or closing and opening. By closing, Xiong means that reality has the tendency to integrate, to momentarily be what we call matter. By opening, he means that reality has the tendency to maintain its own nature, to be its own master, what we can temporarily call mind.

When Mao Zedong (1893–1976) and his Communist followers won the civil war in 1949, Confucianism and Confucius were strongly attacked. Feng, Xiong, and all other scholars were forced to denounce Confucius and their own decadent views. The Communist Party became far more tolerant of Confucianism after the Mao's death, such that by the 1990 party propaganda began to cite the ideas of Confucius or his followers. In addition, there are still in both Taiwan and the West practicing Confucianists.

James D. Sellmann

Further Reading

Allan, Sarah. (1997) *The Way of Water and Sprouts of Virtue.* Albany, NY: State University of New York Press.

Ames, Roger T., and Henry Rosemont, Jr., trans. (1998) *The Analects of Confucius: A Philosophical Translation.* New York: Ballantine Books.

Chan, Wing-tsit. (1963) *A Source Book in Chinese Philosophy.* Princeton, NJ: Princeton University Press.

Fung, Yu-lan. (1952) *History of Chinese Philosophy.* Trans. by Derk Bodde. Princeton, NJ: Princeton University Press.

Graham, Angus C. (1986) "The Background of the Mencian Theory of Human Nature." In *Studies in Chinese Philosophy & Philosophical Literature*, edited by Angus C. Graham. Singapore: The Institute of East Asian Philosophies, 7–59.

———. (1989) *Disputers of the Tao.* La Salle, IL: Open Court.

Hall, David L., and Roger T. Ames. (1987) *Thinking through Confucius.* Albany, NY: State University of New York Press.

Hsiao, Kung-chuan. (1979) *A History of Chinese Political Thought.* Trans. by Frederick Mote. Princeton. NJ: Princeton University Press.

Ivanhoe, P. J. (1993) *Confucian Moral Self-Cultivation.* New York: Peter Lang.

Jensen, Lionel M. (1997) *Manufacturing Confucianism: Chinese Traditions and Universal Civilization.* Durham, NC, and London: Duke University Press.

Lau, D. C., trans. (1979) *The Analects.* Middlesex, U.K.: Penguin Books.

———, trans. (1970) *Mencius.* Middlesex, U.K.: Penguin Books.

Legge, James, trans. (1960) *The Chinese Classics.* Reprint ed. Hong Kong: University of Hong Kong.

Munro, Donald J. (1979) *Concept of Man in Contemporary China.* Ann Arbor, MI: University of Michigan Press.

Nivison, David S. (1996) *The Ways of Confucianism: Investigations in Chinese Philosophy*, edited by Bryan W. Van Norden. Chicago and La Salle, IL: Open Court.

Tu, Weiming. (1979) *Humanity and Self-Cultivation: Essays in Confucian Thought.* Berkeley, CA: Asian Humanities Press.

———. (1985) *Confucian Thought: Selfhood as Creative Transformation.* Albany, NY: State University of New York Press.

———. (1996) *Confucian Tradition in East Asian Modernity.* Cambridge, MA: Harvard University Press.

CONFUCIANISM—JAPAN The ideas of the great Zhou-dynasty Chinese philosopher Kong Qiu (551–479 BCE), or Confucius, as he is known in the West, diffused to the Korean kingdoms nearly a millennium later, in the early fourth century CE. A century after that, in 405, these ideas were brought to Japan by scholars from Paekche, the southernmost of the Korean kingdoms. It was not until the latter part of the next century, however, as the Yamato state began to solidify its rule, that Confucianism really took hold in Japan. Confucian scholars accompanied the Buddhist missionaries sent by the king of Paekche to the Yamato court, and by the reign of Empress Suiko (593–628), the Confucian classics, in combination with Mahayana Buddhist theology preached by the Korean missionaries, had become the foundation of the nascent imperial regime. The man who accomplished this synthesis was one of the most important figures in Japanese history, Suiko's regent and kinsman, Shotoku Taishi. Prince Shotoku's famous "Seventeen-Article Constitution," the goal of which was to provide the basis for a harmonious and hierarchical political system centered on the imperial monarchy, was in large measure based on Confucian precepts.

The *Junzi* and the Ideal of *Ren*

The essential idea of Kong Qiu's teachings is that the source of all morality is filial piety, that is, a child's absolute respect for and loyalty to his parents. This, in turn, is reflected in the relationship between the ruler and his subjects, with the ruler the equivalent of the morally upright father. One must cultivate virtue at all times so as to become a "superior man," or *junzi*. The most important component of the "superior man" was *ren* (or *jin* in Japanese), which can be defined as benevolent altruism. The virtuous ruler is one whose behavior is suffused with *ren* and who commands the loyalty and obedience of his subjects, not by terror, but by example and by enlightened benevolence. Moral training was to be exclusively the province of the father/male ruler; indeed, women play hardly any role in traditional Confucianism.

These ideas are contained in a series of classical texts, including the *Yi jing* (Book of Changes), an ancient divinatory manual that Confucius was believed to have edited; the *Shu jing* (Book of Documents); the *Shi jing* (Book of Songs); the *Chun qiu* (Spring and Autumn Annals); and, most importantly, the *Lun yu* (Analects), a collection of sayings by Confucius and his disciples. Until modern times, when they were finally translated into the vernacular, these texts were studied by Japanese scholars in classical Chinese.

Confucianism in Ancient Japan

In addition to contributing to the Seventeen Article Constitution, Confucian ideas influenced the Taika Reform (646), which abolished all private ownership of rice lands and called for the establishment of a permanent capital and an elaborate administrative bureaucracy on the Chinese model. Indeed, several of the scholar monks who engineered the coup d'etat of 645 had spent time in China studying Confucianism, as well as Buddhism, and the resulting *ritsuryo* system, in which land was periodically redistributed according to need, was based on Confucian principles. So was the Taiho Code of 701, which set up a bureau that was charged with performing divinatory rituals according to the Confucian model. Another manifestation of Confucianism in ancient Japan was the appearance of historical chronicles, such as the *Kojiki* (Record of Ancient Matters, 712) and *Nihonshoki* (Chronicle of Japan, 720). Chinese Confucianism placed great value on historical scholarship, as it could provide lessons on proper statecraft and the moral behavior of rulers. By ordering the compilation of national histories, Japan's newly established Nara regime (710–794) sought to establish its authority and legitimacy.

Neither China's intensely patriarchal family structure nor the Chinese model of a bureaucratic elite steeped in the Confucian classics ever took firm root in Japan; however, filial piety and a profound respect for education and the teacher *(sensei)* became integral elements of Japanese culture and have continued to shape the Japanese worldview.

Medieval Japan and the Tokugawa Period

During China's Song dynasty (960–1279) Confucianism underwent a radical reformation. The chief figures were the Cheng brothers: Cheng Hao (1032–1085), Cheng Yi (1033–1107), as well as Zhu Xi (1130–1200) and Wang Yangming (1472–1529), who shifted the focus of Confucianism from ritualism and virtuous rulers to individual ethical and spiritual enlightenment and, in the process, added a mystical, quasi-religious aspect to the tradition. This reformed Neo-Confucian tradition was transmitted to Japan in the late twelfth and early thirteenth centuries, primarily by Zen monks who had studied in China, and it soon came to play a role in the samurai-based society that took shape during the Kamakura (1185–1333) and Muromachi (1333–1573) periods. The spiritual aspect of Neo-Confucianism helped reinforce the warrior mystique, as well as the ideal of absolute loyalty to one's master.

After the establishment of the Tokugawa shogunate in 1603, Neo-Confucianism received state sponsorship and became the official ideology of the *bakufu* (shogunal government). The Neo-Confucian emphasis on spiritual discipline, hierarchy, and social harmony was ideally suited to Tokugawa policy, the cornerstone of which was to rebuild Japanese unity under the benevolent but absolute authority of the *bakufu*, after centuries of internal strife. The Tokugawa also drew heavily on the concept of *ren*, as prolonged peace caused the samurai to evolve into a class of gentlemen bureaucrats broadly analogous to those who traditionally managed affairs in China and Korea. The Confucian ideal of the scholar-administrator led the regime to subsidize schools in each of Japan's feudal domains; there local samurai could study the Confucian classics. In 1632, the third Tokugawa shogun,

Iemitsu, established a shrine to Confucius in the capital, and in 1704, the *bakufu* constructed the only Confucian temple in Japan in what is now the Hongo district of modern Tokyo.

The Confucian Legacy

After the Meiji Restoration in 1868, when the center of power in Japan shifted once again to the imperial monarchy and Japan began to absorb Western philosophical, religious, and ethical ideas, the importance of Confucianism waned briefly. However, as the new regime crystalized, especially after the Imperial Rescript on Education (1890), Confucianism once again came to play an important role by defining the filial relationship between the emperor and the nation. Indeed, in the early 2000s it still permeates almost every aspect of Japanese culture, at least to some degree, from the persistence of filial piety and respect for teachers to the way corporations are organized and business conducted. Together with people in China, Korea, and Vietnam, the Japanese continue to be inspired by the teaching of Kong Qiu and his disciples.

C. Scott Littleton

See also: **Confucianism—China; Confucianism—Korea; Confucius; Neo-Confucianism; Zhu Xi**

Further Reading

Bellah, Robert. (1970) *Tokugawa Religion: The Values of Pre-Industrial Japan.* Boston: Beacon Press.

Creel, Herrlee Glessner. (1960) *Confucius and the Chinese Way.* New York: Harper & Row.

De Bary, Wm. Theodore. (1988) *East Asian Civilizations: A Dialogue in Five Stages.* Cambridge, MA: Harvard University Press.

De Bary, Wm. Theodore, and Donald Keene, eds. (1958) *Sources of Japanese Tradition.* New York: Columbia University Press.

Earhart, H. Byron. (1982) *Japanese Religion: Unity and Diversity.* 3d ed. Belmont, CA: Wadsworth Publishing Company.

McMullen, James. (1983) "Confucianism." In *Kodansha Encyclopedia of Japan*, edited by Gen Itasaka. Tokyo: Kodansha, 1: 352–358.

Nivison, David S., and Arthur F. Wright, eds. (1959) *Confucianism in Action.* Stanford, CA: Stanford University Press.

Hall, John Whitney. (1970) *Japan: From Prehistory to Modern Times.* New York: Dell Publishing Company.

Reader, Ian. (1991) *Religion in Contemporary Japan.* Honolulu, HI: University of Hawaii Press.

Smith, Warren W., Jr. (1973) *Confucianism in Modern Japan: A Study of Conservatism in Japanese Intellectual History.* 2d ed. Tokyo: Hokuseido Press.

Waley, Arthur, trans. (1966) *The Analects of Confucius.* New York: Random House.

CONFUCIANISM—KOREA

Koreans are fond of bragging that Korea is the most Confucian country on earth. They note that over 230 Confucian academies are still open south of the border that divides North Korea from South Korea. They also boast that Confucianism has been an important part of Korean culture for at least 1,600 years. However, the Confucianism found in South Korea in the twenty-first century differs from the Confucianism that existed on the Korean peninsula a millennium and a half ago. Moreover, both forms of Confucianism differ from the Confucianism that dominated Korea during the five centuries of the Choson dynasty (1392–1910).

Early Confucianism in Korea

Confucianism originally entered Korea from China as an administrative tool. In the fourth century, two of the three kingdoms on the Korean peninsula at that time, Koguryo (37 BCE–668 CE) and Paekche (18 BCE–663 CE), established Confucian academies to teach lower-level government officials how to keep historical records and write diplomatic documents in the format and language used by Confucian government officials in China. The third kingdom, Shilla (57 BCE–935 CE), did the same in the seventh century.

This Confucianism was for government clerks. High government officials were not expected to have a Confucian education until the Koryo dynasty (918–1392). A substantial percentage of upper-echelon Koryo officials passed the Confucian civil-service examination after they had embarked on their careers in government. This suggests that a Confucian education had become an aid to promotion, although it was not yet required for an initial appointment.

The Koryo civil-service examination system was a modified version of the civil-service examination sys-

JONGMYO—WORLD HERITAGE SITE

A UNESCO World Heritage Site since 1995, Jongmyo in South Korea is the oldest remaining Confucian royal shrine in existence. Unchanged since the sixteenth century, sacrificial song, dance, and music rituals are still performed at Jongmyo.

Women musicians in traditional Korean Confucian costume perform at the Grand Ceremony at Chongmyo, the Royal Ancestral Shrine in Seoul. (NATHAN BENN/CORBIS)

tem of Tang-dynasty China (618–907). The men who took the Koryo examinations could choose to be tested either on their ability to analyze classical Confucian texts or on their ability to write essays and poems in the style of revered Chinese Confucian writers. Because most who sat for the examinations chose the composition track, Confucianism remained primarily a guide to good writing.

Neo-Confucianism in the Choson Dynasty

This approach changed in the Choson dynasty, which replaced the Koryo at the end of the fourteenth century. The Choson dynasty was Korea's first and only Confucian dynasty, and most entry-level government officials were required to pass a Confucian civil-service examination. This examination focused on policy and morality more than on literary style. In the preceding periods, Buddhism had dominated court ritual and ethical discourse. Confucianism was confined primarily to defining how official histories, government documents, and literary compositions should be written.

Confucian influence on Korean moral thinking before the fourteenth century, however, was not insignificant. Confucian moral rhetoric, particularly terms such as loyalty and filial piety, had penetrated Korea via the texts taught to government clerks in earlier periods. Confucian virtues had become an inextricable part of the Korean ethical discourse, but they existed alongside, and often as a supplement to, the ethical principles of the official state religion, Buddhism.

During the Choson dynasty, Neo-Confucianism replaced Buddhism both inside and outside government as the principal arbitrator of how human beings should live. Neo-Confucianism, which Koreans called "the learning of human nature and principle," insisted that Confucian moral principles not only defined how human beings should interact with one another, but also defined what human beings were when they realized their full human potential. In other words, moral principles constituted human nature.

In order to help human beings realize that full potential, Neo-Confucianism offered two tools to replace the sutra study, chanting, and meditation Buddhism had offered. The first was ritual and etiquette, detailed prescriptions of how to behave in specific situations. The second was practical moral psychology, techniques for cultivating a moral character that could follow those prescriptions.

One of the more important guides to proper behavior during the Choson dynasty was *House Rules of Master Zhu*, a guide to household ritual and etiquette by the great Chinese Neo-Confucian Zhu Xi (1130–1200). Koreans became aware of this work near the end of the Koryo dynasty, but only in the Choson dynasty did it assume so much importance that family relationships were restructured to bring them more in line with its prescriptions. According to Zhu Xi, only eldest sons could host ancestral memorial services. This contradicted the Koryo practice of letting younger sons and even daughters lead rituals honoring their parents and of letting younger sons and daughters inherit the property that provided enough income to host such rituals. In order to bring Korean ritual practices in line with Neo-Confucian ritual prescriptions, the Choson dynasty redefined the family to give priority to the eldest son, reducing the inheritance rights of younger sons and depriving daughters of any inheritance rights whatsoever.

Korean Neo-Confucians accorded as much importance to the cultivation of a proper mental attitude for such rituals as they did to the rituals themselves. The most effective approach to such character cultivation became a hotly debated issue in the sixteenth century. For the next three centuries, Koreans argued about whether to follow the advice of Yi Hwang (1510–1570, pen name T'oegye) or Yi I (1536–1584, pen name Yulgok). T'oegye recommended sitting in quiet concentration to rid the mind of disturbing self-centered emotions. Yulgok, on the other hand, encouraged his followers to cultivate an attitude of sincerity so that they always acted appropriately in whatever situation they found themselves, whether hosting an ancestral memorial service or advising their king.

Confucianism in Korea Today

When the Choson dynasty fell in 1910, Neo-Confucianism lost its institutional base and could not maintain its hegemony over government, ritual, philosophy, and ethics. Nevertheless, a century later, Korea still shows traces of its Confucian past. Koreans continue to mourn their ancestors with Confucian ritual, albeit modernized and simplified. And they continue to wield Confucian terminology in debates over ethical issues. Sixteen hundred years after Confucianism became established in Korea, Korea remains in many ways a Confucian country.

Don Baker

Further Reading

Deuchler, Martina. (1992) *The Confucian Transformation of Korea: A Study of Society and Ideology.* Cambridge, MA: Harvard University Press.

Duncan, John. (2000) *The Origins of the Choson Dynasty.* Seattle, WA: University of Washington Press.

Kalton, Michael. (1988) *To Become a Sage : The Ten Diagrams on Sage Learning.* New York: Columbia University Press.

Palais, James. (1996) *Confucian Statecraft and Korean Institutions: Yu Hyongwon and the Late Choson Dynasty.* Seattle, WA: University of Washington Press.

Palmer, Spencer. (1984) *Confucian Rituals in Korea.* Berkeley, CA: Asian Humanities Press.

CONFUCIUS

CONFUCIUS (551–479 BCE), Chinese philosopher. Confucius, whose family name was Kong and personal name was Qiu (stylized as Zhongni), is recognized as China's greatest teacher. He was eventually given the title "Kong the Grand Master" (Kong Fuzi), which has been Latinized as Confucius. He was born in the state of Lu (in Shandong Province), during the Zhou dynasty (1045–256 BCE). His father died when he was three; by seventeen, he supported his mother. Confucius married at nineteen, had two daughters and a son, and held a minor office in Lu. He dedicated his life to teaching, but believed he was called to reform the decaying Zhou culture. At the age of fifty-one, Confucius was promoted to magistrate and subsequently to minister of justice. Discouraged by conditions in Lu, at the age of fifty-six, Confucius and his closest disciples traveled to other states in search of a worthy ruler to implement his teachings. After almost thirteen years, Confucius returned to Lu to teach. Tradition claims that he wrote or edited the Five Classics *(Shujing, Shijing, Yijing, Chunqiu,* and *Liji)* and the now-lost classic of Music. Of the traditional three thousand students, only seventy-two mastered his teachings, and only twenty-two were close disciples.

After his death, Confucius's reputation underwent a process of apotheosis. By the time of Mencius (371–289 BCE), he was called a sage. Emperors of the Han dynasty (206 BCE–220 CE) made offerings at his tomb, which became a shrine and later a temple. He was given the imperial title "duke" in 1 CE, "foremost teacher" in 637, "king" in 739, and "perfect sage" in 1013. By 1906, the ritual for the "emperor on high" was performed in the name of Kong Fuzi.

Details of Confucius's life and teachings are found in the Four Books; among them, the *Analects* is most important. With typical "Chinese" humility, Confucius claims in the *Analects* to be a transmitter, not an innovator. This is certainly not the case, but it displays the importance of maintaining historical precedent, namely, following the example of the ancient sages for self-cultivation, to sacrifice personal needs and wealth for the good of the community and to rule by virtue rather than law.

Confucius was an innovative teacher. His school was open to all serious students, even commoners, transforming aristocratic values into collective moral values. His methods went beyond vocational training, emphasizing moral cultivation, which institutionalized the literati class and influenced Chinese history.

An undated portrait of Confucius. (BETTMANN/CORBIS)

Confucius emphasized literacy *(wen)* and demanded that his students be enthusiastic, serious, and self-reflective. His teachings are of a practical nature. He held that all persons, but especially the ruling class, must develop their moral integrity by practicing ritual action *(li)* to express person-to-person-care or humanity *(ren)* to become a consummate person *(junzi)*. Empathy *(shu)*, defined in the *Analects* as "never do to another what you do not desire," summarizes his teachings in one word. With the renewed interest in Confucius even in the People's Republic of China, his teachings continue to influence Chinese and Asian cultures.

James D. Sellmann

Further Reading

Ames, Roger T., and Henry Rosemont Jr., trans. (1998) *The Analects of Confucius: A Philosophical Translation.* New York: Ballantine.

Dawson, Raymond. (1981) *Confucius.* Oxford: Oxford University Press.

Hsiao Kung-chuan. (1979) *A History of Chinese Political Thought.* Trans. by F. Mote. Princeton, NJ: Princeton University Press.

CONNECTIONS. See **Guanxi.**

CONSTITUTION—INDIA

One of the longest and most comprehensive documents in the history of modern Asian legislature, the Indian constitution has twenty-two parts, 395 articles, and twelve schedules that provide an enormous body of instructions and provisions that affect almost every aspect of Indian life.

Most of the framers of the Indian constitution had extensive experience in constitutional law during the British rule in India. Soon after India gained independence on 15 August 1947, its Constituent Assembly started working on constructing a constitution for a country beset by the centuries-old socioeconomic inequities of the caste system and the unsatisfactory postcolonial sharing of political powers between the central and provincial authorities. Ironically, the committee that wrote the constitution worked under an untouchable leader of India, Dr. Bhimrao Ramji Ambedkar (1893–1956), a law graduate from Columbia University, New York. The first draft constitution was published in February 1948. Its final version was officially adopted on 26 November 1949 but went into effect on 26 January 1950. Mohandas K. Gandhi (1869–1948) was not there to guide the framers of India's constitution while it was being written, but the ideals for which he had struggled were enshrined in it: liberty, equality, justice, and fraternity.

The Contents of the Constitution

The preamble states the solemn resolution of the people of India: that of turning the country into a sovereign socialist secular democratic republic that will secure social, economic, and political justice for all its citizens. It guarantees liberty of thought, expression, belief, faith, and worship; equality of status and of opportunity; and promotion of fraternity, securing the dignity of the individual, and the unity and integrity of the nation.

Articles in the twenty-two parts of the constitution mainly deal with the Indian union and its territories; citizenship; fundamental rights; principles of state policy; fundamental duties; the union government; the state governments; the *panchayat* (village council) system; city municipalities; tribal areas; relations between the central and state governments; finance, property, contracts, and suits; trade; commercial dealings within the territory of India; services under the union and the states; tribunals; elections; special provisions relating to certain classes; official languages; emergency provisions; miscellaneous matters; amendments to the constitution; temporary, transitional, and special provisions. The authoritative text of the constitution is in Hindi.

Redressing Historical Inequity

India's constitution provides equal opportunity for all citizens regardless of their creed or color. Article 16 promises equal opportunity in matters related to employment or appointment for any office under the state. No citizen, therefore, shall be considered ineligible or discriminated on the bases of religion, race, caste, sex, descent, place of birth, or residence. Since the government of India, through its military and bureaucracy, is the largest economic provider in the country, Article 16 opened public positions to lower-caste members of the society who had hitherto been excluded from pursuing economic and political opportunities.

Abolition of untouchability was the crowning achievement of the Indian constitution. India's vast majority of untouchables—whom Gandhi called Harijan, or "children of God"—were among the most oppressed people in the world. Article 17 declares the practice or enforcement of untouchability in any form as an offense punishable in accordance with the law. The constitution not only did away with special powers for the privileged social and economic classes such as the feudal lords but also provided special protection and quotas for the historically oppressed castes and tribes. With these leveling measures, the constitution changed for the better the social, political, and economic conditions of India's 1 billion people. Reservation of seats and quotas for depressed classes in union and state governments—and especially in educational institutions—brought about revolutionary changes in India. And even though there were calls to end such reservations, they were extended in 1952.

Although discrimination against women is unconstitutional, it has been rampant in every aspect of Indian life. Thanks to the growing women's rights movement and the rise in female education in India, politicians are now more responsive to women's needs. Although the socioeconomic and political conditions of women in rural India are far from satisfactory, the status of the educated and liberated women in cities and urban centers is a spectacular success story. India is a signatory to the worldwide women's resolution to set aside 33 percent of national and state legislative assembly seats for women, and in Indira Gandhi (1917–1984) has already had a powerful female prime minister.

National and Local Government

Central and state powers are balanced by organizing India into a federal democratic republic of twenty-five states headed by governors and seven union territories administered by ministers, all appointed by the president. India has a bicameral parliament composed of two bodies: the Rajya Sabha, or Council of States; and the Lok Sabha, or House of the People. The Rajya Sabha has 250 members, of which 238 are elected by their state legislative assemblies every second year. The president nominates the other twelve members, who are known nationally for their sound knowledge and experience in the fields of arts, literature, social sciences, and natural sciences. The Lok Sabha has 550 seats, with 530 members from the states and twenty members from the union territories.

Amendments

With more than eighty amendments as of 2000, India's constitution stands as one of the most frequently amended documents. Jawaharlal Nehru (1889–1964), the first prime minister of India, insisted that India's constitution must be flexible and responsive to new changes in the country. There are three ways to pass amendments to the constitution. First, a simple majority of both houses of the legislature can amend only those articles that are related to matters in the schedules—those parts in the constitution that deal with states and union territories, state governors, allocation of seats in the state councils, administration of tribal areas, and state languages, and so forth. Second, a two-thirds majority in both houses of the parliament is required for amending articles that deal with important matters, such as fundamental rights, citizenship, state policies, duties of the executive, constitution of parliament and state legislatures, legislative powers of the president, state governors, relations between the union and the state, and elections under the union and the states. Third, in addition to the two-thirds majority in each house of parliament, an amendment related to the distribution of legislative authority between the central and state government also must be passed by 50 percent of the state legislatures.

Checks and Balances

The Indian Supreme Court and Election Commission are recognized as the bedrock of Indian democracy; these two bodies stand up to the enormous powers that the constitution invests in the central government in general and to the unbridled powers of the Indian prime minister in particular. The checks and balances that are provided by the constitution also smooth out the strained relations between the central government and the states by limiting the central government's ability to interfere in the states' affairs. Usually, either the state government or a political party may file an appeal or a writ petition in the Supreme Court against a policy or practice of the union or a state.

Although India's constitution follows the British parliamentary system, it is the constitution and not the parliament of India that reigns supreme. As in the United States, the Indian courts interpret the constitution and adjudicate the laws passed by the parliament. Although the parliament has the authority to amend the constitution, India's courts have made sure that the parliament does not change its fundamental structure, which guarantees economic opportunities, social justice, and religious and political freedom to all its citizens. Although political corruption and coercion are rampant in India—as they are in other developing countries—the courts are judiciary guarantors of India's freedom from oppression.

Abdul Karim Khan

Further Reading

Awasthi, S. K. (1999) *The Constitution of India.* Allahabad, India: Dwivedi Law Agency.

Basu, Durga Das. (1994) *Shorter Constitution of India.* 11th ed. New Delhi: Prentice-Hall of India.

Jain, C. K., ed. (1992) *Constitution of India in Precept and Practice.* New Delhi: CBS.

CONSTITUTION, IRAN—ISLAMIC

The Iranian Islamic Constitution was approved by a national referendum in December 1979. The concept of *vilayet-i faqih* (rule of religious jurisprudence) is at the core of this constitution.

Soon after Ayatollah Khomeini (1900–1989) rose to power in Iran in January 1979, he gave the task of drafting a new constitution to the provisional government. The latter prepared a draft constitution, which was ready for national referendum in June of that year. However, several prominent figures insisted that an expert panel should review the draft constitution before it was put to a vote. Ayatollah Khomeini agreed and appointed an Assembly of Experts to review the draft constitution. The Assembly of Experts, made up of seventy-three members, was heavily weighted in favor of religious leaders and supporters of Ayatollah Khomeini's vision. The result was a substantially modified constitution, which institutionalized the role of clerics in the government. Reportedly, it was approved with over 98 percent of the vote.

The Islamic Constitution established the role and functions of the *faqih* (spiritual leader) as well as the executive, legislative, and judiciary branches of the government. The *faqih* is given oversight responsibility over the other three segments of the government in order to make sure they are operating within the tenets of Islam. He or she has the right to declare war or peace based on the recommendation of the Supreme Defense Council, over half of whose members the *faqih* nominates. He or she can depose the president if either the Supreme Court or the *majlis* (parliament) considers it appropriate. In addition, the *faqih* is responsible for selecting the supreme judge, the chief of the general staff, and half of the members of the Guardian Council. Ayatollah Khomeini was named the first *faqih* of the Islamic Republic and was given this position for life. The Islamic Constitution makes provisions for an Assembly of Experts, which is composed entirely of clerics, in order to choose successive *faqih*s based on constitutional criteria.

The executive branch of the government is composed of the president and cabinet. The president is elected for a four-year term. The legislative branch is represented by the *majlis*, 270 members who are also elected for four-year terms. The *majlis* handles the budget, general policy matters, and the introduction and passage of bills. However, any bill passed by the *majlis* must be reviewed by the Guardians Council, a group of six lawyers and six judges who verify that all new legislation and laws do not contradict Islamic principles.

Houman A. Sadri

Further Reading

Algar, Hamid. (1991) "Religious Forces in Twentieth-Century Iran." In *Cambridge History of Iran*, 7: *From Nadir Shah to the Islamic Republic*, edited by Peter Avery, Gavin Hambly, and Charles Melville. Cambridge, U.K.: Cambridge University Press, 732–764.

Kamali, Masoud. (1998) *Revolutionary Iran: Civil Society and State in the Modernization Process.* Brookfield, CT: Ashgate.

Khomeini, Ruhollah. (1981) *Islam and Revolution: Writings and Declarations of Imam Khomeini.* Trans. by Hamid Algar. Berkeley, CA: Mizan Press.

Sadri, Houman A. (1999) "An Islamic Perspective of Non-Alignment: Iranian Foreign Policy in Theory and Practice." *Journal of Third World Studies* 2, 16 (Fall): 29–46.

Schirazi, Asghar. (1997) *The Constitution of Iran: Politics and the State in the Islamic Republic.* New York: I. B. Tauris.

CONSTITUTION, JAPAN—POSTWAR

Drafted by the staff of General Douglas MacArthur (1880–1964) in 1946, Japan's constitution created a democratic, pacifist nation. Japan gives more per capita support to the United Nations than any other nation but cannot use military force to defend the U.N. Charter. Despite North Korean missile threats, growing Chinese dominance in East Asia, and nuclear bombs in South Asia, Japan still depends on American forces for its national security.

On 15 August 1945, Japan surrendered to the Allies. American occupation forces under General MacArthur, the supreme commander of the Allied powers, ordered Japan's demilitarization and democratization. To Americans, revising the Japanese constitution was the best assurance of democracy. The Japanese favored limited constitutional change preserving the imperial institution. Government proposals in September and October 1945 seemed promising but never reached the cabinet; a committee led by Prince Konoe Fumimaro (1891–1945), which MacArthur initially encouraged and then denounced, ended in Konoe's suicide in December; the cabinet's conservative effort led by the state minister Matsumoto Joji (1877–1954) failed in January 1946, partly because of lack of support and advice from MacArthur.

By early February 1946, several developments had convinced MacArthur of the need to draft a "model" constitution for Japan. Emperor Hirohito (1899–1989), fearing Allied retribution, sought MacArthur's protection by cooperating and revealing an interest in Christianity, which MacArthur saw as the foundation of democracy. The Allied powers attempted to gain control over Japan's constitutional reform, and Australia and the Soviet Union wished to try the emperor as a war criminal. On 25 January 1946, MacArthur warned the U.S. government of the dangers of this course of action. On 1 February, the Japanese press leaked the Matsumoto committee's conservative proposals for revising the constitution.

Two days later, MacArthur ordered his government section, under General Courtney Whitney (1899–1969), to draft a new constitution for Japan in one week, making the emperor the head of state without power and prohibiting Japan from having military forces or war potential, even for self-defense. Whitney presented the draft to Matsumoto and to the foreign minister Yoshida Shigeru (1878–1967) on 13 February. The stunned Japanese ministers had only an hour to look over the draft in English. Whitney said MacArthur wanted the cabinet to produce a Japanese draft, quickly, using this model.

The cabinet reluctantly accepted the draft constitution on 26 February and rushed an unfinished Japanese draft to Whitney's office on 4 March. Thirty hours of nonstop debate, translating, and redrafting ensued, ending shortly before MacArthur published the document on 6 March as a draft produced by the Japanese government and approved by himself and the emperor. An election was scheduled for 10 April to elect representatives to adopt Japan's new constitution. Thirty-one days had passed since MacArthur's order to write a model constitution for Japan.

The liberal provisions of the draft surprised many Japanese: the antiwar article: a powerless emperor as a symbol of the state; guarantees of basic freedoms, universal education, and equality of women with men; a true parliamentary system; and a powerful supreme court. The cabinet independently rewrote the document in vernacular Japanese. Prime Minister Yoshida, eager to end the military occupation, urged a quick approval.

Historians have understated the role of Japanese constitutionalists and politicians in the debate. Despite vigilant American monitoring, members of the national diet (created in 1889) engaged in spirited debate, refashioning a distinctly Japanese understanding of the draft, particularly about the role of the emperor; reshaping the peace clause; expanding the bill of rights; elevating the supreme court; and generally developing a sense of proprietorship over the text. Approved by both houses of the diet, the new constitution was promulgated on 3 November 1946 and took effect on 3 May 1947.

Movements for constitutional revision have roiled Japanese politics since the end of the American occupation in 1952. Again in 2000 Japan was engaged in a public debate over the relevance of the antiwar article. According to Article 9 and court rulings, Japan can use its self-defense forces, which are never called the army, navy, or air force, only to defend itself. So far, however, Japan has not felt that it can legally commit these forces to take part in U.N. peacekeeping missions or to help the United States in its self-proclaimed war on terrorism.

Ray A. Moore

Further Reading

Inoue, Kyoko. (1991) *MacArthur's Japanese Constitution.* Chicago: University of Chicago Press.

Koseki, Shoichi. (1997) *The Birth of Japan's Postwar Constitution.* Ed. and trans. by Ray A. Moore. Boulder, CO: Westview Press.

McNelly, Theodore H. (2000) *The Origins of Japan's Democratic Constitution.* Lanham, MD: University Press of America.

Moore, Ray A., and Donald L. Robinson. (1998) *The Constitution of Japan: A Documentary History of Its Framing and Adoption, 1945–1947.* Text-based CD-ROM. Princeton, NJ: Princeton University Press.

Tanaka, Hideo. (1987) "The Conflict between Two Legal Traditions in Making the Constitution of Japan." In *Democratizing Japan,* edited by Robert E. Ward and

Sakamoto Yoshikazu. Honolulu, HI: University of Hawaii Press, 107–132.

CONSTITUTION—TURKEY

Since the Turkish Republic was founded in 1923, it has adopted three different constitutions and a series of constitutional revisions. A common characteristic of Turkish constitutions is that all of them were developed in reaction to the political problems of a previous period, and each successive constitution tried to prevent recurrences of these problems through constitutional restrictions.

The First Constitution of 1920

The first constitutional document of modern Turkey was created by the Turkish Grand National Assembly (TGNA) during the war for independence. The Law of Constitution, dated 20 January 1920, designated the TGNA as the supreme organ of the state. It was given executive, legislative, and judicial powers. The executive power was exercised by a council of ministers, or cabinet, which the TGNA elected from among its members through direct vote. The ministers of the council were individually responsible to the TGNA, which also resolved executive disagreements in the council.

The First Constitution of the Republican Era of 1924

Problems associated with the concentration of power in the hands of the TGNA led to a change in the Law of Constitution. In 1924, the newly elected members of the TGNA, then dominated by the Republican People's Party (RPP) under the strict control of Mustafa Kemal (later Ataturk), developed the first constitution of the Republican era. The 1924 constitution maintained the supreme status of the TGNA by vesting the sovereignty fully and unconditionally in the nation; the TGNA was empowered to exercise its sovereignty on behalf of the nation (Article 5). The constitution did, however, transfer the exercise of executive power to the president and the Council of Ministers, so-called after 1924. The Council of Ministers was accountable to the TGNA under the principle of "collective responsibility." The president, however, was kept out of the principle and was not vested with political responsibility.

The Constitutional Amendments of 1934

The 1924 constitution was amended in 1934, and the six principles of the ruling RPP's program—republicanism, nationalism, populism, secularism, etatism, and reformism—were included in it as the defining characteristics of the state. Although the 1924 constitution had recognized civil liberties and social and political rights, it failed to put them under constitutional protection. The constitution had also lacked effective check-and-balance mechanisms over the legislative and executive bodies, which became extremely damaging after the transition to the multiparty period in 1950. The unlimited rule of the majority party, the Democrat Party (DP), finally led to the collapse of the first Turkish Republic in 1960.

The Second Republican Constitution of 1961

A military coup was carried out in 1960 by a group of junior officers, who declared their intention to create a democratic constitution and to transfer power to civilian rule. Unlike the 1924 constitution, which had been developed by the popularly elected TGNA, the 1961 constitution was prepared by a bicameral Constituent Assembly. The junta, which called itself the National Unity Committee, constituted the first chamber. Members of the second chamber included representatives of various social groups and political parties, chosen either by indirect election or by appointment. Exclusion of the supporters of the banned DP from the Constituent Assembly clouded the legitimacy of the 1961 constitution for the coming decades.

The 1961 constitution, which was approved by 60.4 percent of the popular vote, was a reaction to the problems of the DP era of the 1950s. It aimed to prevent the hegemony of an elected parliamentarian majority over the political system. The constitution foresaw a complete separation of powers and implemented a strong mechanism of checks and balances over government and parliament. The new system had a strong bicameral legislature, a weak executive, and an autonomous and strengthened judiciary.

Distrust of political bodies led to the establishment of the Constitutional Court, empowered to review the constitutionality of legislation. The 1961 constitution also renamed the National Unity Committee; it became the National Security Council—a permanent advisory body to assist the cabinet in issues related to national security, which legitimized the role of the military in government. The 1961 constitution was considered progressive because it expanded civil liberties and social rights and put them under constitutional protection. The constitution also granted administrative autonomy to various public organizations and civil-society institutions (nongovernmental, nonmilitary institutions). Although the 1961 constitution was liberal in tone, it still restricted participation of certain political groups and ideologies in the political arena. Progressive aspects of the constitution were later blamed for the country's woes and were curtailed by the 1971 and 1973 constitutional amendments. These amendments also strengthened the executive body by granting it power to use government edicts and increased the institutional autonomy of the military.

The Third Republican Constitution of 1982

The third constitution was developed after the 1980 military coup. The new constitution created in 1982 restricted civil rights, freedoms, and political expression even further. It was prepared by a bicameral Constituent Assembly established for the purpose, but even less representative than the previous one. The National Security Council was given more power than it had been granted in 1961; it now constituted the first chamber. The second chamber, handpicked by the National Security Council, excluded members of all political parties and all social groups of the previous period. Unlike the 1961 constitutional referendum, which allowed the expression of opposing views, the 1982 referendum campaign did not allow any debate on the draft constitution.

Identifying weakness of the executive as the root of the problem with the 1961 constitution, the 1982 constitution aimed to provide a strong executive and a weak unicameral legislature. Distrust of elected politicians and civilian institutions led to strengthening the powers of the presidency and the National Security Council. The president was given substantive powers in appointing heads of public organizations and could also dismiss the prime minister and other cabinet members, dissolve parliament and call for a general election, and declare a state of emergency. Under the 1982 constitution, individual rights and freedoms were limited; freedoms of association and of political participation were restricted; the privileges and autonomy of civil-society institutions were reduced; and the powers of the judiciary were limited.

The 1982 constitution has been criticized for its undemocratic nature. Although constitutional change has been on the agenda of every political party in the 1990s, political dynamics in the country have delayed any amendment of the constitution. Since 1995, some articles of the constitution, related mostly to freedom of association and freedom of political participation, have been amended. These amendments, however, have brought little improvement in the protection of civil rights and liberties in Turkey.

The Constitutional Court

The Constitutional Court was introduced in the 1961 constitution as a body to review the constitutionality of legislation and to prevent arbitrary and partisan rule by the elected bodies and governments and domination of the political system by the majority party. The Court was empowered as a high council to try senior members of the state, to prevent the abuse of political power, and to outlaw political parties that acted outside constitutional limitations. The rulings of the Court were final and binding on all the organs of the state.

A wide range of political and social institutions were given the right to request review of the constitutionality of laws by the Court. The president, the parliamentary groups of political parties, political parties that had won at least 10 percent of the popular vote in a general election, or one-sixth of the members of the TGNA, as well as civil and public organizations as long as the matters submitted for review dealt with these groups' functions, could exercise this right.

The Constitutional Court consisted of fifteen regular and five substitute members. Two members of the court were appointed by the president. The remaining members were chosen by the Court of Account (one regular), the TGNA (five regular and two substitute), the High Court of Cassation (four regular and two substitute), and the Council of State (three regular and one substitute) from among their members.

The Court was under constant attack by political parties in the 1961 constitutional era. It was accused of usurping the prerogatives of parliament and obstructing the government's performance of its executive duties. The Court was also criticized for closing down the Turkish Workers' Party and the National Order Party because of their ideologies.

Under the 1982 constitutional regulations, the function and scope of the Constitutional Court have been remarkably restricted. Review of the constitutionality of laws and decrees issued by the National Security Council during the interim period is no longer under the Court's authority. Its membership is reduced to eleven regular and four substitute members, and all members are appointed by the president. Only the president, the parliamentary group of the governing party or the main opposition party, or one-fifth of the members of the TGNA may request review of the constitutionality of laws. Presidential decrees are kept out of the Court's jurisdiction. The Court's status as a high council to try senior members of the state and to outlaw political parties acting outside constitutional limitations remains intact.

Ayla Kilic

Further Reading

Kili, Suna. (1971) *Turkish Constitutional Developments and Assembly Debates on the Constitutions of 1924 and 1961.* Istanbul, Turkey: Robert College Research Center.

Ozbudun, Ergun. (2000) *Contemporary Turkish Politics: Challenges to Democratic Consolidation.* London: Lynne Reinner.

CONSTITUTIONAL CRISIS OF 1881

The revolutionary changes introduced by government leaders during the Meiji period (1868–1912) provoked a great deal of uncertainty and unrest throughout Japan. For a variety of different reasons—from unfair taxation to reduced incomes and loss of political status—the samurai and farmers were extremely dissatisfied with the direction in which the new government was headed. Amid such growing turmoil, the Popular Rights movement *(minken)* evolved, one of whose leaders was Itagaki Taisuke (1836–1919). In 1874, Itagaki and other like-minded political leaders gained enough influence to submit a proposal to the government calling for the establishment of a national assembly. Cronyism and despotism were rotting the country, they complained. If Japan had any hope of keeping pace with the West, free public discussion must be permitted, and the best way to do that was to establish a national assembly.

In mid-1878, the home minister Okubo Toshimichi (1830–1878) was assassinated. Okubo had singled out a politician, Ito Hirobumi (1841–1909), to succeed him, but another Okubo favorite, Okuma Shigenobu (1838–1922), had also developed a strong following. Meanwhile, the Popular Rights movement was sweeping the country, and pressure to establish a national assembly intensified. Various councilors and politicians submitted proposals favoring a gradual movement toward a constitutional government, but in March 1881 Okuma startled them by presenting a paper calling for the speedy drafting of a constitution on the English model. This threw the principal parties into immediate conflict.

The political upheaval reached a boiling point in summer 1881, when Okuma and his followers refused to approve a proposal to sell at a huge discount the government's holdings in a Hokkaido project (Hokkaido Colonization Commission) to a business consortium headed by a former official, calling it the most blatant form of favoritism. Angered by Okuma's condemnation, not to mention his attempt to bypass their constitutional proposals, the councilors insisted in August that he and his followers be expelled from the government. Okuma and his cohorts resigned their official posts shortly afterward.

In an effort to calm the political agitation that the government knew would come with Okuma's ouster, the councilors agreed that a constitution would be granted by the emperor within the next decade. Ito was given the task of drafting it, but took Prussia as his model rather than England or the United States. Eight years later, on 11 February 1889, the Meiji Constitution was proclaimed.

Craig Loomis

Further Reading

Hane, Mikiso. (1972) *Japan: A Historical Survey.* New York: Scribner's.

Jansen, Marius B. (2000) *The Making of Modern Japan.* Cambridge, MA: Harvard University Press.

Yanaga, Chitoshi (1949) *Japan since Perry.* New York: McGraw-Hill.

CONVEYANCE ARTS

The tradition in South Asia of conveyance arts—decorating vehicles of all kinds—can be traced to the classical periods of Indian history. This article focuses mainly on conveyance arts in Bangladesh and Pakistan, with a brief discussion of the phenomenon in India and Afghanistan.

Bangladesh

Contemporary artisans in Bangladesh who decorate the three-wheeled cycle rickshas or pedicabs with elaborate pictures, scrollwork, calligraphy, and fancy machine-sewn, appliquéd, and painted plastic hoods are drawing on a long tradition. In past centuries, palanquins and pleasure boats were beautifully ornamented, often with gilt and colorful designs; animal transports were also lavishly decorated. Cycle rickshas became popular modes of transport by the mid- twentieth century. Ricksha art began to appear in Bangladesh a few years later, by the mid-1950s.

Today's rickshas are designed and hand-painted by special ricksha artists *(shilpakars)*, or decorations are handmade by ricksha artisans *(mistris)* who assemble rickshas to order for customers. Many of the artists speak and read some English; they often designate themselves as "artist" or "painter," adopting the English terms. Most ricksha artists either learn by working under an artist master or are self-taught. The main image on a ricksha is the backboard picture panel *(chobi)*. It is separately painted and hangs behind the ricksha, at the base of the cab between the rear wheels. Since the 1990s, commercial mass-produced photo prints have appeared as decoration on some ricksha backboard panels, possibly indicating a future trend toward the decline or even the elimination of hand-painted art.

A man with his decorated ricksha in Dhaka, Bangladesh. (EYE UBIQUITOUS/CORBIS)

The range of content of conveyance arts is both exuberant and varied. The artists denote certain picture themes by special names: for example, *jongler shin* (jungle scene), *shohorer shin* (city scene), *poshu shin* (animal scene), *filmi shin* (movie scene), *goromer shin* (village scene), and *mukti joddha shin* (liberation war scene), to name the most common selections. Movie scenes (or *manusher chitra*—people pictures) are mainly drawn from foreign, Indian, or local films. These may feature Tarzans, Rambos, and Bengali heroes or danger women sporting weapons, such as the real-life bandit queen Phulan Devi of India, who inspired popular films in India and Bangladesh. Glamorous actresses and actors from Dhaka and Calcutta films often are depicted, as well as political heroes—for example, the Bengali schoolboy Khudiram Bose, of Indian independence fame; Saddam Hussein, of Gulf War vintage; or the Awami League Prime Minister Sheikh Hasina. In the 1970s, jungle scenes of animals congregating at a waterhole, animal-human impersonations, and fantastic courting birds were predominant.

Overall decor on a costly ricksha includes intricately handsewn appliquéd hoods, which fold or unfold like umbrellas. These are decked with medallions in which they place shiny gold, silver, black, or pink peacock cutouts applied to a central white, red, or yellow field. Sometimes hand-painted red roses, butterflies, candles set within lotuses, or flowers are inserted in the medallions instead of peacocks. Hood designs, together with certain other features, can usually identify the city or region from which a ricksha originates. The seat base, ornamented by variably shaped recessed niches and bordered by gleaming nail heads, was filled with painted paired birds—peacocks or pigeons—signifying love or sexual fulfillment, or inserted view cards of movie stars. The footboard bore geometric or curvilinear designs (hearts pierced by arrows were popular). Painted conventional floral designs covered the ricksha's metal frame. Hand-painted designs on plastic, artfully cut and installed, upholstered the seatbacks and arm rests. The passenger's seat cover bore a conventional lotus design, suggesting (ironically, perhaps) that the rider is a petty deity, since deities are seated on lotuses.

The driver's seat was dotted with colored plastic flower cutouts. Handlebars sported small brass flower vases containing plastic flowers and colored plastic streamers. In Bangladesh, a nation with a Muslim majority, undecorated rickshas or imagery featuring only scenery or birds were favored by pious owners who observed the traditional Islamic prohibition on graven images, a practice based on several *hadith* (traditions of the Prophet). Birds are messengers of Allah in the Qur'an, and emblems of the soul in Sufi thought. They are thus not offensive to piety, although they might subversively suggest the motif of male desire, which is a foundation of this popular art form.

Ricksha arts are part of the male public culture. In the late twentieth century, a few women ricksha artists emerged, but women usually participated as family members in some artist's or ricksha maker's shop. Made to be seen "at a glance," the significations of ricksha art seems to be male desire in its major forms: for sex, competitive power and wealth, for one's home village, for the blessings of religious devotion, for new things. After the United States put a man on the moon in 1969, a few rickshas featured a man, in a spacesuit, planting a Bangladesh flag on the moon. In the late 1990s, auto taxis featured travel-poster images of far-flung places such as Sydney Harbor, Mt. Fuji, European-style palatial mansions with red sports cars in the driveway, and Tower Bridge in London, a prime emigration goal of many Bangladeshis.

India

In India, various conveyances, such as auto taxis and trucks, also tend to be decorated. The auto taxis, however, are usually not as fully decorated as they are in

Bangladesh, nor are the trucks as flamboyant as those found in Pakistan. In Rajasthan during the 1998 Diwali festival, trucks sported multiple glittering tinsel streamers and garlands in gold and colors, but hand-painted décor on the sides or on truck bodies was sparse. The state of Kerala boasts some of India's most outstanding conveyance art; the décor seems to reflect a regional style. Colorful boards with carved edges that suggest painted garlands of flowers and birds, surmounted by a rectangular name board, are installed above the cab. The names on the name board may be women's names (such as Sajna), inspirational names (Sunrise, for example), or Muslim names, (Nizamol, for example). Painted in blocky calligraphy, the truck names are spelled out either in English or romanized Malayam. The hood often sports apotropaic eyes; a demon mask may be hung below the front bumper—both intended to ward off evil. The sides of the cab are built up to the headboard above the cab door, and painted with dense millefleur designs interest with small, conventional landscape cameos. Here one might find slogans amidst the posies: "Do for India; Die for India," for example. Behind the cab (at the cab end of the truck bed) is a large square picture; common themes are the Taj Mahal or Lord Ganesa, the Hindu god who is the remover of obstacles; also popular are parrots or a gigantic red rose, all popular images throughout the subcontinent. Floral styles surrounding the truck door resemble those found in other Keralan fold arts in their large scale and sculptural-mimesis painting technique, especially as compared to floral representations on trucks in other parts of the subcontinent.

Pakistan

The decoration of trucks in Pakistan resembles the decoration of rickshas in Bangladesh in many ways, although the artists tend more assiduously to avoid depicting people, favoring instead scenic landscapes, complicated geometric designs, fantastic gardens, pillared mansions, rockets, airplanes, wild animals and birds, and calligraphy. Pakistani trucks began to be decorated with flamboyant art design in the mid-twentieth century, a period when interprovincial transport began to expand, truck owners were getting rich, and display became competitive. As in the rest of the subcontinent, royalty traditionally decorated both human-carried palanquins and animal transports, including camels, which still today sometimes sport elaborate necklaces of bells and colored plush tassels. Truck art today is a fulsome elaboration from earlier conventional geometric and floral designs as well as from banners (now devolved into plastic streamers) and camel or donkey necklaces with pendants, which have evolved into ornamental chain pendants that hang below a truck's front and rear bumpers. Since approximately the 1970s Pakistani motorized three wheeler transports (auto taxis) have also been decorated with designs and movie material, but their overall impression is not as outstanding as that made by the trucks.

A decorated truck hauling ice in Karachi, Pakistan. (NIK WHEELER/CORBIS)

Pakistan truck art—most of which originally was produced in Rawalpindi but now is made in other cities as well—is also handmade. Like the ricksha artists, Pakistan truck artists may use cheap printed calendars and illustrated paper books from the bazaar as reference material for their designs. They do not copy these but redesign them to suit their own taste or the truck's structure. Several men, the master artist and helpers, work on one truck.

Pakistan truck designs since the 1950s have become increasingly more elaborate geometrically, such that almost the entire surface is decorated, an old tradition in Islamic arts. The style at beginning of the twenty-first century emphasized vertically stacked horizontal friezes of fish, birds, and geometric designs, on which contrasting designs or framed picture scenes, and pious calligraphy are superimposed. As with the Bangladesh ricksha arts, in gender-segregated Pakistan all the artists are men. The pious inscriptions include such wisdom as "Before going on this journey, pray for forgiveness for your sins. This might be your last trip." Pakistan trucks—commonly, English Bedfords—show architectural propensities in the built-out decorated crown *(taj)* towering above the cab and projecting forward over the motor hood. In addition to the *taj*, gigantic pictures applied to the back slats of the truck bed or to the round rear end of a tanker truck and multiple panel or scenic medallion designs on the sides are central decorative features, imposing in size and astonishing in overall lavishness.

The truck crown is built up to twice the height of the truck below the cab, providing a grand billboard for colors and designs. Every color in the usual palette is used, with red, gold, silver, and green (the heraldic color of Islam) being favorites. Sculpted and painted fish or peacock framing devices might overlay bands of repeated geometric figures, or square boards bearing calligraphic proverbs or Qur'anic verses might be placed front and center on the taj and draped with cloth scarves.

Motorbuses are also elaborately painted and decorated, often with flat or three-dimensional multicolored scenic medallions, peacocks, hearts, and birds. One motif found repeated on the side of panels (under the windows) of a bus was a delicate woman's hand with polished fingernails holding up pearl necklaces and flower garlands, juxtaposed with a flower vase holding a lighted candle.

Afghanistan

Decorated trucks have been found in Afghanistan for several decades. Most of them were painted in Rawalpindi, Pakistan, once the only site of truck art decoration in the general area and a city on a main route between Afghanistan and Pakistan. These trucks originally resembled Pakistani trucks in style and picture themes; at that time, the crown over the Afghan truck cab was not built up as high as it now is in Pakistan. Under the Taliban, in power in Afghanistan from 1996 through late 2001, truck decorations were most likely restricted to purely geometric and calligraphic designs, in compliance with the Taliban's prohibition against representations, in home or in public, of humans or animals.

Joanna Kirkpatrick

Further Reading

Blanc, Jean-Charles. (1976) *Afghan Trucks.* New York: Stonehill Publishing Co.

Gallagher, Rob. (1992) *The Rickshaws of Bangladesh.* Dhaka, Bangladesh: University Press Ltd. Kirkpatrick, Joanna. (1984) "The Painted Ricksha as Culture Theater." *Studies in Visual Communication* 10, 3: 73--85.

———. *Transports of Delight: The Ricksha Arts of Bangladesh.* CD-ROM. Forthcoming.

Kirkpatrick, Joanna, and Kevin Bubriski. (1994) "Transports of Delight." *Aramco World* (January–February): 32–35, 41.

Rich, George W., and S. Khan. (1980) "Bedford Painting in Pakistan: The Aesthetics and Organization of an Artisan Trade." *Journal of American Folklore* 93, 369 (July–September): 257–295.

COOMARASWAMY, ANANDA KENTISH

(1877–1947), Sri Lankan art historian. Anada Kentish Coomaraswamy was an art historian who, in a series of influential books, greatly advanced the understanding of Hindu and Buddhist iconography. Originally trained as a geologist, he gained a Doctorate of Science in that subject from London University (1905). On returning to Ceylon, he felt that the traditional culture had been corroded by Western influences and was in need of a spokesman, which he then became. After about a decade in Ceylon, he left for the United States, where he founded the first museum department of Indian art at the Boston Museum of Fine Arts in 1917.

In his writings, Coomaraswamy presented South Asian art as a form of knowledge strongly imbued with a religious feeling. He was strongly influenced by mystics and metaphysicians, considering art "an effective expression of metaphysical theses." He was thus profoundly concerned with the communicative characteristics of art, viewing traditional art not from an aesthetic so much as an inspirational position, in which technical function was fused with symbolic meaning. He discovered the Rajput school of painting, and related it to Indian literary forms. Perhaps his most remarkable achievement was his demonstration of the way in which the Hindu temple represented the body and house of God. He was a pioneer in presenting South Asian art within a similar intellectual framework to that which had long been applied to Western art. In this, he set his thinking in opposition to the conventional dismissals of Indian art that had come from European critics such as Hegel (1835) and Ruskin (1859), who had considered it irrational and unnatural.

Paul Hockings

Further Reading

Lipsey, R. (1977) *Coomaraswamy: His Life and Work*. Princeton, NJ: Princeton University Press.

CORDILLERA CENTRAL The Cordillera Central is the centrally located mountain range on Luzon island in the Philippines. It consists of three parallel mountain ranges. These ranges are the Malayan, Central, and Polis. Mount Pulog, which is the highest peak on Luzon and the second highest in the country, is within the Polis range. These mountains vary greatly in width—from 58 kilometers to 86 kilometers (36 miles to 54 miles). The average height of its peaks is about 1,800 meters (5,900 feet). The Philippine mountain ranges typically are oriented in the same direction as the islands on which they are located. This is approximately north to south for the Cordilleras.

This mountain range connects with the Sierra Madre Range and the Caraballo Mountains. Located between these ranges is the Cagayan Valley. Several rivers' headwaters begin on the slopes of Mount Data, which is located within this mountain range. The Abra and Agno rivers in particular are controlled by the massive Cordillera Central mountains until they reach the sea. The metamorphic rocks that form these mountains are exposed. For this reason, much of the Philippine metals mining (for ores such as copper and gold) is concentrated in the Cordillera Central.

Linda Dailey Paulson

Further Reading

Wernstedt, Frederick L., and J. E. Spencer. (1967) *The Philippine Island World: A Physical, Cultural, and Regional Geography*. Berkeley and Los Angeles: University of California Press.

CORMORANT Cormorant, or shag, refers to any of about thirty species of the family Phalacrocoracidae, a family of dark-colored water birds. The large cormorant *(Phalacrocorax carbo)* is one of the most widespread of birds, occurring near rivers, lakes, cliffs, and seashores throughout Eurasia, as well as in eastern Canada and Iceland to the west, parts of Africa to the south, and Australia and New Zealand. In the Himalayas it is found in Ladakh, a region of Jammu and Kashmir, up to 3,000 meters. Friar Odoric (c. 1265–1331; a Franciscan monk who traveled from Italy to the East) reported seeing cormorant fishing from boats in China.

The young are easily trained to fish. The large cormorant and the slightly smaller Japanese cormorant *(Phalacrocorax capillatus)* are the two species that have been domesticated in eastern Asia for fishing, mainly in China, Vietnam, and Japan; the large shag was once used in France and England in the same way.

A speedy swimmer, the cormorant catches a fish underwater and brings it to the surface in its gular (throat) pouch. It then tosses the fish in the air and swallows it—unless a fisherman-owner has put a strap round the bird's neck. In one day it can eat up to half a kilogram of fish. The birds nest communally in great colonies with other water birds. The body of the adult bird may be 80 centimeters or even one meter long. Its remarkable agility underwater depends on the webs between the four toes, the long, stiff tail, and in adults the absence of external nostrils. The cormorant numbers over half a million in Europe alone (2001), where it is now seen as a threat to inland fisheries. In Asia, its numbers are probably much greater.

Paul Hockings

CORRUPTION Corruption, a serious problem in many Asian countries today, refers to "the misuse of public power, office, or authority for private benefit—through bribery, extortion, influence peddling, nepotism, fraud, speed money, or embezzlement" (United Nations Development Programme 1999: 7). (See Table 1.)

In Table 1, the higher the rank, the worse the corruption. The table shows that, except for the city-states of Singapore and Hong Kong, corruption is rampant in many Asian countries, with Pakistan and Indonesia being perceived as among the most corrupt nations in the world. Why has corruption been minimized in Singapore and Hong Kong on the one hand, and why is it rampant in Indonesia and Pakistan on the other hand?

The extent of corruption in Asian countries depends on two factors: the causes of corruption and the

TABLE 1

Ranking of Twelve Asian Countries on Transparency International's Corruption Perceptions Index from 1995 to 2001

Country	1995	1996	1997	1998	1999	2000	2001	Average
Singapore	3	7	9	7	7	6	4	6
Hong Kong	17	18	18	16	15	15	14	16
Japan	20	17	21	25	25	23	21	22
Taiwan	25	29	31	29	32	28	27	28
Malaysia	23	26	32	29	32	36	36	31
South Korea	27	27	34	43	50	48	42	39
Thailand	34	37	39	61	68	60	61	52
China	40	50	41	52	58	63	57	52
Philippines	36	44	40	55	54	69	65	52
India	35	46	45	66	72	69	71	58
Pakistan	39	53	48	71	87	-	79	63
Indonesia	41	45	46	80	96	85	88	69
Sample (N)	41	54	52	85	99	90	91	73

SOURCE: Data from Transparency International (2001).

degree to which government anticorruption measures are effective. Governments that have correctly diagnosed the causes of corruption and taken appropriate measures to eliminate them are more effective than governments that do not observe the same logic of corruption control.

There are three patterns of corruption control in Asian countries, depending on the types of anticorruption agencies and laws employed. The first pattern is adopted in Mongolia, which introduced the Law of Anti-Corruption in April 1996, but has no independent anticorruption agency. The task of controlling corruption is shared among the police, the general prosecutor's office, and the courts. The second pattern of corruption control can be found in China, India, and the Philippines, which employ many anticorruption laws and rely on multiple anticorruption agencies.

The third and most effective pattern of fighting corruption is the combination of comprehensive anticorruption laws impartially implemented by an independent anticorruption agency. Singapore and Hong Kong demonstrate this pattern, and it is not surprising that they are both perceived to be the least corrupt countries in Asia.

Causes of Corruption

In his comparative study of bureaucratic corruption in Hong Kong, India, and Indonesia, Leslie Palmier identified three important causes of corruption: opportunities for corruption, which depend on the degree of involvement of civil servants in administering or controlling lucrative activities; salaries; and policing or the probability of detection and punishment. He contended that the combination of these factors accounts for the level of corruption in a country. When there are few opportunities, good salaries, and effective policing, there is little corruption, and when there are many opportunities, poor salaries, and weak policing, there is considerable corruption.

Low Salaries Political leaders and civil servants who are poorly paid are more vulnerable to corruption, as they are more likely to succumb to temptation by making use of their position or authority for their personal benefit. Singapore's former prime minister, Lee Kuan Yew (b. 1923), justified raising the salaries of political leaders in March 1985 when he noted that political leaders and civil servants should be paid the top salaries that they deserve to ensure a clean and honest government. If they were underpaid, they would succumb to temptation and be corrupt.

In Indonesia and the Philippines, corruption was a serious problem during the colonial period under the Dutch and Spanish, respectively, as civil servants were poorly paid and had many opportunities for corruption. In 1971, the salaries and allowances of Indonesian civil servants constituted about one-third of their monthly income. In the Philippines, civil servants are paid starvation wages and are forced to sell goods in the office, hold a second job, teach part time, practice their profession after office hours, work as researchers and consultants, and resort to petty corrupt practices. Finally, in contemporary Mongolia, which has a per capita gross domestic product of $390, the major cause of corruption is the low salaries of civil servants and politicians; the highest monthly salary is $71, and the lowest monthly salary is $35.

Ample Opportunities for Corruption David J. Gould and Jose A. Amaro-Reyes observed that the expansion of the government's role in developing countries contributed to the bureaucracy's monopolistic position and increased the opportunities for administrative discretion. Red tape and enhanced bureaucratic discretion provide ample opportunities for corruption, as civil servants extract bribes from individuals or groups competing for access to such goods and services. Thus, Hong Kong's experience shows that when the government must control certain activities, there is ample room for corruption.

According to Donald Warwick, the opportunities for corruption in Indonesia depend on whether an agency is "wet" or "dry": "Wet" agencies, such as the police, customs, immigration, and internal revenue, provide more opportunities for corruption than "dry" agencies, such as research and administrative departments, which do not interact with the public. Radius Prawiro, the Indonesian coordinating economics minister from 1989 to 1993, identified the tax office and customs service as the most lucrative "wet" government agencies in Indonesia.

Low Risk of Detection and Punishment As corruption is illegal in all countries, individuals convicted of corruption should be punished. However, in reality, the probability of detection and punishment of corrupt offenses varies in Asia. Corruption thrives in those Asian countries where the public perceives it to be a low-risk, high-reward activity and is not a serious problem in countries where it is perceived as a high-risk, low-reward activity.

For the population in a country to perceive corruption as a high-risk, low-reward activity, the government must publicize through the mass media the detection of corrupt behavior among civil servants and politicians and their punishment according to the law if they are found guilty. Such adverse publicity serves as an effective deterrent against corruption. Conversely, those governments that muzzle the media, such as Indonesia under President Suharto (b. 1921) or India during the emergency of the 1970s, actually encourage corruption.

Pattern 1: Anticorruption Laws without an Independent Agency

Mongolia became the first Communist state in Asia in July 1921 and was dependent on the former Soviet Union for foreign aid, technical assistance, and a large market for its exports until the departure of the Soviet advisers in 1991. Corruption existed in Mongolia during its seven decades of Communist rule. However, the transition from a Soviet-style command economy to a market economy since 1991 has increased the opportunities for corruption and made the environment conducive for corruption for three reasons: the poverty of the population, the low salaries of public officials, and the lack of enforcement of the anticorruption laws.

The Law of Anti-Corruption (LAC) requires all Mongolian public officials to declare their incomes and assets and those of their families within a month of assuming their positions and thereafter to submit their annual declarations during the first two weeks of February. Failure to submit such declarations results in fines of between $6 and $29. Officials who do not monitor the declarations are fined between $24 and $35. Failure to declare gifts or foreign bank accounts results in fines of between $35 and $47. Finally, corrupt officials are discharged or displaced according to the procedure provided in the law.

The LAC is ineffective; only three members of Parliament have so far been convicted of corruption since its enactment in April 1996. The LAC's first weakness is that no specific agency is responsible for its implementation; Article 5 indicates that all state organizations are required to perform four common duties to prevent corruption. Second, the penalties imposed on officials for their failure to submit or monitor their annual income and assets declarations are too low to be effective deterrents, and there is no imprisonment.

Corruption offenses are first handled by the Criminal Police Department, which investigates and refers the cases to the Investigation Department. Both departments investigate complaints of corruption against public officials, and if there is evidence to substantiate these complaints, the cases are handed over to the General Prosecutor's Office (GPO). From the GPO, the cases are processed by three levels of courts.

This lengthy procedure for dealing with corruption offenses itself provides opportunities for corruption among the officials involved as each can interpret the law differently. For example, a bribery case by the police can be interpreted as a smuggling offence by the GPO and as illegal crossing of borders by the courts. As judicial salaries are low, individuals can pay the poorly paid judges to make decisions in their favor.

Pattern 2: Anticorruption Laws with Many Agencies

China, India, and the Philippines are examples of this pattern. China's battle against corruption has intensified as economic reform presented more opportunities for corruption; India has battled corruption since its independence in 1947, and the Philippines began fighting corruption in the 1950s.

China As corruption was endemic in China during the post-1978 reform period, the regime of Deng Xiaoping (1904–1997) relied on the Criminal Law of 1979 as the major law for curbing corruption. This law was amended twice: in 1982, to impose heavier penalties for corruption; and in 1997, to link the penalty for corruption to the amount involved. For example, a person found guilty of corruption involving more than 100,000 yuan ($12,000) is punished by ten years' imprisonment or the death penalty.

The various anticorruption agencies in China are organized along three sectors. The Supreme People's Procuratorate (SPP) was formed in 1978 to combat corruption in the judicial sector. Below the SPP, the Bureau for Embezzlement and Bribery of the People's Procuratorate handles and prevents cases of embezzlement and bribery. Given China's vast domain, it is not surprising that there are 3,563 agencies for embezzlement and bribery. In December 1986, the Ministry of Supervision (MOS) was reorganized to curb corruption and maladministration in the civil service. Finally, the Central Disciplinary Inspection Committee (CDIC) was created in 1978 to check corruption among the Chinese Communist Party (CCP) members.

Even though the MOS had received more than 700,000 reports in 1993, both the CDIC and MOS failed to reduce corruption because of the lack of political will to deal with corruption among senior party members. Until recently, few senior party officials have been convicted of corruption because they can seek help from their protectors in the CCP hierarchy. However, since 1999, Premier Zhu Rongji (b. 1928) has waged a crusade against corrupt officials; in March 2000, Hu Changqing, the deputy governor of Jiangxi province, became the highest-ranking public official to be executed. One month later, the deputy mayor of Guigang city, Li Chenglong, was executed for taking $478,000 worth of bribes.

India The Prevention of Corruption Act of 1947 is implemented by the Central Bureau of Investigation (CBI), the Central Vigilance Commission (CVC), the state anticorruption bureaus, and the state vigilance commissions. The CBI was created in April 1963 to investigate cases of bribery and corruption, but it could do so in a state only with the consent of the local government. This requirement became a problem after the decline of the Congress Party, as some state governments withdrew the consent given by their predecessors. The CVC was formed in February 1964 to investigate complaints of corruption against civil servants. Apart from requesting reports from ministries, departments, and public enterprises to check and supervise their vigilance and anticorruption efforts, the CVC can also request the CBI to investigate a case.

The CBI, however, is perceived by the public as ineffective; only 300 of the 1,349 cases (22.2 percent) in 1972 and 164 of the 1,231 cases (13.3 percent) in 1992 resulted in conviction. The CBI tends to concentrate on minor wrongdoers; its record in investigating more important cases is dismal: There have been no convictions.

The Philippines The Philippines has relied on seven laws and thirteen antigraft agencies since its fight against corruption began in the 1950s. The Forfeiture Law of 1955 authorizes the state to acquire property illegally obtained by corrupt officials, but there were no convictions after four years. The most important law is the Anti-Graft and Corrupt Practices Act of 1960, which identifies eleven types of corrupt acts among public officials and requires them to file every two years a detailed and sworn statement of their assets and liabilities. The other laws are the presidential decrees (PD) issued by President Ferdinand Marcos (1917–1989) after the establishment of martial law in September 1972. For example, PD No. 6, which identifies twenty-nine administrative offenses and empowers heads of departments to dismiss guilty officials immediately, has resulted in the termination of nearly 8,000 public officials.

The large number of anticorruption agencies in the Philippines can be attributed to the frequent changes in political leadership; such agencies are either created or abolished by the president. During May 1950 and January 1966, five anticorruption agencies were formed and dissolved, during five changes in political leadership. President Marcos created another five anticorruption agencies, the most important of which were the Sandiganbayan (Special Anti-Graft Court) and the Tanodbayan (Ombudsman), which were established in July 1979.

Similarly, President Corazon Aquino (b. 1933) created the Presidential Commission on Good Government (PCGG) and the Presidential Committee on Public Ethics and Accountability (PCPEA) during her term of office. However, both agencies were ineffective. The PCGG itself was accused of favoritism and incompetence as five of its agents faced graft charges and thirteen more were under investigation, and the PCPEA lacked staff and funds. Aquino's anticorruption stance was honest, but she lacked the political will to punish corrupt officials.

In 1994, President Fidel Ramos (b. 1928) formed the Presidential Commission against Graft and Corruption (PCAGC). In June 1997, the Inter-Agency Anti-Graft Coordinating Council was set up to control graft in government through the sharing of information and resources among the Commission on Audit, the Civil Service Commission, the National Bureau of Investigation, and the PCAGC. However, the Philippines' sixty-fifth ranking on Transparency International's 2001 Corruption Perceptions Index reflects the ineffectiveness of its anticorruption strategy. Eufemio Domingo, the head of the PCAGC, concluded that the anticorruption agencies in the Philippines were not working because the anticorruption laws were not implemented.

Pattern 3: Anticorruption Laws with an Independent Agency

Singapore and Hong Kong, the two Asian countries that show relatively low levels of corruption, are examples of this pattern. In both cases, severe corruption was overcome through the implementation of this pattern.

Singapore The Prevention of Corruption Ordinance (POCO) was Singapore's first anticorruption law, introduced in December 1937, and it was implemented by the Anti-Corruption Branch (ACB) of the Criminal Investigation Department (CID) within the police force. The ACB was ineffective as it did not have sufficient staff and resources, and it failed to deal impartially with police corruption. The discovery by the British colonial government that police officers were involved in the theft of S$400,000 of opium in October 1951 demonstrated clearly the ACB's inability to curb corruption. The British authorities realized the importance of creating an independent anticorruption agency that was separate from the police. Accordingly, the ACB was dissolved and replaced by the Corrupt Practices Investigation Bureau (CPIB) in October 1952.

When the People's Action Party (PAP) government assumed office in June 1959, corruption was a way of life in Singapore and was perceived to be a low-risk, high-reward activity. To minimize corruption and change the public perception of corruption to a high-risk, low-reward activity, the PAP leaders initiated a comprehensive anticorruption strategy in 1960 by enacting the Prevention of Corruption Act (POCA) and strengthening the CPIB. As Singapore was a poor country with a per capita gross domestic product of S$1,330 ($443) in 1960, the PAP government could not afford to raise the salaries of civil servants. Accordingly, it was left with the alternative of strengthening the existing anticorruption laws to reduce the opportunities for corruption and to enhance the penalty for corruption.

The POCA of 1960 removed the POCO's weaknesses, increased the penalty for corruption to five years' imprisonment and/or a fine of S$10,000, and gave the CPIB more powers to perform its duties. The penalty for corruption was increased to S$100,000 in 1989. The CPIB has grown from eight officers in 1960 to its current size of seventy-seven staff. While the CPIB investigates corruption complaints in both the public and private sectors, its emphasis is on misconduct by public officials; it also examines the practices and procedures in the civil service to reduce opportunities for corruption. The CPIB can perform its duties without a large staff as its location within the prime minister's office and its legal powers enable it to obtain the required cooperation from both public and private organizations.

Hong Kong Following Singapore, the POCO was introduced in Hong Kong in 1948 and implemented by the ACB of the CID of the Royal Hong Kong Police Force. The ACB was separated from the CID in 1952, but it kept its name and remained within the police. In 1968, the ACB reviewed the POCO and recommended a scrutiny of the anticorruption laws of Singapore and Ceylon (now Sri Lanka). A study team visited the two countries during 1968 to examine how their anticorruption laws worked in practice. The study team was impressed with the independence of the anticorruption agencies in these countries and attributed Singapore's success in minimizing corruption to the CPIB's independence from the police. The knowledge gained from the study tour contributed to the enactment of the Prevention of Bribery Ordinance (POBO) on 15 May 1971.

The introduction of the POBO in May 1971 led to the upgrading of the ACB into an Anti-Corruption Office (ACO). The escape to England of a corruption suspect, Chief Superintendent P. F. Godber, on 8 June 1973, angered the public and undermined the ACO's credibility. The governor, Sir Murray MacLehose, decided to form a new anticorruption agency that was independent of the police.

The Independent Commission Against Corruption (ICAC) was formed on 15 February 1974 with the enactment of the ICAC Ordinance and was entrusted with two tasks: to stop corruption and to increase public confidence. The ICAC is independent in terms of structure, personnel, finance, and power. Before the handover of Hong Kong to China in July 1997, the ICAC was directly responsible to the governor, and its commissioner reported directly to him and had easy access. Since July 1997, the ICAC reports directly to the chief executive of Hong Kong Special Administrative Region and is directly responsible to him.

Corruption in Asia Today

For anticorruption measures to be effective, they must be properly designed to attack the causes of corruption and must be supported by the political leadership. This explains why the third pattern is more effective than the first two; the experiences of Singapore and Hong Kong have shown the critical importance of political will in curbing corruption. The political leaders in a country must be sincerely committed to the elimination of corruption by demonstrating exemplary conduct and adopting a modest lifestyle themselves. Those found guilty of corruption must be punished, regardless of their position or status in society. Political will is absent when the rich and famous are protected from prosecution for corruption, and only ordinary people are caught.

Political will is the most important prerequisite for implementing a comprehensive anticorruption strategy. It ensures the allocation of adequate personnel and resources and the impartial enforcement of the anticorruption laws by the anticorruption agency. Thus, even though the Philippines has the most anticorruption laws and agencies in Asia, it has been ineffective in curbing corruption because of the lack of political will among the political leaders. Similarly, the anticorruption strategies in China, India, and Mongolia are ineffective because of the absence of political will in those countries.

In addition to political will, Pattern 3 is also more effective because the anticorruption agency is a specialized agency dedicated to the task of minimizing corruption. The agency is not distracted by other competing priorities. For example, India's CBI is not only concerned with fighting corruption but also with organized crime and terrorism. In contrast, Singapore's CPIB and Hong Kong's ICAC focus their resources on curbing corruption.

Jon S. T. Quah

Further Reading

Alfiler, Maria Concepcion P. (1979) "Administrative Measures against Bureaucratic Corruption: The Philippine Experience." *Philippine Journal of Public Administration* 23, 3–4 (July–October): 321–349.

Balgos, Cecilia C. A. (1998) "Ombudsman." In *Pork and Other Perks: Corruption and Governance in the Philippines*, edited by Sheila S. Coronel. Metro Manila, Philippines: Philippine Center for Investigative Journalism, 244–269.

Burns, John P. (1994) "Civil Service Reform in China." *Asian Journal of Political Science* 2, 2 (December): 44–72.

Chan, Kin-Man. (1999) "Corruption in China: A Principal Agent Perspective." In *Handbook of Public Administration in the Asia-Pacific Basin*, edited by H .K. Wong and H. S. Chan. New York: Marcel Dekker, 299–324.

Corpuz, Onofre D. (1957) *The Bureaucracy in the Philippines.* Quezon City, Philippines: Institute of Public Administration, University of the Philippines.

Day, Clive. (1966) *The Dutch in Java.* Kuala Lumpur, Malaysia: Oxford University Press.

De Speville, Bertrand. (1997) *Hong Kong: Policy Initiatives against Corruption.* Paris: Organization for Economic Cooperation and Development.

Gill, S. S. (1998) *The Pathology of Corruption.* New Delhi: HarperCollins.

Gould, David J., and Jose A. Amaro-Reyes. (1983) *The Effects of Corruption on Administrative Performance: Illustrations from Developing Countries.* Washington, DC: World Bank Staff Working Papers, No. 580.

Kuan, Hsin-Chi. (1981) "Anti-Corruption Legislation in Hong Kong—A History." In *Corruption and Its Control in Hong Kong*, edited by Rance P. L. Lee. Hong Kong: Chinese University Press, 15–43.

Lethbridge, Henry J. (1985) *Hard Graft in Hong Kong: Scandal, Corruption, the ICAC.* Hong Kong: Oxford University Press.

Luo, Ji, Miao Chunruim, and Guo Hua. (n.d.) *The Work against Embezzlement and Bribery in the People's Procuratorates of the People's Republic of China.* Beijing: Procuratorial Department for Embezzlement and Bribery.

McPhail, Stephanie. (1995) *Developing Mongolia's Legal Framework: A Needs Analysis.* Manila, Philippines: Asian Development Bank.

Narasimhan, C. V. (1997) "Prevention of Corruption: Towards Effective Enforcement." In *Corruption in India: Agenda For Action*, edited by S. Guhan and Samuel Paul. New Delhi: Vision Books, 251–285.

Padilla, Perfecto L. (1995) "Low Salary Grades, Income-Augmentation Schemes, and the Merit Principle." In *Public Administration by the Year 2000: Looking Back into the Future*, edited by Proserpina Domingo Tapales and Nestor N. Pilar. Quezon City, Philippines: College of Public Administration, University of the Philippines, 186–214.

Palmier, Leslie. (1985) *The Control of Bureaucratic Corruption: Case Studies in Asia.* New Delhi: Allied.

Prawiro, Radius. (1998) *Indonesia's Struggle for Economic Development: Pragmatism in Action.* Kuala Lumpur, Malaysia: Oxford University Press.

Quah, Jon S. T. (1982) "Bureaucratic Corruption in the ASEAN Countries: A Comparative Analysis of Their Anti-Corruption Strategies." *Journal of Southeast Asian Studies* 13, 1 (March): 153–177.

———. (1999) *Combating Corruption in Mongolia: Problems and Prospects.* Singapore: Department of Political Science, National University of Singapore, Working Paper, No. 22.

———. (1995) "Controlling Corruption in City-States: A Comparative Study of Hong Kong and Singapore." *Crime, Law, and Social Change* 22: 391–414.

———. (1999) "Corruption in Asian Countries: Can It Be Minimized?" *Public Administration Review*, 59, 6 (November–December): 483–494.

———. (1989) "Singapore's Experience in Curbing Corruption." In *Political Corruption: A Handbook*, edited by Arnold J. Heidenheimer, Michael Johnston, and Victor LeVine. New Brunswick, NJ: Transaction, 841–853.

Root, Hilton. (1996) "Corruption in China: Has It Become Systemic?" *Asian Survey* 36, 8 (August): 741–757.
Smith, Theodore M. (1971) "Corruption, Tradition, and Change." *Indonesia* 11 (April): 21–40.
Straits Times (1999) 22 October: 23; (2000a) 9 March: 30; (2000b) 24 April: 2.
Timberman, David G. (1991) *A Changeless Land: Continuity and Change in Philippine Politics*. Singapore: Institute of Southeast Asian Studies.
Transparency International. (2001) "Global Corruption Reports 2001: Regional Reports—East Asia and the Pacific, Southeast Asia, South Asia." Retrieved April 2002 from: http://www.globalcorruption report.org
United Nations Development Programme. (1999) *Fighting Corruption to Improve Governance*. New York: UNDP.
Warwick, Donald P. (1987) "The Effectiveness of the Indonesian Civil Service." *Southeast Asian Journal of Social Science*, 15, 2: 40–56.
Wong, Jeremiah K. H. (1981) "The ICAC and Its Anti-Corruption Measures." In *Corruption and Its Control in Hong Kong*, edited by Rance P. L. Lee. Hong Kong: Chinese University Press, 45–72.

CORRUPTION—CHINA

The Chinese term *tanwu* is similar to the Western term "corruption," meaning the abuse of a public position to line one's own pocket. Opinion polls in the 1980s and 1990s show that the population regards corruption as the most important social problem. Even the party leadership realized that the phenomenon was seriously threatening its legitimacy, and has repeatedly started anticorruption campaigns. China is now accused of being one of the most corrupt countries in Asia.

Corruption has a long history. Even in early classical documents, affairs covered by the current meaning were regarded as moral depravity on the part of the government (and consequently also of society), as errors that violated the prevailing moral code. An emperor who was "corrupt" in this sense of the word had betrayed his Mandate of Heaven. Excessive public corruption was often the cause of rebellions and uprisings such as the Taiping rebellion in the nineteenth century. In this early period there were already criminal punishments for what is today referred to as corruption. The criminal code of the Qin dynasty (221–206 BCE) included a catalog of strict punishments for all offenses related to "dereliction of duty in office."

In the People's Republic, corruption has been defined differently in each period according to the political aims. In politically radical times it was identified as ideological deviation, supposedly antisocialist or bureaucratic behavior. In public, however, the topic was mainly taboo. Only at the end of the 1970s, as reform policies began to emerge, was the press permitted to report cases of corruption again. To begin with, the "Gang of Four" were held responsible, but the dramatic increase in corruption in the 1980s made new explanations necessary.

There are factors embedded in the system that favor corruption, for example overcentralization of the economy, the Chinese Communist Party's (CCP) monopoly position, lack of a clear division between public and private spheres, bureaucratic planning, and state control of resources. In addition, there are psychological factors such as the failure of the revolutionary model, changes in values, and development deficiencies such as shortages of goods and resources, and the town-country divide. The introduction of reforms (decentralization, openings to the outside world, extension of market mechanisms, migration, and diversification of property structures) has led to increases in corruption in some areas. Since the CCP's monopoly on power has not been affected, and since no instruments to control cadres have been introduced, functionaries can use the CCP's monopoly on power and their right to distribute goods and resources quite freely to line their own pockets. Some officials, however, have been accused of corruption and subsequently punished—including Chen Xitong, the former party secretary and member of the Political Bureau of the CCP, who was sentenced to many years in prison in 1998; and Chen Xitong, the vice-chairman of the National People's Congress, who was executed in August 2000.

Thomas Heberer

See also: **Guanxi; People's Republic of China; Qin dynasty**

Further Reading

Heberer, Thomas. (1991) *Korruption in China. Analyse eines Politischen, Ökonomischen und Sozialen Problems*. Opladen, Germany: Westdeutscher Verlag.
Kwong, Julia. (1997) *The Political Economy of Corruption in China*. London: M. E. Sharpe.
Lo Tit Wing. (1993) *Corruption and Politics in Hong Kong and China*. Buckingham, U.K.: Open University Press.

CORRUPTION—KOREA

Known as the "Korean disease," corruption pervades South Korean society and has manifested itself in many forms in everyday life. Widespread corruption, such as influence peddling, cronyism, and bribery, has long been a part of Korean culture and has served as a catalyst for change in Korean history as far back as the Koryo dynasty (918–1392 CE), when corruption among Buddhist monks eventually led to the downfall of the dynasty and the adoption of neo-Confucianism in the following Yi dynasty (1392–1910). More recently, the April Students' Revolution of 1960 was a revolt against Republic of Korea President Syngman Rhee's corrupt administration.

Although corruption occurs worldwide, corruption in Korea has exhibited unique characteristics. The centralization of power and the abuse of power within the governmental and bureaucratic structure of South Korea have provided opportunities for individuals to accrue power and influence.

Interestingly enough, preventing widespread corruption has been the focus of successive presidential administrations as the lethal effects of corruption have created a public backlash. During the 1990s, a series of accidents was blamed on corrupt bureaucrats and inspectors. Yet changing the entrenched culture where gift-giving and kickbacks are routine has proved difficult as corruption and graft have been tied to the highest levels of government, with many of the politicians and bureaucrats charged with curbing corruption having themselves become corrupt. Moreover, governmental agencies charged with investigating corruption have often failed to investigate wrongdoing and indict those responsible in criminal corruption cases.

Things may change in the Republic of Korea with the passage in 2001 of legislation that tightens anticorruption laws by protecting whistle-blowers, requiring civil servants to report wrongdoing, and allowing for the confiscation of bribes.

Keith A. Leitich

Further Reading

Caiden, Gerald E., and Jung H. Kim. (1993) "A New Anti-Corruption Strategy for Korea." *Asian Journal of Political Science.* 1, 1 (June): 133–151.

Kim, Byong-Seob. (1998) "Corruption and Anti-Corruption Policies in Korea." *Korea Journal* 38, 1 (Spring): 46–69.

Kim, Yong-jong. (1997) *Korean Public Administration and Corruption Studies.* Seoul: Hak Mun Publishers.

Oh, Suek Hong. (1982) "The Counter-Corruption Campaign of the Korean Government (1975–1977)." *In Korean Public Bureaucracy: Readings*, edited by Bun Woong Kim and Rho Wha Joon. Seoul: Kyobo Publishers.

COURTYARDS The courtyard house is the archetypal form of traditional Chinese dwelling. Its basic design of a central courtyard surrounded on four sides by buildings or pavilions parallels the basic model of traditional Chinese-built environments, including cities and gardens: a central open space enclosed by buildings. The buildings face the courtyard, which provides outdoor space for leisure activities, work, air circulation and ventilation, water drainage, and storage. Access to the enclosed courtyard house is provided through a south or east entrance. Carved arches or ornate door lintels signify the class and trade of the resident, and many entrances are flanked by stone lions. A courtyard complex may be expanded by adding more courtyards in front, in back, or on either wing. Different regional variations cater to local environmental conditions. In Beijing and other northern cities, courtyards are large in area to admit more sunlight, while in southern cities they are smaller so that more shade and better ventilation are provided.

During the chaotic Cultural Revolution of 1966–1976, many families were evicted from their courtyard homes in Beijing because of their "bad class backgrounds." Following the Tangshan earthquake of 1976, refugees poured into the city and took shelter in the courtyard gardens, and many stayed. With the current economic boom in China, land prices have skyrocketed, and urban renewal programs to clear neighborhoods of one-story courtyard houses to make room for multistory buildings are under way. Courtyard houses are becoming mere memories.

Robert Y. Eng

Further Reading

Blaser, Werner. (1979) *Courtyard House in China: Tradition and Present.* Basel, Switzerland: Birkhauser.

Wu Liangyong. (1999) *Rehabilitating the Old City of Beijing: A Project in the Ju'er Hutong Neighbourhood.* Vancouver, Canada: University of British Columbia Press.

CRAM SCHOOLS "Cram school" is the English translation for *juku*, the Japanese word for a wide range of private, after-school schools. During the Edo period, *juku* included the highly academic private academies organized around one scholar who was renowned in a particular field. Some offered instruction in Japanese musical instruments, abacus, calligraphy, martial arts, and tea ceremony. When the modern education system was introduced into Japan at the end of the nineteenth century, academic *juku* almost disappeared.

In the latter half of the twentieth century, *juku* has meant private classes, usually intended as preparation for entrance exams to high school and university, or a type of remedial education. Nonacademic *juku*, also known as *okeiko*, provide instruction in traditional arts and defensive skills, as well as enrichment classes such as music lessons. *Juku* range in size from home-based operations to large nationwide corporations.

Education in Japan has been described as having a dual structure. The cram-school industry is the informal side, and public and private schools comprise the formal side. In public schools all students must learn at the same pace, but it is widely acknowledged that entrance exams to the best high schools, and therefore the top universities, require more advanced instruction. Students from both public and private schools, therefore, attend *juku* to maximize their chances in the examination competition. If students fail the entrance exam to the university of their choice, then they may also attend an intensive one-year exam preparatory school known as *yobiko*.

In 1998, the Education Ministry reported that 37 percent of public elementary students, 72 percent of public junior high, and 35 percent of high school students were attending cram schools. The increasing role of *juku* as a supplement to the formal education system in Japan was acknowledged for the first time in the early 2000s by the Education Ministry. On a final note, while the *juku* phenomenon is sometimes seen as typically Japanese, similar cram schools exist in Korea and Taiwan, where they fulfill similar functions.

Tetsuya Kobayashi and Diane Musselwhite

See also: **Japan—Education System**

Further Reading

Cutts, Robert L. (1997) *An Empire of Schools, Japan's Universities and the Molding of a National Power Elite.* Armonk, NY: Sharpe.

Leestma, Robert, et al. (1987) *Japanese Education Today.* Washington, DC: U. S. Department of Education.

Marshall, Byron K. (1994) *Learning to be Modern, Japanese Political Discourse on Education.* San Francisco: Westview Press.

Okano, Kaori, and Motonori Tsuchiya. (1999) *Education in Contemporary Japan, Inequality and Diversity.* New York: Cambridge University Press.

Shimizu, Kazuhiko, ed. (2000) *Kyoiku Data Land.* Tokyo: Jijitsuushinsha.

CRANGANUR

CRANGANUR (2002 est. pop. 36,000). Cranganur (Cranganore, Kadungalloor) is a small city on the Alwaye river estuary in northern Kerala state, India, lying 26 kilometers to the north of Cochin. While of minor economic importance, exporting some timber and peppers, in ancient times it was the site of one of the great entrepôt centers of the East, the Roman emporium of Muziris (its Greek name).

Muziris was the best harbor on the Kerala coast (before silting occurred). Saint Thomas is thought to have founded a church there in 52 CE. Muziris in 341 CE was the seat of government of Cheraman Perumal, a king of the early ninth century, who sanctioned the first settlement of Jews and Christians on this coast. The town has a synagogue three centuries old, and a Portuguese tomb dating to 1551.

In classical times the port exported tropical lumber, pearls, ivory, silk, diamonds, sapphires, and pepper. The town was so important to the Romans that they maintained a legion of soldiers here, around five hundred to one thousand men, and the city boasted a temple to Augustus (undiscovered, but probably submerged in the estuary). An ancient Tamil poem captures the bustle of the ancient port: "Agitating the white foam of the Periyaru [River] the beautifully built ships of the Yavanas [Ionians] come with gold and return with pepper, and Muziris resounds with the noise."

Paul Hockings

Further Reading

Schoff, Wilfred H. ([1912] 1974) *The Periplus of the Erythraean Sea.* Reprint ed. New Delhi: Munshiram Manoharlal.

CRICKET

CRICKET A sport originating in a small Hampshire village in seventeenth-century England, cricket was introduced to South Asia by the British in the early eighteenth century. The first recorded cricket match in South Asia took place in 1721 in Cambai, western India, between the officers and men of a British ship. Although at first played only by the British, cricket eventually gained a following among local populations. Indians formed their first cricket club, the Orient Cricket Club, in Bombay in 1848. Today cricket is immensely popular throughout the subcontinent and is regarded as a national sport in several South Asian countries.

Cricket is a bat-and-ball game played between two teams of eleven players each. Each side takes turns at bat, while the fielding and bowling side attempts to get the opposing batsmen out for the least number of runs. The team with the highest number of runs wins. Most cricket matches are concluded in one day, but games at higher levels of competition may last longer. For example, Test matches (international matches between the top ten cricket-playing nations) are played over five days.

The subcontinent has produced world-famous cricketers, such as Ranjitsinhji (1872–1933), after whom India's Ranji trophy is named, and the Nawab

CRICKET

As this notice in a Bombay newspaper of 1825 illustrates, it was important to find "amusements" for "the ladies" who would not be among the cricket players.

> There will be tents for the ladies, and as the cricketers are all to be dressed in an appropriate uniform, we anticipate one of the most gay and animated scenes that has ever graced our island.
>
> We feel infinite pleasure in announcing amusements which tend to counteract the effects of this enervating climate, by raising the spirits from apathy, and the physical powers from that feminine indolence which is generally rewarded by premature old age, skin hanging in drapery, and muscles reduced to pack thread.

Source: Hilton Brown. (1948) *The Sahibs.* London: William Hodge & Co, 184–185.

of Pataudi (1910–1952). Both of these players represented England before India was accorded Test status.

In the modern era, India and Pakistan have been the traditional cricketing powers of Asia. In 1983, with stars such as Kapil Dev and Sunil Gavaskar, India won the Cricket World Cup, becoming the first country from South Asia to win this major international competition. Current players such as Sachin Tendulkar are national heroes in India. Pakistan, too, has fielded some excellent national teams, especially in the early 1990s under its legendary captain Imran Khan. Waqar Younis, Shoaib Akhtar, and Wasim Akram are among the current Pakistani stars. In recent years Sri Lanka has performed well in international competition, while Bangladesh attained full Test status in the summer of 2000 (the International Cricket Council determines which countries compete at this highest level of cricket). India, Pakistan, Sri Lanka, and Bangladesh play regular series against other Test nations (England, the West Indies, South Africa, Zimbabwe, Australia, and New Zealand). These games create intense interest among fans of cricket in South Asia and are widely regarded as highlights of the sporting calendar.

Deryck O. Lodrick

Further Reading

Wright, Graeme, ed. (2001) *The Wisden Cricketers' Almanack.* Guildford, U.K.: John Wisden & Co., Ltd.

CUI JIAN (b. 1961), Chinese singer and musician. Cui Jian is China's first rock and roll star. Born to musician parents of Korean descent, Cui was raised in Beijing during the Cultural Revolution (1966–1976). He began learning trumpet at age fourteen and in 1981, joined the Beijing Philharmonic Orchestra as a trumpet player. In his spare time he explored popular music.

While Cui's first album was a largely unnoticed collection of pop music covers (*Lanzigui*, 1984), he soon began writing his own music and lyrics and developing his trademark gravel-voice style, drawing inspiration from Western rock bands like the Beatles, the Rolling Stones, and the Police. In Beijing in May 1985, Cui performed one of his first rock songs, "Nothing to My Name," a disconsolate ballad melding western rock with traditional Chinese melodies and instrumentation. The performance rocketed him to stardom and the song remains his signature hit and an anthem of loss for the Tiananmen generation, the youth who witnessed the bloody crackdown on student democracy activists on 4 June 1989.

Cui's albums include *Rock and Roll on the New Long March* (1987), *Solution* (1991), *Balls Under the Red Flag* (1994), and *Power of the Powerless* (1998).

Alexa Olesen

Further Reading

"Cui Jian." (2001) Retrieved 9 January 2002, from: http://www.cuijian.com.

Jones, Andrew F. (1992) *Like a Knife.* Ithaca, NY: Cornell East Asia Series.

CUISINE—AFGHANISTAN Afghani cuisine blends the flavors and ingredients of Central Asia, the Middle East, South Asia, and China. Afghanistan's lo-

An Afghani girl carrying bread on a street of damaged buildings in Kabul. (BACI/CORBIS)

SAMOOS-I-YIRAKOT

Samoos (or samosas) are a popular dish in Afghanistan and South Asia. Samoos are fun to make and are a good appetizer or hors d'oeuvre.

1 tbs. corn oil
1 medium onion; chopped
1 garlic clove; chopped
1 potato; peeled and cut into small pieces
½ cup cauliflower; chopped
½ cup carrot; chopped
½ cup green peas, fresh or frozen
½ cup thin-sliced green beans
¼ tbs. salt
¼ tbs. freshly ground black pepper
1 cup corn oil, for deep-frying

Mix the meal, egg and salt together, adding just enough water to make a moist dough that holds together. Set aside. Heat the oil in a skillet, add the onion and garlic, and stir-fry over moderate heat until light brown, about 3 minutes. Set aside. Take the potato and ½ cup each of any other 3 vegetables and blanch in boiling water for 5 minutes. Drain well. Add these to the pan with the onion and garlic and stir-fry over moderate heat for 3 minutes, to mix well. Add salt and pepper. Cool. Take 1 heaping tablespoon of the dough and press it out on a flat surface into a 2½-inch square. Put 1 tablespoon of the vegetable mixture on the bottom half of the square and fold it over into a triangle. Prepare all the samoosi this way. Heat the oil in a wok or skillet and brown the turnovers over moderate heat for about 3 minutes. Drain on paper towels. Serve warm. Makes about 20 turnovers.

Source: Afghan Cooking Channel. Retrieved 15 March 2002, from: http://www.afghan-network.net/Cooking.

cation at the hub of the Silk Road accounts for the wide range of culinary influences on the country, with typical dishes ranging from traditional Indian breads to meat kabobs that are the staples of Middle Eastern cuisine.

Breads (such as nan and chapattis) and noodles are central to meals. Short-grain rice is used for *bata* (sticky rice), and long-grain rice is the basis for a wide variety of flavorful pilafs. Fried turnovers stuffed with potatoes (*boulanee*) or vegetables (*samoosi*) are popular

THE TRADITIONAL AFGHAN DIET

"Necessity compels the Afghans to live soberly and frugally, and they subsist on fruit nearly half the year. Meat, unless swimming in grease, is not approved; and no meat may be eaten unless it is *halal*, that is to say the animal must have had its face turned towards Mecca and its throat cut in a particular part, to the accompaniment of certain words of prayer. Rice and wheaten bread are consumed by the well-to-do, the former generally cooked with meat and fat in the shape of *pilao*. The principal food of the villagers and nomads, out of the fruit season is *krut*, a kind of porridge made of boiled Indian corn, bruised between two stones, or simply unleavened bread, with which rancid grease is eaten."

Source: Imperial Gazetteer of India: Afghanistan and Nepal. (1908) Calcutta: Superintendent of Government Printing, 28.

appetizers. Spices such as saffron, cumin, mint, cardamom, orange peel, cinnamon, and Chinese chives are part of many dishes; yogurt, nuts, and raisins are often-used ingredients as well.

Vegetables are more widely available than meat. Pumpkin is used as the main ingredient for turnovers and soups, and eggplant and spinach figure prominently in many dishes. Lamb is the most popular meat and is used in curries, kabobs, and stews (*korma*). Recipes also include ground beef, chicken, and goat. Although spices in these dishes are wide ranging and exotic, Afghan cooking is considered to be somewhat mild compared to other Asian cuisines.

Seasonal fresh fruits such as melons and grapes are often served at the conclusion of a meal. Sweet treats are considered an extravagance and are not routinely served, but such foods as *firnee* (a milky pudding flavored with rose water and pistachios), baklavah, and halvah would be among the dessert items for special occasions.

Marcy Ross

Further Reading

Saberi, Helen. (2000) *Afghan Food and Cookery*. New York: Hippocrene.

CUISINE—CENTRAL ASIA Central Asian cuisine encompasses the traditional culinary practices of the region's five countries, whose methods of food preparation can be divided into two groups. Historically, Kazakhstan and Kyrgyzstan were populated primarily by nomadic peoples, who for centuries herded sheep, camels, and horses. Their constant movement left no time for agriculture or complex cooking; the people of these countries relied mainly on the meat and milk provided by their herds, with very little else to diversify their diet. In contrast, inhabitants of the more settled regions of Uzbekistan, Tajikistan, and Turkmenistan cultivated crops and developed sophisticated cooking techniques, thanks to greater availability of produce as well as their ability to spend time at the hearth.

Central Asia's largely harsh and arid climate meant that even in the agricultural regions people relied heavily on meat and cultured dairy products, with relatively few vegetables beyond hardy root crops. Beginning in the late nineteenth century, however, many new crops were introduced, and as the traditional nomadic way of life began to disappear, more garden crops were sown, a process accelerated by the use of widespread irrigation during the Soviet period. Today, after more than a century of change and outside influence, the differences among the Central Asian countries are far less pronounced than they once were, and it is possible to make certain generalizations about the foods of the region.

Meats and Meat Dishes

Meat remains an important food source throughout Central Asia. Lamb is the most popular, although the Turkmens favor mountain goat or kid, while Kazakhs are partial to organ meats. The Kyrgyz consider horsemeat sausage a delicacy. The two most widespread methods for preparing meat are grilling and boiling (or steaming). Uzbekistan is renowned for its many varieties of kabob (skewered grilled meat, either in whole pieces or ground). The excellent *kiyma* kabob is made by shaping seasoned ground lamb around a skewer.

Two women in Old Town, Khiva, Uzbekistan, make flatbread in an outdoor oven. (WOLFGANG KAEHLER/CORBIS)

Turkmen and Tajik meat cookery also depends on the grill, but in Kazakhstan and Kyrgyzstan boiled meats are more common. An ancient dish still eaten today is *kavurdak*, meat that has been stewed in its own fat and then stored in vessels for long keeping. Meat is also preserved by drying it on tall poles in the sun. Both methods reflect the necessities of itinerant life.

Meat is used to flavor a variety of soups; especially prized is the *lagman* found throughout Central Asia, a hearty soup of lamb, carrots, and noodles. Unlike many clear European and Asian soups, the soups of Central Asian are nearly always stew-like, enriched with thickeners like potatoes, chickpeas, or mung beans. These soups tend to be rich and filling from the addition of the prized fat from fat-tailed sheep.

Domestic fowl is not as popular as red meat; more highly appreciated are wild fowl such as pheasant and quail. Since pork is proscribed under Islamic law, it is consumed solely by the minority non-Muslim population. Fish is regularly eaten only in regions that have a significant water source, such as western Turkmenistan and Kazakhstan bordering on the Caspian Sea.

Dairy Products

The second most important component of Central Asian cuisine is the wide array of cultured dairy products made from the milk of sheep and camels and, to a lesser extent, goats and cows. These include *koumiss* (slightly fermented milk), *ayran* (yogurt mixed with water), *kaymak* (clotted cream), and *suzma* (yogurt cheese). Uzbek cuisine in particular boasts numerous milk-based soups, one of the best being *shirkovok* (milk soup with pumpkin and rice). Eggs are not significant in Central Asian cookery.

Grains, Legumes, and Breads

Central Asian cuisine is perhaps best known for its extensive variety of rice pilafs (*palov*). Uzbekistan alone is said to have one hundred different types, and their proper preparation is considered an art. Often legumes such as chickpeas (*nut*) and mung beans (*mash*) are mixed with the rice for extra protein. Pilafs are also made from other grains including millet, barley, and sorgo. All of the Central Asian countries enjoy tasty flatbreads, dumplings, and pies made with wheat-flour dough. *Manty* (large steamed dumplings filled with meat or vegetables), *chuchvara* (small boiled dumplings), and *samsa* (baked or fried pies filled with meat or vegetables) are encountered throughout the region. Kazakhstan is also known for its *beliashi* (open-faced pies fried in a skillet). Central Asian flatbreads are baked in a *tandyr*, a clay oven similar to the Indian tandoor. *Non*, a large, flat round bread pricked in a decorative pattern with a special instrument, is the most popular. These round breads were originally baked to mimic the shape of the sun. They are eaten out of hand or used as a plate to hold meat or vegetable stews.

Seasonings

Although different regions favor different spices and seasonings, certain flavors characterize Central Asian cuisine as a whole. Onion is used abundantly, as is the fat of the fat-tailed sheep, which lends intense flavor to meat and vegetable dishes. Hot red pepper and black pepper add heat to a wide variety of dishes. *Zira* (cumin), sesame seed, nigella, basil, dill, cilantro, parsley, and mint are all used to enliven foods from soups to salads to pilafs. Cinnamon and saffron are used less widely. Garlic adds intensity to many dishes, while dried barberries contribute a sour tang.

Beverages

Tea, either black or green, is the most popular beverage of Central Asia; the preference for one type over the other depends on the locale. Kazakhs tend to drink more black tea, while the Kyrgyz enjoy green tea served with milk or cream and slightly salted. In Uzbekistan black tea is drunk more often than green. Black tea, often in traditional pressed brick form rather than loose leaf, is boiled with milk and served as a rich beverage. Central Asians drink tea from a *pialy*, a bowl-like cup without a handle, and serve it as a ritual part of their hospitality. Other beverages include the aforementioned *koumiss* and *ayran* as well as a variety of refreshing fruit drinks with sugar (*sherbet*).

Fruits and Vegetables

Kazakhstan is the birthplace of the apple (the name of the capital city, Almaty, means "father of apples"), and Uzbekistan and Tajikistan produce exceptionally sweet melons. Other fruits include apricots, peaches, cherries, quince, persimmons, and pomegranates; Central Asian raisins and dried apricots are among the best in the world. The most frequently encountered vegetables are root crops such as carrots, turnips, radishes, onions, and garlic. Carrots alone come in a surprising variety of shapes and colors and have a rich, sweet flavor. Pumpkins and squash are frequently used in soups and as fillings for dumplings and pies. Typically, vegetables are not served alone but are added to soups or paired with meats or pilafs.

Sweets

Traditional Central Asian sweets consist of fruits or nuts simmered in a sugar- or honey-based syrup, served either as a compote or allowed to dry and crystallize. Often fruits are boiled down to make *bekmes*, a concentrated syrup. Other desserts include halvah, made from ground sesame seeds, and dough fried in coils or balls and sweetened with syrup. Although European-style cookies and cakes were introduced under Russian rule, they never displaced the traditional Eastern sweets that still constitute the best ending to a Central Asian meal. Ice cream, however, is extremely popular.

Two centuries of Russian domination did little to change the traditional foodways of the region, and Central Asian cuisine today still reflects a historical reliance on meats and cultured dairy products. The local foods also reveal the influence of centuries of trade, from Chinese noodles to tandoor-baked flatbreads to Persian-style pilafs. Central Asian cuisine is much more diverse now than it was in the past, with vegetables and fruits making up a larger part of the diet. One thing that has remained constant over the centuries, however, is Central Asia's great tradition of hospitality, which is still very much alive in the region's many *chai-khanas* (tea houses) as well as in private homes.

Darra Goldstein

Further Reading

Pokhlebkin, Vil'iam Vasilevich. (1978) *Natsional'nye kukhni nashikh narodov* (National Cuisines of Our Peoples). Moscow, Russia: Pishchevaia promyshlennost.

Visson, Lynn. (1999) *The Art of Uzbek Cooking*. New York: Hippocrene.

CUISINE—CHINA

China's cuisine has spread to all corners of the earth, and the lavishness and variety of Chinese meals is legendary. Yet, through most of history, the vast majority of Chinese have eaten very simple fare, and have considered themselves lucky if they had enough of that. Dense population, unpredictable weather, poverty, and progressive environmental damage combined to give the country a reputation in literature as a land of famine. Only since about 1970 has China been free of major food shortages. The cuisine developed its sophistication partly through the constant need to use every possible resource with maximum efficiency.

History

Early humans populated East Asia approximately one million years ago. They lived by hunting, fishing, and gathering plants and shellfish. Agriculture began before 8000 BCE in China. Recent finds have shown that by this time rice agriculture was well established along the Chang (Yangtze) River and agriculture based on foxtail millet *(Setaria italica)* was established in the drier, cooler drainage basin of the Huang (Yellow) River. By 4000 BCE, cultivation or domestication of many of the basic elements of Chinese food was already widespread: rice, Chinese cabbages, pigs, chickens, sheep, cattle, and various fruits and nuts. Hunting and fishing were still important, however. Archeological finds have revealed that by 3000 BCE a wealth of sophisticated cooking implements and eating utensils existed. Inequalities in wealth were also well established by this time. Perhaps wheat and barley had also arrived from the Near East. They appear by 2000 BCE, but were rare until later.

Chinese cuisine enters the written record in the Zhou dynasty (1045–256 BCE), when recipes begin to appear in ritual texts. Supernatural beings and human elders had to have food prepared according to specific rules. The *Book of Songs (Shi Jing)* , a collection of folk and popular songs from about 1000–500 BCE, includes the names of most of the commonly eaten plants and animals. Although the record of ritual cooking runs primarily to meat—always a luxury and feast food—and grain, with liberal amounts of *jiu*, mildly alcoholic drinks brewed from fermented grains (usually translated "wine," but technically beer or ale), the *Book of Songs* gives a wider perspective, with mentions of vegetables, fruits, nuts, herbs, fish, and game. Grain was the staple food, with vegetables a very long second in importance. The basic distinction between *fan* (cooked grain) and *ts'ai* (vegetables, or any dish eaten with grain) was already being made. It continues to be basic in Chinese food. Soybeans were known, but not much used.

In the Han dynasty (206 BCE–220 CE), contacts with West and South Asia brought new things, including grapes and wine, but, more important, advanced milling technology. This enabled the Chinese to do far more with wheat and soybeans, both of which need to be ground to be useful. It is probable that China's enormous wealth of wheat products—noodles, dumplings, breads, steamed buns, fermented pastes, sauces, gluten products, and more—began its evolution at this time. Soybeans were used for soy sauce and pastes, and probably for tofu (bean curd), though the evidence is thin.

In the next several centuries, Chinese cooking became more elaborate. In the Song dynasty (960–1267), growing prosperity and the arrival of new foodstuffs led to the development of the complex, sophisticated cuisine we know today. Crucial to this, according to modern scholars, was the development of a middle class. Unable to afford the sheer quantity of game and domestic meat that dominated the tables of the nobility, the middle class developed complex culinary techniques, making small amounts of ordinary ingredients into refined, elegant fare. Buddhism, which values simplicity, contributed to this development. In the northwest, Persian and Central Asian influences were particularly strong, due to trade along the Silk Road.

When the Mongols conquered China and founded the Yuan dynasty (1267–1368), influences from western Asia flowed into China, profoundly shaping court cuisine. Dishes from Baghdad and Kashmir were served along with Mongol and Chinese foods. Such influences remained primarily in the north and west. The east developed a highly complex cuisine that made much use of fish, shellfish, and vegetables.

The Ming dynasty (1368–1644), a native Chinese dynasty, reasserted Chinese traditions, partly because of new nationalism. Cuisine perceived as central Asian became steadily less popular. Dairy products, for instance, were popular in west and north China during the entire period of Asian influence but lost ground during the Ming dynasty. Animal herding was displaced by grain agriculture in many areas as the population rose. Most East Asian adults cannot digest lactose (milk sugar) and get indigestion from fresh milk, but they once consumed much yogurt and similar products in which the lactose is destroyed by fermentation.

The Ming dynasty saw the arrival of new foreign influences. Portuguese and Spanish traders introduced New World crops domesticated by Native American peoples. China's economy was radically transformed by maize, sweet potatoes, peanuts, tomatoes, chili peppers, tobacco, and minor crops from pineapples to guavas. Maize and sweet potatoes (and, later, white potatoes) became famine staples and animal feeds; peanuts were a new source of protein and oil.

The Qing dynasty (1644–1912), China's last imperial dynasty, saw a steady increase in European influence on China. The expansion of the tea trade integrated China into the expanding world trade in foodstuffs. After the fall of the Qing dynasty, the incorporation of China into the global economy pro-

CHA XIAO BAO (ROAST PORK DUMPLINGS)

Dim sum or yum cha dates back to the tenth century when little dumplings began to be served with tea. These treats have evolved considerably since then and are one of the most delicate and complex Chinese dishes.

Dough
20 oz. flour
1 cup sugar
6 tsp. baking powder
1½ tsp. white vinegar
2 tbsp. lard
6 oz. lukewarm water
wax paper
2 egg whites

Filling
10 oz. roast pork
1 clove garlic
1 sprig scallion
5 tbsp. cornstarch
6 tbsp. water

Sauce
4 tbsp. sugar
4 tbsp. light soy sauce
1 tbsp. dark soy sauce
2 tbsp. oyster sauce
1 tsp. sesame oil
dash of pepper
⅔ cup water

For the filling, start by frying the garlic and scallion in 2 tbsp oil. Add the sauce ingredients and the roast pork. Thicken with the starch and water.

For the dough, sift the flour with the baking powder. Heap the flour, making a crater in the middle. Add sugar, beaten egg white, vinegar, lard, and water. Mix the ingredients together and knead into a ball. Leave dough to rest for half an hour. Then roll the dough between your palms into a long cylinder about 1½-inches wide. Cut into 20 pieces.

Flatten each piece of dough into a disk and add the filling. Bring the edges up and gather at the center. Put each dumpling on a piece of wax paper and put into a steamer. Bring the water to a rolling boil. Put the steamer over the boiling water, cover and let steam for 10 minutes over high heat.

Source: "John Sui's Recipes by Request." Retrieved March 15 2002, from http://www.galaxylink.com.hk/~john/food/cooking/canton/chaxiaobao.htm.

ceeded apace. China has taken advantage of the global economy to spread Chinese cuisine worldwide. Such items as soy sauce and tea are known and used throughout the world.

Current Changes

Chinese food continues to evolve and change. One change—deplored by traditional gourmets—is the coming of monosodium glutamate, which was isolated from seaweed in Japan in the early twentieth century and only since 1960s spread into Chinese cooking. Another addition is the "fortune cookie," invented by a Chinese bakery in California in the late nineteenth century; it reached East Asia in the mid-twentieth century. Western food, including the fast food offered at McDonald's, has come to China. Another recent development has been the spread of the Cantonese custom of making a leisurely breakfast of dim sum. The Cantonese phrase *dim sam* (Mandarin *dienxin*) literally means "dot the heart" but may more idiomatically be translated "hits the spot." Dim sum are small, savory, high-calorie snacks, most often various kinds of stuffed and steamed dumplings and buns. They are eaten with endless cups of tea. Traditionally a breakfast for workers or for weekend outings, dim sum have become exceedingly popular in urban China, and in many distant urban centers to which Chinese have migrated.

General Characteristics

Chinese cuisine shows similarities with other cuisines of East Asia, partly because of China's influence in the region. Throughout East Asia, meals are typically boiled grain with some form of mixed topping involving vegetables, spices, and soy products. Soup is

BOK CHOY SOUP

This recipe is adapted from Ken Hom's *Easy Family Recipes from a Chinese-American Childhood.* Hom recalls that his neighbors would grow bok choy and other traditional Chinese vegetables in small garden plots in Chicago's Chinatown.

4 cups chicken stock or reduced-salt canned broth
1 cup bok choy, cut up
1 egg
2 tsp. sesame oil
1 tsp. sugar
1 tsp. salt
¼ tsp. freshly ground white pepper
1 tbs. light soy sauce
3 tbs. finely chopped scallions, white part only
3 tbs. finely chopped green scallion tops (for garnish)
1 cup shredded iceberg lettuce

Put the chicken stock in a pot and bring it to a simmer. Separate the leaves and stalks of the bok choy, and cut the leaves into 2-inch pieces. Peel the stems, cut them into diagonal slices, and wash them well in several changes of water.

Lightly beat the egg and then mix with the sesame oil in a small bowl. Toss the sugar into the simmering stock, taste, then add salt, pepper, and soy sauce and give the stock several good stirs. Next toss in the bok choy and scallions and then drizzle in the egg mixture in a very slow thin stream. Using a chopstick or fork pull the egg slowly into strands.

Remove the soup from the heat and toss in the shredded lettuce, stirring all the while. Garnish with the finely chopped scallion tops and serve at once.

Source: Ken Hom (1997). *Easy Family Recipes from a Chinese-American Childhood.* New York: Alfred E. Knopf, 51–52.

abundant and important. The grain is most often rice, simply boiled (often miscalled "steamed"). Boiled rice (or a substitute such as millet or cracked maize) is topped with a mixed dish, usually involving a good deal of highly flavored sauce that can soak into the rice. Next most common, especially in China itself, are noodles—usually made of wheat, often of rice or other grains. These are most often cooked in soup, but they are frequently boiled and then fried with vegetables and flavorings (the familiar "chow mein"—more correctly *chao mien*—and its relatives). Steamed buns, small breads, dumplings, and other products, usually made of wheat but often of maize, buckwheat, or other grains, are common. These are usually eaten by themselves, as snacks or quick meals. In some of the poorest parts of China, heavy flat cakes of maize or buckwheat were staples. They have since been replaced by wheat and rice products over the last thirty years.

Within China, pork is the commonest meat. China is home to two-thirds of the world's domesticated pigs. Chickens—native to China—come second. Fish and shellfish abound wherever there is water. Thousands of species of marine life are used. Most fish are now supplied by pond farming. This practice was invented in China at least 2,000 years ago and continues to increase. Hundreds of species of vegetables and fruits are eaten.

Traditionally, oils were most often made from cabbage seeds (rapeseed oil). Later came unrefined sesame, maize, and peanut oils, whose marked tastes added much to the cuisine. Today, rapeseed and soy oils are common; maize and peanut oils continue to flourish; all are refined and essentially tasteless.

Food is usually boiled, steamed, or fried. Soup is traditionally present at virtually every meal, and often is the entire meal. Water was (and still often is) highly polluted, and had to be boiled; making it into soup or tea thus made good sense. Frying usually involves the famous process called *chao* in Chinese and "stir-frying" in English: Food is cut into small pieces and stirred in a small amount of extremely hot oil. This process spares oil and fuel. The custom of eating with chopsticks *(kuayzi)* was already established by the Zhou dynasty (1045–256 BCE).

The mix of spices and flavorings distinguishes Chinese food from other cuisines of East Asia. Flavorings in a Chinese meal almost always contain at least some of the following: Soy sauce, fermented soybean paste (or whole beans), garlic, onions (often small green onions), chili peppers, fresh ginger, Chinese "wine," and Chinese vinegar. The latter two are made by fermentation of grain, using special strains of fungi and bacteria that yield complex and distinctive flavors. In impoverished or climatically stressed areas, food flavorings may be little more than garlic and onions and a bit of soy sauce. In overseas restaurants that cater to non-Chinese, the flavorings are usually reduced.

Chinese cooking evolved as a cooking of scarcity. Several characteristics of the cuisine follow from this. First, food, especially meat, is cut into small pieces. This allows it to cook more quickly and go farther in serving, and to make it manageable by chopsticks. Second, dishes and stoves are designed to use little fuel. This, with the thin slicing, allows ordinary people to cook a meal on a handful of grass or splinters; until recently, this was all the fuel available for many or most families. Third, by putting small dishes of cut-up vegetables and meat on the rice, in a closed pot, cooks can produce a three- or four-course meal in one pot, cutting back still further on fuel use. These are only a few of many tricks for saving fuel and food.

Another type of efficiency is gained by using almost everything edible. Tough leaves can be boiled for soup. Frogs, small shellfish, and minnows are consumed. Wild herbs and berries are sought out. Many crops are grown, the choice governed by what grows best in each local habitat—streamsides, rice paddy banks, groves, pots, even roofs. The result is an enormous variety of foodstuffs and of dishes. Restaurants often have 400 dishes on their menus and can make many more on request.

Most important of all, Chinese cuisine is based on foods that produce an adequate diet on a minimum of land. Rice is the highest yielding of all grains. Sweet potatoes and other root crops extend the range of cultivation. Soybeans are high in protein that complements rice protein in the diet. Chinese cabbages and other popular vegetables are high in vitamins and minerals.

Many foods are eaten solely for their high nutrient value. An example is *kou ji cai (Lycium chinense)*, "the poor people's vitamin pill," whose leaves and berries are among the richest sources of vitamins known. Long before anyone analyzed vitamins, the leaves and dried fruits of this plant were known to be nutritious and strengthening. Handfuls of the fruits *(kou ji zi)* are used in soups for women recovering from childbirth or for persons convalescing from sickness.

Regional Variations

Within these general guidelines, Chinese cuisine varies greatly by region. The basic divide is between north and south. The north is dominated by wheat, with maize, sorghum, millet, and rice playing minor parts. The south is dominated by rice. The northern limit of the Jiang River basin is the approximate dividing line; the Jiang drainage basin grows both rice and wheat (and now a great deal of maize). Maize is produced in large amounts almost everywhere in China, but it is usually used for animal feed and is not popular with humans.

In the north, distinctive subtypes have evolved in the major geographic divisions. Particularly famous are the cuisines of Shaanxi (centered on Xi'an), Hebei (centered on Beijing and Tianjin), and Shandong. All are characterized by the dominance of noodles, dumplings, and steamed breads. All use a great deal of onions and garlic. Lamb, very rare southward, is used in the northwest. Shaanxi food is simple and often flavored with local vinegar. Beijing is more elaborate and has its own elite tradition in the form of the cuisine of the Forbidden City; the disappearance of the imperial court led to great reduction of this cuisine, but it survives in a few restaurants and banquet halls. Shandong food uses many vegetables, soybean products, seafoods, and dumpling varieties.

The classic centers of the south are Hunan-Sichuan, the Chang delta, and Guangdong. Hunan and Sichuan have always had a spicy cuisine. Until chilies arrived from the Americas, the "heat" came from smartweed (*Polygonum* spp.), Sichuan "pepper" (actually a prickly ash or fagara, *Xanthoxylum* spp.), and black pepper and relatives (*Piper* spp.). Chilies gave local cooks a chance to escalate the heat level. This spicy style has spread to, or has influenced, most of southwest China.

Life in the Chang delta originally centered around several great cities: Hangzhou, Suzhou, Ningpo, Shanghai (recently), and others. Each city has its own variant of a general style characterized by sweet-sour dishes, much oil, a smooth and mellow texture, and very heavy use of vegetables and seafoods.

Guangdong (Cantonese) cuisine is marked by its enormous variety of ingredients (even by Chinese standards) and its heavy use of various fermented soybean products, including the distinctive fermented "black beans" (Mandarin *dou shi*, Cantonese *tausi*). Seafoods are intensively used, and are often made into salty pastes and sauces; these resemble similar Southeast Asian products.

Several other important southern styles exist, including Chaozhou (Teochiu, Chiuchow), Fuzhou, and others. Distinctive cuisines also characterize the many minority groups that speak non-Chinese languages. The largest of these, the Zhuang minority (speaking languages very close to Thai), is noted for heavy vegetable use and for certain fermented products. Some Zhuang villages are characterized by high life expectancies, due in large part to their healthy diet of relatively unprocessed grains and varied local vegetables.

Issues for the Twenty-First Century

Overuse of wild foods, especially rare animals (with the distinction between medicine and cuisine blurred), is now a serious problem. Erosion, deforestation, spread of cities and roads onto farmland, and other processes are destroying much of the landscape. Unless conservation is taken far more seriously, China will again be the land of famine.

Gene Anderson

Further Reading

Anderson, E. N. (1988) *The Food of China.* New Haven, CT: Yale University Press.

He Bochuan. (1991) *China on the Edge.* San Francisco, CA: China Books and Periodicals.

Simoons, Frederick J. (1991) *Food in China.* Boca Raton, FL: CRC Press.

Watson, James L., ed. (1997) *Golden Arches East: McDonald's in East Asia.* Stanford, CA: Stanford University Press.

GADO-GADO (INDONESIAN VEGETABLE SALAD)

2 cups sliced lettuce
2 cups sliced steamed cabbage or cauliflower florets
2 cups steamed bean sprouts
1 boiled potato, thinly sliced
½ cucumber, thinly sliced
1 large tomato, thinly sliced
Arrange the vegetables in a platter

For garnish:
1 hard boiled egg, sliced
crushed *krupuk* (prawn crackers)

Peanut Sauce
1 cup crunchy peanut butter
2 tbs. sweet soy sauce
1 tbs. fried onions
2 tbs. brown sugar
1 tbs. lime/lemon juice
1 cube chicken bouillon
1 cup boiling water
salt to taste

Simmer ingredients for the sauce over low heat. Cool and pour over salad, garnish with sliced egg and prawn crackers.

Source: Catharina Purwani Williams

CUISINE—INDONESIA Indonesian cuisine is as distinct and diverse as the many thousands of islands that make up the archipelago. On the routes of commerce between India, China, and the Middle East, Indonesia developed a cuisine that reflects these foreign influences in its curries and stir-fries. In the basic Indonesian staples of rice *(nasi)* and vegetable dishes, fish, and occasionally beef or pork, the cuisine also reflects local products. Rice is grown in places with rich volcanic soil, either by terraced, wetland cultivation or by dry cultivation in eastern Indonesia.

The Wallace line divides the Indonesian archipelago into two parts with distinctly different fauna and flora. The west consists of the larger islands of Sumatra, Java, Bali, and Kalimantan, while the east consists of Sulawesi, Maluku, the Lesser Sunda Islands, and West Papua. The differences in produce and cuisine roughly follow this biological division. Another dividing factor is the proximity to coastal areas, which are known for many fish and coconut dishes combined with spices and vegetables and complemented with tropical fruits.

Javanese, Sumatran, and Balinese cuisine represent the dominant Indonesian cuisines and are widely available across the archipelago because of interisland migration. Beef *rendang* is well known internationally.

SAMBAL DENDENG (SPICY SHREDDED BEEF)

This spicy, deep-fried shredded beef dish is typical of Indonesian cuisine. A blend of Chinese and Southeast Asian influences, sambal dendeng is a good dish for entertaining or for exploring the culinary pleasures of Southeast Asia

1 lb. beef round, cut into ¼-inch-thick pieces
salt as needed
oil as needed
4 Holland red peppers (fresh cayenne may be substituted)
8 garlic cloves
½ tsp. shrimp paste
1 tsp. minced zedoary (ginger can be substituted)
2 thinly sliced galangal (ginger can be substituted)
2 tbs. lime peel
½ tsp. tamarind (the pulp from a lemon or lime can be substituted)
½ cup coconut milk
1 cup water

Sprinkle some salt on beef pieces then deep fry them in oil for 7 minutes. Drain on a paper towel then let cool. Shred beef into small pieces. If they are too tough or rubbery, pound them with a meat tenderizer before shredding.

Grind Holland red peppers, garlic cloves, shrimp paste, zedoary, and galangal to a fine paste. Heat a deep frying pan, add 2 tablespoons of oil. Sauté spice paste for about 5 minutes then add lime peel, tamarind, coconut milk, and water. Bring sauce to a boil then lower heat to simmer. Add beef to the sauce, then simmer, covered, until beef is tender and sauce is almost dry. Season with salt. Serve with steamed rice.

Source: Indokitchen.com. Retrieved 15 March 2002, from: http://www.indokitchen.com.

From West Sumatra, this dish is a beef curry cooked in spices, chilies, and coconut, simmered until dry. It is purchased in tiny stalls (*warung* Padang) in remote regions of the eastern islands of Indonesia and together with *nasi goreng* (fried rice) has become a café-style take-out food all over the world and in upmarket Asian restaurants in the Netherlands, United States, and Australia. During the centuries before air travel, the mainly Muslim inhabitants of West Sumatra brought *rendang* with chilies and spices as preservatives on their long pilgrimages to Mecca.

Javanese *tempe* (tempeh) and *tahu* (tofu), both made from soybeans, are the basis of many Javanese dishes. In the West, they are often sold in health shops and Asian groceries. They have become popular daily foods throughout Indonesia because of their high nutrition, low cost, easy storage, and delicious taste. Eastern Indonesia, which is partly non-Muslim, offers pork-based dishes.

Meals

In prosperous times, people expect to eat rice three times a day, accompanied by a main dish and side dishes. In Java, it is customary to offer to share food with others, and this practice has been adopted throughout Indonesia as a social gesture of inclusion: *selamat makan* or *bon appétit.* Guests arriving around mealtime are invited to share the meal. The food is placed on the table or floor mat where the diners serve themselves. In a middle-class home, a plate, spoon, and fork are used, while others use banana leaves as plates and eat with their right fingers.

Rice and a variety of dishes based on vegetables, fish, poultry, beef, pork, and pulses (beans) are cooked in a wok or a pot. The main ingredient is mixed, marinated, broiled, fried, or simmered with spices. Spices include pepper, nutmeg, coriander, lesser galingal, turmeric, candlenuts, garlic, onions, and chilies, which are crushed using pestle and mortar. During feasts, such as weddings and *Lebaran* (the Muslim celebration at the end of the fasting month of Ramadan), a variety of dishes are served: for instance, yellow (turmeric) rice accompanied by fried chicken, fried fish, chicken curry, or prawn curry and garnished with thinly sliced omelettes and greens. This combination is the basis of the internationally acclaimed rijstafel (rice and a set of special dishes), a Dutch colonial's gastronomic adaptation of the typical East Indies (as Indonesia used to be known) feast.

Everyday cooking relies on vegetables, such as cabbages, *kang-kung* (a kind of watercress), Chinese cabbages, snake beans, a variety of bean sprouts, and summer squash, available daily in the market. *Gado-gado*, a famous Indonesian vegetarian dish, consists of vegetables, including tomatoes, garnished with thinly sliced boiled eggs and crushed *krupuk* (prawn crackers), and complemented with peanut sauce as a dressing. This low-cost but healthy dish is popularly eaten as a snack or main meal during midday, competing with chicken *satays* (cubed meat on a skewer), both of which are available in street food stalls or from hawkers and restaurants.

Sweets and Beverages

Indonesians eat sweets as snacks, not as desserts. Dessert is commonly a selection of tropical fruits in season, particularly bananas, which are available all year. Cakes, puddings, biscuits, and pastries have been much influenced by the Dutch, while traditional sweets are made of cassavas, sweet potatoes, glutinous rice, palm sugar, or grated coconut or a combination of these. The mainly Muslim population does not drink alcohol with meals; however for feasts and special occasions in some areas, people may drink a locally produced fermented palm wine, known as *tuak*, *moke* (palm wine or *lontar* palm), *arak* (distilled liquor from sugar palm), or *brem* (fermented rice). People usually drink hot or iced tea or water with their meals.

Today Indonesian cuisine also reflects the Western influence of fast foods such as breads and hamburgers and the Chinese influence of noodles, along with the traditional foods based on fresh tropical produce with various tastes: spicy, sweet, savory, sour, pungent. The home of a wide range of spices, Indonesia became famous during three and a half centuries of colonial rule for these condiments and since then for its cuisine.

Catharina Purwani Williams

Further Reading

Marahimin, Hiang, and Roos Djalil. (1995) *Indonesian Dishes and Desserts*. Jakarta, Indonesia: Gaya Favorit Press.

Marks, Copeland. (1994) *The Exotic Kitchens of Indonesia: Recipes from the Outer Islands*. New York: M. Evans and Company.

Owen, Sri. (1995) *Indonesian Regional Cooking*. New York: St. Martin's Press.

Reid, Anthony. (1988) *Southeast Asia in the Age of Commerce, 1450–1680*. Vol. 1: *The Lands below the Winds*. New Haven, CT: Yale University Press.

CUISINE—IRAN Because of its relatively large size and diverse climates (from the Persian Gulf in the south to the Caspian Sea in the north), a history of several thousand years, and the many ethnic groups that populate it, Iran has a rich variety of foods that differ from region to region and sometimes even season to season. The national cuisine of Iran, however, which has spread to and influenced the cuisines of other cultures and countries in South and Central Asia and the Middle East, consists of ethnic and regional foods that have been refined and perfected over the course of many centuries, particularly by the master chefs of the royal courts. To Western tastes, Iranian food seems both exotic and familiar: exotic because the many combinations of vegetables, herbs, spices, and fruits are new; familiar because almost all the ingredients are commonly used in the West. What characterizes this cuisine is essentially its emphasis on flavors.

Based on the ingredients used and methods of preparation, Iranian foods are categorized in a dozen or so main groups, some of which are *polo* (rice mixed with other ingredients such as legumes, meats, vegetables, and herbs), *khoresh* (stew-type dishes that are usually served over *chelo*, plain rice), *kabab* (skewered meats), *ash* (thick pottage-like dishes), *abgusht* (soups), *dolmeh* (stuffed vegetables and grape leaves), *kufteh* (meat and/or rice balls), and *kuku* (vegetable or other soufflé-type dishes). Rice is one of the most important staples in the Iranian diet and is often the main dish. The most popular way of making rice in Iran, which is quite different from that of most other cuisines, results in fluffy, separated grains of rice. For this kind of dish, a high quality, long grain rice such as basmati is used, which has a unique flavor and aroma. Rice dishes are usually

DOLMEH-YEH FELFEL

An Iranian classic, the flavor-infused rice and dense but delicate taste and textures characteristic of Iranian foods are wonderfully presented in this recipe. Adapted from the Iranian culinary "bible," Rosa Montazemi's *Honar-e Aashpazi* or *Art of Cooking*, dolmeh-yeh felfel or stuffed peppers are relatively simple to make and absolutely delicious.

2 medium onions, finely chopped
cooking oil
1/2 lb. ground lamb or beef
salt
black pepper
3–4 tsp. tomato paste
1/3 cup parsley, finely chopped
1/3 cup mint, finely chopped
1/2 cup spring onions, finely chopped
1/3 cup garlic chives, finely chopped
1/3 cup tarragon, finely chopped (optional)
3 1/2 oz. of long-grain or basmati rice
4 large green or red peppers
2–3 tsp. sugar
3–4 tbs. fresh lime juice

Fry onions in cooking oil over medium heat until golden. Add ground meat and fry further until meat changes color. Add 1/2 cup water, salt, pepper and most of tomato paste. Mix and cook further until water boils off.

Fry prepared herbs and spring onions in cooking oil over medium heat until wilted. Boil 2 cups of water in a small pot. Add 1 teaspoon of salt and rice and boil further until rice softens. Drain the water and let cool slightly.

Cut a circle at the top of the peppers and remove seeds. Boil 2 cups of water in a large pot. Add 1 teaspoon of salt and the peppers. They should be placed side by side (make sure not to stack them). Cook until they soften slightly. Take care not to overcook or they might fall apart later on. Drain the water and let cool.

Mix well-prepared meat, vegetables, most of the lime juice, most of the sugar, and rice. Sprinkle some salt inside peppers, fill them with the mix and close the tops. Again place the peppers side by side (avoid stacking them) in a large pot. Prepare sauce by mixing 1/2 cup of hot water with the rest of sugar, lime juice and tomato paste. Pour the sauce in over the peppers and simmer for 5–10 minutes. Serve this dolmeh hot with the sauce. Makes four servings.

Source: Iranian/Persian Recipes. Retrieved 17 March 2002, from: http://www.ee.surrey.ac.uk/Personal/F.Mokhtarian/recipes.

decorated with saffron-flavored grains of rice. Traditionally, red meat (usually mutton) and poultry are not consumed in the quantities that are customary in the West. Meats are often used to flavor dishes, as are other ingredients. Iranian foods are by no means bland, which is not to say that they are spicy, as is Indian cuisine. What distinguishes an Iranian table is the subtlety of the combination of flavors. A typical Iranian meal may consist of a rice dish with a meat sauce; yogurt; fresh herbs such as mint, basil, and tarragon; and freshly baked bread, of which there are many varieties available on every street corner.

M. R. Ghanoonparvar

Further Reading

Batmanglij, Najmieh. (1992) *New Food of Life: Ancient Persian and Modern Iranian Cooking and Ceremonies.* Washington, DC: Mage Publishers.

Ghanoonparvar, M. R. (1981) *Persian Cuisine, Book One: Traditional Foods.* Lexington, KY: Mazda Publishers.

———. (1984) *Persian Cuisine, Book Two: Regional and Modern Foods.* Lexington, KY: Mazda Publishers.

Mazda, Maideh (1960) *In a Persian Kitchen: Favorite Recipes from the Middle East.* Rutland, VT: Charles E. Tuttle.

CUISINE—IRAQ Iraq's rich and varied cuisine reflects the nation's long history. Located at the geographic center of the Middle East, modern-day Iraq also encompasses ancient Mesopotamia, the so-called land between the rivers. On the rich soils between the Tigris and Euphrates Rivers, some of the world's first agriculturalists started domesticating livestock and raising crops ten to twelve thousand years ago. From these earliest origins came a number of the staples of modern Iraqi cuisine: dates from palms that dotted the oases; wheat, rice, and barley from lush, intensively cultivated fields; and meat from lambs, sheep, goats, cattle, and camels that served as the basis of nomadic Iraqi life.

Iraq's location has also made it a crossover point for cuisines. Along the Silk Road from China came ingredients such as peas and apricots, as well as techniques for combining sweet and sour flavors. Mongol invaders brought tea, a drink popular to this day. Periods of rule by the Sumerians, Babylonians, Assyrians, Persians, Greeks, Romans, Arabs, Ottomans, and the British also left their marks.

Baghdad served as a center for culinary mixing as well as a center for gastronomic extravagance. Medieval Islamic caliphs, for instance, threw lavish banquets in which their guests feasted for days and wrote poetry exalting their food bounty.

From the neighboring Persians, Iraqi cooks learned to create sweet and savory dishes combining meats with dried and fresh fruits. Like their Turkish neighbors, Iraqis enjoy stuffed vegetable dishes, including stuffed grape leaves (dolma). Well-traveled Jewish chefs also left their mark, introducing French and Italian influences in the eighteenth century, notably a pizza-like dish consisting of flat yeast bread coated with a tomato sauce and ground meat.

Formal meals consist of multiple courses, starting with appetizers that might include kebabs (skewered grilled meats) or yogurt dishes. Flavored rice dishes serve as the foundation of meals and also mark a cook's skill. The most common meats include lamb and mutton, but the meat of cows, goats, chickens, and even camels is still used. Pork is prohibited by Muslim law throughout the region. Fish, however, forms the basis for perhaps the country's most famous dish, *masgoof,* a skewered river fish barbecued and spiced with salt, pepper, and tamarind. Pickled vegetables *(turshi)* link Iraqi cuisine to that throughout northeast Africa and the Middle East.

Abroad and at home, Iraqi cooks continue to adapt their cooking techniques, responding to new influences while retaining millennia of traditions.

Ann DeVoll Brucklacher

OVEN BARBECUED FISH WITH TRADITIONAL STUFFING

A traditional Iraqi method for preparing fish with a pungent but delicious stuffing.

1 whole fish (approx. 3 lbs.), cut open lengthwise head to tail through the back
4 tbs. vegetable oil
8 chopped onions
12 garlic cloves, minced or pressed
2 tsp. curry powder
2 tsp. salt
2 tbs. tamarind paste (can substitute pulp of lemon or lime)
1 cup warm water

Place the open fish skin down on a cookie sheet. Broil for 3–4 minutes until partially cooked. Heat oil in a saucepan, and sauté the onion and the garlic, stirring until the onions are tender. Add curry powder and salt. Stir. Dissolve the tamarind in the warm water, then add it to the onion mix. Let cook on medium heat until the mixture is a thick paste (about 30 minutes). Spread the onion mixture on the broiled fish.

Bake the fish in a 350° oven for 15–30 minutes or until done. Place the fish under the broiler for few minutes until a thin crust has formed on the stuffing. Serve with rice and green salad.

Source: Saleh's Iraq. Retrieved 15 March 2002, from: http://www.mecookbook.com/Book_Maklooba.html.

Further Reading

"Iraq." (1998) *Worldmark Encyclopedia of Cultures and Daily Life*. New York: Gale.

Rosgov, Daniel. (2002) "Iraqi Cuisine." Retrieved 11 January 2002. from: www.us-israel.org/jsource/Food/iraq.html.

CUISINE—JAPAN The basic characteristics of Japanese foodways may be traced to its ecological and historical contexts, above all, to the conditions related to island life and to the periods of isolation and borrowing from Asia and European culinary influences. Reliance on the products of the sea made fish, shellfish, and sea vegetables preeminent in the Japanese diet, and the suitability of Japanese soil to rice growing made rice the staple carbohydrate. Rice is the center of any meal; in fact, most older Japanese would not consider a meal complete without rice. Other dishes, such as pickles, cooked vegetables, and small amounts of salted fish and egg are flavor accompaniments to the main dish of rice. Before modern transportation permitted a more varied diet, people ate whatever their regions afforded.

Legendary Times Through the Nara Period

Prehistoric evidence from archaeological sites demonstrates the dominance of seafoods, especially shellfish—*asari* (short-necked clam), *hotategai* (scallop), and *awani* (abalone)—as represented in ancient shell mounds. It is probable that fish such as *tai* (sea bream), *suzuki* (sea bass), *koi* (carp), and *unagi* (eel) were also central to the diet during the Jomon culture (10,000 –300 BCE). In addition, the diet may have included deer, crane, duck, boar, and rabbit. There is evidence too of other foods such as nuts and melons. Pottery and tools indicate that boiling and grilling were the main cooking methods. By the third century BCE, mainland Asian rice, millet, and wheat had come to Japan. Salt extraction from seawater permitted the pickling, preserving, and fermenting of foods; it is in this period that the standard meal evolved, consisting of a central grain dish accompanied by small portions of pickles and vegetables.

Rice growing depends on the cooperation of many people and the coordination of irrigation systems. By the seventh century, reliance on rice cultivation helped to create a political and social system in which mutual dependency for labor and irrigation was managed and controlled by a landlord class that gained economic and political power. Taxation of agricultural production was managed by a bureaucracy that could reach every farm worker and tie local organizations and authorities to the imperial capital, which by the eighth century was established in Nara. The court at Nara received the bounty of the outlying regions, and a more diversified and elite cuisine became the object of courtier connoisseurship. Along with the refinement of taste, preparation methods were codified. Artisan tableware developed and an aesthetics of dining manners was created for courtiers. Class distinctions in diet and manners were apparent. Chopsticks *(hashi)* were used by aristocrats, while common people ate with their fingers. Peasants, agricultural producers of the aristocratic rice, ate less refined grains such as millet.

Heian and Kamakura Periods

During the Heian period (794–1185), court life featured elaborate presentations based on Chinese cooking methods. At the same time, the variety of foodstuffs declined under the influence of Chinese Buddhism, which prohibited the use of animal products. Japanese culinary historians look to this period as a time when the ubiquitous soup stock, dashi, was developed. Literature of the time includes details of dining. While rice was clearly the staple food, noodles were also prepared. A banquet might include raw fish, a soup, boiled foods, grilled and fried foods, followed by more boiled and steamed foods and ending with pickles and rice. Murasaki Shikibu, author of the Heian-period novel *The Tale of Genji*, records that the meals were taken at midmorning and midafternoon, supplemented by snack foods during the day and evening.

In the Kamakura period (1185–1333), the dominance of the warrior class spread a culture of simplicity and tough frugality, in which it became a virtue to simplify one's meals. Indeed, going without a meal was seen as a sign of good character. The need for foods transportable to battle sites and campgrounds may have been the origin of the *bento*, prepared foods that would keep longer. The *umeboshi* or pickled plum is said to have been created in this period; it became a necessary accompaniment to rice and other grains. In the court and in temples, however, refinements were based on Zen Buddhist simplicity, rather than warrior sensibilities, and on the tea ceremony, which was developed and practiced by Buddhist priests. The development of a Zen Buddhist cuisine elevated frugality and vegetarianism to an art in which "eating with the eyes" *(me de taberu)* was a value, and the aesthetics of food preparation and presentation became a tenet of Buddhist culinary practice.

The Tokugawa Period

The influences of European foodways began in Japan in the 1500s, when traders and missionaries from Spain, Portugal, and Holland brought methods of preparation such as breading and deep frying, as well as new foodstuffs such as leavened bread. Most of these *namban ryori* (southern barbarian cooking) foods, however, did not influence local diets beyond the more cosmopolitan samurai and official classes. Moreover, there were as yet no routes to disseminate these novelties, and most people's diets were still determined by locally available foodstuffs.

By the Edo or Tokugawa period (1600/1603–1868), the elaborate cuisine attached to the tea ceremony *(chakaiseki ryori)* defined an order of service and mode of eating. *Kaiseki* cuisine emerged as the most refined eating, and evolved as a formal meal independent of the tea ceremony from which it derived. Seasonal fresh foods were emphasized, and the quality of ingredients was highly regarded. *Kaiseki* service stipulated that each element in the meal be prepared separately to ensure freshness and that it be prepared according to its own nature. The idea of separate courses in a meal was established by this principle. As a correlate, the appearance of each dish became very important and serving ware and implements had to be designed to reflect color and taste, as well as to present each element of the meal to its best advantage. The order of service, as established and elaborated from the Heian period banquet, began with *sakizuke* (appetizers), tiny portions of elegantly prepared fish. Second was *chinmi*, a kind of salad, tofu, or wheat gluten. Third was a soup, often a simple and elegant clear broth with a tiny vegetable, fish or clam decorating the bottom of a dark lacquer bowl, perhaps suggesting a miniature landscape. Next was *mukozuke*, a portion of sashimi or raw fish, followed by *takiawase* (a vegetarian simmered dish).There followed *mushimono*, steamed items flavored with a sauce based on soy sauce and garnished with grated *tororoimo* (mountain potato), a *yakimono* or grilled dish, a vinegar *sunomono* (salad), and finally rice with *miso* soup and pickle. Variations on these themes abound, and *kaiseki* came to include a wide variety of ingredients and preparations, combining the virtues of Buddhist simplicity with elaborate aesthetics.

A Japanese woman assists a man who is eating a sashimi meal of *fugu* in Fukuoka in 1995. (JAMES MARSHALL/CORBIS).

During the Edo period, peace and bureaucratic centralization allowed for the flowering of arts and the development of an urban culture. The rise of the merchant class and a money economy meant the creation of a new urban consumer culture, which included an emphasis on entertainment and eating. Restaurants such as noodle shops, tempura shops, and grill houses became popular in the entertainment section of the cities. There were also *yatai*, stalls where workers could stop for a stand-up or sit-down meal. New foodstuffs continued to diversify the diet of the townspeople, and foreign ingredients and modes of preparation were introduced. Chinese tradition also continued to influence the diet. The bureaucratic centralization of the nation included compulsory sojourns in Edo (present-day Tokyo) for local *daimyo* (feudal lords); the frequent travel this system demanded helped to establish regular routes to the capital along which restaurants and teahouses sprang up. As ever, social class distinctions were reflected in food consumption patterns. Elaborate entertainment focusing on food were popular among the aristocracy and some members of the merchant class. Among commoners and peasants, a much simpler diet prevailed.

Meiji and Taisho Periods

Western food traditions continued to influence Japan even in the *sakoku jidai* (closed country) of the Tokugawa period. It was in the Meiji period (1868–1912), however, that full exposure to foodstuffs and cultures of the West occurred. At first many people were reluctant to try exotic substances, but the diffusion of a sophisticated cosmopolitan urban culture through media such as women's magazines that included recipes for roast meats and dairy-based dishes like custards, puddings, and butter cakes spread the fashion of eating foreign foods. Many older people, however, rejected the meals based on bread, potatoes, and starches other than rice. Meat eating had arrived in Japan much earlier, when Spanish and Portuguese missionaries had made beef eating part of the Christian conversion experiences of nobles in the sixteenth century. Ordinary people, however, did not eat beef until the Meiji era. Some Meiji leaders encouraged beef eating as a means for strengthening Japanese physically. The Meiji Emperor proclaimed the suitability of beef for the Japanese diet, and dishes like sukiyaki became popular. Western dining habits began to influence home meals. A dining table and chairs took the place of a traditional low *kotatsu* table and sitting on the floor. Using Western cutlery was also a novelty, and etiquette books be-

POUK CUTLET ON RICE *(KATSUDON)*

This dish, adapted from a recipe by master chef Shizuo Tzuji, is a staple in homes and restaurants throughout Japan.

6–8 cups hot cooked short-grain white rice
4 6-ounce pork loin cutlets (pork tenderloin steaks or chops without bone)
salt and pepper

Breading

6 tbs. flour
2 eggs, beaten
2 cups breadcrumbs
vegetable oil for frying (peanut or corn oil works well)

Onion-and-Egg Topping

1 small onion
2½ cups *dashi* (Japanese soup stock; vegetable broth can be substituted)
7 tbs. *mirin* (rice wine or sake)
6 tbs. soy sauce
4 green onions, cut into 1½-inch lengths
6 eggs, beaten

Pound cutlets with a mallet or bottle to flatten slightly. Remove fat at the edge of the cutlets to keep the meat from curling during frying. Salt and pepper both sides.

Dust with flour, dip in beaten egg, and coat both sides thickly with dry or fresh breadcrumbs. Let stand 2 or 3 minutes before frying. Note: Alternatively, the frying can be done in 3/4 inch of oil in an ordinary skillet

Heat a generous amount of oil in a heavy-bottomed pot or deep-fryer to a medium temperature (340°F/170°C), and deep-fry cutlets one at a time, turning once, till golden brown, about 6 minutes each. Remove and drain on absorbent paper, and cut crosswise into ½-inch slices. Keep hot.

Meanwhile slice onion into rounds or half moons and, in a large frying pan in a scant amount of oil, sauté onion over high heat till transparent and soft. Add the *dashi*, *mirin*, and soy sauce to the pan. Simmer, and add the green onion lengths.

Finally, pour the beaten egg over the simmering onions. Stir when the egg begins to set. The egg is done when it is a little runny and juicy.

To serve, put a single portion of hot rice, 1½ to 2 cups, into a *donburi*-type bowl. Arrange one of the cutlets so it covers half the rice. Use the fried onion-and-egg topping to cover part of the cutlet and the rest of the rice. Use all the liquid. Serve immediately. Makes 4 servings.

Source: Shizuo Tsuji. (1981) *Japanese Cooking: A Simple Art.* Tokyo: Kodansha International, 445–446.

came popular describing the precise fork and spoon to use with a course or dish.

In the Taisho period (1912–1926), the Japanese began to create uniquely Japanese versions of adopted foodstuffs, as with the Japanese versions of British versions of Indian curries *(kare raisu)*. Pork dishes like *tonkatsu*, using the Portuguese method of deep frying the meat and serving it with shredded cabbage salad, became ordinary urban restaurant food, as did *korokke* (croquettes), torpedo-shaped fried mixtures of potato, chicken, and other foods, derived from French and other European dishes.

Food technology also changed since the beginning of the Meiji period. Industrialization involved changes

FRIED *FUGU* WITH POTATO SALAD

Oddly enough, the potentially poisonous effects of *fugu*—the ovaries and liver are toxic and require removal by a licensed chef before the fish can be prepared—make it a rare delicacy. This recipe allows you to substitute other fish, chicken, or pork for *fugu*, which can cost up to $200 when served in a fine restaurant in Japan.

Thinly sliced *fugu* (or any other white fish, chicken, or pork)
Thinly sliced potatoes
Watercress
Red pepper or soy sauce

Fry *fugu* slices. In place of *fugu*, you can use any white fish, chicken, or pork.

Slice potatoes very thinly and place in water. Take potatoes out of water and spread on a plate. Place *fugu* on top, and decorate with cress. Season lightly with red pepper. If you prefer, serve with Chinese-style dressing or soy sauce.

Source: Sake Bar. Retrieved 15 Mach 2002 from: http://www.sakebar.net/special/foods/food5.html

in household technology, as well as changes in agricultural and food processing technologies. Refrigeration in food locations, as well as in transport vehicles for fresh foods, meant a greater distribution of fresh foodstuffs and better preservation without salting, pickling, drying, and fermenting. In the post–World War II era, more people had refrigerators at home, allowing the purchase of foods for several days' use, and daily shopping was no longer necessary. Home ovens also began to appear after World War II, but only became popular after 1970. Other domestic equipment began to appear such as electric mixers, toasters, and later, food processors have become popular as well.

Globalization produced new influences on the daily diet of most Japanese people. Fresh and frozen seafood and produce can be transported to Japan from anywhere in the world within twenty-four hours. In the early twenty-first century, Japan became the buyer of about 55 percent of the tuna caught in the world. At dockside in many small harbors along the Maine Coast, lobster buyers from Japan are ready to purchase catches as they come in, and local fishermen know the rigid specifications they must adhere to if the lobsters and fish they catch are to be acceptable to Japanese buyers.

Conversely, foods from Japan also have penetrated the foreign markets, and sushi is eaten in every major city in the world by people who have never been to Japan, but who now know words like *maguro*, *toro*, *uni*, and *unagi*. Instant ramen is recognizable in most of the world too, though it is not seen as a Japanese product. In fact, it is a modern version of a Chinese food that was thoroughly assimilated in Japan and then sold as a convenience food everywhere.

Fast foods and family restaurants are everywhere in Japan. There were local fast food places in Japan before the advent of hamburgers, fried chicken, and donuts, but these tended to be unique operations, run by a family who lived above the shop and catered to a local clientele that might drop by after work to pick up prepared food such as yakitori, sushi, and soba.

The extraordinary period of economic boom demonstrated the full diversification and spread of the Japanese diet, as restaurants of high quality prospered and food trends became more elaborate. Eating as entertainment of clients, family, and friends became expensive propositions, and meals of delicacies such as *fugu* (the poisonous blowfish that requires preparation by a licensed chef) could cost as much as $300 per person. Indeed, single cups of coffee at one Ginza coffee shop could cost that much—because of the pure gold leaf that was served in them.

The bursting of the bubble economy did not slow development of new food trends. In the 1990s, restaurant eating continued to be popular, although the business expense account for dining significantly diminished. Consumers continued to explore new cuisines and ethnic restaurants became popular. The leading new cuisine in the early twentieth century has been Italian, but other trends include Thai, Vietnamese, African, Indian, and Sri Lankan foods, American regional cuisine, and refinements of regional French and Spanish dishes. There is almost no food that cannot be obtained in Japan. Food-related television programs such as the hit show "Ryori no Tetsujin" (Iron Chef) became popular in the 1990s, along with food and cooking-related magazines. These included not only women's magazines, but also magazines for men, young people, and the elderly, who have joined women in taking cooking classes. Food tourism also has become a prominent travel industry, with small groups of connoisseurs visiting vineyards, restaurants, food-preparation establishments, and cooking schools all over the world.

Merry Isaacs White

Further Reading
Ekuan Kenji. (1999) *The Aesthetics of the Japanese Lunchbox*. Cambridge, MA: MIT Press.
Field, George. (1989) *The Japanese Market Culture*. Tokyo: Kodansha International.
Kumakura Isao. (2000) "Table Manner Then and Now." *Japan Echo* (February): 58–62.
———."Tea and Japan's Culinary Revolution." *Japan Echo* (April): 39–43.
Seligman, Lucy. (1994) "The History of Japanese Cuisine." *Japan Quarterly* (April–June): 165–179.
Tamura Shinpachiro, and Kishi Asako. (1999) "The Impact of Technology on the Japanese Diet." *Japan Echo* (December): 51–56.
Tsuji Shizuo. (1980) *Japanese Cooking, A Simple Art*. Tokyo: Kodansha International.

CUISINE—KOREA As was the case with other aspects of Korean culture, Korean cuisine developed under the strong influence of its powerful neighbor, China. Rice and fermented soybean products (soy sauce, soybean paste, and soybean curd, or tofu) occupy a prominent place in the diet of the Korean people. The use of chopsticks is another indicator of Chinese influence. The emphasis on five elements in Korean cuisine, for example, five flavors (salt, sweet, sour, hot, bitter) and five colors (red, green, yellow, white, black) has Chinese origins as well.

Rice and Meat

The technology of rice cultivation was brought to the northern parts of the Korean peninsula from China probably late in the second millennium BCE, but rice became a staple of the Korean diet only in the Shilla period (668–935). Earlier staples had been buckwheat, millet, and barley. Before the late twentieth century, furthermore, rice was not the staple for everyone, but was rather a symbol of wealth. The old phrase "White rice with meat soup," for example, connotes the good life, while tacitly acknowledging that not everyone could afford either rice or meat.

Buddhist influences in Korea did not have much impact on meat eating. (According to Buddhist principles, Buddhists should be vegetarians, although nowadays this is not always the case. Buddhism forbids the eating of animal flesh, which is closely connected to killing

SPICY PORK STIR-FRY (*JAE YOOK BOKUM*)

This hefty Korean side dish goes well with kimchi.

20 oz. thin cut pork meat
1 onion
½ carrot
2 thick green onions
3 smaller green onions
2 tbs. red bean paste
1 tbs. ground red pepper
2 tbs. soy sauce
3 tbs. sugar
2 tbs. chopped green onion
1 tbs. chopped garlic
1 tbs. ginger juice (or ginger powder)
2 tbs. rice wine
1 tbs. sesame oil
ground black pepper
oil

Pork meat should be as thin as possible, about 1 inch. Use meat tenderizer and lightly beat the meat. Cut onion and carrot into thin strips and cut green onions diagonally. In a large bowl, mix red bean paste, red pepper, soy sauce, sugar, chopped green onion, chopped garlic, ginger juice, rice wine, sesame oil, and black pepper. If your pork meat is too big, cut them the way you want.

Marinate pork meat and vegetables with the seasoning mixture for about 30 minutes. Coat a large skillet with oil, and stir fry meat and vegetables until meat is completely cooked. Serve over rice.

Source: Julia's Cook Korean Site. Retrieved 15 March 2002, from: http://www.geocities.com/ypmljulia/images/Stir-Fry/spicy_pork_stirfry.htm.

a living organism; some vegetarians exclude milk and eggs as well.) Beef, pork, lamb, chicken, and various types of game were regularly consumed by the Korean upper classes. Still, before the economic growth of the 1970s, for common people in Korea, the eating of meat was a luxury. Farmers, who formed the majority of the Korean population, rarely ate meat apart from the three days in summer when dog stew was served and a special day in winter when sparrows, wild boar, or wild rabbit was prepared. In both cases, the eating of meat, which was not part of the daily fare, was intended to strengthen physical resistance against extreme weather conditions.

Fermented and Pickled Products

The techniques of wine making and *chang* (a semiliquid predecessor of soy sauce and soybean paste) making were also introduced from China and by the seventh century were already highly advanced. This was also the time when fermented seafood *(chotkal)* developed, along with vegetables preserved in salt. The latter eventually evolved into kimchi—the spicy pickled cabbage that is nowadays a symbol of Korea and Korean culture.

Kimchi is considered to be quintessentially Korean by Koreans and foreigners alike. Yet, in the form we know it today, it matured only a hundred years ago, after chili pepper and *chotkal* were added to the fermentation process. The addition of chili pepper took place in the mid-eighteenth century and gave kimchi its characteristic red color and pungent taste. *Chotkal*, which has been included in the pickling from the late nineteenth century onward, not only enriched the taste of kimchi, but also increased its regional diversity. While at the end of the seventeenth century only eleven types of kimchi were classified, the regional varieties of *chotkal* (some regions use shellfish, others anchovies or other fish), which is now one of kimchi's vital ingredients, contributed to the development of several hundred varieties of kimchi. The vegetables that are pickled have also changed. Gourd melon and cucumber have been used since ancient times, followed by eggplant and Chinese radish. The Chinese cabbage that is most commonly used for making the popular *paech'u* kimchi was introduced only about a hundred years ago.

Chili pepper was brought to Korea at the end of the sixteenth century, most probably via Japan. It began to be widely cultivated a century later and by the twentieth century had become an integral part of Korean cuisine. In addition to being an indispensable component in kimchi, chili pepper contributes to the flavoring of the majority of Korean dishes through chili pepper powder and chili pepper paste *(koch'u-jang)*. Both are not only used extensively in the kitchen, but often appear as a relish at the table.

Street vendors prepare a batch of kimchi on a sidewalk in Kyoonggi-do, South Korea. (MICHAEL FREEMAN/CORBIS)

KIMCHI

This powerful smelling, fiery dish provides much of the vegetable content of Korean cuisine. Most recipes require at least a week of fermentation for the lactic acids to break down the cabbage or radish, but this recipe only needs about a day. Kimchi may be a bit of an acquired taste for some, but its enormous nutritional content and purported anticancer properties make it a good addition to any diet, even if you don't eat the half pound a day the average Korean does.

1 lb. Napa or Peking cabbage
½ tbsp. salt
1 tbsp. chopped spring onions
½ tbsp. minced ginger
½ tbsp. minced garlic
½ tbsp. chili flakes
¼ cup light soy sauce
¼ cup white vinegar
¾ tsp. sugar
sesame oil

Coarsely chop the cabbage and place in a glass dish (metallic dishes can discolor and contaminate the kimchi). Sprinkle the cabbage with salt and let stand for 3–4 hours, or until the cabbage is thoroughly wilted (the high salt content breaks down the cell walls of the cabbage and makes it easier for the bacteria to digest). Remove the cabbage from the brine and squeeze out the excess liquid, and then add the next 7 ingredients. Transfer the mixture to sterilized jars to ferment, seal, and leave in a cool place for at least 24 hours. The kimchi should keep for a few weeks in the refrigerator, but will be best if eaten within a few days. Sprinkle the kimchi with sesame oil before serving. Yields 1 pound.

Source: Jacki Passmore. (1991) *Asian Food & Cooking*. Singapore: Kyodo Printing, 151.

The Typical Korean Meal

Throughout the ages, Korean cuisine developed two distinct types of cooking: home cooking of the common people, matured within the family and the province of the housewife, and the more refined cuisine of the royal court, with its intricate cooking methods and elegant presentation. With the economic and social modernization that took place during the twentieth century, the distinction between the two became increasingly blurred. The twentieth century was also the time of Westernization of Korean cuisine. This process was initiated during the Japanese occupation (1910–1945), when Western food and drink, such as bread, confectionery, and beer, became popular in Korean cities, and a Western-style food processing industry in Korea began. Some Japanese food items were also adopted into Korean cuisine at that time, such as *tosirak* (the assorted lunch box) and sushi rolled in sheets of seaweed, which was popular in Korea under the name of *kimbap*.

A contemporary Korean meal is structured around plain boiled rice, accompanied by soup *(kuk)* and side dishes *(panch'an)*. The number of side dishes varies, from three at ordinary meals to as many as twelve at more elaborate occasions. Stews *(tchigae)* and greens (blanched or sautéed and then mixed with a dressing) constitute the majority of *panch'an*. A variety of seafood and a wide selection of vegetables, along with beef, pork, and chicken, are the major foodstuffs. Seaweed is also used, but less extensively than in Japan. Chili pepper, soy sauce, soybean paste *(toenjang)*, sesame oil, garlic, and green onions in various combinations give Korean dishes their characteristic flavor.

Eating Utensils and Eating Habits

A spoon and metal chopsticks are used while eating. Rice, soup, and other liquids are eaten with the former, side dishes generally with the latter. Soup and rice are served in individual bowls, but side dishes can often be shared by more than one diner. Nowadays, bowls are usually made of stoneware, steel, or plastic, but for special occasions white porcelain is used. In the past, the tableware of the upper classes changed depending on the season: brass bowls were used in the winter and white porcelain ones in the summer. It is considered inelegant to lift bowls from the table (contrary to the rest of East Asia, where it is customary to lift bowls up to the mouth).

The majority of eating-out facilities in Korea have two dining areas: one with Western-style tables and chairs and one with an elevated floor where customers, seated on cushions, dine at low tables. Similarly, most Korean households use Western-style tables with chairs on a daily basis (with the table usually in the kitchen) but share meals seated on cushions on the floor, at a low table with short legs, when guests are entertained. The most traditional dining device is a small table designed for one or two persons. In upper-class households, such tables were once laid in the kitchen and then carried to different parts of the house where family members dined, divided according to age, gender, and position.

Fast Food

In recent decades, dairy products, confectionery, and a variety of Western-style dishes that are available at restaurants and fast-food outlets have become increasingly important items in the diet of the Korean population. Various noodles *(kuksu)* and stuffed dumplings *(mandu)* are popular and quick lunch dishes. Noodles are usually served in soupy liquids; stuffed dumplings are steamed, fried, or simmered in soups *(manduguk).*

Although Korean family meals still remain relatively uncontaminated, the share of commercially prepared foods is rising, as opposed to the pattern of home processing that prevailed before the 1970s. It may be surmised that further changes will take place in the decades to come. However, change rather than stability characterizes Korean cuisine, as any other.

Katarzyna J. Cwiertka

Further Reading

Bak, Sangmee. (1997) "McDonald's in Seoul: Food Choices, Identity, and Nationalism." In *Golden Arches East: McDonald's in East Asia,* edited by James L. Watson. Stanford, CA: Stanford University Press, 136–160.

Kim, Joungwon, ed. (1997) *Korean Cultural Heritage.* Vol. 4, *Traditional Lifestyles.* Seoul: Korea Foundation.

Korean Overseas Information Service. (1997) *Korean Cultural Heritage.* Seoul: Korean Overseas Information Service.

Pemberton, Robert W. (2002) "Wild-Gathered Foods as Countercurrents to Dietary Globalisation in South Korea." In *Asian Food: The Global and the Local,* edited by Katarzyna Cwiertka with Boudewijn Walraven. Honolulu, HI: University of Hawaii Press, 76–94.

Walraven, Boudewijn C. A. (2002) "Bardot Soup and Confucians' Meat: Food and Korean Identity in Global Context." In *Asian Food: The Global and the Local,* edited by Katarzyna Cwiertka with Boudewijn Walraven. Honolulu, HI: University of Hawaii Press, 95–115.

CUISINE—MALAYSIA

Malaysian cuisine reflects the rich multicultural heritage of the nation. When the port sultanate of Malacca (1400–1511) was founded, it attracted traders from both the East and West. Later culinary traditions were brought by Portuguese (1511–1641), Dutch (1641–1876), and English (1876–1957) colonists, as well as merchants from China, India, Saudi Arabia, and the Indonesian archipelago.

The dietary staples of rice and noodles reflect in part geography and native plant life, while the spice trade left an indelible impression on present-day tastes. The cuisines of Malaysia's three main ethnic groups, the Malays, Chinese, and Indians, form the core of Malaysian cuisine.

Various manifestations of rice dishes abound, and accompanying dishes are highly spiced in traditional Malay cuisine. Coconut cream features prominently. Malay food is ever evolving as old recipes for curries, *sambal*s (spicy chili-pepper-based paste), and chutneys (spicy fruit- or vegetable-based paste) reappear. The best-known forms of Malay cuisine are *satay,* meat kebabs served with a spicy peanut sauce, cucumbers, onions, and rice cooked in coconut fronds; and *nasi lemak,* rice cooked in coconut cream and served with various condiments.

Malaysian Chinese cuisine can be categorized as Cantonese, Hainanese, Hakka, or Hokkien. Again,

A Malaysian steamed fish dish served in Penang in 2001. (MACDUFF EVERTON/CORBIS)

SOTO AYAM (CHICKEN SOUP)

Chicken soup is a Malaysian classic. This particular recipes makes heavy use of some of the Malaysia's more Indian culinary influences, such as cumin, turmeric, and fennel and stirs it up into something uniquely Malaysian.

1 packet compressed rice (or noodles)
4 cloves
1 stick cinnamon
several tbsp. ghee (unsalted butter may be substituted)
2 liters chicken stock (either from bones or cubes)
pandan leaves (also known as screw pine leaves)
1 chicken cut into big pieces
salt
MSG
bean sprouts

Grind the following:
10 shallots or 1 red onion
½ inch ginger
3 cloves garlic
1 tsp. fennel seeds
1 tsp. cumin seeds
1 tbs. coriander seeds
1 tsp. black pepper
3 candlenuts (Be sure to cook them well as they are toxic when raw. Macadamia nuts may be substituted.)
½ tsps turmeric powder

Boil compressed rice packet in water till cooked, take out and leave to cool.

Fry ground ingredients, cloves, and cinnamon in a little ghee till fragrant, add stock, pandan, and chicken. Cook till chicken is done. Remove chicken and shred. Strain soup, season with salt and MSG. (Reduce the stock if necessary)

To serve, pour hot soup over rice, bean sprouts, and chicken in a large bowl.

Source: Thian's Mom. Retrieved 15 March 2002, from: http://www.makantime.com

rice and noodles are staples in the offerings of one-dish meals. Seafood and vegetables as well as meats are served with rice, and noodles are prepared in many different ways. Notables include hawker fare from the northern island-state of Penang and Cantonese offerings in the Klang Valley situated in the state of Selangor, and the city of Ipoh in the state of Perak.

Indian food, contrary to popular belief, is not always spicy. Vegetarian offerings are plentiful in Malaysian Indian cuisine, and the most popular dishes include rice with various curries served on a section of banana leaf, in south-Indian style. Indian-style breads are numerous, among them *roti canai* (local name for *paratha*, a crispy bread with several thin layers), chapati (a thicker whole-wheat bread), nan (a thick bread of northern Indian origin), and *thosai* (a thin pancake made from the paste of ground lentils). Styles of preparations of accompanying dishes differ according to India's various regions and states, and there are distinctions between Indian Muslim and South Indian cuisines.

Overall, with constant exposure to cuisine from around the world, Malaysia's cuisine goes through a continual process of metamorphosis. The rise in "self-consciousness" about Malaysian cuisine also plays a large role in its evolution, exemplified by the plethora of Malaysian cookbooks and the mushrooming of Malaysian restaurants in Western cities during the last decade.

Mark Stephan Felix

Further Reading

Hutton, Wendy, ed. (1995) *The Food of Malaysia: Authentic Recipes from the Crossroads of Asia.* Intro. by Wendy Hutton. Singapore: Periplus Editions; Watsonville, CA: Crossing Press.

Leinbach, Thomas R., and Richard Ulack. (2000) *South East Asia Diversity and Development.* Upper Saddle River, NJ: Prentice-Hall.

Malaysian Festival Cuisine. (1995) Kuala Lumpur, Malaysia: Berita.

Marks, Copeland. (1997) *The Exotic Kitchens of Malaysia.* New York: Donald I. Fine Books.

Traditional Malaysian Cuisine. 1983) Kuala Lumpur, Malaysia: Berita.

CUISINE—MONGOLIA Traditional Mongolian foods have been and remain whatever the Mongols can obtain from their flocks (above all, milk, usually consumed fermented; more rarely, meat, generally boiled) and by hunting or gathering (or today, by importing). In general, these foods are monotonous, and access is highly seasonal and uneven. The Mongols also eat a number of bread foods when they can get access to flour. These foods are often in forms borrowed from a larger Eurasian world, e.g., the varieties of *boov* (from the Chinese *baozi*, meaning bread or bread food) that range from pastry to steamed dumplings

A woman cooking in a large piot in her yurt in Hovd Province, Mongolia, in 1996. (STEPHEN G. DONALDSON PHOTOGRAPHY)

HORSHOOR

Mutton and beef should taste just fine in this traditional Mongolian recipe, since goat, camel, and horse tend to be a little stringy—not to mention being difficult to find in supermarkets.

2 lbs. meat (mutton or beef; camel, horse, or goat for the true Mongolian dish)
chopped cabbage and onion
vegetable oil
water
3 cloves minced garlic
1 tsp. salt
2 cups flour

Partially fry meat, vegetables, and garlic and set them aside. Make a pastry dough of flour, the salt, and enough water to make a pie-like dough. Mix the pastry ingredients together and knead until well blended. Let the dough sit for 10 minutes, roll out into little circles and fill with the meat mixture. Either place another circle atop the first and seal the edges or bring the sides together and pinch closed.

Fry the *horshoor* in about an inch of oil on medium-high until golden brown.

Source: Chicago Area Peace Corps Association Newsletter. Retrieved 15 March 2002, from: http://www.capca.org.

MONGOLIAN BEEF

A slightly Westernized version of Mongolian beef, this fairly easy recipe evokes notes reminiscent of true nomadic Mongolian cuisine.

4 cups peanut oil
15 green onion tops
1 tbs. minced ginger
2 lbs. flank or sirloin steak
1½ tbs. water chestnut flour
2 egg whites
cornstarch paste

½ tsp. salt
1 tsp. chili paste with garlic
¼ cup chicken stock
2 tbs. soy sauce
¼ tsp. sugar
1½ tbs. of dry sherry

Cut tops of green onions into 2-inch-long pieces. Combine sauce ingredients (at right) in small bowl and stir thoroughly. Cut steak across the grain into thin slices, about ½-inch deep by 2-inch long. In a large bowl, combine egg whites, salt, and water chestnut flour. Beat with chopstick until frothy. Add steak and use fingers to coat each slice.

In a wok, heat oil to moderately hot. Fry meat in small batches; drop in 1 slice at a time to avoid sticking. Cook until lightly brown, about 1 minute. Drain on a paper bag.

Next, remove all but 2 tablespoons of oil from wok. With wok at medium heat, quickly stir-fry green onions and ginger for about 20 seconds. Add sauce; bring to boil on high heat while stirring. Add beef all at once, and toss with sauce until beef is hot and coated. Push beef out of sauce, dribble in cornstarch paste to lightly thicken. Recombine. Serves 4.

Source: Food Down Under. Retrieved 15 March 2002, from: http://fooddownunder.com/cgi-bin/recipe.cgi?r=34250.

similar to those eaten in China. Mongols also directly use grain, ground or semiground, in such dishes as *tsampa* (buttered grain). Tea is now ubiquitous, most popularly as *suutei tsay* (Mongolian tea), made by long boiling of compressed bricks of tea in milk, with various additives, including butter or cream. Elites living a more completely sedentary life have often assimilated the foods of neighboring Russians and Chinese. In Inner Mongolia, for example, urban Mongols and the best-educated often serve foods that are more North Chinese than Mongolian, strictly speaking, but these North Chinese foods themselves have been heavily assimilated from central Eurasia by centuries of contact.

Mongolian cuisine was not always so dull as this description implies; the Mongols were once briefly arbiters of international taste, as is evidenced by the rich cuisine of the *Yinshan zhengyao* (Proper and Essential Things for the Emperor's Food and Drink), presented to the Mongolian court in China in 1330 by its author, the Sino-Uighur dietary physician Hu Sihui. In this work, whose recipes for traditional foods run the gamut from roast wolf to a Kashmiri curry eaten with a fennel yeasted bread, there is an underlying foundation of *shulen* (banquet soups). These are exquisite blends of lamb, spices, and ingredients from one end of Asia to the other, melded in an attempt to create a cuisine that has a little something for everyone but is, at the same time, firmly based in a Mongolian love of boiling.

Paul D. Buell

Further Reading

Buell, Paul D. (1990) "Pleasing the Palate of the Qan: Changing Foodways of the Imperial Mongols." *Mongolian Studies*, 13: 57–81.

———, and Eugene N. Anderson. (2000) *A Soup for the Qan: Chinese Dietary Medicine of the Mongol Era as Seen in Hu Szu-hui's Yin-shan Cheng-yao*. Appendix by Charles Perry. London: Kegan Paul International.

CUISINE—PHILIPPINES The cuisine of the Philippines reflects its complex history of colonialism and its geographic location. Beginning in 1521, three hundred years of Spanish colonization were followed by fifty years of American rule. These events have left their indelible marks on the foodways of the Philippines, making it one of the "centers for gastronomic change" (Sokolov 1991, 14–25). Combined with these influences is a history of commerce with Chinese and Malay neighbors, and the result is a dynamic cuisine where no one dish can properly represent the country. *Sinigang*, a broth of fish or shrimp paired with vegetables and flavored with tamarind, guava, or citrus fruits, may be the most indigenous dish, which best symbolizes the sour-salty combination preferred by Filipinos. *Adobo*, made with chicken or pork cooked in vinegar and garlic, originates in Mexican-Spanish influences, while *pancit* (noodles crowned with meat, vegetables, or local ingredients) and *lumpia*, a spring roll fried or served fresh, derive from Chinese cuisine.

Lunchtime at a Jollibee fast-food restaurant in Manila in April 2000. The company controls 46 percent of the fast-food business in the Philippines. (REUTERS NEWMEDIA INC./CORBIS)

Composed of 7,000 islands, the Philippines is surrounded by the sea. Fresh seafood is a must, especially in *kinilaw*, where fresh fish is marinated in vinegar and immediately eaten. Fish and a jar of palm wine were the first gifts to greet Magellan and his party. Today, fish served with rice is a Filipino meal boiled down to its essence. There are at least 160 words relating to rice and its prominent role as the staple grain, although in some areas corn or sweet potatoes are preferred. Beloved for its versatility, rice not only makes a meal but is used for rice cakes called *puto* as well as numerous sweets. The coconut is a close second to rice; its juice and meat are consumed fresh or used to flavor cooking, while the heart of the tree is enjoyed as a delicacy. Reliance on nature is another trademark of Filipino cuisine, seen in the use of cooking utensils that flavor food. The hollow of a bamboo pole can be made to boil rice while banana leaves steam fish or meat as well as flavor *bibingka* (rice cakes topped with sugar and native cheese).

Each province or region is known for its specialties. In Pampanga, a province reputed to harbor good cooks, cured meats are among the specialties. *Tocino* is made from thin slices of seasoned pork and served with eggs over fried rice for breakfast, or sometimes it is *longanisa*, a slightly spicy and sweet pork sausage. *Pinakbet*, a vegetable dish of bitter melon, eggplant, and *bagoong*, a popular condiment made from fermented tiny shrimp or anchovies, typifies Ilocano foodways. Down south, in Muslim Mindanao and Sulu, pork is avoided. Instead, goat, beef, and seafood cooked with coconut milk and spicy red chilies are favored.

SINIGANG SHRIMP

5–7 cups water
1 onion, sliced
2 jalapeño peppers or 2 whole chilies (optional)
long string beans, cut into bite-size pieces
1–2 taro root, peeled and sliced into chunks.
1 packet Sinigang tamarind mix (if unavailable, use a few teaspoons tamarind paste)
1 pound whole raw prawns, unshelled (fish or pork can be used)
2 tomatoes
kangkong (swamp cabbage) or substitute spinach or other leafy vegetable

Boil water with onion. Add peppers, string beans, taro root, and tamarind mix. Simmer until taro root is done. Add shrimp and tomatoes; cook for a few minutes. Add kangkong or leafy vegetable. When vegetables are barely cooked, just before serving, smash the tomatoes. Serve with hot rice and fish sauce.

Source: Margaret Magat

TINOLA (CHICKEN WITH GREEN PAPAYA)

2–4 garlic cloves
1 tbs. minced ginger
1 medium onion, sliced
1 green papaya, sliced into chunks
chicken pieces, skinless and defatted
6–7 cups water
chili pepper leaves (if unavailable, whole chilies)

In a deep pot, sauté garlic, ginger and onions. Add chicken, sauté until the outside is barely cooked. Add water and boil until chicken is tender, then add papaya and simmer. Minutes before serving, add chili leaves. Serve with hot rice and fish sauce.

Source: Margaret Magat

Fiestas and special occasions like Christmas call for rich Spanish-based dishes, such as *lechon* (roasted pig), *paella* (saffron-flavored rice seasoned with tomatoes and garlic and topped with meats and seafood), and chicken or fish *relleno* (stuffed chicken or fish), with *leche flan* (an egg custard) for dessert. For everyday meals, lower and middle classes prefer Malay- and Chinese-influenced dishes. *Merienda* is the afternoon snack, as simple as a mango or as elaborate as *puto* and *dinuguan* (pork blood stew). Favorite *pulutan* or snacks like fertilized duck eggs called *balut* are both street food as well as snacks eaten during drinking sessions, and are believed to be an aphrodisiac for men. Despite foreign influences, the liberal use of flavoring condiments like *bagoong*, chilies, crushed garlic, and vinegar can be said to indigenize Filipino cuisine, making dishes unique to that country.

Margaret C. Magat

Further Reading

Fernandez, Doreen. (1994) *Tikim: Essays on Philippine Food and Culture*. Pasig, Philippines: Anvil Publishing.

Fernandez, Doreen, and Edilberto Alegre. (1988) *Sarap: Essays on Philippine Food*. Manila, Philippines: Mr. & Mrs. Publishing.

———. (1991) *Kinilaw: A Philippine Cuisine of Freshness*. Makati, Philippines: Bookmark.

Lopez, Mellie. (1984) "A Study of Philippine Folklore." Ph.D. diss. University of California, Berkeley.

Sokolov, Raymond. (1991) *Why We Eat What We Eat: How the Encounter between the New World and the Old Changed the Way Everyone on the Planet Eats*. New York: Summit Books.

CUISINE—SOUTH ASIA

Like Europe, South Asia has a variety of sophisticated local, regional, and ethnic cuisines. The most familiar and recognizable cuisine of the subcontinent is Indian cuisine, but some of what passes for Indian food is actually Bangladeshi or Pakistani cuisine. The cuisine of each locality and ethnic group in the subcontinent was usually inspired by local ingredients, and each region boasts distinct specialties and recipes handed down from generation to generation.

However, until the Green Revolution of the 1970s, certain regions in India and Bangladesh regularly suffered from overpopulation, which, along with drought and floods, led to pronounced and repeated food scarcity. Today India is self-sufficient in food grains and suffers no major shortages, but the same is not true for all of South Asia.

Some of the distinctive culinary regions of South Asia are the Punjab area in the central Indo-Gangetic plain, including parts of Pakistan, dominated by spicy baked meats (such as tandoori chicken) and flat breads made of wheat flour; the Bengal region to the east, including Bangladesh, known for mustard-spiced fish dishes and *rossogollas* (cottage-cheese sweets); the Tamil/Kerala area in the south, including Sri Lanka, known for rice-based meals, snacks such as *idli* (steamed rice cakes), and meat and vegetables cooked in rich coconut sauces *(sambhal);* and the Kashmiri region in the Himalayas, influenced by Afghani cuisine, with meat and rice cooked Persian fashion with raisins and nuts.

The use of spices and sauces is the unifying thread of an otherwise diverse cuisine, as is the variety of unleavened flat breads made with wheat flour, rice, and ground legumes. Dairy products, such as ghee (clarified butter), buttermilk, curds (yogurt), along with dals (dried peas and beans) and vegetables, are dietary staples. Vegetables are generally fried to make curry (Tamil *kari)* or are served with gravies or in legume-based soups.

A traditional meal *(thali)* for lunch or dinner is eaten with the fingers. Originally served on a leaf, now commonly served on a stainless-steel platter, a typical meal includes several vegetable dishes, rice, puris or chapatis (fried unleavened bread), pickles, *papads* (lentil wafers), salads, dessert, and yogurt. The *thali* can be vegetarian or can include meat dishes. The meal is usually accompanied by tea, coffee, or hot water and followed by a *paan* (betel leaf and nut, eaten as a digestive).

South Asian cuisine also offers much in the way of vegetarian and nonvegetarian snack foods. These are usually savory dishes served with chutneys and pickles and eaten at any time of day.

Cooking in the subcontinent was traditionally associated with religious practices and moral beliefs. For example, India has a centuries-old tradition of cooking highly sophisticated and elaborate ritual food *(prasadam)* for sacred offerings to temple deities and for life-cycle rituals of devotees. This tradition is still alive today, and there is a vast resource of indigenous cooking knowledge and expertise in the subcontinent.

Diets and dietary restrictions in the subcontinent are closely linked to religion. India is predominantly Hindu, and while it is believed that all Hindus are vegetarian, the practice is usually confined to the Hindu upper castes; lower castes eat meat such as poultry and mutton, but no beef. Muslims of India, Pakistan, and Bangladesh eat mutton, beef, poultry, and seafood, but no pork. Christians of the subcontinent eat poultry, fish, pork, mutton, and beef on a regular basis.

Historical Influences

South Asia was a destination of spice traders from the second through fourteenth centuries, so that foreign elements inevitably seeped into the culinary culture and modified local cuisines. The major influences were the Mughals, the Portuguese, and the British.

In 1527 the Mongol emperor Zahir-ud-Din Muhammad (Babur) invaded India and established the Mughal dynasty (1526–1857). The Mughals created the "Mughlai" court cuisine, heavily influenced by Afghani and Central Asian cuisine. Spices were added to cream and butter, rice was cooked with meat, and dishes were garnished with nuts. India was also introduced to kebabs and pilafs, as well as a variety of sweets made of wheat, cream, honey, and nuts. Today Mughlai cuisine is the core of the cuisines of India, Pakistan, and Bangladesh.

The Portuguese had traded in Goa on the southwestern coast of India as early as 1510, and Portuguese rule in Goa lasted for 450 years. Portuguese traders introduced such New World crops to Goa as potatoes, tomatoes, chilies, pineapples, yams, tobacco, and guavas, transforming the cuisine of the entire subcontinent.

In 1600 the British East India Company was established under a royal charter of Queen Elizabeth I for a fifteen-year period of spice trading. That event marked the beginning of the British empire's rule, which lasted three centuries on the subcontinent. With the British came a new cuisine called Raj—a compromise between British cuisine and that of the subcontinent. Bombay duck (native dried fish) replaced kippers at the colonial British breakfast table, and Bengali breakfast foods such as kedgeree (steamed rice and pulses) were exported from the subcontinent to the British table.

Kashmiri chefs in Srinagar, India, preparing a wedding banquet in an outdoor kitchen. (EARL & NAZIMA KOWALL/CORBIS)

MASALA DOSAI

The *masala dosai* is the traditional south Indian lunch dish. The *dosai* is a large rice flour pancake often filled with the rich but refreshing spicy coconut chutney and spicy potato curry described here. *Dosai* are very versatile and can be filled with a variety of different foodstuffs, although these by far the most common.

2 cups par boiled rice
2 cups raw rice - 1 cup *urud dal* (yellow lentils)
1 tsp. fenugreek seeds

Rinse the above ingredients in water for about 2–3 hours. Then grind in a blender (with adding water in steps) into a very fine flour. Add salt and keep it aside (to get sour) for 12 hours.

Heat the pan and spread a drop of oil on it. When the pan is fully heated, take some flour and spread it on the pan into a round shape. Turn it over so that both sides are cooked well. When it is almost cooked spread a teaspoon of coconut chutney over it. Place some potato curry and roll the *dosai* on both sides and move it to a plate.

Coconut Chutney
1 cup grated coconut
2 green chilies
¼ tsp. salt
pinch of *asafetida* (garlic or onion powder may be substituted)
pinch of tamarind (lemon or lime pulp may be substituted)

To the coconut, chilis, and salt, add a pinch of tamarind and grind everything into a thick paste. Splatter with mustard seeds and *urud dal.*

Potato curry
1 lb. potatoes
3 ½ oz. onions
3 ½ oz. green peas
1 tsp. mustard seeds
1 tsp. *urud dal* (lentils)
3 small green chilies
1 twig of curry leaves
½ tsp. of salt

Boil the potatoes fully, peel and mash them. Heat some oil and add mustard seeds and urud dal. Add finely cut onions, fresh green peas and fry until the onions turn transparent. Add some fine pieces of green chillies and add the mashed potatoes, salt and fry. Add some curry leaves.

Source: India Tastes—South Indian Recipes—Masala Dosai. Retrieved 15 March, 2002, from: http://www.indiatastes.com/categories/22.html.

The British also introduced the word "curry," which people today associate with food from the subcontinent. British cooks ground spice powders to season meats and vegetables and cooked them into a kari, a stir-fried preparation with gravy. The British called the ground spices "curry powder" and took it back to Britain, where it became popular. In 1997 Britain declared curry Britain's national dish, and in a

THE COLONIAL DIET

"You ask what shops we have. None at all; the butler buys everything in the bazaar in his bill every day. One of the Court native writers translates it into English, and very queer articles they concoct together! Such as, 'one beef of rump for biled;'—'one mutton of line beef for *alamoor estoo*,' meaning *à-la-mode stew*;—'mutton for curry pups' (puffs);—'eggs for saps, snobs, tips, and pups' (chops, snipes, tipsycake, and puffs);—'medication (medicine) for ducks;'—and at the end 'ghirand totell' (grand total, and 'howl balance')."

Source: Julia C. Maitland. (1846) *Letters from Madras during the Years 1836–39*. London: Wm. Clowes & Sons.

countrywide survey 51 percent of people claimed they were "curryaholics," a word that may soon be listed in the Oxford English dictionary.

Vegetarianism

Toward the end of the Vedic period (1500–500 BCE), the concept of vegetarianism arose in the subcontinent primarily as a reaction to the dissolute upper castes who ate meat and drank liquor. The Buddhist notion of ahimsa (nonviolence) forbade the killing of animals as food, and this idea further influenced the Hindus not to eat meat. Asoka (d. 238 or 232 BCE), the Buddhist ruler of three-fourths of the subcontinent, further contributed to the development of vegetarianism by banning meat eating in his empire. Upper castes adopted vegetarianism soon afterward, and today vegetarianism is linked with upper-caste diet and behavior. Lower castes adopted vegetarianism as part of the process of Sanskritization (emulation of higher castes). Many vegetarian dishes of contemporary South Asia, especially of India, have been exported to the West, especially for those cultivating a healthful alternative lifestyle.

Contemporary South Asian Food

Today in South Asian cities like Delhi and Dacca, multinational companies such as McDonald's, KFC, Wimpys, and Pizza Hut offer pizzas, hamburgers, fried chicken, and other American and European foods. However, the indigenous food industries on the subcontinent compete with multinational interests in anticipating the needs of South Asian consumers.

In the indigenous food industry, Indian, Pakistani, Bengali, and other regional recipes are simplified for fast production, which decreases preparation time and costs for consumers. Food products include those for immediate consumption, as well as prepared foods such as snacks, spice powders, lentil wafers, pickles, and chutneys. Many of these prepared foods are exported to Britain and the United States for consumption by the South Asian diaspora, and today foods from various parts of the subcontinent are popular all over the globe.

Tulasi Srinivas

Further Reading

Achaya, K. T. (1994) *Indian Food: A Historical Companion*. Delhi: Oxford University Press.

Appadurai, Arjun. (1988) "How to Make a National Cuisine: Cookbooks in Contemporary India." *Society for the Comparative Study of Society and History* 4175/88/1193-0110: 2–23.

Burton, David. (1993) *The Raj at Table: A Culinary History of the British in India*. London: Faber and Faber.

Khare, R. S. (1976) *The Hindu Hearth and Home*. Durham, NC: Carolina Academic Press.

Marriott, McKim. (1968) "Caste Ranking and Food Transactions: A Matrix Analysis." In *Structure and Change in Indian Society*, edited by M. Singer and B. S. Cohn. Chicago: Aldine.

Srinivas, M. N. (1972) *Social Change in Modern India*. New Delhi: Orient Longman.

Srinivas, Tulasi. (2002) "A Tryst with Destiny: Cultural Globalization in India." In *Many Globalizations*, edited by Peter L. Berger and Samuel P. Huntington. New York: Oxford University Press.

CUISINE—THAILAND Thai cuisine is defined by its balance of four flavors: spicy, salty, sweet, and sour. Preserved fish or seafood generally provides the

Bowls with an assortment of spices to make Thai curry. (MACDUFF EVERTON/CORBIS)

LAAP KAI (MINCED CHICKEN SALAD)

2 chicken breasts (approximately 1 pound)
2 cloves garlic, minced
2 ½ tbs. fish sauce
3 tbs. lime juice
1 tsp ground cayenne pepper
1 tbs. roasted rice powder*
2 tbs. chopped scallions, ends only
½ cup fresh mint leaves, roughly chopped
lettuce leaves
1 cucumber peeled and sliced

Cook chicken in a covered skillet over medium heat until done, about 20 minutes. Add 1–2 tablespoons of water to prevent chicken from sticking to the pan while cooking if needed. Let the chicken cool and then chop it by hand or in a food processor into small chunks.

Transfer the meat into a mixing bowl. Add garlic, fish sauce, and 2 tablespoons of lime juice and mix well. Add more lime juice according to taste. Mix in ground pepper and rice powder, and then toss in chopped scallions and mint leaves.

Transfer mixture to serving plate lined with lettuce and arrange cucumber slices. Serve with steamed sticky rice.

*Roasted rice powder may be purchased at Asian grocery stores or made at home. Roast 1 tablespoon of uncooked sticky rice in a dry pan. When the rice granules turn brown, remove from heat and pound in a mortar and pestle.

Source: Linda McIntosh

salty flavor, while the spiciness originates from chilies and peppercorns. Palm sugar and coconut milk lend sweetness, and the sour or citrus flavor comes from sources such as lemon grass, kaffir lime, and tamarind. Indian, Chinese, and Western cooking has influenced Thai cuisine, which also shares similarities with the cuisine of Thailand's neighboring countries—Malaysia, Myanmar (Burma), Laos, and Cambodia. Despite these external influences, Thai cuisine is distinguished by its combination of fresh ingredients and its relatively short cooking time.

The foundation of Thai food is rice. Jasmine rice is the staple in central Thailand, while people living in the north and northeast prefer a glutinous or sticky rice. Various Thai noodle dishes were adopted from the Chinese. Abundant rivers and coastal areas make fish and seafood, either fresh or in a preserved form such as fish sauce, shrimp paste, or fermented fish, another staple of Thai diets.

Thailand's four regions offer distinct cuisines. Central Thai food, the regional cuisine most commonly found in Thai restaurants, is known for its coconut-based curries. The people of north and northeast Thailand eat sticky rice and *laap*, a salad dish made from minced raw or cooked meat, including that of water buffalo and catfish, flavored with garlic, chilies, lime juice, and mint. In the northeast, Thailand's poorest region, exotic foods such as ant eggs are frequently eaten. Southern Thai cuisine, heavily influenced by Malay and Indian cooking, uses many spices. The majority of the south's population is Muslim and of Malay descent, so the influence from these countries comes naturally. Seafood is a common dish in the south, where the primary occupation is fishing.

KHAO NIEO MAMUANG (MANGO AND STICKY RICE)

8 oz. (1 cup) sticky rice
6 oz. coconut milk
1½ tbs. sugar
pinch of salt
2 ripe mangoes
4 tbs. coconut cream

Soak sticky rice in water for at least 4 hours. Drain rice and steam for 20 minutes or until tender, stirring occasionally while cooking. Transfer steamed rice to a bowl.

In a small mixing bowl, combine coconut milk, sugar, and salt. Combine the coconut milk mixture with the rice. Mix well and let rice sit for 30 minutes or until the milk mixture is absorbed.

Peel and slice the mangoes. Slice the two halves of the mango alongside its pit. Slice each half into diagonal, ½-inch-wide slices.

To serve, divide the rice and mango slices among four plates. Dribble 1 tablespoon of coconut cream onto the rice on each plate.

Source: Linda McIntosh

A typical Thai meal consists of several dishes, including a soup, a curry, a fried dish, and a spicy salad accompanied by rice. A fork and spoon are the usual Thai eating utensils; chopsticks are reserved for noodles. Fresh fruit to cleanse the palate typically follows the meal. Sweets are generally eaten as snacks throughout the day. Traditional Thai sweets include sweetened sticky rice with mango or durian and a custard called *sangkhaya*. Thai cuisine has received international attention as Thai restaurants have spread across North America and Europe. Thai ingredients are now found on the shelves of Western supermarkets. Thai cuisine is likewise thriving in its homeland with endless food stalls, markets, and restaurants, despite the popularity of foreign—especially Western "fast food"—restaurants.

Linda McIntosh

Further Reading

Bhumichitr, Vatcharin. (1998) *Vatch's Thai Cookbook*. London: Pavilion.

Cummings, Joe. (2000) *World Food: Thailand*. Victoria, Australia: Lonely Planet.

CUISINE—TURKEY

Turkey, the unique Muslim Republic with a democratic and secular regime, located in the eastern Mediterranean where it bridges Europe and Asia, has always been a bridge between European and Middle Eastern cultures with its historic and contemporary customs and traditional cuisine.

The richness and diversity of Turkish cuisine is a result of the Ottoman empire (453–1922), which reigned for centuries over a varied geography and landscape combining characteristics of Europe, Africa, and Asia, and which interacted with different cultures throughout the centuries. Thus Turkish cuisine has many specialties and variations, and it is understandable that people from Greece or Lebanon can claim that moussaka, for instance, is a Greek or Lebanese dish.

Meals at Home and in Restaurants

Turkish cuisine generally consists of soups; salads; sauced dishes prepared with cereals, vegetables, and meat; pastries with meat and vegetable fillings; cold vegetable dishes cooked in olive oil; and flour- and semolina-based desserts.

A typical Turkish breakfast consists of white cheese, fresh tomatoes, black or green olives or both, honey and jam, boiled eggs, fresh bread from the bakery, and tea. New healthy eating habits imported from Europe and the United States, such as consuming cereals and fruits, are welcomed by Turkish families. However, consumption of meat products such as ham or sausage is still not popular.

Families and working people who lack the time to get together tend to skip lunch. However, in restaurants, the lunch served includes soup, seasoned lamb or chicken with vegetables, a rice- or bulgur- (cracked and boiled wheat) pilaf dish, and salad. Milk desserts are preferred for lunch.

Most Turkish dinners start with appetizers called meze. Mezes are a category of food, consumed in small quantities, at the start of a meal and traditionally intended to accompany alcoholic drinks, especially raki, an anise-flavored liqueur. White-bean salad, smoked eggplant puree, green salads, pickles, feta cheese, fresh vegetables drenched in yogurt sauce and garlic, pastrami (dried tenderloin or sirloin), *tarama* (fish puree), humus (chickpea puree), and fava (broad-bean puree) are served as mezes. The main course that follows is grilled or fried fish or meat with fried tomatoes, green pepper, and sautéed potatoes. Fruits and desserts are served before enjoying Turkish coffee.

SHISH KEBABS

A classic Turkish dish, shish kebabs are basically meats on a stick. These barbecued meats are gently marinated and, while cooking, infuse with flavors from the peppers and onions.

Marinade

1 whole squeezed lemon
1 tsp. coarse sea salt
6 cloves garlic
1 tsp. mint
1 tsp. oregano
Dash olive oil

Kebabs

1½ lbs. lamb (or beef) cut into 1½-inch pieces
button mushrooms
cherry tomatoes
yellow bell pepper cut in 2-inch pieces
red bell pepper cut into 2-inch pieces

To make the marinade, add together squeezed lemon, garlic, coarse sea salt, mint, oregano, and olive oil. Coat the lamb chunks and refrigerate for about 2 to 3 hours. Thread the meat onto one set of skewers and the vegetables on a separate set of skewers. Cook the lamb over medium-high fire until done (about 6 minutes). Cook the vegetables until slightly charred (about 8 minutes). Serve with tahini, pita, and lemon.

Source: Adapted from *Food and Wine*. Retrieved 25 March 2002, from: http://www.foodandwine.com.

Vegetables

Vegetables are consumed in large quantities. Generally they are not boiled in water or used as garniture. It is customary to cook vegetables with meat, onions, tomatoes, or tomato paste. Vegetables are also cooked in olive oil. A specialty of Turkish cuisine is the *zeytinyagli* or olive-oil course. Oil is important in Turkish cuisine: Vegetables, such as root celery, green string beans, artichokes, leeks, eggplants, or zucchini can be cooked in olive oil and served at room temperature. Vegetables such as peppers, eggplants, carrots, or zucchinis can also be fried and served with a tomato-garlic or yogurt-garlic sauce.

Onions and tomatoes are the main ingredients of almost all dishes. Chopped onions fried in oil and fresh tomatoes (or tomato paste) are added to dishes and are also chopped into most salads.

"Dolma" is the term for stuffed vegetables. There are two kinds of dolmas: those filled with ground meat and eaten with a yogurt sauce, and those with seasoned rice mix and cooked in olive oil. The former is a frequent main-course dish. Any vegetable that can be filled with or wrapped around these mixes can be used to prepare dolma: zucchini, pepper, tomato, cabbage, grape leaf, and eggplant are examples of such vegetables. Eggplant (or aubergine) has a special place in Turkish cuisine.

Meat

Sheep, lamb, beef, and veal meat are generally consumed with vegetables in dishes served hot at home. However the real taste and flavor of meat can be best appreciated by tasting kebabs at restaurants. Kebab is widespread in many Mid-Eastern countries, but is originally Turkish. Shish kebab is grilled cubes of skewered lamb or veal. *Doner* kebab is made by stacking layers of ground meat and sliced leg of lamb on a large upright skewer, which is slowly rotated in front of a vertical charcoal fire. As the outer layer of the meat is roasted, thin slices can be cut and served with rice pilaf. Southern and southeastern cities of Turkey are famous for the variety of their kebabs.

Pilaf

Pilaf is another specialty of Turkish cuisine. The most common types are cracked-wheat pilaf and rice pilaf. Pilaf is made of rice boiled in beef stock with cubed onions and tomatoes and green peppers

ALMOND BAKLAVA

This Turkish delight is sticky, crisp, and rich, yet surprisingly easy to make. Be warned, though, that baklava is very rich and dense, so unprepared diners may need a jolt of mud-thick Turkish coffee to keep them from napping after eating it.

Pastry
¼ cup sugar
2 tsp. cinnamon
4 cups almond slivers
filo dough
1¼ cups butter, melted

Syrup
4 cups sugar
3 cups water
½ cup honey
1 stick cinnamon
6 whole cloves

Mix together ¼ cup of sugar, the cinnamon, and the almond slivers. On a medium-size buttered pan lay out one of the sheets of filo dough, butter it, and layer on another five or six buttered sheets of filo. Try and keep the dough covered for as long as possible, as the paper-thin pastry tends to dry out.

Lay out another sheet of filo dough, without buttering it this time. Spread on some of the almond mix, enough to cover it evenly, about a sixteenth of an inch. Keep doing almond layers until all the mix is gone.

Fold in the dough that hangs from the side of the pan. Some of the edges will be dry, so just cut them and discard them. Continue layering the remainder of the filo dough (about 5 sheets), making sure to butter each one and fold in the edges before adding the next one. Butter the top sheet very well, and sprinkle a little bit of water on it so the top doesn't burn in the oven.

Bake at 375° for about 20 minutes or until golden. Remove from oven, slice into small rectangles and serve dripping with syrup. To make the syrup, combine the remaining sugar, water, honey, cinnamon and, cloves in a small sauce pan and heat, stirring frequently over medium heat until the mixture is thick and syrupy. Remove cloves before serving.

Source: Botherless Baklava. Retrieved March 21, 2002, from: http://www.geocities.com/NapaValley/2267/baklava.html

sautéed in butter and usually served with vegetable and meat dishes.

Bread and Pastries

Accompanying the main dishes is a variety of bread made of wheat and corn flour. Pita, a flatbread with various toppings, *simit,* ring bread with sesame seed, and *manti* (Turkish ravioli) are some examples of breads and pastries. But the true specialty is the *borek,* a special pastry of thin sheets of homemade dough *(yufka).*The pastry sheets are layered or folded into various shapes after being filled with cheese, vegetable, meat, or other mixes, and then are baked or fried.

Spices and Seasonings

Various spices are used in Turkish cooking, the most common being red pepper, cinnamon, thyme, and cumin. Widely used seasonings are dill, mint, parsley, and garlic. Fresh or dried mint is also consumed.

Yogurt and Ayran

Yogurt, a contribution of Turkish cuisine to the world, is a popular food and a staple in the Turkish diet. Turkish chefs can cite at least hundred recipes in which yogurt is used as an ingredient or a sauce. *Ayran,* a widely consumed national nonalcoholic drink, is a diluted and salted sour yogurt, served with meals or with snacks.

Desserts and Beverages

The best-known sweets associated with Turkish cuisine are Turkish delight *(lokum)* and baklava. *Lokum* is a jelly sweet often mixed with walnuts or pistachios, cut into cubes, and rolled in powdered sugar. Baklava is the paper-thin pastry sheets that are brushed with butter and folded, layered, or rolled after being filled with ground pistachios, walnuts or heavy cream, baked, then soaked with a thick syrup.

Muhallebi, made with milk, sugar, and rice flour, is a traditional dessert in Turkish cuisine, as is halvah, made by pan-sautéing semolina and pine nuts in butter before adding sugar, milk, or water and briefly cooking until these are absorbed.

Turkish traditional drinks include Turkish coffee, preferred after meals, and Turkish tea, with its deep red color and unique taste. *Cay*, Turkish tea, is brewed over boiling water; it is served in special small, thin-walled glasses.

Among alcoholic drinks, raki is usually mixed with water at the table; in everyday language, it is called lion's milk. *Sherefe* (cheers) is a common toast.

Eating is taken seriously in Turkey. It is inconceivable for family members to eat alone, or eat and run, while others are at home. The concept of having a potluck meal at someone's house is also entirely foreign to the Turks. Despite the increasing presence of frozen and canned foods and fast-food chains in the big cities, Turkish cuisine is resisting the new habits of eating, both in domestic settings and in restaurants.

Emel Yilmaz

Further Reading

Basan, Ghillie. (1997) *Classic Turkish Cooking*. New York: St. Martin's Press.

Baysal, Ayse. (1993) *Samples from Turkish Cuisine*. Ankara, Turkey: Historical Society.

Eren, Neset. (1969) *The Art of Turkish Cooking, or Delectable Delights of Topkapi*. Garden City, NY: Doubleday.

CUISINE—VIETNAM

The most common Vietnamese word for food has the basic meaning of "cooked rice" *(com)*. Vietnamese has many words for rice, depending on whether it is husked or unhusked, cooked or uncooked, plain white rice or sticky (glutinous) rice. At most Vietnamese meals, a bowl filled with white rice sits in front of everyone present. Platters of food, sauces, and condiments are shared family style, with small helpings added on top of the rice. If enough rice is available, several bowls of steamed white rice form the foundation of almost every meal. Fish, meat, and even vegetables are used mainly as condiments to be eaten with the rice. Without adequate rice, many people feel they are hungry, even if other food is available.

When rice is scarce, people add substantial amounts of corn, manioc, yams, or sweet potatoes to their diet to make their rice supply last longer. These foods are sometimes boiled and eaten separately and sometimes mixed in with the rice. But rice is almost always preferred. With certain dishes or for ceremonial offerings, glutinous rice is preferred. There are many kinds of both regular and sticky rice, depending on whether the grain is short or long, heavy or light. Ordinary rice is also pounded into powder to make different kinds of noodles and cakes, while glutinous rice is used for certain pastries.

Meat and Fish

Most Vietnamese eat little meat; the meat eaten is mainly pork and chicken. Beef is not often eaten; it is scarce, expensive, and poor in quality. Almost all parts of slaughtered animals are eaten, including organs and intestines. Bones are used to make soup. Most people eat more fish than meat. Fish come from rice fields, ponds, rivers, lakes, streams, and the sea. People also eat meat from goats, ducks, and geese. Crab, shrimp, snail, and eel are also eaten where available. In the north, some people eat field rats and dogs, the latter dish being usually preferred by older men. A few restaurants in and around major cities and resort areas specialize in snake meat; others serve exotic game dishes.

Shrimp rolls ready for eating in Ho Chi Minh City. (CATHERINE KARNOW/CORBIS)

TET ROAST BEEF SALAD WITH SPRING ONION OIL

This special dish is one of the foods often served during Tet, the Vietnamese New Year.

Salad

1 large cucumber, peeled
1 large carrot, peeled
2 limes
½ tsp. sugar
½ tsp. crushed red pepper flakes
½ tsp. toasted sesame oil
1 clove garlic, minced
1 piece ginger, ½ inch in length, peeled and minced
½ lb. spinach, washed, trimmed, and dried
½ lb. roast beef, thinly sliced
3 tbs. crushed toasted peanuts
cilantro sprigs
fresh cracked pepper

Spring Onion Oil

¼ cup canola oil
4 large chopped green onions, including green part
¼ tsp. salt

Slice the cucumber into thin rounds. Lightly salt the rounds and leave in a colander to drain for at least 15 minutes. Slice the carrot into thin rounds and set aside. When the cucumbers have drained, squeeze out the excess water with your hands.

Cut 1 lime into wedges and set aside. In a small bowl, mix together the juice of the remaining lime, sugar, red pepper flakes, sesame oil, garlic and ginger. Toss the cucumbers and carrots with this sauce and let them sit 5 minutes.

Toss the spinach with 2 tablespoons of the spring onion oil, or amount to taste. Arrange on a platter. Pour the cucumber and carrot mixture, with the dressing, on top of the spinach. Arrange the roast beef slices around the edges of the salad. Spoon 1 to 2 tablespoons of the remaining spring onion oil (with toasted onion bits) on top of the roast beef. Serve topped with the toasted peanuts, sprigs of cilantro, fresh cracked pepper and the reserved wedges of lime on the side.

To make the spring onion oil, heat the oil in a saucepan on high until very hot. Add the onions and salt. Fry the onions until they become crisp and the edges begin to brown. Turn off the heat and let the onions continue to cook in the hot oil until they become very brown. Drizzle sparingly on salads, cooked chicken, noodles, soups, and other dishes, sprinkling a bit of the onion bits on top.

Source: Adapted from Kate's Global Kitchen. Retrieved 15 March 2002, from: http://www.globalgourmet.com/food/kgk/2000/0200/onion.html.

Sauces and Garnishes

Dipping sauces and garnishes are important parts of Vietnamese cuisine. Meat and vegetable dishes are often highly seasoned (with garlic, chili peppers, lemon grass, ginger, or any of a number of herbs) and heavily garnished with mint, basil, dill, slices of chili peppers, bean sprouts, or crushed peanuts. Most meat dishes, even whole chickens, are chopped (bones and all) into bite-size pieces that are dipped into one or another of half a dozen common dipping sauces. The most prevalent of these is a sauce made from fermented fish *(nuoc mam)*, which is also used in cooking. For dipping, the fish sauce is mixed with crushed garlic, lime juice, sugar, and chili pepper, then slightly diluted with water. It is often served in individual dipping bowls, to which chili peppers can be added to taste.

Vegetables and Fruits

Vegetables include a spinach-like green grown in water *(rau muong)* and many different kinds of beans, squash, pumpkins, cabbages, lettuce, eggplant, turnips, cucumbers, both regular and green onions, carrots, and tomatoes. These are eaten fresh, boiled, sautéed, or fried. Some are pickled, and some are dried for use in cooking. There are also many varieties of corn, yams, sweet potatoes, Western white potatoes, manioc, and other tuber crops.

Fruits are abundant, and most Vietnamese eat a lot of fruit. Common fruits include papaya, mango, orange, lime, pomelo, tangerine, watermelon, jackfruit, litchi, rambutan, custard apple, jujube, persimmon, plum, dragon fruit, milk apple, star fruit, and mangosteen. Some Vietnamese like durian very much; others, not at all.

Beverages and Soups

Most Vietnamese drink large quantities of tea, usually warm green tea with nothing added. A thermos of hot water is often kept at the ready in homes and offices for making a pot of tea or topping up a pot that has been sitting and has got cold. Many varieties of tea are available: black, green, lotus, and jasmine. Tea bags can now be found in quite a few urban homes. Most Vietnamese do not drink much coffee, and they tend to drink it very strong with a generous dollop of sweetened condensed milk in it. Limeade is popular, and vendors sell drinks of juice from crushed sugarcane in the streets.

Most Vietnamese drink alcoholic beverages only moderately and mainly at social and ritual occasions, although some men are heavy drinkers. Locally distilled rice whiskey *(ruou de)* is a common and affordable drink throughout Vietnam, and beer is very popular. Inexpensive, locally produced draft beer of variable quality is readily available in all cities and most towns. Canned and bottled beer, both imported and domestic, has recently become popular, but is expensive for many people. Western-style wine made from grapes was once largely imported and expensive, but the quality of domestic wines has been improving. A growing but still small number of Vietnamese can now afford to buy an occasional bottle of wine or champagne. Many ethnic minority groups make wine from fermented rice or sometimes from manioc. Brandy is popular among those who drink hard liquor. Some people have developed a taste for imported scotch, bourbon, or blended whiskey. Gin and vodka are less popular but are readily available in shops and stalls in major urban centers.

Soup and noodle dishes are also important parts of Vietnamese cuisine. The most popular Vietnamese soup is *pho*, which contains flat rice noodles in either beef broth or chicken broth, with small amounts of meat. Another popular soup is made with a different kind of flat rice noodle *(bun)*. Often this noodle is served in a bowl of broth containing grilled and seasoned meat *(bun cha)* or with snails *(bun oc)*. Another common soup is rice porridge *(chao)*, a rice gruel to which may be added chicken, fish, pork, shrimp, organ meat (heart, liver), or even eel. Other soups are made with Chinese wheat noodles *(mi)*, which are also sometimes served sautéed with vegetables, meat, or seafood. Most of these soups are commonly eaten in small restaurants or soup stands or purchased from sidewalk vendors. Soup is eaten at all hours of the day, as a meal or a snack. Clear, light soups *(canh)* are often served with meals both in homes and in restaurants. In cities, one can find wonton soup, eel soup, crab and asparagus soup, and many others.

Desserts

Vietnamese normally do not eat much dessert. A meal may end with tea and perhaps a little fruit. Sometimes a kind of pudding or custard *(che)* may be served. These desserts usually contain glutinous rice, soy beans, black beans, green beans, tapioca, or lotus seeds. They usually contain no milk products, but are made with plenty of sugar and one of a variety of flavorings (ginger, sesame, or others). Such dishes may be called dessert dishes, but they are commonly eaten as snacks.

Regional Specialties

There are hundreds of regional specialties, but some are common all over Vietnam. One of the best-known Vietnamese dishes is the distinctive Vietnamese version of a spring roll, known as *nem* or *cha gio*. Another dish, *chao tom*, is made by pounding shrimp, garlic, and other ingredients into a paste and wrapping the paste around a thick stick of the inner portion of a sugarcane and then grilling it. Another dish *(banh xeo)* is something between a pancake and an omelet. Ingredients include eggs, rice flour, coconut milk, green onions, beans, and bean sprouts, fried in a hot skillet.

There are hundreds of special dishes associated with a region, a city, or even a particular street. In Hanoi, a famous fish dish *(cha ca)* is associated with one small street, and shrimp cakes *(banh tom)* are sold mainly in a short strip along West Lake. Ho Chi Minh City cuisine features a sumptuous meal of "seven kinds of beef" *(thit bo bay mon)*. Hue cuisine includes many varieties of distinctive cakes and dumplings and an astonishing variety of vegetarian dishes.

In Vietnam, what people eat and how they prepare it depend on social class, region, and the seasons. In winter in the north, people eat more meat and more fried dishes, and they season the food more. In summer, people eat more fruit and vegetables and more soups and puddings. Throughout the year, people take advantage of whatever produce is fresh and at the peak of its season.

Food and the Theory of Yin and Yang

Vietnamese cuisine was influenced by the ancient East Asian model of yin and yang, the two primordial forces from which everything in the world was created. A balance between yin and yang was necessary in all things. Illness was thought to be caused by a lack of balance between yin and yang, either within a person or between a person and the environment. It was believed that diet could disrupt or restore harmony. All foods were thought to have an essential nature, to be hot, warm, cool, or cold. Hot and warm foods were yang; cool and cold foods, yin. Depending on weather, environment, and symptoms of illness, one would eat certain foods and avoid others to preserve or regain good health.

Neil Jamieson

Further Reading

Ngo, Bach, and Gloria Zimmerman. (1979) *The Classic Cuisine of Vietnam.* Hauppauge, NY: Barron's Educational Series.

Routhier, Nicole, Martin Jacobs, and Craig Claiborne. (1989) *Foods of Vietnam.* New York: Stewart, Tabori, and Chang.

Trang, Corinne, Christopher Hirsheimer, and Martin Yan. (1999) *Authentic Vietnamese Cooking: Food from a Family Table.* New York: Simon and Schuster.

CUKONG

CUKONG Derived from the Chinese word *hokkien* (master), *cukong* is a pejorative term in the Indonesian language for a clever Chinese businessman who plays a role as a middleman with connections and cooperation with those in power. The figure is not unique to Indonesia but occurs in other Southeast Asian countries as well.

The concept of the Chinese businessman as *cukong* arose from the nature of Dutch colonial policies in the eighteenth and nineteenth centuries in Indonesia. These policies estranged the Chinese minority from the rest of the population. Forbidden government jobs, the Chinese were forced into roles as traders. As traders, they established networks and developed their management skills.

A broadening of the concept of *cukong* began in 1965 when the army took over political power in Indonesia and asserted control over the country's economic resources. Lacking skills, experience, and trading networks, some army officers authorized Chinese businessmen to run the army's businesses and manage their economic interests.

These army officers believed that their collaboration with the Chinese businessmen, coupled with discriminatory laws and the weak political base of the Chinese minority in Indonesia, would maintain the army's political and economic power more effectively than it would be maintained if the officers collaborated with indigenous, or *pribumi*, businessmen. This system has developed into what is known in Indonesia today as the "*cukong* system," a web of collusion and corruption among Chinese businessmen, bureaucrats, and military officers. The *cukong* specialize in administering business affairs while the bureaucrats and military officers provide them with government funds, facilities, and security protection.

Andi Achdian

Further Reading

Mackie, J. A. C., ed. (1976) *The Chinese in Indonesia.* Singapore: Heineman Education Books.

Seagrave, Sterling. (1999) *Para Pendekar Pesisir: Sepak Terjang Gurita Bisnis Cina Rantau.* Jakarta, Indonesia: Alvabet.

Suryadinata, Leo. (1978) *Pribumi Indonesians: The Chinese Minority and China.* Kuala Lumpur, Malaysia: Heineman Education Books.

CULT OF MAITREYA The cult of Maitreya (Mile) in China was originally associated with the vows of monk-scholars to be reborn in what they called Tusita heaven. The goal was that they might hear the dharma directly from the mouth of the future Buddha Maitreya and thus attain Buddhahood. These elite monks, and the aristocrats and royalty who patronized them, commissioned images of Maitreya, both standing and seated in meditation, as objects of worship and as aids for visualization and contemplation. Standing images of Maitreya were indicative of his preaching in Ketumati, and seated images portrayed Maitreya's waiting in Tusita. Both styles are found closely connected in the art of the Northern dynasties (220–589 CE) and the Tang dynasty (618–907 CE) and demonstrate that these two aspects of the cult of Maitreya were interrelated in early medieval China.

The origins of the monastic aspect of the cult of Maitreya in China may be traced to the exegete Daoan (312–385), whose worship was focused around his desire to be reborn in Tusita heaven in the presence of Maitreya so that his doubts concerning the scriptures could be resolved. The famous Buddhist pilgrim Xuanzang (Hsuan-tsang, c. 596–664) was a fervent devotee of Maitreya who desired rebirth in Tusita, so the cult became closely associated with his school of Chinese Yogacara.

The Maitreya cult was an important focus of Buddhist belief in early medieval China. Since the sutras about Maitreya suggested that he would descend from Tusita to inaugurate a peaceful Buddhist millennium after years of warfare and the decline of the Buddhist teaching *(mofa)*, worship of Maitreya spread throughout Chinese society. During the chaos that ensued at the end of the Sui dynasty (581–618 CE) and rise of the Tang, a few Buddhist monks and laymen justified their rebellions by claiming to be Maitreya, thus drawing upon the imagery and beliefs common to the cult. Later, Empress Wu Zetian (624–705) justified her usurpation of the Tang throne and declaration of her short-lived Zhou dynasty (690–705) by identifying herself with Maitreya. Followers of Maitreya rebelled frequently through the Song (Sung) period (960–1279), and rebels drew upon Maitreya cult imagery to lend authority and religious fervor to their uprisings.

The image of Maitreya and his cult have gone through many transformations in Chinese society. Maitreya was eventually reinterpreted iconographically, going from the slim and sleek figure of the Northern dynasties period to the roly-poly figure of Budai (Pu-tai) during the Song. The "Laughing Buddha," as he is commonly known, spread throughout Chinese popular culture during the late imperial Chinese period (1368–1912) and is a staple image of traditional Chinese culture that has been exported to the West through immigrant Chinese communities.

Richard D. McBride II

Further Reading

Ch'en, Kenneth. (1964) *Buddhism in China: A Historical Survey.* Princeton, NJ: Princeton University Press.

Forte, Antonino. (1976) *Political Propaganda and Ideology in China at the End of the Seventh Century.* Naples, Italy: Istituto Universitario Orientale Seminario di Studi Asiatici.

Lee Yu-Min. (1984) "Ketumati Maitreya and Tusita Maitreya in Early China." Part 1: *National Palace Museum Bulletin* 19, 4 (September–October 1984): 1–11; Part 2: *National Palace Museum Bulletin* 19, 5 (November–December 1984): 1–11.

Sponberg, Alan, and Helen Hardacre, eds. (1988) *Maitreya, The Future Buddha.* Cambridge, U.K.: Cambridge University Press.

CULTURAL REVOLUTION—CHINA

The Chinese Cultural Revolution (CR), the full title of which was the Great Proletarian Cultural Revolution, was the largest and most important of the ideological campaigns of Mao Zedong (1893–1976). Because of the political movement's length, scale, and destabilizing effects, its significance for the history of China under Mao and the Chinese Communist Party (CCP) he led was enormous. There is general agreement that Mao was by far the single most important figure in the campaign and that the Cultural Revolution gave rise to a massive personality cult surrounding him. Yet it was also a mass movement, involving many millions of people and considerable struggle between different sectors of Chinese society over the movement's control and direction. There was consequently much violence and even periods of localized civil war. However, Mao and his followers presented the CR to the people in Marxist ideological terms, the central feature being an extreme emphasis on class struggle, dubbed "the key link."

What Caused the Cultural Revolution?

Mao, the CCP chairman from the early 1940s until his death, had both ideological and political reasons for initiating the CR. He opposed the moderate economic policies that his former comrades in the CCP leadership had implemented following the failure of his own radical Great Leap Forward economic campaign, begun in 1958. He regarded the CCP as beginning to display the characteristics of a new ruling class and feared that the growing elitism and bureaucratization of the CCP would, if left unchecked, spell the end of his radical notions of revolution and result in a "capitalist restoration." The CR was thus both an ideological campaign and a struggle for power. Mao was supported by Lin Biao (1908–1971), Mao's chief deputy until 1971, and by his own wife, Jiang Qing (1913–1991). Their opponents in the CCP hierarchy were led by Liu Shaoqi (1898–1969), who in April 1959 had replaced Mao as China's president, and by Liu's chief supporter, Deng Xiaoping (1904–1997).

For Mao, the outcome of the CR would determine fundamental questions of policy regarding China's

To celebrate the Cultural Revolution, thousands of Red Guards wave Mao's Little Red Book on 1 May 1969 in Tiananmen Square, Beijing. (AFP/CORBIS)

economic and political direction. He believed in the need for an increasing socialization of China's economy and society and for continual revitalization of the revolution through a campaign-style of politics that both mobilized the masses and prevented the party and its cadres from becoming elitist. Liu, conversely, believed in the importance of careful economic planning under the control of the CCP. He also believed a retreat from the radical economic policies of the Great Leap Forward was necessary, and he reintroduced measures, such as rural markets and private farm plots for the peasants, which encouraged production through offering material incentives to the Chinese people. Mao believed Liu's policies facilitated the emergence of a new bourgeoisie, and it was consequently those "persons in authority taking the capitalist road" such as Liu and his supporters who were to become the main targets during the CR.

The Early Stages of the Cultural Revolution

Opposed by most of the party leadership, Mao turned to China's students and the People's Liberation Army under the control of Lin Biao for support in his struggle against the "capitalist roaders" within the CCP. Frustrated by attempts by the mayor of Beijing, Peng Zhen (1902–1997), to limit the CR's scope to strictly cultural affairs (Peng was initially put in charge of the movement), Mao had Peng purged and established a Cultural Revolution Group under the control of Jiang Qing and Chen Boda (1904–1989). This group encouraged and directed much of the radical activity over the next few years. In late May 1966, secondary and university students began to organize themselves into groups called Red Guards, which were central to the mass struggles and violence that characterized the CR. The first official party document on the CR was the sixteen-point "Decision" adopted by the Eleventh Plenum of the Eighth Central Committee (August 1966). The "Decision," which set the intensely ideological tone of the CR and provided guidelines to run it, declared the CR to be a new stage in China's revolution, one that "touches people to their very souls." It emphasized the need to struggle against and overthrow those in authority taking the capitalist road and endorsed the struggle in education against "bourgeois" academic authorities. The "Decision" did, however, caution against violence as a means of resolving contradictions or differences among the people. It also declared that the "great majority" of cadres—party administrators and professionals—were "good" or "comparatively good," suggesting that Red Guards should not attack them without good reason. In the event, the commands against both violence and attacking "good" cadres were frequently disregarded, as Red Guard factions attempted to outdo one another in demonstrating their devotion to Chairman Mao.

On 18 August 1966, Mao, Lin Biao, and other CR leaders reviewed a mass rally of over 1 million Red Guards in Tiananmen Square in central Beijing. Some half-dozen such mass rallies were held in the square from then until late November. Rallies were also held in other cities. These helped to spawn a one-sided revolutionary atmosphere that brooked no view on any topic but the one supposedly authorized by Mao, with the result that fanaticism became commonplace.

The Red Guard organizations spread through society and across China, believing they had a duty to destroy old culture and habits, including anything traditional, and to establish new, supposedly socialist, things in their place. The Red Guards subjected teachers to often-violent criticism and effectively closed down the education system. They frequently spearheaded the attack against the "capitalist roaders" within the CCP, ransacking party offices, parading cadres through the streets wearing dunce hats, and subjecting these persons to humiliating criticism sessions that often ended in violence. The ideological orientation of the Red Guard organizations was variable, and in the hothouse atmosphere of the CR, fueled by the cult of personality surrounding Mao, these ideological differences often ended in pitched battles between rival Red Guards, resulting in numerous casualties. From August 1966, Red Guards also destroyed or damaged religious buildings and attacked and humiliated their clergy.

In September 1966, *Mao zhuxi yulu* (Sayings of Chairman Mao Zedong), usually described as The Little Red Book, was published. This book, which became an icon for Mao's followers, especially the Red Guards, contained the nucleus of his thought. According to official figures, 350 million copies had been printed by the end of 1967. The obsession with following Mao's thought saw an emphasis on class struggle and "serving the people" (the title of Mao's most popular article) rather than on oneself or one's family, and on demanding sacrifices from ordinary people on behalf of socialism and the revolution. Meanwhile, the attacks on "old culture" created an extraordinarily narrow and restrictive cultural environment. Very few books were published other than those expressing Mao's thought or the CCP or revolutionary history. Many literary figures were humiliated and even persecuted to death, notably the famous fiction writer and playwright Lao She, who died 24 August 1966. All traditional theater was banned, and Jiang Qing imposed a theory of "model" dramas, based on a forum held in February 1966, which insisted that all literature and art should reflect and propagate the class struggle and revolutionary heroism.

CHAIRMAN MAO ON IDEOLOGICAL AND POLITICAL PURITY

"Recently there has been a falling off in ideological and political work among students and intellectuals, and some unhealthy tendencies have appeared. Some people seem to think that there is no longer a need to concern oneself with politics or the future of the motherland and the ideals of mankind. It seems as if Marxism was once all the rage but it is currently not so much in fashion. To counter these tendencies, we must strengthen our ideological and political work. Both students and intellectuals should study hard. In addition to the study of their specialized subjects, they must make progress both ideologically and politically, which means that they should study Marxism, current events and politics. Not to have a correct political point of view is like having no soul . . .

"All departments and organizations should shoulder their responsibilities in ideological and political work. This applies to the Communist Party, the Youth League, government departments in charge of this work, especially to heads of educational institutions and teachers."

Source: Mao Zedong. (1966) *Quotations from Chairman Mao Tsetung*. Beijing: Foreign Language Press, 142–143.

Developments to the Ninth CCP Congress

The Red Guards' failure to observe the injunction against violence as well as the heightened radicalism and fanaticism of late 1966 and early 1967 led the CR leaders, in January 1967, to command the People's Liberation Army to restore order, extending its control to many civilian institutions. "Revolutionary committees" were then set up in the whole country from every province down to every factory, school, and people's commune to take over the power of old administrative authorities. These committees were a new administrative model regarded as appropriate for a mass revolutionary movement like the CR. They contained representatives of the military, the Red Guards (the masses), and experienced cadres who had survived the CR relatively unscathed. However, the military soon occupied a prominent leadership role in these revolutionary committees.

A mid-1967 resurgence of radical Red Guard activity led to violent conflict between the Red Guards and the military in several areas. The most serious was a three-week civil war in July and early August in and around Wuhan, the capital of Hubei province central China. Fanned by Jiang Qing, this war ended in a victory for Mao and the Red Guard forces when the commander of the Wuhan military region, Chen Zaidao, was dismissed. In the international arena, Red Guard–inspired disturbances flared in Hong Kong, and there was a savage attack on the British chargé d'affaires office in Beijing on 22 August.

After another period of relative order, a further resurgence of fighting occurred from April to July 1968, with many small-scale civil wars in southern China, especially in the Guangxi Autonomous Region, bordering Vietnam. A war in April and early May in Wuzhou, in far-eastern Guangxi, brought about large-scale destruction in the city and the torture and deaths of several thousand Red Guards. Ultra-leftist groups plundered trains taking weapons to Vietnam, where the Vietnam War was raging.

Seeing that a continuation of this situation would throw the country into civil war, Mao moved to end the chaos. Early in the morning of 28 July 1968, Mao, Lin Biao, Jiang Qing, and other leaders interviewed several Red Guard leaders, condemned them, and began the process of sending large numbers of Red Guards to the countryside. This was carried out supposedly to broaden the revolutionary experience of the Red Guards, but the real motive was to get them out of the cities, thereby reducing the level of conflict and violence.

In October 1968, a CCP Central Committee plenum condemned Liu Shaoqi as a traitor and sent him to prison, where he died on 12 November 1969. Not until February 1980 was his death revealed to the world. After this revelation, he was rehabilitated by the post-Mao leadership of Deng Xiaoping, which adopted an extremely hostile view of the CR.

The Ninth Party Congress, held in April 1969, ended the most important and radical phase of the CR and stressed unity and the need to rebuild the CCP. Appearing as a total victory for Mao, it even declared Lin Biao his "close comrade-in-arms and successor" as well as the sole CCP vice-chairman. However, challenges to the CR's line were far from over.

The Lin Biao Affair and the Later Stages of the Cultural Revolution

The years from the Ninth Party Congress to Mao's death were characterized by a retreat from the radicalism of the early years of the CR, as the party rebuilt itself and reasserted its authority. Victims of this process were often those who had most ardently supported Mao's radical line. A campaign against Mao's erstwhile ally Chen Boda was initiated in September 1970, and the following year saw the Lin Biao affair, probably the most unusual example of intra-elite political conflict during the CR. According to official accounts, Lin and his main followers, including his son and wife, had concocted a plot to assassinate Mao but were killed in an air crash in September 1971 while fleeing from China after their attempt was exposed. Lin's death in the air crash is not in doubt, but there have been many explanations of his fate, and Western scholars are generally skeptical that he had tried to assassinate Mao. What is clear is that to have Mao's "close comrade-in-arms and successor" condemned as the chairman's would-be assassin severely undercut the power of the Left. It also raised serious doubts among many Chinese about the validity of the CR and whether Mao's judgment was as reliable as the almost godlike status accorded him implied.

At the same time as the Lin Biao affair, enormous changes were taking shape in the field of China's foreign relations. Following the largely self-imposed isolation of the early phase of the CR, China moved to rejoin the international community. In October 1971, China was admitted into the United Nations, and in February 1972, the U.S. president Richard Nixon visited China. The first half of the 1970s saw China establish full diplomatic relations with numerous countries, including several major Western countries.

Signs of the relatively relaxed atmosphere continued in 1973, although factional struggles within the CCP leadership persisted. Deng Xiaoping was again referred to as vice-premier in April, after seven years in disgrace. The Tenth CCP Congress of August 1973 saw the trusted premier Zhou Enlai (1898–1976) replace Lin Biao as Mao's first deputy and CCP vice-chairman. On the other hand, Wang Hongwen, a radical young worker (and later a member of the Gang of Four) from Shanghai, emerged among the other vice-chairmen, showing that the influence of the CR was still alive. A series of ideological campaigns, initiated by either Mao or his radical supporters, followed. These were aimed at keeping alive enthusiasm for the CR. The last of these, beginning in February 1976, saw Deng Xiaoping condemned as an "arch unrepentant capitalist roader still on the capitalist road" and ousted once again from his leadership positions.

With Mao's death in September 1976, the CR lost its major source of inspiration. According to the Resolution of the 1981 Sixth Plenum of the Eleventh Central Committee of the CCP, the arrest the next month of the Gang of Four (Mao's widow Jiang Qing and three of her influential radical supporters, including Wang Hongwen) signaled the end of the CR.

The Cultural Revolution Assessed as a Setback to Development

The 1981 Resolution was unequivocal in its judgment, roundly condemning the CR and claiming that the CR had "led to domestic turmoil and brought catastrophe to the Party, the state, and the whole people." However, despite the authoritative status of the

Resolution, there are numerous divergent views, from both Western scholars and Chinese commentators, of the causes, course and consequences, and even the dates, of the CR. Yet most agree that the CR caused much suffering to millions of people and set back China's development for several years.

Deng Xiaoping returned to power in July 1977 and, from December 1978, was able to dictate an economic policy that was hostile to the spirit of the CR in nearly all respects. The condemnation of "old culture" gave way to a major revival of traditional arts. The revolutionary committees were dismantled, along with almost every other idea and practice spawned by the CR. It is thus evident that the CR failed to achieve the radical socialist objectives Mao had set for it. The CR nevertheless provided one of the most important chapters in the political and economic history of contemporary China, and it is only against its backdrop that the increasingly pro-market economic reforms introduced by Deng Xiaoping after 1978 can be understood.

Nick Knight and Colin Mackerras

See also: **Deng Xiaoping; Gang of Four; Great Leap Forward; Lin Biao; Liu Shaoqi; Mao Zedong; Red Guard Organizations; Zhou Enlai**

Further Reading

Daubier, Jean. (1974) *A History of the Chinese Cultural Revolution.* Trans. by Richard Seaver. New York: Random House.

Gao Yuan. (1987) *Born Red: A Chronicle of the Cultural Revolution.* Stanford, CA: Stanford University Press.

Hunter, Neale. ([1969] 1988) *Shanghai Journal: An Eyewitness Account of the Cultural Revolution.* Reprint. Hong Kong: Oxford University Press.

Joseph, William A., Christine P. W. Wong, and David Zweig, eds. (1991) *New Perspectives on the Cultural Revolution.* Cambridge, MA: Harvard University Press.

Leys, Simon. (1981) *The Chairman's New Clothes, Mao, and the Cultural Revolution.* Trans. by Carol Appleyard and Patrick Goode. London: Allison and Busby.

Liang, Heng, and Judith Shapiro. (1983) *Son of the Revolution.* New York: Knopf.

MacFarquhar, Roderick, and John K. Fairbank, eds. (1991) *The Cambridge History of China.* Vol. 15: *The People's Republic,* Pt. 2: *Revolutions within the Chinese Revolution, 1966–1982.* Cambridge, U.K.: Cambridge University Press.

Teiwes, Frederick C., and Warren Sun. (1996) *The Tragedy of Lin Biao: Riding the Tiger during the Cultural Revolution, 1966–1971.* London: Hurst.

White, Lynn T. (1989) *Policies of Chaos: The Organizational Causes of Violence in China's Cultural Revolution.* Princeton, NJ: Princeton University Press.

Yan Jiaqi, and Gao Gao. (1996) *Turbulent Decade: A History of the Cultural Revolution.* Translated and edited by D. W. Y. Kwok. Honolulu, HI: University of Hawaii Press.

CURZON, GEORGE NATHANIEL (1859–1925), Viceroy of India.

CURZON, GEORGE NATHANIEL (1859–1925), Viceroy of India. After brilliant undergraduate years at Oxford, George Nathaniel Curzon prepared himself for a grand political career. He traveled through most of the countries of North America and Asia, including Russia, China, and Afghanistan, and produced three solid books on contemporary Asian political affairs. He was elected to Parliament in 1885 and later served as undersecretary for India (1891– 1892), undersecretary for foreign affairs (1895–1898), and ultimately as viceroy of India (1899–1905). In this position he behaved more like the president of a republic than the queen's representative in Calcutta. Ever fearful of Russian expansion, he dealt with the Dalai Lama in Lhasa, and the Amir Abdur Rahman in Kabul, and reorganized military operations in the new Northwest Frontier Province so as to maximize British influence along India's northern borders. He even sent an unsuccessful commercial mission into Tibet.

Within India, Curzon did much to rectify previous administrative errors, setting up commissions to deal with irrigation, railways, agricultural banks, and police. He even succeeded at currency reform and at reducing the amount of governmental paper flow. While much of this was quite popular in India and rather less so in London, his decision to split Bengal Province in two in 1905 was universally condemned, and the two parts had to be reunited in 1911—only to be split permanently in 1947.

Curzon made no attempt to involve the Indian public in his reforms. He clashed with Lord Kitchener, then commander-in-chief of the Indian army, and repeatedly clashed with statesmen in London. The disfavor he brought upon himself affected the positions he held after his return to Britain: chancellor of the University of Oxford, Lord Privy Seal, and president of the Air Board (1916); but then he became foreign secretary (1919–1924). He was elevated to the House of Lords, but was shattered when, in 1924, his old dream of becoming prime minister ended with the selection of Stanley Baldwin, and he died within a year.

Paul Hockings

Further Reading

Dilks, David. (1969, 1970) *Curzon in India.* 2 vols. London: Hart-Davis.

Zetland, Lawrence John. (1972) *The Life of Lord Curzon; Being the Authorized Biography of George Nathaniel Curzon of Kedleston.* Freeport, NY: Books for Libraries Press.

CUSTOMARY LAW. See **Adat.**

DA NANG (2002 pop. 446,000). Da Nang is a large city located on the central coast of Vietnam 973 kilometers (603 miles) north of Ho Chi Minh City and 30 kilometers (17 miles) north of Hoi An. It became an important port city at the end of the nineteenth century after Hoi An's access to the ocean, via the Thu Bon river, was filled in by silt runoff. In 1888, the French seized control of Da Nang, which they called Tourane, from Vietnamese emperor Gia Long after he reneged on a promise to assist them in Vietnam. During the first part of the twentieth century, the city was second only to Saigon as Vietnam's busiest port and most cosmopolitan city. Da Nang received much attention from both France and the United States during the ensuing wars in Vietnam. Da Nang, only 200 kilometers (124 miles) south of the Demilitarized Zone, was the first place U.S. military forces landed in Vietnam in 1965 and was the home of a large U.S. Air Force base from which bombing missions were launched against the Democratic Republic of Vietnam (DRV). The influx of thousands of military personnel brought about rapid growth to the city both in population and in various businesses. Many South Vietnamese refugees used Da Nang as a staging area for escape from the country when the DRV took over the surrounding areas in 1975. Today Da Nang, still with its French and American vestiges in the form of wide avenues, old villas, and diverse entertainment, is only a remnant of its former bustling self.

Richard B. Verrone

Further Reading

Admiralty, Naval Intelligence Divison, Great Britain. (1943) *Indo-China*. London: Her Majesty's Stationery Office, Geographical Handbook Series, B.R. 510.

Cima, Ronald J., ed. (1989) *Vietnam: A Country Study*. Washington, DC: U.S. Government Printing Office.

Guillon, Emmanuel. (2001) *Cham Art: Treasures from the Da Nang Museum Vietnam*. Bangkok, Thailand: River Books.

DADRA AND NAGAR HAVELI UNION TERRITORY (2001 pop. 220,000). The Union Territory of Dadra and Nagar Haveli, located in western India, is surrounded by the states of Gujarat and Maharashtra. It is a predominantly rural area and has seventy-two villages. Its capital city is Silvassa, and the principal languages spoken are Gujarati and Hindi.

Originally a part of the Maratha Confederacy, Dadra and Nagar Haveli became the scene of prolonged skirmishes between the Portuguese and the Marathas in the eighteenth century. In December 1779, the Maratha government, in an effort to ensure the friendship of the Portuguese, assigned to them the revenue of a few villages of the region. Since then the Portuguese ruled over the territory until its liberation on 2 August 1954. Subsequently it merged with the Indian Union on 11 August 1961 as a Union Territory.

Agriculture is the major occupation of the people of the region, paddy rice and millet being the most important crops cultivated. Fruits, especially mango and banana, are also produced. Nearly 40 percent of the total geographical area of Dadra and Nagar Haveli is under forest cover, which provides a livelihood to the tribal population.

Traditional crafts of the region include pottery, bamboo, and leather goods. The establishment of a cooperative industrial estate by Dan Udyog Sahakari

Sangh Limited introduced industrialization in 1967–1968. Since then, modern industries have sprung up in the cities like Silvassa, Masat, and Khadoli. At present, the region boasts 988 cottage, village, and small-scale industries and 312 medium-scale industries in textiles, engineering goods, plastics, chemicals, and pharmaceuticals. A multiple-development project, the Damanganga Irrigation Project, a joint venture of the Union Territories of Dadra and Nagar Haveli and Daman and Diu and the state of Gujarat, is nearing completion. Despite its advantages, it has also caused hardship and displacement to some. The village of Kothar has been submerged, and four others partly submerged due to its construction.

Tourism is well developed in the region. Sites include the Tadkeshwar Siva temple, the Vanganga Lake, Dadra, Bindrabin, and the Tribal Cultural Museum and Hirvavan garden at Silvassa. Usually all Hindu, Muslim, and Christian festivals are celebrated in the territory. Members of the significant tribal population celebrate their own festivals. The Dhodia and Varli tribes celebrate Diwaso; Varlis and Koli celebrate Bhawada. Almost all the tribes perform Khali Puja after harvesting crops and Gram Devi before the harvest.

Sanjukta Das Gupta

Further Reading

Research, Reference and Training Division, Government of India. (2001) *India 2001: A Reference Annual.* New Delhi: Publications Division, Ministry of Information and Broadcasting.

Singh, K. S. (1994) *Dadra and Nagar Haveli.* People of India, vol. 18. Chennai, India: East West Publishers.

DAENDELS, HERMAN WILLEM (1762–1818), Dutch colonial governor. Herman Willem Daendels's brief term as governor-general of the Dutch East Indies marked the beginning of a new era of direct colonial intervention and ambitious social and political engineering in the colony. After commanding the revolutionary "Patriots" who overthrew the oligarchic Dutch Republic in 1795, Daendels, who was born in Hattem, the Netherlands, rose to become commander of Dutch military forces under King Louis Napoleon (1778–1846). He took office as governor-general of the Dutch East Indies in 1808, after the Dutch government had dissolved the Dutch East Indies Company (VOC) and placed the colony under metropolitan authority. His rule was energetic and autocratic. He incorporated Javanese "regents" *(bupati)* into the colonial bureaucracy, annexed new territories in Java, and reduced sultans to the rank of vassals. He banned officials from receiving private income and moved the center of administration from old Batavia to a new suburb, Weltevreden. Daendels reformed the judicial system, establishing different courts for different population groups. He conscripted laborers to construct fortifications against an expected British attack and, at the cost of many lives, to lay down a postal road running the length of Java. To fund his reforms and defense works, he sold vast areas of land to Chinese and European investors and speculators. He was recalled to the Netherlands in 1811 and the following year served as marshal in the Napoleonic invasion of Russia. He was governor of the small Dutch colonies in West Africa from 1815 to 1818.

Robert Cribb

Further Reading

Day, Clive. (1904) *The Policy and Administration of the Dutch in Java.* New York: Macmillan.

Vlekke, Bernard H. M. (1943) *Nusantara: A History of the East Indian Archipelago.* Cambridge, MA: Harvard University Press.

DAGESTAN (2002 est. pop. 2.2 million). A southern Russian republic, Dagestan is bordered by Azerbaijan to the south, Georgia to the west, and the Caspian Sea to the east. Although Dagestan translates as "land of the mountains," the republic actually consists of three general geographic zones. First, there is an elevated southern region situated in the northeastern Caucasus that descends to foothills and mixed forests in the north. Second, there is an arid and sparsely vegetated northern region located in the Nogai Steppe. Third, there are narrow coastal lowlands in the east that run along the Caspian Sea, which include saline wetlands in their northernmost extreme. Although increasingly endangered, Dagestan is one of the leading hearths of biodiversity within the Russian realm.

Renamed after the revolutionary Dagestani leader Makhach, Makhachkala is the capital of Dagestan; the port city, on the site of a nineteenth-century Russian fortress, is located roughly in the middle of the republic's coastal zone. The city's chief industries are related to oil and gas refineries and pipelines, chemical factories, and manufacturing. Although there are considerable oil and gas resources in the republic, they remain relatively unexploited due to inaccessibility. Derbent, the other major city, dating to a fifth-century fortress, lies in the south at a narrow point on the coast between the Caspian Sea and the Caucasus

Mountains; Derbent translates as "gateway." However, the majority of Dagestanis (about 60 percent) live in rural areas.

The Dagestani population is characterized by extreme ethnic diversity. Although in the late 1990s the republic's population was estimated at fewer than 2.2 million, it includes many different national groups—between twenty and forty (although some sources put it as high as eighty). The largest of these, the Avars, constitute roughly 30 percent of the total population. Although Russian is employed as a common language, Avar is the most common local language, and is also the common medium for communication between those indigenous to the republic. The majority of the population is Islamic, and the Dagestanis are world-renowned for their carpet weaving and colorful, geometric designs.

Long before becoming a Russian republic Dagestan was legendary for its resistance to external powers (e.g., Arab/Islamic, Seljuk Turk, Mongol-Turkic, Ottoman Turk, and Persian armies). This image is personified in the histories and legends of Shamil, the nineteenth-century Imam of Dagestan. Reportedly an Avar, he established a Dagestani state and led Dagestanis and Chechens against the czarist empire, preventing pacification of the region by the Russians for over twenty-five years. Dagestan was designated an autonomous republic of the Soviet Union in 1921; it became a Russian republic in 1991. The stability of the republic is tenuous due to extreme instability in neighboring Chechnya, with Chechen rebels entering the republic in an attempt to unite with Dagestanis in a larger separatist movement, and Russian troops entering Dagestan to prevent such an escalation. There is also increasing activism among Islamists (both homegrown variations of Sufism and Wahhabism as fostered in the Middle East), Chechen rebels, cleavages between ethnic groups, and separatist movements, especially among the Lezgin peoples living on both sides of the Azeri-Dagestani border.

Kyle T. Evered

Further Reading

Chenciner, Robert. (1997) *Daghestan: Tradition and Survival.* New York: St. Martin's Press.

Gammer, Moshe. (1994) *Muslim Resistance to the Tsar: Shamil and the Conquest of Chechnia and Daghestan.* London: Frank Cass.

Ware, Robert Bruce, and Enver Kisriev. (2000) "The Islamic Factor in Dagestan." *Central Asian Survey* 19, 2: 235—252.

DAI QING (b. 1941), Chinese journalist and environmental activist. Dai Qing is the adopted daughter of Ye Jianying, who was a high-ranking government official. Raised in a privileged revolutionary family, she was trained as a missile engineer and worked in military intelligence before starting her career in journalism. She came to prominence in the early 1980s for a series of investigative reports, written for the *Guangming Daily*, about persecution within the Chinese Communist Party in the early days of the revolution.

Dai went on to become the most outspoken critic in China of the Three Gorges Hydroelectric Dam. In 1989 she published a collection of essays condemning the $30 billion project titled *Yangtze! Yangtze!* Later that year, Dai publicly denounced the 4 June 1989 Tiananmen Square massacre and on 5 June 1989 quit the Chinese Communist Party. As a result, she was fired from the *Guangming Daily*, jailed for ten months, and her writing was banned in China.

Dai was awarded the Harvard University Nieman Fellowship for journalists in 1991, the Golden Pen for Freedom Given by the Paris-based International Federation of Newspaper Publishers in 1992, and the Goldman Environmental Award in 1993. In 1997 Dai published a second volume of critical essays on the Three Gorges project titled *The River Dragon Has Come!*

Alexa Olesen

Further Reading

Dai Qing. (1994) *Yangtze! Yangtze!* Toronto: Earthscan Publications.

———. (1997) *The River Dragon Has Come!* Armonk, NY: M. E. Sharpe.

Kristof, Nicholas D., and Sheryl Wudunn. (1994) *China Wakes: The Struggle For the Soul of a Rising Power.* New York: Times Books.

DAI VIET SU KY *Dai Viet Su Ky*, also known as *Dai Viet Su Ky Toan Thu*, designates a collection of historical chronicles written by several different authors over a period extending from the thirteenth to the fifteenth centuries. Le Van Huu (1230–1322), considered the father of Vietnamese history, wrote the first narrative, relating events occurring between the years 207 BCE and 1225 CE. Phan Phu Tien (fifteenth century) continued Le Van Huu's account to 1446. Both of these works no longer exist as independent works. Ngo Si Lien, an official historian of the court of emperor Le Thanh Tong (1460–1497), reproduced them while comparing them with Chinese official histories, Vietnamese nonofficial accounts, as well as other historical material such as biographies, genealogies, and eyewitness reports. He also added his own commentaries. In the presentation of his work to the emperor, Ngo Si Lien informs us about his conception of history: "History records events; whether good or bad, they can serve as examples for posterity." As for his method, he followed the footsteps of Sima Qian in his *Shi Ji* and Confucius in his *Qun Qiu*, which means that events are recorded year by year—earning for these histories the common title of annals—listed under the names of successive rulers.

Truong Buu Lam

Further Reading

Ngo Si Lien. (1998) *Dai Viet Su Ky Toan Thu*. Hanoi, Vietnam: Khoa Hoc Xa Hoi.

Qen Jing He. (1984–1986) *Kogobon: Daietsu Shiki Zensho*. Tokyo: Tokyo University.

DAIGAKU *Daigaku*, the Japanese word for universities and colleges, has its origins in the earliest academic institutions of higher learning in Japan, centers of scholarship that developed at influential temples not only in Kyoto but in the Kanto region (eastern Japan) as well. The curriculum of these primarily secular institutions, which took their name from the Chinese term for schools that trained government officials, was centered primarily on Confucian texts and Chinese histories and literary anthologies that were transmitted to Japan beginning in the sixth century CE. Two types of schools of higher learning were established for the nobility: the Daigakuryo, a Confucian college for nobility in the capital, and branch schools for nobility in the provinces.

During his stay in Japan in the mid-sixteenth century, Francis Xavier noted that in addition to the university in the capital city of Kyoto there were five other significant universities with enrollments of over 3,500. Of these, the largest and most representative was the Ashikaga Gakko (Ashikaga School), located in the Kanto region.

After completing basic education at one of the numerous local temple schools, students would set out to further their education at centers of higher learning where they could gain the training that would lead to a successful career. Many students completed their training at the Ashikaga School, studying both Buddhist and Confucian texts.

During the Sengoku period (c. 467–1568), when rival clans were continually in a state of war, the university offered a curriculum that came to include medicine, military science, and astronomy, along with the ancient study of divination—all subjects essential to medieval warfare. During the Edo period (1600/1603–1868), there were *han* (domain) schools for the samurai, as well as private schools that provided advanced instruction to both commoners and samurai in a variety of disciplines, notably "Western" studies. Prior to and immediately following the Meiji Restoration of 1868, desire for knowledge about the West grew rapidly, and institutions of higher education flourished.

In 1872 the Fundamental Code of Education delineated standards for a modern educational system. The first of the modern universities to be established was Tokyo Daigaku in 1877, a merging of two existing shogunal schools. National universities were later founded in Kyoto (1897), Tohoku (1907), and Kyushu (1910). Institutions such as Keio University (founded as a private academy by Fukuzawa Yukichi in 1858) and Waseda University (founded by Okuma Shigenobu in 1882) went through several transformations before becoming full-fledged universities. Several of the most prestigious universities were founded as Christian missionary schools; these include Doshisha, Sophia, and International Christian University. Today there are about 450 public and private four-year universities.

James M. Vardaman, Jr.

Further Reading

Beauchamp, Edward R., and Richard Rubinger. (1989) *Education in Japan: A Source Book*. New York: Garland Publishing, Inc.

Government of Japan. (1980) *Japan's Modern Educational System: A History of the First Hundred Years*. Tokyo: Ministry of Education, Science, and Culture.

Ohto Yasuhiro. (1999) "Schools and Learning in the Medieval Period." *Journal of Japanese Trade and Industry* November/December: 52–55.

DALAI LAMA The Dalai Lama is the spiritual and temporal leader of the Tibetan Buddhist peoples, by whom he is regarded as the earthly manifestation of Chenrezi, the bodhisattva ("incarnating deity") of compassion. Each Dalai Lama is regarded as being the reincarnation of his predecessor, and after the death of a Dalai Lama, a search is made for the young boy in whom he is considered to have taken rebirth. Tenzin Gyatso (b. 1935), the present Dalai Lama, is the

THE PALACE OF THE DALAI LAMA

The following text written by two French missionaries in the mid-nineteenth century provides a positive impression of the home of the Dalai Lama in Tibet, despite mainly critical comments about Buddhism in general found throughout their report.

> The palace of the Talé-Lama merits, in every respect, the celebrity which it enjoys throughout the world. North of the town, at the distance of about a mile, there rises a rugged mountain, of slight elevation and of conical form, which, amid the plain, resembles an islet on the bosom of a lake. This mountain is entitled Buddha-La (mountain of Buddha, divine mountain), which upon this grand pedestal, the work of nature, the Talé-Lama have raised the magnificent palace wherein their Living Divinity resides in the flesh. The palace is an aggregation of several temples; that which occupies the centre is four stories high, and overlooks the rest; it terminates in a dome, entirely covered with plates of gold, and surrounded with a peristyle, the columns of which are, in like manner, all covered in gold. It is here that the Talé-Lama has set up his abode. From the summit of this lofty sanctuary he can contemplate, at the great solemnities, his innumerable adorers advancing along the plain or prostrate at the foot of the divine mountain.
>
> *Source:* Huc Evariste-Regis and Joseph Gabet. ([1851] 1987) *Travels in Tartary, Thibet and China, 1844–1846.* New York: Dover Publications, 171.

fourteenth in a line of succession originating in a fourteenth-century disciple of the founder of the Gelugpa sect, the leading school of Tibetan Buddhism.

Commonly referred to in English by the title "His Holiness," the fourteenth Dalai Lama was born into a peasant family in the village of Takster, in the northeastern Amdo Province of Tibet (now part of China's Qinghai Province). His predecessor had "passed to the heavenly fields" in 1933, and Tenzin Gyatso was recognized as his reincarnation in 1937. He was taken to Lhasa, the Tibetan capital, in 1939 and was enthroned in the Potala Palace in February 1940. While a regent ruled Tibet in his name, he began the lengthy course of studies that culminated in his being awarded the *Lharampa Geshe* degree (roughly equivalent to a doctorate in Buddhist studies) in 1959.

Due to the crisis caused by the Communist Chinese invasion of Tibet in October 1950, the sixteen-year-old Tenzin Gyatso assumed temporal power in Tibet on 17 November 1950. He remained there under Chinese authority until the excesses of the Communist regime prompted him to flee Lhasa in March 1959. Although closely pursued by Chinese forces, he succeeded in reaching India. There, with around one hundred thousand of his followers, the Dalai Lama established a Tibetan government-in-exile in Dharamsala, in the Himalayan foothills of north India. He has since become the primary ambassador of the Tibetan cause as well as a world-renowned spokesman for nonviolence and for the Buddhist ideal of "universal compassion." In October 1989 he was awarded the Nobel Peace Prize.

The fourteenth Dalai Lama remains the focus of Tibetan identity in the world. A charming and modest, yet charismatic figure, with a great appeal in the West, he prefers to be known as "a simple Buddhist monk." His leadership has been characterized by an openness to change, the promotion of dialogue be-

The Dalai Lama at a news conference in New Delhi, India, in May 1999 at which he announced a series of concerts entitled the "World Festival of Sacred Music." (AFP/CORBIS)

tween religions and science, and a steadfast belief in the principles of nonviolence.

Alex McKay

Further Reading

Avendon, John. (1985) *In Exile from the Land of the Snows.* New York: Wisdom Publications.

Hicks, Roger, and Ngakpa Chogyam. (1984). *Great Ocean—An Authorised Biography.* Shaftesbury, U.K.: Element Books.

Gyatso, His Holiness Tenzin. (1962) *My Land and My People.* New York: McGraw-Hill.

———. (1990) *Freedom in Exile.* London: Hodder and Stoughton.

Snellgroves, David, and Hugh Richardson. (1968) *A Cultural History of Tibet.* London: Weidenfeld and Nicolson.

DALAT (2002 pop 125,000). Dalat is a small city located in the central highlands of Vietnam 205 kilometers (127 miles) southwest of Nha Trang and 308 kilometers (191 miles) north of Ho Chi Minh City. Named for the "River of the Lat Tribe" after the native Lat ethnic group who live in the area, Dalat, with its cool climate, has been used by the Vietnamese and eventually the Europeans in Vietnam as a vacation spot that allowed an escape from the extreme heat of the cities and the Mekong Delta area. The Frenchman Dr. Alexander Yersin (1863–1943), a protégé of Louis Pasteur, is credited with "discovering" Dalat for such purposes. During Vietnam's war with the United States, high-ranking North and South Vietnamese officials used Dalat as a nonpartisan resting locale before it was captured officially by the North Vietnamese on 3 April 1975. Dalat's most famous former resident was the last Nguyen emperor, Bao Dai, whose summer palace exists today as a tourist attraction. Today Dalat is used by Vietnamese as a favorite honeymoon destination and, with its many former colonial villas as guest houses, nice restaurants, and eighteen-hole golf course, is in the process of being transformed by the Vietnamese government into an international tourist destination.

Richard B. Verrone

Further Reading

Admiralty, Naval Intelligence Divison, Great Britain. (1943) *Indo-China.* London: Her Majesty's Stationery Office, Geographical Handbook Series, B.R. 510.

Cima, Ronald J., ed. (1989) *Vietnam: A Country Study.* Washington, DC: U.S. Government Printing Office.

DAMAN AND DIU UNION TERRITORY (2001 est. pop. 200,000). Daman and Diu Union Territory, comprising two separate districts, lies within the Gujarat state of western India. It was a part of Goa Union Territory until Goa achieved statehood in 1987. Goa, along with Daman and Diu, had made up Portuguese India *(Estado da India)* until it became part of the India in December 1961. The Portuguese acquired Daman and Diu from Bahadur Shah (1506–1537) of Gujarat in 1534.

Daman (formerly Damao), 170 kilometers north of Mumbai (Bombay), is on the east side of the Gulf of Cambay (Khambhat), while Diu, 270 kilometers northwest of Mumbai, lies at the southern tip of the Kathiawar Peninsula. Both districts—Daman and Diu—are coastal enclaves on the Arabian Sea. Fishing and shipping are common activities for both, but a water depth of only one or two fathoms is insufficient to accommodate large vessels. Both Daman and Diu have small airports. The Gujarati language is common to both settlements. Their crops include rice, groundnuts, pulse, beans, wheat, banana, mango, coconut, and sugarcane.

Daman

Daman has two forts: Little Daman, with a picturesque main gate in an aquatic motif, inside which is the church, Nossa Senhora do Mar ("Our Lady of the Sea"); and Big Daman, which has a small park, houses, shops, and the remains of a seventeenth-century church and convent. The Damanganga River separates the two forts. The population of Daman in 1991 was 62,101. The area covers 78 square kilometers.

Diu

The coastal city of Ghoghla (formerly Gogolá) faces an island 11 kilometers long that contains the Fortaleza, the largest Portuguese fortress in Asia. In the channel between Ghoghla and the island is a "water fort" or *panikota* in Gujarati, *fortim do mar* in Portuguese. Built in 1536, the Fortaleza was besieged by Turks in 1538 and 1546. Today it holds a small garrison and is a local tourist attraction. Another tourist attraction is Nagoá Beach. On the island are several ancient homes, about 150 Hindu temples, and several mosques and churches, including the Sé Matriz Cathedral, which was built in 1601 and was formerly a Jesuit college.

East of Ghoghla is Simbor, where there is another *panikota*, S. António, in the estuary of a river. It was at S. António that in December 1961 the last European flag to fly over Indian territory was finally lowered. In addition to tourism, industries include salt processing and fishing. The population of Diu in 1991 was 39,485. The area covers 52 square kilometers.

Henry Scholberg

Further Reading

Singh, K. Suresh, B. R. Solanki, N. K. Sinha, and Jaime F. Pereira. (1994) *People of India: Daman and Diu.* Mumbai (Bombay): Popular Prakashan.

DAMDINSUREN, TSENDIYN (1908–1986), Mongolian writer. Tsendiyn Damdinsuren, one of Mongolia's most distinguished writers, was born in what is now Dornod Province and grew up in the era of Mongolian autonomy and early Communism and became politically active in the Mongolian Revolutionary Youth League. He gained election to its Central Committee in 1926 and later became editor of its publications. Subsequently Damdinsuren became chairman of the Council of Mongolian Trade Unions and later was involved in the forced collectivizations and seizures that brought Mongolia close to civil war. Young Damdinsuren had to tread carefully to avoid being purged or executed. In 1932, he joined the Communist Party while continuing his editorial work but in 1933 went to Leningrad to further his education, returning only in 1938.

Once back in Mongolia, Damdinsuren became increasingly allied with Yumjaagiyn Tsedenbel, Mongolia's future premier and president, and his circle. Damdinsuren became involved in efforts to adapt the Cyrillic script to write Mongolian. Prior to that time Mongolian had been written with the Uighur script, which was both difficult to learn and use and divorced from spoken Mongolian. The new script and orthography, on the other hand, closely reflected living usage and were a common element in the rest of the Soviet world. According to some sources, it was Damdinsuren who proposed the change in the first place, and he later became one of its most active proponents. In connection with his linguistic work, Damdinsuren later worked on the first large Russian-Mongolian dictionary and between 1942 and 1946 was editor of the party newspaper *Unen.* In 1950, he served as chairman of the Committee of Sciences and between 1953 and 1955 as chairman of the Writers Union. By this time Damdinsuren was becoming increasingly famous for his literary works, above all his poetry, but also his prose, including literary studies and a translation of the *Secret History of the Mongols* into modern Mongolian.

Damdinsuren's style is lucid and readable, and he was a master of writing in the new Khalkha literary language that he helped create. He was a vivid storyteller, particularly when his stories focus on everyday Mongol life. Although he did not suffer as much as his contemporary B. Rinchen, Damdinsuren fell afoul of party authorities more than once. Unlike the academician Bazaryn Shirendev, he did not live long enough to see the triumph of the new Mongolia after the decline and collapse of Communism. His works remain in demand and have been frequently reprinted after his death.

Paul D. Buell

Further Reading

Sanders, Alan J. K. (1968) *The People's Republic of Mongolia: A General Reference Guide.* London: Oxford University Press.

Shirendev, Bazaryn. (1997) *Through the Ocean Waves: The Autobiography of Bazaryn Shirendev.* Trans. by Temujin Onon. Bellingham, WA: Center for East Asian Studies, Western Washington University.

DAMKOENG, AKAT (1905–1932), Thai prose writer. M. C. Akat Damkoeng Raphiphatna was born in 1905 at Rajaburi Palace as the sixth of eleven children of Phra-ong Chao Raphiphatnasak Kromluang Rajaburi-direkruethi. The royal title M. C. *(Mom Chao)* was given to Akat Damkoeng as a relative of the king.

Though in poor health from his early childhood on, Akat Damkoeng was an extraordinarily good pupil, who—together with Kulap Saypratisth and Ja-eam Antrasen—engaged in writing and publishing as editor of the "Srithep Journal" of the Thep Sirindra High School in Bangkok. In 1924 he went to London to study legal science, but failed the examinations because of being more interested in literature and his own writing. Then he matriculated at Georgetown University, Washington, D.C., for foreign studies. However, due to a serious ophthalmic disease he had to go back to Thailand in 1928 without a degree.

In Bangkok, Akat Damkoeng began to work at the Ministry of Interior, Department of Public Health, where he met his former fellow student Ja-eam Antrasen, who encouraged Akat to write.

In 1929, the first novel of Akat Damkoeng, *The Circus of Life*, was published and became a best-seller at once. A sequel to this novel, *Yellow Skin or White Skin*, was published in 1930. Only one year later, a collection of short stories and the manuscript of the novel *East or West* (in English) were finished. Permanently in poor health—physically as well as mentally—Akat Damkoeng died in 1932 of malaria. His short stories were published after his death in Thailand and Hong Kong, but *East and West* remains unpublished.

Jana Raendchen

Further Reading

Muanmil, Prathip. (1999) *100 nakpraphan Thai* (100 Thai Writers). Bangkok, Thailand: Chomromdek.

Raphiphatna, Akat Damkoeng. (1998) *Lakorn haeng chiwit* (The Circus of Life). Bangkok, Thailand: Sanam-luang.

———. (1999) *Phiu luang ruu phiu khao* (Yellow Skin or White Skin). Bangkok, Thailand: Double Nine.

Sutthisakorn, Orasom. (1987) *Lakorn chiwit chao jay nak praphan* (The Circus of Life and Its Author). Bangkok, Thailand: Dok-nya.

DANCE—BALI Dance is integral to Bali's cultural life, and includes sacred temple dances that are indispensable to religious rituals, adaptations of old temple or court dances now chiefly performed for tourists, and social folk dances. Balinese dance is rooted in the Hindu-Javanese culture that predates the coming of Islam in the fourteenth and fifteenth centuries, but the repertory has been continually augmented and developed. After Java's conversion to Islam, Balinese dance continued to develop in a sacred, temple setting, while Javanese dance was centered in the royal courts. Balinese choreography generally tended to be more dynamic than Javanese choreography. Balinese choreography emphasizes controlled animation of the entire body, with stance, and leg, arm, hand, and eye movements all carefully defined and positioned.

Visitors to Bali can easily become confused by the plethora of regional variations and dance styles. The following descriptions are generic; details of costume, repertory, and performance vary widely among regions and villages. In Bali, it is customary to classify the dance repertory according to the division of the Balinese temple into three courtyards. The main dance repertory is thus divided between sacred dances traditionally performed in the *jeroan* (inner temple), less sacred dances performed in the *jaba tengah* (middle courtyard), and secular dances which belong in the *jaba*, or outer courtyard.

Jeroan Dances

The main *jeroan* dances are the *pendet*, *rejang*, and *baris gede*. The *pendet* is a dance of welcome for the gods, and is danced by a group of girls or women, each wearing ordinary traditional dress (as opposed to a special dance costume) and carrying an offering in her right hand. *Pendet* is widely taught to girls in Bali today, and has a more or less standardized form. The *pendet* is accompanied by a gamelan gong ensemble. The *rejang* is a stylized procession to entertain visiting spirits. *Rejang* is danced by a group of women and girls of all ages, wearing traditional temple dress along with a gold headdress decorated with flowers. *Baris gede* is a stylized warrior dance performed by a group of men, who form the personal guard of the visiting spirits. The dancers carry weapons—usually pikes, but sometimes *kris* (traditional daggers) or even firearms—and wear distinctive helmets decorated with pieces of shell. The dance represents military actions, including a mock battle. The *sanghyang* dance also belongs to the inner temple group, as does, by extension, the *kecak*. *Sanghyang* is a ritual trance dance accompanied by gamelan gong or chanting, performed to repel evil influences. The dancers are young girls of around eight to ten years old. *Kecak* is a modern offshoot of *sanghyang* developed in the 1930s, which uses the chanting of traditional *sanghyang* as an accompaniment to theatrical dance using stories from the *Ramayana* epic.

Jaba Tengah Dances

The *jaba tengah* dances are mostly narrative. The most important is the *gambuh*, which, like the *jeroan* dances, functions to welcome the spirits. The *gambuh* has pre-Islamic Javanese court origins, and is generally held to be the source of all Balinese narrative dance forms in terms of movement vocabulary, character types, costume, plot development, dramatic conventions, and musical accompaniment. *Gambuh* performances originally lasted for several days, though today they rarely exceed an hour or two. Most *gambuh* performances tell stories from the early Javanese *Panji* romance cycle, often placing the central character in Bali rather than Java. Dialogue is in *Kawi* (Old Javanese), though the comic characters keep up a running commentary in Balinese.

The *topeng pajegan* and *wayang wong*—both masked dramatic forms—also take place in the *jaba tengah*. In *topeng pajegan*, a single dancer performs the entire story, changing masks and voices to represent the various characters, while in *wayang wong* a number of dancers present an episode from the Ramayana epic, again with dialogue in *Kawi*. There is also an outer courtyard masked dance known as *topeng panca* (masked dance of five), in which five dancers represent different characters.

Jaba Dances

Jaba (outer courtyard) dances can be performed outside the context of religious ceremony as purely secular, artistic events. Some of these are dramatic forms, while others, like the *legong* and *baris* dances, are choreographic character studies. *Legong* is performed by three young girls, and has a dramatic structure when performed in its entirety. Today, however, it is usually excerpted, the point being the grace and elegance of the choreography. *Legong* is normally the first dance taught to young girls when they start to study dance. *Baris*, in contrast, is a vigorous male dance style representing a warrior preparing for and engaging in combat. *Baris* is normally taught to all male dance students in Bali, as it contains all the fundamentals of Balinese male choreography. A modern development of the *legong* is the *kebyar duduk*, in which the dancer sits at an instrument of the gamelan gong *kebyar* (modern-style gamelan) ensemble, and the choreography, while based on *legong* style, incorporates playing the instrument.

Outside the temple are a number of genres of social dance, such as *joged bungbung* and *janger*. *Joged bungbung* is similar to the Javanese *tayuban*, and features a number of young female dancers paid to dance flirtatiously with male guests, usually inviting the man to dance by placing a sash around his waist. *Janger* resembles a secular version of the *sanghyang*, and features a group of performers split evenly between the sexes. They sit facing each other in lines and sway rhythmically to their own chanting.

Balinese dance has been widely admired by foreign artists and scholars as a vibrant and vital strand of Balinese culture. Some of these, like German artist Walter Spies, contributed to the development of dance in Bali itself. The continued popularity of traditional dance with Balinese performers themselves should ensure the survival of the tradition even as Indonesian society changes around it.

Tim Byard-Jones

Further Reading

Eiseman, Fred B., Jr. (1990) *Bali: Sekala and Niskala*. Vol. 1: *Essays on Religion, Ritual, and Art*. Hong Kong: Periplus Editions.

Yousouf, Ghulam-Sarwar. (1994) *Dictionary of Traditional South-East Asian Theatre*. Kuala Lumpur, Malaysia: Oxford University Press.

Zoete, B. van, and Spies, Walter. (1973) *Dance and Drama in Bali*. Oxford: Oxford University Press.

DANCE—BANGLADESH

Folk dancing in Bangladesh has to be viewed in the context of the history of the Indian subcontinent. Bangladesh is among the youngest nations of the world; it became a nation in 1971, following its independence from Pakistan, which itself became a nation in 1947. Bangladesh, as former East Pakistan, was far removed socially and culturally from West Pakistan and was closer in every respect to the neighboring Indian province of West Bengal. With its very strong emphasis on cultural preservation, Bangladesh has retained the majority of folk dances that were practiced in Bengal, drawing also from other Indian states such as Orissa and Bihar, with which there have been strong interactions for centuries. It is to be noted that even though a large number of folk dances have been inspired by Hindu rituals, they have been well preserved in Bangladesh, even though since 1947 that region has been predominantly Muslim. If some of the traditional folk dances have gone out fashion, then it is more due to the constraints of urbanized living than to any religious censure.

Mask Dances

The most prominent among the folk dances are mask dances, originally from the Mymensingh district but later performed in various other parts of Bangladesh as well. These dances, usually held after the harvest in March–April, are enactments of myths of the cult of the Hindu god Siva and the goddess Kali.

The wooden masks for the dancers are made by the village carpenter and painted by the potter. All the roles—male and female—are played by village boys. The local drum, the *dhaka*, is played dexterously, and the audience usually joins the performer in singing the chorus of the songs. In these dances, Siva is always shown as a bare-bodied ascetic. The dancer performing as Siva enters and dances; the songs begin in a slow rhythm, progressing toward a faster beat. In the second part of the performance, Kali, the consort of Siva, represented in a terrible form causing destruction, enters and circles around, while Siva lies prostrate on the ground. Kali stands for a while with one foot on the chest of Siva and then proceeds to perform the main section of the dance. These dances are largely improvised, and the songs are composed locally.

The Bara-buri ("old couple") dance also uses masks, but it is very different from the religious dances. The songs and demeanor of the masks depict a good-humored celebration of married life in old age. This dance is performed for fun at social and family functions. The actors are usually males and amateurs.

Other Popular Folk Dances

The most popular form of dancing associated with all Bengali territory is the Kirtana dance. This is a purely devotional dance for the worship of Krishna, started four centuries ago by the saint Caitanya (1485–1583). The movements of this dance are very simple, consisting of raising the hands above the head and clapping to the beat of the *khol*, an elongated wooden drum. Part of the dancing company vigorously plays the *khol*, and everybody sings "Hare Krishna" ("Hare" is the vocative case for "Hari," the name of Vishnu as Krishna). This dance has become known all over the world since the 1960s as part of the Hare Krishna movement.

A spectacular activity is the incense dance, held at the end of the Bengali year during dark, moonless nights. The dancers hold earthen incense pots containing glowing charcoal and throw incense at the end of the refrain while singing, creating a shower of sparks and smoke.

Because smallpox was a major threat in the subcontinent before the advent of modern medicine, regular worship was held for the goddess Sheetala, who was believed to prevent the disease or at least mitigate its fury; she was also believed to cure infertility in women. This worship, which is still used for curing infertility along with modern medicine, is a community effort in which the ritual lead is taken by one woman at whose house other village women gather before proceeding through the village to the riverbank. The leader carries a pitcher of water placed on a winnowing fan on her head, and all the women make loud ululations, a sound that marks many sacred activities in this region. After a ritual bath in the river, the company returns to the house of the leader, where songs and dances are held around the pitcher and fan. The next day, the pitcher and the winnowing fan are taken to various homes in the village, and dances are held in each house around these objects. A drummer of the lower caste plays the *dhak*, a small drum, and women perform ring dances accompanied by simple chants.

The Rayibeshe dances preserve the memory of a past martial tradition. They are no longer very common. Features include a gong called *kansi*, the *khol* drum, and dancing bells worn only on one foot. Rayibeshe dances were manly and vigorous, full of war cries, acrobatics, swordsmanship, and duels with knives and spears. They required long and special training. A similarly martial dance was the Dhali, albeit different in style.

The Shi'a sect of the Muslims holds a period of mourning, called the *Muharram*, in memory of the death of Hussain and Hassan, the sons of Ali (the Prophet Muhammad's son-in-law) at the battlefield of Karbala. During this period, when Shi'ite Muslims avoid most song and dance, mourning songs—*marsia* and *jari*—are sung with deep emotion and great finesse during nights in community gatherings. A special dance performed by men is held, in which they hold one end of their white undergarments (dhoti) in one hand and a piece of scarlet cloth in the other. Slow and mournful movements are made to the chiming of bell-anklets used to create sad rhythms.

Professionally Performed Dances

Khemta, another form of dance, is performed by professionals (for example, courtesans or prostitutes) in family and community gatherings and in religious processions. As most celebrations, including birth, child naming, marriage, and initiation of males, are occasions for dancing, the courtesan class are invited to add to the gaiety. The dance also serves the purpose of providing some extra income to courtesans. Family members, however, only watch; they do not dance along with the courtesans. These dances are usually accompanied by songs on the love dalliance of the god Krishna and his beloved Radha. Intricate footwork and certain features of refined dancing such as complex eye movements are also used. A typical feature of the costume of the main courtesan is a big necklace called *sinthi*. The supporting instruments are tabla (small hand drums) and *sarangi* (an instrument similar to a violin). These are not folk instruments but are used by classical singers only, indicating a close connection with formal dance.

The professional dance that is best known is the Baul, performed by male, rarely by female, members of the Baul community. Simple but full of abandon, this dance has distinctive music and can be performed at any time for recreation. The Bauls are usually traveling mendicants.

Dance in the Twenty-First Century

Folk dances in Bangladesh, as in the rest of the subcontinent, are threatened in the twenty-first century, as the social climate in which they once flourished has changed with the modernization of society. Reduction of community activity such as harvest festivals, extended marriage feasts, lengthy personal and family rituals and loss of patronage from rich landowners and merchants have diminished their frequency. Amateur performers have migrated to big cities, so that training in the village communities is difficult. The new patronage given by academies and art centers is located in the cities and does not promote dances as part of the social fabric of everyday life but only as cultural entertainment. As a result, the folk dances are not only withering, they are becoming more contrived under city patronage, far removed from their native vitality.

Bharat Gupt

Further Reading

Banerji, Projesh. (1959) *The Folk Dances of India*. Allahabad, India: Kitabistan.

Gaston, A. (1997) *Krishna's Musicians*. Delhi: Manohar.

Vatsyayan, Kapila. (1976) *Traditions of Indian Dancing*. Delhi: Indian Book Company.

DANCE—CENTRAL ASIA

Located at the heart of the great Silk Road, Central Asia is crossed by an ancient network of caravan routes that linked China with the Mediterranean. The dances of the region reflect the rich legacy of many cultures, both indigenous and foreign. Through commerce and conquest, Iranian, Turkic, Indian, Arabic, Chinese, and Mongolian elements entered dance styles of the region. The spiritual traditions of Zoroastrianism, shamanism, Hinduism, Buddhism, Christianity, and Islam had an impact on dance. The great division between steppe and oasis that characterizes Central Asian geography influenced cultural development; as a result, the music and dances of nomadic people were less elaborate and varied than those of the settled oasis dwellers.

Dance has long been integral to Central Asian peoples. On the territories of present-day Uzbekistan, Kazakhstan and Azerbaijan, rock paintings known as petroglyphs depict dancing figures and date back to as early as the Bronze Age. Later objects, such as sculptures, frescoes, ornaments, ossuaries, and serving vessels, also portray dancing figures.

General Characteristics

Central Asian dance is often of a solo, improvisational nature, although line and circle dance also exist. Women, or young boys imitating them, usually perform the most celebrated dances. Men and women do not typically dance together and, if they do, they rarely touch.

Typical characteristics encountered in Central Asian dance include head slides and circles. Hands and arms are especially expressive. Wrist circles, hand undulations, and shifting arm patterns create intricate spatial designs around the body and above the head. Shoulder isolations can include up and down lifts, back and forth pushes, and sustained shimmies. The relatively uncomplicated footwork patterns create constant traveling steps over which intricate movements of the upper body are layered. Rhythmic accents occasionally punctuate some dances with stylized hand clapping, finger snapping, and foot stomping by the performer.

Traditionally, many dances were performed almost completely in place because they were done within a household, with guests seated around the perimeter of a room. In Persia, temporary wooden stages covered with carpets were created on top of the decorative ponds that were the central feature of courtyard gardens—another factor that limited performance space. Portions of the dance often took place with the performer kneeling on the floor, requiring a graceful ascent and descent. Spins and turns, ranging from simple to complex, have long been identified with the dance of the area. Folk dances sometimes included hops but rarely high leaps. Unlike Arabic dance, Central Asian dance has virtually no true pelvic isolations, although Persian and Azeri dance sometimes has simple hip twists. Acrobatic components, such as deep backbends or spins ending in a sudden drop to the floor, are usually encountered only in the dance of professionals.

Facial expressions of great emotional range play a central role in the dance performances of women and girls. In the *yalla* dance genre, which is accompanied by song, the dancer must mirror the content of the lyrics in her movements and gestures.

With the exception of some ritual dances, performers wore traditional clothing from the region of a dance's origin. Professional dancers favored more opulent fabrics and jewelry, which were sometimes bestowed by a patron. (This practice continues even today.) Contemporary costumes frequently consist of stylized garments, sometimes from synthetic textiles, which more tightly fit a dancer's body than the voluminous robes of the past.

Ritual, Spiritual, and Healing Dances

Ritual, spiritual, and healing dances reflect a close spiritual relationship with the yearly cycle of nature and the animal world. The Iranian and Turkic peoples of Central Asia celebrated the New Year at the spring equinox with a pre-Islamic festival known as No Ruz (New Day). In ancient times it represented the sacred marriage between Innana, the queen of heaven, and her consort Tammuz, the shepherd god who represented the creative powers of spring. This ritual promoted the fertility of crops, animals, and humans for the coming year. Women still engage in the all-night ritual of making *sumalak*, a special dish of seven grains, singing and dancing while they take turns stirring a large cauldron. No Ruz continues to be celebrated and has enjoyed a revival in the Central Asian republics that were once part of the Soviet Union.

Vestiges of Central Asian shamanism can be linked to the incantational dances of medicine men and fortune-tellers that were still common at the beginning of the twentieth century but that largely died out under the Stalinist persecutions of the 1930s. Traces of the shaman's dance can be discerned in *lazgi*, a traditional healing dance from the Khorezm region that contains trembling movements common to trance dances, as well as gestures imitating animals such as birds or fish.

Some of the earliest references to dance reveal links to religious and spiritual practices. The cult of Mithra, widespread throughout Central Asia, included ritual dance. Zoroastrianism had a fire dance. The so-called whirling dervish traditional dance may have derived from the Tocharian spinning dance and was possibly brought to Asia Minor by Jalal ad-Din ar-Rumi (c. 1207–1273), who was born in the city of Balkh in present-day Afghanistan.

Another ritual was *suskhotin*, a dance entreating "the Lady of Waters" for rain. In the *zikr*, a ritual from the Sufi tradition of Islamic mysticism, dancers travel in a circle with repetitive movements accompanied by chanting and percussion. The dance is still performed. Other folk dances depict daily chores, seasonal work, or important events. Some dances relate to ceremonies such as weddings and funerals.

Combat or War Dances

Martial dances not only developed agility but also aided warriors in achieving a frenzied state that banished fear. The Greek historian Xenophon (430–c. 355 BCE) in his work *Anabasis* described a Persian war dance in which the performer clashed shields together, crouched on one knee, and sprang up again—all accompanied by flute. Afghan men, before going into battle, traditionally performed the *atan milie*. The *atan* still figures in Afghan holidays and wedding festivities. The dancers hold swords and scarves, executing vigorous turns and twisting jumps, as they travel in circles around the musicians, who play the *dohl* (a drum) and *bajakhana* (double-reed oboe).

Court and Professional Dance

From the fourth to the eighth century, the professional dancers of the Samarqand, Bukhara, and Tashkent region enjoyed popularity at the court of the Chinese emperor. During the Tang dynasty (618–907 CE), the celebrated Chinese poet Bo Juyi (772–846 CE) compared the movements of these dancing girls to the whirling of snowflakes. Silver and gilt ewers (pitchers or jugs) dating from the eighth century and discovered in Iran and Uzbekistan depict nude or thinly garbed females, adorned with jewelry, dancing with veils and finger cymbals.

The adoption of Islam subsequent to the Arab invasion of Central Asia in the seventh century promoted sexual segregation and the practice of veiling. Public entertainers suffered from a low social status; female dancers were often linked with prostitution. Respectable women danced for each other in the *ich kari* or *andaroon*—the women's quarters—away from the eyes of strange men.

Generally, public performance of dance became the domain of the *batcha* (dancing boy), who dressed in women's clothing, wore makeup, and danced in a decidedly effeminate style. Rulers and well-to-do merchants kept troupes of these dancing boys. Sometimes several men pooled resources to become patrons of a troupe, which then would entertain at parties.

In the rarefied setting of the court, female dancers entertained, as depicted in the miniature paintings that illustrated manuscripts produced in Central Asia and

Persia from the Middle Ages until the nineteenth century. Many of these dancers came from the non-Muslim population, such as Greek and Armenian Christians and Bukharan Jews.

The clownlike *maskharaboz* were traveling players who performed in bazaars, wearing white-face makeup, tall hats, and patched coats. They developed a humorous dance form known as *gul ufari*, in which the mannerisms associated with various elements of society (wealthy aristocrats, for example) were lampooned.

In Bukhara, a tradition of female wedding performers known as *sozanda* developed. These women sang and danced while wittily improvising poetic verses in praise of the guests.

Social Dances

Important Central Asian festivals and celebrations have long featured dance. When Alexander of Macedon (356 BCE–323 BCE) visited Sogdiana, he was entertained by dancers at a wedding banquet. Line dances, common in the Caucasus and Asia Minor, especially among Kurdish and Azeri populations, are encountered less frequently than circle dances in Central Asia. Turkmen women and men dance in circle formation together in the *kush-depte*. Generally, dancers do not touch each other as they travel in a circular pattern. Solo improvisational dance is more typical, with several persons sharing the performance space but dancing as individuals.

Musical Accompaniment

Music for dance ranges from a purely rhythmic accompaniment to simple folk tunes and songs. Classical art dances are performed to intricate compositions, or *maqam*s, played by ensembles of traditional instruments with singers. At times the dancers themselves create the rhythm by snapping their fingers or clapping their hands. Rhythm can also be provided by *zang* (wrist bells), worn by female dancers, and *kairok* (smooth river stones played somewhat in the manner of castanets). Dances in which the dancers provide their own rhythm range from simple folk dances to sophisticated art dances in which the performer moves to complex and constantly changing rhythm patterns. Even everyday objects of domestic life, such as saucers, thimbles, teacups, and teapots, become potential percussion instruments.

Traditional instruments include the *nai* (reed flute), *zurnai* (double-reed oboe) and *karnai* (long trumpet), *chang* (hammer dulcimer), *gidzhak* (spike fiddle) and *kemanche* (three-string fiddle), *doire* (frame drum), and *davul* (double-headed drum.)

Western Influences

The Russian empire expanded into portions of Central Asia and the Caucasus in the nineteenth century. Although it made some effort to convert the local populations to Russian Orthodox Christianity, the government left most traditions and customs undisturbed. In the early twentieth century, pan-Turkist ideas of the Young Turks, led by Mustafa Kemal (later Ataturk; 1881–1938), reached Central Asia. Another important intellectual current was the Jadid movement of Crimean Tatar educational reformer Ismail Bey Gaspirali (1851–1914), which encouraged the merging of Western advances with traditional Islamic values. The Bolshevik Revolution of 1917 and the subsequent creation of the Soviet Central Asian republics introduced additional Western influences. Perhaps of greatest impact were universal education for both genders and the *khujum* campaign to eliminate the custom of veiling.

With the increased freedom brought about by unveiling, public performances of dance by women and girls followed. In the 1920s, Tamara Khanum (1906–1990) became one of the first women to defy tradition and perform unveiled, often courting death at the hands of reactionaries. The brother of another dancer, Nurkhon, murdered her for dishonoring the family by dancing in public.

The Soviet government promoted the establishment of "national" dance ensembles in each republic and the creation of ballet companies. With state support, Soviet Central Asian republics developed professional folk-dance and ballet ensembles. If indigenous people did not have a significantly developed dance culture, specialists were sent to the area to create one. Elizavetta Petrosian, sister of Tamara Khanum, developed Karakalpak dance, inventing movements based on traditional carpet designs. These state folk-dance companies, following the Soviet dictum of "national in form, socialist in content," adopted Western staging techniques, creating choreographies based on politically approved themes. Some Central Asian performers and choreographers trained in Moscow.

Huge Soviet-style celebrations with mass dance presentations in large public spaces, popular from the 1930s to the end of the Soviet period, robbed dances of delicate, nuanced gestures. The advent of television brought back the intimacy of traditional performance settings; close-ups could reveal the subtle facial expressions and small movements that had been the hallmark of traditional styling. Televised dance concerts became prominent in Central Asia in the 1960s, and increased in popularity in the following decades. Special dance programming bestowed celebrity status on leading female dancers. Expanded contact with the outside world, especially in the 1980s, encouraged Western dance forms to flourish in Central Asia, including ballroom dance, break dance, aerobics, and hip-hop.

After the collapse of the Soviet Union in 1991, the Central Asian republics embraced dance as an expression of national identity and included it in Independence Day celebrations. Nonindigenous forms were sometimes seen as unwelcome foreign imports. In March 2001, Turkmen President Saparmurat Niyazov announced that he would abolish the National Ballet of his country because the Turkmen people "have no ballet in their blood."

Contemporary Western influence continues through the media of television and movies and the incursion of foreign business people and tourism. Traditional dance has become more commercial in nature, abandoning many of the older classical dances in favor of more lively numbers performed to ethno-pop-style music on stages replete with fog machines and laser lights. Arabic and Turkish style dances, with pelvic movements and more revealing costumes, have also been incorporated into popular concerts and nightclub performances.

Central Asian dance continues to gain popularity with Western audiences; some foreign dancers have even mastered folk and classical repertoires. Uzbekistan, and specifically the capital Tashkent, continues to serve as the unofficial cultural center for the Central Asian republics. Leading performers such as Qizlarhon Dustmuhamedova, proclaimed the "People's Artist of Uzbekistan," instruct at dance seminars and work with professional Western dance companies, and similar developments are occurring throughout the Central Asian republics.

Laurel Victoria Gray

Further Reading

Al Faruqi, Lois Ibsen. (1987) "Dance as an Expression of Islamic Culture." *Dance Resource Journal* 10, 2: 6–17.

Avdeeva, Lyubov' Aleksandrovna. (1989) *Tanets Mukarram Turgunbaevoi* (The Dance of Mukarram Turgunbaeva). Tashkent, Uzbekistan: Matbuot Publishing House.

Chardin, Sir John. ([1927]1988) *Travels in Persia: 1673–1677*. Reprint ed. New York: Dover.

Karimova, Rozia. (1970) *Bukharskii tanets* (Bukharan Dance). Tashkent, Uzbekistan: Gafur Gulyam Literature and Art Publishing House.

———. (1973) *Ferganskii tanets* (Ferghana Dance). Tashkent, Uzbekistan: Gafur Gulyam Literature and Art Publishing House.

———. (1975) *Khorezmskii tanets*. (Khorezm Dance). Tashkent, Uzbekistan: Gafur Gulyam Literature and Art Publishing House.

———. (1979) *Tantsy Ansambl'a Bakhor* (Dance of the Bakhor Ensemble). Tashkent, Uzbekistan: Gafur Gulyam Literature and Art Publishing House.

———. (1986) *Uzbekskiye Tantsy v postanovke Isakhara Akilova* (Uzbek Dances in the Choreographies of Isakhar Akilov). Tashkent, Uzbekistan: Gafur Gulyam Literature and Art Publishing House.

Levin, Theodore. (1996) *The Hundred Thousand Fools of God: Musical Travels in Central Asia (and Queens, New York)*. Indianapolis, IN: Indiana University Press.

Schuyler, Eugene. ([1876] 1966) *Turkistan: Notes of a Journey in Russian Turkistan, Kokand, Bukhara and Kuldja*. Reprint ed., New York: Praeger.

Shirokaya, O. I.. (1973) *Tamara Khanim*. Tashkent, Uzbekistan: Gafur Gulyam Literature and Art Publishing House.

Tkachenko, Tamara. (1954) *Narodny Tanets* (Folk Dance). Moscow: Isskustvo.

DANCE, EAST ASIA—MODERN

Modern dance in East Asia—Japan, Korea, China, and Taiwan—has a complex and varied history in the twentieth century. It is characterized by four main directions: (1) the work of pioneers who were influenced by the West, (2) the transformation of indigenous dance forms, (3) the introduction of foreign styles of modern dance, and (4) the introduction, assimilation, and creation of new works in the classical ballet genre. In addition, many traditional forms have been maintained and continued in new contexts.

Modern Dance in Japan

Modern dance pioneers in Japan were Ishii Baku (1886–1962), Eguchi Takaya (1895–1929), and Ito Michio (1892–1961). Ishii studied with Mary Wigman (1987–1973), a German modern dance pioneer. He then toured in East Asia and influenced dance there. Eguchi also studied with Mary Wigman and was influenced by Êthe eurythmics teacher Émile Jaques-Dalcroze (1865–1950). Ito worked in the United States and Europe. He also assisted the Irish poet and dramatist W. B. Yeats (1865–1939) with his work on Noh theater.

In 1948, Nihon Geijutsu Byoka Kyokai (NGKB, Japan Dancing Artists Association) was founded with Ito Michio as president. In 1958, ballet members of this society joined the then-established Japan Ballet Association. In 1971, NGBK renamed itself Gendai Buyo Kyokai (Modern Dance Association). In the late

1990s, a National Modern Dance Company was established at the new National Theater for Opera and Dance in Tokyo, which became a focal point to bring modern dancers together in a culture where cooperation among groups has been elusive.

Creative expression was curtailed by the military in Japan during the 1930s, but modern dance developed rapidly after World War II. Whereas the pioneers were influenced primarily by the German school, the postwar dancers looked to Martha Graham, musical theater, and later Merce Cunningham for inspiration. Major artists of this period included Fuji Mieko and Wakamatsu Miki. Orita Katsuko, Kanai Fumie, and Takeya Keiko are also notable. In 1985, Teshigawara Saburo founded a group called Karas. He was trained as a visual artist, and set design is an important part of his creations. Butoh, an indigenous Japanese genre, has influenced the development of dance artists worldwide. After its defeat in World War II and the devastation of the atomic bomb, Japan entered a period of social unrest; neo-Dada art was in fashion. Butoh artists rejected Western influences and expressed the spirit of postwar Japan in a way that was sometimes provocative and violent. There was an interest in the old, the ill, and criminals, and in how body memory can be reflected in postures and movements. The result has been called grotesque, shocking, humorous, poetic, and hypnotic. Training for Butoh dancers involves various strenuous activities, discipline, and a lifestyle similar to that of monks. Movement style became increasingly slow, focusing on basic emotional gestures. Often, the general atmosphere is one of chaos.

Three dancers influential in developing the Butoh style are Hijikata Tatsumi, Kasai Akira, and Ohno Kazuo. The dances of all three were characterized by an androgynous quality.

Ohno (b. 1906), the best-known Butoh dancer today, studied with Japanese pioneers Ishii and Eguchi. Ohno's signature work, "Admiring La Argentina," was first performed in 1977 when he was seventy years old. It has since been performed all over the world and is typical of the delicate and transient nature of Ohno's fragile and ascetic art. Ohno has also starred in films and is a writer.

Hijikata, who began to work in the 1950s, was endorsed by the writer Mishima Yukio. Hijikata's work started the trend of naked shaved-head dancers covered in white body paint. In 1963, he called his dances "Ankoku (dark) Butoh (dance)," and the word Butoh has been used since to refer to this style.

Kasai, a follower of Ohno, founded a group called Tenshi-kan in 1971. He came from a Christian background, but also studied Shintoism and Rudolph Steiner's mysticism; some of his works had a spiritual intensity. There was also an erotic element arising from his interest in the writers Jean Genet and the Marquis de Sade.

The two major Butoh companies are Dairakudakan and Sankaijuku. Dairakudakan, founded by Maro Akaji in the early 1970s, uses large-scale sets and huge casts to create spectacular effects. The basically male group works in a comic and exaggerated style borrowed from cabaret theater. Sankaijuku, founded by Amagatsu Ushio in the late 1970s, is known for its solemn reflective atmospheres. Both companies have toured extensively and are credited with making this uniquely Japanese art form known abroad. Major solo Butoh artists include Tanaka Min, Goi Teru, Ashikawa Yoko, and Ono Man. Butoh is now being seen and appreciated more in Japan after having gained recognition abroad, and many young artists are experimenting with this genre.

Two recent trends in dance in Japan can be seen in the work of Condors, an all-male group dressed in school uniforms, which satirizes Japanese pop culture and integrates film, speech, and visual gags into its format. The second trend is to look to Europe for new directions. Japan and its artists are known for continually searching for new trends in the arts and public culture.

Modern Dance in Korea

In 1922, Japan's Ishii Baku visited Seoul and performed a work titled "Dance Poem." After this, several Korean students went to Tokyo to study with Ishii. One of these was Choi Seung-hee (1910–?), a dance pioneer who returned to work on a new dance style for Korea. She later toured the West under the management of Sol Hurok, then spent her later years in North Korea, though little is known of her work there.

In 1962, a modern dance course was introduced at Ewha Women's University by Yuk Wan-sun, who trained in the United States with Martha Graham and is called the godmother of Korean modern dance. Ewha's is considered the top university dance program in Korea, and the university continues to graduate dancers who become leaders in the modern dance world there. Modern dance is taught in about forty universities in Korea, and many small companies have been established in recent years.

After World War II and the end of the Japanese occupation, many Koreans began to look to their own cultural history for inspiration. One of the major artists in this effort was Kim Mae-ja, a master teacher of traditional Korean dance, who creates modern works based on that tradition. She teaches and performs frequently in China and has established the Chang Mu Arts Center in Seoul where her company performs along with other Korean and international dance groups. Kim Myong-sook, a professor in dance at Ewha University, also creates contemporary works based on traditional Korean genres and organized the Nuri Dance Company in 1996.

Many outstanding modern dance choreographers are active in Korea: Choi Chung-ja expresses the emotional intensity of pain and spirituality in her work; Park Myung-sook works with women's issues and inner feelings; Ahn Ae-soon deals with the Asian idea of opposites and suggestion in movement and in life; Nam Jeong-ho studied in France, and her works are called fresh and innovative; and Ahn Song-soo worked in New York and London and creates technically demanding choreography. Working in a more avant-garde style, Hong Shin-ja creates work that stems from a natural outdoor environment and traditional spirituality.

Modern Dance in China

Dance pioneers in mainland China were Wu Xiaobang (1906–1995) and Dai Ailien (b. 1916). Wu trained in Japan and returned to China to establish his own school in Shanghai in 1931. In the 1930s his dance creations expressed his patriotism, and after World War II he worked in many institutes in the new China and wrote about theories and methods for his adaptations of Western modern dance to create a new Chinese dance tradition. Dai was born in Trinidad, studied ballet in London, and went to China in the 1940s to take part in the building of a new China. She helped to establish the Beijing Dance Academy, the Central Ballet Company, and after 1949 was one of the first dancers to go into the villages and study the dances of minority peoples. She was made to do hard labor during the Cultural Revolution, but after that traveled abroad as an ambassador for dance in China.

Around 1949, with the help of Russian ballet artists, a new classical Chinese dance was created that is a hybrid of classical ballet and Chinese opera movement. This newly created classical Chinese dance is taught at all the major dance academies in mainland China and in Hong Kong. In recent years this style has been expanded, with many new choreographic works in a contemporary style.

In 1987, Yang Meiqi led the establishment in Guangdong of the first school and company for modern dance in China. Choreographers and teachers from the United States have contributed to the development of the Guangdong Modern Dance Company, which tours internationally and has received glowing press reviews. One of the first choreographers for this company was Wang Mei, head of the Modern Dance Program at the Beijing Dance Academy. Resident choreographers Liang Xing and Sang Jija create works that illumine an experimental aspect of the spirit of the modern China.

In Hong Kong, City Contemporary Dance Company (CCDC), founded by Willy Tsao in 1979, is the major voice for modern dance. Tsao has been a major figure in Chinese circles as a producer and promoter of contemporary dance and is now working in Beijing as director of the Modern Dance Company. Other important Hong Kong choreographers, all connected with CCDC, are Helen Lai, who choreographs for many groups in Asia; Mui Cheuk-yin, best known for her innovative solos stemming from Chinese tradition; Poon Siu-fai, creating avant-garde pieces; and Yuri Ng, who works in a modern ballet style. CCDC has a strong education and outreach program that contributes to the growth of interest in dance as a career and to the raising of dance standards in Hong Kong. Since 1980, CCDC has made fifty-one international tours to over thirty major cities in Asia and the West. Also in Hong Kong, the School of Dance at the Academy for Performing Arts, founded in 1984, has become a major training center for modern dance (and for ballet and Chinese dance), and its graduates have established many small groups in Hong Kong and overseas.

Modern Dance in Taiwan

Modern dance in Taiwan was first introduced during the Japanese occupation by touring companies in the early 1930s. A young dancer, Tsai Ryueh, then went to Japan to study with Ishii Baku after the latter visited Taiwan, and Tsai returned to Taiwan to pioneer modern dance. In 1966, Al Huang Chung-liang came to Taiwan to conduct modern dance workshops at the Chinese Dance Arts Institute founded by Tsai. In 1967, Liu Feng-shueh began a modern dance center.

The best-known dance artist in Taiwan is Lin Hwai-min, who founded the Cloud Gate Dance Theatre in 1973. Cloud Gate, with Lin's choreography, draws heavily on Chinese culture, its legends, and its folklore. In the early years, his work was a synthesis of Chinese opera movement, ballet, and Graham technique; in recent years, however, the primary source of movement inspiration and training has been tai chi and improvisation. Lin was also instrumental in 1983 in establishing the Dance Department at the National Institute of Arts in Taipei, now the main training center for modern dance in Taiwan. Cloud Gate tours internationally and is the best-known Asian modern dance company. Before his dance career, Lin was famous as a writer in Taiwan and was known for his astute political sense and deep concern for the Taiwanese people.

Taiwan's many modern dance artists include Henry Yu, former member of the Graham company; Heng Ping, who established a dance center and the Taipei Dance Forum with resident choreographer Sunny Pang of Hong Kong; and Liou Shaw-lu, a former Cloud Gate member who directs the Taipei Dance Circle, which tours extensively and performs Liou's unique art of oiled bodies sliding around and over each other on large plastic floor cloths. Two others of note are Lo Man-fei, who formed a company of mature dancers, many of whom had danced with Cloud Gate, and Lin Hsiu-wei, who developed a modern theatrical dance style that draws heavily on Chinese opera tradition.

General Trends

For many years, East Asia has been exporting modern dancers and choreographers who have had successful careers around the world. A notable example from China is Chiang Ching, who worked in the United States and Europe in the 1970s. H. T. Chen of Taiwan has worked in New York's Chinatown for the past twenty years. From the 1960s through the 1980s, several dance artists from Japan came to the United States to pursue their careers. Kanda Akiko, Takako Asakawa, and Yuriko Kimura were soloists with the Martha Graham Company. In 1969, Takei Kei did her first group work, "Light," which began a life-long journey exploring the theme of an imaginary family of man in his ceremonies though time and nature.

The development of modern dance in East Asia is expanding at a phenomenal rate. Modern dance programs have been established in many secondary and tertiary educational institutions, and graduates are participating in a variety of ways in their local dance worlds. Moreover, many excellent new choreographers and companies are emerging and making important contributions to dance communities in Asia and around the world. In the near future, there is likely to be continued growth and exciting new trends in the modern dance of East Asia.

Carl Wolz

Further Reading

Benbow-Pfalzgraf, Taryn, ed. (1998) *International Dictionary of Modern Dance*. Detroit, MI: St. James Press.

Fraleigh, Sonda Horton. (1999) *Dancing into Darkness*. Pittsburgh, PA: University of Pittsburgh Press.

Korean National Commission for UNESCO, ed. (1983) *Korean Dance, Theater, and Cinema*. Seoul: Si-sa-young-o-sa Publishers.

Solomon, Ruth and John Solomon, eds. (1995) *East Meets West in Dance*. Amsterdam: Harwood Academic Publishers.

Strauss, Gloria B. (1977) "Dance and Ideology in China, Past and Present: A Study of Ballet in the People's Republic." In *CORD Research Annual 8: Asian and Pacific Dance*. New York: CORD.

DANCE—INDIA

DANCE—INDIA Dance in India is as diverse as the multiethnic society from which it stems. Each region, with its own language, literature, customs, costume, and cuisine, has its own dance forms, some of which are traced through wall paintings, ancient manuscripts, and temple sculptures to well over three thousand years ago. There are dances in which everyone participates, at religious festivals or private celebrations, and those performed only by specialists who undergo rigorous training from childhood. Some forms are considered classical, while others are classified as folk; each is part of larger theater, music, religious, and even cinema traditions.

Indian dancers gesture with the eyes, head, neck, and hands. With wrists bent and arms flowing, the dancer interprets the lyrics of accompanying songs, telling stories through facial expression and hand gesture; with bare feet, rhythms are beat on the ground to complement percussion instruments like drums, sticks, and cymbals. Indian classical dances have influenced court and temple dance in most of Southeast Asia—Myanmar (Burma), Thailand, Indonesia, and Cambodia. Dance sequences in modern Indian films, choreographed to extremely popular songs, have captivated peoples all over the world.

Ancient and Classical Dance

Detailed descriptions of ancient Indian theater and dance are found in Sanskrit texts like the *Natya Sastra* (Treatise on Dramaturgy, second century BCE) and the *Abhinaya Darpana* (Mirror of Gesture, thirteenth century CE), which present the theory and technique of a highly developed art. Elaborate lists of eye, neck, head, and hand movements, and of walks and turns, include the various meanings that can be conveyed. Sections are devoted to the performers, music, costume, and stage, as well as to the sacred and aesthetic purposes of dance performance.

THE ESSENCE OF DANCE IN INDIA

"Wherever the hand moves, there the glances follow; where the glances go, the mind follows; where the mind goes, the mood follows; where the mood goes, there is the flavor."

Source: Ananda Coomaraswarmy and Gopala K. Duggirala, trans. ([1917] 1970) *The Mirror of Gesture: Being the Abhinaya Darpana of Nandikesvara.* Reprint ed. New Delhi: Munshiram Manoharlal.

By the end of the nineteenth century, both the texts and the dances they described had fallen into obscurity due to lack of patronage and also to attitudes introduced by the British about the immorality of dance. Dance was associated with *nauch* (dancing) girls, many of them *devadasi*s (female servants of gods) attached to temples who performed at temple festivals and palace parties. Regarding them as prostitutes, some outraged British women led an anti-*nauch* movement and sought to ban dance.

The rediscovery and translation of ancient manuscripts, the birth of Indian nationalism, and growing pride in indigenous art forms led to a revival of many dance forms. The first dance form to be revived in the 1930s, that of the *devadasi*s from temples in south India, was renamed *Bharata Natyam* (Theater of Bharata) after the legendary author of the *Natya Sastra*.

With the ascendance of other forms like *Kathak, Odissi, Kathakali* and *Kuchipudi*, dances performed by men, and dances originating in royal courts, *Bharata Natyam* remains the paradigm of Indian classical dance. Traditionally taught by hereditary male gurus (maestros), who rarely performed, classical dance training includes the study of ancient texts on theater, aesthetics, mythology, and music. Many universities offer academically rigorous degrees in dance.

Folk and Popular Dance

While classical dances are presented by specialists and associated with elite social groups (the ideal spectator is learned, noble, and refined), everyone can participate in folk dances. Like one's mother tongue, these are learned while growing up in a community. Each region and ethnic group has its own dances, as various as the dances of warriors carrying spears and the dances of women in swirling skirts with several water pitchers balanced on their heads. When dancers from all over India come to the nation's capital to participate in the annual Republic Day parade, their nationally televised performances require a sports stadium.

People dance at village fairs, street festivals, and in homes during marriages. They carry their dances with them when they emigrate to other provinces, or even abroad. Folk dances from different regions are now taught in high schools, and in many cities, when one ethnic group dances during its festivals, members of other ethnic groups join in. Traditional dances to a disco beat are popular among young and old, from Mumbai (Bombay) to London. Dance dramas or ballets, modeled on Western and indigenous forms in which a story is enacted through dance, are also popular among professional and amateur dance groups.

Most popular of all are *filmi* dances that accompany the many songs that characterize Indian cinema. Clips of these dance sequences, in which stars lip-sync the lyrics while performing hip-jerking movements in an array of romantic settings and while wearing a range of form-revealing costumes, are a major part of television programming. Street children in many countries break into the more famous routines the minute they see an Indian tourist. Commercially produced extravaganzas, at which cinema icons perform live, are extremely successful in India.

Music and Costume

Musical accompaniment for dance is as varied as the dances. In general, dances from the south are allied to the Carnatic musical tradition, and those of the north to the Hindustani system and so follow their distinctive musical modes (ragas) and rhythmic cycles (talas). Beyond that, each dance form—folk, popular, or classical—has its own melodies, rhythms, and instruments. A *chenda* double-headed drum signals an all-night dance theater from Kerala, whereas a *pungi* double clarinet with a gourd reservoir accompanies a gypsy dancer from Rajasthan. As with the rest of Indian music, the leading instrument is the human voice, and, even within a single form, individual dances are defined by specific songs.

Apart from percussion instruments and feet with bells, rhythms are also expressed by vocalized syllables, like *tat, dhit, gadhi ghena dhaa.* In classical dance these syllables are chanted by the leader of the musical ensemble and accompany sequences of rhythmic dance. Songs can be set just to Indian musical syllables—sa, re, ga (the Indian do, re mi)—or to poetic texts or both. Poetic texts are interpreted with mimed as well as abstract movement. Lyrics usually refer to deities and characters from Hindu scriptures who, particularly in female temple-dance forms, are directly addressed in passionate love songs through which the dancer expresses a human's yearning for union with the divine soul.

Dancers' costumes are usually the festive wear of the communities from which they stem, characterized by colorful fabrics and elaborate ornaments. In keeping with their earlier ritual status as "brides of a deity," temple dancers are dressed as brides; actor-dancers of theatrical forms sometimes wear masks or masklike makeup, especially in Kathakali dance. Traditional dance and theater rarely employ scenery or props.

Dance in the Early 2000s

As India modernizes, becomes more urban, and is influenced by a world economy, the traditional dance ethos is changing. Dance festivals, organized by the government or supported by businesses, are held at ancient ruins and in foreign countries. Dance is becoming increasingly prestigious and performers are highly valued; they win national awards and receive government land to start academies. A new generation of spectators is encouraging dancers to update the form and style of dances and to experiment with nontraditional themes.

Indian dancers travel widely; many live, choreograph, and teach abroad. Each artist subtly adds to and even changes the traditional forms, whether working within those forms or breaking away to find a more contemporary idiom. Fusion is a growing trend—*Kathak* and Flamenco, *Bharata Natyam* and jazz, *Kathakali* and ballet, *filmi* dance and Western disco. Yet the fount remains the traditional, particularly the classical, forms with which most dancers, including film stars, are familiar. Indeed, it is this interplay between popular and classical that has characterized Indian dance throughout the ages and makes it a vibrant expression of Indian culture.

Rajika Puri

Further Reading

Ambrose, Kay. (1983) *Classical Dances and Costumes of India*. 2d ed. New York: St. Martin's Press.

Coomaraswarmy, Ananda, and Gopala K. Duggirala, trans. ([1917] 1970) *The Mirror of Gesture: Being the Abhinaya Darpana of Nandikesvara.* Reprint ed. New Delhi: Munshiram Manoharlal.

Ghosh, Manmohan. (1967) *The Natyasastra (A Treatise on Ancient Indian Dramaturgy and Histrionics) Ascribed to Bharata-Muni.* Calcutta, India: Granthalaya.

Puri, Rajika. (1985) "Paradigm of India's Classical Tradition: Bharatanatyam as Performed Today." *Journal for the Anthropological Study of Human Movement* 3, 3: 117–138.

Ragini Devi. (1990) *Dance Dialects of India*. 2d ed. New Delhi: Motilal Banarsidass.

Vatsyayan, Kapila. (1987) *Traditions of Indian Folk Dance.* New Delhi: Clarion Books.

DANCE—KOREA

DANCE—KOREA Traditional dance in Korea can be divided into two categories, folk dance and court dance. Ritual folk dance is performed by women and men, although originally only men performed the sacred dances within Confucian shrines. Ritual dance in North Korea tends to be more athletic, with jumps and quicker tempos, while South Korean ritual dance is more meditative and slow. Also known as "shaman dancing," ritual dance is used in some cases to exorcise bad spirits. The *Salp'uri* is a slow/fast, joyful, often bewitching and entrancing style of dance. Ritual dances honoring various deities as well as the folk dances celebrating the various agricultural seasons of the earth and the farmer's festivals were also used in the training of peasant militia groups during ancient times.

Music and dance associated with the agricultural aspects of Korean life are called *nongak. Nongak* is one of the oldest traditional forms of Korean dance, tracing its roots back to the period of tribal states (first century BCE) and before. Although *nongak* was performed during the course of everyday farm work as well as festivals, professional musicians and dancers also performed the style for entertainment. These performers also wore masks. *T'al'ch'um* is the Korean form of a masked dance drama. The masks themselves represent the five geographic directions: Yellow = center, red = south, blue = east, white = west, and black = north. *T'al'ch'um* was originally a style of Buddhist morality plays from China. The Korean style of the form evolved a comic sense, making light of everyday situations, and at times could be quite racy with theme and dialogue.

Court dance in Korea is much more reserved than folk dance. This style is often described as *chong'joong'-dong* or "motion within stillness." The movements are elegant, graceful, flowing, and restrained, with the movement controlled by the dancer's inhalation and exhalation. The costumes cover the entire body: long full skirts and tops with extended sleeves that help to augment the small delicate movements of the hand and forearm, making the dancer appear to float weightless during performance.

Dance continues to evolve in Korea through contemporary modern styles. Young dance artists such as

Dancers participate in a folk dancing competition in Aanyan, South Korea, in 1989. (STEPHANIE MAZE/CORBIS)

Hong Sin-cha, Nam Jeong-ho, Lee Kyung-ok, Kim Hyon-ok, Kim Mae-ja, and Ch'ang Mu Hoe explore both the traditional spirituality, breaking the boundaries established by their predecessors, while finding their own unique movement vocabularies.

Stacey Fox

Further Reading

Kendall, Laurel (1985) *Shamans, Housewives, and Other Restless Spirits: Women in Korean Ritual Life*. Honolulu, HI: University of Hawaii Press.

DANCE—MALAYSIA Dances in Malaysia are categorized into court-classical dances, folk dances, ethnic-tribe dances, and dances from immigrant communities such as Chinese, Indian, and Portuguese, as well as modern dance. Although Malaysia is a Malay-dominated nation, it is multiethnic.

Court and folk dances are mainly Malay. Even though Malaysia has thirteen states plus the federal territory of Kuala Lumpur and Labuan, Sabah, only nine sultanates survived—Perlis, Kedah, Perak, Kelantan, Terengganu, Pahang, Selangor, Negeri Sembilan, and Johor. Melaka, regarded as the beginning of Malay civilization in the fifteenth century, was captured by the Portuguese in 1511. The fall of Melaka resulted in the birth of other sultanates such as Johor and Perak. The Malay court dances originated from these courts. The courts of the northern Malay states of peninsular Malaysia are perceived as culturally richer. The best-known court dance is Asyik from Kelantan.

Other dances include *inai* of Perlis, *gamelan* of Terengganu, and *mak yong* of Kelantan, the latter being dance theater that encompasses many dances within it, such as Mengadap Rebab and Belan-belan Bejalan. Some of the Malay folk dances were also performed at court for special social functions, either as presentation or as social dance, such as *joget*. The word *joget* could actually be translated as "dance" but is commonly translated as "folk dance." The court-classical dances are normally much slower and performed by women, which is one of the reasons why the court dances disappeared after these courts became more Islamic. The folk dances are normally performed as social dance in villages for special occasions such as weddings and engagements. The ethnic-tribe dances are common among ethnic groups in Sabah and Sarawak as well as among the Orang Asli (Original People) of peninsular Malaysia. Most of the ethnic-tribe dances are related to rituals of tribes, such as the harvest festival.

Other dances include ballet, modern, and contemporary dance. Contemporary dance in Malaysia is not restricted to Western modern and contemporary dance, but includes contemporary Malaysian dances

Dayak women performing in a costumed dance drama in Sarawak, Borneo, Malaysia. (CHARLES & JOSETTE LENARS/CORBIS)

that include Chinese, Indian, Malay, and ethnic issues. Perhaps the early contemporary dances could be traced to dances created for films in the 1950s and 1960s. In the 1970s, contemporary dances developed further when dance and theater groups collaborated for new works. Today, the contemporary dances continue to be developed by incorporating Malaysian issues (that is, issues that affect all citizens of Malaysia, not just ethnically Malay citizens) rather than Malay issues, especially with new performance venues and the Malaysia Dance Society and National Arts Academy teaching both traditional and contemporary dances. Traditional Malay and ethnic dances continue to be performed for tourists.

Zulkifli Mohamad

Further Reading

Brandon, James R., ed. (1993) *Cambridge Guide to Asian Theatre.* New York: Cambridge University Press.

Brandon, James R. (1967) *Theatre in Southeast Asia.* Cambridge, MA: Harvard University Press.

Nasaruddin, Mohamed Ghouse. (1994) *Malay Dance.* Kuala Lumpur, Malaysia: DBP.

———. (1991) *Malay Music Tradition* Kuala Lumpur, Malaysia: DBP.

Winstedt, Richard O. (1950) *The Malays, a Cultural History.* New York: Philosophical Library.

DANCE, SRI LANKA—KANDYAN Kandyan dance is a style of classical dancing that flourished under the patronage of the rulers of the kingdom of Kandy (1597–1815), in central Sri Lanka. Kandyan dance is known as *uda rata natam;* it is one of three distinct styles of traditional dance in Sri Lanka. (The other two are *pahatha rata natum* and *sabaragamuwa* dance.) Kandyan dance is characterized by very elaborate costumes and by a highly developed rhythmic system *(tala)*, which is carried by drums and tiny cymbals *(thalampataa)*.

Drumming is such an integral part of Kandyan dance that the very act is surrounded by sanctity. The basic drum scale is made up of the drum syllables *tha - ji - tho - nun*, and these individual notes are considered a salutation to, respectively, the Buddha, the gods, the master or teacher, and the audience. Of several drums that are used, the most important for dance is the *gete-bere*, which is played on all festive occasions in Sri Lanka. It consists of a single piece of wood hollowed out to form a cylinder, with a drumhead on each end: one is made of monkey skin, the other of oxhide. The drum is slung round the drummer's waist so that he can play it with both hands.

The term "Kandyan dance" actually embraces five distinct types. *Ves* dance is derived from an ancient purification rite and is still performed as propitiation, by

Kandyan dancers performing at the Esala Perahera festival in Kandy, Sri Lanka, in 1981. (TIM PAGE/CORBIS)

male dancers only. The elaborate dance costume is thought sacred, as belonging to the deity Kohomba, and it has only been a century since the dancers were first permitted to perform outside the Kankariya Temple in Kandy.

Another of the dance types is *uDekki* dance. This uses a small, lacquered, hand-held drum called *uDekki*, the parts of which are believed to have been given to humankind by various gods. It has strings that can be tightened to change its pitch. It is difficult to play, especially as the dancer is singing while playing it.

Pantheru dance employs an instrument called *pantheruwa*, which resembles a tambourine but without a skin. This dance is believed to have come down from the time of the Buddha (c. 566–486 BCE). The gods are said to use this particular instrument to celebrate their victories in battle, and Sinhalese kings used to use *pantheru* dances in the same way.

The *naiyaaNDi* dance is performed during preparations for the Kohomba Kankariya festival and other religious festivals. It is characterized by a special dance dress.

Vannam dance derives from the Sinhalese word *varNana* ("descriptive praise"). Originally these *vannams* were only sung, but later they were adapted for solo dancing, each one expressing a single dominant idea. There are eighteen principal *vannams*, and the songs are said to have been composed by the sage Ganithalankara. They take their inspiration from many different themes, and bear titles like "elephant," "precious stone," "lion," "arrow," and "peacock."

Paul Hockings

Further Reading

Kotelawala, Sicille P. (1974) *The Classical Dance of Sri Lanka: The Kandyan Dance.* New York: Performing Arts Program of the Asia Society.

DANCE DRAMA, MASK—KOREA Korean mask dance drama, *t'alch'um (sandae nori)*, dates back to prehistoric Korean shaman rituals. Mask dance dramas were performed to propitiate the spirits during the agricultural year, repel evil, honor ancestors, and ensure bountiful harvests. With the introduction of Buddhism to Korea, influences from India via China were adopted, as noted in the lion dance. Performed at New Year's, Buddha's birthday, and the Tano and Ch'usok festivals, the dramas were a lively folk tradition. Today, the dance dramas, in reality short skits, are a combination of music, dance, song, and narrative combined with humor.

The dramas, handed down as part of an oral tradition, were always performed outdoors at night by firelight. The performers were exclusively men, usually farmers, until recently, when women began to participate. Drumming and music were a crucial component, with a different rhythm introducing each new character. The characters included humans, gods, spirits, and animals. The masks (made of wood, gourds, or paper) were exaggerated and brightly colored to compensate for the low light. Colors have special significance; black is used for the faces of the elderly, red for a young man, and white for a young woman. Most of the masks are backed with black cloth to signify hair and to secure the mask. Some masks have movable parts, such as the eyes or lower jaw. Some of the roles are acted in pantomime and dance alone. Performances can last the entire night or only a few hours. Improvisation often is used. The artistic masks used in traditional dance dramas were often destroyed after performances.

Performances are often opened with a ritual ceremony to ensure the success of the play. The most common theme of dance dramas is social satire. Many of the satires ridicule the ruling classes, wayward Buddhist monks, and shrewish women. Broad humor is a strong component. The *Kosong ogwangdae*, a mask dance drama from southeastern Korea, has five scenes including a leper, a disreputable Buddhist monk, and a ruined aristocrat. Complicated love triangles between a man, his proper wife, and his courtesan abound. Traditionally, masks depicting the *yangban* (ruling classes) usually were given unattractive features such as a harelip or lopsided leer. Such entertainment enabled the common people to voice social criticisms and rebellious sentiments safely.

In the 1980s, interest was revived in this folk art form, and many small troupes were formed. Modern *t'alch'um* performances can be seen in Seoul at the Chong-dong Theater.

Noelle O'Connor

Further Reading

Lee, Hye-Gu. (1977) *Introduction to Korean Music and Dance.* Seoul: Royal Asiatic Society, Korea Branch.

Van Zile, Judy. (2001) *Perspectives on Korean Dance.* Middleton, CT: Wesleyan University Press.

DANCHI During the Meiji period (1868–1912), Japanese cities rapidly industrialized, bringing large numbers of people from rural areas to urban centers. Some neighborhoods in Tokyo became virtual tenements, with almost 200 percent occupancy in some dwellings. However, the situation in Japan never approximated the slum conditions of industrializing urban areas in America and Europe due to the nature of labor migration. Most early factory workers lived in dormitory-like accommodations, established by factories for *dekasegi rodo*—young people (especially women) brought for a contracted term to live in the cities but to return to the rural areas after a fixed period, with their wages sent home to the countryside, and their housing and food provided by the employers. Thus a permanent urban working class was slow to form in Japan, compared to the earlier industrializing nations. However, with the devastation of the 1923 Tokyo earthquake, many workers needed housing, and *danchi*—large-scale apartment dwellings—were constructed to meet these needs. Some of these complexes were envisioned by their developers as communities, with a central plaza or square in the center of the surrounding buildings, and with facilities for residents held in common. In general, these large buildings were relatively clean and hygienic and provided reasonable accommodations in close quarters. Construction was suspended in wartime, when bombings and fire destroyed many homes.

In postwar Japan, the remaining housing was overcrowded and lacked amenities. Many families doubled or tripled up, sleeping took places in shifts, and workers sometimes stayed at their place of employment rather than return "home." The enormous apartment complexes built on city fringes since the war also create bedroom towns in suburban areas. These *danchi* may contain as many as 400 or more units. They were first built in the late 1950s to accommodate workers migrating to urban industrial areas, and workers displaced from war industries or from former colonies. Soon, burgeoning white-collar workplaces brought more educated young people from the countryside and provincial cities to the capital. The residents of *danchi* were often young couples living on their own, away from their rural or provincial extended households. During this period very few of these young wives worked outside the home, though some older wives and mothers did *naishoku* (take-home employment) as piecework for small-scale enterprises contracting out light manufacturing or assembly work. Because of the isolation from their natal families, young women with small children and little contact with adults during the day, sometimes fell victim to *danchibyoo*, or "apartment complex sickness," a syndrome characterized by depression and neurasthenic symptoms—similar to suburban housewives' depression-related symptoms in postwar America.

Some *danchi* are private apartments and some are rented at highly subsidized rents to workers, with most of the cost covered by the employer. *Danchi* continue to be built, some resembling small towns, with community services, shopping, and day-care centers included. Some *danchi* now are specially built to accommodate the increasing number of elderly, who living alone or in couples, away from caregiving children or other relatives, are provided with some assistance, such as visiting home aides, meals on wheels, and telephone chain contact.

A typical *danchi* apartment is known as a "2LDK," because it has two "living areas" and a kitchen-dining room, along with a separate toilet and a bathroom. It is also likely to have a small balcony with a washing machine and clothes drying lines. Such an apartment may have one large Western style room with a carpeted floor. Frequently, the other "living" area will be tatami matted. New buildings may have no tatami-matted rooms at all. These two large rooms will have large closets on one side where futons (sleeping mats, mattresses, etc.) are kept during the day, and brought out at night. Most families with young children tend now to have a designated "children's room" once the children are of kindergarten age (before that age, children tend to sleep next to their parents on futons), and there may be bunk beds or fixed furnishings, less flexible than the older style of mobile bedding.

Merry Isaacs White

Further Reading

Allinson, Gary. (1979) *Suburban Tokyo.* Berkeley and San Francisco: University of California Press.

Dore, Ronald. (1958) *City Life in Japan*, Berkeley and San Francisco: University of California Press.

Robertson, Jennifer. (1991) *Native and Newcomer: Making and Remaking a Japanese City.* Berkeley and San Francisco: University of California Press.

Sofue, Takao. (1984) "Urbanization and Changing Human Relations in Japan. In *Proceedings; International Symposium on Metropolis.* New York: Japan Society.

DANGREK RANGE The Dangrek Mountains, known in Khmer as the Chuor Phnum Dangrek, divide Thailand and Cambodia along an east-west axis. The range is located along the northern Tonlé Sap Basin and is primarily a steep escarpment. The average elevation of the escarpment is about 500 meters. Its peaks range from 450 to 700 meters in height.

The Dangrek escarpment is located on the southern edge of the Khorat Plateau. The mountains extend west from the Mekong River to approximately San Kamphaeng, Thailand. This watershed serves as the boundary between Thailand and Cambodia, running about 800 kilometers in length. Although there is a main road in the area connecting these two nations, travel and communications are difficult. The Mekong valley, located at the eastern end of the range, and the Mekong Delta, in the southeast, provide land and water access between Cambodia and Laos.

Because this geographic feature has served as a border between nations, it has also been a region in which military activity has taken place during periods of civil unrest and war. The Dangrek Mountains have a place in history as having been where Pol Pot (1925–1998), the leader of the Khmer Rouge, died.

Linda Dailey Paulson

Further Reading

Hoskin, John. (1992) *Cambodia: A Portrait.* Hong Kong: Elsworth Books.

DAOISM. See **Taoism.**

DARDANELLES The Dardanelles is a 61-kilometer-long strait separating European and Asian Turkey, linking the Aegean Sea with the Sea of Marmara. Its widest point is 7 kilometers, its narrowest only 1,600 meters. During classical antiquity the strait was known as the Hellespont, and its modern Turkish name is Canakkale Bogazi. The Dardanelles, together with the Bosporus Strait farther north, has been a major crossing point between Europe and Asia and also controls navigation between the Black and Mediterranean Seas.

The ancient city of Troy was located near the Dardanelles, and both Xerxes I of Persia (c. 519–465 BCE) and Alexander of Macedon (356–323 BCE) crossed the strait during their military campaigns. During the Byzantine and Ottoman empires, the strait was used in the defense of Constantinople (now Istanbul) and was fortified for this purpose. In World War I, the Allied powers attempted to pass through the strait, but two early attempts, in 1915, were unsuccessful. The second of these, the Gallipoli campaign, resulted in great loss of life. In 1918, the Allies passed through the strait and took Constantinople. Following the war, several international treaties demilitarized and internationalized the Dardanelles, but the Montreux Convention of 1936 allowed Turkish remilitarization while guaranteeing access to foreign vessels. The strait remains important as a shipping lane for Black Sea nations.

Michael Pretes

Further Reading

Luce, John Victor. (1998) *Celebrating Homer's Landscapes: Troy and Ithaca Revisited.* New Haven, CT: Yale University Press.

A cruise ship docks in the harbor at Canakkale on the Dardanelles. (WOLFGANG KAEHLER/CORBIS)

Zurcher, Erik Jan. (1993) *Turkey: A Modern History.* London: I. B. Tauris.

DARHAN (2000 pop. 66,000). The city of Darhan (elevation 700 meters) located some 219 kilometers north of Ulaanbaatar, Mongolia, on the Trans-Mongolian Railway, is the third largest city in Mongolia. Before 1961 the site where Darhan now stands was nothing but rolling pastureland in Selenge Province. What sets this site apart from other regions of Mongolia, however, is its proximity to the country's only transnational rail line and a surplus of raw materials, including coal, marble, and limestone. For these reasons, the Mongolian government and its former economic partner, the Union of Soviet Socialist Republics, envisioned locating a fledgling industrial complex here and in 1961 began building the city from the ground up. Beginning with the building of a reinforced concrete factory, which contributed to further development, the city grew quickly and by 1990 had reached a population of 70,000. The population is as young as the city, with 90 percent of all inhabitants under the age of thirty-five (in 1990). Construction workers and specialists from other socialist countries—as far away as Czechoslovakia, the German Democratic Republic, Poland, Bulgaria, and Hungary—played a large part in the city's rapid growth. For this reason, Darhan is known as the "town of international friendship."

Daniel Hruschka

Further Reading

The MPR Academy of Sciences. (1990) *Information Mongolia.* Oxford: Pergamon Press.

DARI Dari, a language of Indo-Iranian origin, is one of the official languages spoken in Afghanistan (Pashto is the other official language of Afghanistan). Dari is a dialect of Farsi (or Persian), the official language of Iran, and the two languages are so similar in their structure, syntax, and lexicon that Iranians and Afghans can communicate with each other with little difficulty. Nevertheless, there are some distinctive differences between the two. The accent in Dari is not quite as stressed as in Farsi; the vowel systems of the two languages differ; and Dari employs more consonants than Farsi. Finally, when a designation is specified, Dari adds a suffix, *ra.*

Dari uses a modified Arabic script with thirty-two alphabetic characters, and the language has many loanwords from Arabic as well as Persian. There is a formal and more proper version of the language as well as an informal one. In fact, the word "Dari" originates from the word *"dar,"* or *"darbari,"* which means "court language." Dari, like Pahlavi Middle Persian, is thought to have been spoken in the eastern Iranian royal courts. The language, however, may have originated as common people's speech, which later became formalized to bring it to the level required for use in the royal courts. Today the language has evolved to a stage where the formal style is more closely associated with Farsi, while the informal one resembles more the language spoken in Tajikistan.

Dari is spoken by approximately 5 million people in Afghanistan. Several ethnic groups, including the Chahar Aimak, Hazara, and Tajik, speak Dari as their main language. In Afghanistan Dari is spoken when people who speak different languages come together.

Dari has a rich literary tradition and history. It was the language chosen by several prominent ancient and modern literary figures to weave an epic tale or compose a touching poem. Poets who wrote in the Dari language include Abu Hafs-I Sughdi, Abu al-Abbas-I Marvarzi, and Yazid Ibn-I Mifraq. A modern Afghani poet, Ustad Khalilullah Khalili, also writes in Dari, and many critics consider his use of the Dari language to be brilliant. Khalili has written almost fifty literary works, which include poems, fiction, history, and Sufi studies, all representing some of the finest literary points of the Dari language.

Houman A. Sadri

Further Reading

Adamec, Ludwig W. (1997) *Historical Dictionary of Afghanistan.* 2d ed. Lanham, MD: Scarecrow Press.

Norton, Augustus Richard, ed. (1996) *Civil Society in the Middle East.* Leiden, Netherlands, and New York: Brill.

DARJEELING (2002 est. pop. 110,000). Celebrated as a hill resort and tea-producing center, Darjeeling is a city in India situated along a ridge in the Himalayan foothills of northern West Bengal State, 500 kilometers north of Calcutta. Its name is derived from the Tibetan Dorje-Ling, "place of the thunderbolt," and much about the city is Tibetan in sensibility. It has three parts, joined by flights of steps and steep narrow streets; highest are hotels, shops, private schools, and entertainment for visitors and the wealthy, near the ridge line; lower, homes of residents, smaller hotels, and shops; at the bottom, the main market and bazaars. The rajas of Sikkim controlled Darjeeling intermittently until 1816, when the British

DARJEELING HIMALAYAN RAILWAY—WORLD HERITAGE SITE

The Darjeeling Himalyan Railway was designated a UNESCO World Heritage Site in 1999 for its singular demonstration of the profound sociological and economic impact railroads had on the nineteenth-century world. The railroad still provides transportation to and from the hilltop tea-producing city of Darjeeling.

gained use of the area. In 1835, the British established a sanatorium in Darjeeling. Tea arrived in 1856, and within twenty years 113 estates were producing 4 million pounds of tea per year. By the early 1900s, Darjeeling was considered among the most glamorous outposts of the British empire. After World War I, it became a staging ground for expeditions to Mount Everest. From the 1980s through the 1990s, the local population called for political autonomy from West Bengal. Attractions are the "toy train" (a narrow-gauge extension of the North Bengal State Railway); Tiger Hill, with its magnificent view of Kanchenjunga and, occasionally, Mount Everest; botanical gardens; Buddhist monasteries; and museums.

C. Roger Davis

Further Reading

Michell, George, and Philip Davies. (1989) *The Penguin Guide to the Monuments of India*. Vol. 2. New York: Viking.

DARUL ISLAM Darul Islam (House of Islam) was a revolutionary Islamic movement that fought between 1948 and 1963 to make Indonesia an Islamic republic. The Darul Islam arose from Muslim militias formed to fight the Dutch during Indonesia's independence war (1945–1949). It was founded in West Java by S. M. Kartosuwiryo (1905–1962) in May 1948, after the Indonesian Republic agreed to surrender that region to the Dutch. Kartosuwiryo proclaimed himself imam of an Islamic State of Indonesia, which was to replace the Republic. The Darul Islam continued its struggle after the Dutch were defeated and the movement was loosely allied with Islamic rebels in South Sulawesi from 1952 under Kahar Muzakkar (1921–1965) and in Aceh from 1953 under Daud Beureueh (1899–1987).

The movement controlled only rural areas, but its operations extended to the fringes of many towns and cities, including Jakarta. The movement's administration was based on Islamic law as interpreted by Islamic teachers *(kyai)*, but in many areas its forces were little more than rural bandits. In 1957 the Indonesian authorities pacified Aceh with an offer of special status for Islamic law in the region, but the Java and Sulawesi movements were suppressed by the army, which captured and executed Kartosuwiryo in 1962 and killed Kahar Muzakkar in battle in 1965.

Robert Cribb

Further Reading

Dijk, C. van. (1981) *Rebellion Under the Banner of Islam: The Darul Islam in Indonesia*. The Hague, Netherlands: Martinus Nijhoff.

DASHT-E MARGO Dasht-e Margo (Desert of Death) is located in the southwestern part of Afghanistan. Sometimes referred to as the Western Stony Desert, it is dry, dusty, and full of sharp, windblasted pebbles. The Iranian border with Afghanistan and the Iranian desert are in the western part of Dasht-e Margo. To the north lies the base of the Hindu Kush (killer of the Hindus). It is approximately 900 meters above sea level, very hot during the day, and freezing at night. The only plants to be found are deep rooted and generally have very sharp thorns. The only possible food source comes from the sap of the razor-sharp camel grass found in certain parts of the cracked earth.

The harsh climate, barren landscape, and waterless earth have left this region relatively unexplored. However, Afghanistan is home to a hardy group of pastoral nomads called the Kuchis. The Kuchi nomads have been crossing the Dasht-e Margo two times a year for generations during their migration seasons as they search for water for their flocks.

Jennifer L. Nichols

Further Reading

Elphinstone, Mountstuart. ([1815] 1998) *An Account of the Kingdom of Caubul*. Reprint ed. Columbia, MO: South Asia Books.

DASTAN, TURKIC Traditionally, there are three epic genres in Asia: Altaic, Persian, and subcontinental (of the Indian subcontinent). While the latter two have been studied to a certain extent, the Altaic genre, the origin of Turkic *dastans*, has been largely inaccessible until recently.

The term "*dastan*" is relatively new to the Turkic epic genre and was first recorded in the twelfth century. Some six to eight centuries earlier, oral composers, reciters, and owners of this genre among the Turks either used only the name of the work, which intrinsically referenced the genre, or employed specific autonomous terms such as *chorchok*, *jir*, and *sav*. Though in various dialects, all refer to the same concept, that is, the words of the forefathers.

Performers of and Occasions for *Dastan*s

Therefore, a *dastan* is thought to contain the words of the forefathers, embellishing the story of how a particular Altaic lineage and polity gained independence. The reciter, called an *ozan*, or, depending on geographic location, an *akin*, *ashik*, *bahshi*, or *kam*, performs the work, while accompanying him- or herself on a traditional stringed instrument. The occasion of such a performance is an event itself. Apart from that, the recitation is a standard requirement for momentous anniversaries: births, burial ceremonies of rulers, annual festivals, marriages.

The Epic Hero

The main character of the epic is an *alp*, or epic hero, who endures the worst possible scenarios in life to save his or her people from military defeat and slavery. The work is usually known by the *alp*'s name. He or she is fully supported by a sizable cast of characters and is opposed by powerful and treacherous foes and villains. Regardless of the hopelessness of the circumstances, the *alp* can never be subjugated and can never abandon the fight. In the end, under appalling conditions, the *alp* and his followers triumph.

The villains are generally punished lightly. Usually their shame is made public, but they are allowed to wander the earth searching for forgiveness. The victorious ending is celebrated by a grand feast, during which, of course, the *chorchok*, *jir*, *sav*, or *dastan* is joyfully recited by the *ozan*.

Cultural Values in *Dastan*s

Apart from the messages of independence, the genre is also a repository of identity. As such, *dastans* are carriers of early cultural values, including ancient spiritual values, such as the Tengri belief system—one of the earliest monotheistic religions. Because the genre contains immutable linkages to the past, it is common to quote from older *dastans*. This assures and reminds the audience and owners of the works that they are the same people, sharing common goals. The genre is alive and well across Asia, with dozens of original plots, each replete with several dozen variants.

H. B. Paksoy

Further Reading

Carrie, K. S. ([1992] 1994) "Z. V. Togan: On the Origins of the Kazaks and the Ozbeks." Reprint in *Central Asia Reader: The Rediscovery of History*, edited and translated by H. B. Paksoy. New York and London: M. E. Sharpe.

Hatto, A. T., ed. and trans. (1977) *The Memorial Feast for Kokotoy-khan (Kokotoydun asi): A Kirghiz Epic Poem.* London Oriental Series, no. 33. Oxford and New York: Oxford University Press.

Kostina, R. A. A., ed. (1986) *Bashkirskie bogatirskie skazi* (Bashkir Hero Stories). Ufa, Bashkortostan: Baskkirskoe knijnoe izdatelstvo.

Marazzi, Ugo, ed. and trans. (1986) *Maday Qara: An Altay Epic Poem.* Naples, Italy: Istituto Universitario Orientale Dipartimento di Studi Asiatici.

Paksoy, H. B. (1989*) Alpamysh: Central Asian Identity under Russian Rule.* Hartford, CT: Association for the Advancement of Central Asian Research.

Radloff, V. V. (1967) *South Siberian Oral Literature.* Edited by Denis Sinor. Indiana University Uralic and Altaic Series, no. 79, 1. Bloomington, IN, and The Hague, Netherlands: Indiana University Press.

Sumer, Faruk, Ahmet E. Uysal, and Warren S. Walker, trans. and eds. (1972) *The Book of Dede Korkut: A Turkish Epic.* Austin, TX: University of Texas Press.

Tekin, T. (1968) *A Grammar of Orkhon Turkic.* Indiana University Uralic and Altaic Series, no. 69. Bloomington, IN: Indiana University Press.

Valikhanov, Chokhan Chinghizovich. (1984–1985) *Sobranie sochnenii v piiati tomah* (Collection of Works in Five Volumes). 5 vols. Almaty, Kazakhstan: Akademiia Nauk Kazakhskoi SSR, Institut Istorii, Arkheologii, i Etnografii Imina Ch. Ch. Valikhanova.

DAUD, MUHAMMAD

DAUD, MUHAMMAD (1909–1978), Afghan political figure. Muhammad Daud belonged to the royal family of Afghanistan. Educated in Europe (1921–1930) while his father was in temporary exile, he joined the army on his return to Afghanistan. In 1934 he married the sister of the new Afghan king (and his cousin), Zahir Shah.

A resolute supporter of the modernization of Afghanistan, though not of its democratization, and a tough Pashtun nationalist, Daud became minister of defense in 1946, but in 1948, after a disagreement with the prime minister, he was sent to Paris as ambassador. A year later, he became minister of the interior and, in 1953, prime minister, holding that position until 1963.

During this period (the so-called Daud decade), he exacerbated the question of Pashtunistan—the creation of a single state for all the Pashtun—which poisoned relations with Pakistan, since that state had a strong Pashtun minority. For his policy of modernization, he looked for military aid and economic assistance from both the U.S.S.R. and the United States, cunningly playing on their rivalry.

In 1963 he was forced to resign in order to prevent a serious confrontation with Pakistan and was excluded from active political life. Nevertheless, Daud maintained strong ties with the army and the communist activists. In 1973 he seized power with a bloodless coup, declaring Afghanistan a republic and becoming its president. The worsening of his relations with the Afghan communist activists and with Moscow weakened his position. In April 1978 he was killed, along with his family, during the communist coup, which paved the way for the Soviet invasion of 1979.

Riccardo Redaelli

Further Reading

Adamec, Ludwig W. (1987) *A Biographical Dictionary of Contemporary Afghanistan.* Graz, Austria: Akademische Druck-u. Verlagsanstalt.

DAUYLPAZ The *dauylpaz* is a small kettledrum used by the Kazakhs in falconry. Falconry was one of most popular and entertaining forms of hunting in Kazakhstan and other parts of Central Asia from the earliest times. For fowling they used sparrow hawks and goshawks; for hunting wolves, foxes, and mountain goats, the *berkut* (golden eagle) was irreplaceable. The *dauylpaz* has similar names among the Turkic peoples: The Kyrgyz call it *doolbas*, the Uighur *tevilvaz*, and the Azerbaijanis *tebl-baas*, which all derive from the Arabo-Persian *tabl-baz* (where *tabl* stands for drum, and *baz* for falcon). Falconry scenes were often depicted in the Islamic miniatures of the sixteenth and seventeenth centuries.

The *dauylpaz* had a helmet-shaped body with a leather head (diameter about 300 millimeters, height 160 millimeters) and was often beautifully ornamented. A flat leather strap, a beater, or sometimes a hand was used to produce sound. The instrument was attached to the saddle under the left hand of a horseman, while the falcon rested on his other hand. The *dauylpaz* could also be held in the hands. The *dauylpaz* was used as a signaling instrument in military activities as well.

Another term in Kazakh used for this instrument is *shyndauyl* (similar to the Uzbek *chindaul*). Some experts believe the only difference between a *dauylpaz* and a *shyndauyl* is that the body of the latter was of metal (copper), while the body of the *dauylpaz* was of wood. Both these kinds of kettledrums have not been used since the end of the nineteenth century. Modified forms of the *dauylpaz* are used in the Kazakh folk instrument orchestras.

Aygul Malkeyeva

Further Reading

Sarybaev, Bolat. (1978) *Kazakhskie muzykal'nye instrumenty* (Kazakh Musical Instruments). Almaty, Kazakhstan: Zhalyn.

Vertkov, K., G. Blagodatov, and E. Yazovitskaya. (1975) *Atlas muzykal'nykh instrumentov narodov SSSR* (Atlas of Musical Instruments of the Peoples Inhabiting the USSR). 2d ed. Moscow: Muzyka.

Vyzgo, T. S. (1980) *Muzykal'nye instrumenty Srednei Azii: istoricheskie ocherki* (Musical Instruments of Central Asia: Historical Studies). Moscow: Muzyka.

DAVAO (2000 est. pop. 1.1 million). Davao, an important commercial, educational, and cultural center of the southern Mindanao region, is one of the largest seaports in the Philippines. Davao lies on the southeast side of Mindanao Island, occupying a total area of 2,440 square kilometers, with an average population density of 491 persons per square kilometer. Davao port services interisland and international shipments. The city is situated 974 kilometers south of Manila, on the shore of Davao Gulf. "Davao" also refers to three provinces: Davao del Norte, Davao del Sur, and Davao Oriental. Davao City is located in Davao del Sur but is politically and administratively independent of the province.

When Spaniards first visited Davao in 1528, they found thriving communities of various ethnic groups, such as Bagobos, Mandayas, B'laans, and Manobos. Some of these later embraced Islam and were called Moros or Moors by the Spanish. The modern history of Davao began in the mid-nineteenth century, when Spanish colonizers defeated a rebellion of Moros and established a Roman Catholic settlement on the strategically important bank of the Davao River. Thus the Spanish gained leverage over the flourishing and lucrative regional trade, yet they were unable to establish full control over many parts of Mindanao Island.

A community of buildings on stilts in Davao. (YANN-ARTHUS-BERTRAND/CORBIS)

The American occupation of Davao began after the Spanish were defeated in the Spanish-American War (1898). Davao grew further in the twentieth century. In addition to the rich agriculture on Mindanao Island, mining flourished, and international trade grew to supply a strong worldwide demand (especially from the United States) for abaca hemp (from the banana leafstalk), cotton, coffee, and rubber. During this time, a large Japanese community settled in Davao and became one of the most influential communities in the city. In 1937, Davao was formally inaugurated as a city.

World War II arrived to Davao in 1941; the Japanese made Davao the regional headquarters of the imperial army. The city was heavily damaged in heavy fighting between Japanese and American troops in 1945.

Davao was extensively rebuilt after the war, with its economy now based on food processing, textiles, mining, and regional and international trade. During this era, most of the forest in and around Davao was destroyed, damaging Davao's status as a city in a jungle. Between the 1960s and 1990s, Davao experienced a new wave of industrialization and population growth, although in the early 1980s its business environment was heavily damaged by kidnappings and attacks by guerrillas and leftist groups such as the Communist New People's Army.

In response, citizens of Davao formed Alsa Masa, a vigilante group organized with the support of the Philippine military. Some view this organization as exacerbating the already-volatile situation in Davao by focusing its vigilante justice on the New People's Army and Muslim separatists. The political situation in Davao is still unstable, although after the fall of the regime of Ferdinand Marcos (1917–1989) in 1986 most guerrillas ceased their operations in the city. Public officials still tolerate the existence of self-defense groups that engage in extrajudicial killings, ostensibly to fight crime, drug trafficking, and Communists and Muslim extremists, but Davao City is more peaceful than it was during the height of Alsa Masa activity. At the turn of the century, Davao had become one of the fastest-growing cities in the Philippines, with a population growth of 3.23 percent; its population doubled between 1980 and 1999. If the city maintains peace and order through the rule of law, its economy will become even more successful.

Rafis Abazov

Further Reading

Abinales Patricio. (2000) *Making Mindanao: Cotabato and Davao in the Formation of the Philippine Nation-State.* Manila, Philippines: Ateneo De Manila University Press.

"Davao City." Retrieved March 2002, from: http://www.davaocity.gov.ph/.

DAVID, COLLIN (b. 1937), Pakistani painter. Born in Karachi, Pakistan, Collin David produces minimalist paintings that are complex studies of line and structure, which question the very humanity of the women who inhabit them. David first attended the National College of Art and then the Fine Arts Department, Punjab University, from which he graduated with a master's degree in 1960. David studied under the tutelage of the landscape artist Khalid Iqbal, but found his own forte in portraiture and figurative art. After attending the Slade School of Art in London for one year, he joined the faculty of the National College of Art, Lahore, in 1964, where he has continued to teach.

David's art focuses primarily on women, but he is unconcerned about the social or psychological dimension of his subjects. The bodies, nude or clothed, form part of the spatial composition of his canvases. Artistic trends of the 1960s like op art influenced his early work to some degree, as in the 1970 painting *Ghazala*, which depicts a woman in the center of a concentric grid, her striped clothes interacting and colliding with the background in an optical pas de deux.

Kishwar Rizvi

Further Reading

Sirhandi, Marcella Nesom. (1992) *Contemporary Painting in Pakistan*. Lahore, Pakistan: Ferozsons.

DAWAI, ABDUL HADI (1894–1982), Afghan poet and diplomat. A native of Kabul, Afghanistan, Abdul Hadi Dawai belonged to the Pashtun tribe, a group that predominates in southern Afghanistan.

In 1912, at the age of eighteen, he graduated from Habibia High School and became the assistant editor of the magazine *Seraj*, a Persian-language journal, where he published his first poems and articles. In 1920, he moved on to edit *Aman-e-Afghan*, another Persian-language journal. In his writings, he critiqued society and politics from a socialist point of view and expounded on the beauties and strengths of Afghan culture. He published his poems in Dari (Persian as spoken in Afghanistan) under the pen name Pareshan, meaning "perplexed."

In addition to his writing career, Abdul Hadi Dawai became a diplomat and was present at the peace conferences held in Rawalpindi, modern Pakistan (1919), and Mussoorie, India (1920), when Britain and Afghanistan formally signed a peace accord that ended years of hostility between the two nations. Thereafter, from 1922 to 1933, he served in various diplomatic posts in London, Berlin, and Afghanistan.

From 1933 to 1946, he was imprisoned for his support of the former Afghan king Amir Amanullah Khan (1892–1960), who had been forced into exile because of his policy of modernization. After Abdul Hadi Dawai's release, he again entered Afghan politics, was elected to parliament, and became speaker of the house. He also served as secretary to King Muhammad Zahir (b. 1914) and tutored the crown prince, Mohammad Akbar Khan, from 1933 to 1942. After 1958, he retired from political life and devoted himself to writing. He died in Kabul in 1982.

Nirmal Dass

Further Reading

Ewans, Sir Martin. (2001) *Afghanistan: A New History*. Richmond, Surrey, U.K.: Curzon Press.

Vogelsang, Willem. (2002) *The Afghans*. Oxford and Malden, MA: Blackwell.

DAZAI OSAMU (1909–1948), Japanese writer. Born into a wealthy family in Tsugaru, Aomori prefecture, Dazai Osamu showed a strong interest in writing as a student. Feeling alienated from his family, which had political connections at the national level, and attracted to a bohemian lifestyle and left-wing politics, he failed in his studies. Nonetheless, in 1929, following the first of several attempted suicides, he gained admittance to Tokyo Imperial University. In Dazai's seminal work, "Omoide" (Recollections), published in 1933, he employed his characteristic method of autobiographical storytelling; in "Omoide" the narrator struggles to find some worth in his existence. Plunging into the literary life, he failed to graduate from university, attempted suicide two more times, suffered from peritonitis, became addicted to painkillers, and failed to win the first Akutagawa Prize (a prestigious literary award), which he desperately craved. Encouraged by his mentor Ibuse Masuji (b. 1898), he married and achieved a new stability that allowed him to write short stories and gain recognition. Commissioned to write a travel book about his home province, he published *Tsugaru*, a masterpiece of reminiscence and anecdote, in 1944. Gradually, he slipped back into his self-destructive ways, and this provided him with the stimulation for his great novel *Shayo* (The Setting Sun, 1947), which depicts a determined heroine struggling to survive in postwar Japan. In the following year, he published *Ningen shikkaku* (No Longer Human), a reworking of earlier themes. Only a few weeks later he committed suicide with Yamazaki Tomie, one of his disciples.

James M. Vardaman, Jr.

Further Reading

Lewell, John. (1993) *Modern Japanese Novelists: A Biographical Dictionary*. Tokyo: Kodansha.

Lyons, Phyllis I. (1985) *The Saga of Dazai Osamu*. Stanford, CA: Stanford University Press.

O'Brien, James A. (1975) *Dazai Osamu*. Boston: Twayne Publishers.

DAZU ROCK CARVINGS Dazu County, located 160 kilometers (100 miles) west of Chongqing, Sichuan Province, in central China, contains an exceptional series of rock carvings, most dating from the ninth to the thirteenth centuries CE. Construction of the Dazu carvings began during the early period of the Tang dynasty (618–907 CE) and continued until the late Song dynasty (960–1279). Buddhist, Daoist, and Confucian influences are evident in the fifty thousand individual statues found in grottoes and shrines at seventy-five major sites across the mountainous county. The largest and most spectacular grottoes are found at Beishan and Baodingshan. Built during the Song dynasty, the Baodingshan Grotto is carved beneath the overhang of a horseshoe-shaped cliff. The grotto, known as the "Great Buddha Bend," stretches for 500 meters (1,640 feet) and houses over ten thousand sculptures. The Dazu sculptures depict religious and secular life in China and are noted for their diverse subject matter. Many bear inscriptions asking people to embrace moral and religious principles. Dazu County has attracted pilgrims and other travelers for over a thousand years. The rock carvings were inscribed on the World Heritage List in 1999.

Daniel Oakman

Further Reading

Mizuno Seiichi. (1960) *Bronze and Stone Sculpture of China: From the Yin to the Tang Dynasty*. Tokyo: Nikon Keizai.

Ziran Bai, ed. (1984) *Dazu Grottoes*. Beijing: Foreign Language Press.

DEFENSE INDUSTRY—CHINA Upon its establishment in 1949, the People's Republic of China was faced with a hostile Western world and came to rely on the Soviet Union for military and technological assistance. This resulted in the adoption of the Soviet organizational model, compelling each factory and industrial sector to be as self-sufficient as possible, even at the expense of efficiency. In 1960, the abrupt end of Soviet assistance forced China's defense research and production to stand alone, adversely affecting the country's overall industrial development.

Perceived threats from abroad between 1965 and 1971 led to a massive "third-front" (or third-line) construction model, an effort to build a huge self-sufficient industrial base in the remote southwestern and western regions. (The "first front" usually refers to coastal areas, which would be hard to defend; the "second front," inland from the first front, might have to give way to the third front, still farther inland and thus more suitably defended in a protracted war.) Approximately 50 to 55 percent of China's defense industry was located in provinces such as Sichuan, Shanxi, Hubei, Yunnan, and Guizhou. By 1975, the percentage of domestically manufactured weapons was 71, 75, 89, and 97 percent, respectively, for tanks, aircraft, naval ships, and cannons.

In 1977, after the Cultural Revolution, the defense industry adopted the policy of "combining the military with the civilian" and "using the civilian to support the military" to fulfill the overall goal of economic reform and modernization. Under the joint supervision of the Central Military Commission and the State Council, the Commission of Science, Technology, and Industry for National Defense (COSTIND) was established in 1982 to ensure better coordination in defense-industry leadership. In that year as well, the machine-building ministries were renamed to indicate their functional responsibilities. For example, the Second Machine Building Ministry became the Ministry of Nuclear Industry. The 1980s also witnessed the production of some civilian goods by the defense industry, thus involving it in dual functions and profit-making activities.

The significance of high-tech weapons during the Persian Gulf War (1990–1991) renewed China's interest in technological development. In March 1998, COSTIND was headed for the first time by a civilian bureaucrat, a change regarded as an attempt to avoid the military's heavy-handed interference in China's defense industry's operation. While the General Armaments Department, newly created within the People's Liberation Army, now oversees weapons research, the military is expected to pay more for weapons and equipment from COSTIND's defense factories, due to further involvement in the nuclear economy. On 1 July 1999, corporations in the main defense industrial sectors were split for further specialization. For example, the nuclear industry was divided into the China National Nuclear Corporation and the China Nuclear Engineering and Construction Group Corporation.

CHINA'S NATIONAL DEFENSE IN 2000

On 16 October 2000, the State Council of the People's Republic of China issued a white paper, "China's National Defense in 2000." The foreword to that paper, which follows, stresses China's commitment to peace even as it pursues a strong national defense.

> "The turn of the century has opened a new chapter in the development of human society.
>
> "When we look back on the twentieth century we notice that mankind created enormous material and spiritual wealth never seen before. We also experienced two world wars, hundreds of local wars and the Cold War that lasted for nearly half a century, suffering tremendously from the scourge of wars or the menace of wars. The Chinese nation has gone through many hardships. The Chinese people have fought bravely for their national independence, liberation, democracy and freedom. They have finally brought the country onto the road toward modernization. The Chinese people know full well the value of peace.
>
> "Humanity is facing a rare chance for development as well as tough challenges in the new century. To safeguard world peace and promote the development of all are the themes of the times and the common aspirations of people all over the world. China is engaged wholeheartedly in its modernization drive. A peaceful international environment and a favorable surrounding environment serve China's fundamental interests. China steadfastly follows an independent foreign policy of peace and is committed to a new world of peace, stability, prosperity and development. China firmly pursues a defensive national defense policy and is determined to safeguard its state sovereignty, national unity, territorial integrity and security. The Chinese people are ready to work together with other peace-loving people of the world and contribute their wisdom and strength to world peace and development, and a more beautiful future for mankind.
>
> "At this important point in history—the turn of the century—we publish this white paper, China's National Defense in 2000, to express the Chinese people's sincere aspirations for peace and to help the rest of the world better understand China's national defense policy and its efforts for the modernization of its national defense."

Source: Information Office of the State Council of the People's Republic of China. "China's National Defense in 2000." Retrieved 21 February 2002, from: http://www.chinadaily.com.cn/highlights/paper/ndefence.html.

Achievements

China claims that its military-industrial complex, which is composed of thirty thousand state-owned entities engaged in the aerospace, aviation, ordnance, shipbuilding, and nuclear industries and which builds everything from warships to washing machines, produced and exported $7 billion worth of goods in 1997.

The Chinese defense industry's nearly unrivaled access to supplies and its rarely challenged methods of marketing have gradually been forced to change, however, and to respond to market trends. In the 1980s, a shift in emphasis from preparation for war to preservation of peace necessitated the reorganization of the defense industry. Conversion to civilian production mitigated the pain caused by the cuts in military spending and symbolically showed China's willingness to contribute to global peace. While data vary for different sectors, civilian goods in the late 1990s approached 80 percent of the gross output value of China's defense industry. In 1997, for example, China's defense industry claimed credit for producing 50 percent of motorcycles and 30 percent of color televisions in the domestic market. The goal is for the defense industry to be increasingly self-sustaining, efficient, and innovative. In addition, loosening state control has given defense factories flexibility in interaction with foreign business communities.

Another phenomenon of the 1990s was the formation of big-business conglomerates to link firms vertically and horizontally so that they could participate in economies of scale. One such conglomerate is the China North Industries Corporation, reported in 1997 to have more than three hundred affiliated units with fixed assets of at least $7.5 billion.

Indigenous efforts and access to foreign know-how may enable the defense industry to close technological gaps between China and the world's other major powers. China's defense industry has been working on advanced weapons systems such as cruise missiles and satellite-positioning systems. In 1999, China successfully launched and recovered an unmanned spacecraft. As long as China's economic boom continues and the government increases the budget for military procurement, the defense industry has great potential for growth.

Challenges

The legacy of central planning has hurt the economic vitality of China's defense factories. Many defense plants have found themselves with duplicate production, oversupply, and brain drain to lucrative private enterprises. For the "third-front" defense factories, inconvenient sites and worn-out infrastructure have scared off new investors. Although defense factories have been successful in joint-venture deals with companies like Mercedes-Benz (now Daimler Chrysler), Suzuki, and McDonnell Douglas, by 1998 fewer than six hundred joint ventures had been forged, despite years of courtship.

Overall, the viability of China's defense industry relies as much on public-policy design, the political will of leaders, and military circumstances as on economic development. Problems like a bloated labor force and ever-increasing costs for technological innovation must be solved. Most important, a defense industry long accustomed to government planning must make a difficult shift to a market mentality in consolidating and rationalizing its industrial layout and operation.

With recipients like Armenia, Iran, Pakistan, Turkey, and Brazil, China's aggressive arms-transfer policy made China the sixth largest supplier for the 1993–1997 period. Although China had a new arms-export statute in place in 1998, its nontransparent practices have occasionally violated certain international agreements and norms governing global arms transfers. Even with the 1999 structural separation of COSTIND from the military, the image of the defense industry's symbiotic association with China's military persists. This mammoth military-industrial complex poses a hindrance to the central authority. Eventual loosening of military control over the defense industry and more transparent arms-transfer procedures seem to be the main task for the healthy development of the defense industry. The detachment of COSTIND from military control was just the first step.

Wei-chin Lee

See also: **People's Liberation Army**

Further Reading

Brömmelhörster, Jör, and John Frankenstein, eds. (1997) *Mixed Motives, Uncertain Outcomes: Defense Conversion in China.* Boulder, CO: Lynne Rienner.

Feigenbaum, Evan A. (1999) "Soldiers, Weapons, and Chinese Development Strategy: The Mao Era Military in China's Economic and Institutional Debate." *China Quarterly* 158 (June): 285–313.

Folta, Paul Humes. (1992) *From Swords to Plowshares? Defense Industry Reform in the PRC.* Boulder, CO: Westview Press.

Frankenstein, John, and Bates, Gill. (1997) "Current and Future Challenges Facing Chinese Defense Industries." In *China's Military in Transition*, edited by David Shambaugh and Richard H. Yang. Oxford: Clarendon Press, 130–163.

Gurtov, Melvin, and Byong-Moo Hwang. (1998) *China's Security: The New Roles of the Military.* Boulder, CO: Lynne Rienner.

DEFORESTATION For millennia people have known the importance of trees. The Sumerians described in their tablets how the forest canopy shades the earth and moderates the climate. The authors of the Old Testament realized that trees were necessary for year-round springs and rivers. Plato told how forests prevented flooding and runoff, thereby preserving the earth's fertility. Today it is known that forests and their soils absorb great quantities of car-

A dirt road cuts into the rain forest in remote West Kalimantan, Indonesia, to provide access for loggers. When the land is cleared, it will be occupied by migrants from Java. (ECOSCENE/CORBIS)

bon dioxide, and that the forest canopy exudes oxygen and provides living space for a myriad of creatures.

Throughout history people have plundered forests to obtain the wood needed for construction and fuel. Until the late nineteenth century, all ships were built from hull to mast of timber. The spokes, wheels, and chassis of almost every cart, chariot, or wagon were made of wood, as were the bridges they crossed. Transportation would have been impossible without wood. Timbered beams and rafters held up ancient palaces and propped up the world's mines. Wherever trees have abounded, people invariably build their homes of wood, and wood has been used for uncountable tools and domestic items; more trees have been lost to fuel than have been lost to lumber.

When civilization first arose in Asia, so too did large-scale deforestation. Today, Asia still leads the world in the aggregate amount and percentage of forestland lost. Since the rise of the first great civilizations, the continent had a little over 15 million square kilometers of forest; today, only around 4 million square kilometers of forested land remain.

The first accounts of humanity's attack on forests come from ancient Mesopotamia, China, and India. The *Epic of Gilgamesh*, the world's first written saga, tells of Mesopotamia's founding king and his entourage stripping the mountains of their forests. Mesopotamian kings of the third millennium BCE boast in cuneiform script preserved on clay tablets how they made paths in cedar mountains and cut its cedars with their great axes.

Likewise, deforestation dominates the founding legend of historical China. According to the ancient Chinese philosopher Mencius (c. 372–289 BCE), the legendary emperor Yao (c. twenty-fourth century BCE) felt great anguish to see the land overgrown by vegetation and crowded by swarming birds and beasts. Yao's handpicked successor, Shun, acted to rid the landscape of what had so offended his mentor. He ordered his forester, Yi, to set fire to the forests and vegetation on the mountains and in the marshes so that the birds and beasts fled away and grain could be planted. Over the centuries the mountains and plains of China underwent a similar transformation.

The policies of Mao Zedong (1893–1976), the leader of China's Communist revolution, continued the destruction of forests. His Great Leap Forward resulted in tens of thousands of villages cutting down nearby timber stands to fuel their backyard iron furnaces. A loss of over 100,000 square kilometers of forest resulted from Mao's other initiative: "Taking Grain as the Key Link." That program converted 700,000 square kilometers of forestland to agricultural uses.

The topic of forest destruction also comes up in the *Mahabharata*, the national epic of India. The ancient Aryan heroes Krishna Vasudeva and Arjuna help the fire god devour the great Khandava Forest in northern India and make sure none of the fleeing creatures survive. They want the forest cleared so that the new kingdom they have fought for will be assured of sufficient farmland. In India's other ancient epic, the *Ramayana*, the hero Rama shows no compunction in ordering the felling of whole forests to build a great causeway for his troops to cross. Thousands of years later, the British continued the destruction of India's woodlands. Independence did nothing to ameliorate what the British had done to India's forests; in fact, deforestation accelerated. Taken together, only 20 percent of China and India's original forests remain.

The accelerated deforestation of China and India's neighbors to the east and south has more recent origins. As late as 1919, almost 70 percent of the original forests in the Philippines were intact, but as of 1989, that figure had dropped to 20 percent. Other recent deforestation flash points include eastern Myammar (Burma), northern and northeastern Thailand, Vietnam, the state of Sarawak in eastern Malaysia, and Sumatra and East and South Kalimantan in Indonesia. This rapid loss of forests coincides with an almost twelve-fold increase in logging in the region since 1950 and the population explosion that began in the 1960s. Loggers cull hardwoods from among other trees in the forest. To gain access to these trees and to haul the logs overland for export, they build roads that allow the landless masses to enter the forests. Once there, the landless burn down what trees are left, and plant what crops they can. When that patch inevitably gives out, they move deeper into the forests and continue to slash and burn. In this fashion, more and more forested land turns barren.

Deforestation in Asia follows a world pattern. Between 1990 and 1995, the developing world has cleared 65 million hectares of forestland. Deforestation in Asia as well as in the rest of the developing world ranks along with global warming among the world's gravest environmental problems faced in the new millennium.

John Perlin

See also: **Forest Industry—Mongolia; Forest Industry—Southeast Asia; Mangroves**

Further Reading

Bryant, D., Nielsen, D. and L. Tangley. (1997) *The Last Frontier Forests: Ecosystems & Economies on the Edge*. Washington, DC: World Resources Institute.

Myers, N. (1980) "The Present Status and Future Prospects of Tropical Moist Forests." *Environmental Conservation*, 7, 2: 101–114.

Perlin, J. (1991) *A Forest Journey: The Role of Wood in the Development of Civilization*. Cambridge, MA: Harvard University Press.

Smil, V. (1984) *The Bad Earth*. London: Zed Press.

Stebbing, E. P. (1982) *The Forests of India*. 4 vols. New Delhi: A. J. Reprints Agency.

Tucker, R. P., and J. F. Richards, eds. (1983) *Global Deforestation and the Nineteenth-Century World Economy*. Durham, NC: Duke University Press.

———. (1988) *World Deforestation in the Twentieth Century*. Durham, NC: Duke University Press.

DEHRA DUN

DEHRA DUN (2001 est. population 448,000). A city in northwestern Uttar Pradesh state, India, Dehra Dun is a popular retirement area in the Himalayan foothills, known for elite private schools and long-grain Basmati rice. It was founded in 1699 when the heretical Sikh Guru Ram Rai, driven out of the Punjab, built a temple there. During the eighteenth century it was occupied by successive invaders, culminating in the Gurkhas. At the end of the Gurkha War in 1816, it was ceded to the British.

Tea processing is the main industry, along with wheat, millet, and timber. Dehra Dun is home to the Forest Research Institute and headquarters of the Survey of India, which has produced maps of Indian cities, states, and regions since 1767. It is an important railhead on the Northern Railway. The city was once known for its exquisite climate, lush green forests, and clean environment. Building and mining have denuded the hillsides and wrought other unwelcome changes. Since 1988, however, Supreme Court rulings have sought to restore the environment, and the government plans to develop a technology center to encourage Dehra Dun's emergence as a major center for higher education, including medicine and engineering.

C. Roger Davis

Further Reading

Davies, Philip. (1989) "Dehra Dun." In *The Pelican Guide to the Monuments of India*. Vol. 2. London: Viking, 117–118.

DEKKAN

DEKKAN The Dekkan (or Deccan) Plateau, in Sanskrit Dakshin (meaning "south"), is a triangular plateau covering central India, at an average elevation of 450 to 600 meters, with a gentle sloping toward the east, which drains several major rivers in that direction. The northern boundary is the Vindhya range or the Narmada Valley, while to the south it reaches to the Kaveri River, the Malabar Coast, and the Coromandel Coast, tapering off in the plains of Tamil

Nadu. A more restricted use of the term Dekkan applies to the land between the Narmada and the Kistna rivers. In its broad usage Dekkan has been contrasted with Hindustan, an old term for the Indo-Gangetic Plain to the north. In the Puranas and other Sanskrit texts the region was referred to as Dakshinapathi or Dakshinatya.

Between the mid-fourteenth and the late-seventeenth centuries, six Indo-Islamic sultanates were established in several parts of the region, each evolving a distinctive art style and culture, and all known collectively as the Deccan Sultanates. Otherwise the Dekkan has historically been a Hindu preserve for the most part. Today the region encompasses most of the states of Maharashtra, Madhya Pradesh, Andhra Pradesh, Chhattisgarh, and Karnataka. Three major inland cities are Hyderabad, Pune, and Bangalore; and the main agricultural produce includes cotton, sugarcane, and food grains.

Paul Hockings

Further Reading

Yazdani, Ghulam, ed. (1960). *The Early History of the Deccan*. New Delhi: Oxford University Press. 2 vols.

HUMAYUN'S TOMB—WORLD HERITAGE SITE

Humayun's Tomb—the Mughal empire's first garden tomb and precursor to the Taj Mahal—was designated a UNESCO World Heritage Site in 1993 for the profound effect its beautiful geometric style had on Mughal architecture.

DELHI UNION TERRITORY (2002 est. pop. 14 million). India's third-largest city (after Calcutta and Mumbai) and a union territory, Delhi has served as the capital of various regimes for over ten centuries. Jawaharlal Nehru (1889–1964), India's first prime minister after achieving independence, called it "the symbol of old India and new." The union territory (federal district) includes the area known as Old Delhi, the population center, with many mosques, museums, and forts, and New Delhi, built as the imperial capital by the British, with wide avenues, many embassies, government buildings, and research centers. The population of the city of Delhi (Old and New) was approximately 10 million in 2002.

Situated in north-central India at the intersection of the route from the Khyber Pass to the Ganges-Yamuna valley, the Aravalli hills, and the south-flowing Yamuna River, Delhi has always been a transportation, trade, and communications center. It was the central place for regimes aspiring to hold the Punjab, Afghanistan, Rajasthan, and the Gangetic plains east of the Yamuna. The area survived much rebuilding and much devastation. The earliest settlement Indraprastha (est. 1400 BCE) is featured in the epic poem *Mahabharata*, though none of its archaeological remains have been found. From the twelfth to the fourteenth century CE, royal enclaves were located ten miles west of the river. Rainwater tanks were then supplemented by elaborate canals. The Tomar Rajputs built Lal Kot, the core of the first of Delhi's eight successive cities, in 736. Qutb-ud-Din-Aibak made Delhi his capital in 1206 and built the Quwwat ul Islam mosque and the towering Qutb Minar. After the sack of Baghdad in 1258, Delhi's court and *madrasahs* (Islamic seminaries) made it the most important cultural center of the Muslim east.

Allaudin Khilji established Siri, the second city, in 1304. The third Delhi was Tughlagabad (1321); the fourth, Jahanpanah (1325); the fifth, Firozabad, was famous for its Ashokan pillar; and Purana Qila was the sixth. Shajahanabad was the seventh Delhi, serving as the Mughal capital from 1639 to 1771, when Hindu Maratha princes held it off and on until 1803—after which time Delhi came under British rule. The Red Fort remains as a reminder of the Mughal period. The writings of Delhi's Persian and Urdu poets from the fourteenth to the nineteenth century—Amir Khusrau, Mir, Ghalib—became widely known.

Delhi was a center of the Indian Mutiny. In 1857 revolting Indian soldiers (sepoys) seized Delhi for several months where fighting ensued between the British army and mutineers. The imperial capital New Delhi was completed by 1931. Delhi became a union territory in 1956. With twenty-five daily newspapers and 125 weeklies, Delhi continues to be both daunting and alluring, an intellectual and tourist center as well as a political and administrative one. Besides its stunning architectural backdrop and overall scale, attractions include Delhi University; Delhi Zoo; many religious celebrations and secular festivals; and the National Museum, with paintings, sculptures, manuscripts, weapons, jewelry, pottery, and relics dating back four thousand years.

C. Roger Davis

Further Reading

Frykenberg, Robert E., ed. (1986) *Delhi through the Ages: Essays in Urban History, Culture, and Society.* Delhi: Oxford University Press.

Michell, George, and Philip Davies. (1989) "Delhi" and "New Delhi." In *The Penguin Guide to the Monuments of India.* 2 vols. New York: Viking, 1: 123–128; 2: 119–145.

DEMIREL, SULEYMAN (b. 1924), Turkish political leader. Suleyman Demirel is a major political figure in contemporary Turkey. He was born in a modest peasant family in the village of Islamkoy, located in the Isparta province of central Anatolia. Benefiting from government scholarships, he obtained a degree in civil engineering from Istanbul Technical University in 1949 and went to the United States for further study on a Eisenhower Exchange Fellowship. In return for the scholarships, Demirel completed his obligatory service in the Turkish State Statistical Institute and the State Hydraulic Works. The prime minister, Adnan Menderes (1899–1961), appointed him the director-general of the State Hydraulic Works, in 1955, when Demirel was thirty-one.

After the 1960 military coup, he joined the newly founded Adalet Partisi (Justice Party). In 1964 following the death of the party's first chairman Ragip Gumuspala (1897–1964), Demirel was elected chairman, and he held this post until the dissolution of the party in 1980, when all political parties were dissolved following another military coup. His first cabinet post was as the deputy prime minister in the 1965 cabinet of Prime Minister Suat Hayri Urguplu (1903–1981). Following the victory of the Justice Party in the 1965 general elections, he was appointed the prime minister at the age of thirty-nine. He held the post for seven different terms, from October 1965 to April 1993.

Demirel was largely blamed for the unstable political coalitions of the Turkish government during his tenure as prime minister in the 1970s, which pushed Turkey into economic crises and urban violence. His reign was interrupted by military intervention in 1971 and again in 1980. Following the 1980 coup, he was banned from politics together with other political leaders of the pre-1980 era. He returned to active politics as the chairman of the Dogru Yol Partisi (True Path Party) after a 1987 referendum, which removed the political ban. His party won 27 percent of the popular vote in the 1991 general elections, and Demirel was appointed the prime minister for a seventh time.

In 1993, after the death of President Turgut Ozal (1927–1993), Demirel was elected as the ninth president of the Turkish Republic. His term of office ended in May 2000. During his presidency, he played a pivotal role as an arbiter between the army and the politicians, especially through the Refah Partisi (Welfare Party) crisis.

Ayla H. Kiliç

Further Reading

Turgut, Hulusi. (1992) *Demirel'in Dunyasi* (Demirel's World). Istanbul, Turkey: ABC Ajansi Yayinlari.

Uraz, Abdullah. (1993) *BABA: Demirel'in Buyuk Turkiye Kavgasi, Demokrasi ve Kalkınma* (FATHER: Demirel's Great Crusade, Democracy, and Development). Ankara, Turkey: Desen Ofset.

DEMOCRAT PARTY—TURKEY The Democrat Party (Demokrat Parti; DP) was the first party in Turkey to challenge successfully the rule of the Republican People's Party (RPP). The DP ruled the nation from May 1950 to May 1960, when it was overthrown and shut down by the Turkish military.

During the single-party period of the RPP (1923–1945), some members of the RPP increasingly opposed a political system that was seen as inflexible, unresponsive to the people, and undemocratic; they also opposed the power of the party leader, Ismet Inonu. In late 1945 Celal Bayar (1884–1987), Adnan Menderes (1899–1961), Fuat Koprulu (1890–1966), and Refik Koraltan (1889–1974) were expelled from the RPP for criticizing the leadership and calling for changes. In May 1946 the four joined to form the DP. As the new party's leaders recruited members and began to set up a national organization, the party immediately attracted widespread support from businesspeople, merchants, and manufacturers, among others. Despite calls to boycott early elections set for 1946, the DP issued a platform supporting a program of liberalism, including lowering taxes, shrinking the public sector in favor of private enterprise, having less state control of cultural matters, and showing greater respect for Islam. In 1946 the DP gained 65 of the 465 seats in the Turkish Grand National Assembly (the RPP won 390 seats), where members continued to demand reform of the electoral system.

In 1950 the Democrat Party won 53 percent of the vote and took control of the National Assembly. President Bayar named Menderes prime minister. During the 1950s the DP encouraged growth of the private sector and development of agriculture, as well as close relations with the United States. In 1954 and again in 1957, the DP was returned to power. By the end of the 1950s, however, the party's popularity was waning, and Menderes began to adopt more authoritarian policies in a bid to retain power. In May 1960 a group of officers overthrew the DP government. The DP was shut down, and Bayar and Menderes were both tried for charges ranging from corruption to crimes against the nation. Menderes was convicted and executed; Bayar served six years in prison. The DP's agenda was adopted by the Justice Party, which held power in the late 1960s and 1970s.

John M. VanderLippe

Further Reading

Feroz, Ahmad. (1977) *The Turkish Experiment in Democracy, 1950–1975.* Boulder, CO: Westview.

Ozbudun, Ergun. (2000) *Contemporary Turkish Politics: Challenges to Democratic Consolidation.* Boulder, CO: Lynne Rienner.

DEMOCRATIC SOCIALIST PARTY—JAPAN

DEMOCRATIC SOCIALIST PARTY—JAPAN In 1960 the right wing of the Japan Socialist Party (JSP) split off, and the Democratic Socialist Party (DSP) was formed. Three issues divided the left and right wings of the JSP. One was the far-left faction's continued adherence to the goals and tactics of Marxism, such as the elimination of capitalism and the establishment of a workers' state by means of violent revolution. The second issue was the right's support for the existence of the Japanese military (the Self-Defense Force), and the third was its interest in an expanded security role for Japan in international affairs by being a more active partner with the United States and by taking a more visible role in international organizations.

The DSP moved away from doctrinaire socialism and toward centrism, accepting private enterprise instead of public ownership of the means of production and emphasizing welfare issues. It saw its role primarily as a coalition partner with other moderate parties such as the Clean Government Party. The DSP drew support from labor and in particular the federation of unions representing industrial and trade workers mostly from the private sector.

In several elections, the DSP tried to present itself to voters as an alternative to the Liberal Democratic Party. The strategy worked in that LDP losses translated into DSP gains and vice versa. In the party realignments of the 1990s, the DSP was unable to make headway. Smaller parties were joining with each other to form new parties and the DSP was no exception. In 1993, the party disbanded and its members joined the New Frontier Party.

Louis D. Hayes

Further Reading

Hrebenar, Ronald J. (2000) *Japan's New Party System.* 3rd ed. Boulder, CO: Westview Press.

DEMOCRATIZATION—SOUTH KOREA

South Korea's movement from authoritarian rule toward a more democratic form of government has been a record of irregular progress since the nation developed political independence in 1948. The movement toward democracy has been interrupted by the involvement of high-ranking military officers who have seized power in times of crisis, but a central group of opposition candidates have, over time, led the nation from authoritarian rule to a more democratic system.

Korea's First Elections

Korea's first elections were held in 1948. In that year, United Nations–sponsored elections were to be held in all of Korea, but the election was not permitted to be carried out in the Soviet-controlled north. The election, held in the U.S.-controlled south, chose a National Assembly that wrote a constitution and appointed Korea's first president, Yi Seung-man, known in the West as Syngman Rhee (1875–1965). While the president was indirectly chosen in this first election, he governed, according to the constitution, at the will of the National Assembly. When the Assembly sought to remove Rhee from office in 1952, however, he declared martial law and forced into effect a revision to the constitution that called for direct election of the president.

Rhee was elected by popular vote in 1952, and in 1954 the constitution was revised to permit him to run for an unlimited number of terms. He was reelected in 1956 (after his opponent died of a heart attack ten days before the election) and again in 1960 (when another opponent died just before the election); however, because of widespread suspicion over balloting, Rhee resigned, and a new constitution, placing executive power in the hands of a prime minister, was drafted. In July 1960, Chang Myon (John Myon Chang) was chosen as the prime minister of the Second Republic.

Political Difficulties in the 1960s and 1970s

Economic difficulties in 1960 led to political difficulties for the new regime, and in May 1961 General Park Chung Hee (1917–1979) seized power in a coup organized by Colonel Kim Jong-pil (b. 1926). A new constitution approved in late 1962 returned power to the president (who was to be elected by popular vote) and diminished the power of the National Assembly.

Park left the military to seek election in 1963 and was elected that year and subsequently reelected in 1967 and 1971. In the 1971 election, Park was nearly defeated by the opposition leader Kim Dae Jung (b. 1925), who received 45 percent of the vote. Kim Dae Jung lost votes to another opposition candidate, Kim Young-sam (b. 1927). President Park named Kim Jong-pil as his prime minister.

President Park subsequently declared martial law in South Korea and in October 1972 instituted the Yushin (Revitalization) constitution, which provided for election of the president through an electoral college, ending direct election of the president.

During this period of martial law, Kim Dae Jung was in Japan; in 1973, he was kidnapped from a Tokyo hotel by agents of the South Korean government and smuggled back to South Korea, where he was placed under house arrest. He was arrested for subversive activities in 1976 and sentenced to five years in prison but was released in 1978 for health reasons.

President Park was elected by an electoral college in 1978 for a six-year term, but was assassinated by the head of his own Korea Central Intelligence Agency in 1979. In accordance with the Korean constitution, Prime Minister Choe Kyu-ha (b. 1919) became acting president and declared martial law. Within a few days, President Choe began the release of political prisoners (including Kim Dae Jung) from house arrest and prison and subsequently pardoned hundreds.

Political Repression in the 1980s and the Beginning of Democracy

The officer in charge of the investigation of Park's assassination, Lieutenant General Chun Doo Hwan (b. 1931), began to consolidate his power within the military and seized power from Choe in May 1980; Choe retained his position as president, but Chun held actual power, leading to massive protests in the city of Kwangju. Chun authorized the use of the military to put down the riots and retake control of the city. Hundreds of citizens were killed in the fighting, and Kim Dae Jung was arrested and sentenced to death as a protest leader (his sentence was later commuted to twenty years, and he was released in exile to the United States). Chun rose to four-star rank, retired from the military, and was named president by the electoral college in August 1980.

Under a new constitution, President Chun was reelected to a single seven-year term in February 1981. Kim Young-sam, was placed under house arrest for two years. Kim Dae Jung returned to Korea in 1985 and was placed under house arrest with his civil rights suspended. As this political repression was taking place, South Korea hosted the 1986 Asian Games and prepared for the 1988 Olympic Games.

In October 2000 South Korean students protest and block the arrival of former president Kim Young-sam at Korea University. They hold pictures of people who died during his presidency. (REUTERS NEWMEDIA INC./CORBIS)

South Korea's democratization is often said to have started with the election of President Roh Tae Woo (b. 1932) in 1987. A new constitution that year provided for the first direct election of a president since 1971, the others having been conducted with an electoral college similar to that in the United States. However, Roh was a former army general, a classmate of Chun Doo Hwan at the Korean Military Academy, class of 1955, and had been in charge of the military forces that had put down the protests in Kwangju in 1980.

The 1987 electoral campaign was hotly contested, and the primary opposition candidate, Kim Young-sam, led in some polls late in the campaign. In what was claimed to be an act of good will, President Chun restored Kim Dae Jung's civil rights late in the campaign. Kim Dae Jung declared himself a candidate for the election, which split the opposition vote between himself, Kim Young-sam, and Kim Jong-pil. This division of the opposition vote allowed Roh to win the election with 8.2 million votes. Kim Young-sam received 6.3 million, while Kim Dae Jung received 6.11 million. Once again, a former general had come to power, although this time by more democratic means. During Roh's administration, his former political rival Kim Young-sam brought his political party into a coalition with Roh's.

South Korea's Government in the 1990s

In 1992, South Korea elected its first president since Syngman Rhee who had not been in the military, and Kim Young-sam won with 42 percent of the vote. Kim's main competitors were Kim Dae Jung, who received 34 percent of the vote, and Chung Ju-young, the founder of the Hyundai Group, an industrial conglomerate. President Kim initiated a campaign against corruption in government, asserting that no official should profit from his or her position. To this end, in 1995, the former presidents Chun and Roh were tried and convicted of mutiny, treason, and corruption. Chun was sentenced to death (later reduced to life in prison) and Roh to twenty-two years in prison (later reduced to seventeen years).

In the national elections of 1997, Kim Dae Jung was elected president, winning over 40 percent of the popular vote. Kim's popularity was based largely on his continued role in opposition to past administrations, despite accusations of his being pro-North Korea. One of his first actions was to pardon the former presidents Chun and Roh, who were present at his inauguration.

Kim Dae Jung held a summit meeting with North Korea's leader, Kim Jong Il (b. 1941) in June 2000, the first summit ever between the leaders of North and South Korea, and reestablished cross-border family reunions. Advances in public welfare, human rights, and the economy were primary goals of his administration. However, he has been criticized for his government's hard line on labor issues.

Thomas P. Dolan

Further Reading

Breen, Michael. (1998) *The Koreans.* New York: St. Martin's Press. Rev. ed. Boston: Houghton Mifflin.

Korean Overseas Information Service. (1993) *A Handbook of Korea.* Seoul: Samhwa Printing.

Reischauer, Edwin O., Albert Craig, and John Fairbank. (1989) *East Asia: Tradition and Transformation.*

Saccone, Richard. (1993) *Koreans to Remember: 50 Famous People Who Helped Shape Korea.* Seoul: Hollym Corporation.

DENG XIAOPING (1904–1997), leader of the Chinese Communist Party. Deng Xiaoping, head of the Chinese Communist Party (CCP) during the 1980s, survived the purges of the Cultural Revolution of 1966–1976 to assume the party leadership. The eldest son of a prosperous landlord, he was born on 22 August 1904 in Paifang Village, Sichuan Province. Like many of his contemporaries, Deng went to France through the work-study program, where he became involved with what would be the future leadership of the CCP. Following his time in France, Deng went to Moscow, where he trained as a political activist and organizer. After working briefly as Communist Party organizer in Southwest China, Deng moved to the Kiangsi Soviet to be with party leader Mao Zedong (1893–1976). From 1938 to 1952, Deng served in the forerunner of what would later be the People's Liberation Army, where he led forces against

A billboard in Shenzhen features Deng Xiaoping and reads: "Uphold the party's fundamental line—we will not waver in a hundred years." (EYE UBIQUITOUS/CORBIS)

the Japanese and later against nationalist forces during the Chinese civil war.

Following the Chinese civil war, Deng's loyalty to the CCP was rewarded when he was named vice premier. Deng primarily worked in the ministry of finance, where he would formulate economic policy. He later was appointed to the Politboro, where he eventually became general secretary. He held that post until 1966, when he was denounced for his opposition to Mao's Socialist Education Movement (1962–1965) and removed from his post by Mao, Lin Bao, and Chen Boda. In 1973 Deng was rehabilitated and returned to office. In 1975 he once again was denounced and removed from office, this time by the Gang of Four, a group of radical leaders who sought to seize control of the CCP. Following Mao's death and the arrest of the Gang of Four, Deng again assumed the mantle of leadership within the Communist Party and maintained this position until his death on 19 February 1997.

Keith A. Leitich

Further Reading

MacFarguhar, Roderick, ed. (1997) *The Politics of China: The Eras of Mao and Deng*. New York: Cambridge University Press.

Yung, Benjamin. (1998) *Deng: A Political Biography*. Armonk, NY: M. E. Sharpe.

Zhang, Wei-Wei. (1996) *Ideology and Economic Reform Deng Xiaoping, 1978–1993*. New York: Columbia University Press.

DENKI ROREN

Denki Roren, or the Japanese Federation of Electric Machine Workers' Unions, was the sector-level labor-union federation for Japan's workers in the electrical machinery, electrical appliance, and electronics industries between its May 1953 formation and its July 1992 conversion into Denki Rengo (Japanese Electrical, Electronic, and Information Union).

Formed out of remnant enterprise unions in the electrical sector following the late 1940s purge of Communists and other militant elements, Denki Roren pursued a "neutral" brand of unionism that steered clear of the political rivalry between Sohyo (General Council of Trade Unions of Japan) and Domei Japanese Confederation of Labor) and was the leading industrial federation in Churitsu Roren, or the Federation of Independent Unions (formed September 1956). While actively participating in Sohyo's annual wage offensive (*shunto*) and sharing with Sohyo support of "unarmed neutralism" in foreign policy, Denki Roren simultaneously championed an enterprise-oriented cooperative approach to labor-management relations that overlapped with that of Domei unions and the International Metalworkers Federation Japan Council (IMF-JC), in which it took an active part. It was thus quite fitting that when the Japanese labor movement began to move toward consolidation during the late 1970s, Denki Roren was at the forefront of the efforts to merge Sohyo and Domei, and that Denki Roren's president, Tateyama Toshifumi, was selected as the Rengo's first president in 1987.

Lonny Carlile

Further Reading

"Denki Rengo." (2002) Retrieved 18 January 2002, from: http://www.jeiu.or.jp/index-e.html.

DEPARTMENT STORES—EAST ASIA

In East Asia, department stores are more than just glittering showplaces for merchandise. They have reflected and helped propel urban development, the growing middle classes, and the transition to consumer lifestyles. Pivotal in the transition to a Westernized and internationalized lifestyle, East Asian department stores have introduced foreign goods, customs, and holidays. Conversely, they have also helped preserve traditional customs and activities. They have mediated historic transitions, addressing issues these changes have brought for consumers. Further, they have provided education and entertainment and have been primary promoters of art and culture.

Japan

Japan's department stores boast a four-hundred-year history. These stores stem from two traditions. The older historic tradition is the development of department stores from *gofukuya*, clothing and drapery stores, which originated as large merchant houses during the Edo or Tokugawa period (1600/1603–1868). These accompanied the rise of Japan's early cities and the new middle classes that emerged from the formerly lowly ranks of artisans and merchants. Early in the twentieth century, some decades after Japan opened to the outside world, these stores expanded into *hyakkaten*, "one-hundred-things stores," or department stores. The second tradition for the development of department stores in Japan is with railroad companies, which built department stores at stations at urban intersections and in outlying suburban areas as railroads became prominent in commuting within

Ornate light fixtures in Lotte department store in Seoul, South Korea, in 1998. (CATHERINE KARNOW/CORBIS)

cities and in connecting cities to the outlying areas where many urban employees lived. These stores were called *tetsudo depaato* ("railroad department stores"). Over time both types of department stores came to be referred to as either *hyakkaten* or *depaato. Depaato* is more common in colloquial speech, while *hyakkaten* is used more in official store titles.

Japanese department stores played a major role in introducing the West to Japan. One of the earliest department stores, Mitsukoshi, established ties to British stores and British royalty while also promoting American connections. Department stores brought in Western goods and taught people how to use them. Specialized employees taught the Japanese how to put on Western-style clothing with buttons, which were very unfamiliar to a populace who daily wore kimonos wrapped or tied into place. Department stores also promoted foreign holidays, such as Christmas, Valentine's Day, Mother's Day, and Father's Day. After a fire at the Mitsukoshi department store in Tokyo, several shoes went missing in the rush to exit the store, and the store began requiring its employees and customers to wear shoes in the store, ending the previous Japanese business custom of removing outside footwear and wearing slippers in shops. Several kimono-clad women died in another fire at the Shirokiya department store because they would neither jump nor slide down chutes for fear their clothing might become disarrayed and embarrassingly revealing. The store joined the Tokyo municipal fire department in promoting the adoption of Western-style underpants so both lives and honor could be saved in a fire.

Japanese department stores proffered entertainment with concerts, craft fairs, and recreational facilities inside stores and on rooftops. They offered education in the form of seminars, health and medical guidance for new parents, and in-store science fairs and educational contests for children. Typically, such seminars and other free information services did not involve the expectation that customers would buy anything on that occasion, but were geared toward developing loyal patronage through an ongoing relationship with the store. Stores also sent educational specialists into schools. Tokyo's Seibu department store started a "community college" (requiring course fees) with over four hundred course offerings, a major innovation in personal-interest education in Japan. Most department stores have exhibit and gallery spaces for art and folk craft displays. Isetan and Seibu department stores inaugurated legally designated museums of art within their stores. These museums, galleries, and exhibit halls have been pivotal in circulating Japanese and foreign art. In the last few decades of the twentieth century in Japan more international art circulated through department store museums than through government and private museums. These stores also responded to Japanese nostalgia for lost Japan by sponsoring Japanese traditional crafts and hosting calendrical festivals associated with a rural agrarian past.

South Korea

Department stores in the Republic of Korea (South Korea) have also been pivotal in introducing foreign culture by popularizing Western customs and trends from Japan. Seoul department stores became focal arenas of fashion couture, while department stores in other areas disseminated these new trends to smaller cities. In Seoul the rise of a middle-class consciousness was strongly associated with frequenting the city's glistening new department stores as opposed to shopping in traditional market districts like Namdaemun (South Market) or Tongdaemun (East Market). Among status-oriented female consumers, shopping for daily family goods at department stores rather than at open markets became a sign of rising family status.

South Korean department stores have hosted entertainment and educational offerings within stores and in addition have established other amusement centers. The department store conglomerate Lotte built the entertainment theme park Lotte World, an amusement park similar to Disneyland in concept but featuring Lotte's own characters, in a Lotte department store on the outskirts of Seoul.

China

Chinese department stores also mirror historical changes, further development of urban centers, and the rising middle class. The immense early-twentieth-century entrepreneurial development in China's main cities was reflected in the rise of department stores. Shanghai in particular became a major industrial and commercial center after the end of the Sino-Japanese war in 1895. Nanjing Road, Shanghai's version of New York's Fifth Avenue, saw the birth of glamorous department stores that offered the increasing numbers of middle-class customers a different shopping experience from traditional shops and markets. Along with the visible array of a wide spectrum of goods, fixed prices, and extensive services, these Chinese department stores provided rooftop tea gardens, music recitals, and dancing parties. Sincere department store had an attached hotel, showing that a trip to Shanghai for shopping had itself become a vacation objective. Chinese department stores mediated the transition to Westernization and modernization, tutoring customers on issues of style and essentials of modern life. As in Japan, department stores were linked to the development of railroads and involved a reinterpretation of the merchant classes. Whereas traditionally merchants had been seen as unproductive to society, merchants were increasingly seen as entrepreneurs whose economic activity could be advantageous to society, partly because of the rising prominence of department stores.

Regional Trends

East Asian department stores have influenced women's employment and domestic roles. In 1900 Sincere department store caused a sensation with the opening of a Hong Kong branch with female shop clerks; previously women were employed only in family shops. Due to the public outcry over this public employment of women at that time, these women were laid off, but by the late 1930s female sales clerks were an accepted part of Chinese department stores. In Japan, even before the Equal Employment Opportunity Law of 1985, department stores promoted more women to managerial positions than did other private or government concerns because the overwhelming proportion of both department-store employees and walk-in customers were women.

Another trend has involved the establishment of large Japanese and Chinese retailing concerns in Europe, North America, and Australia. Some of these stores, such as Yaohan, were considered extended supermarkets in their home countries but have been perceived as department stores in the foreign context. These stores primarily cater to Asian customers abroad and to Asian-descent populations, but they also appeal to non-Asian Westerners. Where East Asian department stores have long introduced Western goods and culture to Asian countries, now the reverse is also true. Stores originate in East Asia, and they transmit food, styles, fashions, culture, and trends from their Asian countries of origin to the Western countries where they do business, thereby acting as mediators between culture and consumption.

Millie Creighton

Further Reading

Cochran, Sherman, ed. (1999) *Inventing Nanjing Road: Commercial Culture in Shanghai, 1900–1945.* Cornell East Asia Series, no. 103. Ithaca, NY: Cornell University East Asia Program.

Creighton, Millie. (1991) "Maintaining Cultural Boundaries in Retailing: How Japanese Department Stores Domesticate 'Things Foreign.'" *Modern Asian Studies* 25, 4: 675–709.

———. (1994) "Edutaining Children: Consumer and Gender Socialization in Japanese Marketing." *Ethnology* 33, 1: 35–52.

———. (1998) "Pre-Industrial Dreaming in Post-Industrial Japan: Department Stores and the Commoditization of Community Traditions." *Japan Forum* 10, 2: 1–23.
MacPherson, Kerrie, ed. (1998) *Asian Department Stores*. Surrey, U.K.: Curzon Press.
Nelson, Laura C. (2000) *Measured Excess: Status, Gender, and Consumer Nationalism in South Korea*. New York: Columbia University Press.
Philips, Lisa A., et al. (1992) "Hong Kong Department Stores: Retailing in the 1990s." *International Journal of Retail and Distribution Management* 20, 1: 16–24.
Redding, Stanley Gordon. (1990) *The Spirit of Chinese Capitalism*. New York and Berlin: Walter de Gruyter.
Tobin, Joseph, ed. (1992) *Re-Made in Japan: Everyday Life and Consumer Taste in a Changing Society*. New Haven, CT: Yale University Press.

DEV, NANAK GURU (1469–1539), founder of Sikhism. Nanak Dev, who laid the foundation of Sikhism, endeavored to synthesize both Hinduism and Islam in the new religion and combat social inequality. Born in the village of Talwandi in western Punjab to Kalyan Das Meheta and Tripta Mahal, Nanak was attracted to spiritualism from childhood and contributed monetarily to charitable works. His marriage at the age of eighteen to Sulakhani Devi did not deter him from spiritual pursuits, and he traveled throughout India and even to Mecca, Medina, Tibet, and Sri Lanka.

Nanak rejected the prevailing social system based on caste and class. Identifying with the downtrodden, he declared, "I am lowliest of the low." He was also averse to rituals and idol worship. Holding woman in high esteem, he asked, "Why denounce her form [of] whom even kings and great men are born?" One of the important aspects of Nanak's teaching was monotheism, and to him God was timeless and everlasting. He advocated an honest livelihood and shared earnings. His simple and universal message had widespread appeal. Nanak's followers were known as Sikhs, and after his death in 1539, Sikhism became an important religion.

Patit Paban Mishra

Further Reading

Bhattacharyya, Narendra Nath. (1999) *Medieval Bhakti Movements in India*. New Delhi: Munshiram Manoharlal.
Majumdar, R. C., ed. (1989) *The Delhi Sultanate (1300–1526 ad)*. Vol 6. Bombay, India: Bharatiya Vidya Bhavan.

DEVELOPMENT ZONES—CHINA The creation of development zones in China since 1984 marked the intensification of an open-door policy and a wider engagement of China with the outside world. By 1988 China had designated fourteen development zones: Dalian, Qinhuangdao, Ningbo, Qingdao, Yantai, Zhanjiang, Guangzhou, Tianjin, Nantong, Lianyungang, Fuzhou, Minxing, Hongqiao, and Caohejing. These development zones were located in close proximity to coastal cities and placed major emphasis on export processing, technology development, and foreign investment. With tax incentives and preferential policies, development zones function as new growth poles of the economy. This in turn results in their quick development and diversification.

Concept and Characteristics of Development Zones

The idea of development zones did not originate in China. Development zones became popular following World War II in such forms as free ports, free trade zones, export-processing zones, science and industry parks, and border trade zones. China modeled its own development zones on this international experience, treating them as new means to open China to the outside world. It aimed to create an attractive business and investment environment to encourage foreign investment, joint ventures, and technology development and transfer and to learn advanced management skills.

China's development zones are similar in many respects to special economic zones (SEZs) but they have some distinct features. First, SEZs are relatively independent in administration; their administrative rank is equivalent to that of a province. Development zones, by contrast, are managed by local governments through a development zone committee. Second, SEZs are encouraged to develop into a cross-sector comprehensive economic structure; development zones focus on export-led industry and technology or other special sectors. Third, all types of investment enjoy tax incentives in SEZs, while development zones are only intended to offer tax incentives for investment in industry and technology or in other designated sectors.

Development zones have advantageous locations. Economic and technological development zones and tax-free zones are normally located in coastal cities and ports. Border cooperative zones are located in inland border trade areas. High-tech development zones are located in large or medium-size cities across the country. In short, they have easy access to transport networks. They are often in or close to areas with well-developed industrial foundations or an advanced economy. Development zones are provided modern infrastructure and high standard services.

History of China's Development Zones

In 1983 China opened up fourteen coastal cities to the outside world, and in late 1984 and early 1985, the government designated eleven development zones in eleven coastal cities. Shanghai was approved to establish two development zones in 1986 and a further one in 1988. The main work during this initial period (1984–1988) included: (1) the establishment of an administrative committee to oversee the development zones, as well as the establishment of the Economic and Technological Development Corporation; (2) the planning of the development zones; (3) the preparation and creation of regulations and policies relating to the development zones; and (4) the construction of physical infrastructure.

The forms of development zones have been diversified since 1988. The first high-tech development zone was established in Beijing in 1988, and tax-free zones were created in 1990. Development zones have received unprecedented rapid development since 1992, when paramount leader Deng Xiaoping (1904–1997) toured south China and called for further opening up of China's economy. After that, even small cities, counties, and townships began to create their own development zones.

Achievements and Problems of the Development Zones

Although development zones only account for 0.004 percent of China's land, they account for about 10 percent of the total national foreign investment. More than two hundred giant international corporations have invested in China's development zones, which are particularly effective in advancing technology development and in facilitating national economic restructuring. In most of the development zones, more than 60 percent of the industrial projects are high-tech or new technology projects.

Development zones have created extremely rapid growth and high productivity. The gross industrial product in the first thirteen development zones increased about 450 times within ten years and had grown to 135 billion yuan (China's currency) in 1996. The per capita productivity in Minxing, Tianjin, Dalian, Hongqiao, Beijing, and Kunshan exceeded 200,000 yuan in 1996; Minxing, in particular, recorded a high of 419,000 yuan. Problems include a lack of strategic coordination and effective control in the development of development zones. For example, 1992 saw the sudden creation of more than two thousand new development zones, which were more than twenty times the total number created before 1992. Among these, only 1.1 percent were approved by state, province, or city governments. Counties, small cities, and townships were also striving to establish development zones. This led to uncontrolled expansion of such zones to occupy 33.34 billion square meters of land, of which 80 percent was arable land. This resulted in the wasteful use of land resources and the abuse of preferential policies by local authorities.

The Future

After more than two decades of open-door policies, China is turning its attention to establishing a fair competition environment throughout the country. This will result in the gradual reduction and eventual abolition of tax incentives and preferential policies enjoyed by development zones.

Xing Quan Zhang

Further Reading

Gao Shangquan, and Chi Fulin. (1997) *New Progress in China's Special Economic Zones.* Beijing: Foreign Language Press.

Ge Wei. (1999) *Special Economic Zones and the Economic Transition in China.* Singapore: World Scientific.

Li B. H., ed. (1996) *China Development Zones.* Beijing: China Building Material Industry Press.

Tai H. H. (1989) "Moving Forward on the Road of Open-Door Policy." In *Yearbook of China's Special Economic Zones and Coastal Economic and Technological Development Zones (1980–1989).* Beijing: Reform Press

DEVI, PHOOLAN (1964?–2001), Indian political figure. In contemporary India, Phoolan Devi's name is intimately connected to the country's history of caste and class animosities. Born in a north Indian village, Devi grew up amid extreme poverty. At a young age, she was abducted, repeatedly assaulted, and raped. Although a great deal of controversy surrounds the exact details of her early life, it is generally believed that she reacted to her harrowing upbringing by participating in the "Valentine's Day Massacre" in 1981, in which twenty people of an upper caste background were killed. After leading life as a bandit for three years, she surrendered in 1983, and was incarcerated for the next eleven years.

Following the release of her biography by Mala Sen in 1991 and the film *Bandit Queen*, directed by Shekhar Kapoor and released in 1994, Phoolan Devi became a well-known public figure. She was released from prison in 1994 and subsequently went on to become a successful politician. With support from lower caste groups and women, she was elected twice to the Indian parliament. In 1995 she converted to Buddhism, an act viewed by many as a political move. In July 2001 she was shot dead by unidentified assailants outside her Delhi home on her way back from Parliament.

Vivek Bhandari

Further Reading

Sen, Mala. (1993) *India's Bandit Queen: The True Story of Phoolan Devi*. London and San Francisco: Pandora.

Devi, Phoolan, with Marie-Thérèse Cuny and Paul Rambali. (1997) *I, Phoolan Devi: The Autobiography of India's Bandit Queen*. London: Warner.

DEVIL DANCING. See **Possession.**

DHAKA (2002 est. pop. 8.5 million). Located in central Bangladesh, Dhaka (formerly Dacca) lies on an alluvial terrace above the northern bank of the Buriganga River, which offers access to several of the major regional rivers, including the Brahmaputra, the Meghna, and the Padma. Dhaka's early history is linked to the prominence of the nearby administrative urban center of Sonargaon, which lay to the east along the Buriganga. Dhaka grew as a result of the commercial and political prominence of Sonargaon from the late thirteenth to the sixteenth centuries, as indicated by the names of neighborhoods in the old town, which point to a pre-Mughal Hindu presence there. The old town is bounded by the Dulai River, a waterway coming from the north and curving eastward as it joins the Buriganga.

In 1610, the Mughal governor Islam Khan (ruled 1608–1613) chose Dhaka as the regional capital. He built an artificial canal joining the Dulai to the Buriganga, thus forming a western boundary for the old town. The Mughals expanded Dhaka to the west and north along the Buriganga, building two large forts and several major mosques. Dhaka was the center of the eastern Mughal empire, hosting diplomatic and commercial visitors from around the globe, including Sebastian Manrique, Jean Baptiste Tavernier, and Thomas Bowrey, each of whom published an account of his visit. During the late seventeenth and early eighteenth centuries, the Mughals allowed Europeans to build factories along the river; these structures were still extant when James Rennell's *Bengal Atlas* was published in 1780. An Armenian community grew in the old town, and the Portuguese built a small church and community in the northern suburb of Tejgaon. Dhaka remained the regional capital until 1717, when the Mughal prince Azim Shah (1697–1712) shifted the capital to Murshidabad.

During the eighteenth century, Dhaka's population and urban infrastructure declined; paintings of the city emphasize its decay, as evidenced by Charles D'Oyly's *Antiquities of Dacca* series, done between 1814 and 1827. In the nineteenth century, the British East In-

A crowded ferryboat in Dhaka in 1996. (TIZIANA AND GIANNI BALDIZZONE/CORBIS)

dia Company built the residential area of Wari in the old town and cleared Ramna Park to the north. Between 1905 and 1911, Dhaka was the capital of the short-lived province of East Bengal and Assam. After Independence and the partition of British India into Pakistan and India in 1947, Dhaka served as the capital of the East Pakistan province. In 1971, a bloody civil war led to the creation of the independent state of Bangladesh, with Dhaka as its capital. The American architect Louis Kahn (1901–1974) designed its striking parliament building (completed 1974). Dhaka has preserved its pre-Mughal, Mughal, and European histories in its contemporary urban fabric.

Rebecca M. Brown

Further Reading

Ahmed, Sharif Uddin. (1986) *Dacca: A Study in Urban History and Development.* London: Curzon Press.

———, ed. (1991) *Dhaka: Past Present Future.* Dhaka, Bangladesh: The Asiatic Society of Bangladesh.

DHAMMAYUT SECT Founded by King Mongkut (1804–1868) of Siam during his twenty-six years of monkhood, the Dhammayut sect (Thammayut or Dhammayuttikanikaya, those attached to the dharma, or Buddhist teachings/doctrines) is distinguished from the other order of Theravada Buddhism in Thailand: Mahanikaya (the great congregation). Both sects cooperate in some ways and for some rituals and are united in Thailand under the nationwide Council of Elders, or Sangha Supreme Council. While the laity rarely pay attention to the differences between the two sects, each sect has its own rituals and emphases, and the Dhammayut sect is known for its greater orthodoxy and closer relationship with royalty and the aristocracy.

After Mongkut was ordained in 1824, he became the principal religious figure in Siam at the time. Studying the Pali (the language of the Theravada Buddhist canon) scriptures and the strict discipline of Mon monks, he became convinced that Siamese Buddhism had gone astray and came to demand from his followers more serious study of Pali and the Vinaya (the Buddhist scriptures pertaining to monastic rules) and more dedication to and proficiency in meditation. He sought to put aside superstitions and tried to discern the most accurate pronunciation of Pali, demanding monks learn this. He also insisted that laypeople perform tasks such as cleaning, robe-washing, and distributing monk's food so the monks could adhere more strictly to their discipline. The most visible sign of the difference in Mongkut's order at its founding was the style in which monks wore their robes. At the founding of the order, Mongkut insisted that the robes cover both shoulders, allowing the right arm freedom. (Later, when he became king, Mongkut would allow monks to choose for themselves what style of robe they preferred.) Other changes in monastic practice included ordination rituals, daily routines, and observance of different religious days. When Mongkut left Wat Bowonniwet, the center of the sect, in April to be crowned king in May 1851, he vowed to support both Dhammayut and Mahanikaya.

During the reign of Mongkut's son Chulalongkorn (1853–1910; reigned 1868–1910), Prince Vajiravudh (1881–1925), who was another of Mongkut's sons and a half brother of Chulalongkorn, led the Dhammayut sect to a period of particular influence. Prince Vajiravudh eventually headed the entire *sangha.* Chulalongkorn unified Siamese Buddhists into a national organization, and monks throughout the country helped determine its policies and programs. While originally the Dhammayut sect made up an elite group, the demand for rigor and study led to standardization of discipline, education, and rituals throughout the country. A standard monastic curriculum was established and a state-sponsored Buddhist nationalism arose without the diversity found previously in customs, practices, and emphases. In 1864 a Khmer monk who had studied in Siam brought the sect to Cambodia, leading to a similar division between Mahanikaya and Dhammayuttikanikaya devotees in that country.

Sid Brown

Further Reading

Kamala, Tiyavanich. (1997) *Forest Recollections: Wandering Monks in Twentieth-Century Thailand.* Honolulu, HI: University of Hawaii Press.

Kirsch, A. Thomas. (1975) "Modernizing Implications of Nineteenth Century Reforms in the Thai Sangha." *Contributions to Asian Studies* 8: 8–23.

Reynolds, Craig J. (1973) *The Buddhist Monkhood in Nineteenth Century Thailand.* Ithaca, NY: Cornell University Press.

Reynolds, Frank E. (1977) "Civic Religion and National Community in Thailand." *Journal of Asian Studies* 36, 2: 267–282.

DIKIR BARAT *Dikir barat* is a form of popular Islamic-oriented musical entertainment particularly associated with the northern Malaysian state of Kelantan. It may be derived from the Arabic *zikir*, which generally refers to a form of Islamic chanting in which the various names of Allah are repeated, leading the reciter into a state of trance. In Malaysia, however, this practice has evolved into a popular form of poetic debate, *dikir barat*. Originating among the Malays of the northern state of Kelantan, it is usually sung by teams in a responsorial (solo-chorus) fashion.

A team consists of a chorus (*awok-awok*) of ten to fifteen singers, who sit cross-legged on the floor and sing in unison; a lead singer (*tok juara*); and a second solo singer (*tukang karut*), who spontaneously creates and sings lyrics. The *tok juara* begins the performance by chanting a *pantun* (four-line quatrain of Malay origin) in free rhythm, while the chorus repeats a fixed verse, interjecting syncopated shouts, clapping their hands, and making dancelike movements with their hands, arms, and upper torsos. The *tok juara* and chorus alternate until the final chorus, when the *tukang karut* takes the lead, spontaneously creating new lines of text and singing in a responsorial style with the chorus.

The vocalists are accompanied by a small ensemble of frame drums (*rebana*), a bossed gong (*tetawak*), a pair of small knobbed gongs suspended over a wooden resonator (*canang*), and maracas. The *rebana* and maracas establish a recurring rhythmic pattern, while the *tetawak* and *canang* mark larger two- or four-beat units.

Contemporary *dikir barat* texts often have heavy religious or political content. Competitions are common, and performances are frequently broadcast on television to increase public awareness of social issues. Originally performed only by male vocalists, female *dikir barat* choruses have become popular.

Margaret Sarkissian

Further Reading

Matusky, Patricia, and Tan Sooi Beng. (1997). *Muzik Malaysia*. Penang and Kuala Lumpur, Malaysia: The Asian Centre

———. (1998) *Pengantar Muzik Malaysia*. Penang and Kuala Lumpur, Malaysia: The Asian Centre.

DILI (1999 pop. 250,000). Dili is the largest town and capital of East Timor, with a premier seaport located on the northern coast of the island of Timor on Ombai Strait. Dili was once the capital of Portuguese Timor where Portuguese traders arrived as early as 1512. The population is mostly Timorese and Atonese with minorities of Eurasians and Arab Muslims. The importance of Dili as a trading post has been in decline since the 1920s, as the sandalwood trade declined and Portugal fell into depression. Dili's modest prosperity is derived from the production and export of coffee.

An East Timorese woman and her child stand in front of a destroyed home in Dili in October 1999. (REUTERS NEWMEDIA INC./CORBIS)

After the end of the dictatorship in Portugal and fighting in East Timor between groups favoring integration with Indonesia and proindependence groups, the last Portuguese soldiers left Dili in 1975. With Indonesia's invasion and East Timor's formal integration into Indonesia on 17 July 1976, Dili became the capital of Indonesia's twenty-seventh province. After the announcement of the United Nations–sponsored public consultation on the future of East Timor in September 1999, Dili was rampaged and destroyed by pro-Indonesian militia forces, and most of its inhabitants fled. Since 1999, Dili has been rebuilt and as of 2001 is the administrative center of an independent East Timor.

Frank Feulner

Further Reading

Dunn, James S. (1996) *Timor, A People Betrayed*. Sydney: ABC Books.

Taylor, John G. (1999) *East Timor: The Price of Freedom*. New York: Zed Books.

DILI MASSACRE The Dili Massacre, also known as the Santa Cruz Massacre, took place on 12 November 1991 in East Timor. This event became a turning point in the search for a final political status for the territory. Since Indonesia's military invasion in December 1975, the military's behavior was characterized by a pattern of human-rights violations. However, this became a major international news issue only in 1991.

On 12 November, a memorial mass was held for Sebastião Gomes, a proindependence East Timorese, killed on 28 October by the Indonesian military. In the procession from the Church of Motael to the Santa Cruz cemetery, there was a small clash between the participants in the mourning and Indonesian soldiers. Later, when the crowd had reached the cemetery, the military opened fire against the crowd, began beating them, and bayoneted those inside the cemetery.

Contrary to other human-rights violations committed before in the territory, this time there were seven foreigners present—one of them was killed—at the cemetery when the events took place. The English cameraman Max Stahl recorded what happened and was able to smuggle the videotape showing the events out of East Timor. On 13 November, the European community condemned Indonesia's behavior, and in the next few days several governments suspended their aid programs to Indonesia.

A first official Indonesian version of what happened admitted only nineteen deaths. The East Timorese estimated that the true number was at least five times higher. Owing to the international criticism, Indonesia was compelled to form a national commission to investigate the facts. On 26 December, the commission admitted the occurrence of fifty deaths. Two days later, President Suharto replaced the East Timor military commander Brigadier General Rudolf Warouw and his immediate superior based in the Bali Udayana Command, Major General Sintong Panjaitan. Moreover, he also ordered the army chief of staff Edi Sudrajat to form a military tribunal—a Council of Military Honor—to recommend whether any officers should face court-martial. The Council operated from 2 January to 20 February 1992. On 27 February, it became public that six officers had been disciplined, but their names were never made public.

The Dili Massacre triggered a rare instance of public criticism of the Indonesian military, the need for an allegedly independent report, and, especially, a response by Suharto. It was the first time that Indonesia was compelled to appease international criticism since its invasion of East Timor. In fact, the Indonesian foreign affairs minister Ali Alatas would later describe those events as a turning point in Jakarta's international support.

Paulo Gorjão

Further Reading

Inbaraj, Sonny. (1995) *East Timor: Blood and Tears in ASEAN.* Chiang Mai, Thailand: Silkworm Books.

Kohen, Arnold S. (1999) *From the Place of the Dead.* New York: St. Martin's Press.

Schwarz, Adam. (2000) *A Nation in Waiting: Indonesia's Search for Stability.* Boulder, CO: Westview Press.

DIN MOHAMMAD, MUSHK-E-ALAM (1790–1886), Afghan hero. Din Mohammad is a national hero of Afghanistan, renowned for his undying enmity to the British. He was a mullah (Islamic cleric), whose grandfather came from India and settled in Ghazni, a city southwest of Kabul.

Din Mohammad studied with various religious teachers, one of whom gave him the name Mushk-e-Alam ("Musk of the World"), because of his erudition. He was a militant mullah and in time opened his own religious school where he propounded his aggressive views. This ensured him a following of like-minded mullahs, many trained by him, and he became a man of considerable influence among the Ghilzais, the clan that inhabited Ghazni and the surrounding area. He was given an allowance by Shir ʿAli Khan (1825–1879), the amir of Afghanistan from 1863 to 1879.

Din Mohammad openly preached jihad or holy war against the British during the Second Anglo-Afghan War (1878–1881). When ʿAbdorrahman Khan (c. 1844–1901), the ruler of Afghanistan from 1880 to 1901, tried to limit his influence and his rhetoric, Din Mohammad incited the Margul and Ghilzai tribes to open rebellion in 1886. Din Mohammad died during this revolt, but his son, the mullah Abdul Karim, took up his father's cause and led the Margul and Ghilzai uprising; it was only with great difficulty that the amir ʿAbdorrahman suppressed the rebellion.

Nirmal Dass

Further Reading

Gulzad, Zalmay. (1994) *External Influences and the Development of the Afghan State in the Nineteenth Century.* New York: P. Lang.

O'Balance, Edgar. (1993) *Afghan Wars, 1839–1992: What Britain Gave Up and the Soviet Union Lost.* London and New York: Barssey's.

DING LING (1904–1986), Chinese novelist. Born in Hunan Province, Ding Ling studied at several schools in Shanghai and Beijing. She began to publish short stories in 1927 and quickly emerged as the country's foremost woman writer. After she joined the Chinese Communist Party in 1932, she was arrested by the Guomindang government and held in detention for three years. Her husband Hu Yepin was killed secretly by the Guomindang.

In 1936 she went to Yanan, the capital of the Soviet government of China. There she published the well-known essay "Thoughts on the March 8 Festival (Women's Day)," in which she examined women's situation and sharply criticized discrimination against them. This made her a target of the Yanan Forum in 1942. Though she held senior official positions for several years after the establishment of the People's Republic of China, she was once again criticized in 1955. From that time on, she was either in jail or in labor camps in north China until the end of the Cultural Revolution. She died in 1986.

Ding Ling always maintained a sincere interest in Chinese women. She was the first writer to portray women liberating themselves in Chinese society. From her maiden effort, "Mengke," to such representative works as "Miss Sophie's Diary" and "Mother," she described how the first generation of new women struggled to get free from the yoke of feudalism.

She Xiaojie

Further Reading

Feuerwerker, Yi-tsi Mei. (1982) *Ding Ling's Fiction: Ideology and Narrative in Modern Chinese Literature*. Cambridge, MA: Harvard University Press.

DISEASE, TROPICAL Tropical diseases are those found in the tropics, which is the climatic region that lies between 30 degrees north latitude and 30 degrees south latitude. People living in the tropics are prone to the same infections that are found in other parts of the world, but tropical diseases are more prevalent in the tropics. Tropical diseases vary in time and space. Factors such as population distributions, cultural patterns, political circumstances, economic situations, and the physical environment determine the spatial and temporal distribution of these diseases. The countries of Asia that are in the tropics include India, Pakistan, Bangladesh, Sri Lanka, Nepal, Myanmar (Burma), Laos, Vietnam, Cambodia, Thailand, Taiwan, Philippines, Brunei, Malaysia, Indonesia, Singapore, and parts of Japan and China. Most tropical countries have high average temperatures and humidity, and these conditions are conducive to the prevalence of many tropical disease vectors. Some diseases, such as African sleeping sickness, are confined to tropical areas because the transmission of these diseases can occur only in tropical climates.

Most of the tropical countries of Asia are poor and therefore diseases caused by nutritional deficiencies are common. Many tropical countries have inadequate

SURVIVING IN THE TROPICS

This account indicates the horrors that awaited many Europeans who traveled to tropical regions of Asia. In India, there was the two-season rule: if one survived two tropical seasons, the chances were good that one would survive in the future.

> The Common Distemper that destroys the most in *India*, is Feavers, which the *Europeans* with difficulty escape, especially if they have boild up their Spirits by solemn Repast, and been ingag'd in a strong Debauch. Besides this, the Mordechine is another Disease of which some die, which is a violent Vomiting and Looseness, and is caus'd most frequently by an Excess in Eating, particularly of Fish and Flesh together. It has been Cur'd by Red-hot Iron clapt to the Heel of him that is sick, so close that it renders him uneasie by its nearness, whereby it leaves a Scar behind it.

Source: John Ovington. (1690) *A Voyage to Suratt in the Year 1689* (1690), as quoted in *The Sahibs*, edited by Hilton Brown (1948). London: William Hodge & Co., 37.

public health systems and a poorly educated population, two factors that contribute to the spread of disease. Increased international travel has facilitated a rapid increase in the spread of tropical diseases into temperate countries by refugees, immigrants, tourists, and business people. Development itself may also introduce new health problems. The construction of dams and irrigation canals may create breeding sites for the vectors of malaria, yellow fever, and schistosomiasis.

Factors Contributing to Tropical Diseases

A hot, wet, tropical climate is an ideal habitat for many microbial agents, parasites, insects, and rodents. Insects and other arthropods serve as vectors for disease agents. Numerous species of animals, especially rodents, live near humans and are reservoirs for diseases. Close contact with animals exposes humans to a wide range of zoonotic diseases (diseases that are transmissible from animals to humans). Genetic factors also contribute to the spread of tropical diseases. For instance, leprosy is more prevalent in Caucasian and East Asian populations than in Africans because of genetic predispositions. While natural immunity can explain why some people do not suffer from certain infections, immunity acquired during childhood by being exposed to a disease or by getting a vaccine against it is a more usual explanation. Vaccines control the spread of diseases that were once highly prevalent worldwide. Efficient vaccines exist for many diseases, including yellow fever, polio, measles, and tetanus. However, they have made little impact in many developing countries of the tropics because vaccine programs are expensive and difficult to administer. Exposure to certain tropical diseases, such as onchocerciasis does not lead to meaningful immunity against them, and therefore vaccines for these diseases do not exist.

Diseases of malnutrition are related to the availability and cost of food, which are dependent on the economic and political circumstances in a particular region. Malnutrition is also associated with the prevalence of gastrointestinal infections as well as traditional practices and taboos that may limit the use of available food. Acute infectious diseases, especially respiratory infections, measles, and gastroenteritis, still account for the high infant mortality in some parts of the tropics, where up to 40 percent of children die before five years of age. Acute infections such as measles may cause specific forms of malnutrition including protein deficiency (kwashiorkor). The absence of a clean water supply and sewage disposal system, especially in the urban slums of the tropics, leads to a high prevalence of gastrointestinal infections. Poor sanitary conditions contribute to the spread of diarrheal diseases, especially among children.

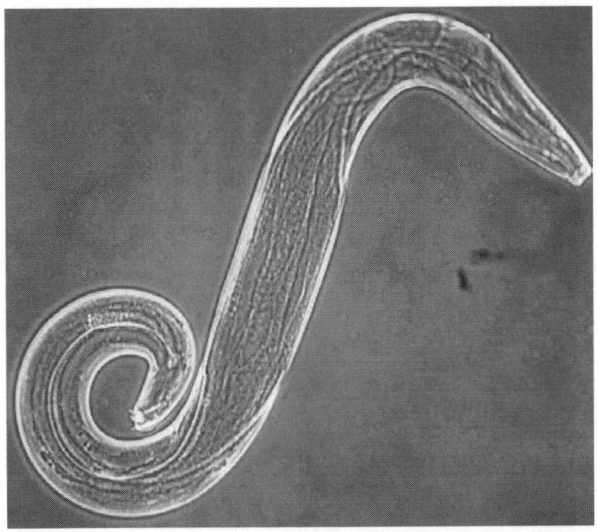

The *Plasmodium falciparum* parasite, which causes malaria, one of the most common and most deadly diseases in the tropics. (LESTER V. BERGMAN/CORBIS)

Prevalent Tropical Diseases in Asia

Tropical diseases that lead to the highest number of deaths in tropical Asia include respiratory infections and diarrheal diseases. Other diseases that lead to a high number of deaths include measles, nutritional deficiencies, tetanus, pertussis, AIDS, sexually transmitted diseases, leishmaniasis, and dengue fever. Acute respiratory infection is the most common cause of childhood death in the world. Bacterial pneumonia and tuberculosis are the most common respiratory infections in Asia. Chronic bronchitis is rare in most rural areas of Asia, although it is common in North and Central India, where it is attributed to smoke from wood fires in dwellings.

Worldwide, 10 million people die each year from diarrheal diseases, and children who live in the tropics are at highest risk. Many different disease agents are responsible for diarrheal diseases; common agents are cholera, rotavirus, *Escherichia coli*, salmonella, shigellosis, and giardia. Diarrhea is often associated with bottle-feeding when baby formula is mixed with contaminated water. Most diarrhea attacks are self-limiting within several days, but if diarrhea is severe and treatment is not available, severe dehydration and death may result, as is common with cholera. Infantile diarrhea is also the single most important cause of malnutrition in infants in the tropics. The most important treatment for diarrhea is rehydration, which can be accomplished

THE EPIDEMIC GHOST

In many Asian cultures, indigenous beliefs about disease exist alongside Western scientific medicine. In Central Thailand, rural villagers often attribute serious outbreaks of disease to a supernatural force—the epidemic ghost.

> Until the Twentieth Century, Thailand was visited by terrifying epidemics of cholera, smallpox, and other devastating diseases. The physiological and psychological consequences of these sudden epidemics were shattering, and it is not at all surprising that the culture has evolved a specialized ghost that is considered peculiarly responsible for these visitations. Since buffaloes and other farm animals are also of vital importance in the livelihood of the Bang Chan farmer, this same ghost is considered responsible for epidemics of rinderpest and other economically disastrous animal diseases.
>
> One frequently hears the world haa (epidemic) in everyday speech, usually of a rough sort. Taaj haa means to die of an epidemic disease. Aaj haa is an insulting term implying that the person spoken about derives from, or is associated with, the hated and feared haa ghosts.
>
> The sole effect of Epidemic Ghost is to inflict sickness in the form of epidemic diseases. Conversely, diseases of epidemic proportions are caused only by Epidemic Ghosts, among all the S-s found in the culture. If a person is stricken by a disease which, at the time, is endemic rather than epidemic or nearly so, then the diagnosis will invariably be rendered in terms of other S other than Epidemic Ghost.
>
> Although there are no standardized notions as to the derivation of Epidemic Ghost, it is not surprising that idiosyncratic notions tend to define this S as deriving from an out-group. Thus, Monk Doctor Marvin told me that Epidemic Ghost derives from a dead Muslim or Lao—explaining that those ethnic groups like to eat fresh raw meat. The Laos do in fact like raw meat prepared in certain ways. Nai Sin, on the other hand, believes that this S derives from a Muslim who, before death, specialized in slaughtering buffaloes and chickens, and who now, as a ghost, continued to indulge in killing those animals. Muslims around Bang Chan do in fact engage disproportionately in slaughtering, a service which they render commercially to their Buddhist neighbors, whose Merit-Moral system includes a firm prohibition against the taking of animal life.
>
> *Source:* Robert B. Textor. (1973) *Roster of the Gods: An Ethnography of the Supernatural in a Thai Village.* New Haven, CT: HRAFLex Books, 391–392.

by drinking oral rehydration solution or through the administration of intravenous fluids.

Several diseases can be caused by nutritional deficiencies of total calories, protein, iodine, vitamin A, vitamin C, and iron. Calorie deficiency, or marasmus, causes emaciation and can lead to death. Protein deficiency, or kwashiorkor, makes its victims more susceptible to other infections and can cause mental deficiency. Iodine deficiency may lead to enlargement of the thyroid gland, or goiter, which leads to various complications. Vitamin A deficiency leads to blindness, and vitamin C deficiency, or scurvy, leads to anemia, bleeding of the gums, and bleeding under the skin. Iron deficiency also leads to anemia, which causes weakness and other complications.

Two especially deadly tropical diseases are visceral leishmaniasis and dengue fever. They are both diseases that are transmitted by insects. Visceral leishmaniasis is caused by a protozoan and is transmitted to humans by the bite of a sand fly. It causes damage to the spleen, liver, and bone marrow of its victims and has a high fatality rate. Prevention of leishmaniasis includes both control of the sand fly vector and control in humans through treatment. The sand fly vector has been successfully controlled by spraying insecticides on the walls of homes. Dengue fever is a viral disease that is transmitted by mosquitoes. It causes severe fever, headache, muscle pain, and a rash. Severe cases of dengue fever result in a syndrome called dengue hemorrhagic fever, which can lead to death. The only way to control the disease is to control the mosquito population.

Another tropical disease that is not responsible for large numbers of deaths in Asia but is a serious health problem is schistosomiasis. Schistosomiasis is a parasitic disease that is caused by blood flukes belonging to the genus *Schistosoma*. Infection occurs when a person wades or bathes in water that is infested with snails that transmit the blood flukes. The parasite infects an individual's blood vessels and is characterized by blood in the urine. The disease is associated with irrigation development schemes in many parts of the tropical world.

Fighting Tropical Diseases

Fighting tropical diseases involves not only diagnosis and treatment but also health education, environmental management, provision of a clean water supply, and development of a health-care infrastructure. However, many tropical countries in Asia have limited health budgets, making a comprehensive approach difficult.

Michael Emch, Aliya Naheed, and Mohammad Ali

Further Reading

Behrman, J. N. (1980) *Tropical Diseases: Repsonses of Pharmaceutical Companies*. Washington, DC: American Enterprise Institute for Public Policy Research.

Biggam, A., and F. J. Wright. (1964) *Tropical Diseases*. Baltimore: William and Wilkins.

Bradshaw, M. (2000) *World Regional Geography: The New Global Order*. 2d ed. Boston: McGraw Hill.

Chulay, Jeff. (1991) "Leishmaniasis: General Principles." In *Hunter's Tropical Medicine*, edited by G. T. Strickland. Philadelphia: W. B. Saunders Company, 638–643.

Desowitz, Robert. (1998) *Who Gave Pinta to the Santa Maria? Tracking the Devastating Spread of Lethal Tropical Diseases into American*. San Diego, CA: Harvest Books.

Felsenfeld, O. (1966) *The Epidemiology of Tropical Diseases*. Springfield, IL: Charles C. Thomas.

Kean, B. H., K. E. Mott, and A. J. Russell. (1978) *Tropical Medicine and Parasitology: Classic Investigations*. Ithaca, NY: Cornell University Press.

MacLeod, J., C. Edward, and I. Bouchier. (1990) *Davidson's Principles and Practice of Medicine*. 15th ed. London: Churchill Livingstone Medical Division of Longman Group.

Manson-Bahr, P. (1943) *Synopsis of Tropical Medicine*. Baltimore: William and Wilkins.

Peters, W., and H. M. Gilles. (1989) *A Colour Atlas of Tropical Medicine & Parasitology*. 3d ed. Weert, Netherlands: Wolfe Medical Publications.

Warren, Kenneth, and Adel Mahmoud. (1984) *Tropical and Geographical Medicine*. 2d ed. New York: McGraw-Hill.

World Health Organization (2000) *World Health Report 2000: Health Systems-Improving Performance*. Geneva: World Health Organization.

Wright, W. H. (1962) *Tropical Health: A Report on a Study of Needs and Resources*. Publication 996. Washington, DC: National Academy of Sciences, National Research Council.

DIWALI

DIWALI Although the religious practices of India are numerous and diverse, the festival of Diwali (array of light) is celebrated in most parts of India, primarily by Hindus. Diwali occurs on the new moon day of Kartik (a month during October and November).

The festival is celebrated by putting oil or ghee (clarified butter) lamps (*diyas*), wax candles, and sometimes colored electric bulbs around the house and setting off firecrackers during the night. The goddess of wealth, Lakshmi, is worshiped at night. Houses are cleaned and painted, and colored decorations *(rangoli)* adorn the doorways and courtyards to welcome the goddess. The trader community *(Banya)* begins the new financial year after Diwali.

According to popular stories about the origins of this ancient festival, *diyas* are lit to welcome Lord Rama, his wife Sita, and his brother Lakshmana to their kingdom of Ajodhya (former city in northern India) after a fourteen-year exile. Another story is that Diwali is observed to commemorate Krishna's killing of the demon Narakasura and the rescue of 16,000 women held captive by him. In southern India, Diwali celebrates the killing of the demon Hiranyakashipu by Vishnu in the form of a man-lion.

Hrushikesh Panda

Further Reading

Sharma, Brijendra Nath. (1978) *Festivals of India*. Delhi: Abhinav Publications.

Underhill, Muriel Marion. (1921) *The Hindu Religious Year.* Calcutta, India: Association Press; London: Oxford University Press.

DIYARBAKIR (2002 pop. of province 1.4 million). Diyarbakir (formerly Diyarbekir, ancient Amida, capital of the province of Diyarbakir) is located in southeastern Turkey on a basaltic plateau on the right bank of the Tigris River. Its old name, Black Amida, came from the black basalt walls surrounding the city. Diyarbakir is a very ancient city, dating back 5,000 years. Assyrians and Persians ruled there until Alexander of Macedon's conquests. The city walls, originally Roman (297 BCE), were rebuilt by the Byzantines. Arabs arrived around 638 CE and renamed the city Doyarbakir, "abode of [the tribe of] Bakr."

The collapse of the Byzantine empire in 1071 enabled the Seljuks to annex the city. Many nomadic pastoral tribes, especially Turkmens and Kurds, then settled in the area. The city was conquered by the Kara-Koyunlus in the fifteenth century, was occupied by the Safavids in 1507, and finally fell into Ottoman hands in 1515. The Ottomans organized the newly conquered territories into the province of Doyarbakir, centered on the city of Amida. One of the largest provinces of the Ottoman empire, it had special importance because of its position near the Persian frontier. In 1923 the city was officially named Diyarbakir under the new Turkish Republic. Today Diyarbakir is a largely Kurdish town and is the major center of trade, industry, culture, and education in southeast Anatolia.

T. Isikozlu-E.F. Isikozlu

DOAN THI DIEM (1705–1748), Vietnamese poet. A brilliant exponent of the Vietnamese *nom* (demotic script) verses, Doan Thi Diem was born in 1705 in the village of Gia Pham in Hai Hung Province, northern Vietnam, into a family of teachers. When she was twenty-five years old, her father died, and, as she was unmarried, she went to live with her brother, who held a doctor's degree. It was under his tutelage that Doan Thi Diem continued her education and writing career. Tragedy struck a few years later when her brother died. She then had to shoulder the responsibility of providing for her mother and her brother's family by engaging in two professions unprecedented for a Vietnamese woman: she practiced medicine and taught. She excelled in both while also pursuing her writing. She published collections of poems, but she was most famous for her translation into *nom* of a long poem, *Chinh Phu Ngam* (Lament of the Soldier's Wife). The original version of this poem was written in classical Chinese by a Vietnamese scholar, Dang Tran Con (1710–1745), a contemporary of Doan Thi Diem. Her translation equaled its Chinese version in grace and elegance but surpassed it in sensitivity, as it was able to communicate to its audience in their own tongue the pain, distress, and anguish of a wife whose husband has gone to war. Doan Thi Diem died of a severe cold, contracted while accompanying her husband, an official, to his new post in the province of Nghe An, south of Hanoi.

Truong Buu Lam

Further Reading

Dang Thai Mai. (1992) *Giang van Chinh Phu Ngam: cua Doan Thi Diem.* (Literary Explication: Lament of the Soldier's Wife, by Doan Thi Diem). Hanoi, Vietnam: Truong Dai Hoc Su Pham.

Dang Tran Con and Doan Thi Diem. (1959) *Lament of the Soldier's Wife.* Trans. by Rewi Allen. Hanoi, Vietnam: Foreign Languages Publishing House.

DOGRA DYNASTY The Dogra dynasty (1820–1947) was a lineage of Rajputs who ruled much of Kashmir and adjacent valleys. Dogra was in fact the name given to the country surrounding the small state of Jamma; the word meant "two lakes," in reference to the inhabitants' ancestral home between the lakes Siroensar and Mansar. During the First Sikh War (1845–1846) the Dogras won a high reputation as soldiers fighting on the British side, and during their later service in the Indian Army, they distinguished themselves in several operations late in the nineteenth century. Dogras were of mixed culture: Hindus, Muslims, and even Sikhs, all claiming Rajput status. They still have a dominating position in the state of Jammu and Kashmir.

The first ruler of the Dogra line, Gulab Singh (1792–1857), was appointed raja of Jammu in 1820 by the Sikh ruler of the region. He became a mediator rather than a participant in the First Sikh War, and was rewarded by the British with the province of Kashmir. It was in this way that a largely Muslim state came to have a Hindu ruler, down to independence in 1947. In that year Hari Singh, the great-grandson of Gulab Singh, acceded to the union of Kashmir with India.

Paul Hockings

Further Reading

Gough, Charles, and Arthur D. Innes. (1897) *The Sikhs and the Sikh Wars: The Rise, Conquest, and Annexation of the Punjab State.* London: A. D. Innes & Co.

DOI INTHANON Doi Inthanon (known as the Roof of Thailand) is the highest mountain peak in Thailand at 2,565 meters. The mountain is located in northwestern Thailand near the upper Ping River in the Chiang Mai province. On its summit rests the pagoda built by King Kue-Na in the fourteenth century that is said to house relics of Buddha.

Doi Inthanon, also designated a national park, covers more than 48,000 hectares. The park is splendent with mountains from the Shan Hills range, waterfalls and limestone rock formations and caves in the eastern end of the park. Forest floras include plants that grow in the park's temperate climate, such as rhododendron, pine, and laurel. Epiphytes can be found here, mainly orchids. Lichens, lianas, and fern are also abundant. The park has the largest number of bird species in Thailand. The Center for Wildlife Research at Mahidol University has recorded more than 360 species, making the park a popular destination among birdwatchers from around the globe.

Linda Dailey Paulson

Further Reading

"Doi Inthanon National Park: 'The Roof of Thailand.'" (2002) *Welcome to Chiangri & Chiangmi* magazine. Retrieved 14 January 2002, from: http://www.welcome-to.chiangmai-chiangrai.com/int-park.htm.

DOI MOI *Doi moi*, which means "renovation" in Vietnamese, is a set of political and economic reforms that were instituted in Vietnam by the Central Committee of the Vietnamese Communist Party (VCP) during the Sixth Party Congress in December 1986 in response to severe economic problems and a lack of confidence in the government.

Economic Crisis

After Vietnamese reunification in 1975, an economic crisis and serious food shortages became increasingly problematic for the VCP. This was mainly due the U.S.-imposed trade and aid embargo and the difficulties that the government had converting the agricultural sector in the south to socialist collectivism. In response, the Vietnamese government instituted a series of economic reforms which can best be described as a trial-and-error process. Initially, the government recognized contracts signed without a legal basis by some state enterprises with other state enterprises and private entrepreneurs to address the insufficient supply of production tools and fertilizer. The agricultural contract system and the industrial three-plan system (a three-fold production plan: Plan A was the general state plan with highest priority, Plan B authorized the purchase of production means and their autonomous use, and Plan C authorized the sale of products of lower value) were intended to increase private initiative, strengthen market functions, and intensify material production incentives. Between 1981 and 1985, low productivity, insufficient quality standards, and energy and material shortages, as well as inefficient management, further paralyzed economic development. Although policy papers recognized the important role agriculture played in the development of the country, state subsidies were allocated primarily to heavy industries. Despite this, in 1983 family agricultural production already accounted for 50–60 percent of the income and 90 percent of foodstuffs available in agricultural areas. It also provided 30–50 percent of the entire foodstuffs of the country.

Instituting *Doi Moi*

Initial discussion of the *doi moi* program occurred at the Eighth Plenary Session of the Vietnamese Central Committee in June 1985. At this session, members agreed that the main cause for the further deterioration of living standards were two basic concepts of the DRV model: bureaucratic centralism and the state subsidies system. These, they argued, led to large disparities between public and private prices. Further, the agricultural contract system was still inefficient because the state was not able to fulfil the provision of seeds, crops, and fertilizer. Consequently the Central Committee decided on currency, price, and salary reforms, as well as increased autonomy for the state enterprises and the abolition of the state subsidies system and the twofold price system (the official state prices and the free prices of the private market). When these reform measures resulted in a further decline of living standards, popular confidence in the VCP's economic competence began to suffer. Inflation, corruption, and smuggling only worsened the situation. During the Sixth Party Congress in December 1986, liberal reformers such as Nguyen Van Linh, Vo Chi Cong, and Vo Van Kiet gained decisive influence within the Party.

The rather vaguely formulated *doi moi* program also resulted in a restructuring of the government, which was publicly announced in February 1987. Twenty-two ministries were filled with new personnel and the National Assembly developed a more debate-oriented approach. In addition to making these personnel changes, the Party cited bureaucratic centralism, state subsidies, and international isolation as the major reasons for economic deterioration. Consequently the

Party's ideologically derived foreign policy changed, and in May 1988 the Politburo Resolution No. 13 codified the need for a "multidirectional foreign policy orientation." After the end of the Cambodian conflict, Vietnam succeeded not only in reestablishing relationships with member countries of the Association of Southeast Asian nations (ASEAN), but also in reestablishing diplomatic and economic relations with the United States and Europe. Vietnam became a member of ASEAN and the United States removed its trade and aid embargo.

Despite these efforts, however, the economic sector was affected by further decline and confusion for various reasons, including the national budget deficit, a patchwork of reform measures, tremendously high inflation rates, and the lack of a clearly defined *doi moi* policy. Controversy about the future role of the private sector led to ongoing discussions among the leadership and in the media. Then, in 1988, the reforms seemed to succeed partially. Substantial cuts of subsidies for state enterprises, the abolition of the central state price system, and a further devaluation of the Vietnamese currency resulted in a short-term economic recovery. The short-term nature of this recovery was due to the fact that financial reallocation from the industrial sector to the agricultural sector could not be effectively organized, even after the Sixth Party Congress. Although agricultural production increased in 1986, it decreased again in 1987 and the state-owned media admitted that about ten million people in the northern provinces suffered severely from starvation.

In April 1988, two new laws, one addressing agricultural management renovation and another dealing with land disputes, led to various reactions among the population. South Vietnamese peasants publicly argued about their right to take back confiscated parts of land. Early in 1988 a new contract system guaranteed peasants at least 40 percent of their harvest. During the second half of 1988 foodstuff production increased considerably and Vietnam even became one of the world's leading rice-exporting countries. According to Gerd Trogemann, this was not only due to the new contract system but also to better energy supplies and favorable weather conditions. As before, however, economic achievement did not prove to be sustainable. Cuts in subsidy programs and bad weather conditions were responsible for low productivity in 1991. Decentralization measures and the promulgation of efforts to develop a multicomponent economy accompanied an overall reform of state enterprises and efforts to reallocate budgets from heavy to light industries.

While *doi moi* was easily understood as renovation of the economic structure, political reforms still lagged behind societal development. Since the introduction of *doi moi*, however, political liberalization has gained a certain dynamism, especially among the mass media, which have shown more willingness to publish criticism and openly unveil cases of severe corruption among state officials. When intellectuals and artists have contributed to this political criticism, however, the government has reacted with political repression. Because civil society is still underdeveloped in Vietnam and an overall public consensus about the necessity of smooth and uninterrupted economic development prevails even among the opponents of the VCP, political reforms are still limited.

The Future

By the early 2000s, it has become clear that the renovation program is irreversible and that economic development is inevitably accompanied by certain structural changes within society. More freedom to participate in privately financed foreign exchange programs, as well as the increasing access to information from the Internet will certainly contribute to more open-mindedness in Vietnam. Time will tell how important a role the emerging middle class and private entrepreneurs will play in the future political liberalization process of the country.

Ursula Nguyen

Further Reading

Desbarats, Jacqueline. (1990) "Human Rights—Two Steps Forward, One Step Backward?" In *Vietnam Today: Assessing the New Trends*, edited by Thai Quang Trung. New York: Taylor & Francis, 47–66.

Diehl, Markus. (1993) *Stabilization Without Crisis: The Case of Vietnam*. Working Paper no. 578. Kiel, Germany: Kiel Institute of World Economics.

Duiker, William J. (1996) *The Communist Road to Power in Vietnam*. Boulder, CO: Westview Press.

Elliott, David W. P. (1993) "Dilemmas of Reform in Vietnam." In *Reinventing Vietnamese Socialism: Doi Moi in Comparative Perspective*, edited by William S. Turley and Mark Selden. Boulder, CO: Westview Press.

Fforde, Adam, and Stefan de Vylder, eds. (1996) *From Plan to Market: The Economic Transition in Vietnam*. Boulder, CO: Westview Press.

Forbes, Dean K., David Marr, et al., eds. (1991) *Doi Moi: Vietnam's Renovation, Policy, and Performance*. Canberra, Australia: Panther Publishing and Press.

Goodman, Allan E. (1995) "Vietnam in 1994: With Peace at Hand." *Asian Survey* 35, 1 (January): 92–99.

Kerkvliet, Benedict J. Tria, ed. (1995) *Dilemmas of Development: Vietnam—Update 1994*. Canberra, Australia: Panther Publishing and Press.

Porter, Gareth. (1990) "The Politics of 'Renovation' in Vietnam." *Problems of Communism* 39, 3 (May–June): 72–88.

———. (1993) *Vietnam: The Politics of Bureaucratic Socialism.* Ithaca, NY: Cornell University Press.

Stern, Lewis M. (1995) "Party Plenums and Leadership Style in Vietnam." *Asian Survey* 15, 1 (October): 909–921.

Than, Mya, and Joseph L. H. Tan, eds. (1993) *Vietnam's Dilemmas and Options: The Challenge of Economic Transition in the 1990s.* Pasir Panjang, Singapore: Singapore National Printers Ltd.

Thayer, Carlyle A., and Ramses Amer, eds. (1999) *Vietnamese Foreign Policy in Transition.* New York: St. Martin's Press.

Trogemann, Gerd. (1997) *Doi Moi—Vietnam's Reformpolitik in der Retrospektive.* Passauer Beiträge zur Südostasienkunde, vol. 1. Passau, Germany: Passau University Press.

Turley, William S., and Mark Selden, eds. (1993) *Reinventing Vietnamese Socialism: Doi Moi in Comparative Perspective.* Boulder, CO: Westview Press.

DOKMAI SOT (1905–1963), Thai novelist. Dokmai Sot ("Fresh Flower") is the pen name of M. L. Buppha Kunjara Nimmanhemin. Born into an aristocratic family, she began writing in her early twenties. Her first four novels were published in installments in one of the major literary magazines of the day, but thereafter she published her novels herself, producing eleven novels between 1929 and 1940. Of these, the most famous is *Phu di* (A Person of Quality), first published in 1938, in which she intended to demonstrate that a person of quality was defined not by social status or wealth but rather by Buddhist qualities of patience, wisdom, and self-sacrifice.

Dokmai Sot's novels are mostly domestic dramas, admired for both their use of language and their content. Her novels were among the first to be accepted in literature syllabi at secondary- and tertiary-education level in Thailand. The author's penchant for including Buddhist epithets at the beginning of each chapter led the writer and critic Nilawan Pinthong to describe her as a preacher.

At the age of forty-nine, Dokmai Sot married Sukit Nimmanhemin, a former minister of industry who later briefly held the position of deputy prime minister; she accompanied him to India when he was appointed ambassador in 1959. Her health was never robust, and she died of a heart attack in Delhi, India, in 1963.

David Smyth

Further Reading

Barang, Marcel. (1994) *The 20 Best Novels in Thailand.* Bangkok, Thailand: Thai Modern Classics.

DOLL FESTIVAL. See **Hina Matsuri.**

DOMBRA The *dombra* belongs to the family of two-stringed lutes that are widespread in Central Asia and especially associated with pastoral nomadic peoples. They include the Kazakh *dombura*, the *dambura* of Turkestan and Badakhstan, and the Uzbek and Uighur *dutar.* The instrument consists of a rectangular or oval body usually hewn out of a single piece of wood, covered by a wooden soundboard, with a long, slender neck. It is usually unfretted, although modern versions of the instrument have added frets set at chromatic intervals. The *dombra* is strung by a single gut, or nylon string, which passes from a wooden tuning peg at the end of the neck, looped around a pin at the base of the body and up to a second peg to make two tunable strings. The strings are most commonly tuned a fourth apart—the higher string is physically below the other when the instrument is played—and they are plucked with the thumb and two fingers and held together with a sweeping back-and-forth movement.

The *dombra* is commonly used to play dance tunes, solo programmatic pieces, or to accompany songs and epic tales. Typically *dombra* music alternates between double and triple rhythms and has a general emphasis on fourths and fifths as basic structural intervals, with the widespread use of melody plus drone.

Rachel Harris

Further Reading

Slobin, Mark. (1976) *Music in the Culture of Northern Afghanistan.* Tucson, AZ: University of Arizona Press.

DOST MUHAMMAD (1793–1863), founder of the Pashtun Barakzai dynasty in Afghanistan. Dost Muhammad, the twentieth son of the chief of the Pashtun Barakzai clan, spent his early years living with his mother's relatives, part of a Turkish nomadic tribe. After 1810, thanks to the favor of his powerful eldest brother, Fath Khan, he held important political and military offices in Kuhistan, Kashmir, and Herat, at that time part of the Afghan kingdom. Dost Muhammad demonstrated his military skills by capturing the Afghan cities of Kabul, Ghazna, and Jalalabad in 1818, after the king of Afghanistan, Mahmud Shah, had blinded his eldest brother. In 1826 Dost Muhammad became the effective ruler of Afghanistan, although he formally took the title of emir (king) only in 1834.

During the first years of his reign Dost Muhammad tried to secure the position of his ethnic confederation, the Durrani, against the rival Pashtun group of the Ghilzay, and to recover lost Afghan territories. However, he was hindered by a Persian attack against the city of Herat in 1837 and the British invasion of Afghanistan in 1839. Dost Muhammad escaped toward Central Asia, where he was arrested and deported to India with part of his family.

The British crowned Shah Shuja (d. 1842) as the new puppet emir of Afghanistan. Ethnic outbreaks, however, continually challenged the British army, which was forced to retreat in the winter of 1841–1842 and was almost entirely slaughtered by Ghilzay tribes. Dost Muhammad returned to Kabul in 1843 and was restored as emir by the new British governor-general of India, Lord Ellenborough, who had decided to quit the country. Dost Muhammad dedicated the last twenty years of his life to consolidating Durrani authority, recovering the northern territories and the cities of Qandahar, Balkh, and Herat.

Riccardo Redaelli

Further Reading

Noelle, Christine. (1997) *State and Tribe in Nineteenth-Century Afghanistan: The Reign of Amir Dost Muhammad Khan (1826–1863).* Richmond, U.K.: Curzon Press.

DOUMER, PAUL (1857–1932), governor-general of Indochina. Paul Doumer was governor-general of French Indochina from 1897 to 1902. Born in Aurillac, France, Doumer worked as a journalist before embarking on a political career. He was first elected to the French National Assembly in 1888 and served as minister of finance (1895–1896) just before his appointment as governor-general of Indochina.

During his five-year mandate in Indochina, Doumer instituted a number of reforms. He created a general budget for Indochina and established monopolies on salt, opium, and alcohol to finance colonial development projects. He promoted the construction of a railway line from Saigon to Yunnan (the Yunnan Railway project), and sanctioned public works projects, such as the building of roads, bridges, canals, and communications lines. Doumer also systematized the colonial civil service by creating departments of public works, customs, and agriculture and commerce. In 1898 he founded the Ecole Française D'extrême Orient, whose purpose was the study of East Asia.

Doumer returned to France in 1902 and was elected senator of Corsica (1912–1931). He eventually was elected president of France in 1931 but was assassinated one year later by a Russian immigrant who accused him of siding with Bolsheviks.

Micheline R. Lessard

Further Reading

Bouche, Denise. (1991). *Histoire de la colonisation française.* Paris: Fayard.

Meyer, Jean, Jean Tarrade, Annie Rex-Goldzeiguer, and Jacques Tholie. (1991) *L'Histoire de la France coloniale des origines à 1914.* Paris: Armand Colin.

DRAGON BOAT FESTIVAL The annual Dragon Boat Festival, commemorating the dead, is observed primarily in central and southern China. It occurs on the fifth day of the fifth lunar month and falls between 28 May and 25 June in the Western calendar. During this festival, people along the seacoasts and major rivers compete in races in boats made from wooden planks and carved with dragon heads and tails.

A team of young adult males rows the boats, directed by a team leader who synchronizes their action with a big drum. While racing dragon boats in competition, the competitors occasionally toss triangular-shaped rice cakes, typically made from glutinous rice with meat or sweet bean paste stuffing and wrapped in bamboo leaves, into the water. Popular folktale attributes this festival to the patriotic poet Qu Yuan, who lived in the third and second centuries BCE in the southern kingdom of Chu during late Zhou dynasty (1045–246 BCE). According to legend, Qu was dissatisfied with the ineptness of the Chu king. When the king spurned his repeated advice, Qu threw himself into a river in today's Hunan Province. The boat racing is said to have originated from the attempt to recover his body. Throwing rice cakes symbolizes a sacrificial offering to Qu.

Huang Shu-min

Further Reading

Bodde, Derk. (1975) *Festivals in Classical China: New Year and Other Annual Observances during the Han Dynasty, 206 B.C.–A.D. 220.* Princeton, NJ: Princeton University Press.

Eberhard, Wolfram. (1958) *Chinese Festivals.* New York: Abelard-Schuman.

———. (1968) *The Local Cultures of South and East China.* Leiden, Netherlands: E. J. Brill.

Men row a dragon boat in Xishuangbanna, Yunnan, China, in c. 1996. (KEREN SU/CORBIS)

DRAMA—CHINA Chinese drama has a long tradition. Generally, the highly developed structure of dramatic text created in the Yuan dynasty (1279–1368) is considered to have influenced later traditional theater literature, and therefore the Yuan dynasty often cited as the age in which Chinese drama began. Dramatic influences on Yuan drama, however, go back many centuries, beginning in the earliest courts of record—the Zhou (1045–256 BCE).

Drama during the Zhou Dynasty

One of the most important elements of Chinese drama, the performance synthesis of song, dance, and music, first appeared in the Zhou courts. The *Liji* (Book of Rites) describes performance synthesis as the inherent, correlative relationship between music, movement, emotion, and other aspects of performance wherein the sum of the parts creates a greater whole. Throughout Chinese theatrical history, the aesthetic of melding into a singular totality the skills of singing, dancing, acrobatics, special speaking techniques, and use of costuming, props, and dramatic storytelling has been an identifying feature. Both the Zhou court ritual dance-dramas and some of the acts staged by court jesters featured performance synthesis as an inherent element of the dramatic basis of their presentations.

Drama during the Qin and Han Dynasties

In the Qin (221–206 BCE) and Han (206 BCE–220 CE) eras, the court ritual of the Zhou was assumed for new purposes, although quite likely revised, and new forms of dramatic entertainment arose in both the countryside and urban areas. Two of the most important forms were based on popular stories; in the dramatically enacted combat scenario of *chiyouxi*, or Chi You theater, one finds the epic myth of the cosmic battle between the demonic rogue Chi You and the Yellow Emperor (the legendary founder of the Chinese empire). In the second skit, *Donghai Huanggong* (Duke Huang of the Eastern Sea), a drunken shaman is overpowered by a tiger and killed after displaying a series of magical acts. These dramatic pieces, as well as others, were often performed as part of enormous variety shows (*baixi*, "hundred acts") staged by the courts as part of expensive displays intended to impress foreign envoys; they took the form of circus-like entertainments with costumed performers singing, dancing, and playing musical instruments among equestrian, acrobatic, and magic acts.

Drama during the Tang Dynasty

During the Tang dynasty (618–907 CE), such skits as *Donghai Huanggong* continued to be popular presentations in the marketplaces, at court, and in temples, as well as in the homes of patrons. Other favored dramatic sketches of the Tang included *Tayaoniang* (Singing-Stepping Woman), in which male and female actors employed song and dance to comically portray the plight of a battered woman married to a drunken, egotistical official. In another favorite, *Botou* (Setting Matters Right), a son mourns his father, killed by a tiger while journeying through some mountains, using a mixture of monologue and conventionalized movement patterns to portray the father's ill-fated trip. Similar to these entertainments was *canjunxi* ("adjutant theater"), wherein two actors enacted a comic scenario about a corrupt official who steals bolts of silk.

Also during the Tang period, Buddhist monks began to dramatize sermons with the aid of scrolls illustrating Buddhist teachings; this form was called *bianwen*, or transformational tales, and exhibited not only religious but also historical and social or political contemporary themes. All topics were presented through a mix of literary and vernacular styles, using song, prose, verse, and idiomatic speech. Additionally, *chuanqi*, or marvel tales, a more literary form composed of short stories with dialogue, originated during the Tang dynasty and initiated a greater interest in using literary stylization in the dramas of developing theatrical forms. Puppet performances may have also played a significant role in the evolution of drama at this time.

Drama during the Song Dynasty

During the Song dynasty (960–1279), dramatic developments began to take place that would distinguish northern from southern forms until the present day. Song *zaju* ("miscellaneous theater"), popular in both the north and south, included on a much smaller scale some of the variety-show characteristics found previously in Han *baixi*, but the primary focus of the presentation was on a central play or sketch. By the Southern Song dynasty (1126–1279), Song *zaju* was composed of three parts: (1) a curtain raiser, (2) the main comedy, and (3) a comic or variety-show act. A variation of early *zaju*, known as southern theater *(nanxi)*, also developed at this time, as did ballad forms such as *daqu* ("great song set") and *zhugongdiao* ("various palace tones"), which, using direct speech rather than description, alternated song and speech. The Mongol Jin dynasty, operating in the north while the Southern Song continued in the south, developed *yuanben* ("courtyard literature"), instigating a tradition of crafting texts through writing guilds that collectively worked to craft their scripts of words, song, and music.

Drama during the Yuan Dynasty

During the Yuan dynasty, drama flourished. Some theorize that this resulted when the many unemployed literati, ousted from court office in the Mongol conquest and the subsequent political shift against Confucianism, used their free time to write drama to attack the new government. *Yuanben* continued in the northern courts, but the most important form to evolve was that of Yuan *zaju*. The writing guilds of the court infused tremendous literary breadth into *zaju*, and the compositional form encouraged further development of actor technique, especially in singing. Yuan *zaju* was divided into four acts, each featuring a soloist. Every act contained several songs, all in a single key, giving the acts a musical unity. Metrical rules were set for the alternation of prose and poetry, with over 80 percent of the ends of lines rhyming. Each act, however, had a rhyme scheme differing from that of the other acts in the play. Additionally, a "wedge" (a simple song of one or two stanzas) could be placed between acts. Although the song sets *(qu)* were a primary element, the plots and dramatic dialogue were also rich; plays often contained forty or more acts and could have been staged in their entirety only over several days. The length of such scripts has strongly influenced presentation until this day; most modern performances stage only highlights of a drama instead of performing the whole story. In the south, *nanxi* continued to develop, employing duets and trios to present the alternating lines of sung and spoken dialogue.

Drama during the Ming and Qing Dynasties

In the Ming dynasty (1368–1644), various forms of music were combined with dramatic features of pronunciation, rhyming patterns, and regional singing fashions (alternating song and speech was a common trait), producing new forms. The dramatic texts for these forms included song and musical scores; some plays were shared, but altered, between forms. *Kunqu* (Kunshan opera) evolved in this age and is still performed by five major troupes located in both the north and south of modern China.

In the Qing dynasty (1644–1912), musical systems continued to be melded with regional songs and stories to produce forms such as Beijing Opera, now performed by hundreds of professional and amateur troupes. Between 1895 and 1905, plays using Western themes and traditional Chinese performance form were introduced and called New Theater (*xinju* or *xinqu*); an example is Liang Qichao's *Xin Luoma* (New Rome) staged in *kunqu* form with a theme relating the contemporary government to that of the Italian risorgimento (the nineteenth-century political movement toward Italian unity and the formation of a nation-state), with the characters of Dante and Cavour quoting Confucius and Tang poetry. *Huaju* (spoken drama), essentially Western nonmusical drama, was then imported and translated into Chinese, with favorites being works of Brecht, Shakespeare, and

Chekhov. Chinese authors, such as Cao Yu and Lao She, wrote their own plays using this dramatic style.

Drama in the People's Republic of China

During much of the Cultural Revolution (1966–1976), all theater was banished except for eight plays and one ballet. The plays, focused on concerns of workers, were performed in the style of traditional opera but without its elegant costuming. In 1972, the ban on theater was lifted, with traditional and new performances again becoming significant aspects of Chinese culture.

After the 1976 fall of the Gang of Four (the four people held responsible for implementing the Cultural Revolution), the "model" operas of the Cultural Revolution were no longer performed. During the next ten years, an open-door policy initiated an influx of foreign drama and theatrical personnel into China as well as an opportunity for Chinese artists to bring Chinese opera to America and Europe; Arthur Miller directed *Death of a Salesman* in Beijing in 1983, and the Shanghai Kunqu Troupe toured Europe with a *Kunqu*-styled production of *Macbeth* in 1988. Dramatic developments focused on experimental and social-problem plays. A Jia and other theorists began to elaborate on the result of combining Western schools of acting, especially the Stanislavsky method, with traditional Chinese drama form and with artistic elements taken from ancient Chinese poetics and painting. The result is an evolving style of drama, uniquely Chinese, combining realism and well-defined characters with performative techniques that focus on the actor's presence.

Although many of China's new works have developed under the auspices of major institutions, such as the Beijing People's Art Theater, China's minority groups have also actively produced works of their own. Two well-recognized productions are *The Battle of Potala Palace* by the Tibet Autonomous Regional Drama Troupe and *Hello, Standard-Bearer* by the Inner Mongolia Autonomous Drama Troupe. In 2000, the Nobel Prize for Literature was awarded to Chinese dissident Gao Xingjian, author of *Chezhan* (The Bus Stop) and *Bi An* (The Other Shore).

Dallas L. McCurley

See also: **Beijing Opera; Gao Xingjian; Lao She; Liang Qichao; Xiqu**

Further Reading

Crump, James Irving. (1990) *Chinese Theater in the Days of Kublai Khan*. Ann Arbor, MI: Center for Chinese Studies, University of Michigan.

Dolby, William. (1976) *A History of Chinese Drama*. London: P. Elek.

Shih, Chung-wen. (1976) *The Golden Age of Chinese Drama, Yuan tsa-chu*. Princeton, NJ: Princeton University Press.

DRAMA—INDIA India has a long tradition of dramatic forms dating as early as Mauryan times (c. 324–c. 200 BCE). The *Natya Sastra* of Bharata (flourished second century CE), a treatise on dance and acting, became the bible of Indian performers. Regional folk traditions like *kathakali*, *yatra*, and *yakshagana* enriched Indian drama. Indian theater as it exists today, however, appeared in India in the nineteenth century, as did European drama.

During the nineteenth century traditional Indian plays were written and acted to highlight the evils of society and the consequences of British rule. There were also dramatic presentations of plays translated from Western sources, particularly Shakespeare. The National Theatre of Calcutta, the first public theater in India, was created in 1872. Itinerant Parsi drama companies also attracted large crowds due to the plays' humor and grand spectacle. The *Krishnakumari* (1861) of Madhusudan Dutt, the *Niladarpan* (1860) of Dinabandhu Mitra, the *Kanchi Kaveri* (1880) of Ramshankar Ray, and the *Lalita Dukh Darsak* (1864) of Ranchodbhai Udayram were some notable nineteenth-century plays.

In the beginning of the twentieth century, powerful dramatic literature began to appear not only in English, but in many Indian languages. The playwrights Sri Aurobindo, T. P. Kailasham, and Harindranath Chattopadhyay wrote in English. Iswar Chandra Nanda wrote plays in the Panjabi tongue, highlighting social problems. Imtiaz Ali's *Anarkali* was much acclaimed. P. Sambandha Mudaliyar brought new direction to the Tamil-language stage. Annapurna Theater kept the Oriya-language dramas alive. The *Gayopakhyana* of Chilakamarti Lakshminarasimgha was well received by Telugu-speaking audiences. K. M. Munshi, Jayashankar Prasad, and D. L. Ray wrote plays in Gujarati, Hindi, and Bengali, respectively. The *Rakta Karabi* of Rabindranath Tagore is a landmark in Indian theater.

In 1943, the Indian People's Theatre Association began a progressive trend encompassing all of India. In the 1950s, new names came on the scene. Badal Sircar earned fame by introducing new forms. Instead of writing in regional languages, Girish Karnad, Vijay Tendulkar, Mohan Rakesh, and Adya Rangachari became all-India figures. *Ghashiram Kotwal* by Vijay Tendulkar was acclaimed throughout the country.

The Kendirya Sangeet Natak Academy and National School of Drama gave new direction to Indian drama. B. V. Karnath, Habib Tanvir, and Rattan Thiyyam directed many modern plays. The *Bitter Harvest* by Manjula Padmanvan received international acclaim. By then there was a strong interplay between drama and film; many well-known film actors got their start on the stage.

Patit Paban Mishra

Further Reading

Anand, Mulk Raj. (1950) *The Indian Theatre.* London: Denis Dobson.

Benegal, Som. (1967) *A Panorama of Theatre in India.* New Delhi: Indian Council of Cultural Relations.

Das, Sisir Kumar. (1991) *A History of Indian Literature, 1800–1910.* New Delhi: Sahitya Akademi.

———. (1995) *A History of Indian Literature, 1911–1956.* New Delhi: Sahitya Akademi.

George, K. M., ed. (1984) *Comparative Indian Literature.* 2 vols. New Delhi: Macmillan.

Richmond, Farley P., et al., eds. (1990) *Indian Theatre: Traditions of Performance.* Honolulu, HI: University of Hawaii Press.

DRAMA—JAPAN

This article deals with Western drama in Japan; traditional dramatic forms, such as Kabuki, are covered under their own names.

Modern theater in Japan began as an attempt to import wholesale Western drama and theater of the late nineteenth and early twentieth centuries. Its development occurred in three stages, characterized first by adaptation, then borrowing, and finally rejection of Euro-American models. When Japan was forcibly opened to foreign commerce and diplomacy in the early Meiji period (1868–1912), the arts of Europe, and later America, flooded into Japan along with political, social, and economic ideas. Learning from Ibsen, Chekhov, Shaw, and Stanislavsky, young playwrights and directors staged Japanese versions of contemporary European drama that represented the present world in contrast to the ancient and feudal worlds dramatized by Noh, Kabuki, and Bunraku. Many producing companies emerged in the 1920s and 1930s, only to be suppressed during World War II for being too Western in orientation. In the half-century following Japan's wartime defeat, modern drama flourished, and in the early 2000s hundreds of troupes perform in newly built, state-of-the-art theaters.

Shinpa

In 1899, the young politically active actor-director Kawakami Otojiro (1864–1911) and his wife, Sadayakko (1871–1946), embarked on the first of four trips to the United States and Europe, where they performed before elite Western intellectuals. Sadayakko received ecstatic reviews. More important than their success in bringing Japanese theater to the West was the opportunity their travels gave them to see Henry Irving, Ellen Terry, and Sarah Bernhardt onstage. Returning home, they performed *Hamlet* and *Othello* with contemporary Japanese settings. The style of performance, in which Western and Japanese theaters and cultures melded, was called Shinpa (new school) to contrast it with old-school Kabuki, which was rooted in the feudal age. Through the 1920s several Shinpa troupes staged newly written plays that dramatized urban life in Japan, mixing actresses and *onnagata* (men playing women's roles). The major Shinpa star before and after the war was the actress Mizutani Yaeko (1905–1979). Today a single Shinpa troupe continues under the management of the Shochiku Theater Company.

Shingeki

In contrast to diluting European art through adaptations, directors and actors of the Shingeki (new theater) movement attempted to replicate European plays as authentically as possible. In 1906, scholar Tsubouchi Shoyo (1859–1935) formed the Literary Arts Society (Bungei Kyokai) at Waseda University in Tokyo; it was dedicated to training students in Western realistic acting. The group's star, Matsui Sumako (1886–1919), was Japan's first modern actress. Director Osanai Kaoru (1881–1928) and Kabuki actor Ichikawa Sadanji II (1880–1940) founded the Free Theater (Jiyu Gekijo), in which professional Kabuki actors and young amateur actresses joined in epochal productions of Ibsen and Gorky. Kabuki actors, especially *onnagata*, found it difficult to abandon stylized acting, and the Free Theater was able to take only a few steps toward a genuinely modern theater. Authors in their twenties, such as Kikuchi Kan (1888–1948), Yamamoto Yuzo (1887–1974), and Tanizaki Junichiro (1886–1965), who went on to became famous novelists and playwrights, were stimulated to write plays in the style of Ibsen, Shaw, and Chekhov.

The construction of the 500-seat Tsukiji Little Theater (Tsukiji Shogekijo) in 1924 marked a major step in breaking away from traditional theater. The first theater in Japan expressly designed for modern drama, it was the brainchild of Hijikata Yoshi (1898–1959) and Osanai Kaoru. Hijikata and Osanai directed more than one hundred recent plays by O'Neill, Strindberg, Capek, Pirandello, and other Western playwrights, largely ignoring newly written

Japanese plays. Osanai's sudden death in 1928 precipitated a breakup of the theater into progressive and artistic factions; Hijikata became a leader of the progressive camp and later established the New Tsukiji Troupe (Shin Tsukiji Gekidan).

Shingeki was severely suppressed during World War II. In August 1940, the police arrested more than one hundred Shingeki artists, and thereafter most troupes were ordered to disband. Following Japan's defeat in the war, the American Occupation supported Shingeki as a means of conveying democracy and liberal ideas. During the 1950s, Shingeki was a major cultural force, and scores of troupes contributed to its reinvigoration. Socially concerned theater artists formed the People's Art Theater (Gekidan Mingei) to bring serious drama to village audiences and workers. Members of the Advance Theater (Zenshinza), who joined the Communist Party en masse, brought both Kabuki and modern drama to youth audiences throughout the country. Postwar playwrights whose works can be read in English include Mishima Yukio (1925–1970), Kinoshita Junji (b. 1914), Tanaka Chikao (b. 1905), and Abe Kobo (1924–1990).

The 1960s saw an abrupt rejection of the values of Western-based, realistic Shingeki and an explosion of experimentation in new theatrical and dramatic forms, known variously as *angura* (underground), *han*-Shingeki (anti-Shingeki), or *shogekijo* (little theater). Ohta Shogo (b. 1939) exposed the existential nature of human life in wordless dumb shows in his "theater of silence." Hijikata Tatsumi (1928–1986) and Ohno Kazuo (b. 1906) created a profoundly unsettling "dance of darkness," Ankoku Butoh, in which naked performers appear as tortured ghosts from another world.

During Japan's bubble economy of the 1980s, more than forty high-tech theater complexes were built throughout the country, and theater companies found generous subsidies. Despite a severe economic slowdown in the 1990s, the modern theater scene is diverse and active. On any given day in Tokyo, more than 150 performances of modern drama and theater are staged. Performance art, high-tech staging, and video art reflect Japan's digital age. Collaborations among contemporary and traditional performers are increasingly common. The latest teen idols of the music industry crossing over into theater compete with old-line Shingeki troupes; new productions by Suzuki, Ohta, and Ninagawa; and explorations in Butoh. Each holds a segment of a diverse audience for contemporary theater.

James R. Brandon

See also: **Bunraku; Kabuki; Noh-Kyogen**

Further Reading

Mishima Yukio. (1957) *Five Modern No Plays.* Trans. by Donald Keene. New York: Alfred A. Knopf.

Rimer, J. Thomas. (1975) *Toward a Modern Japanese Theater: Kishida Kunio.* Princeton, NJ: Princeton University Press.

Rolf, Robert T., and John K. Gillespie, eds. (1992) *Alternative Japanese Drama: Ten Plays.* Honolulu, HI: University of Hawaii Press.

Toyotaka Komiya. (1956) *Japanese Music and Drama in the Meiji Era.* Trans. by Edward G. Seidensticker and Donald Keene. Vol. 3, *Japanese Culture in the Meiji Era.* Tokyo: Obunsha.

DRAMA—KOREA

DRAMA—KOREA Although scores of court and folk dances and dance-dramas are known in Korea, no forms using dramatic scripts evolved until the twentieth century. Masked-dance dramas (dramas or farces featuring masked performers) are especially characteristic of Korea and were performed throughout the Three Kingdoms era (37 BCE–935 CE), which includes the kingdoms of Koguryo, Paekche, and Shilla. The earliest records mention annual or biennial festivals honoring heaven; people danced and sang at these events to cement their tribal identities and may have used specific themes or stories to dramatize the dances.

Early Forms

In the later years of the Koguryo kingdom (37 BCE–668 CE), an influx of music and dance entered the central courts from the foreign courts of the Sui (581–618) and Tang (618–907) dynasties of China and from Central Asian sources, profoundly affecting the development of elite entertainment. In the neighboring kingdom of Paekche (18 BCE–663 CE), a presentation developed called *kiak* ("skill performance"). *Kiak* seems to have been a pantomime consisting of ten scenes with Buddhist ceremonial characteristics. It was probably performed by a masked dancer and no doubt aimed to promote Buddhism.

While essentially no evidence of drama survives from the Shilla kingdom (57 BCE–935 CE), theatrical presentations in the Unified Shilla (668–935) had probably existed, perhaps in a simpler form, in earlier times as well. One such form, *choyong kamu* ("to-tolerate-punishment song and dance") evolved through stages from the worship of mountain and dragon deities to entertainments that became a verse-drama form by the Koryo (918–1392) and Choson dynasties (1392–1910). In the courts of these dynasties, skits satirizing corrupt officials were often presented; one skit concerned a loyal soldier of the twelfth century, Ho Kong Jin.

Masked Drama and the Rise of Professional Organizations

In the Koryo and Choson eras, an important genre of dance-drama featuring masked performers began to be performed on upper-level stages, a practice that gave the name of the stages, *sandae* ("mountain platform"), to the presentations. Also in these eras, professional associations of performers, assembling to perform various specialties, aided dramatic development. New political ideas, and especially the dictate to reject Buddhism and respect Confucianism, influenced writings.

Furthermore, as a result of the schism between the aristocratic and common classes beginning in the Koryo period and continuing through the Choson era, performers began to specialize in particular skills. The *p'ansori*, or narrative song, became a popular entertainment under this continuing evolution of dramatic song and dance forms. Puppet plays staged by traveling performers were also a favorite attraction in the countryside. The dramas staged in many of the puppet plays are like those of the masked dance-dramas, and the same characters found in the *sandae* forms appear again as puppets.

Modern Korean Drama

In the twentieth century, Korea adopted Western realistic drama forms. Yi In-jik, returning from studying in Japan, wrote and staged the so-called New Dramas at the Wongaksa Theater in Seoul beginning in 1908. He was followed in 1911 by Im Song-gu, who focused on popular romantic sentiments in what became known as New-School Plays. The Drama Arts Society was organized in 1921, mostly by students returning from Japan, and the T'owolhoe (Earth-Moon Society) was formed in 1923 by students then studying in Japan. Though an amateur society, the T'owolhoe was consistently acclaimed for its high artistic standards and for introducing realistic themes. Its repertoire consisted mostly of original works written by its membership, but it also included translations and adaptations of world masterpieces. In 1931, the Society for the Study of Dramatic Arts was organized by the elite of Korea's theatrical and literary circles. This group presented great works of world drama as well as original scripts by its members.

Japanese authorities closed theater after theater during its rule over Korea (1910–1945), but the establishment of the Republic of Korea (1948) paved the way for a National Theater in 1950. The Drama Center of the Seoul Institute of Arts was established in 1962 by the dramatist Yu Chi-jin. Numerous young writers in the 1970s adapted traditional theatrical forms such as the masked dance-dramas, shamanic rituals, and *p'ansori* into new works, a trend that influences theatrical practice to this day. O T'ae-sok is the most celebrated of the playwrights who have achieved national prominence. Drama in the 1990s has continued to flourish in Seoul with a growing interest in staging musicals.

Dallas L. McCurley

Further Reading

Lee, Du-Hyun. (1981) *Masks of Korea.* Seoul: Korean Overseas Information Service, Ministry of Culture and Information.

Pihl, Marshall R. (1994) *The Korean Singer of Tales.* Cambridge, MA: Harvard University Press.

Yoh, Suk-kee. (1970) "Traditional Korean Plays and Humor: With Special Reference to Sandae Mask Play." *Korea Journal* 10, 5 (May): 19–22.

Yoo, Min-young. (1996) "Fifty Years of Korean Drama since Liberation." *Korea Journal* 36, 2 (Spring): 115–143.

DRAMA—SOUTH ASIA

Dance-dramas, both classical and folk or popular, have long been a part of South Asian culture. Many of these forms draw on the epics of the *Ramayama* (c. 300 BCE) and the *Mahabharata* (c. fifth century BCE) for their story lines. Performance styles of folk forms vary greatly, often reflecting the diverse religious traditions of each region. Classical forms evolved out of the system of dramatic theory and practice found first in the Sanskrit theater and are still present in the South Asian region.

Sanskrit Theater (c. 1000 BCE–Twelfth Century CE)

The oldest dramatic form, Sanskrit theater, is often considered to have had its origin in the dialogues of the Vedic hymns of the Rig Veda (c. 1000 BCE); the Vedic ritual performances featuring song, dance, chant, and impersonation that were staged for various deities; or to have developed from epic recitations. The earliest extant critical work on Sanskrit drama, the *Natya Sastra* (attributed to Bharata; flourished second century CE), reflects a highly sophisticated tradition of dramaturgy and theatrical activity already in practice by this time.

Although scholars disagree, the *Natya Sastra* is generally held to reflect a theatrical tradition that began in the ancient Gandhara region, covering areas now located in Afghanistan, northern India, and Pakistan. A prescriptive work, it describes a rigidly fixed system of theatrical presentation, according to which staging was crafted and plays constructed throughout the lengthy history of Sanskrit drama. At its base are four styles of performance—the Verbal, the Grand, the Energetic, and the Graceful—which are further divided into specific varieties of action. According to the *Natya Sastra*, from out of these styles derive ten dramatic classifications ranging from elaborate multiact plots of the *nataka* (concerned with stories and characters out of legends) and *prakarana* (requiring an "original" plot from the author) to simple balladlike forms performed by a single performer. All classifications work toward an aesthetic sharing of emotions (categorized into eight primary *rasa*, or "flavors") between the actor and audience. The remarkably persistent use of these presentational guidelines continued until the decline of Sanskrit drama, which began in the tenth century CE and was complete by the twelfth century CE.

On reading a Sanskrit drama for the first time, a reader is most immediately impressed by the melding of prose and poetry in the language of the play. The remarkably descriptive passages lead the audience to imagine the environment and, therefore, stage settings—necessary in traditional Western theater—can be dispensed with. The extant scripts were only a part of the complicated performance activity; because the staging of a play was considered in its totality a visual sacrifice in the *Natya Sastra*, ritual acts of dance, chant, and song were integral to the performance.

According to Bharata, a Sanskrit drama performance began with eighteen preliminary actions, the first nine involving various prescriptive means of tuning instruments and preparations for dancers and singers. A curtain was removed and the presentation began, according to the *Natya Sastra*, with a series of songs, ritual actions, and recitations. The ritual preliminaries continued with a short scene played between the stage manager, a clown, and an attendant. Finally, a brief synopsis of the play and an appeal for the success of the presentation were made by the stage manager.

The major Sanskrit playwrights include Asvaghosa (80?–150 CE), Bhasa (c. third century CE), King Sudraka (c. fifth century), Kalidasa (c. fifth century), Bhavabhuti (flourished 700), Harsa (c. 590–647), and Visakadatta. It is important to note that of the primary authors of Sanskrit drama, all except Bhasa (of whom the least is known) were members of court environments (two, Harsa and Sudraka, were kings). Sanskrit drama was written and performed by professional troupes for court audiences, and their authors, at least, were members of the highest social class. The royal patronage of Sanskrit drama certainly contributed to its lengthy history, providing a sheltered environment for its traditions of highly codified activity to develop. The essence of Sanskrit performance, as dictated by the *Natya Sastra*, is still alive in the tradition of classical forms of South Asia.

Classical Theater Forms

The *kuttiyatam* of Kerala, the oldest extant theatrical form in India (and, quite possibly, in the world), probably began as a regional derivation of Sanskrit theater and became well-developed in its own terms prior to the tenth century. Performed by male actors born into a special caste of performers, *kuttiyatam* presentations originally took place only in theaters constructed in temple compounds, but they now may be seen occasionally in more commercial venues. Performances still include extensive preliminary ritual preparations and require a lifetime of training to achieve a level of virtuosity in various verbal and physical techniques that closely resemble those discussed in the *Natya Sastra*.

Classical Indian forms such as *bharata natyam* and *kathakali*, among others, owe much to the traditions formed in Sanskrit theater. *Bharata natyam*, while often classified as a dance form of South India, requires an increasingly dramatic portrayal from the solo performer throughout the course of an evening's performance. *Kathakali*, perhaps the most internationally known theater form of India, dramatizes the epics using a particularly vivacious style of acting melded with singing and dancing. *Chau*, a dance-drama form (masked in two of its three forms), is found only in three districts of western India and is considered a classical form by the elite of one district who once served as patrons. The *yaksa gana* of Mysore is a dance-drama form featuring not only actor-dancers but also a narrator who uses both song and recitation to establish elements of the story. The *kandyan* dramatic dance of Sri Lanka also demonstrates many Sanskrit features.

Folk and Popular Forms

While many of the numerous folk and popular dramatic forms of the South Asian region are related, most are specifically associated with a single region and, in many cases, linked to a particular urban or rural area. It has been argued that the sophisticated presentation of the Sanskrit theater developed out of popular forms, and, with its decline, various forms of popular theater reemerged from the remnants. While this may be true for some folk and popular theater forms, many others developed out of tribal practices.

The Bengali *jatra* originally focused on stories of Krishna but now characteristically presents social and political commentaries to enthusiastic audiences in Bangladesh and the Indian states of West Bengal, Orissa, and Bihar. *Svang*, a narrative, operatic form of North India, has influenced variant forms, such as the northern *nautanki*, the *khyal* of Rajasthan, and the *maach* of Madhya Pradesh. Amateur rural theater, performed in regional languages and focusing on social issues, has become especially important in Bangladesh, Kashmir, and Pakistan in recent years. Parsi theater, dating to the second half of the ninteenth century and featuring large-budgeted productions, toured the subcontinent—beginning in the 1870s, peaking in the 1890s, and dwindling after 1925—influencing the growth of similar theatrical enterprises.

The urban theater of Mumbai (Bombay) and Calcutta is well developed; over three thousand troupes are registered in Calcutta and over five hundred in Mumbai, while only a few dozen exist in each of the other major urban areas of Delhi, Colombo, and Dhaka. Most plays presented in the urban areas are realistic. The generally middle- and upper-middle-class audiences see Western plays in translation as well as farces, social dramas, and experimental productions in regional languages. Few actors or directors are able to sustain a living on the salaries earned for stage performances; many (especially young actors in Mumbai) hope to secure passage into the more lucrative Hindi film industry through their participation in plays.

Dallas L. McCurley

Further Reading

Baumer, Rachel Van M., and James R. Brandon, eds. (1981) *Sanskrit Drama in Performance*. Honolulu, HI: University of Hawaii Press.

Bharatamuni. (1967) *Natyasastra*. 2d rev. ed. Vol. 1. Edited and translated by Manmohan Ghosh. Calcutta, India: Manisha Granthalaya.

———. (1961) *Natyasastra*. Vol. 2. Edited and translated by Manmohan Ghosh. Calcutta, India: Asiatic Society.

Richmond, Farley P., Darius L. Swann, and Phillip B. Zarilli, eds. (1990) *Indian Theatre: Traditions of Performance*. Honolulu, HI: University of Hawaii Press.

DRAMA—SOUTHEAST ASIA

Numerous theatrical genres developed in Southeast Asia as a result of influences coming from India, the Islamic nations, and China. Additionally, as indigenous theater practices crossed national borders in the Southeast Asian region, they influenced new developments in adjoining countries. Finally, in many of the individual nations that collectively compose the region of

A man operates shadow puppets in a shadow theater in Wayang Kulit, Java, Indonesia, in 1992. (CHARLES & JOSETTE LENARS/CORBIS)

Southeast Asia, local forms evolved as specific responses to political and social conditions.

While primary elements of form differ between theater genres from area to area, certain dramatic elements are shared by most types of plays. Epic stories, often featuring the fall of kingdoms or great battles involving kings and gods, make up the dramatic text of performances throughout the region. Comic, serious, and farcical sentiments are collectively present in most plays, and most drama serves a didactic purpose, demonstrating the victory of good over evil.

Indonesia

Many ancient forms of theater are still popular in the Javanese-speaking area of the island of Java. *Wayang kulit* (leather shadow-puppet theater), the most popular form of theater in Southeast Asia, was well established by the time of its inclusion in twelfth-century court literature. Rulers patronized performances that took place during religious events. In *wayang kulit*, a *dalang* (a person functioning as a puppeteer, orchestral conductor, priest, and narrator combined) manipulates up to two hundred puppets in a drama beginning at dusk and continuing until dawn. A gamelan orchestra, composed of multiple chimelike instruments struck in repetitive rhythms, accompanies the action. The elegant puppets, intricately incised with cutout designs and subsequently coated with colored paint and gold, developed their current form between the thirteenth and seventeenth centuries. The movable arms of the puppets, especially effective in the display of battle actions, were added during the final period of this development. During the eighteenth century, puppet sets included up to 400 puppets. By the nineteenth century, puppet shapes and coloring had become fixed.

During the performance, the *dalang* sits on one side of a white screen *(kelir)*, originally lit by the flickers of an oil lamp but today usually by electric light. Audiences may sit on either side of the *kelir*, the side opposite where the *dalang* sits being favored to see the shadows on the screen. By sitting on the *dalang's* side, however, his skilled puppet manipulation and his tour-de-force vocal performance can be more clearly observed. The cycles of plays performed in *wayang kulit*, collectively known as the *purwa* (old) cycle, feature Java's most ancient myths, including those borrowed from the *Ramayana* and the *Mahabharata*.

Several forms developed out of *wayang kulit*, each practiced almost exclusively in court environments. A derivative known as *wayang madja* (middle theater) employs leather puppets to tell stories of legendary Ja-

A Thai dancer performing traditional costumed dance. (CORBIS)

vanese kings. The shadow-puppet form of *wayang gedog*, created in the sixteenth century, dramatizes stories of the Javanese prince Panji. *Wayang klitik* uses wooden puppets enacting the rise of Damarwulan from village youth to national hero during the Majapahit era (1293–c. 1520). *Wayang dupara* depicts historic events from the central Javanese trade and cultural center of Surakarta. The Java War of the early nineteenth century provides the leather-puppet dramas of the *wayang Djawa*, and the period of Dutch rule is portrayed in the *wayang wahana*. *Wayang beber*, a puppetless form originally performed as a religious ritual, features a *dalang* punctuating his presentation by referring to illustrations painted on long scrolls, which he unwinds to musical accompaniment.

Wayang orang (literally, "human theater") also sprang up in the courts at some time prior to the fourteenth century. Stories taken from the mythology of early kingdoms were enacted by an unmasked human cast using dance and song, which was at times improvised by the actors. Another form featuring human performers is *wayang topeng* (masked theater), which probably developed as a result of the influence of Indian dance dramas on indigenous animistic rituals. The *wayang Menak*, also known as *wayang tengul*, which uses leather puppets, depicts stories of the Islamic hero Amir Hamzah of the late sixth–early seventh century.

Developed in the twentieth century, *ketoprak* and *ludruk* are popular attractions. *Ketoprak* originated in central Java as a dramatic form based on stamping rhythms from rice-planting activities and uses dance-acting to dramatize Javanese legends. Performances today are fairly naturalistic and exclude dance, although both song and dance may precede the central play. Improvised dialogue is used by both male and female performers, and wing-and-drop scenery is conventionally employed. *Ludruk*, commonly associated with the city of Surabaya, developed in eastern Java. Although it traces its origins to an animistic form called *ludruk lerog*, today it is a realistic, spoken entertainment concerned with modern life; domestic comedies are particularly popular. Song and dance may be performed in the intervals between scenes, and a traditional dance known as *ngremo* precedes every *ludruk*. An unusual feature of *ludruk* is the appearance of female impersonators, rarely found in realistic theater forms in which women are included as cast members.

The western Sundanese region of Java developed a doll-puppet form called *wayang golek*. Because daytime performances were more popular than evening ones in this region, the doll-puppets supplanted the newly introduced *wayang kulit* during the nineteenth century. While Islamic themes with a proselytizing function initially supplied the dramatic content of *wayang golek*, present-day stories are intended primarily to entertain. The *dalang* has been replaced in most presentations by a female singer who performs popular songs. Sundanese theater also includes theatrical stagings called *sandiwara*, which may include dramatizations of scenes from the *Ramayana* and the *Mahabharata* in the style of *wayang orang*, history plays presented in the style of *ketoprak*, or more realistic dramas depicting contemporary life.

Balinese *wayang kulit* is similar to its Javanese model, but simpler: the performance lasts only four hours, the puppet designs are less intricately patterned, and there are only sixty or seventy puppets in a set. Plots continue to be taken from the *Ramayana* and the *Mahabharata*, but significant legends of the Balinese are also dramatized. In *wayang wong*, a Balinese derivative of *wayang orang*, characters often wear masks. Since *wayang wong* was developed in the villages, the overall environment of a presentation contrasts greatly with the sophisticated court atmosphere of a *wayang orang* production. Only stories from the *Ramayana* are staged in *wayang wong*. Most important, where in *wayang orang* dance is featured, in *wayang wong* performers emphasize poetic recitation.

Wayang topeng is also popular in Bali, its masked performers remaining silent throughout the dance-drama in contrast to the presentation of Javanese *topeng*, in which characters may employ dialogue. A theatrical ritual known as the *barong* dance-drama presents a cosmic story relating the balance between good and evil. Chaos is magically ousted from the community through the reenactment of a fight between the lion-like figure of the *barong* and a witch named Rangda. Villagers, wielding sharp knives in a state of trance, join in the fight but neither Rangda nor the *barong* can be destroyed: the play's conclusion is a balance demonstrated between the forces of good and evil.

Thailand

Traditional Thai theater consists of several performance genres. The two most important classical forms are the *khon*, a masked court dance-drama in which scenes are staged from the *Ramayana* (called *Ramakien* in Thailand), and the *lakon*, a term covering various forms of dance-dramas. In addition, there is *likay*, a rural folk play in which actors boisterously improvise comic or melodramatic dialogue interspersed with dance and music, as well as *nang yai* or *nang talung* shadow-plays, found in southern Thailand.

The *khon* masked drama adopted movements from Indian temple dancing. During the Ayutthaya period (1350–1767), the *khon* was enacted by male court retainers playing both male and female roles. By the mid-1800s, men and women were performing together. *Khon* performances are characterized by their combination of song, dance, and acting. Actors and actresses are masked, and only clown characters speak onstage; narrative verses are usually recited and sung by a chorus sitting with the accompanying woodwind and percussion musical ensemble.

Generally in *lakon* and *khon*, little scenery is used, but costumes and props can be very elaborate. The oldest form of *lakon*, and indeed of all Thai theater, is the *lakon jatri* or "sorcerer theater." Beginning as animistic ritual, *lakon jatri* developed into a dramatic form after Indian dance traditions were introduced into the telling of the Buddhist *jataka* tale of Manora; the theatrical form itself came to be known as *manora*. During the fourteenth century, *lakon jatri* arrived in the central capital and evolved into *lakon nok* (also called *manora),* which relies less on dance and more on contemporary dialogue and bawdy humor.

Likay, a popular theater genre, developed at the beginning of the twentieth century. *Likay* is found primarily only in Bangkok today, but during the 1920s and 1930s hundreds of *likay* troupes attracted audiences throughout Thailand. A solo singer initiates the performance; then an actor engages the singer in a dialogue and introduces the drama. Common stories are taken from literature or history.

The puppet theaters of Thailand include both doll and shadow-theater forms. The *nang yai* shadow-theater is an ancient form that influenced the development of *khon.* Scenes from the *Ramakien* are performed to musical accompaniment.

Under King Chulalongkorn, Western forms of drama began to be popular. Shakespeare's *Romeo and Juliet, As You Like It,* and *The Merchant of Venice,* as well as a number of English, French, and classical Sanskrit plays were translated by King Vajiravadh. Today many playwrights produce dramas written in the form of Western spoken drama or in a fusion of Western spoken drama and traditional Thai forms. One of the most widely produced playwrights is Supa Devakul, a writer of popular novels and of plays for stage and screen.

Laos

While few, the theater forms of Laos are diverse. *Moh lam* (literally, "singer of *lam*") is a folksinging performance originally involving a duet composed of a singer and a *khene* (reed organ) player. Developing out of the Buddhist melodic storytelling popular since the first millennium CE, early forms of *moh lam* included topics such as accounts of local and court news, bawdy ditties, and epic stories from the *Rama Jataka* (the Laotian *Ramayana,* containing strong Buddhist elements). Today, the popular presentations feature two singers competitively improvising love poems, according to strict traditional formulas.

In another form of *lam, lam luong,* the *moh lam* originally enacted all the roles, changing costume and movement with each character. Now, influenced by Thai *likay,* as many as thirty people perform the various roles.

Modeled after Khmer court performance in the fourteenth century, Laotian court theater *(lakon phrarak phraram)* included female dance, masked male dance, shadow-theater, and musical presentations. Patronized by the court, the elegant presentations were refashioned to favor Thai stylistic elements after the Thai conquest of the Khmer kingdom. Remnants of *lakon phrarak phraram* are now occasionally staged in Laos and in overseas areas to demonstrate traditional culture.

Modern spoken drama *(lakon wau)* was introduced to Laos during the early 1980s. Today the National Drama Company presents works derived mainly from improvisations or adapted from Laotian legends, as well as translations of Western classics.

Cambodia

Thirteenth-century reliefs found at Angkor Wat testify that a form resembling Indian dance existed in the Khmer courts. Indian dance, and possibly dance-drama, probably accompanied Buddhism into Cambodia between the fourth and ninth centuries. Javanese dance-drama was also brought into the Khmer court by its Javanese founder, Jayavarman II (802–869). The court asserted its cultural identity by evolving an elegant classical dance-drama tradition maintained until the fall of Angkor in 1431. At this time, Siamese (Thai) forces transplanted the Khmer court along with its theatrical forms to Siam. During the nineteenth century, Thai classical dance, modeled after the transplanted Khmer dance-drama, was carried back into Cambodian courts; further developments created a repertoire of dance-dramas performed until the Pol Pot massacre of court performers. The government of Cambodia now cultivates this traditional dance, previously restricted to the court, at the National Theater Company, which also features Khmer shadow-puppetry and circus. Her Royal Highness Bopha Devi, a former classical dancer and the daughter of King Sihanouk, is now the minister of culture and is actively seeking to restore the vitality of Cambodian arts, including drama.

Popular twentieth-century theater forms include *lakon yike* and *lakon bassac. Lakon yike* resembles Thai *likay* in that both mix classical and contemporary choreography and instrumentation. *Lakon bassac,* featuring traits found in classical Vietnamese theater, Khmer theater, and even Hindi and Western movies, developed as traveling performers of different styles stopped at villages along the Bassac River. Modern spoken drama, originally in French, entered Cambodia in the 1940s. Plays focus on Khmer society.

Myanmar (Burma)

Sixteenth-century traveling entertainers performed Burmese spirit-plays, wherein a clown played the primary role. The existing *nat pwe,* in which a medium performs Indian-like dance movements, descends from this form.

Captured Thai prisoners brought Thai classical dance-drama into the Burmese courts in 1767. At first presenting the Thai *Ramayana*, Burmese dramatists soon crafted their own adaptations and wrote new plays based on Burmese stories, until the demise of the court dance-drama with the British conquest a century later. Musical and dance characteristics of the Burmese courts continue, however, in the classical *zat pwe* musical plays found in central and southern Burma.

Vietnam

From the thirteenth through the early twentieth centuries, Chinese opera was reconfigured to please Vietnamese courtiers. While the new plays reflected Vietnamese concerns, performance elements continued to use costuming and makeup, conventionalized action, and symbolic use of scenery found in traditional Chinese opera. Popular throughout central Vietnam until the end of the nineteenth century, *hat boi* has practically disappeared since losing its court support. In the twentieth century, two popular variations of *hat boi* evolved: *tuong tau* and *cai luong*. Each adopted Vietnamese melodies, replacing the Chinese musical system of *hat boi*. Both added scenery and sought new dramas from Vietnamese history and love stories. The *tuong tau* repertoire was eventually subsumed into *cai luong*, effectively combining the two forms into one.

Modern spoken drama *(kich)* began in the cities with the introduction of French plays. It developed a variety-show format in which a half-hour play follows two hours of musical entertainment.

One of the most unusual forms of puppetry in the world is also found in Vietnam. Puppeteers stand on one side of a body of water and by using long strings operate puppets located on an island or a boat between the operators and their audiences. The spectators gather on the banks of the opposite shore to watch.

Malaysia

Javanese *wayang kulit* was introduced into Malaysia prior to the sixteenth century. Presented in Malay, stories came from Hindu and Islamic sources. An ensemble of Malaysian instruments replaced the Javanese gamelan. Some regional dance-dramas resemble Thai *likay* in their combination of dance, drama, opera, and comedy.

Bangsawan originated in Penang in the late nineteenth century. An operatic theater form, it combines improvised dialogue, singing, dancing, martial combat, music, poetry, and comedy. Chinese opera is also popular with the Chinese community, although it is now in danger of losing its audiences since many younger Malaysian Chinese do not speak Chinese.

The Philippines

Epic recitations, brought by early Malay and Indonesian settlers and possibly also emerging from the early Negrito culture of the indigenous population, date to the pre-Hispanic era in the Philippines. In the seventeenth century, Spanish missionaries created the *moro-moro* play, or *komedya*, dramatizing through marches, stage combat, and music the Christian conquest of the Moors. A passion play, known as *sinakulo*, is still enacted during Lent.

During the period of U.S. colonization (1898–1945), the operetta form of the *zarzuela* was played before officials and traders. Anti-American sentiments and other social concerns fueled new dramas. Subsequently, companies turned primarily to Western drama, staging Shakespeare and musicals. Noted modern Filipino playwrights include Wilfrido Ma, Guerrero, Severino Montano, and Bienvenido Noriega.

Singapore

Reflecting its ethnically diverse population, Singaporean theater includes nonprofessional Chinese opera, called *wayang* by the Singaporeans; *bharata natyam* and *kathakali* (Indian classical dance forms), danced by committed amateurs in the Indian community; and Western dramas, musicals, and experimental forms staged by young directors. Singapore is home to Southeast Asia's largest performing arts complex, the Esplanade-on-the-Bay, and interest in theater has steadily grown since the early 1990s, when the government reversed its previous stance opposing theater and acknowledged theater as economically important to the community.

Brunei

Since the nation of Brunei Darussalam achieved independence from Britain in 1983, both government and nongovernment organizations have been established to support the preservation of traditional theater forms and the development of new dramas and musicals. Primary producing groups include the Senandung Badaya Groups (KKBS), Rusilia, Darah Kedayan, Putera Seni, Kastea, and Astrawani. Traditional performances are generally dramatic pieces featuring various combinations of song, dance, humorous banter, trance, and martial arts display. The most popular forms are performed on special occasions such as marriages *(alus jua dindang*, song-dance), harvests *(aduk-aduk*, dance and the martial art form of *silat)*, coronations *(alai sekap*, dance), festivals *(henari*, dance and humorous banter), or as cures for sicknesses *(anding*, trance dance).

Dallas L. McCurley

See also: **Drama—Thailand; Literature—Laos; Literature—Myanmar; Music—Southeast Asia; Ramakien**

Further Reading

Brandon, James, ed. (1967) *On Thrones of Gold: Three Javanese Shadow Plays*. Honolulu, HI: University of Hawaii Press.

———. (1967) *Theatre in Southeast Asia*. Cambridge, MA: Harvard University Press.

Miettinen, Jukka O. (1992) *Classical Dance and Theatre in South-East Asia*. New York: Oxford University Press.

DRAMA—THAILAND

The principal traditional dramatic genres of Thailand are *khon* (masked drama), *lakhon* (dance-drama), *likay* (folk opera), *nang* (shadow theater) and *hun* (puppet theater). While there is a secondary school that specializes in training children to become classical performers, opportunities to pursue a career in traditional theater are extremely limited, for public performances are few and far between. Thai scholars writing in the 1930s often lamented the decline of traditional theatrical genres. Attempts to revive and revitalize the traditions have had limited success, although drama continues to be widely promoted as a symbol of national identity. Images of Thai classical drama are represented widely in advertisements and greeting cards in the form of souvenir dolls, ornamental *khon* masks, and miniature shadow puppets, while much-abbreviated performances are staged in restaurants for the benefit of foreign tourists.

A Buddhist puppet used in Thai drama. (WERNER FORMAN/CORBIS)

Khon

The origins of *khon* are uncertain, but the prototype is generally believed to have existed in the fourteenth century CE. The most distinctive feature of *khon* performances is that nearly all the actors, with the exception of those taking female roles, wear elaborately painted masks. Performances are based on episodes in the *Ramakien* (the Thai retelling of the Hindu epic the *Ramayana*), with battle scenes in which the hero Phra Ram vanquishes the villain Thotsakan particularly popular. It is a convention of Thai theater, however, not to portray Thotsakan's death onstage, as it is believed to bring misfortune. The story is narrated in verse by a chorus and there is an accompanying musical ensemble. The style of dancing and martial posturing, unlike the *lakhon* style mentioned below, puts emphasis on leg and body movements rather than refined hand gestures. Until the 1930s all parts were taken by male actors.

Lakhon

Lakhon emerged during the Ayutthaya period (1351–1767). It is subdivided into *lakhon nok* (dance-drama of the outside), performed outside the royal court, and *lakhon nai* (dance-drama of the inside), performed within the royal court. The differences between the two lie in the stories performed, style of dancing, musical accompaniment, and costume. The stories performed in *lakhon nai* are taken from the epic poems known as the *Ramakien*, *Inao*, and *Unarut*. Traditionally, and as still practiced, women took both male and female parts, with men confined to playing the part of clowns. Performers do not wear masks unless taking the part of monkeys or demons; graceful arm movements and elaborate hand gestures are the outstanding characteristics of the dance movements, which are accompanied by an offstage chorus and a small orchestra. By contrast, *lakhon nok* is a folk dance–drama that employs faster dance movements, more action, and scenes of comedy and melodrama; its repertoire is drawn from the *jataka* tales (tales of the past lives of the Buddha). *Lakhon nok* was traditionally performed by an all-male cast but later by mixed casts.

Likay

Likay is a part of traditional popular "low culture." It appeared toward the end of the reign of Rama V (1868–1910), blending elements of *lakhon nok* with music, singing, and dancing of Indian or Malay origin. A *likay* troupe traditionally consisted of a mixed cast of between twelve and forty players and musicians. It would normally perform on a makeshift stage at temple fairs, markets, and other public gatherings, using garishly painted backdrops for scenery. Its repertoire was drawn from well-known historical tales, folktales, and literary works, featuring an array of kings, clowns, and star-crossed lovers. The *likay* audience, which tended to be made up largely of lower-class women, did not expect highly stylized and polished performances from the comically overdressed and gaudily made-up cast. *Likay*'s charm came from its brashness, its vulgarity, the amateurishness of the untrained performers' movements, and the often-bawdy improvised dialogue; and at the same time it provided a relaxed backdrop for gossiping, eating, drinking, and chewing betel. Today *likay* is a rapidly dying art form; although it could still be seen and heard regularly on the television and radio in the 1980s, it faces ever increasing difficulty in competing to attract young audiences away from newer, more sophisticated forms of entertainment.

Nang

Nang is the traditional Thai shadow play, developed during the Ayutthaya period; it employed large, elaborately drawn figures or scenes, usually taken from the *Ramakien*, which were embossed on dried buffalo hide and painted. They were then mounted on two sticks so that they could be held up, either in front of or behind an illuminated white sheet, which served as background. A chorus narrated the story while the shadow puppets were moved across the screen by men who adopted dancing postures and steps to fit in with the story. It has been speculated that the shadow theater was a possible precursor of the *khon* masked drama, which was likewise originally performed before a screen, and in which the masked characters still try to present a side profile to the audience rather than a full face. Another kind of shadow theater, *nang talung*, which originated in southern Thailand, employed much smaller figures, each of which had one arm that moved. The first surviving references to *nang talung* are during the reign of Rama V, when it was introduced to Bangkok, but its origin was doubtless much earlier.

Hun

Now resurrected only occasionally, this traditional puppet theater, which dates from the nineteenth century, was confined to the royal elite. The string puppets were beautifully crafted and dressed in elaborate costumes; unlike Western puppets, their legs and arms were manipulated from below. Plays were taken from classical tales. A new form of puppet theater, *hun krabok*, emerged during the reign of Chulalongkorn (Rama V; reigned1868–1910) in which the puppets' arms and legs were manipulated by bamboo rods; plays performed in this style usually offered scope for slapstick humor and the genre continued to enjoy some popularity up to the late 1940s. In recent years university drama departments have played an important role in trying to preserve the dying art of *hun krabok*.

During the reign of Chulalongkorn there was an attempt to introduce a "sung drama," *lakhon rong*, imitating Western operetta, while Rama VI (reigned 1910–1925) actively wrote and promoted Western-style plays, termed *lakhon phut*, as a means of promoting patriotism. In the 1930s the nationalistic plays of Luang Wichitwathakan were given government support, while less didactic plays began to appear during the 1940s when the import of foreign films was banned. Today, live Western-style plays are produced almost exclusively in university drama departments and reach only a very limited audience.

David Smyth

Further Reading

Rutnin, Mattani. (1975) *The Siamese Theatre: A Collection of Reprints from the Journals of the Siam Society*. Bangkok, Thailand: The Siam Society.

Rutnin, Mattani Mojdara. (1993) *Dance, Drama, and Theatre in Thailand: The Process of Development and Modernization*. Tokyo: The Centre for East Asian Cultural Studies for UNESCO.

DRAVIDIAN LANGUAGES In terms of the number of speakers the Dravidian language family is the fourth or fifth largest in the world. It consists of at least twenty-three languages spoken primarily in South Asia by about 230 million people. Zvelebil's 1997 survey enumerated eighty-eight languages, most of which are unwritten (nonliterary, preliterary), and many of which are probably dialects of other known languages. Some of these languages are reportedly spoken by 350 speakers (Allar or Chatan in Kerala) or even fewer (Vishavan or Malarkuti, 150 speakers, in Kerala; Cholanaickan of Nilambur forest, Kerala, 20 speakers).

The Indian Constitution (1951) established the creation of states in the Indian Union along linguistic lines. Four Dravidian languages, Telugu (55 million) in the state of Andhra Pradesh, Tamil (48 million) in Tamil Nadu, Kannada (27 million) in Karnataka, and Malayalam (27 million) in Kerala, were recognized as official languages. All of them have written literature of high quality and great antiquity, with early inscriptions in all four dating to between the third century BCE and the ninth century CE. In each language literary composition began one or two centuries after the first inscriptions. Each of these four literary languages developed a distinctive writing system (so-called alphasyllabic scripts), which can be traced back to southern varieties of the Asokan Brahmi script (used in India from around 250 BCE). A number of Dravidian words have made their way into English (e.g., rice, pepper, ginger, mango, coir, curry, cheroot, catamaran, carborundum).

Languages of the Family

The Dravidian linguistic family is usually described in terms of four subgroups: South Dravidian, South-Central Dravidian, Central Dravidian, and North Dravidian. These subgroups were established according to typological similarities and diachronic or historical reconstructions.

Apart from the three great literary languages of Tamil, Malayalam, and Kannada, South Dravidian encompasses a number of nonliterary or preliterary languages, including Kota, Toda, Irula, Kurumba, Kodagu, and Tulu. Tamil is one of India's two classical languages, alongside Sanskrit, and the only one of the two with continuity between classical and modern forms. Tamil has a number of regional and social dialects and is also spoken outside India, in Sri Lanka, Malaysia, South Africa, and elsewhere.

Between 800 and 1200 the western dialects of Tamil developed into Malayalam, spoken mostly in Kerala; Malayalam speakers boast the highest literacy rate in the Indian Union. The Nilgiri Mountains are home to a number of nonliterary languages such as Badaga, Kota, Toda, Irula, and Kurumba. Despite the small number of speakers, these languages have attracted linguistic, anthropological, and cultural interest. Kodagu is spoken only in the Coorg district of Karnataka. Tulu is probably the first language to have branched off from proto-South Dravidian; traditionally described as a nonliterary language, it has been written down for about the last 250 years in Malayalam and Kannada scripts.

South-Central Dravidian includes a great literary language, Telugu, and six nonliterary languages spoken in parts of central India: Gondi with numerous dialects, Koya, Konda, Kui, Kuvi, Pengo, and Manda. Telugu is the Dravidian language spoken by the greatest number of speakers (more than 60 million) and has four regional dialects and important ancient and modern literature. Among the other languages, Konda seems to be the most phonologically conservative of the group. Kui, Kuvi, Pengo, and Manda, are closely related and, unlike other Dravidian languages, have devised a system of object-verb agreement.

Central Dravidian includes five nonliterary languages, Gadaba, Kolami, Naiki, Ollari, and Parji, spoken in central India. Whereas South Dravidian languages developed the use of the auxiliary verb *iru* "be," Central Dravidian has not lost the ancient perfect tense auxiliary verb *man* "be."

North Dravidian languages include Brahui, spoken in Baluchistan, a province of Pakistan, and considered the first to branch off from the Dravidian protolanguage. Kurux (alias Oraon) is spoken in northeastern India and Bangladesh. It is also spoken in Nepal, where it is known as Dhangar or Jhangar. Striking in its grammar is a distinction between men's and women's speech, found also in the third language of the group, Malto (northeastern India, Bangladesh).

The count of the number of Dravidian languages and their speakers has steadily increased. The "father" of Dravidian linguistics, Robert Caldwell (1814–1891), listed nine languages in 1856, while a 1997 survey listed about ninety. Because of the absence of adequate description, it is impossible to decide whether all these languages are new or merely various forms of known languages. However, new Dravidian languages are likely to be discovered, particularly in central India and the mountains and forests of southwestern India.

Historical Dimension

Nothing definite is known about the ancient domain of the Dravidian ancestral speech. Dravidian speakers must have been widespread throughout India because numerous features of Dravidian vocabulary and grammar appear in the Rig Veda, the earliest known Indo-Aryan literary composition. Proto-Dravidian probably existed as a single language as late as 4000 BCE, when the linguistic unity of Dravidian began to disintegrate, and distinct branches and individual languages began to develop.

The divergence of the last major branch, South Dravidian, might have taken place around 1500 BCE. The arrival of Dravidian speakers in India is shrouded in mystery, but linguistic evidence suggests that the present locations of Dravidian languages resulted from several distinct movements. Brahui, Kurux, and Malto may represent surviving islands of a speech once extant all over northern India and Pakistan. A widely accepted hypothesis proposes that ancient Dravidian speakers traveled from the mountains of eastern Iran to south India and ultimately to Sri Lanka, "dropping off" groups of languages along their way. This movement might have taken place between c. 4000 and 1500 BCE. Along the route various Dravidian speech-forms peeled off the main stock, and some of them may have played an important role in the ethnolinguistic composition of the Indus Valley (Harappan culture).

Dravidians continued to move until the southernmost part of the peninsula was reached by the proto-Tamils, who, between c. 600 and 400 BCE, established the first historically recognizable literate and cultured Dravidian-speaking civilization, with the adaptation of Emperor Asoka's (reigned c. 265–238 BCE) Southern Brahmi script to preliterary Tamil.

Characteristics of Dravidian Languages

The morphology of Dravidian languages is agglutinating and exclusively suffixal. An agglutinative language incorporates separate formal units of distinct meaning into a single word, but Dravidian morphology also distinguishes between so-called free and bound forms. Free forms are "words," and bound forms are "clitics." There are some elements of internal flexion (the alternation of short and long vowels in derived words) as well as regular alternation in vowel and consonant qualities in the root. Relatively low receptivity to change resulted in a slower rate of diachronic (historical) development than in Indo-European languages. The degree of phonetic divergence among the Dravidian languages is not very great; hence etymologies are not too difficult to discover. Proto-Dravidian seemed to have had just two parts of speech, noun and verb, identified by their characteristic inflectional morphology. The reconstruction of further parts of speech such as adjectives and adverbs in the protolanguage is controversial, but the daughter languages originated other parts of speech (word classes). In any study of Dravidian both evolution and diffusion must be taken into account.

The Sounds of Dravidian

The two most striking features of the proto-Dravidian sound-system are the surprising number of apical stop (plosive, obstruent) phonemes (perhaps the world's maximum) and the total absence of sibilants. The protolanguage contained five pairs of vowels, both short and long: *a, ā, i, ī, u, ū, e, ē, o, ō*.

There is no evidence for the reconstruction of diphthongs. The most important vowel developments are the gradual elimination of the contrast between short and long *ē̆* and *ō̆* in Brahui and the merger of proto-Dravidian *ī̆* and *ū̆* with *ē̆* and *ō̆* in South Dravidian before a consonant plus *ā̆*). The proto-Dravidian set of stops exhibits a six-way contrast: voiced stops are allophones of their voiceless counterparts in the protolanguage. Most consonant clusters appear only at morpheme boundaries; hence no consonant clusters occur in root morphemes, which are essentially monosyllabic. The prosodic structure of Dravidian is quantitative rather than qualitative. Only a limited number of syllabic structures can occur in the protolanguage. Several important and regular prosodic alternations have been reconstructed for the protolanguage. Stress occurs in many Dravidian languages but is not distinctive. It typically falls on the first syllable of a word. Some languages developed, after the loss of vocalic peaks, long consonant clusters: for instance the Kota *anžrčgčgvḓk* "because of the fact that (someone) will cause (someone) to frighten (someone)."

Grammatical Features

Dravidian words consist of two or more morphemes strung together in the agglutinating process in a linear fashion from left to right with minimum morphophonemic intervention. Morphemes appear in the order (lexical root [+ derivative suffix] + inflectional suffix). Nouns are inflected for case and number and secondarily for person and gender. There are two numbers, unmarked singular and marked plural. The proto-Dravidian gender system apparently distinguished between human (animate) and nonhuman (inanimate) nouns. Animate nouns were often further divided into masculine and feminine. First person plural of pronouns distinguished between inclusive plural "we and you" and exclusive plural "we but not you."

Proto-Dravidian verbs distinguished two tenses, past and nonpast. The present tense developed independently in various languages. Verbs also distinguished between affirmative and negative forms. All verbs were either finite or nonfinite (these last do not mark subject-verb agreement). A characteristic derivation is that of "pronominalized" (alias "personalized") nouns, for example, Tamil *iḷai* "youth": *iḷai-y-am* "young-we."

In a sentence, however complex, only one finite verb occurs (normally at the end), preceded (if necessary) by a number of nonfinite forms: for instance Tamil *rāmaṉ vantu eṉṉai-p pārttu ōṭi-p pōṉāṉ* "Raman came, saw me, and ran away." The determining member always precedes the determined: Tamil *poṉ* "gold" + *nakaram* "town": *poṉṉakaram* "golden town." Word order follows certain basic rules but is relatively free; however, the most frequent normal word order is subject-object-verb.

Vocabulary

Different Dravidian languages were receptive to loanwords in differing degrees. The existence of many cognate words of Dravidian origin (i.e., exhibiting no "outside" etymological relationships) and systematic correspondences among them enabled scholars to establish a Dravidian linguistic family, based on a comparative lexicon.

Among the literary languages Tamil has the lowest number of Indo-Aryan loanwords (18–25 percent, according to the style), although the modern spoken language adopts loanwords from English and other non-Indian languages. In Malayalam, Kannada, and Telugu the percentage of loanwords is higher. The most important sources of loanwords have been Sanskrit, Pali, Prakrits, and later Urdu, Portuguese, and English. There was not much lexical borrowing from one Dravidian language to another. Brahui was obviously most influenced by borrowing, mainly from Indo-Aryan and Iranian. In contrast Toda of the Nilgiris was probably least influenced by any other language.

At the beginning of the twentieth century a movement called "Tamil Only" was initiated to remove Sanskritic elements from the Tamil vocabulary and replace them with Tamil ones. This linguistic purism is still active, but similar movements have not occurred in the other cultivated languages.

Writing

Tamil, Malayalam, Telugu, and Kannada have phonologically based writing systems and are written from left to right. All these scripts are derived from South Indian Brahmi, used from around 250 BCE as the medium of Buddhist inscriptions, carved at the orders of Emperor Asoka (reigned c. 265–238 BCE). In the script each consonant is represented by a consonantal symbol; a following short vowel *a* is considered inherent in each consonantal symbol. All other vowels are written as obligatory diacritics; a vowel in an initial position has an independent symbol. Consonants may also occur in sequences, particularly in words borrowed from Sanskrit (e.g., *str*). Writing systems of this Indic type, which indicate consonant-vowel combinations by vowel diacritics obligatorily attached (above, below, in front, or behind) to the consonants, are rather rare in the world. Such systems are usually called alphasyllabic, suggesting similarities with both alphabets and syllabic systems. The traditional order of symbols in all South Indian scripts is based on articulatory phonetics as developed from Sanskrit (i.e., *a ā i ī u ū e ē o ō* . . . etc.).

External Links of Dravidian

The Dravidian linguistic family is what is usually called an isolate; that is, no external (non-Indian) linguistic genetic kinship has so far been convincingly proved. As soon as Dravidian became known to Western scholarship and recognized as an independent linguistic family, the question arose of its origin and possible genetic kinship with other languages and language families. Among the possible candidates for such genetic relations were Scythian, Nubian, Finno-Ugric, and Japanese. The most plausible candidates are Elamite and Ural-Altaic. A few scholars explain Ural-Altaic and Dravidian affinities by actual genetic relations; however, although the typological and even material similarities may be striking, they can probably be explained by widespread diffusion and borrowing due to multilingualism, ethnic mixture, conquests, dominance movements, or accidental events somewhere in Central Asia—an area of prolonged and ancient contacts—rather than by genetic relations. Several scholars, particularly archaeologists, have accepted the Elamo-Dravidian hypothesis as almost a fact, but it too seems dubious for several valid reasons. Even less convincing is the Japanese connection. The most provocative hypothesis is the Indus Valley (Harappan) connection, which maintains that the language on the (as yet undeciphered) Harappan seals was an early form of Dravidian. None of the hypotheses of genetic relations is to be rejected without further rigorous study. There are still no adequate descriptive studies of most Dravidian languages, particularly their historical development, and no critical editions of the earliest texts in Dravidian. The reconstruction of proto-Dravidian itself is fragmentary and provisional.

As long as it remains so, the external links and possible genetic affiliations remain in the realm of typological and etymological speculations. This presents Dravidianists with a great challenge and opportunity. Among the tasks ahead is, above all, the full descriptive study of the various languages (including their dialects); a full diachronic, historical treatment of their development; and a new, revised etymological analysis and description of their respective lexica.

K. V. Zvelebil

Further Reading

Burrow, Thomas, and Murray B. Emeneau. (1984) *A Dravidian Etymological Dictionary*. 2d ed. Oxford: Clarendon Press.

Caldwell, Robert. (1976) *A Comparative Grammar of the Dravidian or South-Indian Family of Languages*. 3d ed., repr. rev. by J. L.Wyatt and T. Ramakrishna Pillai. Madras, India: University of Madras Press.

Emeneau, Murray B. (1984) *Toda Grammar and Texts*. Philadelphia: American Philosophical Society.

Hockings, P., and Christiane Pilot-Raichoor. (1992) *A Badaga-English Dictionary*. Berlin: Mouton de Gruyter.

Zvelebil, K. V. (1990) *Dravidian Linguistics: An Introduction*. Pondicherry, India: Pondicherry Institute of Linguistics and Culture.

———. (1997) "Language List for Dravidian." *Archiv Orientalni* 65: 175–190.

DRUG TRADE Asia has a long history of dealing with psychoactive substances. Many of them have existed from time immemorial all over the continent. Various places established traditional uses for some drugs and even integrated them into social codes. However, today's drug trade in Asia threatens the health and safety of its population as well as the stability of its countries. The drug trade is shaped and spurred by mercantilism and grows on the fertile and complex terrain of poverty and armed conflicts. In fact a direct relation between drug production, poverty, and war appears to exist. Thus drug production and trafficking can be perceived as the outcomes of economic as well as political events.

History

The first stage in the Asian commerce in drugs was probably the opium trade along the numerous and far-reaching precursors of the Silk Road and the early Chinese maritime trade that reached Africa by the first century BCE. However, the opium poppy, *Papaver somniferum L.*, most likely a European plant, was spread throughout Asia mainly by the Arab traders who transmitted it to the Indians in the seventh century and to the Chinese a century later. It is questionable whether the Arabs themselves actually introduced the opium poppy into these areas, since early Indian traders or Buddhist pilgrims may have done it, but Arab traders undoubtedly were the main contributors to its commercial spread as a cash crop.

The next stage in the opium commerce was taken by European maritime colonial powers, who used it to balance their trade in spices and tea with Southeast Asia and China: first by the Venetians (in the fourteenth century), then by the Portuguese and the Dutch in the sixteenth century, and finally by the British from the seventeenth century and on. Through their powerful East India Company (founded 1600), the British brought to China opium originating in the poppy fields of India, where it had long been produced by the Mughal rulers. This led, in the mid-nineteenth century, to China's two Opium Wars, first with the British and second with a British-French coalition. The treaty of Nanjing (1842), which ended the first war, gave Hong Kong to the British; it went on to become the world's heroin hub. China, confronted with exploding opium consumption, eventually fostered local poppy production as a way to balance its growing trade deficit.

After the southern migration of some opium growers from Yunnan, pressured by imperial political repression and, later, by the enforcement of communist prohibition, opium production spread from China into Southeast Asia, which became the Golden Triangle (Burma, Laos, and Thailand), a precursor to the Southwest Asian Golden Crescent (Afghanistan, Iran, and Pakistan). Opium was integrated as a trade commodity, but it needed improvements to increase its global marketability. Consequently, after heroin was synthesized from opium in 1898, producers were able to transform opium into heroin, a product with a greater efficacy that was easier to trade than the bulky opium.

The Twentieth Century

Opium poppy production expanded to almost everywhere in Asia, from Turkey in the Near East to Japan in the Far East, along the succession of mountain ranges that stretch across Iran, Afghanistan, Pakistan, India, Burma (Myanmar), Laos, Thailand, Vietnam, and China, as well as in Russia and the Central Asian republics. Nonetheless, the opium poppy is of course not the only psychoactive plant thriving in Asia. *Cannabis sativa L.*, consumed as either marijuana or hashish, is prevalent as well. In fact Lebanon, Turkey, Afghanistan, Pakistan, India, Nepal, Thai-

THE TREATY OF NANJING

The Treaty of Nanjing between China and Great Britain marked the conclusion of the Opium War and the opening of trading ports to Britain. The Treaty heavily favored Britain.

Victoria, by the Grace of God, Queen of the United Kingdom of Great Britain and Ireland, Defender of the Faith, etc., etc., etc. To All and Singular to whom these Presents shall come, Greeting! Whereas a Treaty between Us and Our Good Brother The Emperor of China, was concluded and signed in the English and Chinese Languages, on board Our Ship the Cornwallis, at Nanking, on the Twenty-ninth day of August, in the Year of Our Lord One Thousand Eight Hundred and Forty Two, by the Plenipotentiaries of Us and Our said Good Brother, duly and respectively authorized for that purpose; which Treaty is hereunto annexed in Original:

Article I. There shall henceforward be Peace and Friendship between Her Majesty the Queen of the United Kingdom of Great Britain and Ireland, and His Majesty the Emperor of China, and between their respective Subjects, who shall enjoy full security and protection for their persons and property within the Dominions of the other.

Article II. His Majesty the Emperor of China agrees, that British Subjects, with their families and establishments, shall be allowed to reside, for the purpose of carrying on their Mercantile pursuits, without molestation or restraint at the Cities and Towns of Canton, Amoy, Foochow-fu, Ningpo and Shanghai, and Her Majesty the Queen of Great Britain, etc., will appoint Superintendents or Consular Officers, to reside at each of the above-named Cities of Towns, to be the medium of communication between the Chinese Authorities and the said Merchants, and to see that the just Duties and other Dues of the Chinese Government as hereafter provided for, are duly discharged by Her Britannic Majesty's Subjects.

Article III. It being obviously necessary and desirable, that British Subjects should have some Port whereat they may careen and refit their Ships, when required, and keep Stores for that purpose, His Majesty the Emperor of China cedes to Her Majesty the Queen of Great Britain, etc., the Island of Hongkong, to be possessed in perpetuity by Her Britannic Majesty, Her Heirs and Successors, and to be governed by such Laws and Regulations as Her Majesty the Queen of Great Britain, etc., shall see fit to direct.

Article IV. The Emperor of China agrees to pay the sum of Six Millions of Dollars as the value of Opium which was delivered up at Canton in the month of March 1839, as a Ransom for the lives of Her Britannic Majesty's Superintendent and Subjects, who had been imprisoned and threatened with death by the Chinese High Officers.

Article V. The Government of China having compelled the British Merchants trading at Canton to deal exclusively with certain Chinese Merchants called Hong Merchants (or Cohong) who had been licensed by the Chinese Government for that purpose, the Emperor of China agrees to abolish that practice in future at all Ports where British Merchants may reside, and to permit them to carry on their mercantile transactions with whatever persons they please, and His Imperial Majesty further agrees to pay to the British Government the sum of Three Millions of Dollars, on account of debts due to British Subjects by some of the said Hong Merchants (or Cohong), who have become insolvent, and who owe very large sums of money to Subjects of Her Britannic Majesty.

Article VI. The Government of Her Britannic Majesty having been obliged to send out an Expedition to demand and obtain redress for the violent and unjust proceedings of the Chinese High Authorities towards Her Britannic Majesty's Officers and Subjects, the Emperor of China agrees to pay the sum of Twelve Millions of Dollars on account of the Expenses incurred, and Her Britannic Majesty's Plenipotentiary voluntarily agrees, on behalf of Her Majesty, to deduct from the said amount of Twelve Millions of Dollars, any sums which may have been received by Her Majesty's combined Forces as Ransom for Cities and Towns in China, subsequent to the 1st day of August 1841.

Source: Treaties, Conventions, etc. between China and Foreign States. (1908) Miscellaneous Series, no. 30. Shanghai, China: Imperial Maritime Customs, vol. I: 159–160.

land, and Cambodia are among the most internationally renowned producers and exporters of cannabis. Kazakhstan for its part boasts the world's largest area of wild cannabis.

In Asia the production, trade, and consumption of opiates always have combined national and international issues and stakes. In fact the spread of drug trafficking in Asia and elsewhere is linked to its international prohibition. The 1955 Persian prohibition stimulated production in Afghanistan and Pakistan and affected even the distant Golden Triangle. In another example, Turkey began a long legal and power struggle with the United States in the early 1960s. In Turkey, poppies were grown legally for pharmaceutical purposes, and a large quantity of illicit opium was smuggled to France, where it was processed into heroin and subsequently shipped to the U.S. drug market. The United States pressured Turkey to institute a national prohibition against opium production, which, after many setbacks, Turkey instituted in 1972. The 1960s were bounded by two significant events that shaped the way all narcotic phenomena were addressed. In 1961 the United Nations Single Convention on Narcotic Drugs reinforced the previous multilateral agreements that had followed the 1909 Shanghai Convention. The main international concern then was heroin. In 1971 the administration of U.S. President Richard Nixon declared a "war on drugs," setting up the "carrot and stick" system that conditioned U.S. financial aid on drug eradication and thus favoring a bilateral, biased approach over the multilateral approach of the United Nations. Turkey's compliance in 1972 had deep repercussions in Asian trade, spurring the Golden Crescent's production and further linking Asia's various poppy-growing areas.

These pressures on the drug trade were nevertheless counteracted by the U.S. Central Intelligence Agency (CIA), which played a significant role in the drug trade in both Southeast Asia and Southwest Asia. Its anti-Communist covert actions benefited from the participation of some drug-related combat units who, to finance their own struggle, were directly or indirectly involved in drug production and trade. Considering the involvement of different groups in the drug trade (for example, the Hmong in Laos, the Nationalist Chinese [Guomindang] in northern Burma, and the Islamic mujahideen resistance [the party of Gulbuddin Hekmatyar, notably] in Afghanistan), their backing by the CIA implied that the agency condoned the use of drug proceeds and considerably increased opiate production in Asia. Hence the Golden Triangle and the Golden Crescent remain the world's two major opium production areas. The Golden Triangle led world production until 1991, with Myanmar ranking at the top. After that date the Golden Crescent took the lead, with Afghanistan breaking previous records in 1999. (In 2001 the Taliban government forbade opium growing, and production plunged.) Opium production in these two areas can be attributed to the protracted civil wars that have plagued Myanmar since 1948 and Afghanistan since 1979. The atmosphere of conflict during the Cold War also contributed. In the late twentieth century Thailand, Iran, and Pakistan, former important opium producers, coped with growing narcotics trafficking and, even more disrupting, local epidemics of narcotic addiction. Conservative estimates in Iran and Pakistan show 2 million opiate addicts in each country, and the number continues to grow. Afghanistan, mainly a producer, is likely to become an important consumer, as indicated by the spillover in Central Asia. In fact Iran, previously the primary trading route, has succeeded in partially diverting Afghan smuggling toward Central Asia.

Thailand, Myanmar's neighbor, faces the same problems and has reoriented trading routes toward China, Laos, and Vietnam. Thailand is now emerging as a pioneer in new drug consumption patterns as amphetamine-type stimulants overtake heroin in the kingdom, with Myanmar massively producing such synthetic drugs in its Shan states.

Drug production and trade in Asia thus evolve and adapt to the market, be it opium, heroin, amphetamines, or ecstasy. These types of trade and consumption, ancient phenomena, have benefited from world globalization and conflicts. Rooted in poverty, the drug trade quickly grows on the ruins of development and its related political conflicts. Wars have proven to nurture the drug trade, and drug profits prolong wars.

Pierre-Arnaud Chouvy

Further Reading

Booth, Martin. (1998) *Opium: A History*. New York: St. Martin's Press.

Labrousse, Alain. (1999) *Drogues, un marche de dupes*. Paris: Editions Alternatives.

McCoy, Alfred. (1991) *The Politics of Heroin: CIA Complicity in the Global Drug Trade*. New York: Lawrence Hill Books.

Observatoire Géopolitique des Drogues. (1996) *Atlas mondial des drogues*. Paris: Presses universitaires de France.

Stares, Paul B. (1996) *Global Habit: The Drug Problem in a Borderless World*. Washington, DC: Brookings Institution Press.

Tullis, Lamond. (1996) *Unintended Consequences: Illegal Drugs and Drug Policies in Nine Countries*. Boulder, CO: Lynne Rienner Publishers.

DU FU (712–760), Chinese poet. Du Fu, who was also known as Zimei, is commonly recognized as the greatest poet in Chinese history and is referred to as the "Poet-Historian" or "Poet-Sage." The Tang dynasty (618–907 CE) was beset by the An Lushan rebellion just as Du Fu was seeking advancement as an official, so he experienced firsthand the decline of China's greatest dynasty. His own failures and frustrations in official life, criticism of the wrongdoings of those in power, praise of good officials, and sympathy for the common people became the main themes of his poetry, which presents a vivid picture of his troubled times. A prolific writer, with over 1,400 surviving poems, Du Fu was proficient in various poetic forms. He rigidly complied with the rules for regulated verse, but he also composed in various "ancient style" formal types, as well as creating new forms. Seen as exemplary in both prosody and morality, with his poems the focus of the attentions of generations of scholars and commentators, Du Fu became a paragon in traditional China for readers and poets alike.

Timothy Wai Keung Chan

Further Reading

Chou, Eva Shan. (1995) *Reconsidering Tu Fu: Literary Greatness and Cultural Context.* New York: Cambridge University Press.

Davis, A. R. (1971) *Tu Fu.* New York: Twayne Publishers.

Hung, William. (1952) *Tu Fu, China's Greatest Poet.* Cambridge, MA: Harvard University Press.

DUCK AND GOOSE, DOMESTICATED

Along with swans, ducks and geese belong to the Anatidae family of large waterbirds characterized by webbed feet. Ducks differ from geese in having shorter necks and legs, but both are at home on lakes and ponds; geese commonly graze on grassland even at some distance from water.

The mallard (*Anas platyrhyncos*, about 60 centimeters long) was domesticated in Eurasia and was the ancestor of most domestic breeds of duck worldwide; today wild mallards live throughout the Northern Hemisphere. Ducks were domesticated in China probably as early as the seventh millennium BCE; there are ten native species in that country. From northern China and Japan came the small Mandarin ducks *(Dendronessa galericulata)*, first introduced to Europe in 1830. The goose was also domesticated in China from the Chinese, or swan, goose *(Cygnopsis cygnoides)*, the largest living goose, today native to Siberia and eastern Mongolia.

Both ducks and geese are farmed for their meat and eggs, and sometimes their down. Centuries ago, the Chinese had invented incubators made of pottery that were capable of hatching a thousand eggs.

Paul Hockings

DUJIANGYAN Dujiangyan is one of the world's greatest water engineering operations, dating from the Qin dynasty. For over 2,000 years the Dujiangyan complex has provided water to millions of Chinese citizens while protecting them and their farms from flooding, a situation rarely if ever achieved anywhere else. The complex is located near the city of Guanxian, 56 kilometers (35 miles) from Chengdu in Sichuan Province, central China. The name Dujiangyan means "the dam on the capital's river." Construction of the project began in 256 BCE and was directed by the engineer Li Bing and his son Li Erlang. Dujiangyan incorporates a dike of piled stones that divides the Min River, a tributary of the Chang (Yangtze) River, into inner and outer channels. The inner channel is diverted for irrigation, allowing, at the time of its construction, about 1 million hectares of the Chengdu Plain to be irrigated without danger of flooding, supporting a population of 5 million. The complex has been in continual use since its construction, and expansion of the project in later years, along with annual silt removal, allows about 3 million hectares to be irrigated today. The role of the two engineers is commemorated in the Fulong Guan, or Temple of the Harnessed Dragon (referring to the river), a place of veneration for Li Bing, and the Erwang Miao, or Two Kings Temple, memorializing Li Erlang. Dujiangyan was inscribed on the World Heritage List in 2000.

Michael Pretes

Further Reading

Luo, Zhewen, and Peng Shen, chief compilers. (1986) *Through the Moon Gate: A Guide to China's Historic Monuments.* Hong Kong: Oxford University Press.

Needham, Joseph. (1971) *Science and Civilisation in China,* Vol. 4, Part III, Sections 28–29. Cambridge, U.K.: Cambridge University Press.

DULATOV, MIRZHAQYP (1885–1935), Kazakh writer, poet, dramatist, social activist. Mirzhaqyp Dulatov was born in 1885 in Turgai province to a poor family. His father and mother died while he was still young. His education started with a local mullah, and when he was twelve years old he enrolled in the second class of the Russian-Kazakh school in Turgai. The education regime included studies in mathematics, history, geography, physics, philosophy, and other subjects. He quickly demonstrated talents as a skilled debater and musician. After graduating, he moved to Omsk to teach at a local school. He joined an underground Kazakh political organization and quickly established himself in local social movements. He became a staunch critic of the czarist government's policies and actively pursued reform that would alleviate the suffering among those Kazakhs who were forced to settle and give up their former nomadic way of life. In 1909 he published a book that was among the most important influences on the development of Kazakh national identity and consciousness. *Oian, Qazaq!* (Awake, Kazakh!) was a small collection of poems that attempted to rally Kazakhs to oppose the increased Russian migration to the steppe while identifying the internal disintegration of Kazakh society. For Dulatov and many other Kazakhs, the seizure of land came to symbolize colonial oppression and national humiliation. The work was criticized by czarist authorities and Dulatov was arrested several times for illegal political activities. In 1912 he published *Baqytsyz Zhamal* (Unhappy Zhamal), the story of a poor Kazakh girl forced to marry against her will. It is regarded by many scholars to be the first novel in the Kazakh language. In 1913 he joined Akhmet Baitursynov on the editorial board of the Kazakh-language newspaper *Kazak*, contributing many articles during the next five years. In 1917 he became an essential leader of the Kazakh national movement Alash Orda (The Horde of Alash). Following the Bolshevik victory in the Russian Civil War, he joined the Communist Party and vigorously worked for Kazakh cultural autonomy, particularly in education. During the 1920s he published many more works about Kazakh history and culture and worked for the Soviet-Kazakh newspaper *Engbekshi Kazak* (Kazak Worker). In 1928 he was arrested for bourgeois nationalism and spent the next several years under constant surveillance. In 1935 he was arrested again and incarcerated in Solovetsk prison, dying of an illness while imprisoned.

Steven Sabol

Further Reading

Absemet, Marat Oralbaiuly. (1995) *Mirzhaqyp (Omiri men shygharmashylyghy)*. Almaty, Kazakhstan: Kenzhe Press.

Dulatov, Mirzhaqyp. (1991) *Shygharmalary*. Almaty, Kazakhstan: Zhazushy

Dulatuly, Mirzhaqyp. (1996) *Shygharmalary-2 kitap*. Almaty, Kazakhstan: Ghylym.

———. (1991) *Oian, Kazak!*. Almaty, Kazakhstan: Altyn Orda.

DUNGANS

DUNGANS Dungan is the Turkic name for Chinese-speaking Muslims living in various parts of Central Asia. Significant Dungan communities in the Central Asian republics of Kyrgyzstan, Kazakhstan, and Uzbekistan came to Central Asia from China in the nineteenth century. A Dungan population living along the Myanmar (Burma)-China border is known as Pathay, their Burmese name.

Dungans are descended from communities of Muslim merchants, soldiers, artisans, and scholars who established themselves in China under the Tang dynasty (618–907) and later under the Yuan dynasty (1206–1368). These groups intermarried with Han Chinese and adopted the Chinese language, and today they are physically indistinguishable from the rest of the Han population.

The Dungan communities of Kyrgyzstan, Kazakhstan, and Uzbekistan arrived in two waves in the late nineteenth century. The first group crossed the Tian Shan range in the winter of 1877–1878, fleeing to the Russian empire after the suppression of a Muslim revolt in southwest China. The second group was invited to resettle in the Russian empire after the Treaty of Peking adjusted the Russo-Chinese border in 1881. Many Dungans who had been Russian subjects chose to remain part of the Russian empire rather than pass under the authority of the Manchu emperors of China.

Andrew Sharp

Further Reading

Dyer, Svetlana. (1994) "Dungans." In *Encyclopedia of World Cultures*. Vol. 6, *Russia and Eurasia/China*. Edited by Paul Friedrich and Norma Diamond. New York: Macmillan, 107–111.

DUONG VAN MINH

DUONG VAN MINH (1916–2001), last president of the Republic of Vietnam. Duong Van Minh was born in 1916 in My Tho in the Mekong Delta. He received military training in France and in 1955 became an army officer in the Republic of Vietnam. Known as "Big Minh" because of his size (he was over six feet tall), he gained notoriety in 1956 when he captured Hoa Hao sect leader Ba Cut and had him publicly guillotined. Later that year, President Ngo Dinh Diem stripped him of military power by making him a "special adviser."

On 1 November 1963, Duong Van Minh headed the Revolutionary Military Council that ousted Ngo Dinh Diem (1901–1963) from power. The following day, Diem and his brother Nhu were assassinated, reportedly on Minh's orders. In January 1964, Minh was overthrown in a coup led by General Nguyen Kahn. In 1971, Minh ran for the presidency of the Republic of Vietnam but withdrew because he could not seriously challenge Nguyen Van Thieu (1923–2001).

In April 1975, President Thieu resigned and Vice President Tran Van Huong appointed Minh president. He was the Republic of Vietnam's last president. On 30 April 1975, he was arrested when North Vietnamese army forces marched into the presidential palace. In 1983, he immigrated to France.

Micheline R. Lessard

Further Reading

Duiker, William. (1981) *The Communist Road to Power in Vietnam*. Boulder, CO: Westview Press.

Kahin, George McT. (1987) *Intervention: How America Became Involved in Vietnam*. New York: Anchor.

Karnow, Stanley. (1983) *Vietnam: A History*. New York: Viking.

DURRANI Durrani was the dynasty that ruled Afghanistan from 1747 to 1842. It was founded by Ahmad Shah Abdali (1722?–1773), who gained his power and prestige through successful raids on India. He was elected king by a tribal council in Kandahar and adopted the title Durr-e-Durran (the pearl of pearls); from the title the dynasty acquired its name "Durrani."

It was during Ahmad Shah's rule that Afghanistan became an empire. By uniting the various warring factions, he was able to extend Afghan rule from Delhi, Kashmir, and the Punjab to Meshed and from the Amu Dar'ya River to the Arabian Sea. Thus, Afghanistan became the second-largest Muslim empire, surpassed in size only by the Ottoman empire to the west.

After Ahmad Shah's death in 1773, rule passed to his son Timur Shah (reigned 1773–1793), who spent most his reign suppressing uprisings. The fifth and last ruler of the dynasty, Shah Shoja (1780–1842), concluded a treaty with the British in India by which he agreed to oppose any passage of foreign troops through Afghanistan. This move was to negate Napoleon's plan to invade India with the help of Russia from the north. Eventually, Shah Shoja was overthrown by the Barakzai brothers, who in 1826 founded their own dynasty, which lasted until 1973, when Zahir Shah (b. 1914) abdicated. The Barakzai dynasty may once again play a role in Afghanistan, now that Zahir Shah has returned to Kabul, his old capital.

Nirmal Dass

Further Reading

MacMunn, George Fletcher. (1929). *From Darius to Amanullah*. London: G. Bell.

Singh, Ganda. (1959) *Ahmad Shah Durrani: Father of Modern Afghanistan*. London: Asia Publishing House.

DUSHANBE (2002 est. pop. 581,000). Formerly named Stalinabad (1929–1961), Dushanbe is the administrative, industrial, and cultural center of Tajikistan, a small republic adjacent to Afghanistan, China, and other Soviet Central Asian successor states. The site appears to be level, but it is actually a series of gently sloping and rocky alluvial fans at the base of the Pamir and Hissar mountains in Southwest Tajikistan. The Varzob and Kofanihon Rivers flow through the city. Rough roads connect it to Tashkent, Uzbekistan (314 kilometers to the north), and the Afghanistan frontier post of Termez (230 kilometers to the south). The city's 690-meter elevation and interior Central Asian location produce a long, hot summer lasting from May until September, where many days exceed 38° C. Mountain breezes ameliorate the intense July and August heat. The cold winter (0° C January mean) lasts from November through February. An average 85 millimeter (3.3 inches) of precipitation arrives during heavy spring rains or sporadic winter snowfall.

Dushanbe began as three small settlements of modest single-story rock and mud structures that served as the eastern administrative center of the Bukhara khanate until 1920 when Soviet troops toppled the emir. The heavy fighting destroyed many buildings. In 1924 the Soviets designated Dushanbe the capital of the new Tajik Autonomous S.S.R. They combined the three settlements and initiated rapid development and population growth that lasted until Tajik independence in 1991. The Transcaspian railroad linked Dushanbe with Turkmenistan in 1929, transforming the Monday bazaar into a daily event that remains its commercial and social heart. The city center offers broad tree-lined streets bounded by multistory Soviet-era government buildings. The many fountains, shaded plazas, and *chaikhanas* (teahouses) invite much bicycle and pedestrian traffic. Elsewhere, high-rise concrete apartment blocks alternate with pre-Soviet mud and brick structures designed to mitigate the severe earthquake hazard.

Dushanbe is also the financial and commercial center of Tajikistan. Aluminum and cement factories, large textile combines, and manufacturing plants for looms, electric cable, and appliances are nearby. It was the primary staging and supply center for the 1979–1989 Soviet-Afghan war. It remains an important military crossroads. Since independence, Dushanbe has been the center of a prolonged civil war between competing ethnoreligious and political factions. The violence severely damaged the infrastructure and discouraged most foreign investment. The manufacturing sector is facing an uncertain future.

There are many fine parks; a zoo; two live theaters and an opera house; hospitals; medical, teacher-education, agricultural, and polytechnic institutes; the Tajik Academy of Sciences (1951); and the Tajik State University (1948). The Firdowsi Library houses an impressive collection of medieval Islamic manuscripts. The abrupt termination of Soviet support is jeopardizing these institutions. The predominantly Tajik and Russian population includes Kirghiz, Kazakh, Uzbek, Tatar, and Ukrainian minorities. Since 1991 *ostravechnio* (outmigration of Russians) and persistent refugee movements inside and outside of Dushanbe have altered the demographic profile.

Stephen F. Cunha

Further Reading

Allworth, Edward. (1994) *Central Asia: 130 Years of Russian Dominance, A Historical Overview.* Durham, NC: Duke University Press.

Djalili, Mohammad-Reza, ed. (1998) *Tajikistan: The Trials of Independence.* Richmond, U.K.: Curzon Press.

The insignia of the Dutch East India Company on a building in the Netherlands in 1997. (DAVE BARTRUFF/CORBIS)

DUTCH EAST INDIA COMPANY The Dutch East India Company, or Vereenigde Oostindische Compagnie (VOC), was formed in 1602. VOC consisted of sixty companies aimed at monopolizing the spice trade, expanding Dutch colonial influence, and reducing competition from other commercial powers. The government of the Netherlands supported VOC financially, as well as giving it immense powers, including the right to trade, maintain military forces, take possession of territories, declare war, and make peace. At the height of its power, the company had roughly 150 trading vessels, 40 warships, and 10,000 soldiers.

With such power and authority, VOC dominated the spice industry, especially the cinnamon, clove, and nutmeg trade in the East Indies during the seventeenth and eighteenth centuries. The company's Asian base was in Batavia (modern Jakarta), which came under Dutch control in 1619. In 1650, VOC merchants became the first Europeans settlers in South Africa on the Cape of Good Hope; in 1652, the Cape of Good Hope became a Dutch colony, remaining so until taken over by Great Britain in 1814. The company's influence extended to Cape Town, which emerged as a key supply point for provisioning Dutch ships with food, water, and other goods. By 1670, VOC was the richest company in the world, controlling trade from the Cape of Good Hope to the Straits of Magellan.

In the Malay archipelago, VOC controlled the spice trade in Banda, Ternate, Grisek, Patani, Aceh, Johore, and Bantam. After its capture in 1605, Amboina (now Ambon) became the first Dutch possession in the East. Subsequently, VOC controlled and colonized local rulers, and drove the British and Portuguese from the Malay archipelago and Ceylon. The Anglo Dutch Treaty of 1824, which divided the Malay archipelago into British and Dutch spheres of influence, further enabled VOC to establish Dutch rule in Indonesia.

Throughout its existence, however, VOC had trouble maintaining its monopoly, as strong competition came from other European powers; the English, Portuguese, and Spanish challenged the Dutch whenever possible, as they too wanted a share of the spice trade. By the late eighteenth century, Chinese tea and textiles were more in demand than spices, and in 1789 VOC was disbanded, due in part to corruption, rising debts, and competition from other traders. VOC was not merely a company that monopolized world trade, but was also the sole representative of Dutch political power in the East Indies for nearly 200 years.

Geetha Govindasamy

Further Reading

Boxer, Charles Ralph. (1979) *Jan Compagnie in War and Peace, 1602–1799: A Short History of the Dutch East India Company.* Hong Kong: Heinemann Asia.

Lewis, Dianne. (1995) *Jan Compagnie in the Straits of Malacca 1641–1795.* Athens, OH: Ohio University Center for International Studies.

Lohuizen, Jan van. (1961) *The Dutch East India Company and Mysore.* The Hague, Netherlands: M. Nifhoff.

Prakash, Om. (1985) *Dutch East India Company and the Economy of Bengal 1630–1720.* Princeton, NJ: Princeton University Press.

Vos, Rentouit. (1993) *Gentle Janus, Merchant Prince: the VOC and the Tightrope of Diplomacy in the Malay World.* Leiden, Netherlands: KITLV Press.

DUTCH IN SOUTHEAST ASIA

In the early 1600s, two maritime nations, Britain and the Netherlands, were emerging as powerful players in the world economy. Seeking to challenge the network of the Portuguese and the Spanish, who had divided the non-European world between them under the authority of a Papal Bull (edict), the two emerging Protestant nations sought to control the spice trade. In 1602 the Vereenigde Oostindische Compagnie (VOC, or the Dutch East India Company) was formed to gain a share of this lucrative spice trade. Britain and the Netherlands, although rivals in many senses, came to an agreement to divide trade with Asia. The Dutch, notably under Batavia-based governor-general Jan Pieterszoon Coen in the early 1600s, aimed to achieve a stranglehold on the spice trade. In 1641, with the help of the Sultan of Aceh, the Dutch captured Melaka (Malacca) from the Portuguese and at this point the strategic balance shifted in favor of the Netherlands.

Dutch Ascendancy

Like the Portuguese before them, the Dutch initially sought to take control of small strategic ports, while local potentates were left undisturbed to rule over the hinterlands. Initially this involved a series of processing factories scattered around India and what is now Indonesia, as well as the seizure of territory in Taiwan (Formosa), Sri Lanka, the west coast of Malaya (including Melaka), and Batavia, Flores, and Maluku

A Dutch trading building in the former colony of Sulawesi, Indonesia. (JEREMY HORNER/CORBIS)

in the Dutch East Indies (later known as Indonesia). The VOC forced local rulers to deliver spices at fixed prices and banned any trade with other outside powers in order to ensure the Dutch monopoly. Regular patrols were mounted to police these rules. The strategic possessions the VOC held in Southeast Asia were to enable the export of such spices as nutmeg and mace, cloves, and pepper.

Dutch control over Indonesia, from their arrival in the early seventeenth century, took more than three hundred years to complete and largely occurred without resort to large-scale conventional warfare, although rebellions were commonplace. There was no actual strategic decision or plan to assume control over the entire archipelago, but the Dutch found it necessary to control more and more of the hinterlands to prevent rebellions and attacks. After interfering in rivalry and dynastic disputes among the various Javanese kingdoms, the Dutch commercial empire had authority over Java by 1800. The empire of the Netherlands grew as far as possible within the geographical confines of neighboring empires. However, this imperial overstretch, which required funding a growing administration and military campaigns, meant that by 1799 the VOC was bankrupt and was subsequently abolished. In the first half of the nineteenth century the Dutch military fought a series of wars of against local resistance in Sumatra, Java, and Bali.

After 1800, pressure grew in the Netherlands to improve the livelihoods of the people of the Dutch East Indies. Pressure in the Netherlands, coupled with demands for greater self determination inside the Dutch East Indies, led to the development of the "Ethical Policy" to devolve authority to Indonesia, provide health and education, and develop infrastructure. The Netherlands came to have far greater contact with the Indonesian people, but ultimately failed to keep vague promises of independence. The Ethical Policy helped unify the disparate ethnic groups into a collective consciousness. Significant gains were made in public health, resulting in the biggest population explosion that maritime Southeast Asia had ever seen—Java alone increased from a population of 4.5 million in 1815 to nearly 35 million a century later. One major reason for this exponential increase was the end, under the authority of Dutch overlordship (the so-called Pax Neerlandica), of regular warfare between the smaller feudal kingdoms. However, this belated attempt at development could not alter the fact that the rationale for the Dutch presence was the exploitation of natural resources and labor to generate capital for the Netherlands. It did nothing to undermine calls for independence; on the contrary, young Indonesian intellectuals such as independence leaders Sukarno (1901–1970) and Mohammad Hatta (1902–1980) trained in the Netherlands and learned about democracy, nationalism, and self-determination. Powerful nationalist (and religious) movements emerged in the Dutch East Indies from the first half of the nineteenth century until the Japanese invasion, in contrast to the localized rebellions of earlier times in Sumatra and Java.

Japanese Occupation and Its Aftermath

Japanese forces arrived in Indonesia in January 1942, primarily to seize the oilfields of the coastal areas of Sumatra and Kalimantan. Many Indonesians welcomed the Japanese as liberators but soon discovered that their new master was both far more ruthless and not serious about promises of independence. However, it was the Japanese invasion that broke Dutch rule; nationalists, led by Sukarno (later to be the first president of Indonesia) cooperated with the Japanese authorities as a means of gaining independence.

The Japanese left Indonesia in August 1945, and Sukarno and Hatta announced independence and the creation of the Republic of Indonesia. The return of Dutch administrators, initially backed by British troops, sparked a rebellion in Java and Sumatra. Against the advice of the British, who were preparing the Indian subcontinent and Burma (now Myanmar) for independence, in July 1947, the Dutch had marshaled enough forces (after tricking the Indonesian leaders through a peace agreement) to launch a "police action" to retake West and East Java, followed by a second police action in December 1948 to retake the remaining territory. With Sukarno and Hatta imprisoned, the Indonesian army of former Dutch officers and Japanese-trained troops under General Soedirman decided that armed revolution was the only solution and launched a fierce counterattack. This time, the United Nations condemned Dutch actions, while large numbers of Dutch soldiers, themselves former victims of the Nazi occupation, had no will to enforce Dutch imperial rule. The Dutch left Indonesia on 27 December 1949. They left behind a country of more than two hundred ethnic groups that had little in common except the experience of Dutch colonial rule and bonds forged between the intelligentsia as a result of the Ethnical Policy, which had done little to prepare for independence. By attempting to recolonize Indonesia after World War II, the Dutch helped enshrine the Indonesian army as the "protector of society" that continues to be the justification for its interference in civil affairs.

Anthony L. Smith

Further Reading

Dixon, Chris. (1991) *South East Asia in the World-Economy*. Cambridge, U.K.: Cambridge University Press.

Hyma, Albert. (1942) *Dutch in the Far East: A History of the Dutch Commercial and Colonial Empire*. Ann Arbor, MI: George Wahr Publishing Co.

Vlekke, Bernard H. M. (1945) *The Story of the Dutch East Indies*. Cambridge, MA: Harvard University Press.

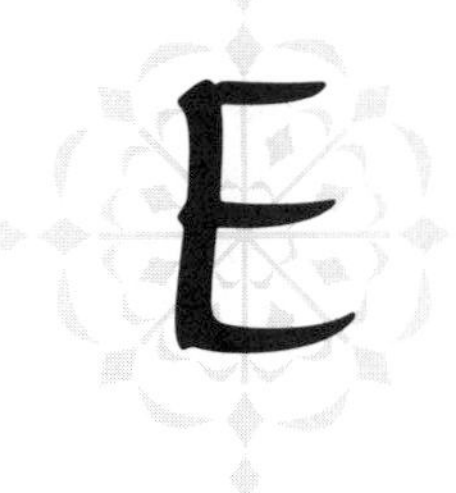

EARTHQUAKES Earthquakes are the result of rocks breaking under stress. The constant movement of the tectonic plates that cover the earth's thin outer crust, or lithosphere, causes stress to build up in the rocks beneath the earth's surface. Rocks adjust to this stress over time by folding, but occasionally the stress is released, creating seismic or energy waves that cause the sudden and sometimes disastrous vibrations known as earthquakes. Earthquakes occur throughout the world, but mainly along narrow belts marking the boundaries of the earth's major tectonic plates. Ninety percent of all earthquakes take place at these plate boundaries, and about two-thirds of all large earthquakes are located in the circum-Pacific belt. This tectonic collision zone is one of the most active in the world and stretches from the Aleutians in the North Pacific through Japan, Taiwan, the Philippines, and Indonesia to the Himalayas in northern India. Although there are hundreds of earthquakes in this belt each year, few are felt by the population. However, there have been more than sixty large earthquakes registering 7.0 or higher on the Richter scale in the last

An elderly women walks in the ruins of Kobe following the 1995 earthquake which destroyed much of the city and killed over 6,000 people. (REUTERS NEWMEDIA INC./CORBIS)

EXPLAINING EARTHQUAKES IN SOUTH ASIA

Throughout human history and across cultures, earthquakes have been terrifying events that are beyond human control. Numerous explanations have been set for earthquakes. The following is the explanation of the Andaman Islanders, the indigenous people of the islands of the same name in the Bay of Bengal.

> The Andaman Islands are occasionally visited by earthquakes. An Aka-Kede account of how earthquakes are caused is that when a man dies he goes to the spirit world which is beneath the earth. The spirits hold a ceremony. My informant spoke of the ceremony as Kimil, which is the name of the initiation ceremonies. At this ceremony they have a dance similar to the peace-making dance . . . but instead of erecting a screen such as is used in that ceremony, they make use of the rainbow. As they shake the rainbow in dancing this causes earthquakes. The ceremony which newly-arrived spirits have to undergo in the world after death is a *poroto kimil*, i.e., the initiate eats *poroto* (Caryota sobolifera).

Source: A. R. Radcliffe-Brown. (1922) *The Andaman Islanders: A Study in Social Anthropology.* Cambridge, U.K.: University Press, 146–147.

quarter century, the largest of which released twenty times more energy than the annual energy consumption of the United States. Significant property damage and loss of life can result from earthquakes and the secondary hazards associated with these events, especially when they occur near urban centers or areas of high population density.

Earthquakes occurring at weak points in the interior of plates, away from the major plate boundaries, are more difficult to explain. They do not occur according to well-defined patterns like those at plate boundaries. Scientists have not yet been able to model their occurrence so that forecasts of time, place, and size of future earthquakes could be made. China, for example, experiences numerous intraplate earthquakes hundreds of miles toward the interior of the country. Since 1990 eight major intraplate quakes of 5.2 to 7.1 on the Richter scale have been recorded in Yunnan, Hebei, Sichuan, and Menglian provinces in China.

The vibrations, or seismic waves, from an earthquake travel outward in all directions from the fault and, if the earthquake is large enough, are recorded around the world on special measuring instruments called seismographs. A seismograph measures the amplitude of the energy (or seismic waves) released; the measurement is expressed on the Richter scale. The most severe earthquakes recorded to date have not exceeded 9.0 on this scale, although there may be hundreds of low-magnitude quakes measuring 3 or 4 in Asia alone in a single year. Energy release and earthquake magnitude can be poor guides to the hazardous impact of earthquakes, however, because the duration of ground shaking is not accounted for in this scale. The extent of that hazard depends on many other factors, such as distance from the epicenter, rock and soil conditions, population density, and types of building construction.

Although ground shaking is the primary earthquake hazard and the cause of much structural damage and human injury, there are also important secondary hazards. Liquefaction, which happens when loosely packed, waterlogged sediments lose their strength in response to strong shaking, can damage structural foundations of buildings and highways, cause buildings to settle or tilt, and produce submarine avalanches that can destroy harbor facilities and break underwater telecommunication cables. Landslides and rock and snow avalanches can also result from earthquakes. Landslides triggered by earthquakes often cause more destruction than the quakes themselves. Since 1964 landslides resulting from large-magnitude earthquakes in Japan have accounted for more than half of all earthquake-related deaths. The most characteristic secondary earthquake-related hazard is the seismic sea wave, or tsunami. Most tsunamis result from tectonic displacement of the seabed associated with large shallow-focus earthquakes under the oceans, but can also be caused by exploding volcanic islands. These waves may reach 100 feet or higher and can travel across the ocean at speeds as great as 150 kilometers per hour. The 1883 volcanic eruption of Krakatau Island in Indonesia generated a tsunami that killed more than thirty-six thousand people in nearby Java and Sumatra. More than 370 tsunamis were observed in the Pacific from 1900 to 1980; Japan is particularly vulnerable to these events, especially on the eastern margins of the large island of Honshu.

Twentieth-Century Occurrences

More than one-half of the most destructive earthquakes in the twentieth century, those causing five thousand or more deaths, have taken place in Asia.

The three largest of these occurred in China, each with more than 200,000 deaths. The 1923 Tokyo-Yokohama earthquake resulted in 143,000 deaths. Indonesia, located astride the boundaries of the Indo-Australian and Eurasian plates, records hundreds of quakes each year; between 1994 and 2000 twelve registered 4.7 to 7.6 on the Richter scale. India had at least five major quakes of 6.2 to 8.4 magnitude in the twentieth century, each resulting in tens of thousands dead and injured. When earthquakes take place near urban centers or more densely settled areas, the impact can be catastrophic. The 1995 Kobe, Japan, earthquake, for example, was measured at a relatively moderate level of 6.9 but caused significant damage and loss of life because it took place in a densely populated port and industrial city. More than 5,500 people were killed and more than 300,000 left homeless due to shock waves, fires, and the collapse of housing built to withstand tropical cyclones but not earthquakes. A similarly disastrous earthquake registering 7.6 on the Richter scale hit northwestern Taiwan in June 2000, causing millions of dollars in property damage, killing 2,100 people, and injuring more than 8,000.

Programs for earthquake disaster preparedness and management in countries throughout the Asia Pacific region are quite varied. The 1990s saw a shift away from local disaster relief activities to increased preparedness and preventive strategies in how regional governments and disaster management organizations respond to earthquake hazards. Enhanced preparedness measures should be augmented with preventive strategies to mitigate earthquake hazards, link rehabilitation with sustainable human development, and focus on community-based disaster management (CBDM) approaches. For CBDM approaches to gain wider support and be more effective, however, there must be greater acceptance by national governments throughout the region. A number of international agencies, regional disaster training groups, and private philanthropic and nongovernmental organizations are increasingly engaged in discussing and planning new earthquake and disaster management strategies in this part of the world. Groups that are involved include the Asian Disaster Preparedness Center, the ASEAN Earthquake Information Center, the United Nations Development Program, the United Nations High Commission for Refugees, CARE, and Save the Children, among others. Information and lessons learned from other earthquake-prone areas of the world help to improve earthquake forecasting, disaster preparedness, and mitigation for this region of the world. This level of international collaboration is an encouraging development for the millions of people who are vulnerable to the social and economic consequences of earthquakes in Asia.

James Hafner

Further Reading

Merrits, Dorothy, Andrew Dew Wet, and Kristen Menking. (1998) *Environmental Geology: An Earth System Science Approach*. New York: W. H. Freeman and Company.

Smith, Kenneth. (1996) *Environmental Hazards: Assessing Risk and Reducing Disaster*. London and New York: Routledge.

Strahler, Alan, and Arthur Strahler. (1994) *Introducing Physical Geography*. New York: John Wiley & Sons, Inc.

EAST CHINA SEA The East China Sea (Dong Hai) constitutes part of the Western Pacific. It is 1,296 kilometers long from the north to the south and 740 kilometers wide from the east to the west and covers an area of 790,000 square kilometers. In the north, it borders on the Yellow Sea (Huang Hai), and in the east it borders on Jiangsu, Zhejiang, and Fujian provinces of the Chinese mainland. In the south, the East China Sea is connected to the South China Sea (Nan Hai) through the Taiwan Strait. The southern Japanese archipelago with the Ryukyu Islands constitutes the eastern border. Except for an area around the Ryukyu Islands, where depths up to 2,700 meters have been measured, the East China Sea is on a shallow continental shelf most of which is less than 200 meters deep. The Chang (Yangtze) River flows into the East China Sea, leaving huge deposits of sediment. The climate is subtropical, and monsoon winds with summer rain predominate in the area. The East China Sea is China's most important marine fishing area, and the catches of hairtail, small and large yellow croaker, and cuttlefish account for two-thirds of China's total catch. Shanghai, just south of the mouth of the Chang River, is the largest port bordering the sea and also is the center for food processing.

Bent Nielsen

Further Reading

Choi, B. H. (1980) *A Tidal Model of the Yellow Sea and the Eastern China Sea*. Seoul: KORDI report.

Morgan, Joseph, and Mark J. Valencia, eds. (1992) *Atlas for Marine Policy in East Asian Seas*. Berkeley and Los Angeles: University of California Press.

EAST INDIA COMPANY. See **British East India Company; Dutch East India Company; French East India Company.**

EAST TIMOR—PROFILE (2001 est. pop. 800,000). On 20 May 2002, the former Portuguese colony of East Timor, occupied by Indonesia in 1976, became the world's newest independent state. East Timor burst into world attention on 30 August 1999, following a flawed U.N.-supervised referendum on independence that left Indonesian armed forces in charge of security. When almost 80 percent of registered voters rejected integration with Indonesia, a full-blown campaign of terror orchestrated by the Indonesian led to the destruction of 70 percent of East Timor's infrastructure. Many Timorese were murdered, kidnapped, or disappeared. As many as 500,000 were displaced from their homes. In response to international outrage, the U.N. Security Council mandated an Australian-led international force (INTERFET) to restore security and supervise the withdrawal of Indonesian occupation forces. Deemed successful, INTERFET was subsequently transformed on 25 October 1999 into a U.N. blue beret force (United Nations Transitional Administration for East Timor) to provide security pending a transition to full independence.

Topography and People

Of recent geological formation, the island of Timor features a mountainous interior, with its highest peak, Tata Mai Lau, rising 3,000 meters above sea level. Situated at the extreme east of the Lesser Sunda chain, Timor island is subject to great climatic contrasts between monsoon seasons, and is ecologically more vulnerable than islands to the west. The southern coast supports an extensive coastal plain, which is more restricted in the north, where mountain spurs extend to the sea. The diverse landscape is matched by a variety of climatic zones and supports a diversity of vegetation: swamps on the plains, pockets of tropical rain forest, and extensive eucalyptus forests on the mountain slopes.

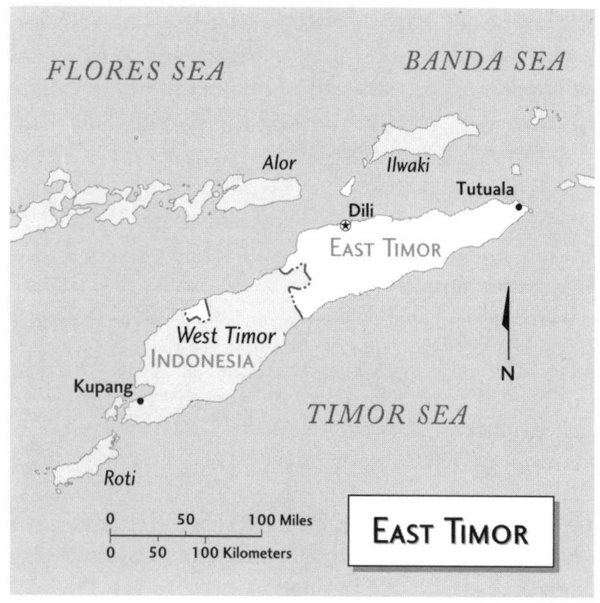

While anthropologists differ as to specifics, there is broad agreement that eastern Timor was populated by successive waves of Malays and proto-Malays, and also Papuan elements, although none exist today in pure form. The linguistic situation is no less complex: there are sixteen distinct languages in the whole of Timor, thirteen of which are spoken in East Timor. Most of these fall into either the Austronesian or Papuan language families. Tetum, also spoken in parts of West Timor, serves as lingua franca in East Timor.

The Traditional Political System

Sharing cultural and political traditions with other islands and societies in the Lesser Sunda Islands, Timor's traditional political system conforms to what Dutch anthropologist F. A. E. van Wouden calls a "segmented society" (one divided along ethnic lines). Not directly touched by Indian or Islamic influences, Timor never developed a centralized government, aside from a highly mythologized center believed to have been located in Wehale, in West Timor, in what would eventually become Dutch territory. In fact, geography and the complex peopling of the island bequeathed many competing and warring societies, often in conflict with each other and with outsiders who came in search of Timor's coveted sandalwood. Real power was in the hands of the *"liurai,"* a Portugalized term meaning "little king." While the traditional lineage of the *liurai* was ruptured by the Portuguese after the Boaventura rebellion of 1911–1912 in order to win and cement new alliances, they continued to wield considerable local influence, surviving even the Indonesian occupation.

The Portuguese Colonial System

First reached by Portuguese traders and missionaries in the early 1500s, the island of Timor was ruled from the early 1700s by Portuguese governors sent first to the enclave of Oeccuse, and then, with the transfer of the seat of government in 1776, to Dili, the present capital. Although Timor was distant and neglected within its empire, Portugal nevertheless developed a successful coffee plantation system, as well as bequeathing the Timorese a Catholic and Portuguese heritage.

In the modern period, notably after the 1911–1912 rebellion, the Portuguese introduced new forms of local government around military posts centered on districts, but in a classical colonial system that saw little Timorese representation in the upper echelons of colonial administration. The rising tide of anticolonial nationalism in Southeast Asia bypassed eastern Timor. The major threat to the status quo was always Indonesia, as proven by an Indonesian separatist rebellion in the Viqueque district of eastern East Timor in 1959, suppressed with much loss of life.

Treated as part colony, part protectorate, a system that saw metropolitan Portugal subsidize only a meager developmental budget—which left most Timorese outside the coffee economy living in an unmonetized or subsistence economy—there is a sense that Portugal actually conserved rather than dissolved feudal bonds and cultural forms.

Portuguese political life atrophied under the premiership of Antonio de Oliveira Salazar (1932–1968) and his successor, Marcello Caetano (1968–1974), but with Lisbon's "flower revolution" of 25 April 1974, in which reformist soldiers replaced the dictatorship, the independence of Timor was placed squarely on the table, and political parties sanctioned. But just as East Timor's majority Fretilin party prevailed in a short civil war against its adversary, União Democratica Timorenses, and proclaimed a democratic republic on 28 November 1975, Timor was robbed of its short-lived independence by invading Indonesian forces. After successfully waging a guerrilla war of resistance against the Indonesian occupier, the armed wing of Fretilin (Falintil) only grew in stature with the capture and incarceration of its leader, José "Xanana" Gusmão (born 1946 in Manatuto district of East Timor), in 1992. As leader of CNRT, an umbrella front conjoining Fretilin and other parties and personalities, Gusmão, along with countrymen Bishop Carlos Ximenes Belo and José Ramos-Horta (recipients of the 1996 Nobel Peace Prize), became an international symbol of East Timor's struggle for freedom and justice.

The Indonesian Colonial System

Following an invasion on 7 December 1975, East Timor was annexed as the twenty-seventh province of the Republic of Indonesia. The Jakarta government reproduced in East Timor all branches and agencies of its own central and provincial governments. In a classic case of internal colonialism in which most East Timorese were economically and politically marginalized, Indonesian rule was supported not only by a cadre of collaborators, but also by an iron fist. The foremost Indonesian achievement in East Timor was undoubtedly the introduction of a universal education system that saw large numbers of Timorese students rise through the educational hierarchy, some attending universities in Indonesia. The other tangible achievement of Indonesian rule was the expansion of the infrastructure bequeathed by the Portuguese. Both education and infrastructure served the counterinsurgency aims of the Indonesian military, as did such forms of population control as resettlement villages and the introduction of large numbers of Indonesian settlers. Sustained and repressive military actions, however, not only led to the deaths of up to one-third of the population of East Timor, but also destroyed the fabric of traditional Timorese society.

Rule under the United Nations Transitional Administration

Headed by a Brazilian diplomat, Sergio Vieira de Melo, answering directly to the U.N. secretary-general, and staffed by some one thousand international civil servants, the United Nations Transitional Administration for East Timor (UNTAET) formed the de facto government in East Timor from early 2000 until its dissolution in May 2002. UNTAET was also backed by eight thousand international peacekeepers, along with hundreds of civilian police. UNTAET was empowered to make and enforce laws, to enter into international agreements (such as the renegotiation of the Timor Gap Treaty), and to supervise all aspects of governance. UNTAET decrees covered the establishment of a central banking system, the nomination of the U.S. dollar as official currency, the creation of a police force, the rebuilding of the justice system, the creation of a civil-service commission, and the recruitment of a seven-thousand-member civil service. Nevertheless, in deference to East Timorese opinion, and sometimes frustration owing to disagreement with East Timorese over administrative issues, UNTAET sanctioned the establishment of a transitional National Consultative Council alongside a parallel East Timor Transitional Administration, thereby speeding up the "Timorization" process.

In mid-2001 UNTAET focused on drawing up electoral laws and the norms for the creation of political parties. An election in which sixteen political parties took part was conducted on 30 August 2001 for a second transitional Constitutional Assembly; Fretilin emerged victorious. Fretilin Vice President Mari Alkatiri was appointed the country's first chief minister. The main task of the transitional assembly was to debate and approve the new nation's constitution.

Having adopted both Portuguese and Tetum as official languages, the new Democratic Republic of East Timor remains true to its long history under European colonialism. Under East Timor's new constitution, East Timor will be governed by a mixed presidential and cabinet system; church and state will be separated. East Timor vows to uphold a democratic system with free institutions, but as a desperately poor country, it will remain dependent upon the goodwill of international donors for years to come. The United Nations maintains a scaled-down presence in East Timor to further assist in capacity building and to guarantee East Timor's security.

Geoffrey C. Gunn

See also: **United Nations in East Timor**

Further Reading

Dunn, James. (1983) *Timor: A People Betrayed.* Milton, Australia: Jacaranda Press.

Gunn, Geoffrey C. (1997) *East Timor and the United Nations: The Case for Intervention.* Lawrenceville, NJ: Red Sea Press.

———. (1999) *Timor Loro Sae: 500 Years.* Macau, China: Livros do Oriente.

EASTERN GHATS The Eastern Ghats are a somewhat fractured mountain range running down much of eastern India and thus forming the eastern border of the Dekkan Plateau. The geological formation is granite, with gneiss and mica slate. The Eastern Ghats rise in the northern part of Orissa and then strike in a south-southwesterly direction, parallel to the coast and at a distance of from 80 to 250 kilometers from it. There is thus a broad and fertile coastal plain, much of it devoted to rice and coconut cultivation. However, in the Ganjam and Visakhapattinam areas, the Ghats nearly abut on the coast; here too are found the highest peaks. With several wide breaks to allow the eastward passage of some major rivers, the Godavari, Kistna, and Kaveri, the chain continues in the same direction until it reaches South Arcot district in Tamil Nadu. Then, adopting a more westerly direction, the Eastern Ghats finally merge with the Western Ghats in the high Nilgiri Plateau. Outliers are found further south in Tiruchirappalli and Tinnevelli Districts. The average elevation of the Eastern Ghats is about 450 meters; they are thus considerably lower than the Western Ghats. In Orissa, Chhattisgarh, and Andhra Pradesh, the hills are inhabited mainly by tribal people who have a mixed farming economy supplemented by some hunting and gathering.

Paul Hockings

EASTERN LEARNING. See **Tonghak.**

EASTERN ORTHODOX CHURCH The Eastern Orthodox (from Greek "right believing") faith is directly descended from the spiritual communities established by the apostles of Jesus Christ in the eastern Mediterranean region; Eastern Orthodox Christianity officially separated from the Western (Roman Catholic) branch of the Christian church in 1054, though the split had begun centuries earlier with the division of the Roman empire. Today Eastern Orthodoxy flourishes in Greece as the Greek Orthodox Church. The Russian, Bulgarian, Romanian, Serbian, and Georgian Orthodox churches have also reemerged following the collapse of Communism in Eastern Europe in the 1980s and 1990s. Sizable Orthodox populations also exist in America and Australia.

The majority of early Christian communities, founded by St. Paul or his followers, shared common beliefs and liturgy, but worship was conducted in different languages. However, Syrian beliefs, originating from St. Thomas, emphasized the humanity of Christ. After the Roman emperor Constantine I (324–337) first adopted Christianity, he assumed the secular leadership of the Church and the patriarch of Constantinople (his capital) laid claim to religious authority over the whole church. Constantinople remained the center of Eastern Orthodoxy until the city fell to the Turks in 1453. Even today the patriarch of Constantinople has authority over the Greek communities in Turkey, the Greek islands, northern Greece, and the rest of the world. The other spiritual leaders of the early Christian church were the patriarchs of Rome, Alexandria, Antioch, and Jerusalem.

THE ORTHODOX CHURCH

"The Church also possesses the great tradition of the Hesychastic and ascetic fathers, the liturgical tradition, the immutable tradition of theological experience and thought, and the cultivation of letters and fine arts, particularly Byzantine iconography and music, as well as the equally important tradition of social philanthropy and conciliatory spirit."

Source: Patriarch Bartolomeos, reported by the *Turkish Daily News*, April 2000.

An Orthodox priest with prayer candles in the Phokas Orthodox Church in Istanbul in 1997. (DAVE BARTRUFF/CORBIS)

Early Offshoots of Eastern Orthodoxy and the Advent of Islam

Eastern Orthodoxy recognizes the authority of seven ecumenical councils, starting with the first Council of Nicaea (325), which were convened to decide matters of doctrine. Constantine imposed his personality on the council of Nicaea, but subsequently interpatriarchal rivalry emphasized differences. At the third council (the Council of Ephesus, 431), the Nestorian church diverged, and at the fourth council (the Council of Chalcedon, 451), dispute about the nature of Jesus caused the Armenian, Syrian, and Coptic churches to secede. The other councils were the first, second, and third Councils of Constantinople (381, 553, and 680) and the second Council of Nicaea (787).

From the sixth century many Asian and Mediterranean Christians came under Persian and then Islamic Arab rule. The conquerors divided the Orthodox population into separate self-governing communities led by their own patriarchs. Except during times of war, Arab occupation did not cut cross-border contacts; the three Eastern patriarchs (of Alexandria, Antioch, and Jerusalem) and bishops were able to attend church councils; pilgrims continued to visit the shrines in the Holy Land. The Orthodox church in Asia was at its maximum extent in around 901, with 405 bishops, including fifty-four metropolitans and fifty autocephalous (independent) bishops; Orthodox missionaries also converted the Slavs, Bulgars, and Russians.

The Split between Eastern and Western Christianity

Eastern and Western Christianity diverged gradually. In 800 Pope Leo III anointed Charlemagne as Holy Roman Emperor, thus placing the Western church under the protection of France; from this time forward Western Christianity regarded the Roman pope as the prime religious authority. The Eastern Church, however, asserted its historical precedence, and differences between East and West eventually led to a complete schism in 1054. Among the doctrinal differences dividing Eastern Orthodox and Western believers is the nature of the relation of elements of the divine trinity (Father, Son, and Holy Spirit.) The Nicene creed adopted by the Western Church says that the Holy Spirit proceeds "from the father and the son," but the Eastern Church believes that the Holy Spirit proceeds from the Father alone. The final insurmountable issue was a dispute over who had jurisdiction where: Pope Leo IX and Michael Cerularius, the patriarch of Constantinople, mutually excommunicated each other. Rome and Byzantium cooperated to some degree during the Crusades, but in 1204, during the Fourth Crusade, Westerners besieged and looted Constantinople.

Eastern Orthodoxy under Ottoman Rule

After the fall of Constantinople Sultan Mehmed II (1432–1481) set fairly generous rules for the surviving fifty thousand members of the Orthodox community and recognized the patriarch as the head of all the Christians in the Turkish empire. Saint Sophia, the central church in Orthodoxy, was immediately dedicated to Islam, but most churches remained in use. (Today, most surviving Orthodox churches in Turkey have become museums.) Superior training and knowledge of languages enabled much of the Orthodox community to monopolize the Turkish diplomatic service. The Orthodox patriarchate thus survived in Constantinople partly by collaboration with the Muslim overlords.

Informal leadership of Orthodoxy in time moved to the Russian church; in 1589 it received its own patriarch, but in 1721 Peter the Great (1672–1725) abolished it (it was reestablished in 1917). In the nineteenth century, when the Orthodox peoples of Asia were freed from Turkish rule, the Balkan states and Greece won church and state independence, and the patriarchate of Constantinople lost whatever religious powers it had enjoyed.

During World War I and the War of Turkish Independence Greco-Turkish animosities led to atrocities. The burning of Izmir is still referred to by Orthodox Greeks as the Catastrophe. In 1923 about 800,000 Greek Christians (Orthodox and Catholic) living in Turkey were exchanged with a population of

1.2 million Muslims living in Greece; about 100,000 Greek Christians, protected by the Treaty of Lausanne, remained in and around Istanbul. Today only an estimated 3,000 Greek Orthodox remain in Turkey.

Distinctions between Eastern Orthodoxy and Roman Catholicism Today

Orthodox doctrines have always lacked precision, partly due to the conviction that it is presumptuous to define God, partly because, in Byzantine times, theology was a universal intellectual hobby. Few doctrinal differences separate Orthodoxy from Catholic Christianity; the dividing issues remain the governance of the church, papal versus conciliar authority, and a married priesthood. The seven sacraments of Catholic Christianity (baptism, confirmation, marriage, holy orders, penance, anointing of the sick, and the Eucharist) are augmented in Eastern Orthodoxy by others for special occasions. Both churches rescinded the mutual excommunications of 1054 in the twentieth century, and following Roman Catholicism's Second Vatican Council (1962–1964), ecumenical dialogue between the Eastern Orthodox Church and the Roman Catholic Church was undertaken.

Kate Clow

Further Reading

Alexandris, Alexis. (1992) *The Greek Minority of Istanbul and Greek Turkish Relations, 1918–74.* Athens, Greece: Center for Asia Minor Studies.

Herrin, Judith. (1987) *The Formation of Christendom.* Princeton, NJ: Princeton University Press.

Runciman, Steve. (1968) *The Great Church in Captivity.* Cambridge, U.K.: Cambridge University Press.

EBINA DANJO (1856–1937), Japanese Christian leader and educator. Ebina Danjo, a native of Yanagawa in Japan's Chikugo Province (now a part of Fukuoka Prefecture), was a Christian leader and educator of the Meiji (1868–1912), Taisho (1912–1926), and Showa (1926–1989) periods. In 1872 Ebina attended the Kumamoto Yogakko, a school that was established in 1871 for Western studies, where he came under the influence of an American educator, Leroy Lansing Janes (1838–1909). He was then baptized. Thus, in 1876, converted to Christianity, he became a member of the Kumamoto Christian Band. He went to study at Doshisha (Doshisha University since 1920) in Kyoto under Niijima Jo (1843–1890). In 1879 Ebina became a pastor of the Annaka Church in Gumma Prefecture and traveled around Japan to spread Christianity. He was also engaged as a pastor in Kobe in 1893. It was especially when he was a pastor of the Hongo Church in Tokyo from 1897 to 1920 that he became known as a preacher and evangelist. In 1920 he also founded a Christian journal entitled *Shinjin* (New Man) and educated younger people such as Yoshino Sakuzo (1878–1933) and Suzuki Bunji (1885–1946). At Hongo, and as the head of Doshisha from 1920 to 1928, Ebina was a leading figure in the congregational church in Japan.

Nathalie Cavasin

Further Reading

Scheiner, Irwin. (1970) *Christian Converts and Social Protest in Meiji Japan.* Berkeley and Los Angeles: University of California Press.

Yoshinare, Akiko. (1982) *Ebina Danjo Seijishiso* (Political Thoughts of Ebina Danjo). Tokyo: Tokyo University Press.

ECONOMIC PLANNING AGENCY OF JAPAN Until January 2001, the Economic Planning Agency (Keizai Kikakucho) of Japan was an agency under the jurisdiction of the prime minister's office. One of its key responsibilities was to act as secretariat to the Economic Council (Keizai Shingikai), an advisory council to the cabinet. While the EPA was not a cabinet ministry, its director-general was officially a cabinet member. In January 2001, its offices and functions were reassigned to the newly organized Cabinet Office (Naikakufu, the successor to the prime minister's office), where they function as secretariat to the Council on Economic and Fiscal Policy (Keizai Zaisei Shimon Kaigi, which replaces the old Economic Council). The title of director-general has changed to minister of state for economic and fiscal policy.

The EPA was established on 20 July 1955, but its direct antecedents date back to 12 August 1946, when the Economic Stabilization Board (Keizai Anteibu) was established at the behest of the Allied Occupation forces. When the occupation ended, the board was officially renamed the Economic Deliberation Agency (Keizai Shingicho) on 1 August 1952 and became the Economic Planning Agency on 20 July 1955.

The EPA was responsible for preparing national economic plans and for compiling a variety of economic statistics and providing projections. In its early years, its planning functions were at the forefront. Based on assessments of potential output in different industries and of the barriers to achieving that potential, long-term (generally five-year) plans laid out a series of investment, employment, and production targets. These plans were primarily recommendations, since the Japanese government had limited authority to shape private-sector activities. However, private firms would take into account EPA plans and predictions of supply-and-demand conditions in their own planning.

EPA plans also affected government behavior. In the 1950s and 1960s, the lending programs of government financial institutions, such as the Japan Development Bank, were based on EPA plans. Public investment also reflected those plans to some extent. Over time, the plans changed their focus from postwar reconstruction to high-speed growth to social amenities. In the 1990s, many plans tended to focus either on responding to economic stagnation or on economic restructuring.

The most famous of the various EPA economic plans was undoubtedly the Income Doubling Plan (Kokumin Shotoku Baizo Keikaku). Promulgated under Prime Minister Hayato Ikeda in 1960, the plan called for a doubling of Japan's gross national product within a decade. Though widely considered unrealistic at the time, the goal was realized in slightly over seven years. While considerable government investment did result from the Income Doubling Plan, for the most part the plan's writers recognized the latent potential of the Japanese economy: a skilled but still underutilized workforce, rapid capital accumulation, and an ability to gain access to and assimilate technological improvements. Public investment was aimed mainly at transportation and regional development.

The EPA continued to engage in long-term planning, but the practical effects of the plans decreased in importance as the government's role in the economy declined. In the 1980s and 1990s, the most influential documents produced by the EPA were the annual cabinet economic forecasts (*Economic Outlook and Basic Policy Stance on Economic Management*, or *Keizai mitoshi to keizai un'ei kihonteki taido*). The macroeconomic projections in those forecasts provided the basis of budget and tax debates. In the 1990s, these predictions became controversial, outsiders deriding them as overoptimistic. Indeed, the predictions regularly exceeded actual growth rates.

The EPA produced a variety of publications based on statistical analysis and forecasting. Notable publications included the annual *Economic White Paper (Keizai hakusho)* and *White Paper on the National Lifestyle (Kokumin seikatsu hakusho)*. The EPA collected some of the original data itself through surveys, but relied on other ministries for much of its data. One of its main roles was to produce statistics on the economy and government finance that conformed to the internationally accepted System of National Accounts (SNA). The SNA was introduced by the Organization for Economic Cooperation and Development in 1953. After spending several years investigating how best to meet those standards, the EPA began publishing such figures in 1966 and continues to do so. In the late 1990s, the EPA began to release many of its publications and statistical series in electronic form on the Internet.

While the EPA's responsibilities were important, it was considered to be weak politically. Its subordinate position was reflected in its agency rather than ministry status. Many of its staff were seconded from the powerful Ministry of Finance (MOF) and Ministry of International Trade and Industry (MITI). In the 1960s, the EPA was the site of a well-known turf battle between MOF and MITI; career EPA staffers backed MOF, and the result was that MITI's role was sharply reduced. Subsequently, the Ministry of Finance was seen as particularly influential in the EPA.

The EPA was not in a political or administrative position to control forecasting and planning functions, despite its official mandate to do so. Line ministries such as MITI, the Ministry of Agriculture, Forestry, and Fisheries, and the Ministry of Posts and Telecommunications have had the greatest control over those functions for industries under their jurisdictions. Similarly, while the EPA was the official compiler of economic stimulus packages, these were actually put together largely by the Ministry of Finance, which has responsibility for fiscal policy. The EPA's role was thus mostly technical, although in its early years it did participate in coordinating the various ministries' plans so as to match Japan's limited resources.

Career EPA officials have positioned themselves as technocrats and have worked to improve their expertise in econometrics and measurement. Additionally, the agency's Economic Research Institute was a resource for academic economists investigating public finance and various economic phenomena, and constructed sophisticated computer models such as the EPA World Econometric Model. Despite the EPA's origins as a central planning agency, its officials have been regarded as strong advocates of greater liberalization of the Japanese economy since at least the 1970s.

William W. Grimes

Further Reading

Calder, Kent. (1993) *Strategic Capitalism.* Princeton, NJ: Princeton University Press.

Economic Planning Agency. (1996) *Sengo Nihon keizai no kiseki: Keizai kikakucho 50 nenshi* (The Trail of the Post-War Japanese Economy: EPA 50-Year History). Tokyo: Ministry of Finance Printing Bureau.

Council on Economic and Fiscal Policy. (2002) Retrieved 18 January 2002, from: http://www5.cao.go.jp/keizai/index-e.html.

Johnson, Chalmers. (1983) "Economic Planning Agency." In *Encyclopedia of Japan.* New York: Kodansha, 167–168.

Kosai Yutaka. (1987) "The Politics of Economic Management." In *The Political Economy of Japan, Volume 1: The Domestic Transformation*, edited by Kozo Yamamura and Yasukichi Yasuba. Stanford, CA: Stanford University Press, 555–592.

ECONOMIC STABILIZATION PROGRAM After World War II, the United States initiated programs to demilitarize and democratize Japan. These were followed by additional initiatives designed to reform the Japanese economy. The main tasks were combating inflation and boosting production, with factions in both Japan and the United States divided over which was more important. In 1949, President Harry Truman appointed Joseph Dodge, president of the Detroit Bank, to spearhead an economic reform package. Dodge reluctantly accepted the position of "Financial Adviser" to the Supreme Commander of Allied Powers (SCAP), but once in Japan he wasted no time drafting the Economic Stabilization Plan.

The "Dodge Line," as the plan is better known, aimed to balance the national budget, establish the U.S. Aid Counterpart Fund, fix a single foreign exchange rate, and decrease government intervention in the economy. Short-term successes were immediate: inflation dropped from 80 percent in 1948 to 24 percent in 1949, and the number of goods on the black market fell. Laid-off workers expressed discontent, however, a likely reason why Douglas MacArthur did not want to lead the economic recovery himself. Scholars debate the extent to which the Dodge Line contributed to Japanese economic recovery in the long run, especially since the Korean War, which began the year after Dodge's arrival, boosted Japanese production.

Marie Thorsten

Further reading

Sugita Yoneyuki, and Marie Thorsten. (1999). *Beyond the Line: Joseph Dodge and the Geometry of Power in U.S.-Japan Relations.* Okayama, Japan: University Education Press.

EDA SABURO (1907–1977), Japanese politician. Born in Okayama Prefecture, Eda Saburo left college to participate in the leftist farmer's movement. Those activities led to his becoming a member of the central executive committee of the National Farmers' Party and service in Okayama Prefecture's prefectural assembly. An activist for socialist causes all his life, he spent time in prison in the 1930s for his activities and worked for the North China Political Council in Beijing in the 1940s. He joined the Japan Socialist Party (JSP) after returning to Japan in 1946 and served several terms as party secretary-general in the 1960s. With Asanuma Inejiro (1898–1960), the head of the JSP, Eda led the movement opposing the renewal of the U.S.-Japan Security Treaty, which let the United States retain military bases in Japan. After Asanuma's assassination in October 1960, Eda took over leadership of the party; he then stood for election as the party head, but lost, despite his platform of structural reform. In 1976 he lost a bid for election to the lower house of Diet, and the following year he left the JSP.

William Nelson Ridgeway

Further Reading

Dore, Ronald. "The Japanese Socialist Party and Structural Reform." In *The Japan Reader*. Vol. 2, edited by Jon Livingston, Joe Moore, and Felicia Oldfather. New York: Random House, 500–502.

Ushio Shiota. (1994) *Eda Saburo: hayasugita kaikakusha* (Eda Saburo: Reformer Ahead of His Time). Tokyo: Bungei Shunju.

EDIGE The epic *Edige* has as its historical nucleus the emir of the Golden Horde Edige (also called Edigu, Idiga, Idiku, d. 1419) and his wars against Khan Tokhtamysh (d. 1406/1407) and the Russians. The epic is shared by a number of Turkic peoples who trace their origins back to the tribal confederation of the Golden Horde. The earliest known version is a Kazakh text that was written in the nineteenth century by the Kazakh prince Chokan Valikhanov (1835–1865). In the twentieth century the epic was recorded mainly from Kazakh, Karakalpak, Noghay, and Tatar singers. In the epic, Edige is presented as both a wise man and a hero who fights against an unjust khan and helps his tribe to survive and prosper in a hostile environment. The epic is important as a testimony to the transformation of history into heroic poetry and for exemplifying one of the main functions of the heroic epic, the celebration of a glorious tribal past.

Karl Reichl

See also: **Alpamish**

Further Reading

Medeuubekuly, Saghatbek, et al. (1996) *Edige Batyr* (Hero Edige). Almaty, Kazakhstan: Ghylym.

Reichl, Karl. (2000) *Singing the Past: Turkic and Medieval Heroic Poetry*. Myth and Poetics. Ithaca, NY: Cornell University Press.

Schmitz, Andrea. (1996) *Die Erzählung von Edige: Gehalt, Genese und Wirkung einer heroischen Tradition* (The Tale of Edige: Content, Genesis and Impact of a Heroic Tradition). *Turcolologica* 27. Wiesbaden, Germany: Harrassowitz.

EDIRNE (2002 pop. 128,000). Edirne is the capital of the province of Edirne in northwestern Turkey, near the border with Greece and Bulgaria and the confluence of the Tundzha, Maritsa, and Arda rivers. The city is the gateway from the Balkans to the east. The first settlers were most likely Thracian tribes, succeeded by the Macedonians and later by the Romans under the emperor Hadrian (76–138 CE), who named the city Hadrianopolis or Adrianopolis. The city was captured by the Ottoman sultan Murad I (1326?–1389) in 1362, after which it became Edirne, the second capital of the Ottoman empire after Bursa. From here Fatih Sultan Mehmed planned his attack on Constantinople in 1453. Due to Edirne's importance as one of the first capitals of the Ottoman empire, many Ottoman monuments, mosques, and palaces adorn the city. Most notable is the Sultan Selim Mosque, commissioned by Sultan Selim II (1524–1574), built between 1568 and 1574 by the distinguished Ottoman architect Mimar Sinan (1489–1588). The mosque's dome has a diameter of 31.5 meters, a few centimeters larger than the Saint Sophia dome in Istanbul, and has the second-highest minarets in the world, surpassed only by those in Mecca.

The Sultan Selim Mosque in Edirne in the 1990s. (Chris Hellier/Corbis)

Edirne was occupied by the Russians during the Russian-Turkish wars in 1829 and 1878–1879, and by the Bulgarians in 1913. After World War I the Greeks laid claim to Edirne from 1920 to 1922. Edirne officially became part of the Turkish Republic in 1923 under the Treaty of Lausanne. Each summer Edirne hosts the popular Kirkpinar Festival, a 600-year-old competition of greased wrestling.

T. Isikozlu-E.F. Isikozlu

Further Reading

Statistical Yearbook of Turkey, 1998. (1998) Ankara, Turkey: Devlet I Statistik Enstitusu.

EDOGAWA RAMPO (1894–1965), Japan's first modern mystery writer. Edogawa Rampo (whose real name was Hirai Taro) graduated from Waseda University in 1916. He worked alternately as a clerk, accountant, and editor, but in 1923 found himself unemployed. An avid reader of foreign mystery stories, he penned *Nisen doka* (The Two-Sen Copper Coin) and submitted it to the only mystery magazine in Japan, *Shin seinen*, which published translations of Western mysteries. Edogawa's short mystery was accepted, and it became the first original Japanese mystery story to be published. He chose as his pen name Edogawa Rampo, after the Japanese pronunciation of Edgar Allen Poe.

With the subsequent publication of *Shinri shiken* (The Psychological Test) in 1925 and *Yaneura no samposha* (The Attic Stroller) in 1925, he became the leading Japanese writer in the mystery genre. Gradually turning to longer mysteries, he published *Inju* (Dark Beasts, 1928), *Kumootoko* (Spider Man, 1930), and *Ogon kamen* (Golden Mask, 1931), which found a large audience. As founder of the Japan Mystery Writers' Club and the Edogawa Rampo Prize, he encouraged young writers and wrote critical essays of works in the mystery genre.

James M. Vardaman, Jr.

Further Reading

Edogawa Rampo. (1956) *Japanese Tales of Mystery and Imagination*. Trans. by James B. Harris. Tokyo: Charles E. Tuttle.

EHIME

EHIME (2002 est. pop. 1.5 million). Ehime Prefecture is situated in the northwest region of Japan's island of Shikoku. It occupies an area of 5,672 square kilometers. The main geographical features include a mostly mountainous terrain, western Japan's tallest peak, Ishizuchisan, various coastal plains and river valleys, and a rugged shoreline in the south with many small offshore islands. Ehime Prefecture, once the ancient province of Iyo, is bordered by the Inland Sea and by Kochi, Kagawa, and Tokushima Prefectures.

The prefecture's capital is the centrally located port city of Matsumaya, Shikoku Island's largest city. Matsumaya Castle is one of the few feudal fortresses to survive relatively intact. The city's traditional crafts include *iyogasuri* (an indigo-dyed textile) and *tobeyaki* (blue and white porcelain). The larger industries include petrochemicals, soda factories, and wood pulp processing. Nearby is Dogo Onsen, one the nation's oldest hot spring spas. Matsumaya also is the site of eight of Shikoku's eighty-eight pilgrimage temples. The other important cities of Ehime Prefecture are Niihama, Saijo, Yawatahama, and Uwajima.

Ehime's warm temperatures make it the major source of Japan's mandarin oranges and other citrus fruit. Commercial fishing now has given way in part to shellfish fishing, pearl culture, and the production of *nori* (edible seaweed). Along the northeast coast is an industrial zone of plants for processing metals, chemicals, paper, textiles, and petrochemicals. Among the other tourist attractions are the Inland Sea National Park and the Ichizuchisan area.

E. L. S. Weber

Further Reading

"Ehime Prefecture." (1993) In *Japan: An illustrated Encyclopedia*. Tokyo: Kodansha.

EKAPHAP

EKAPHAP *Ekaphap* (unity) is a word found in both Thai and Lao languages. Unity and preservation of a distinctive national identity have been important priorities of both the Thai and Lao states. *Ekaphap* is one of the five major political slogans of the Lao government. The challenge to unity in both the Thai and Lao cases has been the existence of considerable ethnic diversity. Only 52.5 percent of the Lao nation is ethnically lowland Lao. Thailand also has considerable ethnic diversity, though less than that of Laos.

Thailand's leadership has been remarkably successful in creating national unity, primarily through the institution of the monarchy and a uniform, standardized modern educational system, which has required all to learn and use standard Thai, the national language and a unifying factor. His Majesty King Bhumibol Adulyadej has been brilliant in using the institution of the monarchy to create solidarity and unity among all Thais. The king travels to all regions of the country on a regular basis to help build national unity. With the abolition of the Lao monarchy in 1975, Lao unity has been achieved primarily through the promotion of standard Lao language and the institution of the revolutionary party that led the long Lao struggle for political independence.

Gerald W. Fry

Further Reading

Barmé, Scott. (1993) *Luang Wichit Wathakan and the Creation of a Thai Identity*. Singapore: Institute of Southeast Asian Studies.

Ngaosyvathn, Mayoury and Pheuiphanh. (1994) *Kith and Kin Politics: The Relationship between Laos and Thailand*. Manila, Philippines and Wollongong, Australia: Journal of Contemporary Asia Publishers.

ELBURZ

ELBURZ Elburz is a mountain range located between the Caspian Sea and the central Iranian plateau. The range serves as a natural border for Iran and its northern neighbors (Azerbaijan, Armenia, and Turkmenistan) in the Caucasus. The extinct volcano of Mount Damavand is the peak of the Elburz Range, rising to about 5,600 meters. Elburz is covered by an ice cap of about 140 square kilometers, with seventy-seven minor and steadily retreating glaciers radiating from it, some reaching 400 meters in thickness. Lakes are mostly of glacial origin, small in area, but deep.

The range consists of steep, narrow, parallel ridges crossed only by the Safid River, whose valley forms the main trans-Elburz route. The northern slope of the Elburz is rainy and forested, and the southern slope is semiarid. Snowcapped water peaks provide seasonal flow used for irrigation and industry. Elburz is composed of both hard crystalline rocks and magma. In the surrounding valleys, mineral springs are common and in a few places, sulfurous fumes escape through fissures, often deep under the ice cover. Pine forests mingled with birch and mountain ash cover the north of the main ridge valleys and lower mountain slopes of Elburz. In higher elevations, forests have been replaced by alpine meadows rich in flowers. The foothills of Elburz, lying to the north of Tehran, act as a major recreational attraction for both alpinists and nature enthusiasts.

Payam Foroughi and Raissa Muhutdinova-Foroughi

Women assemble the electronic components of a high-tech toilet at the Toto Toilet Company in Miyazaki, Japan, in the early 1990s. (MICHAEL S. YAMASHITA/CORBIS)

ELECTRONICS INDUSTRY—JAPAN

After being opened to the West in the mid-nineteenth century Japan quickly adopted the electrical technologies of the time. By the early decades of the twentieth century the Japanese military and some Japanese researchers had attained world-class levels in many areas of electronics. Japan's electronics industry, however, remained largely dependent on U.S. and European firms for technology and capital throughout the prewar era.

After World War II, Japanese firms effectively used, and often improved, foreign technology to become world leaders in electronics. For some time, the Japanese electronics industry has been second only to that of the United States. At the beginning of the twenty-first century, however, the Japanese electronics firms have been handicapped by the slow growth of the Japanese market.

The Introduction of Electrical/Electronics Technology in Japan

Despite being relatively isolated from the West until the middle of the nineteenth century, the Japanese were aware of important developments in Western science and technology. This was thanks to Japanese scholars who painstakingly translated science books acquired from Dutch traders into Japanese. Information on the telegraph, for example, was translated in 1848, ten years after Samuel Morse had demonstrated the device to the U.S. government.

In 1853 and 1854, a U.S. naval squadron under Commodore Matthew Perry (1794–1858) visited Tokyo Bay. Crew members demonstrated a telegraph and other modern Western technology. Perry's visit demonstrated the inability of the ruling government to protect Japan from the Western powers that had already colonized most of Asia. It also suggested that Japan needed to adopt Western technology to maintain its national sovereignty. After some years of internal conflict, a new government determined to "modernize" Japan was formed in 1868. Just a year later, telegraph service was inaugurated between Tokyo and Yokohama.

In the 1870s, the government started a university-level program in electrical engineering and established electrical research laboratories. Now that Japan was more fully open to information flows from the West, the Japanese were quick to master the new electrical technologies. Japanese made a telephone receiver in 1878, only two years after Alexander Graham Bell. They started producing electric light bulbs in 1884. An electric lighting system was established in Tokyo in 1887, only five years after Edison established his first system in New York. That same year Japan built its first electric power plant and Tokyo Electric Lighting started supplying electricity to factories. General telephone service was introduced in Tokyo and Yokohama in 1890. In 1905 the Japanese Navy used wireless telegraphy to defeat a Russian fleet at the Battle of Tsushima. Radio broadcasting began in 1925, initiating modern electronics engineering in Japan.

The Japanese also made significant original contributions to electronics technology. The Yagi antenna, which became the world's most widely used radio and television antenna, was invented in 1926 by Yagi Hidetsugu and Uda Shintaro. Also in 1926, Takayanagi Kenjiro was one of the first in the world to successfully produce an all-electronic television image. Toshiba demonstrated Japan's first televison set in September 1939, only eight months after RCA first demonstrated its television technology.

Origins of Major Private Firms

Japan's first firms in the electrical/electronics industry were established in the late nineteenth century. Many of these firms soon experienced severe difficulties. Electrical technology was advancing rapidly in the West and was becoming increasingly complex. After Japan joined the International Patent Convention in 1899, Japanese firms were less free simply to copy foreign technology. Another problem was that economic conditions in Japan made it difficult for the new electronics firms to get adequate capital.

Foreign firms often provided the solution to both the technology and capital shortages. In 1899, the U.S. company Western Electric established the firm that became NEC. In 1905, another U.S. company, General Electric (GE), acquired 51 percent of Tokyo Electric Lighting, and provided it with light bulb manufacturing technology. With GE's capital and technology, Tokyo Electric soon dominated light bulb production in Japan. In 1910 GE took 24.5 percent of the equity of Shibaura Engineering Works in exchange for technology. This allowed Shibaura to become Japan's largest producer of generators and other heavy electrical equipment. In 1939 Tokyo and Shibaura merged to form Tokyo Shibaura Electric, today's Toshiba. Westinghouse Electric of the United States and Mitsubishi formed Mitsubishi Electric in 1921; Germany's Siemens and Furukawa Electric formed Fuji Electric in 1923 (one of the spin-offs from Fuji Electric is Fujitsu).

A few Japanese electronics firms have always been independent from foreign firms. Hitachi, which started out as a mine repair shop in 1908, became a separate electrical/electronics firm in 1920. The company long prided itself on its independence from Western technology. Matsushita (also known by its Panasonic and National brand names) was founded in 1918. The firm that became Sharp was established as a metal-processing firm in 1912; it grew based on its founder's invention of a mechanical pencil (the Ever Sharp) and began making radios in 1925.

In the late 1930s, the Japanese government restricted the production of home appliances, and the electronics industry concentrated on producing electronics for the military. The foreign firms were increasingly forced to withdraw. Toshiba shared the technology it had gotten from General Electric with Hitachi, NEC, and other companies, but during the war years the Japanese electronics firms suffered from their loss of contacts with the rest of the world. Military electronics research in such areas as radar, however, was nearly equal to that in Western countries.

Postwar Recovery: Radio and Television

The environment facing the Japanese electronics firms changed drastically with the end of World War II. During the postwar occupation of Japan (1945–1952), U.S. authorities banned research in radar and other areas considered to be of military significance. One of Japan's premier centers of electronics research, the Naval Research Institute, was dismantled. And, of course, there was no longer a market for military electronics. One consequence of this was that talented researchers shifted their interest to consumer electronics. Masaru Ibuka (1908–1997) and Akio Morita (1921–1999), for example, left their positions as naval researchers and went on to found Sony in 1946. Other wartime researchers moved into leading positions at the other electronics firms.

The U.S. Occupation authorities regarded the development of commercial radio and television broadcasting as a way to build support for democratic institutions in Japan. High priority was given the establishment of commercial stations and the manufacture of radios. With this encouragement, around two hundred firms of various sizes began producing radios by 1949. Television broadcasting was begun in 1953. Sharp (then called Hayakawa Electric) put the first Japanese-made television receiver on sale in January 1953. By the end of the 1950s, there were 3.3 million television sets in Japan.

Technology Imports

Although Japanese technologies were being developed that might eventually have served as the basis for Japan's television industry, the faster route of using American standards and relying on foreign technology was chosen. Nearly forty Japanese firms quickly entered into license agreements for foreign television technology, most often with the dominant American firm at the time, RCA. Meanwhile Japanese electronics firms, beginning with Sony, quickly signed licensing agreements for the transistor technology developed at Bell Laboratories in the United States. Although U.S. firms were the first to market transistor radios, Sony developed a radio of the right size and price to appeal to a mass market. The production of transistors for transistor radios also established Japanese firms in the new semiconductor industry.

By 1959, more than one hundred Japanese companies were making transistor radios, and Japan was the world-leading producer of transistors. In 1960 transistor radios were Japan's second largest generator of export earnings, after ships. Although Sony and other Japanese firms deserve credit for developing transistor radios that were popular with consumers, there was another reason for Japan's success with these products. These products were highly labor intensive at the time and Japanese firms were able to hire thousands of female factory workers for about ten cents per hour.

In the late 1960s, the integrated circuit (IC) and the LSI (large-scale integrated circuit) calculator played a role similar to that of the transistor and the transistor radio in the 1950s. While Sony had been the catalyst for the early technology, Sharp was the key early mover with the LSI calculator. In 1969 Sharp introduced a calculator based on U.S.-developed LSIs. Some fifty other Japanese firms quickly brought out versions of this product. Japanese semiconductor firms quickly developed the technical expertise to meet the needs of the calculator producers. This supported Japan's growing strength in the world semiconductor industry throughout the 1980s.

Japan continues to spend $2 billion a year on imported electronics technology, but Japan's electronics firms are now also leading suppliers of technology, with annual receipts for technology exports of more than $1.5 billion.

Developing a Japanese Technological Capacity in Electronics

Although imported technology was essential to the Japanese electronics industry, much more was needed. First of all, the Japanese firms needed to build a strong capability to absorb the technology. Secondly, creative adaptations in product design or production methods, as with the transistor radio and LSI calculator, were needed to make the technology a success. In some instances it was necessary to create new markets for products, such as Sony's Walkman, that had not previously existed. Some of these capabilities were developed through heavy spending on research. In some instances government provided funds and coordinated the activities of firms to develop technology and markets.

The Electronics Industry Law of 1958, for example, provided government subsidies for research and development. Special loans and tax policies encouraged investment in efficient new plants and equipment. Another major policy measure encouraged the formation of research associations—groups of firms subsidized by government and exempted from antitrust laws that worked on specific new technologies. The first of these in the electronics industry, the Japan Electronics Industry Promotion Association, was established in 1958 as the first major cooperative research program. Although it is not clear how many of the research associations can be characterized as successful, the VLSI (Very Large Scale Integration) Consortium is often credited with helping Japan catch up with the United States in this technology and there may have been other successes in the electronics industry.

Evolving Domestic Market

While Japanese electronics exports attracted attention around the world and sometimes have been the subject of heated trade disputes, a major factor in the Japanese electronics industry's growth has been Japan's increasingly affluent and sophisticated domestic market. Black and white television helped propel the rapid growth of the Japanese electronics industry in the 1950s, but it was not long before the market for this product became saturated. By the time of the Tokyo Olympics, in 1964, about 90 percent of Japanese households had black and white television sets. The electronics firms quickly moved to the production of color television sets. In 1970 color televisions accounted for one third of total electronics industry sales. While a similar transition occurred in the United States and Europe, it extended over a much longer period.

As the Japanese market for color televisions neared saturation in the mid and late 1970s the electronics firms began introducing home video recorders. This time the Japanese domestic market received large volumes of a new electronic product ahead of the United States and Europe, giving an added advantage to the Japanese in export markets. By 1985 Japanese firms and their affiliates accounted for some 80 percent of world video recorder production. In 1979 Sony created another hit product, the Walkman. Other consumer products such as room air conditioners and compact disc (CD) players quickly sold in the Japanese market, contributing to the rapid growth of the Japanese firms.

The demand for increasingly sophisticated consumer products, added to that for calculators and computers, also meant lucrative new markets for Japanese semiconductor producers. Through most of the 1980s five and sometimes six of the world's ten largest semiconductor producers were Japanese. In 1987 Japanese firms had more than half the world's semiconductor market.

The 1990s and 2000s

By the beginning of the 1990s, Japan's household market for consumer products was largely saturated. Worse yet for the electronics firms, Japan's economy had entered a long-term period of stagnation at the end of the 1980s. During the 1990s, although there was some growth in industrial electronics, sales in the consumer electronics segment of the industry dropped almost in half. The weakness in consumer markets also caused problems for Japanese semiconductor producers. At the end of the 1990s, more than a third of the demand in Japan for semiconductor products came from consumer products, compared to about 5 percent in the United States. Often the consumer applications required analog products, so semiconductors designed for these markets could not be used in the faster-growing computer market.

Another problem facing the Japanese electronics firms in the late twentieth century was the high level of Japanese wages. Beginning in the mid-1980s Japanese electronics firms began moving their facilities offshore to reduce their labor costs. In 1998 these firms had about eight hundred production facilities in Asia and another four hundred in other parts of the world. By the late 1990s, Japanese firms were producing about 40 million color television sets per year, but only about 10 percent of these were actually being made in Japan. Offshore production of video recorders was more than double domestic production. Similar patterns were being seen in the production of stereos, car stereos, and other consumer electronics products.

Despite their success in reducing labor costs by moving offshore, in the late 1990s and early 2000s Japan's "big five" industrial-electronics firms, Toshiba, NEC, Hitachi, Fujitsu, and Mitsubishi Electric (together accounting for 5 percent of Japan's GDP and more than a quarter of its exports) and Japan's largest consumer electronics firm, Sony, were all experiencing serious difficulties. Toshiba, for example, was experiencing its first losses in nearly a quarter of a century. The firms were all being widely criticized for a lack of focus and all were announcing moves to restructure their businesses. Vertically integrated single-nation electronics firms seem to be losing competitive advantage to multinational alliances of more specialized firms. In response to this trend, Japanese firms are increasingly entering into international alliances, most often with U.S. partners.

Leonard Lynn

Further Reading

Anchordoguy, Marie. (1989) *Computers Inc.: Japan's Challenge to IBM.* Cambridge, MA: Harvard University Press.

Aoyama, Yoshiyuki. (1991) *Kaden* (Home Electronics). Tokyo: Nihon Keizai Shimbun.

Goto, Hiroyuki, and Akira Goto. (1996) *Technology and Industrial Development in Japan.* New York: Oxford University Press.

Lynn, Leonard. (1998) "The Commercialization of the Transistor Radio in Japan: The Functioning of an Innovation Community." *IEEE Transactions on Engineering Management* 45 (August): 220–229.

———. (2000) "Technology Competition Policies in the Semiconductor Industries of Japan and the United States: A Fifty-Year Retrospective." *IEEE Transaction on Engineering Management* 47.

Methe, David. (1991) *Technological Competition in Global Industries.* New York: Quorum.

Nakayama, Wataru, William Boulton, and Michael Pecht. (1999) *The Japanese Electronics Industry.* Boca Raton, FL: Chapman and Hall/CRC.

Partner, Simon. (1999) *Assembled in Japan: Electrical Goods and the Making of the Japanese Consumer.* Berkeley and Los Angeles: University of California Press.

ELEPHANT, ASIAN

ELEPHANT, ASIAN The Asian elephant *(Elephas maximus)*, also known as the Indian elephant, inhabits the forests and grasslands of Southeast Asia, from India and Sri Lanka to Thailand, Malaysia, and Sumatra. Enormously strong, Asian elephants are also intelligent and easily tamed. Asian elephants were first tamed over 5,000 years ago and can be trained to a very high standard. They are usually captured in the wild as young adults and the initial breaking in and taming process takes only a few weeks. Each elephant is assigned a handler known as a mahout who trains the animal according to detailed traditional procedures and may use tame elephants to calm the new captive and to teach by example. An unbreakable, lifelong bond often develops between a mahout and his elephant. They have served people as beasts of burden, as draft animals, in warfare, and for ceremonial purposes for several thousand years.

Males (bulls) stand three to four meters high and weigh up to six tons. Females (cows) are smaller. Their thick gray skin is wrinkled and almost hairless and their

An 1849 illustration of the Asian elephant in South Asia. (MICHAEL MASIAN HISTORIC PHOTOGRAPHS/CORBIS)

trunk, a fleshy, boneless nose, acts as a hand. Bulls have large ivory tusks, used for digging and fighting. Elephants have poor eyesight, but extremely keen hearing and sense of smell. They are herbivores, feeding primarily on leaves, grasses, bark, and roots. They also enjoy bananas and sugarcane. Food is ground down with their four huge molar teeth.

Elephants live and migrate together in herds and are very social animals. They have a lifespan of up to sixty years. Following a twenty-two-month pregnancy, a cow gives birth to a single calf.

Asian elephants are generally gentle, curious, and friendly creatures. However, enraged or stampeding elephants will trample everything in their path and have occasionally been known to kill people, usually those threatening or hunting them.

Asian elephants are seriously endangered due to loss of habitat and poaching, despite a ban on trading ivory. Most remaining wild elephants are in special reserves.

Lucy D. Moss

Further Reading

DeLort, Robert. (1992) *The Life and Lore of the Elephant.* New York: Harry N. Abrams.

Shoshani, Jeheskel, and Frank Knight, eds. (2000). *Elephants: Majestic Creatures of the Wild.* New York: Checkmark Books.

ELEPHANT RANGE The Chuor Phnom Damrei (Elephant Mountain Range) is an extension of the Chuor Phnom Kravanh (Cardamom Mountains) of western Cambodia. Extending 110 kilometers south and southeast from the capital city of Phnom Penh to the Gulf of Thailand, with an average elevation of 500 meters, the name is literally translated as "the mountains around which the clouds turn." The Elephant Range was the principal center of Cambodia's pepper-growing industry until the Khmer Rouge, also referred to as Red Cambodians, took power in 1975. The heavily forested western slopes receive nearly 5,000 millimeters of rain each year from the southwest monsoons. The rainfall in the eastern hills, however, rarely exceeds 1,520 millimeters, because they lie in the rain shadow.

The highest point in the Elephant Range is Mount Bokor (1,081 meters), located near the coast between the towns of Kampot and Kampong Saom (Sihanoukville). Now a national park, the mountain contains the abandoned ruins of the Bokor hill station, once a popular retreat for the French administrators who sought to escape the summer heat of Phnom Penh. More recently, it was controlled by Khmer Rouge guerrilla soldiers. Today, both visitors and residents seek out the mountain for its forested surroundings and scenic, panoramic views of the sea.

Greg Ringer

Further Reading

Ringer, Greg. (2000) "Tourism in Cambodia, Laos, and Myanmar: From Terrorism to Tourism?" In *Tourism in South and Southeast Asia: Issues and Cases*, edited by C. Michael Hall and Stephen Page. Oxford: Butterworth-Heinemann, 178–94.

World Commission on Protected Areas. (1998) *Mountain Protected Areas Update*. Geneva, Switzerland: International Union for the Conservation of Nature.

EMAKIMONO *Emakimono (emaki)*, meaning literally "pictures rolled," is a uniquely Japanese painting format in which a narrative is presented in both words and pictures through a long horizontal handscroll. *Emakimono* illustrate texts that can be either religious or nonreligious; the emphasis is always on the narrative and thus continuous landscape paintings, for example, cannot be considered *emakimono*.

The scroll, made of paper or silk, is attached to a wooden dowel at the far left end so that the picture may be rolled up for storage, secured by a braided silk cord. The *emakimono* is backed by silk to protect it and give it strength. Once rolled, the scroll can be placed on a shelf or in a large box if the work is comprised of several scrolls.

An *emakimono* is best seen by a single viewer who unrolls and rolls the scroll with both hands. The act of touching the scroll creates an intimate relationship between the painting and the viewer, who is able to control the action of the narrative by moving quickly along some parts of the scroll and pausing at others. As both the Chinese and Japanese languages are traditionally read from right to left, these illustrated handscrolls are intended to be viewed by unrolling the scroll from right to left as well. Typically, an *emakimono* begins with a frontispiece of decorated paper, and then proceeds to the main work where passages of text alternate with illustrations. There is no set length for either the illustrations or the text, but in general, the scenes of battle stories are longer because they convey intense drama.

A number of subjects are found in *emakimono* and include romances, famous battles, legends, and Buddhist themes, such as biographies of eminent monks and histories of temples. *Emakimono* were especially

A scene from the *Tale of Genji.* (ARCHIVO ICONOGRAFICO, S.A./CORBIS)

popular from the twelfth to the fourteenth centuries when stories of this nature were enjoyed. Although the subject matter varied considerably, there are in essence only two types of *emakimono*—those composed of small scenes alternating with sections of text, which include Buddhist treatises and courtly romances, and those with long and dramatic scenes that are unbroken by passages of text, such as the fiery stories of military events.

At the end of the fourteenth century, the vogue for *emakimono* declined, largely due to the growing popularity of Zen-inspired ink paintings and later a market for decorative paintings to adorn sixteenth-century castles and palaces.

Catherine Pagani

Further Reading

Murase Miyeko. (1983) *Emaki: Narrative Scrolls from Japan.* New York: The Asia Society.

Okudaira Hideo. (1973) *Narrative Picture Scrolls.* Translated by Elizabeth ten Grotenhuis. New York: Weatherhill.

EMEI, MOUNT Mount Emei is a 3,099-meter mountain located 200 kilometers southeast of Chengdu in Sichuan Province, China. Dramatic cliffs provide excellent views of the Himalayan Plateau to the west. It is notable for its very diverse vegetation, including a rare plant called the "dove tree." Monkeys heckle pilgrims for food on the trail, and bearded toads, tree frogs, silver pheasants, and a small species of panda inhabit the undisturbed wilderness of the mountain.

The site has been sacred for over 2,000 years. The Taoists practiced on the mountain during the Eastern Han dynasty (25–220 CE). The first Buddhist temple was said to have built there in the first century CE. Mount Emei is one of the four sacred Buddhist mountains in China. Imperial support of Buddhist institutions at Mount Emei came at the end of the Tang dynasty (618–907 CE) and during the Song dynasty (960–1279). The most remarkable was the Giant Buddha of Leshan, carved out of a hillside in the eighth century and looking down on the junction of three rivers. At 71 meters high, it is the largest Buddha in the world. Another famous image on the mountain is an enormous bronze statue cast in 980. This statue was mounted on a white ceramic elephant during the Ming dynasty (1368–1644), which saw a revival of imperial patronage for the mountain's Buddhist monasteries. In the fourteenth century, over one hundred temples and thousands of monks and nuns could be found there; only twenty temples remain today. The mountain (in Tibetan: *Glang chen 'gying ri*), which is located within the sight of the cultural Tibetan border, is currently a pilgrimage destination for Chinese and Tibetan Buddhists. In 1996 the mountain, including the Leshan Giant Buddha scenic area, was listed as a UNESCO World Heritage site.

Gray Tuttle

Further Reading

Emei shan tu zhi (Mount Omei: Illustrated Guide). (1967) With a translation by Dryden Linsley Phelps. Hong Kong: University Press Reprint.

Fojiao Xiehui. (1990) *Emei Shan* (Mount Emei). Chengdu, China: Sichuan Renmin Chubanshe.

EMERALD BUDDHA The Emerald Buddha is the most sacred Buddha image in Thailand, which prior to 1939 was Siam. It rests in its own chapel within the Wat Phra Keo, the royal palace and temple complex in Bangkok. Carved out of green jasper, the image is 66 centimeters (26 inches) high and is in *virasana mudra* (sitting with hands on the lap). The Emerald Buddha is an object of national veneration and is believed to protect Thailand. Its origins, however, are mysterious. The *Chronicle of the Emerald Buddha*, an anonymous text of unknown date, relates a legend suggesting that the Emerald Buddha was sculpted in India by Nagasena and the god Vishnu. The *Chronicle* tells that the image then traveled to Sri Lanka, Burma, Cambodia, Laos, and Thailand. The Emerald Buddha was discovered, encased in stucco and inside a stupa (dome-shaped Buddhist shrine), in Chiang Rai, Siam, in 1434. The image later traveled to Lampang, Chiang Mai, and Vientiane. It was brought to Siam in 1778, after the Siamese army sacked Vientiane at the command of King Taksin, the expansionist ruler who united Siam. The Emerald Buddha was first brought to Thonburi and then, in 1784, to Bangkok, where it was installed in its current location by King Rama I when he moved the national capital to Bangkok. Rama I used the image to legitimize his reign. Successive members of the Chakri dynasty (1782–present) have used the image in a similar way. The most important ceremony associated with the Emerald Buddha is the dressing of the image, which takes place three times each year, marking the beginning of the hot, rainy, and cool seasons. The king of Thailand cleans the image and changes its headdress, and then prays while a royal attendant changes the image's garments. The Emerald Buddha is Bangkok's most important treasure and is part of the Thai language name of Bangkok.

The Temple of the Emerald Buddha in Bangkok, Thailand. (TIM PAGE/CORBIS)

Michael Pretes and Daniel Oakman

Further Reading

Anonymous. (1932) *Chronicle of the Emerald Buddha.* Trans. by Camille Notton. Bangkok, Thailand: Bangkok Times Press.

Narula, Karen Schur. (1994) *Voyage of the Emerald Buddha.* Kuala Lumpur, Malaysia: Oxford University Press.

Roeder, Eric. (1999) "The Origin and Significance of the Emerald Buddha." *Explorations in Southeast Asian Studies* 3, 1:15–34.

ENCHI FUMIKO (1905–1986), Japanese novelist. Enchi Fumiko was born Ueda Fumi, daughter of the well-known linguist Ueda Kazutoshi. She received a good education, including private tutoring in English, French, and Chinese classics. From childhood, she absorbed the Kabuki plays and Japanese classics, such as *The Tale of Genji* (eleventh century) and late Edo tales of the supernatural, which, combined with her knowledge of Western literature, formed the foundation for her writings. Her literary debut as a playwright occurred in the late 1920s. After marrying the journalist Enchi Yoshimatsu in 1930 and having a daughter, she began writing fiction but fell into relative silence. Her unsatisfactory marriage provided her the emotional energy that fueled many of her powerful writings. Her mastectomy (1938) and hysterectomy (1946, from which she nearly died) also deepened her insight into women's psychology and sexuality. Her short story "Himojii Tsukihi" (Hungry Years, 1953) brought her public recognition. Her masterpiece, *The Waiting Years* (1949–1957), depicts the unhappy marriage of a persevering woman, inspired by the life of Enchi's grandmother. It garnered the Noma Literary Prize (1958). Enchi's works often feature strong, suffering, and tenacious women. Recurrent themes from classical literature, such as spirit possession, shamanism, or blending of the real and the supernatural, also characterize her works. She also translated *The Tale of Genji* into modern Japanese, in ten volumes (1972–1973). In 1985 she received the Order of Culture.

Nobuko Miyama Ochner

Further Reading

Carpenter, Juliet Winters. (1990) "Enchi Fumiko: A Writer of Tales." *Japan Quarterly* 37, 3 (July–September): 343–355.

Mulhern, Chieko Irie. (1993) "Women Writers Past and Present: A Comparison of Lady Murasaki and Enchi Fumiko." In *Japan: A Literary Overview*, Vol. 18, edited by John K. Gillespie. New York: Griffon House Publications: 137–164.

Rieger, Naoko Alisa. (1986) *Enchi Fumiko's Literature: The Portrait of Women in Enchi Fumiko's Selected Works.* Hamburg, Germany: Mitteilungen der Gesellschaft für Natur- und Völkerkunde Ostasiens.

Vernon, Victoria V. (1988) *Daughters of the Moon: Wish, Will, and Social Constraint in Fiction by Modern Japanese Women.* Berkeley, CA: Institute of East Asian Studies, University of California Press.

ENDANGERED SPECIES

Tropical Asia and Australia appear to have a large number of endangered species and particularly high extinction rates. In the face of this global crisis, international treaties to control trade in wildlife and wildlife products, government education and species protection programs, and efforts by wildlife conservation programs have been developed and expanded.

Asia's Endangered Species

In twenty-six Asian countries stretching from Japan to Afghanistan, a total of 2,022 species of mammals, birds, reptiles, amphibians, fish, and invertebrates were identified as endangered in 1996 by the International Union for Conservation of Nature and Natural Resources (IUCN). Among these countries, Indonesia, China, India, the Philippines, and Vietnam are among the richest in species and yet have the largest number of endangered species.

The 2000 IUCN Red List of Threatened Species reported that Indonesia harbors the highest number of threatened mammals (135 species), while India (80 species), China (72 species), and Thailand (32 species) rank among the top ten. In the Philippines, which has a large number of endemic species or mammals found nowhere else, 32 percent of those mammals are endangered.

A similarly discouraging profile of endangered bird species is also typical of Asia. Of the twenty countries with the largest number of threatened avian species, 50 percent are from Asia. According to the Red List, the Philippines, a biodiversity hot spot that has lost 97 percent of its original vegetation, has more critically endangered birds than any other country. Endangered species of doves, parrots, and perching birds (passerines) found in Southeast Asia have also shown marked declines due to continued deforestation. Indonesia and China, with some of the largest numbers of bird species in the world, are also countries with large numbers of threatened species. As is the case with the mammals, the countries with the most threatened species also have extremely high human populations. Since 1966, the number of threatened reptiles has grown more slowly, but the populations of freshwater turtles and tortoises are deteriorating rapidly in Southeast Asia. Their decline is due to heavy exploitation for food and medicinal use and to unregulated hunting. As these populations disappear in Southeast Asia, there are signs that this trade is shifting to the Indian subcontinent. Other Asian species, such as snakes and salamanders, are heavily exploited for use in traditional Chinese medicine, but the effects of this and other pressures on most of these species have not yet been assessed.

Various plant species, especially tropical timber trees, are also endangered in large areas of Southeast Asia. Malaysia, for example, has the most threatened number of plant species (681), followed closely by Indonesia with 384.

Preservation and Conservation

In 1975 the CITES treaty, or the Convention on International Trade in Endangered Species of Wildlife Fauna and Flora, was approved to control the trade in wildlife and wildlife products. Over 151 countries have signed this treaty, which identifies species and species products that are illegal to purchase or sell for profit or whose sale is allowed only if it will not harm their survival. Other actions have been taken to protect endangered species and their habitats from one of the main factors driving their decline: humans. In Nepal, a second home for the endangered greater one-horned rhino was created in Royal Bardia National Park, helping that population grow to over 550 animals. China's giant panda, a universal symbol of endangered wildlife, has benefited in the past two decades by the creation of thirty-two reserves protecting more than 15,540 square kilometers (6,000 square miles) of panda forest habitat from timber harvesting. And similar efforts are under way to provide protected habitats for the endangered Asian elephant in Sumatra, Indonesia. These government efforts are often undertaken in cooperation with such organizations as the World Wildlife Fund (WWF), the World Conservation Society (WCS), and the IUCN to provide training in conservation methods, conduct surveys of endangered species, and develop long-term species conservation and protection programs.

While there has been some success in species conservation over the last twenty years, these have come too infrequently and generally have been achieved through large investments that tackle immediate threats. There have been very few attempts to address the underlying driving forces that contribute to species endangerment or extinction. For this crisis to be addressed effectively, greater action is needed to remove the immediate threats to species and the driving forces causing their decline. These issues will be tackled only if there is much greater support for lifestyle changes, and this involves the political will of governments.

James A. Hafner

Further Reading

Baillie, Jonathan. (1996) "Analysis." In *1996 IUCN Red List of Threatened Animals.* Geneva: International Union for Conservation of Nature and Natural Resources.

International Union for Conservation of Nature and Natural Resources (IUCN). (1996) "Confirming the Global Extinction Crisis." *1996 IUCN Red List of Threatened Animals.* Geneva: International Union for Conservation of Nature and Natural Resources.

———. (2000) *2000 IUCN Red List of Threatened Species.* Geneva: International Union for Conservation of Nature and Natural Resources.

World Wildlife Fund. (2000) *The Global 200 Ecoregions.* Washington, DC: World Wildlife Fund.

ENDO SHUSAKU

ENDO SHUSAKU (1923–1996), Japanese writer. As a boy, Tokyo-born novelist and playwright Endo Shusaku, was baptized into the Catholic Church. After majoring in French literature at Keio University, in 1950 he was selected as the first Japanese to study abroad. Endo spent two and a half years in France, reading especially French Catholic writers. Upon his return to Japan he began writing fiction, publishing in 1955 *Shiroi hito* (White Man), for which he won the Akutagawa Prize, followed by *Kiiroi hito* (Yellow Man). In these works he contrasted the Western and Japanese views of faith, guilt, and sin.

In 1958, Endo published *Umi to dokuyaku* (The Sea and Poison), which dealt with the vivisection of captive American soldiers. In *Ryugaku* (Foreign Studies, 1965) he examined the difficulties that Japanese have in absorbing the essence of Western culture, particularly Christianity. Perhaps his most well-known work is *Chinmoku* (Silence, 1966), concerning the martyrdom of Christians in Japan beginning in the late-sixteenth century. With *Samurai* (The Samurai, 1980), critics began to write of Endo as an eventual candidate for the Nobel Prize. While a devout adherent to Christian faith, to the end of his life he pursued as his subject the human psyche in its sometimes disturbing complexity.

James M. Vardaman, Jr.

Further Reading

Lewell, John. (1993) *Modern Japanese Novelists: A Biographical Dictionary.* Tokyo: Kodansha.

Williams, Mark B. (1999) *Endo Shusaku: A Literature of Reconciliation.* New York: Routledge.

ENERGY—CENTRAL ASIA

ENERGY—CENTRAL ASIA Among the many regions suddenly opened to the outside world with the end of the Cold War are the five countries of Central Asia—Kazakhstan, Kyrgyzstan, Tajikistan, Turkmenistan, and Uzbekistan. These new nations, home to 55 million people in an area 40 percent the size of the United States, are best known in the West as lands of the ancient Silk Road that connected the European, Islamic, and Asian civilizations. But beneath the steppes, deserts, mountains, and river valleys, abundant energy resources lie waiting for investment and development.

Energy—including oil, natural gas, coal, electricity generated from these and hydroelectric sources, and nontraditional sources—is the most abundant and valuable natural resource of Central Asia. Kazakhstan has large reserves of oil and coal, Turkmenistan and Uzbekistan have significant reserves of gas, and Kyrgyzstan produces important amounts of hydroelectric power. Only Kazakhstan has an operating nuclear power station, but plans to build a new plant were abandoned in 2000 over safety and cost concerns. All of these energy reserves form a basis for economic growth and development, with energy exports promising to generate foreign-exchange revenues. Central Asia is, in fact, poised to become a major world supplier of energy, especially in the oil and gas sectors.

To develop and restructure the energy sector in the Central Asian republics, energy planners are addressing two key issues: (1) overcoming periodic energy shortages and (2) reducing dependencies on unreliable sources of energy. All governments in the region are trying to develop new international markets that provide stable supplies of foreign exchange as they internationalize and develop ties with countries in the West and with their neighbors.

Oil

Oil is the most valuable commodity traded in the world; billions of dollars' worth of oil are globally traded daily. As such, oil serves as the economic foundation of many countries. Yet in Central Asia oil is only the second most important resource: on an energy-equivalent basis, Central Asia is still a gas-producing region, although this could change in the near future with the tremendous oil potential of places such as Kazakhstan.

Central Asia now produces more oil than it consumes, as a result of a dramatic increase in output during the second half of the 1990s. Production will probably continue to grow in the first decades of the twenty-first century as major projects are developed. Output from the entire region—50 million metric tons—amounts to about one-seventh that of Europe or Central and South America.

Kazakhstan is the main producer of oil in the region (35.3 million metric tons or 745,000 barrels daily in 2000), with proven reserves of 8 million barrels, or 1.1 billion metric tons. Uzbekistan has modest oil reserves (0.6 billion barrels, or 0.1 billion metric tons) and produces 7.5 million metric tons of oil and condensates each year. It could increase output relatively easily if a viable external market were identified. Like Uzbekistan, Turkmenistan has limited oil reserves, totaling 0.5 billion barrels in 2000. Kyrgyzstan and Tajikistan produce only small quantities of oil, with oil balances in these two countries likely to worsen in the immediate future if economic development proceeds briskly and demand for energy increases.

Natural Gas

Central Asia is predominantly a gas-producing region, with proven gas reserves amounting to 6.6 trillion cubic meters—2.9 trillion cubic meters in Turkmenistan, 1.9 trillion cubic meters in Uzbekistan, and 1.8 trillion cubic meters in Kazakhstan. This represents slightly more than one-tenth of the known gas reserves of the former Soviet Union, which total 56.7 trillion cubic meters. Combined, Central Asia's output—106.7 billion cubic meters or 96.2 million metric tons oil equivalent—represents about half that of the Middle East.

Uzbekistan and Turkmenistan are the two leading gas producers, although Kazakhstan, too, has significant deposits. Until 1991 Turkmenistan produced nearly 80 billion cubic meters of gas per year, but output has fallen dramatically since then because of difficulties in paying for Turkmen gas in the Ukraine and harmful actions by Gazprom, the Russian gas line company. Turkmenistan's production totaled 43.8 billion cubic meters in 2000. Uzbekistan produced 52.2 billion cubic meters in 2000 and estimates it will export between 5 billion and 10 billion cubic meters per year in the future.

Gas from the region is generally high in sulfur, containing corrosive properties, as is also the case with oil from Kazakhstan and other parts of Central Asia. The pipelines therefore have to be well maintained and fuels cleaned before transportation.

As the economies in the region continue to develop, the demand for natural gas as a source of both heat and electricity will increase. Conversion from coal to gas for thermal power production would result in less pollution and reduce the cost of energy. But in spite of significant gas deposits, gas shortages are a continuing problem in some areas because of the inadequate gas pipeline network, inadequate energy policies, payment difficulties, and unstable government structures.

Coal

In spite of the importance of oil and gas in the region's export economy, coal remains the most common source of energy in Central Asia. It is the primary source of electricity in Kazakhstan, for example, and is a major source of heat in both Kazakhstan and Kyrgyzstan. Many thermal power plants in Uzbekistan are fired by coal, although an effort is being made to convert coal-fired power plants to gas in that country.

The biggest coal producer in Central Asia is Kazakhstan, with an estimated 120 billion metric tons of coal in Karaganda and other areas, but the quality is generally poor, and the deposits are far from major industrial locations. The quality can be enhanced, however, if it is mixed with higher-quality coal from other areas, just as oil and gas can be enriched. There is such a tremendous coal base in Kazakhstan that the government is considering converting coal to synthetic oil in the eastern part of the country, where it is economically feasible.

Electricity

Electric power is essential for economic development. The countries of Central Asia generate power by various means. Kyrgyzstan, which has large hydroelectric potential, generates most of its electricity through hydroelectric power stations. Uzbekistan relies primarily on thermal power stations fueled by natural gas, although cheaper energy produced by hydropower electric plants exists. The country also draws significantly on hydropower produced by power stations in Kyrgyzstan and Tajikistan. Kazakhstan depends primarily on coal to generate electricity.

With the exception of Turkmenistan, electricity shortages are a major problem in the region, particularly in Kazakhstan. To alleviate the power shortage, the Kazakh government has implemented a privatization program aimed at rejuvenating the entire electric power industry. Turkmenistan has excess electric generation capacity, and the country has the potential to boost its electricity exports.

Nontraditional Energy Resources

Some of the countries in Central Asia have made substantial commitments to support development of nontraditional energy sources such as solar energy and wind power. In Kyrgyzstan, for example, the Kyun government agency is entirely devoted to examining alternative energy supplies, including solar, wind, geothermal, and coal-bed methane gas. Kyun is one of four key energy agencies or ministries in Kyrgyzstan directly under the Cabinet of Ministers and has the same level of authority and prestige as the other energy ministries.

In Kazakhstan, government officials have mapped alternative energy resources across the country to determine the feasibility of developing these resources. Kazakhstan's southern and northern tiers annually receive an abundance of sunshine and possess significant potential for solar energy. Potential wind and biogas resources have been identified in the west. Both southern and northeastern Kazakhstan have potential for geothermal energy. Kyrgyzstan, Kazakhstan, and Uzbekistan have formed a joint venture to produce solar batteries and panel components for export to India and the People's Republic of China.

AN INTERCONNECTED POWER GRID

A fairly reliable regional electricity grid serving Uzbekistan, Kyrgyzstan, Tajikistan, Turkmenistan, and five districts in the southern territory of Kazakhstan was established in 1960, under Soviet administration. During the first years of independence, there were relatively few problems with the region-wide system. Rainfall was abundant and Kyrgyzstan's Toktogul Reservoir was full. However, between 1992 and 1997 rainfall was less than average, and hydroelectricity generation from Kyrgyzstan became less reliable. As a result, shortages plaguing Central Asia's entire electric power system caused serious disagreements among the countries.

Major Trends in the Energy Sector

After decades of closed economies in Kazakhstan, Kyrgyzstan, Tajikistan, Turkmenistan, and Uzbekistan, local government officials are now encouraging rapid development of their oil, gas, coal, electricity, and nontraditional sectors. To do this, governments in the region are actively restructuring their energy sectors to improve efficiency, streamline operations, and internationalize. In both Kazakhstan and Kyrgyzstan, for instance, privatization is changing the agencies involved in energy production, transportation, and utilization. Government ministries involved in energy exploration, development, and use are being reorganized; large state enterprises are being disaggregated and their component parts converted to joint stock companies. In Kazakhstan, the government ministerial systems, including those engaged in energy development, have been restructured repeatedly over the past several years.

In addition to privatizating state enterprises, countries in Central Asia are soliciting foreign investment to facilitate rapid development of their energy reserves. Central Asian leaders now view their energy resources as a long-term source of revenue, and the nations, especially Kazakhstan, Turkmenistan, and Uzbekistan, are revising investment and taxation codes to woo foreign investors. To date, most private foreign investor interest in Central Asia has focused on providing technology and expertise for the development of the region's potentially huge oil and gas fields. Investment opportunities include refinery and pipeline construction, enhanced oil recovery, and development of a regional pipeline system to distribute natural gas resources from wells to surrounding areas and neighboring republics.

James P. Dorian

See also: **Oil and Mineral Industries—Central Asia**

Further Reading

Asian Development Bank. (1998) *Regional Economic Cooperation in Central Asia*. Manila, Philippines: Asian Development Bank.

Dorian, James P. (2001) *Oil and Gas in Central Asia and Northwest China*. London: CWC Group.

Dorian, James P., Pavel A. Minakir, and Vitaly T. Borisovich, eds. (1993) *CIS Energy and Minerals Development: Prospects, Problems, and Opportunities for International Cooperation*. Dordrecht, Netherlands: Kluwer Academic.

Dorian, James P., Utkur Abbasovich Tojiev, Mikhail S. Tonkopy, Alaibek Jumabekovich Obozov, and Qiu Daxiong. (1999) "Energy in Central Asia and Northwest China: Major Trends and Opportunities for Regional Cooperation." *Energy Policy* 27, 7 (May): 281–297.

Gleason, Gregory. (1997) *The Central Asian States: Discovering Independence*. Boulder, CO: Westview Press.

Munro, Ross H. (1994) "Central Asia and China." In *Central Asia and the World*, edited by Michael Mandelbaum. Washington, DC: Council of Foreign Relations.

Riva, Joseph P., Jr. (1994) *Petroleum Exploration Opportunities in the Former Soviet Union*. Tulsa, OK: PennWell Books.

ENERGY INDUSTRY—CHINA

China is the biggest producer and consumer of coal in the world. Some 1.4 billion metric tons are produced each year. This means that coal industries, rather than petroleum or natural-gas industries, have played the most significant role in energy production and industrial development to date.

The use of coal to heat buildings and smelt metals began in China at least as early as the fourth century, when coal was simply excavated from surface deposits. Coal was a leading fuel by the year 1000, a time when settlements in Europe still preferred to use wood and charcoal (a fuel made from wood). Coal continued to dominate energy use in China for the next thousand years. In the 1960s, however, increasing concerns about the security of the domestic energy supply, as well as market demands for alternatives to coal, led to major initiatives in oil and gas exploration, including the development of the famous Daqing oil field. Proven oil and gas reserves on the mainland and offshore, however, will not meet increasing domestic demand. China has become and will continue to be a net importer of oil and gas. Other diversification initiatives beyond oil and gas include developing untapped hydroelectric potential and the decision, in particular, to create the Three Gorges hydroelectric dam by blocking the Chang (Yangtze) River, the world's third-largest river after the Amazon and the Nile.

The sources of electricity production provide one key insight into the Chinese energy industry. Of the 1.16 trillion kilowatt-hours of electricity produced in 1998, 80 percent was supplied by coal industries. The balance came from hydroelectric and nuclear-power industries at about 18 percent and 1 percent, respectively. Other sources, including renewable sources, are insignificant. The amount of coal used in electricity production is 24 percent of total coal consumption. Industries such as iron and steel, armaments, cement, and chemical fertilizers also use significant amounts of coal.

Energy use by fuel type provides another key insight into the energy industry. Coal accounts for 74 percent of all energy use in China, ensuring the dominance of coal industries. Oil, at 20 percent of all energy use, is a distant second. Hydroelectric power, natural gas, nuclear, and renewable-energy sources account for 6 percent, 2 percent, 0.1 percent, and 0.1 percent, respectively.

Industrial Restructuring

The shift toward a market economy in energy in China has been fraught with difficulties. National-security concerns over the control of energy policy and the difficulty of separating government and enterprise functions in the energy sector represent two overarching challenges at the domestic level. At the international level, the Asian financial crisis of 1997, combined with low prices for oil and coal in the late 1990s, has made the economic climate for reforms more difficult.

The restructuring of the energy industry varies by sector, with the level of competition significantly less than that in the United States, Canada, and Europe. In January 1994, coal prices were deregulated and gradually allowed to float. This led to the closure of 31,000 unprofitable mines in 1999 and another 18,000 mines in 2000. Some 420,000 miners were laid off in 1998 alone.

The oil and gas industries, like other industries, were centrally controlled by the government. Since the economic reforms of the 1980s, however, state-owned oil and gas companies have been created to increase productive capacity through joint ventures with foreign oil companies. The fact that oil consumption has outpaced domestic production since 1993 has further spurred efforts to increase domestic production. To this end, exploration licenses are now awarded to state-owned (but slightly privatized) companies on a competitive basis to meet national production targets. The energy reforms also saw the creation of two vertically integrated and publicly traded companies from government-controlled organizations that previously had to serve public-policy and regulatory functions. By creating two "market-based" companies, PetroChina and Sinopec, the Chinese government sought to have greater efficiency in energy production and to prepare the way for the competitive pressures that would arise from greater foreign direct investment in domestic-energy projects.

PetroChina was created from the China National Petroleum Corporation (CNPC) in 1999 with 480,000 of its 1.5 million workers. CNPC allocated the majority of its best assets to PetroChina while retaining the excess workforce and welfare obligations. At the outset, PetroChina ranked fifth in the world in estimated reserves, produced 68 percent of China's total oil, operated 3,400 gas stations, and owned pipelines transporting 84 percent of China's natural gas. A second company, Sinopec, followed in 2000. This company operates more than 20,000 gas stations, 1,100 bulk-storage facilities, and a number of refineries. A significant aspect of this restructuring has been the dismissal of excess staff. PetroChina laid off 38,000 employees by January 2001, and Sinopec is expected to cut its workforce of 500,000 by 20 percent by 2005.

Changes planned in hydropower production are also significant. A number of large hydropower dams are under construction. The Three Gorges dam, the largest of these, is scheduled for completion in 2009, when it will generate 84.7 billion kilowatt-hours a year.

Of the remaining sources of energy—natural gas, nuclear energy, and renewable energy—natural gas will probably be the most significant. China has significant domestic reserves of natural gas and a plan to deliver up to three times the amount currently consumed by 2010. A "West to East" natural-gas pipeline could involve partnership with Western companies. Nuclear-power capacity will also expand. There are currently two nuclear-power facilities, the first in Zhejiang Province south of Shanghai and the second in Guangdong province near Hong Kong. Several new nuclear-power facilities are under construction to expand electricity production from just over 1 percent to 3 percent. Of the renewable-energy sources, only hydropower plays a significant role. Other sources of renewable power, such as biomass, wind, solar, geothermal, and tidal power, are minor in China compared with levels of 3 percent in nations such as Denmark and the United States. Their potential for development, however, is considerable.

China relies heavily on coal as a source of energy as with this coal-fired power plant in northern China. (EYE UBIQUITOUS/CORBIS)

Eco-efficiency

China's reliance on coal has led to serious energy-efficiency and environmental problems and makes the development of less harmful sources of energy a pressing challenge. Environmental problems created by burning coal include acid rain, smog, and greenhouse gases such as carbon dioxide. Each of these problems has specific impacts on the environment and human health. Acid rain, for example, damages forests, croplands, and lakes. Smog, made up of particulate matter and sulfur dioxide emissions, covers many cities and affects people's health. In certain parts of China, the concentration of total suspended particles is two to three times the level specified as safe under World Health Organization guidelines. Carbon-dioxide emissions (the main cause of greenhouse-effect climate change) in China are second only to emissions in the United States. On a per-person basis, however, the average American creates 7.5 times more carbon dioxide than does the average Chinese.

Energy production is no longer a simple matter of economic efficiency, narrowly defined. Because energy production can have significant impacts on employment and the environment, capital markets are increasingly required to consider environmental, labor, and human-rights ramifications before they make their investment decisions.

Energy industries, whether they are publicly or privately owned, not only have to produce more energy from existing natural resources, they also have to produce it in environmentally responsible ways. Improving energy efficiency while linking energy production to environmental goals is part of a larger challenge China shares with other nations.

Robert Gale

See also: **Three Gorges Dam Project**

Further Reading

Andrews-Speed, Philip, and Stephen Dow. (2000) "Reform of China's Electric Power Industry: Challenges Facing the Government." *Energy Policy* 28: 335–347.

Chang, Felix K. (2001) "Chinese Energy and Asian Security." *Orbis* 45: 211–241.

United States Energy Information Administration. (1997) "Country Reports: China: An Energy Sector Overview." Retrieved 4 December 2001, from: http://www.eia.doe.gov/emeu/cabs/china/china97.html

Zhang, Shi-qiu. (2000) "China's Energy, Environment, and Policy Perspective." *Journal of Environmental Sciences* 12: 270–275.

ENGLISH IN ASIA

ENGLISH IN ASIA English is an Asian language. That may sound strange at first, but the facts are clear. English has been used in various parts of Asia for almost two hundred years. It is the first language of two countries in Asia (Australia and New Zealand), the second language of seven others (Bangladesh, India, Malaysia, Pakistan, the Philippines, Singapore, and Sri Lanka), and the first foreign language in the remaining Asian countries. More fluent users of English can be found in Asia (estimated at 350 million) than on any other continent; English is used predominantly to communicate with fellow Asians. Locally published English newspapers can be found in practically every metropolitan city across Asia. Conferences frequently are conducted in English (and their proceedings published in English) when only a few, if any, of the participants are native English speakers. English is the language of the Association of Southeast Asian Nations (ASEAN), even though it is not the first language of any of the member countries. More students are studying English in this region than in any other part of the world. China alone has 100 million people learning English. Although most people in Asia do not speak English, Asian leaders in many fields (the arts, business and commerce, education, diplomacy, law, the military, space exploration, and tourism) usually do. English sometimes enables different ethnic groups in the same country to communicate with one another, helping to establish a sense of nationhood.

The Debate on the Use of English

Ongoing articulate debates about English in Asia have continued for some time. One side takes the position that English is an instrument of cultural imperialism and neocolonialism. They argue that linguistic diversity is greatly diminished by the spread of English, which adversely affects minority languages. The other side does not see English as an alien language or as an instrument of Western hegemony. This group maintains that English belongs to those who use it, not only to native speakers, and that it also expresses Asian culture. They point out that leaders such as Mohandas K. Gandhi (1869–1948) and Jawaharlal Nehru (1889–1964) wrote in English to reach a national audience and to promote a national agenda. They make the point that English has no claims to intrinsic superiority but that it has a preeminent role in Asia because it is a medium for science, technology, literature, and law. English has borrowed from the languages of Asia as well. A few examples include "bungalow" from Bengali, "pajama" from Hindi, "sugar" from Sanskrit, "serendipity" from Singhalese, "kowtow" from Mandarin, "ketchup" from Malay, "boondocks" from Tagalog, and "tycoon" from Japanese.

Features of Asian English

There are also national coinages in English, which are familiar primarily to a local population. These include "dirty kitchen" (in the Philippines, the room in a home where the real cooking is done), "minor wife" (in Thailand, a wife who is secondary to the major wife), "lah" (in Singapore and Malaysia, a mark of informality), "field chickens" (in China, frogs), "sayonara home run" (in Japan, the winning run), and "crow and sparrow story" (in India, a "cock and bull" story).

Pronunciations vary across Asia, but intelligibility of the different varieties of English is no more of a problem in Asia than it is in other parts of the world. As in the United States, grammar use across Asia ranges from pidgin to an international standard. Discourse patterns are frequently different in different varieties of Asian English.

Showing politeness is important in every culture, but it is done differently in the various forms of Asian English. Because the Japanese are reluctant to say "No" directly, a person from Osaka may say "I will consider it," or a person from Tokyo may say, "That will be difficult," when they mean "No." Nodding the head and saying "Yes" do not always mean agreement from an Asian speaker of English; neither do "I'm sorry" and "I apologize" necessarily mean an acceptance of guilt or responsibility for a mistake. Often each of these means "I regret there is some unpleasantness here. I wish it were not so."

One way to learn about the use of English in Asia is to read creative writing by Asians. Talented authors include Anita Desai, Wimal Dissanayake, Ha Jin, Minfong Ho, F. Sionil Jose, Catherine Lim, Shirley Geok-Lin Lim, R. K. Narayan, Arundhati Roy, Raja Rao, Bienvenido N. Santos, Pira Sudham, and Edwin Thumboo. There are also academic publications devoted to the topic of English in Asia.

The future of English in Asia is one of growth and variation. In almost every Asian country the percentage of the population fluent in English is increasing rapidly, and it is predicted that 30 to 35 percent of the population will use English on a daily basis by the year 2010. English will doubtless continue to be the language Asians use to represent their personal aspirations and public policies in the international workplace, the global media, and for Internet communication.

Larry E. Smith

Further Reading

Bautista, Ma. Lourdes S., ed. (1997) *English IS an Asian language: The Philippine Context*. New South Wales, Australia: Macquarie Library.

Honna Nobuyuki, ed. (1998) *Asian Englishes: An International Journal of the Sociolinguistics of English in Asia/Pacific*. Tokyo: ALC Press.

Kachru, Braj B., ed. (1992) *The Other Tongue: English across Cultures*. Urbana, IL: University of Illinois Press.

Smith, Larry E., and Michael L. Forman, eds. (1997) *World Englishes 2000*. Honolulu, HI: University of Hawaii Press.

ENOMOTO TAKEAKI

(1836–1908), Japanese government official. Enomoto Takeaki was a naval officer and diplomat who served the Tokugawa shogunate (known then by the name of Kamajiro) and later the Meiji government. Born in Shitaya, Edo prefecture, he studied at the Shoheiko (Shogunal College) and learned navigation from the Dutch in Nagasaki. Appointed director of the Shogunate naval school, in 1862 he went to Rotterdam to study military services and to supervise construction of the warship *Kaiyo Maru*, which was commissioned by the shogunate. After six years in Europe, he became vice commander-in-chief of the shogunate navy. When the rule of the house of Tokugawa was overthrown and power was restored to the Meiji emperor, Enomoto, with a small army of supporters, took eight ships of the Tokugawa navy to the northern island of Hokkaido to establish an independent republic. He surrendered to imperial forces in 1869, spent three years under house arrest, and was pardoned in 1872. Restored to favor, he later received many important ministerial appointments within the Meiji government, including envoy to Russia (1873–1876). He concluded the Treaty of St. Petersburg (1875), by which Japan abandoned its claim to Sakhalin Island in exchange for the northern Kuril Islands. Enomoto was subsequently appointed navy minister (1876–1882), minister to China (1882–1884), and he held cabinet posts in communications, education, foreign affairs, agriculture, and commerce He was made a viscount in 1887 and named adviser to the Privy Council in 1890.

William Nelson Ridgeway

Further Reading

Morris, J. (1906) *Makers of Japan*. London: Methuen.

ENVIRONMENTAL ISSUES.

See **Air Pollution; Aral Sea; Bhopal; Deforestation; Earthquakes; Endangered Species—Asia; Green Revolution—South Asia; Green Revolution—Southeast Asia; Maldives—Profile; Mangroves; Narmada Dam Controversy; Nuclear Arms; Soil Loss; Sustainability—Asia; Three Gorges Dam Project; Typhoons; Volcanoes.**

ERDENET

(2000 pop. 68,000). Erdenet (1,300 meters above sea level), located 240 kilometers northwest of Ulaanbaatar, Mongolia, is the second largest city in the country. Erdenet is also one of Mongolia's youngest cities. Its establishment began with the discovery of massive copper and molybdenum deposits in Erdenet Mountain in the 1960s. By 1974, an ore-processing plant began operating in the area under a Mongolian-Soviet joint venture—the Erdenet Copper and Molybdenum Mining and Concentrating Combine. In 1975, the industrial complex, located in a valley between the Selenge and Orhon Rivers, was officially declared a town.

Although the city has several industries—including a carpet factory, a food-processing plant, and a timber-processing plant—its economy revolves around copper and molybdenum mining. By 1990, the city boasted Asia's largest copper-molybdenum ore-processing plant and accounted for up to 90 percent of the total output of Mongolia's mining industry. The city also supplies 30 percent of the country's tax income and 60 percent of its exports.

Daniel Hruschka

Further Reading

The Academy of Sciences Mongolian People's Republic. (1990) *Information Mongolia.* Oxford: Pergamon Press.

ERSHAD, H. M. (b. 1930), President of Bangladesh. Born in the Rangpur District of modern-day Bangladesh, Hussain Muhammad Ershad became a career officer in the Pakistan army, reaching the rank of lieutenant colonel by 1971. Stationed in Pakistan when Bangladesh and Pakistan split, he was interned there (as an East Pakistani he was believed to be disloyal to a united Pakistan) and did not return to Bangladesh until 1973, when he was included in the Bangladesh army. Ershad succeeded Ziaur Rahman (Zia) as chief of staff in 1978. From that position, he overthrew the Bangladesh Nationalist Party government of Abdus Sattar, who had succeeded to the presidency on the death of President Zia. He assumed the title of president in December 1984, having earlier ruled as chief martial-law administrator. Although an unpopular and unelected leader (he did win an obviously rigged referendum in 1986), Ershad continued many of the development programs of Zia and was rather successful in reducing the rate of population growth, receiving a citation from the United Nations for this. Opposition, which was endemic, peaked in the last months of 1990, resulting in his resignation in December 1990. He had formed a party, the Jatiya (People's) Party, which contested in the 1991 and June 1996 elections, finishing third each time. In 1996 the Jatiya Party supported an Awami League–led coalition, but the party has since split and the faction led by Ershad has withdrawn support from Sheikh Hasina and joined Khaleda Zia in opposition.

Former President Ershad at a Jatiya Party rally in Dhaka in March 1997. (AFP/CORBIS)

Craig Baxter

Further Reading

Ahmed, Moudud. (1995) *Democracy and the Challenge of Development: A Study of Politics and Military Intervention in Bangladesh.* New Delhi: Vikas Publishing House.

Baxter, Craig. (1997) *Bangladesh from a Nation to a State.* Boulder, CO: Westview.

ERZURUM (2002 est. pop 333,000). Erzurum is one of the most important cities in eastern Turkey. The capital of the province of Erzurum, it is located between the Karasu and Aras valleys at an altitude of nearly 2,000 meters. Due to its geographic location, Erzurum has always held military and economic significance. Its strategic location also means it was often fought over in the past, despite the high frequency of earthquakes. The city first became significant in 415 when the Byzantine emperor Theodosius fortified and renamed it Theodosiopolis. For the next 500 years, it was held, alternately, by the Byzantines, Arabs, and Armenians (who called it Karin). The Byzantines reigned until the Battle of Manzikert (1071), which left Erzurum under Seljuk rule. It later fell to the Mongols, after which it was conquered by Sultan Selim I (1467–1520) in 1514 and incorporated into the Ottoman empire. Erzurum became the capital of the new province in 1534 and served as the primary military base for campaigns to Iran and Georgia throughout the sixteenth and seventeenth centuries. During the Ottoman-Russian wars, Erzurum was occupied by the Russians in 1829, 1878, and 1916. On 23 July 1919 Mustafa Kemal Ataturk (1881–1938), founder of the Republic of Turkey, held the first meeting of the National Congress in Erzurum. The city was linked to the country's rail system in 1939 It is the location of the 3rd Army and Ataturk University, which opened in 1958. Erzurum is often used as a base for outdoor expeditions to nearby Mount Ararat.

T. Isikozlu-E.F. Isikozlu

Further Reading

Inalcik, Halil. (1960) "Erzurum." In *The Encyclopedia of Islam.* 2d ed. Leiden, Netherlands: Brill.

Statistical Yearbook of Turkey, 1998. (1998) Ankara, Turkey: Devlet Istatistik Enstitusu.

ESFAHAN (2002 pop.1.4 million). Esfahan, an ancient city located in central Iran, has played a significant role in Iranian history, as it was often the battleground between warring tribes and dynasties, undoubtedly because of its strategic position. Not much is known about the city before the Sasanid dynasty (224/228–651 CE). Its location, however, at the intersection of several important roads, suggests that it may have been a cultural and financial center. Some believe that Esfahan was the residence of a few Achaemenid royals, who called it either Gaba or Gi. In 642 CE the city was conquered by the Arabs, who made Esfahan the capital of al-Jibal Province. Esfahan was controlled by various rulers over the years and its prosperity depended upon their whims. When the Seljuk dynasty began in the eleventh century, Toghril Beg named Esfahan the capital of his realm. During this time the city flourished, increasing in size and population. With the demise of the Seljuk dynasty, however, Esfahan endured neglect and difficulty.

Esfahan experienced a renewal in the late sixteenth and seventeenth centuries when it was designated the capital city of the Safavid ruler Shah Abbas I the Great, who used his riches to improve the city's sanitary conditions and architectural landscape. After the Safavid dynasty (1501–1722/1736) fell, however, Esfahan once again became the target of various warring factions. Political and economic stability did not return to Esfahan until the Qajar dynasty (1794–1925) rose to power in the eighteenth century. This stability continued through the Pahlavi dynasty. Toward the end of the Pahlavi dynasty (1924–1979), the people of Esfahan were active in their opposition to the shah's policies and instrumental in the establishment of the Islamic Republic of Iran in 1979.

Esfahan is currently home to Esfahan University, which was founded as part of a program to bring higher education to the provinces of Iran. Due to its ancient roots, Esfahan is also home to several famous architectural sites: Meydan-i Shah (Royal Square), Masjid-i Shah (Royal Mosque), Masjid-i Shaykh Lotfollah (Lotfollah Mosque), A'li Ghapo (Royal Palace), the Great Bazaar, and Sadr Boulevard. These sites make Esfahan a beautiful Iranian city, which also enjoys the greenery that the Zayandeh River and its channel system bring. Esfahan is also an important manufacturing center, home to Iran's modern steel industry, and pipe-building, helicopter assembly, among others.

Houman A. Sadri

Further Reading

Barthold, W. (1984) *An Historical Geography of Iran.* Trans. by Svat Soucek. Princeton, NJ: Princeton University Press.

ESTRADA, JOSEPH (b. 1937), president of the Philippines, 1998–2001. The thirteenth president of the Republic of the Philippines, Joseph Estrada was born José Ejercito. Against his parents' wishes, he became a movie actor, adopting the stage name Joseph Estrada and the nickname "Erap." In his thirty-two–year acting career, Estrada starred in 107 movies,

President Estrada with a baby in a Manila slum neighborhood in October 2000. (REUTERS NEWMEDIA INC./CORBIS)

often portraying Robin Hood–type roles. This endeared him to the masses, and he became a popular and recognizable personality.

His popularity served him well when in 1969 he ran for mayor of the Manila suburb of San Juan and won. During his sixteen years as mayor, he earned a reputation as a champion of poor people. Although he initially ran as an independent, he later became identified with the former president Ferdinand Marcos (1917–1989). In 1986, following the ouster of Marcos through popular demand, Estrada was unseated, along with other local officials, as a result of the massive governmental reorganization that Corazon Aquino (b. 1933) embarked on when she assumed the presidency.

The following year, Estrada successfully campaigned for a senate seat and was one of only two candidates who won under an opposition ticket allied with old Marcos forces. Elected vice president in May 1992, he used that position as a launching pad for his presidential campaign. In May 1998, he was elected president by the largest electoral margin in Philippine history.

Though poor people believed him to be their champion, Estrada did little to mitigate poverty or address land reform, and his presidency was short lived. Amid allegations of rampant corruption, he was criticized for giving lucrative business contracts and concessions to former Marcos cronies. He was later accused of receiving $80 million in bribes from illegal gambling operators, as well as kickbacks from tobacco excise-tax receipts.

In 2000, as the house of representatives voted to impeach Estrada, the groundswell for his resignation heightened. The Philippine senate then began the impeachment trial, but after a close vote of eleven senators to ten, which in effect suppressed evidence supposed to prove Estrada's guilt, senate president Aquilino Pimentel and the entire house prosecution team resigned. Mass rallies took place, and in January 2001 several cabinet officials and senior military officers withdrew their support for him in favor of the vice president Gloria Macapagal-Arroyo (b. 1947).

When Estrada left Malacanang, the presidential residence, the supreme court regarded him as having resigned from his position and declared the presidency vacant. It then swore in Macapagal-Arroyo as president. Estrada was arrested in May 2001 and continues to be detained at a military hospital. He faces charges of perjury, corruption, and economic plunder and could receive the death penalty for the latter offense.

Zachary Abuza

Further Reading

Doronila, Amando. (2002) *The Fall of Joseph Estrada: The Inside Story.* Manila, Philippines: Center for Investigative Journalism.

ETATISM—TURKEY

Etatism (statism), derived from the French word *état* (state), was adopted as one of six ideological principles of Kemalism, the founding ideology of the Republic of Turkey, named after Mustafa Kemal (later Ataturk). The others are republicanism, secularism, nationalism, reformism, and populism. The Republican People's Party (RPP), which was founded in 1924 and ruled until 1950 as the single and, therefore, dominant party, incorporated the principle of etatism into its program as the term defining the official economic strategy at its 1931 congress. In 1937 the principle was incorporated into the Turkish constitution.

Definitions of Etatism

Etatism has two interrelated meanings. Broadly, it referred to the state-centric component of Kemalist ideology, which stressed the autonomous role of the state in shaping policy outcomes and societal forces. It reflected the Kemalists' intentions to use the state as a pioneering and active agent of modernization. Etatism gained a more limited meaning after the fourth RPP congress, which was held in 1935. There the term was used to refer specifically to the economic strategy of the ruling RPP, which called for state involvement in the economy to advance the nation's welfare and prosperity. The state's involvement in the economy did not mean the abolishment of private initiative, as was the case of Soviet-style collectivism. Private enterprise was to play a fundamental role in the economy, but coordinated government intervention was considered to be essential to accelerate the accumulation of initial capital necessary for rapid economic development, since the private sector was too weak to undertake this task. Etatism encouraged indigenous capitalist development by shielding the local infant industries through various protectionist policies.

Turkish Economic History

The Republic of Turkey was founded in 1923, the same year in which the Allies recognized Turkey as an independent state with the signing of the Lausanne Treaty. Successive wars since the Ottoman Empire's entry into World War I in 1915 and the War of Independence between 1919 and 1922 had had a devastating impact on the economy of the Anatolian peninsula. The Lausanne Treaty contained some restrictive clauses that set the tone for the economic policies of the new republic. Turkey was not required to pay war reparations, but it agreed to pay the debts of the former Ottoman empire—the last installment was paid in 1953. The treaty also prohibited Turkey from adopting a protective customs regime until 1929. The underlying rationale was to protect the rights of the foreign firms operating in Turkey. In exchange for its recognition as an independent state, Turkey agreed to that term, but the state then gave support to Turkey's weak private sector through a complex system of incentives and subsidies in line with the guiding principles adopted at the Izmir Economic Congress of 1923. The passage of the Law for the Encouragement of Industry in 1927 was the first sign of the expansion of state control over industry.

Having faced the aftereffects of the Great Depression of 1929, which signaled a collapse of liberal laissez-faire economics in Europe and the United States, republican governments began to formulate conscious etatist policies. Having been influenced by the interventionist trend in Western European economic theory and the practical insights drawn from the successes of the planned industrialization efforts (1928–1933) of the Soviet Union, the Kemalist elites, in search of some alternatives to laissez-faire economics, revised their earlier liberal economic policies along etatist lines. One of the first measures they imposed was the nationalization of foreign companies operating in such various sectors as infrastructure and the service sector. The nationalization program, completed in 1939, paved the way for further state control of the economy through expanding public ownership into different branches of the economy. In addition to the failure of laissez-faire liberalism in the late 1920s, the lack of initial capital formation and entrepreneurial spirit, as well as the need for protectionism, can be counted as three basic reasons for the state's turn to etatism in the 1930s.

The state took two crucial steps that constituted the backbone of etatist policies: first, large state-owned or -controlled companies, known as state economic enterprises (SEEs), were founded; second, industrial development plans were formulated. The state's active involvement in the economy under the guise of etatism created the earliest patterns of an inward-looking industrialization strategy in which the SEEs such as Sumerbank (1933) and Etibank (1935) would play a leading role. These were giant state companies, specialized in diverse manufacturing industries such textiles, mining, and extraction and founded for the production of intermediate, consumer, and producer goods. The foundation of People's Bank of Turkey (1935) and the reorganization of Agricultural Bank of Turkey (1937) on etatist principles signaled the state's expansion in the financial sector through a network of credit facilities, grants, and subsidies.

To coordinate public and private industrialization efforts, the state launched comprehensive plans. The First Five-Year Industrial Plan was launched in 1934. The second one, launched in 1938, became obsolete with the outbreak of World War II in 1939. Some minor plans were also designed on a sectoral basis, as in the case of mining. Centrally planned industrialization strengthened etatist control over the economy, since the state began to intervene intensely in industry, commerce, and finance to achieve the objectives set in the plans.

Effects of Etatism on the Turkish Economy

Under etatist policies, the public sector had a pioneering role in the economy; etatism also provided a new basis of political legitimacy for Kemalism by making the state the most active institution, one that would lead the nation to the highest levels of material welfare. Etatist policies in effect from the 1930s until 1980 made the state a significant economic actor in Turkey.

After Turkey's transition to multiparty politics in 1950, all the major parties on both the left and the right supported the etatist policies that the RPP had launched in the 1930s. Therefore, vestiges of etatism survived until the 1980s in the form of central planning, protectionism, and the state's pioneering role in the import-substitution method of industrialization. These vestiges impeded the development of a full market economy. Etatist practices created an economic system that suffered from weak export capacity, chronic trade deficits, shortages of foreign currency, and balance-of-payment deficits.

Influenced by the West's popular supply-side economic policies, the Turkish economy was reoriented at the beginning of the 1980s and moved from a state-led model of industrialization to an export-oriented growth strategy. The etatist policies that the state had followed since the 1930s were severely challenged as the Turkish economy embarked on a journey of restructuring according to liberal principles.

Nazim Irem

Further Reading

Barlas, Dilek. (1998) *Etatism and Diplomacy in Turkey: Economic and Foreign Policy Strategies in an Uncertain World, 1929–1939*. Boston, MA: Brill Academic Publishers.

Boratav, Korkut. (1974) *Turkiye'de Devletcilik* (Etatism in Turkey*)*. Istanbul, Turkey: Gercek Yayinlari.

Heper, Metin. (1985) *The State Tradition in Turkey*. Walkington, U.K.: The Eothen Press.

Koker, Levent. (1990) *Modernlesme, Kemalizm ve Demokrasi* (Modernization, Kemalism, and Democracy). Istanbul, Turkey: Iletisim Yayinlari.

Landau, M. Jacob, ed. (1984) *Ataturk and the Modernization of Turkey*. Boulder, CO: Westview Press.

Lovatt, Debbie, ed. (2001) *Turkey since 1970: Politics, Economics and Society*. New York: Palgrave Publishers Ltd.

Parla, Taha. (1989) *Ziya Gokalp, Kemalizm ve Turkiye'de Korporatizm* (Ziya Gokalp, Kemalism, and Corporatism in Turkey). Istanbul, Turkey: Iletisim Yayinlari.

Singer, Morris. (1977) *The Economic Advance of Turkey, 1938–1960*. Ankara, Turkey: Ayyildiz Matbaasi A.S.

Tekeli, Ilhan, and Selim Ilkin. (1982) *Uygulamaya Gecerken Turkiye'de Devletciligin Olusumu* (Development of Etatism in Turkey in Transition to Implementation). Ankara, Turkey: Middle East Technical University.

———. (1982) *1929 Dunya Buhraninda Turkiye'nin Iktisadi Politika Arayisi* (Turkey's Search for an Economic Policy during the World Depression of 1929*)*. Ankara, Turkey: Middle East Technical University.

Tuncay, Mete. (1981) *Turkiye Cumhuriyetinde Tek Parti Yonetiminin Kurulmasi, 1923–31* (The Establishment of One-Party Regime in the Turkish Republic: 1923–31*)*. Ankara, Turkey: Yurt Yayinlari.

ETHNIC COLONIAL POLICY—INDONESIA

For most of the long period of Dutch involvement in Indonesia, colonial authorities made clear administrative distinctions between ethnic groups. The sharpness of these distinctions and the extent to which it was possible to cross the boundaries varied, however, over time.

The Dutch East India Company (VOC) avoided having direct administrative control over non-Europeans, preferring to rule via traditional elites or by appointing other Asians—especially Chinese—to be agents, often called *kapitan*. Because few European women traveled to the Indies, many Europeans married or cohabited with local women, though from time to time laws were introduced to ban such practices. Their descendants were seen as European if they were Christian and recognized by their fathers; consequently, European society in the Indies was very much mestizo (of mixed ancestry) in culture and appearance. Christian Indonesians were close to Europeans in status.

After the end of rule by the VOC in 1795 and the imposition of direct rule by the Netherlands, a formal legal distinction between Europeans and "natives" *(inlanders)* began to harden. This distinction enabled the Dutch to restrict land ownership to natives, and after about 1830 it was almost impossible for any European to buy land. This was partly to protect the native population, partly to enable natives to be tied to the land for tax purposes, and partly to preserve many elements of traditional law, culture, and social structure. It also allowed discrimination against Indonesians in employment conditions and in civil and political rights (especially in criminal procedure). This discrimination contributed to the eventual emergence of nationalism. As in VOC times, legitimate children produced by marriages of Europeans and natives followed the heritage of their fathers, while illegitimate children followed their mothers'. Those who were neither European nor native were attached to one category or the other for different purposes until a third category, "foreign Orientals" *(vreemde oosterlingen)*, was developed in the late nineteenth century. Natives and foreign Orientals could legally acquire European status if they were culturally Europeanized or had legal need of the status, for example, as owners of businesses. In the late nineteenth century, many Dutch policy makers proposed abandoning such classifications to encourage modernization, but they were blocked by conservatives and supporters of traditional law.

In 1899, Japanese diplomatic pressure forced colonial authorities to grant Japanese subjects European status. There was increasing pressure from China to do the same for resident Chinese, especially in the 1930s. This led to a gradual change in emphasis from "racial" categories to various categories of citizenship.

The Dutch also distinguished among native ethnic groups, such as the Javanese, Balinese, and Timorese, particularly in matters of civil law and recruitment into the colonial army. These legal distinctions were, however, never legislatively defined and disappeared with Indonesian independence.

Robert Cribb

Further Reading

Cribb, Robert, ed. (1994) *The Late Colonial State in Indonesia: Political and Economic Foundations of the Netherlands Indies, 1880–1942*. Leiden, Netherlands: KITLV Press.

Taylor, Jean Gelman. (1983) *The Social World of Batavia: European and Eurasian in Dutch Asia*. Madison, WI: University of Wisconsin Press.

ETHNIC CONFLICT—AFGHANISTAN

Ethnic differences are strongest when other significant differences—religious, ideological, economic, geographic, linguistic—reinforce distinctions between one ethnic group and another. Although Afghanistan is a complex country in terms of ethnic composition, the importance of ethnicity in explaining conflict has varied significantly throughout its history.

In the original state named Afghanistan, dating back to 1747, the Pashtun ethnic group constituted an overwhelming majority. Until the late nineteenth century, Afghanistan was a fragile confederation of Pashtun tribes, and the word "Afghan" was used as a synonym for Pashtun. As part of a nation-building project early in the twentieth century, it increasingly came to imply "citizen of Afghanistan." The borders of the territory that now form Afghanistan were established toward the end of the nineteenth century, when the British and Russian empires were competing for control of the region. The Pashtun population was split, one part living in British India and the Pashtun majority in Afghanistan being reduced to around half the total population.

During his monarchy, Abdur Rahman Khan (reigned 1880–1901) attempted to build a stronger, more modern state, less dependent on shifting tribal alliances. Trying to establish authority throughout the country, particularly where ethnic minorities were dominant, the king battled several contentious groups, with especially harsh implications for the Hazara and Nuristani peoples. Whereas Afghanistan's majority are Sunni Muslims, the Hazara are Shiʿa, and the Nuristani practice their own religion. Religion was used to legitimize warfare and ethnic persecution. Abdur Rahman Khan also forcibly moved large numbers of noncomplying Pashtuns to minority-dominated areas in the north, thus forming people who were formerly a threat into an effective instrument for strengthening his rule in non-Pashtun areas. Pashtun nomads were granted privileges such as access to pastures in the Hazara-inhabited central region.

Twentieth-Century Events

Habibullah (reigned 1901–1919) and Amanullah (reigned 1919–1929) introduced constitutional reforms and outlawed slavery and other discriminatory practices that affected primarily minorities. King Amanullah fell in 1929, replaced by the sole non-Pashtun ruler in Afghan history, Bacha-e-Saqao—"son of the water-carrier." A Tajik from the Kohistan region north of Kabul, his position was based less on ethnicity than on support from a religious network.

Nader Shah (reigned 1929–1933), representative of a tribal Pashtun confederation, deposed Bacha-e Saqao after only nine months. After Zaher Shah (reigned 1933–1973) inherited the throne, the country was relatively calm for several decades. A short era of liberalization in the late 1940s was strangled by the ruling family in 1953, when Prince Daud Khan, the king's cousin, became prime minister. Daud, a strong proponent of Pashtun nationalism, wanted to expand Afghanistan to include the Pashtun population of Pakistan. This led to tense relations between the two countries and to the eventual ouster of Daud in 1963.

The constitution of 1964 allowed freedom of the press, and political parties were established. The pro-Soviet communist party, the People's Democratic Party of Afghanistan (PDPA), was dominantly Pashtun, but split into the Parcham branch of urban intellectuals with a tendency toward ethnic accommodation and the rural, authoritarian, and nationalist Khalq branch. The major Maoist party, Shula-e Jawid, arose in 1967 from divisions in PDPA. Faced with a variety of parties seeking to place ethnic discrimination squarely on the political agenda, the king responded by unofficially ensuring that minorities were represented in the cabinet, but the basic attitude toward ethnic differences was that economic modernization would lead to their gradual erosion.

When former prime minister Daud Khan regained power in 1973, the "new democracy" of the past ten years came to an end. He established an authoritarian rule that was overturned in a PDPA coup in 1978. PDPA immediately announced a Soviet-style nationality policy that addressed four areas: government participation, education, newspapers, and culture. PDPA's credibility was severely undermined by Pashtun dominance of the party and its attempts to foster Pashtun support by launching ethnic appeals.

With the 1978 coup and the Soviet invasion of 1979, Afghani resistance parties were established in Pakistan and Iran. The Pakistan-based parties were, with the exception of Jamat-i Islami, dominated by Pashtuns, and all had some form of Sunni Islamic orientation. Iran became the major backer of the groups active among the Hazara. The resistance based its legitimacy on various forms of politicized Islam, and ethnicity was low on the political agenda of the exiled parties in the early 1980s. Nonetheless, the fact that the resistance leadership was overwhelmingly Pashtun was problematic from the perspective of the non-Pashtun population. Resistance-based shadow cabinets were notoriously weak and fragmented, mainly because the resistance leaders could not accommodate Afghanistan's ethnic variety.

Once in power, the PDPA went on to announce a Soviet-style nationality policy. In practice, the will to implement such reforms was limited, and PDPA's credibility was severely undermined by its Pashtun dominance. When President Najib took power in 1986, there was a change of approach. First, Najib's government was designed as a massive project in political accommodation. Second, the government realized that Soviet military presence in Afghanistan was on the wane, and ethnic and tribal loyalties were exploited to establish local militias to fill the gap. The so-called Uzbek militia of General Dostum and the Ismaili militia of Sayyed Mansoor developed into major military units. Ethnicity, for many, became an avenue to privileges. Military groups of different origins opposed or supported one another, as when Uzbek militias were used to reinforce the defense of threatened government garrisons in the Pashtun south.

The ethnic dimension was brought to the limelight as the resistance took power in Kabul in April 1992. Jamat-i Islami and its key commander, Ahmed Shah Massoud, were a major force, but different groups in the resistance soon split Kabul into separate sections, and the ethnic definition of the conflict gained in prominence. Alliances between resistance groups and sections of the old government army that shared ethnic identity emerged as key forces in the battle for controlling the capital. Alliances rapidly shifted; political and military leaders used ethnic arguments to build support, and common people had little alternative but to seek protection with their own group.

The Taliban emerged in late 1994 in reaction to the strife in Kabul and the lawlessness in the rest of the country. Based on traditionalist networks of Islamic scholars and village mullahs, the Taliban found supporters mainly in the Pashtun population. At first the organization avoided ethnic rhetoric, but gradually it began using pro-Pashtun as well as anti-Shiʿa arguments. In the aftermath of armed confrontations with other groups, the Taliban often arrested and harassed people only for ethnic reasons. The movement's dominantly Pashtun membership and the frequency of ethnic violence have only contributed to further manifest ethnicity as a central component of the conflict in Afghanistan. It remains to be seen how the Taliban's removal from power in late 2001 will affect the complex ethnic conflicts in the country.

Kristian Berg Harpviken

See also: **Hazara; Pashtun; Taliban**

Further Reading

Dupree, Louis. (1980) *Afghanistan*. 2d ed. Princeton, NJ: Princeton University Press.

Harpviken, Kristian Berg. (1997) "Transcending Traditionalism: The Emergence of Non-State Military Formations in Afghanistan." *Journal of Peace Research* 34: 271–287.

Naby, Eden. (1980) "The Ethnic Factor in Soviet Afghan Relations." *Asian Survey* 20: 237–256.

Rashid, Ahmed. (2000) *Taliban: Islam, Oil, and the New Great Game in Central Asia*. London: I. B. Tauris.

Roy, Olivier. (1986) *Islam and Resistance in Afghanistan*. Cambridge, U.K.: Cambridge University Press.

ETHNIC CONFLICT—MYANMAR

Ethnic conflict has been a central feature in the political life of Myanmar (Burma) since independence from Great Britain was obtained in 1948. Located on the crossroads between East, South, and Southeast Asia, Myanmar is one of the most ethnically diverse countries in the region. But the failure of successive governments to resolve the issues of insurgency and equitable representation for the various ethnic nationalities is a major factor behind the country's long-standing malaise.

A Land of Diversity

Burma's 1974 constitution (the country did not become Myanmar until 1989) set aside states for the seven largest ethnic minority groups in the country: the Chin, Kachin, Karen, Kayah, Mon, Rakhine, and Shan. The situation, however, is rather more complicated in the field. Minority ethnic groups, speaking a total of over one hundred languages and dialects, make up a third of the total population. These groups range in diversity from the Salum (Moken) sea-gypsies of the subtropical Tenasserim (Tanintharyi) division to the Nung-Rawang crossbow hunters in the mountains of Kachin state.

Under British colonial rule (1826–1948), the different peoples of Myanmar were kept on largely different roads of political and economic development. While minority ethnic groups in the borderlands remained under their traditional rulers in the Frontier Areas Administration, the Burman majority was governed separately under Ministerial Burma, in which a limited form of parliamentary democracy was introduced. Relations became dangerously inflamed during World War II, when many ethnic minority groups remained loyal to the British, while the Burma Independence Army (BIA) initially fought on the Japanese side and changed to the British side only in 1945. As a result, there were disturbing outbreaks of intercommunal violence, including the killing of Karen villagers and, during 1941–1942, the expulsion of ethnic Indians from the country, after BIA members accused them of supporting British colonialism.

In the hasty run-up to Burma's independence, many issues of ethnic social and political rights, territorial divisions, and legacies of the war were never fully resolved. A general agreement of principles was established at the Panglong Conference in February 1947, but a number of important groups were missing. As a result, the 1947 constitution was full of anomalies. While the Shan and Karenni (subsequently Kayah) states were granted the right of secession after a ten-year period, many other ethnic groups—such as the Mon, Rakhine, and Pao—went unrecognized. It also was decided to leave the controversial question of the designation of territory for a Karen state until after independence.

A State of Insurgency

Burma gained independence in January 1948 against a backdrop of political violence. This was tragically highlighted by the assassination of Aung San (1915–1947) and most of his cabinet in July 1947 by the gang of a political rival. Aung San was widely regarded as the one Burman leader who had the trust of most ethnic minority peoples. Even before the British departure, ethnic Rakhines and Muslims had begun guerrilla actions in Arakan (present-day Rakhine state). The situation deteriorated rapidly following an attempt to seize power by the Communist Party of Burma (CPB), beginning in March 1948. The CPB's insurrection was supported by widespread desertions from the fledgling armed forces of the new government.

Myanmar's ethnic nationalities were soon pulled into this spiral of conflict. The Karen National Union (KNU) took up arms in January 1949, rapidly followed by various Mon, Karenni, Pao, and Kachin forces. At one stage, as insurrections swept the country, the cabinet of the prime minister U Nu (1907–1995) became known as the "Rangoon six-mile government," as this was the only territory it controlled. A further descent into chaos took place at the end of 1949, when Chinese Guomindang remnants from Yunnan Province seized large areas of territory in Shan state.

In the late 1950s, a number of peace talks were held with different ethnic forces, but these groups failed to gain countrywide momentum. During the "Military Caretaker" administration (1958–1960) of General Ne Win (b. 1911), the rights of the traditional Shan and Karenni rulers were abolished. In 1961, U Nu attempted to make Buddhism the country's official state religion. Such moves only fueled disquiet in the Shan and Kachin states (the latter, especially, is home to many Christians), where a new generation of nationalist movements was now getting under way.

In March 1962, Ne Win seized power, and the former Shan president of Burma, Sao Shwe Thaike (1894–1962), and many other minority leaders from the parliamentary era (1948–1962) were arrested. An unsuccessful "peace parley" was then held during 1963–1964, but virtually all opposition groups rejected Ne Win's "Burmese Way to Socialism." Subsequently, Ne Win embarked on a twofold strategy: he conducted intensive counterinsurgency operations in rural areas while seeking to impose a one-party system under the Burma Socialist Programme Party (BSPP), which would radiate out from Rangoon (now Yangon) into the ethnic minority states.

Such tactics endured for a quarter-century, but they did not end armed resistance. As the Burmese economy declined, insurgency became a virtual way of life in many ethnic minority areas. Opposition groups were able to finance their struggles through control of the black-market trade in everything from luxury goods and medicines to teak, opium, and jade. Military supplies were also plentiful, both through illicit purchases in Thailand and also from the insurgent CPB, which was given military backing by China after 1968.

During the BSPP era (1962–1988), two main ethnic coalitions emerged: those allied with the CPB in northeastern Burma, who looked to the "autonomous region" system of China as their political model; and the eleven-party National Democratic Front (NDF), established in 1976, which sought the formation of a federal union of Burma. Together they maintained under arms some fifty thousand troops who controlled substantial "liberated zones" around all of Burma's borders.

Changes after 1988

Ethnic politics then underwent a dramatic reorientation during the epoch-making events of 1988–1990. The collapse of Ne Win's BSPP during the pro-democracy protests in 1988 was followed by mass ethnic mutinies from the fifteen-thousand-strong People's Army in 1989. The atmosphere of impending change was further enhanced by the flight of thousands of democracy activists into NDF territories following the assumption of power by the military State Law and Order Restoration Council (SLORC). This momentum was then maintained by the landslide victory of the National League for Democracy (NLD) and nineteen ethnic parties in the 1990 general election. A fundamental realignment in Myanmar's politics appeared imminent.

Not for the first time, however, events now moved in directions that few observers predicted. Following the CPB mutinies, four new ethnic armies emerged in northeast Myanmar, spearheaded by the United Wa State Party. These forces quickly agreed to cease-fires with the beleaguered military government, which unexpectedly announced a new peace policy toward all armed ethnic groups. Under these agreements, cease-fire forces would be allowed to administer their territories and join political discussions until Myanmar's new constitution was introduced. Subsequently, the Shan, Pao, Palaung, Kachin, and Mon nationality members of the NDF—as well as the Mong Tai Army of Khun Sa—all made peace deals with the SLORC government.

Underpinning these changes of strategy was a growing war weariness after more than four decades of fighting in which it is estimated that over a million people had died. In the process, many communities had been devastated, and as many as two million people had been displaced from their homes. Also prompting minority leaders was the desire to be on the inside of the political process at a rare moment of reorientation and transition in the country's history.

The importance of the ethnic issue was taken up by the United Nations, which called for "tripartite dialogue" between the military government, the NLD, and the ethnic minority groups as an essential element in the reform process. Differences, however, remained in all political camps. Among ethnic nationality groups, there were disagreements between cease-fire forces, which advocated a "peace through development" strategy, and the remaining non-cease-fire forces, centered around the KNU in southeast Burma, which continued to work with exile groups and underground opposition parties allied in the Democratic Alliance of Burma and the National Council Union of Burma. Following abortive peace talks with the SLORC in 1995–1996, the KNU in 1997 announced support for the NLD and called for "politics first" agreements as the only way forward.

This resulted in intensive Burmese army offensives against remaining KNU bases, the defections of more Karen guerrillas to the government side, and the continuing exodus of refugees into Thailand, where official refugee numbers passed the 100,000 mark. Fighting continued in Shan, Kayah, and also in several other borderland areas.

By the beginning of the twenty-first century, this situation created an ambiguous picture of life in ethnic lands. Whereas peace had returned to many areas for the first time in decades, there were many regions in which conflict continued. All sides agree that only inclusive dialogue and reform will bring about the stable peace that the peoples of Myanmar desire. To help achieve this, during 2001, efforts were stepped up by Razali Ismail, the special representative of the United Nations secretary-general, to try to bring together representatives of the military government, the NLD, and the ethnic minority groups.

Martin Smith

Further Reading

Falla, Jonathon. (1991) *True Love and Bartholomew: Rebels on the Burmese Border*. Cambridge, U.K.: Cambridge University Press.

Leach, Edmund. (1954) *Political Systems of Highland Burma: A Study of Kachin Social Structures*. London: G. Bell & Son.

Lintner, Bertil. (1990) *Land of Jade: A Journey through Insurgent Burma*. Edinburgh, U.K.: Kiscadale.

McCoy, Alfred. (1972) *The Politics of Heroin in Southeast Asia*. New York: Harper Torchbooks.

Silverstein, Josef. (1980) *Burmese Politics: The Dilemma of National Unity*. New Brunswick, NJ: Rutgers University Press.

Smith, Martin. (1999) *Burma: Insurgency and the Politics of Ethnicity*. 2d ed. London: Zed Books.

———. (1999) "Ethnic Conflict and the Challenge of Civil Society in Burma." In *Strengthening Civil Society in Burma: Possibilities and Dilemmas for International NGOs*, edited by Burma Center Netherlands. Chiang Mai, Thailand: Silkworm Books, 15–53.

———. (1994) *Ethnic Groups in Burma: Development, Democracy, and Human Rights*. London: Anti-Slavery International.

Tzang Yawnghwe, Chao. (1987) *The Shan of Burma: Memoirs of an Exile*. Singapore: Institute of Southeast Asian Studies.

Yan Nyein Aye. (2000) *Endeavours of the Myanmar Armed Forces Government for National Reconsolidation*. Yangon, Myanmar: U Aung Zaw.

ETHNIC CONFLICT—SOUTH ASIA

Until the renewal of violent conflict in Central and Eastern Europe, and more spectacularly in the Balkans, at the end of the twentieth century, postindependence South Asia seemed more prone to violent conflict linked to nationalism and ethnicity than most other parts of the world. The terms "nationalism" and "ethnicity" have eluded the efforts of generations of scholars to define them precisely. The common assumption—stemming largely from the Central and Eastern European and Balkan situations—is that the two terms are so closely intertwined as to be interchangeable. The South Asian record shows that they are often intertwined, but clearly not interchangeable.

"Ethnicity" has many facets; scholars treat groupings as varied as communities, cultures, language groups, and even corporations as ethnic groups, under certain circumstances. The castes in South Asia, particularly

INDIA AND THE TAMIL-SINHALESE CONFLICT IN SRI LANKA

In 2002 the conflict between Sri Lankan Tamils (a people of Indian origin resident in Sri Lanka for centuries) and the dominant Sinhalese remains one of the longest-lasting and bloodiest ethnic conflicts in the world. The resolution which follows was passed by the Indian National Congress party in January 1953. It failed to prevent the conflict and some Sri Lankans place partial blame on India, which has been accused of supporting the Tamils.

> This Congress views with grave concern the latest developments in Ceylon in regard to the people of Indian origin, who have long been resident there and who have not been or who are no longer citizens of India. The administrative measures and economic sanctions taken against these people have not only caused them considerable hardship but intend to make them stateless and thus create a grave situation. The Congress is of opinion that these measures of the Ceylon Government are not in conformity with justice or international practice, and appeals to the Government of Ceylon to give further consideration to this question which is not only important because it affects large numbers of people, but comes in the way of friendly and cooperative relations which should exist between such near neighbours as India and Ceylon which have had so much in common from immemorial times.
>
> *Source:* Jagdish Saran Sharma. (1965) *India's Struggle for Freedom: Select Documents and Sources*. Vol. II. Delhi: S. Chand, 222.

Hindu India, for example, can be considered ethnic groups. There is no pure form of ethnicity, and definitions of ethnicity are therefore prone to circular reasoning. Scholars generally agree that ethnicity functions as a way to bind individuals to a group. An ethnic group becomes one because and when it successfully presents itself as one and, having secured acceptance of this identity by its own members, gains recognition by others. An essential feature of a mature or maturing ethnicity is an awareness of the common identity. Ethnic identities often carry with them deep-rooted historical memories that link ethnicity and nationalism.

South Asia offers many examples of identities that have withstood the passage of time and form part of the consciousness of people, whether such consciousness is linked to religion, as is the case with the Sikhs in India, or rooted in language and culture, as with the Ahoms of Assam. Nevertheless, despite the remarkable powers of survival that ethnic identities possess, they are not immutable. They are changeable and have changed through the centuries. The core of most communities' ethnic identity is the traits that set them apart from others, primarily language and culture and often religion; as with castes in Hinduism a distinctive identity may be linked to a ritual status imposed and sustained by religious sanctions.

In the politicization of ethnicity, a process transforms an ethnic group into a political one. The South Asian experience shows that transformation of an ethnic group or community into a nationality or nation can be a dual process, partly cohesive and partly divisive. A new state faces the threat of separatist activity waged by ethnic groups; it often resorts to violence to prevent the separation, as in India, Pakistan, and Sri Lanka.

Language and Ethnicity

In the early years of independence in South Asia, disputes about language policy were a more divisive source of political instability in India, Pakistan, and Sri

Sri Lankan soldiers patrol the outskirts of Jaffna in September 2000 following weeks of fighting that left 160 soldiers and about 600 Tamil Tiger separatists dead. (AFP/CORBIS)

Lanka than were religious tensions. When the terms of the transfer of power were being negotiated in the then-undivided India and in Sri Lanka, the assumption was that English, the official language of colonial rule, would be replaced after independence by indigenous languages or language. The political elite in all these countries, as legatees of colonial powers, viewed the replacement of English by an indigenous language as easily accomplished, but they soon learned how difficult it was.

The first overt threat to the stability of the newly independent Indian state came from linguistic nationalism, or ethnic identity based on language. Like the political leadership in both Pakistan and Sri Lanka, Jawaharlal Nehru (1889–1964), first prime minister of India from 1947, was ill prepared for the challenge posed by the forces of linguistic nationalism, but he handled these problems better than his counterparts in Pakistan and Sri Lanka. In Pakistan the challenge to the integrity of the state from 1947 came from the Bengalis in East Pakistan (now Bangladesh), who resisted the attempt to impose Urdu as the national language in Pakistan.

The partition in 1947 of the British Raj into India and Pakistan had demonstrated that the religious divide between Hindu and Muslim was too deep for accommodation in a single state; twenty-five years later Pakistan was divided, showing that religion alone was not enough to bind a state together when ethnic identities based on language and culture divided it. The state of Bangladesh emerged independent.

Sri Lanka provides a classic example of the destabilizing effects of linguistic nationalism in a multiethnic society. Disputes about language policy were the focal points of tension between the Sinhalese majority and the Tamil minority in the 1950s and 1960s, each identifying themselves on the basis of language loyalties. Sri Lanka was unique in South Asia in the repudiation of the language settlement that had been agreed on before independence. Substantial progress had been made in the implementation of that policy, which envisaged the replacement of English by Sinhala and Tamil by the mid-1950s. The two languages were to have parity of status. Instead this policy was repudiated in 1956, and Sinhala was elevated to the status of sole official language in the country. Just as the Bengali majority in East Pakistan opposed the imposition of Urdu, so too in Sri Lanka the Tamil minority opposed the elevation of Sinhala. The upshot of this conflict was that the decade of peace and stability that the country had enjoyed since independence was over for many years to come.

Ethnicity and Separatism

In India as in other parts of South Asia, ethnic identities linked to language, culture, and religion, dating from precolonial times and acting separately or in combination, threatened the stability of the postindependence state. India confronts more separatist and autonomy movements than any other state in the world, with the exception of Russia in its present form, and many of these movements originated in the colonial expansion and consolidation under the British Raj. Thus Indian separatism and autonomy movements are rooted in two processes: first, colonial expansion and consolidation in the territories that now constitute India; second, the revitalized precolonial forces with identities linked to language, culture, and religion.

India has kept these latter forces at bay by a number of policies. One was the redemarcation of state boundaries, with the adoption of the recommendations of the Report of States Reorganization Commission in the mid-1950s and 1960s, on the basis of linguistic identities. Another is the creation of new states to meet the pressure of regional forces seeking autonomy in existing states. Thus the number of states in the Indian union has increased since the 1950s and 1960s. In a country as large and populous as India, where some states are larger than many independent countries in other parts of the world, demarcation of new states in response to agitation for regional autonomy can be unending. Another policy was the use of force to crush separatism when the integrity of the Indian state was seen to be threatened.

There have been very few successful separatist movements in the postcolonial societies of the third world. Bangladesh is generally considered the product of the only successful separatist movement in postindependence South Asia and therefore a unique development. Even in Bangladesh's case the separatist struggle might not have succeeded but for India's intervention on behalf of the separatists.

Having lost its eastern unit to a successful separatist movement, Pakistan faced two other secessionist movements, in the frontier province and in Baluchistan, which reemerged under the government of Zulfiqar Ali Bhutto (1928–1979) in the 1970s. The military involvement first in putting down the guerrilla warfare in Baluchistan and later in running the government directly for almost a decade under General Mohammad Zia-ul-Haq (1924–1988) alienated various communities in the smaller provinces—the Baluchis in Baluchistan and the Sindhis in Sind—even if these separatist aspirations were effectively thwarted. Thus ethnolinguistic identity emerged as an important issue in Pakistan's national politics in the 1980s and 1990s. The continuing ascendancy of Punjab in the state system of Pakistan, and the alliance between the Punjabi elite and their preferred partners, whether Urdu-speaking *mohajirs* (immigrants from India) in the past or the Pashtuns now, cause tensions in other provinces and among other communities.

In the mid-1980s the *mohajirs* themselves engaged in a struggle against a political system they had dominated from the time of the establishment of Pakistan in 1947. Their struggle has many peculiar features. The *mohajirs*, as a group, lack a common geographical, historical, or cultural identity; and they are differentiated internally along lines of class and sectarian loyalties, linguistic identities, and areas of origin. Yet they provide an unusual example of the deliberate construction of ethnicity for political purposes, the welding of a heterogeneous mass of people who had chosen to leave India at the time of the partition of the Raj, into a distinctive group. Their transformation into an ethnic group is by no means complete, and their rights to claim such a status do not remain unchallenged by others, especially the Sindhis, among whom a great many *mohajirs* live, especially in the city of Karachi.

Sri Lanka's separatist agitation is postcolonial; its strength, in recent times, owes a great deal to Indian intervention on behalf of the Tamil separatists. Indian intervention failed in most if not all of its objectives, and the Tamil separatist movement ranks as one of the most thwarted in South Asia. Early expressions of separatist sentiments (in the late 1940s and early 1950s) developed into a full-fledged movement over a period of twenty-five or more years. That transformation resulted from several factors: a perceived threat to the ethnic identity of the Tamils from political, economic, and cultural policies; perceived grievances of a political or economic nature or both; and a sense of relative deprivation at the loss or imminent loss of the privileged position the Tamil minority enjoyed under British colonial rule.

Bangladesh is virtually unilingual; between 95 and 98 percent of the population speaks Bengali (or Bangla, as it is called in Bangladesh). Moreover, apart from a small Hindu minority of about 10 percent, almost everybody is Muslim. A tiny minority (about 1 percent) are Buddhists and animists living in the Chittagong Hill Tracts (CHT). Yet this minuscule minority is at the center of international attention as Bangladesh's most persistent minority problem and one that touches on every aspect of ethnic identity, separatism, and separatist agitation reviewed here. The crux of the problem is that the CHT constitutes 9 percent of the land area of Bangladesh but has only 1 percent or less of the population. Bangladesh, the most densely populated country in South Asia, has around twice the land area of Sri Lanka but more than six times Sri Lanka's population. Thus the temptation to disregard the special status conferred on the CHT by the British and the interests of the tribal population has been great, and resistance to that temptation has been little. Separated from the predominantly Bengali Muslim population of Bangladesh by language, culture, religion, and forms of livelihood, the tribal people have had little choice but to fight back.

In its more constructive form the combination of ethnicity and nationalism has been an instrument of national integration in South Asia. Nevertheless the record is somewhat ambiguous. Pakistan, as it was in 1947, lasted just twenty-four years. The Indian polity, on the other hand, has remained intact, with virtually the same territorial boundaries if not the same form, as it had at partition. In every South Asian country the combination of ethnicity and nationalism or the politicization of ethnicity has a historical dimension. Thus while the political establishments and political elites have some justification for their claim that the linkage between ethnicity and nationalism has been, more often than not, a stabilizing influence, they would have to concede that the same combination of forces is also the principal cause of internal disharmony and discord in all the states of South Asia.

K. M. De Silva

See also: **Jammu and Kashmir; Nagaland**

Further Reading

Ahmed, Feroz. (1998) *Ethnicity and Politics in Pakistan.* Karachi, Pakistan: Oxford University Press.

Amin, Tahir. (1993) *Ethno-national Movements of Pakistan.* 2d ed. Islamabad, Pakistan: Institute of Policy Studies.

De Silva, Kingsley M. (1998) *Reaping the Whirlwind: Ethnic Conflict, Ethnic Politics in Sri Lanka.* New Delhi: Penguin Books.

Gupta, Dipankar. (1996) *The Context of Ethnicity: Sikh Identity in a Comparative Perspective.* Delhi: Oxford University Press.

Lamb, Alistair. (1991) *Kashmir: A Disputed Legacy, 1846–1990.* Hertingfordbury, Hertfordshire, U.K.: Roxford Books.

Rahman, Tariq. (1996) *Language and Politics in Pakistan.* Karachi, Pakistan: Oxford University Press.

Schofield, Victoria. (1996) *Kashmir in the Crossfire.* London: Taurus,

Van der Veer, Peter. (1996) *Religious Nationalism: Hindus and Muslims in India.* Delhi: Oxford University Press.

Verghese, George. (1996) *India's North-East Resurgent: Ethnicity, Governance, and Development.* Delhi: Konark.

A Karen child in a refugee camp in Thailand near the Myanmar border. (HOWARD DAVIES/CORBIS)

ETHNIC RELATIONS—SOUTHEAST ASIA

ETHNIC RELATIONS—SOUTHEAST ASIA Southeast Asia consists of the ten nation-states of Brunei, Cambodia, Indonesia, Laos, Malaysia, Myanmar (Burma), the Philippines, Singapore, Thailand, and Vietnam. The people in each are of mixed ethnic backgrounds since they are composed of groups descended from indigenous people as well as migrant Chinese and Indians. These migrant groups settled in the region in large numbers during the colonial administration of many countries in Southeast Asia.

The population in Malaysia, for example, is 58 percent Malay and other indigenous peoples, 26 percent Chinese, 7 percent Indian, and 9 percent other ethnic origins. Similarly, Singapore's 4 million population is 77 percent Chinese, 14 percent Malay, 8 percent Indian, and 1 percent people of other ethnic origins. This multiethnic mix is a characteristic of all Southeast Asian countries.

A Chinese student is attacked by Indonesian youths at Republican University in Jakarta in October 1965. (BETTMANN/CORBIS)

Colonization brought Western political and social influences to Southeast Asia. Western institutions of government and social organization were superimposed on indigenous structures and traditions. With independence from the Western colonial powers, emerging nation-states formed along the lines of the former colonies. The boundaries of these nation-states straddle territories long inhabited by indigenous tribes, migrant groups, and dominant ethnic groups. Even the concept of the nation-state is one derived from the West, and the governments in the Southeast Asian nation-states have faced major challenges in shaping a common national identity among their multiethnic citizenry. Former colonies of European industrialized nations were challenged with what must have seemed like an impossible task on independence—the construction of a national identity that would be simultaneously unitary and racially plural. The birth of the nation-state in Southeast Asia has been associated with ethnic strife and conflicts. These included racial riots in Malaysia, Singapore, and Indonesia.

With the assumption of independence and the end of colonial rule, former colonies such as Singapore basically had to shape nation-states out of what were then considered as immigrant societies—different ethnic groups comprising immigrant groups mixed with indigenous and local groups but sharing relatively little apart from the territory on which they had settled. Indeed, many of the immigrants had continued to maintain strong links with kin and family in their countries of origin. In a similar manner, the hill tribes and other such groups residing in the mainland Southeast Asian states of Myanmar, Thailand, Laos, Cambodia, and Vietnam have had to adapt to the new territorial identities that the imposition of national boundaries required. What it means to ethnic groups that straddle the borders of several nation-states to be citizens of just one of those states remains in question. Being nationals of several emerging nation-states has meant that ethnic groups such as the Karen, like the earlier immigrant Chinese and Indians, now belong to different nationalities depending on which side of the national borders they are living.

Interethnic differences have been accentuated by the coincidence of social and economic divisions with ethnic groups. In Indonesia as well as Malaysia, the Chinese have been perceived to be economically more successful than the indigenous people. This has led to the imposition of a preferential policy favoring the Malays and other indigenous people in Malaysia. Until the end of the Suharto regime in Indonesia, the Chinese were not allowed the use of their language or to celebrate their festivals.

Interethnic tension runs high in the region, with the Karen waging a separatist war in Myanmar, the Acehnese people in northern Sumatra contesting the legitimacy of the government in Indonesia, and Muslim separatists active in southern Philippines and also southern Thailand. Since 1997 and the onset of the Asian economic crisis in the region, there have been armed conflicts between Christians and Muslims in Indonesia as well as between groups indigenous to the outer territories and other ethnic groups who have been resettled in these territories as part of the transmigration program meant to ease population pressures in and around Java. The growing popularity of an Islamic political party in Malaysia has been of concern given the decades of moderate Muslim leadership in both Malaysia and Indonesia, the two countries with the largest Muslim groups in Southeast Asia.

Given the national policies introduced to manage interethnic relations in the countries of Southeast Asia that have tended to favor one ethnic group over others, stability in these relations has been of major concern. With weakening of the unitary state that had earlier brooked no challenge to its policies on interethnic relations, there is great concern that race and religion will once again become the rallying platforms for the people in Southeast Asia who are discontented with the outcome of development.

Ooi Giok Ling

Further Reading

Cleary, D. (1999) *Race, Nationalism, and Social Theory in Brazil: Rethinking Gilberto Freyre*. Oxford: School of Geography and the Environment Working Papers, Oxford University.

Ho, K. L. (1997) "Political Indigenisation and the State in Peninsular Malaysia.'" In *ASEAN in the Global System*, edited by H. M. Dahlan, H. Jusoh, A. Y. Hing, and J. H. Ong. Bangi, Selangor, Malaysia: Penerbit Universiti Kebangsaan Malaysia, 210–224.

Hodder, B. W. (1953) "Racial Groupings in Singapore." *Journal of Tropical Geography* 1: 25–36.

Keyes, C. F., ed. (1979) *Ethnic Adaptation and Identity: The Karen on the Thai Frontier with Burma*. Philadelphia: Institute for the Study of Human Issues.

Lee, K. H. (1997) "Malaysian Chinese: Seeking Identity in Wawasan 2020." In *Ethnic Chinese as Southeast Asians*, edited by L. Suryadinata. Singapore: Institute of Southeast Asian Studies, 72–114.

Mee, W. (1998) "National Difference and Global Citizenship." In *Southeast Asian Identities: Culture and the Politics of Representation in Indonesia, Malaysia, Singapore, and Thailand*, edited by J. S. Kahn. Singapore: Institute of Southeast Asian Studies, 227–259.

Ooi, G. L., S. Siddique, and K. C. Soh. (1993) *The Management of Ethnic Relations in Public Housing Estates*. Singapore: Institute of Policy Studies and Times Academic Press.

Rajah, A. (1990) "Ethnicity, Nationalism, and the Nation-State: The Karen." In *Ethnic Groups across National Boundaries in Mainland Southeast Asia*, edited by G. Wijeyewardene. Singapore: Institute of Southeast Asian Studies, 102–133.

Tønneson, S., and H. Atlöv, eds. (1996) *Asian Forms of the Nation*. Richmond, Surrey, U.K.: Curzon Press.

ETO JUN

ETO JUN (1933–1999), Japanese writer and critic. Eto Jun was one of the most outspoken critics of postwar Japanese culture, society, and politics, who over the course of his long career dissented from both right and left wings. Born in Tokyo, he achieved recognition with his debut book in 1956 on novelist Natsume Soseki (1867–1916). The book, which casts Soseki in the light of Meiji period (1868–1912) historical contexts, disputes the critical consensus of Soseki as an individualist. After receiving recognition for his work on writer Kobayashi Hideo (1902–1983), Eto traveled to the United States and taught and researched at Princeton University.

In reflections on his cross-cultural encounters published as *Amerika to watashi* (America and Myself, 1965), Eto critiqued the problematic relationship between Japan and the United States. For the next three decades, Eto developed and sustained the notion that the Japanese defeat in World War II and subsequent U.S. occupation led to an unrecoverable loss of Japan's autonomy and understanding of history. From 1979, Eto began to consider the long-term effects of the occupation, making his most controversial arguments that the militarists alone, not Japan as a whole, unconditionally surrendered, and that the imported "false" taboos of occupation censorship imprisoned all of postwar literature in a linguistic space closed off from true freedom. In his view, Japanese democracy today carries the taint of its undemocratic inception. Shortly after the death of his wife, Eto took his own life in 1999.

J. Abel

Further Reading

Olson, Lawrence. (1992) "Intellectuals and the Search for Cultural Identity in Postwar Japan: On Eto Jun." In *Ambivalent Moderns: Portraits of Japanese Cultural Identity*. New York: Rowman and Littlefield.

Eto Jun. (1982) "The Civil Censorship in Occupied Japan." *Hikaku bunka zasshi* 1 (Journal of Comparative Cultures) Trans. by Jay Rubin.

ETOROFU ISLAND (Est. pop. 6,000). Etorofu Island (Russian: Iturup) is the largest of the Kuril Islands. A volcanic island 3,000 square kilometers in size, Etorofu is located 110 kilometers from the northeast of Cape Nosappu-Misaki on the northern extremity of the Nemuro Peninsula in Hokkaido, between the Sea of Okhotsk and the Pacific Ocean. Until the end of the eighteenth century, the population was exclusively autochthonous (Ainu). At the time of the Russian occupation in August 1945, the population, mainly Japanese, was expelled, and Soviet citizens were encouraged to settle on the island.

In 1941, the Japanese sailed from the Gulf of Hitokappu, located in the middle of the island on the Pacific Ocean side, to attack Pearl Harbor. Etorofu is one several islands (Kunashiri, Shikotan, and the Habomai group of islets) of the Northern Territories for which Japan asserted a claim in 1955, when Japan and the Soviet Union began negotiations toward a peace treaty. In 2001, it was still administered by the Russian Federation and the territorial dispute was not yet resolved.

Among the twelve volcanoes on the island, the highest is Chirippu-date (Chiriporupuri, 1,587 meters). The average annual temperature on the island is 4.3°C, and in winter, it drops to minus 5°C. The main products are salmon, trout, codfish, crabs, and seaweed. There was an active mining industry (sulfur) before World War II. Mineral deposits include tin, zinc, lead, copper, nickel, sulfur, and metallic sulfides.

Nathalie Cavasin

Further Reading

Hasegawa Tsuyoshi. (1998) *The Northern Territories Dispute and Russo-Japanese Relations: Between War and Peace 1697–1985*. Vol. 1. Berkeley and Los Angeles: University of California Press.

———. (1998) *The Northern Territories Dispute and Russo-Japanese Relations: Neither War Nor Peace*. Vol. 2. Berkeley and Los Angeles: University of California Press.

Kenichi Ohmae. (1990) "Calmer Waters: Ambitious Plan May Transform Contested Islands." *Far Eastern Economic Review* 30 (August): 28–30.

Stephan, John J. (1974) *The Kuril Islands: Russo-Japanese Frontier in the Pacific*. Oxford: Clarendon Press.

EUPHRATES RIVER The Euphrates River is the longest river in West Asia, crossing a distance of 2,700 kilometers. (The Euphrates is known in the Bible as Perath, in Arabic as al-Furat, and in Turkish as Firat.) It originates in the Armenian Mountains of eastern Turkey and flows southeast across northern Syria and southern Iraq to merge with the Tigris River

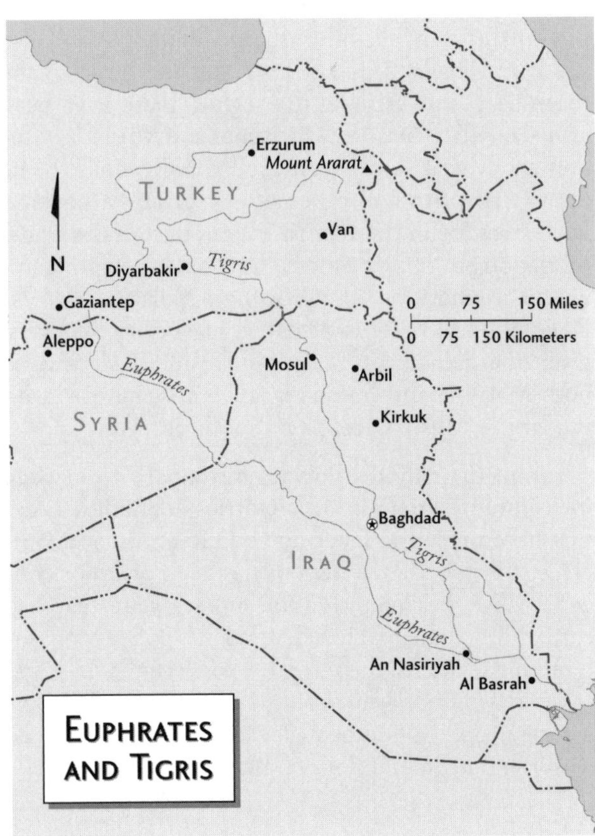

and form the Shatt al-Arab River, which enters the Persian Gulf.

The Euphrates is formed by the confluence of the Karasu stream, rising close to the city of Erzurum, and the Murat stream, rising close to Mount Ararat. The river flows through the Taurus Mountains of southern Turkey and descends to the plains of Syria and Iraq. In Syria, the Euphrates flows south-southeast into Iraq through entrenched valleys and collecting waters from its two main left-bank tributaries.

In its lower course, the Euphrates enters the Mesopotamian alluvial plain. The mainstream meanders slowly in braided channels with waters rapidly decreasing through seepage, evaporation, and irrigation. Depositing sediment along the vast plain, the river raises its bed level and becomes prone to seasonal overflow and spontaneous course changes. Just below the town of al-Fallujah, close to Baghdad, the Euphrates approaches the Tigris River at a distance of approximately 30 kilometers before it divides into two branches. The branches reunite after a distance of 175 kilometers near the town of al- Samawah, and the river continues downstream to join the Tigris and empty into the Persian Gulf.

To control the varied flow of the river and to draw water for irrigation and the generation of power, Iraq has developed a system of diversion and storage, including the drainage canal, the "Third River," 563 kilometers long, flowing between the Tigris and Euphrates. Since the 1970s, however, the construction of a series of large dams in Turkey and Syria has intensified rivalry among the riparian states over water usage.

Flowing almost parallel to the Tigris River, the Euphrates water is the source of life in Mesopotamia giving rise to the most ancient civilizations. On its banks emerged the great civilizations of Sumer, Akkad, and Babylonia, which drew sustenance from its waters through extensive irrigation schemes.

Manat H. al Shawi

Further Reading

Hillel, Daniel. (1994) *Rivers of Eden: The Struggle for Water and the Quest for Peace in the Middle East.* New York: Oxford University Press.

Kolars, John. (1994) "Problems of International River Management: The Case of the Euphrates." In *International Waters of the Middle East: From Euphrates-Tigris to Nile*, edited by Asit K. Biswas. Oxford: Oxford University Press, 44–94.

Soffer, Arnon. (1999) *Rivers of Fire: The Conflict over Water in the Middle East.* Lanham, MD: Rowman & Littlefield Publishers.

EUROPE–ASIA RELATIONS

Relations between Asia and Europe have come a long way since the colonial and postindependence periods in Asia. For the last thirty years, Europe has been building a constructive relationship with the Association of South East Asian Nations (ASEAN). The European Commission-ASEAN (EC-ASEAN) ministerial meetings established in 1980 are a forum for regular dialogue between the two entities. In February 1996, a Europe-Asia Meeting process (ASEM) was launched, thanks to Goh Chok Tong, the president of Singapore. ASEM hopes to promote political, cultural, and people-to-people dialogue along with traditional economic exchange.

The Missing Link

When compared with the involvement of the United States in the Asia-Pacific region, the involvement of Europe has been weaker, despite strong historical links and growing economic interdependence. Strengthening the weak leg of the U.S.–Asia–Europe relationship—that is, the Asia–Europe relationship—provided the major rationale for the creation of ASEM. In July 1994, the EC published a discussion paper entitled "Towards a New Asia Strategy," which shed light on the necessity to upgrade European relations with all Asian countries, while continuing to emphasize ASEAN's centrality to Europe. In the 1980s, there had already been some concern about Japan–U.S. relations. Although Japan and Europe have made significant efforts to enhance their interchange, no formal relation had been established between Europe and East Asia before ASEM. Launched to balance the U.S.–Asia relationship and enhance the Europe–East Asia relationship, the ASEM process had no clear common vision, except the shared principle that regional cooperation and dialogue help regional stability.

The ASEM Process Meetings

The ASEM process brings the leaders of ten countries of East and Southeast Asia together with leaders from the fifteen member states of the European Union (EU). The inaugural meeting at Bangkok (1–2 March 1996) clearly reflected a shared enthusiasm, while the second meeting held in London (3–4 April 1998) stressed the necessity to elaborate materials to give stronger credit to the interregional relationship. The ASEM Trust Fund, established after the London summit, was a useful creation in the context of the Asian financial crisis. The Trust Fund, which became operational in June 1998, for two years, provides technical assistance and financial and social training. In 1997 and 1998, almost all Asian countries faced financial and economic turmoil, leadership crises, and intraregional tensions. There was strong sentiment in these Asian countries that Europe was not doing enough to help: the London summit, in a sense ASEM's first test, showed that Europe's multilateral and bilateral contributions to the numerous international financial packages to Asian countries ranked second after those of Japan. The European financial and economic commitment to the recovery of Asia was reconfirmed with the ASEM Trust Fund. The launch of the Euro has also changed Asian perceptions of the European Union, since a successful Euro offers the possibility of diversifying Asia's debt structure and debt servicing, reducing vulnerability to major fluctuations in the dollar exchange rate.

Yet at the London meeting, the political and people-to-people dialogues were unsuccessful. At the Seoul meeting (20–21 October 2000), the countries issued the "Asia-Europe Co-operation Framework for the First Decade of the New Millennium"; this framework set the principles, aims, priorities, and mechanisms of the ASEM process for the ten following years and stressed the sociocultural intention of promoting both interregional political dialogues and economic partnerships. Among the mechanisms established were informal human-rights seminars, the last one of which occurred in Denpasar in July 2001, and the trade facilitation action plan, which began in 2001 and aims to remove trade obstacles between the two regions.

The Asia–Europe Foundation (ASEF), based in Singapore, is the body in charge of promoting cultural, intellectual, and people-to-people exchanges. ASEF was created in February 1997, after the Bangkok summit. It organizes workshops on education, human rights, and the position of the individual, and strengthens cultural exchanges. Yet it remains to be seen whether the Foundation, with a staff mainly of career bureaucrats and with limited personnel and financial resources, can meet the challenge.

Problems Facing ASEM

The EU is a highly regulated area with its Commission, Council, and Parliament, while ASEAN is an informal structure based on consensus policy making and noninterference in member states' business. Northeast Asian countries (Japan, China, South Korea) are still trying to solve historical disputes and achieve cooperative interchange. The lack of unity in Asia, and also in a Europe still looking for a common foreign-security policy, makes it difficult to promote basic cooperative schemes.

Obviously, the first pillar of the ASEM process—political dialogue—takes longest to bear fruit, since cultural sensitivities act as stumbling blocks. The issue of Myanmar (Burma) is a good example: Myanmar challenged the long-established EC-ASEAN relationship when it was admitted as a member of ASEAN in 1997. European criticism of Myanmar's record on human rights made official meetings between the EU and ASEAN virtually impossible for three years. Yet at the thirteenth EU-ASEAN ministerial meeting, held in Vientiane on 11–12 December 2000, with Myanmar attending, all sides showed some willingness to look beyond their differences.

Another problem is that Europe, lacking strategic interest in Asia, finds it difficult to play a significant role in security issues and in promoting regional stability, yet regional stability is probably one of the main concerns of both Europe and Asia. In 1995, ASEAN countries launched the ASEAN Regional Forum, the only structure in Asia in which all the Asian countries, together with the United States, Russia, and Europe, meet to discuss a security agenda. Europe has already showed commitment toward helping resolve such Asian crises as the aftermath of Cambodia's civil war, tensions between North and South Korea, and the struggles of East Timor for independence from Indonesia. Europe's increased interest in the security of the Asia-Pacific region mainly follows the "comprehensive security" theory, which emphasizes, among other concepts, political stability, economic prosperity, and environmental safety. Europe's experience in preventive diplomacy, confidence-building measures, and reconciliation has an appeal to its Asian partners. Learning from European expertise is perhaps preliminary to deeper cooperation on security issues between the two regions.

Although ASEM still lacks a clear vision or a shared philosophy of what the Asia–Europe relationship should be, it has enhanced the regionalization processes in Asia. The launch of ASEM coincided with the enlargement of the ASEAN ministerial meetings in Northeast Asia (Japan, South Korea, and China—a process called the "ASEAN plus three"), and there are signs of a possible dialogue among Northeast Asian countries. Whether the regionalization processes lead to more unified regions will be important for determining ASEM's future relevance. The invisible third party at the table, the United States, will also have a decisive impact.

Régine Serra

Further Reading

Bobrow, Davis. (1999) "The US and ASEM: Why the Hegemon Didn't Bark." *Pacific Review* 12, 1: 103–128.

Bridges, Brian. (1999) *Europe and the Challenge of the Asia-Pacific*. Cheltenham, U.K.: Edward Elgar.

Brittan, Leon. (1999) "Europe/Asia Relations." *Pacific Review* 12, 3: 491–498.

Cho, Hong-sik. (2000) "Social and Cultural Cooperation under ASEM." *Korea Focus* 8, 6: 133–150.

European Commission. (2000) *Perspectives and Priorities for the ASEM Process (Asia-Europe Meeting) into the New Decade*. Working Document COM(2000)241final. Brussels, Belgium: EU.

Hanggi, Heiner. (1999) *ASEM and the Construction of the New Triad*. MARC Occasional Papers No. 15, IUHEI-IUED. Geneva: University of Geneva.

Maull, Hanns, Gerald Segal, and Jusuf Wanandi, eds. (1998) *Europe and Asia-Pacific*. London: Routledge.

Yeo, Lay Hwee, and Latif Asad, eds. (2000) *Asia and Europe: Essays and Speeches by Tommy Koh*. Singapore: World Scientific Publishing Company.

EUROPEAN UNION AND TURKEY The European Union (EU) is a multinational organization for economic and political integration in Europe, instituted on 7 February 1992 with the signing of the Treaty on European Union (known as the Maastricht Treaty).

History

Since 1870 three increasingly destructive wars were waged in western Europe. To bring stability and prosperity to Europe and to settle the historical feud between France and Germany (major contenders in all three wars), European powers agreed that a cooperation mechanism, including these two countries and other Western European powers, should be created.

In 1946 Winston Churchill called for the United States of Europe, and one year later he fostered the creation of the United European Movement. The French Council for a United Europe was created by Socialist parliamentarian René Courtin on 1 July 1947, and the Socialist United States of Europe was established in the same year. While the Council for a United Europe was absorbed by the United European Movement in 1953, the Socialist United States of Europe was renamed the European Left in 1961.

When the Marshall Plan for European reconstruction was launched in 1947, sixteen European states formed the Organization for European Economic Cooperation to coordinate the distribution of American economic aid. On 7–11 May 1948, the Europe Congress, fostered by the International Coordination of Movements for the Unification of Europe, met in the Hague and agreed to establish a European Deliberative Assembly and a European Special Council. France, Great Britain, Belgium, the Netherlands, Luxembourg, Denmark, Ireland, Italy, Norway, and Switzerland then formed the Council of Europe in 1949.

On 25 March 1957, the treaties establishing the European Economic Community (EEC) and the European Atomic Energy Community were signed in Rome by Belgium, France, Germany, Italy, Luxembourg, and the Netherlands. The European Parliament was established in March 1958. The Merger Treaty of 8 April 1965, which came into force on 1 July 1967, brought all these organs and institutions together and established a single executive called the European Community (EC).

In the 1970s and 1980s the EC was enlarged: in 1973 by granting membership to Denmark, Ireland, and the United Kingdom; in 1981 by the addition of Greece; and in 1986 by Spain and Portugal. In 1986 the Single European Act, which planned the institution of a common market no later than 31 December 1992, was signed. The Maastricht Treaty (7 February 1992) produced a clear timetable for further progress on the road to economic and monetary union, including the introduction of a European Central Bank and a single currency no later than 1999. From 7 February 1992, the European Community (EC) became known as the European Union (EU).

Austria, Finland, and Sweden joined the EU in 1995, and the EU started negotiations with thirteen other European countries interested in membership: Hungary, Poland, the Czech Republic, Slovakia, Slovenia, Estonia, Cyprus, Romania, Bulgaria, Latvia, Lithuania, Croatia, and Turkey.

The European Parliament

The European Parliament, the EU's public forum, has 626 members, elected for five-year terms. Parliament members form political rather than national groups. Parliament's main power is to vote for the EU's budget. The distribution of the seats is as follows: Germany ninety-nine; France, Italy, and the United Kingdom eighty-seven each; Spain sixty-four; the Netherlands thirty-one; Belgium, Greece, and Portugal twenty-five each; Sweden twenty-two; Austria, Denmark, and Finland sixteen each; Ireland fifteen; and Luxembourg six.

The European Commission

The Commission, consisting of twenty commissioners, including the president and members who are nominated and appointed by the consensus of EU countries, proposes policies and is the only body allowed to initiate legislation, with exceptions in the fields of common foreign and security policies, justice, and home affairs. It is also responsible for administration and ensures that the provisions of the treaties and the decisions of the institutions are properly implemented.

The European Council

The European Council is the EU's legislative body for a wide range of EU issues. It exercises its legislative power in co-decision with the European Parliament. It also coordinates general economic policies, concludes international agreements on behalf of the EU, with the parliament constitutes a budgetary authority that adopts the EU's budget, takes decisions necessary for defining and implementing common foreign and security policy, coordinates the activities of member states, and adopts measures in the fields of police and economic and judicial cooperation in criminal matters.

The council is composed of ministers representing the national governments of the fifteen member states, with a total of eighty-seven votes distributed according to the size of the countries. The numbers are as follows: Germany, France, Italy, and the United Kingdom ten each; Spain eight; Belgium, Greece, the Netherlands, and Portugal five each; Austria and Sweden four each; Ireland, Denmark, and Finland three each; and Luxembourg two.

The European Court of Justice

The court provides judicial safeguards necessary to ensure that the laws are observed in the interpretation and application of the treaties and in all of the activities of the EU. The Court is composed of fifteen judges, assisted by nine advocates-general. The judges and advocates-general are appointed by common accord of the governments of the member states and hold office for a renewable term of six years. They are chosen from jurists whose independence is "beyond doubt" and who are of recognized competence.

The Ankara Agreement

Turkey first applied to join the EEC in 1959. The EEC's response was to suggest a loose association until Turkey's circumstances permitted it to join. Ensuing negotiations resulted in the signature of the Ankara Agreement on 12 September 1963, which entered into force on 1 December 1964. It aimed at securing Turkey's full membership in the EEC through the three-phase establishment of a customs union that would serve to bring about integration between the EEC and Turkey. The Ankara Agreement still constitutes the legal basis of the association between Turkey and the EU.

Turkey's Application for Full Membership

Turkey applied for full membership in 1987. The request underwent the normal procedures, and the commission's opinion was completed on 18 December 1989. It underlined Turkey's eligibility for membership, yet deferred the in-depth analysis of Turkey's application until the emergence of a more favorable environment. Although the commission argued that the EU was not ready at the time to accept and digest additional members, refusal of Turkey's application was, in fact, unofficially based on economic and political arguments. Turkey's democratic credentials, its high rates of inflation and unemployment, and the possibility of an influx of population to EU countries were points of concern. On the other hand Greece's resistance to Turkey's membership was also an effective factor in the decision. The commission stressed the need for a comprehensive cooperation program and added that the Customs Union should be completed in 1995 as envisaged.

Customs Union

Talks for the envisaged Customs Union (CU) began in 1994 and were finalized on 6 March 1995 at the Turkey-EU Association Council. Although basic agricultural products were excluded from the initial package, a preferential trade regime for those products was adopted on 1 January 1998.

Apart from technical provisions related to the establishment and proper functioning of the CU, the package also included an Association Council resolution providing for the intensification of cooperation between Turkey and the EU in areas not covered by the CU, such as industrial cooperation, trans-European networks, energy, transport, telecommunications, agriculture, environment, science, statistics, matters relating to justice and home affairs, consumer protection, cultural cooperation, and information. These provisions demonstrated that, despite predictions to the contrary, the Turkish economy was able to withstand EU competition.

The EU Enlargement Process and Turkey

In the Association Council of 29 April 1997, the EU reconfirmed Turkey's eligibility for membership and asked the commission to prepare recommendations to deepen Turkey-EU relations, while claiming that the development of this relationship depended on factors relating to Greece, Cyprus, and human rights. The commission, however, excluded Turkey in its report entitled "Agenda 2000." While the report conceded that the CU was functioning satisfactorily and that it had demonstrated Turkey's ability to adapt to the EU norms in many areas, it repeated the same political and economic arguments against Turkey and made no reference to Turkey's full membership objective. The commission proposed measures that would reinforce the current relationship and complemented these measures with the idea of inviting Turkey to the European Conference.

After Turkey's rejection of the invitation and EU's various proposals, the Helsinki European Council held on 10–11 December 1999 produced a breakthrough in Turkey-EU relations. At Helsinki Turkey was officially recognized without any precondition as a candidate state on an equal footing with the other candidate states.

Mustafa Aydin and Cagri Erhan

Further Reading

Eichenberg, Richard C. (1993) "Europeans and the European Community: The Dynamics of Public Support for European Integration." *Integration Organization* 47, 4: 507–534.

El-Agraa, Ali. (1998) *The European Union: History, Economics, and Policies*. London: Prentice-Hall.

Howard, Michael, and Roger Louis, eds. (1998) *The Oxford History of the Twentieth Century*. New York: Oxford University Press.

Muller, Pierre, and Jean Louis Quermonne, eds. (1996) *Adjusting to Europe: The Impact of the European Union on National Institutions and Policies*. New York: Routledge.

Piening, Christopher. (1997) *The European Union in World Affairs*. London: Rienner Publishers.

Redmond, John, ed. (1997) *The 1995 Enlargement of the European Union*. Brookfield, MA: Ashgate.

Richardson, Jeremy, ed. (1996) *European Union Power and Policy Making*. New York: Routledge.

Taylor, Paul. (1975) "The Politics of the European Communities." *World Politics* 27, 3: 366–390.

Tsebelis, George. (1994) "The Power of the European Parliament as Conditional Agenda Settler." *American Political Science Review* 88, 1: 128–142.

EVEREST, MOUNT Mount Everest, known in Tibetan as Chomolungma ("mother goddess of the land") and in Nepali as Sagarmatha ("peak of the heavens"), is located in the Himalayan Range on the border between Nepal and Tibet. It is 8,848 meters high and thus the world's highest mountain. Its English name honors Sir George Everest (1790–1866), the surveyor-general of India from 1830 to 1843. Although it had been surveyed from a distance and flown over, in 1921 George Mallory was the first European to attempt to climb it. He lost his life there in 1924. Sir Edmund Hillary (b. 1919), a New Zealand mountaineer, and Tenzing Norgay (1914–1986), a Sherpa, finally reached the summit in 1953. Subsequently many adventurers have made the ascent from several directions with the help of modern equipment. Six deaths on the mountain during an ill-fated climb in

CLIMBING MOUNT EVEREST—JUST A JOB

To the Sherpas of Nepal, guiding tourists up and down Mount Everest is just a job and the mountain itself a source of income.

> Eight of Khumbu's most experienced and illustrious *sardars* unanimously agreed that virtually the only reason they climb is that they need the high income they cannot earn any other way. As one put it, if he had the education to qualify for a good office job, he would unhesitatingly choose that line of work. Sherpas see no intrinsic point in climbing; neither fame (though that is welcome since it helps them get their next climbing job more easily; it also accounts for the multiple ascents of Everest), nor challenge, nor adventure. Climbing is simply a high-paying job. None of the eight *sardars* expressed much enthusiasm for a hypothetical all-Sherpa expedition because they could not imagine any earnings accruing from it. Even though they enjoy the camaraderie and the scenic views and take pride in a job well done, these reasons alone would never motivate them to move up a mountain. Plans for a "First Sherpa Youth Mt. Everest Expedition 91" indicate contrary sentiments, but if skilled Sherpa climbers are paid on such an expedition, the view of the eight *sardars* will stand unchallenged.

Source: James F. Fisher. (1990) *Sherpas: Reflections on Change on Himalayan Nepal.* Berkeley and Los Angeles: University of California Press, 129.

Snow-capped Mount Everest in Gokyo, Nepal. (ALISON WRIGHT/CORBIS)

1996 were seen as a consequence of increasingly novice climbers tackling the mountain. In 2000 a Slovenian mountaineer, Davo Karnicar, ascended to the summit in four days and became the first person to ski down.

Paul Hockings

Further Reading

Hagen, Toni. (1963) *Mount Everest*. New York: Oxford University Press.

Hillary, Edmund. (1955) *High Adventure*. London: Hodder.

SAGARMATHA NATIONAL PARK—WORLD HERITAGE SITE

Home of Mount Everest, Sagarmatha National Park's deep glacial valleys teem with pandas and snow leopards. The park was designated a UNESCO World Heritage Site in 1979 for its ecological significance and indigenous Sherpa culture.

EXPORT-LED DEVELOPMENT

"Export-led development" refers to the experience of nations in which strong export growth has been the leading factor driving strong overall economic growth. Such development has come to characterize the exceptional growth performance of Asian nations, especially Japan, South Korea, Taiwan, and Singapore. Export growth has been credited as the main contributor to their high overall growth rates in the 1970s and 1980s.

Theoretical Considerations

Rigorous theoretical models link economic growth to factor accumulation (labor, capital) and productivity improvements. In these models, exports enter as a source of foreign exchange to finance capital accumulation or as a learning opportunity to assimilate more productive foreign know-how.

Exports as a channel to generate foreign exchange for investment in foreign capital goods has been the focus of the traditional growth literature, which focuses on the limited availability of capital in developing nations. In this way, available resources are channeled from domestic consumption to investment. Exports may also serve as a signal to foreign investors that external debts incurred today can be serviced in the future and thereby allow foreign savings to be tapped for further investments.

Exports as a channel toward rising productivity have been the focus of the new growth literature focusing on knowledge spillovers. Exports are much less effective for adopting foreign know-how than are imports or inward foreign investment. But a strong export performance can finance imports of advanced foreign goods. It can increase a location's profile as an export platform and thus attract foreign investments that tend to imply knowledge transfer into the economy.

More qualitative concepts, such as Michael Porter's "diamond" framework, incorporate factor conditions, the context for firm strategy and rivalry, demand conditions, and supporting and related industries in order to study factors driving productivity and productivity growth. In these concepts, export-led development affects, for example, the context for firm strategy and rivalry through companies' exposure to competition on international markets and to management practices at foreign business partners, as well as demand conditions through exposure to world-class customer needs.

The theoretical welfare implications of export-led growth are ambiguous. Moving from a closed economy to an open economy with exports unambiguously raises prosperity. Moving further to actively promoting exports in an otherwise undistorted economy, however, creates welfare losses in traditional growth models. In the new growth models and the competitiveness framework, as well as in traditional growth models with distortions, the welfare implications are ambiguous.

Development Policy Implications

The export-led growth performance of Asian nations had a major impact on policy discussions. The apparent success of the export-led model has refuted the earlier import-substitution development model. The role of government in the export-led model has unleashed a vigorous debate on the merits of government intervention. Moreover, the observation that export-led growth was driven by factor accumulation rather than productivity increases has shed doubts on the long-term sustainability of the export-led model.

The export-led growth model was preceded by earlier attempts in many parts of the world to use import substitution as an engine of development. Proponents of import substitution argued that companies from advanced economies had advantages over potential competitors from developing economies based on existing scale and thus would dominate industries with high potential for growth and value creation, absent government intervention. To counter these scale advantages of advanced economy companies, import-substitution policies closed developing nation markets to imports and encouraged the creation of domestic companies to serve these markets. The experience with this approach—especially in Latin America, where it was pushed in the 1960s and 1970s by the U.N.'s Economic Commission for Latin America—was disappointing. Under the cover of import tariffs local companies remained inefficient and consumers had to put up with high prices and low-quality domestic goods.

The role of the government in export-led development has been debated since the success of Japan. In many nations associated with export-led development the government has played a role through, for example, export targets for individual companies, the allocation of credits for export-oriented investments, or a consciously undervalued currency. But did growth materialize because of government intervention, or in spite of it? Initially, the success of Japan and the other Asian nations that followed in its footsteps was credited to institutions such as Japan's Ministry of International Trade and Industry (MITI). Over time, however, it was pointed out that many of the most successful Japanese export industries had flourished against the advice of MITI, whereas industries that had been targeted, like the aircraft industry, turned out to be failures. Other nations such as Taiwan and Thailand also achieved success based on export-led development but with less interventionist economic policies. An emerging third view argues that government interventions had a positive impact when they encouraged exports and competition on world markets across companies and industries but had a negative impact when they targeted individual companies or industries for export success.

The long-term sustainability of the export-led development model has come into focus more recently. In an influential article, Alwyn Young pointed out that the growth performance of the Asian "tigers" following in Japan's footsteps can be almost exclusively accounted for by the increased use of factor inputs. The productivity of factor input use, however, has stagnated. Low productivity has two effects: It limits the growth potential for catch-up at increasing income levels, and it limits the prosperity that nations can enjoy as a consequence of growth.

Growth at higher income levels is limited because further factor accumulation becomes harder and less effective. In the past, the Asian nations were able to increase their industrial labor force by increasing female labor force participation and moving people from agriculture into industrial jobs. They were also able to increase their capital stock through heavy investment. Now, however, the labor pool is largely exploited, and further capital investments face diminishing returns.

Growth without productivity improvements also limits the level of prosperity that nations can enjoy. As the returns of further capital accumulation diminish, further wage growth can be supported only by productivity improvements. To turn wage growth into prosperity, nations need to have an efficient domestic sector in order not to diminish the real value of wages. High retail, real-estate, and local-service costs have, for example, limited prosperity in Japan despite high wage levels in the 1990s.

Status of the Current Debate

The debate on the implications of export-led growth, especially in Asian nations, continues: On one side of the spectrum export-led development and the Asian experience are seen as evidence for the merits of a more directive government role that sets clear sectoral priorities. On the other side of the spectrum it is argued that the Asian growth experience can be explained by traditional factor accumulation. Export orientation had a role within a procompetition policy agenda that also opened up internal markets and refrained from sectoral interventions. Although the debate is far from over, more recently the majority view seems to shift in the latter direction.

Christian Ketels

Further Reading

Eatwell, John. (1996) "Import Substitution and Export-Led Growth." In *The New Palgrave: A Dictionary of Economics.* Vol. 2. New York: Grove's Dictionaries, 737–738.

Grossman, Gene M., and Elhanan Helpman. (1991) *Innovation and Growth in the Global Economy.* Cambridge, MA: MIT Press.

Krugman, Paul R., and Maurice Obstfeld. (2000) *International Economics: Theory and Policy.* 5th ed. Boston: Addison Wesley.

Porter, Michael E. (1998) "The Competitive Advantage of Nations." In *On Competition*, edited by Michael E. Porter. Boston: Harvard Business School Press, 155–196.

———, Hirotaka Takeuchi, and Mariko Sakakibara. (2000) *Can Japan Compete?* London: Macmillan.

World Bank. (1993) *The Asian Miracle: Economic Growth and Public Policy.* Oxford: Oxford University Press.

Young, Alwyn. (1995) "The Tyranny of Numbers: Confronting the Realities of the East Asian Growth Experience." *Quarterly Journal of Economics* (August): 641–680.

FA NGOUM (1316–1374?), founder of the Lan Xang kingdom of Cambodia. Fa Ngoum or Fa Ngum was born in Muang Sawa, a Lao principality located on the site of present-day Luang Prabang, and founded the Lan Xang Hom Khao (better known as Lan Xang) kingdom in Laos in 1353. Phraya Khampong, ruler of Muang Sawa and Fa Ngoum's grandfather, banished Fa Ngoum and his father, Chao Fa Ngiew, to the Khmer kingdom of Angkor in the 1320s due to his father's indiscretion with one of the grandfather's wives. Fa Ngoum subsequently married a Khmer princess, Keo Keng Nya. With the support of Angkor, Fa Ngoum returned to Muang Sawa with a Khmer army to gain control and consolidate his kingdom, Lan Xang Hom Khao—"land of one million elephants and a white parasol." The elephants symbolized military power since most battles were fought using elephants, and the white parasol symbolized royalty, particularly a Buddhist monarch. Fa Ngoum further legitimized his rule by enshrining the Prabang Buddha image as the spiritual protector of the kingdom in Viang Chan Viang Kham (present-day Vientiane). He made Xiang Dong Xiang Thong (later renamed Luang Prabang) his capital. Fa Ngoum is credited with introducing the Theravada Buddhist sect to the region when the Khmer monks who accompanied the image of the Prabang Buddha established a monastery in Lan Xang. Political turmoil ensued, and Fa Ngoum's son Oun Hueun (Sam Sene Thai, 1356–1417) succeeded the throne in 1368. Fa Ngoum died in Muang Nan in 1374 or 1375.

Linda S. McIntosh

Further Reading

Stuart-Fox, Martin. (1998) *The Lao Kingdom of Lan Xang: Rise and Decline.* Bangkok, Thailand: White Lotus.

FAIZ AHMAD FAIZ (1911–1984), modern Urdu poet of Pakistan. Born in Sialkot, Pakistan, Ahmad Faiz symbolizes the heights that progressive poetry reached on the Indian subcontinent. He employed all the devices of classical Urdu lyrical poetry to convey a modern sensibility. The heady combination of ideological commitment and romanticism ensured his wide popularity. A recipient of the Lenin Prize for his work on behalf of the downtrodden and for peace, Faiz wrote eight volumes of poetry and six volumes of prose, as well as other works. His poetry represents the high point of progressive literature in the Urdu language.

Faiz's early poems were concerned with love and were written in the idiom and imagery current in Urdu poetry in the early decades of the twentieth century. His formative phase ended when Urdu poets were divided into three categories, depending on their ideological-artistic inclinations: first, those writing in the orthodox classical tradition who regarded any deviation in matters of style and prosody blasphemous; second, those who styled themselves progressives (whose objective was to work for social uplift rather than for aesthetic reasons) or their sympathizers; and third, the group called "Circle of Men of Good Taste," who claimed to write pure poetry, unencumbered by any social(ist) concerns. These distinctions were drawn in the 1940s and 1950s by the Circle of Men of Good Taste. Faiz belonged to the second group, though he did not share the extreme views of some of its members. The catholicity of taste, lyricism, and perfect blending of tradition and modernity in his poetry made him acceptable to all, encompassing ideological divides.

The first collection of his poems, *Naqsh-i Faryaadi* (Supplicant's Prayer), was published in Urdu in 1941.

His earliest poems, written mostly in the *ghazal* form, speak of love in the traditional vein. However, the poem *Mujh se pahli si muhabbat meri mahboob na maang* (My Beloved, Do Not Ask of Me My Former Kind of Love) marks the beginning of a new consciousness in which love for an earthly beloved is suffused with awareness of suffering humanity.

The poems in his second collection, *Dast-i Saba* (Fingers of the Morning Breeze, 1952), reflect his commitment to the progressive ideology at its height so much so that he characterized Indian independence in 1947 as a "much-stained radiance" in his justly famous poem *Subh-e azad* (Freedom's Dawn), which expresses Faiz's dissatisfaction with mere political freedom unaccompanied by economic freedom. In his inimitable style Faiz gave expression to a feeling of disillusionment with the false dawn of India's freedom from colonial domination, as well as feelings of resolve to continue the struggle against all oppressive regimes. Many of the poems in *Dast-i Saba* and all the poems in his third collection, *Zindan Nama* (Prison Writings; 1956), were composed during his imprisonment from 1952 to 1955 for opposing imposition of martial law in Pakistan and have an urgency about them. They speak of the need to fight against capitalism and dictatorship and to safeguard freedom of speech, the isolation of prison life, and undaunting courage in the face of suffering, imprisonment, even execution. At the same time Faiz also wrote poems about human feelings that are universal in nature, including "Tanhaai" (Solitude) and "Yaas" (Despair).

Faiz's diction is often consciously literary and decorative. He moved from the traditional rhymed verse in his early phase to free verse in his middle and later phases. In matters of style he blended the old with the new; his adherence to the traditional symbols and imagery of the *ghazal* is traditional, whereas his espousal of social themes is new. Innovation and experimentation for their own sake had no appeal for him.

M. Asaduddin

Further Reading

Ali, Agha Shahid. (1992) *The Rebel's Silhouette.* Delhi: Oxford University Press.

Kiernan, Victor. (1971) *Poems by Faiz.* London: George Allen & Unwin.

Lazard, Naomi. (1988) *The True Subject.* Princeton, NJ: Princeton University Press.

FALUN GONG Founded by Li Hongzhi (b. 1952) in 1992 in China, the Falun Gong, or Falun Dafa, is the fastest-growing religious and social movement in recent history. The Chinese government estimates the number of Falun Gong followers as between 2 and 10 million in China, but Li claims there are 100 million adherents in thirty countries. The movement first attracted the world's attention with a series of well-organized protests in Beijing in early 1999. Li left China in 1998 for New York City, probably in anticipation of his trouble with Chinese authorities. Alarmed by Falun Gong's organizational prowess and its challenge to the official ideology, the Chinese government declared Falun Gong a "heretical organization" on 23 July 1999 and launched a full-scale propaganda campaign against Li and his followers. Falun Gong has responded to the official ban with more protests and its own publicity crusade carried out mostly through Western news media and on the Internet.

The rapid rise of Falun Gong has as much to do with Li's charisma as with his message. All established religions in China have seen significant growth in their membership, and many new quasi-religious sects associated (like Falun Gong) with *qigong* were established there in the 1980s. *Qigong* is a three-thousand-year-old natural-healing discipline involving exercises and meditation. Like other *qigong* masters, Li emphasizes its spiritual element, but he distinguishes himself by linking *qigong* with Buddhist and Taoist cosmologies.

Falun Gong has spread through Li's many books and lectures and the testimonials of practitioners. Despite its proven capability of mobilizing people, Falun Gong remains a loosely organized movement as determined by Li's teaching. Practitioners can participate at exercise centers or cultivate on their own. Li is the only "teacher," or "master," in the religion.

Dian Li

Further Reading

Li Hongzhi. (1999) *Revolving the Law of Wheel.* 2d ed. New York: The Universe Publishing Co.

———. (2000) *China Falun Gong.* 2d ed. New York: The Universe Publishing Co.

Schechter, Danny, ed. (2000) *Falun Gong's Challenge to China.* New York: Akashic Books.

Wong, John, and William T. Liu. (1999) *The Mystery of China's Falun Gong: Its Rise and Its Sociological Implications.* Singapore: World Scientific Publishing Co. and Singapore University Press.

FAMINE—CHINA Famine is a result of multiple political, economic, social, and ecological disorders that combine to produce an increase in the number of deaths from starvation and epidemic disease. An ex-

A crowd at a government facility providing rice during the famine of 1948. (BETTMANN/CORBIS)

amination of Chinese famines and Chinese official responses to famine conditions reveals universal features that apply to both traditional and modern times. Famine descriptions punctuate China's historical records. One survey noted that eighteen hundred famines were recorded between 108 BCE and 1929 CE. Chinese record keepers were careful to note that, in most cases, actual famine conditions did not result directly from drought, flood, war, or neglected infrastructure, but rather from failures of official intervention in the face of widespread popular distress.

Traditional Relief and Prevention

Famine relief and prevention traditionally formed an inherent part of Chinese official responsibility for popular welfare. Historical literature describes different episodes of famine and explains direct, indirect, and long-term measures for dealing with famine conditions. Lists of precipitating events point to differences between so-called heavenly calamities, such as drought or flood, and calamities linked to human causes, such as political ineptitude, rebellion, or war. Scarcities produced by grain transfers or extractions and failure to maintain irrigation works, dikes, and transport networks are classified as human causes.

A guiding principle for relief efforts called for them to be administered according to circumstances. Local investigators described famine conditions in terms of degrees of hunger or the amount of food available per person during a given period. Immediate, or direct, relief measures included food and cash distributions to halt starvation. Indirect measures included tax relief, seed distributions to restore agricultural productivity, and work-relief projects to repair famine-related damage. Long-term relief measures included plans for water conservancy and programs to help settle famine refugees on unused land. Officials often planned projects ahead of actual needs so that they could be implemented quickly and without controversy.

An examination of Chinese official responses to famine conditions reveals that, overall, relief efforts succeeded best when China had a strong central order to mobilize physical and economic resources on behalf of popular welfare. When the central order was weak, millions were doomed. A hallmark of Chinese famine intervention called for grain storage to protect against the effects of crop failures. China's "ever normal granaries" served the dual goals of price stabilization and food relief by permitting officials to sell grain at reduced prices and to arrange grain transfers to avert hoarding and price gouging.

Historical data reveal that, by the mid-nineteenth century, the Chinese state could not mobilize resources necessary to carry out effective famine relief and that famine conditions occurred somewhere in China almost every year throughout the first half of the twentieth century.

Foreign Intervention

Foreigners in China during the late nineteenth and first half of the twentieth centuries made repeated attempts to provide famine relief, but they confronted a system in decline, and their efforts never evolved into coherent programs. Foreign efforts did, however, yield themes that were reiterated by a variety of relief agents and agencies in China. One was foreign insistence that China needed long-term physical and economic improvements before the constant threat of famine could be eliminated. A second proposed that the necessary improvements be instituted and run by foreign agencies and personnel. A third theme took form in negative reports that discouraged foreign donors and governments from contributing to Chinese official relief efforts.

Chinese officials regularly accepted foreign food and money for short-term relief and, with equal regularity, rejected long-term relief proposals for projects designed to be owned and run by foreigners. Ultimately, foreign relief efforts emulated Chinese trends. They succeeded best when they had strong external political support. They failed when foreign governments determined that conditions for relief were hopeless and refused to support agents and agencies operating in China.

China and the Great Leap Famine

Establishment of the People's Republic of China in 1949 brought dramatic improvements in medical care, disease prevention, and agricultural production. For a time it seemed as if official priority given to eliminating famine would bring positive results. Food production and distribution came under strict central controls, and the state gave high priority to increasing food supplies and improving transport networks. However, state collectivization policies produced disaster as outside assistance was halted, agriculture became collectivized, demands for huge quotas could not be met, and limited resources could not be distributed equitably. An estimated 30 million people died of starvation and disease during the Great Leap Famine of 1958–1962. It is now referred to as the worst famine in human history. A consensus holds that it was human made and that it resulted primarily from political failures associated with the Great Leap Forward, Mao's abortive effort to encourage rural industrialization at the expense of agriculture.

Since the death of Mao in 1976, China has gradually liberalized its economic policies and allowed for private control of agricultural land while maintaining firm centralized control of the government. It is to be hoped that these measures have put famine firmly in China's past.

Arline Golkin-Kadonaga

Further Reading

Becker, Jasper. (1966) *Hungry Ghosts: Mao's Secret Famine.* New York: Henry Holt.

Bohr, Paul Richard. (1972) *Famine in China and the Missionary: Timothy Richard as Relief Administrator and Advocate of National Reform, 1876–1884.* Cambridge, MA: Harvard University Press.

Chang Chung-li. (1974) *The Chinese Gentry.* Seattle, WA: University of Washington Press.

Golkin, Arline T. (1987) *Famine: A Heritage of Hunger.* Claremont, CA: Regina Press.

———. (1990) "American Missionaries and the Politics of Famine Relief to China" In *United States Attitudes toward China: The Impact of American Missionaries,* edited by Patricia Neils. New York: M. E. Sharpe.

Tawney, R. H. (1932) *Land and Labour in China.* New York: M. E. Sharpe.

Will, Pierre-Etienne, and R. Bin Wong. (1991) *Nourish the People: The State Civilian Granary System in China, 1650–1850.* Ann Arbor, MI: University of Michigan Center for Chinese Studies.

FARID, KHWAJA GHULAM (1845–1901),

South Asian Sufi poet. Khwaja Ghulam Farid was a great Sufi poet, mystic, and literary figure who remains revered and beloved by millions to this day all over the India-Pakistan subcontinent. Khwaja Ghulam Farid composed in the *kaafi,* the favored poetic genre of his native Multan in present-day Pakistan, to bring spiritual enlightenment to Muslim contemporaries, considered during that period to be in the throes of political, economic, and spiritual decline that manifested itself in widespread drug use, social ills, superstition, and debased religious practices.

Farid's poetry reflects his great love and knowledge of music and his homeland. He chose to compose in the regional language of Siraiki rather than Persian or Urdu, the courtly and scholarly languages of the time. He added a romantic, ecstatic flavor and new musicality to the more ascetic devotional poetry of his predecessors. Effortlessly he takes the reader/listener through explanations of the highest mystical matters as well as charming depictions of everyday lives of simple folk. As a result, to this day, his mystical expressions of wonderment, love, humility, and gnosis bring delight to both the lover of poetry and the illiterate villager, while edifying the student of theology.

Like other Sufis of the subcontinent, Farid's expansive spirit of tolerance endeared him to Muslim, Hindu, and Sikh alike. Even today, his shrine in Kot Mithan is visited by thousands each year on the occasion of his *urs* (death anniversary).

Shabana Mir

Further Reading

Durrani, Jamilah. (1996) *Khwaja Ghulam Farid: shakhs aur sha'ir* (Khwaja Ghulam Farid: The Man and His Poetry). Jampur, Pakistan: Kitab Sarai.

Haq, Mehr Abdul. (1988) *Fard-e-Fareed: Hazrat Khwaja Ghulam Farid ke kaam-o-paigham ka tehseeni ja'izah* (The Unique Individual: Critical Appreciation of Hazrat Khwaja Ghulam Farid's Work and Message). Multan, Pakistan: Saraiki Adabi Board.

FARMERS' MOVEMENTS

FARMERS' MOVEMENTS Japanese farmers face demographic and economic challenges. Their political strength of the early post–World War II period has waned due to a demographic shift away from rural areas. Deregulation of the agricultural commodity trade has put further pressure on Japanese farmers.

Comprehensive taxation on farmers was introduced from Tang dynasty China during the seventh century. Farmers faced an additional burden as drafted foot soldiers during the warring states period of the late-fifteenth to mid-sixteenth centuries. Their repeated rebellions against local lords resulted in confiscation of all swords from the farmers in 1588 by Toyotomi Hideyoshi and their complete separation from the warrior class.

Heavy tax burdens, especially during poor harvests, prompted farmers to rebel against domain lords. During the Edo period (1600/1603–1868), the decentralized and more sophisticated taxation on farmers by local domains and the ban on land transactions kept most farmers small-scale and poor. While most rebellions were quickly suppressed by the domain forces, the widespread rebellion by mostly Christian peasants in Shimabara (1637–1638) required intervention by the central government. Frequent famines after the late-eighteenth century and the development of urban commerce and industrial activities prompted informal transfer of land titles, dividing the farmers into a few rich landowners and many poor tenant farmers.

The two-tiered structure of the farmers largely continued throughout the pre–World War II period, despite limited land reforms, and the dual burdens of taxation to fuel state-led industrialization and military draft fell heavily on the tenant farmers. Some Marxist intellectuals, like Kawakami Hajime and his followers, and anarchists insisted on a political alliance of industrial workers and tenant farmers but had limited success due to state suppression. Farmers took part in the prewar proletariat movements in the stream of worker-farmer parties, such as Rodo Nominto, Nihon Ronoto, and Zenkoku Rono Taishuto. However, the military government and its control of agriculture through the Food Control Law of 1942 tightly incorporated farmers into the war efforts.

More than half the Japanese population was engaged in agriculture at the end of World War II. The American-led occupation forces implemented a major land reform program, breaking large land holdings into small independent farms. The collective support of these small farmers became a backbone of the ruling Liberal Democratic Party. The government used the Food Control Law for encouraging production and orderly distribution of rice under its monopoly during the food shortage following the war. The farmers set up the Central Union of Agricultural Cooperatives and successfully pressured the government into raising its purchase price of rice until the mid-1980s. Government efforts to deregulate the rice distribution system and discourage rice production through crop diversion programs had limited success. In other commodities, such as oranges and beef, quota-based imports started in the 1980s.

In the face of U.S. demands that Japan open its rice market to imports, Japanese farmers launched political campaigns to block imports and promote quality domestic rice. The former campaign delayed the opening of the rice market until 1994, when Japan agreed to institute a quota-based import program. In 1999, a tariff replaced the quota system. Meanwhile, the "quality rice" campaign networked farmers, environmentalists, and quality-conscious consumers and may provide a way for innovative farmers to compete successfully with imported rice. By the late 1990s, less than 10 percent of the Japanese population was engaged in agriculture, and half Japan's farmers produced commodities other than rice. The monolithic political strength of the farmers has vanished.

Yoichiro Sato

Further Reading

Donnelly, Michael W. (1984) "Conflict over Government Authority and Markets: Japan's Rice Economy." In *Conflict in Japan*, edited by Ellis S. Krauss, Thomas P. Rohlen, and Patricia G. Steinhoff. Honolulu, HI: University of Hawaii Press, 335–374.

George, Aurelia. (1988) *Rice Politics in Japan*. Food Policy Study no. 54. Tokyo: Agricultural Policy Research Center.

Karube, Kensuke. (1997) *Nichibei Kome Kosho: Shijo kaiho no shinso to saikosho he no tenbo* (U.S.–Japan Rice Negotiation: The Truth About the Market Opening and the Vision Toward Renegotiation). Tokyo: Chuokoron-sha.

Sato, Yoichiro. (1996) "Sticky Efforts: Japan's Rice Market Opening and U.S.–Japan Transnational Lobbying." In *Japan Engaging the World: A Century of International Encounter*, edited by Harumi Befu. Denver, CO: Center for Japan Studies, Teikyo Loretto-Heights University, 73–99.

Soda, Osamu. (1994) *Kome wo kangaeru* (Thinking of Rice). Tokyo: Iwanami Shoten.

FARS (2002 pop. 4.2 million). Fars, in southern Iran, is one of the largest Iranian provinces, with an area of 133,294 square kilometers; it is a region with great historical significance. The nucleus of the ancient Persian empire (c. 550–331 BCE), it was called Persis and was the seat of the royal cities of Pasargadae and Persepolis. An evolved version of the ancient Persian tongue (called Farsi or Parsi after the region) is still spoken today in Iran and is the official language of the country.

The Iranian-speaking Aryans first came to northern Fars; later the valleys of the Kur and Pulwar rivers became centers and remained so until the time of the Sasanid dynasty. Darius the Great (reigned 522–486 BCE) built Persepolis where the Pulwar flows into the Kur on the plain of Marwdasht. Another town on the banks of the Pulwar, called Istakhr in the Middle Ages, was the focal point of the Sasanid dynasty. Other cities of Fars later outshone Istakhr in terms of size and activity (namely Shiraz, Fasa, Siraf, and Arrajan).

Throughout history, Fars flourished and waned according to the fortunes of the dynasty in power. Shiraz was the capital of various dynasties, but eventually power, money, and prestige shifted from this area to the northerly cities of Tehran and Isfahan. Fars nevertheless remained a significant commercial and cultural center. Today Shiraz is not only the bustling hub of commerce for the Fars region, but is also one of the most industrialized cities in Iran. It is a major destination for tourists who appreciate historical sites and art centers and wish to visit the tombs of the poets Sa'di and Hafez.

Ruins of the Persian capital of Persepolis in Fars. (CORBIS)

Several nomadic ethnic groups, including the Qashqais, inhabit Fars as they did in past centuries. Nomads mounted on horses or camels may spend summers on the high plateaus and move south to the Persian Gulf in the winter to search for pastures for their herds; others spend winters in a city. These groups represent not only an economic mode of production, but also a lifestyle that has strong cultural and traditional roots in many parts of Iran.

Houman A. Sadri

Further Reading

Barthold, W. (1984) *An Historical Geography of Iran.* Trans. by Svat Soucek. Princeton, NJ: Princeton University Press.

Ghirshman, Roman. (1978) *Iran.* Middlesex, U.K.: Penguin Books.

FARSI-TAJIKI The Farsi-Tajiki or Tajiki language, the name given to one of the Iranian languages spoken in Central Asia, is also called Persian, Tajik, or Tajik Persian. This variety of names reflects the rather complicated history of the language.

Forms of New Persian

Farsi-Tajiki belongs to the Western branch of the Iranian language group (of the Indo-Iranian branch of the Indo-European language family), in which it is usually classified as New Persian. Today there are three standardized forms of New Persian: Farsi-Tajiki, Farsi, and Dari. In their standard forms, these three are to a large extent identical, although there are many regional spoken variants, which may differ considerably from the standard forms. Since 1989, Farsi-Tajiki has been the official language of Tajikistan, but it is also spoken in large parts of the neighboring republic of Uzbekistan and in Afghanistan. Farsi is the official language of Iran, and Dari the official language of Afghanistan.

History of Farsi-Tajiki

Farsi means "Persian," and Tajiki is derived from *Tajik*, a word with an obscure etymology, once implying "Muslim," but nowadays referring to the people of the Central Asian republic of Tajikistan. Farsi-Tajiki evolved from the classical New Persian language that gradually emerged as a new written language, replacing Middle Persian and other Iranian languages in the centuries following the Muslim Arabs' conquest of Iran and Central Asia in the seventh century. (Iranian languages had long been spoken in Central Asia.) Classical New Persian, like the modern New Persian (Farsi) of today, is written in an adaptation of the Arabic script and is characterized by a large number of loanwords from Arabic. Farsi-Tajiki also has a relatively large number of Turkic loanwords. With the coming of the Turkic tribes from the tenth century on, Turkic languages, such as Uzbek, gradually superseded the Iranian languages once spoken in the area of Central Asia. More recently, Russian has deeply influenced Farsi-Tajiki.

The term "Tajik" began to be used widely from the sixteenth century onward to refer to speakers of New Persian in the area of the Oxus River (the modern Amu Dar'ya, in central and western Central Asia) basin and present-day northeastern Afghanistan, to distinguish them from speakers of Turkic languages in that area. The expansion of Turkic peoples, mainly Uzbeks and Turkmen, from the north to the south of Central Asia, in combination with the stabilization of national frontiers in the sixteenth century, separated the Iranians of the Iranian plateau from the Iranians to the northeast. From then on, the spoken Persian of the northeast developed separately from that of Iran.

However, the written Persian, in use for administrative and literary purposes in India as well as Central Asia, remained the same as the Persian used in Iran until the first quarter of the twentieth century. This language was called Farsi or Parsi (Persian, or more specifically New Persian) in the whole of the Iranian cultural area, which stretched from India to western modern Iran. The term "Farsi-Tajiki" or "Tajiki" came into use under Soviet influence around 1925.

Emergence of Farsi-Tajiki

The development of standard Farsi-Tajiki was instigated by the poet and novelist Sadriddin Aini (1878–1954), considered the founder of modern Tajik literature. He was trained in the medieval cloisters of a Bukharan *madrasah* (Muslim religious school), but he used his talents in the service of reform and revolution.

When Soviet rule was established in Central Asia in the 1920s, it was decided that the region should be divided into national republics. The republics were named after their dominant ethnic groups, whose languages had to be developed as tools for educating the proletariat. This division into national republics was artificial, not only since there were many more ethnic groups than national republics, but also because different ethnic groups had been living together in the same areas for centuries. A seemingly neat division was nevertheless carried through, and the newly appointed national languages were turned into modern Soviet-era languages by introducing elements from the vernacular to replace classical expressions. Sadriddin Aini was among the intellectuals who created the reformed Persian, which was called Tajiki. Aini apparently invented the term "Farsi-Tajiki," to mark the language's close relationship with the classical Persian heritage and with the Persian spoken in Iran and Afghanistan. Although this language was based on the spoken forms of Persian around Bukhara and Samarqand in present-day Uzbekistan, it was imposed as a new literary language on the inhabitants of the newly founded republic of Tajikistan, which was situated farther east and did not include Bukhara and Samarqand, the Tajik centers of old. Until then the area of Tajikistan had been only sparsely populated, and those who lived there mainly spoke different forms of Tadjiki or other Iranian languages, although Uzbek and Kirghiz were also spoken in western and northern present-day Tajikistan.

One of the first steps in transforming the allegedly old-fashioned and feudal image of the Persian language used in Central Asia was the adoption of a new alphabet. First, around 1930, the Latin alphabet was adopted. In 1940 the introduction of a modified Cyrillic alphabet facilitated the adoption of many Russian loan words, and the Russian language gradually gained importance in Tajikistan, marginalizing and Russianizing Farsi-Tajiki. This process ended in the late 1980s under the influence of glasnost and perestroika.

Since the disintegration of the Soviet Union in 1991, the people of Tajikistan have tried to reintroduce the Arabo-Persian script and to decrease the use of Russian and Russian loan words in Tajiki. However, so far the poor economic situation prohibits an effective reintroduction.

In short, Farsi-Tajiki in its present form is a relatively new language, but it has a long history. Its direct ancestor is classical New Persian, which had been spoken in Central Asia since the emergence of Islam. Whereas the Soviets increasingly tended to isolate Farsi-Tajiki from the Persian (Farsi) of Iran and Afghanistan, since independence Tajiks have tried to emphasize Farsi-Tajiki's similarity to Farsi and Dari. Both Farsi-Tajiki and Farsi have a common heritage, although political and historical circumstances through the centuries have resulted in considerable differences in grammar and vocabulary, particularly in colloquial language.

Gabrielle Van den Berg

Further Reading
Lazard, Gilbert. (1970) "Persian and Tajik." In *Current Trends in Linguistics*, 6, edited by Thomas A. Sebeok. The Hague, Netherlands, and Paris: Mouton, 64–96.
———. (1975) "The Rise of the New Persian Language." In *The Cambridge History of Iran*. Vol. 4, edited by R. N. Frye. Cambridge, U.K.: Cambridge University Press, 595–633.
Perry, John R., and Rachel Lehr. (1998) *The Sands of the Oxus: Boyhood Reminiscences of Sadriddin Aini*. Costa Mesa, CA: Mazda.
Rastorgueva, Vera Sergeevna. (1963) *A Short Sketch of Tajik Grammar*. Trans. by Herbert Paper. Bloomington, IN: Indiana University Center for Anthropology, Folklore, and Linguistics.
Rzehak, Lutz. (1999) *Tadschikische Studiengrammatik*. Wiesbaden, Germany: Reichert Verlag.
Schmitt, Rüdiger. (1989) *Compendium Linguarum Iranicarum* (Iranian Language Compendium). Wiesbaden, Germany: Reichert Verlag.

FAZILET PARTY. See **Refah and Fazilet Parties.**

FAZL, ABU'L (1551–1602), Indian historiographer. Born in Agra in 1550, Abu'l Fazl, the second son of Shaikh Mubarak, was a learned man of north India who became the faithful secretary and adviser of the Mughal emperor Akbar. His great scholarship as a historiographer is evidenced in his famous but adulatory book, the *Akbarnama* (Book of Akbar, 1590s), which chronicles the history of India in the time of Akbar, and in its supplement, the *Ain-i-Akbari* (Institutes of Akbar, 1593), a statistical account of the Mughal empire. The *Akbarnama* is the most important of all Mughal-era documents. Both books were written in an elegant style of Persian, the court language. Abu'l Fazl's brother Faizi was a noted court poet at the time.

After many years of service Abu'l Fazl was murdered at the instigation of Prince Salim while he was returning from a mission to the Dekkan (a plateau in southern India); the killer was a Bundella chief. (The Bundellas were a dominant clan in the region.) That prince, who had become jealous of the minister's influence, afterward became the emperor Aurangzeb.

Paul Hockings

Further Reading
Wade, Bonnie C. (1998) *Imaging Sound, an Ethnomusicological Study of Music, Art, and Culture in Mughal India*. Chicago: University of Chicago Press.

FEDERAL TERRITORIES—MALAYSIA
Malaysia has a federal system of government that is made up of thirteen states and three federal territories that are under the direct control of the federal government. Wilayah Persekutuan, the national capital region (often called the Kuala Lumpur Federal Territory) was created in February 1974 from part of the state of Selangor and includes the city of Kuala Lumpur and the surrounding area. Putrajaya is the newly built national capital and was declared a federal territory on 1 February 2001. The third federal territory is the island of Labuan, which the government is trying to promote as an international offshore banking center. When the Federation of Malaya was founded in 1957, the federal territories also included Pulau Pinang and the city of Malacca, in addition to Kuala Lumpur. Pulau Pinang and Malacca, however, became states in 1957.

The federal territories have a different political structure from the thirteen other Malaysian states. There is a cabinet-level minister of federal territories, who is assisted by an advisory board for the general administration of each of the three federal territories. The mayors of Kuala Lumpur, Putrajaya, and Labuan are appointed by the king of Malaysia on the advice of the prime minister.

Zachary Abuza

Further Reading
Andaya, Barbara Watson, and Leonard Y. Andaya. (2001) *A History of Malaysia*. 2d ed. Honolulu, HI: University of Hawaii Press.
Crouch, Harold. (1996) *Government and Society in Malaysia*. Ithaca, NY: Cornell University Press.

FEDERALLY ADMINISTERED TRIBAL AREAS—PAKISTAN (2002 est. pop. 3.5 million). Home to Pashtun tribes, the strip of territory along Pakistan's northwestern border with Afghanistan has retained a degree of autonomy since the territories' inception as a buffer zone during British colonial rule (1757–1947). Encompassing seven tribal areas (Khyber, Kurram, Orakzai, Mohmand, Bajaur, North Waziristan and South Waziristan), the region makes up some 27,220 square kilometers of Pakistani territory.

Pakistan's constitutional agreement with the Pashtun tribes, who are the ethnic majority in neighboring Afghanistan, is much more than a mere formality. The Pashtun have successfully resisted occupation for centuries, and until pressure from the United States forced the Pakistani government to mount a helicopter expedition into the area in 2002 to look for the Saudi terrorist Osama bin Laden, the last national military intrusion was by the British in 1897. That expedition never returned. The disastrous mission put an end to British colonial designs on the area, and instead of seizing and settling it (the British pattern for other problematic provinces), the British officially incorporated it into their North-West Frontier Province, but designated it a tribal area and stayed away from it.

When Pakistan gained its independence in 1947, the tribal areas voluntarily swore allegiance to the new government but stopped short of any actual integration and rejected the imposition of any governmental apparatus that might have threatened their autonomy. The tribes were granted a seat in the parliament, and technically universal suffrage applies to them, but with tribal law forbidding political parties, only the tribal elders vote.

The tribal areas have always been a center of smuggling in the region and refuge for some of Pakistan's worst criminals. The situation worsened in the 1960s, when worldwide demand for heroin increased (the tribal areas are centers of opium production, heroin processing, and distribution), and the Soviet invasion of Afghanistan in 1979 further exacerbated the situation. Always a center of arms production, with tribal law and custom dictating that every man should own a gun, the influx of arms from the Soviet invasion of Afghanistan exponentially increased the availability and sophistication of the arms available to the Pashtun, particularly when the United States began covert sales of arms to the Mujahadeen rebels. The area came to be known as *ilaqa ghair* ("the land without laws"), and is a big contributer to instability in the region. With the U.S.-led invasion of Afghanistan in 2001, international pressure to bring the rule of law to the region is growing and will probably succeed, even if only temporarily.

James B. McGirk

Further Reading

Frei, Matt. (2002) "Time Stands Still at Khyber Pass." BBC News (13 January). Retrieved 28 March 2002, from: http://news.bbc.co.uk/hi/english/world/from_our_own_correspondent/newsid_1756000/1756957.stm

McCarthy, Rory. (2000) "Generals Target Arms Bazaar: Pakistan Bids to Silence Village's Replica Rocket Launchers and Copy Kalashnikovs." International Action Network on Small Arms (15 December) Retrieved 28 March 2002, from: http://www.iansa.org/news/2000/dec_00/gen_target.htm.

Shahin, Sultan. (2001) "Taliban Find Safe Haven in Pakistan's Wild West." Asia Times Online (27 November). Retrieved 28 March 2002, from: http://www.atimes.com/ind-pak/CK27Df01.html.

United Nations Office for Drug Control and Crime Prevention. (2002) *Pakistan Profile*. Retrieved 28 March 2002, from: http://www.undcp.org/pakistan/country_profile.html.

FEDERATED MALAY STATES

The Federated Malay States (FMS) was a former federation of the states of Perak, Pahang, Selangor, and Negeri Sembilan on the southern part of the Malay Peninsula. British colonial administrator Frank Swettenham (1850–1946) suggested the idea, and the FMS was established 1 July 1896 and terminated in 1946. With the inclusion of the unfederated Malay States, the Federation of Malaya was formed in 1948.

The British Resident system had previously overseen local administration in the various states. However, Swettenham and other British officers, felt that a central government was needed for greater unity, uniformity, and cooperation between these states. The FMS headquarters were established in Kuala Lumpur, where a Federal Civil Service consisting of departments such as Justice, Communications, Finance, and Public Works was set up. A council of Malay rulers for the FMS was instituted to discuss matters of importance with the British rulers. The first conference of Malay rulers, popularly known as the Durbar (royal display), was held in July 1897 at Istana Negara, Kuala Kangsar, Perak. The Durbar conference was held nine times until the year 1939.

With the formation of the Federation of Malaya in 1948, the Durbar membership increased with the inclusion of the unfederated Malay States of Johor, Kedah, Perlis, Kelantan, and Trengganu. On 18 February 1948 its first conference was held in Kuala Lumpur. The Conference of Rulers was held fifty times from February 1948 until August 1957.

Khai Leong Ho

Further Reading

Heussler, Robert. (1981) *British Rule in Malaya: The Malayan Civil Service and Its Predecessors, 1867–1942*. Oxford: Clio Press.

Ryan, N. J. (1976) *The Making of Modern Malaysia and Singapore*. Kuala Lumpur, Malaysia: Oxford University Press.

Sidhu, Jagjit Singh. (1980) *Administration in the Federated Malay States, 1896–1920*. Kuala Lumpur, Malaysia: Oxford University Press.

FEDERATION OF MALAYSIA

The Federation of Malaysia was the name given to the 1963 political union of several British colonies on the Malay

Peninsula, as well as Singapore and the island of Borneo. In 1946, Britain had separated Singapore, which remained a crown colony, and organized the nine sultanates and two federal territories on the peninsula into the Malay Union. Sarawak and British North Borneo (Sabah) were brought under direct colonial control at that time. There was considerable opposition to the Malay Union, which the local leaders felt consolidated British control. After protracted negotiations with Malay rulers, the British established the Federation of Malaya on 1 February 1948. In this agreement, the British committed themselves to preparing for the Federation's independence. A federal government headed by a British High Commissioner was established in Kuala Lumpur.

Local-level elections were established in 1951, and the first federal elections were held in 1955. Soon after these elections, the coalition government dominated by the United Malays National Organization (UMNO) began negotiations with the British over independence, while Singapore was granted internal autonomy. As a result of an agreement between the British and ethnic Malay, Chinese, and Indian communities, on 31 August 1957, the independent Federation of Malaya was established. This compromise agreement gave ethnic Chinese and Indians citizenship rights but tacitly preserved the leadership role of ethnic Malays in government and constitutionally recognized the "special position and needs of the Malays," creating an affirmative action program. The agreement set up a parliamentary democracy with a bicameral parliament, composed of a nonelected upper house made up of the nine Malay sultans among whom the position of head of state, or paramount ruler, rotated, and an elected lower house.

On 12 May 1961, Prime Minister Tunku Abdul Rahman proposed that the Federation of Malaysia absorb Singapore and the British-controlled territories in northern Borneo, Brunei, Sabah, and Sarawak to create a united Malaysia. The proposal was well accepted in peninsular Malaya and Singapore, but was less popular in the three Borneo territories. The proposal infuriated the Philippines, which asserted a claim over Sabah until 1987, and Indonesia, which viewed it as a neocolonialist plot and began a low-intensity conflict as part of President Sukarno's policy of Konfrontasi from 1963 to 1965. Elections were held for the first time in 1962 in Sabah and Brunei, and an Anglo-Malay commission visited the three territories in 1962, where it reported that following a September referendum a majority of the population was in favor of integration. Although Brunei opted to remain outside the Federation, on 16 September 1963, Sabah, Sarawak, and Singapore were constitutionally added to peninsular Malaya to create the Federation of Malaysia. Under the constitution, the state governments have only limited autonomy and internal security; nation defense, foreign policy, and fiscal policy are prerogatives of the federal government.

Despite the founding of the Federation of Malaysia, there was little attempt to integrate Singapore into the Federation. UMNO extremists feared giving their Singapore counterparts economic advantages and government contracts, yet Kuala Lumpur demanded an increased percentage of Singapore's revenues. The creation of the Federation also radically changed the racial makeup of the country. Though there was a large increase in the number of Chinese, there was a similar rise in the number of indigenous peoples from Sabah and Sarawak. The UMNO campaigned in Singapore's September 1963 elections, and Singapore's ruling party, The People's Action Party (PAP), campaigned in Malaysia's April 1964 elections, causing mistrust. In May 1965, the PAP and four other Chinese-dominated opposition parties founded the Malaysian Solidarity Convention, which convinced many in the UMNO that there was a Chinese plot to take over the country. Communal tensions continued, and on 6 August 1965, the Tunku notified the Singapore chief Lee Kwan Yew that Singapore would be expelled from the Federation. On 9 August 1965, without any Singaporean representatives in attendance, the Malaysian parliament passed a bill favoring separation by 126 to 0. The Republic of Singapore was founded that day. The Federation of Malaysia then adopted the official name Malaysia.

Zachary Abuza

Further Reading

Andaya, Barbara Watson, and Leonard Y. Andaya. (2001) *A History of Malaysia.* 2d ed. Honolulu, HI: University of Hawaii Press.

Crouch, Harold. (1996) *Government and Society in Malaysia.* Ithaca, NY: Cornell University Press.

FELTING—CENTRAL ASIA

Felt is one of the earliest and most important textiles used by the nomads of Central Asia. For over two thousand years, felt has been used to make tents, furniture, and clothing. Through the influence of the nomads, the textile spread out of Asia and into Europe, where it remains an influence.

Materials and Techniques

Felt is a textile usually made from sheep wool or goat hair, but it can sometimes be made from fur.

The exterior of a traditional yurt in Kyrgyzstan covered by decorated felt siding that can be removed and rolled for storage during travel. (JANET WISHNETSKY/CORBIS)

Throughout Asia, wool is the most common material used for felt. The most prevalent sheep of this region are those of the family called fat tailed, because of their large, fat-filled tails. These sheep produce wool that is coarse and easy to felt. The felt made from this wool is stiff and holds up well under heavy use. The outside walls of the Central Asian *ger* (yurt) are made of thick sheets of this stiff felt. Carpets of felt are folded and rolled to be used as furniture inside the *ger*. In addition, felt is used for cloaks, boots, hats, and saddle blankets. Mohair, from Angora goats, is also used to make felt. (The "whirling dervishes" of Turkey wear tall hats of mohair felt.)

The sheep are shorn twice a year, in the spring and at the end of summer. It is the summer fleece that is used for making felt. (The spring fleece is spun into yarn and used for weaving.) After shearing, the wool is laid onto a large piece of cloth on the ground and is beaten with long, flexible sticks. This causes the clumps of fiber to open up and become fluffy.

The fluffy wool is laid out on reed mats in a pile that is about 35 centimeters deep. Boiling water is sprinkled on top of the wool. A long stick is laid on one end of the reed mat, and the mat is rolled up with the wet wool inside it. Sometimes the roll is covered with a piece of canvas or tarp, and then the whole bundle is tied with strong cord in several places. In Turkmenistan, Kyrgyzstan, and Kazakhstan, a long cord is put around the roll, and it is pulled in such a way that it makes the roll rotate. Then a group of people walks arm and arm and kicks the top of the roll as it is rotating. In Mongolia and parts of China, the roll is attached to a rope behind a horse or camel. When the animal is guided forward, the mat-roll turns and hits against the ground, causing agitation. The agitation caused by this action, along with the moisture, causes the wool fibers to expand and contract until they are tangled together. This tangled mass of fiber is what we call felt.

With each method, after a half hour or so, the roll is untied, more hot water is added, and the whole thing is rolled up again from the opposite end of the mat. This rolling process can go on for several hours. At this point, because the felt is still not quite hard enough to function well, it is removed from the reed mat, heated with boiling water, and rolled up on itself, without the center rolling bar. The workers roll it back and forth with their forearms for ten to fifteen minutes. The felt is then unrolled and rerolled from another direction; the process is repeated until it has been rolled from all directions and on both sides. When it is finished, the edges are trimmed and it is allowed to dry.

Felt Decorations and Carpets

Asian felt is often used for carpets. These carpets fall into two major categories: decorated single-layered felts and double-layered felts. Single-layered felts are known by various names and have various surface-decoration techniques. In Kashmir, the carpets are called *numdah,* and the decorations are embroidered onto the finished piece of felt. The edges of these felts have a fleece fringe. In Mongolia, the carpets are usually quilted and sometimes have additional motifs cut from felt and appliquéd onto them. The carpet edges are cut, and a piece of wool rope is sewn to them for added durability. Kyrgyz people make a carpet called *alla kijiz,* in which all the designs are added as the felt is being made. In Europe and North America, this method of creating motifs in felt is called inlay.

Inlay techniques are a common method of decorating felt in Central and Western Asia. The design is created by laying bits of colored fleece either onto a background layer of wool or onto the reed mat before the background layer is placed on it. A variation is to use a sheet of partially made soft felt. Shapes are cut from this soft felt and used like the colored fleece bits mentioned above.

The double-layered felt carpets are among the most prized of Central Asia. Called *shirdak* by the Kyrgyz and *syrmak* by the Kazakhs, these carpets have a patchwork-felt top layer and a solid felt bottom layer, which are quilted together. In English, these types of carpets are called mosaic felts.

Socioeconomic Context

In most parts of Central Asia, the women of nomadic tribes make felt, usually for the family's use. They work together to make the felt, since it is a labor-intensive activity. In some cases, men help by leading the animals that drag the felt rolls. In the nonnomadic community, however, men make felt as a business. These city dwellers work in shops, with master felters doing the layout and design of the felt carpets and apprentices doing the heavy labor. Because felting is so laborious, the master felters find it difficult to find apprentices. This, together with the lack of commercial interest in felt carpets, has caused many felt businesses to close.

During the time of the Soviet Republics (1920s–1991), many nomadic people were relocated onto collective farms and could no longer travel along their nomadic routes. They raised sheep not for their own felting, but so that the wool could be exported to the carpet factories of Russia. As a consequence, people in some areas forgot their traditional methods of making felt. Since the fall of the Soviet Union, there has been a resurgence of felting, and government agencies are sending teachers out to the countryside to help as people try to resume their traditional way of life.

History

Until recently, the earliest known pieces of felt were found in frozen grave mounds *(kurgans)* in Siberia. These felt artifacts included wall hangings, stuffed animals, saddle blankets, and cloaks, dating from 600 to 100 BCE. The Siberian finds were ornately decorated with many of the same inlay techniques used by Asian felters today. The State Hermitage Museum in Saint Petersburg has a wonderful collection of these artifacts. However, in the late 1980s, Western scientists found some very old mummies in western China. These mummies, dating from 2000 to 500 BCE, in many cases were dressed in felt boots and hats. While these objects had simple ornamentation, their shapes were complex, and they were made in a sophisticated three-dimensional felting technique. Also of note are the felt carpets in the Shosoin Repository, in Nara, Japan. Dating from 618 to 906 CE, these items were collected from all over Asia to be part of the Japanese emperor's treasure. Their intricate motifs show a complexity that is unrivaled today.

While felting has been an important part of the culture of Central Asia for over two thousand years, the twentieth century was a troubled time for the craft. With the collectivization of the nomads, many people lost their knowledge of the technique. In the cities, felt carpet businesses shut down. In the early 2000s, however, there has been an effort across the region to help people reconnect with their past and bring this craft back to life.

Patricia Spark

Further Reading

Barber, Elizabeth Wayland. (1999) *The Mummies of Urumchi.* London: W. W. Norton.

Burkett, Mary E. (1979) *The Art of the Feltmaker.* Kendall, U.K.: Crafts Advisory Committee.

Hayaski Ryoichi. (1975) *The Silk Road and the Shoso-in.* Heiboncha Survey of Japanese Art, no. 6. New York: Weatherhill.

Levine, Louis. (1977). "Notes of Feltmaking and the Production of Other Textiles at Seh Gabi, a Kurdish Village." In *Studies in Textile History,* edited by Veronika Gervers. Toronto: Royal Ontario Museum.

Mallory, J. P., and Victor H. Mair. (2000) *The Tarim Mummies: Ancient China and the Mystery of the Earliest Peoples from the West.* New York: Thames & Hudson

Rudenko, Sergei. (1970) *Frozen Tombs of Siberia.* Berkeley and Los Angeles: University of California Press.

Sjöberg, Gunilla Pateau. (1996) *New Directions for Felt, an Ancient Craft.* Loveland, CO: Interweave Press.

Spark, Patricia. (1996) *Fundamentals of Feltmaking, Enlarged Edition.* Petaluma, CA; Shuttle-Craft Books/Unicorn Books.

FEMININE LANGUAGE Sex differentiation in language has long been noted as a feature of some non-Western languages. It was only after the worldwide women's movement gained momentum in the 1960s and 1970s, however, that researchers in the United States, Europe, and other parts of the world seriously investigated various gender-related linguistic phenomena.

Scholars assume that differences exist between the way men and women speak in most languages, reflecting the universality of gender-based role divisions in human societies. Women generally speak in what is characterized as a feminine way, that is, more deferentially and less assertively than men. Although in most contemporary societies feminine language is less conspicuous than it has been in the past, some Asian languages preserve grammatical features strongly associated with feminine language. Japanese, the most well-known example, marks femininity through pitch, excessive politeness, hesitation, deletion of declarative predicates, and avoidance of final particles with strong assertion. Thai and Korean, although not as pronounced as Japanese, also are sensitive to the gender of the speaker.

Studies show that the feminine language is a social stereotype, that is, an idealized version of women's talk represented in literature and mass media (for example, television dramas) and that it is not as consistent in actual interaction as is often implied in existing literature on the subject. Studies also indicate that younger speakers tend to obscure the boundary between men's language and women's language, and some researchers predict that feminine language will gradually become more subtle than it is at present.

Katsue Akiba Reynolds

Further Reading

Bak, Sun-Yun. (1983) "Women's Speech in Korean and English." *Journal of Korean Studies* 7: 61–75.

Bodine, Ann. (1975) "Sex Differentiation in Language." In *Language and Sex*, edited by Barrie Thorne and Nancy Henley. Rowley, MA: Newbury House, 130–151.

Lakoff, Robin. (1975) *Language and Women's Place*. New York: Harper and Row.

Reynolds, Katsue Akiba. (1998) "Female Speakers of Japanese in Transition." In *Language and Gender: A Reader*, edited by Jennifer Coates. Oxford: Blackwell Publishers.

FENG SHUI Feng shui is an ancient Chinese art of site orientation based on the belief that the human dwelling or tomb can be situated physically to take advantage of invisible currents of energy within the environment. This energy, called *qi (ch'i)*, is the same force that is affected by the pierce of the acupuncture needle. The human body is an analogue of the Earth, such that the blood veins of one correspond to "dragon veins" of the other. When a tomb is excavated or ground is broken for a house, such action taps into these dragon veins. Whereas arteries and veins bring oxygen and nutrients to the cells of the body, the *qi* brings good fortune to those residing in a dwelling.

THE ORIGINS OF THE NAME "FENG SHUI"

"*Qi* rides the wind (*feng*) and scatters, but is retained when encountering water (*shui*). The ancients collected it to prevent its dissipation, and guided it to assure its retention. Thus it was called *feng shui*. According to the laws of *feng shui*, the site that attracts water is optimum, followed by the site that catches wind.

"Where forces cease and features soar high, with a stream in front and a hill behind, here hides the head of the dragon. The snout and forehead are auspicious; the horns and eyes bring doom. The ears obtain princes and kings; the lips lead to death or injury from weapons. Where terrain winds about and collects at the center, this is called the belly of the dragon. Where the navel is deep and winding, descendants will have good fortune. If the chest and ribs are injured, burial in the morning will bring sobbing that night."

Source: Zangshu, or *Book of Burial*, attributed to Guo Pu (276–324), translated by Stephen Field.

Seeking the Dragon Veins

The Chinese developed two different procedures for locating *qi*. One approach, first outlined in a fourth-century text, though it undoubtedly originated earlier, was based on the idea that water collects and stores *qi*, while wind captures and scatters it. So the auspicious site would be bordered on three sides by mountains to block the wind and fronted by a pond or nestled in the crook of a stream to attract *qi*. Practitioners of this technique are collectively called the Form School. Another approach, elements of which date back to the second century BCE, was based on the theory of *wu xing* (the five phases), which analyzes *qi* as a force alternating between the poles of yin and yang

FENG SHUI AND ONE'S FATE

In traditional rural Chinese society, the effective use of feng shui was thought to bring prosperity to the family. This account of the use of feng shui by the Miao people of southern China in 1937 before the government repressed the practice indicates its importance in controlling fate.

> The Miao believe in feng shui. When I was in Ang-chi village, Lu Tsun-ying, the chia-ch'ang, told me that the reason the Miao people there were so poor was because the feng shui was not good there. He also pointed out how the feng shui was poor. The mountain peaks were too sharp, there was a lack of springs, and the aspect was too narrow, so that there was nothing from which wealth could issue. His cousin, a pao-ch'ang, also asked whether I knew how to practice feng-shui. I gave him a negative answer. He said he would save more money to enable him to engage a good master of feng shui, who would find for him a place of prosperity.
>
> *Source:* Hsing-ju Wang. (1948) *The Miao People of Hainan Island*. Canton, China: Chu-hai University Press, 68.

as it progresses through the five elemental phases of earth, metal, water, wood, and fire. Each year has an elemental designation, as does each direction. Since each of these phases produces one of its fellows and is simultaneously destroyed by another, it is possible to avoid destructive *qi* by orienting dwellings or tombs toward productive directions according to one's year of birth. Practitioners of this technique became the Compass School.

Feng Shui in the West

Feng shui became accessible to the English-speaking world only at the end of the nineteenth century, when the British missionary Ernest Eitel published his landmark study of feng shui in 1873. But only in the last quarter of the twentieth century did the public at large discover this ancient system. One of the earliest proponents in the United States was Thomas Yun Lin, who founded a temple for American Black Sect Tantric Buddhism in 1986. His brand of feng shui dispensed with many of the traditional practices and relied on intuition and mystical knowledge. Subsequently every major city in the United States attracted its own community of feng shui consultants, many of them trained by Lin or his school. There are now institutes of traditional feng shui—as opposed to the Black Sect variety—all over the Western world. Outside the United States, the practice of feng shui is most popular in England, Brazil, the Netherlands, and Australia.

Ironically, the practice of feng shui is no longer popular in China, where it was labeled a superstition and banned by the Communist Party; its practitioners there work mostly underground. The practice continues in Hong Kong, Taiwan, and Singapore, however, and it is from there that feng shui has spread rapidly to the West.

Stephen L. Field

See also: **Five Phases**

Further Reading

Eitel, Ernest John. (1873) *Feng-Shui: or, The Rudiments of Natural Science in China*. Hong Kong: Lane, Crawford.

Feuchtwang, Stephan D. R. (1974) *An Anthropological Analysis of Chinese Geomancy*. Vientiane, Laos: Editions Vithagna.

Field, Stephen L. (1999) "The Numerology of Nine Star Fengshui." *Journal of Chinese Religions* 27: 13–33.

Walters, Derek. (1991) *The Feng Shui Handbook*. London: Aquarian.

Wong, Eva. (1996) *Feng-shui*. Boston: Shambhala.

FERGANA VALLEY The Fergana (Farghona, Farghana) Valley, on the Syr Dar'ya River with an area of 22,000 square kilometers (8,494 square miles), is a fertile, densely populated irrigated valley in the southeastern part of Central Asia. As a result of the Soviet demarcation (1924), the Fergana Valley is divided between three Central Asian states—Uzbekistan, Tajikistan, and Kyrgyzstan. The largest portion is in Uzbekistan.

The valley, which is 300 kilometers (186 miles) long and 170 kilometers (106 miles) wide, ranges from 330 to 1,000 meters above sea level. The Tian Shan and Pamir ranges enclose the valley on the north, east, and south. The valley is mainly accessible through the western Khudzhand Pass.

The Fergana Valley, as an important center of Central Asia, was first mentioned by Chinese sources in the fourth century BCE. The ancient Great Silk Road linking China with the Mediterranean crossed the valley and contributed substantially to the valley's prosperity. Islam was introduced in the eighth century. Starting from the late sixteenth century, the Fergana Valley was

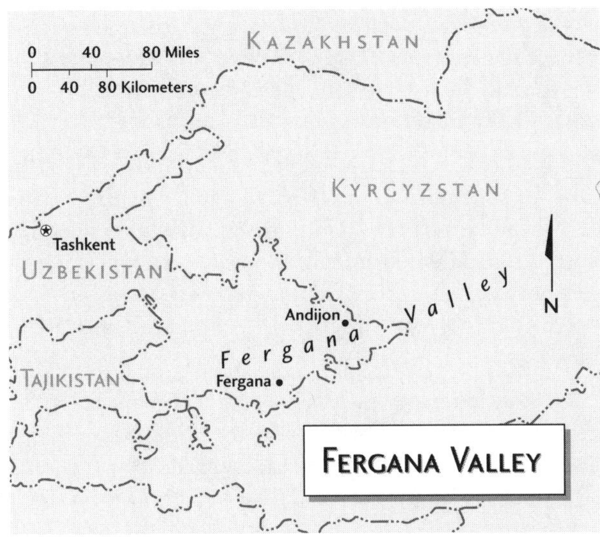

part of Bukhara and Kokand khanates (principalities) until it was fully incorporated into Russia in 1876.

The Fergana Valley is irrigated by the Syr Dar'ya River, one of the two major Central Asia streams, and a wide network of canals. The major dams in the Fergana Valley are the Nurek dam (constructed in 1980), which at 300 meters is the tallest dam in the world; the Baypaza dam (1968); the Rogun dam (1983), all in Tajikistan; and the Toktagul dam (1974) in Kyrgyzstan.

The Fergana Valley is the most densely populated area in Central Asia. The average density in the central Andizhan Province of Uzbekistan is 465 inhabitants per square kilometer (1,203 per square mile). It is an important regional center of irrigated agriculture, silk production, and industry.

Natalya Yu Khan

Further Reading

Allworth, Edward, ed. (1994) *Central Asia: 130 Years of Russian Dominance: A Historical Overview*. 3d ed. Durham, NC: Duke University Press.

Lubin, Nancy, and Rubin, Barnett. (1999) *Calming the Ferghana Valley: Development and Dialogue in the Heart of Central Asia*. New York: The Century Foundation Press.

Roy, Oliver. (2000) *The New Central Asia: The Creation of Nations*. New York: New York University Press.

FERTILITY Human fertility is the number of births contributed to a population. Historically, in Asia as a whole, the average levels of births and deaths have been relatively in balance and have been more significant than levels of migration; consequently, population growth has been slow.

Two measures based on annual births are sensitive to year-by-year changes. The first is the crude birthrate (CBR), usually calculated as annual births per thousand midyear population. In 1999 Asian crude birthrates ranged from nine in Hong Kong and ten in Japan to forty-three in Afghanistan and Oman. The second measure is the total fertility rate (TFR), the sum of the birthrates for each single age of women of reproductive age. When fertility is stable for decades, the TFR approximates completed fertility. Even when fertility is changing, the TFR provides a good index, and it also shows what completed fertility would be if the changes ceased. In 1999 Asian total fertility rates ranged from lows of 1.1 in Hong Kong, 1.3 in Georgia, and 1.4 in Japan and Taiwan to highs of 6.7 in Yemen and 7.1 in Oman. Most societies that have not attempted to control the number of births have recorded total fertility rates around six to seven, limited by early widowhood without remarriage, sterility, and the cessation of sexual activity within marriage. Crude birthrates were rarely higher than forty-five. A total fertility rate of around 2.1 is considered population replacement. In the absence of immigration, sustained periods below this level lead to population decline, even with low mortality levels.

A woman with twin babies in Shanghai, China, in 1996. (STEPHEN G. DONALDSON PHOTOGRAPHY)

TABLE 1

Total fertility rates, 1950–2000

	1999 population (millions)	TFR immediately before decline	Period of TFR decline	1999 TFR
Asia	3,637	5.9	1970–1975	2.8
Subregions				
East Asia	1,481	5.7	1970–1975	.8
South Central Asia	1,451	6.1	1975–1980	3.6
Southeast Asia	520	6.1	1970–1975	2.7
West Asia	186	6.4	1970–1975	3.9
Largest countries				
China	1,254	6.1	1970–1975	1.8
India	987	6.0	1975–1980	3.0
Indonesia	212	5.7	1970–1975	2.5
Pakistan	147	7.0	1985–1990	4.9
Japan	127	5.7	1930–1935	1.4
Bangladesh	126	7.0	1985–1990	3.0
Vietnam	80	6.1	1980–1985	2.5
Philippines	75	7.3	1965–1970	3.5
Iran	66	7.3	1985–1990	2.9
Turkey	66	6.9	1960–1965	2.4
Myanmar (Burma)	48	6.0	1975–1980	2.7
South Korea	47	6.3	1965–1970	1.7

Note: East Asia includes China, Hong Kong, Japan, Macao, Mongolia, North Korea, and South Korea; South Central Asia includes Afghanistan, Bangladesh, Bhutan, India, Iran, Kazakhstan, Maldives, Nepal, Pakistan, Sri Lanka, Tajikistan, Turkmenistan, and Uzbekistan; Southeast Asia includes Brunei, Cambodia, East Timor, Indonesia, Laos, Malaysia, Myanmar (Burma), Philippines, Singapore, Thailand, and Vietnam; and West Asia includes Armenia, Azerbaijan, Bahrain, Cyprus, Gaza, Georgia, Iraq, Israel, Jordan, Kuwait, Lebanon, Oman, Qatar, Saudi Arabia, Syria, Turkey, United Arab Emirates, and Yemen.

SOURCE: Department of Economic and Social Affairs, Population Division (1999: 408–839); Population Reference Bureau (1999); United Nations Economic and Social Commission for Asia and the Pacific (1999).

The problems associated with land inheritance and food production during famines forced some agrarian societies to limit the number of children. Between 1500 and 1800, Western Europeans delayed or forwent marriage, and total fertility rates dropped to 5.5 or lower. Without lowering fertility, infanticide produced a similar effect in Japan, China, and northern India. In spite of these checks, economic growth during those centuries produced a considerable population increase in Japan and China, in the latter due to intensified cultivation and the migration of farmers to South China.

Fertility in the Second Half of the Twentieth Century

Table 1 shows the 1999 total fertility rates for Asia, its subregions as defined by the United Nations Population Division, and the area's twelve largest countries, which account for almost 90 percent of Asia's population. Demographers consider a fertility rate drop of 10 percent from a higher stable rate to be a fertility transition. In some countries fertility levels rose immediately before the fertility transition because modernization brought a decline in widowhood, a shortened breast-feeding period, and possibly increased sexual activity.

Fertility transition in Japan began in the early 1930s, only to stall until after World War II. In the rest of Asia, population growth rates rose as mortality declined with unprecedented steepness, and many governments responded with national family planning programs, but there were no signs of fertility decline until the 1960s.

Fertility began to fall widely in Asia in the mid- to late 1960s following early signs of an incipient fall in Sri Lanka, Singapore, Turkey, and the Philippines in the late 1950s and in South Korea, Taiwan, Malaysia, and Thailand in the early 1960s. The beginning of fertility transition was delayed in Oman, Bhutan, Laos, and, among the larger countries, in Pakistan particularly.

At the end of the twentieth century, fertility in East Asia was below replacement level (TFR 2.1) except in Mongolia. In Southeast Asia fertility was below replacement in Singapore and Thailand; moderate (TFR 2.2–2.9) in Indonesia and Vietnam; moderately high (TFR 3.0–3.9) in Malaysia and the Philippines, where political and religious forces opposed fertility control; and very high in Cambodia and Laos, which were relatively underdeveloped. In South Asia fertility was moderate in Sri Lanka; moderately high in India, Bangladesh, and Iran; and very high elsewhere. In West Asia fertility was very high, except in Turkey, Lebanon, and Bahrain, where it was moderate. In the Asian states of the former Soviet Union fertility rose with the proportion of Muslims, from below replacement level in Armenia and Georgia to very high in Tajikistan, with the exception of Azerbaijan, which was 93 percent Muslim but had replacement-level fertility.

The Asian fertility decline of the late twentieth century was central to control of the global population explosion. Between 1995 and 2000 worldwide births numbered only three-fifths of the births that could have been expected if the fertility levels of 1955 to 1960 had continued. Asia was responsible for 70 percent of the birth decline, and three Asian countries—China, India, and Indonesia—were responsible for 50 percent of the decline.

The Causes of the Asian Fertility Decline

Underlying the Asian fertility decline were profound economic, demographic, and social changes, including rising per capita income, declining mortality, increasing urbanization and nonfarm employment, and dramatically rising educational and literacy levels. As a consequence the average age of female marriage rose at least two years. While a minor factor in the fertility transitions of most areas, the delay in female marriage, to almost twenty-five years of age by 1981, was largely responsible for the beginning of the fertility transition in Sri Lanka.

The decrease in marital fertility was the major factor in the fertility decline in Asia, the only continent where nearly all fertility occurs within marriage. The decline likely was hastened by national family-planning programs. First initiated in India in 1952, these programs were confined largely to the Asian continent. Combining free or inexpensive access to contraception with information and moral suasion to control family size, they were most effective in Turkey and the arc of countries from South Asia to East Asia, where Brahman, Confucian, military, and communist elites encouraged family planning amid little social or religious opposition. Compared with elsewhere in the world, the resulting fertility declines began at lower per capita income levels and within lower levels of the Human Development Index, a measure of income, literacy, and mortality devised by the United Nations Development Program. The relative importance of socioeconomic changes and family planning programs in lowering fertility have been debated, especially with regard to Bangladesh.

Several individual national experiences are notable. China in the 1970s and India during the emergency of 1975–1977 showed that people could be coerced into adopting fertility control, while Indonesia successfully employed subtler pressures during that period. China reduced its TFR by over two-thirds in twenty-five years, from 6.1 in the late 1960s to 1.9 in the early 1990s. A comprehensive family planning program begun in Bangladesh in the late 1970s halved fertility in two decades. Iran, which experienced a TFR of almost seven after its 1979 revolution, began to facilitate family planning in the 1990s and subsequently halved its fertility level during that decade. Political and religious opposition at times slowed the fertility decline in the Philippines and reversed the decline among the Malay population of Malaysia. A diverse range of contraceptive methods, including sterilization, the intrauterine device (IUD), the birth-control pill, the condom, and traditional methods such as withdrawal and rhythm, effected the Asian fertility declines. Abortion, both legal and illegal, also became more widespread.

United Nations Projections

The United Nations medium-range population projections show Asia reaching the long-term fertility replacement level (TFR 2.1) around 2020 and slow population growth (under 0.5 percent per annum) in 2035. The long-range population projections suggest the Asian population will be stationary, that is, with fertility and mortality equal (TFR 2.1 or a little lower), by 2150, amounting to 6.1 billion people out of a world population of 10.8 billion people. Accordingly, Asia's population would constitute 56 percent of the world's population, a reduction from 61 percent at the end of the twentieth century.

John C. Caldwell

Further Reading

Caldwell, John C., and Bruce K. Caldwell. (1997) "Asia's Demographic Transition." *Asian Development Review* 15, 1: 52–87.

Department of Economic and Social Affairs, Population Division. (1998) *World Population Projections to 2150*. New York: United Nations.

———. (1999) *World Population Prospects: The 1998 Revision*. Vol. 1. New York: United Nations.

Freedman, Ronald. (1995) "Asia's Recent Fertility Decline and Prospects for Future Demographic Change." *Asia-Pacific Population Research Reports*, no. 1. Honolulu, HI: Program on Population, East-West Center.

Leete, Richard, and Iqbal Llam, eds. (1993) *The Revolution in Asian Fertility: Dimensions, Causes, and Implications*. Oxford: Clarendon Press.

Liu, Ts'ui-jung, ed. (2000) *Asian Population History*. Oxford: Clarendon Press.

Population Reference Bureau. (1999) *1999 World Population Data Sheet*. Washington, DC: Population Reference Bureau.

United Nations Economic and Social Commission for Asia and the Pacific. (1999) *1999 ESCAP Population Data Sheet*. Bangkok, Thailand: Population Division of the United Nations Economic and Social Commission for Asia and the Pacific.

FINANCIAL CRISIS OF 1927

The financial crisis of 1927 in Japan was characterized primarily by a large-scale collapse of banks, both large and small, that resulted in greater financial control of the economy by the biggest banks, which took over the assets of bankrupt firms. The crisis originated in the latter stages of World War I, when companies had to decide whether to reduce commitments in view of an expected slowdown after the war or to expand investments to exploit an anticipated postwar recovery. Many Japanese companies chose the latter option, fueling their expansion with credit. When Japan's stock market crashed in March 1920, the superstructure of this expansion collapsed. Furthermore, now debt-ridden companies lacked the competitive power to engineer a recovery. Their prices had risen more rapidly during the war than those of their Western competitors but had declined more slowly after it due to the underdeveloped state of Japan's technology and the higher costs faced by Japanese companies seeking to manufacture comparable products.

Initial government countermeasures were undermined by the massive Tokyo earthquake of 1923. The financial aftershock of the earthquake created an insurance crisis and greatly expanded the debt held by banks that took out loans to invest in the stock market and in industrial enterprises during the short-term boom after World War I. The government sought to ameliorate the situation with "earthquake bills," a second round of special credit. A key institutional feature of Japanese finance in this era was the "organ bank." Many banks had lent so much to related industrial firms whose fortunes were so precarious that cutting off credit would bankrupt both the firms and the banks. The largest such linkage, and the one that resulted in the biggest disaster, was between the Bank of Taiwan (which was a Japanese bank), and Suzuki Trading Company. In late March and early April 1927, the Finance Ministry warned the Bank of Taiwan to cut back on its loans to Suzuki. Mitsui Bank then called in some of its loans to the Bank of Taiwan, precipitating the closure of both Suzuki and the Bank of Taiwan, with the latter subsequently being reorganized. As a result of this crisis and the consequent short bank moratorium, many banks and the industrial firms that they had financed went bankrupt. Their assets were then acquired by the large *zaibatsu* (family-owned financial and industrial groups). With their consequent broader control over the banking sector, the top five banks increased their share of national deposits from 24 percent in 1926 to 40 percent in 1930.

The 1927 financial crisis can be placed within the larger patterns of Japan's modern history. At least through the 1980s Japan was credited with dealing exceptionally successfully with economic crises. A frequently cited example is its response to the energy crisis of the 1970s. That, however, was primarily a crisis of inflation. By contrast, the era immediately preceding the 1927 crisis was one of wealth (produced by the wartime boom) and deflation (meaning the decline in prices after the war). There is a striking similarity between that crisis and the prolonged financial crisis beginning in 1990. The latter manifested a similar sequence of boom (generated by inflated asset prices in real estate and stocks) and deflation (the bursting of the financial bubble followed by long-term price decline). This comparison suggests that in the twentieth century Japan has been singularly inept at handling problems of wealth and deflation.

William Wray

Further Reading

Cho Yukio. (1974) "Exposing the Incompetence of the Bourgeoisie: The Financial Panic of 1927." *Japan Interpreter* 8, 4 (Winter): 492–501.

Patrick, Hugh. (1971) "The Economic Muddle of the 1920s." In *Dilemmas of Growth in Prewar Japan*, edited by James Morley. Princeton, NJ: Princeton University Press, 211–266.

Yamamura Kozo. (1972) "Then Came the Great Depression: Japan's Interwar Years." In *The Great Depression Revisited*, edited Herman van der Wee. The Hague, Netherlands: Martinus Nijhoff, 182–211.

FINE ARTS—CENTRAL ASIA

FINE ARTS—CENTRAL ASIA The art of Central Asia has always been the consequence of the contacts of local cultures with neighboring great civilizations. Being at the crossroads of the Persian, Hellenic, Indian, Arabic, Mongol, and Turkic worlds and later influenced by European culture, Central Asia was a melting pot of aesthetic systems, producing local schools that are interesting for more than their own aesthetic discoveries. The interaction of Hellenistic and Buddhist or Persian and Turkic elements, and the later meeting of West and East, brought about unprecedented intercultural penetration.

Prehistory to Middle Ages

The first artifacts known from Central Asia are rock paintings (showing the hunting scenes and magic symbols characteristic of prehistoric cultures) such as those of Zaraut-Sai, Uzbekistan, dating from the Mesolithic period (eleventh–sixth millennia BCE). The Neolithic period and the early Bronze Age (sixth–third millennia BCE) are represented by ornamental paintings preserved in the ruins at Iassydepe, Anau, in Turkmenistan. During the Bronze Age, when two types of civilization (sedentary-agricultural and nomadic-stockbreeding) existed in the region, two trends of artistic metal treatment were defined. The first, connected with early town culture, presented figures of oriental mythology in a local style. The second, the so-called animal style involving the symbolic depiction of animals, originated with the Sako-Scythian nomadic tribes of northern Central Asia. Prior to its conquest by Alexander of Macedon, this region belonged to the Achaemenid empire (559–330 BCE). Little is known of Achaemenid art in Central Asia apart from the scarce artifacts of the so-called Amu Dar'ya hoard, some animal-style artifacts, and a few preserved architectural structures (Kyzyltepa and Kutlugtepe, Uzbekistan). Historians accompanying the campaign of Alexander left accounts of numerous images of epic personages displayed in the homes of the people of Sogdiana (now in Uzbekistan and Tajikistan).

The Greek conquest (330–328 BCE) opened a new and important period in Central Asian art history. According to Galina A. Pugachenkova, this period was initially characterized by the rapid Hellenization of the art of Bactria (the region between the Hindu Kush mountains and the Amu Dar'ya river) between 323 and 140 BCE, evident in temple paintings of the Dioscuri found in Dilberdzhin north of Afghanistan and in the development of Hellenistic sculpture in North Bactria (Ai Khanum, Afghanistan). Between 100 BCE and 100 CE, a diversified Bactrinization of Hellenism took place (seen in artifacts from Dilberdzhin, Afghanistan, and Khalchayan, Uzbekistan). Sculpture of this period was especially distinctive in its synthesis of Greek masterpieces and its tendency to psychological expression in the depiction of local ethnic personages. Similar processes took place in neighboring Parthia (now northeastern Iran), where the Greek style was interpreted on the basis of Persian-Parthian traditions, evident in the statue *Rogoduna* and drinking vessels from Nisa (Turkmenistan, 200 BCE). A final phase known as the Kushanization of Bactrinism (100–300 CE) began with the rise of the Kushan empire (30–370 CE) and was characterized by the interaction of antique and Buddhist elements with local traditions (for example, the sculpture, painting, and architecture of Dalverzintepe, Fayaztepe, and Afrasiab in Uzbekistan).

The early medieval period (500–722 CE) was the height of mural painting of the Sogdian school, whose best-known frescoes are the Red Hall in Varakhsha Palace, Uzbekistan, and the so-called *Procession of Ambassadors* in Afrasiab, Uzbekistan, and especially the frescoes in Pedjikent, Tajikistan. These were characterized not only by an original graphic style that defined oriental miniature painting for several centuries but also by the depiction of figures from Central Asian folklore, later represented in the poetry of Firdawsi (c. 935–c. 1020).

The Arab invasion (late 700s–800 CE) prohibited the creation of sculpture and considerably limited the development of representational painting because of Islamic prohibitions. Visual art was mostly ornamental, and architecture became the dominant art form. Inventive bricklaying was the primary means of expression in the pre-Mongol period. The most interesting buildings in Bukhara are the mausoleum of Ismail Samani (Samanid era, 864–999) and the Kalyan minaret (Karakhanid era, twelfth century); in Merv, the mausoleum of Sultan Sanjar (Seljuk era, 1038–1157) is prominent. During the first half of the thirteenth century, the development of Bukhara and Khorezm as artistic centers was halted by the Mongol invasion (1220).

Much of the fine arts of Central Asia shows an Islamic influence. This tile mosaic of a vase with flowers is from a mosque in Kazakhstan. (BUDDY MAYS/CORBIS)

The high point of the art of Central Asia was reached in the epoch of the Timurids (fourteenth–fifteenth centuries). Historical documents reveal that fresco painting was revived, and architecture, miniature painting, decorative applied arts, and calligraphy all achieved a unity and harmony that have led some scholars to speak of a Timurid Renaissance. The highest achievements in architecture were created in Samarqand, center of the Timurid empire: the Bibi-khanum mosque, the memorial complex Shakhi-Zindah, Gur-Emir (Timur's mausoleum), and the *madrasah* observatory of Ulugh Beg. Significant structures were also built in Turkistan (the mausoleum of Khoja Ahmaf Yassavi) and in Shakhrizyabs (Ak-Sarai, the palace of Timur). Miniature painting was highly developed in Samarqand and especially in Herat, where the renowned schools of Kamal al-Din Behzad (1455?–1536?) and the calligrapher Sultan-Ali Mashhadi (1442–1520) flourished during the reign of Sultan

Hussein (1438–1506). Miniature painting now took many forms: genre painting, portraiture, painted chronicles, and the lyric genre.

Another considerable phase in the development of medieval culture in Central Asia began in the era of the Shaybanid dynasty (sixteenth century) as the center of artistic life gradually shifted to Bukhara. The sixteenth and seventeenth centuries were the height of miniature painting and architecture in Bukhara and Samarqand, where Tajik and Uzbek artistic interaction took place, generating new schools of art and architecture. In this period, the main architectural monuments are Registan Square in Samarqand, the Kalyan mosque, and *madrasah* Abdulaziz Khan in Bukhara. With the nineteenth century a long period of stagnation in the art of this region began.

Modern Period

The modern phase of Central Asian art was initiated with the Russian colonization that began in the second half of the nineteenth century. Central Asia experienced three cultural interventions: European, Russian, and Soviet. Initial imitation of the Russian-European artistic tradition later gave way to transformation, which ultimately led to a regional reaction to Europeanization in the 1970s and 1980s. The art of Europeans resident in Central Asia developed alongside local art, and the two interacted with each other.

Colonial Period to 1917 Russian colonization triggered a wave of Orientalism in the art of Central Asia. This phenomenon was a consequence of the interest of Russian artists in the exoticism and ethnography of the East. Several Russian painters visited Russian Turkistan immediately after its colonization (1865), among them Vasilii Vereshchagin (1842–1904) and Nikolai Karazin (1842–1908), active participants in military campaigns who developed the principles of naturalism and interest in the ethnography of the region. Vereshchagin's works expressed a contradictory aspiration to justify the imperialistic ambitions of Russia and at the same time created symbolic images of the calamities of war (*Apotheosis of War*, 1870–1871). Other Russian artists, such as Rikhard Zommer (1866–1939), Sergei Iudin (1853–1933), Ivan Kazakov (1873–1935), and Lev Bure (1887–1943), adhered to the traditions of the late Wanderers (a Russian artistic group at the end of nineteenth century), painting landscapes and architectural studies. The Orientalism of Central Asia was defined by its descriptive nature and the tendency to cultural realism. In architecture, the colonial style was not aesthetically uniform. In the Caspian region the so-called Russian style predominated, whereas a provincial modernism predominated in Tashkent and Quqon. Colonial urbanism differed markedly from the traditional dwellings, and traditional and European artistic cultures coexisted in relative independence.

Soviet Period, 1917–1991 The Russian Revolution was both a social and a cultural event with grave consequences for life in Central Asia as an ideologically indifferent czarism gave way to a Communist ideology envisioning radical social reconstruction. The East became one of the main regions of revolutionary transformation in which Soviet Central Asia was eventually divided from a larger cultural and geographical region called the Central East.

After new states came into existence in Central Asia following the disintegration of the Soviet Union in 1991, there were persisting discussions on the significance of the Soviet period in their history. According to popular opinion, characteristic of the official institutions of the new states, the local elite managed to return to the ethnicity-oriented path around the 1970s, and Sovietization did not stop but merely delayed the development of local ethnic cultures; its consequences were predicted to be quickly overcome when independence was achieved. However, the Sovietization of Central Asia meant the radical Europeanization of the local elite's consciousness, and it cannot be overcome by the surface changes in political ideologies. The twentieth-century art of Central Asia has been the arena of broad interaction of European and Asian spiritual paradigms.

Artistic institutions of a European cast emerged in Central Asia from the 1920s through the 1950s. Local institutions were founded to train artists, professional theater groups, philharmonic societies, and researchers in traditional and modern art. Two opposite tendencies followed: the Orientalization of the Russian avant-garde and the Europeanization of Central Asian thought and education. The most significant phenomenon of that period was the development of a moderate Central Asian avant-garde, represented by Ruvin (Il'ya) Mazel (1890–1967), Aleksandr Nikolaev (1897–1957), and Aleksandr Volkov (1886–1957), almost all connected with key members of the Russian avant-garde.

Developing in two principal directions, the Central Asian avant-garde sought to apply to Central Asian material the artistic principles of modern Russian European art (constructivism, decorativism, and primitivism), a trend seen in painters such as Volkov (*Pomegranate Tea-room*, 1925) and the photographer Max Penson. They also sought a synthesis of oriental painting (mostly miniatures) with the broader European tradition (the Russian icon, the Italian Renaissance, and the twentieth-century European avant-garde), as seen in *Friendship, Love, Eternity* (1929) by Nikolaev (also known as Usto-Mumin).

During the 1920s various artistic groups appeared: the shock school of Eastern art (under Ruvim Mazel and Aleksandr Vladychuk, 1920–1926) was founded in present-day Turkmenistan; a local affiliate of the Association of Revolutionary Russian Artists opened in Turkistan in 1922 and has functioned ever since; and the group called Masters of the New East (Volkov, Nikolaev, Mikhail Kurzin, Vera Markova, Semen Malt, and others) was founded in 1929.

In the critical period of Stalinization (late 1920s through early 1930s), some members of the Central Asian avant-garde turned to new subjects and independently cultivated a style close to the Mexican muralists around Diego Rivera (Volkov, Nikolai Karakhan, and others), whereas others turned to the more stereotypical forms of socialist realism. Numerous members of the avant-garde were persecuted during the Stalinist repression of the 1930s (Kurzin, Nikolaev, and others). At the same time, an official aesthetic doctrine that emphasized the national character of art, promoting works that were ethnic in form and socialist in content, lent significance to folk art. Orientalism could now develop within Socialist realism, and Chingiz Akhmarov cultivated the principles of oriental miniature in monumental paintings from the end of the 1940s.

Constructivist ideas were popular in the architecture of Central Asia of the 1920s and 1930s. New building types were seen in such structures as communal housing. The most significant constructivist structures were government buildings by Moisei Ginzburg (1929) in Alma-Ata (present-day Almaty in Kazakhstan) and by Stepan Polupanov (1931) in Tashkent (the capital of present-day Uzbekistan). When criticized in the mid-1930s for using "bourgeois" and "anti-popular" styles, constructivist architects attempted a synthesis of Stalinist classicism and traditional architecture, chiefly expressed in opera and ballet theaters in Alma-Ata (by Nikolai Prostakov, 1941) and Tashkent (by Alexei Shchusev, 1947), in which buildings were decorated by masters of applied folk art.

The period from the 1960s to the 1980s was characterized by an open confrontation between Europeanism and an aspiration toward ethnic identity. During the 1960s, a European openness prevailed in the so-called strict style in painting and in a post-impressionist style in portraiture and still life (Iurii Taldykin and Grigorii Zilberman in Uzbekistan; Salikhitdin Aitbaev and Tokbulat Tugusbaev in Kazakhstan; A. T. Amindzhanov, A. Ahunov, V. Boborykin, and K. Zhumagazin in Tajikistan; Chary Amangeldyev, S. Akmuhamedov, S. Babikov, and D. Bairamov in Turkmenistan; and Myrza Omorkulov and Altymysh Usumbaliev in Kyrgyzstan). A new specifically Central Asian international style evolved in architecture (the Public Library in Ashkhabad, Turkmenistan, by Abdula Ahmedov, 1961–1975; the Uzbek Communist Party Central Committee Building and Panoramic Cinema in Tashkent by Sergo Sutiagin, Vladimir Berezin, Dmitrii Shuvaev, and others, 1964). Urban planning showed the influence of European principles, such as the garden city utopia (Navoi, Uzbekistan, 1970; downtown Tashkent, 1966). By the end of the 1960s, however, artists increasingly rejected cosmopolitan doctrines and sought new artistic means among local traditions.

In the 1970s, a search for local specificity prevailed, giving rise to a national romanticism in which artists adapted motifs from ancient and medieval Central Asian art (an influence of active archaeological excavations) to the present. Thus the *pandzhara*, an added sunshade, which was a modernization of the traditional geometrical ornamental lattices, became popular in architecture. Ceramic art was the most developed of the decorative arts and appeared not only in walls but also sculpturally in urban architecture. Painting and sculpture interpreted and used numerous sources: European Orientalist paintings of the early twentieth century, local oriental material, and the adoption of "ethnic" motifs from the Central Asian avant-garde of the 1920s. The influence of Latin American art was also evident.

Postmodernism was the prevailing style of the 1980s and 1990s. The 1980s witnessed the disintegration of official Soviet art and was the first period since the 1920s in which new artistic ideas were spontaneously formed. Postmodernism had two branches: that of the Central Asian Europeans, who turned mostly toward Western art, and that of the ethnic modernists, who turned to traditional art, local folklore, and the mythology of Islam, Buddhism, and Zoroastrianism. The two branches interacted, but whereas the Europeans situated their work in the context of modern and past (Asian) cultures, the traditionalists developed an individual style in which tradition was reflected. Painting dominated over other visual arts, and Central Asian art became known abroad through the work of Maksim Vardanian, Daima Rakhmanbekova, and Gairat Baimatov. Notably, the leaders of European art in Central Asia, after leaving Asia, became new Orientalists (Maksim

Vardanian, Konstantin Titov), whereas former leaders of the traditional movement of the 1980s, after leaving Central Asia in the 1990s, refused to use "oriental" motifs in their work and became "international" artists (Abduhakim Turdyev, Fayzula Shakirov). Thus the cultural preferences of both groups were polyvalent and could be converted reciprocally in other circumstances—one consequence of Europeanization.

Modern Period, 1991 to Present The independence of the Central Asian republics has had an ambivalent influence on the development of art in the region. The developing art market has been a positive consequence and has led to the secularization of artistic life and the formation of local art schools. At the same time, state regulation of art has intensified. In Turkmenistan and Uzbekistan, new official art has returned to the socialist realism of the 1940s and 1950s. By the end of the 1990s, many European artists had left the region, along with some local artists who founded small Central Asian art communities in Russia, Europe, and the United States. The architecture of this period has a clearly expressed Western character, whereas buildings that tried for an Oriental feel have a kitsch quality (Timur Museum, Tashkent, mid-1990s). The number of genres and types of art practiced in Central Asia has diminished, but some maintain the level apparent at the end of the 1980s.

Boris Chukhovich (Translated by E. Romanova)

Further Reading

The Art of Central Asia. (1996) Bournemouth, U.K.: Parkstone.

Chuvin, Pierre. (1999) *Les arts de l'Asie centrale.* Paris: Citadelles & Mazenod.

Khakimov, Akbar. (1988) *Sovremennoe dekorativnoe iskusstvo respublik Sredney Asii: probleme traditsiy o novatorstva* (Modern Decorative Art of Central Asian Republics: To the Problem of Tradition and Innovation). Tashkent, Uzbekistan: Fan.

Knobloch, Edgar. (1972) *Beyond the Oxus: Archaeology, Art and Architecture of Central Asia.* Totowa, NJ: Rowman & Littlefield.

Kovtun, Evgueniy, Marinika Babanazarova, and El'mira Gazieva. (1989) *Avangard ostanovlennyj na begu* (Avant-Garde, Stopped at a Run). Leningrad, Russia: Aurora.

Lentz, Thomas, and Glenn Lowry. (1989) *Timur and the Princely Vision: Persian Art and Culture in the Fifteenth Century.* Los Angeles: Los Angeles County Museum of Art.

Coudé-Gassen, Geneviève, Véronique Schiltz, Marinika Babanazarova, Jean-Claude Marcadé, Anne Coldefy-Faucard, and Pierre Chuvin. (1998) *Les survivants des Sables Rouges: art russe du Musée de Noukous, Ouzbékistan, 1920–1940.* Paris: Conseil Régional de Basse-Normandie.

Pugachenkova, Galina, and Akbar Khakimov. (1988) *The Art of Central Asia.* Leningrad, Russia: Aurora.

Pugachenkova, Galina, and Lasar' Rempel. (1965) *Istoriya iskusstv Uzbekistana s drevneyshikh vremen do seredini XIX veka* (Uzbekistan Art History since Prehistory until the Middle of the Nineteenth Century). Moscow: Iskusstvo.

———. (1982) *Ocherki iskusstva Srednei Azii: drevnost' i srednevekov'e* (Essays on Central Asian Art: Prehistory and Middle Ages). Moscow: Iskusstvo.

Rempel, Lasar'. (1978) *Isskustvo Srednei Vostoka* (The Art of Central Asia). Moscow: Sovetskiy khudojnik.

———. (1987) *Tsep' vremen: vekovye obrazy i brodiachie siuzhety v traditsionnom iskusstve Srednei Azii* (Bond of Ages: Ancient Images and Migrant Subjects in Traditional Art of Central Asia). Tashkent, Uzbekistan: Izdatelstvo literatury i iskusstva imeni G. Guliama.

FIRDAWSI. See **Shahnameh Epic.**

FISH-FIGHTING

Thailand is notable for indigenous sports that involve nonhuman competition including cockfighting, kite-flying, and fish-fighting. Fish-fighting is now a mainly rural sport, as it is banned in Bangkok. It involves placing two male Thai or Siamese fighting fish *(Betta splendens)* in a bottle and watching them tear at each other with their mouths until one dies or is severely injured. The spectators, including the owners of the fish, bet on the outcome throughout the match. *Betta*, which are native to Thai canals, are raised and bred by their owners to be ferocious fighters and those who win a match but are injured will be nursed back to health to fight again. Only males, generally no more than 5 centimeters long and 1 centimeter across, are used for fighting. It takes about six or seven months to raise a fish for fighting. Part of the appeal of the sport is the fighting and gambling and another is the bright colors of the *Betta*, one of the most popular tropical fish among fish enthusiasts around the world.

David Levinson

Further Reading

Tourism Authority of Thailand. (2000) *A Traveller's Guide to Thailand.* Bangkok, Thailand: Tourism Authority of Thailand.

FISHING INDUSTRY—CHINA

The Chinese fishing industry has led world production since 1989. It produces primarily for domestic consumption and helps to absorb surplus labor in rural areas. It is divided into four sectors: marine fishing, mariculture, freshwater fishing, and freshwater culture.

The Traditional Fishing Industry

The Chinese have practiced fish culture for over 3,000 years; the first pisciculture manual, by Fan Li, dates from around 475 BCE. Polyculture (the raising of multiple species) was introduced in the Tang dynasty (618–907 CE), when the consumption of common carp was forbidden because its name *(li)* had the same sound as the surname of the imperial family. Farmers responded by moving from monoculture based on common carp to polyculture. Compared to intensive monocultural systems with reliance on carnivorous fish species practiced today in developed countries, polyculture not only requires much less labor but also releases much less waste and is much more efficient in the conversion of biological energy. Up to nine different species of fish (primarily herbivores), each feeding on different resources, are spawned in the artificial and balanced ecosystem of a fishpond.

A distinctive method for pond fishing, integrated culture, was developed in the Pearl River delta in South China around 1400. In a complex dike-pond ecosystem, crops such as mulberry, sugarcane, fruits, and rapeseed are grown on the dike banks. These crops are used for fish feed in the ponds, and the fishes' waste in turn is used to fertilize the plants on the dikes.

The practice of paddy fish farming, first documented in the third century CE, probably evolved from the catching of wild fish in ponds that had been dug in the rice fields for water storage, irrigation, and water control. The most productive species, which can help to control rice weeds and harmful insects as well as provide fertilizer for rice fields, are selected for breeding.

The Modern Fishing Industry

Fisheries took off after the onset of economic reform in 1978. The government gave households greater freedom in managing aquaculture production, deregulated purchase and sales prices in 1985, and provided support through research and extension. Fisheries production rose rapidly: total aquatic production expanded more than eightfold between 1978 and 1998, from 4.7 million to 39.1 million metric tons. Fisheries' share of gross output value of primary food industries in China has risen from 1.6 percent in 1978 to 9.9 percent in 1998.

Marine capture fisheries dominated production until the 1980s, when the government focused on the development of aquaculture in response to the depletion of many major marine fishery resources. In 1978, the share of capture production was 73.9 percent of total aquatic production, but that share declined steadily thereafter even as total quantity continued to grow. By 1993, aquaculture contributed over 50 percent of total fish production. China became the first major fisheries country with aquacultural production exceeding wild fishing.

Marine fishing has expanded in recent years primarily through the increase in number of motorized vessels, from around 50,000 to 274,000 vessels between 1980 and 1995. China fields over 1,600 oceangoing fishing vessels. The government has supported capture fisheries production through an extensive program of fishing vessel building, modernizing, and purchasing from abroad.

Mariculture, or marine culture in intertidal zones, small bays, and shallow seas, accounted for a negligible 5.8 percent of total catches in 1970. But production increased almost twenty times between 1978 and 1998, from 0.45 to 8.6 million metric tons. Seaweed, fish, crustaceans (especially prawns), and mollusks (particularly scallops) are its major products. Mariculture has benefited recently from the application of the principle of integrated culture. For example, some species of mollusks may be bred in prawn ponds or along with cultivated seaweed.

Varieties of carp continue to be the most important component of freshwater culture. Recently, however, over twenty foreign species, most notably the Nile tilapia, have been introduced into Chinese fish culture. Since the 1950s fish culture has spread from the original core areas of the Chang (Yangtze) and Pearl River deltas to virtually all provinces, and even lakes and reservoirs in remote regions and paddy fields in mountainous areas have been increasingly exploited. Nonetheless, output in freshwater fish culture has expanded primarily through the improvement and popularization of modern and traditional technologies rather than by enlarging the area under cultivation.

Before 1960, fish culture depended on fry (immature fish) originating from the natural reproduction of wild stock. The availability of fry increased greatly with the successful development from 1958 to 1960 of techniques for hormonally induced spawning of the four common species of carp. Subsequently, artificial propagation techniques, including induced breeding and hatching and larval breeding, were further developed and introduced for additional varieties of fish. The expansion of fry production by artificial propagation was especially rapid after 1978. By the 1990s most counties had at least one fingerling (fish up to a year in age) farm to supply local fish farmers, many of whom also reared fingerlings in their ponds and rice paddies.

After a period of rapid growth, the industry has encountered serious resource constraints. Already by 1990 average yields (per units of effort) in capture fisheries had dropped to less than 50 percent of 1950s levels. Some traditional species have been overexploited, and increasingly harvests shifted towards juvenile fish and lower-value species. Uncontrolled industrial effluent and domestic discharge have contaminated many lakes, rivers, and coastal areas. Red tides—massive concentrations of microscopic algae that flower and multiply rapidly—have caused serious losses in maricultural production along the South China coast.

The government first formulated a sustainable development strategy for its marine program in 1996. The revised Marine Environmental Protection Law of 2000 seeks to curb marine pollution and to conserve marine resources. Amendments to the 1986 Fishery Law promulgated in 2000 regulate the number of fishing permits and quantity of fish and strive to protect China's rights in its exclusive economic zones while maintaining stable relations with neighboring countries.

Competition over fishing rights and claims to territorial waters and associated marine resources had become a serious security issue in the western Pacific by the 1990s. China's Territorial Sea Law of 1996 claims sovereignty over islands and reefs also claimed by other countries. However, China also ratified the U.N. Convention on the Law of the Sea in 1996 and signed bilateral fisheries agreements with Japan and South Korea in 2000.

Robert Y. Eng

Further Reading

Rana, K. J. (1997) "China." In *Review of the State of World Aquaculture*. FAO Fisheries Circular, no. 886. Rome: Food and Agriculture Organization of the United Nations. Retrieved 18 January 2002, from: www.fao.org/docrep/003/w7499e/w7499e11.htm.

Zhong, Yiguang, and Geoff Power. (1997) "Fisheries in China: Progress, Problems, and Prospects." *Canadian Journal of Fisheries and Aquatic Sciences* 54: 224–238.

FISHING INDUSTRY—JAPAN Japan's fishing industry is divided into four types: coastal fishing, distant-water fishing, aquaculture, and recreational fishing. Coastal fishing of various species has continued since the country's premodern era, whereas distant-water fishing beyond its present exclusive economic zones (EEZ) started around the 1920s and increased dramatically during the food shortage of the immediate post–World War II period. Aquaculture has long been another feature of the Japanese fishing industry, the oldest form being the farming of seaweed. Japan's recreational fishing industry is probably the largest in volume of sales and most diverse in the world, including everything from charter boat businesses and equipment and bait production and sales, to various fee-based fishing park operations.

The coastal fishing sector has been characterized mainly by small-scale independent boat owners organized into township fishery cooperatives that collectively deal with wholesale fish dealers. Japan's coastal fishing has suffered since the 1970s from both depletion of resources and the lack of successors. In recent years, the removal of trade barriers on fishery products and the reduction of government subsidies to the fishing industry have also forced coastal fishermen to change careers. Japanese trading companies and supermarket chains have bypassed the wholesale dealers, thereby increasingly challenging the hierarchically organized domestic fish distribution networks of the cooperatives.

Since the late 1970s, distant-water fishing has experienced the twin blows of unilateral proclamations by many coastal states of 200-nautical mile fishery zones and the adoption of the EEZ concept in the United Nations Convention on the Law of the Sea (UNCLOS) in 1982. Coastal states' extended control over fishery resources in adjacent seas reduced Japan's free access to distant-water fish stocks.

UNCLOS also laid the legal foundations for the management of anadromous species (species that travel between fresh water and sea, such as salmon). Jurisdiction for the management of such species was given to the coastal states in whose rivers such species originated. Japan's offshore salmon fishing ceased as negotiations with the then Soviet Union failed. Highly migratory species (such as tuna) were placed under joint management by coastal states, which resulted in the imposition of international catch quotas and regulations on tuna fishing practices. Japan is a member of all such international tuna management bodies. According to the *GGT Newsletter* of 25 March 1999, the number of Japanese tuna boats declined from about 1150 in 1980 to 661 in 1997.

Japan's major fishing companies have transformed themselves into trading companies dealing in fishery products and have invested in the fishing industries of other countries. The high costs of operating Japan-based ships contributed to this trend. Retired tuna boats have been sold to owners in other countries, who in turn have registered their boats in countries such as Taiwan and Korea that do not belong to the international management bodies. The "flag-of-convenience"

Two sea bass fishing boats in Tokyo Bay in 1994. (MICHAEL S. YAMASHITA/CORBIS)

fishing operations by these boat owners continue to supply tuna to the Japanese market through the trading companies. Japan's Fishery Agency and the Fishery Division of the Ministry of Foreign Affairs consider access to distant-water fishery resources a matter of national security, and work jointly to defend the sustainable use of fishery resources in international waters against both unmanaged "pirate" fishing and dogmatic conservationists.

The declining coastal fishing industry is being replaced by aquaculture. Japan has a long history of aquaculture, from the farming of seaweed, pearl, and carp to more modern fish farming of yellowtail, snapper, jack mackerel, flat fish, and eel. In addition, coastal waters have been stocked with farm-raised juvenile snapper, flat fish, crayfish, abalone, and other species, to be later harvested. This has created conflicts between professional and recreational fishermen, the latter being accused of stealing and free riding. The aquaculture industry has suffered from the growth of toxic planktons and algae caused by nutrient-rich household wastewater. The industry has also been accused of destroying reef ecosystems with organic wastes from fish feed. Consumers are increasingly alarmed by the industry's use of antibiotics in fish feed.

The recreational fishing industry is growing fast. While recreational fishing in general has been considered an activity for older males, several developments have gradually altered this perception. American bass fishing using artificial lures has become popular with a large number of younger Japanese, and increasing social independence and disposable income have contributed to the rising numbers of women in recreational fishing. Charter boat businesses provide exclusive charter, casual booking, and nonbooked individual services, targeting various species of fish. Operators of such businesses have joined environmentalists in opposing various land reclamation projects.

Japanese-made fishing equipment enjoys worldwide popularity. Computer-based high technology (using computer-assisted design techniques as well as microcomputers in fishing reels) and basic composite material are lavishly applied to reels and rods, and countless minor fishing devices have been patented.

Japan's fishing industry, like many other industries, is going through a major transformation to achieve higher added value. The era of fishing as a primary and commodity industry is passing, and the growing industrial aquaculture, manufacture of recreational fishing gear, and fishing-related services characterize the diversifying Japanese fishing industry.

Yoichiro Sato

Further Reading

Akaha, Tsuneo. (1985) *Japan in Global Ocean Politics*. Honolulu, HI: University of Hawaii Press and Law of the Sea Institute, University of Hawaii.

Asada, Yohoji. (1983) *Fishery Management in Japan*. Rome: Food and Agriculture Organization of the United Nations.

Bergin, Anthony. (1991) *Japan's Distant Water Tuna Fisheries: Retrospect and Prospect*. Hobart, Tasmania, Australia: Institute of Antarctic and Southern Ocean Studies, University of Tasmania.

Food and Agriculture Organization of the United Nations. (1999) *Marine Ranching: Global Perspectives with Emphasis on the Japanese Experience*. Rome: Food and Agriculture Organization of the United Nations.

Howell, David Luke. (1995) *Capitalism from Within: Economy, Society, and the State in a Japanese Fishery*. Berkeley and Los Angeles: University of California Press.

Mottet, Madelon Green. (1981) *Enhancement of the Marine Environment for Fisheries and Aquaculture in Japan*. Olympia, WA: State of Washington, Department of Fisheries.

Ruddle, Kenneth. (1987) *Administration and Conflict Management in Japanese Coastal Fisheries*. Rome: Food and Agriculture Organization of the United Nations.

FISHING INDUSTRY—KOREA Korea is among the world's leading fishing countries (sixth in 1995 in terms of gross registered tonnage). Of the many varieties caught, the major ones by tonnage are squid, saury pike, Alaska pollack, shrimp, yellow corvina, sabre fish, mackerel, and anchovy.

Fishing was regarded as a plebeian business during the Yi (Choson) dynasty (1392–1910). Under the Japanese occupation, fishing in Korea started its modernization process, which was made possible by more modern ships, equipment, and technology. The industry was devastated by the Korean War (1950–1953) but has recovered rapidly. Over the long term, the rise in the catch has been closely matched by the tonnage of the fishing fleet, which increased from 262,079 tons in 1967 to 991,955 tons in 1999. During the 1990s the number of fishery workers dropped slightly, from 176,123 in 1995 to 170,590 in 1999, whereas the number of fishing vessels rose in the same period from 76,801 to 94,852. Nonmotorized vessels constituted only 6 percent of the total number in 1999. Of 535 Korean-registered deep-sea fishing vessels, approximately 65 percent were more than sixteen years old in 1999.

Increases in wages and reduced fishing territories created significant problems after the mid-1980s. For example, Korea's deep-sea catch reached a peak in the mid-1970s and then declined sharply due to rising fuel costs and the declaration of 200-mile economic sea zones by many nations. The total production has gone down considerably during the 1990s, from 3,348,184 metric tons in 1995 to 2,190,450 in 1999. Also contributing to this decline are the serious ecological problems affecting the coastal fishing industry and inland waters that Korea currently experiences as the result of land reclamation projects, industrial water effluents, and waste disposal. The ecosystem surrounding the Republic of Korea is very vulnerable to the coastal activities of adjacent nations. The primary sources of sea-based pollution of the marine environment are oil spills, aquaculture, and dredging. The decline mentioned above encompasses distant waters fisheries, adjacent waters fisheries, shallow-sea cultures, and especially inland waters fisheries. The production of aquaculture from inland waters, for example, dropped

THE SOCIAL ROLE OF FISHING

A major economic activity, fishing also plays a major role in the social interaction in Korean fishing communities. The account below shows how these social responsibilities can be more important that the economic issues.

> Fish are an important medium of exchange in many social transaction within the village. "Gifts" of fish expressing the fulfillment of various obligations or an attempt to gain favors are frequent. Sokyp'o fishermen resort to considerable subterfuge in order to safeguard this traditional outlet for their catch from the demands of buyers. On four occasions I spent the entire day out fishing, each time on a different sailing junk. In three cases the boat owner put more than half of the choicest fish in a relatively inaccessible compartment on top of which lines and other heavy gear were piled as we approached the beach. Then when the buyer (or buyers) came scrambling aboard, the owner and crew, bewailing their small catch, showed them only the remainder of the fish that had actually been caught. Not until the dealers had been ferried off to the other shore were the rest brought out. Some were divided among the crew, and I was always given one. The rest was either distributed on the spot to villagers who had been alerted by some mysterious communications network that I never understood, or they were delivered by members of the boat owner's family directly to certain houses. Invariably the supply seemed insufficient to satisfy the demand.
>
> *Source:* Vincent S. R. Brandt. (1971) *A Korean Village between Farm and Sea*. Cambridge, MA: Harvard University Press, 63.

from 20,365 metric tons in 1995 to 11,529 in 1999—that is to say, more than 40 percent. Korea's share in the world's commercial catches of fish, crustaceans, and mollusks dropped from 2.54 percent in 1993 to 2.07 percent in 1999.

The fishing industry remains an important source of revenue. Exports of fish and other seafood stayed stable in the1990s, whereas imports went up sharply. To a great extent the future of the fishing industry depends upon Korea's success in negotiating fishing rights with other nations and improving processing methods.

Dimitar L. Dimitrov

Further Reading

Griffin, Trenholme J. (1988) *Korea, the Tiger Economy.* London: Euromoney Publications.

Moreddu, Catherine. (1999) *Review of Agricultural Policies in Korea.* Paris: Organization for Economic Cooperation and Development.

FISHING INDUSTRY—SOUTHEAST ASIA

Many Southeast Asian countries have extensive coastlines and river systems. Hence, commercial, local-market, and subsistence fishing have long been important economic activities. The region's total catch was estimated at nearly 86 million metric tons in the 1980s; Indonesia alone accounted for 2.8 percent of the world's total fish production, followed by Thailand (2.5 percent) and the Philippines (2.2 percent).

Southeast Asian waters are believed to be home to more different fish species than any other part of the world. Most of these live in shallow water, and because the coastlines in much of this region are fringed by wetlands, the fishing industry continues inland—in swamps, flooded rice fields and their canals, lakes, lagoons, and rivers. Until the 1960s, nearly three-quarters of Southeast Asian sea fishing was done at depths of less than 3 meters. Deepwater fish in Southeast Asia were only exploited commercially by Japanese trawlers; local fishermen were usually too poor to equip themselves for deepwater trips.

Among the most important commercial fish are anchovy, shrimp, and tuna. The primary tuna fishing grounds are found in the Pacific Ocean east of the Philippines and north of the eastern islands of Indonesia; anchovy fishing grounds are primarily found in the Celebes Sea; shrimp fishing grounds are in the shallow waters of the South China Sea extending into the Gulf of Thailand. In common with fisheries elsewhere, overexploitation is the greatest threat to commercial fisheries in the region. Such overfishing is particularly serious in the Gulf of Thailand and off the coast of peninsular Malaysia.

Fishing boats docked in a lagoon beside the small fishing village of Kuala Paka, Malaysia. (ECOSCENE/CORBIS)

TABLE 1

Marine and freshwater catches and aquaculture

(in metric tons)

Average Annual Marine Catch		Average Annual Freshwater Catch	Average Annual Aquaculture 1993–1995			
Country	1993–1995	1993–1995	Freshwater Fishes	Diadromous Fishes	Marine Fishes	Mollusks and Crustaceans
Indonesia	3,277.5	611.5	292,635	161,268	9,273	139,936
Cambodia	31.8	76.4	7,940	-	-	597
Malaysia	1164.6	16.1	14,468	5,970	3,111	93,812
Myanmar	610.6	220.7	70,987	-	-	7
Philippines	1,961.9	305.3	95,931	147,934	1,283	127,670
Singapore	13	-	22	239	315	2,203
Thailand	3,081.8	332.5	138,224	3,128	1,080	335,820
Vietnam	362.4	287.6	141,667	-	-	58,300

SOURCE: World Resources Institute (1998): 314–315.

Subsistence fishing is carried out in coastal waters and rivers. It is estimated that 3 million people fish for a living, although that number may be on the conservative side. Much of this catch finds its way to local village markets.

Commercial aquaculture in Southeast Asia has so far been limited, mainly for economic reasons. Such commercial aquaculture has been focused mostly on shrimp ponds and prawn farms in Thailand, Indonesia, the Philippines, and, increasingly, in Vietnam. (See Table 1.) These produce mostly for export to cities, as well as to countries such as the United States and Japan. Southeast Asian countries, however, are far behind industrialized countries in their output for world markets.

A traditional form of aquaculture is still practiced in conjunction with wet rice cultivation in Java, Bali, Thailand, and Vietnam: rice farmers set aside a deep-water area for raising fish, or introduce fish, such as paddy eel, directly into the wet fields. Due to the Green Revolution, when it became common to plant high-yield varieties of rice that required the increased use of pesticides, it became very difficult to continue these traditional aquacultural practices, as the pesticides harmed the fish. In addition, many believe that the heavy exploitation of coastal areas for tourism and the development of other industries is contributing to declining fishing yields and major environmental problems. Both may have a major impact on aquaculture as well as on the region's marine fisheries.

Regional Survey

In Vietnam, investment by the state in the fisheries sector increased fivefold between 1996 and 2000, with additional plans to convert 300,000 hectares of rice fields into aquaculture breeding farms in an attempt to earn $3 billion in seafood export revenue over the next four years. This implies a yearly catch of 1.4 million tons, while fish farm stocks could reach 1.5 million tons.

Due to ongoing deforestation in Cambodia, the water quality of Tonle Sap (Cambodia's largest lake) and rivers in some provinces has been affected, and many fish species have been threatened with extinction. Other species are faced with degraded habitats that no longer support spawning and reproduction. This means the potential for fishing is declining in Cambodia.

Commercial fishing in Myanmar is small in scale and takes place in major rivers, as well as off the long Arakan and Tenasserim coasts. Much of the total catch, which amounts to nearly 389 million kilograms a year, is provided by part-time fishermen. Traps are commonly used in standing water and rivers. Farm families may also supplement their diets by fishing with nets or hooks and lines. In 1990, the total catch was 743,818 metric tons, which made Myanmar the twenty-third most productive fishing nation in the world. The catch suggests a per-capita annual consumption of about 17 kilograms, slightly more than in the United States, although a large proportion of this is in the form of a fish paste taken with rice.

As is the case in most Southeast Asian countries, in Indonesia fish remains the single most important source of animal protein. Nearly 75 percent of the catch is taken from marine fisheries off the western coast of Sumatra, the northern coast of Java, and the southern coasts of Kalimantan and Sulawesi, Bali, Nusa Tenggara, the Moluccas, and Irian Jaya. Inland fisheries, however, employ more people. More than 1 million families engage in inland fishing, while fewer than 500,000 families engage in marine fishing. Inland fisheries in Indonesia include open-water fishing in lakes and rivers, as well as the aquacultural cultivation of fish, shrimp, and prawns in freshwater ponds *(kolam)* and bamboo cages placed in streams and rice fields, brackish coastal ponds *(tabak)*, and paddy fields. In 1989, Java contributed 44 percent of inland tonnage and 23 percent of marine tonnage. Overfishing in marine waters and a decline in the rate of fish production were sufficiently alarming to lead to a presidential decree banning trawling in marine waters.

Fishing accounts for 5 percent of the gross national product of the Philippine economy and supplies 60 percent of the animal protein in the Filipino diet. The Philippine archipelago has long been known for the availability of a wide variety of fish. Two million metric tons were caught in 1989; of this, inland fishing accounted for about a half million metric tons, and marine fishing the rest. More than half the catch came from subsistence fishing; one-third came from commercial fish ponds. Although production has been steadily increasing over the years, the industry has not been able to cope with the growing demand in the Philippines and the rest of Southeast Asia. Export revenue, mainly from shrimp, tuna, and dried seaweed, amounted to nearly $500 million in 1990 alone.

Ooi Giok Ling

Further Reading

Dutt, Ashok K. (1996) *Southeast Asia: A Ten Nation Region.* Dordrecht, Netherlands: Kluwer.

Dwiponggo, A. (1987) "Indonesia's Marine Fisheries Resources." In *Indonesian Marine Capture Fisheries*, edited by Conner Bailey, A. Dwiponggo, and F. Marahudin. Jakarta, Indonesia: Directorate General of Fisheries.

Fischer, Charles A. (1964) *Southeast Asia*. London: Methuen.

Guerrero, Rafael D. (1993) "Economic Policies for Sustainable Management of Fisheries Resources: The Philippines Experience." In *Economic Development and the Environment in ASEAN Countries*, edited by Praipol Koomsup. Bangkok, Thailand: The Economic Society of Thailand, 89–94.

Ling, Shao-Wen. (1977) *Aquaculture in Southeast Asia: A Historical Overview*. Seattle: University of Washington Press.

Wernstedt, Frederick L., and J. E. Spencer. (1967) *The Philippine Island World.* Berkeley and Los Angeles: University of California Press.

World Resources Institute. (1988) *World Resources 1998–1999.* New York and Oxford: Oxford University Press.

FIVE CLASSICS The Five Classics (Wujing) were lengthy collections of prose and poetry that formed the core of the Chinese Confucian canon from the Western Han dynasty (206 BCE–6 CE) through the Southern Song dynasty (1127–1279), when another collection, the Four Books, began to gain prominence through the influence of Neo-Confucianism. The Five Classics were the following: *Shijing* (Book of Songs; also called Classic of Poetry or Book of Odes), the *Shujing* (Book of Documents), the *Li* (Rites), the *Yijing* (Book of Changes, often known in English under its Wade-Giles romanization: *I-ching*), and the *Chunqiu* (Spring and Autumn Annals). A sixth, the *Yue* (Music), is no longer extant.

Although literate elites in China and elsewhere celebrated the Five Classics as primary expressions of Confucian thought, each of the classics had roots in traditions and practices far older than the era of Confucius (551–479 BCE) himself. The *Shijing* is made up of 305 verse texts of varying length, the earliest dating from the tenth century BCE and the latest from the sixth. Contents range from sacrificial hymns to folk songs. The *Shujing* purported to record key speeches of sage rulers; the earliest chapters dated to the tenth century BCE, and the latest were fourth-century CE forgeries. The *Li*, as codified in three distinct texts (the *Liji* [Record of Rites], the *Yili* [Ceremonies and Rites], and the *Zhouli* [Rites of Zhou]), detailed ritual prescriptions for a range of public events, from governmental entertainments to funerals and mourning, and defended the role of ritual propriety as a tool of social control. The *Yijing*, originally a divination manual constructed around sixty-four hexagrams and associated early Zhou mantic texts, came to include much cosmological and political philosophy in the form of commentaries. The *Chunqiu*, a terse chronicle of the years 722 to 479 BCE, was accompanied by three commentaries containing more extensive historical and exegetical material: the Zuo commentary *(Zuozhuan)* and the commentaries of the Gongyang and Guliang schools *(Gongyangzhuan, Guliangzhuan)*.

By 136 BCE, when Han Emperor Wu (reigned 141–87 BCE) elevated the five works by appointing official teachers for them at the capital, the texts were strongly associated with Confucius, who was believed to have had edited or written parts of each of them. The Five Classics's canonical status was cemented in later centuries by the frequent appearance of new commentaries and by the court's expectation that most prospective candidates for government office would be able to demonstrate a basic knowledge of the works in their essays for civil service examinations. Confucian courts in Japan, Korea, Vietnam, and elsewhere also promulgated the Five Classics as a basis for moral philosophy and political practice. In contemporary China, debate over the antiquity and importance of the Five Classics continues to serve as an index of cultural continuity.

David Schaberg

Further Reading

Legge, James, trans. (1960) *The Chinese Classics.* Hong Kong: Hong Kong University Press.

Loewe, Michael, ed. (1993) *Early Chinese Texts: A Bibliographical Guide.* Berkeley and Los Angeles: The Society for the Study of Early China and the Institute of East Asian Studies, University of California Press.

Nylan, Michael. (2001) *The Five "Confucian" Classics.* New Haven, CT: Yale University Press.

FIVE PHASES Zou Yan (c. 305–240 BCE) is traditionally regarded as the systematizer of the philosophy of the yin-yang (bipolar forces of the universe; yin is the dark, passive female force, and yang is the light, active male force) five phases *(wuxing)*, namely, wood, fire, earth, metal, and water. Despite the pervasive affect of the five-phases concept on the philosophy of the Han dynasty (206 BCE–220 CE) and on subsequent Chinese science, cosmology, and medicine, little is known of Zou Yan's teachings.

The *Yingtong* (Responding in Kind) chapter of *Master Lu's Spring and Autumn Annals* is usually cited as the standard elucidation of Zou's ideas. In this chapter, the five phases are used to explicate a cosmological order to explain historical political change according to the conquest cycle of the five phases. This influenced the justification of the "first emperor" of the Qin dynasty for adopting the symbols of "water" to show he had vanquished the "fire" of the Zhou dynasty (1045–256 BCE). Subsequently, the idea was hotly debated by Han philosophers, some of whom sought to use it to justify Han rule.

The five phases explain the processes of change in terms of conquest and productive cycles. In the conquest cycle, earth is conquered by wood, wood is vanquished by metal, metal is melted by fire, fire is extinguished by water, and water is obstructed by earth—and thus the process continues. In the productive cycle, wood produces fire, fire's ashes generate earth, earth begets metal, from metal drips water, and water nourishes wood—and thus the cycle continues. The five phases are bound up with the nondual correlative thinking of yin and yang, and they are correlated with the myriad aspects of nature and human experience.

The philosophy and classification system of the five phases left a lasting impression on Chinese science, medicine, and alchemy, on and the art of placement (feng shui). Because the five phases are correlated with every aspect of the natural world and human life and are believed to explain and predict change, they became indispensable tools for taxonomy and for un-

THE FIVES PHASES AND THEIR ASSOCIATIONS

In Chinese cosmology, each of the five phases is linked with specific manifestations of different categories of natural phenomenon. Knowledge of these associations is important to diviners who use them in formulas that help them predict and control the future.

Associations	Wood	Fire	Earth	Metal	Water
Seasons	Spring	Summer	Late Summer	Autumn	Winter
Directions	East	South	Center	West	North
Colors	Green	Red	Yellow	White	Black
Tastes	Sour	Bitter	Sweet	Acrid	Salty
Virtues	Benevolence	Wisdom	Faith	Righteousness	Decorum
Disease	Insomnia	Heartache	Stomach	Lungs	Sex Organs

Source: John L. McCreary. (1983) *The Symbolism of Popular Taoist Magic.* Ann Arbor, MI: University Microfilms, 60.

derstanding transformation. Five-phases philosophy is still used in the practice of Chinese medicine and the art of placement. In Chinese medicine, the organs, acupuncture points, and herbs are correlated with the five phases. Thus, a weak heart correlated with the fire phase is treated by administering herbs correlated with fire and stimulating acupuncture points correlated with fire. In placement, the sink should go on the north wall and the stove on the south side of the kitchen, because water is correlated with the North and fire with the South.

James D. Sellmann

Further Reading

Connelly, Dianne M. (1994) *Traditional Acupuncture: The Law of the Five Elements.* 2d ed. Columbia, MD: Traditional Acupuncture Institute.

Ni, Maoshing, trans. (1995) *The Yellow Emperor's Classic of Medicine.* Boston, MA: Shambhala.

Rossbach, Sarah. (1983) *Feng Shui: The Art of Placement.* New York: Arkana/Penguin.

FIVE POWER DEFENCE ARRANGEMENTS The Five Power Defence Arrangements (FPDA), which came into effect 1 November 1971, refer to a collective agreement between Australia, Britain, Singapore, Malaysia, and New Zealand to maintain ongoing consultations and an agreement to consult in the event of external attack against Singapore and Malaysia. A series of exercises evolved from this framework. A tandem arrangement also saw the stationing of ANZUK (Australia, New Zealand, the United Kingdom) forces in Singapore and Malaysia, although in time they were withdrawn. The FPDA replaced the Anglo-Malayan ("Malaysian" from 1963) Defence Agreement (AMDA), which lasted from 1957 to 1971 and contained a far more overt commitment to assist Malaysia and Singapore in the event of a security threat. Thus, forces from Australia, New Zealand, and the United Kingdom had fought, during the Malayan Emergency and *Konfrontasi*, in order to guarantee Malayan/Malaysian and Singaporean security. While the ANZUK forces were gradually withdrawn in phases—Britain by 1976, Australia by 1986, and New Zealand by 1989—FPDA has continued. This loose military alliance has evolved from one that initially intended to give confidence to Malaysia and Singapore to one of interoperability and joint military exercises. By the 1990s major sea and air exercises were held—often involving thirty warships and fifty aircraft in comprehensive exercises including all aspects of land, sea, and air defense and electronic warfare systems (Rolfe 1995: 9).

The FPDA has been criticized by those who view it as a product of either British colonialism or the Cold War, and by those who see it as contrary to greater Southeast Asian multilateralism and self-reliance. Some Indonesian officials and commentators have wondered aloud if the alliance is maintained with Indonesia firmly in mind (Methven 1992:126–130). Malaysia did briefly suspend participation in exercises in the late 1990s, most probably because of bilateral tensions with Singapore, while New Zealand has sometimes scaled back its participation due to budgetary reasons. However, the alliance members seem committed to FPDA, which shows no signs of being shelved. All members seem to view the alliance as useful for the following reasons: (1) all benefit from the utility of defense exercises with historical allies; (2) Malaysia and Singapore have additional assurance; (3) Australia and New Zealand are able to participate in the security of an area seen as important to regional security, as well as being in the last military alliance that includes traditional ally Britain; and (4) Britain is able to continue its presence and influence in Southeast Asia.

Anthony Smith

Further Reading

Chin Kin Wah. (1974) *The Five Power Defence Arrangements and AMDA.* Singapore: Institute of Southeast Asian Studies, Occasional Paper No. 23.

Leifer, Michael. (1995) *Dictionary of the Modern Politics of South-East Asia.* London: Routledge.

Methven, Philip. (1992) *The Five Power Defence Arrangements and Military Cooperation among the ASEAN States: Incompatible Models for Security in Southeast Asia?* Canberra Papers on Strategy and Defence No. 92. Canberra, Australia: Australian National University.

Rolfe, Jim. (1995) *Anachronistic Past or Positive Future: New Zealand and the Five Power Defence Arrangements.* Working Paper 4/95. Wellington, New Zealand: Centre for Strategic Studies.

FLORES SEA The Flores Sea or Laut Flores, with a surface area of around 240,000 square kilometers (93,000 square miles), is located off the eastern part of the Indonesian archipelago. It is a portion of the western South Pacific Ocean bordered on the south by the Lesser Sunda Islands of Flores and Sumbawa and on the north by the island of Sulawesi (Celebes). Part of Laut Flores is preserved in the Taman Nasional Taka Bonerate, a national park including a series of twenty-one coral atolls that cover a vast area of around 220,000 hectares, the third largest coral atoll network in the world after Maldiva and Kwadifein. Laut Flores is also well known for its beauty and the richness of its underwater life. It has a greater diversity of submarine life than the other nearby shallow-water sea, the Java Sea (Laut Jawa).

Andi Achdian

Further Reading

Ensiklopedi Nasional Indonesia. (1994) Vol. 4. Jakarta, Indonesia: PT Cipta Adi Pustaka.

FOLK OPERA—BANGLADESH. See **Jatra**.

FOLKLORE—CENTRAL ASIA Through oral folklore the peoples of Central Asia express their identity in speech and song while renewing and refashioning links with their past. The numerous Central Asian verbal art genres are as diverse as life's varied situations, yet share common features owing to regional cultural contacts and common origins. The forms of folklore expression are intimately tied to language. The Karakalpaks, Kazakhs, Kyrgyz, Turkmen, Uighurs, and Uzbeks all speak Turkic languages and have a shared stock of oral traditions; the Tajiks speak an Iranian language and have distinct traditions, but their Persian cultural heritage has influenced the folklore of their Turkic neighbors, especially the Turkmen, Uighurs, and Uzbeks.

"Oral tradition" refers not only to a body of tales, epics, songs, proverbs, and legends, but also to the ways in which these verbal materials are created and transmitted. Texts are rarely handed down verbatim through the generations; each successive bearer of the tradition, as an active practitioner of oral folk art, recreates an expression by using patterns, styles, and performance situations as traditional as the words themselves. Central Asian peoples have contributed significantly to folklorists' understanding of the worldwide phenomenon of oral composition-in-performance and of oral tradition in general. With the help of various techniques, specialists may even study the oral or oral-derived aspects of written texts hundreds of years old.

Written Records

The oldest records of Central Asian folklore are preserved in a dictionary of the Middle Turkic language, *Diwan Lughat at-Turk*, written around 1075 by Mahmud al-Kashghari. The numerous specimens of popular poetry and songs that Kashghari cited display a range of rhythms, assonances, rhymes, imagery, and word combinations found even today in the oral poetry of contemporary Central Asian Turkic peoples. Many of the specimens in the *Diwan Lughat at-Turk* are of heroic poetry, and other records of Turkic folklore from the Middle Ages, such as the *Kitab-i Dede Qorqut* (Book of Grandfather Qorqut), also attest to heroic and epic traditions with links to Central Asian nomadic peoples.

Speakers of a dialect of Persian, the Tajiks carry on Iranian oral traditions known in writings from medieval greater Iran. An early written folklore specimen from the region inhabited by the Tajiks is a partial Arabic translation of a satirical song composed in Balkh in modern Afghanistan in 725 CE. Tajik oral poetry before the twentieth century is discerned mainly through the abundant folk motifs in literary poetry, as in the Persian *Shahname* epic.

The search for national origins, which peaked in Europe in the nineteenth century, stimulated a generation of European and European-trained folklore collectors to study Central Asia, and the work of documenting oral traditions has continued through the czarist and Soviet eras to the present day. Thus there are numerous written records of Central Asian folklore from the last century and a half, including the nineteenth-century collections and translations of Chokan Valikhanov (Kazakh and Kyrgyz), Arminius Vámbéry (Khivan dialect of Uzbek), Wilhelm Radloff (Kazakh, Kyrgyz, and Taranchi), and Abubekir Divaev (Kazakh and Karakalpak). Much early collecting work was done in the name of linguistic investigation.

After 1918 the Soviet government took an active role in preserving certain folk traditions for the sake of their content, and projects to collect folktales, epics, songs, and many other genres went hand in hand with concerted scholarly study and publication. Similar efforts have been carried out among the Uighur, Kazakh, and Kyrgyz populations of the Xinjiang Autonomus Region of China. Today Central Asians themselves are responsible for most of the work being done to document and analyze Central Asian folklore. Western researchers, influenced by theories of verbal art performance, have introduced an emphasis on studying audio and audiovisual recordings of actual folklore events.

Genres and Practitioners

Folklore may be classified into prose and poetic genres. Central Asian legends and tales—folklore in prose—are heard in everyday situations that make up the context of traditional culture. Legends are short narratives in ordinary language about what people believe to be true events of the past, whether mundane or supernatural. Central Asian legends share material with epic poetry; some feature giants, sprites, and magical feats. Miracles play a prominent part in legends connected with Sufi saints and their shrines. Ethnic groups have legends about their origins, and in some cases these refer to a divine progenitor or an animal such as a dog or doe that suckled the ancestor of the tribe. Numerous Central Asian legends mention local heroes who have a basis in historical fact. One of the oldest of these is Iskandar, or Alexander of Macedon, whose conquests in Bactria and Sogdiana in 329–328 BCE placed part of Central Asia under short-lived Hellenistic dominion.

Tales are stories that the teller and audience know are untrue. Tales about human beings typically have a happy ending. The hero or heroine of a Central Asian tale may be of noble or low birth; if the former, often the character begins poor and in reduced circumstances and only later learns the truth and regains a destined high position. The sovereign (khan or *padishah*) with whom the hero or heroine deals may be good, generous, and a just arbiter, or wicked, greedy, and a jealous antagonist. Some common stories are romantic tales, often about a poor girl who wins her "prince charming" by means of her intelligence or beauty, and animal tales, which usually have a moral lesson. The humorous tales (Tajik and Uzbek *latifa*) of the "wise simpleton" Nasruddin Hoja are enjoyed throughout much of the Islamic world, and Central Asia is no exception. One of the most popular facets of this humble figure is his gift for exposing and subverting the pretensions of the rich, powerful, and vain. The Uzbeks know him as Nasreddin Apandi or Afandi, the Kyrgyz as Apendi, and the Kazakhs as Khoja Nasr. Facetious tales about the deceptive, malicious, and cruel figure *Kose* (Beardless) occur in Uzbek, Kazakh, and Turkmen traditions.

Central Asian folk poetry is sung poetry. Thus, renowned practitioners of this art go by the general terms "singer" (Uzbek *bakhshi*, Turkmen *bakhshy*, Karakalpak *baqsy*, Kazakh *olengshi* or *zhyrshy*, Kyrgyz *yrchy*, Kazakh and Karakalpak *zhyrau*) or "poet" (Uzbek and Tajik *shoir*). Other terms highlight genre specializations, such as the Turkmen *ozan* (epic bard) or Kyrgyz *manaschy* (singer of the *Manas* epic). Kyrgyz *akyn* means simply a poet, whether literary or oral, but in the context of oral tradition, *akyn* refers to a highly skilled songster who performs with an instrument, usually the lute. Good singers gain fame and enduring reputations, such as the eighteenth-century Kazakh bard Buqar-zhyrau or the Kyrgyz *akyn* Toktogul (1864–1933), who essayed his traditional poetic mastery in the new field of Communist propaganda.

The Central Asian folksinger entertains audiences with a wide variety of poetic genres, including epics, lyrics, plaints, admonitions, didactic verses, even insults and denunciations; in several of the Turkic languages, any improvised song is called *terma* or *terme*. Epic *(dastan)*, the art of long narrative poetry (or mixed poetry and prose), is both widespread and diverse in Central Asia and is esteemed as a special repository of the people's identity and culture. Epic singers may perform other genres as well. Kazakh, Karakalpak, and Kyrgyz singers excel at virtuosic song-contests (Kazakh, Karakalpak *aitys*, Kyrgyz *aytysh*) in which two *akyn*s match wits in impromptu composition while performing topical songs, with liberal doses of self-praise and jibing at their opponents. Genealogies (Kazakh *shezhere*, Kyrgyz *sanzhyra*) in the form of oral poetry and legends are a feature of the folklore of Central Asian peoples with a nomadic tribal past.

Folk songs are often classified without regard to the professional and specialist performance spheres, in such categories as work, ceremonial, lyrical, and children's genres. Work songs may reflect agricultural or pastoral work or a specific trade. Songs sometimes have ties to a specific socioeconomic group, as in the Tajik *gharibi* genre of plaintive songs about the difficulties of life, sung originally by transient laborers. Professional mourners, usually women, compose and perform long, eulogistic laments at funerals. The Uzbek and Turkmen *yar-yar* (Kazakh *zhar-zhar*) is a sometimes mournful, sometimes playful wedding-lyric sung by the bride, her parents, the groom's friends, and other participants, all linked by a common phrase in the refrains, *yar-yar* or *zhar-zhar* (beloved). Love lyrics are popular. The Tajik and Uzbek *lapar* is a dialogue-song sung by a boy and a girl in a competitive style; the dialogues, sometimes improvised, range from urgent expressions of love to satirical taunting as the singers attempt to outdo each other in witty repartee.

Proverbs, sayings, and riddles are concentrated folk expressions. Their brevity often belies artful structure and profound cultural reference. Proverbs, loosely defined, are distillations of popular wisdom in the form of simple idiomatic sayings or figures of speech ("To pour saltwater over a burn"—Tajik) or observations ("A knife wound will heal; a tongue wound will not heal"—Kazakh) or admonitions ("Don't throw your coat in the fire in annoyance at the fleas"—Karakalpak). Proverbs are highly portable bits of folklore, appearing as embedded elements in lyric and didactic poetry, epics, tales, and many other genres. Central Asian riddles may be no more than a phrase, such as the Kashgari (Uighur) riddle *Ishttin pes attyn igiz* (Lower than a dog, higher than a horse. Answer:

saddle), or they may constitute tiny poems in a symmetrical style, as in this Kashgari example:

Qulaqy quiruqynyng qashita,	Its ears on the side of its tail,
Ucheii qosaqynyng tashita	Its guts outside its belly
(dutar)	(Answer: *dutar*, a lute with two gut strings)

Poetics

The quantitative meters of Persian oral and literary poetry dominate Tajik folk verse, and Islamized Turkic peoples have used Persian-based verse structures for oral poetry. In quantitative verse, the fundamental linguistic principle used to organize sounds into verse is the length (quantity) of the syllables: a long syllable usually has the same metrical length as two short syllables. The ʿarudh system of metrics in Persian literature has had an influence on oral metrics. In turn, two popular literary verse-forms are believed to originate from oral models. The *ghazal*, a lyric miniature somewhat analogous to a sonnet, consists of five to fifteen *beits* (distychs or double lines) in a single rhyme, in which the first line sets the theme of the poem and the final line gives a concluding image or idea. The *rubaʿi* is a quatrain of *beits* in an *aaba* rhyme scheme.

In contrast to the quantitative poetics of Tajik folk poetry, the traditional Iranian meter for epic recitation is syllabic, or organized by the number of syllables in a line. The *Shahname*, *Farhad and Shirin*, and other Tajik epics follow an eleven-syllable verse scheme in rhymed couplets.

Turkic folk verse forms have found particularly rich development in Central Asia. The older Turkic meter is syllabic; this meter is common to the oral poetry of all Central Asian Turkic peoples. In Turkic syllabic poetry the basic poetic form derives from a combination of two fundamental features of Turkic grammar, the "agglutinative" principle of word formation (common to all Turkic languages), where meaning is built by stringing suffixes onto base words; and "vowel harmony," or rules by which the base vowel of a word governs the shape of the vowel in succeeding syllables (these rules are absent in most dialects of Uzbek). In poetic composition these principles of word morphology and phonology produce a class of effects known as rhythmico-syntactic parallelism. Kyrgyz, with clear-cut vowel harmony, affords a rich illustration of these effects in a few lines from the epic *Manas:*

Aryp-darbyp miniship,	Greatly excited, mounting (horses),
Aikyryp zholgo kiriship,	Shouting and getting under way,
Toogo chapty toptoshup,	They galloped to the mountains en masse,
Adyrga chapty antalap,	They galloped to the hills in a group,
Boksogo chapty bolunup,	They galloped to the foothills breaking up,
Talaaga chapty dabyrap.	They galloped thunderously to the steppe.

Rhythmico-syntactic parallelism is found in poetic passages as far back as the *Diwan Lughat at-Turk* and subsequently in most oral poetic forms among the Central Asian Turkic peoples. It is also used in proverbs and riddles, as in this Turkmen riddle:

Aghyr haly kakylmaiar	The heavy carpet cannot be shaken;
Kakylsa da dokulmeiar	even if it shakes, they won't fall off
(jildiz)	(Answer: the sky and stars)

In addition to the seven- and eight-syllable lines seen in the examples above, compositions in eleven- and twelve-syllable lines are also common. In the early system, verses were loosely organized with respect to one another. The easygoing feel of the resulting rhythms is exemplified in two Kazakh and Kyrgyz verse-forms named after the gaits of horses: *zhorgo soz* (pacing speech) and *zheldirme* (jog-trot). Strophic structure, or organization of verses into stanzas, was a later development and is found in the folklore of most Central Asian Turkic peoples.

Folklore and Society

People's oral traditions preserve many aspects of their self-images and aspirations. Folklore performers know and exploit this situation by singing and speaking to their specific audiences. For example, a singer performing for a rich and powerful personage may improvise lines alluding to the preeminence of the patron or the patron's ancestors; this may even elicit a material reward from a happy patron. Other audiences may need to be consoled for their lot in life or reminded of their people's proud history or inspired to act for the good of the group.

Because folklore is an ideological phenomenon, Central Asian folklore traditions became the focus of ideological debate and struggles in Soviet society, especially during the 1930s to the 1950s. The Communist Party actively embraced folklore as a means of promoting approved values of the working classes, such as love of the land and the nation, respect for hard work, and enmity toward religion and the exploitative classes. This emphasis went together with the forcible suppression of other popular traditions, such as religious legends and poetry connected with Sufism. Epic poetry was entwined with the sensitive issue of national identity and tended to espouse religious themes and a positive attitude toward ruling elites. For this reason numerous Central Asian epics were banned by the Soviet authorities around 1951. They were later rehabilitated, but the Soviet period of cultural indoctrination affected Central Asian peoples' views on the nature of folklore in general.

Today Central Asians are taking advantage of national independence and openness to revitalize their folklore traditions. While economic and political transition and globalization create challenges for Central Asians interested in recovering and preserving their cultural memory, folklore traditions may now advance to positions of unprecedented preeminence in society. For example, in 1995 the government of the Kyrgyz Republic recognized the epic *Manas* as the official basis of state ideology, and basic rules of social conduct devised by President Askar Akayev in the name of the hero Manas are taught in the schools.

D. Prior

Further Reading

Beliaev, Viktor. (1975) *Central Asian Music: Essays in the History of the Music of the Peoples of the U.S.S.R.* Ed. by Mark Slobin, trans. by Mark Slobin and Greta Slobin. Middletown, CT: Wesleyan University Press.

Bogdanova, M. I., ed. (1960) *Istoriia literatur narodov Srednei Azii i Kazakhstana* (History of the Literatures of the Peoples of Central Asia and Kazakhstan). Moscow: Moskovskii gosudarstvennyi universitet.

Boratav, Pertev N., Ilhan Basgoz, and Helga Uplegger. (1965) "Die Volksliteratur." In *Philologiae Turcicae Fundamenta* (Fundamentals of Turkic Philology). Vol. 2, edited by Louis Bazin, Alessio Bombaci, Jean Deny, Tayyib Gökbilgin, Fahir Iz, and Helmuth Scheel. Wiesbaden, Germany: Franz Steiner, 1–170.

Cuiyi Wei and Karl W. Luckert, eds. and trans. (1998) *Uighur Stories from along the Silk Road.* Lanham, MD: University Press of America.

Dor, Rémy. (1982) *Chants du toit du monde: Textes d'orature kirghiz suivis d'un lexique kirghiz-français.* Paris: G.-P. Maisonneuve & Larose.

Feldman, Walter R. (1988/1980) "The Uzbek Oral Epic: Documentation of Late Nineteenth and Early Twentieth Century Bards." Ph.D. diss., Columbia University, 1980; photocopy reproduction: Ann Arbor, MI: UMI Dissertation Information Service, 1988.

Jarring, Gunnar. (1946) *Materials to the Knowledge of Eastern Turki: Tales, Poetry, Proverbs, Riddles, Ethnological and Historical Texts from the Southern Parts of Eastern Turkestan.* 4 vols. Lund, Sweden: CWK Gleerup.

Prior, Daniel. (2000) *Patron, Party, Patrimony: Notes on the Cultural History of the Kirghiz Epic Tradition.* Papers on Inner Asia 33. Bloomington, IN: Indiana University Research Institute for Inner Asian Studies.

Radloff, Wilhelm (Radlov, Vasilii V.). (1885) *Dialect der Kara Kirgisen: Proben der Volkslitteratur der nördlichen türkischen Stämme* 5 (texts and German translations). St. Petersburg, Russia: Imperatorskaia Akademiia nauk.

Reichl, Karl. (1985) *Karakalpakische Märchen.* Bochum, Germany: N. Brockmeyer.

———. (1970) *Kirgisische Mundarten: Proben der Volkslitteratur der türkischen Stämme Süd-Sibiriens* 3 (texts and German translations). St. Petersburg, Russia: Imperatorskaia Akademiia nauk.

———. (1986) *Märchen aus Sinkiang: Überlieferungen der Turkvölker Chinas.* Cologne, Germany: E. Diederichs.

———. (1992) *Turkic Oral Epic Poetry: Traditions, Forms, Poetic Structure.* New York: Garland.

———. (1982) *Türkmenische Märchen.* Bochum, Germany: N. Brockmeyer.

———. (1978) *Usbekische Märchen.* Bochum, Germany: Studienverlag N. Brockmeyer; St. Petersburg, Russia: Imperatorskaia Akademiia nauk.

Tietze, Andreas. (1966) *The Koman Riddles and Turkic Folklore.* Berkeley and Los Angeles: University of California Press.

Voorter, Thomas. (c. 1999) "Kyrgyz Heroes: Songs of Sanzyra and Tales of Batyrlar." Retrieved 1 October 2001 from: http://www.vic2000.net/heroes/.

Winner, Thomas G. (1958) *The Oral Art and Literature of the Kazakhs of Russian Central Asia.* Durham, NC: Duke University Press.

Zhirmunsky, Viktor M. (1985) "Rhythmico-Syntactic Parallelism as the Basis of Old Turkic Folk Epic Verse." In *Selected Writings: Linguistics, Poetics*, edited by Viktor M. Zhirmunsky, translated by Sergei Ess. Moscow: Progress Publishers, 320–352.

FOOD CRISIS—NORTH KOREA

It has been reported that more than 3 million people out of 23 million have died from hunger in North Korea since 1995, the first of two consecutive years during which North Korea suffered floods. The flooding was followed by a serious drought, and the nation was hit by tidal waves in 1997. The succession of misfortunes brought about widespread famine. There have been reports of people surviving by eating the bark of pine trees and grass roots, or by selling items like clothing and furniture to buy food. The condition of the children has been compared to that of the children of Ethiopia during the famines of the mid-1980s. The World Food Program (WFP) continued through 2001 to warn that without food grain aid from outside, the most vulnerable people were still in danger of starvation.

Since North Korean authorities have provided no reliable data on demographics or the nation's criteria for food rationing, it is difficult to evaluate the food situation in North Korea. According to a report of the North Korean Flood Damage Rehabilitation Committee in March 1998, annual demand for food grain was shown to be as much as 7 million metric tons, while actual production in 1997 was 2.3 million metric tons. However, the Ministry of Unification in South Korea estimates that the north's total demand for grain is 5.5 million metric tons, while grain output was 3.9 million metric tons in 2001. According to these figures, a shortage of 1.6 million metric tons remains. An assessment by the WFP and other U.N. food assistance groups puts North Korea's annual grain demand at 4.8 million metric tons, with 2.9 million metric tons of grain harvested, also leaving a shortage of 1.9 million metric tons in 2000. However, this shortage should be eased by food assistance from the U.N., grain secured through the North Korea's bartering activities, and Chinese relief efforts. While it is hard to judge the accuracy of these figures, the general view is that North Korea suffers a food shortage of 2 million metric tons of grain annually.

Causes of the Food Shortage

The food shortage in North Korea has continued unabated because of the structural deficiencies of its socialist economy, combined with natural disasters and the disappearance of entire markets within the international socialist bloc. North Korea's cooperative farm system reduced farmers' incentive to work and dampened their productivity. Further, the cutting off of North Korea's oil supply, which had been provided largely by the former Soviet Union; a sharp drop in foreign trade; and the collapse of socialist countries, particularly the former Soviet Union, dealt a heavy blow to all sectors of the North Korean economy. Moreover, the government's expansion of farmland to hillside regions through bench-terraced farming was a major factor in the destruction of forestland, which increased the destructive force of the floods. The country's inadequate transportation system also compounded its deepening food crisis by making it difficult to ship food to where it was needed.

As the food crisis has worsened, the North Korean government has tried to minimize its responsibility to supply food grain through the central distribution system. It launched a national campaign, the "Arduous March" (1996–1997), in order to overcome the worsening food crisis. Grain rationing by the central government was curtailed to the minimum level, leaving local authorities and institutions to make up the bulk of the shortage. Although there are regional variations in food shortage due to the regional self-supply system, food grain rationing by the central government was reduced to 300 grams (half a bowl) per day in most areas of North Korea, except the capital city Pyongyang.

It is not easy to confirm how many people starved to death during the "Arduous March" campaign. Based on interviews with 1,694 North Korean "food refugees" in northeast China, the Buddhist Chapter of the Movement for Mutual Help of Our Nation estimated that 3 million people (27 percent of the entire population of North Korea) died from hunger between August 1995 and March 1998. Before he defected to South Korea, Hwang Jang Yup, the former secretary of international affairs of the North Korean Worker's Party, claimed to have heard from a reliable source that 1.5 million people had starved to death by the end of 1996. The Council on Foreign Relations of the U.S. Congress estimates that the total number of deaths from starvation to date ranges from 1 million to 2 million.

In addition to those who have lost their lives due to food shortages, many people are suffering from malnutrition and a lack of adequate health care. According to a World Vision report of July 1997, out of 547 North Korean children of two years and under in five nursery schools in the cities of P'yongyang, Wonsan, Sariwon, Haeju, and P'yongsan, 85 percent were malnourished and 29 percent were severely malnourished. Although it is hard to forecast how the food crisis is going to be resolved in the near future, there seems no way out without a fundamental reformation of the sluggish economy.

Byounglo Philo Kim

Further Reading

Choi, Sooyoung. (1996) *A Study on Agricultural Policy and Food Problems in North Korea*. Seoul: Korea Institute for National Unification.

Kim, Byounglo Philo. (1999) "The Sociopolitical Impact of Food Crisis in North Korea." *Korea and World Affairs* 23, 2 (Summer): 207–224.

FOOT BINDING A practice that might have originated in the court of a decadent, late-tenth-century emperor with a fetish for small feet, foot binding spread through China from the end of the eleventh century and was a common practice by the time of the Ming dynasty (1368–1644). Girls between the ages of five and seven years were subjected to the practice, in which their toes and heels were bound together with tight bandages, so that their feet would ideally be about eight centimeters long. Originally an emblem of femininity and a marker of social status for upper-class women, foot binding spread to lower-class women, for whom the possession of feet resembling "golden lotuses" represented opportunities for upward mobility in the marriage and service markets.

By keeping women largely confined to inner chambers (since it was difficult to walk any distance with bound feet), foot binding maintained the chaste roles prescribed for women by Neo-Confucianism, yet at the same time turned them into objects of erotic desire. Foot binding thus became a symbol for feminine beauty, social and sexual hierarchy, and Confucian morality.

By the early twentieth century Chinese reformers campaigned against foot binding and saw it as a source of national shame and weakness. For the reformers, foot binding symbolized China's vulnerability to Western imperialism, as it left a large portion of the population capable only of hobbling. Natural feet became the sign of feminine beauty. The anti–foot binding efforts of Chinese natural-foot societies and Western women and Christian missionaries living in China—combined with the fierce criticism of the May Fourth intellectuals (who favored the adoption of Western science and philosophy for the strengthening of China) and laws prohibiting foot binding and rewarding those who turned in women's binding cloths and lotus shoes—brought about the demise of the 900-year-old custom by the 1920s.

Robert Y. Eng

Further Reading

Jackson, Beverly. (1997) *Splendid Slippers: A Thousand Years of an Erotic Tradition*. Berkeley: Ten Speed Press.

Levy, Howard. (1967) *Chinese Footbinding: The History of a Curious Erotic Custom*. New York: Bell.

Wang, Ping. (2000) *Aching for Beauty: Footbinding in China*. Minneapolis: University of Minnesota Press.

FORBIDDEN CITY. See **Imperial Palace.**

FOREST INDUSTRY—MONGOLIA Forests occupy only 8.1 percent of Mongolia—a total of 17.5 million square hectares. Most forest reserves are pine, birch, and other conifers and are located in the northern uppermost corridor, which borders Siberian Russia. Forests are found mainly in Selenge Aimag (province), but also in the northern provinces of Bulgan, Khubsgul, and Hentii, and even in the Gobi Desert to the south near China. Although small, Mongolian forests provide ecological balance, soil protection, and water collection. As of 1997, total forest resources were 1.337 billion square meters, with an annual growth rate of 5.6 million square meters.

Mongolia's first forest utilization/preservation law was passed in 1940; from 1970 to 1990, 1.7 million square meters of forest were cut annually; 270,000 hectares of forest were destroyed by fire, and another 70,000 hectares were lost to insects and diseases. At the end of the Socialist era in 1990, there were twenty-three small state-owned wood-processing companies. With the complete privatization of these companies in the past decade, in 2000 there were about fifty shareholding companies, mainly exporting nonprocessed wood to China. This represents about 6 percent of Mongolia's total industrial output. According to the Mongolian Ministry of Nature and Environment, Mongolia's few wood-processing plants have cut down almost half of the national timber resources over the last few decades and, if the pace continues, in seventy years Mongolia will have no forests.

The Mongolian government is concerned about deforestation and believes that the export of nonprocessed wood has an adverse impact on the price of domestic wood products. At the beginning of 1999, the government began limiting nonprocessed wood exports and imposing timber export taxes under the National Program on Forests. Nevertheless, the amount of exported timber in 1999 exceeded the limits set by Ministry of Nature and Environment. The government, to discourage additional logging, imposed a tax of 150,000 tugrik ($1,500) per cubic meter of export timber. Also, a reforestation plan has been implemented: in 1999, young trees were planted over 6,000 hectares, and projects with foreign export partners are under development. The tax policy on timber has hurt an already-declining local industry. Many workers have lost their jobs, especially in Selenge Province. Wood-processing factories have gone bankrupt because the tax policy on timber has decreased Chinese market demand.

The Mongolian government is promoting development in three areas of the forest industry: (1) production of tincture for medicinal use, powdered vitamins, and oils from conifers and pine resins; (2) production of construction materials, cut board, and tree particle board; and (3) production of furniture and birch floor and construction materials.

Alicia J. Campi

Further Reading

Government of Mongolia. (1998) "Agro-Industry Investment Project Profiles." 24–26 June.

FOREST INDUSTRY—SOUTHEAST ASIA

An important source of raw materials and revenues, the forests of Southeast Asia have played a key role in the development of trade and commerce in this region for more than two millennia. Since World War II the forest industry in Southeast Asia has become an increasingly significant player in the international forest-products trade. The effects of many years of overcutting and forest conversion are transforming this sector. Forestry institutions as well as the forest industry are changing as concern for the social and environmental role of forests grows.

Historical Basis

Forest produce, as trade or tribute, has formed the basis of economic and political relationships between neighboring societies in this region since earliest times. Indian, Arab, and Chinese vessels plied southern seas conducting a thriving trade for more than a thousand years before Europeans arrived in Southeast Asia in the late fifteenth century. Historically important trade goods have included spices, aromatics (e.g., sandalwood and aloeswood), medicines, dyes, and decorative woods (e.g., ebony), plus a great variety of gums, resins, fruits, and various wild animals and animal products, all from the forest. Expansion of commerce has been instrumental in the domestication of several forest species, including pepper, cloves, and cinnamon, while products less easily cultivated (e.g., sandalwood) have been pressed to the brink of extinction.

As tropical timber was too heavy and cumbersome to haul long distances, industry tended to establish itself close to the sources, as in the case of teak and shipbuilding. With timber clearly of strategic importance in commercial and military terms, extensive forest clearing for agriculture, construction materials, and fuel in the early 1800s prompted fears of a timber famine and the introduction of "scientific" forest management into first India and later Southeast Asia by midcentury. Well into the twentieth century, however, the so-called "minor," or nontimber, forest products remained a primary source of revenues, and in volume terms nearly 60 percent of total wood removals in Asia ended as fuel.

Development of the Modern Forest Industry

With most countries in Southeast Asia achieving independence soon after World War II, government focus shifted to reconstruction and economic development. Nations looked to their forest reserves to play an important role in providing the resources, both physical and fiscal, for nation building. At the middle of the twentieth century, the area of productive forest in Asia was about 0.3 hectares per person, approximately the same as Europe. Only about half of this area was accessible. Southeast Asia was generally considered well forested, with Indonesia alone harboring three to four times the forest area of any its neighbors. With extraction costs high, the primary market for tropical wood products was seen to be the richer, industrialized nations.

Technological advances in logging equipment soon brought previously inaccessible forests into production. Led initially by multinational firms, logging contractors advanced through the Philippines, Malaya, Borneo, and Sumatra in the 1960s. Technical and financial aid from bilateral and multilateral development assistance agencies promoted forest-industry development. Enticing foreign investors with low royalty fees, tax holidays, export credits, and tariffs on competing imports, governments promoted the establishment of manufacturing facilities to process rather than export logs. Manufacturers formed industry associations to improve bargaining power in international trade and nations cooperated under the auspices of the Association of Southeast Asian Nations (ASEAN) to develop and share information on economics, silviculture, and other management issues. In 1986 the International Tropical Timber Organization (ITTO) was established to provide a framework for consultation and cooperation between producer and consumer countries on production, trade, and conservation of tropical timber worldwide.

The success of these efforts is seen clearly in the statistics. In 1950 little more than 30 percent of the 93.6 million cubic meters of total wood production in Asia was saw logs, veneer logs, or squared timber. According to the Food and Agriculture Organization's *Yearbook of Forest Products, 1993–1997*, in 1997 Southeast Asia accounted for nearly 41 percent of the 960 million cubic meters of industrial roundwood produced in Asia. A variety of finished products, including furniture, doors, molding, and parquet as well as lumber are produced from tropical hardwoods. Increasingly, industrial roundwood is being processed domestically with greater emphasis on fiber processing, especially for panel products such as particle board. The comparatively higher growth in processed goods indicates significant gains in utilizing raw materials and processing them efficiency. In 1994 Southeast Asia was the Asian leader in the export of sawed wood and wood-based panels. Indonesia remains the clear leader in absolute volume of roundwood produced, with 1997 output of 201.6 million cubic meters at approximately seventy times 1950 levels and more than four times that of any of its neighbors, according to the *Yearbook of*

Forest Products, 1993–1997. The financial crisis beginning in late 1997 severely affected tropical timber trade. Although the weakened Southeast Asian currencies made Southeast Asian timber more competitive, the industry suffered sharp declines in prices—some as much as 50 percent—for logs, sawed wood, and plywood. Global trade in wood pulp fell as well in 1998, reflecting the sharp drop in demand from East and Southeast Asia as well as global oversupply.

The Negative Impact of Industrial Development

The development of Southeast Asia's forest industry has not been an unqualified success. There have been both environmental and social consequences. Low stumpage fees have led to wasteful use of timber, and badly designed timber contracts have undermined sound forest management. Degradation of residual forests has resulted from unregulated harvesting and deliberate fires, as well as from the normal insect, pest, and disease problems. Subsidized factory installation has resulted in excess capacity and poor profitability for some products and inadequate investment in research has handicapped forestry vis-à-vis competing enterprises including plantation crops such as oil palm. Poor coordination of the broad spectrum of government policies has led to conflicts among the various sectors of the forest-products industry, and loss of forest land to often less productive uses. Logging bans instituted to protect forest often shift the burden of demand to neighboring countries where unstable political conditions or economic needs are conducive to overcutting. For example, Thailand's ban on logging teak resulted in increased cutting of teak in Cambodia, Laos, and Myanmar. At home these laws may actually accelerate forest destruction, because they have the effect of devaluing it (since it can no longer be regarded as a source of income).

From a socioeconomic perspective forest industry development in most instances has failed to produce the desired multiplier effects. Rather than training local people, contractors have brought in guest workers to operate the new technology, thus reducing benefits to local communities. Forests traditionally used by local communities to provide a myriad of useful and commercial products were assigned to logging companies who so badly mangled these areas that they became virtually useless and the target for illegal wood cutting and land clearing. Ignoring local community needs has resulted in social conflict detrimental to all. Swidden (slash-and-burn) agriculture, long decried as a threat to forests, reflects the failure of government development policies to deal effectively with a growing rural population. Reorientation of forest administrations to incorporate local community interests in forest planning and management, a process begun in the 1980s, still has far to go.

A boat pulls logs on the Chao Phraya River to Bangkok, Thailand, in 1996. (JAMES MARSHALL/CORBIS)

Prospects for the Future

Southeast Asia contains approximately 8.4 percent of the world's population. Rapid rates of economic growth, rising incomes, and rising expectations throughout Asia will mean continued strong demand for forest products. China's imports of tropical logs between 1996 and 1998 grew nearly as much as Japan's imports fell between 1997 and 1998. Although tropical-hardwood log and sawed-wood production fell worldwide in 2000, veneer and plywood production increased, led by Malaysia and Indonesia respectively. Malaysia supplied nearly half of the world's tropical log exports for 2000. The gap between recorded exports and imports in 2000 amounted to 3.6 million cubic meters, three times the level in the previous year, reflecting the rising rate of illegal logging in Southeast Asia, especially Indonesia. Thailand contributed significantly to the increase in sawed-wood exports in 2000, while Indonesia and Malaysia together provided more than 90 percent of the tropical plywood exports. Exports of finished or secondary processed wood products rebounded in 1999, led by exports from Indonesia, Malaysia, and Thailand. Although Japan retains first position as tropical plywood importer, China, now the leading importer of tropical logs, sawed wood, and veneer, the majority of which come from Southeast Asia, is likely to remain the strongest influence on the Southeast Asian forest products market for the foreseeable future (ITTO 2000, Table 2, pp. 115–118).

Southeast Asia contains 65 percent of Asia's remaining tropical forest and is one of richest areas of biological diversity in the world: Indonesia alone is estimated to have a greater variety of animal life than all of Africa. Over the past two decades concern over the fate of tropical forest has transformed it into a global resource. As forests in Southeast Asia are being lost at an estimated rate of 1.5 percent of forest area annually—and more than that in some areas—the services or nontangible benefits derived from forests, such as watershed protection, recreation, preservation of cultural heritage and biological diversity, habitat protection, and climate mitigation (carbon sequestration) are becoming of increasing interest and are expected to play a more important role in shaping future development of the forest industry.

The wave of new wood supplies—largely from plantations in New Zealand, Australia, and Chile—projected to enter Asia-Pacific markets by 2005, possibly meeting 10 to 15 percent of regional demand, will undoubtedly affect the world supply-demand balance. By some estimates this resource could meet some 70 percent of the world's present needs for industrial wood. The implications for industry are significant. The present market for timber and pulpwood-based products is already fiercely competitive; if estimates are correct, from about 2005 onward the tropical timber industry will face an oversupplied and even more intensively competitive market. We may well see production shift to specialty and decorative timbers and nontimber forest products.

With large-diameter logs of the old-growth, natural forests being replaced by smaller materials and plantation output, we are seeing a fundamental change that should affect all levels of the industry. Consumer demands for "certified" wood produced in a sustainable, environmentally friendly system will push up production costs and prices. Greater materials recovery, utilization of more species, and genetically improved stock should mean enhanced productivity per unit area of managed forest.

With the devolution of forest administration to local authorities in many countries in the region, there will be a trend toward community forest management, in which case we may find an increasing number of small-scale sawmills harvesting and preprocessing logs, such as are now seen in Indonesia.

Policy makers struggle with pleas for favoritism from this historically protected sector. Although a significant foreign-exchange earner for many countries (and source of political support for many in this region), the industry is often laced with corruption and is a poor environmental citizen. Issues that governments must deal with include devolution of authority; decentralization and participatory management; recognition of historical claims, traditional-use rights, and indigenous knowledge in the context of changing national priorities; and increasing competition in the global marketplace; as well as an increasing list of international commitments, economic and environmental. The demand for wood products, whose beauty and mechanical and structural qualities are broadly appreciated worldwide, will undoubtedly endure. For the forestry industry the essential challenge remains how to balance the demand for raw materials with the need to preserve and conserve forest areas.

Deanna G. Donovan

See also: **Cambodia—Economic System; Deforestation; Indonesia—Economic System; Laos—Economic System; Malaysia—Economic System; Myanmar—Economic System; Thailand—Economic System; Vietnam—Economic System**

Further Reading

Dauvergne, Peter. (1997) *Shadows in the Forest: Japan and the Politics of Timber in Southeast Asia.* Cambridge, MA: MIT Press.

Dawkins, H. Colyear, and Michael S. Philip. (1998) *Tropical Moist Silviculture and Management: A History of Success and Failure.* Wallingford, U.K.: CAB International.

Food and Agriculture Organization of the United Nations (FAO). (1951) *Yearbook of Forest Products Statistics.* Rome: FAO.

———. (1998) *Asia-Pacific Forestry towards 2010.* RAPA Publication 1998/22. Bangkok, Thailand: FAO Regional Office for Asia and the Pacific.

———. (1999a) *Commodity Market Review, 1998–1999.* Rome: FAO.

———. (1999b) *State of the World's Forests.* Rome: FAO.

———. (1999c) *Yearbook of Forest Products, 1993–1997.* FAO Forest Series no. 32. Rome: FAO.

Gray, Denis, et al. (1991) *National Parks of Thailand.* Bangkok, Thailand: Industrial Finance Corporation of Thailand.

International Tropical Timber Organization (ITTO). (1999) *Annual Review and Assessment of the Timber Situation, 1998.* Yokohama, Japan: Division of Economic Information and Marketing Intelligence, ITTO.

Leslie, Alf. (2000) *For Whom the Bell Tolls: What Is the Future of the Tropical Timber Trade in the Face of a Probable Glut of Plantation Timber?* Yokohama, Japan: International Tropical Timber Organization.

Repetto, Robert, and Malcolm Gillis, eds. (1988) *Public Policies and the Misuse of Forest Resources.* Cambridge, U.K.: Cambridge University Press.

Stewart-Cox, Brenda. (1995) *Wild Thailand.* London: New Holland, 1995.

FORSTER, E. M. (1879–1970), British novelist and essayist. A prolific British writer of the twentieth century, Edward Morgan Forster was born in London on New Year's Eve in 1879 to Morgan and Alice Forster. His father died when Forster was near two years old, and his mother raised him. Educated at Tonbridge School and Kings College, Forster had been to Italy, Greece, Germany, the United States, Egypt, and India. He began his literary career with short stories, which he published in *Independent Review*, a literary journal that Forster along with Lowes Dickinson (1862–1932) started in 1903. Forster wrote his first novel, *Where Angels Fear to Tread*, in 1905 and the autobiographical work *The Longest Journey* two years afterwards. *A Room with A View* (1908), *Howards End* (1910), and *A Passage to India* (1924) brought him literary fame. *Maurice*, dealing with homosexuality, was published posthumously in 1971.

Forster's most famous novel, *A Passage to India*, was viewed as an indictment of British colonial rule in India and played an important part in molding Western perceptions of Britain's presence there. Published in 1924, *A Passage to India* is a discourse on the British Raj with a liberal-humanist touch, portraying cross-cultural friendship. Forster has been accused by some critics for succumbing to "Orientalism," the term generally associated with the study of non-Western culture by scholars from the West and their motivations. Although Forster writes about the failure of British rule in India, he also shares certain myths concerning Indian culture and people, which were hallmarks of the "Orientalists" of the nineteenth century.

Patit Paban Mishra

Further Reading

Furbank, P. N. (1978) *E. M. Forster: A Life.* New York: Harcourt Brace Jovanovich.

Tambling, Jeremy, ed. (1995) *E. M. Forster.* London: Macmillan.

FOUR BOOKS Zhu Xi (1130–1200 CE), the great synthesizer of neo-Confucianism, was an innovator in standardizing educational methods by compiling what came to be known as the Four Books. Before Zhu Xi, Confucian education focused on the Five Classics, that is, the books of *History*, *Poetry*, *Changes*, *Rites*, and the *Spring and Autumn Annals*, supplemented by the *Analects*, *Mencius*, *Xunzi*, Dong Zhongshu's (179–104 BCE) *Chunqiu fanlu*, and such other texts as the *Classic on Filial Piety* and *Ceremonies and Rites (Yili)*. Zhu Xi streamlined the educational process with the Four Books, namely, the *Analects*, *Mencius*, *Great Learning (Daxue)*, and *Centrality and Commonality* (*Zhongyong*, often rendered as the *Doctrine of the Mean)*. The latter two were extracted from the book of *Rites*.

Zhu Xi wrote special commentaries on these four books, reinterpreting their contents in the light of his syncretic approach, and used them as the basis of his moral, social, and political philosophy. His innovation had a lasting impact on Confucian education and Chinese bureaucracy, in that the Four Books were used as the basis of the civil-service examinations from 1313 to 1905. By emphasizing the Four Books, Zhu Xi removed many Buddhist and Taoist tendencies from neo-Confucianism. It is not an overstatement to claim that the Four Books influenced Chinese culture more than any other classics during the last six hundred years of the dynastic period.

The *Analects* contains the teachings of Confucius, which advocate moral self-cultivation and rulership based on virtue. The *Mencius* describes the teachings of Mencius, which expand Confucius's ideas, emphasizing the inner quality of the virtues and advocating humanitarian rulership. The *Great Learning* explicates the chain reaction that begins with the "investigation of things," initiating a process of moral cultivation that regulates the family and brings order to the state and ultimately peace on earth. *Centrality and Commonality* is usually mistakenly translated as the *Doctrine of the Mean*, which wrongly implies that it is similar to Aristotle's Golden Mean or the Buddha's Middle Way. Whereas Aristotle sought a balance between extremes and the Buddha proposed a way to extinguish extremes, the Confucian concept of "centrality" is defined as the natural condition "before the feelings of pleasure, anger, sorrow, and joy come forth."

James D. Sellmann

Further Reading

Ames, Roger T., and Henry Rosemont, Jr., trans. (1998) *The Analects of Confucius: A Philosophical Translation.* New York: Ballantine Books.

Fung Yu-lan. (1952) *History of Chinese Philosophy.* 2 vols. Trans. by Derk Bodde. Princeton, NJ: Princeton University Press.

Graham, Angus C. (1989) *Disputers of the Tao.* La Salle, IL: Open Court.

Hsiao Kung-chuan. (1979) *A History of Chinese Political Thought.* Trans. by F. Mote. Princeton, NJ: Princeton University Press.

Jensen, Lionel M. (1997) *Manufacturing Confucianism: Chinese Traditions and Universal Civilization.* Durham, NC: Duke University Press.

Lau, D. C., trans. (1979) *The Analects (Lun Yu).* Middlesex, U.K.: Penguin Books.

———. (1970) *Mencius.* Middlesex, U.K.: Penguin Books.

Legge, James. (1960) *The Chinese Classics.* 5 vols. Hong Kong: Hong Kong University Press.

Munro, Donald J. (1969) *Concept of Man in Early China.* Stanford, CA: Stanford University Press.

Sung, Joseph H. C. (1976) *The Extensive Learning and the Practice of Impartiality and Harmony in Life.* Taipei, Taiwan: Commercial Press.

Tu, Wei-ming. (1989) *Centrality and Commonality: An Essay on Confucian Religiousness.* Albany, NY: State University of New York Press.

FRANCO–VIET MINH WAR

The Franco–Viet Minh War (1946–1954) began following skirmishes between French and Viet Minh (Vietnamese Liberation League) troops in Haiphong and Hanoi. The war lasted eight years and marked the end of French colonial rule in Indochina (Vietnam, Cambodia, and Laos).

Background

Although the war began in 1946, the conflict between France and Vietnam can be traced back to 1885, when France colonized Vietnam and divided it into three separate administrative areas: Cochin China, Annam, and Tonkin. Vietnamese resistance to French colonial rule was immediate and constant. In 1930 the Vietnamese independence movement reached a decisive turn, when Ho Chi Minh (1890–1969) helped create the Vietnamese Communist Party. The party later changed its name to the Indochinese Communist Party in order to include Laos and Cambodia. The party provided an organizational framework for obtaining independence from France. In 1941, at the suggestion of Ho Chi Minh, the Viet Minh was formed. This was a Communist-led and -dominated alliance of various nationalist groups, Communists and non-Communists alike. Viet Minh strategy called for a struggle for independence on both military and nonmilitary fronts. In 1944 the Viet Minh created its first armed units while also sending some of its members into the Vietnamese countryside to politically "educate" the general population. Most of the Viet Minh's activities were restricted to Vietnam's northern and central areas (Tonkin and Annam), but Viet Minh units also operated in the southern area (Cochin China). By 1945 the Viet Minh had made significant headway in securing the northern part of Vietnam, and it prepared itself to fill the power vacuum that would follow the end of World War II. Following Japan's unconditional surrender in August 1945, Ho Chi Minh and the Viet Minh mounted a general insurrection (the August Revolution), and on 28 August 1945 Viet Minh general Vo Nguyen Giap and his troops marched into Hanoi. By 2 September Ho Chi Minh had formed his administration and proclaimed the Democratic Republic of Vietnam.

In Paris, one of the postwar aims of the French government was to reestablish a measure of colonial rule in Indochina. The first obstacle was to remove the defeated Japanese troops from Vietnam. An agreement between France and her allies in July 1945 at the Potsdam Conference called on China's nationalist army to supervise the departure of Japanese troops in Tonkin and Annam. In Cochin China, this task was given to British troops. Although Britain's military had been ordered not to allow France to reclaim sovereignty in Vietnam, French troops previously arrested by the Japanese were armed and used to police the area. By October 1945 more French troops poured into Cochin China from France, commanded by General Jacques LeClerc. On 8 February 1946 French troops arrived in Tonkin. On 25 March 1946 French admiral Georges Thierry D'Argenlieu established an autonomous French-ruled republic in Cochin China.

There were numerous French and Viet Minh attempts to negotiate a political settlement. Viet Minh and French representatives met in Dalat, Vietnam, in April and May 1946, but negotiations failed. The two parties were unable to agree to a definition of Vietnamese independence. In addition, no resolution was reached to the problem posed by France's creation of a separate republic in Cochin China. Negotiations failed also at the Fontainebleau Conference of July and August 1946. As in Dalat, an obstacle at Fontainebleau was the question of Vietnamese integrity, of reuniting Tonkin, Annam, and Cochin China into one nation.

The Conflict Heats Up

By the fall of 1946, the autonomous republic established by France in Cochin China had failed. Viet Minh guerrillas had made their way into Cochin China, and the French high command in Vietnam now decided it needed to retake Tonkin and defeat the Viet Minh in order to maintain the colony. On 23 November the French navy bombed the port of Haiphong, killing thousands of Vietnamese. French troops were able to retake the northern port city of

VICTORY AT DIEN BIEN PHU

In the excerpt below, General Vo Nguyen Giap describes the Vietnamese effort that led to victory at Dien Bien Phu in 1954.

> Truck convoys valiantly crossed streams, mountains and forests; drivers spent scores of sleepless nights in defiance of difficulties and dangers, to bring food and ammunition to the front. . . .
>
> Thousands of bicycles from the towns also carried food and munitions to the front. Hundreds of sampans of all sizes, hundreds of thousands of bamboo rafts crossed rapids and cascades to supply the front.
>
> Convoys of pack-horses from the Meo highlands or the provinces headed for the front. Day and night, hundreds and thousands of porters and young volunteers crossed passes and forded rivers in spite of enemy planes and delayed-action bombs.
>
> Near the firing line supply operations had to be carried out uninterruptedly and in the shortest possible time. Cooking, medical work, transport, etc., was carried out right in the trenches, under enemy bombing and cross-fire.
>
> Such was the situation at Dien Bien Phu. . . . Never had so many young Vietnamese travelled so far and become acquainted with so many distant regions of the country. From the plains to the mountains, on roads and jungle trails, on rivers and streams—everywhere there was the same animation.

Source: General Vo Nguyen Giap. (1962) *People's War—People's Army*. New York: Praeger: 183–184.

Haiphong and then the northern city of Lang Son. On 19 December Viet Minh troops mounted an attack in Hanoi, killing thousands of French residents there, and officially declared war on France.

The Viet Minh strategy of political mobilization had been effective. In March of 1945 there were approximately 1,000 Viet Minh armed soldiers, but they numbered an estimated 50,000 by the end of 1945, and 100,000 by the end of 1946. In addition to its regular army, the Viet Minh could count on guerrilla and regional and local self-defense forces throughout Tonkin, Annam, and parts of Cochin China. As for the French high command, in 1946 it could count on approximately 67,000 soldiers. Although French forces were able to retake Hanoi shortly after the 19 December Viet Minh insurrection, General Giap and his troops retreated to the northern countryside (the Viet Bac) and enjoyed the support of an estimated 800,000 members of the general Vietnamese population. In the hills of the Viet Bac, the Viet Minh leadership prepared for a prolonged war against France.

China's Role

The war took a decisive turn in 1949 after Mao Zedong's Communist forces won China's protracted civil war. From this point, what had been primarily a colonial war now also became an international Cold War conflict. Once in power, Mao's government soon officially recognized the Democratic Republic of Vietnam. The Soviet Union and the Eastern Bloc countries quickly followed suit. On 1 April 1950 a Sino–Viet Minh aid agreement was reached, and Chinese military matériel and advisers poured into the Viet Bac. Mao's military also contributed by training Viet Minh soldiers in China. Meanwhile, France received substantial financial aid from the United States.

It is estimated that by 1952, 40 percent of France's war effort in Vietnam was funded by the United States.

Chinese aid allowed the Viet Minh to change tactics, and the Viet Minh was able, for the first time, to engage in a direct attack, successfully overrunning a French military post at Pho Lu. In addition, Ho Chi Minh increased the size of the Viet Minh by declaring in May 1950 that all Vietnamese males in Tonkin and Annam between the ages of sixteen and fifty would be conscripted.

In early 1953 General Henri Navarre became commander of French forces in Indochina. Navarre's strategy was first to attack Viet Minh strongholds along the Red River delta in Tonkin. Rather than face French units head on, Giap's troops retreated to the hills. Viet Minh units focused instead on the northwest area of Tonkin and on the Lao border. Navarre decided that in order to counter this Viet Minh initiative, French troops needed to secure and hold a base in the area. He chose Dien Bien Phu, believing that the surrounding mountains made the area impenetrable. Navarre had underestimated the Viet Minh. By November 1953 French paratroopers controlled the garrison, but over the course of the winter, Giap's forces surrounded the area. The Viet Minh managed to position approximately fifty thousand soldiers around the French garrison, while hundreds of thousands of Vietnamese civilians helped by building roads and transporting food and equipment into the mountains.

Viet Minh forces, now known as the People's Army of Vietnam (PAVN), began their attack on Dien Bien Phu on 13 March 1954. They managed to damage the airfield, crippling French supply lines. Their siege of Dien Bien Phu lasted almost two months. French supplies ran out, and PAVN forces dug trenches in order to approach the French garrison. On 7 May 1954 the PAVN, in a horrendous battle, took Dien Bien Phu. An estimated 8,000 Viet Minh soldiers were killed. On the French side, an estimated 2,200 were killed. The fall of Dien Bien Phu was a serious setback for France and resulted in its permanent withdrawal from Indochina. The terms of withdrawal, the Geneva Accords, were drawn up between 8 May and 21 July 1954.

Micheline R. Lessard

Further Reading

Duiker, William J. (1981) *The Communist Road to Power in Vietnam.* Boulder, CO: Westview Press.

Hémery, Daniel. (1990) *Ho Chi Minh de l'Indochine au Vietnam.* Paris: Gallimard.

Kolko, Gabriel. (1985) *Anatomy of a War.* New York: New Press.

MacDonald, Peter. (1993) *Giap.* New York: Norton.

FRENCH EAST INDIA COMPANY Although originally established by a charter that King Henry IV granted in 1604, the French East India Company lacked funds and soon went out of business. In 1664, however, Jean-Baptiste Colbert (1619–1683), the finance minister of Louis XIV, infused new spirit into the company through state funding and the granting of trade monopolies. He also equipped the company with guns and soldiers, so that it could compete with the Dutch and British East India Companies for raw materials and markets in Asia and Africa. To encourage French merchants and aristocrats to support the company, Louis XIV himself started investing in it and gave it his royal patronage. In 1674, headed by François Martin, the company established its headquarters in South India at Pondicherry and set up subsidiary factories at Surat north of Mumbai (Bombay) and at Chandarnagar near Calcutta and the Hughli River. In 1722 the company brought the islands of Mauritius and Bourbon in the Indian Ocean under its military control.

The French East India Company gained further military and financial strength in 1742 under Joseph-François Dupleix (1697–1763), the French governor-general of Pondicherry. Dupleix easily captured Madras on the southeast Indian coast in 1746. When challenged by Anwar-ud-Din, the ruler of Carnatic in southern India, for the possession of Madras, Dupleix led 230 French soldiers supported by 700 Indian sepoys (soldiers) to victory over a 10,000-man Indian army and gained control of Carnatic.

With such easy conquests Dupleix came to believe that India was ripe for French imperialism, and he became a de facto ruler in the south of India. To secure the French East India Company's position against the British East India Company, Dupleix acted as a kingmaker by aiding pro-French and anti-British Indian rulers. He also interfered in the dynastic problems of contending Indian rulers. When in 1748 the old Nizam (ruler) of Hyderabad died, Dupleix placed his own nominee on the throne against the Nizam's wishes. In the ensuing war Dupleix's French forces defeated the army of Nizam's nominee, whom the British favored. In 1754, however, the British East India Company, under Robert Clive (1725–1774), defeated the French forces of Dupleix, and Dupleix was recalled to France.

Dupleix had gained an enormous knowledge of India. But his expensive warfare against Indian rulers, and the Seven Years' War (1756–1763) between

France and England, led to the company's bankruptcy and ultimately to its complete collapse during the French Revolution in 1789.

Abdul Karim Khan

Further Reading

Malleson, George Bruce. (1984). *History of the French in India: From the Founding of Pondicherry in 1674 to the Capture of That Place in 1761*. Delhi: Renaissance.

Subramanian, Lakshmi, ed. (1999) *French East India Company and the Trade of the Indian Ocean*. New Delhi: Munshiram Manoharlal.

FRETILIN Fretilin is an acronym derived from the Portuguese Frente Revolucionária do Timor Leste Independente (the Revolutionary Front for an Independent East Timor). It is the most important political movement in East Timor and enjoys strong support from the local population.

Fretilin was founded on 20 May 1974 in Dili, East Timor, in the wake of the revolutionary armed forces movement in Lisbon, which advocated that Portugal grant independence to its overseas possessions. Established by a seminary-trained elite of intellectuals and civil servants, Fretilin's program called for immediate participation of Timorese in government, an end to racial discrimination, and an offensive against corruption.

Together with the Timorese Democratic Union (UDT) it campaigned for independence from Portugal, but Fretilin's more radical stand attracted a growing number of politicized East Timorese. The radical rhetoric alarmed the leadership of neighboring Indonesia, which governed the western part of Timor. After fighting between Indonesian-sponsored groups and Fretilin ended in 1975 and negotiations failed, Fretilin declared a unilateral independence for East Timor on 28 November 1975.

Following a brutal invasion by Indonesia and East Timor's formal integration into Indonesia on 17 July 1976, Fretilin carried out a sporadic insurgency throughout the 1980s. In 1992 the commander of the Fretilin Armed Forces (Falintil), José "Xanana" Gusmão, was captured and imprisoned in Jakarta. Represented by an observer at the United Nations, which had refused to recognize the annexation of East Timor by Indonesia, Fretilin refrained from retribution against Indonesian troops during the U.N.-sponsored consultation on the future of East Timor in August 1999.

Frank Feulner

Further Reading

Dunn, James S. (1996) *Timor, a People Betrayed*. Sydney: ABC Books.

Taylor, John G. (1999) *East Timor: The Price of Freedom*. New York: Zed Books.

FU BAOSHI (1904–1965), Chinese painter. Fu Baoshi was one of the most influential figures in early-twentieth-century Chinese painting. Born into an impoverished family in Nanchang, Jiangxi, Fu studied art history and sculpture at the prestigious Tokyo Academy of Fine Arts from 1933–1935. Upon his return to China, Fu developed his own distinctive painting style, integrating his studies in Western, Japanese, and Chinese painting. Although most famous as a figure painter, Fu also excelled at landscape painting. He composed his landscapes out of free interweaving broken ink brushstrokes and light washes rather than traditional calligraphic lines. His works are remarkable for their poetic eloquence and mood, and they emphasize a personal response to nature, rather than the physical appearance of the landscape. Fu was also one of the first historians of Chinese painting. His famous works include "Such Is the Beauty of Our Mountains and Streams," the large officially commissioned wall painting in the Great Hall of the People in Beijing, jointly painted by Fu and Guan Shanyue in 1959.

Ying Chua

Further Reading

Fu Baoshi. (1988) *Paintings of Fu Baoshi/Fu Baoshi Huaji*. Jiangsu, China: Jiangsu Fine Arts Publishing Company.

Sullivan, Michael. (1996) *Art and Artists of Twentieth-Century China*. Berkeley and Los Angeles: University of California Press.

FUGU Fugu is a globefish or blowfish from the family *tetraodontidae*. When these fish swell up, they puff their bodies into a nearly square shape. They are cultivated in cages in the sea off the coast of Japan, where they are a delicacy in the Japanese diet, cited in early records of cuisine. Part of the attraction is that the fugu contains a deadly poison. Since the Meiji Period (1868–1912), prohibitions and restrictions limit its sale, and only licensed chefs can prepare this fish as it is necessary to remove the ovaries and liver wherein the poison resides. A lethal dose, one milligram, can fit on a pinhead, and one typical mature fugu contains thirty times that amount. The poison acts by blocking sodium channels in nerve tissues, paralyzing muscles and causing eventual respiratory arrest. No antidote exists, but fisherman lore says that burying the victim up to his or her head with sand will reverse the poison's course.

In spite of this hazard, connoisseurs enjoy fugu prepared as sashimi. It is a white fish, usually sliced in paper-thin translucent wafers and eaten in soups or arranged on a platter in the shape of a flying crane, the symbol of longevity. It is frequently served with *ponzu*, a mixture of citrus juice and soy sauce. Some daring (or foolhardy) gourmands like to include a tiny dot of the liver as they eat it, savoring the "high" of the numbness just short of dangerous ingestion—though no licensed chef would prepare it this way.

Winter is the best time to eat fugu, when its flavor is most delicate. The price is the highest between October and March. A fugu meal at a good restaurant will cost about $200. In Shimonoseki, known as "fugu city," 80 percent of Japan's fugu catch is sold and a fisherman can make up to $100,000 in an hour's auction. The sales rates of fugu, which decline in times of recession, are said to be an indicator of the economic climate.

Merry Isaacs White

Further Reading

Hosking, Richard. (1996) *A Dictionary of Japanese Food: Ingredients and Culture.* Rutland, VT: Charles E. Tuttle.

FUJI, MOUNT Mount Fuji rises on the border of the Shizuoka and Yamanashi prefectures in central Honshu, Japan, near the Pacific Coast. Identified as a conical stratovolcano, it is the highest peak in Japan at 3,776 meters above sea level. Mount Fuji has a complex history of growth. A group of overlapping volcanoes rather than a single structure, it is composed of Komitake, Ko-Fuji (Older Fuji Volcano), and Shin Fuji (Younger Fuji volcano). Shin Fuji experienced a period of lava flows from 11,000 BCE to 8,000 BCE that account for four-fifths of its current volume. The base of the volcano is about 125 kilometers in circumference with a diameter of roughly 40 to 50 kilometers. The summit is a circular crater about 500 meters across and about 250 meters deep below the highest point.

The volcano has erupted approximately sixteen times since 781 CE. An eruption from 16 December 1707 to 22 January 1708 contributed to the formation of a large, new crater on the east flank. This is known as Mount Hoei. The summit vent released steam between 1780 and 1820, and despite remaining dormant since then, the mountain is classified as an active volcano.

The temperature at the top of Mount Fuji averages –19.2°C in January and 5.9°C in August. At the foot the temperature averages 2.2°C in January and 23.8°C

Mount Fuji in November 1972. (CHARLES E. ROTKIN/CORBIS)

in August. Precipitation is important at the foot, where the annual rainfall reaches 2,000 millimeters. Flora and fauna are abundant. The more than 1,300 plant species include alpine varieties, and more than 130 bird species are native to the region. Many rivers flow through the area, including the Kisegawa, Ayusawagawa, Uruigawa, and Shibagawa. The eruptions of Mount Fuji have formed five small lakes at the mountain's northern foot. From east to west they are Lake Yamanaka, Lake Kawaguchi, Lake Sai, Lake Shoji, and Lake Motosu. The abundance of groundwater and streams around Mount Fuji has encouraged farming and has facilitated the establishment of paper and chemical industries.

A feature of Fuji-Hakone-Izu National Park, Mount Fuji is a popular tourist attraction and climbing site. Since early times the summit has been considered a sacred peak. In 1994 Mount Fuji was considered for registration as a World Natural Heritage site, and subsequent measures toward nature conservation have been significant issues in Japan.

Nathalie Cavasin

Further Reading

Association of Japanese Geographers, eds. (1980) *Geography of Japan*. Tokyo: Teikoku-Shoin.

Simkin, Tom, and Lee Siebert. (1994) *Volcanoes of the World: A Regional Directory, Gazetteer, and Chronology of Volcanism during the Last 10,000 Years*. Tuscon, AZ: Geoscience Press.

Suwa Akira. (2001) *Fujisan* (Mount Fuji). Tokyo: Mainichi Shimbun Sha.

FUJIAN (2002 est. pop. 36.2 million). Located on China's southeastern coast, Fujian Province covers an area of 121,400 square kilometers and is bordered by the Taiwan Strait to the east and the Wuyi Shan mountain range to the west. As of 1996, Fujian's capital, Fuzhou, had a population of 1.4 million. Xiamen is the second largest city of the province, with a population of 600,000.

Fujian has a long history and can trace its origins to the Warring States period (475–221 BCE), when it was a part of the kingdom of Yue. Yue was conquered by the kingdom of Chu, which was then conquered by China's first emperor, Qin Shi Huangdi, who annexed Fujian during his reign (221–210 BCE). Following the overthrow of the Tang dynasty (618–907 CE), a short-lived Yue kingdom was reestablished but lasted only a few years, until 946. Fujian was also the last stronghold of the Ming dynasty (1368–1644 CE) before its downfall and the emergence of the Qing dynasty (1644–1912 CE).

Owing to its proximity to the sea, Fujian has long been a center of shipbuilding and trade. During the Song and Ming dynasties, shipbuilding and trade were the primary sources of income in Fujian Province, as ships laden with silk, porcelain, and tea sailed for Japan and Korea as well as Southeast Asia and the Middle East and brought back spices and herbal medicines. Foreign traders have also long plied the waters off of Fujian. As far back as the eleventh century, Muslim traders settled in the southern Fujian city of Quanzhou to trade ivory and spices for silk and tea. The sixteenth century saw the arrival of Dutch and Portuguese traders, who exported porcelain, silk, and tea from China.

Today, Fujian has a broad and varied economic base, producing bananas, fish, fruits, pears, rice, rubber, seafood, sugar, and tea. Fujian's nearness to Taiwan has also made it the center of the growing cross-strait trade between China and Taiwan as the two sides seek closer economic ties. Fujian Province is also tied linguistically to Taiwan, because about half of all current Taiwanese hail from Fujian and speak a dialect native to southern Fujian.

Keith A. Leitich

Further Reading

Clark, Hugh R. (1991) *Community, Trade, and Networks: Southern Fujian Province from the Third to the Thirteenth Century*. New York: Cambridge University Press.

Hook, Brian, ed. (1996) *Fujian: Gateway to Taiwan*. New York: Oxford University Press.

Lyons, Thomas P. (1995) *The Economic Geography of Fujian: A Sourcebook*. Ithaca. NY: East Asia Program, Cornell University.

FUJIEDA SHIZUO (1908–1993), Japanese novelist. Fujieda Shizuo is the pseudonym of Katsumi Jiro. Born in Shizuoka Prefecture, Fujieda graduated from Chiba Medical College and became an ophthalmologist. He published his first short story at the age of thirty-nine in the magazine *Kindai Bungaku* (Modern Literature). He wrote principally in the genre of autobiographical fiction *(watakushi shosetsu)* favored by Shiga Naoya, whose writing he most admired. Major works include *Iperitto-gan* (Eyes of Mustard-Gas, 1949), based on his experience as a medical doctor; *Inu no chi* (Dog's Blood, 1956); *Kuki atama* (Head of Air, 1967), a detailed account of his wife's recovery from tuberculosis and his own musings on a bizarre medical experiment; *Kyoto Tsuda Sanzo* (Outlaw Tsuda Sanzo, 1961), a nonautobiographical work based on the attack on the Russian crown prince in 1891; and *Kanashii dake* (Only Sadness, 1979), a requiem for his deceased wife. Beset by senility and self-loathing, he continued writing spare and poignant novels, such as *Kyokai* (Empty Longing, 1983), until his death in 1993.

William Ridgeway

FUJISAWA TAKEO (1904–1989), Japanese novelist. Born in Osaka, Japan, Fujisawa Takeo began writing short stories as a high school student. He published in small *dojin zasshi* (literary coterie magazines) and soon won acclaim from established writers of the Shinkankaku-ha (Neo-Sensationalist School) such as Yokomitsu Riichi (1898–1947) and Kawabata Yasunari (1899–1972). He turned to writing proletarian fiction while a student at Tokyo University; *Kizudarake* (Song of the Bruised and Battered, 1930) is his best known work in that genre. He contributed to the left-wing magazines *Daigaku Saha* (University Left Wing) and *Senki* (Battle Flag, a major leftist literary journal) during the late 1920s.

After being institutionalized for tuberculosis treatment from 1930 to 1933, Fujisawa shifted his focus to popular fiction. His later fiction is characterized not by the autobiographical style favored by the naturalists but by a bright, cosmopolitan flair. As a town native, Fujisawa became the toast of the Osaka literary world. His novel of love and romance, *Shinsetsu* (Fresh Snow, 1941–1942), was made into a film in 1942. His autobiography, *Osaka Jijoden* (Osaka Autobiography), was published in 1974.

William Ridgeway

FUJITA TSUGUHARU (1886–1968), Western-style Japanese painter. A native of Tokyo, Fujita Tsuguharo was also named Fujita, Tsuguji, or Leonard Foujita. After graduation from Tokyo Bijutsu Gakko (now the Tokyo School of Fine Arts and Music) in 1910, Fujita went to France in 1913. He became associated with the École de Paris, developed his own style, and gained a considerable reputation in Parisian artistic circles through works such as *My Studio* (1921), and *Five Nudes* (1923). In 1931 he traveled in the Americas, before going to Japan in 1933. He became a member of the Association of Artists *(Nikakai)* and started to paint several murals such as *Early Events in Akita* (1933), and *The Festival of the Four Seasons in Akita* (1937). World War II brought him back to Japan, and he was appointed to the Imperial Art Academy. He painted war zones in China and Southeast Asia, and received the Asahi Culture Prize for *The Last Days of Singapore* (1942) and other paintings. He left Japan and went back to France, taking French nationality in 1955. He converted to Catholicism and was christened Leonard, which led him to design the stained glass windows and murals for the chapel of Notre-Dame-de-la-Paix built in Reims.

Nathalie Cavasin

Further Reading

Buisson, Sylvie, and Dominique Buisson. (1987) *La vie et l'oeuvre de Leonard-Tsuguharu Foujita.* (The Life and Work of Leonard-Tsuguharu Foujita). Paris: ACR.

Tanaka, Jo. (1969) *Fujita Tsuguharu (Fujita Tsuguharu).* Tokyo: Shincho sha.

FUKUCHI GEN'ICHIRO (1841–1906), journalist, politician, and playwright. Fukuchi, who was also known by the pen name Ochi Fukuch, was born in Nagasaki. The son of a doctor, he studied the Dutch language during his youth. When he was eighteen, he went to Edo (now Tokyo) to study English, and in the early 1860s he was a translator for the Tokugawa government and acted as interpreter on Bakufu missions to the United States. In the same year as the Meiji Restoration, 1868, he was jailed for the publication of an antigovernment newspaper, *Koko Shimbun.* In 1870 he joined the new government and accompanied Hirobumi Ito (1841–1909) and Tomomi Iwakura (1825–1883) on missions abroad (1871–1872). From 1874 to 1888 he worked as an editor of the *Tokyo Nichi Nichi* newspaper. Later, he held a short tenure in the Finance Ministry. After becoming a leading journalist in Japan, he founded and led the pro-government *Rikken Teiseito* (Constitutional Imperial Party) in 1881–1883. He started to write novels, historical works, and Kabuki plays, and from 1887, he helped to build the Kabuki Theater. In 1904 he was elected to the Diet (legislature).

Nathalie Cavasin

Further Reading

Fukuchi Gen'ichiro. (1989) *Bakumatsu seijika* (Politician at the End of the Edo Period). Tokyo: Heihonsha.

Huffman, James. (1980) *Politics of the Meiji Press: The Life of Fukuchi Gen'ichiro.* Honolulu, HI: University Press of Hawaii.

FUKUDA HIDEKO (1865–1927), pioneer of Japan's women's liberation and socialist movements. Born Kageyama Hideko in Okayama prefecture, Japan, Fukuda was first inspired to join the women's liberation and democratic rights movements by a speech made by the women's rights advocate Kishida Toshiko (1864–1901) in 1882. The following year, she took an active part on behalf of the Liberal Party in Okayama by founding a private night school for girls. She ran the school until it was ordered closed in 1884. In 1885, Fukuda was arrested in Tokyo for her involvement with a group of radicals advocating the Korean reformation movement. She was later released from prison under the amnesty of 1889.

Married to a radical socialist for eight years, Fukuda became more deeply involved with well-known socialist groups of the times. She then became a socialist herself, particularly concerned with raising the status of women. In 1907, Fukuda began publishing the feminist journal *Sekai fujin* (Women of the World), which introduced Japanese readers to the activities of the women's suffrage movement around the world. Though Fukuda labored under financial difficulties and political suppression throughout her life, she continued to educate women and to advocate women's political and economic independence. She also supported various social and political movements. In 1904, she wrote an autobiography titled *Warawa no hanseigai* (My Life Thus Far).

Kyoko Murakami

Further Reading

Fukuda Hideko. (1988) "People's Rights and National Rights." In *Reflections on the Way to the Gallows: Rebel Women in Prewar Japan*, edited and translated by Mikiso Hane. Berkeley and Los Angeles: University of California Press, 29–50.

Sievers, Sharon L. (1983) "Women in the Popular-Rights Movement." In *Flowers in Salt: The Beginnings of Feminist Consciousness in Modern Japan*. Stanford, CA: Stanford University Press, 26–53.

FUKUDA TAKEO (1905–1995), prime minister of Japan. Fukuda Takeo was born in Gumma Prefecture and graduated from Tokyo University. A career bureaucrat in the Ministry of Finance and a member of the House of Representatives from 1952 until his death in 1995, Fukuda held cabinet posts under various prime ministers; he served as minister of agriculture, of finance, and of foreign affairs. As foreign minister in the cabinet of Prime Minister Sato Eisaku (1901–1975), Fukuda handled negotiations with the United States during the conclusion and ratification of the 1971 agreement on the return of Okinawa. He successfully challenged Miki Takeo for presidency of the Liberal Democratic Party (LDP), resulting in his becoming president of the LPD and prime minister of Japan in 1976. Unable to stabilize the economy and faced with declining public trust in his leadership, he was forced to dissolve his cabinet in 1978 when party members were implicated in the Lockheed bribery scandal, in which government and business colluded to purchase aircraft in exchange for kickbacks.

William Ridgeway

FUKUI (2002 est. pop. 829,000). Fukui Prefecture is situated in the western region of Japan's Honshu Island. Occupying an area of 4,192 square kilometers, it is divided into a more populous northern district of mountain ranges intercut with river valleys and coastal plains and a narrow rocky strip extending southward along Wasaka Bay. Its main rivers are the Kuzuryugawa, Hinogawa, and Asuwagawa. Fukui is bordered by the Sea of Japan and by Ishikawa, Gifu, Shiga, and Kyoto prefectures.

The capital of the prefecture is Fukui City, which grew around a castle built in 1575 by Shibata Katsuie (1522?–1583), the future governor of Echizen Province (subsumed into Fukui Prefecture in 1881). Severely damaged by bombing during World War II and by a 1948 earthquake, the city has since been rebuilt. Traditionally a weaving center, it now produces synthetic fiber as well as foodstuffs and machinery. Among its attractions are the former site of Fukui Castle; the remains of the Asakura family fortress, Ichijodani; and Asuwayama Park. Other important cities of the prefecture are Takefu, Sabae, and Tsuruga, the last near the Hokuriku Tunnel, the second longest in Japan.

Fukui's many archaeological sites are evidence of early human settlement. Rice culture, commercial fishing, and textile mills are the main economic activities. Modern chemical and machinery industries operate alongside more traditional producers of lacquer ware and cutlery. Fukui also supplies the Kansai region, comprising the cities of Osaka, Kyoto, Kobe, and Nara, with nuclear power. Visitors are drawn to Fukui by the ancient Buddhist temple complex of Eiheji and by Hakusan National Park and other parks along the coast.

E. L. S. Weber

Further Reading

"Fukui Prefecture." (1993) *Japan: An Illustrated Encyclopedia*. Tokyo: Kodansha.

FUKUMOTO KAZUO (1894–1983), Japanese Marxist intellectual. The most influential ideologue of

Japanese Marxism in the 1930s, Kazuo Fukumoto introduced the question of subjectivity into Marxist thought with his postulate that the class struggle was a matter of self-transformation. He was born in Tottori Prefecture, graduated from Tokyo University in 1920, and taught at Matsue Higher School. In 1922, he went to study Marxism in Germany and France.

After returning to Japan in 1924, Fukumoto joined the Communist Party. With the support of his students, he criticized the theories of established Marxists such as Yamakawa Hitoshi (1880–1958) and Kawakami Hajime (1879–1946), and attempted to reorganize the Communist Party. In 1926 he became the head of the party's political section, but was forced to resign in 1927 due to increasing criticism from the Comintern and other Japanese Communists, who felt his ideas alienated the party from the masses, and that Fukumoto didn't understand the correct role of the party as distinct from the labor unions. This marked an end of Fukumoto's prominence. He was arrested in June 1928 and sentenced to ten years at hard labor but was imprisoned for fourteen.

After the Second World War, he joined the Communist Party again but was expelled in 1958 for disagreeing with other party members. In his sixties, Fukumoto turned to the study of economic history and Japanese culture, focusing on the Edo Period (1600–1868).

Nathalie Cavasin

Further Reading

Allinson, Gary D. (1999) *The Columbia Guide to Modern Japanese History.* New York: Columbia University Press.

Langer, Paul F. (1972) *Communism in Japan: A Case of Political Naturalization.* Stanford, CA: Hoover Institution Press.

Seki, Yukio. (1992) *Yamakawa izumu to fukumoto izumu* (Yamakawaism and Fukumotoism). Tokyo: Shin Nihon Shuppan Sha.

FUKUOKA (2002 est. pop. 5 million). Fukuoka Prefecture is situated in the north of Japan's island of Kyushu. Once a conduit for the transmission of culture from ancient China by way of Korea, it occupies an area of 4,963 square kilometers. Its main geographical features are the central Tsukushi Mountains, the river Chikugogawa surrounded by broad plains in the south, and the northwestern Fukuoka Plain. Fukuoka is bordered by Oita, Kumamoto, and Saga Prefectures, and by the Inland, Ariake, Genkai, and Hibiki Seas. The prefecture assumed its present name and borders in 1876; it subsumed the former provinces of Chikuzen, Chikugo, and Buzen.

The capital of the prefecture is Fukuoka city, situated on Hakata Bay. It is Kyushu Island's largest city as well as its cultural, commercial, and political center. Fukuoka city began as the seventh-century port of Hakata; close by was Dazaifu, the administrative center for all Kyushu. In the thirteenth century the Mongols tried to invade Japan along the Fukuoka coast. Hakata flourished through trade with Ming China (1368–1644). In 1601, a castle was erected in Hakata and named Fukuoka. The city of Fukuoka resulted from the merger of the new castle town and Hakata in 1889. Following destruction in World War II, Fukuoka was rebuilt on a grid plan.

Today its cultural institutions range from Kyushu University to numerous shrines and temples, notably the Shofuku Buddhist temple, founded in 1195 by Eisai (1141–1215), the monk who established the Rinzai sect of Zen Buddhism in Japan. Kyushu's oldest Shinto shrine, Sumiyoshi Jinja (1623), is also located in Fukuoka. Among the city's traditional crafts are silk weaving and dyeing and the manufacture of dolls. It is noted for one of the largest fish catches in Japan, and its modern industries include chemicals, textiles, electrical equipment, machinery, printing, and food processing. The other important cities of Fukuoka Prefecture are Kita, Kyushu, Kurume, and Omuta.

The prefecture's rich coal deposits fueled Japan's industrialization around the beginning of the twentieth century, although the coal output declined after World War II. Today the prefecture's larger industries include steel, glass, and ceramics. The agriculture of rice, vegetables, fruit, tea, and livestock remains productive. Visitors are drawn to scenic Inland Sea National Park and to the area's quasi-national parks, as well as to the Kofun tombs around the capital.

E. L. S. Weber

Further Reading

"Fukuoka Prefecture." (1993) *Japan: An Illustrated Encyclopedia.* Tokyo: Kodansha.

FUKUSHIMA (2002 est. pop. 2.1 million). Fukushima Prefecture is situated in the northern area of Japan's island of Honshu. A prime agricultural region and the transportation link between northeastern and southwestern Honshu, it occupies an area of 13,784 square kilometers. Its primary geographical features are the Abukuma, Ou, and Echigo mountain ranges that separate the coastal plains and central river basins. The main rivers are the Abukumagawa, Nippashigawa, and Tadamigawa. The region's highest peak is Hiuchigadake, rising 2,356 meters. The prefecture is bordered by the Pacific Ocean and by Yamagata, Miyagi, Ibaraki, Tochigi, Gumma, and Niigata Prefectures. Once part of Mutsu Province, Fukushima assumed its present name and borders in 1876.

The capital of the prefecture is Fukushima city. During the fifteenth century, it grew as a castle town and a post station town. Today it is home to Fukushima University and Iizaka Hot Spring. The prefecture's other important cities are Aizu Wakamatsu, Iwaki, Koriyama, and Sukagawa.

In the late nineteenth century the prefecture was a hotbed of popular resistance against the high taxes and conscript labor of the Meiji government. In the Fukushima Incident of 1882, some one thousand peasants assembled to demand the release of their leaders from jail. The leaders had opposed the public auction of the property of peasants unable to pay taxes, and the event came to symbolize commoners' resistance against unjust rulers.

Today, half of the prefecture's arable land is devoted to rice. Cucumbers, tomatoes, peaches, pears, and apples also are grown, as is tobacco. Nuclear energy powers such industries as the processing and production of chemicals, metal, machinery, and textiles. Visitors are drawn to Bandai-Asahi National Park and to the prefecture's many hot spring resorts.

E. L. S. Weber

Further Reading

"Fukushima Prefecture." (1993) *Japan: An Illustrated Encyclopedia*. Tokyo: Kodansha.

FUKUZAWA YUKICHI (1835–1901), Japanese intellectual. Of all the intellectuals associated with Japan's late-nineteenth-century transformation, none has earned more scholarly and popular attention than Fukuzawa Yukichi, a man whose name evokes the ideology of "civilization and enlightenment" that engulfed the country during the 1870s. Fukuzawa was born in the city of Osaka but raised in a samurai family of modest standing in the small domain of Nakatsu in Kyushu. Schooled in the Confucian classics, Fukuzawa, at age nineteen, ventured out in pursuit of "Western learning" first in Nagasaki, then Osaka, and finally Edo (Tokyo). The move to Edo in 1858 was precipitated by the request of the local domain officials that Fukuzawa open his own Dutch (soon to become English) academy. Over the next decade, this school, which eventually evolved into Japan's leading private institution for higher learning (Keio University), served as the institutional foothold for Fukuzawa's career as the nation's preeminent pedagogue of Anglo-American culture and thought. Fukuzawa's credentials were further enhanced when he joined missions to the United States and Europe during the 1860s that were sponsored by the Tokugawa *bakufu* (shogunate). From 1866, when he published the first volume of his famous *Conditions in the West*, until his death in 1901, Fukuzawa's writings on education, economics, government, and social etiquette circulated more widely than those of any other contemporary writer. Fukuzawa Yukichi's legacy, however, remains a subject of controversy. Fukuzawa was a man of striking ambivalence: an egalitarian liberal and iconoclast in some respects, but also a conservative bureaucrat with distinctly aristocratic pretensions. Among scholars of "Western learning," he stood at the progressive forefront in his call for individual freedom and independence, the universal pursuit of utilitarian learning, and the equality, at least in regard to property rights, of wives and husbands within the family. Still, for all of his celebrated disdain for "feudal" privilege and custom, Fukuzawa was himself a *bakufu* employee between 1860 and 1867 and, for the most part, remained an enduring defender of the old regime during its Restoration struggles between 1858 and 1868. Nevertheless, within the context of his times, Fukuzawa stands out as an innovative educator who helped to navigate the nation through its historical transition from the Tokugawa period (1600/1603–1868) to the Meiji period (1868–1912).

Donald Roden

Further Reading

Blacker, Carmen. (1964) *The Japanese Enlightenment: A Study of the Writings of Fukuzawa Yukichi*. Cambridge, U.K.: Cambridge University Press.

Craig, Albert. (1968) "Fukuzawa Yukichi: The Philosophical Foundations of Meiji Nationalism." In *Political Development in Modern Japan*, edited by Robert E. Ward. Princeton, NJ: Princeton University Press.

Hane, Mikiso. (1984) "Fukuzawa Yukichi and Women's Rights." In *Japan in Transition*, edited by Hilary Conroy. Rutherford, NJ: Fairleigh Dickinson University Press.

Kinmonth, Earl. (1978) "Fukuzawa Yukichi Reconsidered: *Gakumon no susume* (The Encouragement of Learning and Its Audience)." *Journal of Asian Studies* 37,4 (August): 677–696.

Kiyooka Eiichi, trans. (1969) *The Autobiography of Fukuzawa Yukichi*. New York: Columbia University Press.

Pyle, Kenneth. (1989) "Meiji Conservatism." In *The Cambridge History of Japan*. Vol. 5. Cambridge, UK: Cambridge University Press.

FUNAKOSHI GICHIN (1868–1957), father of modern karate. Funakoshi Gichin was born in Shuri, Okinawa, Japan, to a *Shizoku* (gentry) family. He was raised by his grandfather, a Confucian tutor to the Okinawan royal family. Funakoshi also became an educator, but is more popularly known as a master of Okinawan martial arts. He studied with a number of legendary Okinawan teachers such as Matsumura Sokon (1809–1901) and Kanryo Higaonna (1853–1917), but his closest teachers were Azato Yasutsune (1828–1906) and Itosu Yasutsune (1831–1916).

Funakoshi is considered today to be the father of modern karate. He was not the first proponent of the Okinawan martial arts to teach in mainland Japan, but he is remembered as the Okinawan master who popularized karate in Japan. Between 1917 and 1921, he was involved in a number of martial arts demonstrations, including one for Crown Prince Hirohito. In 1922, Funakoshi was selected by his teachers and peers to attend the Ministry of Education's National Athletic Exhibition in Tokyo, where he demonstrated various self-defense techniques and lectured about the health benefits of the Okinawan martial arts. At the request of a number of important Japanese officials, Funakoshi agreed to remain in Tokyo and teach his art.

Before these demonstrations most people in Japan had never heard of Okinawan martial arts. Within a few short years, however, Funakoshi had organized martial arts clubs at all of Tokyo's most prestigious universities and authored a number of books on the martial arts of Okinawa. It was around this time that Funakoshi popularized the name *karatedo* (empty hand way) to describe the practice he was teaching. Before this, the martial arts of Okinawa were usually referred to as "Chinese hand" or "Okinawan hand." By 1936, with the help of his third son Gigo (1907–1945), Funakoshi was able to open a private dojo (training hall), which his students named the Shotokan in honor of the Master's pen name Shoto (pine waves).

The interwar years were a dark time for Funakoshi. Not only did he suffer from dire poverty and hunger, as did most of Japan, but he also lost his wife, his son Gigo, and the Shotokan. In 1949, during the U.S. occupation of Japan, Funakoshi's students helped him to pick up the pieces and formed the Japan Karate Association with Funakoshi as its chief advisor. From this point, he began to teach once again, and karate began to gain popularity around the world.

Funakoshi continued to teach and write until his death in 1957. He dedicated his life to promoting an understanding of what he referred to as "the true meaning of *karatedo*." He felt that karate was grossly misunderstood and misused by most practitioners. He often commented that the practice of karate is best used for combating sickness and old age rather than people and that the highest goal in karate is to diffuse a potentially dangerous situation before it escalates into violence.

Matthew F. Komelski

Further Reading

Draeger, Donn F. (1974) *Modern Bujutsu and Budo*. New York: Weatherhill.

Funakoshi Gichin. (1975) *Karatedo: My Way of Life*. Tokyo: Kodansha.

———. (1994) *Karatedo Nyumon*. Tokyo: Kodansha.

Stevens, John. (1995) *Three Budo Masters*. Tokyo: Kodansha.

FUNCINPEC A Cambodian political party, the National United Front for an Independent, Neutral, Peaceful, and Cooperative Cambodia is known by its French acronym, FUNCINPEC. The party traces its origins to the non-Khmer Rouge political faction associated with King (then Prince) Norodom Sihanouk (b. 1922), which fought for control of the country from a base near the Thai-Cambodian border against the incumbent People's Republic of Kampuchea during the 1980s.

The FUNCINPEC returned to mainstream politics in the aftermath of the 1991 Paris Peace Agreements, when it emerged as one of the dominant parties contesting the 1993 national elections. Capitalizing on its royalist heritage, it won the majority of seats at those elections, with the party's leader, Prince Norodom Ranariddh (b. 1944), a son of Sihanouk, assuming the title of first prime minister. Since the FUNCINPEC's political infrastructure was poorly formed at local levels, its power-sharing coalition with the Cambodian People's Party (CPP) soon became inequitably weighted in favor of the latter, former rulers of the People's Republic of Kampuchea, who controlled much of the country's security forces and administration, and were therefore particularly influential in much of the rural countryside.

In 1997 problems between the coalition partners reached the boiling point, with CPP leader Hun Sen (b. 1952) ousting Ranariddh. Many FUNCINPEC officials fled the country, leaving the party in shambles. Those officials slowly returned to the country in late

1997 and 1998, when the FUNCINPEC again contested the national elections. The party came in second to the CPP in the national vote and assumed the role of junior coalition partner. FUNCINPEC leader Prince Ranariddh became the president of the legislature, the National Assembly.

David M. Ayres

Further Reading

Brown, Macalister, and Joseph Zasloff. (1998) *Cambodia Confounds the Peacemakers, 1979–1998.* Ithaca, NY: Cornell University Press.

Corfield, Justin. (1991) *A History of the Cambodian Non-Communist Resistance, 1975–1983.* Clayton, Australia: Monash University Centre of Southeast Asian Studies.

FURUKAWA ICHIBEI (1832–1903), Japanese entrepreneur. Born in Kyoto, Furukawa was engaged in the silk trade business for the Ono Group, a merchant company based in Kyoto. In 1874, Ono went bankrupt and Furukawa started independently in the same activities. After raw silk exporting became unprofitable, he turned to mining ventures. He went to manage a mining company that was operated by the Soma family in the Tohoku region. In 1877, with a loan and the aid of the financier and entrepreneur Eiichi Shibusawa (1840–1931), Furukawa purchased the Ashio copper mine from the government. His innovations in Ashio produced commercial success. By 1885, Ashio's production reached 4,131 tons annually, which represented 39 percent of Japan's total copper output. Furukawa extended the purchase of mines by acquiring in 1885 the Great Innai and Ani silver mines. He possessed by 1900 eighteen metal mines and four coal mines. In 1897, Furukawa's operations passed to his adopted son, Junkichi. After the death of Furukawa Ichibei in 1903, the enterprise was reorganized, to take the form in 1905 of a *zaibatsu,* one of the pyramid-type business conglomerates that dominated the Japanese economy until their dissolution in 1945.

Nathalie Cavasin

Further Reading

Hirschmeier, Johannes. (1964) *The Origins of Entrepreneurship in Meiji Japan.* Cambridge, MA: Harvard University Press.

Nishimura Kazuo. (1997) *The Ashio Riot of 1907: A Social History of Mining in Japan.* Translated by Terry Boardman and Andrew Gordon. Durham, NC: Duke University Press.

Sunakawa Yukio. (2001) *Undonkon no otoko furukawa ichibei no shogai* (The Life of Ichibei Furukawa). Tokyo: Shobunsha.

FUTABATEI SHIMEI (1864–1909), Japanese novelist and translator. Futabatei Shimei (pseudonym of Hasegawa Tatsunosuke) was born in Edo (now Tokyo) to a samurai family. He is the author of Japan's first modern novel, *Ukigumo* (The Drifting Cloud, 1887–1889), which he began while still a student at Tokyo Gaikokugo Gakko (now Tokyo University of Foreign Studies). Futabatei's studies in Russian language and literature resulted in many fine translations, which he continued to produce until his death, including those of Turgenev, Tolstoy, Dostoevsky, Goncharov, and Chekov. He was able to achieve a literary style appropriate to the realistic fiction of contemporary Japan known as *gembun itchi* ("fusion of spoken and written language"). Futabatei also accomplished a psychological realism that his mentor, Tsubouchi Shoyo, had originally proposed in his *Shosetsu shinzui* (Essence of the Novel, 1885–1886) but could not himself realize. Futabatei had little trust in the public reception of his art and, unable to make a living from writing, took up a government post in 1889, withdrawing from literary circles but continuing to devote his time to writing. His ambivalence toward being a novelist is reflected in his choice of a pseudonym that sounds like the profanity *kutabatte shimae,* "go to hell." In the last years of his life, he again received critical attention for a novel on the common Japanese practice of adopting a son-in-law into a family that has no heir, *Sono omokage* (An Adopted Husband, 1906). The author's bitter attitude toward his literary milieu is summed up in his final novel *Heibon* (Mediocrity, 1907), a semiautobiographical study. Hired as a newspaper correspondent in Russia, he took ill soon after arrival and died on his return trip to Japan.

William Ridgeway

Further Reading

Lewell, John, ed. (1993) *Modern Japanese Novelists: A Biographical Dictionary.* Tokyo: Kodansha.

Ryan, Marleigh Grayer, trans. (1965) *Japan's First Modern Novel:* Ukigumo *of Futabatei Shimei.* New York: Columbia University Press.

GADJAH MADA UNIVERSITY In December 1949, Gadjah Mada University (Universitas Gadjah Mada, or UGM), in the city of Yogyakarta, located in the quasi-provincial area of Yogyakarta (Daerah Istimewah Yogyakarta, or DIY), became Indonesia's first national university. It superceded the Gadjah Mada Institute of Higher Learning, previously established on 3 March 1946 by, among others, Hamengku Buwono IX, Sultan of Yogyakarta, in the then capital of the newly proclaimed Republic of Indonesia.

To form the university, the Institute merged with the School of Engineering (founded by the Indonesian Department of Education), the staff and students of which were recruited from an engineering institution in Bandung, West Java. Also joining in the merger was the College of Political Science, a training center for bureaucratic and diplomatic staff run by the Department of the Interior. The new university was named after a fourteenth-century Javanese statesman.

The state-run UGM has eighteen faculties, including medicine, law, education, philosophy, engineering, animal husbandry, and forestry. It offers sixty-three undergraduate programs, sixteen diploma programs, and several nondegree programs. Its Graduate Studies Faculty comprises fifty-two programs. UGM has nineteen specialized research centers, five interuniversity centers and six community centers. With over 38,000 students and first-class academic and research facilities, UGM is one of Indonesia's largest universities.

Andi Faisal Bakti

Further Reading

"Gadjah Mada University." (2002) Retrieved 23 January 2002, from: http://www.gadjahmada.edu.

Sardjito. (1959) *The Development of Gadjah Mada University*. Yogyakarta, Indonesia: Gadjah Mada University.

GAFUROV, BOBOJAN GAFUROVICH (1908–1977), Tajik politician and scholar. Bobojan Gafurovich Gafurov led the Tajikistan Soviet Socialist Republic from 1946 until 1956 as the first secretary of the Communist Party. Born in Ispisar (a remote northern province of the republic) in 1908, he began his career as a journalist and lecturer before joining the Communist Party apparatus and climbing up to the highest political post in the republic under Josef Stalin (1879–1953), then Soviet leader. In 1956 he left the republic to become the director of the Institute of Oriental Studies of the Soviet Academy of Science in Moscow.

However, it was his works on the history of Central Asia, and particularly on the history of Tajikistan and Tajiks, that won him nationwide recognition in Tajikistan and a reputation as one of the founders of the Tajikistani oriental school and Tajikistani nationalism. In his publications, including two versions of *Tarikhi Mukhtasari Halki Tochik* (The History of Tajik People), he put forward the idea that the beginning of the Tajiks could be in ancient civilizations of Central Asia. This interpretation of history was widely used in the consolidation of the Tajik identity in the territory of modern Tajikistan.

Rafis Abazov

Further Reading

Abdullaev K., and Shahram Akbarzadeh. (2002) *The Historical Dictionary of Tajikistan*. Metuchen, NJ: Scarecrow Press.

Djalili, Mohammad-Reza, Frédéric Grare, and Shirin Akiner, eds. (1997) *Tajikistan: The Trials of Independence*. New York: St. Martin's Press.

Gafurov, B. G. (1947) *Tarikhi Mukhtasari Halki Tochik* (History of the Tajik People). Part 1. Stalinabad, U.S.S.R.: Gosudarstvennoe Izdatelstvo.

Gafurov, B. G., and B. A. Litvinskii. (1963–1965) *Istoriia tadzhikskogo naroda* (History of the Takik People). 3 volumes. Moscow: Izdatelstvo vostochnoi literatury.

Shashi Bhushan. (1977) *Academician Babajan Gafurov*. New Delhi: Progressive Peoples Sector Publications.

GAJAH MADA (d. 1364), Javanese military leader. The Hindu-Javanese kingdom of Majapahit, established in 1293 by the East Javanese king Vijaya (d. 1328), experienced its golden age in the fourteenth century CE, owing to the military prowess and political cunning of Gajah Mada. Born a commoner, Gajah Mada rose to fame when he was still an officer of the royal bodyguard. After he overcame an insurrection against Vijaya's son, King Jayanagara (reigned 1309–1328), he was elevated to the rank of minister. His loyalty, however, waned when Jayanagara laid claim to Gajah Mada's wife. After successfully plotting the death of the king, he ascended to the height of his power under the reign of Jayanagara's daughter Tribhuvana (reigned 1328–1350), who appointed him as prime minister after he quelled another rebellion. True to his oath that he would conquer the whole archipelago, he subjugated Bali in 1343 as well as other smaller kingdoms. These conquests are related in the *Nagarakertagama* (Sacred Book of the Prosperous State), a Javanese epic that was written in 1365 under his sponsorship by the poet Prapancha. Tribhuvana, who abdicated in 1350, was succeeded by her son Hayam Wuruk (reigned 1334–1389). During his reign, Gajah Mada extended Majapahit's influence even further, up to mainland Southeast Asia. Gajah Mada died in 1364 under mysterious circumstances.

Martin Ramstedt

Further Reading

Bernet Kempers, A. J. (1991) *Monumental Bali. Introduction to Balinese Archaeology and Guide to the Monuments*. Singapore: Periplus.

Coedès, Georges. (1964) *Les États Hindouisés d'Indochine et d'Indonésie*. Paris: E. de Boccard.

Pigeaud, Theodore G. (1963) *Java in the Fourteenth Century. A Study in Cultural History. The Nagara-Kertagama by Rakawi Prapanca of Majapahit, 1365 A.D.* 5 vols. The Hague, Netherlands: Martinus Nijhoff.

Vlekke, Bernard H. M. (1959) *Nusantara: A History of Indonesia*. The Hague, Netherlands, and Bandung, Indonesia: W. van Hoeve.

Zoetmulder, P. J. (1974) *Kalangwan. A Survey of Old Javanese Literature*. No. 16. Leiden, Netherlands: KITLV.

GAKUREKI SHAKAI *Gakureki* is the Japanese word for an individual's educational record or history, and *gakureki shakai* describes the characteristics of Japanese society that make such a record crucial to a student's future social status. With the rapid expansion of enrollment in senior high schools and universities between the early 1960s and the late 1970s, not only the level of education obtained but also the rank or status of a person's alma mater became a major factor in determining his or her initial labor-market position.

The Japanese education system is generally considered meritocratic and egalitarian because of the open competition of the entrance exams. However, empirical studies show a consistent link between parents' educational or social status and the level of schooling attained by their offspring. Nevertheless, the Japanese educational selection system is widely regarded as legitimate among students and parents despite the severe academic competition.

Three characteristics of Japanese culture and society may explain this enduring legitimacy. First, no overt link exists between middle-class values and the knowledge tested on entrance exams. Unlike many European nations, which emphasized elite forms of social capital in schools and in interviews for job entry, Japan has historically emphasized Japanese national culture. This continued in modern education. Second, most Japanese do not believe in innate differences in either intelligence or ability. Most people view success as the product of individual effort. This belief is reinforced by the fact that students who do not study hard risk failure in the intense competition for high school or university entrance, even if they are gifted with academic ability. Third, education in high schools and universities and the transition to the job market revolve around competition. Students are faced with the constant possibility of losing or winning, and the status of past winners in future competitions is ambiguous, promoting a cycle of status anxiety and increased aspirations.

In the mid-1980s, concerns about intense academic competition and an eruption of school problems, including bullying, violence, and students refusing to go to school, engendered support for a series of educational reforms focused on individual differences, freedom in education, and creativity. Multiple selection criteria for admission to high schools and universities, including interviews and evaluations of extracurricular activities, were introduced in the 1990s. However, these reforms were implemented without parallel changes in the job market, thereby increasing the popularity of *juku* (cram schools) and private schools that fuel competition. In addition, some argue that the introduction of the new criteria in the selection system creates inequality between students from different social classes, as disadvantaged students will have fewer opportunities to participate in extracurricular activities and may experience discrimination during interviews. *Gakureki shakai* will continue to flourish, even after a series of educational reforms to suppress competition, as long as no dramatic changes occur in the job market and in its legitimacy among participants.

Motoko Akiba

Further Reading

Kariya Takehiko. (1995) *Taishu kyoiku shakai no yukue* (The Future of the Mass-Education Society). Tokyo: Chuko Shinsho.

LeTendre, K. Gerald. (1996) "The Evolution of Research on Educational Attainment and Social Status in Japan." *Research in Sociology of Education and Socialization* 11: 203–232.

Takeuchi Yoh. (1995) *Nippon no Meritokurashi* (Japan's Meritocracy). Tokyo: Tokyo Daigaku Shuppankai.

GAMA, VASCO DA (c. 1460–1524), Portuguese explorer. Vasco da Gama discovered the sea route to India from Europe and established a Portuguese presence in India, which lasted until 1961. He was born in Simes, Portugal, around 1460. In 1497 King João II of Portugal sent him on a mission to India; da Gama was to find a route that would circumvent the Middle East, where travel and commerce were difficult for European traders. Da Gama sailed from Lisbon with four ships on 8 July and rounded the Cape of Good Hope in November, arriving in Calicut, in southwest India, on 20 May 1498.

The Zamorin of Calicut welcomed him, but because of Muslim opposition da Gama was unable to conclude a treaty. He returned to Lisbon in 1499 and was granted a triumphal homecoming; King Manuel I granted him the title of Dom (Sir) and named him Admiral of the Indian Ocean. He also received a large pension from the king.

In 1502, he was sent back to India to avenge the destruction of a factory the Portuguese had built in Calicut. He sank a ship sent against him, killing all on board; then bombarded the city. After concluding a treaty with the ruler of Cannanore, he returned to Portugal and retired to Évora. He was made Conde de Vidigueira in 1519. In 1524, he was appointed viceroy of India and arrived there in September 1524, only to die in December in Cochin. His discovery of the route around South Africa was commemorated by the poet Camões.

Henry Scholberg

Further Reading

Stanley, Henry E. J., ed. (1869) *The Three Voyages of Vasco da Gama by Gaspar Correa*. London: Hakluyt Society.

Subrahmanya, Sanjay. (1997) *The Career and Legend of Vasco da Gama*. Cambridge, U.K.: Cambridge University Press.

GAMBANG KROMONG *Gambang kromong* refers to a type of ensemble, based in and around Jakarta, that combines Indonesian and Chinese instruments and styles. Its name derives from two of the instruments played: the *gambang*, a xylophone, and the *kromong*, a set of kettle-gongs on a rack. These are combined with instruments originating from China: a two-stringed fiddle and a side-blown flute. The remaining instruments in the core ensemble are percussion (hanging gongs, drums, and a set of clashing metal plates). Male and female singers, who sing lyrics in the popular Malay form of pantun, round out the ensemble. Western instruments may also be added, including electric guitars, trumpets, clarinets, saxophones, and electronic keyboards.

The music is performed and patronized by two groups who live in and around Jakarta (in Bekasi, northern Bogor, and Tangerang): Peranakan, people of mixed Chinese and Pribumi (native Indonesian) ancestry; and Betawi, who are considered Pribumi. Ensembles accompany male-female dancing at Peranakan weddings and other family celebrations. In this context, female dancers are hired as partners for men. Ensembles also accompany a form of popular theater called *lenong*.

Ethnomusicologist Philip Yampolsky has identified two repertoires that are part of modern performance practice: *lagu lama*, older songs oriented toward Chinese musical features; and *lagu sayur*, newer songs that tend to be based in Malay musical idioms. *Lagu lama* melodies were probably brought from the Fujian province of southern China to the Dutch colonial city of Batavia, presumably in the seventeenth and early eighteenth centuries. At that time, *gambang kromong* groups played for private weddings and parties. During the latter part of the nineteenth century, as the music became part of a more public sphere, the instrumentation embraced Indonesian instruments, including drums, gongs, and *kromong*. The *lagu sayur* repertoire emerged at this time, and in the early twentieth century embraced popular songs in the region around Batavia. The music became even more hybrid in the 1920s and 1930s, as it blended with U.S. and European popular music and jazz. A genre called *gambang moderen* ("modern gambang [kromong]"), associated with the actor and popular music composer Benyamin S. (1939–1995), is an important marker of Betawi cultural identity in contemporary Indonesia.

Andrew Weintraub

Further Reading

Yampolsky, Philip. Recording notes to *Music from the Outskirts of Jakarta: Gambang Kromong Music of Indonesia, 3.* Smithsonian Folkways SF 40057.

GAMBUH

GAMBUH The classical Balinese dance drama *gambuh* probably originates from the last eastern Javanese Hindu kingdom of Majapahit. Majapahit fell to the coastal kingdom of Demak—then mostly Muslim—around 1520, but its dance drama tradition continued in Bali. *Gambuh* was traditionally performed on secular and ritual occasions in temples, palaces, or villages, and related the life in the ancient Hindu-Javanese courts—the ancestral home of the Balinese nobility. Nowadays, *gambuh* is predominantly staged during rituals, and is flourishing after almost vanishing between the 1930s and the 1980s. Plots draw on the old-Javanese mythical epic, *Malat*, narrating the adventures of Prince Panji and Princess Candra. The old-Javanese historical epic, *Rangga Lawe*, is another source. The knowledgeable audiences appreciate the refined performance, complicated choreography, and accomplished dancing and singing. *Gambuh* is considered the basis for all the other classical dance forms. The dancers-cum-singers are accompanied by a *gamelan gambuh* orchestra consisting of bamboo flutes, a bowed lute, drums, cymbals, bells, and gongs.

Performers getting ready for a *gambuh* dance performance at Besakih Temple in Bali in 1997. (CATHERINE KARNOW/CORBIS)

Martin Ramstedt

Further Reading

Bandem, I. Made, and Fredrik E. de Boer. (1995) *Balinese Dance in Transition: Kaja and Kelod.* Kuala Lumpur, Malaysia: Oxford University Press.

De Zoete, Beryl, and Walter Spies. (1973) *Dance and Drama in Bali.* Kuala Lumpur, Malaysia: Oxford University Press.

Formaggia, Maria Cristina. (2000) *Gambuh: Drama Tari Bali.* Jakarta, Indonesia: Yayasan Lontar.

GAMELAN

GAMELAN The term "gamelan" refers to various indigenous music ensembles of Java and Bali, the core instruments of which are usually drums, variously tuned bronze gongs, different sets of bronze metallophones, cymbals, and flutes. The bas-reliefs of some of the ancient Hindu and Buddhist temples in Central and East Java, dating from the eighth to fourteenth centuries CE, depict many examples of instruments similar to some of those used in contemporary gamelan orchestras, such as drums, flutes, small knobbed gongs, cymbals, and xylophones. Most contemporary instruments, however, are not represented on these reliefs. They actually much more resemble those used in traditional court orchestras throughout mainland Southeast Asia. The largest of the Javanese court gamelan, usually accompanying the sophisticated court dances (e.g., *bedaya, serimpi, wayang wong)* and shadow plays *(wayang kulit)*, consist of various sets of metallophones *(demung, sarong, slentem, gender)*, differently sized horizontally or vertically suspended gongs *(kenong, kempyang, ketuk, bonang, gong)*, and spoon-shaped, cymbal-like instruments *(kemanak)* made of bronze, as well as drums *(kendang)*, flutes *(suling)*, plucked *(celempung)* and bowed *(rebab)* string instruments, xylophones *(gambang kayu)*, and singing *(pesinden, dalang)*.

In Bali, a variety of gamelan ensembles have been in use for centuries, both in village life and at the various courts, accompanying rituals as well as dance dramas and shadow plays. They, too, are usually different sets of bronze metallophones *(gangsa, kantilan, calung, jegogan, gender)*, vertically and horizontally suspended gongs of different sizes *(gong, kempur, kemong, kempli, reyong, trompong)*, cymbals *(ceng-ceng)*, drums *(kendang)*, and flutes *(suling)*. Some of the ensembles

Musicians perform in a gamelan orchestra in Bali. (CHRISTINE OSBORNE/CORBIS)

also include a bowed string instrument *(rebab)* and singing.

Among the most conspicuous instruments of both the Javanese and Balinese gamelan are the various metallophones. Their bronze plates, struck with mallets, are vertically suspended over either a wooden resonance trough or resonance tubes made of bamboo. Each gamelan is unique in tone color and pitch, fine tuned by master gong-smiths in accordance with the seven-tone *pelog* tonal system, consisting of unequal intervals, or the five-tone *slendro* tonal system, consisting of equal intervals. Javanese gamelan are, in fact, composed of both a *pelog* and a *slendro* set of instruments, whereas in Bali the *slendro* scale is reserved for the ensembles *(gender wayang)* that accompany the shadow plays. Both *pelog* and *slendro* are determined by their respective relative intervals, that is, independently of absolute pitch. Each tonal system allows for different scales, which are classified according to different modes (in Java called *patet* and in Bali *tetekep*).

Martin Ramstedt

Further Reading

Bakan, Michael B. (1999) *Music of Death and New Creation: Experiences in the World of Balinese Gamelan Beleganjur.* Chicago: University of Chicago Press.

Hood, Mantle. (1984) *The Evolution of Javanese Gamelan.* Vol. 2: *The Legacy of the Roaring Sea.* New York: Edition Heinrichshofen and C. F. Peters.

———. (1954) *The Nuclear Theme as a Determinant of Patet in Javanese Music.* Groningen, Netherlands, and Jakarta, Indonesia: J. B. Wolters.

Kunst, Jaap. (1973) *Music in Java: Its History, Its Theory, and Its Technique.* The Hague, Netherlands: Martinus Nijhoff.

Suryabrata, Bernard. (1987) *The Island of Music: An Essay in Social Musicology.* Jakarta, Indonesia: Balai Pustaka.

Tenzer, Michael. (1991) *Balinese Music.* Berkeley: Periplus.

Toth, Andrew. (1980) *Recordings of the Traditional Music of Bali and Lombok.* Society of Ethnomusicology (Special Series no. 4).

Wisnusubroto, Sunardi. (1997) *Sri Lestari: An Introduction to Gamelan.* Yogyakarta, Indonesia: Gajah Mada University Press.

GANDAN LAMASERY Gandan lamasery, nestled in the modern city of Ulaanbatar, is the seat of Mongolian Buddhism and the largest monastery in the Mongolian People's Republic. Founded at nearly the same time as Ulaanbaatar, in the seventh century CE, Gandan lamasery shares a common history with the nation's capital. In 1651 Gandan lamasery was established at the behest of Dalai Lama Ngawang Lobsang Gyatso (1617–1682) in the young nomadic religious settlement of Orgoo in Mongolia. For over a century, the lamasery moved with Orgoo and became the center of the settlement's religious activities. Orgoo and Gandan lamasery settled in 1778 on the site of modern-day Ulaanbaatar, and gradually a city of merchants and craftsmen formed around the religious center. By 1900 Gandan lamasery boasted a majority of the city's 25,000 inhabitants. This changed with the beginning of socialist rule in the 1920s, when the government instituted strict rules against the practice of Buddhism and destroyed most of the monasteries in Mongolia. Due to its special status, Gandan was preserved as a religious museum during this time, but the number of lamas in its service decreased dramatically. With Mongolia's transition to democracy beginning in 1989, Gandan monastery reopened as a center of the Buddhist faith and has grown to include several thousand monks.

Daniel Hruschka

Further Reading

Bawden, Charles R. (1968) *The Modern History of Mongolia.* London: Weidenfeld & Nicolson.

Center of Gandantegchilin Studies. (1981) *Buddhism in Mongolia.* Ulaanbaatar, Mongolia: State Publishing House.

GANDHI, INDIRA (1917–1964), prime minister of India. Indira Gandhi, daughter of Jawaharlal Nehru (1889–1964), the first prime minister of independent India, married Feroze Gandhi, a Parsi (not related to Mohandas [Mahatma] Gandhi); their sons were Rajiv (who also served as India's prime minister, 1984–1989) and Sanjay. She joined the Indian

Indira Gandhi with her sons Rajiv and Sanjay in New Delhi in 1967. (HULTON-DEUTSCH COLLECTION/CORBIS)

National Congress (INC) in 1938 and was its president from 1959 to 1960. She was a minister in Prime Minister Lal Bahadur Shastri's cabinet from 1964 to 1966 and succeeded him in 1966. As prime minister, she concluded a friendship treaty with the Soviet Union and backed the secession of Bangladesh from Pakistan. In 1974 she ordered the test of a nuclear device. When she nearly lost her mandate due to petition for early elections, she proclaimed a national emergency in 1975 and postponed the elections of 1976. In the elections of 1977 she was defeated, but she returned to power in 1980. When Sikh separatists occupied the Golden Temple of Amritsar, a site sacred to Sikhs, she ordered the army to capture the temple, resulting in 450 Sikh deaths. She was shot fatally by her Sikh bodyguards in October 1984.

Dietmar Rothermund

Further Reading

Sahgal, Nayantara. (1982) *Indira Gandhi: Her Road to Power.* New York: Ungar.

MOHANDAS GANDHI ON THE IMPORTANCE OF LAND OWNERSHIP FOR THE PEOPLE OF INDIA

"Real socialism has been handed down to us by our ancestors who fought: *'All land belongs to Gopal, where then is the boundary line? Man is the maker of that line and he can, therefore, unmake it.' Gopal* literally means shepherd; it also means God. In modern language it means the State; the People. That the land to-day does not belong to the people is too true. But the fault is not in the teaching. It is in us who have not lived up to it.

"I have no doubt that we can make as good an approach to it as it possible for any nation, not excluding Russia, and that without violence. The most effective substitute for violent dispossession is the wheel with all its implications. *Land and property is his who will work on it.*

"Unfortunately the workers are or have been kept ignorant of this simple fact.

"Continuous unemployment has induced in the people a kind of laziness which is most depressing. Thus whilst the alien rule is undoubtedly responsible for the growing pauperism of the people, we are more responsible for it. If the middle-class people, who betrayed their trust and bartered away the economic independence of India for a mess of pottage, would now realize their error and take the message of the wheel to the villagers and induce them to shed their laziness, and work at the wheel, we can ameliorate the condition of the people to a great extent."

Source: Jagdish Saran Sharma. (1962) *India's Struggle for Freedom: Select Documents and Sources.* Vol. 1. Delhi: S. Chand, 29

GANDHI, MOHANDAS K. (1869–1948), Indian nationalist and promoter of nonviolent resistance. Mohandas Karamchand Gandhi grew up in Porbandar, Gujarat, the son of a minister of a princely state. His father became a judge at a special court in Rajkot, Gujarat, settling disputes among princes. In such a court, nobody could be sentenced: the judges had to bring equitable compromises between the princes. Gandhi's father was good at this, and young Mohandas admired him for it. His mother was a pious woman who often took vows and observed them religiously. These parental virtues left a deep impact on him.

Gandhi was sent to London at the age of eighteen to study law. After obtaining his degree, he returned to India in 1891, but did not do well as a lawyer, as he was too shy. A Muslim businessman sent him to South Africa to resolve a legal dispute between two rich Muslims. Gandhi persuaded them to settle the issue out of court. He was about to return to India when he noticed that Indian immigrants in South Africa were about to be deprived of their right to vote. He organized the Natal Indian Congress to fight against this measure. Soon he became involved in more issues affecting the civil rights of the Indian minority. He stressed that rights also implied duties and, during both the Boer War and the Zulu rebellion, he organized an Indian ambulance corps. The white militia's brutal massacre of the Zulus brought about a fundamental change in Gandhi's life. He renounced his profession, took a vow of chastity and decided to devote his life to political and social work. In this new capacity, he developed *satyagraha* ("holding on to the truth"), a strategy of nonviolent resistance to unjust laws. He empowered the Indian minority by organizing campaigns along these lines. He also wrote his manifesto *Hind swaraj* ("Freedom of India"), which was published in 1909. He stated that the British ruled India only because they could rely on the cooperation of the Indians. Nonviolent noncooperation would thus put an end to colonial rule.

When Gandhi returned to India in 1915, there was no scope for political campaigns. During World War I, the British-Indian government was armed with emergency powers. Gandhi devoted himself to local issues such as oppression of peasants by British indigo planters in Champaran, Bihar. After the war, the British extended their wartime emergency powers by means of an act that became known by the name of Justice Rowlatt, who had drafted it. In 1919, Gandhi organized a *hartal*, a kind of general strike of all traders, in protest. To his dismay, the campaign did not remain nonviolent, and the strike was brutally repressed by the British. When he launched his *satyagraha* campaign in 1920, he restricted it to a series of boycotts (for example, of elections, of the schools and law courts, and of foreign cloth). Gandhi also drafted a new constitution of the Indian National Congress, the political party agitating for India's independence. The participation of rural India in Congress politics and the creation of the Working Committee as a permanent leadership for agitation were the main features of this new constitution. Through his hold on the Working Committee, Gandhi controlled the Congress, even when he had no official position in the organization.

The British hesitated to arrest Gandhi during the noncooperation campaign for fear of adding fuel to the fire. In 1922, Gandhi terminated the campaign, as an outbreak of violence in a remote village had alarmed him. He was then sentenced to six years of rigorous imprisonment but was released for health reasons in 1924. Most people thought at that time that he was a spent force. When the Congress planned another political campaign in 1930, however, Gandhi was again its main strategist. This time, he found the unjust salt law to be a proper target for *satyagraha*. The law gave the government a monopoly over the production of salt; Gandhi organized a march to the sea to collect sea salt. When agrarian prices dropped by half due to the Great Depression, peasants who had to pay revenue and interest at their old rates flocked to the Congress. The British viceroy, Lord Irwin, fearing a peasant rebellion, concluded a pact with Gandhi, who hoped that he could arrive at a similar pact with the British prime minister to secure substantial concessions for India. In this, he was to be disappointed. In subsequent years Gandhi devoted himself to constructive work in Indian villages and to the uplift of the untouchables.

Mohandas K. Gandhi praying in December 1949. (BETTMANN/CORBIS)

Gandhi was only once more called on to launch a major campaign, when the Congress rejected the offer that the British minister, Sir Stafford Cripps, had taken to India in 1942, promising independence after World War II if Congress would back the British war effort. Gandhi asked the British to "Quit India" immediately, but before he could organize a campaign, he and all other Congress leaders were imprisoned.

On the eve of Independence, Gandhi had to be reconciled to the partition of India into two states, India and Pakistan, which he had opposed. The new Indian government was reluctant to agree to this, as India was already at war with Pakistan over Kashmir. Gandhi saw to it that Pakistan got its share, and for that he was shot fatally by a radical Hindu nationalist, five months after India's independence. Beloved by millions of Indians and admired by people worldwide, he became known as the Mahatma, or Great Soul.

Dietmar Rothermund

Further Reading

Brown, Judith. (1989) *Prisoner of Hope*. New Haven, CT: Yale University Press.

Conrad, Dieter. (1999) "Gandhi's Egalitarians and the Indian Tradition." In *Zwischen den Traditionen*, edited by Jürgen Lütt. Stuttgart, Germany: Franz Steiner.

Rothermund, Dietmar. (1992) *Mahatma Gandhi: An Essay in Political Biography*. New Delhi: Manohar.

GANG OF FOUR The Gang of Four (*siren bang*) is the name given to the four most influential supporters of the Chinese Cultural Revolution in its later stages, other than Mao Zedong (1893–1976). The group's main focus of activities was in Shanghai. There were three men, Zhang Chunqiao (1917–1991?), Yao Wenyuan (b. 1931), and Wang Hongwen (1935–1992), and one woman, Jiang Qing (1914–1991). According to the official Chinese Communist Party (CCP) version of history since the early 1980s, it was their arrest and overthrow on 6 October 1976 that signaled the end of the Cultural Revolution (1966–1976).

The term "gang of four" was actually coined by Mao. It was first used publicly in a speech given by Beijing CCP First Secretary Wu De (1910–1995) on 24 October 1976 to an enormous crowd in Tiananmen Square in central Beijing. After Wu's speech, the term was widely used in China, with these four being blamed for virtually all the ills of the Cultural Revolution.

All except Wang Hongwen had been members of the CCP Politburo since April 1969. In August 1973, Zhang Chunqiao was added to the Politburo Standing Committee, the most powerful governing body in China, while Wang Hongwen became not only a member of the standing committee but a CCP deputy chairman as well. In July 1977, the CCP Central Committee dismissed all four from all posts, accusing them of being "bourgeois careerists, conspirators and counterrevolutionary double-dealers."

Jiang Qing, Mao's wife, had been extremely powerful since 1966 as a member of the Cultural Revolution Group, the body Mao set up that year to guide the Cultural Revolution, and she also gained power by being the person who transmitted instructions from Mao. Her best-known initiative was the reform of the Chinese theater, involving elimination of traditional items among many other changes. Zhang Chunqiao was noted as a radical ideologue, and it was he who led the abortive Shanghai People's Commune of January 1967. In November 1965, Yao Wenyuan wrote an article in a Shanghai newspaper that at the time was credited with launching the earliest stage of the Cultural Revolution.

The members of the gang of four were tried by a special court toward the end of 1980. They were accused of a range of crimes, especially of persecuting large numbers of people, including CCP and state leaders. Jiang Qing was most vocal in her own defense, arguing that she was simply carrying out Mao's wishes, despite which all four were convicted. Actually, she was right in the sense that none of the four could have done what they did without Mao's support, and it was he, not they, who was leading the Cultural Revolution. However, the Chinese press went to considerable lengths to clear Mao of any criminal motivation or action, instead laying blame on the gang.

The court issued its verdicts against the gang on 25 January 1981. It sentenced Jiang Qing and Zhang Chunqiao to death with two-year reprieves. As it happened, neither was executed, and Jiang committed suicide in May 1991. Zhang Chunqiao died in prison, probably in 1991. Wang Hongwen was sentenced to life imprisonment, dying in 1992, while Yao Wenyuan was given twenty years but was released in October 1996.

Colin Mackerras

Further Reading

Bonavia, David. (1984) *Verdict in Peking: The Trial of the Gang of Four*. London: Burnett Books.

Hsiung, James C. ed., with documents prepared by Hongdah Chiu. (1981) *Symposium: The Trial of the "Gang of Four" and Its Implication in China*. Baltimore, MD: School of Law, University of Maryland.

GANGES RIVER The Ganges River, or Ganga, as it is known to Hindus, is the great river of India. By the fourth century BCE, the fame of the Ganges had reached the West. Alexander of Macedon (356–323 BCE), who regarded the river as the farthest

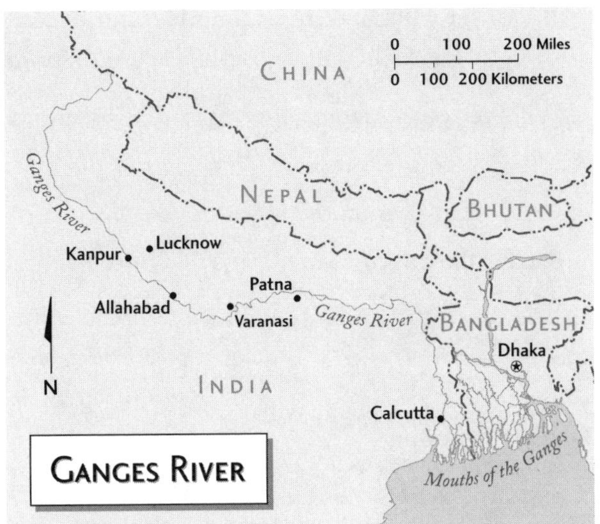

increasingly became a part of the Indian ethos. With the flourishing of commerce and agriculture, its water performed a thousand functions. Just as few can resist someone who is utterly devoted, so people came to worship the river that offered them so much.

Beginning with the Hindu scriptures of the third century CE, the Ganges has played a vital role in religious ceremonies, especially in rituals of birth, initiation, and death. As a goddess the river has appeared with the great celestials of Hinduism, at times the child of Brahma, the wife of Shiva, or the metaphysical product of Vishnu. Always conferring a benediction, the river shares none of the destructive qualities of some other Indian goddesses or the sepulchral

limit of the Earth, hoped to reach the Ganges and, by continuing east, to return to Europe through the Pillars of Hercules. However, he never reached his destination. Virgil, Ovid, and Dante all mentioned the Ganges, and the river held a unique position in medieval thought. In a curious blend of scripture and classical geography, Christian church leaders came to regard the Ganges as the Phison, the first river of paradise. Accepted by such notable figures as Saints Augustine, Ambrose, and Jerome, that belief prevailed throughout the Middle Ages.

What about the river so kindled people's imaginations? The sanctity of water has been a part of the Indian tradition from its beginnings in the Indus Valley well over four thousand years ago into the twenty-first century. At the start of the plowing season, before the seeds are sown, farmers in the Indian state of Bihar place water from the Ganges in a pot in a special place in the field to ensure a good harvest. Newly married women unfold their saris to the Ganges and pray for children and for long lives for their husbands. In the Ganges Valley and along the Bengal Delta, the Ganges is known as Ganga Mata or Mother Ganges. The image of the Ganges echoes throughout Indian history in the many tales of its generative powers: giving birth, restoring life, conferring immortality.

Historically the Ganges Valley was an entry point into the subcontinent for the first Indo-European invaders, who probably moved into India starting around the eleventh or twelfth century BCE. To these early wanderers the river loomed massive and omnipresent. Its current held the thread of contact with other settlements, old and new, and its route pointed ever eastward toward some unknown destination. As civilization grew on its banks and cities arose, the Ganges

HARNESSING THE GANGES

"A new development of the irrigation system is the Ganges Canal hydro-electric scheme in the United Provinces, of which the power stations were opened towards the end of 1937. This supplies power both for agricultural and industrial purposes. It protects 1 1/2 million acres against famine; it provides 88 towns with power for electric lighting, electric fans, and industrial undertakings; and it assists rural development by mechanizing agricultural processes and energizing industrial activities by means of the cheap power provided for local sugar-mills, oil-crushing plants, flour-mills, &c. By substituting electric power for manual and animal labour, the electric grid is transforming the social economy of the area which it serves. Flour used to be ground by hand; sugar-cane was crushed by primitive stone crushers operated by bullocks going slowly round and round in a circle; the water required for irrigating the fields was raised from wells, tanks, and ditches by bullocks pulling it up in leather bags or men swinging it up in baskets. These operations are now performed by electricity, and the labour of millions of hands has been released for more profitable work."

Source: Jagdish Saran Sharma. (1962) *India's Struggle for Freedom: Select Documents and Sources.* Vol. 1. Delhi: S. Chand & Co., 38.

SUNDARBANS—WORLD HERITAGE SITE

Stretching across the border of India and Bangladesh, and containing the world's largest region of mangrove forest within its ten-thousand-square kilometers; Sundarbans National Park was designated a World Heritage Site in 1987 for its fragile ecosystem and abundant Ganges Delta wildlife.

goddesses of Greece. Even in mythical travels in the underworld, the Ganges forever points the way to paradise.

The river itself is born in the Gangotri glacier in the high Himalayas, and it flows 2,510 kilometers to the Bay of Bengal. The Gangotri glacier is a mountain of ice 32 kilometers long and close to 4 kilometers wide surrounded by peaks six or seven thousand meters high. From there the river's two main sources, the Alakananda and the Bhagirathi, flow past the sacred villages of Gangotri and Badrinath, revered centers of pilgrimage. The two streams merge just above Rishikesh and enter the plains at Haridwar (Hardwar), the Gate of Vishnu (Hari is a name of Vishnu; *dvara*, the Sanskrit word for "door" or "gate").

Pilgrims gather at Haridwar in May and September to provision for the long journey north. The water at Haridwar and at Rishikesh is considered the river's holiest, and people travel great distances to fill their vessels for special occasions, such as marriages, deaths, or when they must call on the Ganges to remind them of the dreams that have faded from their hearts.

In the Ganges Valley the river is joined by another sacred river, the Jumna (Yamuna). Legend has it that the two rivers are joined by a third, invisible course, the Sarasvati, which can be seen only through the eye of wisdom. This point where the three rivers meet, known as *triveni* (the three braids), is the place of oneness, where opposites cease to exist and the true believer steps beyond time.

Bengal, more than elsewhere along the river's course, feels the power of the Ganges. In Bengal its restless current has created and destroyed great cities, and its shifting silt has devastated entire regions. No wonder the river is so prominent in the literature and religion of the delta. The folk poet Phatik Chand sang:

On a river without water, a lotus blossom floats
while gazelles leap silver in the moonless night.
Whoever can surmount the vortex of Triveni,
where three rivers meet,
will float forever on the waves of time.

Such is the dream of the Ganges that people carry in their hearts.

Steven Darian

Further Reading

Darian, Steven. (1970) *The Ganges in Myth and History*. Honolulu, HI: University of Hawaii.

———. (1988) *A Ganges of the Mind: A Journey on the River of Dreams*. Delhi: Ratna Sagar.

GANGTOK (2001 pop. 29,000). The capital of Sikkim State in northeastern India, Gangtok ("top of the hill") is wedged between Tibet, Nepal, and Bhutan on a long ridge flanking the Ranipul River, with breathtaking Himalayan views. It was the government seat of the kingdom of Sikkim until the area was annexed by India (1975). Tradition, hospitality, and ceremony prevail over speed in this version of Shangri-la, where steep slopes are striped with rice terraces and plantations of tea or cardamom, and temples and fairytale towns hang on the faces of sheer cliffs.

The capital is an active market center for corn, rice, oranges, spices, subtropical fruits, Nepalese silver spread on sarongs, and the work of tribal weavers; gardens bloom with hundreds of varieties of orchids and rhododendron. Gangtok has a hospital, secondary school, law court, and modern shops, hotels, and cinemas, along with the former royal palace and chapel, Enchey Monastery, and the Namgyal Institute of Tibetology, including a library and museum. The Buddhist monastery of Rumtek lies to the southeast. Mask dances performed by lamas in the monastery courtyards are among the most colorful in the world. Gangtok's spectacular scenery has made the city a popular vacation destination among Bengalis, especially during the ten-day Durga Puja holiday in September and October.

C. Roger Davis

Further Reading

Lama, Mahendra P., ed. (1994) *Sikkim: Society, Polity, Economy, Environment*. London: Thames & Hudson.

GANSU (2002 est. pop. 27.1 million). Gansu (Kansu) Province is located in northern China at the upper reaches of the Huang (Yellow) River. In the west, the province borders on Qinghai and Xinjiang, in the north on Mongolia, in the east on Ningxia and Shaanxi, and in the south on Sichuan. Gansu covers an area of 454,000 square kilometers and divides into three distinct topographical regions. The western region composes part of the Gobi desert and the so-called "Gansu corridor," a more than 1,000 kilometer-long and only 50 to 70 kilometer-wide east-west passage between the Tibetan Plateau in the south and the Gobi Desert in the north. The Gansu corridor was an important part of the ancient silk route, and agriculture in the oases here depend on the glacial streams from the Tibetan Plateau. The main crops are wheat, sugar beets, and cotton. The central region is part of the great loess plateau of northern China, an extremely eroded area, parts of which are the poorest districts in China. The southern region is a mountainous earthquake area rising between 2,000 and 4,000 meters above sea level.

About 90 percent of Gansu's population is Han Chinese. The remaining 10 percent is distributed over a number of minority nationalities who are either Muslims or who belong to Tibetan religions. The capital of the province, Lanzhou (1996 estimated population of 1.5 million), is situated in the rich agricultural area of the Huang River valley in the central region.

Gansu has been under Chinese control and influence on and off since the third century BCE and has played a continuously important role in trade between Central Asia and China. When China was strong, Gansu constituted the western frontier of China, and the Great Wall ends here. During the Yuan dynasty (1279–1368), Gansu became part of the empire along with Xinjiang and Qinghai. The suppression of a Muslim rebellion in 1862–1878 almost devastated the area, and in 1928 Xinjiang and Qinghai became independent provinces. The present borders of Gansu changed several times in the twentieth century, and in 1958 a large part was cut out to become Ningxia Hui Autonomous region. In the fertile river valley of the central region, agricultural products such as millet, wheat, tobacco, melons, and fruit dominate. Gansu mainly has heavy industry, which is concentrated in and around Lanzhou, and manufactures heavy machinery, petrochemical products, and nonferrous metals. The pollution of the industrial center is high.

Bent Nielsen

Further Reading

Lipman, Jonathan N. (1997) *Familiar Strangers: A History of Muslims in Northwest China*. Seattle, WA: University of Washington Press.

Schran, Peter. (1976) *Guerrilla Economy: The Development of the Shensi-Kansu-Ninghsia Border Region*. Albany, NY: State University of New York Press.

GAO XINJIANG (b. 1940), Chinese writer and Nobel Laureate. Gao Xinjiang, the first Chinese-language writer awarded the Nobel Prize in literature, in 2000, was born in 1940 in Ganzhou, Jiangxi Province, China, and grew up in a family that encouraged his interest in art, literature, and music. He studied French literature at the Beijing Foreign Language Institute from 1957 to 1962 and worked after graduation as a French translator for a bookstore.

During the Cultural Revolution (1966–1976), along with numerous other intellectuals in China, he had to destroy all his writing and go to the countryside for "rehabilitation." After the Cultural Revolution, however, he emerged on the literary scene as an important writer for his short fiction, plays, novels, and literary criticism. His essay entitled "Preliminary Exploration into the Techniques of Modern Fiction" contributed to the demolishing of "socialist realism," the then-regnant method of literary representation under Mao Zedong (1893–1976). But on the whole, Gao's voice was heard in China not so much for his fiction or literary criticism as for his works in such experimental plays as *Bus Stop*, a work highly reminiscent of Samuel Beckett's *Waiting for Godot*.

After he left China to settle in Paris in 1987, Gao supported himself mainly by painting. Meanwhile, he continued to write his novels and plays, which gradually gained recognition in France and Australia, though remaining less studied in Britain and the United States. His winning the Nobel Prize "for an oeuvre of universal validity, bitter insights and linguistic ingenuity," as the Swedish Academy stated, and his claim in his Nobel speech that literature is an apolitical enterprise, were not received without a sense of irony, since his selection and his award of the prize are felt by many to be unavoidably a political statement.

Jian Xu

Further Reading

Gao Xingjian. (1999) *The Other Shore: Plays by Gao Xingjian*. Trans. by Gilbert C. F. Fong. Hong Kong: Chinese University Press.

———. (2000) *Soul Mountain*. Trans. by Mabel Lee. New York: HarperCollins.

Tam Kwok-kan, ed. (2001) *Soul of Chaos: Critical Perspec-tives on Gao Xingjian.* Hong Kong: Chinese University Press.
Zhao, Henry Y. H. (2000) *Towards a Modern Zen Theatre: Gao Xingjian and Chinese Theatre Experimentalism.* London: School of Oriental and African Studies.

GARABIL PLATEAU Situated mainly in southeastern Turkmenistan, the Garabil (also spelled *Karabil*) plateau is a geological curiosity whose deposits of rock salt are among the largest in the world. The plateau marks the end of the sandy Turkmen Karakum Desert, between the Murgab and Amu Dar'ya Rivers. This area represents the foothills of the Paropamisus Mountains, part of the Hindu Kush, located in northern Afghanistan.

The plateau is rather low (only 832 meters at its highest point) and is semidesert; it is highly eroded, with large ancient valleys and basins. The region is known for its great variations in temperature and its rare precipitation. Savanna and groves of wild pistachio are the most common vegetation. However, the ecoregion has a wealth of plant and animal life, with more than 1,100 species of vascular plants (ferns) and a variety of birds, reptiles, urials (wild sheep), onagers, and gazelles.

Mainly used for pastures and for a little agriculture, the Garabil plateau is also of great economic importance because of large deposits of rock salts, estimated at 4 billion tons. Since Turkmenistan's independence, these deposits have begun to be cataloged and exploited.

Patrick Dombrowsky

Further Reading

Ovezov, Balych. (1960) *Le Turkménistan, pays de "l'or blanc."* Paris: Éditions Études soviétiques.
United Nations Development Programme. (1999) *Animals.* Vol. 1 of *The Red Data Book of Turkmenistan.* Ashkhabad, Turkmenistan: United Nations Development Programme.
———. (1999) *Plants.* Vol. 2 of *The Red Data Book of Turkmenistan.* Ashkhabad, Turkmenistan: United Nations Development Programme.

GARCIA, CARLOS P. (1896–1971), fourth president of the third Philippine republic. Garcia was born in the town of Talibon on the island of Bohol. His father served as mayor of the town for four terms. Garcia earned a law degree from Philippine Law School in 1923 and taught high school for several years after that. Due to his poetic abilities, he was known as the "Bard from Bohol." He entered politics in 1925 as a member of the Nacionalista party and served as congressman of the third district of Bohol until 1931, when he became governor of Bohol. In 1941, he was elected senator, and was reelected after World War II. He became vice president in 1953. He assumed the presidency when President Ramon Magsaysay died in a plane crash on 17 March 1957. He subsequently won the presidency in his own right in elections of November of that year.

When Garcia won the presidency, his running mate, Speaker of the House Jose Laurel, Jr., was defeated by Diosdado Macapagal, marking the first time in Philippine politics that the president was elected with a vice president from the opposition. (Macapagal was from the Liberal Party.)

With serious economic problems confronting the Philippines, Garcia advocated fiscal austerity. He opposed a return to free enterprise in the Philippine economy and put forward the Filipino First policy, seeking economic independence from foreign dominance for the Philippines. His administration was tainted by corruption and, along with the dissatisfaction in some quarters with his nationalistic Filipino First policy, this led to his defeat in 1961 by Diosdado Macapagal.

Garcia was a delegate from his home district to the 1971 Constitutional Convention. He was elected president of the Constitutional Convention on 11 June 1971, but died three days later.

Damon L. Woods

Further Reading

Bananal, Eduardo. (1986) *The Presidents of the Philippines.* Manila, Phillipines: National Book Store.
Gagelonia, Leticia S. Guzman. (1976) *Presidents of the Philippines.* Manila, Phillipines: National Book Store.

GARDENING—CHINA The Chinese garden is in essence an encapsulation of nature in a prescribed framework. Gardens are considered venues for spiritual and artistic endeavors, loci for celebrations, and themselves works of art. The history of Chinese gardens is complex and divergent, and it is important to understand not only their design principles, but also the spiritual basis of their construction.

History of Chinese Gardens

Two main garden traditions in China evolved over time: the vast imperial gardens, emblematic of the power and wealth of the empire; and the scholar, or literati, gardens, built as retreats from the onerous world of officialdom. The earliest references to gardens in China are found in Zhou-dynasty (1045–256 BCE) records describing vast tracts of land to be reserved for hunting parks for kings and princes. Success in the hunt was a metaphor for a successful reign. Later, in the *Chu ci* (Songs of Chu), a fourth-century BCE text, a shaman singer attempts to entice the soul of a dying king back to life with a description of the beauties of a garden with winding streams, lotus lakes, and distant views of the mountains. In the Shanglin park of China's first emperor, Zheng (Shi Huang Di) (259–210 BCE), were countless animals, birds, and exotic plants gathered as tribute from vassal states, thus creating a living replica of his entire domain. Poets such as the famed Tao Yuanming (365–427 CE) recorded in verse the pleasures of strolling though one's garden. Both the Sui (581–618) and Tang (618–907) dynasties saw the further development of imperial and individual gardens. Wang Wei (699–759) created his Wangchuan villa in Lantian County, Shaanxi, a rustic retreat immortalized in poetry and paintings for centuries as the epitome of the scholar's retreat.

The Song dynasty (960–1279) gave rise to the proliferation of urban literati gardens, and at Kaifeng, Song Huizong (1082–1135) erected the Gen Yue mountain, an artificial construct approximately seventy-seven meters tall, including many famous garden rocks. Kublai Khan (1214–1294) of the Yuan dynasty (1279–1368) built at Beijing an extravagant city complete with lakes and hunting parks. The subsequent Ming dynasty (1368–1644) revised and embellished the Forbidden City with myriad courtyards and gardens and developed the Park of the Sea Palaces, a vast complex of gardens and retreats for the imperial family. The most famous of the gardens of the Qing dynasty (1644–1912) was the imperial Yuan Ming Yuan, commissioned by the Qianlong emperor (1711–1799), within the precincts of which were countless watercourses, pavilions, libraries, farms, training fields for the emperor's soldiers, and European-style fountains and buildings.

Gardens and pagoda at the Yu garden in Shanghai, China, in 1996. (STEPHEN G. DONALDSON PHOTOGRAPHY)

Cosmology of Chinese Gardens

The unique character of Chinese gardens has its roots in Chinese philosophy, most notably Taoism. A garden was seen as a mirror of the natural world. Everything in the universe was created from and a conduit for *qi* (vital energy, or life force). The universe was understood to be a combination of yin (female) and yang (male) elements in a state of constant fluidity. A balance of opposites in the construction of buildings, natural features, and plantings was a goal of the garden designer. Recreating the natural world in a garden was thought to replicate the benefits of immersing oneself in nature, a belief similar to ideas about the benefits of landscape painting. Scholars whose official duties prevented them from visiting the mountains could enjoy the benefits of nature in their own gardens. The ancient practice of feng shui (literally, "wind-water," often translated as geomancy) consisted of situating homes, buildings, graves, and gardens properly in a landscape to receive the optimum benefit.

Elements of the Garden

The two main elements of a garden are rocks and water, symbolizing the yang and yin, respectively. Traditional Chinese gardens are constructed in a series of walled outdoor courtyards, joined by walkways or doorways. Use of garden rocks (yang) at strategic locations within a garden brings to mind the mountain ranges and peaks of nature. Incorporation of a watercourse, pool, lake, or cascade adds the water (yin) and all its mutable forms. Plants are included for literary and cultural references, for seasonal suitability, and for aesthetic reasons, such as the beauty of their shadows against the light garden walls, or the harmony of the sound of wind and rain in their foliage. Buildings such as *ting* (pavilions with open sides), *xie* (gazebos), *tang* (formal halls), and covered walkways make accessible the featured sites in the gardens and the effects of the changing hours of the days and seasons.

Such garden structures are named with references to classical literature, and the addition of calligraphy adds another layer of appreciation to the garden. Often potted plants are placed in courtyards at the peak of their blooming seasons, and pools and lakes house water lilies, lotus, and fish. Gardens also include rockeries that are constructed of aggregates of bizarrely shaped rocks made into miniature mountains or roofs for artificial caves, both symbolic of the entrance to the realms of immortals and useful as an escape from the heat of summer.

Yuan Ye (The Craft of Gardens, datable to 1631–1634), written during the late Ming dynasty by Ji Cheng (late sixteenth–early seventeenth century), is considered the classic text on garden design. Encompassing both practical and aesthetic advice, the manual advises the garden designer to be sensitive to the proper use of contrasts and juxtapositions of elements and to seek the essence lying behind the forms. Details concerning window lattice patterns, doors and wall openings, brickwork for paths, and suitable alignment of the garden with existing landscape features are included.

Chinese Gardens Today

Beihai Park in Beijing in the Forbidden City, which was first built in the tenth century as a hunting lodge, currently encompasses approximately 67 hectares of lakes and artificial islands. There an example of a prerevolutionary walled garden, the Limpid Mirror Studio (Jing Qing Zhou), once housed the Qing-dynasty princes. The West Lake in Yangzhou had its origins in the Sui and Tang dynasties. Suzhou's gardens include the Shizi Lin (Stone Lion Grove), built around 1336 for a Buddhist monk, Tian Ru, and the Wang Shi Yuan (Garden of the Master of the Fishing Nets), first constructed there in 1440.

Suzhou also contains the Zhouzheng Yuan (Garden of the Unsuccessful Politician). The Zhouzheng Yuan has antecedents dating back to the Tang dynasty. It has been variously a Confucian scholar's home, a garden, a Buddhist monastery, and a warlord's headquarters. It has changed hands many times and once was even sold to pay gambling debts. It is most renowned for its association with the Ming artist Wen Zhengming (1470–1559), who lived there for a time and recorded it in paintings. Wen Zhengming, a Wu School artist and one of the so-called four masters of the Ming, was an unsuccessful politician who after many failed attempts at success in the imperial examination system finally secured a minor post but quickly relinquished it to devote himself to artistic pursuits and teaching.

Hangzhou's West Lake is one of China's most beloved parks. Many new Chinese gardens have been built within the last twenty years in America, notably the Astor Garden Court at the Metropolitan Museum of Art in New York City and the Chinese scholar's garden at the Staten Island New York Botanical Garden.

Noelle O'Connor

See also: **Architecture—China; Architecture, Vernacular—China**

Further Reading

Cheng Ji. (1988) *The Craft of Gardens.* Trans. by Alison Hardie. New Haven, CT: Yale University Press.

Keswick, Maggie. (1986) *The Chinese Garden.* New York: St. Martin's Press.

GARO The Garo are a tribal people of India, about half a million of whom live in the Garo Hills of Meghalaya, northeastern India. Others live in neighboring West Bengal, Assam, Nagaland, and Tripura. In Meghalaya they are the major Scheduled Tribe (an ethnic subgroup that has faced discrimination and economic privation). They are well known as a matrilineal society who practice shifting cultivation. Being so numerous, they are divided into several dialectal and cultural groups, but nonetheless there is a strong sense of Garo identity, and the culture is still fairly uniform. The biggest distinction today is between Christian and non-Christian Garo, who live in separate villages.

The Garo have uxorilocal households; that is, a man usually finds himself living with his wife, her parents, her sisters, and all their children. The oldest of the sisters is recognized as the heiress. Neolocal residence (establishment of a new household rather than residence with a spouse's parents) also occurs today.

The society is divided into five matrilineal descent groups, or phratries. The clans that make up each phratry are exogamous; that is, members are required to find a spouse who is not a member of the same clan. Within each clan the most significant unit is called the *machong*, a group of close matrilineal relations who play a key role in the formation and maintenance of each household, and in controlling the cross-cousin marriages. Only an heiress is expected to marry her father's sister's son, while other girls are free to marry more distant cross-cousins. In common with a number of other Indian tribes, the institution of the bachelor's dormitory—a building where young unmarried men lived—was until quite recently an important social institution.

The traditional Garo religion is Sangasarek, which recognizes a supreme being, but is much concerned with the propitiation of spirits that may otherwise bring misfortune. Today, however, about 70 percent of the population is Christian, an effect of British missionary work in the late nineteenth and early twentieth centuries that followed upon British seizure of the area in 1873.

Several centuries ago the Garo were infamous as headhunters. The isolation this fostered gave way to numerous trade links with the plains, usually through bartering goods with Koch, Bengali, and various other Hindu or Muslim traders. Garo still go to the plains to sell baskets, ginger, chilies, and bamboo mats, getting rice in exchange. The traditional form of shifting cultivation, called *jhum*, is still practiced by about half the Garo today. Other land is farmed on a permanent basis, and is losing some of its fertility thereby.

Paul Hockings

Further Reading

Burling, Robbins. (1963) *Rengsangri: Family and Kinship in a Garo Village.* Philadelphia: University of Pennsylvania Press.

Playfair, I. A. (1909) *The Garos.* London: David Nutt.

GAWAI DAYAK

Gawai, a ritual festival, is celebrated by the Dayak people (a collective name for the native ethnic groups of Borneo, an island in the Malay Archipelago). *Gawai* is a form of communication with the spirit world. It is important to communicate with the spirit world in order to obtain blessings and to thank the spirits that have aided the Dayaks in agriculture or in healing an ailment. This ritual, involving chants and incantations, is a way to show gratitude to the spirits for the good harvest and health of the Dayak people.

There are four main *gawai:* rituals connected with cultivation of rice; with health and longevity; with acquisition of wealth; and with headhunting and prestige. The celebration of all *gawai* involves a series of rites—first, sacrificial offerings *(piring)* are made; second, there is a cleansing ceremony *(biau)*, which involves a summoning of spirits by incantation and a slaughter of cockerels and waving them as another sacrificial offering to the spirits; and third and most important, prolonged sacred chanting (*timang* or *pengap*) by ritual experts or bards *(lemambang)*.

Today, a *gawai* is usually a festival celebrating the Dayaks' bountiful harvest. (The other types of *gawai*, especially related to healing and head-hunting, are rarely practiced today due to modernization and mass conversion of the Dayaks to Christianity.) The festival marks the end of one paddy-harvesting season and the beginning of another. It is a time to show gratitude to the gods for the good harvest and to ask for their blessings for the coming season. The contemporary Gawai Dayak is a statewide celebration in Sarawak (a state on the island of Borneo), and is also an occasion to renew communal and cultural ties as well an opportunity for the Dayaks to share their festive mood with other communities.

Shanthi Thambiah

Further Reading

Freeman, J. D. (1955) *Iban Agriculture: A Report on the Shifting Cultivation of Hill Rice by the Iban of Sarawak.* London: Her Majesty's Stationery Office.

Jensen, Erik. (1974) *The Iban and Their Religion.* London and Oxford: Clarendon Press.

Kedit, Peter Mulok. (1969) "Gawai Betambah—Bulu." *Sarawak Museum Journal* 18, 34–35: 120–122.

———. (1969) "A Gawai Kenyalong (Bird Festival) at Wong Pandak, Lubuk Antu." *Sarawak Gazette* 95 (30 June): 137–143.

GAZIANTEP

(2002 pop. 795,000). Gaziantep, previously Aintab ("good spring") and commonly referred to as Antep, is the capital of Gaziantep Province in southeastern Anatolia, Turkey, forty-five kilometers from the Syrian border. Situated where important routes converge and first settled by the Hittites, Antep assumed importance only after the Byzantines captured Duluk (Doliche, now Dulukbaba) in 962. During the First Crusades (1096–1099) Antep was ruled by Armenian Philaretus and fell to the Byzantines in 1150 only to be captured by the Seljuks of Konya in 1151. After falling to various peoples, it became part of the province of Aleppo in 1153.

Timur (Tamerlane, 1336–1405) captured Antep in 1400, and various Turkmen dynasties conquered it before it fell to the Ottomans in 1516. Antep was occupied by the English in 1919 and by the French from

1920 to 1921. Mustafa Kemal Ataturk (1881–1938), founder of the Turkish Republic, renamed it and added the prefix *Gazi* ("Muslim warrior for the faith") in honor of the Turkish nationalist forces who withstood a ten-month siege by French troops at the end of World War I.

Today Gaziantep is renowned for its pistachio nuts (*antep fistigi*) and the grape preserve called *pekmez.* Economically the city has benefited from the GAP Project (*Guneydogu Anadolu Projesi*, Southeastern Anatolia Project), a massive hydroelectric project under construction since 1974.

T. Isikozlu-E.F. Isikozlu

Further Reading

Statistical Yearbook of Turkey, 1998. (1998) Ankara, Turkey: Devlet Istatistik Enstitusu.

Geishas laughing at a party in the Gion district of Kyoto, c. 1993. (MICHAEL S. YAMASHITA/CORBIS)

GEISHA Geisha are professional entertainers and hostesses, skilled in the traditional Japanese arts. They are found throughout Japan; the largest and most highly respected geisha districts, however, are in Kyoto and Tokyo. The Western tendency to associate geisha with prostitution is based on a misunderstanding. The word "geisha" literally means "arts person," and a geisha must undergo rigorous training in the traditional arts—playing *shamisen* and koto (traditional Japanese stringed instruments) and dancing *nihon buyo*. Her job is to create a convivial atmosphere for her customers, typically wealthy businessmen and politicians, and entertain with music, dance, and intelligent conversation.

Male entertainers in the seventeenth century were the first to call themselves geisha. By the mid-eighteenth century they were outnumbered by female geisha, who were looked to as trendsetters and fashion icons. Bound by a code of secrecy, geisha became the confidants of important men and were influential in political affairs. The numbers of women who became geisha decreased during the twentieth century, although there are still several thousand and the profession shows no immediate signs of dying out.

Prior to World War II, geisha began their training before puberty and many girls were sold to geisha houses *(o-kiya)* by their impoverished parents. Those showing aptitude would be permitted to commence training as *maiko* (novice geisha), bound to the adoptive geisha mother by a strict contract. In the early 2000s, girls may apply to join a geisha house and become a *maiko* upon completing middle school. A *maiko* accompanies senior geisha to parties, wearing an ornate long-sleeved kimono, an elaborate hairstyle, and distinctive thick white makeup. After several years of intensive artistic training, she must decide whether to become a geisha or to leave the geisha world. Transition to geisha status is marked by a ceremony and the adoption of more sober dress. Geisha may eventually leave their geisha house to set up their own establishment. Lesson fees and clothing costs are very high and many geisha receive financial support from a patron. A geisha must give up her profession upon marriage.

Geisha entertain at special teahouses *(o-chaya)*, where Japanese-style rooms may be rented and food and drink is served. An air of exclusivity is an essential aspect of the geisha world, and accordingly, new patrons must be recommended by established customers and fees are extremely high. The geisha world has inspired numerous plays, films, and novels, including *Madam Butterfly* (1904), Nagai Kafu's *Geisha in Rivalry* (1917), and Arthur Golden's *Memoirs of a Geisha* (1997).

Lucy D. Moss

Further Reading

Dalby, Liza. (1998) *Geisha*. Berkeley and San Francisco: University of California Press.

Downer, Lesley. (2001) *Women of the Pleasure Quarters: The Secret History of the Geisha*. New York: Broadway Books.

GENGHIS KHAN (c.1162–1227), Mongolian ruler. Genghis Khan, also known as Chinggis or Chinghiz Khan, was born with the name of Temujin. After surviving tribal wars in Mongolia following the death of his father Yesugei, Temujin built a tribal confederation that dramatically restructured Mongolia.

After rising to power in 1185, Temujin experienced numerous setbacks and eventually victories. By 1206 Temujin was the paramount power in Mongolia and received the title Genghis Khan (thought to mean Oceanic Ruler). The years between 1185 and 1206 were, without doubt, the most difficult years for one of the most feared and respected men in history.

After uniting the various tribes of Mongolia into the Mongol supra-tribe, Genghis Khan went on to conquer much of northern China and Central Asia. In 1209, the Uighurs voluntarily submitted to Genghis Khan. Later in that year, the Mongols began their conquest of the Tangut kingdom of Xi-Xia, located in northwestern Gansu Province of China. After the Tanguts submitted in 1210, hostilities erupted between Genghis Khan and China's Jurchen Jin dynasty (1125–1234). Although the Jin were not defeated until seven years after Genghis Khan's death, the Mongols conquered much of northern China during his lifetime.

Genghis Khan led his army toward Central Asia in 1219. In fighting with the Khwarazmian empire, the Mongols utterly devastated most of Central Asia and eastern Iran. After the destruction of the Khwarazmians, the Mongols withdrew to deal with their disobedient vassal Xi-Xia, which had refused to send troops for the campaign in Central Asia. It was during this campaign that Genghis Khan died from internal injuries suffered after he fell from his horse while hunting in August 1227.

His wars were as often a matter of retaliation as they were for territory or riches. Genghis Khan's organizational and strategic genius created one of the most highly disciplined and effective armies in history, but this same genius gave birth to the core administration that ruled it. Even after his death, the Mongol armies dominated the battlefield until the empire stretched from the Pacific Ocean to the Adriatic Sea.

His nonmilitary achievements include the introduction of a writing system to the Mongols, the ideal of religious tolerance throughout the empire, and unity among the Mongols. Genghis Khan's accomplishments should not be seen in terms of territory or military victories but in the presence of a Mongol nation and culture. Mongols still venerate him as the founding father of Mongolia.

Timothy M. May

Further Reading

Cleaves, F. W., ed. and trans. (1982) *The Secret History of the Mongols.* Cambridge, MA: Harvard University Press.

Juvaini, ʿAta Malik. (1997) *Genghis Khan: The History of the World-Conqueror.* Seattle, WA: University of Washington Press.

Martin, H. D. (1950) *The Rise of Chingis Khan and his Conquest of North China.* Baltimore: Johns Hopkins Press.

Morgan, David. (1986) *The Mongols.* Oxford: Blackwell.

Ratchnevsky, Paul. (1992) *Genghis Khan: His Life and Legacy.* Trans. by Thomas Nivison Haining. Cambridge, U.K.: Blackwell.

GERINDO Gerindo (Gerakan Rakjat Indonesia, Indonesian People's Movement), an Indonesian national political party, was formed in May 1937. Its leaders included A. K. Gani (1905–1958), Muhammad Yamin (1903–1964), and Amir Sjarifuddin (1907–1948). Like the earlier Partai Nasionalis Indonesia Baru (New Indonesia Nationalist Party), Gerindo's aim was to raise public consciousness of nationalist ideas by organizing the people. Gerindo's foundation, however, also reflected a growing willingness on the part of many left-wing Indonesian nationalists to cooperate with the Dutch. This willingness arose both from despair over the prospects for organizing effective nationalist resistance in the face of Dutch military and police power and from a conviction that collaboration against fascism (especially Japanese fascism) had the highest priority in world affairs. Gerindo hoped to achieve from this collaboration a full parliament for Indonesia. Shortly before the Japanese attack on Java, Amir Sjarifuddin received funds from the Dutch authorities to organize underground resistance. This movement was quickly ended by the Japanese, however, who also banned Gerindo along with all other political parties.

Gerindo's willingness to work with the Dutch prefigured the postwar strategy of the Socialist Party—including that of Amir Sjarifuddin as defense minister and later prime minister of the Indonesian Republic—in making far-reaching concessions to the Dutch to obtain international recognition of Indonesia's sovereignty.

Robert Cribb

Further Reading

Abeyasekere, Susan. (1976) *One Hand Clapping: Indonesian Nationalists and the Dutch, 1939–1942.* Clayton, Victoria, Australia: Centre of Southeast Asian Studies, Monash University.

Leclerc, Jacques. (1986) "Underground Activities and Their Double: Amir Sjarifuddin's Relationship with Communism in Indonesia." *Kabar Seberang Sulating Maphilindo* 17: 72–99.

GERMANS IN CENTRAL ASIA Germans were first invited to settle in the Russian empire by Empress Catherine II. Large German communities on the lower Volga, the Black Sea coast, the Transcaucasus, and other areas prospered and soon sent out their own settlers. Several thousand Germans made their way to various parts of Russian Central Asia. By the outbreak of World War I, more than 50,000 settlers were living there and were cultivating more than 300,000 hectares.

Following the Russian Revolution the Soviet government initially seemed to favor the German minority, which received the first autonomous area (ASSR) in 1924. Things changed quickly, though, and the collectivization campaigns saw thousands of Germans sent into exile to Siberia and Central Asia. After Nazi Germany's invasion of the Soviet Union in June 1941, ethnic Germans were immediately suspected of collaboration. Mass deportations of German communities in Russia, the Ukraine, and the Caucasus began on the day the Germans invaded. Hundreds of thousands were deported to Central Asia. By 1945 more than 400,000 ethnic Germans had been deported to Kazakhstan alone. Though many Germans opted to emigrate after they were granted the right to leave their places of exile in 1972, substantial German communities remain in Central Asia, especially in Kazakhstan.

Andrew Sharp

Further Reading

Fleischhauer, Ingeborg, and Benjamin C. Pinkus. (1986) *The Soviet Germans: Past and Present*. London: Hurst.

Pohl, J. Otto. (1999) *Ethnic Cleansing in the USSR, 1937–1949*. Westport, CT: Greenwood.

GESER KHAN Although Geser Khan may have been a historical personage, he is primarily known as a protective deity of warriors and herds in Mongolian religion, both Buddhism and Shamanism, as well as in literature. The numerous epics concerning Geser Khan are rich sources of information about Mongol mythology and cosmological beliefs. He is particularly revered among the Buryat Mongols of Russia. It is thought that the worship of Geser Khan did not enter Mongolia until the early seventeenth century.

The Geser Khan of the Mongols may be the same figure as the Geser Khan of the Tibetans. They share many characteristics, both as cult and literary figures. Despite Geser Khan's possible Tibetan origin, the Mongol epics are distinct from their Tibetan counterparts. For example, whereas the Tibetans deified some of the companions and opponents of Geser, this appears less frequently in the Mongolian cult of Geser.

In the Mongol tradition, Geser Khan comes into the world to rid it of evil for the betterment of humankind. Throughout time, Geser Khan's importance in Shamanism and Buddhism has remained constant for the Mongols, and special shrines to him existed into the 1940s. Some shrines may remain today; however, Soviet influence, whether overt or covert, seriously undermined not only the Buddhist religion among the Mongols but also the folk religion so that many traditions died out. Whether the Geser cult remains today is uncertain but probable, as more and more Mongols have begun to seek out their past religious systems. The epic certainly remains a vital part of Mongolian literature.

Timothy May

Further Reading

Curtin, Jeremiah. (1909) *A Journey in Southern Siberia*. Boston: Little, Brown.

David-Neel, Alexandra, and the Lama Yongden. (1959) *The Superhuman Life of Gesar of Ling*. Trans. with the collaboration of Violet Sydney. London: Rider.

Heissig, Walther. (1980) *The Religions of Mongolia*. Trans. by Geoffrey Samuel. Berkeley and Los Angeles: University of California Press.

———. (1984) "Shamanic Myth and Clan-Epic." In *Shamanism in Eurasia*, pt. 2, edited by Mihaly Hoppal. Göttingen, Germany: Herodot.

GESTAPU AFFAIR The Gestapu affair was an ambiguous and abortive leftist coup on 1 October 1965, which triggered the end of Indonesia's Guided Democracy period. The term "Gestapu" is an acronym of Gerakan September Tiga Puluh (September Thirtieth Movement); Indonesians now generally use the term "G-30-S."

Troops under Lieutenant Colonel Untung, commander of the Presidential Guard, allegedly conducted the coup, ostensibly to prevent an expected rightist coup by pro-Western generals. Six senior generals, including the army commander General Achmad Yani, were killed, though the defense minister General A. H. Nasution escaped. Plotters seized radio and telecommunications buildings and formed a Revolutionary Council but otherwise failed to follow up their actions. The coup was suppressed within twenty-four hours by Strategic Reserve troops under General Suharto.

Contemporary observers believed the coup was directed by the Indonesian Communist Party (PKI). The failed coup provided a pretext for a massacre of party members in which perhaps 500,000 people were killed, mainly in North Sumatra, Central and East Java, and Bali. Hatred of the Communists was exacerbated by the deliberate spreading of false rumors that the generals were tortured before being killed. More than a million people were detained for longer or shorter periods on grounds of "involvement" in the coup, though the events of 1 October were clearly the work of a small group of conspirators. Even in the early 1990s, family or other connections with those "involved" could mean exclusion from sensitive jobs, including teaching. Most of the conspirators themselves were tried in 1965–1966 in special military tribunals and then executed.

Evidence of PKI involvement in the coup is slight, and the leftist officers involved possibly acted mainly on their own initiative, though they would have expected approbation from the PKI and perhaps from President Sukarno, who feared a rightist military coup. Circumstantial evidence suggests that Suharto may have encouraged, or at least known of, the coup plans, which he was then in a position to foil and exploit to his advantage. Lack of evidence still makes it impossible to reach a conclusion on the origins of the coup, but the general scholarly consensus is that the PKI was too weak to take power and that the coup was a pretext for rather than a cause of the military takeover.

Robert Cribb

Further Reading

Anderson, Benedict R., and Ruth T. McVey. ([1971] 1991) *A Preliminary Analysis of the October 1, 1965, Coup in Indonesia*. Reprint ed. Ithaca, N.Y.: Modern Indonesia Project, Cornell University.

Crouch, Harold. (1978) *The Army and Politics in Indonesia*. Ithaca, N.Y.: Cornell University Press.

GHALIB, MIRZA ASADULLAH KHAN

(1797–1869), Indian poet. Ghalib (Mirza Asadullah Khan), commonly regarded as the greatest Urdu poet, also wrote poetry and prose in Persian and was a great wit and conversationalist. Born to a noble family of Mughal descent in Agra, India, he migrated to Delhi around 1813 and later became the poetic mentor of the last Mughal emperor, Bahadur Shah Zafar (1837–1858). As he was accustomed to living like an aristocratic nobleman, his needs far outstretched his means, so that he was forced into a life of penury.

Ghalib started writing poetry at a very early age under the pen name Asad, which he later changed to Ghalib. A study of his earliest manuscripts demonstrates that he produced most of his significant verses before he was twenty-one. He spent much of his youth writing poetry in Persian, putting together his Persian Diwan (*Diwan-e Farsi*, c. 1835) at least three years before the Urdu Diwan (*Diwan-e Ghalib*, c. 1838). His two collections of letters, *Ud-e Hindi* (Indian Harp) and *Urdu-e Mua'lla* (High Urdu), show him to be a classic writer of Urdu prose. *Dastanbu* (Persian, Pellet of Perfume, 1858) records his impression of the 1857 upheaval (the Sepoy Mutiny; also regarded by some as the first war of Indian independence), while *Mihr-e Nim Roz* (Persian, Midday Sun, 1854–1855) is the first volume of a projected multivolume history of the Timurid dynasty (ruled in India 1513–1857, with a brief interruption of Pathan rule).

However, Ghalib's Urdu Diwan, containing 1,458 verses, has been most instrumental in establishing his reputation as a great writer. Each generation reads the poetry of Ghalib for its own reasons; the metaphysical cogitations and the tough intellectual content strike a chord in every mind.

The themes of Ghalib's poetry are varied—love, the nature of human life and existence, people's role in the universe, free will versus predestination. However, love between a man and a woman, the traditional subject of the *ghazal* (Arabic, a poetic genre), does not substantially engage his mind, and he views this transcendental passion with profound skepticism. Ghalib was a product of the Sufi tradition and had a highly eclectic mind and an attitude of cheerful irreverence toward God and institutionalized religion. If he asserted the dignity and self-respect of people in their relationship with God, he also advocated the value of humans as human, regardless of their religion and race.

To Ghalib the poet, sorrow and pain are essential conditions of human life. He does not neglect or underplay any experience but savors each to the full, even if it is painful. To him every experience becomes an ontological end in itself, regardless of the attendant pain or pleasure. In one of his couplets, he yearns for the inclusion of hell in heaven, as that would provide greater scope for his mind and imagination. In another verse, he exhorts his heart to find solace even in sorrow's song, because one day the body would be deprived of even this sensation, having become insensate and inert. This insatiable appetite for new experiences remains the driving force behind much of his poetry and imparts to his images a private significance and an illuminating power.

Mohammad Asaduddin

Further Reading

Ahmad, Aijaz. (1971) *Ghazals of Ghalib*. New York: Columbia University Press.

Bijnori, Abdur Rahman. (1925) *Mahasin-e Kalam-e Ghalib* (An Appreciation of Ghalib's Poetry). Aurangabad, India: Anjuman Taraqqi Urdu Hind.

Mujeeb, Muhammad. (1969) *Ghalib*. New Delhi: Sahitya Akademi.

Russell, Ralph, and Khurshidul Islam. (1969) *Ghalib: Life and Letters*. Cambridge, MA: Harvard University Press.

GHAZNA (2002 pop. 39,000). Ghazna is the old name of the present town of Ghazni, situated 145 kilometers southwest of Kabul in east-central Afghanistan at an altitude of 2,220 meters. The town is the administrative center of the province of Ghazni.

The early history of Ghazna is obscure. The town was probably the political center of the region of Zabulistan, invaded during the seventh century CE by the Arabs. In 977 CE, a slave commander of the Samanid dynasty, Sebuktigin, established himself in the city and founded the dynasty of the Ghaznavids. Under Mahmud of Ghazna (971–1030), it became the core of a vast empire, stretching from western Persia to the Indian subcontinent. With the decline of Ghaznavid power, Ghazna was sacked by the Ghurids in 1150–1151 and finally lost in 1163. Afterward, different kingdoms and empires, such as the Mongols, Timurids, and Mughals, contended for the city, but it never regained its old glory.

In 1747 Ghazna became part of the new Afghan kingdom of Ahmad Shah Durrani (1722–1773). During the first Anglo-Afghan War (1838–1842), the town was captured by the British, due to its important strategic position on the way to Kabul. During the twentieth century, Ghazni became the form in use for its name; the town rose again in importance as one of the main Afghan centers, mainly due to its geographical position along the Kabul-Kandahar road.

Riccardo Redaelli

Further Reading

Dupree, Luis. (1980) *Afghanistan*. Princeton, NJ: Princeton University Press.

Raverty, Henry George. (1995) *Ghaznin, and Its Environs: Geographical, Ethnographical, and Historical. An Account Extracted from the Writings of the Little Known Afghan and Tajik Historians, Geographers, and Genealogists*. Rev. and enlarged ed. Lahore, Pakistan: Sang-e-Meel.

GIFU (2002 est. pop. 2.1 million). Occupying an area of 10,596 square kilometers, Japan's Gifu Prefecture is situated in central Honshu Island in the middle of the so-called Japan Alps region. Its primary geographical features are the Hida and Ryohaku mountain ranges and the Nobi Plain in the south. Gifu's main rivers are the Nagaragawa, Kisogawa, and Ibigawa. It is bordered by Shiga, Fukui, Ishikawa, Toyama, Nagano, Aichi, and Mie Prefectures.

The capital of the prefecture is Gifu, on the Nagara (Nagaragawa) River. The prefecture's other important cities are Ogaki, Tajimi, Kakamigahara, and Takayama. Gifu evolved from Inokuchi, the castle town of the Toki family during the Muromachi period (1333–1573). The warlord Oda Nobunaga (1534–1582) assumed control of the town in the late sixteenth century and changed its name to Gifu. During the Edo, or Tokugawa, period (1600/03–1868), Gifu flourished as a post station along the Nakasendo route, one of the five main highways that traversed Japan. Traditional crafts associated with the city include fans, paper lanterns, and paper parasols. A major attraction is cormorant fishing (*ukai*), the use of trained and collared birds to catch small river fish, which is carried out on moonless nights.

Present-day Gifu Prefecture was created from Hida and Mino provinces in 1876. As a historic crossroads of inland and marine routes, the region became the locus of such military encounters as the 1600 Battle of Segikahara, in which Tokugawa Ieyasu (1542–1616) defeated his enemies to become shogun, the paramount military leader of the newly reunified Japan.

As part of the Chukyo industrial zone, the prefecture produces lumber, pulp and paper, textiles, ceramics, and transportation equipment. Visitors are drawn to the scenic national parks and to the highland town of Takayama, known as "little Kyoto" for its fine old architecture and crafts, as well as for its Sanno Matsuri and Yahata Matsuri festivals.

E. L. S. Weber

Further Reading

"Gifu Prefecture." (1993) In *Japan: An Illustrated Encyclopedia*. Tokyo: Kodansha Ltd.

GINSENG *Panax ginseng* (Chinese *renshen*), popularly known as ginseng, is China's best-known medicinal product and has been highly sought after both in China and abroad. The swollen root is used (usually the whole root) after careful cleaning, drying, and wrapping in paper. Also used are medicinal extracts made primarily with alcohol and, primarily to suit Western tastes for medicinal teas, ginseng powders. Ginseng belongs to the Araliaceae family and is one of a number of related plants used primarily for their effects on the brain and nervous system. In China, ginseng is most prized because of perceived benefits to the urogenital systems of aging males, whose sexual problems were a major focus in traditional Chinese medicine.

The natural range of ginseng is comparatively limited. In China it grows principally in the lush forests of Manchuria. It is also cultivated to replace and expand root sources in areas where wild ginseng has died out. By the nineteenth century, interest in ginseng as a cure-all had also grown in the West, and the remotest parts of Manchuria were soon penetrated from end to end by ginseng hunters. They advanced far into Siberia as Manchurian resources were depleted, and by the late nineteenth century, China was even importing ginseng from the United States and Canada, a trade that still continues to a limited extent, although both of these countries are now net importers of ginseng, mostly from South Korea.

Paul D. Buell

Further Reading

Perry, Lily M., and Judith Metzger. (1980) *Medicinal Plants of East and Southeast Asia: Attributed Properties and Uses.* Cambridge, MA: MIT Press.

GION MATSURI Kyoto's Gion Matsuri, or Gion Festival, is one of Japan's grandest festivals, consisting of a series of major and minor events throughout July. Dedicated to the deity of the Yasaka Shrine in the Gion district of Kyoto, the festival has a history of more than 1100 years. It originated as a purification ritual *(goryo-e)* to placate angry spirits. The highlight occurs on 17 July, when thirty-two magnificent festival floats, some as much as twenty-four meters in height and twelve tons in weight, decorated with sumptuous textiles and figures are paraded through the city, accompanied by dancers and musicians.

In 869 CE, when plagues were raging across the country, the emperor ordered that special prayers be offered at Yasaka Shrine. The plagues abated, and a thanksgiving procession was held. The procession was repeated later, and in 970 CE it was decreed an annual event. The procession gradually became more and more splendid with large and increasingly elaborate floats. By the sixteenth century Kyoto's prosperous merchants competed to create the most spectacularly decorated floats, donating mechanical figures and fine tapestries from China, Persia, and Europe.

The thirty-two floats, each belonging to a Kyoto neighborhood, are of two types. The nine massive *hoko* floats, roofed and topped by a long pole, are hauled by teams of forty men and carry musicians who play distinctive folk tunes. The twenty-three smaller *yama* floats display historical and mythological figures and sacred pine branches. Following construction by traditional methods, the floats and art treasures are displayed for a three-day "eve of the festival" period *(yoi-yama)* prior to the Grand Procession *(yamaboko-junkô)* on 17 July. The order of the floats is determined by drawing lots, and the lead float has the honor of carrying the *chigo*, a young boy chosen to represent the "celestial child." He is entrusted with the task of severing a sacred straw rope stretched across the procession route, symbolically allowing the floats to enter the realm of the gods. Following the parade the floats are returned to their neighborhoods and are taken apart quickly to banish any unlucky spirits the festivities may have attracted.

While retaining its importance as a purification rite, the Gion Matsuri has become a celebration of Kyoto's heritage and a source of enormous civic pride. The greatest of Kyoto's three foremost festivals, it is designated an Intangible Cultural Asset by the Japanese government and attracts more than a million spectators.

Lucy D. Moss

Further Reading

Haga Hideo. (1970) *Japanese Folk Festivals Illustrated.* Trans. by Fanny Mayer. Tokyo: Miura.

Vilhar, Gorazd, and Charlotte Anderson. (1994) *Matsuri: World of Japanese Festivals.* Tokyo: Shufunotomo.

GOA (2002 pop. 1.4 million) The Indian state of Goa is approximately 400 kilometers south of Mumbai (Bombay). The states of Maharashtra and Karnataka lie to the north and southeast, respectively, and the Arabian Sea to the west. Goa occupies 3,702 square kilometers and has a population of 1,169,793. It is 62 percent Hindu, 34 percent Christian, 3 percent Muslim, and 1 percent "other." Divided into eleven *talukas*

The Dom Bosco Church in Goa. (EYE UBIQUITOUS/CORBIS)

(districts), Goa is governed by its chief minister. The union government in New Delhi appoints the governor, whose function is largely ceremonial. Its legislature is unicameral.

In addition to Goa University, there are numerous schools and colleges. The population of Goa is 77 percent literate, far above the national average of 52 percent. Goa's principal languages are Konkani (the state language), Marathi, and Kannada. Twenty newspapers have been published in English, Marathi, Konkani, and Portuguese. English is the dominant language of journalism in Goa.

CHURCHES AND CONVENTS OF GOA—WORLD HERITAGE SITE

These beautiful manifestations of the spread of Portuguese Catholicism in Asia were designated a World Heritage Site in 1986. The most famous of the churches, the Church of Bom Jesus, is popular with pilgrims all over the world who marvel at the mysteriously undecomposed corpse of Saint Francis-Xavier, the Apostle of the Indies.

Goa is an agricultural state, rice being the principal crop. Coconuts, mangoes, and cashew nuts are also grown. The principal industries are iron mining and tourism. Although Goa is India's smallest state, it produces one-third of India's iron ore: annually, 14 million metric tons of iron ore are mined. Sandy beaches, temperate weather (25–30° C), and historical monuments make Goa a major tourist attraction.

The city of Old Goa is famous for the Sé Cathedral, the Basilica of Bom Jesus (which houses the sarcophagus of Saint Francis Xavier, the patron saint of Goa), and the Church of Saint Cajetan. Ponda is noted for the Mangesh, Mhalasa, and Mahalakshmi Hindu temples and the Safa Muslim mosque. Vasco connects Goa to the rest of India by rail, and the Dabolim airport is reached by domestic flights.

Panaji (population 43,165), the capital, is a port city on the Mandovi River. The origin of the name is uncertain. There are two possible meanings: *panalkhalli* ("place of running water") and *ponnje* ("marshy, fertile place"). The city of Old Goa was the original capital. When its population was decimated in 1759 following plagues, the viceroy moved his residence to Pangim (as it was known then). Pangim was renamed Nova Goa in 1843 and made the capital city.

Mormugao (population 83,200), at the estuary of the Zuari River, is the chief shipping center of Goa

THE SIGHTS OF COLONIAL GOA

"*Goa*, the Metropolis of *India*, under the Dominion of the Crown of *Portugal*, stands on an Island about 12 Miles long, and 6 broad. The City is built on the North Side of it, on a Champain Ground, and has the Conveniency of a fine salt Water River, capable to receive Ships of the largest Size, where they ly within a Mile of the Town. The Banks of the River are beautified with noble Structures of Churches, Castles and Gentlemens Houses; but in the City, the Air is reckoned unwholsom, which is one Cause why at present it is not well inhabited. The Vice-roy's Palace is a noble Edifice, standing within Pistol Shot of the River, over one of the Gates of the City, which leads to a spacious noble Street, about half a Mile long, and terminates at a beautiful Church, called *Misericordia*. The City contains many noble Churches, Convents, and Cloisters, with a stately large Hospital, all well endow's, and well kept. The Market-place stands near the *Misericordia* Church, and takes up about an Acre square, where most Things of the Product of that Country are to be sold; and, in the Shops about it, may be had what *Europe*, *China*, *Bengal*, and other Countries of less Note furnish them with. Every Church has a Set of Bells, that one or other of them are continually ringing, and, being all christned, and dedicated to some Saint, they have a specifick Power to drive away all Manner of evil spirits, except Poverty in the Laity, and Pride in the Clergy; but, to those that are not used to nocturnal Noises, they are very troublesome in the Nights."

Source: Alexander Hamilton. (1702) *A New Account of the East Indies*, as quoted in *The Sahibs* (1948), edited by Hilton Brown. London: William Hodge, 23–24.

and, after Mumbai, India's largest port. Margao (population 58,500) is the chief industrial city of Goa, specializing in electronics, textiles, pharmaceuticals, plastics, and metals.

From the second century CE until 1312, Goa was under the Kadamba rulers, and for most of the fourteenth century Goa was dominated by Muslim invaders. It was annexed by Vijayanagar and later conquered by the Bahmanis, who subdivided it in 1382, making it a part of the Bijapur kingdom, which it remained until the coming of the Portuguese. Alfonso de Albuquerque conquered Goa in 1510 and made it the headquarters of Portuguese possessions in India. Daman and Diu were added later. After India gained independence in 1947, a freedom movement led to the annexation of Goa by force in December 1961. Goa became a union territory in 1962 and a state in 1987. Daman and Diu have remained union territories.

Henry Scholberg

Further Reading

Census of India, 1991. (1996–1998) New Delhi: Controller of Publications.

Fonseca, Nicolau da. (1878) *A Historical and Archaeological Sketch of the City Goa, Preceded by a Short Statistical Account of the Territory of Goa.* Mumbai, India: Thacker.

Rao, R. P. (1963) *Portuguese Rule in Goa, 1510–1961.* Mumbai, India: Asia Publishing House.

Whiteway, Richard Stephen. (1899) *The Rise of the Portuguese Power in India.* Westminster, U.K.: A. Constable.

GOAT The goat *(Capra hircus)*, an even-toed hoofed animal that chews a cud, was probably domesticated in the area of present-day Iran in the mid-eighth millennium BCE and from there spread towards Southeast Europe. Its wild progenitors were three species: the markhor *(C. falconeri)*, the pasang *(C. aegagrus)*, and the extinct Balkan *C. prisca.* In recent times, domesticated goats have been kept throughout West Asia, South Asia, and northwestern China, as well as in the Mediterranean basin and Africa.

Being herded animals, sheep *(Ovis aries)* and goats are sometimes farmed together, with a goat serving as the leader of a flock of sheep. Yet their distribution is not identical, because sheep require dry grassland, whereas goats can flourish in a much wider variety of settings, including India and tropical Africa. Goats do better than sheep in the most marginal of dry lands.

Like other ruminants, goats have complex four-part stomachs in which vegetable food is slowly digested by a process of regurgitation and chewing the cud. They are about one meter in length, with hollow, curved horns, and are covered in long hair useful for spinning into thread. They produce one or two young at a birth; and the udders have two teats. Goat's milk is widely used for food, including cheese making, and goat meat is easily transported to market on the hoof.

Paul Hockings

Further Reading

Watt, George. (1966) "The Goats and Sheep of India." In *The Commercial Products of India*. New Delhi: Today & Tomorrow's Printers & Publishers, 743–749.

GOBI DESERT The Gobi Desert, 1.3 million square kilometers (500,000 square miles) of rugged plains crossing Mongolia and northeastern China, extends roughly from the Great Khingan Mountains (Da Hinggan Ling) in the east to the Tian Shan in the west and from the Altun Shan, Qilian Shan, and Yin Mountains in the south to the Altay Shan and Hangai Mountains in the north. Under this definition the Gobi Desert extends approximately 1,600 kilometers from east to west and 480 to 960 kilometers from north to south. In the Mongolian language the term "gobi" refers to any vast, flat, dry area where people are scarce and where sand and coarse pebbles cover the ground. In fact several deserts on the Central Asian Plateau bear the name, including Gaxun Gobi, Junggar Gobi, Trans-Altay Gobi, and Eastern or Mongolian Gobi.

The Gobi Desert's chalky plateaus consist of bare rocks with intermittent areas of shifting sand. The climate is continental and dry, with severe winters and hot summers. Annual precipitation varies from 6.9 centimeters (2.7 inches) in the west to 20 centimeters (8 inches) in the east. The average lows in January drop to –40°C (–40°F), and the average highs in July reach 45°C (113°F).

Although the region's harsh terrain is a natural barrier, it would be a mistake to describe the land as lifeless. Shrubs and bushes grow on plains watered by mountain streams. Sandy desert occupies only 3 percent of the total area, and much of the Gobi is high mountains and dry grasslands. These areas are home to wild camels, sheep, ibex, snow leopards, lynx, and steppe foxes. The Gobi was also home to the modern world's last remaining wild horse species, Przewalski's horse, which disappeared from the Mongolian steppe in the 1950s but has been reintroduced to the region since 1992. Animals, grazing lands, and subterranean wells are abundant enough to support sparse human populations of one person per square kilometer.

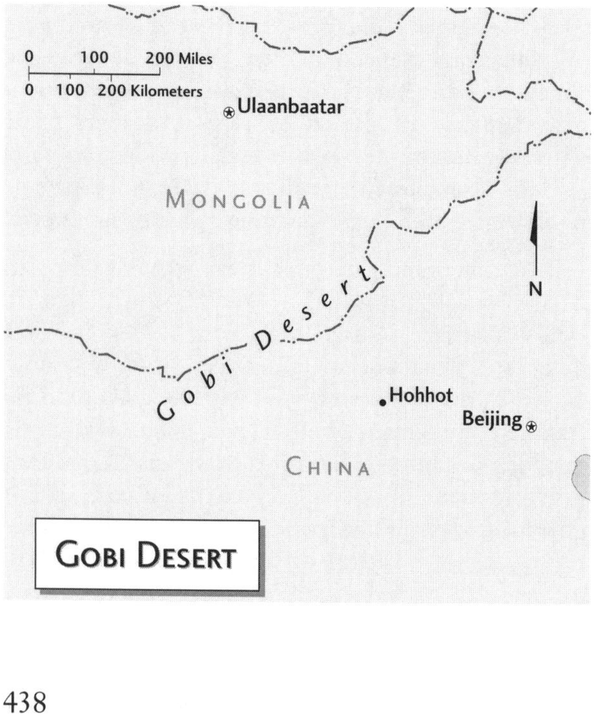

In the twentieth century the Gobi became noted for its wealth of dinosaur fossils. In 1922 the Central Asiatic Expedition under the direction of Roy Chapman Andrews (1884–1960) first discovered the fossilized remains of dinosaurs in the region, and subsequent researchers found the remains of hundreds of dinosaurs in the Gobi Desert. Many of these finds, including *Oviraptor*, *Stegoceras*, *Protoceratops*, and *Velociraptor*, were the first of their kind. In some instances the fossils were lying on the desert floor, covered only by a thin layer of dust.

Although the Gobi region has supported a rich variety of flora and fauna from prehistoric to present times, increasing urbanization, livestock grazing, and agricultural development in the last century have upset the Gobi's delicate ecological balance in many areas. For example, the outskirts of cities, such as Sainshand, Mongolia, have seen brushy and grazable land turn to infertile shifting sands as herds overgraze near the city and motorized vehicle traffic increasingly tears up the Gobi's delicate surface. Both the Chinese and the Mongolian governments have instituted projects to counter this man-made degradation, but only time will tell if the Gobi desert is destined to become in actuality the wasteland that many outsiders think it is.

Daniel Hruschka

Further Reading

Cable, Mildred. (1984) *The Gobi Desert.* London: Virago.

Man, John. (1999) *Gobi: Tracking the Desert.* New Haven, CT: Yale University Press.

GODAVARI RIVER The Godavari (or Godavery) River, 1,445 kilometers long, originates in India's Western Ghats, in Nasik District, and then flows in a southeasterly direction across Maharashtra and Andhra Pradesh, bisecting the Deccan Plateau, and then cutting a valley through the Eastern Ghats in a magnificent gorge only 200 meters wide. Above this, however, the river in parts is 2 to 3 kilometers wide. After crossing a vast fertile delta, the river empties into the Bay of Bengal through three main distributaries in the central part of Andhra Pradesh. Rice is grown on the delta, which benefits from a system of irrigation canals as well as the several distributaries. The main canals are all navigable, totaling some 793 kilometers in length, and irrigating 268,000 hectares. The catchment area of the river has been estimated at 290,600 square kilometers.

Paul Hockings

GODPARENTHOOD—PHILIPPINES

In the Philippines godparenthood based on *compadrinazgo* or *compadrazgo* is known as the *compadre* or *kumpare* system. It is the mechanism whereby new relationships are created through participation in certain rites of passage. Ritual kinship is created through sponsorship at baptisms, confirmations, and marriages required by the Roman Catholic Church. *Compadrinazgo* combines *padrinazgo* or spiritual godparenthood with *compadrazgo* or ritual co-parenthood, with *padrinazgo* emphasizing the vertical relationships, that is between godparents and godchildren, and *compadrazgo* stressing horizontal relationships, that is, between the godparents and the natural parents.

The *compadre* system is not indigenous to the Philippines but an alien institution that has been adapted at different times to meet specific circumstances. Found in Europe as early as the ninth century, the practice was brought to the New World by the Spaniards, where it was quickly accepted and later exported to the Philippines. The *compadrazgo* system includes a mixture of Spanish, Latin American, and Filipino aspects.

In Philippine societies, which were emerging from the kinship stage (Phelan) at the time of the Spanish intrusion, *compadrazgo* represented possibilities for extended kinship systems. Among the features of the *compadre* mechanism are its adaptability to different situations and changing needs. What began as a means of creating extended kinship evolved into a mechanism for survival in a society controlled by colonial powers. Family in the Philippines should be seen as "the strongest unit of society, demanding the deepest loyalties of the individual, and coloring all social activity with its own demands" (McCoy 1995: 1). As such, its responsibilities include providing employment and capital, educating and socializing the young, providing medical care, and sheltering the handicapped and elderly. While blood kinship might not be able to meet all these needs, a system that includes extended kinship has a better chance of doing so. As a result, kinship in the Philippines is not primarily vertical but horizontal and expands within each generation, creating an ever-wider safety net of fictive relationships.

With the emergence of a local elite, the *compadre* system became a tool for reinforcing the patron-client relationship. Both sides of the equation can gain by entering into a *compadre* relationship. The weaker party, the client, seeks the assistance of the stronger, wealthier party. The patron gains the allegiance of others, and can use this for political, social, and economic power.

Damon L. Woods

Further Reading

Foster, George M. (1953) "Cofradia and Compadrazgo in Spain and Spanish America." In *Southwestern Journal of Anthropology* 9, 1 (Spring): 1–28.

Hart, Donn. (1977) *Compadrinazgo: Ritual Kinship in the Philippines*. DeKalb: Northern Illinois University Press.

McCoy, Alfred W. (1995) "'An Anarchy of Families': The Historiography of State and Family in the Philippines." In *An Anarchy of Families: State and Family in the Philippines*, edited by Alfred W. McCoy. Quezon City, Philippines: Ateneo de Manila University Press.

Mintz, Sidney W., and Eric R. Wolf. (1950) "An Analysis of Ritual Co-Parenthood (Compadrazgo)." *Southwestern Journal of Anthropology* 6, 4 (Winter): 341–368.

Phelan, John Leddy. (1959) *The Hispanization of the Philippines: Spanish Aims and Filipino Responses, 1565–1700.* Madison, WI: The University of Wisconsin Press.

GODSE, NATHURAM VINAYAK

(1911–1949), assassin of Mohandas Gandhi. Nathuram Vinayak Godse, perhaps the most notorious assassin of the twentieth century, was the Hindu fanatic who shot Mohandas (Mahatma) Gandhi dead on 30 January 1948 in Delhi. He was a member of the Rashtriya Swayamsevak Sangh (RSS), a political faction angered at what it saw as Gandhi's pandering to the Muslims of India and his "emasculation of the Hindu community" through a long-standing policy of nonviolence *(ahimsa)*. With the end of British rule, this radical faction wanted Hindu Raj, a chauvinistic Hindu government.

In that time of extreme tension between Muslims and Hindus on the subcontinent, a Muslim's attempt on the saintly Gandhi's life would have ignited a bloodbath even greater than the one that had marked the splitting of Pakistan from India. But Godse was, like Gandhi, a Hindu, albeit a militant extremist and

Godse (front row, left) and codefendants at their trial. (BETTMANN/CORBIS)

a Brahmin. He was editor of two magazines published in Pune by the Hindu Mahasabha, another political organization. The immediate cause of Godse's anger was Gandhi's embarking on yet another fast to protest the communal violence that was tearing India apart. A fellow conspirator, Madan Lal, had failed to kill Gandhi the previous day with a bomb explosion. But Godse shot Gandhi at point-blank range after bowing to him, while Gandhi was on the way to evening prayers. Godse was tried, defended himself eloquently, and was sentenced, with his associate Narayan Apte, to execution and was hanged on 15 November 1949.

Paul Hockings

Further Reading

Pyarelal. (1965) *Mahatma Gandhi: The Last Phase.* 2d ed. Weare, NH: Greenleaf.

GOH CHOK TONG (b. 1941), prime minister of the Republic of Singapore. Born in Singapore on 20 May 1941, Goh Chok Tong was educated at the elite Raffles Institution and later earned his B.A. from the University of Singapore in 1964. Upon graduation, Goh joined the Singapore Civil Service. In 1967, he earned a masters degree in economics from Williams College. Goh began his political career in 1976, becoming a member of parliament as a member of the ruling People's Action Party (PAP). In 1977, he became a minister of state for finance, and between 1979 and 1990 he held a variety of cabinet posts, including minister of trade and industry and minister of health. In 1985, Goh became minister for defense and the first deputy prime minister. In 1990, following the

Goh Chonk Tong addressing the United Nations in New York in September 2000. (REUTERS NEWMEDIA INC./CORBIS)

resignation of Singapore's founding prime minister, Lee Kwan Yew (held office 1965–1990), Goh was elected prime minister. In addition to his cabinet posts, Goh has held senior PAP positions since 1979, including the post of secretary general, which he has held since 1992. Goh is a leading voice in the regional organization the Association of Southeast Asian Nations (ASEAN) and has overseen Singapore's consolidation as a regional financial and economic power. A devoted party loyalist, he has ensured the PAP's domination of Singapore politics.

Zachary Abuza

Further Reading

Lee Kwan Yew. (2001) *From Third World to First: The Singapore Story, 1965–2000.* New York: HarperCollins.

GOH KENG SWEE (b. 1918), finance minister and minister of education of Singapore. Goh Keng Swee was born in Melaka to parents of Chinese ancestry. After earning a doctorate from the London School of Economics, he became finance minister of Singapore in 1959. When Singapore became independent in 1965, Goh embarked on a pragmatic program of industrial development, which was to be financed by foreign capital. His program brought prosperity to the island republic while neighboring countries floundered economically.

At the core of his development plan were incentives to foreign corporations. Foreign firms were allowed to operate in tax-free enclaves, exempt from local regulations pertaining to working and other conditions. As a result, Singapore induced many multinational corporations to establish Southeast Asian regional offices there.

In 1979, Goh became minister of education during a crisis in which the government feared that Singapore's students were not ready to meet the challenges posed by an economy based on high technology. In response, Goh revamped the public school system, stressing English as the preferred language of instruction.

Goh retired from politics in 1984. Subsequently, he has served as an advisor to the governments of the People's Republic of China and Singapore on economic matters. His legacy to Singapore is that it became one of the top-ten countries in the world in per capita gross national product, surpassing even Great Britain, by the 1990s.

Michael Haas

Further Reading

Low, Linda. (1998) *The Political Economy of a City-State: Government-Made Singapore.* Singapore: Oxford University Press.

Murray, G., and A. Perera. (1996) *Singapore: The Global City State.* New York: St. Martin's.

GOLDEN CRESCENT The Golden Crescent is the name given to Asia's principal area of illicit opium production, located at the crossroads of Central, South, and Western Asia. This space overlaps three nations, Afghanistan, Iran, and Pakistan, whose mountainous peripheries define the crescent. In 1991, Afghanistan became the world's primary opium producer, with a yield of 1,782 metric tons, surpassing Burma, formerly the world leader in opium production. The Golden Crescent has a much longer history of opium production than does Southeast Asia's Golden Triangle, even though the Golden Crescent emerged as a modern-day opium-producing entity only in the 1970s, after the Golden Triangle did so in the 1950s.

The distribution of opium in the Golden Crescent was a by-product of early commerce along the Silk Road and of Arab maritime trade. Indeed, places such as Kunduz and Kabul in Afghanistan, Peshawar in Pakistan, and the Makran coast of Pakistan served as commercial relays for merchants who undoubtedly traded in opium as early as the first century of the Common Era.

From at least the seventeenth century, the area's main opium-producing state was Persia (later Iran), until the Shah banned all production and consumption in 1955. Only as late as 1979, however, did opiate production really emerge with the establishment of the Islamic Republic of Iran and the Soviet invasion of Afghanistan. During the 1970s, Afghanistan produced a mere 90 to 270 metric tons of opium per year, almost the same yield as neighboring Pakistan, before the latter achieved 720-metric-ton crop in 1979. If Persia's prohibition of opium trade had earlier contributed to Golden Triangle opium production, the 1978 drought that affected Southeast Asia contributed, in turn, to the growth of the Golden Crescent, as shown by the doubling of Afghanistan's opium output in 1983.

Although Pakistan has almost stopped production, it still has a huge addicted population that relies on Afghanistan's opiates. Afghanistan doubled its production again in 1999, reaching a stunning 4,123 metric tons of dry opium. Afghanistan thus emerged as the world's leading producer of opiates before suddenly and dramatically reducing this production by 85 percent in 2001, when it was banned by the Taliban rulers. At the close of 2001, with the Taliban forced from power, opium production is reappearing.

The evolution of opium production in the Golden Crescent was clearly the outcome of the protracted twenty-year Afghan conflict. Afghanistan's current socioeconomic situation makes opium production one of the country's only available economic means of access to land, labor, and credit. Along with the Golden Triangle, the Golden Crescent (with Afghanistan as its preeminent producer) remains one of the world's main areas for the production of illicit opiates. Short-term trends show great irregularities of production, while long-term trends indicate continuing strength in the region's illicit opiates industry.

Pierre-Arnaud Chouvy

See also: **Drug Trade; Golden Triangle**

Further Reading

Mccoy, Alfred. (1991) *The Politics of Heroin: CIA Complicity in the Global Drug Trade*. New York: Lawrence Hill.
Observatoire Géopolitique des Drogues. (1996) *Atlas mondial des drogues*. Paris: P.U.F.
Rashid, Ahmed. (2000) *Taliban, Islam, Oil, and the New Great Game in Central Asia*. New York: I. B. Tauris.
Willems, Peter. (1997) "Afghanistan's Gold." In *The Middle East*. London: IC Publications, 6–9.

GOLDEN HORDE The Golden Horde is best known as that part of the Mongol empire that ruled the lands we now know as Russia from approximately 1237 to 1359. Originally, however, it consisted of those lands that Genghis Khan (1165–1227) bequeathed to his son Jochi (flourished 1184–1225). These consisted of the territories west of the Irtysh River (in modern Kazakhstan) and Khwarizm (in present-day Uzbekistan).

During the reign of Ogodei Khan (d. 1240/1241), the successor of Genghis Khan, the realm exploded in size. In 1237, Jochi's son Batu (reigned 1227–1255), assisted by Genghis Khan's famous general Sabutai (d. 1279), led a large army westward. They destroyed the Bulgar state, pacified the numerous Turkic tribes of the steppes, and conquered Russia's cities. In 1240, Mongol armies invaded Hungary and Poland. As news spread of the ferocity of the Mongol attack, Europe trembled in anticipation of an invasion that never came. In 1241, Ogodei Khan died and the Mongol armies withdrew to elect a new khan.

Batu established the Golden Horde, as his territory was known, as a semi-dependent part of the Mongol empire. The origins of the name Golden Horde are uncertain. Some scholars believe that it refers to the camp of Batu and the later rulers of the Horde. In Mongolian, Altan Orda refers to the Golden Camp or Horde. The golden color *(altan)* also connoted imperial status.

Batu died in 1255 and the next significant ruler of the Golden Horde was his brother Berke (1255–1267). Berke had converted to Islam and focused most of his energies against the Il-Khans of Persia. He completed an alliance with the Mamluks of Egypt, who also were enemies of the Il-Khans. The Il-Khanate collapsed in 1334.

The golden age of the Golden Horde occurred between 1313 and 1341, during the rule of Oz Beg (Uzbek) Khan. During this period, the Golden Horde reached its pinnacle in terms of wealth, trade, influence, and military might. Also during this period Oz Beg Khan forced the conversion of the Golden Horde to Islam. During the mid-fourteenth century, however, the Golden Horde weakened as it, like much of the world, suffered from bubonic plague, civil wars, and ineffective rulers.

Toqtamish (reigned 1379–1391, 1392–1395) restored the Golden Horde to some of its former glory, but he also became embroiled in a series of wars with the Turkic conqueror Timur (Tamerlane; reigned 1369–1404). Timur emerged victorious; Toqtamish died in obscurity. The cities of Sarai and New Sarai were sacked and the trade routes never recovered from Tamerlane's predations. With the death of Toqtamish, the Golden Horde went into a downward spiral and eventually fragmented. By the mid-fifteenth century, it had shattered into the Crimean khanate, the Astrakhan khanate, the Siberian khanate, the Kazan khanate, the Nogai Horde, and the Great Horde.

Timothy M. May

See also: **Mongol Empire**

Further Reading

Fennell, John. (1983) *The Crisis of Medieval Russia, 1200–1304*. New York: Longman.
Halperin, Charles J. (1985) *Russia and the Golden Horde: The Mongol Impact on Medieval Russian History*. Bloomington, IN: Indiana University Press.
———. (1986) *The Tatar Yoke*. Columbus, OH: Slavica.
Hartog, Leo de. (1996) *Russia and the Mongol Yoke: The History of the Russian Principalities and the Golden Horde, 1221–1502*. London: British Academic Press.
Morgan, David. (1986) *The Mongols*. New York: Blackwell.

GOLDEN TRIANGLE The Golden Triangle is one of Asia's two main illicit opium-producing areas. It is an area of around 350,000 square kilometers that overlaps the mountains of three countries of mainland Southeast Asia: Myanmar (Burma), Laos, and Thailand. Along with Afghanistan in the Golden Crescent (together with Iran and Pakistan), it has been one the most important opium-producing area of Asia and of the world since the 1950s.

The term first appeared in 1971, referring to the shape of Myanmar, Laos, and Thailand when taken together. The gold of the triangle is most probably that which the first opium merchants of the region used in exchange for the crops. Although the opium production that exists in the Golden Triangle is frequently and erroneously thought to be an old traditional activity, in fact, opium growing is an altogether recent phenomenon. It is only at the end of nineteenth century that the poppy-growing tribal populations began their southernmost forced migration from China toward the highlands of mainland Southeast Asia. There they scattered and settled, having brought with them the practice and techniques of farming the opium poppy (*Papaver somniferum*).

As World War II drew to a close, this area was producing less than eighty tons of opium per annum. All that changed when China clamped down on opium production and addiction, spurring Southeast Asia to take over production. The sudden suppression of opium production in Iran in 1955 further reinforced the transfer toward Southeast Asia.

Later, due mainly to the internal protracted Burmese conflicts and ethnic and communist rebellions, the Golden Triangle's opium production literally exploded, exceeding 3,000 tons in 1989, with Burma alone producing more than 2,500 tons in 1996. The narcotics trade linked a marginal and isolated Southeast Asian region with principal cities of the Western world. The United States became the main destination of the Golden Triangle's heroin, the so-called China White, or heroin No. 4, renowned for its 98 percent purity.

At the end of the twentieth century, the Golden Triangle was clearly dominated by Burmese production, Thailand had suppressed almost all its poppies, and Laos was still fighting the battle. But a new scourge had arrived in the region: an explosion in amphetamine production in Burma and a large population of addicts in Thailand.

Pierre-Arnaud Chouvy

Further Reading

Boucaud, André, and Louis Boucaud. (1985) *Sur la piste des seigneurs de la guerre*. Paris: L'Harmattan.

Lintner, Bertil. (1994) *Burma in Revolt: Opium and Insurgency since 1948*. Boulder, CO: Westview.

McCoy, Alfred. (1972) *The Politics of Heroin in Southeast Asia*. New York: Harper & Row.

———. (1991) *The Politics of Heroin: CIA Complicity in the Global Drug Trade*. New York: Lawrence Hill.

Observatoire Géopolitiquedes Drogues. (1996) *Atlas Mondial des drogues*. Paris: Presses Universitaires de France.

GOLKAR Golkar (Golongan Karya, or Joint Secretariat of Functional Groups) was a government party in Indonesia during President Suharto's New Order. It was created as an umbrella of anti-Communist civilian associations and trade unions in order to balance the influence of the Indonesian Communist Party (PKI, or Partai Komunis Indonesia), which had grown during the period of Guided Democracy (1959–1965) established by President Sukarno. Golkar was sponsored by the Indonesian army. With Suharto's ascent to power in 1967, Golkar became the electoral organization of the New Order government. At first Golkar lacked the individual membership and special cadre of activists needed to form a strong political party. By 1971, however, it won the national election and subsequently had little competition from the other two political parties—the United Development Party and the Indonesian Democratic Party—that had emerged from Suharto's rationalization of the political system in 1973. By 1983, Golkar was considered a strong political party, widely supported because of Indonesia's economic successes under it but also because opponents were intimidated and election results were manipulated. At the general election of June 1999, Golkar was relegated to second place after Megawati Sukarnoputri's Indonesian Democratic Party, signifying the final demise of the New Order.

Martin Ramstedt

Further Reading

Cribb, Robert, and Colin Brown. (1995) *Modern Indonesia: A History since 1945*. New York: Longman.

Pompe, Sebastiaan. (1999) De Indonesische Algemene Verkiezingen (The Indonesian General Election). Leiden, Netherlands: KITLV Uitgeverij.

Vatikiotis, Michael R. J. (1993) *Indonesian Politics under Suharto*. New York: Routledge.

GOND The Gonds, for the most part located in the state of Madhya Pradesh in central India, are the largest Scheduled Tribe (low-caste tribe) in southern Asia, numbering over 7.3 million in 1981. The more southerly Gonds speak Parji or Gondi, two Dravidian languages, whereas those in the north speak dialects of Hindi or Marathi, which are both Indo-Aryan languages.

The Gonds live, often as extended families, in dispersed housing in villages. Even where other tribes and castes are present, the Gonds tend to remain in separate hamlets. They either farm or work in the forests, collecting timber, honey, or wild plants. Most have been obliged to abandon their former pattern of shifting cultivation for settled farming, in some areas on terraces. Millet, rice, wheat, gram, and other crops are grown, and animal husbandry is practiced. Women play an important role in farming, as well as in collecting fuel and forest produce.

Monogamy is the normal marriage pattern, though polygyny does occur, as well as divorce and widow remarriage. While it has a large population, the tribe was never a political unit. It has always been split into many subgroups, with little or no political influence in modern India. The main authority is the village headman and his council. These traditionally had a judicial role in the society.

The religion of the Gonds may be characterized as Hindu, but with many animistic practices devoted to nature spirits. Gonds believe all humans have two souls. They believe in an almighty god named Bhagwan, but little ritual is directed to him.

Paul Hockings

Further Reading

Fuchs, Stephen. (1968) *The Gond and Bhumia of Eastern Mandla.* 2d ed. Bombay, India: New Literature.

Fürer-Haimendorf, Christoph von, and Elizabeth von Fürer-Haimendorf. (1979) *The Gonds of Andhra Pradesh: Tradition and Change in an Indian Tribe.* New Delhi: Vikas.

GONDAVANA. See **Chhattisgarh.**

GONG LI (b. 1966), Chinese actress. Gong Li was born in Shenyang, Liaoning Province, China, in 1966. She graduated from high school in 1983 and was mentored by Yin Dawei, a stage director with the Jinan Military Drama Troupe, before entering Beijing's Central Drama Academy in 1985. While a student there, she was chosen by director Zhang Yimou to play the lead in his film *Red Sorghum* (1987), which went on to win the Golden Bear award at the Berlin Film Festival.

Zhang and Gong's first creative partnership led to many more films, including *Ju Dou* (1989), *Raise the Red Lantern* (1991), *The Story of Qiu Ju* (1992), *To Live* (1994), and *Shanghai Triad* (1995). For her role in *The Story of Qiu Ju,* Gong was awarded the best actress prize by the Venice Film Festival.

Over her career, Gong has tackled a wide variety of roles from the glamorous to the workaday, always imbuing her performance with tremendous confidence and charisma. She frequently portrays strong, independent women who go against society's grain to pursue their own unshakable convictions.

Gong has also appeared in numerous films by other directors, including Chen Kaige, Wayne Wang, Lu Yue, and Huang Shuqin. In 1998 she became a delegate to the Chinese People's Political Consultative Conference.

Alexa Olesen

See also: **Zhang Yimou**

Further Reading

Zhang Yingjin, and Zhao Zhiwei. (1999) *Encyclopedia of Chinese Film.* London: Routledge.

GORKUT ATA The Gorkut Ata epic, or *Book of Grandfather Korpkut,* is a collection of twelve narratives in a mixture of verse and prose, telling the heroic exploits of the Oghuz, a Turkic tribe from which the modern Turks, Azerbaijanis, and Turkmen arose. The telling of these tales is attributed to Grandfather Korkut, variously called Dede Korkut (Qorqut) or Gorkut Ata, the legendary singer and narrator of the Oghuz. The text of these epic tales is transmitted in two sixteenth-century manuscripts, but the narratives themselves are considerably older. Some may go back to the period when the Oghuz still lived on the Syr Dar'ya River in Central Asia (ninth–eleventh centuries CE). Famous among these narratives are the tales of Basat and Tepe Goz, a variant of the story of Odysseus and the Cyclops, and of Bamsi Beyrek, a version of the Alpamish epic. In spirit and form these narratives can be considered some of the first Turkic epics. The figure of Gorkut Ata is the subject of a number of legends and traditional songs in Central Asia, where he is venerated as the patron saint of epic singers.

Karl Reichl

Further Reading

Ibraev, Sh., et al., eds. (1999) *Korkut Ata: Entsiklopedicheskii sbornik na kazakhskom i russkom iazykakh* (Korkut Ata: An Encyclopedic Collective Volume in Kazakh and Russian). Almaty, Kazakhstan: Qazaq entsiklopediyasy.

Lewis, Geoffrey, trans. (1974) *The Book of Dede Korkut.* Harmondsworth, U.K.: Penguin.

GOTO SHINPEI (1857–1929), Japanese politician. Trained in medicine, Goto made his name as a colonial administrator in imperial Japan's burgeoning empire. He was subsequently influential as a bureaucratic politician in the transition period between oligarchic and political party rule.

Of samurai lineage from the Sendai domain (present-day Miyagi Prefecture), Goto studied medicine in Fukushima and Nagoya and at age twenty-five gained public recognition as the head of Aichi Prefectural Hospital. After two years of study in Germany, he served the empire as chief of the Sanitation Bureau of the Home Ministry (1895–1898), director of the Army Quarantine Office (1895), first head of civilian administration in Taiwan (1898–1906), first president of the South Manchuria Railway Company (1906–1908), and director general, alternately, of the Railway Agency and the Colonization Bureau between 1908 and 1918.

Among Goto's political appointments were membership in the House of Peers (1903–1929), minister of communications (1908–1911, 1912–1913), home minister (1916–1918 and 1923–1924), minister of foreign affairs (1918), and mayor of Tokyo (1920–1923). In addition to his service to the empire, Goto is celebrated for work in reconstruction after the 1923 Tokyo earthquake and his attempt to normalize relations with the Soviet Union in 1923.

Frederick R. Dickinson

Further Reading

Hayase, Yukiko. (1974) "The Career of Goto Shinpei: Japan's Statesman of Research, 1857–1929." Ph.D. diss. Florida State University.

Kitaoka Shin'ichi. (1988) *Goto Shinpei: Gaiko to vuijon.* Tokyo: Chuo koron.

GRAMEEN BANK In 1999, Grameen Bank (GB) distributed $1.5 million in microcredit loans every day. The bank was established in Chittagong, Bangladesh, in 1983 with the belief that credit is a "fundamental human right." The concept is also based on the belief that if poor people are provided with money and a few sound financial principles to live by, such as collective responsibility, close monitoring of repayment of loans, and compulsory and voluntary saving, they will help themselves.

The idea of Grameen Bank became a reality in 1976, when Professor Muhammad Yunus loaned $27 of his own money to forty-two people living in a village in rural Bangladesh. The people to whom he lent the money were stool makers who only needed enough credit to purchase raw materials for their trade.

GB has reversed conventional banking practice by removing the need for collateral and has created a banking system based on mutual trust, accountability, participation, and creativity. Participants, typically small groups of borrowers, are required to set aside 5 percent of a loan as a fund from which all participants can draw, pending group approval. For GB, credit is a cost-effective weapon in the fight against poverty, and it serves as a catalyst in the overall socioeconomic development of the poor, who have been kept outside the banking orbit on the ground that they are not bankable.

Currently, GB is the largest rural finance institution in the country. It has more than 2.3 million borrowers, 94 percent of whom are women. With 1,128 branches, GB provides services in 38,951 villages, covering more than half of the total villages in Bangladesh. The repayment rate of its loans, which average $160, is more than 95 percent. Interest on all loans is currently fixed at 16 percent.

Grameen Bank's positive impact on its poor and formerly poor borrowers has been documented in many independent studies by external agencies, including the World Bank, the International Food Research Policy Institute (IFPRI), and the Bangladesh Institute of Development Studies (BIDS). Grameen Bank has inspired people and institutions throughout the world with its success in poverty alleviation. More than 4,000 people from some 100 countries have gone through Grameen's training programs over the last ten years. Some of those visitors have returned to their countries and replicated the Grameen Bank financial system to help poor people in their own country to overcome poverty. A total of 223 Grameen replication programs in fifty-eight countries have been established during the last decade. Taken together, they have reached several hundred thousand poor borrowers with credit around the world.

Syedur Rahman

See also: **Bangladesh—Economic System**

Further Reading

Holcombe, Susan. (1995) *Managing to Empower: The Grameen Bank's Experience of Poverty Alleviation.* Dhaka, Bangladesh: United Press.

Mueller-Glodde, Ulrike. (1997) *Poor but Strong: Women in the People's Economy of Bangladesh.* Dhaka, Bangladesh: Grameen Trust.

Ray, Jayanta Kumar. (1995) *To Chase a Miracle.* Dhaka, Bangladesh: United Press.

Yunus, Muhammad. (1999) *Banker of the Poor: Micro-Lending and the Battle against World Poverty.* New York: Public Affairs.

GRAND CANAL China's longest canal is the Grand Canal, stretching more than 1,700 kilometers from Beijing in the north to Hangzhou in the south. It is the world's longest man-made waterway and was built over the course of centuries beginning in the fourth century BCE. Major work was undertaken on it during the Sui dynasty (581–618) and the Tang dynasty (618–907); under the Yuan dynasty (1279–1368) the course of the canal was shifted. All China's major rivers run west to east, but the Grand Canal runs north to south, connecting the Chang (Yangtze) River in the south with the Huang (Yellow) River in the north and providing a valuable alternative to overland or sea transport of goods.

The canal's primary use during the Sui and Tang dynasties was to bring grain grown in the fertile south to expanding cities in the north. It became a major trade route, with goods and people flowing in both directions. One important innovation was the invention of the pound lock in the tenth century. The pound lock allowed boats to move along waterways of different levels; the Grand Canal, for instance, rises more than 40 meters above sea level over its course. Currently there are twenty-four locks on the Grand Canal.

The Huang River's flooding and silting have always caused problems for the canal, but it was regularly maintained and used into the twentieth century, when the rise of coastal ports and railroad transportation led sections to fall into disuse. In the 1950s much of the canal was reopened for use, and it is again a major trade route as well as a tourist attraction.

Paul Forage

GREAT GAME The Great Game is the term widely used to describe the bitter nineteenth-century Anglo-Russian rivalry for influence in Central Asia. British and Russian strategists (mainly young military officers) saw the need for influence over Central Asia from a historical perspective. They argued that most military campaigns against the Indian subcontinent were undertaken through the territory of Central Asia, which at that time included Afghanistan and the eastern part of Iran. Thus for the British, primary influence over Central Asia was pivotal to defense of their interests in India against Russian advancement, while it was crucial for Russia to defend its communications lines with Siberia and the Russian Far East, the "soft underbelly" of the Russian Empire in Winston Churchill's words.

Both sides undertook a number of spying and counterspying operations and highly adventurous geographic expeditions in search of allies and routes for troops, all of which were glorified by such writers as Rudyard Kipling. The Russians conducted the first expedition to Khiva in 1839–1840, but the campaign was unsuccessful, and they lost a number of solders and officers in this ill-prepared expedition. Then in 1842, two British officers, Colonel Charles Stuart and Captain Arthur Connolly, were hanged in Bukhara. The Russians collided with the Kokand Khanate when they captured Tashkent (1865), an important economic outpost of the khanate; Khodzhent (1866); and later Kokand (1875), which established their influence over the Bukhara Khanate (1868), advancing all the way to the borders of Afghanistan, the last political barrier before India. Perceiving this as a direct threat to British interests in India, the British advanced northwest in an attempted to establish direct control over Afghanistan.

In the eighteenth century, Ahmad Shah (reigned 1747–1773), the leader of the Abdali tribe of the Pashtuns, had proclaimed Afghan rule as far east as Kashmir and Delhi, north to the Amu Dar'ya, and west into northern Persia. In the nineteenth century, as internal conflicts gradually weakened the Afghan empire, both the British in India and the Russians to the north sought to bring Afghanistan under their control. This resulted in two Anglo-Afghan Wars (1838–1842 and 1878–1880), which the British finally won, establishing their dominance over Afghanistan's foreign relations. Gradually, both sides, British and Russian, accepted Afghanistan as a buffer zone between their respective empires.

The strategic importance of Central Asia was highlighted again in the early twentieth century by Sir Halford John Mackinder, the British political geographer, who in 1919–1920 went as British high commissioner to southern Russia in an attempt to unify the White Russian forces against the Bolsheviks. He produced a simple geopolitical formula: "Who rules the Heartland [which included Central Asia] commands the World-Island [Eurasian Continent]. Who rules the World-Island commands the World."

Since the Soviet Union's dissolution in 1991, a new competition for political influence and a share in the Central Asian market, especially for its natural resources, has emerged between various actors. This competition has often been described in terms of establishing influence over the newly independent Central Asian Republics on a basis strategically similar to the competition between Britain and Russia in the nineteenth century.

Rafis Abazov

Further Reading

Hopkirk, Peter. (1990) *The Great Game: On Secret Service in High Asia.* London: Murray.

Meyer, Karl Ernest, and Shareen Blair Brysac. (1999) *Tournament of Shadows: The Great Game and the Race for Empire in Central Asia.* Washington, DC: Counterpoint.

GREAT LEAP FORWARD The Great Leap Forward was the campaign launched by the Chinese Communist leadership in 1958 to quickly catch up to and leapfrog over Great Britain and the United States. Having become disenchanted with the Soviet-style development strategy that prioritized heavy industry, China's leaders, particularly Mao Zedong (1893–1976), believed that massive social mobilization would allow China simultaneously to develop industry and agriculture. Unfortunately, the campaign ended in utter failure and caused what is today known as the Great Leap famine.

Mao's Successful Promotion of Large Collectives

Any explanation of the Great Leap must begin with the ideological preferences of Mao and his colleagues. Mao's efforts to promote large collectives and communes were based on a belief in economies of scale and a desire to promote social equality. Even though Mao's earlier pursuit of progressively larger rural institutions, ranging from mutual-aid groups to cooperatives and then to collectives, had caused many disruptions in agricultural production, the disruptions were dismissed as temporary. Mao forged on with demands for larger collectives in the late 1950s.

The Chinese political system had no room for dissent at this time. Repeated political campaigns, particularly the Anti-Rightist Campaign of 1957, had banished those who spoke up, primarily intellectuals, to hard labor and even imprisonment. Those who raised questions a little later about Great Leap policy practices, such as the defense minister Peng Dehuai (1898–1974), were persecuted as rightist opportunists. In such a political system, those who aspired to mobility on the political ladder of success watched for cues to Mao's preferences and eagerly supported everything that Mao liked.

Once Mao endorsed the term "people's commune" in early August 1958, local leaders and political activists raced to establish communes and competed to build ever-larger ones. The number of communes proliferated. In just two months, most provinces claimed a successful transition to people's communes. Rural China was organized into 26,500 gigantic communes, each averaging 4,756 households. The communes abolished private property and, in most cases, did away with all economic incentives. The commune mess hall epitomized the frenzy of the Great Leap. Commune members were encouraged to abandon their private kitchens, donate the pots and pans to backyard iron furnaces, and dine in communal mess halls so that women could join the labor force.

The Free-Supply System and Other Wasteful Practices

Amid the euphoria of Communist transition, China's leaders ceased to manage the economy but instead encouraged practices that in hindsight were downright criminal. The state statistical system stopped functioning and was replaced by wild claims of bountiful harvests. Such claims in turn engendered wildly exaggerated output forecasts and prompted prominent regional leaders such as Ke Qingshi (1902–1965) and Tan Zhenlin (1902–1983) to exhort peasants to eat as much as they could. As a consequence, the free-supply system was widely adopted, and the mess hall became the site of communal feasts in many places. The free-supply system induced overconsumption and waste of food, even while state grain procurement was increased sharply on the basis of wildly exaggerated output forecasts. With worsening Sino-Soviet relations, the Chinese leadership increased grain exports, again under the illusion of bountiful harvests, to accelerate China's debt payment to the Soviet Union.

Other practices, including the massive diversion of rural labor to backyard iron furnaces and water-conservation projects, led to gross neglect in harvesting the bumper crops of 1958 and contributed to the ensuing famine. By spring 1959, many communes, caught between higher government procurement and free supply, had exhausted their grain reserves and witnessed a collapse of production incentives. At this point, much could still have been done to avoid the worst of the famine. Unfortunately, during the Lushan Conference of 1959, in which Mao came down hard on Peng Dehuai, Mao unleashed a "second leap" and another push for commune mess halls. This further exacerbated the rural situation and undoubtedly contributed to the jump in China's mortality rates from 12 per 1,000 in 1958 to 14.6 per 1,000 in 1959 and 25.4 per 1,000 in 1960. Statistics reveal that those provinces that had a higher mess-hall participation rate at the end of 1959 also tended to have a higher mortality rate in 1960, the year that China had a net population loss of 10 million people.

Effects of the Great Leap Famine

The Great Leap famine was thus clearly rooted in politics rather than nature. Unfortunately, the peasants who had put their faith in Mao's regime were largely left to fend for themselves when they had exhausted their food supplies. The demographer Judith Banister estimated that the number of excess deaths over 1958–1961 was between 15 and 30 million. In aggregate numbers, the Great Leap famine is the worst famine in human history. The incidence of the famine was emphatically rural, with the grain producers becoming the main victims of famine.

The intensity and magnitude of the Great Leap famine far exceeded the Great Depression in the United States and produced a lasting change in Chinese preferences and behavior. It shattered any nascent beliefs that the rural people might have had about large rural organizations and led them to question government policies. It also prompted Mao and his colleagues to moderate rural policies and scale down the sizes of rural collective organizations. But the famine also induced fissures among the top leaders. As Mao turned his attention away from the economy, he launched the notorious Cultural Revolution in 1966.

While the basic collective institutions were maintained during Mao's lifetime, the famine profoundly undermined popular support for such institutions and laid the foundation for China's eventual decollectivization following Mao's death. Through the early 1980s, the provinces that had suffered more severely during the famine were less likely to adopt radical rural policies and institutions. Following Mao's death in 1976 and the defeat of radical leaders, farmers again turned to household contracting (contracting land to the household), particularly in those areas that had suffered the most during the famine. By the turn of the 1980s, the national leadership, now led by Deng Xiaoping (1904–1997), had embraced rural decollectivization. The Great Leap famine was thus not just a monumental tragedy; it also laid the ground for institutional innovation. It is a great historical irony that the Great Leap Forward, launched to accelerate China's march toward communism, actually served to hasten the arrival of market reforms by precipitating the greatest famine in human history. The tragedy is that China had to go through such a terrible detour.

Dali L. Yang

See also: **Cultural Revolution—China; Mao Zedong**

Further Reading

Bachman, David. (1991) *Bureaucracy, Economy, and Leadership in China*. Cambridge, U.K.: Cambridge University Press.

Banister, Judith. (1987) *China's Changing Population*. Stanford, CA: Stanford University Press.

MacFarquhar, Roderick. (1983) *The Great Leap Forward, 1958–1960*. Vol. 2 of *The Origins of the Cultural Revolution*. New York: Columbia University Press.

Teiwes, Frederick, and Warren Sun. (1999) *China's Road to Disaster: Mao, Central Politicians, and Provincial Leaders in*

A section of the Great Wall at Badaling, China. The wall has been reconstructed in this area and is a popular tourist site. (DEAN CONGER/CORBIS)

the Unfolding of the Great Leap Forward, 1955–1959. Armonk, NY: M. E. Sharpe.

Yang, Dali. (1996) *Calamity and Reform in China: State, Rural Society, and Institutional Change since the Great Leap Famine*. Stanford, CA: Stanford University Press.

GREAT WALL The best-known work of Chinese civil engineering is the Great Wall, a line of fortifications extending for more than 6,324 kilometers, if all the branch walls are counted, and 3,460 kilometers, if the main line alone is measured. As was customary, the wall was built with rubble foundations without binding material and with thin layers of bamboo stems spread between blocks to speed drying. Granite blocks as large as 4.3 meters by 0.9 meters were used in the foundation, and apparently only the simplest of tools were used, though on a vast scale. Reinforcements of wood and iron were used in some sections of the wall. Despite this, during periods of neglect, parts of it collapsed. After the third century CE, there was very little maintenance, though reconstruction was undertaken in later periods, particularly under the Ming dynasty (1368–1644). The wall was not a single massive engineering project, but was the connection of various walls that had been built in previous periods to protect northern Chinese regimes from attacks by the Mongols from the north. In the late twentieth and early twenty-first centuries, with China open to visitors from the West, the Great Wall has become a major tourist attraction, with sections reconstructed for that purpose.

Paul Forage

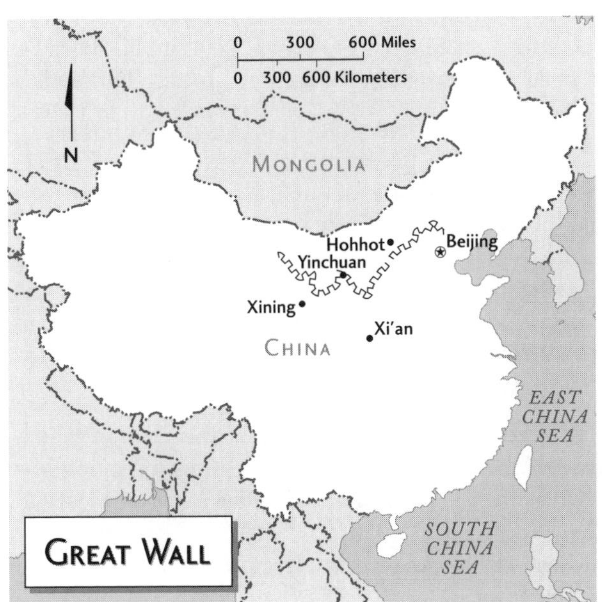

THE GREAT WALL OF CHINA—WORLD HERITAGE SITE

Built to repel the marauding nomadic cavalry of Central Asia, the Great Wall of China was begun in 220 BCE under the Qin dynasty and completed in the Ming dynasty. Clearly visible from outer space, the Great Wall of China became a World Heritage Site in 1987.

GREATER XING'AN RANGE The Greater Xing'an Range (Da Xing'anling) is a crescent-shaped mountain range running 1,400 kilometers from south to north in the northwestern parts of Heilongjiang and Jilin Provinces in northeastern China. The range is divided into a southern and a northern part by the Taoer River near the border between the two provinces. The northern part of the range runs for about 670 kilometers, with peaks rising 1,000 meters above sea level; a few, like Mount Fengshui and Mount Dajiluqina, reach over 1,390 meters. The eastern slopes are steep; the western slopes merge into the Inner Mongolia Plateau, which is about 700 meters above sea level. It is an extremely cold area, with winters lasting more than eight months and an average temperature in January of –28° C. The southern part generally consists of lower mountains and has a slightly warmer climate.

The Greater Xing'an Range is one of China's most important timber areas and has been heavily forested since 1949, which is increasingly threatening the region's ecological balance. The range is sparsely inhabited by minority nationalities, of which the Orogens are most numerous. Their main sources of income are hunting and forestry. Some agricultural products for local consumption are grown in the lower valleys.

Bent Nielsen

Further Reading

Krieg, Renate, et al. (1998) *Provinzporträts der VR China*. Hamburg, Germany: Institut für Asienkunde.

Ma Yin, ed. (1989) *China's Minority Nationalities*. Beijing: Foreign Language Press.

Ren Mei'e, Yang Renzhang, and Bao Haosheng, eds. (1985) *An Outline of China's Physical Geography*. Beijing: Foreign Language Press.

Zhao Songqiao. (1986) *Physical Geography of China*. Beijing: Science Press.

GREEKS IN TURKEY The Greek presence in Turkey and its islands has been continuous since at least the eighth century BCE. The legendary Greek poet, Homer, was from western Turkey, and with the division of the Roman empire into western (Rome) and eastern (Byzantium) portions, Greek culture flowered in the region, with Constantinople (Istanbul) and the Church of Hagia Sophia as the high watermarks of Hellenic civilization.

Although Byzantium endured and flourished for many centuries, its death knell was struck in 1453, when the Ottoman Turks, led by Mehmed II (1432–1481), invaded the region and toppled the eastern Roman empire. They quickly captured Constantinople and converted the Hagia Sophia into a mosque. Thus was established the modern state of Turkey.

The Fall of Byzantium

With the fall of Byzantium, the majority of the Greeks fled either to Greece or westward into Europe. They took with them a vast amount of learning and knowledge, which would provide the incentive for the exuberance of the Renaissance.

However, a large number also remained behind, and they faced the brunt of the ethnic cleansing to which the conquering Turks, who were Muslims, subjected the people. A large number were forcibly converted to Islam, and huge swaths of the nation were ethnically cleansed. Before long, Byzantium, which had been ethnically and linguistically Greek, became Turkish and Muslim.

Persecution of the surviving Greek minority continued through the ages, but in the early twentieth century, it became systematic extermination just after the Armenian genocide by the Turks during World War I and the ensuing Greco-Turkish War of 1922. The latter war ended with the Treaty of Lausanne when the two sides exchanged populations in 1923. Thereafter, a mere 200,000 Greeks remained in Turkey. Because of continuous civil-rights violations, the present Greek population in Turkey is only about 1,500 people, who are concentrated around the Bosporus.

Pogrom of 1955

The worst form of persecution took the shape of a pogrom on 6–7 September 1955. This outburst of violence was directed at the Greek community in Istanbul, with a great loss of personal and commercial property, instances of rape, beatings, and murder. Many churches and schools were torched, houses and businesses looted, and Greek cemeteries desecrated, with some bodies of the patriarchs of the Orthodox Church exhumed and defiled. Also, countless relics were destroyed. In 1995, the U.S. Senate passed a resolution that recognized this pogrom against the Greek community of Turkey and called upon the president to declare 6 September 1955, a day of remembrance of the victims of this state-organized massacre. In 1964, all Greek permanent residents of Istanbul (those who were born in the city but held Greek citizenship) were expelled on a two-day notice.

Religious Persecution

The tiny Greek community that currently resides in Turkey is still persecuted. It faces discrimination, intimidation, threats against its religious leaders, and an ongoing desecration of its holy places. The persecution is immediately discernible in the treatment of the Ecumenical Patriarchate of Constantinople, which is one of the oldest active institutions in Eastern Europe, having been established around 330 CE. It is the spiritual center for Orthodox Christians worldwide, as the Vatican is for Roman Catholics. The Patriarchate's printing facilities have been shut down; the Turkish government will not allow non-Turkish citizens to become bishops, and even the patriarch must be a Turkish citizen. This demand is next to impossible to meet because there are few Greeks left in Turkey, and the Turks themselves are Muslim. Turkey also did not allow the Patriarchate to open a representative office in Brussels, Belgium, in 1994, claiming that the Patriarchate was not a legal body and that thus there was no need for it to be represented in Brussels. In 1995, the U.S. Senate passed a resolution condemning the relentless persecution of the Patriarchate by the Turkish government because it violates international treaties to which Turkey is a signatory.

The Turkish government also closed the Patriarchal Theological School of Chalke, which was the primary educational institute for the Patriarchate clergy; many patriarchs throughout the world graduated from Chalke. Despite requests from the Patriarchate, the Turkish government refuses to reopen the school. In its 1995 resolution, the U.S. Senate also condemned the arbitrary closing of the School of Chalke.

Turkey also refuses to recognize the ecumenical nature of the Orthodox Church and thus will not allow anyone who is not a Turkish citizen to participate in the Patriarchate's affairs in Istanbul; this effectively bars most patriarchs and clergy, who are citizens of other nations.

Denial of Economic and Cultural Rights

Further, in 1986, Turkey revoked the right of ethnic Greeks to buy, sell, trade, or inherit property. This meant that all property once held by Greeks in Turkey eventually passed into Turkish hands. The Greek language is not allowed to be taught at Greek schools, and many young people face discrimination because of their ethnicity.

There are also Greek communities throughout Turkey, and these people have been completely disenfranchised. They live dual lives of sorts, in that they carry on as Turks in the wider society but practice their Orthodox faith secretly; they do not have a right to promulgate their language or culture. There is also a drive toward "Turkification," especially of names. The Orthodox Christians who live to the east of Istanbul cannot worship in Greek, nor can they claim to be Greek Orthodox in official documents and must describe themselves as Turkish; thus even their ethnicity is denied them—which is what the Turkish government hopes to achieve.

The islands of Imvros and Tenedos have been aggressively made Turkish. School property was seized, the thriving meat export industry was shut down, and a large prison was established on Imvros. The government also appropriated property that once belonged to Greeks and turned it over to Turkish settlers from the mainland.

Thus, through a systematic policy of persecution, the ethnic Greek population of Turkey has been driven out, its property turned over to the state, and its freedom to pursue its own culture, religion, and language denied.

Nirmal Dass

Further Reading

Alexandres, Alexes. (1992) *The Greek Minority of Istanbul and Greek-Turkish Relations, 1918–1974.* Athens, Greece: Centre for Asia Minor Studies.

Augustinos, Gerasimos. (1992) *The Greeks in Asia Minor: Confession, Community, and Ethnicity in the Nineteenth Century.* Kent, OH: Kent State University Press.

Gondicas, Dimitri, and Charles Issawi. (1999) *Ottoman Greeks in the Age of Nationalism: Politics, Economy, and Society in the Nineteenth Century.* Princeton, NJ: Darwin.

Halo, Thea. (2000) *Not Even My Name: From a Death March in Turkey to a New Home in America: A Young Girl's True Story of Genocide and Survival.* New York: Picador USA.

Salmone, Stephen D. (1981) *The Greeks and Other Minorities in Turkey: Two Essays.* Buffalo, NY: State University of New York Press.

GREEN REVOLUTION—SOUTH ASIA

The Green Revolution, a transformation in the organization of South Asian agriculture that took place mainly between 1964 and 1978, was attendant upon the adoption of high-yielding varieties (HYV) of major crops, including rice, wheat, maize, and some millets. While farmers traditionally planted seeds selected each year from their own crops, seeds for the high-yielding varieties were created in central facilities by systematic selection, hybridization, and genetic transfer. These HYV cultigens do not breed true to type, and pests and diseases constantly evolve adaptations to the new varieties. Consequently, once farmers adopted them, they became dependent on this large and advanced technological infrastructure. The result is a system of peasant agriculture that combines traditional farm management with some of the world's most advanced agricultural science.

Although the new cultigens are often described as "miracle" varieties, they do not produce increased yields under all conditions. They give increased yields primarily in response to heavier and more regular water, fertilizer, and pest control. Without such inputs, the yields of the new varieties are not consistently better than the yields of the traditional varieties, and they may be worse. Accordingly, even though adoption of the HYV crops has been widespread in South Asia, the benefits have depended largely on the quality of the agricultural-support structure in the several countries. Where yields of HYV cultigens have increased, as a rule the yields of many traditional varieties have increased also (Leaf 1998: 109–112). The transformation has been most widespread and most successful in India, followed by Sri Lanka and Pakistan. The effect has been marginal in Bangladesh and Nepal.

Technology

The core methods for transferring desired characteristics from one species to another were initially developed in two major international laboratories. Beginning in 1942, wheat and maize were developed at the International Maize and Wheat Improvement Center in Mexico under the combined sponsorship of the Mexican government and the Rockefeller Foundation, headed by Norman Borlaug (b. 1914). Beginning in 1960, rice varieties were developed at the International Rice Research Institute (IRRA) in the Philippines, sponsored by the Rockefeller Foundation and the Philippine government and based on the Mexican model. Later, millets were developed in India by the Indian Council for Agricultural Research (ICAR), again in collaboration with the Rockefeller Foundation, with a view toward replicating what had been done to improve the yields of commercial millets in the United States.

Infrastructure

Since the resources on farms are limited in South Asia, much of the infrastructure necessary to provide the required input to HYV plants and to take the resulting crops to market must be created by organizations at or above the village level. The organizations specifically involved with the Green Revolution were primarily government package programs, agricultural universities and research centers, and cooperatives.

Before independence, agricultural research took place in state agriculture departments and a few central institutes, while agricultural colleges aimed almost exclusively at providing departmental staff. These institutions did little to change the historic pattern of a large but poor agricultural population producing only slightly more than it consumed. After independence, the governments of India and Pakistan recognized the contrast between their inherited institutions and the dynamic, productive system of agricultural research and education in the United States. On the basis of agreements between the government of India, the United States Agency for International Development (USAID), and a consortium of five U.S. land-grant universities, signed in 1954 and 1955, India in 1960 began to develop a series of agricultural universities modeled on the American land-grant colleges (Naik and Sankaram 1972: 83, 99).

Concurrently, in 1959, a team from the government of India and the Ford Foundation conducted a study of constraints on agricultural productivity. The result was the formation of the Integrated Agricultural Development Programme, begun in 1961–1962 with support from the Ford Foundation. The main idea was to concentrate development inputs in a few especially promising districts selected from around the country. The newly formed agricultural universities would recommend a package of crops for these districts, based on the best available science, and prescribe the services needed to produce them. The state governments would provide the services (Gill 1983: 205). The plan was successful and was quickly expanded to one district in every state under the new designation of the Intensive Agricultural Areas Programme and to still other districts starting in 1964–1965. Parallel efforts were urged in Pakistan but with little success, largely because Pakistan's rural economy is dominated by a small class of wealthy absentee landholders whose main historical interest has been in maintaining their own power (Sims, 1988: 161–162, 189). A strong district administration responsive to the actual farmers would not serve this end.

TABLE 1

Wheat production for 1965, 1975, 1980, 1995

(in percentages)

	1965	1975	1980	1995
South Asia	100	189	189	258
Bangladesh	100	338	2,382	3,604
India	100	197	197	260
Nepal	100	263	263	349
Pakistan	100	167	167	237

SOURCE: Food and Agricultural Organization of the United Nations.

The package programs demonstrated that the response of traditional crop varieties to increased inputs with increased yields was limited, and this set the stage for the adoption of the high-yielding varieties. In 1962, M. S. Swaminathan (b. 1925), "father" of the Green Revolution in India, urged the Indian Agricultural Research Institute to bring Borlaug to India to arrange a large-scale collaboration, arguing that otherwise it would be impossible to realize the full benefits of the package program (Randhawa 1980–1986: 4:367). The institute agreed, and in 1964 the cooperative effort established new centers that, along with several of the new universities, conducted adaptive research and began testing and multiplying seeds of the most promising varieties.

Results

Results varied according to the crop. Wheat yields in India increased from 9,132 kilograms per hectare in 1965 to 12,384 kilograms per hectare in 1975 and to 14,356 kilograms per hectare in 1980. By 1995, the yield in India was 25,590 kilograms per hectare. The yields in Pakistan were 8,631 kilograms per hectare in 1965, 11,375 kilograms per hectare in 1975, 15,680 kilograms per hectare in 1980, and 20,811 kilograms per hectare in 1995. That is, between 1965 and 1995, wheat yields in India increased about 280 percent, and those in Pakistan increased about 240 percent. Increases in total yields for the four producing countries in South Asia are given in Table 1. All production figures are from the agricultural database of the statistical service of the Food and Agriculture Organization (FAO) of the United Nations. The FAO in turn receives data from the statistical services of the respective countries; therefore data quality varies widely.

TABLE 2

Paddy production in 1965, 1970, 1980, 1985

(in percentages)

	1965	1970	1980	1985
South Asia	100	131	166	193
Bangladesh	100	106	132	143
India	100	138	175	209
Nepal	100	104	112	127
Pakistan	100	167	237	222
Sri Lanka	100	211	279	348

SOURCE: Food and Agricultural Organization of the United Nations.

The impressive proportional gains for Nepal and Bangladesh largely reflect the fact that their calculations start from a particularly small base.

South Asia produces about twice as much rice as wheat. Improvements in rice production have lagged behind those in wheat production but have been sufficient to eliminate substantially the threat of famine. In India, an initiative by ICAR, IRRI, and USAID in 1967 introduced the new varieties through the Central Rice Research Institute in Cuttack, Orissa, and the new All-India Coordinated Rice Improvement Project at Hyderabad, Andhra Pradesh. Several states were involved in the project. In 1965–1966, the entire Indian production of rice was 30.6 million metric tons. By 1976–1977, it was 52.7 million metric tons. The percentage increases in paddy production from 1965 to 1995 for South Asia as a whole and for each major producing country are given in Table 2.

Assessment

In the early 1960s, South Asia faced the threat of severe food shortfalls. The Green Revolution averted that threat. Although hunger still exists in the region, it is the consequence of inequities in distribution rather than insufficient production. The Green Revolution accomplished what its authors promised, and its potential is far from exhausted.

Murray J. Leaf

Further Reading

Food and Agricultural Organization of the United Nations. FAOStats. Retrieved 2–5 January 2000, from: http://apps.fao.org/cgi-bin/nph-db.pl?subset=agriculture.

Gill, Manohar Singh. (1983) *Agriculture Cooperatives*. New Delhi: Vikas.

Goldsmith, Arthur A. (1990) *Building Agricultural Institutions: Transferring the Land-Grant Model to India and Nigeria*. Boulder, CO: Westview.

Leaf, Murray J. (1998) *Pragmatism and Development: The Prospect for Pluralist Transformation in the Third World.* Westport, CT: Bergin and Garvey.

Naik, K. C., and A. Sankaram. (1972) *A History of Agricultural Universities*. New Delhi: Oxford and IBH.

Randhawa, M. S. (1980–1986) *A History of Agriculture in India*. 4 vols. New Delhi: Indian Council of Agricultural Research.

Sims, Holly. (1988) *Political Regimes, Public Policy, and Economic Development: Agricultural Performance and Rural Change in Two Punjabs*. Newbury Park, CA: Sage.

GREEN REVOLUTION—SOUTHEAST ASIA

The term "Green Revolution" is used for big increases in wheat and rice yields in developing countries from the 1960s brought about by new high-yielding crop strains combined with the use of fertilizers and agricultural chemicals. It was launched in Asia in 1960 at the International Rice Research Institute in the Philippines; rice is the staple food for people living in Southeast Asia. Southeast Asia as discussed herein consists of Cambodia, Indonesia, Laos, Malaysia, Myanmar (Burma), the Philippines, Thailand, and Vietnam but excludes Brunei and Singapore. The Green Revolution in Southeast Asia as was a technology package comprising improved high-yielding varieties of rice, irrigation or controlled water supply, improved moisture utilization, fertilizers and pesticides, and associated management skills. Some two decades later, several Southeast Asian countries adopted more of a market approach to rural finance. At the same time, local governments improved rural infrastructures such as transportation, telecommunication, postal, irrigation, and electrical systems to assist large and small farmers previously beyond the reach of technological innovations. The utilization of this technology package in suitable socioeconomic environments has resulted in greatly increased yields and incomes for many farmers in Southeast Asia.

Results

The beneficiaries of the Green Revolution have been the farmers and the consumers. Southeast Asia's population increased by 68.2 percent, or 139.3 million people, between 1970 and 1995. Cereal production in Southeast Asia more than doubled from 33.8 million metric tons to 73.6, and cereal yield increased from 1,352 to 2,237 metric tons per hectare. Food availability (measured as calories available per person per day) increased by 34 percent. Rural incomes (measured as per capita gross domestic product) increased by 193 percent, driven increasingly by urban-industrial growth from the 1980s onwards and by growth in the rural nonfarm economy. Using a benchmark of the international poverty line of US$1 per day (purchasing-power parity, 1985 dollars), the absolute number of poor declined by 41.4 percent from 108 million in 1975 to 40 million in 1995.

Real food prices in Southeast Asia, indeed throughout the world, have steadily declined over the last thirty years as a result of the Green Revolution. Lower real food prices benefit the poor relatively more than they do the rich, since the poor spend a larger portion of their available income on food. Stationary threshers, tube wells, and flour mills have all reduced the drudgery of women. Recent studies of the impacts of the Green Revolution also suggest that it extended beyond the rice producers of Southeast Asia to include other crops and other socioeconomic settings.

The Green Revolution clearly averted a major food crisis in Southeast Asia. Indonesia attained rice self-sufficiency in 1984. Several Southeast Asian countries—Indonesia (pre-1997 crisis) and Vietnam, for example—went from running food deficits in the 1960s to being surplus producers in the late 1980s, despite increasing population. The Green Revolution was the foundation for startling economic growth in Southeast Asia. Since Green Revolution technologies boosted production using less labor without requiring a lot of capital, agricultural labor could easily flow to other sectors. As economies ceased to need to import food, foreign exchange was freed up for other uses. Higher incomes from agriculture caused domestic markets to expand. Indonesia, with the most rapid agricultural growth, has had the most rapid reduction in total poverty. In the Philippines, agricultural growth has been highly inequitable due mainly to the skewed distribution of land holdings and poor rural infrastructure. Overall performance in poverty reduction there has been disappointing because of the unequal distribution of wealth.

The use of high levels of inputs and the achievement of relatively high rice yield in Southeast Asia have made it more difficult to sustain the same rate of yield gains, as yields approach the economic optimum yield levels. Indeed, increased intensity of land use has led to increasing input requirements in order to sustain current yield gains. Environmental pressures are increasing as existing land and water resources come under threat from rapid urbanization, which increasingly withdraws land from agricultural production and create pressure for reallocation of water now used in agriculture.

Furthermore, the Green Revolution technologies were not without their problems. The necessity of using large amounts of agrochemical-based pest and weed control in some crops has raised environmental concerns as well as concern about human health. The chemicals applied as fertilizer and as pest and weed control can pollute rivers and lakes through runoff, and can pollute groundwater through leaching.

The land is increasingly unable to support the burden of intensive agriculture. Intensive farming practices have virtually mined nutrients from the soil. When fertilizers are added to a crop, a plant absorbs not only the extra nitrogen, phosphorus, and potassium from the fertilizer, but also proportionately increased levels of micronutrients from the soil, including zinc, iron, and copper. Over time, the soil becomes deficient in these micronutrients. Their lack, in turn, inhibits a plant's capacity to absorb nitrogen, phosphorus, and potassium. Consequently, crop yields are declining alarmingly. Many farmers are heavily in debt from their investments in new equipment and reliance on chemicals, and rural unemployment is increasing. These are ominous signs of a deteriorating farm economy.

The move to a higher-input environment naturally favored those farmers who had access to capital and skills. They strengthened their roles in society, sometimes at the expense of less well-endowed groups. Many studies have claimed gender bias in the development of the Green Revolution. The established roles of women in the farming systems were challenged by the new technology and the new economic structures, as work performed by women was now handled by machines.

A limitation of the Green Revolution has been its inability to have much direct influence on rain-fed farming systems, whose production may be adversely affected by droughts. As a result, income disparities between irrigated and rain-fed villages and regions have worsened and many rain-fed regions have barely benefited. The prospects for significant technological advances in rain-fed areas are hampered by limited and uncertain rains that often make water a critical constraint in plant growth, and by the diversity of local growing conditions that limits the geographic applicability of improved technologies.

For Indonesian rice farmers, the high costs of high-yielding rice varieties and the chemical nutrients and fertilizers are driving a return to organic farming using organic seeds, minimal fertilizer, and no pesticides. Across Indonesia, about a dozen nongovernmental organizations are seeking to popularize organic farming methods as a sustainable, profitable, and environmentally safe alternative to fertilizers and pesticides.

The Future

In the twenty-first century, the world faces the prospect of a new and complex food crisis that will require better ways of ensuring that the hungry and the malnourished will be able to meet their food needs. To tackle this enormous challenge, a new Green Revolution must be launched that will protect the environment and boost agricultural output. Future agricultural growth will continue to be driven by improvements in crop productivity based on genetic manipulation of plants, and biotechnology will eventually accelerate this process, though genetically modified crop strains have foes in Asia, just as they do in Europe. The need for continuing and aggressive research in all related areas and disciplines is self-evident. Today's farmer requires far more knowledge in order to make environmentally appropriate decisions and to cut production costs. Information resources will need to substitute, in the future, for the currently all-too-frequent excessive use of physical resources.

Kog Yue Choong

See also: **Agriculture—Southeast Asia; Green Revolution—South Asia; Rice and Rice Agriculture; Terrace Irrigation**

Further Reading

Blackman, Allen. (2000) *Obstacles to a Doubly Green Revolution.* Washington, DC: Resources for the Future.

Djalal, Dini. (2000) "Old Ways Return to Favor." *Far Eastern Economic Review* 163, 21 (25 May).

Food and Agriculture Organization (FAO). "Lessons from the Green Revolution: Towards a New Green Revolution." Retrieved 23 April 2001 from: http://www.fao.org/wfs/final/e/volume2/t06-e.htm.

Rosegrant, Mark W., and Hazell, B. R. (2000) "Transforming the Rural Asian Economy: The Unfinished Revolution—Summary." In *Rural Asia: Beyond the Green Revolution.* Manila, Philippines: Oxford University Press, 97–115.

GUANGDONG (2002 est. pop. 74 million). Located in southeast China, Guangdong Province covers an area of 196,891 square kilometers (76,000 square miles). It is bordered to the northeast by Fujian Province, to the north by the provinces of Jiangxi and Hunan, and to the west by the Guangxi Autonomous Region. A coastal province on the northern shores of the South China Sea, Guangdong has long played an important role in China's foreign trade—a role that was expanded after the opening of the country in the 1980s and the creation of the Special Economic Zones at Shenzhen, Shantou, and Zhuhai.

The area was first integrated into the Chinese empire during the Qin dynasty (221–206 BCE), although ethnic Han Chinese did not begin to settle there until the Tang era (618–907 CE). The region experienced a major influx of Han settlers during the Southern Song dynasty (1127–1279), when migrants began to arrive after fleeing the Mongol invasion of northern China. In 1997 the majority (61.6 percent) of the province's population was ethnic Han Chinese, although minority peoples such as the Zhuang, Yao, Shui, Mulam, and Jing are present in sizable numbers, primarily in the mountainous regions of the interior. The main spoken dialect in the region is Cantonese. Another major dialect, Hakka, is the principal spoken tongue in the north and northeastern regions of the province.

Guangdong is also the point of origin for many overseas Chinese in North America and Southeast Asia, whose relatives left the province in search of work or to escape the political turmoil of the nineteenth and twentieth centuries. During the late 1910s and early 1920s Guangzhou (Canton), the provincial capital, served as the headquarters of the Nationalists, first led by Sun Yat-sen (1866–1925), the province's most famous son, and following his death by Chiang Kai-shek (1887–1975). It was from Guangzhou that Chiang Kai-shek launched the Northern Expedition in 1926 to unify China and end the warlord era.

Between the Tang and Qing dynasties (618–1912) Guangdong emerged as an important agricultural province within the empire, producing large volumes of rice, sugarcane, silk, and fruits, and also as a point of contact with the outside world. Guangzhou was one of China's first great trading centers, first visited by Arab merchants during the Tang dynasty and European merchants during the late Ming and early Qing periods. This tradition of commerce was reinvigorated in the post-Mao period, as Guangdong capitalized on its proximity to the former British colony of Hong Kong to become a primary point of entry for foreign investment and trade with the People's Republic of China. Guangdong stands as one of the best examples of China's ability to move from a state-planned to a market economy that is open to the outside world.

Robert John Perrins

Further Reading

Hook, Brian. (1996) *Guangdong: China's Promised Land.* Hong Kong: Oxford University Press.

Johnson, Graham E., and Glen Peterson. (1999) *Historical Dictionary of Guangzhou (Canton) and Guangdong*. Lanham, MD: Scarecrow.

Lin, Alfred. (1997) *The Rural Economy of Guangdong, 1870–1937*. New York: St. Martin's.

State Statistical Bureau. (1998) *China Statistical Yearbook*. Beijing: China Statistical Publishing House.

Vogel, Ezra. (1989) *One Step Ahead in China: Guangdong under Reform*. Cambridge, MA: Harvard University Press.

Yeung, Yue-man, and David K. Y. Chu, eds. (1998) *Guangdong: Survey of a Province Undergoing Rapid Change*. 2d ed. Hong Kong: Chinese University Press.

GUANGXI (2002 est. pop. 50.5 million). The Autonomous Region of Guangxi is located on the southern coast of China. Since 1958 the official name has been the Guangxi Zhuang Autonomous Region. The Zhuang nationality is China's largest minority group and constitutes a third of the region's population of 45.5 million (1996). Guangxi covers an area of 236,661 square kilometers and borders on Vietnam and Yunnan in the west, on Guizhou and Hunan in the north, on Guangdong in the east, and on the Gulf of Tonkin in the south. The region is dominated by mountains with peaks over 2,000 meters above sea level in the far west and the far north. Guangxi is traversed by sixty-nine rivers, most of which are tributaries to the Zhu (Pearl) River.

Guangxi has a subtropical monsoon climate, and the rainy season from April to September accounts for 80 percent of the annual precipitation of 1,250 to 1,750 millimeters. Average temperatures during January lie between 6° and 15°C, while the July average is between 23° and 28°C. The capital, Nanning (1996 estimated population of 1.1 million), is situated in the southern central part of Guangxi. The eastern part of the region became part of the Qin empire (221–206 BCE) in 214, and after a brief period of independence, it was conquered by the Han empire (206 BCE–220 CE) in 112–111 BCE. From the Tang dynasty (618–907 CE) onward, the area has been part of various southern administrative divisions, sometimes divided into a Han Chinese region in the east and a Zhuang region in the west. Throughout the centuries, the region has been marked by rebellions against succeeding imperial governments and tribal warfare between the Zhuang and other minority nationalities that were pushed south by the Chinese migration from the north. The Taiping Rebellion (1851–1864) originated in Guangxi, and later in the nineteenth century, the French colonial power in Indochina extended its activities to the region.

Guangxi is one of China's most diversified areas with regard to population. Although the Han Chinese today constitute 62 percent of the population, there are eleven minority nationalities, of which the Zhuang is the largest by far. Several of these minority groups number fewer than 100,000 people. The most important agricultural crops are rice, millet, and sugarcane, but the region grows a wide variety of crops, including tobacco, tea, fruit, soybeans, sweet potatoes, and peanuts. In the mountains in the northwest, forestry dominates, with pine, fir, oak, and camphor trees. Major industries include textiles, chemicals, machine building, and food and tobacco processing. The scenic areas, with karst mountains and underground caves, around Guilin and Yangshuo in the northeast provide a major source of income through tourism.

Bent Nielsen

Further Reading

Hamberg, Theodore. (1969) *The Visions of Hung-Siu-tshuen, and Origin of the Kwang-si Insurrection*. New York: Praeger.

Lary, Diana. (1974) *Region and Nation: The Kwangsi Clique in Chinese Politics, 1925–1937*. Cambridge, U.K.: Cambridge University Press.

Levich, Eugene William. (1993) *The Kwangsi Way in Kuomintang China, 1931–1939*. Armonk, NY: M. E. Sharpe.

Litzinger, Ralph A. (2000) *Other Chinas: The Yao and the Politics of National Belonging*. Durham, NC: Duke University Press.

GUANGZHOU (2002 pop. 3.4 million). Guangzhou (Canton) is located on China's southeastern coast in the Pearl River Delta. It is the largest city in southern China and the capital of Guangdong Province, which is the main point of entry to China from the Hong Kong Special Administrative Region.

Guangzhou has had a long history as a center of economic activity. As far back as the eleventh century, foreign traders lived in Guangzhou trading ivory and spices for silk and tea. Guangzhou was further opened to the West in the nineteenth century when European nations imposed unequal trade treaties with China that gave European traders access to the Chinese markets. In addition to its importance as a trading center, the city played a central role in the Opium War, the Republican Revolution of 1911, and current economic and political reforms in China.

Following the founding of the People's Republic of China in 1949, Guangzhou achieved notoriety for another reason—families with overseas Chinese relatives. Those with families abroad were either reeducated or punished. During the Cultural Revolution (1966–1976), Guangzhou residents were again attacked, this time by Red Guards for their overseas family connections. Those residents with relatives overseas were either persecuted or endured harassment for their contact with decadent lifestyles.

Buoyed by its liberal economic policies, Guangzhou has played a pivotal role in China's recent modernization effort, attracting foreign capital and investment. Western companies seeking to enter the vast Chinese market have set up factories, shops, and hotels. Yet, despite their investment, overseas Chinese investors account for the majority of foreign capital.

Keith A. Leitich

Further Reading

Victor, F. S., ed. (1985) *Chinese Cities: The Growth of the Metropolis since 1949*. Oxford: Oxford University Press.

Yusuf, Shadid. (1997) *The Dynamics of Urban Growth in Three Chinese Cities*. New York: Oxford University Press.

GUANXI The concept of *guanxi*, or "social relationships," is an important concept in Chinese everyday life. Both individual and group interests are asserted via such relationships. There is a particular image of society behind this concept. Many Chinese see society in the first instance as a hierarchically structured order covered by an interlaced network of relationships. While for many Europeans a person's outward appearance and behavior may be important, for many Chinese, who one knows and to which group or work unit one belongs are of consequence.

Not all interpersonal relations are based on *guanxi*. Relations between members of an immediate family or between spouses are based on other obligations (for example, obedience or respect). *Guanxi* relations arise when people have certain things in common, such as coming from the same local area, mutual experiences, or other social connections, and they are developed first of all with people with whom one is in direct contact.

Tong Relationships

Tong, or having something in common, is the most important basis for *guanxi*. The *tongban* (classmate), *tongbao* (person from the same region), *tonghang* (person in the same business), *tongshi* (colleague), *tongxiang* (person from the same hometown or village), and *tongxue* (person who studied at the same school) all have special relations with one another (*tong* relationships). Relations can also be forged through gifts, personal favors, or mediation by third parties. They include mutual obligations and expectations. For every action, something is expected in return. *Guanxi* is less a private relationship than a role-playing game that on the basis of previous or current situations produces expectations. Those who do favors gain "face" and are recognized by others as people who have respect for those around them.

Friendship and *tong* relationships involve certain obligations, such as constant readiness to help and support not only the person directly involved in the relationship but also his or her family and friends. Refusing to give this help and support was and is seen as negative social behavior, as a complete lack of any kind of human feeling, or alternatively as proof that someone does not love those to whom he or she is naturally linked and therefore obliged to help. In these cases, refusing to help is seen as the highest form of inhumanity and a break with morality.

Guanxi as Connection

To make use of *guanxi*, both sides have to be able to give each other something (influence, protection, access to scarce goods and services, opportunities for promotion or profit). If no connection exists with an influential person, a link is "created" *(la guanxi)*. To do this, a person from the same *guanxi* network is sought who can, via various channels, set up the connection: A requires something from D. However, there is no *guanxi* between them. In A's relationship network, there is B, who is connected with C. And C has *guanxi* with D. A therefore asks B to get in touch with C. B helps A and turns to C; C wants to help B and speaks with D. D wants to do C a favor and therefore helps A. Through this sort chain, new *guanxi* connections develop and with them new mutual obligations. In this way, *guanxi* fulfills the function of a social investment and can be seen as a relationship between people or institutions based on exchange and with a mutual understanding of the rights and obligations of both parties.

Guanxi Versus Corruption

Although there are distinct similarities between *guanxi* and corruption, the two phenomena are not identical, because the social and ethical concepts behind them are (at least theoretically) different. Unlike corruption, *guanxi* is based on real or imagined things in common and is therefore a question of personal emotions. This means that one looks after the person in question personally and is prepared to help him or her. These feelings can be maintained and extended through favors and gifts. Presents of this kind can be found in the traditions of many peoples, and it becomes corruption only within the framework of a rational state form.

Guanxi as Network

There are different degrees of intensity of *guanxi* depending on the degree of emotion involved. The bigger the emotional aspect, the closer the relationship. And if the emotional aspect is less, the relationship is less intense. *Guanxi* relationships based on experiences in common plus emotional connections are therefore stronger than those that came about merely via mediation by a third party. The stronger a relationship, the more social, political, and economic use can be made of it; the more social capital it has.

Guanxi relationships have always played an important role in Chinese history. In premodern China, there was a life-long bond, including mutual political loyalty, between officials who had passed the same top-level exam. At the same time, they were politically loyal to the higher-rank officials who had examined them. This was an important basis for the emergence of "old-boy networks," which today still exist in the form of loyalty to those who studied at the same university or to former political leaders. People from the same village or from the same province clubbed together in areas far from their local region to form regional groups, the members of which are obligated to assist one another (this was still happening in 2002).

In the People's Republic, a system of personal dependencies on superiors developed, because superiors were responsible for hiring, promotion, rewards, punishment, or evaluation of political attitude and therefore could determine the whole life and career of their subordinates. This was encouraged by the fact that the *danwei* (work unit) was responsible not only for work matters but also for political, economical, and social affairs. In this way, an authoritarian culture with relationships based on personal loyalty and "old-boy networks" was encouraged. *Guanxi* relationships are particularly important here, because before the reforms, there were many shortages of goods and services that the state in its monopolist position oversaw, and officials enjoyed privileges that allowed them to use *guanxi* to obtain everything that was officially not available or available only in limited quantities. Friendship and acquaintance with official cadres still help ease some material problems, and political careers and promotion continue to depend on connections with leading functionaries.

Today, *guanxi* still runs through the entire social framework: from employment (retaining or changing jobs) to finance and economics (granting business licenses, loans, tax rates) and everyday life (distribution of housing, access to good medical care), to name only a few examples. Just about everybody has to use *guanxi* to ensure trouble-free living and working. The reform era has even led to a significant expansion of *guanxi* relationships. The strong orientation toward a market economy, combined with the simultaneous retention of the party's monopoly on power, has led to more fostering and development of *guanxi* in the form of an explosion of present-giving and hospitality, which has meant significantly higher costs for individuals and institutions.

Specifically Chinese Institution

The main reason for *guanxi* is social uncertainty, particularly when other security structures such as the clan or the village community are no longer able to provide social protection. Those affected try to obtain personal protection through *guanxi*, particularly when in positions of political and legal uncertainty. In addition, studies have shown that the Chinese (because of their political and social experiences) are a lot more suspicious of other people and of their environment than, for example, Americans are. The conclusion from this is that suspicion and uncertainty make people seek security and trust not in the political sphere but in the private sphere and in *guanxi* relationships—an important factor in the creation of factions and "old boy networks."

Guanxi is an important instrument for contact and communication between social groups and communities (villages, clubs, associations, professional groups) and also between individuals and the state or party, particularly since it eases reciprocal bargaining processes and can lead to decisions that otherwise would not be taken or would be only partially reached. Where there are no formal avenues for participation and the mechanisms for institutional pressure are weak, *guanxi* becomes a means to influence politics and political decisions and serves to link the state (party) with society. However, because individuals and groups use *guanxi* to seek influence, power, or advantages and in doing so disregard state, ethical, moral, social, or political standards, actively breaking with norms when it is advantageous to those involved, this behavior encourages corruption and overlaps with it in part.

Guanxi is neither a "typically Confucian" nor a "typically socialist" concept. It should instead be interpreted as a principle on which society is organized that is explicable in both cultural and political terms and that functions in the People's Republic of China as well as in Taiwan and among Chinese living abroad. For example, in Taiwan, which is more modernized than the mainland, the phenomenon occurs mainly in the *guanxi* networks between entrepreneurs (known as network capitalism or *guanxi* capitalism). In business, families are seen more as hierarchical and weak organizations, whereas *guanxi* guarantees incorporation in a relatively stable network of relationships that go beyond the family.

Thomas Heberer

Further Reading

Kipnis, Andrew B. (1997) *Producing Guanxi: Sentiment, Self, and Subculture in a North China Village.* Durham, NC: Duke University Press.

Oi, Jean. (1989) *State and Peasant in Contemporary China: The Political Economy of Village Government.* Berkeley and Los Angeles: University of California Press.

Redding, S. Gordon. (1990) *The Spirit of Chinese Capitalism.* New York: Walter de Gruyter.

Walder, Andrew G. (1986) *Communist Neo-Traditionalism: Work and Authority in Chinese Industry.* Berkeley and Los Angeles: University of California Press.

Yan Yunxiang. (1996) *The Flow of Gifts: Reciprocity and Social Networks in a Chinese Village.* Stanford, CA: Stanford University Press.

Yang, Mayfair Mei-hui. (1994) *Gifts, Banquets, and the Art of Social Relationships in China.* Ithaca, NY: Cornell University Press.

GUERRERO, FERNANDO MARIA (1873–1929), Filipino patriot and writer. Fernando Maria Guerrero believed that the only way to create a genuine Philippine literature was to draw on Philippine legends, history, and national life. Guerrero was the son of an artist, Lorenzo Maria Guerrero. He studied at the Ateneo Municipal and later at the University of Santo Tomas, where he obtained a law degree. Instead of becoming a lawyer, however, he became a writer for the newspaper *La Independencia* (Independence), writing under the pseudonym Fluvio Gil. His incisive writing made *La Independencia* a dynamic newspaper and brought fame to Guerrero.

In 1900, Pablo Ocampo (1853–1925), newspaper editor and later a member of the Philippine Assembly, employed him to write for *La Patria* (Fatherland), a short-lived newspaper because of the Sedition Law, which banned organs that espoused independence from the United States. Guerrero then tried his hand at running his own newspaper, *La Fraternidad* (Fraternity), but this too was short lived. He later joined *El Renacimiento* (Rebirth) and eventually became its chief editor; during his tenure, it was the most outstanding Spanish-language newspaper in the Philippines.

Guerrero pursued literature with a passion. From 1898 to 1900, he had written several lyric poems and short stories. In 1914, he published *Crisalidas* (Chrysalis), a compilation of poems adjudged one of the ten best books about the Philippines. This was followed by another book, *Aves y Flores* (Birds and Flowers).

Guerrero was also active in politics. He was elected to the first Philippine Assembly in 1907 and later became secretary of the Philippine Senate and then secretary of the Commission on Independence. He was editor of the newspaper *La Opinion* (Opinion) when he died on 12 June 1929.

Aaron Ronquillo

Further Reading

Agconillo, Teodoro. (1990) *History of the Filipino People.* 8th ed. Quezon City, Philippines: Garotech.

Estampador, Jose. (1973) *Fernando Guerrero, Centennial Celebration: 1873–1973.* Manila, Philippines: National Coordinating Council.

Guerrero, Fernando Maria. (1952) *Crisalidas.* Manila, Philippines: Philippine Educational Foundation.

———. (1971) *Aves y Flores.* Manila, Philippines: Solidad Filipino-Hispana.

Quirino, Carlos. (1995) "Guerrero, Fernando Maria." In *Who's Who in Philippine History.* Manila, Philippines: Tahanan, 104.

GUEST HOSPITALITY. See **Qingke.**

GUIZHOU (1999 pop. 37.1 million). "Not three days of weather the same, not three *mu* of flat land, not three *fen* in the pocket." Given that three *mu* is about half an acre and three *fen* is 0.4 U.S. cents, this traditional saying aptly sums up the southwestern Chinese province of Guizhou, located south and east of Sichuan and Yunnan provinces, respectively, and north and west of Guangzi and Hunan. Here some 37 million people are crowded into 176,100 square kilometers, much of which is habitable only at low densities or not at all, for three-quarters of the land is hills and mountains, mostly limestone. So limited is agricultural land that each acre must support seven people; each acre, even on slopes, must be cropped, on average, 1.8 times a year. Population pressure results in two-fifths of the total land being seriously eroded—3 percent of it is bare rock.

Seventy-two percent of Guizhou's workers are employed in the primary sector, mainly in agriculture. The main crops are summer rice and maize, winter wheat and rapeseed, with potatoes as a major subsistence crop at high elevations, plus some apple growing.

Secondary industries produce 43 percent of the wealth from 24 percent of the workers. These are concentrated mainly around the provincial capital, Guiyang, a city of just under a million people (the associated administrative region has a larger population), though there are industrial plants located in smaller towns, such as the large steel works at Anshun in the west, built at the height of the Cold War.

Provincial gross domestic product per person is the lowest in China. Poverty is widespread, exacerbated by relatively high levels of dependency and, for China, high birthrates. These conditions reflect the facts that 24 percent of the population is not Han Chinese, thus not subject to the "one family, one child" policy, and that most Han are rural and are thus allowed two children. Although Guizhou was part of the Chinese empire by the Han dynasty (206 BCE–220 CE), the Han population even in the sixteenth century probably did not exceed a few hundred thousand.

While the province is rich in coal and limestone resources, it will take very large investments to exploit them fully. Although annual rainfall ranges from 800 to 1500 millimeters, surface water is scarce. Limestone landscapes attract tourists mainly from within China, but all kinds of infrastructure in the province are weak. Levels of literacy are low, a quarter of the people being illiterate. Self-supported economic and social development is unlikely in the near term, for poverty extends to government. So long as the central government obtains better returns from development expenditure in the coastal provinces, growth in Guizhou is likely to remain relatively slow, with the province functioning basically as a reservoir of cheap labor. Until transportation infrastructure, especially, is improved, exploitation of that labor reservoir is likely to continue outside the province.

Ronald David Hill

GUJARAT (2001 pop. 50.6 million). The state of Gujarat is located on the west coast of India and is bounded by the Arabian Sea on the west, Pakistan in the north, and the states of Rajasthan in the northeast, Madhya Pradesh in the southeast, and Maharashtra in the south. It covers an area of 196,024 square kilometers, and its principal language is Gujarati. Gandhinagar is the capital city. Other important sites are Ahmedabad, Jamnagar, Rajkot, Junagarh, Bhuj, Cambay, and Surat.

The history of Gujarat goes back to 2000 BCE. It is believed that Lord Krishna left Mathura to settle on the west coast of Saurashtra, which came to be known as Dwarka. Several kingdoms sprang up here at various times. Of these, the Mauryas, Guptas, Pratiharas, and Chalukyas were the most significant. During the medieval period, Gujarat passed under the rule of the Delhi sultans, who were followed by the Mughals, and finally by the British. The present state of Gujarat came into being on 1 May 1960, following the reorganization of the Indian states.

One of the most prosperous states, Gujarat is the main producer of tobacco, cotton, and groundnuts in the country. Other important agricultural products include paddy rice, wheat, and millet. Gujarat is also one of India's leading industrial states and a major center of trade and commerce. It has forty ports, of which Kandla is the most important. Gujarat is famous for industries such as chemicals, petrochemicals, fertilizers, engineering, and electronics. Registered working factories in the state numbered 19,771 at the end of 1999.

Among the annual fairs and festivals of the state is the Tarnetar fair, held at the village of Tarnetar in honor of Lord Siva in the month of Bhadra (mid-August–mid-September). The Madhavrai fair celebrating the marriage of Lord Krishna and Rukmini is held at Madhavpur in Chaitra (mid-March–mid-April). The Ambaji fair, held in the Banaskantha district, is dedicated to the mother goddess Amba. The traditional Hindu festivals of Janmashtami (the birthday of Lord Krishna), Makar Sankranti, and Navaratri are popular throughout Gujarat.

Gujarat attracts a large number of tourists. Tourist spots include sacred Hindu sites such as Dwarka, Somnath, Ambaji, Bhadreshwar, Shamlaji, Taranga, and Girnar. Porbandar, the birthplace of Mahatma Gandhi, Gandhi's ashram at Sabarmati, and archaeological sites at Lothal and Dhabol also draw visitors, as do the beaches at Ahmadpur-Mandvi, Chorwad, and Tithal; the lion sanctuary at Gir Forest; and the wild ass sanctuary at Kutch.

Sanjukta Das Gupta

Further Reading

Sanghvi, Nagindas. (1996) *Gujarat: A Political Analysis*. Surat, India: Centre for Social Studies.

Ward, Philip. (1998) *Gujarat, Daman, Diu: A Travel Guide*. New Delhi: Orient Longman.

GUJARATI Gujarati is the name of both an Indian language and the people who speak it. The language is the official language of Gujarat state, in the west of India and just to the north of Mumbai (Bombay), with a population of 50.6 million in 2001.

Gujarati is an Indo-Aryan language, with considerable amounts of vocabulary borrowed from Sanskrit, Urdu, Arabic, Persian, Portuguese, and English. It is written in its own script, akin to Devanagari, which uses thirty-four consonants and eleven vowels.

The state of Gujarat has the longest coastline of any Indian state, about 1,600 kilometers, and has had strong overseas trade connections ever since the Harappan civilization, over four thousand years ago. The present Gujarat state, with Gandhinagar as its capital, came into existence in 1960 for reasons of linguistic politics, by merging the three former entities of Gujarat, Saurashtra, and Kachchh (Kutch).

Gujaratis of many castes practice farming, the Patidars and Rajputs being especially prominent as landholders. Sorghum, wheat, and rice are the major food crops, but there is also important commercial cultivation of cotton, tobacco, groundnut, and sugarcane. The Gujaratis who are more urbanized have a strong tradition of trading and money lending, especially those groups called Banias. These latter may be Hindu, Jain, or Muslim in religion; all three faiths have a large following in Gujarat.

Some parts of the state are extremely dry and desertlike, so that goat and camel pastoralism is a widespread subsistence practice. In recent times the state government has done a good job of industrializing and attracting foreign capital to support industry. However, many cities suffered a severe setback in 2001 because of a devastating earthquake centered on Bhuj, which was almost completely destroyed.

Foreign investment has been more easily attracted here than to many Indian states because of the large number of Gujaratis who are businesspeople and traders overseas, in East and South Africa, Britain, Canada, and the United States. In the United States today one finds Gujaratis holding a virtual monopoly on the management of certain motel and donut chains and in the running of magazine stalls in the New York City subway.

Paul Hockings

Further Reading

Pocock, David. (1972) *Kanbi and Patidar: A Study of the Patidar Community of Gujarat.* Oxford: Clarendon.

Shah, Arvind M. (1973) *The Household Dimension of the Family in India: A Field Study in a Gujarat Village and a Review of Other Studies.* Berkeley and Los Angeles: University of California Press.

GULF OF OMAN The Gulf of Oman is an extension of the Indian Ocean and the Arabian Sea located between the countries of Oman in the southwest and Iran in the north. The Strait of Hormuz in the northwest links it with the Persian Gulf. The Gulf of Oman is 560 kilometers (350 miles) long and 320 kilometers (200 miles) wide. Summertime temperatures can reach over 49°C (120°F), making this one of the warmest regions of the world. The main ports along its shores are Gwadar Bay in Pakistan, Bandar Beheshti and Jask in Iran, and Suhar, Muscat, and Sur in Oman. For centuries local vessels have carried on a considerable trade across the Gulf of Oman between Iran, Arabia, India, and East Africa. Recently it has become quite important for the shipping of oil from the Persian Gulf region to the rest of the world. Fishing is also a minor industry.

Thabit A. J. Abdullah

GULF OF THAILAND The Gulf of Thailand is west of the South China Sea, surrounded by the Southeast Asian nations of Vietnam, Cambodia, Thailand, and Malaysia. This semienclosed sea of about 320,000 square kilometers is on the Sunda Shelf. It is considered relatively shallow with a mean depth of

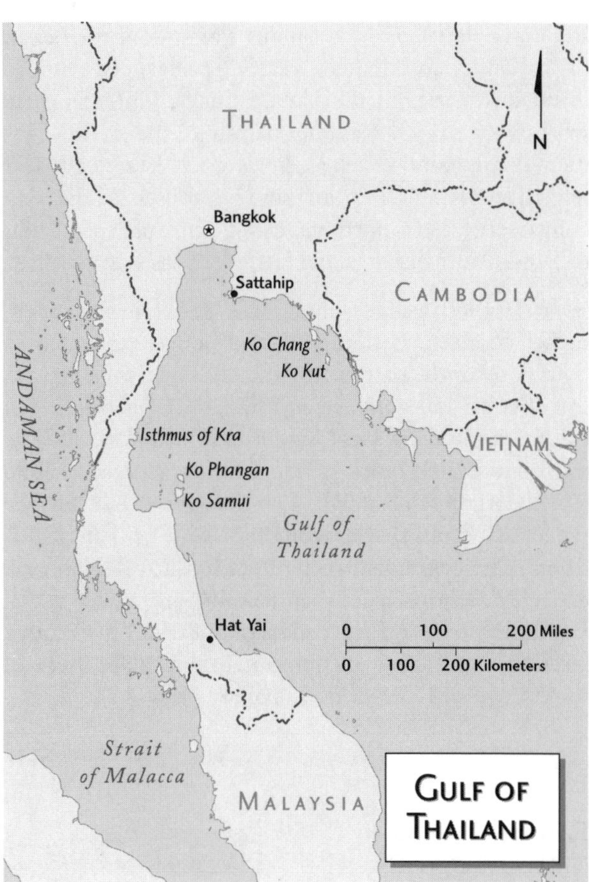

45 meters. The Chao Phraya, Tha Chin, Mea Klong, and Bang Pakong rivers drain into the gulf.

Given its abundance of both living and mineral resources, millions of people derive their livelihoods from the gulf; its environment affects many more. Its ecosystem is of great concern. High demand for food items such as shrimp, crayfish, and prawns, for example, has led to the establishment of aquaculture to supplement those species depleted by overfishing and environmental destruction. The fisheries in 1996 were determined to be near collapse, with fishermen continually experiencing lower catches. There is worry over the presence of petroleum and other contaminants such as mercury in the gulf. Governments are reportedly enacting sustainable-use policies to preserve both resources and the environment; nevertheless, the environmental devastation has created problems for the surrounding population where fish and shellfish are often the only source of dietary protein available.

Linda Dailey Paulson

GULGEE (b. 1926), Pakistani artist. Abdul Mohammed Ismaili, better known as Gulgee, was born in Peshawar in 1926. This famous Pakistani artist began his career as an engineer, receiving advanced degrees from universities in the United States. Gulgee's early works were sketches and oil paintings, mostly government commissions, such as *Afghans*, a 1957 series of 150 portraits of King Zahir Shah and his household. He also composed mosaic portraits, using chips of lapis lazuli, of Saudi Arabian kings and leaders of his Ismaili faith.

In the 1960s Gulgee, like his Western contemporaries, turned to abstract expression, and he has continued in this genre for the past forty years. However, in its vibrant use of color and gold leaf and silver leaf, his painting is clearly inspired by local Sindhi craftsmanship, such as mirror work and block printing. Often, Gulgee's paintings incorporate abstracted Qur'anic verses that further the artist's claim that his paintings mark his Sufi disposition. The generous sweep of his brushstrokes and his dancelike performance when painting are indeed reminiscent of the devotional dances of mystics. The emotive intensity of Gulgee's paintings may thus place them in the context of Islamic devotional art.

Kishwar Rizvi

Further Reading

Sirhandi, Marcella Nesom. (1992) *Contemporary Painting in Pakistan.* Lahore, Pakistan: Ferozsons.

GULISTON (2000 est. pop. 54,000). Guliston is a city in eastern Uzbekistan.. It is the administrative center of the country's Syr Dar'ya Province, famous for its extensive irrigation network and cotton growing. Guliston is situated in the southeastern part of the Mirzachul, formerly the Golodnaia ("hungry") steppe, 120 kilometers southwest of the capital city of Tashkent.

Guliston was founded in the late nineteenth century as a Russian settlement with the name of Golodnaia Step (Hungry Steppe). After Soviet power was established in the region (1921), Golodnaia Step was renamed Mirzachul in 1922. In 1961, it was recognized as a town and received the name Guliston ("flower garden"). From 1963 until the dissolution of the Soviet Union in 1991, Guliston was the administrative center of the Syr Dar'ya subdivision of the Uzbek Soviet Socialist Republic. Since 1991 Guliston has been the administrative center of the Syr Dar'ya Province and the Golodnaia Steppe Economic Region of the republic of Uzbekistan. Present-day Guliston has a railway station, a state university, and cotton processing, mechanical, and construction material plants.

Natalya Yu. Khan

Further Reading

Allworth, Edward, ed. (1994) *Central Asia: 130 Years of Russian Dominance: A Historical Overview*. 3d ed. Durham, NC: Duke University Press.

GUMMA (2002 est. pop. 2 million). Gumma Prefecture is situated in the central region of Japan's island of Honshu. Essentially a satellite of Tokyo, it occupies an area of 6,356 square kilometers. Gumma's main geographical features are a mostly mountainous terrain and a section of the Kanto Plain in the southeast. The Tonegawa, the nation's second longest river (322 kilometers), intersects the prefecture. Gumma is bordered by Saitama, Nagano, Niigata, Fukushima, and Tochigi Prefectures. Once known as Kozuke province, it assumed its present name and borders in 1876.

Gumma's capital is Maebashi, an important provincial town since the eighth century. In the Edo period (1600/1603–1868) it became a castle town and a market center for silk production. Recent decades have seen a greater reliance on lumber production and the development of factories for transportation machinery and electrical appliances. The prefecture's other important cities are Ota, Takasaki, and Shibukawa.

Today Gumma's extensive truck farms produce vegetables for the Tokyo market. The textile industry continues in Kiryu, Isesaki, and Tatebayashi, while the northward encroachment of the Keihin Industrial Zone has fostered chemical, electrical, and machine plants. Visitors are drawn to the Iwajuku archeological site; to the hot spring resorts of Minakami, Ikaho, and Kusatsu; and to skiing and hiking in Nikko and Joshin'etsu Kogen National Parks.

E. L. S. Weber

Further Reading

"Gumma Prefecture." (1993) In *Japan: An Illustrated Encyclopedia*. Tokyo: Kodansha.

GUNEY, YILMAZ (1937–1984), Turkish director and actor. YKlmaz Guney, also known as Cirkin Kral (Ugly King), was one of the most popular directors and actors of Turkish cinema. Born as YKlmaz Putin in rural Adana (Turkey) to poor Kurdish parents, he began his career doing odd jobs on movie sets and worked his way up as an actor, scriptwriter, and director. As a militant Communist, he spent more than eleven years in Turkish prisons. Nevertheless, he acted in 111 films, directed 17, and wrote 53 movie scripts.

Yilmaz Guney set new standards for realism in Turkish cinema. His script for the movie *Suru* (Herd) won the Berlin Film Festival prize in 1979. His most famous work, *Yol* (Path), was filmed according to his script and directions while he was in prison in 1980. *Yol* shared the top prize, the Palme d'Or, at the Cannes Film Festival in 1982, with Costa Gavras's *Missing*.

Guney spent his last few years as an exile in Europe. The military government of Turkey expelled him from citizenship and banned and destroyed his films. *Yol* (Path) was screened in Turkey for the first time in 1999. Guney died of cancer and was buried in Père Lachaise cemetery in Paris. He remains a cult figure in Turkish popular culture.

Aykan Erdemir

Further Reading

Dorsay, Atilla. (2000) *Yılmaz Guney Kitabi* (The Yilmaz Guney Book). Istanbul, Turkey: Guney Yayinlari.

Guney, Yılmaz. (1975) *Selimiye Mektuplari* (Letters to Selim). Istanbul, Turkey: Guney Filmcilik Sanayi ve Ticaret A. S. Yayinlari.

GUNPOWDER AND ROCKETRY The development of gunpowder and the rocket have related histories, and both are believed to have originated in China by the late Song dynasty (eleventh century CE). Gunpowder was the first explosive and propellant and one of world history's most important inventions. It has three ingredients mixed together: potassium nitrate (also called saltpeter), sulfur, and charcoal. Gunpowder, also called black powder, propelled the first bullets and rockets. The rocket used a low nitrate, slower-burning gunpowder and was self-propelled once the powder ignited.

A woman with rockets and fireworks in her shop in Vietnam, c. 1995. (STEVE RAYMER/CORBIS)

Origins

Most likely gunpowder and the rocket were surprise discoveries rather than inventions. For centuries, Chinese Taoist philosophers experimented with chemicals to seek the answer to longevity. One Taoist book, *Zhen yuan miao Dao yao lue* (Classified Essentials of the Mysterious Tao) of around 850 CE, warned not to mix certain ingredients, including sulfur, saltpeter, and other ingredients, because the mixture had been known to flame up, singe beards, and burn a house. This was one of several known Taoist alchemical explosions, and the Chinese of the period do not appear to have understood the true nature of combustion. As late as the seventeenth century, they still believed the combustion of gunpowder was caused by the interaction of the yin, or female element, and yang, the male element.

Early Chinese military terms are often difficult to interpret, but the earliest recognizable gunpowder formulas are found in *Wu jing zong yao* (Essentials of Military Classics), edited in 1044 by Zeng Guangliang. The first true gun appeared about 1260. Many theories have been proposed as to how the rocket appeared. One is that the discovery was made when a Chinese soldier modified an ordinary incendiary "fire arrow."

For certain, Chinese chronicles contain numerous accounts of gunpowder weapons from the late Song dynasty, though it is often unclear whether they refer to rockets. The most famous examples are the flying fire arrows, or more correctly, flying fire spears, used by the Chinese against the Mongols in the siege of Kaifeng in 1232. Some authorities believe the devices were no more than thrown "flying fire" spears, or perhaps handheld lances that merely shot fire into the air; others contend they were true self-propelled rockets.

The term *huo chien* (fire arrow) at first meant simply an incendiary arrow but later came to mean rocket. The earliest known depictions of Chinese rockets, in the *Wu bei zhi* (Treatise on Armament Technology, c. 1628) of Mao Yuanyi, show many variations of arrows with rocket tubes attached, which were therefore true rocket arrows. This may be strongest evidence that Chinese rockets evolved from ordinary incendiary arrows.

Ironically, the clearest early Chinese reference to a rocket device involves fireworks. In 1264, according to *Qi dong ye yu* (Rustic Talks in Eastern Qi, c. 1290) by Zhou Mi, a fireworks display was held in the courtyard of the royal palace. One firework, called a "ground rat," went up the steps of the throne of the empress mother and frightened her. It was thus self-propelled, that is, it was a rocket.

However the rocket appeared, it spread to Arabia by the late 1200s, and apparently from there into Europe, probably to northern Italy first, via maritime trade routes. By the fourteenth century, the first guns appeared in Europe. The spread of gunpowder and the rocket throughout the rest of Asia is less well known. The first rockets in Korea appeared in 1377 and may have been directly introduced from China.

Spread to Southeast Asia and India

One possible way to establish the spread of rocketry in Asia is by tracing the origins of allegedly centuries-old Asian rocket festivals. Northeast Thailand holds the annual Boun Bang Fai festival in which giant, decorated gunpowder rockets with bamboo guide sticks are fired by different villages to please the rain gods and ensure a good rice harvest. Neighboring Laos celebrates the identical animistic and Buddhist festival. A very similar practice is found in the remote Xishuangbanna Dai Autonomous District in Yunnan Prefecture, adjacent to both northeast Thailand and Laos. In Myanmar (Burma), there is the Pa-O Rocket Festival of the Pa-O minority group in the Shan states.

Closer examination shows a definite link between festivals in Thailand, Laos, Yunnan, China, and Burma, whose practitioners are all of the same Tai cultural stock. The actual histories of the festivals are unknown, but one theory advanced is that basic gunpowder and rocket technology started in China, in the eastern, more advanced area of the country, probably in the Song-dynasty capital of Hangzhou.

From this region, knowledge of gunpowder and the rocket probably spread via Chinese maritime trade missions to India in the early fifteenth century CE. In India, gunpowder, fireworks, and especially the rocket became well developed; Indian war rockets were used for centuries. From India, the technology may have spread first to neighboring Burma and from there to Thailand (Siam), Laos, and back again to China, to the more rural agricultural area of Yunnan.

Spread to Japan

In Japan, in several prefectures near Tokyo, annual Ryusei (Ascending Dragon) rocket festivals celebrate good harvests. However, the origin of the rocket festivals in Japan is more problematic. Undoubtedly knowledge of the rockets was imported at an unknown date to Japan and the festival was adapted to local culture. The Japanese had a seventeenth-century colony in Siam that conducted trade in gunpowder between the two countries, but no records have been found mentioning rockets.

Japan was introduced to gunpowder and guns in 1543 by the Portuguese. Fireworks were introduced in 1600, whereas one historian, without verification, claims that Japan imported "rocket arrows" from China about 1595.

Further Areas of Research

More research needs to be done to expand the picture of the overall development and spread of gunpowder in Asia. Information coming out of the rocket festivals presently held in Thailand, Laos, China, Myanmar, and Japan may be a key to determining the origin and spread of the earliest rockets through Asia and elsewhere.

Frank H. Winter

Further Reading

Crozier, Ronald D. (1998) *Guns, Gunpowder, and Saltpeter: A Short History.* Faversham, U.K.: Faversham Society.

Needham, Joseph. (1986) *Science and Civilisation in China.* Cambridge, U.K.: Cambridge University Press.

Partington, J. R. (1999) *A History of Greek Fire and Gunpowder.* Baltimore, MD: Johns Hopkins University Press.

GUO MORUO (1892–1978), Chinese intellectual. Born in Leshan, Sichuan Province, Guo Moruo (or Kuo Mo-jo) studied in Japan from 1914 to 1923 and graduated from Kyushu Imperial University with a medical degree. After returning to China, he began to write and became a famous poet, playwright, paleographer, historian, politician, short story writer, essayist, and translator. His collection of poetry, *Nu Shen* (The Goddesses; published in 1921), is generally regarded as the first significant book of poetry in modern China. His scholarly works on Chinese history and paleography are well regarded.

Guo founded the Chuang Zao She (Creation Society) with a small group of young and idealistic poets and writers who, like him, had recently studied in Japan. But although a writer and historian, Guo was also deeply involved in twentieth-century Chinese politics. During the Northern Expedition (1926–1927), a war that the Nationalists and Communists fought against the northern warlords, he served as a colonel and later a lieutenant general, in charge of public relations. In the Nanchang Uprising of August 1927, which gave birth to the Red Army, he served as director of public relations and during this period joined the Chinese Communist Party. After the establishment of the People's Republic of China on 1 October 1949, Guo Moruo served in many important positions, such as vice premier in charge of culture and education, president of the Chinese Academy of Science, president of the Chinese Writers' Association, vice president of the National People's Congress, and member of the Communist Party Central Committee.

Jian-Zhong Lin

Further Reading

Roy, David Tod. (1971) *Kuo Mo-jo: The Early Years.* Cambridge, MA: Harvard University Press.

Wang Xunzhao, Lu Zhengyan, Shao Hua, Xiao Binru, and Lin Minghua, eds. (1986) *Guo Moruo Yanjiu Ziliao* (Guo Moruo Studies). 3 vols. Beijing: China Social Sciences Publishing House.

GUOMINDANG The Guomindang (Kuomintang), or Chinese Nationalist Party, has its roots in a movement established in 1894 and is China's oldest political party. The history of the Guomindang (GMD) can be divided into six periods. During the first period (1894–1912), before it was known by its current name, it was a movement led by Sun Yat-sen (1866–1925), the so-called father of modern China, aimed at overthrowing the Qing (Manchu) dynasty (1644–1912). Sun changed the movement's name several times, but it was best known in the early days as the Tongmenghui (Revolutionary Alliance).

In the second period (1912–1919), the name Guomindang was used for the first time, and the movement became a parliamentary party active primarily in the new national legislature in Beijing. Then, during the third period (1919–1928), Sun Yat-sen reorganized the Guomindang as an armed political force seeking to overthrow China's warlords and establish a one-party government. During the fourth period (1928–1949), under the leadership of Chiang Kai-shek (1887–1975), who had become the party's leader, the party followed Sun Yat-sen's plan to set up the Republic of China in Nanjing (Nanking) under the tutelage of the Guomindang until China was ready for full democracy. That regime became recognized internationally as the government of China, but it did not control all of Chinese territory.

In the fifth period (1949–1995), the Guomindang's Republic of China withdrew to the island of Taiwan, where it became an authoritarian one-party state allied with United States in the Cold War. For most of the fourth and fifth periods, Chiang Kai-shek (and later his son, Chiang Ching-kuo), occupied both the presidency of the Republic of China and chairmanship of the Guomindang.

Following economic growth in the 1960s, the Republic of China in the early 1980s began a process of political and social liberalization. By the mid-1990s it had developed into a multiparty constitutional democracy. In the 2000 Presidential election, the Democratic Progressive Party candidate, Chen Shui-bian, emerged as the victor with a plurality. This marked the beginning of the Guomindang's sixth period, in which it operates as one party within a multiparty constitutional democracy. This final form fulfills Sun Yat-sen's dream for a full-fledged democracy.

The Guomindang under Sun Yat-sen

Sun Yat-sen's supporters founded the Guomindang in 1912 to represent his views in the legislature of the newly established Republic of China. Sun had intended to serve as president of the new republic but in early 1912 lost out to Yuan Shikai (1859–1916), a general and diplomat formerly in the service of the Qing dynasty. As president, Yuan Shikai opposed parliamentary power and had the Guomindang's parliamentary leader, Song Jiaoren (1882–1913) assassinated.

In the chaotic politics of the next decade, the Guomindang survived as a parliamentary party but had no power. Sun Yat-sen tried to revive the Guomindang in 1919 by moving its headquarters to Guangzhou (Canton), where he cooperated with a local warlord. This effort failed, and in 1923 Sun undertook a further reorganization. Combining assistance and inspiration from the Soviet Union, Sun Yat-sen re-created the Guomindang as a Leninist style party with a clear ideology, limited membership subject to firm party discipline, and a strong army under party control. Sun Yat-sen also permitted members of the tiny Chinese Communist Party to join the Guomindang without giving up their earlier affiliation, so the two parties were allied. Chiang Kai-shek, a military man loyal to Sun Yat-sen, headed the Guomindang's new Whampoa military academy but had no sympathy for Communism or the Soviet Union.

The Guomindang under Chiang Kai-shek

After Sun Yat-sen's death 1925, Chiang Kai-shek emerged as the Guomindang's leader. In the summer of 1926 the Guomindang's newly trained army undertook the Northern Expedition, an effort to end warlordism in China and establish a national government on Sun Yat-sen's model. In April 1927, Chiang Kai-shek's army and local gangs slaughtered Communist members in Shanghai, permanently alienating the Communists.

The Northern Expedition produced a new national government with its capital in Nanjing. Under a provisional constitution, based on Sun Yat-sen's ideas, it was a one-party regime tutoring the Chinese people for democracy. Chiang Kai-shek held both the presidency and chairmanship of the party, which operated along Leninist lines, with top-down control, political commissars, and enforced adherence to the party line. In actuality, however, the Guomindang could never suppress differing agendas within its ranks. Chiang Kai-shek became adept at manipulating factions but could never achieve the total control that Guomindang ideology advocated. In the cities, the Guomindang made alliances with bosses deeply involved in illegal activities. In rural areas, the Guomindang again lacked progressive allies and so had few effective programs. This Guomindang government at Nanjing had many weaknesses including limited territorial control, but promised to evolve into a stable regime that could represent all of China.

In the 1930s, with the rise of fascism in Europe, Chiang Kai-shek promoted some fascist-style organizations, including the New Life Movement, whose goal was to improve public morals, and the Blue Shirts, an organization of young men with ultranationalist ideas. Also in the fascist style, his government asserted control over business and kept the media under close rein. From 1937 to 1945, the Republic of China was locked in war against Japan. During these years the Guomindang atrophied, and the state and military apparatus grew. The party's members, still split into factions, lost both their spirit and a vision for the future. At the war's end bureaucrats and generals, not the Guomindang, ran the regime, and the party lacked broad popular support. These fatal weaknesses in the Guomindang are seen as a major cause of Chiang Kai-shek's defeat in China's 1945–1949 civil war.

On Taiwan after 1950, Chiang Kai-shek established a garrison state committed to recapturing the Chinese mainland. A revived Guomindang had two important functions: As a parliamentary party, it controlled the national legislature. As a mobilizing force, it was intended to spur all levels of society to realize Chiang Kai-shek's dream of returning to rule the Chinese mainland. In practice, Guomindang members came from the ranks of 1.5 million mainlanders who had accompanied Chiang Kai-shek to Taiwan in 1949–1950, rather than from the 11 million Taiwanese. Most Taiwanese had limited interest in Chiang Kai-shek's dream of retaking the mainland. Thus, although the Guomindang had become a more effective party, it still lacked widespread popular support.

The Guomindang under Chiang Ching-kuo and Lee Teng-hui

After Chiang Kai-shek's death in 1975 and under the leadership of his son, Chiang Ching-kuo, the Guomindang underwent important changes. Economic prosperity for all on Taiwan replaced a return to the mainland as the regime's principal goal. Chiang Ching-kuo encouraged youth groups, offering outlets for energies pent up by his father's stifling authoritarian anti-Communism. Also, Taiwan's provincial politics became an arena in which the Guomindang made common cause with some Taiwanese interests. By the late 1980s, the Guomindang, with more than 2 million members in a population of 23 million, had become well integrated into Taiwan on the local and provincial levels. Also, the Guomindang had become exceptionally wealthy through ownership of many of Taiwan's most profitable businesses.

Under the leadership of Lee Teng-hui (b.1923), a Taiwanese who succeeded Chiang Ching-kuo in 1987 as chairman of the Guomindang and president of the government, a sweeping series of political and general reforms gave Taiwanese a real voice in the regime. At the same time, increasing prosperity was accompanied by a general liberalization in Taiwan's social atmosphere. The Guomindang remained in control of politics in Taiwan but in 1986 permitted the emergence of an opposition party, the Democratic Progressive Party (DPP). In elections during the 1990s the Guomindang saw its control over political power erode as the Democratic Progressive Party and the New Party gained more and more positions.

The Guomindang after the 2000 Presidential Election

The Guomindang's dominance in Taiwan was crippled by the March 2000 presidential election, when James C. Y. Soong, a defector from the ranks of the Guomindang, ran as an independent and Lien Chan ran as the official party candidate. They split the party's vote, and the presidency went to the DPP candidate, Chen Shui-bian (b. 1950), who received a plurality but not a majority. Though deprived of the presidency, the GMD retained firm control over the legislature until the December 2001 parliamentary elections. In those elections the GMD's share of seats fell sharply from a majority to less than one-third of the seats, whereas the DPP increased its power to well over one-third. Yet, minority parties, including the People First Party (PFP) led by GMD dissident Soong, collectively won the remaining seats. In this new multiparty era, any government must be based on a coalition. Although the GMD has great financial resources and remains a major player in Taiwan politics, its era of dominance has ended.

David D. Buck

Further Reading

Dickson, Bruce J. (1997) *Democratization in China and Taiwan: The Adaptability of Leninist Parties.* New York: Oxford University Press.

Eastman, Lloyd. (1984) *Seeds of Destruction: Nationalist China in War and Revolution, 1937–1949.* Stanford, CA: Stanford University Press.

Harrison, Henrietta. (2001) *Inventing the Nation: China.* New York: Oxford University Press.

Rigger, Shelley. (1999) *Politics in Taiwan: Voting for Democracy.* London: Routledge.

Shieh, Milton J. T. (1970) *The Kuomintang: Selected Historical Documents, 1894–1969.* New York: St. John's University Press.

Tien, Hung-mao. (1972) *Government and Politics of Kuomintang China, 1927–1937.* Stanford, CA: Stanford University Press.

———. (1989) *The Great Transition: Political and Social Change in the Republic of China.* Stanford, CA: Hoover Institution Press.

Yu, George T. (1966) *Party Politics in Republican China, 1912–1924.* Berkeley and Los Angeles: University of California Press.

GUPTA EMPIRE

GUPTA EMPIRE From the fourth through the middle of the sixth century CE the Gupta empire extended over all of northern India and much of the south. Under the patronage of the Gupta dynasty Indian culture flourished, and the era has rightly been termed the Classical or Golden Age of India.

At the end of the third century, before the rise of the Guptas, the Indian subcontinent was an aggregation of small kingdoms and autonomous states. Around this time a king named Srigupta and his son Ghatotkacha Gupta established an independent kingdom on the eastern Gangetic plain.

The family became preeminent under Chandra Gupta I (flourished c. 320), the son of Ghatotkacha Gupta. Chandra Gupta's son Samudra Gupta greatly expanded the empire and is considered by some to be the real founder. Samudra Gupta (reigned c. 340–380), a formidable warrior, established relations with (and probably some degree of suzerainty over) kingdoms adjoining his frontiers. Samudra Gupta was a patron of learning, a poet, and a musician.

Samudra Gupta's son Rama Gupta probably succeeded him for a short period, followed by another son (or grandson) Chandra Gupta II (reigned 380–c. 415). Under this ruler's long reign the empire flowered. Gupta territory extended in the west beyond the Hindu Kush range into today's Afghanistan and in the east to the western borders of today's Assam and Myanmar (Burma).

Chandra Gupta's son Kumara Gupta (reigned 415–455) had an uneventful and generally prosperous reign. His son Skanda Gupta fought the invading Hunas on the western border on at least three occasions and completely crushed them. Following the death of Kumara Gupta the Gupta empire gradually declined. By the seventh century it was fragmented and reduced in size by the Hunas in the west and by Indian kings on the other three borders.

Nevertheless the Guptas left an indelible mark on subsequent Indian history and culture. They established an efficient administrative system, and under their patronage intellectual and cultural activity flourished as never before. In literature, Sanskrit reached its peak with Kalidasa (drama and poetry), Dandin (poetry and prose), and Subandhu and Banabhatta (prose). Eminent writers from across the country made their ideas universally available through the universal language, Sanskrit. Amara (flourished late fourth and early fifth century) composed the critical Sanskrit lexicon *Amarakosha*, and important explicatory texts in Brahmanic and Buddhist philosophy were created. Brahmanical Hinduism, both Saivism (worship of Siva) and Vaishnavism (worship of Vishnu), was established, while Buddhism and Jainism went into a decline. Much of the Puranic literature (literature reflecting ancient history, laws, and codes of behavior) and the *Dharmasastra*—the basis of Brahmanical Hinduism and Hindu law—took shape. Aryabhata (476–c. 550), one of many astronomers and mathematicians, wrote about quadratic equations and other algebraic rules as well as trigonometry; he also wrote that the earth rotated on its axis and explained solar and lunar eclipses. A great university was established at Nalanda.

The Gupta empire's excellence in metallurgy is evidenced by the outdoor iron pillar near Delhi. This architectural piece, which was erected to glorify the conquests of one of the Gupta kings, remains untarnished to this day.

The Gupta period is also known for the large, beautifully carved figures of Buddha, often with clinging drapery. Sculpture in the form of reliefs on walls of sanctuaries cut from rock was another achievement of this period, as evidenced by the caves at Ajanta; Gupta temple architecture and sculptural decoration are exemplified by the temple of Saranatha. Pillar engravings left intimate details of the empire and emperors. Relations were established with foreign cultures and rulers. Indian kingdoms were established on the subcontinent and across the seas in today's Myanmar, Thailand, Cambodia, the Malayan Peninsula, Java, Bali, and Borneo. The Guptas dominated Indian history and culture for two hundred years after their empire disappeared, and even today they are considered exceptional figures of Hindu India.

Ranès C. Chakravorty

Further Reading

Majumdar, R. C., ed. (1970) *The Classical Age*. Vol. 3 of *The History and Culture of the Indian People*. Bombay (Mumbai), India: Bharatiya Vidya Bhavan.

GURRAGCHAA, JUGDERDEMIDIYN (b. 1947), Mongolian astronaut. Jugderdemidiyn Gurragchaa was the first Mongolian astronaut. He was born 5 December 1947 in the town of Gurvan-Bulak, in the Bulgan province of Mongolia. After attending the Ulaanbaatar Agricultural Institute, he was drafted into the Mongolian army in 1966. In 1973, Gurragchaa attended the Zhukovskiy Air Force Academy in Moscow. Then, in 1978, Captain Gurragchaa trained for three years at the Yuri Gagarin Cosmonaut Training Center in the USSR. In 1981, Gurragchaa and the Soviet cosmonaut Dzhanibekov were launched into space aboard the *Soyuz 39* spacecraft. They spent seven days aboard the *Salyut* 7 space station, performing a variety of tests that focused on mapping Mongolia.

Upon his return to Mongolia, Gurragchaa was promoted to colonel, then major general, and received several honors. He became a deputy of the People's Great Khural (parliament) in 1982, serving until the fall of communism in Mongolia in 1990. During the democratic elections he became the chairman of the electoral commission that organized and supervised the elections. He was also elected the chairman of the Federation of Societies for Friendship between Mongolia and the countries of the Commonwealth of Independent States in 1992.

Timothy May

Further Reading

Cassutt, Michael. (1993) *Who's Who in Space: The International Space Year Edition*. New York: Macmillan.
Sanders, Alan. (1996) *Historical Dictionary of Mongolia*. Lanham, MD: Scarecrow.

GUS DUR. See **Abdurrahman Wahid.**

GUSMÃO, XANANA (b. 1946), East Timorese resistance leader. As the leader of the struggle for independence, Xanana Gusmão became the most important resistance figure of East Timor. Born on 20 June 1946 in Laleia, East Timor, José Alexandre "Xanana" Gusmão was educated at a Jesuit seminary and worked in the civil service. In 1974, he joined the Revolutionary Front for an Independent East Timor (Fretelin) and became its leader in 1978. After years of violent struggle, he was elected commander of Fretelin armed forces (Falintil).

Believing that the fight for independence transcended political loyalties, Xanana developed a policy to unite various pro-independence groups and became the charismatic leader of the national Timorese resistance against Indonesian occupation. In 1992, he was captured by the Indonesian armed forces and imprisoned in Jakarta.

Despite imprisonment, Xanana remained the leader of Timorese resistance. A historic visit by Nelson

Xanana Gusmão arrives at a ceremony formalizing his release on 7 September 1999. (REUTERS NEWMEDIA INC./CORBIS)

Mandela in 1997 raised international awareness of the deteriorating situation in East Timor. In 1999, Xanana was transferred from prison to house arrest but was not allowed to participate in the pro-independence campaign during the process of the U.N.-organized consultation on the future of East Timor. As the president of the National Council of Timorese Resistance (CNRT), he returned to his home country in 1999 and is seen by many observers as the person most likely to lead an independent East Timor.

Frank Feulner

Further Reading

Dunn, James S. (1996) *Timor: A People Betrayed.* Sydney: ABC.

Kingsbury, Damien, ed. (2000) *Guns and Ballot Boxes.* Clayton, Australia: Monash Asia Institute.

Niner, Sarah, ed. (2000). *To Resist Is to Win: The Autobiography of Xanana Gusmão with Selected Letters and Speeches.* Melbourne, Australia: Aurora/David Lovell.

GUWAHATI (2001 pop. 808,000). Formerly Gauhati, Guwahati is the largest city in Assam State, India. It is situated on the Brahmaputra River, 300 miles northeast of Calcutta. As Pragiyotishpura ("the Eastern City of Light"), it was the capital of the Hindu kingdom of Kamarupa around 400 CE and is named in the *Mahabharata*. It was controlled alternately by the Muslims and Ahoms in the seventeenth century; the Ahom raja made it his capital in 1786. The Burmese held it from 1816 until 1826, when it became the British capital of Assam Province.

Guwahati is a busy river port and communications center. It is also the site of one of India's most important Kali temples, Kamakhya and Navagraha, "temple of the nine planets," once a great center of astrology and astronomy. The Siva temple of Umananda stands on an island bluff. Nearby are Hindu pilgrimage centers, a university and law college, the state high court, scientific museums, and a zoological garden. The Srimanta Sankaradeva Kalakshetra opened in 1998, promoting dance, drama, music, and art. Tea is the principal business, and the new Assam Tea Auction Center holds the world's largest tea auctions, supplanting those of Calcutta and London. A large oil refinery on its outskirts symbolizes Guwahati's recent growth.

C. Roger Davis

Further Reading

Michell, George (1989). "Gauhati." In *The Penguin Guide to the Monuments of India*, vol. 1. London: Viking: 234–235.

H

HA LONG BAY Located in northeastern Vietnam 160 kilometers east of Hanoi and 55 kilometers northeast of Haiphong, Ha Long Bay is a 1,500 square kilometer area of water that stretches from the northern Gulf of Tonkin nearly to the Chinese border. In the bay are approximately 3,000 islands of limestone and dolomite that geologists attribute the formation of to sedimentary limestone formed between 300 and 500 million years ago, in the Paleozoic Era. Over millions of years, the water in the bay receded and exposed the limestone to rain, winds, and tidal erosion, resulting in the formation of the uniquely shaped small and large limestone outcroppings that now attract a multitude of tourists each year. The bay has been named by the United Nations Educational, Scientific, and Cultural Organization or UNESCO as a World Heritage Site.

Ha Long literally means "dragon descending" and, according to local myth, the bay and its many islands were formed long ago when the forefathers of the Vietnamese were fighting Chinese invaders from the north. The gods from heaven sent a family of dragons to help defend their land. This family of dragons descended on what is now Ha Long Bay and began spitting out jewels and jade, which, on hitting the sea, turned into the various islands and islets dotting the seascape and formed a formidable fortress against the invaders. The locals were able to keep their land safe and formed what is now the country of Vietnam. The dragon family fell so much in love with this area for its calm water and for the reverence of the people of Vietnam that they decided to remain on earth. The mother dragon lies on what is now Ha Long (her scales forming the rocky islets) and her children lie on Bai Tu Long. The dragon tails formed the area of the beaches of Bach Long Vi. The myth compliments that of the origins of the Vietnamese people, which describes the union between a king (representing the dragon) and his bride (representing a goddess) who gives birth to one hundred children (the ancestors of the Vietnamese people). The myth of Ha Long Bay perpetuates the Vietnamese belief that throughout their history, they have been aided by their ancestors—the dragon and the gods—in the defense of their land.

Richard B. Verrone

HA LONG BAY—WORLD HERITAGE SITE

Ha Long Bay, a beautiful and almost completely uninhabited area off the Gulf of Tonkin in Vietnam, was designated a UNESCO World Heritage Site in 1994 for its thousands of limestone pillars and abundant wildlife.

Further Reading

Admiralty, Naval Intelligence Division, Great Britain. (1943) *Indo-China*. Geographical Handbook Series, B.R. 510. London: His Majesty's Stationery Office.

Cima, Ronald J., ed. (1989) *Vietnam: A Country Study*. Washington, DC: U.S. Government Printing Office.

Taylor, Keith. (1983) *The Birth of Vietnam*. Berkeley and Los Angeles: University of California Press, 38–39.

HABIBIE, B. J. (b. 1936), third president of the Republic of Indonesia. Bacharuddin Jusuf Habibie, known as B. J. Habibie, was born in Pare-Pare in southern Sulawesi (Celebes), Indonesia. The young Habibie has been described as a serious student and strongly religious. Raised in an orthodox Muslim family, he met the future president of Indonesia, Suharto (b. 1921), when the latter was posted to Sulawesi as an army officer. During this period, when Habibie was still a young child, his father passed away. Suharto is believed to have taken a personal interest in Habibie, and the two formed a bond that later led to Habibie's rise in Suharto's government when the latter became the president of the Republic of Indonesia.

B. J. Habibie did his high school diploma course in Java, at the prestigious Bandung Institute of Technology, and got his diploma in 1954. In 1960, he graduated with an engineering degree from the Aachen Institute of Technology in Germany. He received his doctorate in engineering in 1965 from the same institution, graduating summa cum laude.

After completing his education, Habibie worked as a specialized scientist at the Hamburger Flugzügbau in Germany, later known as the Messerchmitt-Bölkow-Blohm company (which had absorbed the company founded by Willy Messerschmitt [1898–1978], the designer of the Messerschmitt fighter aircraft that played so prominent a role in Hitler's Luftwaffe during World War II). Between 1969 and 1973, he headed the methods and technology division for commercial airplanes and military transport at this firm. He was called back to Indonesia in 1974 to develop strategies for achieving Indonesia's technological goals. The then president Suharto backed Habibie's strategy to enable Indonesia to compete technologically with the rest of the world by the end of the twentieth century.

President B. J. Habibie on 5 January 1999 shortly after withdrawing from the election for president. (AFP/CORBIS)

Habibie headed several high-cost ventures supported by the Indonesian state, including the aircraft industry. In 1982, he became a member of the Indonesian parliament as a representative of the ruling party, Golkar. Between 1978 and 1998, he was the state minister of research and technology. In 1990, he became the chairman of the Association of Indonesian Muslim Intellectuals (ICMI); some observers have viewed this as a political role that Suharto gave Habibie to counterbalance the power of the Indonesian armed forces. ICMI also served as an alternative power base to the army.

Habibie was made the seventh vice president of the Republic of Indonesia in March 1998, when the authoritarian president Suharto was fighting for his political survival in the aftermath of the economic crisis in Southeast Asia. In May 1998, Suharto decided to step down after thirty-two years in power. Habibie then assumed the post of president.

Habibie has been described as highly energetic, mercurial in temperament, and excitable, as well as dismissive of criticism. His tenure as president, given the economic problems facing Indonesia, was troubled. In view of the voters' negative reaction to the ruling Golkar Party, which Habibie represented and which was blamed for the country's economic woes, it is not surprising that he lost his election bid in 1999. Habibie now lives in Germany.

Ooi Giok Ling

Further Reading

Castle, James, Percival Manglano, and Richard Howard, eds. (1999) *Who's Who in Indonesia's Political Arena: The Players, the Parties: A Comprehensive Guide.* Jakarta, Indonesia: Castle.

Makmur Makka, A. (1995) *B. J. Habibie—Kisah Hidup and Kariernya.* Jakarta, Indonesia: Gema Insani.

HADOOD Hadood (plural of *hadd*, Arabic for "punishments"), are four Law Ordinances that were ordered by General Zia ul-Haq of Pakistan on 10 February 1979, and passed by the Council of Islamic Ideology in Pakistan. The main purpose of the Hadood Ordinances is to Islamize the laws of Pakistan. The Hadood provide for stoning to death for unlawful sexual intercourse, even if consensual; amputation of hands for theft; and lashing for intoxication and gambling. The Hadood are based on the Qur'an (the holy book of Islam) and Hadith (traditions of Muhammad, the Prophet of Islam) the two sources of the *shari'a*, or the Islamic law. Although no person has been so far stoned to death and no limb amputated in Pakistan, such punishments have been carried out in Saudi Arabia. The Federal Shari'a Court of Pakistan, and the Shari'a Bench of the Supreme Court have the authority to listen to appeals against convictions reached by the criminal courts working under the Hadood Ordinances. According to the Law of Evidence the testimony of one woman, unless corroborated by another woman or man, is not admissible in a court. This provision makes it extremely difficult for a victim of rape, as women have found themselves in jail for the "crime" of naming their attackers.

Abdul Karim Khan

Further Reading

Amin, Dr. Muhammad (1989). *Islamization of Laws in Pakistan*. Lahore, Pakistan: Sang-e-Meel.

Mehdi, Rubya (1994). *The Islamization of the Law in Pakistan*. Richmond, U.K.: Curzon.

HAEJU (2001 est. pop. 260,000). Haeju, the capital of South Hwanghae Province (Hwanghaenamdo), is a port and industrial city on the west coast of the Democratic People's Republic of Korea (North Korea), 140 kilometers south of Pyongyang. The city covers approximately thirty-two square kilometers. The major industries of Haeju are cement manufacturing and chemicals. In addition, the region is emerging as a tourist center because of its historical sites, such as the ancient fort at Suyang Mountain and the 128-meter Suyang waterfall nearby.

Because Haeju is located far to the south (just above 38° N latitude), it has nearly ice-free port conditions throughout the year. For this reason the South Korean companies Hyundai and Samsung plan major joint ventures there.

Haeju is historically significant because it is the birthplace of Kim Gu (1876–1948), a fighter for Korean independence. During the Donghak Rebellion of 1894, Kim led an attack against Japanese soldiers at the fort at Haeju. He was not captured in that attack, but following another the next year, he was imprisoned and tortured in Haeju. Ahn Chung-gun (1879–1910), another independence fighter, was also born in Haeju. Ahn was the assassin of Ito Hirobuni, Japan's resident general over Korea, in 1905.

Thomas P. Dolan

Further Reading

Korea Overseas Information Service. (1993) *A Handbook of Korea*. Seoul: Samhwa.

Saccone, Richard. (1993) *Koreans to Remember*. Seoul: Hollym International.

HAIDAR ALI (1721–1782), Indian warrior. Haidar Ali (or Hyder Ali) was the son of a Panjabi Muslim adventurer. Although not formally educated, Haidar was a sagacious and pragmatic warrior who had many military successes. He learned the skills of warfare during the Anglo-French wars of 1751–1755 in South India and was fighting constantly with his neighbors. His three main enemies were the Marathas to the northwest of Mysore, the Nizam of Hyderabad to the northeast of Mysore, and the British to the southeast in Madras. Haidar would not go to war against any one of them except when confident the other two would not join in against him. He admired the British and French armies in India, and equipped the Mysore army along similar lines.

Haidar became commander of that army in 1759, and in 1761 rose to be chief minister of Mysore State. In 1766 the ruler of Mysore became a mere figurehead, and Haidar assumed complete control of the expanding kingdom. He unified Mysore for the first time since the fall of the Vijayanagar Empire in 1565. In 1766 he controlled the west coast through his conquests, and even organized a small fleet there, one of very few Indian commanders ever to do such a thing.

He then went on to fight the First and Second Anglo-Mysore Wars with great success (1767–1769, 1780–1784), but died before the second war was over. In the first of these wars he dictated terms to the British outside Madras City, and in general demonstrated that the British army was not invincible. When he lost some possessions to the British, however, he hoped that the French would come to his aid, but they never provided sufficient support for him to oust the British from South India; and indeed, when they killed his son Tipu Sultan in 1799, British paramountcy was assured.

Paul Hockings

Further Reading

Sinha, Narendra Krishna. (1969) *Haidar Ali.* 4th ed. Calcutta, India: A. Mukherjee.

HAIKU Haiku is a seventeen-syllable Japanese poetic form divided into three phrases: five syllables, seven syllables, and five syllables. Although the term "haiku" came into common use only after 1892, when Masaoka Shiki (1867–1902) revived and modernized the form, its origins as *hokku,* the opening verse of *haikai* (comic linked verse) date back to the Kamakura period (1185–1333) or even earlier.

Haiku came to maturity in the late sixteenth and early seventeenth centuries. Matsuo Basho (1644–1694) developed what was a trivial form and made it into a serious poetic vehicle. As the opening verse of a linked-verse sequence, this form represents a dynamic movement in two directions simultaneously. It represents a breaking up of the traditional *waka* (a thirty-one syllable poetic form in phrases whose syllable lengths were 5-7-5-7-7) into two smaller units, the 5-7-5 *hokku* and a 7-7 unit, called *waki no ku.* At the same time these smaller units can be linked and repeated to form a longer poetic sequence. Thus *hokku* always implies an incomplete poetic statement to be completed by the reader, and it requires complicity between reader and poet to complete the poem.

Due to its brevity haiku has always been in danger of becoming trivial, and indeed after Basho's life haiku relapsed into a period of easy popularity. Yosa Buson (1716–1783) encouraged a revival of Basho's style, and in the last years of the nineteenth century, after another lapse into triviality, Masaoka Shiki sought both to resurrect Basho's seriousness and to modernize haiku, keeping in step with the modernization of Japanese literature. Shiki insisted that the seventeen-syllable form stand as an independent poetic unit, which he called "haiku."

Early Western students of Japanese literature, such as Basil Hall Chamberlain (1850–1935), who introduced haiku to the world outside Japan, regarded these verses as nothing more than epigrams because of their brevity. Later Ezra Pound (1885–1972) and others recognized haiku as a serious poetic form.

One enduring feature of haiku is the *kigo* (seasonal word), which grounds the poetic moment in a natural context by locating it in the cycle of time. *Kigo* occur in other forms of Japanese poetry and link haiku with its broader cultural context. Another feature of haiku is the *kireji* (cutting word), which acts as a caesura and breaks the already short poem into two parts, making possible a contrast or association that serves both to engage the reader and to allow for poetic complexity. Haiku poetry has flourished in Japan and throughout the world and remains the most popular and well-known form of Japanese poetry.

Stephen Kohl

Further Reading

Blyth, Reginald Horace. (1963) *A History of Haiku.* 2 vols. Tokyo: Hokuseido.

Giroux, Joan. (1974) *The Haiku Form.* Rutland, VT: Tuttle.

Henderson, Harold. (1958) *An Introduction to Haiku.* Garden City, NY: Doubleday.

Ueda Makoto. (1976) *Modern Japanese Haiku: An Anthology.* Tokyo: Tokyo University Press.

Yasuda, Kenneth. (1957) *The Japanese Haiku.* Tokyo: Tuttle.

THREE HAIKU BY BASHO (1644–1694)

Waterjar cracks:
I lie awake
This icy night.

Sick on a journey:
Over parched fields
Dreams wander on.

Lightning:
Heron's cry
Stabs the darkness

Source: "A Haiku Homepage." Retrieved 12 October 2001: http://home.clara.net/pka/haiku/haiku.htm.

HAINAN (1996 est. pop. 7.1 million). Hainan, an island province in the South China Sea off the coast of China's Guangdong Province, covers an area of 34,000 square kilometers. Before 1988, when the island obtained provincial status, it was part of Guangdong Province. The island has a mountainous inland with dense forests. The highest peak, Mount Wuzhi, rises to 1,867 meters above sea level. The coastal regions consist of plains, low hills, and volcanic terraces. The island has a tropical climate, with average temperatures of 22° to 26°C all year, but in extreme cases in the northern part of the island, temperatures may drop to 0°C. Annual precipitation varies; the western parts have an average of 1,000 millimeters, while the southeast, which is frequently hit by typhoons, averages 1,500 to 2,600 millimeters.

Hainan has a population of 7.14 million (1996), 12.8 percent of which belong to the indigenous Li nationality. Another important minority nationality is the Miao. The province's capital, Haikou (406,000, 1996), is situated on the north shore of Hainan, and there are several autonomous counties and townships mainly concentrated in the middle of the island and on the south coast.

Since the Han dynasty period (206 BCE–220 CE), the island has nominally been part of the Chinese empire, but for long periods, the Li evaded government control. During the Song dynasty (960–1279), when immigration from the mainland began, the island became part of Guangdong Province, a status that continued for centuries except for brief periods—during the Yuan dynasty (1267–1368) and in 1912–1921—when Hainan enjoyed independent provincial statues. In imperial China, undesirable officials were commonly exiled to the island. Hainan was occupied by the Japanese from 1939 to 1945, and since 1950 the island has been part of the People's Republic of China.

Hainan is the only part of China with tropical crops. Forestry accounts for almost half of the agricultural output; Hainan has a big rubber production and coconut farming. Other important tropical crops include coffee, pepper, cashew nuts, cacao, pineapples, bananas, carambolas, longans, litchis, and jackfruits. As one of China's special economic zones, Hainan attracted foreign investments and underwent rapid economic growth in the 1990s. The economy is mainly based on light industry and tourism. Industries are concentrated in the area around Haikou, and industrial products include processed rubber and food, electronic articles, and textiles. The tourist industry is located on the south coast in the area around Sanya (145,100, 1996). The flow of outside investment to Hainan subsided drastically toward the end of the 1990s, and many unfinished construction sites have been abandoned.

Bent Nielsen

Further Reading

Feng, Chongyi, and David S. G. Goodman. (1995) *China's Hainan Province: Economic Development and Investment Environment.* Nedlands, Australia: University of Western Australia Press in association with Asia Research Centre on Social, Political, and Economic Change, Murdoch University, Western Australia.

Matsuura, Keiichi. (2001) *Marine Fauna of the Shallow Waters around Hainan Island, South China Sea.* Tokyo: National Science Museum.

Park, Jung-Dong. (1997) *The Special Economic Zones of China and Their Impact on Its Economic Development.* Westport, CT: Praeger.

Schäfer, Bernhard. (1992) *Die Provinz Hainan, ein Beispel für den raumstrukturellen Wandel in der VR China seit Beginn der 80er Jahre.* München, Germany: Weltforum.

HAIPHONG

HAIPHONG (2002 pop. 572,000). Located 103 kilometers (64 miles) east of Hanoi on the coast of northern Vietnam, Haiphong, Vietnam's third-largest city (behind Ho Chi Minh City and Hanoi), is a major seaport and the main hub of northern Vietnam's industrial activity, and has been for more than a century. Haiphong has been a major seaport since the Tran dynasty (1225–1400) and, because of its strategic location, has seen numerous foreign invaders, including the Chinese, the Mongols under Kublai Khan, the Japanese, the French, and the Americans. The French bombing of Haiphong in 1946 precipitated the eight-year First Indochina War. During the Second Indochina War between Vietnam and the United States, Haiphong figured prominently again because of its strategic location and because of its role as an industrial hub and seaport. The United States bombed the city (especially notorious were the 1972 "Christmas bombings") and mined the city's harbor in 1972. In 1979, in the wake of the conflict between China and Vietnam, as many as 100,000 ethnic Chinese fled the city fearing Vietnamese reprisals, taking with them a large percentage of Haiphong's merchant class and economic power. In the last two decades of the twentieth century, Haiphong has sought recovery from its troubled past and has regained much of its economic and political power. Its port remains one of the busiest in Southeast Asia and the city's industry continues to develop.

Richard B. Verrone

Further Reading

Admiralty, Naval Intelligence Divison, Great Britain. (1943) *Indo-China.* London: Her Majesty's Stationery Office, Geographical Handbook Series, B.R. 510.

Cima, Ronald J., ed. (1989) *Vietnam: A Country Study.* Washington, DC: U.S. Government Printing Office.

HAJI, RAJA (d. 1784), Bugis dictator of Riau-Johor. The Bugis were seafarers from the southwest arm of Sulawesi who were known as warriors and enterprising traders throughout the Malay Archipelago. Raja Haji reigned briefly from 1777 to 1784, a period that saw the deterioration of Dutch-Bugis relations.

Raja Haji was the son of Daing Chelak (reigned 1728–1745), one of the five Bugis brothers that fled their homeland of Makassar in Southern Celebes and subsequently imposed Bugis power and influence in the southern Malay Peninsula during the eighteenth century. Raja Haji continued the family tradition by extending Bugis hegemony to the old Malay empire of Johor and the Riau-Lingga Archipelago.

Raja Haji was determined to oust the Dutch in Melaka, the Burgis' rival for control of the archipelago's commerce. To thwart Dutch ambitions in the Riau-Lingga Archipelago, he offered the English a commercial base at Riau. Dutch-Bugis enmity came to the open when they quarreled over the spoils of a captured ship of the English East India Company. The Bugis attacked Melaka and the Dutch in turn raided Riau.

In 1784 Raja Haji and his nephew, Sultan Ibrahim of Selangor, launched an all-out siege of Melaka. A Dutch fleet under Admiral Jacob Pieter van Braam relieved Melaka in June 1784. In the ensuing battle Raja Haji was killed at Telok Ketapang near Melaka. His death marked the decline of Bugis influence in the archipelago, and by October the Dutch had expelled the Bugis from Riau.

Ooi Keat Gin

Further Reading

Andaya, Leonard Y. (1975) *The Kingdom of Johor, 1641–1782.* Kuala Lumpur, Malaysia: Oxford University Press.

Raja Ali Haji Ibn Ahmad. (1982) *Tufat al-Nafis* (The Precious Gift). Trans. by Virginia Matheson and Barbara Watson Andaya. Kuala Lumpur, Malaysia: Oxford University Press.

Trocki, C. (1978) *Prince of Pirates: The Temenggongs and the Development of Johor and Singapore, 1784–1885.* Singapore: Singapore University Press.

HAKATA MATSURI Held from 1 to 15 July in the Hakata district of the city of Fukuoka in Japan, the Hakata Festival is officially named Hakata Yamagasa Gion, linking it to the famous Gion Matsuri in Kyoto. Like that festival, the Hakata Matsuri originated in a purification ritual (*goryo-e*) performed as a plea to the gods to stop a plague ravaging the city.

Dating back to the mid-thirteenth century, the festival marks the start of summer and has long been the highlight of Fukuoka's festival year. A series of purification rituals and festive processions leads up to the climactic high-speed race (*oiyama*) of festival floats that takes place at dawn on the final day. Each of the seven festival district committees selects a team of strong, healthy young men, who must then undergo purification and rigorous training. Participants cleanse themselves with sacred sand, receive an auspicious bamboo branch, and offer prayers for safety during the frenzied race. Each group constructs festival floats (*yamagasa*), which are of two types. *Kazariyama* are extraordinarily ornate, mountain-shaped floats adorned with dolls, ornaments, and lanterns and displayed around the city during the festival. *Kakiyama* floats are smaller but are still elaborately decorated with sacred pine branches and dolls representing heroes from legendary and historical tales. The seven *kakiyama*, each weighing about a ton, are raced through the city streets.

On 12 and 13 July the floats are paraded to Kushida Shrine, where the guardian deity of the city is enshrined. At 4:59 in the morning on 15 July, on the signal of a drumbeat, the first float leaves the Kushida Shrine grounds with the other six following at five-minute intervals. Shouldered by teams of twenty-eight young men in traditional festival dress of loincloths and *happi* coats (light cotton jackets), the floats speed along the five-kilometer course at a furious pace, while thousands of spectators cheer and splash them with purifying (and cooling) water. Many generations of local men have participated in this grueling contest, and the teams have developed fierce rivalries. The average time taken to cover the course is thirty minutes.

After crossing the finish line, the team members fight among themselves to obtain the best of the decorations to keep as souvenirs and talismans. Stripped down to its base, the float is returned to the Kushida Shrine to await use in the following year's festivities.

Lucy D. Moss

Further Reading

Haga Hideo. (1970) *Japanese Folk Festivals Illustrated.* Trans. by Fanny Mayer. Tokyo: Miura.

Vilhar, Gorazd, and Charlotte Anderson. (1994) *Matsuri: World of Japanese Festivals.* Tokyo: Shufunotomo.

HAKKA The Hakka are a Chinese ethnolinguistic minority group. The word "Hakka" means "guest people" or "newcomers" in Yue (Cantonese) and reflects their migration from central to southern China from about the ninth century into the early twentieth century. They tended to settle in distinct Hakka communities. There are about 40 million Hakka in China. Most live in southern China, with Guangdong Province having the greatest concentration, particularly in northern Meizhou Prefecture. There are also sizeable populations in Fujian, Jiangxi, Guangxi, Hainan Island, Hong Kong, and Taiwan. Estimates suggest that there may be more Hakka outside of China than in it, with large overseas communities in Malaysia, the United States, Canada, and Australia. The Hakka language is classified with Yue and Min as a southern Chinese language.

As an ethnolinguistic minority and late arrivals in southern China, the Hakka often had tense and sometimes violent relations with the Yue- and Min-speaking Han. The Han considered the Hakka to be inferior and a tribal people. Research indicates that their origins are Han Chinese, and the government classifies them as Han. Hakka men and women were known as skilled and hardworking farmers who grew sweet potatoes, rice, and vegetables on harsh land ignored by non-Hakka farmers. They also often served in the military and outside China worked in construction and on plantations. In cities, Hakka have been notably successful in academia, politics, and the professions. Well-known Hakka include China's leader Deng Xiaoping, Taiwan's President Lee Teng-hui, Singapore's President Lee Kwan Yew, and Myanmar's President Ne Win.

Both inside and outside China, the Hakka are known for their ethnic solidarity, which may be a product of centuries of discrimination by the Han. Hakka interests are advanced by the Tsung Tsin (Congzheng) Association and the United Hakka Association.

Ooi Giok Ling and David Levinson

Further Reading

Constable, Nicole, ed. (1994) *Guest People: Studies of Hakka Chinese Identity.* Berkeley and Los Angeles: University of California Press.

Leong, S. T. (1997) *Migration and Ethnicity in Chinese History: Hakkas, Pengmin, and Their Neighbours.* Stanford, CA: Stanford University Press.

Pan, L., ed. (1998) *The Encyclopedia of the Chinese Overseas.* Singapore: Chinese Heritage Centre.

HAKKA LANGUAGES Hakka languages are one of the seven major Chinese language groups (the others groups are Mandarin, Wu, Yue, Gan, Min, and Xiang). Although linguists class these as independent Chinese languages, traditionally they have been regarded as dialects, as they will be in this discussion. Native speakers of Hakka are found in Guangdong, Guangxi, Fujian, Xiangxi, Hunan, and Sichuan provinces on the mainland, as well as on Taiwan. Outside of China, Hakka speakers are found in Indonesia, Malaysia, Singapore, Thailand, Brunei, Cambodia, Vietnam, and Laos. The estimated population of the native Hakka dialect speakers in 1988 was 37 million. In some places, Hakka dialects are also called Aihua, Majiehua, Xinminhua, or Tuguangdonghua.

The term Hakka is of Cantonese origin, *hak* meaning "guest", *ka* meaning "family/people." According to Chinese migration history, there were five major migration waves of the Hakka-speaking people, from the central plains of China to the south, beginning during the Eastern Jin dynasty (317–420) and in response to various non-Chinese invasions, civil wars, and other clashes with local peoples. The term Hakka itself, however, did not appear in any Chinese historical documents until the Song dynasty (960–1279). When Hakka-speaking people migrated to the northeastern part of Guangdong Province during the late Ming dynasty (1368–1644) and early Qing dynasty (1644–1912), the local people referred to the new immigrants, with whom they clashed over farmland as Hakka. From 1850 to 1920, the Hakka and the indigenous population clashed, which contributed to the development of the well-known strong sense of ethnic and linguistic identity of the Hakka. The famous family precept of the Hakka, "One would rather to sell one's ancestor's land than to forget one's ancestors' speech," shows this strong loyalty to their mother tongue.

Due to the different destinations of the various waves of Hakka migration, currently several Hakka dialects exist. Among them the Mexian subdialect, spoken in the northeastern part of Guangdong Province, is considered the standard. Chinese uses tone, the musical pitch of the voice, as a distinguishing mark of morphemes (characters or syllables). Traditionally, since Middle Chinese (seventh century CE), Chinese characters have been classified into four tonal categories: *ping* tone (even tone), *shang* tone (rising tone), *qu* tone (going tone), and *ru* tone (entering tone). Each tonal category may have undergone tonal split into two subcategories, *yin* and *yang*. But each tonal category has evolved into different tonal values (different types of pitches) as reflected in modern dialects. Mexian Hakka has six tones: *yin ping* tone (high level), *yang ping* tone (low level), *shang* tone (low falling), *qu* tone (high falling), *yin ru* tone (short low level), and *yang ru* tone (short high level). It has seventeen consonants, the primary of which are: *p*, *p'*, *m*, *f*, *v*, *t*, *t'*, *n*, *l*, *ts*, *ts'*, *s*, *ñ*, *ng*, *h*; six nuclear (main) vowels: *i*, *ï*, *u*, *e*, *a*, *o*; and three pairs of consonant endings: *-m/-p*, *-n/-t*, and *-ng/-k*. The bilabial and velar nasal, *m* and *ng*, may occur alone and form syllabic syllables.

Distinctive Characteristics of Hakka Dialects

The Hakka dialects are set apart from the other major Chinese dialects by unique phonological, lexical, and syntactic characteristics. Phonological characteristics that are typical in Hakka dialects include (1) the fact that Middle Chinese (from around the seventh century CE) voiced obstruent (obstruents are stops and spirants, such as *b*, *d*, *g*, *v*, and *z*) initials are pronounced as voiceless aspirated consonants; (2) Middle Chinese *shang* (rising) tone syllables with nasal, liquid, or glide initials are merged with Middle Chinese *ping* (level) tone syllables with a voiceless initial consonant; and (3) most of the velar fricatives (sounds like voiced *h*) of Middle Chinese are pronounced as *f*. Because the Hakka dialects share some common phonological features and lexical items with Gan, Yue, and Min (to a lesser degree), some scholars have argued that the Hakka dialect should be grouped with Gan to form a major Gan-Hakka group, while others prefer to assign the Hakka dialects to a different group. Some even suggest that the Hakka dialects should be considered subdialects of the Gan-Yue dialect group. Historically, Min dialects are known to preserve several Old Chinese (c. 1000 BCE) characteristics, which distinguish them from other dialects. Therefore, no scholar has ever tried to group Min and Hakka together. Currently, the most popular view is to treat Hakka as a separate group.

Margaret Mian Yan

Further Reading

Hashimoto, Mantaro J. (1973) *The Hakka Dialect: A Linguistic Study of Its Phonology, Syntax, and Lexicon*. Cambridge, U.K.: Cambridge University Press.

———. (1992) "Hakka in Wellentheorie Perspective." *Journal of Chinese Linguistics* 20, 1: 1–49.

Li Rulong and Zhang Shuangqing, eds. (1992) *Ken-Gan Fangyan Diaocha Baogao* (Report on a Survey of the Ke-Gan Dialects). Xiamen, China: Xiamen Daxue Chubanshe.

Li Fang-kuei. (1973) "Languages and Dialects." *Journal of Chinese Linguistics* 1, 1:1–13.

Luo Zhaojin. (1990) *Taiwan de Kejiahua* (The Hakka Dialects in Taiwan). Taipei, Taiwan: Taiyuan Chubanshe.

Norman, Jerry. (1988) *Chinese*. Cambridge, U.K.: Cambridge University Press.

Ramsey, S. Robert. (1987) *The Languages of China*. Princeton, NJ: Princeton University Press.

Sagart, Laurent. (1998) "On Distinguishing Hakka and Non-Hakka Dialects." *Journal of Chinese Linguistics* 26, 2: 281–301.

Wang, William S.-Y., ed. (1991) *Languages and Dialects of China*. Journal of Chinese Linguistics Monograph Series, no. 3. Berkeley, CA: Journal of Chinese Linguistics, University of California.

Yuan Jiahua et al. (1960) *Hanyu Fangyan Gaiyao* (An Outline of the Chinese Dialects). Beijing: Wenzi Gaige Chubanshe.

EDIB ADIVAR, HALIDE

EDIB ADIVAR, HALIDE (1884–1964), Turkish feminist reformer and writer. Halide Edib Adivar was a key figure in the emancipation of women in Turkey. After graduating from the American College in Istanbul in 1901, she married Salih Zeki Bey, with whom she had two sons. She divorced him in 1910 after learning he had taken a second wife. In the following years, she became involved in teaching, social relief work, and nursing. In 1917 Halide Edib married the Turkish politician Adnan Adıvar.

An ardent champion of Turkish independence during the War of Liberation (1918–1922), she supported the movement through writing, mobilizing women, and organizing relief work and is one of the few women to have held military rank during the war. For many years Halide Edib lectured at universities in the United States and India. In 1939 she was appointed chairperson of the English department at the University of Istanbul and in 1950 was elected an independent member of parliament for İzmir. Halide Edib retired from political life in 1954 and died 9 January 1964 at eighty years of age.

Her novels include *Atesten Gomlek* (Shirt of Flame), *Vurun Kahpeye* (Strike the Whore), *Sinekli Bakkal* (Grocery with Flies), and *Akile Hanım Sokagi* (Madame Akile Street). Her works in English include historical writings and memoirs such as *Turkey Faces West*, *Conflict of East and West in Turkey*, and *Inside India*. Her own life served as a model for other women and combined with her advocacy of women's rights made her a pioneer in the women's rights movement in Turkey.

Tipi Isikozlu

Further Reading

Enginun, Inci. (1989) *Halide Edib Adıvar*. Ankara, Turkey: Kultur Bakanlıgı.

HAMADAN

HAMADAN (2002 pop. 409,000). Hamadan (once called Ecbatana), an ancient city in western Iran, was the capital of Media; after the Persians overthrew their Median overlords, the city became the Persian royal summer residence. Alexander of Macedon conquered the city in 330 BCE, while pursuing the last Persian ruler, Darius III. The Seleucids besieged Hamadan, and the Parthians incorporated it into their empire. The Arabs took the city in the seventh century, and the Seljuk Turks in the twelfth century, the Seljuks making Ecbatana their capital. After the Mongols invaded Iran in the thirteenth century, they devastated Ecbatana in 1220; the city of Hamadan rose above Ecbatana's ruins. Timur sacked Hamadan in 1386.

More recently Russians, Turks, and British have held Hamadan for various periods, with the Iranians finally gaining the city in 1918. In the 1980s, the Iran-Iraq war caused much damage to Hamadan.

Hamadan's location explains its history. The city lies on the road between modern Tehran and Baghdad, and whoever controlled the city also dominated north-south and east-west routes—between the Caspian Sea and Persian Gulf and between Europe and China. About one hundred kilometers west of Hamadan, in a mountainous region, is Darius the Great's inscription at Bisitun, meant to impress travelers passing between Assyria and Media. The Persian king's trilingual inscription on the rocky bluff was used to decipher cuneiform in the nineteenth century.

Modern Hamadan is a commercial center noted for fine Persian rugs and leather goods. Ironically Ecbatana's remains are buried beneath modern Hamadan, except for the Sang-e Shir (stone lion), a majestic but time-ravaged guardian of the city gates from the fourth century BCE. The fabled golden treasures of the Median and Persian palaces of Ecbatana await excavation, which is unlikely to occur because the modern city would have to be demolished.

The tomb of Avicenna (Abu Ali al-Husayn ibn 'Abd Allah ibn Sina; 980–1037), a Persian Islamic philosopher and physician, stands in Hamadan; Avicenna's medical text was widely studied in Europe as well as Asia. Also in Hamadan is a tomb said to be that of the biblical Esther and Mordecai; designed in Islamic style, the tomb is guarded by a Jewish family, who serve as custodians and guides.

Houman A. Sadri

Further Reading

Adelkhah, Fariba. (2000) *Being Modern in Iran.* New York: Columbia University Press and Centre d'Études et de Recherches Internationales.

Ghirshman, Roman. (1978) *Iran.* Middlesex, U.K.: Penguin.

HAMENGKU BUWONO IX, SRI SULTAN

(1912–1988), vice president of Indonesia. Sri Sultan Hamengku Buwono IX was Indonesia's vice president from 1973 to 1978 during the New Order under Suharto (ruled 1966–1998). He also was the sultan (1940–1988) and the governor of Yogyakarta (1950–1988). The position of sultan has only a symbolic status in modern Indonesian, but it nonetheless became very influential under Hamengku Buwono IX.

Raden Mas Dorodjatun (his birth name before being appointed as sultan) was born in Yogyakarta on 12 April 1912. He was educated in Indonesia and the Netherlands. As sultan, he mobilized the people's army against the Dutch in the war of revolution in 1945 in central Java and declared that the Yogyakarta kingdom was part of the Republic of Indonesia. He initiated the famous *Serangan Oemum* (General Combat) against the Dutch on 1 March 1949, which showed the world that the new republic still existed.

He served in various ministerial posts after independence, with the exception of the period between 1953 and 1959. His ability to deal with the Dutch during and after the revolution and to mediate conflict between the civilian and the military authorities in the 1950s made him a respected minister of defense during 1949–1953. In the early years of the New Order (1966–1973), together with Suharto and Adam Malik (1917–1984), he was part of a leadership triumvirate, given the task of rehabilitating the economy. As the coordinating minister for economy and finance (1966–1973), he was successful in attracting Western donor countries to the Inter-Governmental Group on Indonesia (IGGI). As the first vice president during Suharto's era (1973–1978), he also held other important positions, including the national head of the Indonesia Sport Committee and the head of the Indonesian Scout Movement. Hamengku Buwono IX passed away in the United States on 3 October 1988. Hundreds of thousands of people lined the twenty-six-kilometer length of road from the palace in Yogyakarta to the sacred Mataram cemetery at Imogiri, where the sultans of both Yogyakarta and Solo are buried.

Abubakar E. Hara

Further Reading

Atmakusumah, ed. (1982) *Tahta untuk Rakyat* (Monarch for the People). Jakarta, Indonesia: Gramedia.

Darban, Ahmad Adaby, ed. (1998) *Biografi Pahlawan Nasional Sultan Hamengku Buwana IX* (A Biography of National Hero Sultan Hamengku Buwana IX). Jakarta, Indonesia: Departemen Pendidikan dan Kebudayaan RI.

HAMHUNG (1993 pop. 709,730). Hamhung is the capital of South Hamgyong Province in North Korea (Democratic People's Republic of Korea). It is located on the Songch'on River on the eastern coast, 315 kilometers (200 miles) northeast of the capital city of Pyongyang. Together with the adjoining outer trade port of Hungnam, this industrial city plays an important role in the country's economy. It was the hometown of Yi Song-gye (1392–1398), founder of the Choson dynasty (1392–1910).

Hamhung is the center of the chemical industry in North Korea (plastic materials, synthetic tar). Chemical factories use local resources such as limestone and anthracite. There are large deposits of magnesite, lead, and zinc. Major industries include heavy equipment (metallurgy, mining, energy, chemical equipment), the electro-technical industry, agricultural machinery, and a hydroelectric power station. The city is also an important center for nonferrous metallurgy (aluminum), textiles (silk and wool), footwear, food, tobacco, fishing, and building materials.

Major industrial plants include the February 8 Vinalon Complex, the Hungnam Fertilizer Complex, and the Ryongsong Associated Machinery Bureau. The Hamhung Branch of the Academy of Sciences founded in 1960 is a general research institute involved in the scientific and technological development of the national chemical industry.

Ariane Perrin

Further Reading

Panorama of Korea. (1999) Pyongyang, North Korea: Foreign Languages Publishing House.

HAN The Han are the majority people among China's fifty-six state-recognized nationalities, and comprise the people usually known worldwide as the Chinese. They are the most numerous of the world's nationalities, approaching 1.2 billion in 2000, and are renowned for their highly distinctive and powerful languages and cultures and for their long and eventful history. The main concentrations of Han Chinese are in the eastern half of China, including Taiwan. Under the People's Republic of China, the state decides who belongs to which nationality. This decision is made according to a rigid definition devised by Joseph Stalin. One group that has, on occasion, requested separate identity is the Hakka, but the state considers them part of the Han nationality.

Population

In the mid-seventeenth century, China's population was about 200 million, the overwhelming majority being Han. The 1953 census showed the Han population at 547 million, which was 93.9 percent of the People's Republic of China (PRC) total. Census figures for 1990 and 2000 put the Han population at 1.04 billion and 1.16 billion, respectively, or 91.99 and 91.59 percent of the PRC total. Since the late 1970s, Han families in the PRC have been subject to a very strict policy rarely allowing more than one child per couple, without which the 2000 Han population would have been somewhat higher than in fact it was. About 98 percent of Taiwan's 1997 population of 21.7 million were Han.

At the end of the nineteenth century there were an estimated 4 million overseas Chinese. In 1990, this figure had grown to about 37 million Chinese living outside China and Taiwan, with 88 percent living elsewhere in Asia. The country with the largest Han population outside China was Indonesia, with about 7.3 million Chinese; the country with the highest Han proportion was Singapore, where the 1990 census showed a total population of 2.69 million, 2.09 million of them (77.7 percent) Han. Hong Kong and Macao, then colonial territories, had about 6 million Han Chinese, the overwhelming majority of both populations. Outside Asia, the country with the largest Chinese population is the United States (about 1.6 million in 1990).

Language

Chinese belongs to the Sino-Tibetan family of languages. The Chinese written language dates at least to the fourteenth century BCE and consists of monosyllabic characters or ideographs. The characters were standardized in the third century BCE and remain essentially unchanged, although the PRC adopted a simplified writing system in the 1950s. Literate Chinese have always been able to understand each other through writing, which has acted as a unifying force throughout history.

Each character represents both a sound and a concept, but meaning is conveyed through characters either singly or in combinations. Chinese is not monosyllabic; objects, actions, or ideas are more likely to be represented through groups of two or three rather than a single character.

Spoken Chinese is sharply regional and divided into several sublanguages and numerous dialects. All of these are tonal and express grammatical relationships through word order, not word endings. The official language is Modern Standard Chinese, or Mandarin, which is based on the pronunciation found in Beijing. The north and southwest of the Han regions (essentially the eastern half of those territories ruled as part of the People's Republic of China, plus Taiwan) of China are dominated by the Mandarin dialects, most of them intelligible to a speaker of Modern Standard Chinese. Sublanguages of the southeast include Yue (Cantonese), Wu (spoken in Shanghai), Hunanese, Jiangxi, North and South Fujian, and Hakka. In the south, even dialects are often mutually unintelligible. Fujian is known for strong dialect differences from one valley to the next.

Approximately two-thirds of Han Chinese speak one of the Mandarin dialects as their mother tongue. In the twentieth century, successive regimes have attempted to have Modern Standard Chinese spoken, or at least understood, by all Chinese through education, radio, and television. Of the southern sublanguages, Wu has the greatest number of speakers, followed by Cantonese.

Culture and Economy

Under Emperor Han Wudi (reigned 140–87 BCE), Confucianism began to dominate the Chinese state, including its ritual, and formed the ideological basis of duty and service for the scholar-official class, which ruled the country. Confucianism laid great emphasis on morality within hierarchical human relationships, on creating and maintaining harmony within society and on the family as the central social unit.

Confucianism accorded greater social respect to men than women and to sons than daughters. Until the twentieth century, marriages were arranged by parents through the aid of matchmakers, and women were very subordinate. Although the revolutions of the twentieth century greatly raised women's status, allowing them to enter the work force, gender equality is nowhere on the horizon among the Han.

Confucian ideology was one primary reason why Han governance was generally far more secular than that found in other great civilizations. In the twentieth century, Confucianism came under strong attack from modernist nationalism and Marxism-Leninism. Modernist nationalists denounced Confucianism as hierarchical, patriarchal, and oppressive, even though Confucianists argued that they were the real nationalists because they upheld Chinese values and traditions. Mao Zedong (1893–1976) orchestrated attacks on Confucian and religious values everywhere in China, but there has since been a revival of Confucian influence in the PRC, and it remains strong in Han communities outside China.

Secularity of governance does not mean the Han are irreligious. To this day, folk religions, which attempt to harmonize relations between humankind and the cosmic order, remain highly influential. Buddhism and Taoism still have Han followers and their places of worship are common, though visitors are more often tourists than believers. However, religions that emphasize belief in a single God have never attained more than minor influence among the Han. Muslims are never classified as Han, but as Hui.

Below the scholar-official, Confucianism prized the peasant. Han society is based on agriculture. The staple in the south is rice and in the north wheat-based products, supplemented by a wide variety of vegetables. The meat most associated with the Han is pork. The Han do not care for dairy products, a taste even extensive Western influence has failed to change. To this day, local markets are important for the economy.

During the Song dynasty (960–1279), China was the world's most technologically developed society. Although Confucianism looked down on the merchant, China underwent a commercial revolution during that time, which produced a degree of prosperity that Marco Polo marveled at in the thirteenth century. However, China later fell far behind technologically and failed to undertake an industrial revolution until the second half of the twentieth century. Under Mao, the Han entrepreneurial spirit was suppressed. But since the late 1970s it has revived, with heavy industry being replaced by more consumer-oriented enterprises and self-reliance by foreign trade.

The commonalities of the Han should not disguise important regional differences. These apply not only to language but also to many aspects of culture and society, including cuisine, festivals, clothing, marriage customs, village architecture, and music and theater. Cuisine provides one example. The Han of the southwest (Hunan, Sichuan, and Yunnan provinces) favor spicy dishes; in the southeast, Cantonese food is noted for its quick cooking and stir-frying at high temperatures, and for rich, sweet dishes.

Unity in the Twenty-First Century

The strength of their culture and the size of their population have made the Han at times inwardly focused, at times outwardly focused. Although there are periods of division in China's long history, and although localist elements remain influential to this day, the Chinese have shown a highly enduring sense of national unity. China's joining the World Trade Organization late in 2001 should reduce isolationist tendencies but will not undermine the essential features of Chinese culture or eliminate nationalism.

Colin Mackerras

Further Reading

Blunden, Caroline, and Mark Elvin. (1990) *The Cultural Atlas of the World: China*. Oxford: Andromeda.

Ebrey, Patricia Buckley. (1996) *The Cambridge Illustrated History of China*. Cambridge, U.K.: Cambridge University Press.

Gernet, Jacques. (1996) *A History of Chinese Civilisation*. 2d ed. Cambridge, U.K.: Cambridge University Press.

Harrell, Stevan. (1991) "Han." In *Encyclopedia of World Cultures*, vol. 6, edited by Paul Friedrich and Norma Diamond. Boston: Hall, 439–449.

Hook, Brian, and Denis Twitchett, eds. (1991) *The Cambridge Encyclopedia of China*. 2d ed. Cambridge, U.K.: Cambridge University Press.

Spence, Jonathan D. (1990) *The Search for Modern China*. New York: Norton.

HAN DYNASTY The Han dynasty (206 BCE–220 CE), which was founded by Liu Bang (256–195 BCE), or Han Gaozu, marks an era of consolidated imperial institutions in Chinese history. After the short-lived Qin regime (221–206 BCE), the Han ruled China for four centuries, governing one of the most successful empires of the time. Conventionally, the dynasty is divided into two periods separated by a short interregnum. The Former, or Western, Han (206 BCE–8 CE) had its capital in Changan; the Latter, or Eastern, Han (25–220) had its capital in the east at Luoyang.

Political Changes

As soon as he established the Han, Gaozu, the first commoner to found a dynasty in imperial China, abolished the brutal laws and heavy taxes of the Qin. With regard to governmental institutions, however, he basically copied the preceding dynasty's system. The imperial throne, whose succession was hereditary, was assisted by a civil bureaucracy. Officials at various administrative levels were recruited through recommendation and examination and appointed by the imperial court. The empire was organized into commanderies *(jun)* and kingdoms *(wangguo);* the former, subdivided into districts *(xian)*, were centrally controlled, while the latter were largely autonomous under enfeoffed kings. Commandery and district officials were responsible for the census of the population and the register of the land, which constituted the basis of the main forms of taxation (the poll tax and the land tax) and military conscription. To relieve the threat from the powerful nomadic peoples of Central Asia known as the Xiongnu (called Huns later in Europe), Gaozu adopted a conciliatory policy, which was continued by his immediate successors. They wooed the Xiongnu leaders by sending valuable gifts and imperial princesses as brides.

Subsequent emperors followed the early Han policy of light labor service and taxation. Due in part to peace and frugal government, the economy expanded, and production soared; as a result, the state treasury was full, and granaries bulged. Meanwhile, the court took steps to isolate the kingdoms and reduce the size of their territories. After 154 BCE, when the imperial court defeated a revolt staged by seven kingdoms, the authority of the central government was further consolidated by splitting the kingdoms' territories and curtailing their powers.

Emperor Wudi (156–87 BCE) oversaw an expansionist era in Han history. Domestically, he sought to expand central power by imposing state monopolies for salt and iron, proclaiming Confucianism the state ideology, and establishing a Confucian imperial university to train officials. In foreign affairs, besides military campaigns, the Han court relied on diplomatic efforts to establish favorable relations with other peoples. As a result, the Han armies advanced to the southwest, into present-day Korea and Vietnam, and to the northeast as far as Dunhuang. It was at this juncture that the trade routes known as the Silk Road were established. The Silk Road connected the Chinese and Roman empires. China imported wool and linen fabrics, amber, wines, acrobats, and gold coins and bullion from the Romans. In imperial Rome, Chinese silk became a major luxury article. Under Wudi, the Han became one of the most powerful empires in the world.

After Wudi, most emperors of the Western Han were young and weak, and regents, eunuchs, and imperial consorts' families dominated court politics. In 9 CE, the regent Wang Mang (45 BCE–23 CE) took imperial power from the Liu family and named his dynasty the Xin (New). Claiming to have received the new Mandate of Heaven, Wang Mang initiated a series of social and institutional reforms. But his attempts antagonized the wealthier members of society and failed to increase the resources of the state. Wang Mang's regime was overthrown by large-scale peasant rebellions.

The Han house was restored by Guangwudi (6 BCE–57 CE), who established the Eastern Han dynasty with its capital at Luoyang. In his efforts to consolidate the government, Guangwudi reestablished the institutions of the Western Han and promoted the cause of scholarship. He also minimized the influences of eunuchs and imperial consorts' families. Under Guangwudi's immediate successors, the Han was once again rich and strong enough to adopt an aggressive foreign policy and assert its influence in Central Asia.

The dynasty started to decline during the time of Hedi (79–105); his reign saw the return of powerful eunuchs and imperial consorts' families in court politics. All ten Han emperors who ruled after Hedi took the throne as minors aged between one hundred days and sixteen years. Political factions manipulated the imperial succession, and factional struggles corrupted politics and weakened the central government.

In local areas, powerful landowners defied the government by evading taxes and enlarging their holdings. Helpless peasants became the virtual serfs of these landowners in return for economic and physical security. The great families converted their manors into fortresses, taking over many of the functions of government in their respective localities. Their estates were largely self-sufficient, so that trade declined and cities shrank correspondingly.

In 184 CE, because of political corruption and land annexation, peasant groups across north China known as the "Yellow Turbans" revolted, severely attacking the great families and shaking the Han house. Cao Cao (155–220), who led the suppression of the rebels, dominated the court after the rebels were put down. He claimed the title of chancellor of the imperial government. In 220, after Cao Cao died, his son Cao Pi (reigned 220–226 as Wendi of the Wei state) forced the last Han emperor to abdicate. China then entered a prolonged period of disunity and disorder similar to that in the West following the collapse of the Roman empire.

CHINA—HISTORICAL PERIODS

Xia dynasty (2100–1766 BCE)
Shang dynasty (1766–1045 BCE)
Zhou dynasty (1045–256 BCE)
  Western Zhou (1045–771 BCE)
  Eastern Zhou (770–221 BCE)
Spring and Autumn period (770–476 BCE)
Warring States period (475–221 BCE)
Qin dynasty (221–206 BCE)
Han dynasty (206 BCE–220 CE)
Three Kingdoms period (220–265 CE)
North and South Dynasties (220–589 CE)
Sui dyansty (581–618 CE)
Tang dynasty (618–907 CE)
Five Dynasties period (907–960 CE)
Song dynasty (960–1279)
  Northern Song (960–1126)
  Southern Song (1127–1279)
Jurchen Jin dynasty (1125–1234)
Yuan dynasty (1279–1368)
Ming dynasty (1368–1644)
Qing dynasty (1644–1912)
Republican China (1912–1927)
People's Republic of China (1949–present)
Republic of China (1949–present)
Cultural Revolution (1966–1976)

Socioeconomic Changes

Han society was largely rural and its economy agrarian. According to the census of 1 CE, the Han population numbered about 60 million. Peasants made up the majority of the population; they paid the government land and poll taxes, rendered labor services, and served in the army. The average peasant family was estimated to consist of five people working about seven hectares of land. Women were significant economic assets to poor peasants: both husband and wife performed hard manual labor in the fields. In the north, millet, wheat, and barley were the grain crops; in the south, rice. Pigs and fowl were the common meat animals. Peasants used a variety of tools, but the most important was the plow. Wooden plows were still used, while cheaply made, yet more effective iron plows grew in popularity. More and more peasants used new tools such as three-legged seeders, iron harrows, and levelers, which were pulled by either draft animals or human laborers. Agricultural production was facilitated by government-sponsored irrigation projects, including reservoirs and canals.

In addition to grains, the Han also promoted sericulture (raising silkworms and spinning and weaving silk cloth). Silks were China's most valuable export commodity, and bolts of silk were used as currency and given as state gifts. Tending silkworms and carding the spinning silk was women's work, and each family was required to pay a tax in silk fabric.

Both manufacturing and commerce flourished. Craftspeople continued the Chinese tradition of excellent metallurgy. By the beginning of the first century CE, China had about fifty state-run ironworks, which smelted iron ore, processed it with chemicals, and fashioned the metal into ingots for tools and weapons. Bronze workers produced jewelry, utensils, and ritual objects. Perhaps the most remarkable product of Han imagination was the invention of paper, which the Chinese traditionally date to 105 CE. By the fifth century, paper was in common use, preparing the way for the invention of printing.

Merchants made tremendous fortunes during the Han. Retail merchants set up shop in stalls in the markets, grouped according to their wares. All the butchers, for example, congregated in one part of the market, each trying to outsell the others. The markets were also the haunts of entertainers and fortune-tellers. The newly developed sturdy carts and wagons as well as networks of roads and waterways facilitated the transportation of goods. Nevertheless, according to government policy, merchants were put at the bottom of the social order, below scholars, peasants, and artisans. Emperor Wudi of the Western Han promulgated sumptuary laws that forbade merchants to flaunt their wealth. He nationalized the iron and salt industries and established a liquor-licensing system, setting up a pattern that persisted into the twentieth century. He also set up state granaries to stabilize grain prices and to discourage speculation. These legal and social restrictions became obstacles for further development of commerce.

Peasants often faced more serious problems. Without reserves to tide them over during times of poor weather or other difficulties, small landholders often went into debt; if they could not pay their debt, they lost their land and had to work as sharecroppers. As sharecroppers, peasants could keep only 50 percent of their yield. Some left the land to become laborers, and the most unfortunate had to sell their children or themselves into slavery to pay off debts. Rich families, meanwhile, accumulated great estates worked by tenants and slaves, and through their political connections they could often evade taxes, which placed a greater strain on the remaining small freeholders. Under these miserable conditions, peasants from time to time revolted. Indeed, it was the large-scale peasant uprisings that destroyed Wang Mang's Xin regime and precipitated the downfall of the Eastern Han dynasty.

Cultural and Intellectual Changes

Han China witnessed dynamic changes in religious and intellectual life. Under the first several emperors, Han thought was dominated by the Taoist notion of "nonaction," which emphasized frugal government and delegation of imperial authority. Han thinkers argued that the emperor must on the one hand uphold basic principles of government and on the other hand leave specific decisions and actions to the care of his officials. Meanwhile, government must adopt the policy of light taxation to alleviate the suffering of the people. Historians attributed early Han prosperity partly to lenient government policies guided by Taoist ideas.

Craving a grandiose empire, Emperor Wudi embraced Confucianism, a belief system that advocated active social participation. To facilitate Confucian learning, the emperor established an imperial university and employed Confucian scholars to prepare future government officials with a curriculum based on Confucian classics. Han Confucianism, however, was influenced by other schools of thought, including yin-yang cosmology, legalism (the doctrine that emphasizes government by legal apparatus), and Taoism. The great synthesizer of Confucian teachings was Dong Zhongshu (c. 179–104 BCE), one of the court advisers of Emperor Wudi. According to Dong's interpretation, the universe consisted of heaven, Earth, and humans, operating on the basis of yin-yang forces and the five agents of water, fire, metal, wood, and earth. Having received the Mandate of Heaven, the human ruler, or Son of Heaven, served as the intermediary between the worlds of humans and spirits. It was his duty to develop his subjects' moral goodness, nourish their livelihood, and maintain social and cosmic harmony. If the ruler failed in such tasks, cosmic portents or even disasters would occur, and Heaven would punish him by revoking the Mandate. While Confucianism strengthened imperial authority, it certainly imposed heavy responsibilities on the emperor.

During the Han, a new form of Taoism—religious Taoism—flourished. Based on popular beliefs, this new trend was concerned primarily with drugs and potions to prolong life and attain immortality, and with alchemy to produce gold from base materials. These interests led to experiments that produced information valuable for chemistry, pharmacology, and other sciences and gave rise to the invention of the compass, which greatly helped navigation, and the discovery of sulfur and saltpeter, the ingredients of gunpowder. By the mid-second century CE, religious Taoists organized themselves into political groups. In 142, Zhang Daoling founded the sect named "Way of the Celestial Masters" in Sichuan. Decades later, Zhang Jue (d. 184) created the sect called "Way of Great Peace" in north China. These Taoist groups, to which peasants belonged, eventually revolted against the Han regime and expedited the fall of the dynasty.

Buddhism was introduced into Han China by Central Asian merchants. During the reign of Emperor Mingdi (28–75), the second ruler of the Eastern Han, some Chinese combined the Buddhist rites and fasts with Taoist practices aimed at physical immortality. In the next century, Buddhist monasteries appeared in the Han empire, and Buddhist texts were translated into Chinese. The Parthian monk An Shigao, for example, reached the Han capital of Luoyang in 148 and began translating a set of texts dealing with meditation practices and the Buddhist worldview. In later dynasties, Buddhism transformed the Chinese cultural landscape.

The Han produced great historians. Sima Qian (c. 145–86 BCE) wrote the first comprehensive history of China entitled *Shiji* (Historical Records). Divided into five sections—basic annals, chronological tables, monographs, hereditary families, and biographies—and 130 chapters, this massive work provided both historical information and moral instruction. Following the example of Sima Qian, Ban Gu (32–92) wrote the first dynastic history of China, *Hanshu* (History of the Han Dynasty). Ban Gu's sister Ban Zhao, the most famous female literary figure of the Han, assisted in the writing of the *Hanshu*. Possessing great historical and literary values, both the *Shiji* and *Hanshu* set the standard for later dynastic histories that continued to the early twentieth century.

Legacy of the Han

The Han dynasty set the pattern of civilization for subsequent Chinese history. It provided future generations with a model of a long-lasting, extensive, and unified empire. It consolidated an effective form of bureaucracy and established a distinguished tradition of political philosophy. It laid a solid foundation of belief system, social structure, and economic form for later dynasties. It also developed a basic mode of thinking and a scheme for dealing with foreign peoples. So strongly did the Han dynasty influence Chinese culture that 95 percent of present-day Chinese call themselves Han, their language the Han language, and their written script Han characters. The Han achievements made China a dominant force in the preindustrial world.

Jiang Yonglin

Further Reading

Loewe, Michael. (1968) *Everyday Life in Early Imperial China: During the Han Period, 202 B.C.–A.D. 220*. New York: Dorset.

Pirazzoli-t'Serstevens, Michèle. (1982) *The Han Civilization of China*. Oxford, U.K.: Phaidon.

Twitchett, Denis, and Michael Loewe, eds. (1986) *The Ch'in and Han Empires, 221 B.C.–A.D. 220*. Vol. 1 of *The Cambridge History of China*, New York: Cambridge University Press.

Yu Ying-shih. (1967) *Trade and Expansion in Han China: A Study in the Structure of Sino-Barbarian Economic Relations*. Berkeley and Los Angeles: University of California Press.

HAN RIVER The Han River flows about 514 kilometers through Seoul, capital of the Republic of Korea (South Korea), rising from a spring in Odae Mountain in Kangwon Province and emptying into the Yellow Sea. Several prehistoric human settlements have been excavated along the river. At present the Han supplies drinking water for 20 million people living within its basin—Kangwon and Kyunggi provinces, including the cities of Seoul and Inchon.

The South Han River, a distinct tributary of the Han River, flows through Kangwon province and North Ch'ungch'ong Province before it joins the North Han at Paldang Reservoir, an artificial dam providing the major source of drinking water for Seoul metropolitan area residents The river also provides water for agricultural and industrial purposes and generates electrical power through three major dams. The Han is a symbol of South Korea's remarkable economic development in the 1970s and 1980s, which is known as the "Han River miracle." The 1988 Seoul Summer Olympic stadium is located along its banks. Other recreational facilities include the Yeouido Han Riverside Park, a 36.9-kilometer bicycle trail, swimming pools, and fishing areas. The Han is also popular for water skiing and yachting.

The water quality of the Han River is deteriorating due to increasing nonpoint sources of pollutants from agriculture and rapid urbanization of traditionally rural areas surrounding Seoul. The lack of a buffer zone between the river and increasing human settlement is another cause of environmental concern.

Yearn Hong Choi

Further Reading

Yearn Hong Choi. (1998) "From One Capital to Another." Vol. 10, no. 11 of *Water Environment and Technology*.

HAN YONG-UN (1879–1944), Korean monk, poet, nationalist. Born to a farming family in Chungchong Province, Han Yong-un was originally educated in Chinese classical literature in his village, where he became involved in the Tonghak sect. The Tonghak insurgency led to regional strife and subsequent Japanese intervention. Han went into hiding in the Paektam monastery near Seoraksan in eastern Korea, where he adopted the name Manhae (Ten Thousand Seas).

As a monk, Han traveled to Japan to study Zen Buddhism. When Japan annexed Korea, however, he left for Russia to form a base of resistance against the Japanese. Han returned to Korea and was one of the original signers of the Declaration of Korean Independence, for which act he was imprisoned by the Japanese until 1923. In prison he wrote "A Letter of Korean Independence," which is regarded as one of the founding documents of the 1919 independence movement.

Han's writings are considered among the best of Korean and Zen poetry, and his works have been published internationally. A memorial to him was erected at the site of the 1 March uprising in Tapkol Park (formerly Pagoda Park) in Seoul.

Thomas P. Dolan

HANGAI MOUNTAINS The Hangai (Khangai, Hangayn) Mountains dominate central Mongolia with their rich pastures and forests. The range extends 800 kilometers northwest-southeast and parallels the Mongolian Altai Mountains. Several of the range's snowy peaks reach an altitude of 3,500 meters above sea level, and the highest of these peaks, snow-capped Otgon Tenger (3,905 meters above sea level), remains a central and sacred place in Mongolian folklore. Medicinal herbs and minerals gathered from its slopes are a popular commodity in Ulaanbaatar, Mongolia's capital.

The Hangai Mountains drain into the Arctic basin via the Orhon, Ider, and Selenge rivers, the last being the main tributary of Lake Baikal in Siberia. On the range's southern slopes, the dry beds of occasional watercourses feed into the Valley of Lakes, an arid plateau interspersed with freshwater and saline lakes. The Hangai Range's northern slopes are covered with forest and mountain meadows, while the southern slopes are generally treeless and arid. Frequent earthquakes in the region (the most recent in 1905) have left dramatic fissures referred to as the "trails of a giant snake." In this environment, musk deer, willow grouse, lynx, snow leopard, brown bear, wild boar, golden eagle, and the central Asian viper make their home.

Daniel Hruschka

Further Reading

Mongolian People's Republic Academy of Sciences. (1990) *Information Mongolia*. Oxford: Pergamon.

HANGUL SCRIPT Hangul is a script used in writing Korean, a language of 72 million speakers. It is, like the Roman alphabet, an alphabetical writing, consisting of 24 basic alphabet letters, 14 for consonants and 10 for vowels. Unlike the Roman alphabet in which independent alphabet letters are arranged linearly, for the hangul script, consonant and vowel letters are combined to create syllable blocks.

Whereas the origins of most writing systems are unknown, hangul, originally called *hunminjongum* (meaning "the correct sounds for the instruction of the people"), was invented in 1443 by King Sejong the Great (1397–1450), the fourth monarch (reigned 1419–1450) of the Yi (Choson) dynasty (1392–1910), with his royal scholars.

Although it was promulgated in 1446, it was not until 1894 that the hangul script began to be used in official government documents. The first all-Korean script newspaper, *Tongnip Sinmun* (Independent News), was published in 1896 by Seo Jaepil (1863–1951). The name hangul ("Korean script") was given by Ju Sigyeong (1876–1914), one of the earliest modern Korean grammarians.

The design of the Hangul letters resulted from a deep understanding of phonetic principles and Chinese cosmological philosophy on the part of the king and his scholars. Originally, 28 basic letters (17 consonant letters and 11 vowel letters) were introduced, of which 3 consonant letters and one vowel letter have disappeared in the current writing system.

The consonant letters for *k* (or *g*), *n*, *s* (or *sh*), *m*, and *ng* are designed after the shape of the speech organs when they are pronounced. The other consonant letters are made by adding a stroke or two to these or by extending the initial forms. An extra stroke indicates a different articulatory feature, such as aspiration (extra puff of the air in producing a sound). In this respect, the Hangul Script is unique and more refined in representing sounds than any other script.

Vowel letters are designed based on the yin-yang philosophy of universal complementary forces and the East Asian cosmological belief that heaven, earth, and humanity are the three most fundamental features in the universe. The three initial vowel letters are designed after the round shape of heaven , the flat shape of earth, and the vertical shape of a man standing. The other letters are made by combining the three initial letters, with the combinations being guided by the principles of the yin-yang theory as to how heaven interacts either with the human being or with the earth.

Because of its systematic and scientific organization as well as its sophisticated phonetic representation, the hangul script is regarded as one of Korea's cultural treasures. Its linguistic and cultural value is also recognized by scholars outside Korea as a great intellectual achievement.

Hyo Sang Lee

Further Reading

Ramsey, S. Robert. (1992) *The Korean Alphabet*. In *King Sejong the Great*, edited by Young-Key Kim-Renaud. Washington, D.C.: International Circle of Korean Linguistics, George Washington University, 43–50.

Sampson, Geoffrey. (1985) *Writing Systems*. Stanford, CA: Stanford University Press.

Sohn, Ho-Min. (1999) *The Korean language*. Cambridge, U.K.: Cambridge University Press.

HANGZHOU (2002 est. pop. 1.2 million). Hangzhou was visited by Marco Polo in the thirteenth century. The city is one of the seven ancient capitals of China and today is the capital of Zhejiang province. Hangzhou was first mentioned in 221 BCE during the Qin dynasty (221–206 BCE).

The city prospered after it was linked with the Grand Canal (the world's longest man-made waterway) in 610 during the Sui dynasty (581–618). Under the Tang dynasty (618–907), West Lake, now a famous tourist attraction, was created on the western edge of Hangzhou. An old harbor was also filled in, greatly expanding the size of the city.

At the inception of the Southern Song dynasty (1127–1279), Hangzhou became the dynasty's capital. After the Mongols invaded China in the thirteenth century, Hangzhou continued to prosper through its river and sea trade, ship building, and naval industries. The city was opened to foreigners in 1895 under the terms of the Treaty of Shimonoseki.

Silk production has remained the mainstay of Hangzhou's trade and handicraft industries; the city is also noted for its Longjian (Dragon Well) tea, cotton textiles, steel and chemicals, scissors, hemp, mulberries, and crafts including sandalwood fans, bamboo items, and silk parasols.

Today Hangzhou's primary reputation is as a tourist mecca. West Lake is considered the symbol of Hangzhou, along with the popular Lingyin Si (Temple of Inspired Seclusion).

Carole Schroeder

Further Reading

Hangzhou Wanghu Travel Agency. Retrieved March 2002, from: http://www.wanghuhotel.com/content8-e.htm

Young, Margaret Walsh, and Susan Stetler, eds. (1987) *Cities of the World: Asia, the Pacific, and the Asiatic Middle East*. 3d ed. Detroit, MI: Gale.

HANOI (2002 est. pop. 1.3 million). Hanoi, the capital of Vietnam, is located in the center of the northern part of the country and is bounded by the Red River to the north and east. It is considered one of Asia's most beautiful cities, boasting a number of lakes, including Ho Tay (West Lake) and Ho Guom (Sword Lake), and parks. The Old Town, known for its thirty-six narrow and winding streets named after various trades, is still a vibrant part of the city. Founded in 1010, over the centuries Hanoi bore several names, such as: Dai La, Thang Long, Dong Do, Dong Quan, Dong Kinh, and Hanoi.

In 1009 Ly Cong Uan (974–1028) was proclaimed emperor and founded the Ly dynasty (1010–1225). The following year he decided to move the capital from Hoa Lu to the site of the Dai La citadel, about 70 kilometers to the north. En route, the emperor had a vision in which he saw a golden dragon rising from the Red River. He then decided to change the citadel's name from Dai La to Thang Long, meaning "ascending dragon." The capital city was then developed. The imperial quarters were located near Ho Tay. A civil area was created and divided into artisan, agricultural, and commercial sectors. Both the imperial

The Hanoi Municipal Theater in 1995. (STEVE RAYMER/ CORBIS)

and the civil areas of the city were located within and protected by a citadel. Within a century of its founding, Thang Long had become an important cultural, economic, and political center. Under the Tran dynasty (1225–1400), the imperial quarters were reinforced, and new palaces were built. In addition, administrative units were constructed. By this time the capital city boasted sixty-one quarters. From 1258 to 1288, the city was subjected to three separate, but unsuccessful, Mongol attacks. In 1400 Ho Quy Ly replaced the Tran and founded the Ho dynasty (1400–1407). He moved the capital to Thanh Hoa, which he renamed Tay Do. He also changed Thang Long's name to Dong Do.

In 1407 China invaded Vietnam, and Thang Long was renamed Dong Quan. After Le Loi (flourished 1428–1443) succeeded in liberating Vietnam in 1428, the city changed its name to Dong Kinh. In 1802, Emperor Gia Long (1762–1820) of the Nguyen dynasty (1802–1955) moved Vietnam's capital to Hue, and Dong Kinh became Thang Long once again. Then in 1831 Emperor Minh Mang (1792–1841) changed the city's name to Hanoi, which means "within the river."

In 1884, after France had consolidated its rule in Vietnam, Hanoi was placed under French control. The city became the headquarters of the French administration in Indochina (Vietnam, Laos, and Cambodia). During the French colonial era, the city was expanded, blending French and Vietnamese architecture, and numerous broad avenues and tree-lined boulevards were created. On 2 September 1945, Ho Chi Minh (1890–1969) proclaimed the Democratic Republic of Vietnam, and Hanoi became its capital. Hanoi remained the capital after the country's reunification in 1975.

Micheline R. Lessard

Further Reading

Boudarel, Georges, and Nguyen Van Ky. (1997) *Hanoi 1936–1996.* Paris: Autrement.

Logan, William S. (2000) *Hanoi: Biography of a City.* Sydney: University of New South Wales Press.

Nguyen Vinh Phuc. (1995) *Hanoi, passé et présent.* Hanoi, Vietnam: Gioi.

HANSHIK In Korea the 105th day after the winter solstice is known as Hanshik. This spring observance, falling on or near 5 April, has long been a day for paying homage to one's ancestors. In the most traditional of Korean families, ancestral rites are still observed. In the early hours of the morning, the ancestral rite, *charye*, is performed before tables piled with food offerings to one's ancestors. After sunrise, families make their way to tombs—often located in auspicious spots on the many hillsides—of their most immediate ancestors for another ancestral rite called *songmyo*, which also includes food offerings and bows of respect.

Hanshik literally means "cold food," and traditionally no foods are cooked on this day. Consuming cold foods and performing ancestral rites on Hanshik date back to China's Three Kingdoms period (220–265 CE) and has its roots in Chinese legend. According to the legend, the date of Hanshik was set in commemoration of the ancient Chinese statesman of the Jin dynasty (third–fourth century CE) Jie Jitui (Chieh Chi-t'ui), who elected to die in a forest fire set to capture him rather than surrender and compromise his loyalty to his deposed emperor. Impressed by this act of fealty, the reigning emperor decreed that no fires be kindled and that only cold foods be eaten on this day.

The observance most likely originated out of an ancient spring festival at which new fires were set to symbolize spring. Hanshik became one of the four main observances of the Choson period.

David E. Shaffer

Further Reading

Adams, Edward B. (1995) *Korea Guide.* 8th ed. Seoul: Seoul International Publishing House.

Choe, Sang-su. (1983) *Annual Customs of Korea.* Seoul: Seomun-dang.

Koo, John H., and Andrew C. Nahm, eds. (1997) *An Introduction to Korean Culture.* Elizabeth, NJ: Hollym.

HARA TAKASHI (1856–1921), Japanese politician and statesman. Born in Morioka (in present Iwate Prefecture) into a samurai family, Hara Takashi was an influential figure in Japanese politics in the first decades of the twentieth century. Also known as Hara Kei, he is regarded as one of the principal architects of party government (governing by formation of a cabinet, as opposed to the previous party system dominated by the so-called Meiji oligarchy, mainly former samurai from the clans of Choshu and Satsuma) in modern Japan. In 1918, he became the first prime minister in the history of modern Japan who was a commoner.

Hara was educated in the Nanbu domain school near his place of birth. In 1871, he left for Tokyo, where he joined the law school of the Ministry of Justice. He took a position in the ministry of foreign affairs in 1882. Under the auspices of Mutsu Munemitsu (1844–1897), Hara served as vice minister of foreign affairs and as ambassador to Korea.

After an interlude as a journalist, Hara in 1900 joined the Rikken Seiyukai party and became the party's first secretary general. He ran successfully for the lower house and served as home minister in several cabinets between 1906 and 1913. In 1914, he was elected president of the Seiyukai. After the resignation of Prime Minister Terauchi Masatake (1852–1919) in 1918, Hara formed his own cabinet—the first in Japanese history to be headed by an elected member of the majority party in the lower house.

Hara's popularity declined during his time as prime minister, since he undertook no major institutional reform. He was stabbed to death in Tokyo Station on 4 November 1921 by a right-wing nationalist. His diary continues to be regarded as an important source for historians.

Sven Saaler

Further Reading

Duus, Peter. (1968) *Party Rivalry and Political Change in Taisho Japan.* Cambridge, MA: Harvard University Press.

Najita, Tetsuo. (1967) *Hara Kei in the Politics of Compromise.* Cambridge, MA: Harvard University Press.

Olson, L. A. (1954) *Hara Kei: A Political Biography.* Ph.D. diss. Harvard University.

HARAPPA The Harappan culture, also known as the Indus Valley civilization, is one of the world's first urban civilizations. It thrived between 2500 and 1500 BCE in the fertile floodplains of the Indus River—present-day Pakistan and western India. Archaeologists have discovered two cities, Harappa and Mohenjo Daro, and numerous settlements. Excavations have revealed painted pottery, terra-cotta figures, and inscribed stamp seals. The cities are brick built and feature a high central citadel with public buildings, granaries, and a ritual great bath. The grid layout and extensive drainage and sewerage systems are early evidence of town planning and central administration. The economy appears to have been agricultural, with extensive trading links.

Excavations have uncovered several thousand square soapstone seals. Finely carved with animal images and short inscriptions, they may have served as merchants' signatures. The Harappan script has not yet been deciphered and remains one of archaeology's great enigmas. Little is known about the Harappan religion as well; however, an engraved figure, horned and seated in a yoga position, may be linked to the Hindu god Siva. Other figures have been interpreted as goddesses and high priests. The Harappan culture appears to have declined around 1500 BCE, perhaps because it was conquered by invaders or destroyed by flooding and climatic change.

The ruins of a neighborhood of artisans in the ancient city of Harappa, Pakistan. (PAUL ALMASY/CORBIS)

Lucy D. Moss

Further Reading

Craven, Roy C. (1997) *Indian Art.* The World of Art. London: Thames & Hudson.

Kenoyer, Jonathan Mark. (1998) *Ancient Cities of the Indus Valley Civilization.* New York: Oxford University Press.

HARBIN (2002 est. pop. 2.8 million). Located on the southern bank of the Songhua River, Harbin is the capital city of Heilongjiang Province. Founded as a railway town by Russian engineers in 1895 when czarist Russia began to build the Trans-Manchurian Railway (later named the Chinese Eastern Railway), Harbin became home to the Chinese Eastern Railway's headquarters and tens of thousands of Russian engineers, colonial bureaucrats, soldiers, traders, and their families. It experienced an early boom in its economy and infrastructure during the Russo-Japanese War (1904–1905) when it served as the major supply base and staging area for the Russian armies in Manchuria. Following the Bolshevik Revolution, tens of thousands of new settlers arrived in Harbin—White Russians (supporters of the czar, or people who opposed the new regime). Its population swelled by these new arrivals, in the 1920s, Harbin boasted the largest European community in Asia.

The Japanese Guandong Army occupied Harbin in 1932 and used it as an outpost to observe developments in the far eastern reaches of the Soviet Union until 1945. Harbin was also the location of one of the most notorious branches of the Japanese military during World War II—Unit 731 of the Guandong Army. This unit was responsible for developing and testing chemical and bacteriological weapons using Chinese and Allied prisoners. After the Communist victory in the Chinese Civil War (1945–1949), Harbin continued to play a central role in the transportation network in northeastern China. The city's industrial base was expanded to include tractor, cement, petrochemical, turbine, and machine factories. With the opening of China to foreign trade and investment in the late 1980s and early 1990s, Harbin witnessed a revival, and the city was again at the forefront of Sino-Russian border trade and contact.

Robert John Perrins

Further Reading

Carter, James Hugh. (1998) "Nationalism in an International City: Creating a Chinese Harbin, 1916–1932." Ph.D. diss. Yale University.

Clausen, Soren, and Stig Thogersen. (1995) *The Making of a Chinese City: History and Historiography in Harbin.* Armonk, NY: M. E. Sharpe.

Cohn-Lieber, Zina. (1997) *My Years in Harbin Manchuria.* London: S. S. Graphics.

State Statistical Bureau, comp. (1998) *China Statistical Yearbook.* Beijing: China Statistical Publishing House.

Wolff, David. (1999) *To the Harbin Station: The Liberal Alternative in Russian Manchuria, 1898–1914.* Stanford, CA: Stanford University Press.

HARI RAYA PUASA Hari Raya Puasa literally means "feast of fasting," and refers to 'Id al-Fitr, the celebration marking the end of Ramadan, as it is known to the rest of the Muslim world. This phrase is only known in the Malay world, i.e., Indonesia, Malaysia, Singapore, Brunei, South Thailand, and South Philippines. It represents a return to original purity, after the cleansing of one's sins. It is also known as 'Id al-Saghir (minor feast), as opposed to 'Id al-Kabir (major feast) or 'Id al-Adha (feast of the sacrifice).

Though subject to the sighting of the crescent moon or astronomical calculations *(hisab)*, Hari Raya Puasa always falls on the first of Shawwal. Celebrations start with prayers and a two-part sermon *(khutbah)*, and continue over three days during which Muslims visit family, friends, and neighbors in order to ask their forgiveness for having wronged them. The Hari Raya Puasa sermon closes an intense period of seeking God's forgiveness for past sins by fasting, reading from the Qur'an, reciting prayers, and almsgiving *(zakat al-fitr)* throughout Ramadan. Indeed, after this particular sermon is delivered, the value of almsgiving decreases to that of an act of charity *(sadaqah)*, entailing lesser rewards.

For this feast, it is recommended that Muslims wear their best attire and perfume. In the Malay world, the meals served on this occasion feature traditional Malay-Indonesian food, such as rice wrapped in leaves. Children usually receive presents and special attention.

Andi Faisal Bakti

Further Reading

Abujamin Roham. (1991) *Puasa Perisai Hidup* (Fasting Is the Life Shield). Jakarta, Indonesia: Media Dakwah.

Denny, Frederick M. (1994) *An Introduction to Islam.* 2d ed. New York: Macmillan.

Federspiel, Howard M. (1995) *A Dictionary of Indonesian Islam.* Athens, OH: Center for International Studies, Ohio University.

HARSA (c. 590–647 CE), Indian ruler and poet. Born in Thaneswar, Harsa (also Harsha or Harsavardhana) brought order to northern India when he conquered the region and became king (reigned 606–647). Harsa first ascended the throne of a small kingdom in the state of Haryana, Sthanvishvara (modern Thaneswar), but became the last monarch of classical India to rule an empire covering the Indo-Gangetic Plain from Bengal to Gujarat and from the Himalayas to the Vindhya Range. Kanauj was his chosen capital. To conquer this hard-won territory, Harsa collected a large army and waged incessant war against other kings for six years.

His reign was noteworthy not only for the vast lands he ruled but also for the philosophical change that marked the emergence of medieval Hinduism from the earlier Brahmanic religion. Harsa proved to be as efficient in administration as in war. His court was celebrated by later authors for the king's patronage of art and literature; he himself was a poet and author of three major Sanskrit plays. His own religious practices were eclectic, as he worshiped Siva, the Sun, and the Buddha. In later life he was especially attracted to Mahayana Buddhism.

Paul Hockings

Further Reading

Devahuti, D. (1998) *Harsha: A Political Study.* New York: Oxford University Press.

HART, ROBERT (1835–1911), head of Chinese Maritime Customs Service. Born in Northern Ireland, Robert Hart went to China in 1854. He served in British consulates in Ningbo and Guangzhou (Canton) for several years before he became the second head of the Chinese Maritime Customs Service and a key instrument in the British "informal empire" in China in the latter half of the nineteenth century. In 1863, Hart succeeded Horatio Nelson Lay, whose brusque manner offended many in the Qing dynasty (1644–1912) government. Hart, by contrast, viewed himself as an employee of the Chinese government and urged the foreign employees in the service to learn about China and, indeed, the Chinese language and to respect Chinese customs and values. Chinese officialdom greatly appreciated Hart and looked to him as a trusted foreign advisor.

Under Hart, the Chinese Maritime Customs Service became one of China's few modernized institutions and relatively effectively collected the 5 percent ad valorem tariff permitted by the so-called unequal treaties that China had signed with foreign powers, and this helped provide a dependable and major source of income for the Qing dynasty. Although most of China's tariff revenue was used to pay indemnities to the imperialist powers required by the unequal treaties, some of the revenue did go to support reform efforts in the self-strengthening movement.

For his efforts in China, Hart was knighted by Queen Victoria (1819–1901), and as long as he was alive, the Qing dynasty appointed no other inspector-general for customs. Hart even declined an opportunity to serve as British minister to China in order to remain with his beloved Customs Service.

Charles Dobbs

Further Reading

Bruner, Katherine F., John K. Fairbank, and Richard J. Smith, eds. (1986) *Entering China's Service: Robert Hart's Journals, 1854–1863.* Cambridge, MA: Harvard University Press.

Wright, Stanley F. (1950) *Hart and the Chinese Customs.* Belfast, U.K.: Queen's University Press.

HARVEST MOON FESTIVAL. See **Ch'usok.**

HARYANA (2001 est pop. 21 million). With the partition of 1947, the Muslim part of the Punjab was assigned to Pakistan, and the Sikh and Hindu parts to India. In 1966 the mostly Sikh, Punjabi-speaking area became Punjab, and the primarily Hindi-speaking area became Haryana. Haryana is said to mean "home of Hari," a name of the god Vishnu. The state has a proud history dating to the Vedic age. It was home to the legendary Bharata dynasty. The battle between the Kauravas and the Pandavas, described in the Sanskrit epic poem the *Mahabharata,* is believed to have been fought on the site of the modern Kurukshetra (a plain in the northern part of Haryana). Here Lord Krishna is said to have delivered to the warrior Arjuna the teachings of the Bhagavad Gita, venerated by Hindus as the highest code of ethics.

Epigraphic evidence indicates that Haryana was part of the Maurya empire in the third century BCE, and that a string of empires controlled the city after, including rulers from the Kushan, the Gupta, and the Harsha empires. In 1192 the region became part of the Delhi sultanate and remained so until 1526, when the city was seized by Mughals. With the decline of the Mughal empire in the seventeenth century, the region was claimed alternately by the Marathas and the Sikhs, and the British East India Company took control in 1803. In 1858 the region became part of the new province of Punjab and began to be overshadowed by a shift of power to Lahore in the Sikh-dominated, northern area. Well before India's independence from the Britain and the subsequent partition of Pakistan, strong sentiment existed among the region's Hindu residents for a separate statehood, due to cultural and linguistic differences. Increasingly fierce and violent calls were made for Sikh independence, so that the creation of a new state in 1966 was widely welcomed by both sides.

The state occupies a fertile tract of river plain and is the "bread basket of the nation," with irrigation canals and modern crop technology producing nearly a quarter of India's wheat, along with millet, rice, corn, sugar cane, and cotton, and one-third of its milk and dairy foods. Machine tools, electrical goods, cement, paper, and bicycles are manufactured. Passing through Haryana are the Northern Railroad and the Grand Trunk Road, the most famous highway in India. Described by Rudyard Kipling in his novel *Kim,* it stretches 2,000 kilometers from Peshawar to Calcutta. Haryana has a network of forty-three tourist complexes named after birds. The state boasts several colleges, temples, and archaeological sites. Annual fairs and festivals preserve Hindu religious and cultural traditions.

C. Roger Davis

Further Reading

Gupta, L. C., and M. C. Gupta. (2000) *Haryana on the Road to Modernization.* New Delhi: Excel.

HASINA WAJID, SHEIKH (b. 1947), Bangladesh prime minister. Sheikh Hasina Wajid, the elder daughter of former Bangladesh president and prime minister Shiekh Mujibur Rahman (Mujib) (1921–1975), was born 28 September 1947 at the family's home in Tungipara, Gopalganj district. She had been generally uninterested in politics and was absent from Bangladesh when Mujib and many of his family were assassinated on 15 August 1975. However, when political activity was fully revived following the 1979 parliamentary election in which her father's Awami League fared badly, the party was left without a strong and well-known leader. Hasina was called back to Bangladesh and assumed leadership of the party on 17 May 1981. She opposed the Hussain Muhammad Ershad (b. 1930) regime, and she participated in the 1986 election, leading the Awami League. Despite a strong rivalry with Khaleda Zia (b. 1945) of the Bangladesh Nationalist Party (BNP), Hasina joined hands with Zia in a movement that led to Ershad's fall in December 1990. Following the February 1991 election, the Awami League became the principal opposition, a position from which the party and Hasina harassed the BNP government. In June 1996, the Awami League, in coalition with Ershad's Jatiya Party, formed a government, and Hasina became prime minister. Ershad himself left the coalition, but a faction of the Jatiya Party remains in Hasina's government. The lack of cooperation between the government and the opposition since the restoration of parliamentary government has hindered political development in Bangladesh.

Craig Baxter

Further Reading

Ahmed, Moudud. (1995) *Democracy and the Challenge of Development: Study of Politics and Military Intervention in Bangladesh.* New Delhi: Vikas.

Baxter, Craig. (1997) *Bangladesh from a Nation to a State.* Boulder, CO: Westview.

HASSANAL BOLKIAH (b. 1946), Brunei ruler. Born on 15 July 1946, Hassanal Bolkiah Mu'izzaddin Waddaulah II had his early education in Brunei. On 14 July 1961, he became crown prince. He continued his studies in Kuala Lumpur, Malaysia, at the Gurney Road School and the Victoria Institution. He left for Britain in 1966 to enroll at the Royal Military College, Sandhurst. He returned to Brunei in 1967, when he was installed as ruler.

Hassanal Bolkiah ascended the throne of Brunei Darussalam ("Brunei abode of peace") upon the sudden voluntary abdication of his father, Sultan Omar Ali Saifuddin III (d. 1986). Concurrently sultan and Yang Di-Pertuan ("He Who Is Made Lord," supreme ruler) of the kingdom of Brunei, from 1984 onward he has held numerous posts, among them prime minister, minister of defense, and minister of finance. Since 1967 he has been head of the Islamic faith in Brunei. He is also inspector-general of the Royal Brunei Police, commander-in-chief of the Royal Brunei Armed Forces, and the chancellor of Universiti Brunei Darussalam.

Sultan Hassanal Bolkiah addressing the United Nations Millennium Summit on 8 September 2000. (AFP/CORBIS)

Hassanal Bolkiah concluded two treaties with Britain, one in 1971 whereby Brunei became a self-governing kingdom with full internal sovereignty, another, the Anglo-Brunei Treaty of Friendship and Cooperation (1979), that set forth a five-year schedule for full independence. A sovereign and independent Brunei came into being on 1 January 1984.

Keat Gin Ooi

Further Reading

Bartholomew, James. (1989) *The Richest Man in the World: The Sultan of Brunei.* London: Viking.

Chalfont, Lord Alun. (1989) *By God's Will: A Portrait of the Sultan of Brunei*. London: Weidenfeld and Nicolson.

HASTINGS, WARREN (1732–1818), governor of Bengal and governor-general of British India. Born in Churchill, Oxfordshire, in England, Warren Hastings was the son of a clergyman who abandoned him at an early age. Hastings was educated by his uncle at the Westminster School in London, but his education was cut short by his uncle's death, and Hastings sailed for India in 1750 to become a "writer" (junior clerical employee) for the East India Company. Directly or indirectly, he played a role in the transition of the East India Company from a commercial to a political power in the third quarter of the eighteenth century.

In 1765 disputes forced Hastings to leave service, but he returned to Bengal as the chief administrator in 1771. The administration of Bengal was then awkwardly shared between the nominally sovereign nawab of Bengal, in charge of governance, and the East India Company, in control of the finances. Hastings moved to take control of governance and reformed the administration of justice and the fiscal system, serving as governor of Bengal from 1771 to 1773. His tenure was weakened by corruption and bitter rivalries. From 1774 until his return to England in 1784, Hastings served as governor general of British India, and was mainly occupied in trying to contain belligerent Indian regimes perceived to be dangerous to British power. His method of financing wars in India, by politely forcing his allies to pay, was the subject of an inquiry and a trial (1788–1795) in which he was honorably discharged. Aside from his controversial but critical political role, Hastings is significant for his curiosity about Indian traditions in literature and scholarship, which led the way to a flourish of European studies of these subjects.

Tirthankar Roy

Further Reading

Moon, Penderel. (1947) *Warren Hastings and British India*. London: Hodder and Stoughton.

Trotter, L. J. ([1890]1972) *Warren Hastings*. Reprint, edited by W. W. Hunter. London: Ayer.

HATOYAMA ICHIRO (1883–1959), prime minister of Japan. Hatoyama Ichiro was born in Tokyo, the first son of Dr. Hatoyama Kazuo, a legal scholar, lawyer, and (later) leading politician, and Hatoyama Haruko, a pioneer in women's education. After graduating from Tokyo Imperial University in 1907, Hatoyama served in the Tokyo City Assembly and then in 1916 was elected to the Diet as a member of his late father's party, the Rikken Seiyukai (Friends of Constitutional Government). He was elected a total of fifteen times.

Hatoyama was a nationalist, dismissing liberal professors from Kyoto University when serving as education minister from 1931 to 1934, and writing in support of Hitler and Mussolini in a book published in late 1938 following a trip to Europe. After the war, Hatoyama formed the Liberal Party, heading it until his purge by Allied Occupation forces in early 1946. Allowed to return to politics in August 1951, Hatoyama succeeded Yoshida Shigeru as party president and then prime minister in late 1954. During his time as prime minister (1954–1956), Hatoyama restored diplomatic relations with the Soviet Union and subsequently secured Japan's entry into the United Nations. Domestically, he brought the Liberal Party and the Democratic Party together in 1955 to form the Liberal Democratic Party in what become known as the "1955 System," which pitted the conservative Liberal Democratic Party against the leftist Socialist Party.

Robert Eldridge

Further Reading

Masumi Junnosuke. (1985) *Postwar Politics in Japan, 1945–1955*. Trans. by Lonny E. Carlile. Berkeley, CA: Institute of East Asian Studies, University of California.

HATTA, MOHAMMAD (1902–1980), Indonesian nationalist leader and politician. Born in West Sumatra, Mohammad Hatta studied economics in the Netherlands, where he led the student group Perhimpunan Indonesia (Indonesian Association, or PI) from 1922. In 1927 he was tried in the Netherlands for sedition but was acquitted. His thinking was strongly influenced by socialism, but by 1931 Communists dominated the PI, and he was expelled. He returned to Indonesia in 1932 and led the PNI-Baru (the "New" Indonesian National Education), a nationalist party that aimed to build a large but unobtrusive cadre party. In 1934, however, he was exiled, first to Boven Digul in Dutch New Guinea, and then in 1936 to the Banda Island of Indonesia. In 1942 he reluctantly agreed to work with the Japanese occupation, and in August 1945 he became vice president of the independent Indonesian Republic.

Although the vice presidency had no power, Hatta became a rallying point for opposition to the left, and from January 1948 he led a nonparliamentary cabinet

Vice President Mohammad Hatta in 1949. (HULTON-DEUTSCH COLLECTION/CORBIS)

that suppressed the Communist Party following its participation in an abortive revolt in the East Java town of Madiun in September–October 1948. He was a member of the Indonesian delegation that concluded negotiations with the Dutch for the formal transfer of sovereignty in December 1949. In the 1950s he again attracted those opposed to President Sukarno (1901–1970) and the left, but when he resigned as vice president in 1956, he was unable to marshal enough support to return to executive power.

Robert Cribb

Further Reading

Hatta, Mohammad. (1972) *Portrait of a Patriot: Selected Writings*. The Hague, Netherlands; Paris: Mouton.

Rose, Mavis. (1987) *Indonesia Free: A Political Biography of Mohammad Hatta*. Ithaca, NY: Cornell University Press.

HAWKINS, WILLIAM (1560-1613), first Englishman to reach the court of the Mughal emperors. William Hawkins, thought by some to be related to the famous sea-faring family of Plymouth, commanded the British East India Company's ship *Hector*, which reached Surat on India's western coast on 24 August 1608. In his possession were gifts and a letter from King James I of England (1566–1625) to the Great Mughal of India, Jahangir (1569–1627). Hawkins survived several assassination plots by the Portuguese—who were already present in India—and journeyed overland to the court of Jahangir at Agra. Hawkins, who spoke fluent Turkish, soon became a favorite of the emperor, who granted him the title "Khan." Jahangir also granted Hawkins permission to set up an English factory (trading post) at Surat.

The Portuguese, feeling their interests in the region threatened by this, convinced Jahangir to reverse his decision allowing the English to trade in India. Unable to persuade Jahangir to change his mind, Hawkins left Agra for Surat in November 1611. He and his wife—an Armenian Christian whom Hawkins had married at Jahangir's insistence—sailed for England via Java on 26 January 1612. Hawkins died at sea on 20 May 1613. Although he was unsuccessful at opening India to English trade, he led the way for the English mercantile venture that eventually resulted in Britain's Indian empire.

Deryck O. Lodrick

Further Reading

Foster, William. (1921) *Early Travels in India 1583–1619*. London: Oxford University Press, 60–121.

HAYASHI As a small ensemble typically consisting of a flutist and three drummers, the *hayashi* is the main source of music for Japanese festivals. The term refers to both the musical accompaniment and the ensemble itself. The flute is a simple bamboo pipe with six or seven holes. The *o-daiko*, large drum, has a convex wooden body and two tacked heads and may be set on a crate or tipped with one head toward the player who strikes it with two blunt sticks. The smaller *taiko* drums consist of two heads lashed together with rope and tightened by a second encircling rope, through which a stick is inserted to tip the drum toward the player. A fourth addition is the voice of the drummers used instrumentally at a rhythmical highpoint. An occasional fifth component is a small brass gong, *atari-gane*, suspended or held in the hand. The music tends to be casual and somewhat repetitive, and its primary function is to spur on folk dances.

In Noh accompaniment, the *hayashi* ensemble consists of one flute and two or three drums—*taiko*, *kotsuzumi*, or *o-tsuzumi*—the latter two of which have two heads lashed together and resemble an hourglass. In Kabuki, a similar ensemble performs onstage together with singers and shamisen players, while another group provides additional music backstage.

James M. Vardaman, Jr.

Further Reading

Harich-Schneider, Eta. (1973) *A History of Japanese Music*. London: Oxford University Press.

Malm, William P. (1959) *Japanese Music and Musical Instruments*. Rutland, VT: Tuttle.

HAYASHI RAZAN (1583–1657), Japanese Neo-Confucian scholar. Hayashi Razan, known also as Doshun, was one of the foremost Japanese Neo-Confucian scholars and an influential adviser during the Edo period (1600/1603–1868) in Japan.

Hayashi was born in Kyoto and trained himself as a Buddhist priest during his childhood. Later he abandoned Buddhism and studied Confucianism, devoting himself to the doctrines of Zhu Xi (1130–1200). In 1605, he met Tokugawa Ieyasu (1543–1616), who served as the first shogun of the Edo period from 1603 to 1605, at Nijo Castle in Kyoto. The meeting became a vital encounter for both men, as well as the basis for changes in the Japanese social order.

Ieyasu's main concern was the restoration of peace and order to the war-ravaged society. In order to accomplish this, Ieyasu turned to China and Confucianism, particularly Hayashi's thoughts on Neo-Confucianism.

Hayashi introduced the Confucian stress on loyalty and obligations that provided a standard code of conduct with which the Edo shogunate could govern autonomous territories and still maintain social order. Furthermore, he emphasized that the understanding of things can be derived only from understanding the Confucian principle of *li* (universal natural law) operating behind them. This led to the development of an empirical science in Japan, a method of knowledge that stressed the observation and study of material and human things. In addition, he emphasized the study of history and inaugurated several centuries of great Japanese history writing. Supported by Ieyasu, many social changes based on the teaching of Zhu Xi, such as establishing prohibitions for samurai families, occurred in Japan.

Hayashi continued to serve as an adviser until the fourth shogun, Ietsuna (1651–1680). Because of his position in the government, Hayashi Razan established a dynasty of Neo-Confucian philosophers in the Edo court. He, his son, and then his grandson built the uniquely Edo version of Chinese Neo-Confucianism in Japan; the Hayashi family ultimately headed Daigaku-no-kami, the state university, until 1906.

Unryu Suganuma

Further Reading

De Bary, William Theodore, Donald Keene, and George Tanabe, eds. (2001) *Sources of Japanese Tradition.* Vol. 1. 2d ed. New York: Columbia University Press.

Nakai, K. W. (1997) "Tokugawa Confucian Historiography: The Hayashi, Early Mito School, and Arai Hakuseki." In *Confucianism and Tokugawa Culture*, edited by Peter Nosco. Honolulu, HI: University of Hawaii Press.

HAZARA The Hazaras, an isolated group of Shiʿa Muslims who lived in the mountainous regions of central Afghanistan until political upheavals forced them to scatter, were once the second-largest, although least-known, ethnic group in the country. Many scholars believe that the Hazaras are descendants of the Mongol army of Genghis Khan (c. 1162–1227), which invaded this area of Afghanistan in the thirteenth century. According to other theories, the Hazaras' ancestors were Buddhist monks who lived in the city of Bamian in central Afghanistan, when it became a center of Buddhism some two thousand years ago, but this explanation ignores the fact that the Hazaras are now Shiʿa Muslims. Their physical characteristics suggest a Mongol ancestry, yet their language, called Hazaragi, is a unique, archaic version of Persian, albeit with remnants of Mongolian vocabulary.

Hazara children stand in front of the alcove that housed a statue of Buddha destroyed by the Taliban government of Afghanistan. (REUTERS NEWMEDIA INC./CORBIS)

The Hazaras lived mainly as sheepherders in the center of the Hindu Kush mountain range. In recent Afghan history, they have become an oppressed minority, partly because of their Shiʿite beliefs. Due to the lack of arable land in this harsh, mountainous region, as well as the recent political developments limiting their access to trade routes in the Hindu Kush, many moved to the cities to work as menial laborers to provide food for their families.

During the Taliban regime in Afghanistan, the Hazaras suffered massive losses from starvation and massacres by the Taliban, who brutally slaughtered thousands of Hazaras in an attempt to eradicate Shiʿa Muslim believers. Most Hazaras now live as refugees in Pakistan, India, China, and Mongolia.

Jennifer L. Nichols

Further Reading

Elphinstone, Mountstuart. ([1814] 1972) *An Account of the Kingdom of Caubul.* 3d ed. New intro. by Sir Olaf Caroe. Karachi, Pakistan: Oxford University Press.

Ewans, Martin. (2002) *Afghanistan: A Short History of Its People and Politics.* New York: HarperCollins.

Ghobar, Mir Gholam Mohammad. (2001) *Afghanistan in the Course of History.* Trans. by Sherief A. Fayez. Alexandria, VA: Hashmat K. Gobar.

Mousavi, Sayed Askar. (1998) *The Hazaras of Afghanistan: An Historical, Cultural, Economic, and Political Study.* Richmond, U.K.: Curzon.

HEALTH AND ILLNESS. See **Acupuncture; Aging Population—Japan; AIDS—Asia; Fertility; Massage; Medicine, Ayurvedic; Medicine, Traditional—Central Asia; Medicine, Traditional—China; Medicine, Traditional—West Asia; Medicine, Unani; Moxibustion.**

HEBEI (2002 est. pop. 70.4 million). Hebei (Hopei, Hopeh) Province in northern China covers an area of 187,700 square kilometers, borders in the west on Shanxi, in the north on Inner Mongolia and Liaoning, in the east on the Bohai Gulf—part of the Yellow Sea—and Shandong, and to the south on Henan. The province surrounds the self-governed municipalities of Beijing (8,400 square kilometers) and its seaport, Tianjin (3,900 square kilometers). To the west, the Taihang mountain range, with peaks up to 2,870 meters above sea level, form a physical barrier between Hebei and Shanxi, and in the north the Yanshan range, rising to 1,500 meters, constitutes the traditional frontier between China and the nomads in the north. It is here that the eastern extension of the Great Wall is located. Southern Hebei, covering an area of about 78,000 square kilometers, is part of the north China plain, most of which is lowland under 50 meters above sea level.

The province has a temperate continental monsoon climate. Winters are cold and dry, and in January temperatures may drop to −21°C in the north (a minimum of −42.9°C has been recorded). It is less cold in the south. The rainy season stretches from June through August, and temperatures in July average 18° to 27°C, but most regions have recorded temperatures over 40°C. The capital, Shijiazhuang (1.6 million, 1996), is situated in the southern lowlands, which is also where the majority of Hebei's 64.6 million (1996) people live.

Hebei is divided into 10 regions, 142 counties, and 2 autonomous counties between Beijing and Tianjin that are inhabited by the Hui Muslims, who are the largest minority group in the province. There also are Manchu and Mongolian people in the northeast, but the Han Chinese make up 98 percent of the population. Traces of agriculture date back to 4000 BCE, but the marshy lowlands of southern Hebei were first drained and settled during the Han dynasty (206 BCE–220 CE), and for centuries this densely populated area was one of the most productive in the empire. During the Tang dynasty (618–907 CE), the area declined as the Chang (Yangtze) River valley was developed. Hebei was incorporated into a number of foreign dynasties, the Liao (916–1125) and the Jin (1115–1234). Beijing became the capital of the Yuan empire (1279–1368), and with brief interruptions, Beijing has remained capital of China.

The economy of Hebei has for centuries been dependent on Beijing, and the intensive agriculture in the lowlands has supplied the capital with wheat, corn, vegetables, and fruit. Light industry is distributed over the province, with major textile centers in Shijiazhuang and Handan. In 1976 a major earthquake (7.8 on the Richter scale) devastated the city of Tangshan in eastern Hebei.

Bent Nielsen

Further Reading

Li Zongmin. (1993) *Changes in the Role of Rural Women under the Household Responsibility System: A Case Study of the Impact of Agrarian Reform and Rural Industrialization in Dongyao Village, Hebei Province, North China.* Madison, WI: Land Tenure Center.

Myers, Ramon H. (1970) *The Chinese Peasant Economy: Agricultural Development in Hopei and Shantung, 1890–1949.* Cambridge, MA: Harvard University Press.

Pomeranz, Kenneth. (1993) *The Making of a Hinterland: State, Society, and Economy in Inland North China, 1853–1937*. Berkeley and Los Angeles: University of California Press.

HEIAN PERIOD The Heian period (794–1185) started with the transfer of the capital from Nara to the new imperial city of Heian-kyo (Kyoto) and ended with the establishment of a warrior government in Kamakura. This period was the peak of Japanese aristocratic and court life, a time during which literature and the arts flourished.

The *Ritsuryo* System

The *ritsuryo* system, first established in the Nara period (710–794 CE), was modeled on the political and economic system of Tang-dynasty (618–907 CE) China, which was composed of both a centralized government dominated by the emperor and nationally controlled estates. Although various attempts were made to preserve and augment the system, the expansion of *shoen* (private landed estates) and their exemption from taxation encroached on public land and reduced the authority of the central government. The creation of extra-statutory officials, such as *sessho* (regent) and *kampaku* (chief councillor), opened the way to power for non-imperial families among the nobility.

From the mid-ninth century, members of the Fujiwara family dominated the court and controlled the imperial line as *sessho* or *kampaku* by marrying their daughters to imperial successors. The rise of the Fujiwara family proved the failure of the *ritsuryo* emperor-dominated political system. From the late ninth century to the first half of the tenth century, however, emperors controlled the court without the Fujiwara regents. Emperor Uda (867–931), having no connection to the Fujiwara family, singled out Sugawara Michizane (845–903) to balance Fujiwara authority. But in 901, a member of the Fujiwara family, envious of the influence of Michizane, deceptively reported that Michizane was plotting against the emperor. Michizane was exiled to Kyushu and died there two years later. Emperor Daigo (885–930), Uda's successor, also avoided Fujiwara influence.

The Aristocracy

In the tenth and eleventh centuries, the Fujiwara ruled the court by reestablishing the tradition of regents. The period from 967 to 1068 was called *sekkan seiji* (Fujiwara regency government). Emperors were born of Fujiwara mothers and were completely dominated by their uncles, fathers-in-law, or grandfathers. Their influence reached its peak under Fujiwara Michinaga (966–1028), who dominated the court from 995 to 1027. Michinaga's son Yorimichi, a high-ranking

The entrance to Phoenix Hall, Byodo-in Temple, Honshu, Japan. (ARCHIVO ICONOGRAFICO, S.A./CORBIS)

JAPAN—HISTORICAL PERIODS

Jomon period (14,500–300 BCE)
Yayoi culture (300 BCE–300 CE)
Yamato State (300–552 CE)
Kofun period (300–710 CE)
Nara period (710–794 CE)
Heian period (794–1185)
Kamakura period (Kamakura Shogunate) (1185–1333)
Muromachi period (1333–1573)
Momoyama period (1573–1600)
Tokugawa or Edo period (Tokugawa Shogunate) (1600/1603–1868)
Meiji period (1868–1912)
Taisho period (1912–1926)
Showa period (1926–1989)
Allied Occupation (1945–1952)
Heisei period (1989–present)

noble for three-quarters of a century, continued Fujiwara glory until the accession of emperor Go-Sanjo in 1068, when the Fujiwara declined and a succession of non-Fujiwara emperors came to power.

This period was characterized by the development of a truly Japanese culture in art and literature, after having absorbed Chinese values. The *kana* script, one of the most important inventions in Japanese cultural history, contributed to the creation of great quantities of verse and prose. Murasaki Shikibu's *Genji Monogatari* (*The Tale of Genji*, c. 1000), is not only a brilliant record of life among the aristocracy, but also a masterpiece of world literature. *Waka*, or Japanese poetry, was a crucial part of aristocratic daily life, and proficiency in making *waka* was regarded as essential for nobles. In religion, the secret sects of Tendai and Shingon Buddhism continued to flourish, but they lost their purely religious goals by connecting Buddhism to formalistic court rituals. Instead, the doctrines of the Jodo (Pure Land) sect, which emphasized simple faith in Amida Buddha, grew in popularity in the late Heian period. These doctrines offered consolation to the common people during the social disturbances that occurred in this period.

Age of *Insei*

The accession of Go-Sanjo, the first emperor in one hundred years whose mother was not of the Fujiwara regents' line, initiated the last part of the Heian period, which extended until the establishment of the Kamakura shogunate (military government) in 1185. This last phase was dominated by three successively powerful retired emperors—Shirakawa, Toba, and Go-Sanjo—who replaced the reigning emperors of the earlier period and the regents of the mid-Heian period as the supreme political figures. It was a time of imperial revival.

Emperor Shirakawa (1053–1129) retired early, became a nominal Buddhist monk, and established *insei* (often translated as "cloistered government," because it was government by retired emperors who had taken the monk's tonsure) to rule behind the throne. His successors continued the system off and on until the late Kamakura period. *Shoen* continued to expand, with the imperial family under the active leadership of retired emperors replacing the Fujiwara as the largest *shoen* holders in the land. The imperial family developed a strong household organization that attracted a number of clients among the nobility, and the fortunes of the imperial house increased immensely.

During this time, however, the *ritsuryo* system almost faded away. In the absence of central authority in the provinces, powerful local individuals, banding together in *bushidan* (large military groups), caused confusion. Meanwhile, the Buddhist temples in the capital collected large armies and fought against one another, against the nobles, and against the court, for both economic and religious prizes. The general anarchy led many to believe that the world had entered *mappo* ("latter days of the law"), the final phase of human decline according to Buddhist doctrine.

With the outbreak of civil disturbances in 1156 and 1160, caused by conflicts over political power in both the imperial and the Fujiwara families involving two warrior clans, the Taira and the Minamoto, the military or warrior class became essential to the maintenance of civil government in the capital and indispensable to court politics. The warrior-noble Taira Kiyomori (1118–1181) maintained tenuous control over the court until 1185, but lost power eventually to the powerful Minamoto clan, which established the Kamakura *bakufu* and ushered in a new era in Japanese history.

Hirohisa Yamazaki

Further Reading

Borgen, Robert. (1986) *Sugawara no Michizane and the Early Heian Court*. Cambridge, MA: Harvard University Press.

Hall, John W., and Jeffrey P. Mass, eds. (1974) *Medieval Japan: Essays in Institutional History*. Stanford, CA: Stanford University Press.

Hurst, G. Cameron, III. (1976) *Insei: Abdicated Sovereigns in the Politics of the Late Heian Japan, 1086–1185*. New York: Columbia University Press.

McCullough, William H., and Helen Craig McCullough. (1980) *Tale of Flowering Fortunes: Annals of Japanese Aristocratic Life in the Heian Period.* Stanford, CA: Stanford University Press.

Shively, Donald H., and William H. McCullough, eds. (1999) *The Cambridge History of Japan: Heian Japan.* New York: Cambridge University Press.

HEILONGJIANG (2002 est. pop. 38.3 million). Lying in the northernmost part of Northeast China, Heilongjiang Province has a total area of 453,900 square kilometers, of which 60 percent is made of mountains, 10 percent rivers, and 30 percent farmland. It has a common boundary with the Inner Mongolia Autonomous Region and Jilin Province. In the north, it borders on the Russian Federation. Within its population are 2 million people of minority nationalities, including Manchus, Koreans, Huis, Mongolians, Daurs, Hezhens, Oroqens, and Evenkis.

Heilongjiang has a cold-temperate continental climate and a mean annual temperature of 3° to –2°C, an ice-bound period of five to six months, and a frost-free period of 120 days. It has warm, rainy summers with an annual rainfall of 400 to 650 millimeters and long hours of sunshine, which is favorable to crop growth.

Named after its longest river, Heilongjiang—the Black Dragon River—has five large river systems: the Heilong, Songhua, Wusuli, Nenjiang, and Suifen rivers. Rivers and lakes provide good-quality water resources for agriculture, industry, and human consumption. It has vast expanses of flatland and wide areas of fertile back soil and is one of China's major commodity grain growers. It is nicknamed "the Great Northern Granary," denoting its abundant production of soybeans, maize, wheat, millet, sorghum, sugar beets, flax, and sunflower seeds.

Its land area also includes the country's largest known oil reserve. The Daqing oil field is not only the biggest one in China, but it also is one of the largest known oil fields in the world. The province is rich in coal, gold, copper, aluminum, lead, zinc, silver, molybdenum, bismuth, and cobalt. Heilongjiang has a forest area of close to 210,000 square kilometers, or 49 percent of the province's total area, and leads the country in timber reserves. The mountains and forests abound in alpine weasels, sables, otters, deer, and musk deer. Ginseng is cultivated.

Rail is the principal means of transport in Heilongjiang, with Harbin as the central hub. Heilongjiang has the most developed inland shipping among the northern provinces.

Harbin, the provincial capital (with an estimated population of 2.8 million in 2002), is located on the south bank of the Songhua River and is the economic, cultural, and communications center of the province. The city used to be called "Little Moscow," as a result of colonialism, cooperation with, and immigration from nearby Russia. The town looks a little like the last threadbare outpost of imperial Russia. Harbin is also famous worldwide for its annual Winter Ice Festival.

Di Bai

Further Reading

China Handbook Editorial Committee. (1992) *Geography, China Handbook Series.* Trans. by Liang Liangxing. Beijing, China: Foreign Languages Press.

Hsieh, Chiao-Min, and Max Lu, eds. (2001) *Changing China: A Geographical Appraisal.* Boulder, CO: Westview.

HEISEI PERIOD With the death of Emperor Hirohito (b. 1901) in January 1989, the Showa period, which had taken Japan from 1926 through the postwar recovery, came to an end. In its place came a new emperor, Akihito (b. 1933), and a new period, Heisei. Already the Heisei period has seen dramatic changes. The tremendous Heisei economic boom has taken a precipitous turn into lasting recession. Faltering financial institutions, crashes in land prices, and the erosion of the lifetime employment tradition have altered Japan's economic and social climate. International conflicts have thrust Japan onto the geopolitical stage, while domestic political changes have begun to rattle the established bureaucracy and disasters such as the great Kobe earthquake and the Tokyo subway sarin gas attack have further shaken the nation's nerves.

The Heisei Boom

The Heisei period started out with a boom, riding in on a period of economic prosperity that had begun in 1986 and would last until early 1991. Not since the Izanagi Boom (1965–1970) had the Japanese economy experienced such a long, uninterrupted period of economic expansion. Domestic consumer demand, helped by government monetary policy, boosted the economy. With the signing of the Plaza Accord in 1985, the Japanese government had pledged to encourage consumer demand, let the value of the yen better reflect the strength of the Japanese economy, and regulate against inflation. In 1986, the government had cut the official discount rate. By February of the next year, the rate had fallen to 2.5 percent, the lowest in the post–World War II period. Spurred by lowered

JAPAN—HISTORICAL PERIODS

Jomon period (14,500–300 BCE)
Yayoi culture (300 BCE–300 CE)
Yamato State (300–552 CE)
Kofun period (300–710 CE)
Nara period (710–794 CE)
Heian period (794–1185)
Kamakura period (Kamakura Shogunate) (1185–1333)
Muromachi period (1333–1573)
Momoyama period (1573–1600)
Tokugawa or Edo period (Tokugawa Shogunate) (1600/1603–1868)
Meiji period (1868–1912)
Taisho period (1912–1926)
Showa period (1926–1989)
Allied Occupation (1945–1952)
Heisei period (1989–present)

interest rates, investors snapped up land and property and bought more durable goods and machinery. This economic momentum continued into the early years of the Heisei period.

A strengthened yen, likewise, brought more buying power to individuals and corporations looking to invest abroad. From a record low of 240 yen to the dollar in 1986, the yen strengthened steadily to 130 yen to the dollar just two years later. By 1991, the last of the boom years, the yen stood at around 140. The yen went to 99 to the dollar in January of 1995, reaching 84 to the dollar in June 1995 and continuing to hold below 100 until September. The strengthened yen did little to curb Japan's export competitiveness abroad, as manufacturers could import raw materials at lower costs. A strengthened yen also helped government efforts to curb Japan's wide trade deficits and the associated "Japan bashing" that had arisen with trading partners abroad, particularly the United States.

During the same period, land prices soared as more and more investors turned their capital to real property. Prices nationwide, but particularly in Japan's largest cities (Tokyo, Yokohama, Osaka, and Nagoya), rose to a peak in 1990. Golf course development, along with other resort development initiatives, also gained steadily during the wealthy years of the Heisei boom. Concurrently, golf course memberships themselves were looked to as indicators of the economy's health. A golf membership fees index tracked the exorbitant prices that Japan's corporate wealthy were willing to pay for the privilege of belonging to and networking at the nation's most prestigious golf courses. When Japanese investors bought the famed Pebble Beach Golf Course in California (along with a host of other high-publicity real estate purchases such as Carnegie Hall and Columbia Pictures movie studio), business professionals worldwide began to study the Japanese "economic miracle." Indeed, with Japan's gross domestic product (GDP) averaging about 4.5 percent growth, including a peak of over 6 percent growth in 1989, and unemployment rates at an all-time low, it looked as though the Japanese economy would increasingly dominate the twenty-first century.

Recession

However, as heady as the late 1980s and early 1990s were for many, there were signs that Japan's rising economy was, in fact, an overinflating bubble, filled with emptiness and ready to burst. By the middle part of the 1990s, it had. The overheated land prices with which the bubble had been inflated dropped precipitously. Corporations and financial institutions that had overextended themselves, often on risky investments and real estate ventures, found that they could not repay their loans or collect from bankrupt creditors. In August 1995, Hyogo Bank, the nation's thirty-eighth largest, and Kizu, the nation's largest credit union, shut their doors. Larger banks were to follow: in November two years later, Sanyo Securities, Yamaichi Securities, and Hokkaido Takushoku Bank announced financial collapse.

During the same period, eight of the country's mortgage lending companies *(jusen)* revealed 6 trillion yen ($67.5 billion) of debt caused mainly by investments in high-priced real estate that had since lost value. When the Ministry of Finance (MOF) stepped in to prop up bad *jusen* loans, more controversy ensued. Historically reluctant to give out money, the MOF spent 685 billion yen ($6.52 billion) of taxpayer money to recover investor losses. When rumors circulated of poor investment practices by *jusen* managers (a number of whom were retired MOF bureaucrats) and possible underworld involvement, the public labeled the incident the *jusen* scandal. Confidence in the Ministry of Finance declined, and greater public cries for transparency in financial institutions ensued. Further turmoil erupted when agricultural cooperative credit unions that had also extended real estate investment loans experienced similar troubles and demanded similar government bailouts.

To relieve the fears of depositors, in 1996 the national government committed itself to unlimited guarantees on all deposits at failed banks. Some critics, however, complained that the government was not prompting bankers to change faulty policies rapidly enough. So-called Big Bang measures to bring more transparency, oversight, and accountability to financial bureaucracies were also introduced in 1996 and have been instituted with varying degrees of success.

In addition to propping up failing institutions, the government continued past policies aimed at priming the economy through government-funded development projects. Giving money to transportation infrastructure and resort and rural development projects, the government hoped to promote work throughout the country. However, although the construction industry flourished and the economy had made signs of recovery with GDP growth at slightly over 4 percent in 1996, by 1997 the GDP had once again begun to fall. By the following year, the GDP had slipped into negative numbers, and although slight growth rates were recorded in the following years, recession continued.

Not only company accounts suffered. Workers who once assumed lifetime employment and company-subsidized benefits found their jobs less secure. Companies began to trim excess workers from their payrolls, creating thousands of new jobless. Japan's jobless rate reached a record 6 percent in October 2001. In conjunction, the rate of homelessness has also risen.

The Asian Economic Crisis

The strength of the Japanese yen in the beginning of the Heisei period had prompted investment in neighboring nations. When the economic bubble burst, however, many companies began to restrict cash flow to overseas holdings and to withdraw capital from overseas banks. As regional currencies lost value, Asian banks struggled to meet dollar-denominated foreign debts. Japan's economic crisis directly contributed to economic crises in Southeast Asia and Korea at the end of the 1990s (particularly in 1997 and 1998, when various Asian nations struggled with plummeting currency values and bank failures).

In turn, Asia's poor economic performance has hindered Japan's recovery. In the late 1990s, nearly 38 percent of Japan's exports were aimed at Southeast Asia, but devastated currency values stopped many Southeast Asian consumers from buying higher-priced Japanese exports. Although the region has rebounded, economic performance is not yet what it was in the boom years of the "Asian Miracles."

Political Changes

Great changes have also taken place in Japan's political arena during the Heisei period. For the first time in thirty-eight years, the long-ruling Liberal Democratic Party (LDP) was knocked out of power in 1993 and joined a coalition government with various opposition parties. Although the LDP regained power the next year, significant political restructuring has followed.

Most sweeping has been electoral reform. In a large-scale effort at demographically based redistricting not seen since the end of World War II, Japan created three hundred new electoral districts. The newly drawn districts were designed to alleviate disparities between rural and urban voting power that disproportionately favored rural districts. Under the new system, the Lower House membership consisted of three hundred single-seat constituencies and two hundred proportionate seat constituencies elected from eleven regional districts (in proportionate seat elections, voters vote for a party slate whose members then proportionately fill the number of seats allotted to their party). The number of proportionate seats was reduced to 180 in 2000.

Although political reform was aimed at creating a two-party adversarial system similar to that in the United States, the LDP, along with its coalition partners, has continued to dominate national politics. In the summer 2001 election, for instance, the LDP, helped by the wave of popularity surrounding Prime Minister Junichiro Koizumi, won the national election handily and was able to continue its rule along with its New Komeito and New Conservative coalition parties. Moreover, the new electoral system has not kept smaller parties from entering into the political process. In fact, over thirty new political parties have been created since 1994, and more voters are describing themselves as independent. Similarly, redistricting has not alleviated rural-urban voting disparities and differences. Although rural support for the LDP has lessened somewhat (from what was once an assured support for the LDP's generally protectionist policies toward farmers and small business owners), rural districts still vote primarily for the LDP and its allies.

Peace and Conflict Abroad

Political challenges have not happened only on the domestic front, however. During the Heisei period, the bounds of Japan's postwar constitution have come under international scrutiny. Article 9, the constitutional "peace clause" that forbids Japan's involvement in acts of foreign aggression, has been overwhelmingly popular with the Japanese public. International allies, however, severely criticized Japan for not promptly sending more support during the 1991 Gulf War. A belated $13 billion in monetary support did little to bolster Japan's image as an international player.

To maintain better diplomatic ties with the United States and European allies, Japan committed financial aid and elections observers in support of U.N. efforts in the Bosnia-Herzegovina region in 1996. Following East Timor's independence in 1999, Japan contributed similar forms of aid and development personnel to peacekeeping and reconstruction projects.

More recently, after the 11 September 2001 terrorist attacks in the United States, Japan took its largest steps yet into the arena of international conflict. Pushing to the limits of Article 9 and banking on his great popularity, Prime Minister Koizumi pledged not only money, but also noncombatant support troops from Japan's Self-Defense Force (SDF) to war and rebuilding efforts in Afghanistan. SDF personnel would be able to provide medical aid, intelligence-gathering support, and refugee relief in the Afghan and Middle East region. The move is significant and controversial because it sent SDF troops to an area of active conflict.

Agriculture

Debates on agricultural markets have also continued throughout the Heisei period, with intense controversy over the extent to which Japan should open its markets to foreign produce. At issue are questions of price, selection, health, rural economics, and food security.

Through quotas, tariffs, and rigid quarantines, Japan managed to buffer its small farmers from the brunt of international competition for decades. With small farm sizes (on average, 1 to 1.5 hectares), high operating costs, and an aging farm population, Japan's farmers have long feared unchecked imports and unsubsidized farming. However, as electoral politics began to shift and as more farmers began to retire, popular support for large farm subsidies began to decline. Price supports for rice fell, and more and more imported goods began to find their way into Japanese markets.

With the signing of the Uruguay Round of the General Agreement on Tariffs and Trade (GATT) in September 1993, Japan agreed to limited imports of its most symbolic and most protected grain: rice. The agreement was a shock to rice farmers, who had suffered poor harvests in 1993 but had recovered with bumper crops by 1994. Angry farmers publicly derided the quality of imported rice, feeding it to their livestock on national television. However, the agreement stood, committing Japan to yearly increases in rice imports.

Besides rice, Japan has been increasingly importing other food products from abroad, including apples and various vegetables, as well as meat and preprocessed products. At the beginning of the twenty-first century, it is possibly China that causes the most concern. Controversy has already raged over the import of Chinese leeks, garlic, ginger, mushrooms, and reed matting (tatami).

Proponents of continued agricultural protections point to the likelihood of exacerbated economic disparities between rural and urban regions if Japan's small farms go under. Japan must also consider issues of food self-sufficiency and national security. At present, Japan has the lowest food self-sufficiency ratio in the industrialized world, with only 40 percent of average caloric intake provided from domestic sources.

Shocks

Two particularly infamous events will forever mark the Heisei period. On 17 January 1995, an earthquake measured at 7.2 on the Richter scale rocked the city of Kobe in the early morning, killing 6,425 people. Fires raged around the city, highways and buildings lay toppled, and rescue teams had a difficult time reaching the wounded. In addition to the horrific human costs, the Kobe earthquake was Japan's costliest in economic terms. The earthquake also toppled the nation's feeling of security because many "earthquake-proof" structures crumbled.

Although all Japanese know that their land will shake, most had assumed that they remained relatively safe from crime and domestic terrorism. That peace, as well, was shattered a few months after the Kobe earthquake when, on 20 March 1995, members of the Aum Shinrikyo cult released sarin gas inside a Tokyo subway. The attack killed twelve and injured six thousand. Communities and law enforcement moved to squelch the cult, and membership is reportedly down from the ten thousand members it had acquired by 1995. The cult's leader, Asahara Shoko (b. 1955), has been jailed. The subway attack, however, painfully revealed Japan's vulnerability. It also revealed an alienated segment of Japanese society that some scholars say grew in number after the economic bubble collapsed.

What Will Come Next?

In December 2001, the nation celebrated the birth of Imperial Princess Aiko, the daughter of Crown

Prince Naruhito and Princess Masako. Many hope that the imperial family will revise current rules that permit only male heirs to take the throne. The idea of reform in imperial succession in the years to come cheers many in the current era of dim economics and uncertain international politics.

The Heisei period has already seen significant changes and challenges. The outcome of the period remains to be seen, but the events of its first years have already made a lasting imprint on Japan's modern history.

Ann D. Brucklacher

Further Reading

Allinson, Gary D. (1999) *The Columbia Guide to Modern Japanese History.* New York: Columbia University Press.

Callen, Timothy, and Warwick J. McKibbin. (2001) "Policies and Prospects in Japan and the Implications for the Asia-Pacific Region." IMF Working Paper, no. 01/131. Washington, DC: International Monetary Fund.

Kristof, Nicholas, and Sheryl Wu Dunn. (1999) *The Japanese Economy at the Millennium: Correspondents' Insightful Views.* New York: Foreign Policy Association.

Metraux, Daniel A. (1999) *Aum Shinrikyo and Japanese Youth.* Lanham, MD: University Press of America.

Muta, Shohei. (1996) "The Fall of the Mighty MOF? Lack of Accountability in the Japanese Bureaucracy." *NIRA (National Institute for Research Advancement) Review* (Spring). Retrieved 11 January 2002, from: http://www.nira.go.jp/publ/review/96spring/muta.html.

Otsuma, Mayumi, Ken Ellis, Todd Zaun, Andrew Morse, and Norie Kuboyama. (1996) "Lenders' Crisis." *Japan Policy Research Institute Critique* 3, 2. Retrieved 9 April 2002, from: http://www.jpri.org/public/crit3.2.html.

Schiff, Anshel J., ed. (1995) *Hyogoken-Nanbu (Kobe) Earthquake of January 17, 1995.* Lifeline Performance Technical Council on Lifeline Earthquake Engineering Monograph, no. 14. Reston, VA: American Society of Civil Engineers.

HENAN

HENAN (2002 est. pop. 100.8 million). Located in north-central China, Henan Province covers an area of 167,000 square kilometers and is bordered by Hebei, Shandong, and Shanxi Provinces. Today, Henan has a population of 92 million; its capital is Zhenzhou. Located on the North China Plain and with its close proximity to the Huang (Yellow) River, Henan Province has had a long history of flooding. For thousands of years, the Chinese have built dams and dikes here in an effort to stem the devastating effects of these yearly floods. Yet the floods have also deposited large quantities of rich silt, leaving Henan one of China's most fertile regions. The temperature is hot in the summer and cold in the winter, and annual rainfall averages 1,250 to 1,750 millimeters.

The province, known as the cradle of Chinese civilization, is one of the oldest inhabited regions of China. Archeologists have found evidence that Henan was inhabited as far back as the Neolithic period. Recent excavations have unearthed artifacts dating back to the Shang dynasty (1766–1045 BCE). Several cities in Henan have served prominently in Chinese history. Anyang, located in northern Henan, was the first capital of the Shang dynasty, while Luoyang served as imperial capital of the Eastern Zhou dynasty (770–221 BCE), and Kaifeng was the imperial capital during the Five Dynasties period (907–960 CE) as well as the Northern Song dynasty (960–1126 CE).

The province is known as a major producer of wheat, tobacco, and cotton. Textile, electricity, and other industries developed recently. The provincial capital, Zhenzhou, located at the crossroad of several major railroad lines that transverse China, is one of the key points of China's national transportation system.

Keith A. Leitich

Further Reading

Domenach, Jean Luc. (1995) *The Origins of the Great Leap Forward: The Case of One Chinese Province.* Trans. by A. M. Berrett. Boulder, CO: Westview.

Wou, Odoric Y. K. (1994) *Mobilizing the Masses: Building Revolution in Henan.* Stanford, CA: Stanford University Press.

HENG SAMRIN

HENG SAMRIN (b. 1934), president of the People's Republic of Kampuchea. Heng Samrin, president of the People's Republic of Kampuchea (PRK) from 1979 to 1991, was born in Kompong Cham Province in 1934. He became involved in Communist activity in the 1950s and later rose to become a Khmer Rouge division commander in the Eastern Zone. He fled to Vietnam with Hun Sen and others during the Khmer Rouge purges of 1978. On 3 December 1978 Radio Hanoi announced the formation of a united front of the National Salvation of Kampuchea under the leadership of Heng Samrin. Weeks later Vietnamese forces entered Phnom Penh, defeated the Khmer Rouge, and began their occupation of the country. On 10 January 1979 they formed the PRK and named Heng Samrin president. The PRK government was formed from the top down by recruiting those who both strongly opposed the return of the Khmer Rouge and were willing to work within the Vietnamese political structure. The Heng Samrin government was never widely recognized as the legitimate government of Cambodia. It was not seated at the United Nations, was refused

U.N. aid, and was boycotted by the United States. In the mid 1980s, power moved to Hun Sen, who became prime minister in 1985. Heng Samrin remained head of state until Sihanouk returned in 1991. Following the election of 1998, he became first vice chairman of the National Assembly.

Jeanne Morel

Further Reading

Chandler, David. (1996) *A History of Cambodia.* 2d ed. Boulder, CO: Westview.

Heder, Steven, and Judy Legerwood. (1996) "Politics of Violence, an Introduction." In *Propaganda, Politics, and Violence in Cambodia: Democratic Transition under United Nations Peace-keeping.* Armonk, NY: M. E. Sharpe.

Kiernan, Ben. (1985) *How Pol Pot Came to Power: A History of Communism in Kampuchea, 1930–1975.* London: Verso.

HENGDUAN RANGES The Hengduan region in northwest Yunnan Province in China, extending into neighboring Tibet and Sichuan, is China's longest and widest mountain system. The area is transversed by several big rivers running from north to south: the Nu, Lancang, Yalon, and Jinsha. The river valleys are 1,500 to 2,000 meters above sea level, while peaks in the southern part reach 4,124 meters (Tiancang); Guangmao in the eastern part reaches 4,023 meters. The peaks stand close together, and the area is almost without plateaus and broad valleys. There is a relative high annual precipitation, up to 2,500 millimeters on the western slopes of the mountains while the eastern slopes receive markedly less rain, about 900 millimeters annually. The region is sparsely populated. Most inhabitants belong to minority nationalities like the Yi, Lisu, Bai, and Tibetans, and the majority of the region is divided into autonomous districts. The main city of the area is windswept Xiaguan, situated at the southern end of Lake Erhai. Main sources of income are forestry, cattle, and sheep. Since tea plants were introduced in the nineteenth century, the region has become a major tea producer. The area is also one of China's important nonferrous metal industrial bases.

Bent Nielsen

Further Reading

Li Heng. (1981) *Geological and Ecological Studies of Qinghai-Xizang Plateau.* Beijing: Science Press.

Zhao Songqiao. (1986) *Physical Geography of China.* Beijing: Science Press.

HENTII MOUNTAINS Located in northeast Mongolia, the Hentii (Khentii) range consists of smooth, rounded mountains covered by large stretches of well-watered virgin forest. The range lacks the high mountaintop relief that one observes, for example, in the Rockies of North America. The highest point is located at Asralt Hairhan (2,751 meters above sea level).

The Hentii mountain range is one of the wettest regions in Mongolia, with a total annual precipitation of 250 to 300 millimeters at altitudes higher than 1,000 meters. Water collects in the range's glacial lakes or drains into one of two oceanic basins—the Pacific Basin via the Herlen and Haraa Rivers, and the Arctic Basin, via the Tuul, the Yoroo, and the Onon, a tributary of the Amur River.

Mountain forest, or taiga, covers a large portion of the lower Hentii range. Cedar and cedar-larch are the most commonly found tree species in the taiga-dominated areas. At higher elevations, low-lying shrubs and rocky outcroppings predominate. A variety of animals make the mountains their home. These include lemmings, sable, glutton (wolverine), northern pika, musk deer, elk, bear, Manchurian deer, and the Hentii mountain stout.

Daniel Hruschka

Further Reading

The Academy of Sciences of the Mongolian People's Republic. (1990). *Information Mongolia.* Oxford: Pergamon.

HERAT (2002 est. pop. of province 1.3 million; 2002 est. pop. of city 167,000). An important historical, commercial, and cultural center in Central Asia, Herat (ancient Aria) is a city on the Hari River in northwest Afghanistan and the capital of Herat Province. Herat played an important role in the military and cultural history of the Central Asian region due to its strategic location on the Silk Road from China and Central Asia to Western Asia and Europe. According to historical records, a large settlement in this area had existed at least since the fifth century BCE; Herat Province may be the ancient homeland of Aryan-speaking people, and Aria was a satrapy of the Persian empire (sixth–fourth centuries BCE). Alexander of Macedon (356–323 BCE) destroyed the Persian citadel and the city around 328 BCE, during his conquest of the Persians. Nonetheless, the city was rebuilt and continued to serve the flourishing trade on the Silk Road, surviving turmoil and frequent wars.

In the eleventh century, Herat was captured by the Seljuks, and in the twelfth century, it was taken over by the powerful Khwarizm empire centered on the valley of the Amu Dar'ya River. In the thirteenth century, Herat was destroyed by Mongols led by Genghis Khan (c. 1162–1227), who ordered the slaughter of all 80,000 citizens of the city, yet it was rebuilt again. In 1381, Timur (Tamerlane, 1336–1405) conquered the city, but his son, Shah Rokh (1377–1447), rebuilt Herat and made it his capital and an intellectual and cultural center. During this time, Herat was famous for its poets, painters of miniatures, and architecture.

From the seventeenth to nineteenth centuries, Herat was fought over by various regional powers, and only in 1863 did Abdorrahman Khan (c. 1844–1901), the Afghan ruler, finally integrate it into Afghanistan with British support. During the last quarter of the twentieth century, the city experienced decay due to political turmoil, the Soviet occupation in 1980, and civil war. Presently it remains a commercial center that relies on agriculture and small-scale manufacturing, including food processing and textile and carpet manufacturing.

Rafis Abazov

Further Reading

Allen, Terry. (1983) *Timurid Herat*. Wiesbaden, Germany: Reichert.

Dupree, Louis. (1980) *Afghanistan*. Princeton, NJ: Princeton University Press.

Ewans, Sir Martin. (2002) *Afghanistan: A Short History of Its People and Politics*. New York: HarperCollins.

Tumanovich, N. N. (1989) *Gerat v XVI–XVIII vekakh* (Herat in the Sixteenth to Eighteenth Centuries). Moscow: Nauka.

HIGASHIKUNI NARUHIKO

(1887–1990), prime minister of Japan. Higashikuni Naruhiko was Japan's first prime minister following its surrender to the U.S. on 15 August 1945; he served from 17 August to 9 October 1945. An uncle to Emperor Hirohito by marriage (Higashikuni's wife, Toshiko, was the ninth and youngest daughter of the Meiji emperor), Higashikuni acted in the role of caretaker prime minister to peacefully turn over control of Japan to the Allied Occupation armies.

Higashikuni was born in Kyoto in 1887. As a member of the nobility, following the custom of the times, he entered the attached Primary School of the Imperial Army, followed by Officers' School and Army College. After graduation, Higashikuni married and in 1920 went to France to study, staying for seven years. While in France, Higashikuni developed affection for Impressionist art and had a wide circle of friends, including Claude Monet and Georges Clemenceau. Through these acquaintances, Higashikuni learned about Western social and political thought and developed a reputation as a liberalist among the nobility.

Upon his return to Japan, Higashikuni rose to the rank of field marshal. After the fall of the Konoe Fumimaro cabinet in October 1941, he was recommended to become prime minister in the belief that he could prevent the march toward war, but Army Minister Tojo Hideki took the post instead. In August 1945, Higashikuni became prime minister; his main tasks were preparing for the official surrender and the start of the Allied Occupation. In October of that same year, Higashikuni and his Cabinet resigned due to policy differences with the Occupation authorities. In 1950, Higashikuni formed his own religious sect, Higashikunikyo. In 1990, one year after the death of Emperor Hirohito, he died at the age of 103.

Robert Eldridge

Further Reading

Masumi Junnosuke. (1985) *Postwar Politics in Japan, 1945–1955*. Trans. by Lonny E. Carlile. Berkeley, CA: Institute of East Asian Studies, University of California.

HIGH-TECHNOLOGY INDUSTRY

Asian development strategies typically have three stages. Initially, low-cost labor attracts labor-intensive and low value-added assembly businesses. Second, countries attempt to increase value-added capabilities to sustain economic development as wage rates rise. Finally, successful development requires that local firms expand operations into the global marketplace. Industry growth requires competitive economies of scale, which means that firms must obtain global market shares. Long-term leadership requires brand names to ensure global brand recognition and acceptance.

Electronics' Low-Cost Imperative

Less-developed countries such as China, India, and many Association of Southeast Asian Nations (ASEAN) countries with low-cost labor attract companies with labor-intensive operations. In the 1970s and 1980s South Korea, Taiwan, Hong Kong, Singapore, and Malaysia benefited from such foreign direct investments; they are now newly industrialized economies (NIE). Unfortunately, per capita incomes have increased to only $11,100 for Malaysia but to $26,800 for Hong Kong. (See Table 1.) To stay competitive, NIE firms are moving operations to

TABLE 1

Comparative economic statistics

	Malaysia	Hong Kong	Singapore	South Korea	Taiwan
GDP per capita	$11,100.00	$26,800.00	$24,600.00	$13,700.00	$14,200.00

SOURCE: AsiaSource (2001).

less-developed countries (LDCs) such as Indonesia, the Philippines, Vietnam, and China. China received nearly 80 percent of all foreign investments in Asia.

Hong Kong's Shift to Mainland China Hong Kong's wages are among the highest in Asia. Between 1982 and 1994, Hong Kong's manufacturing firms lost cost competitiveness and moved labor-intensive operations to China; Hong Kong's industrial base declined nearly 10 percent annually between 1988 and 1991.

Hong Kong now lacks technical competitiveness with mainland China as well as with other NIEs, including South Korea, Taiwan, and Singapore. Mainland China's successful attraction of leading-edge electronics firms has usurped Hong Kong's role in technology transfer. Today Hong Kong struggles to find a new competitive strategy that fits its high labor costs. Hong Kong continues to provide China with logistics support and capital, but these roles will be diminished as China builds its own capital markets, deregulates markets, and builds its infrastructure. However, in 2000 Hong Kong's gross domestic product (GDP) increased by 10.5 percent, the highest growth rate in thirteen years.

Taiwan's Search for Lower-Cost Labor Taiwan also found its competitiveness dwindling in labor-intensive businesses. To address the problems of increasing wage rates, the Taiwanese government allowed firms to import foreign workers for up to two years. Twenty-five percent of Taiwan's manufacturing workforce was foreign by 1996; the majority were well-educated and hard-working Filipinos.

Taiwanese firms also sent labor-intensive operations to countries like the Philippines, Vietnam, and China. (See Table 2.) Companies producing products such as power supplies, keyboards, and computer mice had been moved offshore by the late 1990s. Trade, investment, and travel restrictions between Taiwan and mainland China were rapidly lifted as Taiwan became the largest investor in China.

Singapore's Off-Shore Industrial Parks Singapore became a corporate headquarters center, with the strategy of helping firms stay competitive by means of labor-intensive operations. Both domestic and foreign companies were encouraged to minimize overall costs by maintaining management and research functions in Singapore while shifting production and marketing operations to less-developed economies. Singapore created the first economic-development triangle in Southeast Asia in 1989. The Indonesian province of Riau and the Malaysian state of Johor supplied low-cost land and labor, while Singapore provided technology and capital. Singapore has built high-tech industrial parks in China, Vietnam, and India. The China-Singapore Suzhou Industrial Park (CS-SIP), initiated in 1995, provided revenue of 1.63 billion yuan ($196 million) to China in 2000, with an import and export value of $3.4 billion.

Singapore's Vietnam Industrial Park was launched near Ho Chi Minh City in 1996. The International Tech Park in Bangalore, India, was officially opened in January 2000, with 150 infotech companies and 5,000 computer specialists. By 1999 India's software industry had reached revenues of $3.9 billion and was projected to reach $50 billion by 2008. In 1999 India had more than 160,000 programmers.

China's Mastery of Industrial Parks China has five special economic zones (SEZs), which are in Shenzhen, Zhuhai, Xiamen, Shantou, and Hainan. Across the border from Hong Kong, Shenzhen has 1,500 factories producing computer components. Thirty-six of the world's top-500 companies and 150 large multinationals have set up high-tech businesses in the city. Shenzhen bested larger Chinese cities in revenue from the high-tech sector, turning out high-tech products worth nearly $10 billion.

The "Torch Program," established in 1988, promotes commercialization, industrialization, and the internationalization of China's high-tech achievements. By 1995 the central government had approved fifty-two high-technology development zones, which integrate research institutions like universities with start-up incubator facilities and firms that are committed to using the technologies. Six high-tech devel-

TABLE 2

Countries with low labor costs

	China	India	Indonesia	Philippines	Vietnam
Population	1,236,914,658	984,003,683	212,941,810	77,725,862	76,236,259
GDP per capita	$3,460.00	$1,600.00	$4,600.00	$3,200.00	$1,700.00

SOURCE: AsiaSource (2001).

opment zones have been established in the cities of Shanghai, Najing, Wuxi, Changzhou, Suzhou, and Hanzhou.

The Beijing Zhongguancun Science and Technology Park was the first science and technology industrial park in China, approved by the State Council in May 1988. In June 1999 the central government approved a ten-year construction plan for this park, now called China's "Silicon Valley" because it houses more than 4,000 high-tech enterprises. It is near Tsinghua University and Beijing University—the two leading seats of learning in China—and the Chinese Academy of Sciences.

The Chang (Yangtze) River Delta is one of China's economic powerhouses. One of the high-tech development zones in the area is Shanghai's Caohejing High-Tech Development Zone. It is six square kilometers in size, with 500 companies, of which 150 are funded from overseas. Major multinationals, including AT&T, General Electric Company, 3M, ICI, Philips, Toshiba, and DuPont, have subsidiaries there. High-tech firms in the zone are in microelectronics, bioengineering, new materials, automation, aviation, and space technology.

The Shanghai Pudong Jinqiao Export Processing Zone is nineteen square kilometers in size and is located in the middle of the Pudong New Area. Pudong attracted $6.13 billion of overseas investment for 661 projects in 2000 alone and accounted for $20 billion in foreign trade. In microelectronics Pudong projects added ten production lines of integrated circuit chips and more than one hundred ventures for chip design, production, testing, and assembling.

The government plans to create about twenty industrial zones in inland regions during the next five-year plan, with more than 60 percent of resources earmarked for investment in western China to ease the tensions arising from economic disparity. The plan is to shift more capital-intensive industries into coastal areas as labor-intensive industries move inland.

Upgrading Electronics Technologies

Asian NIEs are upgrading their technologies. Strategies include developing government research institutes, targeting growth industries, and building technologies and components needed for next-generation products.

Building Research Centers Government-supported research institutes (GRIs) "prime the pump" for technology development. They focus on basic problems relating to technology development and transfer. Through the 1970s Korean GRIs carried out high-risk research in low-profit areas and in areas where universities lacked research capabilities. Private research focused on the imitation of foreign products and the licensing of foreign technology. Between 1982 and 1989 the number of private Korean industrial research institutes increased from 46 to 749 through the government's cooperative research and development (R & D) programs. By 1992 the number was 1,435 as a result of government support and tax incentives.

Singapore established the National Science and Technology Board (NSTB) in 1991 to promote R & D. NTSB initiated five programs for (1) partnering with industry; (2) recruiting and training of R & D personnel; (3) establishing and maintaining national research institutes and centers; (4) providing R & D infrastructure; and (5) building international alliances and cooperative agreements. Its GRIs encourage development in microelectronics, wireless communication, data storage, manufacturing technology, information technology and multimedia technology, neural networks, and artificial intelligence.

Taiwan has similar institutes. In electronics the Industrial Technology Research Institute (ITRI) has been the dominant player, with more than 6,000 engineers.

Building the Microelectronics Infrastructure The government of Taiwan has targeted electronics as a growth industry requiring component and product developments. Integrated circuits (IC) fabrication, IC

TABLE 3

Taiwan IC industry growth

(in millions of dollars)

	2000	1999	00/99 Growth rate
Industry revenue	16,480	12,512	31.7%
Design	2,660	1,973	34.8%
Fabrication	10,609	1,973	33.3%
Foundry	6,322	4,525	39.7%
Packaging	2,474	1,995	24.0%
Domestic-owned packing	2,103	1,707	23.2%
Testing	736	585	25.9%
Product revenue	6,947	5,407	28.5%

SOURCE: Industrial Technology Information Services (2001)

module packaging, printed wire board assembly, liquid crystal (LC) module assembly, and final systems assembly were considered the critical capabilities. Each component and technology was systematically targeted for development. By 2000 the electronic-components industry reached revenues of more than $16 billion. (See Table 3.) IC fabrication approached $11 billion in revenues, and IC packaging was projected at nearly $2.5 billion.

Taiwan's share of global IC capacity grew from 11.9 percent in 1999 to 13.4 percent in 2000. The first IC fabrication facility was established in 1979, and Taiwan had forty such facilities by 2001. The four leading firms had twenty-five facilities with eight-inch wafer production and had announced plans to build advanced twelve-inch fabs. In IC fabrication, wafers are the silicon disks that are used for water fabs. The largest firm, Taiwan Semiconductor Manufacturing Corporation (TSMC), had revenues of $5.3 billion, with net income of more than $2 billion in 2000.

Building Essential Components and Products Taiwan continues to be a one-stop shop for electronic products and components and has led the world in information-technology production in fourteen product categories. (See Table 4.) Taiwan held 49 percent of the world market share in notebook computers, surpassing Japan's 40-percent share in 1999, with $10.2 billion in sales, a trend that continues today. Other figures are equally impressive, with Taiwan holding more than 50 percent of the market share in computer monitors, motherboards, keyboards, scanners, video cards, and power supplies. Taiwanese firms have become original design manufacturers that sell "ready-to-go" products to original equipment manufacturers. With growing strength in product design and new product development, Taiwanese companies have continued to strengthen their global market position.

China's IC Industry According to the Ministry of Information Industry, the output value of China's electronics industry was expected to reach $110 billion in 2000. China's electronic equipment production is expected to continue growing at a compounded annual rate of 16.8 percent to 2003, when it will reach about $100 billion. China's $7 billion semiconductor market has been growing annually at an average of 37 percent since 1992. Table 5 shows the breakdown between demand for metal oxide semiconductor (MOS) memory and logic ICs and analog devices. With only 10 percent of those chips made locally, the government had recruited foreign investment to establish IC facilities

TABLE 4

1999 Sales of Taiwan's major information-technology (IT) hardware products

(Value in millions of dollars; volume in thousands of units or thousand of cards)

Ranking	Product	Value	Value growth	Volume	Volume growth
1	Notebook PC	10,198	21.1%	9,355	53.7%
2	Monitor	9,330	24.0%	58,729	17.7%
3	Desktop PC	7,188	11.2%	19,457	35.7%
4	Motherboard	4,854	12.6%	64,378	21.0%
5	SPS	1,744	16.4%	80,221	36.6%
6	CD/DVD	1,740	25.4%	48,690	58.8%
7	Case	1,423	18.4%	75,768	22.3%
8	Scanner	925	13.1%	21,901	43.7%
9	Graphics card	848	44.3%	18,583	7.0%
10	Keyboard	512	2.8%	79,445	31.3%
11	UPS	370	15.6%	3,008	27.3%
12	Mouse	155	-9.0%	68,160	19.8%
13	Sound card	78	-41.4%	8,481	-39.7%
14	Video card	33	-17.0%	1,102	49.3%

SOURCE: Industrial Technology Information Services (2001).

TABLE 5

China semiconductor consumption*

(in millions of dollars)

	1998	1999	2000	CAGR
MOS memory IC	1,504	2,136	3,033	42%
MOS logic IC	1,180	1,651	2,312	40%
Analog devices	1,796	2,388	3,177	33%

*Not including Hong Kong

SOURCE: Wilson (1999).

to supply the local market. China produces less than 1 percent of the world's ICs, and the Chinese government added favorable policies to support the development of the microelectronics industry. Such overseas giants as Motorola, NEC, Philips, Siemens, and Toshiba are transferring technology, building wafer fabs, and forming joint ventures with Chinese partners. The Shanghai Grace Semiconductor Manufacturing Company plans a $1.63 billion facility in Zhangjiang High-Tech Park, Pudong New Area, in Shanghai.

China's leading-edge semiconductor facility was NEC Corporation's $1.2 billion fab, a joint venture with the Shanghai Hua Hong Group known as the government's "Project 909." Hua Hong invested $250 million, a sum matched by Shanghai's local government. NEC put up $200 million, and a Japanese bank and some Chinese banks will lend the remaining $500 million. Although NEC is a minority equity partner, it keeps management control of the fab. NEC has been running a small Beijing foundry that has had modest success in the low-end market, producing 8,000 six-inch wafers per month at the 0.5-micron level.

Building Globally Competitive Brands

To sustain developing world-class technologies and products, firms must invest heavily in R & D. To support the high cost of R & D, a firm must expand sales beyond its home market, building global market recognition and brand names. Successful global competitors create a national dilemma in which global competitiveness requirements supersede national priorities. This becomes especially difficult in countries where industrial development policies are closely tied to company success.

Of the leaders outside Japan, Korean conglomerates (called *chaebol*) like Samsung, LG Goldstar, and Daewoo have built global brand names. By 2000 Taiwanese electronics firms had surpassed some of the leading Korean firms. (See Table 6.)

Promoting Local Enterprises Singapore's Economic Development Board has supported local enterprises with strong core capabilities, clear vision, and high growth potential—enterprises that could become multinational companies with strong brand names. Success stories include Aztech Technology, which has had the leading share of the world's sound card market. Chartered Semiconductor Manufacturing (SCM) and IPC Corporation have established international market niches in ICs. SCM, Singapore's largest government-backed semiconductor foundry, has produced application-specific integrated circuits.

China's State-Owned Enterprises With deregulation and opening markets, China's state-owned enterprises (SOEs) must become profitable and competitive. China has 305,000 state enterprises, 118,000 of which are industrial. World Bank statistics report that 50 percent of SOEs lost money in 1996 and that debt ratios reached 80 to 90 percent of assets. More than half of the SOEs were operating in the red in 1999. The government encouraged restructuring of SOE debts into equity holdings of banks and government. In 1996 three hundred Chinese firms were targeted to go global, becoming joint-stock companies with improved technological capabilities. The most likely candidates are firms that hold strong national brands. Some Chinese brands have moved into the international market on the back of competitive pricing, while Haier, one of China's leading home-appliance producers, has competed on product quality and efficient distribution and after-sales service. SOEs have improved management practices, acquired advanced technologies, entered joint ventures and strategic alliances, and commercialized research. To upgrade and modernize state-owned enterprises, China has reduced barriers to foreign venture with them.

TABLE 6

Leading Asian electronics firms

Rank 2000	Rank 1998	Company	Country
5	14	Taiwan Semiconductor	Taiwan
6	53	Samsung Electronics	South Korea
7	29	United Micro Electronics	Taiwan
26		Infosys Technologies	India
34		Hyundai Electronics	South Korea
39	79	Acer	Taiwan
42		Quanta Computer	Taiwan
50		Chartered Semiconductor	Singapore

SOURCE: Financial Times (2000)

In 1999 Telecom equipment maker Shenzhen Huawei Technology had $1 billion in revenue. The television firm Konka Electronics exported its own brand-name televisions into the U.S. market. China's leading personal computer (PC) vendors, Legend and Founder, dominated the domestic PC business. Legend has been China's leading domestic information-technology vendor, with production of 1.3 million units in 1999, a share of more than 20 percent. To become one of the world's top-ten PC makers in 2000, Legend increased capacity to 3 million units in 2000. In 1999 Legend surpassed Changhong, China's dominant television supplier, to rank as China's largest electronics firm in that year. Legend's goal was to reach $10 billion in sales (five times its 1998 sales level) by 2004, the twentieth anniversary of its founding.

Future Considerations

Asian countries continue to aggressively build a strong competitive base in electronics. China is now the country to beat because it provides the largest potential market in Asia and captures nearly 80 percent of foreign direct investment. It provides an attractive low-cost labor force supported by special incentives and infrastructures such as high-technology industrial parks. At the same time, China is building nationally successful corporations that are beginning to move into the global marketplace. This evolution has been supported by heavy foreign direct investments by leading global players. Taiwan, with its leadership in information technologies, is the top investor in China and will probably be the primary long-term funnel of advanced technologies. Hong Kong continues to struggle to find a competitive strategy, but still provides capital and logistics support to mainland China. As the remainder of Asia continues to recover from the Asian financial crisis, countries must also compete for investment with China—a battle that they have been losing.

William Boulton

Further Reading

AsiaSource. (2001) "Asia Profiles." Retrieved June 2001, from: http://www.asiasource.org/profiles/ap_mp_05.cfm.

Boulton, William R., and Michael J. Kelly. (1999) *Information Technologies in the Development Strategies of Asia.* Washington, DC: U.S. Department of Commerce.

ChinaOnline. (2001) "Hong Kong Sets Economic Record in 00." Retrieved February 2001, from: http://www.chinaonline.com/issues/econ_news/NewsArchive/cs-protected/2001/January/C01011911.asp.

Financial Times. (2000) "Global 500—Section One." Retrieved June 2001, from http://specials.ft.com/ln/specials/global5002a.htm.

Hall, Chris. (2000) "Shape Up or Ship Out." Retrieved June 2001, from: http://www.eb-asia.com/registrd/issues/0011/0011c-story.htm.

Industrial Technology Information Services. (2001) "2000 Taiwan Industrial Outlook—Hardware Industry." Retrieved June 2001, from: http://www.itis.org.tw/english/rep0007.html.

———. (2001) "2000 Taiwan Industrial Outlook—IC Industry." Retrieved June 2001, from: http://www.itis.org.tw/english/rep0002.html.

Isaka Satoshi. (1997) "Hong Kong Keeping 'Brain' Functions." *The Nikkei Weekly*, 23.

The People's Daily. (2001) "Suzhou Industrial Park Sees Fast Growth." Retrieved June 2001, from: http://english.peopledaily.com.en/200102/02/eng20010202_61477.html.

Taiwan Semiconductor Industry Association. (2000) *The Current Status in Taiwan IC Industry.* Taipei, Taiwan: Taiwan Semiconductor Industry Association.

TSMC Press. (2000) "Announce First Functional 0.13-Micron Processor Wafers." Retrieved June 2001, from: http://www.tsmc.com/press/20001212.html.

Wilson, Drew. (1999) "China's New Chip Roadmap." Retrieved June 2001, from: http://www.eb-asia.com/registrd/issues/9912/1299c-story.htm.

HIKAYAT AMIR HAMZA

The *Hikayat Amir Hamza* is a legendary prose story in the Malay language, based upon a Persian romance, which has Hamza, the paternal uncle of the Prophet Muhammad, as its main protagonist. The historical Hamza presented a highly suitable Muslim hero for tales of chivalry and courage. As the quest for fame, respect, and honor was a major preoccupation in Malay literature, the battlefield takes pride of place in this story. Its translation from Persian into Malay may well have taken place not much later than the fourteenth century because the story, in both its Persian and Malay forms, mentions firearms, which first became known in the Muslim world in the 1380s. The *Hikayat Amir Hamza* was certainly written before 1511 because it is mentioned in the so-called *Sejarah Melayu* (Malay Annals). The Malay version was adapted in Buginese, Macassarese, Balinese, and Javanese, whereas the Sundanese version seems to be based on the Javanese one. The Javanese work is generally known as the *Menak*, after a noble title given to the hero Amir Hamza. The adventures of Amir Hamza also form part of the repertoire of the Javanese and Sundanese rod-puppet theater (*wayang golek*).

Edwin Wieringa

Further Reading

Wieringa, Edwin. (1996) "Amir Hamzah, the All Too Human Hero." *Kajian Malaysia* 14, 1–2: 183–193.

HIKMET, NAZIM (1902–1963), Turkish poet, playwright, and novelist. Nazim Hikmet Ran is considered Turkey's foremost modern poet. A socialist whose humanistic views transcended national borders, he gained international acclaim for his writings. Nazim Hikmet was born in Thessaloniki, in today's Greece, then part of the Ottoman empire, into an upper-class family of bureaucrats. During the Turkish war of independence, he left the Turkish naval academy and worked in Anatolia as a teacher. He joined the Turkish Communist Party, which was founded in Ankara in 1920. The appeal of the Russian Revolution and its promise of social justice led him to Moscow, where he studied economics and political science. After returning to Turkey in 1926, he was soon arrested for his leftist activities. He escaped to Russia, where he stayed for two years; he returned to Turkey following the general amnesty of 1928. For the next ten years he was in and out of prison on a variety of political charges.

In 1938, Nazim Hikmet was arrested for inciting the Turkish armed forces to revolt through his writings and was sentenced to twenty-eight years in prison. While in prison, he published numerous novels and plays, as well as poems that revolutionized Turkish poetry, including his epic masterpiece, "Memleketimden Insan Manzaralari" (Human Landscapes from My Country.) In 1949, an international committee formed in Paris to agitate fo his release; it included Pablo Picasso and Jean-Paul Sartre. His name was finally included on the political amnesty list of the Democratic Party in 1950. Following his release, however, at the age of forty-nine, he was drafted for military service in Korea. Fearing for his life, he fled from Turkey for the second time. He spent the rest of his life as a political refugee in Poland, Bulgaria, and the Soviet Union. Stripped of his Turkish citizenship in 1959, he chose to become a citizen of Poland. He died of a heart attack in Moscow at the age of sixty-one.

Although Nazim Hikmet's works have been translated into more than fifty languages, none were published in Turkey between 1938 and 1965. The ban on his books was lifted only after his death. Since the late 1960s his poems, novels, and plays, as well as a vast number of biographical works about him, have been published in Turkey.

The main themes of his works were universalism, social justice, and compassion. He expressed a passionate love for his native country in his poetry. Although he used his writings in the service of his political beliefs, his brilliant use of Turkish lyrics in almost-musical compositions saved his verse from becoming a propaganda tool.

Ayla H. Kilic

Further Reading

Hikmet, Nazim. (1993) *Selected Poetry of Nazim Hikmet.* Trans. by Randy Blasing and Mutlu Konuk. Persea Series of Poetry in Translation. New York: Persea.

HILL TRIBES OF INDIA The term "hill tribe" was long and inexactly applied to the indigenous inhabitants of upland and mountain areas in South Asia. The hill tribes are and were culturally distinct groups, usually endogamous social units, bearing a tribal name and having a distinct material culture, including, very often, characteristic styles of housing and dress. Often the isolated hill tribes speak their own languages.

The term "hill tribe" is little used today by anthropologists, yet it is not disappearing altogether, because the concept is enshrined in some national legislation. In India the two broad social categories of disadvantaged people, known since independence as the Scheduled Tribes and the Scheduled Castes, have incorporated nearly all of those groups formerly known as hill tribes.

Hill tribes are characterized by great diversity of culture. While early census officials often designated them as "Animists," many in fact follow a variety of "universal" religions, including Islam, Hinduism, Buddhism, and Christianity. Most practice some form of agriculture, but there are groups like the Todas who are pastoralists, others like the Kotas who are craftsmen, and some groups who are itinerant peddlers, magicians, or entertainers.

Paul Hockings

Further Reading

Fuchs, Stephen. (1973) *The Aboriginal Tribes of India.* New York: St. Martin's.

Singh, K. S. (1994) *People of India: The Scheduled Tribes.* New York: Oxford University Press.

HIMACHAL PRADESH (2001 est. pop. 6.1 million). Crowned by the "snowy mountains" from which comes its name, Himachal Pradesh is a state in northwestern India originally constituted in 1948, after independence, as an administrative unit of thirty hill states. It grew to include the former states of Bilaspur, Kulu, Simla, Lahaul-Spiti, and Kangra before achieving full statehood in 1971. A region of scenic splendor, with an area of 55,673 square kilometers, it is surrounded by Jammu and Kashmir, Uttar Pradesh, Haryana, Punjab, and Tibet, enveloped by the Pir

Panjal and Dhauladhar ranges in the northwest, and dominated by the great Himalayas in the north and east. Five snow-fed rivers provide an estimated 20 percent of India's total hydroelectric potential.

The earliest inhabitants were tribal Dasas who came from the Gangetic plains in 3000 to 2000 BCE. Aryan speakers arrived around 2000 BCE; tribal republics called *janapadas* (territory of the clan) emerged. The Guptas held parts of the region during the second to fifth centuries CE; then came other rulers, including, as early as 550 CE, the Hindu Rajputs. Muslim rulers appeared at the close of the tenth century. By the eighteenth century under Maharaja Ranjit Singh, the Sikhs had gained considerable strength in the west, while the Gurkhas consolidated power in the south. The Gurkhas were succeeded by the British, who made Himachal's capital Simla the summer seat of the viceroy and thus the government headquarters.

Among other distinctions, Himachal proved ideal for growing apples, and modern apple-growers figure importantly in area politics. Each of the state's districts has its own architecture, from rock-cut shrines and *shikhara* temples (a Hindu temple with a spire or tower) to colonial mansions and Buddhist monasteries. Culturally heterogeneous, with 90 percent of the population living outside the main towns, Himachal's districts maintain distinct customs, agricultural methods, and dress. Each village has its own patron saint or god. Hinduism dominates, but there are many Sikhs, Muslims, and Christians, and Lahaul-Spiti, and Kinnaur has been home to Tibetan Buddhists since the tenth century. The approximately two hundred temples are dedicated mainly to Siva, Durga, and Buddha. The capital Simla, India's largest and most famous hill station, is a favorite destination for Indian families and honeymooners with its cool air, crisp light, and superb panoramas.

C. Roger Davis

Further Reading

Parry, Jonathan P. (1979) *Caste and Kinship in Kangra.* London: Routledge and Kegan Paul.

HIMALAYA RANGE The Himalaya Range is the world's highest mountain range, with the fourteen highest mountain peaks in the world; it spans over 2,400 kilometers. It is also one of the world's longest ranges. It runs from the Pamir Mountains in the west to the Indian state of Arunachal Pradesh in the east, in a series of mountain ridges that help designate the border and form a buffer between India and Nepal and also between Nepal and Tibet. The entire mountain system forms the southern boundary of the Tibetan Plateau and divides North and Central Asia from the South Asian subcontinent.

Among the best-known Himalayan peaks are Everest (Qomolangma Feng), the world's highest mountain (8,848 meters), on the border between Nepal and Tibet; and K2 (Qogir Feng), the second highest (8,611

A portion of the Himalaya Range as seen from Nepal. (DAVID SAMUEL ROBBINS/CORBIS)

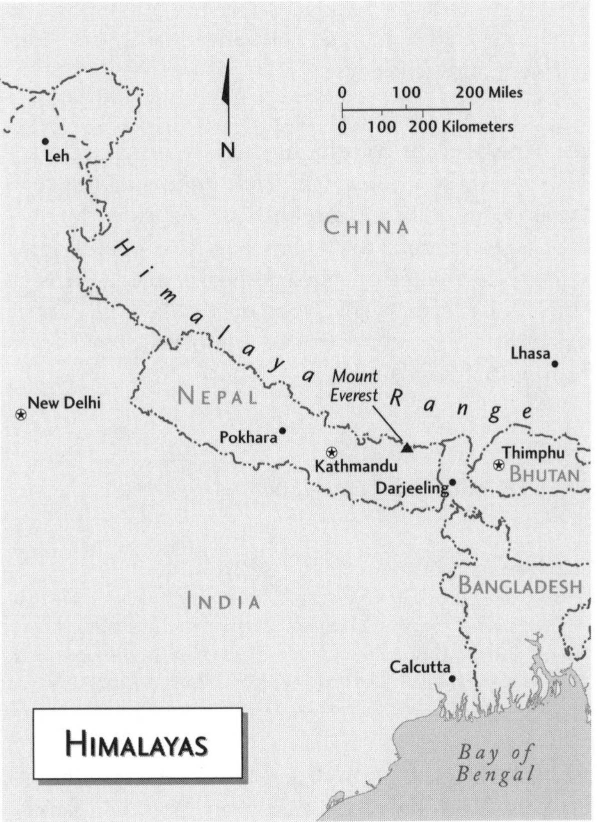

meters), on the border between Tibet and Kashmir. The third-highest mountain in the world is Kangchenjunga at 8,598 meters, on the border between Nepal and India; seventh-highest is Annapurna (8,091 meters) in Nepal. Not until the 1950s were these peaks successfully scaled.

The Himalayas are actually a series of parallel ranges running roughly northwest to southeast, the most important being the Great Himalayas, the Karakoram, the Zaskar, and the Ladakh Ranges. These were thrust upward by the abutment of the Indo-Australian tectonic plate against the Eurasian plate. All of these ranges are over 3,000 meters above sea level, and the highest series, the Great Himalayas, exceed 6,100 meters, with most of the highest mountains being in Nepal and the small Indian state of Sikkim. The Middle Himalayas range between 1,800 and 2,000 meters; to the south of them the low-lying Sub-Himalayas border India and Nepal.

THE FOUR SEASONS AND LIFE IN THE HIMALAYAS

"The Sherpa are one of the peoples of the Himalayas and perhaps the best known in the Western world because of their role as guides on mountaineering expeditions. Their life is governed by the four seasons which are symbolized by colors and marked by festivals.

"Four images of divinity corresponding to the four seasons of the years are generally found in the *gompas*. They have a special importance in the life of a Sherpa. *Ygri-gyemo* is the summer queen of azure colour; *gungi-gyemo* is the yellow winter queen; *tongy-gyemo* is the green coloured queen of autumn; and *chigi-gyemo* the red queen of spring.

"During the four seasons the Sherpa community is called upon to attend and participate in certain ceremonies to be performed at fixed times. The village or the temple is the place where such festivals and ceremonies take place. They take on special importance when the Lama clergy along with a number of representatives participate. They are of great value even from a choreographic point of view. Some festivals last only for a day, others six days. On such occasions the work in the villages comes to a halt and everybody goes to the festival. A responsible person of the village called Lawa is entrusted with the charge of organising such festivals. He collects funds, fixes duties and turns for assistants, regulates various phases of the festival and arranges for the distribution of good among spectators."

Source: Mario Fantin. (1974) *Sherpa Himalaya Nepal.* New Delhi: S. D. Chowdri for the English Book Store, 68.

NANDA DEVI—WORLD HERITAGE SITE

Nanda Devi National Park's rugged terrain, high altitude and remote location have kept this national park in northern India relatively intact. Designated a UNESCO World Heritage Site in 1988, Nanda Devi is home to several endangered species, including the snow leopard and Himalayan musk deer.

The climatic variation is enormous, ranging from below freezing temperatures in the north to a subtropical climate in the south. The range protects the Indian subcontinent from the cold weather of Central Asia and affects seasonal rainfall markedly.

The ancient name of the range was Himavat (Sanskrit for "abode of snow"; in Pali, Hemavata), and there are numerous descriptive references to it in the *Mahabharata*, an ancient Indian epic. The people who have lived in the Himalayas did not scale mountain peaks, which were considered sacred places where gods resided; but they did use the high slopes for grazing yaks, goats, and other cattle. This changed in the late twentieth century, when foreign visitors began to overrun the region, to climb the mountains or to visit Buddhist and Hindu sacred sites. Most famous are the expeditions to Everest, named for Sir George Everest, a surveyor-general of India (1830–1843). From the mid-twentieth century the Himalayas became a major tourist attraction, and nowadays as many as a million people may visit them yearly. So popular has mountain climbing become that wealthy amateurs join expeditions that attempt to reach the summit of Mount Everest; even a blind man succeeded in 2001. The difficult route to the top and the harsh weather conditions sometimes result in injuries or death, even to the experienced climbers who lead these expeditions.

Paul Hockings

Further Reading

Ortner, Sherry B. (1999) *Life and Death on Mt. Everest: Sherpas and Himalayan Mountaineering.* New Delhi: Oxford University Press.

Shirakawa, Yoshikazu, and Kyuya Fukuda (1986). *Himalayas.* New York: Harry Abrams.

HINA MATSURI Hina Matsuri (Doll Festival or Girls' Festival) is a Japanese celebration of girlhood held on the third of March. Girls display special dolls, hold parties for friends and relatives, and receive good wishes for health and happiness.

Baby girls are traditionally presented with a set of ceremonial *hina* dolls with which to celebrate the festival. A full set consists of fifteen dolls: the emperor and empress, three ladies-in-waiting, three guards, two ministers, and five musicians, all dressed in the elaborate court costumes of the Heian Period (794–1185). They are displayed on a tiered stand covered with bright red cloth, accompanied by miniature furniture and household goods. The imperial couple sits on the highest tier, before a golden folding screen with lanterns to either side. Decorations of peach blossom symbolize traditional ideal female qualities of contentment and gentleness.

Girls and their guests drink *shirozake*, a mild, sweet rice wine, and eat colorful diamond-shaped rice cakes *(hishi-mochi)* and other delicacies. Following the celebrations the dolls are carefully packed away, for it is considered unlucky to display them year-round. Hina Matsuri originated in ancient purification rituals in which dolls acted as charms against evil spirits. Today *hina* dolls are greatly treasured and often passed down from mother to daughter.

Lucy D. Moss

See also: **Children's Day—Japan**

Further Reading

Krasno, Rena. (2000) *Floating Lanterns and Golden Shrines: Celebrating Japanese Festivals.* Berkeley, CA: Pacific View.

Vilhar, Gorazad, and Charlotte Anderson. (1994) *Matsuri: World of Japanese Festivals.* Tokyo: Shufunotomo.

HINDI-URDU Hindi and Urdu belong to the Indic branch of the Indo-European language family. Thus they are closely related to other Indic languages spoken in India, Pakistan, Bangladesh, Nepal, and Sri Lanka (for example, Panjabi, Sindhi, Marathi, Gujarati, Bengali, Nepali, and Sinhala) and more distantly related to other Indo-European languages such as English or Russian. Both modern Hindi and Urdu developed from New Indo-Aryan vernaculars spoken in north India around the eleventh to fourteenth centuries CE. With the influx of Turkic- and Persian-speaking peoples in the Muslim courts and armies, first under the Delhi sultanate (1192–1526) and later under the Mughals, Persian and Turkic words began to enter the language. Urdu began to differentiate from the common spoken language of the area as the *Zabaan-e-Urdu-e-Mu'alla* (language of the royal camp), which developed in Delhi after the Mughal court shifted there from Agra in 1648. Modern Urdu was first referred to as "Urdu" by the poet Mashafi (1750–1824) toward the end of the eighteenth century. Since then, Urdu and Hindi have increasingly differentiated over time because of both natural linguistic change and conscious attempts to shape the languages, in particular by the use of quite different scripts. As the Mughal empire declined, an effort was made to exclude Sanskrit words from Urdu and to increasingly Persianize the language. Later, in the nineteenth century, as Hindi and Urdu came increasingly to be associated with religion, attempts were made to Sanskritize Hindi. Similar lan-

CREATING A NATIONAL LANGUAGE

In an effort to create national unity in the face of much cultural, religious, and linguistic diversity, the advocates of Indian independence recommended that Hindi be made the common language and that it be taught in all schools.

> The object of including *Hindustani* as a compulsory subject in the school curriculum is to ensure that all the children educated in these national schools may have a reasonable acquaintance with a common *lingua franca*. As adult citizens they should be able to cooperate with their fellow countrymen belonging to any part of the country. In teaching the language the teacher should in various ways quicken in the students the realization that this language is the most important product of the cultural contact of Hindus and Muslims in India. It is the repository—in its more advanced forms—of their best thoughts and aspirations. They should learn to take pride in its richness and vitality and should feel the desire to serve it devotedly.
>
> In *Hindustani*-speaking areas this language will be the mother-tongue, but the students as well as the teachers will be required to learn both the scripts, so that they may read books written in Urdu as well as in Hindi. In non-*Hindustani*-speaking areas, where the provincial language will be the mother-tongue, the study of *Hindustani* will be compulsory during the 5th and 6th years of school life, but the children will have the choice of learning either one or the other script. However, in the case of teachers who have to deal with children of both kinds, knowledge of both the scripts is desirable.
>
> *Source:* Jagdish S. Sharma, ed. (1965) *India's Struggle for Freedom: Select Documents and Sources.* Delhi: S. Chand, 113.

guage planning efforts continue in the twenty-first century, resulting in the present situation.

The Language Continuum

Hindi and Urdu can be considered as two ends of a language continuum in which the grammar is almost entirely shared, but differences in vocabulary and to a lesser degree in phonology develop in the more formal and literary registers of the languages. The Hindi end of the continuum incorporates many words newly added from Sanskrit, the Indic ancestor language of Hindi, whereas the Urdu end includes many Arabic and Persian words. The middle range of the continuum represents the common spoken language of North India and Pakistan, which is understood by speakers of any variety of these languages. In contrast, the language varieties at each end of the continuum are, to a significant extent, not mutually intelligible. This situation can be schematized as follows:

Urdu	"Hindustani"	(High) Hindi
Many exclusively Urdu words of Perso-Arabic origin	Common vocabulary	Many exclusively Hindi words; Sanskritic words

Phonology

Except where noted, the following description applies to both Hindi and Urdu. The consonant system includes the following contrastive oppositions: (1) voiced versus voiceless (pronounced with as opposed to without vibration of the vocal cords, as in the contrast between English /b/ and /p/); (2) aspirated (including an audible puff of breath immediately after the consonant sound) versus unaspirated (with minimal breath). This difference is like the difference in the /p/ sound in English "pin" (aspirated) and "spin" (unaspirated); (3) dental versus retroflex (position of the tongue touching the front teeth, or at a point farther back in the mouth). Hindi has these consonant phonemes: /k/, /kh/, /g/, /gh/, /c/, /ch/, /j/ /jh/, /T/, /Th/, /D/, /Dh/, /t/, /th/, /d/, /dh/, /p/, /ph/, /b/, /bh/, /m/, /n/, /y/, /r/, /R/, /Rh/, /l/, /w/, /s/, /š/, /h/. (Capital letters represent retroflexes.) Urdu has the additional consonants /q/, /γ/, /x/, /z/, and /f/. The vowel phonemes are /a/, /ā/, /i/, /ī/, /u/, /ū/, /o/, /e/, plus the diphthongs /ai/ and /au/. The vowels have nasalized counterparts.

Hindi is written in the Devanagari script (derived from Brahmi), whereas Urdu script (Nastaliq) derives from Arabic, with modifications introduced to represent Persian and then Urdu sounds not present in Arabic.

Morphology

The noun system distinguishes the grammatical categories of number (singular and plural) and gender (masculine and feminine). Some nouns bear a characteristic mark of grammatical gender, that is, *ā* for masculine nouns like *laRkā* (boy) and *ī* for feminines like *laRkī* (girl), whereas others are not so marked, like *mez* (table, feminine) and *dūdh* (milk, masculine). Similarly, some adjectives bear markers for gender that are the same as those for nouns, for example, *acchī laRkī* (good girl), *acchā laRkā* (good boy), and some do not, for example, *lāl mez* (red table).

Basic verb forms are constructed on the verb stem, the imperfective participle, with characteristic ending *-t-*@; or the perfective participle with characteristic ending -(*y*)@, where @ represents gender/number adjectival marking. Hindi is a "split-ergative" language, in which perfective tenses of transitive verbs agree with an unmarked direct object (rather than with the subject). The normal word order in a sentence is subject, object, verb.

Hindi Speakers

Hindi is the official language of the Union of India and of the following states: Bihar, Haryana, Himachal Pradesh, Madhya Pradesh, Rajasthan, Uttar Pradesh, Andaman and Nicobar Islands, Delhi, and Chandigarh. Because it is spoken over such a vast region, there is much dialectal variation within Hindi. Important varieties include Braj, Bhojpuri, Khari Boli, Awadhi, Bangaru, and Bundeli. It is difficult to give a precise number of Hindi speakers because of differences in the way languages are grouped in census reports and the language that people choose to report as their "mother tongue." But it appears clear that Hindi is spoken by over 180 million as a first language in India and another 2 million worldwide. Including second-language speakers, the total number of users is over 346 million in India and 418 million worldwide. Large numbers of Hindi speakers live in Bangladesh, the United States, Mauritius, South Africa, Yemen, Uganda, Singapore, Nepal, New Zealand, Germany, Kenya, Canada, the United Arab Emirates, and the United Kingdom.

Urdu Speakers

Urdu is the national language of Pakistan, where it is spoken as the first language by about 8 percent of the population (approximately 11 million speakers) and understood as a second language and used as a lingua franca by an increasing majority in all parts of the nation, whose total population is approximately 142.4 million. It is the main language of education and the information media. In India, where there are over 45 million Urdu speakers, it is one of the eighteen designated national languages and is the official language of Indian-held Jammu and Kashmir. A distinctive Dakhini variety of Urdu, which developed from the common language of Delhi carried to the Deccan in the fourteenth century, is spoken around Hyderabad, India. Significant numbers of Urdu speakers live in the United States, the United Kingdom, Canada, the Middle East, Norway, and Germany. The worldwide total of first-language Urdu speakers alone is over 58 million. Taken together, Hindi and Urdu rank fourth in the number of speakers worldwide, after Chinese, Spanish, and English.

Elena Bashir

Further Reading

Kellogg, Samuel H. ([1938] 1989) *A Grammar of the Hindi Language*. 3d ed. New Delhi: Asian Educational Services.

McGregor, Ronald Stuart. (1995) *Outline of Hindi Grammar*. 3d ed. Oxford: Oxford University Press.

Schackle, Christopher. (2000) "Urdu: Language and Literature." In *Encyclopaedia of Islam*. Leiden, Netherlands: Brill.

Schmidt, Ruth Laila. (1999) *Urdu: An Essential Grammar*. New York: Routledge/Summer Institute of Linguistics.

HINDU KUSH The Hindu Kush, a rugged mountain range in Central and West Asia, lies mostly in eastern Afghanistan. The range extends for a total distance of about 965 kilometers, from the plateau of the Pamirs on the east in eastern Tajikistan, along the borders of Jammu and Kashmir, and Pakistan, and west and southwest into Afghanistan as far as the Koh-i-Baba range west of Kabul. It forms a watershed between the Amu Dar'ya River tributaries on the north and the Kabul River on the south. The range is an extension of the Himalayan system, with its main expanse toward the southwest. Several peaks of the Hindu Kush exceed 7,000 meters, and one, Tirich Mir, rises to 7,690 meters.

The range is crossed by several important passes that were ancient trade routes, with the Baroghil Pass, at a height of 3,797 meters above sea level, being the most significant. The Amu Dar'ya, Helmand, Kabul, and Konar Rivers rise in the Hindu Kush.

The local warrior tribes inhabiting the region are collectively called Pathans (in Pakistan) or Pashtuns (in Afghanistan). The modern Salang Tunnel allows the Afghan capital, Kabul, to be linked to the northeastern part of the country and to Tajikistan through this mountain range. At the end of 2001, these mountains saw fierce fighting, including heavy bombing, when U.S., British, Afghan, and other forces were jointly breaking the power of the Taliban and al-Qaeda leadership.

Paul Hockings

Further Reading

Caroe, Olaf. (1958). *The Pathans, 550 B.C.–A.D. 1957.* London: St. Martin's.

Newby, Eric. (1958) *A Short Walk in the Hindu Kush.* London: Secker & Warburg.

HINDU LAW

HINDU LAW Hindu law has several denotations: (1) the whole body of ancient Indian law; (2) under British rule, only those aspects of Hindu civil law not covered by general laws; (3) Hindu law in independent India. In this last sense, it encompasses a series of laws that have radically reformed family law.

Ancient Hindu Law

The all-encompassing term for ancient Hindu law is dharma, which can refer to either a code of conduct or the cosmic law of the universe. The ancient *dharmasastras*, the Hindu law books, prescribe rules of conduct and penalties for misconduct; they also regulate all kinds of rituals, including expiations. The most comprehensive early book of this genre is the *Manusmriti*, which originated between the second century BCE and the second century CE. It was probably preceded by the *Arthasastra*, a treatise on politics and economics, attributed to the Hindu statesman and philosopher Kautilya (flourished 300 BCE). The *Arthasastra* contains a chapter on judges in which Kautilya distinguishes four sources of law: dharma, the traditional law; *vyavahara*, transactions, procedures, and court practice; *caritra*, local customary law; and *rajasana*, the king's edict. According to Kautilya, the order of these sources indicates a ranking, in which the king's edict occupies the highest position.

An Indian king was himself subject to dharma and was obliged to uphold it, but in litigation he was the final court of appeal, and his interpretation of dharma prevailed. The Brahmans who established the norms tried to provide the king with appropriate advice—which might also limit his discretionary powers. In establishing these norms, the Brahmans took care to define the institution of caste and to enshrine their own privileges in Hindu law.

The *Manusmriti* reflects this tendency. It is the subject of numerous commentaries, and with each one arguments were further refined and recommendations for verdicts in special cases increased. This tradition of jurisprudence culminated around 1100 CE with the *Mitakshara* of Vijnanesvara and the *Dayabhaga* of Jimutavahana. (The former originated in western India and the latter in Bengal.) The authors agreed on most legal issues, but fundamentally differed on the law of inheritance. According to the *Mitakshara*, a son is a coparcener (joint heir) in his father's estate from birth; according to the *Dayabagha*, he is not—a son can inherit and divide his father's property only after his father's death. This difference is essential. The *Mitakshara* severely restricts the rights of the father concerning disposal of his property: he must respect the rights of his coparceners. This protects the joint Hindu family as a legal institution.

Hindu Law under British Rule

The British gradually imported an enormous body of their own law—English common law—into India. Early on in their colonial rule, they showed great interest in Hindu law. Sir William Jones (1746–1794), the chief justice of the Supreme Court of Calcutta, requested that Jagannatha Tarkapanchanana, his Brahman associate, compile a code of Hindu law, which was then translated into English by Henry Thomas Colebrooke (1765–1837) and published in 1797. Colebrooke was an excellent Sanskritist and had also served as a judge. The code that he translated was the *Digest of Hindu Law*, known as Colebrooke's Digest, which became the most important reference manual for British courts in India when dealing with Hindu personal law.

By this kind of codification, however, the British reduced the flexibility of Hindu law, freezing it once and for all. There was no attempt to reform the law:

the main aim of the British was to do "justice" to their Hindu subjects and not disturb their "prejudices." In the process, Hindu law was more or less reduced to property relations within the family, everything else being a matter for British civil and criminal law.

Hindu Law in the Republic of India

A uniform civil code was initially sought in independent India, but the idea was dropped so as not to disturb Indian Muslims. Instead, the government concentrated on a reformed "Hindu code." Since this was opposed by orthodox Hindus, the first Indian president, Jawaharlal Nehru (1889–1964), opted for piecemeal reform enshrined in the following acts: the Hindu Marriage Act of 1995, the Hindu Succession Act of 1956, and the Hindu Adoption and Maintenance Act of 1956. Nehru regarded this reform as his major political achievement.

Departure from the old patriarchal order and emphasis on the rights of women were the main features of this reformed Hindu law. Earlier, Hindu men could have had several wives, but now only monogamy was recognized. As long as polygamy had been permitted, divorce was unnecessary; now even women were permitted to sue for divorce. Inheritance had earlier been restricted to men only; now women could also inherit, disrupting the old pattern of the joint Hindu family. The asking for and giving of dowry was also prohibited. The orthodox Hindus particularly resented this, and the practice survived in the form of "gifts."

The act regulating adoption was also seen as violating traditional Hindu custom, which had prescribed the adoption of a son by a man without male issue and permitted a widow without a son to do the same. There was, however, no adoption of daughters. The new act changed all this and permitted men and women to adopt both sons and daughters. Critics predicted that these acts would be repealed after the generation of reformers had passed away, but this did not happen. The new Hindu law had come to stay.

Dietmar Rothermund

Further Reading

Kane, Pandurang Vaman. (1930–1962) *History of Dharmasastra.* 5 vols. Poona, India: Bhandarkar Oriental Research Institute.

Sontheimer, Guenther Dietz. (1977) *The Joint Hindu Family as a Legal Institution.* New Delhi: Manohar.

HINDU NATIONALISM Since the end of the 1980s, Hindu nationalism has emerged as a major political force in India. Although it had played only a marginal role in Indian politics for many decades, the Hindu nationalist Bharatiya Janata Party (Indian People's Party, or BJP) succeeded in gaining more and more votes during the various national elections from 1989 on, ultimately forming the central government of India as leader of a multiparty coalition in 1998. For the first time in the history of modern India, Hindu nationalists had come to power at the national level. Parallel to the growing support for the BJP, the Congress Party lost its former ideological and political hegemony and now finds itself in the role of an opposition party. However, the Hindu nationalists' gradual accession to power was also marked by a high level of militancy, at its worst on 6 December 1992, when Hindu fanatics destroyed the Babri Mosque at Ayodhya and subsequent riots left more than one thousand people dead and many others injured.

History

The origins of Hindu nationalism can be traced back to the 1920s and even further to 1875, when the neo-Hindu organization Arya Samaj (Society of Aryans) was founded by Dayanand Saraswati. In 1915 the Hindu Mahasabha (Hindu General Assembly) came into being, followed in 1925 by the elitist Rashtriya Svayamsevak Sangh (National Volunteer Union, or RSS), which is still the organizational and ideological backbone of Hindu nationalism today. The Bharatiya Janata Party, the political party of Hindu nationalism, was created in 1951 under the name of Bharatiya Jan Sangh (Indian People's Union); it was renamed in 1980. Other important Hindu national organizations include the Vishva Hindu Parishad (All-Hindu Council, founded in 1964) and its youth wing, Bajrang Dal (Bajrangs's Troop, founded in 1984). Together they form the *sangh parivar* (Sanskrit term for RSS family) and play different roles in a common strategy to create a Hindu India. Most BJP leaders are also members of the RSS.

Ideology

The Hindu national organizations all share a common ideology of cultural nationalism—the ideology of *Hindutva*, Hindu-ness. This ideology was expounded first by V. D. Savarkar (1883–1966) and later in a more radical form by M. S. Golwalkar, both Brahmans from Maharashtra. In his booklet *Hindutva*, published in 1923, Savarkar defined what makes an Indian a Hindu and what joins Indians together in a Hindu nation mainly in terms of opposition to others, that is, Muslims and Christians. According to Savarkar, a Hindu is a person who regards India as his or her *pitrabhu* (homeland, land of his or her forefathers) as well as *punyabhu* (holy land). With this definition, Muslims and other minorities are seen as foreign to the Indian nation. Their loyalties are divided, and they do not look on India as their holy land.

In this ideology India is the land of the Hindus; the Indian nation is a Hindu nation. To be an Indian means to be a Hindu, and *Hindutva* is the national identity of India. The inner unity of the Hindus is firmly anchored in this Hindu-ness, which rests on a common homeland *(rashtra)*, a common ancestry *(jati)*, and a common culture *(sanskriti)*, which have existed since time immemorial. In its election manifesto of 1998, the BJP openly referred to the three essentials of *Hindutva* when formulating the slogan: "One nation, one people, and one culture." This exclusiveness leads to the Hinduization of the nation and the nationalization of Hinduism.

This idea of the common territorial, genealogical, and cultural basis of the Hindu nation is central to Hindu national ideology and politics. It first evolved in response to the colonial challenge and is rooted in fears of inferiority, weakness, and domination by others. Hindus, the Hindu nationalists say, are in danger of becoming a minority in their own country, Hindustan, Land of the Hindus.

Hindu nationalists see this deplorable situation as arising from a lack of unity among Hindus. The solution is for Hindus to stand together and to defend themselves against the West and the Muslims. They must resurrect the glorious Hindu past with its timeless cultural heritage, to overcome the misery of the present.

The *sangh parivar*, the RSS family, tries to organize people along ethnic-cultural lines. Since the 1980s, well-orchestrated campaigns have been launched to strengthen Hindu unity and to integrate Hindus into a defensible community against the threatening "others." The overarching goal of the *sangh parivar* is to make India a strong and prosperous Hindu nation where all live in harmony and peace as they do in a large Hindu extended family. Therefore Hindu nationalism rejects the idea of a hierarchical caste system and, in particular, untouchability.

The most prominent of these campaigns was aimed at the "liberation of Rama's birthplace." (The god-king Rama, hero of the epic *Ramayana*, is seen as a perfect incarnation of a righteous Hindu ruler ready to defend a posited Hindu nation.) In December 1992, the campaign led to the demolition of the Babri Mosque in Ayodhya, regarded as the epitome of Muslim conquest and intolerance. This mosque, it is alleged, had been erected in 1528 by the first Mughal ruler, Babur, on the ruins of a great Rama temple marking the birthplace of the beloved god-king. This attack on a religious monument was justified as an act of Hindu self-assertion against Muslim aggressiveness. Only by the reconstruction of a magnificent new Rama temple on this very site would the "liberation" be consummated.

Support from the Middle Classes

The rise of the BJP to the center stage of Indian politics can be attributed to political, socioeconomic, and cultural factors. The self-induced decline of the Congress Party created a political vacuum that gave the BJP the chance to present itself as a disciplined body of principled, selfless politicians and to successfully position itself as a second major national party in India. The mounting political assertiveness of minority groups such as the Sikhs and the Muslims, together with the growth of separatist movements in the Punjab, the northeastern states, and Kashmir, has also contributed to the success of the BJP. The conversion of untouchables to Islam stirred up fears of a Muslim conspiracy supported by the oil-rich Arab countries. The BJP has always criticized the Congress Party for its "pseudosecularism," which conceded special rights and privileges to the minorities at the expense of the Hindu majority.

However, more important factors are the socioeconomic changes resulting from the ongoing modernization process and leading to new constellations in the social fabric of Indian society. The middle classes in particular have been becoming more assertive. Traditional roles and values are eroding and need to be redefined. The new material success has to be legitimized. The growing economic competition in a liberalizing and globalizing economy makes these people fear other competitors and the possibility of becoming a loser. This new situation must be reflected in a meaningful set of explanations offering a firm anchor in a quickly changing, unpredictable social environment.

In the face of this challenge, Hindu nationalism today can be interpreted as an attempt to redefine modernity by reconciling modernity and tradition. Economic progress and material success are embedded in a traditional interpretation of the glorious Hindu culture that must be resurrected. Economic competition is balanced by the idea of a harmonious society of equals where trust, solidarity, and mutual respect prevail. In theory, all people, including the minorities, would be equals in a true Hindu nation.

The *Hindutva* ideology obviously addresses the anxieties and aspirations of Indians who belong mainly to the upward-moving middle classes. Surveys have shown that the majority of the BJP voters are young, male Hindus of high-caste origin, having a good educational background, living in cities, and enjoying a relatively high standard of living. During the recent elections, however, the BJP has also broken new ground among lower castes.

Future Prospects

In its propagation of a strong Hindu nation founded on a uniform Hindu culture, Hindu nationalism is a political attempt at building a national identity based on a highly questionable and selective interpretation of Indian tradition, with a strong Brahmanical bias. It uses religious symbols and beliefs for political ends. The concept of *Hindutva* as the basis of a Hindu cultural nation contradicts the very nature of the Hindu tradition, with its extreme heterogeneity in almost every respect. Moreover this heterogeneity, on the level of the individual, often goes hand in hand with multiple, overlapping identities that change according to context and go beyond a politicized Hindu-Muslim antagonism.

To be successful, the politics of *Hindutva* would need to homogenize a cultural tradition that has evolved over more than three millennia. Furthermore, the *Hindutva* ideology rests on a foreign concept of cultural or ethnic nationalism imported from the West during colonial times, which makes the "Hindu-ness" of *Hindutva* fictitious. The social reality in present-day India, with its extreme hierarchy and social cleavages, openly contradicts the idea of equality and solidarity among all Hindus.

To broaden its electoral base, the BJP has refrained from a radical pro-Hindu, anti-Muslim policy since 1993, so that it seems more liberal. Since then, intraparty differences have surfaced also because of the issue of a strict *svadeshi* (national economic policy). It is doubtful that the RSS and other hard-liners will support this policy of "soft" Hindu nationalism in the long term. The question remains whether the Hindu nationalists can provide convincing answers to the manifold problems India faces at the beginning of the third millennium.

Clemens Jürgenmeyer

Further Reading

Ghosh, Partha S. (2000) *BSP and the Evolution of Hindu Nationalism: From Periphery to Centre.* New Delhi: Manohar.

Gold, Daniel. (1991) "Organized Hinduisms: From Vedic Truth to Hindu Nation." In *Fundamentalisms Observed: The Fundamentalism Project*, Vol. 1, edited by Martin E. Marty and R. Scott Appleby. Chicago and London: University of Chicago Press, 531–593.

Golwalkar, Madhav Sadashiv. (1947) *We, or Our Nationhood Defined.* Nagpur, India: Bharat Prakashan.

Hansen, Thomas Blom. (1999) *The Saffron Wave: Democracy and Hindu Nationalism in Modern India.* Princeton, NJ: Princeton University Press.

Jaffrelot, Christophe. (1996) *The Hindu Nationalist Movement and Indian Politics, 1925 to the 1990s: Strategies of Identity-Building, Implementation, and Mobilisation.* London: Hurst.

Nandy, Ashis, Shikha Trivedy, Shail Mayaram, and Achyut Yagnik. (1995) *Creating a Nationality: The Ramjanmabhumi Movement and Fear of the Self.* Delhi: Oxford University Press.

Savarkar, Vinayak Damodar. ([1923] 1989) *Hindutva: Who Is a Hindu?* Reprint ed. Mumbai (Bombay), India: S. S. Savarkar.

HINDU PHILOSOPHY

HINDU PHILOSOPHY Hindu philosophy is a collective title for the vast number of doctrines and beliefs that evolved in the Indian subcontinent (called *Bharatvarsha* or *Bharatakhanda* in Sanskrit texts) from ancient times to the present. In the first millennium BCE, the Persians used the term "Hindu" for the lands around the Indus River; with the Greeks the word became "India." This initially geographic term was first applied to the religious and philosophical doctrines of India by Arab and Turkish historians in the second millennium CE. In the eighteenth century, European scholars restricted the term "Hinduism" to the beliefs and philosophies following the Vedas (the earliest Hindu sacred writings), thus separating Hinduism from the Buddhist, Jain, and Sikh sects, despite the overlapping of these systems with Vedic beliefs.

The Vedic Foundation

The Rig Veda is the oldest text of religious and cosmic vision in India. Scholars date it anywhere from 1500 to 4000 BCE. Along with the other three Vedas, the Sama, Yajur, and Atharva, it is the only record of the beliefs that existed well before the epic age of the *Ramayana* and the *Mahabharata* (beginning of the first millennium BCE). The Vedas indicate that major deities like Indra, Varuna, Mitra, Prajapati, Sarasvati, Usha, Rudra, Savita, Agni, and many others were worshiped with offerings made through sacrificial fire *(yajna).* These gods were not given iconic form but were prayed to and placated only through various *yajnas*. The Greeks and Iranians also shared this mode of worship through fire.

The Vedic religion did not have a single prophetic founder; the Vedas are a collection of inspired verses

THE SPIRITUAL LIFE OF THE ELDERLY

Across much of Asia, the aged were usually venerated and treated with much respect. Depending on the religious tradition, the elderly were also expected to devote much time to spiritual matters, as with Hindus in India. This particular extract pertains to Tamil Indians in South India in the 1950s.

> As his sons grow into the age of *grahasta* or married adulthood, an old man is customarily expected to retire gradually from the world, to curb his enjoyment of living, and to turn his thoughts still further towards spiritual life. This is ideally the period of *sannyasa* or meditation and chastity in old age. To undertake it fully, a man should surrender his home and property to his sons and wander forth as a stranger begging food and engaging in meditation. As a less extreme course, he may go with his wife to occupy a small hut outside the village, and lead a life of prayer, simplicity, and chastity. One Brahman of the next village had done this. He conducted daily fire-offering to the Vedic gods, and tried by silent meditation to attain union of his soul with the divine soul which he believed to be immanent in all creation but to be personified as Siva. He received young disciples on weekends and instructed them to memorize Sanskrit prayers, to meditate, to perform yogic exercises, to fast periodically, and to gain control over earthly desires. One old man in Kumbapettai lived quietly apart from his family in a separate small house on the street, returning home only for meals. Four others performed regular meditation, prayers and offerings to Siva in their homes, and claimed to live in chastity.

Source: Elizabeth K. Gough. (1956) "Brahman Kinship in a Tamil Village." *American Anthropologist* 58: 838.

or mantras, revealed to seers called *rishis*. The texts have been preserved by oral transmission, a practice that survives even now. Whether written versions of the Vedic text were used to aid this transmission before the tenth century CE is still unknown.

The Vedas postulate that the gods who grant devotees' desires are themselves governed by the cosmic and just principle of truth called *Rit*, which is also called Brahma because it is the universal reality. Other beliefs are explicitly stated or implied in the Vedic hymns. These include beliefs in the existance of the individual soul after death; in the accumulation of merit and demerit in the soul (the theory of karma); the existence of upper and lower worlds (*lokas*); the return of the soul to this world (rebirth); the existence of a world of ancestors; merit in rituals, and moral conduct; purity as a power of soul, mind, body, and environment; word or speech as a psychic force; and obligations or debts to gods, ancestors, teachers, and guests.

No archeological evidence of Vedic civilization has yet been unearthed. The earliest excavated remains are those of the Harappan civilization (ending around 2000 BCE). There is a debate over whether the Harappan culture preceded, succeeded, or equaled the Vedic. Harappan beliefs are virtually unknown, although some motifs in Harappan art recur later.

The ritual aspects of the poetic mantras of the four Vedas were elaborated in later texts called the Brahmanas and Aranyakas. The philosophic kernel was elaborated in the Upanishads, which hold that the ultimate reality is Brahma, manifested as this and other worlds. Brahma can be perceived through inner contemplative knowledge, a practice bringing immortality. Despite intense metaphysical speculation, life was not considered a vale of tears, and subsidiary texts on medicine, archery, grammar, drama, and music (Upavedas, or subsidiary Vedas) were composed to uphold its fullness. The later texts of the classical period stated that a complete life must have four aims *(purusharthas)*: dharma (right action), *artha* (wealth), *kama* (satiation of desire), and *moksa* (enlightenment). The epic and mythic texts called *Itihasa* and Purana connect these values to daily living through the lives of heroes.

Vedic literature also indicates that some faiths neither followed the practice of sacrifice nor revered the pantheon of the Vedic gods. Some sects' members were phallic worshipers; in others, wandering saints preached beliefs scarcely recorded. As they all rejected the authority of Vedic ritual and mantras, they were collectively called *Nastikas* and are supposedly the precursors of the later Jain, Charvaka, Shakta, Tantric, and Buddhist sects.

The Advent of Temple Worship

In the middle centuries of the first millennium BCE, the worship of deities conceived as idols emerged. Major deities, transformations of the earlier Vedic gods, were Brahma the creator (not to be confused with Brahma, the ultimate ground of reality, mentioned earlier), Vishnu the preserver, and Siva the destroyer. The mother goddess of the Harappan age became Shakti, who later developed into different forms such as Uma, Bhavani, or Annapurna the benign, or Kali, Karali, or Chamundi the destroyer. By the third century BCE, temples to Vasudev, Surya the sun god, Kamadeva or Eros, Saraswati, and many other deities proliferated. The elaborate temple rituals, supported by dance and music, which characterize Hinduism to this day, were established as a distinctive feature.

Rules of moral and social conduct were formalized in codes called the *smritis*, of which those of Manu and Yajnavalkya are most prominent. The earlier but looser division of society into four major-castes *(varnas)* was now more rigorously imposed. These four castes—Brahmans (intellectuals), Kshatriyas (rulers), Vaishyas (merchants and farmers), and Sudras (servers)—supplemented by other mixed categories, were primarily an economic order of Hindu society, not part of its crucial religious or philosophic tenets, as is often presumed by non-Indians.

The Six Systems of Philosophy

The story of formal philosophy in India is best told in reference to the *shatdarshanas*, or the six schools. Buddhists, Vaishnavas, Pashupatas, Jain, Charavak, Tantra, Shaktas, and Saivas all developed distinct systems by using the precepts of the *shatdarshanas*.

Nyaya Founded by Gautama, this system defined knowledge as dependent on *pramatri* (subject), *prameya* (object), *pramiti* (cognition), and *pramana* (means of knowledge). The last depends on five things: *pratyaksha* (intuition), *indriya* (senses), *panchamatra* (five elements), *manasa* (mind), and *gyan* (perception).

Vaisheshik Founded by Kanada, this system relied on the text called Vaisheshikasutra, which Kanada composed. The system dwells on the particularity *(visheshatva)* of things. All objects of experience *(padarthas)* fall into six categories of substance: quality, activity, generality, particularity, inherence, nonexistence. The first three are known intuitively; the last three are known by intellectual discrimination. The system propounds nine *tatvas* (primary substances): *prithvi* (earth), *jal* (water), *agni* (fire), *vayu* (wind), *akash* (ether), *kala* (time), *desh* (space), *atma* (self), and *manas* (mind). The system posits a belief in the particularity of everything, including the self. Things are said to be made of *anu* (atoms), which are incapable of further division.

Samkhya In this system, the categories of the cosmos were reduced to basic forces called *purusha* and *prakriti*. There is a constant evolutionary change based on these two principles, and all experience is based on this duality. *Purusha* is the knowing subject, and *prakriti* is objective existence both physical and psychological. The latter is the source of the world of becoming and consists of three qualities that when unbalanced cause evolution. Yoga brings release from ego and leads to salvation. The system was founded by Kapila (flourished 550 BCE), who composed the Sankhyapravachana Sutra. The other basic text is the Sankhya Karika, by Ishwarakrishna (third century CE).

Yoga Yoga is the practical methodology for realization and salvation founded by Patanjali (second century BCE) and given a commentary by Vyasa (fourth century CE). Vachasapati Mishra wrote the Tatvavisharada in the ninth century CE. Yoga relies on Samkhya for its philosophy but accepts Ishwara or God or Brahma as the ultimate reality. The method of achieving *moksha* (liberation) has eight parts: *yama* (precepts), *niyama* (routine), *asana* (postures), *pranayama* (breath control), *pratyahara* (withdrawal), *dharana* (fixation), *dhyana* (meditation), and *samadhi* (highest consciousness). The great masters of all sects and denominations in India have used Yoga in different ways.

Purva Mimamsa This philosophy investigated the definitions of dharma in the Vedas, which are defined as having no maker *(Apaurusheya)*. Mimamsa dwells on the subject of sound and meaning and the ethical code of the Vedic mantras. It accepts the idea of the self and future life. It propounds the idea that all action is done for the sake of fulfilling desires and all *yajna*s for the sake of achieving enjoyment in heaven, or *Svarga-mukti*. In later stages of Mimamsa, around the seventh century CE, the philosopher Prabhakara described liberation as cessation of dharma and nondharma; Kumarila (flourished 730 CE) called it freedom from pain. The system was founded around the third century BCE by Jaimini, the writer of the Mimamsa Sutra, who believed in the existence of various gods but not one supreme god. Kumarila, who wrote the Shlokavartika, argued for the necessity of the supreme god.

Vedanta Founded by Badarayana around the fifth century BCE, this system focused on the Upanishadic teachings about Brahma as opposed to the value of sacrifice *(Karmakanda)* as propagated by Purva Mimamsa. Its basic text is the Vedanta Sutra, also called the Brahma Sutra or Sharirika Sutra. The system was not popular until the seventh century, when Shankaracharya revived it. He postulated that Brahma (the ultimate) and *Jiva* or *Atma* (individual soul) are not two but one. He repudiated the subjectivism of the Buddhist sect of Yogacaras by asserting that the world changes but is not a mental fiction and is also not nonexistent *(Abhava* or *Sunya)*. Brahma appears as *sansara* (the world) through maya (ignorance), just as a rope may appear to be a snake when it is dark. *Vidya* (understanding) through practice of Yoga brings *Moksa*, or freedom from rebirth.

The Non-Vedic Systems

Most other sects followed modified versions of tenets of the Vedic tradition. Except for the materialists, they all accepted karma theory, the existence of the soul, the essentialness of liberation, rebirth, and the moral code of Yama and Niyama.

Charavakas (Lokayatas, Jabalikas) This system of materialist philosophy is referred to only in later schools. It was probably enshrined in the Brihaspati Sutra of the sixth century BCE. It opposed ancestor worship and the concept of life after death. Perception is purely sensory and consciousness a product of chemical reactions. There is no soul or god, and salvation is an illusion. Nature is the only reality, indifferent to good and bad, which are mere social conventions.

Jainism Vardhamana Mahavira (599–527 BCE) consolidated the teachings of twenty-four previous teachers in the Jain tradition. The aim of life is to attain *kaivalya* (the state of ultimate realization of selfhood) by right knowledge, faith, and action. The most distinctive feature of action is total nonviolence, or ahimsa, as living and nonliving objects have souls.

Buddhism Consolidated by Siddhartha Gautama (563–483 BCE), the aim of Buddhism is to attain nirvana (extinction or release). There are four noble truths: (1) the world is sorrow; (2) sorrow is born of desire; (3) freedom from sorrow is attained by freedom from desire; and (4) one ends desire by the eightfold path: right views, right words, right action, right living, right effort, right thinking, right resolution, and right concentration.

The Bhakti Movement

The worship of Vishnu or Vasudeva, which began around the fifth century BCE, acquired great momentum around the seventh century CE with the so-called philosophy of personal and individual *bhakti* (devotion). This sect had two broad divisions: those who worshiped God as an incarnation with human and divine attributes (Saguna) and those who contemplated him as the formless (Nirguna) source of creation, preservation, and destruction. For the former, the life deeds of incarnations like Krishna or Rama were a divine play or a *lila* that must be sung for liberation. The poetry of the saints of this sect was filled with expressions of submission to the divine, chosen as the most desirable form *(ishta)* by the devotee *(bhakta)*. Singing the attributes *(gunakirtana)* of the lord was the chief mode of worship, whether done individually in isolation or in a community of the faithful. For the latter, the formless god (Nirankar) was contemplated by calling or singing only his name, which led to a state of yogic awareness *(samadhi)*. Ramanuja, Ramananda, Kabir, Raidas, Nanak, and a host of others produced poetry that inspired the Nirguna tradition, one of the many sects of the Bhakti movement and philosophy.

Hindu Philosophy in Perspective

Hindu philosophy has adjusted well to a contemporary pluralistic world. Its major doctrines were not contradicted by modern theories of science, humanism, equality, or democracy. Modern exponents of Hinduism such as Ramakrishna, Vivekananda, Dayananda Saraswati, Sri Aurobindo, and Gandhi demonstrated that its ancient beliefs could deliver practical results in the contemporary world. The Hindus and the people of India in general have always believed that there is an underlying ultimate reality behind all beliefs and philosophical systems. This philosophic conviction is reflected nowhere better than in the benedictory verse of the play *Mahanatakam* by the eleventh-century poet Hanuman.

> The One who is worshiped as Siva by the *Saivas*, as Brahma by *Vedantis*, as Buddha by *Buddhas*, as *Karta* by *Naiyayikas* the logicians, as *Arhat* by the *Jainas*, and Karma *(yajna)* by *Mimansakas*; such a Vishnu, the lord of three worlds, may fulfill your desires.

Bharat Gupt

Further Reading

Asvaghosa. (1995) *Buddhacarita.* Trans. by E. H. Johnston. Delhi: Munshiram Manoharlal.

Bhagvadgita. (1997) Trans. by Swami Satyananda Saraswati Vitthalananda Saraswati. Delhi: Motilal Banarsidas.

Dasgupta, S. N. (1988) *A History of Indian Philosophy.* Delhi: Motilal Banarsidas.

Gangrade, K. D., and N. Radhakrishnan, eds. (1998) *Gandhi and the Changing Facets of India.* Delhi: Gandhi Smriti and Darshan Smriti.

Jain, Surender K., ed. (1997) *Glimpses of Jainism.* Delhi: Motilal Banarsidas.

Kinsley, David. (1998) *Tantric Visions of the Divine Feminine: The Ten Mahavidyas.* Delhi: Motilal Banarsidas.

Lokeshchandra. (1998) *Cultural Horizons of India: Studies in Tantra and Buddhist Art and Archeology, Language, and Literature.* Delhi: Aditya Prakashan.

Mahabharata. (1996) Trans. by P. Lal. Calcutta, India: Writers Workshop.

Matilal Bimal, Krishna. (1997) *Logic, Language, and Reality: Indian Philosophy and Contemporary Issues.* Delhi: Motilal Banarsidas.

Rizvi, S. A. A. (1997) *A History of Sufism in India.* Delhi: Munshiram Manoharlal.

Upanishads: English Selections. (1996) Trans. by Eknath Easwaran. Delhi: Penguin.

Warder, A. K. (1998) *A Course in Indian Philosophy.* Delhi: Motilal Banarsidas.

HINDU VALUES

India is home to more religious systems than any other Asian country, implying that it has a more varied range of ethical principles or cultural values than any other part of the continent. Hinduism itself embraces a multiplicity of beliefs, practices, and peoples that emphatically do not fall under the umbrella of one church, one pope, one liturgical system, or one hierarchy of priests or monks.

The word "Hinduism" and even the concept are English, deriving from the Persian Hindu or the Sanskrit Sindhu, names for the Indus River. Indian languages do not have a word that corresponds with *Hinduism*, only such words as dharma (social duty) and karma (fate). Cultural values are pervasive yet difficult to pin down, at the same time a part of behavior, a part of culture, and a part of social structure (Hockings, 1988: 39–46). Moreover they are commonly specified in both sacred texts and secular proverbs.

Ethical obedience is the pathway to salvation. Life should be governed by the discharge of accumulated duties or debts. These debts are diffuse: to the gods, to the seers and sages who discovered truth, to ancestors, and to humanity at large. Debts to the gods can be discharged through sacrifice and *puja* (offering and veneration); to the ancestors by raising good, virtuous children; and to society by acts of hospitality and charity.

Hindu values fall broadly into five categories: moral values (dharma), politico-economic values or concern with worldly affairs *(artha)*, hedonistic values and amorous desires *(kama)*, spiritual values and deliverance *(moksa)*, and absolute reality (brahman). Although categorized thus, values in actual use create a more complex picture altogether. This is readily evident from the corpuses of proverbs, each of which embodies a value: Sebastiao Dalgado (1898) arranged 223 subject headings to present 2,177 Konkani proverbs; Herman Jensen (1897) employed 352 subject headings to present 3,644 Tamil proverbs; and Paul Hockings (1988) used 393 subject headings to analyze some 1,600 Badaga proverbs and 130 other clichés. The Hindu Badagas, for example, have specific cultural values relating to such topics as respect, wealth, exertion, waste, matricide, forgiveness, subjection, and impotence. But just as the complexity of a society based on many hundreds of castes was simplified in ancient times into a model of five *varnas*, or ranked-caste categories, so too the ancient philosophers simplified the multiplicity of values expressed in proverbs and prayers into the neatly comprehensible idea of the fivefold ends of human life outlined above under the headings of dharma, *artha*, *kama*, *moksa*, and brahman.

The Hindu individual is constrained by his or her position in a caste-organized society. The caste into which he or she was born and where he or she will always remain belongs to one of four ranked *varnas* unless that individual is of the very low "untouchable" or tribal status. In that case he or she falls outside this system. The Brahmans are the highest of the four *varnas*, Brahman males traditionally function as priests, teachers, and literati. It is essential that such men and women live in accordance with their dharma and maintain their high level of purity. Kshatriyas are the second-ranking *varna*; Kshatriya males include rulers and warriors. Their duty is essentially concerned with *artha*, the material interests. Next are the Vaisyas who should pursue *kama*, the hedonistic values. These three categories are considered "twice-born" because of their male initiation ceremonies. Sudras, ranked fourth and lowest, are not twice-born. Above the four *varnas* are the few renouncers who abandon the material world for the pursuit of *moksa*, which means deliverance from the cycle of rebirths (samsara). Release from rebirth is the highest apiration.

Paul Hockings

Further Reading

Bishop, Donald H., ed. (1975) *Indian Thought: An Introduction*. New York: Wiley.

Dalgado, Sebastiao Rodolfo. (1898) *Florilégio de Provérbios Concanis Traduizidos, Explicados, Comentados e Comparadoscom os de Linguas Asiaticas e Europeias* (Collection of Konkani Proberbs, Translated, Explained, Commented on, and Compared with Those of Asian and European Languages). Coimbra, Portugal: Imprensa da Universidade.

Fürer-Haimendorf, Christoph von. (1967) *Morals and Merit: A Study of Values and Social Controls in South Asian Societies*. London: Weidenfeld and Nicolson.

Gupta, Shanti Nath. (1978) *The Indian Concept of Values*. Columbia, MO.: South Asia Books.

Hockings, Paul. (1988) *Counsel from the Ancients: A Study of Badaga Proverbs, Prayers, Omens, and Curses*. New York: Mouton de Gruyter.

Jensen, Herman. (1897) *A Classified Collection of Tamil Proverbs with Translations, Explanations, and Indices*. London: Kegan Paul.

Perrett, Roy W. (1998) *Hindu Ethics: A Philosophical Study*. Honolulu, HI: University of Hawaii Press.

Sharma, I. C. (1965) *Ethical Philosophies of India*. Edited and revised by Stanley M. Daugert. Lincoln, NE: Johnsen.

HINDUISM—INDIA

Hinduism, possibly the oldest surviving religion in the world, began well over three thousand years ago in India. A product of a variety of peoples and cultures, it evolved out of the varying faiths in different regions, assimilating all the diverse cultural practices of India. Its original followers knew the faith as *Sanathana Dharma*, or "a way of life"; it was Europeans, who first encountered it being practiced on the banks of the Indus River, who called it "Hinduism," after the Persian name for the river, Sindhu.

Beliefs

Though Hinduism is quite complex and practiced in a variety of ways, it is based on simple tenets, which include a belief in one supreme being who is without forms or attributes; a belief that God accepts everyone's prayer directed towards every form they worship; the espousal of nonviolence *(ahimsa)*; vegetarian

Figures on the frieze of a modern Hindu temple in a small village north of Mysore, India, in 1982. (SHELDAN COLLINS/CORBIS)

MAHABALIPURAM—WORLD HERITAGE SITE

Designated as a UNESCO World Heritage Site in 1984, this group of sanctuaries around Mahabalipuram was hewn into rock off the Coromandel coast in India by Pallava kings in the seventh and eighth centuries CE. The wide variety of temples and statues include the famous open-air relief known as the "Descent to the Ganges," sun chariot ratha temples, and even sanctuaries built into caves.

food habits (where possible); compassion to all lives; divine duty (dharma); activity without attachment (karma yoga); and devotion and surrender to God (bhakti). Hindus also believe in the indestructability of the soul, a cycle of rebirth, and the ultimate liberation of the soul, or *moksa*.

One widespread misperception of Hinduism is that it is a polytheistic religion with pagan rituals. The reality of Hinduism is that there exists *Nirguna Brahman*, or "god without attributes," which we are unable to comprehend. Thus, God appears to us veiled in a *maya* (illusion), as *Saguna Brahman*, or "god with attributes," so that we can relate to it. As a prism of light can be broken down into colors for us to see, Brahman (the ultimate goal of all being) assumes many forms to enable people to understand it. The main three forms of Brahman (also seen spelled Brahma) are Brahma, the creator; Vishnu, the preserver; and Siva, the destroyer. Hindus may worship one form exclusively, as Vaishnavas do for Vishnu, or Saivas do for Siva, or still others do for many, even thousands, of other forms. What is most important is that people from all walks of life and all intellectual levels can worship God; thus, Hinduism espouses tolerance and the freedom to worship God in any form. This tenet of the faith is the foundation for its acceptance of other religions. Whatever form one worships, one is worshiping Brahman.

Hindus understand that in order for a being to live, it must take other lives for nourishment. However, life is put into a hierarchy of sensory perception, with humans having the most sensory perception. To Hindus, the more sensory organs a being has, the more pain it will suffer in the process of being killed. Hinduism does not have specific rules about what to eat and not to eat, but it has the goal of causing the least amount of pain possible when deciding what to consume. Thus, it is believed to be more advisable to kill a plant than to kill an animal for food.

The ultimate goal of a Hindu is to be freed from the cycle of rebirth by *moksa*, or liberation of the soul. Hindus believe the soul is eternal, with no beginning or end. With the ending of each life, the soul leaves a body and enters another, and manifests itself within that body. One's good actions through duty (dharma), and actions having consequences (karma), determine the form of one's next life. If the good done by an individual greatly exceeds any wrongdoing, then the soul may ultimately be liberated from the cycle of rebirth and become one with God.

Development

Hinduism's evolution over time is now denoted by reference to periods that correspond with significant events in Indian history. The earliest period of Indian history is called the Vedic age, dating from roughly 1500 BCE or even earlier, to about 500 BCE. The Vedic age is subdivided by Indian historians into the ages of the Manthras, the Brahmanas, and the Upanishads, all Vedic texts. The second period, during the Maurya empire, from about 324 BCE to 200 BCE, is the age of Vedanga and the Kalpa Sutras. Then, from 200 BCE until 300 CE, around the time of the Gupta empire, is the age of the epics, primarily the *Mahabharata* and the *Ramayana*. The period from 300 CE to 650 CE is the age of the Puranas, Agamas, and Dharsanas, and the period ending around 1000 CE is the age of the later Puranas. The *bhakti* devotional movements started at this time and continued until the eighteenth century. The last four centuries saw the decline and then the renaissance of Hindu religious practice under the Moghul and British rules.

In the twentieth century, Hinduism has been a powerful unifying force in India. In the 1990s it emerged as a political force and was set forth by some political parties as the major unifying and distinctive element of Indian culture.

Paul Hockings

Further Reading

Chaudhuri, Nirad C. (1996) *Hinduism: A Religion to Live By.* Delhi: Oxford University Press.

Stutley, Margaeret, and James Stutley. (1977) *Harper's Dictionary of Hinduism: Its Mythology, Folklore, Philosophy, Literature, and History.* San Francisco: Harper & Row.

Zaehner, R. C. (1972) *Hinduism.* London: Oxford University Press.

HINDUISM—THAILAND In the Buddhist Thai kingdom, the Hindus constitute about one-tenth

Although Buddhism is the major religion across Thailand, Hindu elements are also often present. Here, cleansing water is thrown over a young man in traditional dress at the Thai Buddhist New Year's festival in 1995. (KEVIN R. MORRIS/CORBIS)

of the population. However, various aspects of Hinduism are deeply entrenched in Thai society. Although it sometimes is difficult to distinguish the Hindu elements in Thai culture, Hinduism has survived in Thailand through the concepts of royalty, festivals, music, architecture, the pantheon of Hindu deities, language, and literature.

The Hindu *dharmasastras* (religious scriptures), the concept of kingship, and brahmanical rituals have become essential features of state formation, and rulers have legitimized their position with the help of *brahmans* (priests, *phrams* in Thai). These priests perform various rituals connected with royalty. In the *rajyabhiseka* ceremony (consecration), they invoke the blessings of Hindu deities and present royal regalia to the king, and Thai ceremonies adhere to the tenets of the Satapatha Brahmana and Aitreya Brahmana. The steed of the Hindu God Vishnu Garuda is the royal symbol of Thailand.

The influence of Hinduism is also ingrained in popular Thai culture. Icons of Hindu gods and goddesses have been discovered in ancient excavations, and sculptures of such icons as Parvati, Hanumana, Ganesha, Vishnu, Indra, and Brahma adorn wats (temples) in Thailand. Images of Ganesha, the patron of Thai arts, are sometimes installed in newly constructed buildings. Hindu deities are worshipped along with Buddha and *phis* (spirits). Even to the present, the Thai congregate at the Erawan shrine in Bangkok to invoke Brahma.

The *Ramayana* tradition is important in Thailand. In the process of adoption, the stories of *Ramayana* have been transformed into a Thai version known as the *Ramakien*. Performing arts forms like classical dance, masked plays, theater shows, and shadow plays have continuously used the themes of this classic. The Thai features in these works are so predominant that only the origin of the *Ramakien* remains as a nonindigenous element. An admixture of Hindu and Buddhist elements exists in the popular festivals like *Loh Chingecha* (swing ceremony), *Loi Krathong* (festival of lights), *Baruna Satra* (rain festival), and *Songkran* (astrological New Year). The *brahmans* also have a role in such family ceremonies as births, deaths, purifications, and weddings. The similarities of Thai beliefs in the existence of the other world with such Hindu concepts as *savan* (paradise) and *narok* (hell) and with the Hindu names for deities (*devata*), worship *(pussa)*, and God *(isuan)* point toward the cultural interaction between Thailand and India. Thai society has shown a tremendous capacity to harmonize Hindu elements and yet retain its distinct identity.

Patit Paban Mishra

Further Reading

Chu, Valentin. (1968) *Thailand Today.* New York: Thomas W. Crowell.

Coedes, George. (1968) *The Indianized States of Southeast Asia.* Honolulu, HI: East-West Center Press.

Dawee Daweewarn. (1982) *Brahmanism in South-East Asia.* New Delhi: Sterling.

Desai, Santosh N. (1994) *Hinduism in Thai Life.* Mumbai, India: Popular Prakashan.

Promsak Jermsawatdi. (1979) *Thai Art with Indian Influences.* New Delhi: Abhinav.

HIR RANJHA STORY The story of Hir and Ranjha is an important part of Punjabi cultural life. A seminal part of the region's vibrant oral tradition from at least the sixteenth century, the story is also prominent in the Punjab's print culture from the mid-nineteenth century onward. Composed in many languages, among them Arabic, Hindi, Persian, Rajasthani, Sindhi, and Urdu, and famous beyond the geographical boundaries of the Punjab, the Hir Ranjha story is considered the region's premier epic romance.

The story concerns Dhido, known throughout the tale by his clan name Ranjha, the favored son of a landowner in the village of Takht Hazara (Punjab, Pakistan). Upon his father's death, Ranjha is cheated of his inheritance by his brothers and leaves home in search of a renowned beauty, Hir, a member of the prominent Sial clan and the daughter of an important landowner in the area of Jhang (Punjab, Pakistan). Upon his arrival in Jhang, Ranjha and Hir fall in love. Hir's family objects to the relationship because of Ranjha's perceived inferior social status and insists that she marry Seido of the Khera clan, a match that her family considers more suitable. Hir is forced to marry Seido, and, depending on the rendition, Hir and Ranjha are either reunited at the end of the story or die for their love. The story has three primary interpretations: as a temporal love story, as an allegorical tale about divine love (primarily in the Sufi tradition), and as an allegory for stories of Hindu divinities.

That the story was well known in the Punjab as early as the sixteenth century is shown by its inclusion in the compositions of the Sufi poet Shah Hussein (c. 1539–1599) and the Sikh writer Bhai Gurdas Bhalla (c. 1551–1633). Although the first known full-length rendition of the Hir Ranjha story is a Persian composition by Baki Kolabi, dated about 1575, the first rendition of the entire tale in Punjabi is by Damodar, completed about 1605. After Damodar, Ahmad Gujjar composed a version in 1682, Shah Jehan Muqbal in 1746–1747, and Waris Shah in 1766–1767. Although Waris Shah's is the most acclaimed rendition of the story, it has been composed by innumerable poets in both oral and printed forms, each poet giving the story his or her own flavor. Through the early twentieth century the story was always composed in verse (in various genres). Since then the Hir Ranjha story has been adapted to other genres, such as drama and prose, while at the same time continuing to be an important idiom for poetic and cultural expression.

Farina Mir

Hiratsuka Raicho (fifth from the right) with other members of the New Woman's Association at a meeting to discuss gaining the right to vote for Japanese women. (UNDERWOOD & UNDERWOOD/CORBIS)

Further Reading

Sekhon, Sant Singh. (1996) *A History of Panjabi Literature.* Vol. 2. Patiala, India: Punjabi University.

Shah, Waris. (1966) *The Adventures of Hir and Ranjha.* Edited by Mumtaz Hasan; trans. by Charles Frederick Usborne. Karachi, Pakistan: Lion Art Press.

———. (1978) *The Love of Hir and Ranjha.* Trans. by Sant Singh Sekhon. Ludhiana, India: Punjab Agricultural College.

HIRATSUKA RAICHO (1886–1971), Japanese writer and women's rights activist. Born Hiratsuka Haruko, the daughter of a privileged Tokyo family, Hiratsuka graduated from Japan Woman's College in 1906. The college rescinded the diploma in 1908, however, when her relationship with married writer Morita Sohei (1881–1949) became a public scandal. Her notoriety helped launch her writing career in 1911, when Hiratsuka adopted the penname Raicho and, with others, founded the all-women's journal *Seito* (Bluestockings, 1911–1916). Fearless and unconventional, *Seito* gave voice to the desires of the "new woman."

A Zen practitioner, Raicho used *Seito* to urge women to rediscover their creativity, to seek meaningful education and work, and to expand beyond the roles for women extolled by the state. Her most famous essay, the *Seito* manifesto "In the Beginning, Woman Was the Sun," imagines a primordial female courage that paradoxically transcends gender. Raicho brought this boldness into her own life, bearing two children out of wedlock with artist Okumura Hiroshi (1891–1964), who became her lifelong partner and whom she married in 1941.

In 1920 Raicho helped found the Shin Fujin Kyokai (New Woman's Association), which worked to expand women's rights to participate in political organizations and agitated for women's suffrage. From the early postwar years through the 1960s, Raicho was a leading figure in both the domestic and international women's movements for peace.

Jan Bardsley

Further Reading

Bardsley, Jan. (forthcoming) *The Bluestockings of Japan: Feminist Fiction and Essays from Seito, 1911–1916.* Ann Arbor, MI: Center for Japanese Studies.

HIROHITO (1901–1989), Japanese emperor. On 29 April 1901, Michinomiya Hirohito was born as the first son of Japanese Crown Prince Yoshihito (later Emperor Taisho) and Princess Sadako (later Empress Teimei). The lineage of the Japanese emperor system is traced back 2,600 years and is linked with Japanese legend and mythology. Japanese history and legend defined the emperor as a descendant of the sun goddess Amaterasu.

A formal portrait of Emperor Hirohito in 1982. (BETTMANN/CORBIS)

In 1908, Hirohito entered Gakusyuin Elementary School in Tokyo and continued his special training to be emperor. In 1912, after the death of Hirohito's grandfather, Emperor Meiji, Hirohito became crown prince. In the spring of 1921, Crown Prince Hirohito went to Europe for six months, learning of freedom and modernity in European societies through his travels and studies.

Crown Prince Hirohito's reign started in November 1921 because his father, Emperor Taisho, was unable to rule due to illness. In 1924, Crown Prince Hirohito married Princess Nagako, and together they had two sons and five daughters. On 25 December 1926, with Emperor Taisho's death, Crown Prince Hirohito officially took the 124th Chrysanthemum Throne when he was twenty-five years old. Following tradition, Hirohito's ascendance to the throne began a new period, Showa (Illustrious Peace).

Soon after the Showa period started, Japan embarked on militarism, entering a dark period of total war. In 1931, Japan invaded China after the Manchurian Incident, which led to the Sino-Japanese War from 1937 to 1945. In December 1941, Japan entered World War II in the Pacific with the attack on Pearl Harbor. In this period, Emperor Hirohito had supreme authority as the constitutional monarch, in which position he served as the symbol of national unity for the Japanese people and military.

On 15 August 1945, Japan accepted the Potsdam Declaration that ended World War II, after the United States dropped nuclear bombs on Hiroshima and Nagasaki. Under Allied occupation from 1945 to 1952, the emperor was treated as the means of achieving democracy. On 1 January 1946, Emperor Hirohito renounced his divinity under the new constitution (effective in May 1947); the role of the emperor was redefined from "a living god" to "the symbol of the state and of the unity of people." Following this, Emperor Hirohito devoted himself to Japan's postwar recovery by visiting prefectures, making personal appearances in public, and interacting with the Japanese people.

On 7 January 1989, Emperor Hirohito died in the Imperial Palace in Tokyo. This ended the Showa period, a period that saw brutal militarism, the invasion of Asia, World War II, Allied occupation, Japan's recovery from war and poverty, and Japan's economic miracles. Japanese people in the Showa period witnessed a rapid transformation from a military nation to a democratic nation in which Emperor Hirohito took a symbolic role through a dark and prosperous period of Japanese history. The role and image of Hirohito changed over the period due to Japan's political aims and conditions. He was an absolute monarchy and "a living god" to the Japanese before and during the war, and he became a symbol of Japan after the war and was deemed a good man to lead Japan to a modern and democratic society. The emperor system *(tennou-sei)* is deeply integrated into Japanese history, society, and people. Hirohito's birthday is still a Japanese national holiday and is translated as "Green Day."

Hitomi Maeda

Further Reading

Bix, Herbert P. (2000) *Hirohito and the Making of Modern Japan.* New York: HarperCollins.

Irokawa, Daikichi. (1995) *The Age of Hirohito: In Search of Modern Japan.* Trans. by Mikiso Hane and John K. Urda. New York: Free Press.

Large, Stephen S. (1992) *Emperor Hirohito and Showa Japan: A Political Biography.* King's Lynn, U.K.: Biddles.

HIROSHIMA (2002 est. pop. of prefecture 2.9 million). The city of Hiroshima (2002 estimated popula-

The devastation in Hiroshima after the atomic bombing of 6 August 1945. (BETTMANN/CORBIS)

tion 1.1 million) is the capital of Hiroshima Prefecture, situated on Japan's island of Honshu. Today a city dedicated to peace, it was the first to be devastated by an atomic bomb. Now one of the nation's most modern urban areas, the rebuilt Hiroshima is the leading industrial center of the western Honshu region.

Hiroshima grew during the Edo period (1600/1603–1868) as a castle town around a fortress completed in 1593 by the great warrior and Japanese feudal lord Mori Terumoto. After the 1868 Meiji Restoration, the city became an important military, industrial, and transport center. In an attempt to bring World War II to an end, the atomic blast of 6 August 1945 leveled Hiroshima, eventually killing some 200,000 people. Today Hiroshima is a center for world peace. Near the blast epicenter are the Atomic Bomb Memorial Dome, Peace Memorial Park, a museum, and a cenotaph memorializing the victims. There also is a smaller town of Hiroshima outside Sapporo on Hokkaido island; it was settled in 1884 by emigrants from Hiroshima Prefecture.

Hiroshima Prefecture occupies an area of 8,467 square kilometers. Its geography features the Chugoku Mountains, southern highlands, and coastal plains. It is bordered by the Inland Sea and by Shimane, Tottori, Okayama, and Yamaguchi prefectures. Once divided into Aki and Bingo Provinces, it assumed its present name and borders in 1876. In the late twelfth century, the ruling Taira family first developed the region as a commercial and trade center for Inland Sea shipping.

Today rice, citrus fruits, cattle, chrysanthemums, and rushes for tatami mats are produced. The traditional activities of forestry, fishing, and sake brewing continue as well, as do food processing and textile weaving. Heavy industries include steel, petrochemicals, shipbuilding, and automobiles. Visitors are drawn to the island of Miyajima's Itsukushima Shrine, officially one of Japan's three most beautiful views.

E. L. S. Weber

Further Reading

Hersey, John. (1985). *Hiroshima.* New York: Knopf.

Selden, Kyoko, and Mark Selden, eds. (1997). *The Atomic Bomb: Voices from Hiroshima and Nagasaki.* New York: M. E. Sharpe.

HITTITES The Hittite empire dominated the central plateau of Anatolia (the Asian portion of modern-day Turkey) from about 1800 BCE to 1200 BCE, and survived until about 700 BCE as a series of smaller kingdoms based in southern Turkey and northern Syria. During its period of dominance, it was surrounded in the north by Kaska tribes, in the east by the Mitanni, and in the west by several related tribes of which little is known; on the extreme western seaboard were newly founded Mycenaean colonies.

Remains of the Hitite presence are found at the Royal Gate of Hattusa in Bogazkoy, Turkey. (GIANNI DAGLI ORTI/CORBIS)

History

The Hittites seem to have migrated into Anatolia from the Caucasus in around 2000 BCE, and achieved ascendancy over the eastern Anatolian Hurri population. By the eighteenth century BCE their king, Anitta, had conquered neighboring tribes and established a capital at Kussana, in Cappadocia. A century later they had moved the capital to Hattusa, an easily defended citadel 150 kilometers east of what is now Ankara, commanding trade routes from the Black Sea to the Cilician Gates and from the Aegean to Central Asia. Labarnas I (reigned 1680–1650 BCE) and his successors campaigned as far afield as northern Syria; in 1595 BCE Mursilis I captured Babylon from the Hammurabic dynasty, but he was murdered by a pretender to the Hittite throne.

After fifty years of dynastic chaos, the frontiers were consolidated and from the fifteenth century BCE a new dynasty used diplomacy instead of force to dominate client kingdoms. From 1450 BCE, under kings of mixed Hurrian-Hittite lineage, the kingdom again absorbed Aleppo in Syria and Arzawa in southwest Turkey. The kingdom reached its maximum extent under Suppiluliumas I (1380–1340 BCE). The widow of King Tutankhamen of Egypt was so impressed by the deeds of Suppiluliumas I that she asked for his son's hand in marriage.

HATTUSHA—WORLD HERITAGE SITE

Hattusha was designated a World Heritage Site by UNESCO in 1986 because of its historical significance as the former capital of the Hittite empire and its remarkable preservation. Hattusha's ornamented Lion's Gate and the rock art of Yazilikaya still evoke images of the Hittite empire four thousand years after their construction.

In about 1300 BCE the Hittites again encountered the Egyptians, in a battle at Kadesh (Syria), which is described in the poem of the Egyptian poet Pentaus. Maneuvering over hilly ground, the Hittite king, Muwatalli, successfully launched his three-man war chariots crewed by archers at the Egyptian forces, but as the Hittites stopped to plunder, Ramses II counterattacked. The resulting stalemate was formalized in a treaty that is described both on the temple walls at Karnak in Egypt and on cuneiform tablets found at Bogazkoy. To cement the alliance, Ramses married a Hittite princess.

The aggressive Assyrians in the east and the influx of Phrygians from the Balkans led to severe pressure on the Hittite kingdom. In unexplained circumstances the capital, Hattusas, was burned in 1200 BCE. The scattered and defeated Hittites moved southeast under pressure from the Phyrgians and other "sea peoples" and established new kingdoms south of the Anti-Taurus mountains, based on fortified capital cities discovered at Carchemish (Kargamis), near Gaziantep, and Karatepe, north of Adana. These minor kingdoms, which were far less disciplined and centralized than their predecessor, were eventually overrun by the Assyrians in about 700 BCE.

Discovery and Research

The Hittite civilization was discovered from hieroglyphic inscriptions identified and catalogued by Archibald Henry Sayce (1845–1933), an expert in Sumerian and Assyrian. In 1880 he postulated that an extensive civilization, the Hittites, previously only known from the Old Testament, had existed in the wide area between northern Syria and the mid-Aegean Turkish coast, with its capital at Bogazkoy. Hugo Winckler (1863–1913), an archeologist affiliated with the German Oriental Society, obtained the concession to excavate Bogazkoy, and in 1906, within a few days of starting work, he unearthed, in the foundations of a major temple, a library of 10,000 tablets bearing cuneiform, not hieroglyphic, inscriptions. Excavations ceased during World War I, but Bedrich (or Friedrich) Hrozny (1879–1952), professor of Assyriology at the University of Vienna, and others continued to work on decipherment of the cuneiform script. In 1915 Hrozny declared that cuneiform Hittite was an Indo-European language. Based on Sumerian and Akkadian insertions into Hittite texts, scholars were able to postulate a vocabulary, which was more or less complete by 1933. From the tablets, an outline of history complete with rulers was established, although minor controversy over dates remained. The tablets also illuminate the social and legal systems; the ones describing religious ceremonies have proved more difficult to interpret. Much later, in 1947, a bilingual tablet discovered at Karatepe proved to be in Phoenician and the hieroglyphic script. The pictographs were identified as Hittite of a slightly different form to the cuneiform language; probably cuneiform Hittite was the commercial and hieroglyphic Hittite the ceremonial language.

Government

The inscriptions revealed the Hittites as a nationalistic, feudal people with a strong code of justice outlined in over two hundred laws. The priest king was supported by the *panka*, an advisory council (later dissolved); a bureaucratic class; and an underclass of slaves. Councils of elders administered distant areas. The king's duties included serving as both military leader and high priest; his campaigns were sometimes curtailed by the need to attend religious ceremonies. Women appear to have had extensive rights; the queens entered into diplomatic correspondence with foreign rulers, many priestesses are known, and rape was one of the few capital offenses under the law. Equitable laws, mainly based on restitution for wrongs by payment in money or kind, reveal an organized agricultural society whose main crops were barley, wheat, and wine-producing grapes. The wealth of the nation lay in the gold, silver (which provided a currency), and iron, which were probably traded extensively.

Religion

The Hittite religion was based on the Hurri weather god Teshub, who rode a chariot pulled by sacred bulls, and his sun-goddess wife Hebat, referred to as "Queen of the land of Hatti, queen of heaven and earth." The city of Hattusas held many major temples, cleverly constructed so that light from huge windows fell on the sacred statue; an unidentified holy city of Arinna is also mentioned in texts. In the countryside, huge reliefs and inscriptions appear both within and outside Hittite boundaries, often near water sources. The best known religious site, Yazilikaya, 3 kilometers east of Bogazkoy, consists of two adjacent clefts in a hillside, where lines of gods and kings have been carved into the cliffs; a cult building on level ground outside provided a center of worship. This site dates from the reign of King Tudhaliyas IV (reigned 1250–1220 BCE), just before the abandonment of Bogazkoy. The Hittites augmented their pantheon with their neighbors' gods and goddesses; up to a thousand of them were worshipped in local or national festivals with blood sacrifices, or invoked in curses and prayers.

Artifacts

The Hittite culture is represented in the Museum of Anatolian Civilizations in Ankara by many bold reliefs on basalt and limestone blocks and by statues in the round. The motifs are animals (lions, sphinxes, and bulls), the royal family, and the gods. Human figures wear conical hats or helmets, kilts, and boots with turned up toes and are armed; they are usually shown in profile. The Kultepe/Assyrian type of pottery features elegant burnished monochrome pots with long spouts. The museum also houses numerous cuneiform tablets in pottery, silver, and bronze. Hittite writings describe statues made of iron, but it seems that these have not survived. The Turks, supported by the cultural ministry, ascribe great importance to Hittite civilization and in recent years the quest for objects linking the Hittites to sites all over Turkey has become something of a holy grail for Turkish archaeologists.

Kate Clow

Further Reading

Gurney, O. R. (1952) *The Hittites*. Harmondsworth, U.K.: Penguin.

Seton, Lloyd. (1989) *Ancient Turkey: A Traveller's History*. London: British Museum Publications.

———. (1956) *Early Anatolia*. Harmondsworth, U.K.: Penguin.

HIZBULLAH Hizbullah (Arabic: "army of Allah"), an Islamic militia, was founded in December 1944 by Japanese occupation authorities in Java to assist in the island's defense against an expected Allied invasion. It was formally an organ of the Japanese-sponsored central Islamic council, Masjumi or Madjelis Sjuro Muslimin Indonesia (Consultative Council of Indonesian Muslims), and probably numbered about five hundred at the war's end (despite official mention of 400,000 recruits). Its units received only a little Japanese training, but provided a core for many irregular Islamic units that fought the Dutch during Java's nationalist revolution (1945–1949). The Hizbullah high command under Zainal Arifin (1909–1963) remained affiliated with the Masjumi, which had become an Islamic political party in Java, but central authorities had little control over units in the field. In 1947, the Hizbullah and other irregular forces were formally merged with the Army of the Indonesian Republic (Tentara Republik Indonesia, or TRI) to form the Indonesian National Army (Tentara Nasional Indonesia, or TNI), but most units retained their autonomy. The Hizbullah was especially strong in southern West Java and refused to leave their bases when the leaders of the Indonesian Republic formally relinquished West Java to the Dutch in late 1948. Some units became the basis of the armed forces of the Darul Islam rebellion, which first fought the Dutch and then the Republic in West Java from 1948 to 1963 with the aim of establishing an Indonesian Islamic state.

Robert Cribb

Further Reading

Benda, Harry J. (1958) *The Crescent and the Rising Sun: Indonesian Islam under the Japanese Occupation, 1942–1945*. The Hague, Netherlands, and Bandung, Indonesia: W. Van Hoeve.

Van Dijk, C. (1981) *Rebellion under the Banner of Islam: The Darul Islam in Indonesia*. The Hague, Netherlands: Martinus Nijhoff.

HMONG Over the past two centuries, the Hmong people have migrated from the southwestern provinces of China into the foothills of northern Laos and Vietnam, parts of Myanmar (Burma), and Thailand. In China, they form approximately one-third of the minority population officially classified as Miao (a name considered distasteful to Hmong outside China), which numbers over 8 million. The Hmong in China live in remote villages scattered through the provinces of Yunnan, Sichuan, Guizhou, and Guangxi. While at times the Hmong, who are thought to have originated in eastern China, have been able to establish permanent settlements and to practice irrigated agriculture, typically they have been shifting cultivators of upland crops such as dry rice, buckwheat, millet, and maize. As pioneer shifting cultivators, they have migrated great distances from the previous locations of their villages.

History and Economic Development

Rebellious southern people called the Miao, recorded in Chinese annals as having been banished from the central plains around 2500 BCE at the founding of the Chinese state, have existed throughout Chinese history. Although the term was very generally applied to numerous southern populations by the Chinese, ancestors of the Hmong were probably included in many of these references to the Miao. With the great expansion of the Han Chinese people into southern China from the time of the Song dynasty (960–1279 CE) on, increasing pressures were placed on scarce resources of land and water, and the Hmong, together with other minority populations, were further marginalized and forced to the higher altitudes where only shifting cultivation could be practiced. Today, the greatest area of Hmong concentration in China is Wenshan autonomous district on the Vietnam border, although Bijie, in northwest Guizhou, is another area of dense Hmong settlement.

As the Hmong began to migrate into northern Indochina (now the northern parts of Vietnam and Laos) from around 1850, they found themselves inhabiting new nation-states whose borders were eventually formed under the impact of the French colonization of Indochina and the British colonization of Myanmar (then Burma). Colonial encouragement and taxation of opium production created economic improvements that helped solve the chronic shortages of staple foodstuffs and indebtedness to itinerant Chinese traders, which the Hmong had previously suffered. An integrated upland economy developed in the region, based on the cultivation of dry rice in rotation with maize and opium poppy, together with the animal husbandry of swine and poultry, some fishing, hunting of wild animals, and gathering of wild products in the forest. Opium was sold to traders in return for rice.

Hmong involvement in what soon became the global opium trade and their familiarity with remote terrains on the borders with neighboring countries brought them into strategic focus during the struggles between Communists and rightist forces that marked the Indochina wars from 1954 to 1976. Hmong mercenaries fought on both sides and suffered enormous casualties during this period.

Shortly after 1975, over 100,000 Hmong who had fled the Communist victory in Laos were resettled in third countries such as the United States, Canada, French Guyana, Argentina, Surinam, France, Australia, and New Zealand after transiting in refugee camps along the Thai border with Laos. There reportedly are now approximately 1.2 million Hmong living outside China, with some 194,000 overseas and slightly over a million still in Southeast Asia.

Culture and Social Organization

There are two main cultural divisions among the Hmong of Southeast Asia and overseas, which are marked by strong distinctions of dialect, women's costume, domestic architecture, and ritual. These divisions are the Green and the White Hmong (*Hmoob Ntsuab* and *Hmoob Dawb*). Traditionally, Green and White Hmong had difficulties understanding each other, settled in different villages, and rarely intermarried. These distinctions remain strong today, although more intermarriage and co-residence exist than in the past. Other cultural divisions of the Hmong exist in China, such as the Hmong Pua and Hmong Xauv, and still others can be found in Southeast Asia.

All Hmong share a common language and kinship system, with twenty surname groups (*lub xeem*), which reckon descent patrilineally and have names resembling Chinese surnames. At marriage, a woman is expected to leave the household of her natal family and move to that of her husband. While free courtship is customary, the wedding is elaborately celebrated and can be a protracted business, including ceremonial presentations and wedding songs sung by go-betweens representing both parties to the marriage. At marriage, a man is expected to present to his wife's family an expensive bride-price that is traditionally paid in silver and that is said to compensate the bride's parents for their trouble in bringing her up. It may take years to amass a sufficient bride-price to marry, and a young man is often dependent on his father for this. This payment acts as a sanction against divorce, since a wife's family may be reluctant to return this payment unless it can be shown that the wife has given serious grounds for divorce. Strict monogamy is expected of a wife after marriage; a man however may take two or more wives, although this is rare.

In the village, typically located at altitudes of 900–1,500 meters, the local descent group of an exogamous patrilineage—perhaps four or five closely related families—is the main functional social unit. There are no hereditary positions of leadership, and families have considerable autonomy in deciding, for example, where to cultivate fields or whether to move from the village to a new area of cultivation. All adults are farmers, while particular adults may also specialize as blacksmiths or silversmiths, wedding go-betweens, funeral specialists, herbalists, or shamans. The most respected position is that of the shaman (*txiv neeb*). Shamans are consulted in cases of illness, mental stress, or social disturbance.

The Hmong of China and Thailand have now largely abandoned opium production. Many Hmong villages in China have managed to plant small areas of irrigated rice in a way similar to local Chinese villages. In Thailand, however, the Hmong have turned to other cash crops to replace the lucrative opium poppy, and this has led to tensions with lowland Thai, who accuse them of poisoning lowland water sources through the use of chemical fertilizers and pesticides needed for these new cash crops.

The Hmong culture and social system are rich and complex. The elaborations of the wedding ceremony and the beauty of the women's intricate batik and embroidery, the festivities of the Hmong New Year *(noj peb tsaug)*, the shaking of the shaman as she enters the Otherworld to rescue the lost soul of a sick person, and the long mournful chants of the Master of Death as he guides the soul of the deceased back to the village of his or her ancestors at the dawn of historical time are unique and identifying characteristics of Hmong culture.

The Hmong share with the Chinese a system of geomancy *(saib loojmem)* for the siting of villages and graves in which human residences are aligned with the natural contours of rivers and mountains.

For over a hundred years, foreign missionaries have worked among the Hmong, and many Hmong are now Protestants or Catholics, having abandoned ancestor worship, shamanism, and the rites of death. This has led to tensions between traditional and Christian Hmong.

Redefining Traditional Roles

While traditionally Hmong women have had a higher social status than Chinese women, there has been an effective muting of women in Hmong political and ritual affairs, which may have been strengthened by male control of the cash derived from opium sales. Among the overseas Hmong, significant changes have taken place in relations between the generations as well as between men and women. Overseas Hmong communities have debated the changing role of women and elders in their society, how to pay the traditional bride-price, and above all how to preserve the Hmong culture for a younger generation, many of whom show little interest in tradition.

Returning Hmong

Recently some overseas Hmong have begun to revisit their traditional locations in Laos, Vietnam, and Thailand, and even the homes of their more remote ancestors in southern China. New connections between transnational Hmong communities have been formed, aided by the use of videos and the Internet, and some global trading relations have been established along Hmong lines. It is too early to say whether these new contacts will lead to a new kind of diasporic Hmong community, or whether they represent the sentimental nostalgia of a people hopelessly divided and dispersed by the forces of modernity and change.

Nicholas Tapp

Further Reading

Cooper, Robert G. (1984) *Resource Scarcity and the Hmong Response: Patterns of Settlement and Economy in Transition.* Singapore: Singapore University Press.

Geddes, William R. (1976) *Migrants of the Mountains: The Cultural Ecology of the Blue Miao (Hmong Njua) of Thailand.* Oxford, U.K.: Clarendon.

Hendricks, Glenn L., Bruce T. Downing, and Amos S. Deinard, eds. (1986) *The Hmong in Transition.* Minneapolis: University of Minnesota, Center for Migration Studies.

Lemoine, Jacques. (1972) *Un Village Hmong Vert du Haut Laos: Milieu, technique, et organisation social.* Paris: Centre Nationale de la Recherche Scientifique.

Lin Yueh-Hwa. (1940) "The Miao-Man Peoples of Kweichow." *Harvard Journal of Asiatic Studies* 5: 261–345.

Ruey Yih-Fu. (1960) "The Magpie Miao of Southern Szechuan." In *Social Structure in South-East Asia,* edited by George P. Murdock. Viking Fund Publications in Anthropology, no. 29. Chicago: Quadrangle, 143–155.

Tapp, Nicholas. (2000) *The Hmong of China: Agency, Context, and the Imaginary.* Leiden, Netherlands: Brill.

HMONG-MIEN LANGUAGES

HMONG-MIEN LANGUAGES The Hmong-Mien (also known as Miao-Yao—a term now rarely used outside of China) languages, are one of the major independent language families of Southeast Asia. The two branches of the family, Hmong (Miao) and Mien (Yao), respectively, may be described as clusters of dialects, which are scattered over a wide area of southern China and some adjacent Southeast Asian countries. Hmong dialects are spoken by approximately 5.5 million speakers; Mien speakers number approximately 2 million.

The most important variants of Hmong are Western Hmong (2 million speakers in the Chinese provinces of Guizhou, Guangxi, Sichuan, and Yunnan, as well as in northern Vietnam, Thailand, and Laos), Eastern Hmong (1.4 million speakers in Yunnan, Guizhou, and Guangxi), Northern Hmong (750,000 speakers in Hunan Province, China), Hmong Daw, or "White Hmong" (100,000 speakers in Thailand, Laos, and Vietnam), and Hmong Njua, or "Blue Hmong" (200,000 speakers in Laos and Thailand). Considerable numbers of White and Blue Hmong speakers live abroad, at least 70,000 of each group in the United States. The 500,000 speakers of Punu in Guangxi are officially included in the Mien (Yao) nationality but speak a Hmong language. Only a thousand persons of the approximately 350,000 that constitute the She nationality in Guangdong Province, China, speak another Hmong language, generally known as Ho-Nte.

The Mien language is more uniform. Its most important varieties are Mien proper (approximately 850,000 speakers in Guangxi, Guangdong, Yunnan, Hunan, and Guizhou; some 60,000 in Laos; and 30,000 in Thailand), Iu Mien (200,000 speakers in Guangdong), and Mun, spoken in southern China, Laos, and Vietnam.

Hmong-Mien languages are typical Southeast Asian languages, with monosyllabic words, rich systems of tones (up to eight—in some dialects of Mien, more than ten), subject-verb-object word order, etc. Typological differences within the family include the fact that words in Hmong may end only in nasal consonants or no consonant at all, whereas Mien languages mostly tolerate different consonants in this position. In Hmong, modifiers (adjectives, etc.) usually follow the noun they modify, whereas in Mien the opposite order prevails. The She language behaves, in terms of these and other typological features, like a language of the Mien group, but can nevertheless be shown to belong to the Hmong branch.

In terms of genetic relationship, the status of Hmong-Mien as a family of related languages is not in doubt, but external relationships have not been established in a satisfactory way. The formerly widespread inclusion of Hmong-Mien into the large Sino-Tibetan phylum has now generally been abandoned.

Stefan Georg

Further Reading

Harriehausen, Bettina. (1990) *Hmjong Njua: Syntaktische Analyse einer gesprochenen Sprache mithilfe datenverarbeitungstechnischer Mittel und sprachvergleichende Beschreibung des südostasiatischen Sprachraumes.* Tübingen, Germany: Niemeyer.

Mottin, Jean. (1978) *Éléments de Grammaire Hmong Blanc.* Bangkok, Thailand: Don Bosco.

Niederer, Barbara. (1998) *Les langues Hmong-Mjen (Miao-Yao): Phonologie historique.* Munich: Lincom-Europa.

Ramsey, S. Robert. (1987) *The Languages of China.* Princeton, NJ: Princeton University Press.

HO CHI MINH

HO CHI MINH (1890–1969), North Vietnamese president. Born on 19 May 1890 in the village of Kim Lien, in the province of Nghe An in Vietnam, Ho was originally named Nguyen Sinh Cung. At ten, his name was changed to Nguyen Tat Thanh (Nguyen Who Will Be Victorious). In 1911, he left Vietnam for France. In 1919, when U.S. president Woodrow Wilson came to France, Nguyen tried to enlist his support for Vietnamese self-determination; rebuffed, he turned to communism. He became a member of the French Communist Party in 1920 and changed his name to Nguyen Ai Quoc (Nguyen the Patriot). From 1921 to 1929, Nguyen energetically participated in the political activities of the International Communist Party and published a book entitled *Revolutionary Path* in 1927. In 1923, he went to the Soviet Union to win support for his cause among exiled Vietnamese dissidents. His travels also took him to China, Burma, and India. On 3 February 1930, with the approval of

Ho Chi Minh in 1969. (HULTON-DEUTSCH COLLECTION/CORBIS)

Moscow and the support of China, Ho formed the Indochina Communist Party (later referred to as the Viet Minh) in Hong Kong.

Nguyen renamed himself again in 1940, as Ho Chi Minh (Ho Who Aspires to Enlightenment). In 1941, Ho was arrested in China on charges of being a spy for the French. In prison, Ho composed patriotic poems, which expressed his determination and the internal strength to achieve his goal of Vietnamese independence. In 1944, he returned to Vietnam, where he led resistance against both the French and the Japanese. He declared Vietnam's independence from France on 2 September 1945 and named the country the Democratic Republic of Vietnam (DRV). He served as the DRV's first president (1945–1969). The French were unwilling to accept Vietnam's independence, however, and the First Indochina War was fought from 1946 until France's decisive defeat at the battle of Dien Bien Phu in 1954. Vietnam was partitioned at the seventeenth parallel, with the DRV governing the northern portion. Ho, determined to reunite Vietnam, soon found himself fighting the United States; he died before reunification was achieved. The Vietnamese affectionately called him "Uncle Ho." Ho lived in a modest home in Hanoi until his death; that house is on display in Hanoi as part of the mausoleum built in his honor, which is visited by thousands every day. Although highly praised as an outstanding leader, he also received much criticism for to his uncompromising strategies and his willingness to achieve his goals at any price.

Ha Huong

Further Reading

Duiker, William J. (2000) *Ho Chi Minh: A Life*. New York: Hyperion.

Halberstam, David. (1987) *Ho*. New York: Knopf.

Hunt, H. Michael. (1996) *Lyndon Johnson's War: America's Cold War Crusade in Vietnam, 1945–1968*. New York: Hill and Wang.

Kamm, Henry. (1996) *Dragon Ascending: Vietnam and the Vietnamese*. New York: Arcade.

McNamara, Robert. (1999) *Argument without End: In Search of Answers to the Vietnam Tragedy*. New York: Public Affairs.

Nugent, Nicholas. (1996) *Vietnam: The Second Revolution*. Brighton, U.K.: In Print.

HO CHI MINH CITY (2001 pop. 3.3 million). Located on the southern coast of Vietnam near the Mekong Delta, Ho Chi Minh City (Saigon) is a bustling and fast-growing city that has a long and storied history. Bordered by the Ben Nghe Channel to the south, the Thi Nghe Channel to the north, and the Saigon River to the east, the city has been fought over by many groups over the past two thousand years. The area was first settled in the second century BCE by the Khmer empire of Funan (second century CE–sixth century CE), which used the forested area as a trading post and called it Prei Nokor, meaning "Land of Forests." Over the next centuries the trading post attracted merchants from Japan, India, China, the Middle East, Malaysia, and Champa (now part of modern day Vietnam). Over seven centuries, Prei Nokor slowly grew into a small market town and administrative center. Earthen walls were built as protection from the occasional Cham raids on the growing city. By the fourteenth century, Prei Nokor became part of the Angkor empire of the Khmer, sister empire to the kingdom of Champa. In 1674 the Nguyen lords, rulers of southern Vietnam who had defeated the Cham, established a customs post in the city. The Vietnamese, who called the city Saigon, dug a four-mile trench in 1772 on the western edge of the city and, in effect, transferred control of Saigon from the Angkor to the Nguyen. Beginning in 1778, Cholon, the Chinese part of the city, was developed as a second commercial hub in the area. In 1789, the Nguyen moved their government base from Hue to Saigon to escape the Tay Son rebels. In 1802, with French assistance, the Nguyen, under General Nguyen Anh (reigned as emperor 1802–1820), defeated the Tay Son, reunited Vietnam, and moved the capitol back to Hue. The French, after demanding territorial concessions in Vietnam for their assistance to the Nguyen dynasty during the rebellion, attacked and seized Saigon in 1859 and made it the capital of their new colony. After defeat at the hands of the Viet Minh in 1954, the French abandoned Saigon. The city then became the capital of the new Republic of Vietnam (RVN) and remained so throughout the Second Indochinese War between the United States and the Democratic Socialist Republic of Vietnam (DSRV). By 1975, the DSRV had defeated both the Americans and the RVN; when they took over Saigon, they renamed it Ho Chi Minh City after the leader of the Vietnamese independence movement who had died in 1969. Today Ho Chi Minh City, Vietnam's largest, is one of the fastest growing cities in the world, both economically and in population, and remains a city of diverse cultures and influences. The city celebrated its three-hundred-year anniversary in 1998.

Richard B. Verrone

Further Reading

Admiralty, Naval Intelligence Division (Great Britain). (1943) *Indo-China*. London: His Majesty's Stationary Office.

Buttinger, Joseph. (1968) *Vietnam: A Political History*. New York: Praeger.
Cima, Ronald J., ed. (1989) *Vietnam: A Country Study*. Washington, DC: U.S. Government Printing Office.
Sheehan, Neil. (1992) *After the War Was Over: Hanoi and Saigon*. New York: Vintage.
Taylor, Keith. (1983) *The Birth of Vietnam*. Berkeley and Los Angeles: University of California Press.

HO CHI MINH TRAIL The Ho Chi Minh Trail was a 12,000-mile network of jungle roads and trails paralleling the Annamite Cordillera used by the North Vietnamese to transport communications, supplies, and troops to South Vietnam during the Vietnam War. The North Vietnamese began using the system in the late 1950s and quickly expanded and improved the trail's infrastructure in the 1960s as its use increased. A complex communication system arose with underground barracks, repair shops, hospitals, and supply warehouses located at strategic points along the trail. With the trail's improvements, the duration of the trip was shortened from six months to one month, but the travelers still endured dangers such as malaria and wild animals.

It was imperative that the North Vietnamese control the vicinities of the trail, including sections in Laos. The Ho Chi Minh Trail entered Laos at Mu Gia Pass in Bolikhamxai province and traveled south through Attapu province, where the trail branched into Cambodia and South Vietnam. Lao cities located on the system include Pakxong, Salavan, Xekong, and Xepon.

U.S. military aircraft bombed the districts around the trail as well as where communists were active in Laos. The bombings escalated after 1964 when Lao

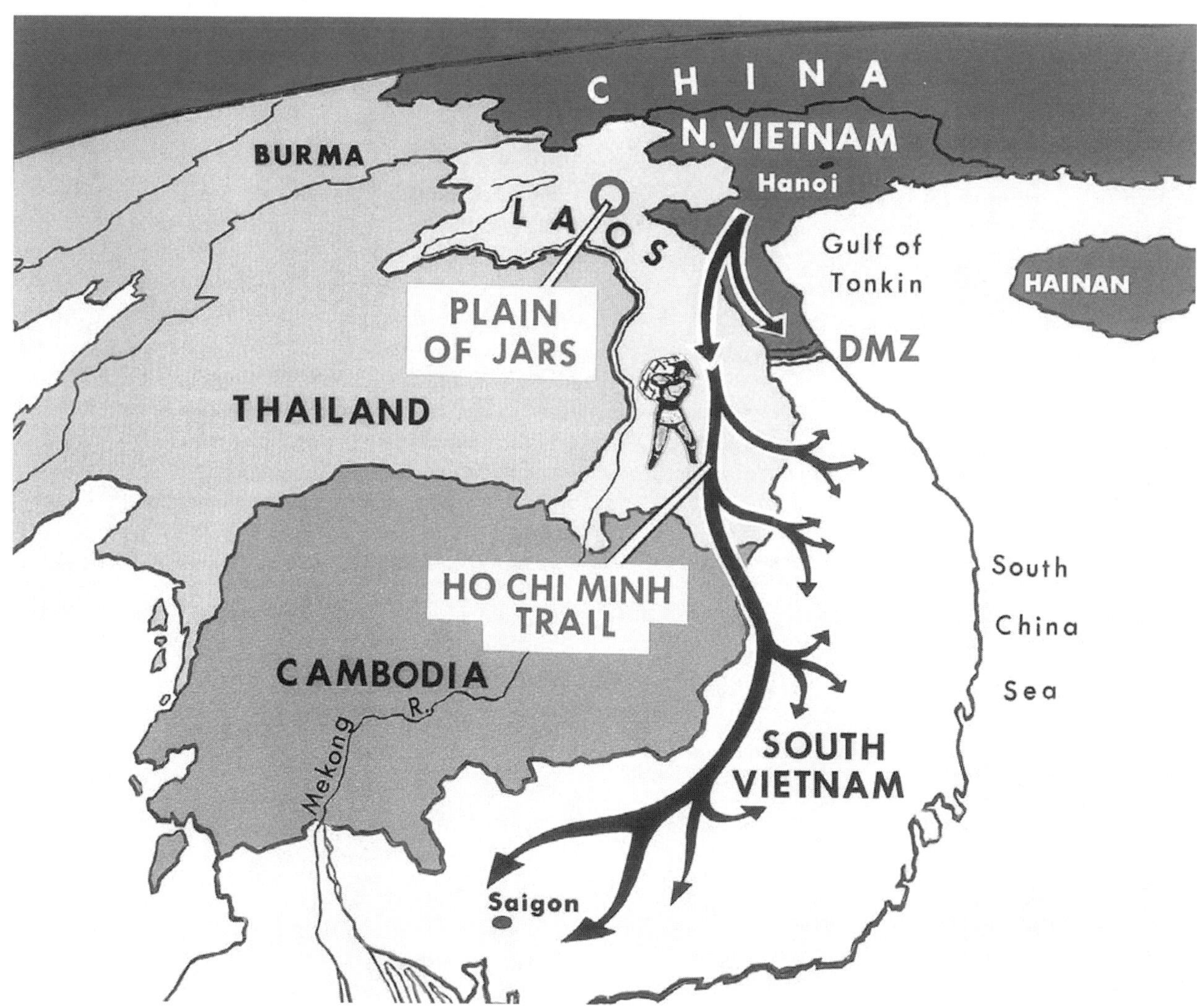

This map from 1970 shows the route of the Ho Chi Minh Trail from North to South Vietnam. (BETTMANN/CORBIS)

prime minister Souvanna Phouma announced his approval for U.S. armed reconnaissance flights over Laos in Operation Steel Tiger. The United States also released defoliants to expose the trail and ground troops in an effort to deter the North Vietnamese. During the Johnson administration the number of bombs dropped increased from three hundred to nine hundred a day. Despite being round-the-clock over a period of years, the bombings failed to stop the North Vietnamese from using the trail.

A major defeat for the United States and South Vietnam was Operation Lam Son 719 in 1971. The target of the operation was Xepon, a major outpost for the communists where the trail diverged into three arteries. The target was never reached, and the South Vietnamese army retreated after suffering over five thousand casualties. The U.S. lost over a hundred aircraft in this failed attempt to shut down the trail.

The effects of the bombings are still felt in Laos. Two million tons of bombs were dropped on Laos during the war, making it the most heavily bombed nation per capita. Accidents involving unexploded ordnance (UXO) occur on average on a daily basis. Teams of UXO detection and demolition specialists continue to comb the countryside in an effort to rid the country of the deadly threats, but the people of Laos will feel the impact of the bombings for decades as more explosives are unearthed.

Linda McIntosh

Further Reading

Nolan, Keith William. (1986) *Into Laos: The Story of Dewey Canyon II/Lam Son 719; Vietnam 1971.* Novato, CA: Presidio.

Prados, John. (1999) *The Blood Road: Ho Chi Minh Trail and the Vietnam War.* New York: Wiley.

Robbins, Christopher. (1987) *The Ravens: Pilots of the Secret War of Laos.* New York: Crown.

HO DYNASTY CITADEL Also known as Tay Do (Capital of the West) or Thanh Nha Ho (Ho Dynasty Citadel), the Ho Dynasty Citadel is located in Tay Giai village in Hoa Binh Province, approximately 150 kilometers west of Hanoi. It was built in 1397 under the rule of Ho Quy Ly. Unlike other Vietnamese citadels, which up until that time had been built of earth, the Ho Dynasty Citadel was made of green block granite. The citadel's shape was square, with walls of 500 meters on each side. The walls were approximately five meters high and three meters thick. On each wall was a stone entrance, and the citadel itself was protected by deep ditches along each of its walls. The citadel did not serve a uniquely military purpose, however, for inside the enclosure the royal palace could be found. For ten years, the Ho Dynasty Citadel served as the seat of the Ho Dynasty's central government. In 1407, the citadel was abandoned and destroyed when Ho Quy Ly was captured and taken prisoner by Ming troops. The only vestiges remaining of the Ho Dynasty Citadel are its south wall and gate, and two carved stone dragons that formerly had been part of the royal palace's structure.

Micheline R. Lessard

Further Reading

Taylor, Keith W. (1991) "The Birth of Vietnam." Berkeley and Los Angeles: University of California Press.

HO TUNG MAU (1896–1951), Vietnamese anticolonial leader. Ho Tung Mau was born in Quynh Doi village in Nghe An Province (in north-central Vietnam) in 1896. The son of a Vietnamese scholar, he obtained a classical education before becoming involved in anticolonial activities. In 1923, along with Ho Chi Minh (1890–1969) (then Nguyen Ai Quoc), Le Hong Phong (1902–1942), and three others, he cofounded the Society of Like Hearts (Tam Tam Xa), a Vietnamese anticolonial organization with anarchist leanings. In 1925 he helped found the Revolutionary Youth League (Viet Nam Thanh Nien Cach Manh Dong Chi Hoi). In March 1926 Ho Tung Mau joined the Chinese Communist Party and worked closely with Ho Chi Minh in China. While in China, Ho Tung Mau was arrested in an anti-Communist sweep in December 1928. He managed to escape from prison in August 1929, and in 1930 he became one of the founders of the Indochinese Communist Party (ICP). French police arrested him once again in China in 1931. Condemned to a life sentence, he was released from prison in 1945. Ho Tung Mau ultimately became a member of the ICP's Central Committee. He was a combat pilot and was reportedly killed in 1951 while engaging in an air attack during the Franco-Vietminh War (1946–1954).

Micheline R. Lessard

Further Reading

Duiker, William. (1981) *The Communist Road to Power in Vietnam.* Boulder, CO: Westview.

Hue Tam Ho Tai. (1992) *Radicalism and the Origins of the Vietnamese Revolution.* Cambridge, MA: Harvard University Press.

HO XUAN HUONG (c. late 1700s–early 1800s), Vietnamese poet and feminist. Although the exact dates of Ho Xuan Huong's life are unknown, she must have lived in the late eighteenth to early nineteenth century. Being the only daughter of a high-ranking civil servant in the Late Le dynasty (1428–1788), she was well educated. She married several times, but for short spans; for some reason, all her husbands died not long after the wedding. She managed a salon frequented by poets and writers; there her talent shone in polished, elegant, but also daring and sexually evocative poems and retorts written in *nom* (Vietnamese demotic script). The following example describes falling down while coming home from school on a rainy day: "I extend my arms to see how high is the sky/ My feet slide to measure the width of the earth!" Another is a reprimand to a close friend who had become too venturesome:

> Scholar, are you sober; are you drunk?
> How dare you discourse about sex in the middle of the day?
> Come here! Come here so that your elder sister may warn you:
> Don't ever finger that place: it is the tiger's den!

Lam Truong Buu

Further Reading

Balaban, John, trans. (2000) *Spring Essence: The Poetry of Ho Xuan Huong*. Port Townsend, WA: Copper Canyon.

Ho Xuan Huong. (1987) *All She Wants: Poetry*. Trans. by David Cevet. London: Tuba.

HOA HAO One of the six officially recognized religions in Vietnam, Hoa Hao is a Buddhist sect founded in 1939 by a mystic from southern Vietnam, Huynh Phu So (1919–1947), who claimed to be the apostle of a famous Buddhist monk. The religion emphasizes personal faith and simplicity of worship and, therefore, has no special places of devotion. Like other Vietnamese religions, Hoa Hao has been highly politicized. The Viet Minh, an umbrella group of communist organizations seeking to expel the French colonial administration of Indochina, considered the Hoa Hao a rival for the support of the poor peasants in the Mekong Delta in their struggle against the French. The Hoa Hao received political and military support from the Japanese during their World War II occupation of Vietnam and then fought alongside French colonial forces against the Viet Minh after political negotiations between the Viet Minh and the French broke down in 1946. As a result, the Viet Minh murdered So in April 1947.

During the U.S. War in Vietnam (1954–1975), the Hoa Hao raised an army and fought both the communist-backed guerrillas and South Vietnamese forces, but their numbers were greatly diminished in the 1950s. With the overthrow of Republic of Vietnam president Ngo Dinh Diem (1901–1963) in November 1963, the Hoa Hao revived as a political and military force in the Mekong Delta and by 1975, claimed to have one million adherents.

Following the reunification of the country in 1976, the relationship between the Hoa Hao and the victorious communist government that disarmed them, confiscated their properties, and banned the religion became tense. Because of their militant anticommunist activities and ties to foreign-based opposition groups, the Hoa Hao arguably have been the most persecuted of all Vietnam's religious groups, and thousands of members have been arrested since 1976. Hoa Hao followers continue to fight for religious freedom and autonomy from government control, including the right to ordain monks, perform rites, proselytize, and control church properties. While in May 1999 the government did allow 160 Hoa Hao delegates to hold a congress and gave the Hoa Hao official recognition, as of 2001 the government continued to limit religious autonomy. Relations between the Vietnamese government and the Hoa Hao remain tense and often deteriorate into armed clashes, such as the December 1999 confrontation between security forces and 300 followers. As of 2001, there were approximately two million adherents, roughly 1–2 percent of the Vietnamese population, though the government put the figure at 1.3 million.

Zachary Abuza

Further Reading

Abuza, Zachary (2001) *Renovating Vietnamese Politics in Contemporary Vietnam*. Boulder, CO: Lynne Rienner.

Tai, Hue-Tam Ho. (1983) *Millenarianism and Peasant Politics in Vietnam*. Cambridge, MA: Harvard University Press.

HOAN KIEM LAKE Located in the center of the Hoan Kiem District in the Old Quarter area of Hanoi, Hoan Kiem Lake (Ho Hoan Kiem or Ho Guom) is the spiritual and social heart of the city and serves as a major gathering point during national holidays such as Vietnam National Day and major festivals such as Tet (New Year's). The small lake is called "The Lake of the Restored Sword," after the legend of Le Loi and his defeat of the Chinese. Under the leadership of Le Loi, a wealthy landowner in the province of Thanh Hoa south of the Red River delta, a movement of national resistance started in 1418 against the Chinese occupiers. After a ten-year struggle, the Chinese were forced to evacuate Vietnam. Le Loi, who ascended the throne shortly thereafter under the name of Le Thai To, became the founder of the third great Vietnamese dynasty, the Later Le (or the Le). Legend has it that Le Loi used a magic golden sword from heaven to vanquish the Chinese invaders. While he was boating on Hoan Kiem Lake in celebration of his successful campaign, a giant tortoise rose from the water and retrieved the sword for its heavenly owner. Real turtles live in the lake and are reported to be a uniquely large species *(Rafetus swimhoei)* that are surfacing for air with increasing frequency as the lake becomes more polluted.

Richard B. Verrone

Further Reading

Cima, Ronald J., ed. (1989) *Vietnam: A Country Study*. Washington, DC: U.S. Government Printing Office.

HOANG NGOC PHACH (d. 1973), Vietnamese writer. Although known as the author who introduced the romantic novel into Vietnamese literature with his work *To Tam*, Hoang Ngoc Phach's biography reads much more like a bureaucrat's than a writer's. Born into a family of scholars in Ha Tinh, Hoang studied the Confucian classics at home until the age of fifteen, when he went to Hanoi to attend a Westernized private school. In 1914 he entered the prestigious French-established high school of the Indochinese Protectorate. In 1922 he graduated from the Superior School of Education. He was appointed teacher, school principal, and superintendent of school districts by the French colonial government and, after 1945, by the government of the Democratic Republic of Vietnam (DRV). After 1954 he joined the Publications Committee of the Ministry of Education of the DRV, where he readied for publication a great number of classical Vietnamese literary works in Hanoi. In 1959, when the Literature Institute of the Social Sciences Committee was founded, Hoang became an active member of that institute and remained there until his retirement in 1963. Hoang is the author of several books and anthologies, but the one that immortalized him was his novel *To Tam*, which he wrote in 1922 and published three years later.

Truong Buu Lam

HOAT, DOAN VIET (b. 1942), Vietnamese dissident. Since 1971, when he returned to Vietnam following the completion of his doctorate in education from Florida State University, Hoat has been a leading dissident intellectual in Vietnam. Hoat was assistant chancellor of Van Hanh University, a private Buddhist university in Saigon, where he became active in the Buddhist peace movement. On 29 August 1976, following reunification of the country and the closure of all private universities, Hoat was arrested for his "ties" to the United States and imprisoned for twelve years. Following his release on 9 February 1988 he began to coedit *Freedom Forum*, an underground newspaper, published between January and November 1990, that called for democracy, an end to the Communist Party's monopoly of power, and religious and press freedoms. He and six others were arrested on 17 November 1990 for the crime of "attempting to overthrow the people's government." Following a closed-door trial, on 29 March 1993, Hoat was sentenced to twenty years in prison. His case attracted much attention from the international human rights community, including Amnesty International and PEN, as well as the U.S. government. He was released in September 1998 in a presidential amnesty and forced into exile in the United States. He has been the recipient of numerous prizes, including the Robert F. Kennedy Human Rights Award and the Golden Pen of Freedom Award.

Zachary Abuza

Further Reading

Abuza, Zachary. (2001) *Renovating Vietnamese Politics in the Era of Doi Moi*. Boulder, CO: Lynne Rienner.

HOI AN (1994 pop. 60,000). Located on the central coast of Vietnam, thirty kilometers (nineteen miles) south of Da Nang, Hoi An, or Faifo, as it was called in previous centuries, is a small, well-preserved riverside town that has a long history built from various foreign influences. From the second to the tenth century CE, the Kingdom of Champa controlled this important port city. Ensuing battles for control of the city between the Cham and the Vietnamese during the fourteenth and fifteenth centuries caused Hoi An to cease its role as a major trading center on the central coast. In the sixteenth century, however, peace between the two sides enabled the city to reestablish its trading role. Ships from Asia and Europe landed here seeking, among other items, lacquer, medicinal herbs, porcelain, and silk. This trade status survived more turmoil (the city was badly damaged during the Tay

Son Rebellion in the 1770s) and traders, particularly the Hainan, Canton, Fukien, and Chaozhou Chinese, built more and more off-season homes. Ethnic Chinese make up a large portion of the present-day Hoi An. After arriving in the late 1800s, the French made Hoi An an administrative post and built a rail line to Da Nang. With the established rail link and the fact that the Thu Bon River was filling up quickly with silt and thus cutting the city's access to the sea, Da Nang eventually eclipsed Hoi An as the region's major trading port. Today Hoi An is fast becoming a major tourist destination with its preserved and varied architectural homes and buildings, clean beach, bustling market, and numerous vendors selling local wares.

Richard B. Verrone

Further Reading

Cima, Ronald J., ed. (1989) *Vietnam: A Country Study*. Washington, DC: U.S. Government Printing Office.

Great Britain Admiralty, Naval Intelligence Division. (1943) *Indo-China*. London: HMSO, Geographical Handbook Series, B.R. 510.

Taylor, Keith. (1983) *The Birth of Vietnam*. Berkeley and Los Angeles: University of California Press.

HOKKAIDO (2002 est. pop. 5.7 million). Hokkaido, the northernmost and second largest of Japan's four main islands (83,519 square kilometers, including the 5,010 square kilometers of the Japanese-claimed but, since 1945, Russian-occupied Southern Kuriles). Hokkaido is bordered by the Sea of Japan on the west, the Sea of Okhotsk on the northeast, and the Pacific Ocean on the south and east. The most densely populated areas are the Ishikari plain in the west and the Oshima Peninsula in the south. Seventy percent of the island is covered by mountains and forests and only 10 percent is agriculturally usable. Sapporo, with an estimated 1.8 million inhabitants (2002), is the capital of Hokkaido and its administrative center. Prehistoric relics have been found on Hokkaido, but the earliest Japanese merchant contacts with the indigenous Ainu on Ezo, as Hokkaido was called before its integration into Japan proper in 1869, date from around the twelfth century. Ainu rebellions against encroaching Japanese economic activities in the seventeenth century were suppressed. The central government organized the development of Hokkaido as a frontier region against an increasing Russian presence in the Far East, following the Meiji Restoration in 1868 until the period of the Hokkaido Colonization Office (1869–1882). At the end of the nineteenth century, American advisers exerted a strong influence on city planning and agriculture. Hokkaido was built up as a Japanese base, mainly for food and natural resources, until the end of World War II.

Although Hokkaido gained some administrative independence in 1948 (with the Local Administrative Law), responsibility for Hokkaido's economic development remained mainly with the central government and the Hokkaido Development Agency (including ten-year development plans). From 1955, the primary sector (agriculture and natural-resources extraction) lost much of its dominant role in Hokkaido (going from 25.2 percent of the island's production in 1955 to 3.8 percent in 2000). A small manufacturing sector developed, but the most important pillar today is the private and government service sector (82 percent). At the start of the twenty-first century, Hokkaido (and, particularly, "Sapporo Valley") was trying to attract information-related industries.

Hokkaido has active intercultural contact with other northern regions in the world through the Northern Intercity Conference. Since the demise of the Soviet Union in 1991, relations with Russia's Far East have intensified (as shown by the 1998 Cultural and Economic Agreement with Sakhalin, the large Russian island to the north of Hokkaido).

Hokkaido's geographic isolation was greatly diminished through the construction of the Seikan Tunnel, for the railway, in 1988, which connected Hokkaido with Honshu. Hokkaido is famous for its beautiful scenery, large national parks, many ski resorts, and its distinct northern flora and fauna, and attracted 9.2 million tourists in 1998.

Wolfgang Bauer

Further Reading

Edmonds, Richard L. (1985) *Northern Frontiers of Qing China and Tokugawa Japan : A Comparative Study of Frontier Policy*. University of Chicago Department of Geography Research Paper, no. 215. Chicago: University of Chicago Press.

Fujita, Fumiko. (1994) *American Pioneers and the Japanese Frontier*. Westport, CT: Greenwood.

Jones, Francis Clifford. (1958) *Hokkaido: Its Present State of Development and Future Prospects*. London and New York: Oxford University Press.

Lensen, George A. (1954) *Report from Hokkaido: The Remains of Russian Culture in Northern Japan*. Westport, CT: Greenwood.

HOLI Holi, the festival of colors, is celebrated especially by Hindus in north, east, and western India.

Only inhabitants of the southern states of India do not mark this festival. Holi occurs on the full moon day of the month Phalguna (falling during February–March). On this day, men, women, and children of different classes and backgrounds join together in the morning and smear *gulal* (colored powder) and spray colored water on one another. Sweetmeats are communally shared. Everybody—rich and poor, powerful and dispossessed—feels equal to everyone else on this occasion.

This festival of colors has been celebrated since ancient times, with pomp and gaiety. According to the most popular story of the festival's origins, the demon-king Hiranyakashipu wanted to be regarded as God himself and set out to kill his son Prahalad, a great devotee of the god Vishnu. Vishnu, however, saved Prahalad, and Hiranyakashipu's daughter, the demon Holika, was burned to death. To celebrate this occasion, people lit bonfires on the night before the full moon.

Hrushikesh Panda

Further Reading

Anderson, Leona M. (1993) *Vasantostsava: The Spring Festivals of India: Texts and Traditions.* New Delhi: D. K. Printworld.

Underhill, Muriel Marion. (1921) *The Hindu Religious Year.* Calcutta, India: Association Press; London: Oxford University Press.

HOLKARS The Holkars were a dynasty of Maratha rulers in eighteenth- and nineteenth-century India. Yashvantrao Holkar (or Jaswant Rao, 1776–1811) was historically the most important. He was an illegitimate son of Tukoji Holkar and a concubine, and rose to prominence in Pune (Poona) during a chaotic period. He gathered some loyal Bhil warriors and began raiding forays until he was powerful enough to seize the territories of Sindhia and challenge Kashi Rao, his own brother, whom he replaced in 1802 after conducting a war against the Peshwa and Sindhia. Then to prevent the British from entering Maratha country to reinstall the Peshwa, their sometime ally, Jaswant Rao placed an adoptive relative, Amrit Rao, on the Maratha throne at Pune.

Jaswant Rao's medieval strategy was to plunder so that war paid for war. He next declared war on the East India Company, but was beaten twice, in 1804 and 1805. Unable to form any alliances with such rulers as Sindhia, the Raja of Jodhpur, or Ranjit Singh, the Holkar ruler was obliged to sign a peace treaty with the British. This (1805) marked the end of the Second Anglo-Maratha War.

Jaswant Rao took a keen interest in the organization of his army, and conducted numerous roving campaigns which kept him in the saddle for long periods. He led a dissipated life, with heavy use of alcohol, and soon was to become insane after poisoning a nephew and his mother. After three years of insanity, Jaswant Rao died at the age of 35.

Paul Hockings

Further Reading

Quanungo, Sudhindra Nath (1965) *Jaswant Rao Holkar: The Golden Rogue.* Lucknow, India: Abhinava-Bharati.

HOMOSEXUALITY When speaking of homosexuality, one must distinguish between male homosexuality and female homosexuality, or lesbianism. Asia has a rich cultural background when it comes to male homosexuality; China and Japan offer abundant historical evidence. Research on lesbianism in Asia has only just begun, but initial results suggest that lesbianism was not uncommon. Throughout Asia, homosexuality is often confused with transvestism (wearing the clothing of the opposite sex), and gay and lesbian individuals have often presented themselves as members of the opposite sex, thereby reinforcing the confusion. This has changed in recent years, however, particularly among middle- and upper-class gay and

GAY JAPANESE COMIC BOOKS FOR THAI WOMEN

Japanese comic books with male homosexual themes have found a new audience—Thai women in Bangkok who are evidently bored with traditional male-female stories and characters. Japanese publishers estimate that Thai women make up about 80 percent of the readership in Thailand. Why women are attracted to the comic books is unclear, although conservatives complain that the comics are offensive.

Source: Pichayanund Chindahporn. (2001) "Manga Goes on a Gender-Bender." *AsiaWeek* (16 November): 16.

lesbian people. In general, gays and lesbians in Asia do not see sexuality as the main determinant of their identity.

Traditional Male Homosexuality in China

In China the oldest-known reports of male homosexuality appear in the earliest poetry anthology of the Zhou dynasty (1045–256 BCE). In this period heterosexual marriages were frequently negotiated for other than romantic reasons, and men were free to search for satisfying sex and romantic love elsewhere, including in homosexual relationships. Homosexuality was typically structured in terms of class, with courtiers seeking the love of powerful men because of the concomitant benefits of such alliances, as in the instance of Lord Long Yang, who made elaborate efforts to prove his devotion to the king of Wei. During the Han dynasty (206 BCE– 220 CE), the emperor's favorites attained enormous prominence at court, and in one instance the dying emperor Ai (reigned 6 BCE–1 CE) even gave the throne to his favorite, Don Xian. Don Xian's enemies, however, forced him to commit suicide and usurped the throne.

The first-known sources on homosexuality outside court life date from the Six Dynasties (220–589). In *Shishui xinyu* (A New Account of Tales of the World) by Liu Qing (403–444), male beauty is a major focus of attention. The Tang dynasty (618–907) provides fewer records of homosexuality at court than did earlier periods, although homosexuality was more often mentioned in literature and particularly in poetry. The first derogatory term connected with homosexuality, *jijian*, usually translated as "sodomy," surfaced during this period in the story of the male prostitute Xue Aocoa.

During the Song dynasty (960–1279), homosexuality apparently continued to be more common outside court circles, and evidence for it increased. Whereas in earlier times patronage consisted of emperors and other high-placed persons bestowing presents and honors on their favorites, in the Song period this patronage took the form of straightforward prostitution in the major cities. Prostitutes rather than patrons were typically seen as passive and anally receptive, whereas in earlier times, the relationship had been one of love.

In the early twelfth century male prostitution was legally prohibited, but the law seems not to have been often enforced. The Ming dynasty (1368–1644) was a time of greater tolerance, with a flowering of literature depicting homosexuality, as ever marked by patronage relationships. During this period clashes over homosexual activity with foreigners occurred, for instance in Manila, where the Spanish arrested and condemned Chinese immigrants, who protested that homosexuality was an accepted custom in their culture.

During the Qing dynasty (1644–1912), literature on homosexuality remained rich, and prostitution was common. In 1860 a Western visitor to Tianjin reported that there were thirty-five brothels and an estimated eight hundred boys engaged in prostitution. Sources of information about male prostitutes largely described actors, who were elite prostitutes. There were sodomy laws at this time, and under Manchurian influence intolerance toward homosexuality began to emerge, though the practice continued to flourish.

Traditional Male Homosexuality in Japan

In Japan, homosexuality has been related to the introduction of Buddhism. Kukai, also known as Kobo Daishi (774–835), the founder of the Japanese Shingon (True Word) sect of Buddhism, was said to have brought male homosexuality from China to Japan. Only from the tenth century, however, is there evidence of homosexual activity in Buddhist monasteries, with novices being seduced by older monks.

Male homosexuality also occurred among the samurai, especially during the Onin War (1467–1600). Male homosexuality was generally thought to be superior to heterosexuality, a view that was probably related to the defilement associated with the female body in both Buddhism and Shintoism. Moreover, love between men was practical during war campaigns, when male lovers could accompany each other.

In the Tokugawa era (1600/1603–1868), a third form of homosexuality came to the fore: that between the patrons and performers of Kabuki theater, an all-male Japanese drama form. The position of *kagema*, or Kabuki trainee, was often a guise for the practice of male prostitution. The popular *Danshoku okagami* (Great Mirror of Male Love) by Ihara Saikaku (1642–1693) provides many insights into the various forms of homosexuality in the Tokugawa period. During the Meiji period (1868–1912), Japan adopted a sodomy law based loosely on the Qing-dynasty legislation. It was, however, little enforced and soon revoked.

Traditional Male Homosexuality in Korea and Vietnam

In Korea, the institution of the *hwarang* (flower of male youth), an elite group of young warriors founded in the sixth century, emphasized such virtues as faithfulness to friends and courage in battle; it was also a seat of male homosexuality. Korea also had theater-related homosexuality, known as *namsadang*.

Little information has been published about homosexuality in Vietnam, but transsexuality and transvestism were apparently linked to shamanistic practices. Homosexuality was reported by Westerners, who reacted with outrage, as had Westerners visiting China and Japan, when they found that Vietnamese did not much object to the practice. Vietnamese legal codes do not mention homosexuality, and Vietnam did not follow the Qing dynasty in criminalizing sodomy.

Traditional Male Homosexuality in Islamic Cultures

As in East Asia, Western observers commented on the prevalence of homosexuality in Islamic cultures, and Islamic culture has a rich literary history of homosexuality. Only in recent years have Islamic people, like other East Asians, overlooked the occurrence of homosexuality. Islamic law in principle condemns homosexual activity as a form of adultery. It is not, however, seen as evil in itself. In practice, it is tolerated in most Islamic countries, as long as it takes place with discretion. Between 1979 and 1984 several men were executed in Iran for homosexual practices, but these events mark an exceptional period, when homosexuality was seen as evil in itself and as representative of Western decadence.

Traditional Male Homosexuality in India

In India the tolerance for homosexuality has been not unlike that in China and Japan. The *Kama Sutra* includes descriptions of men being fellated by eunuchs. According to Hinduism, homosexuality was less of an impediment to escaping the cycle of rebirth than was heterosexuality, although both forms of attachment had to be overcome to achieve immortality. In Indian Buddhism, however, homosexuality, like heterosexuality, was derogated to an extent. Nevertheless, love and friendship between men were considered preferable to similar relationships between men and women, and in monastic life laxity toward homosexuality sometimes existed.

So-called *hijras* (an Urdu word meaning "hermaphrodite," a person with both male and female sexual organs) were considered neither men nor women and were categorized as belonging to a third sex, with institutionalized roles as practitioners of female occupations like singers, dancers, and prostitutes. It was not uncommon for these *hijras* to have their genitalia cut off, but it is surmised that fully equipped gay men sometimes acted like *hijras* to be able to have sex with men. This does not mean, however, that there were not also many gay men who were not *hijras*.

Traditional Male Sexuality in Southeast Asia

Transvestism and homosexuality are confounded throughout Southeast Asia, where, for example, one finds the ladyboy or *kathoey* of Thailand, the *waria* of Indonesia, and the *bakla* of the Philippines. These terms, rooted in local histories and cultures, refer to transgendered males (that is, males who feel feminine and dress as women), often working as prostitutes. Among these types, homosexuality is characterized by femininity, and the masculine partner, supposedly sexually active, is considered a "real" man, straight, not gay.

Female Homosexuality in Asia

The relative scarcity of information about Asian female homosexuality is partly attributable to the predominance of male researchers who have little access to places where women gather together. Islamic harems have been regarded as hotbeds of lesbian activity, but there is little proof of this notion. In Pakistan, female homosexuality has apparently met little opposition, as long as the women properly fulfill their roles of spouses and mothers. In fact a similar view can be discerned throughout Asia. Women's sexuality has not been considered as independent from men, and therefore whatever activities women engage in together are not taken very seriously by men.

Nevertheless there are depictions of women engaging in sexual activity with other women, often involving dildos (artificial penises). Examples include seventeenth-century Indian Mughal paintings and Japanese woodblock prints of the Edo era. In some of the latter, men spy on the women; the prints were probably used by men for their own pleasure and certainly represent a male viewpoint.

Traditional Female Homosexuality in China There is relatively well-documented information about women's communities in imperial China, especially in southern Guangdong. In such communities women could resist social demands that they marry, and particular economic opportunities enabled these women to live largely independently of men. This appears to have been the case in the silk industry. Women in these communities held marriage ceremonies and lived like couples. In Chinese-dominated states, including Singapore, such communities have persisted.

As early as the Han dynasty (206 BCE–220 CE), there is literary evidence of female homosexuality, including a love relationship between two slave women, as well as an empress's servant who dressed in male attire, suggesting a lesbian relationship. The famous

Qing dynasty novel *The Dream of the Red Chamber* also contains depictions of lesbian affairs.

Traditional Female Homosexuality in India In India texts that refer to female homosexuality appeared as early as 1500 BCE. In texts such as pre-Vedic hymns, dual goddesses were fused into twins, and those in female relationships were depicted as mothers, daughters, sisters, lover-maidens, and more, with clearly erotic undertones. Later, in Vedic times, heterocentrism (focus on heterosexuality) occurred in texts in which female relationships were broken up in favor of the formation of heterosexual couples.

Traditional Types of Female Homosexuality in Asia

As with male homosexuality, female homosexuality has often been confounded with transgender phenomena in Asia. In Japan for instance, the term *onabe* refers to a woman who dresses and behaves like a man. Many find employment in specific *onabe* clubs, where they entertain female clients. Most contemporary Japanese lesbian women, or *rezubian*, do not cross-dress, however.

In Indonesia, class differences seem to be expressed in various types of lesbian relationships. Butch *(sentul)*–femme *(kantil)* relationships, where butch women behave like men and femme ones like women, are more typical of poor, lower-class women. As in the case of male transgender types, the *sentul*, also known as *tomboi*, is generally seen as more lesbian than the nontransgendering *kantil*. Elite lesbians, however, have tended to align themselves with Western types of female homosexuality and have thereby found access to international networks denied to lower-class women.

Contemporary Male and Female Homosexuality in Asia

Homosexuality in Asia today continues to be associated with male as well as female transgender practices, but such viewpoints have begun to be questioned. Nowadays the words "gay" and "lesbian" are often used in place of the traditional terms, especially among highly educated people, who tend to distance themselves from the transgender implications of indigenous concepts. In Indonesia, for instance, there has been a clash between the *waria*s and the gays, who see each other as rivals. The same "real men" who paid the *waria*s for sex were paid by the gays to have sex. This matter has been resolved by talks between representatives of the two groups, and the conflict shows signs of dissipating, with gays adopting behavior typical of *waria*s by wearing drag (clothing typical of the opposite sex) and some *waria*s becoming educated and thus equipped to associate with educated gays.

In China as well as Hong Kong and Taiwan, a movement has developed to accommodate this conflict between traditional and contemporary ideas of homosexuality. The common denominator used for gay men, lesbian women, transgender and transsexual people, and even sympathetic and supportive heterosexuals is *tongzhi*, which is the Chinese Communist term for "comrade." The introduction of the term *tongzhi* is a product of the wish to avoid the explicit sexual overtones of other terms for gay men and lesbian women and at the same time to create a network that overcomes the limitations of identity-oriented categories like gay and lesbian. Rather than creating a gay-straight binary, the aim is to question sexuality in general.

In other Asian countries similar attempts to circumvent the pitfalls of identity politics are occurring. Generally people seem to want to be accepted as decent citizens, without an emphasis on sexuality. In Japan there is a division between those who adopt the line of desexualization—a group that, unlike the *tongzhi* movement, does not include transgendered people, let alone heterosexuals—and those who take a more sex-positive approach, explicitly aligning themselves not only with transgendered people but also with sex workers. Members of the first group seem to have largely abandoned the idea of making an impact among Japanese lesbian and gay people and instead mostly direct their attention abroad or toward Japan's politicians and bureaucracy; the other movement is limited in number but is gaining adherents.

In most of Southeast Asia, literature on homosexuality is scarce, and, although the practice is common, it is little spoken of. The discourse of Asian values as promulgated by government leaders of Indonesia, Singapore, and Malaysia denies the existence of homosexuality among Asians, denouncing it as a Western perversion. Ironically this attitude seems to have arisen from an adherence to Western norms according to which homosexuality is a perversion; such norms were introduced during the colonial period and confirmed during the following period of Western cultural dominance. Contrary to the goals of Asian leaders, this denunciation of homosexuality seems to have led to its increased recognition. Gay and lesbian networks have developed throughout Asia and have contacted international organizations, such as the International Lesbian and Gay Organization. While the local branches of these organizations remain somewhat elitist, they are developing Asian perspectives of lesbian and gay liberation and are accepting the various transgender types indigenous to their cultures, rather than simply following Western patterns.

Wim Lunsing

Further Reading

Aronson, Jacob. (1999) "Homosex in Hanoi? Sex, the Public Sphere, and Public Sex." In *Public Sex, Gay Space*, edited by William L. Leap. New York: Columbia University Press, 203–221.

Blackwood, Evelyn, and Saskia E. Wieringa, eds. (1999) *Female Desires: Same-Sex Relations and Transgender Practices across Cultures*. New York: Columbia University Press.

Chou Wah-shan. (2000) *Tongzhi: Politics of Same-Sex Eroticism in Chinese Societies*. New York: Haworth.

Hinsch, Brett. (1990) *Passions of the Cut Sleeve: The Male Homosexual in Traditional China*. Berkeley and Los Angeles: University of California Press.

Ihara Saikaku. (1990) *The Great Mirror of Male Love*. Trans. by Paul Gordon Schalow. Stanford, CA: Stanford University Press.

Jackson, Peter A., and Gerard Sullivan, eds. (2000) *Lady Boys, Tom Boys, Rent Boys: Male and Female Homosexuality in Contemporary Thailand*. New York: Harrington Park.

Leupp, Gary P. (1995) *Male Colors: The Construction of Homosexuality in Tokugawa Japan*. Berkeley and Los Angeles: University of California Press.

Lunsing, Wim. (1999) "Japan: Finding Its Way?" In *The Global Emergence of Gay and Lesbian Politics: National Imprints of a Worldwide Movement*, edited by Barry Adam, Jan Willem Duyvendak, and André Krouwel. Philadelphia: Temple University Press, 293–325.

———. (2001) *Beyond Common Sense: Sexuality and Gender in Contemporary Japan*. London, New York, and Bahrain: Kegan Paul.

Murray, Stephen O. (2000) *Homosexualities*. Chicago: University of Chicago Press.

Murray, Stephen O., and Will Roscoe, eds. (1997) *Islamic Homosexualities: Culture, History, and Literature*. New York: New York University Press.

Nanda, Serena. (1990) *Neither Man nor Woman: The Hijras of India*. Belmont, CA: Wadsworth.

Pflugfelder, Gregory M. (1999) *Cartographies of Desire: Male-Male Sexuality in Japanese Discourse, 1600–1950*. Berkeley and Los Angeles: University of California Press.

Sankar, Andrea. (1986) "Sisters and Brothers, Lovers and Enemies: Marriage Resistance in Southern Kwangtung." In *The Many Faces of Homosexuality: Anthropological Approaches to Homosexual Behavior*, edited by Evelyn Blackwood. New York: Harrington Park, 69–82.

Schild, Maarten. (1992) "Islam." In *Sexuality and Eroticism among Males in Moslem Societies*, edited by Arno Schmitt and Jehoeda Sofer. New York: Harrington Park, 179–187.

Wieringa, Saskia. (1987) *Uw toegenegen Dora D.: Reisbrieven* (Your Devoted Dora D.: Travel Letters). Amsterdam: Uitgeverij Furie.

Zwilling, Leonard. (1992) "Homosexuality as Seen in Indian Buddhist Texts." In *Buddhism, Sexuality, and Gender*, edited by José Ignacio Cabezón. New York: State University of New York Press, 203–214.

HONEN (1133–1212), founder of Jodo (Japanese Pure Land) Buddhism. Honen initially studied the doctrines of the Tendai sect at Enryakuji temple on Mount Hiei near Kyoto. Dissatisfied with the political intrigues of the priests there, he became a mountain ascetic and continued his studies of Tendai teachings and those of the Nara sects. Finally, he came to the realization that few ordinary beings possess the ability to attain enlightenment through their own efforts. To the contrary, such striving is conceitedness that actually impedes emancipation. He concluded that one need only rely on Amida Buddha.

After leaving Mt. Hiei, Honen began preaching the exclusive practice of the *nembutsu*, unceasing meditation on and repeated chanting of the name Amida Buddha in order to obtain rebirth in the Pure Land. The notion that even those who did not devote their lives to Buddhist practice might achieve rebirth had great appeal among the general populace, bringing a sense of crisis to the priests of the older Buddhist sects. These sects appealed to the government to suppress the movement, and in 1207 Honen was banished to Shikoku. The banishment was lifted at the end of that year, and in 1211 Honen returned to Kyoto where he continued to propagate his ideas until his death.

James M. Vardaman, Jr.

Further Reading

Kashiwahara Yusen and Koyu Sonoda, eds. (1994) *Nihon meiso retsuden (Shapers of Japanese Buddhism)*. Trans.by Gaynor Sekimori. Tokyo: Kosei.

Tsunoda Ryusaku, William Theodore De Bary, and Donald Keene. (1958) *Sources of Japanese Tradition*. Vol. 1. New York: Columbia University Press.

HONG KONG (2001 pop. 6.7 million). Hong Kong was part of China's Guangdong Province until it became a British colony in 1842. In 1997, Hong Kong was returned to the People's Republic of China (PRC) and is now known as the Hong Kong Special Administrative Region. During its colonial era, Hong Kong became one of the most important import-export and finance economies in the Pacific region. Today, it remains a vibrant, modern Chinese city with a diverse range of cultural influences and a thriving capitalist economy.

The Dragon Statue and Hong Kong skyline from Victoria Peak in 1997. (Stephen G. Donaldson Photography)

History

Located on the south coast of China near the mouth of the Pearl River, the area that is now known as Hong Kong comprises Hong Kong Island, Kowloon Peninsula, and the New Territories. Until the 1840s, this area was part of Xinan County in the Guangdong Province of the Qing dynasty (1644–1912). The region was populated mostly by Han Chinese and Hakka (a Chinese minority people), and the local economy was dominated by pearl fishing, salt making, incense tree cultivation, and piracy and smuggling.

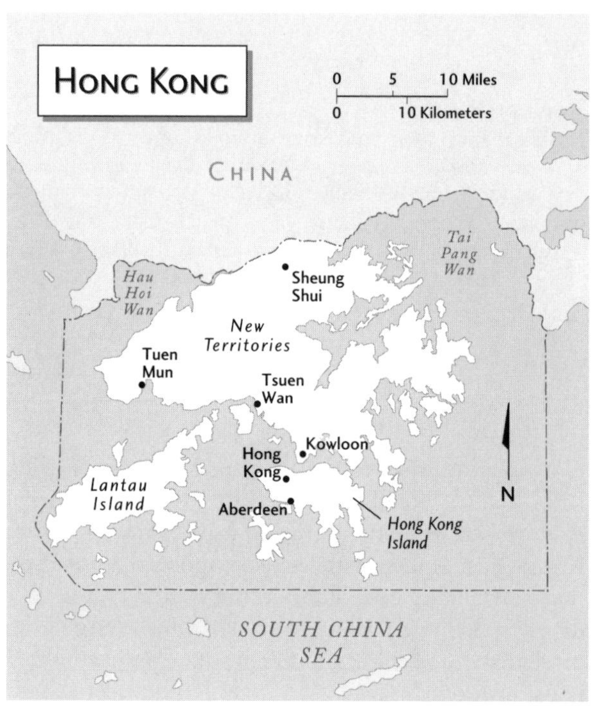

The British, seeking a new location from which to maintain their lucrative opium trade with China, occupied Hong Kong Island in 1841. They were granted formal control of the island by China in 1842 through the Treaty of Nanjing, which ended the First Opium War (1839–1942), and the island became a colony on 26 June 1843. The second Opium War (1856–1860) resulted in Britain's acquisition of Kowloon Peninsula, located across the bay from Hong Kong Island, and in 1898 Britain acquired a ninety-nine-year lease on the New Territories. Britain maintained control of Hong Kong until 1997, except from 1941 to 1945, when the Japanese controlled the territory. The impending end of the lease on the New Territories led to a 1984 agreement between the British and Chinese governments for Hong Kong's return to China as an autonomous region.

Political System

Under the British, the governor, who was appointed, had executive power and was assisted by a Legislative Council, of which a small percentage was elected. This system, which was made somewhat more democratic under the leadership of Governor Chris

PREAMBLE TO THE CONSTITUTION OF HONG KONG

Adopted on 4 April 1990; effective since 1 July 1997.

Hong Kong has been part of the territory of China since ancient times; it was occupied by Britain after the Opium War in 1840. On 19 December 1984, the Chinese and British Governments signed the Joint Declaration on the Question of Hong Kong, affirming that the Government of the People's Republic of China will resume the exercise of sovereignty over Hong Kong with effect from 1 July 1997, thus fulfilling the long-cherished common aspiration of the Chinese people for the recovery of Hong Kong.

Upholding national unity and territorial integrity, maintaining the prosperity and stability of Hong Kong, and taking account of its history and realities, the People's Republic of China has decided that upon China's resumption of the exercise of sovereignty over Hong Kong, a Hong Kong Special Administrative Region will be established in accordance with the provisions of Article 31 of the Constitution of the People's Republic of China, and that under the principle of "one country, two systems", the socialist system and policies will not be practised in Hong Kong. The basic policies of the People's Republic of China regarding Hong Kong have been elaborated by the Chinese Government in the Sino-British Joint Declaration.

In accordance with the Constitution of the People's Republic of China, the National People's Congress hereby enacts the Basic Law of the Hong Kong Special Administrative Region of the People's Republic of China, prescribing the systems to be practised in the Hong Kong Special Administrative Region, in order to ensure the implementation of the basic policies of the People's Republic of China regarding Hong Kong.

Source: International Court Network. Retrieved 8 March 2002, from: http://www.uni-wuerzburg.de/law/home.html.

Patten in the 1990s, has remained essentially intact in the post-1997 era. In March 1990, the PRC's National People's Congress approved a Basic Law, based largely on English law, that constitutes the basis for Hong Kong's current legal system. Under this system Hong Kong has an appointed chief executive who serves for five years, an appointed cabinet, and a legislature that is selected by both direct and indirect elections.

As a condition for the 1997 handover, China agreed to maintain a "one country, two systems" approach to governing Hong Kong for fifty years. Under this system, Hong Kong is to have a high degree of political and economic autonomy from China. Its foreign and military affairs, however, have been taken over by the PRC government. In addition, Hong Kong's chief executive is appointed by the PRC.

Geography

Hong Kong has a tropical monsoon climate. It has an area of 1,097 square kilometers with 733 kilometers of coastline and a large deep-water harbor. The territory consists of a peninsula and over two hundred small islands and is mostly mountainous with a very small percentage of arable land. The hilly terrain provides relatively little living space, and so both Hong Kong Island and Kowloon have been enlarged through land reclamation. Architecturally, Hong Kong is composed almost entirely of large office and apartment blocks. Hong Kong is connected to the rest of China by waterways, such as the Pearl River, as well as railroads and roads.

Demographics

According to Hong Kong's 2001 census, approximately 80 percent of its 6.7 million people live on 8 percent of the land, making Hong Kong one of the world's most densely populated areas. Ninety-five percent of the population is ethnically Chinese, with Filipinos, Indonesians, the British, and Indians constituting the largest other ethnic groups.

Economy

Prior to its colonization by the British, Hong Kong had long been the site of both legal and illegal trade with neighboring Asian nations, Arabs, and some Westerners. Under the British, the colony replaced Guangzhou (Canton) as the principal locus of Anglo-Chinese trade in southern China, much of which, in the nineteenth and early twentieth centuries, was based on opium. This trade was controlled by a few large trading houses, known as *hong*. Following the establishment of the PRC in 1949, Hong Kong experienced a huge influx of refugee industrialists, mostly from the Chinese industrial city of Shanghai. These industrialists, using refugee labor that continued to flow into Hong Kong through the second half of the twentieth century, turned Hong Kong into a center of manufacturing and finance. Hong Kong has limited natural resources, however, and must import most of its food and raw materials. As China increasingly opened up for trade in the 1980s and 1990s, Hong Kong's economy again became more oriented toward China.

Culture

Hong Kong's culture has been influenced by its mostly Chinese population as well as its British colonial past. Its official languages are Cantonese and English. Its population has always been mostly Chinese, and this is reflected in the cuisine, popular culture, and many aspects of the landscape. The British elite who dominated colonial Hong Kong were mostly merchants, civil servants, and missionaries. As the post-1949 Shanghai industrialists established themselves financially, however, Hong Kong's elite culture became increasingly Chinese.

Hong Kong's colonial past led it to develop differently from the rest of China, especially during the period since 1949. Unlike the rest of China, Hong Kong has a thriving, free market, capitalist economy, and the very identity of Hong Kong is rooted in that successful economy. Although the PRC has committed itself to protect Hong Kong's economic and political autonomy until 2047, what, exactly, will be the impact of Hong Kong's reintegration into China remains to be seen. Will Hong Kong remain distinct from China, or will it become just another Chinese city?

J. Megan Greene

Further Reading

Central Intelligence Agency. (2002) *The World Factbook: Hong Kong*. Retrieved 24 April 2002, from: http://www.cia.gov/cia/publications/factbook/geos/hk.html.

Cohen, Warren I., and Li Zhao, eds. (1997) *Hong Kong under Chinese Rule: The Economic and Political Implications of Reversion*. Cambridge, UK: Cambridge University Press.

Lau, Chi Kuen. (1997) *Hong Kong's Colonial Legacy*. Hong Kong: Chinese University Press.

Morris, Jan. (1997) *Hong Kong: Epilogue to an Empire*. London: Penguin.

Welsh, Frank. (1997) *A History of Hong Kong*. London: HarperCollins.

HONG LOU MENG

Hong lou meng (Dream of the Red Chamber, The Story of the Stone) is universally acclaimed as China's greatest work of fiction. It has been hugely influential ever since its appearance in the eighteenth century. A simultaneously realistic and mythical coming-of-age story of a young aristocrat named Jia Baoyu, the novel presents an encyclopedic and lyrical window onto traditional Chinese culture.

Circumscribed by a desire for a transcendent, feminized lyricism and by the need for socially embedded, masculine responsibility, Jia Baoyu's journey from childhood to adulthood probes the limits of self-realization for scions of elite families. A love triangle between Jia and two beautiful, learned, and sensitive young women, Lin Daiyu and Xue Baochai, who embody conflicting ideals of femininity, exacerbates the tensions between sense and sensibility. The story of the rivalry, friendship, and love between Jia, Lin, and Xue is set against the detailed portrayal of over four hundred characters of various social classes.

For all its panoramic scope and its wealth of erudition relating to literature, painting, philosophy, and medicine among other scholarly topics, *Hong lou meng* is a deeply introspective and self-reflexive novel. Playing upon the conventions of Chinese historiography, fiction, poetry, and drama, the simultaneous designation of a stone as the repository of the story itself ("The Story of the Stone") and as the incarnation of Jia Baoyu ("False Precious Stone"), creates an elaborate dialectic between fictionality and reality, with one element continuously destabilizing the primacy of the other. In doing so, the novel slyly affirmed the power of fiction to represent human experience genuinely in an age that valued history as the primary vehicle of truth.

The author, Cao Xueqin (1715–1763), the impoverished and eccentric offspring of a once politically influential family, circulated the first eighty chapters in various manuscript drafts among relatives and friends. In 1791, two men published a version of 120 chapters. Cao is thought to have incorporated autobiographical elements into the text, though his authorship of the last forty chapters remains a subject of debate. Partly due to its adaptation into other popular media, including a highly successful television drama series in the 1980s in the People's Republic of China, the novel and its characters continue to be household names in many Chinese cultural contexts.

Patricia Sieber

Further Reading

Cao Xueqin. (1973–1986) *The Story of the Stone*. 5 vols. Trans. by David Hawkes and John Minford. Harmondsworth, U.K.: Penguin.

Epstein, Maram. (2001) *Competing Discourses: Orthodoxy, Authenticity, and Engendered Meanings in Late Imperial Chinese Fiction*. Cambridge, MA: Harvard University Asia Center.

HONG SHEN (1894–1955), Chinese playwright and director. Hong Shen was born in China's Jiangsu Province and entered Qinghua University in 1912. Four years later, he went to the United States and studied ceramics at Ohio State University. In 1919, after the New Culture Movement started, he studied drama at Harvard University and theater performance and management at Boston Performance School. He was the first person from China to go abroad to study modern drama, which was only introduced to China at the beginning of the twentieth century.

After returning to China in 1922, Hong devoted himself to improving Chinese drama. As a director, he did not follow the traditional Chinese custom of using male actors in female roles. He also established the modern Chinese director and rehearsal systems. Besides constructing directing theories, Hong wrote many plays. In the 1930s, as a main member of a left-wing drama organization, he wrote *Rural Trilogy*, which was composed of *Wukui Bridge*, *Fragrant Rice*, and *Dragon Pool*, and which showed the class struggle in the countryside.

Hong also played an important role in Chinese movie development. He was one of the leaders of the left-wing movie movement and wrote many movie screenplays in his life. After 1949, he became the vice chairman of the Chinese Dramatist Association and also held other leading positions in government. He died of cancer in 1955.

She Xiaojie

Further Reading

Hong Shen. (1954) *Selections of Hong Shen's Dramas*. Beijing: People's Literary Publishing House.

Xu Naixiang. (1986) *Critical Biography of Modern Chinese Writers*. Vol. 2. Jinan, China: Shandong Educational Publishing House.

HONGCUN AND XIDI In 2000 two ancient Chinese villages, Hongcun and Xidi in Anhui Province, were selected for the UNESCO World Cultural Heritage List. The villages and their relics are preserved as a national historical treasure to interpret China's feudal rural past. Founded in 1131 by the Wang family, Hongcun thrived during the Ming (1368–1644) and Qing (1644–1912) dynasties. Xidi was built in the Northern Song dynasty (960–1126). Anhui also has a Neolithic site archaeologists hypothesized might be the origin of Chinese civilization.

Shaped like an ox, Hongcun's design emphasizes waterways. Approximately 140 historical stone buildings, courtyards, and alleys form a living museum. Lexu Hall, the Wang family ancestral temple, is located by a pond. Tourists can visit homes and purchase souvenirs related to village and family history. The village was the location for the 2000 movie *Crouching Tiger, Hidden Dragon*.

The architectural legacy of both villages reveals intricate workmanship, especially carvings, engraved in wooden beams, depicting social activities such as the Lantern Festival. Significant stone masonry includes a memorial archway at Xidi built in 1578.

Another southern Anhui ancient village site, at Lu'an, was discovered in fall 2000. Archaeologists estimated this village existed during the Western Zhou dynasty (1045–771 BCE). Artifacts, including human and animal skeletons and weapons, provide insight into technological developments and the community's agricultural, trading, and military concerns.

Elizabeth D. Schafer

Further Reading

Hongkai Tan. (2001) "Labyrinth to a Distant Past." *China Daily* (6 September).

HONSHU (2001 est. pop.101,000). Honshu is the largest of Japan's four main islands. From northeast to southwest, Honshu is a long, narrow island, 1,500 kilometers in length and 300 kilometers in width, with an area of 230,940 square kilometers. It makes up 62 percent of the total area of the Japanese archipelago and forms the main part of the country. Honshu consists of five regions: Tohoku, Kanto, Chubu, Kinki, and Chugoku; the Fossa Magna fault line separates the northeast from the southwest.

Regional physical features and natural resources are very diversified. Honshu is predominantly mountainous (the Japanese Alps), with plains along the coasts. High peaks that exceed more than 3,000 meters are Mount Fuji (3,776 meters), Mount Shirane (3,192 meters), Mount Okuotakadake (3,190 meters), and Mount Yarigadade (3,180 meters). The mountain ranges influence the climatic differences between the Pacific Ocean and the Sea of Japan. There is little rain on the Pacific Ocean coast in winter, whereas the Japan seacoast is characterized by snowy weather. The climate is temperate, and annual precipitation often exceeds 1,000 millimeters. Lake Biwa is the largest lake on the island. In central and northern Honshu, mixed temperate forests are associated with conifers such as Japanese cypress, Japanese cedar, and pine.

Fishing is an important activity. Agriculture is regionally diversified. In the northern part of Honshu, products include apples, soybeans, cereals, and vegetables. In central Honshu, truck farming is predominant, with the production of vegetables, potatoes, and sweet potatoes. Along the Pacific and the Inland seacoasts, the main products include wheat, sweet potatoes, barley, tobacco, and mandarin oranges.

The major economic activities and most of the population of Japan are concentrated in Honshu. The coastal areas of the Pacific Ocean and the Inland Sea, extending from southern Kanto to Yamaguchi prefecture, are the most industrialized and urbanized regions. This region includes major metropolitan areas such as Tokyo, Yokohama, Nagoya, and the Keihanshin (Kyoto-Osaka-Kobe), where 44 percent of the population is concentrated. Together with northern Kyushu, these districts are called the Pacific coastal belt.

On the other hand, regional differences in economic growth have accentuated regional disparities, particularly on the Japan Sea side. In Hokuriku Prefecture, traditional industries and rice farming are now declining, and depopulation in the Tohoku region is the result of increasing migration of the working population toward the Pacific belt. Due to increasing urbanization, living conditions are not improving, particularly with environmental problems such as noise and pollution.

Nathalie Cavasin

Further Reading

Association of Japanese Geographers, eds. (1980) *Geography of Japan*. Tokyo: Teikoku-Shoin.

Yagasaki Noritaka, ed. (1997) *Japan: Geographical Perspectives on an Island Nation*. Tokyo: Teikoku-Shoin.

SHIRAKANI-SANCHI—WORLD HERITAGE SITE

Shirakani-Sanchi, in northern Honshu, is the site of the last untouched remnants of the beech forests that once covered Japan. Preserved as a UNESCO World Heritage Site in 1993, the forest houses many rare species and is historically significant as a glimpse at the natural forces that shaped Japan.

HORSE, AKHAL-TEKE The Akhal-Teke horse was developed on the southern fringe of the great Kara-Kum Desert of Central Asia, in the foothills of the Kopet-Dag Mountains along the border of modern Turkmenistan with Iran. It is probably the oldest purebred horse in the world; its tall stature, golden color, and beauty were known to the ancient writers. Marco Polo noticed the popularity of Turkmen horses ("Argamaks") among the Turks. Anatomical research shows a great similarity between the modern Akhal-Teke and the English Thoroughbred horse. Some Akhal-Teke characteristics are also recognizable in the conformation of the Syrian Arab horse. Before the Russian takeover of the Transcaspian Region in the 1880s, the nomadic Turkmens of the Teke tribe bred Akhal-Tekes for mercenary raids as well as for racing. Later, in the USSR, Akhal-Tekes suffered heavy losses from mismanagement and direct slaughter. In 1935, Akhal-Tekes were used for a famous marathon trek from Ashgabat to Moscow (around 2,500 miles).

Only about 2,000 Akhal-Tekes now exist in the world, including between 1,200 and 1,300 in now independent Turkmenistan, where the state promotes this horse as a national symbol. "If the carpet is the Turkmen's soul, the horse is his wings," says the Turkmen proverb. A millennium-old cult of the noble Akhal-Teke horse also explains the fact that Turkmens, unlike other Muslim peoples of Central Asia, never use horsemeat for food.

Victor Fet

Further Reading

Klimuk, A. (1999) "The Purebred Akhal-Teke Horse and Its Influence on Other Purebred Breeds." Retrieved 4 February 2002, from: http://www.akhalteke.org.

Maslow, J. (1994) *Sacred Horses: The Memoirs of a Turkmen Cowboy*. New York: Random House.

Witt, W. O., ed. (1937) *Breeds of Horses in Middle Asia*. Moscow: All-Union Research Institute of Horse Breeding.

HORSE, KARABAIR

Also known as Karabairskaya (Russian), the Karabair is one of the most ancient horse breeds of Central Asia. In appearance the Karabair resembles the Arabian, Persian, and Turkmenian as well as the steppe horse breeds. The breed is improved through pure breeding. Karabair horses show good endurance and versatile working qualities. This breed was developed in Uzbekistan and northern Tajikistan (former Soviet republics of Central Asia) under the influence of southern and steppe breeds. It is well adapted to both saddle and harness, and has the typical build of a saddle and harness horse. The coat color is bay, chestnut, gray, or black.

The Karabair horse is distinguished by sound health and average longevity. It is a good horse for long rides. The breed consists of three intra-breed types—basic, heavy, and saddle—as well as eight sire lines and five mare families. The Karabair are currently bred in all zones of Uzbekistan; the main studs are in the Jizak region of Uzbekistan. The Karabair performs very well in sports, mainly in the equestrian game of *kokpar* (similar to the related Afghan sport known as *buzkashi*), in which riders fight over a goat carcass.

Victor Fet

Further Reading

Dmitriev, N. G., and L. K. Ernst. (1989) *Animal Genetic Resources of the USSR*. Animal Production and Health Paper. Rome: FAO.

Porter, V., and I. L. Mason. (2001) *A World Dictionary of Livestock Breeds, Types, and Varieties*. 5th ed. Oxford: C. A. B. International.

HORSE, LOKAI

The Lokai is a mixed breed from Central Asia. At 140–150 centimeters high, it is the shortest of Central Asian horse breeds. Strong and sure-footed, it is a good riding and pack horse, agile and enduring. Its coat is gray, bay, or chestnut (often with a golden tint), sometimes curled. It is an excellent riding horse, well-suited to competitive sports. The Lokai originates from the Pamir Mountains, now in Tajikistan, south of the Tian Shan range. Its name comes from the Lokai tribe of Uzbeks who, starting from the sixteenth century, improved this breed by crossing it with Akhal-Teke, Karabair, and even Arabian horses. The Lokai horse is common in Uzbekistan and Tajikistan, where it is a good, tough saddle and pack pony in its native mountains, at altitudes of 2,000 to 4,000 meters. It can carry a rider eighty kilometers a day over mountain tracks at an average speed of eight or nine kilometers per hour. In a nomadic tradition, the mares are also milked. The tough and swift Lokai is famous for its use by Tajik riders in the equestrian game of *kopar* (*kokpar*) where riders fight over a goat carcass (similar to the related sport of Afghanistan known as *buzkashi*).

Victor Fet

Further Reading

Dmitriev, N. G., and L. K. Ernst. (1989) *Animal Genetic Resources of the USSR*. Animal Production and Health Paper. Rome: FAO

Oklahoma State University. (1996) "Breeds of Livestock—Horse Breeds." Retrieved 4 February 2002, from: http://www.ansi.okstate.edu/breeds/horses.

HORSE, PRZEWALSKI'S

Przewalski's horse *(Equus przewalski)*, or *takhi* in Mongolian, is the last remaining species of wild horse in the world. Przewalski's horse stands around 1.3 meters high, has a large head, a short stocky body, and an upright mane. It has a solid tan coat with a black stripe running along its back, faint zebra stripes on its lower legs, and lighter coloring around the muzzle. Some experts argue that it resembles the common ancestor of all modern horses.

The wild horse was brought to European attention by the Russian naturalist Nikolai Michailovitch Przewalski (1839–1888) after he observed several of the species in Mongolia in 1881. Soon after his sighting, hunting pressure and competition for grazing land and water led to the horse's gradual extinction in the wild. The last reliable sighting in the wild of this horse occurred in 1969 near the Takhin Tal (Wild Horse Mountain) in Mongolia. From a population of thirty to forty Przewalski horses in zoos around the world in 1950, several hundred have now been bred in captivity. In 1992 a breeding group of Przewalski horses was introduced to Mongolia in the hope of later reintroducing the animals to the open steppe.

Daniel Hruschka

Further Reading

Boyd, Lee, and Katherine Houpt. (1994) *Przewalski's Horse: The History and Biology of an Endangered Species.* New York: SUNY Series in Endangered Species, State University of New York Press.

Mohr, Erna. (1971) *The Asiatic Wild Horse.* Trans. by Daphne Machin Goodall. London: J. A. Allen.

HOSEN, IBRAHIM (1917–2001), Indonesian religious figure. Ibrahim, a son of Hosen bin Abdul Syukur, emerged as a colorful religious figure in Indonesia, with bold and unorthodox opinions. He was born in the South Sumatran town of Bengkulu to a Bugis father and a South Sumatran mother. During Ibrahim's early years, his father took the family first to Jakarta and Singapore, where he was in the retail business, and then to Lampung in South Sumatra, where he ran a religious school. Ibrahim's four-year stay in Singapore as a child and pupil at the As-Sagaf School left a strong imprint on his worldview, which tended to be tolerant, open-minded, modern, and pluralist. In 1934 he went to Java for further study of the Qur'an, Islamic law, Arabic literature, and rhetoric. According to his biographers, Ibrahim met and studied under a number of religious scholars and Hadrami (Yemeni Arab) teachers in Java.

After one year of study and travel in Java, Ibrahim returned to South Sumatra. In 1939, for the first time, he successfully represented an established school of Islamic law in a debate, defending its stance on many social and religious issues. During the rapid political disruption in the 1940s, precipitated by the Japanese occupation of Indonesia during the Pacific War and the return of the Dutch, Ibrahim, as a religious scholar-cum-official, energetically took part in socioreligious and political activities in the region of Bengkulu, his native town. He married twice, in 1946 and again in 1948 following the death of his first wife, and had eight surviving children.

In 1955 Ibrahim went to Cairo to study at al-Azhar University. Returning to Indonesia with a degree in Islamic law in 1960, he joined the Department of Religious Affairs in Jakarta. In 1964 he was appointed rector of the newly opened State Institute of Islamic Studies in Palembang.

Following the major political changes in Indonesia in the mid-1960s in the wake of the purge of the Indonesian Communist Party and the rise to power of Suharto, Ibrahim began a major career as a national figure. In 1966 he moved to Jakarta, assuming the post of bureau chief in the Department of Religious Affairs. He continued to occupy an important post in the department until his retirement in 1982. At the same time, capitalizing on his credibility as a religious figure and official, Ibrahim won financial support from many wealthy sponsors to institute and lead two centers of higher learning for Qur'anic studies in South Jakarta, one for men, in 1971, and another for women, in 1977.

Ibrahim was appointed to the chairmanship of the Indonesian Council of Religious Scholars in 1980. Here he found an official platform from which to launch his religious views, considered by many Indonesians to be innovative but also controversial, on account of his toleration of beer drinking, bank interest, the lottery, and contraceptive devices. Although Ibrahim did not write major works detailing his jurisprudential principles, religious philosophy, or reformist ideas, he responded to the religious controversies that occupied the minds of many Indonesian Muslims.

Ibrahim's religious interpretations arose in the context of the nature of Islam in Indonesia, with its often-declared openness, moderation, tolerance, and pluralism. He responded positively to the tolerance and open-mindedness of his countrypeople, and at the same time he saw the religious justification for many practices under scrutiny, such as those mentioned. This religious predilection, not surprisingly, annoyed or even angered many religious leaders who strictly adhered to scripture. At some point, he was even branded a religious scholar who could be hired to issue legal opinions or a religious scholar who always supported government policy.

Ibrahim himself claimed that his approach to any issue was based on the Islamic legal principle of permissibility; that is, that all matters are inherently permissible. Only when there are specific and unequivocal prohibitions in Islam does such permission end. Considering his religious and educational background, Ibrahim can be seen to belong to a scholarly tradition that tackles religious issues on the basis of Islamic jurisprudence, or a legalistic approach. All his references and quotations may be traced to earlier opinions of Muslim jurists or their equivalents. Not surprisingly, he claimed that his legal opinions were not novel, let alone un-Islamic, since his rulings were based on earlier, established scholarly opinion.

Iik A. Mansurnoor

Further Reading

Federspiel, Howard M. (1992) *Muslim Intellectuals and National Development in Indonesia*. New York: Nova Science.

Gibson, Thomas. (2000) "Islam and the Spirit Cults in New Order Indonesia: Global Flows vs. Local Knowledge." *Indonesia* 69 (April): 41–70.

Ratno, Lukito. (1999) "Law and Politics in Post-Independence Indonesia: A Case Study of Religious and *Adat* Courts." *Studia Islamika* 6, 2: 63–86.

HOUSEHOLD RESPONSIBILITY SYSTEM—CHINA The household responsibility system has been a crucial national policy of the Chinese Communist Party (CCP) since 1978. Literally, "responsibility" means that an individual household, or a set of households, assumes the task of production for and payment to the government. As University of Hong Kong scholar Steven Cheung notes, the so-called responsibility contract is "equivalent to the granting of private property rights [sic] through a state lease of land. . . . The duration of the lease may be any number of years or, in principle, it may be in perpetuity. Ownership is not relinquished by the state, but the rights to use and to obtain income are exclusively assigned to the lessee. The right to transfer or to sell the leased resource may take the form of subletting. Various dues exacted by the state may be lumped together in the form of a fixed rent, and since this rent is paid to the state it becomes a property tax" (Cheung 1990: 22).

The household responsibility system was introduced four times in Chinese history: 1957, 1959–1961, 1964, and 1978. In its first three incarnations it was permitted only in extremely poor areas, such as the provinces of Anhui and Sichuan, where it was introduced in an attempt to rescue the provinces from their agricultural crises. A number of Chinese leaders, including Deng Zihui (1896–1972) and Liu Shaoqi (1898–1974), tried to implement the household responsibility system more extensively, but Mao Zedong (1893–1976) crushed their attempts. For instance, in 1961, the secretary of the CCP in Anhui Province tried to employ the household responsibility system throughout the province by requesting permission from the central government. His proposal, if accepted, would have meant a decentralization of power because it would have given provinces more authority to make decisions relating to provincial governance. Along with Liu, many other leaders, including Deng Zihui and Chen Yun (1905–1995), supported reform of the agricultural sector. However, Mao rejected the proposed reforms, accusing these leaders of encouraging capitalist initiatives and widening the gap between rich and poor among Chinese farmers.

Despite prohibitions at the national level, a few areas experimented with the household responsibility system. A village in Guizhou Province adopted the system secretly for more than ten years before 1978. The village did not dare to admit its practice of the official household responsibility system until the new policy was announced. Toward the end of 1978, in Feixi County and Chuxian Prefecture in Anhui Province, a small number of production teams (a communal unit) began to try the system of contracting land, other resources, and output quotas to individual households. However, the practice was restricted to the poor agricultural regions.

Zhao Ziyang (b. 1919) launched the household responsibility system as a reform in Sichuan Province in 1975, during his tenure there as general secretary of the CCP. In 1980, as Deng's protégé, Zhao was made prime minister of China. Subsequently, almost all households in China's rural areas adopted the household responsibility system as national policy by the end of 1983.

Mandatory Production Targets

Prior to 1980, Chinese farms were given mandatory production targets that extended to yields, levels of input applications, and planting techniques. Members of a production team, working under the supervision of a team leader, were credited with work points for jobs they performed. At the end of a year, net team income was first distributed among members according to some basic needs; then the rest was distributed according to the work points that each one accumulated during that year. Work points were supposed to reflect the quality and quantity of effort that each member performed rather than the result of his or her efforts. Therefore, the work point system was not an incentive scheme.

In contrast, under the household responsibility system, land is contracted to individual households for a period of fifteen years. After fulfilling the procurement quota obligations, farmers are entitled to sell their surplus on the market or retain it for their own use. By definition, peasants become residual claimants. The marginal return on their efforts is the marginal product of their efforts. In other words, by linking rewards directly to effort, the contracting system enhanced incentives and promoted efficient production. The most conspicuous effect, however, is the impact on productivity arising from the increased incentive to work. It is estimated that total factor productivity increased 15 percent as a result of the improved incentives inherent in the household responsibility system. The household responsibility system reform was implemented in 1979 and was completed in 1984. During this period, agricultural output increased by 45 percent. About one-third of the output growth between 1979 and 1984, therefore, can be attributed to the household responsibility system reform alone.

The Key to Economic Reform

The household responsibility system symbolized the key to economic reform. Eventually, the system spread to areas other than agriculture. Whereas it took a revolution to abolish private property, the process in reverse may be done through peaceful contracting. The word "private" was scrupulously avoided until March 1988. However, as it turns out, the so-called responsibility contract, with all its modifications and refinements, is a Chinese version of the deed of trust—the right to use and develop land that one does not own outright. The contract is not in perpetuity. Individual households running their own small enterprises can now be found everywhere, and in southern China even state-owned enterprises now refuse to hire state employees; rather, they opt for contract workers. In July 1988, for instance, a Japanese firm won a public auction of land—a first for nonagricultural use in China. Importantly, for the first time since the Communist Revolution, a foreign entity had openly gained a private interest on China's soil.

The responsibility contract as applied to agriculture comes very close to what in the Western world is a grant of private property in land. The main defect of the production system as an institution for agricultural development is its incentive structure. One of the major reasons for the success of China's economic reform today, unlike that of the former Soviet Union, is the household responsibility system. Nevertheless, the household responsibility system faces some problems, including declining arable land area, stagnating grain production, and shrinking income at the rural level. As a result, millions of peasants have migrated to cities such as Beijing and Shanghai to seek employment.

Unryu Suganuma

Further Reading

Cheung, Steven N. S. (1990) "Privatization vs. Special Interests: The Experience of China's Economic Reform." In *Economic Reform in China: Problems and Prospects*, edited by James A. Dorn and Wang Xi. Chicago: University of Chicago Press, 21–37.

Lardy, Nicholas R. (1998) *China's Unfinished Economic Revolution*. Washington, DC: Brookings Institution Press.

Lin, Justin Yifu. (1990) "Institutional Reforms in Chinese Agriculture: Retrospect and Prospect." In *Economic Reform in China: Problems and Prospects*, edited by James A. Dorn and Wang Xi. Chicago: University of Chicago Press, 149–164.

Naughton, Barry. (1995) "Deng Xiaoping: The Economist." In *Deng Xiaoping: Portrait of a Chinese Statesman*, edited by David Shambaugh. Oxford: Clarendon, 83–106.

Pearson, Margaret M. (1999) "China's Integration into the International Trade and Investment Regime." In *China Joins the World: Progress and Prospects*, edited by Elizabeth Economy and Michel Oksenberg. New York: Council on Foreign Relations Press, 161–205.

Sicular, Terry. (1991) "China's Agricultural Policy during the Reform Period." In *China's Economic Dilemmas in the 1990s: The Problems of Reforms, Modernization, and Interdependence*. Washington, DC: U.S. Government Printing Office.

HSIA DYNASTY. See **Xia Dynasty.**

HSUN-TZU. See **Xunzi.**

HU JINTAO (b. 1942), political leader of China. Born in Shanghai in December 1942, with ancestral roots in Anhui Province, Hu Jintao graduated from China's Qinghua University, Department of Irrigation Engineering, in 1965. He joined the Chinese Communist Party (CCP) in April 1964 and became a political/ideological counselor for students while in college. After graduation, he became an engineer at the Liujiaxia Irrigation Works in Gansu Province, northwestern China.

Chosen by Deng Xiaoping (1904–1997) to be the yet-to-be-confirmed paramount leader of the so-called fourth generation of leadership of the People's Republic of China (PRC), Hu has ranked as the fifth and the youngest standing member of the seven-member Political Bureau of the CCP since 1997. His current posts include vice president of the PRC and vice president of the CCP's Military Affairs Committee. He has held the posts of head of the Chinese Communist Youth League (January 1983–July 1985), party secretary of Guizhou Province (July 1985–November 1988), and the eighth party secretary of the Tibet Autonomous Region (December 1988–January 1991).

Hu is known for his deep affiliation with the Chinese Communist Youth League, his longtime supervision of the CCP's ideological work and the training of the CCP's young ideologues, and his crackdown on the Tibetans' uprising in Lhasa, Tibet's capital. He generally evades media coverage and has granted especially little access to the international media.

Wenshan Jia

Further Reading

Li Cheng. (2000) "Jiang Zemin's Successors: The Rise of the Fourth Generation of Leaders in the PRC." *China Quarterly* 161 (March): 1–40.

Ren Zhichu. (1997) *Hu Jintao: China's First Man in the 21st Century.* New York: Mirror.

HU SHI (1891–1962), Chinese intellectual. Born in Jixi, Anhui Province, Hu Shi was China's leading liberal scholar and educator of his time. Hu laid an important foundation for the 1919 May 4th Movement with an essay published in 1917 in the Chinese journal *Xin Qing Nian* (New Youth), which advocated the avoidance of the classical language and the adoption of the vernacular in literature. *Chang Shi Ji* (The Trials), his collection of poetry published in March 1920, was the first noticeable attempt at vernacular poetry in modern China. During the May 4th period, Hu criticized Confucianism and called for individualism and women's liberation. From 1917 to 1948, Hu worked at Beijing University at intervals, serving as the chair of various departments, academic dean, dean of humanities, and university president. The framework he designed in 1922 for the Chinese school system, from primary school to college, remained in practice until the early 1950s. He died as president of the Academia Sinica in Taiwan, which position he had held since 1958.

Hu studied at Cornell (1910–1914) and Columbia (1915–1917, awarded a Ph.D. in 1927), served as China's ambassador to the United States (1938–1942), and resided in the United States from 1949 to 1958. A student of the West, he promoted Western ideas in China in an attempt to better serve the country. However, his advocacy of the total Westernization—reworded later as Internationalization—of China in his earlier years has remained controversial.

Jian-Zhong Lin

Further Reading

Chou Min-chih. (1984) *Hu Shih and Intellectual Choice in Modern China.* Ann Arbor, MI: University of Michigan Press.

Grieder, Jerome B. (1970) *Hu Shih and the Chinese Renaissance: Literature in the Chinese Revolution, 1917–1937.* Cambridge, MA: Harvard University Press.

Zhu Wenhua. (1991) *Hu Shi Pingzhuan* (The Life and Times of Hu Shi). Chongqing, China: Chongqing Press.

HU YAOBANG (1915–1989), Chinese Communist Party reformer in the 1980s. Born in Hunan Province into a peasant family in 1915, Hu Yaobang joined the Red Army and the Chinese Communist Party (CCP) and was included in the 1934–1935 Long March. His career was closely linked with that of Deng Xiaoping (1904–1997). Along with Deng, Hu was purged twice during the Cultural Revolution (1966–1976) and was sent into the countryside for "reeducation." He gained membership in the CCP Politburo in 1978 with Deng's support. Hu organized the rehabilitation of intellectuals disgraced during the Cultural Revolution and presided over a radical liberalization of the party structure between 1982 and 1986.

Hu supported combining economic liberalization with political liberalization. On 16 January 1987, he resigned as general secretary of the CCP after he was forced to accept responsibility for student demonstrations that occurred in December 1986. He went into seclusion, although he remained a member of the Politburo. On 15 April 1989, Hu died of a heart attack. His resignation and subsequent death dimmed the hopes of those who supported political reforms. His funeral sparked student demonstrations that ended with the Tiananmen incident in June 1989.

Elizabeth Van Wie Davis

Further Reading

Pang Pang. (1995) *Death of Hu Yaobang.* Honolulu, HI: University of Hawaii Press.

Yang Zhongmei. (1988) *Hu Yaobang: A Chinese Biography.* Trans. by William A. Wycoff. Armonk, NY: M. E. Sharpe.

HUANG HAI. See **Yellow Sea.**

HUANG RIVER Called "China's sorrow," or Huang Ho in Chinese, the Huang (Yellow) River is the second-largest river in China, flowing 5,954 kilometers from its origins in the Bayan Harshan Mountains on the Qinghai-Tibet Plateau in western China until it empties into the Bo Hai Gulf. The Huang River derives its name from the yellow color of the silt in the water. Each year, tons of silt are deposited on the riverbed, causing annual flooding. The Huang River flows east and then northeast through Qinghai, Gansu, and Ningxia Provinces and then through Inner Mongolia before turning south, forming the border of Shaanxi and Shanxi Provinces. From there, the Huang turns east through Henan and Shandong Provinces before emptying into the Bo Hai Gulf.

Throughout China's long history, the Huang River has overflowed its banks, causing extensive damage to nearby farmland and surrounding communities. Dikes have been built to stem the flooding but have to be continually rebuilt to prevent the river from overflowing its banks. The river has also changed course many times, causing untold damage. During the Yuan dynasty (1279–1368), the Huang River changed its course from northern to southern Shandong Province, flooding 7,769 square kilometers of farmland. Between 1853 and 1855, the river began flowing through northern Shandong Province, destroying large areas of farmland. In modern times, General Chiang Kai-shek (1887–1975) ordered his troops to destroy the dikes along the river in Henan Province, causing disastrous effects, including the drowning of 1 million Chinese civilians.

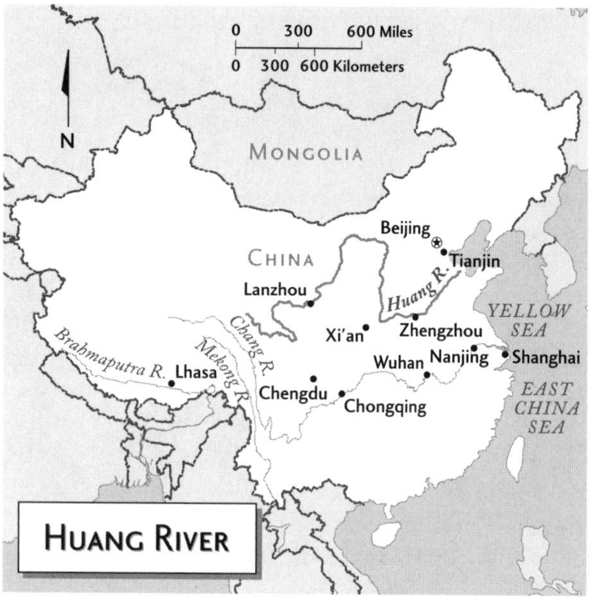

HUANG RIVER

The lower region of the Huang River is considered the birthplace of Chinese civilization, because archaeologists have discovered sites dating as far back as 5000 BCE and have chronicled the emergence of the Yangshao culture (5000–3000 BCE) and the Longshan culture (3000–2200 BCE) on the North China Plain along the Huang River. Since 1949, the Chinese government has accomplished many flood control and reforestation projects to conquer the capricious nature of the river.

Keith A. Leitich

Further Reading

Liu, Jiang. (1980) *China's Largest River.* Beijing: Foreign Language Press.

National Geographic Society. (1982) *Journey into China.* Washington, DC: National Geographic Society.

HUANG SHAN Mount Huang (Huangshan), known as the "most beautiful mountain in China," is located in the southern part of Anhui Province in eastern China. Huang Shan actually is a complex of mountains, covering 154 square kilometers (50 square miles), with seventy-seven peaks above 1,000 meters (3,280 feet). Lotus Flower, the highest peak, reaches 1,864 meters (6,116 feet) above sea level. The mountain has a complex geology but consists mainly of granite rock; the formation derives from faulting and folding processes dating back 100 million years.

HUANG SHAN—WORLD HERITAGE SITE

An important theme in sixteenth-century Chinese Shanshui art and literature, this spectacular granite mountain remains a popular subject for artists and photographers. It was designated a UNESCO World Heritage Site in 1990.

Huang Shan consists of numerous weirdly shaped rock pillars, and frequent fog and mist give the appearance of stone islands rising from a sea of fog. The area also contains waterfalls, lakes, hot springs, and pine forests. From the Tang dynasty (618–907 CE) on it has assumed great importance in Chinese culture, being extolled in art and literature. Huang Shan was proclaimed a site of scenic beauty and historic interest by the Chinese government in 1982 and inscribed on the World Heritage List in 1990.

Michael Pretes

Further Reading

"Huangshan Mountain." (1989) *Information China*. Vol. 1. Oxford: Pergamon.

Kuan, Yu-Chien, and Petra Haring Kuan. (1987) *Magnificent China: A Guide to Its Cultural Treasures*. Hong Kong: Joint Publishing.

Lai Tien Chang. (1979) *Visiting China: A Cultural Guide*. Hong Kong: Swindon.

Munakata, Kiyohiko. (1991) *Sacred Mountains in Chinese Art*. Chicago: University of Illinois Press.

HUANGLONGSI

HUANGLONGSI Huanglongsi, China, and the neighboring ravine to the north, Jiuzhaigou, are two outstanding natural resource areas on the Tibetan plateau. Both areas are national parks and have recently been designated by the United Nations as World Heritage Sites for their extraordinary natural scenery. Jiuzhaigou (Ravine of the Nine Stockade-Villages) is named after the rural Tibetan communities *(sde dgu)* that populate the area and is most notable for dramatic waterfalls and glacier-formed lakes. The limestone geology of the area, combined with hot spring algae growth, has produced an incredible range of colored waters (turquoise, green, yellow, and milky white). Formerly the domain of giant pandas, much of the area was heavily logged in the 1980s. Red pandas, golden monkeys, takins (large ruminants), and water deer are said to still populate the region, but vast areas of rhododendron, wild roses, clematis, and wild ginger are more easily found.

Yellow Dragon Temple (Chinese: Huanglongsi) is a Taoist monastery located in Sichuan Province, China, 35 kilometers from the county seat of Songpan. Because it is located so high (3,430 meters) in the Minshan mountain range, the temple was previously known as the Snow Mountain Temple (Yueshansi). The temple is situated at a pass into a forested valley surrounded by glaciated peaks (up to 5,000 meters) and dotted with over three thousand natural pools of various-colored water, from which the Tibetan name of the temple, Gser mthso lha khang (Yellow Pool Temple), is derived. The existing structure was founded in the Ming dynasty (1368–1644) and is the rear, and only surviving, of three halls built at that time.

Gray Tuttle

Further Reading

Gyurme Dorje. (1996) *Tibet Handbook: With Bhutan*. Chicago: Passport.

Kanamaru, Atsushi. (2000) *Mapping the Tibetan World*. Reno, NV: Kotan.

Sichuan sheng Aba Zangzu Qiangzu zizhizhou difang zhi bianzuan weiyuanhui, ed. (1994) *Aba zhou zhi* (Aba Prefecture Gazetteer). Vol. 3. Chengdu, China: Minzu chubanshe.

Stevens, K. Mark, and George E. Wehrfritz. (1988) *Southwest China off the Beaten Track*. Chicago: Passport.

HUBEI

HUBEI (2002 est. pop. 63.3 million). Hubei (Hupei, Hupeh), a central China province that covers an area of 185,900 square kilometers, borders on Sichuan and Shaanxi in the west, on Henan in the north, on Anhui in the east, and on Hunan and Jiangxi in the south. The province is traversed by the Chang (Yangtze) River from west to east, with the greater part of the province located north of the river. More than three-fourths of the province is hilly and mountainous, with peaks in the western parts reaching to more than 3,000 meters, while the eastern part mainly consists of low-lying plains.

The climate is subtropical, with monsoon rain in spring and summer. Summers are hot and humid; winters generally are mild. The annual average precipitation varies between 700 and 1,700 millimeters, which is the highest average in the southeast. The vast majority of Hubei's population lives in rural areas along the rivers and in the lake district in the eastern part where the capital, Wuhan (4.4 million, 1994), also is situated.

Wuhan was originally three cities separated by the Han and Chang Rivers, but these were joined by bridges in the 1950s. During the Eastern Zhou dynasty (770–221 BCE), the Hubei area was the center of the Chu kingdom, and copper mines were operating near present Daye County, not far from Wuhan. With the unification of China in 221 BCE, Hubei became part of the Chinese empire, but it was not until the Tang dynasty (618–907 CE) that immigration from the north accelerated and the province became a wealthy rice-producing area. In the nineteenth century, the province suffered greatly under the Taiping Rebellion (1851–1864). Cities along the Chang River were opened for trade with the Europeans, and tea became a major commodity. The rebellion that ended the Qing dynasty (1644–1912) originated in Hubei. During the Japanese occupation of eastern China, parts of Hubei were controlled by Japanese troops, and industrial works were bombed.

Large areas of the province are well suited for agriculture; the major crops are rice, wheat, corn, sweet potatoes, cotton, and rapeseed. Products indigenous to Hubei include lacquer, tangerines, tremella, camphor trees, and various sorts of medical herbs and tea. The iron works and steel yards of Wuhan are among the largest in China, and its industry manufactures farm machines, railcars, engines, transport machinery, and so forth. In 1994 the Chinese government initiated the so-called "Three Gorges Dam," a gigantic dam to be built just west of Sandouping, located about thirty-five kilometers west of the river port of Yichang. The project is scheduled to be completed in 2009, by which time the reservoir behind the dam will extend about 500 kilometers upstream, having displaced an estimated 1.9 million people in western Hubei and the neighboring province of Sichuan.

Bent Nielsen

Further Reading

Chen, Anna Gustafsson. (1998) *Dreams of the Future: Communal Experiments in May Fourth China*. Lund, Sweden: Department of East Asian Languages, Lund University.

Esherick, Joseph W. (1976) *Reform and Revolution in China: The 1911 Revolution in Hunan and Hubei*. Berkeley and Los Angeles: University of California Press.

HUE (2001 pop. 262,000). Located thirteen kilometers inland from the South China Sea on Vietnam's central coast and bisected by the Song Huong (Perfume River), Hue is regarded by many as Vietnam's artistic, spiritual, and cultural center. Hue was Vietnam's capital and the Imperial City during the Nguyen dynasty (1802–1955). Even as early as the second century BCE, Hue was home to rulers. From 111 BCE to 222 CE, the Han dynasty (206 BCE–222 CE) Chinese empire occupied Vietnam; during this time, the city (then called Tay Quyen) was headquarters for the Han army. Local chieftains captured the city in the second century CE and renamed it K'ui Sou. The Vietnamese and Cham (who ruled central Vietnam from the second to fifteenth century as the Kingdom of Champa) fought over the city between the tenth and fourteenth centuries. By the fifteenth century, the Vietnamese had captured the city and renamed it Phu Xuan.

In 1847 two French warships bombarded Tourane (Da Nang), to protest the Vietnamese treatment of French missionaries in Vietnam. The attack killed an estimated 10,000 Vietnamese civilians. Emperor Thieu Tri (ruled 1841–1847), recognizing the French technological power advantage, sued for peace, the first step down the road to the establishment of a French protectorate over the country. During the U.S. War in Vietnam, Hue was devastated by the fighting, especially during the 1968 Tet Offensive, which destroyed much of the old Imperial City and Citadel.

Hue continues to adapt itself to different times and circumstances. Today, Hue's main draw is its past. Every year thousands of visitors flock to the ancient Vietnamese capital to soak up its rich history. Elaborate tombs of emperors, ancient pagodas, outstanding cuisine, the Imperial City and Citadel, and a flourishing art business will keep Hue bustling with activity and tourists for years to come.

Richard B. Verrone

HUE—WORLD HERITAGE SITE

A UNESCO World Heritage Site since 1993, Hue was the capital of Vietnam during the feudal Nguyen dynasty. All but abandoned now, the Hue monuments are a poignant reminder of imperial Vietnam.

Further Reading

Admiralty, Naval Intelligence Division, Great Britain. (1943) *Indo-China*. Geographical Handbook Series, B.R. 510. London: His Majesty's Stationery Office.

Cima, Ronald J., ed. (1989) *Vietnam: A Country Study*. Washington, DC: Government Printing Office.

Taylor, Keith. (1983) *The Birth of Vietnam*. Berkeley and Los Angeles: University of California Press.

HUI Hui is a state-recognized nationality of China that is characterized by being Muslim religiously but Chinese culturally. Alternative names include Huihui and Dongan. The Hui are among the most populous of China's minorities. The 1990 census put their population at approximately 8.6 million, third after the

The Great Mosque in Xi'an, one of the oldest and largest mosques in China and spiritual center for the large Hui population in the city. (CARL & ANN PURCELL/CORBIS)

Zhuang and Manchus. The Hui are also the most widely distributed of China's minorities. Although the main concentrations are in the northwest, such as in Ningxia, Gansu, and Shaanxi provinces, communities also exist in Yunnan and elsewhere, and even in Hong Kong, Taiwan, and overseas Chinese communities. Most are Chinese-speaking, retaining Arabic only to read the Qur'an.

Muslims have lived in China since the seventh century CE, notably in the southeast. But it was not until the Mongol conquest of the thirteenth century that many came, gradually becoming settlers, not immigrants, and adopting Chinese culture, speaking Chinese, and marrying Chinese women. To this day, most Hui maintain a belief in a single God, abstain from pork, practice circumcision, and attend mosques in Hui communities. Intermarriage is becoming more common, but it remains infrequent. Hui dedication to Islam is much stronger in the northwest than elsewhere. In the southeast, some people of Muslim descent regard themselves as Hui while following customs and beliefs hardly different from their Han neighbors.

The Hui Muslim tradition is Sunni, but sectarian divisions have been common historically. Relations with the Han Chinese have often been contentious. The nineteenth century saw a high point in Hui rebellions against Chinese regimes. However, since China became a republic in 1912, the Hui have generally been loyal to the Chinese state and fought for it against foreign enemies and even against non-Hui Muslim rebels. During the Cultural Revolution (1966–1976) Muslims were persecuted and mosques were desecrated; the Hui suffered serious religious and ethnic persecution and many hid their identity. However, the Hui remain loyal to China, showing little support for and much opposition to Muslim secession from China. Since the early 1980s, Hui ethnic consciousness has revived strongly.

A tradition of Hui Chinese-language Islamic scholarship developed in China, including in mysticism (Sufism). In addition, the Hui have contributed to such Chinese arts as the Peking Opera. Their tradition of commercial skills remains strong to this day. Over the centuries they have been sinicized, and currently few physical or nonreligious cultural characteristics distinguish them from the Han. The Hui do well socially and educationally, with literacy rates among the highest of the minorities; many urban Hui, including women, enter the professions.

Colin Mackerras

Further Reading

Dillon, Michael. (1999) *China's Muslim Hui Community: Migration, Settlement, and Sects.* Richmond, Surrey, U.K.: Curzon.

Gladney, Dru C. (1991) *Muslim Chinese: Ethnic Nationalism in the People's Republic.* Cambridge, MA: Council on East Asian Studies, Harvard University.

Lipman, Jonathan N. (1997) *Familiar Strangers: A History of Muslims in Northwest China*. Studies on Ethnic Groups in China. Seattle: University of Washington Press.
Wang Jianping. (1996) *Concord and Conflict: The Hui Communities of Yunnan Society*. Stockholm, Sweden: Almqvist and Wiksell.

HUK REBELLION The Hukbalahap, a Tagalog acronym for the Hukbo ng Bayan Laban sa Hapon (People's Anti-Japanese Army), was founded in March 1942 as the military arm of the outlawed Partido Komunista ng Pilipinas (PKP), or the Communist Party of the Philippines. The Hukbalahap (or Huks) sought to defeat Japan, destroy the exploitative landholding system in Central Luzon that for decades had resulted in widespread peasant poverty, and ultimately establish a communist government. As a large and well-organized guerrilla group, the Huks inflicted heavy casualties on the Japanese army, and, significantly, killed an estimated twenty thousand Filipino collaborators, class enemies, or personal rivals. When Japan surrendered, the Huks controlled many local governments in Central Luzon and had appointed governors of Pampanga and Laguna provinces.

Seven Hukbalahap-supported politicians, including Huk Supremo Luis Taruc, were elected to the Philippine Congress in 1946. Their expulsion from congress to ensure the passage of a constitutional amendment favorable to American economic interests and President Manuel Roxas's "mailed fist" policy drove the Hukbalahap underground and into armed conflict with the government. From the four Central Luzon provinces of Bulacan, Nueva Ecija, Pampanga, and Tarlac, the original area of "Huklandia," the Huks increased their political activities in other Luzon provinces and on the island of Panay. The name of the Hukbalahap was changed in November 1948 to Hukbong Mapagpalaya ng Bayan (HMB) or the People's Liberation Army to reflect the PKP's goal of overthrowing the Philippine government.

The turning point in the Huk insurgency was President Elpidio Quirino's appointment of Ramon Magsaysay as secretary of defense in 1950 and an increase in American military assistance to the Philippines. A charismatic former guerrilla leader from Zambales province and a popular congress member with strong ties to the military, Magsaysay was given a free hand in reestablishing law and order. He reorganized the military, retiring or court-martialing corrupt and incompetent officers and soldiers, and worked to regain the confidence of the peasantry. Magsaysay pursued the Huks aggressively and took steps to protect the peasantry from Huk terrorism. He also established the Economic Development Corps (EDCOR) in December 1950 to relocate landless peasants in Hukbalahap-controlled areas to unoccupied land in Mindanao. By 1954, when Huk Supremo Taruc surrendered, the HMB was no longer a threat to the stability of the government. Although remnants of the Huks continued to operate in Central Luzon for more than a decade after Taruc's surrender, the movement was dead by 1970.

Robert L. Youngblood

Further Reading

Kerkvliet, Benedict J. (1977) *The Huk Rebellion: A Study of Peasant Revolt in the Philippines*. Berkeley and Los Angeles: University of California Press.
Lachica, Eduardo. (1971) *HUK: Philippine Agrarian Society in Revolt*. Manila, Philippines: Solidaridad.
Taruc, Luis. (1967) *He Who Rides the Tiger: The Story of an Asian Guerrilla Leader*. New York: Praeger.

HUMAYUN (d. 1556), Mughal ruler. Eldest of four sons, Humayun was the designated successor of Babur, ascending to the throne of the Mughal empire in December 1530 at the age of twenty-three. Humayun inherited an Indian kingdom that was riven by internal dissension and subject to external threats. He had some experience as governor of Badakshan, but as emperor proved a poor replacement to Babur.

A cultivated man, interested in mathematics and astronomy, and with considerable personal valor, Humayun lacked political astuteness. He failed to capitalize on his victories, was indecisive, prone to long bouts of indolence, and addicted to opium. His ambitious brothers were allowed to carve niches for themselves (Kamran, for instance, took control of Kabul and Punjab) and they proved fickle allies, even plotting to overthrow him.

Externally, the two biggest threats came from Bahadur Shah in Gujarat in the west and the Afghan ruler Sher Shah in Bihar in eastern India. In 1535, Humayun defeated Bahadur Shah and established control as far as Cambay on the coast. However, when he marched east to confront Sher Shah, Bahadur Shah recovered his kingdom. Sher Shah inflicted two crushing defeats on Humayun at Chausa (1539) and Kanauj (1540), forcing him into exile. Eventually the Persian emperor Shah Tahmasp helped him recover Delhi and Agra in 1555. Humayun died soon after in January 1556 following a fall in his library in Delhi.

Chandrika Kaul

Further Reading

Lal, Muni. (c.1978) *Humayun*. New Delhi: Vikas.

Richards, John F. (1993) *The Mughal Empire*. Cambridge, U.K.: Cambridge University Press.

HUMOR IN CHINESE HISTORY Humor has a rich history in China. As in other cultures, comedy and humorous literature have often been criticized as immoral by somber ideologues. Nevertheless, playful writing and humorous anecdotes survive from China's earliest times and were produced throughout the imperial era (221 BCE–1912 CE). In Chinese history, humor has been used for a variety of purposes, including entertainment, cultural criticism, personal attacks, and bolstering group solidarity against outsiders. Humor is thus important to study for a full appreciation of the complexity, tensions, and joys of Chinese life over the ages.

Zhuangzi and Confucius

The most famous and influential humorist of ancient China was the philosopher Zhuangzi (Chuang Tzu, 369–286 BCE), whose writings make up one of the two primary texts of Taoism, the other being the mystical Daodejing. Zhuangzi used playful parables, parody, and clever wordplay to ridicule other

SITCOMS COME TO CHINA

Until the 1990s, the government of the People's Republic of China (PRC) exercised tight control over the content of the Chinese television, and TV was used more as a propaganda tool than an entertainment medium. However, in the early 1990s, government subsidies of television were reduced while the number of cable TV stations increased. The government began to allow paid advertising, and marketers saw an opportunity to gain revenues by bringing a different kind of programming to China's 1 billion television viewers. Filmmaker Ying Da thought the time was right to create China's own version of the American situation comedy.

Ying Da, son of the noted Chinese actor Ying Ruocheng, had studied in the United States and worked with U.S. theater and film companies. However, the inspiration for his television career came, appropriately enough, from watching episodes of "The Cosby Show" and "Cheers" during his time in the United States. In 1993, he struck a chord with the sitcom "I Love My Family," about a retired PRC official who has to adjust to the social changes in China. In the late 1990s, he had another hit in "Chinese Restaurant," about the misadventures of Chinese immigrants who make up the staff of a Chinese restaurant in Los Angeles.

Although Chinese television has come a long way, some things remain the same. The government still has ultimate control over the content of programs, so producers have to watch how certain topics are covered. For example, government overseers find it decidedly unfunny to make jokes about authority figures such as teachers or police officers. Even with some restrictions, though, sitcoms have found a happy home in China.

Marcy Ross

Source: Terry McCarthy and Jaime A. Florcruz. (1999) "Uncanned Laughter." *Time Asia* (15 November). Retrieved 14 April 2002, from: http://www.time.com/time/asia/magazine/99/1115/tv.china.html.

philosophers' belief in the power of human reason. According to Zhuangzi, people's understanding of the world is always limited by their limited perspective, just as a frog in a well cannot see more than a small patch of the sky or a sleeping man has no way of knowing that he is not the butterfly he dreams himself to be. Zhuangzi's stories have delighted generations of Chinese readers and served as models of humorous writing.

A chief target of Zhuangzi's joking was another prominent philosopher, Confucius (551–479 BCE). In contrast to Taoists like Zhuangzi, who believed in living in intuitive harmony with the natural order, Confucius promoted a strict ethical code and a hierarchical social order. Confucius is often depicted as a rather stern teacher, but there is some evidence in the conversations with his disciples recorded in the *Analects* that he too had a sense of humor. One of the most amusing images from ancient China was actually produced to illustrate the Confucian ethical principle that one should be filial to one's parents. A stone carving in the Wu Liang shrine, constructed during the second century CE, depicts the well-known story of a seventy-year-old filial son persuading his even more elderly parents that they are still young by acting like an infant.

Confucianism and Humor

Since the Han dynasty (206 BCE–220 CE), Confucianism has tended to reject humor, seeing it as incompatible with sincere devotion to ethical principles. The famous female writer Ban Zhao (c. 45–116 CE) stated that a good woman should shun jests and laughter and solemnly devote herself to serving her husband and his parents. Some Confucian scholars criticized as frivolous all humorous popular novels and plays, which were often banned by the government. Even poetry did not escape the attacks of sterner Confucian critics in the late imperial era (Ming and Qing dynasties, 1368–1912), who saw it as a waste of time that might have been better spent studying history and promoting morality.

The question of the value of humor was never definitively settled within the Confucian tradition, however, and Confucian thought continuously coexisted and interacted with other schools of thought, such as Taoism, that did encourage a humorous sensibility. Buddhism entered China during the Han dynasty, and the Chan school of Buddhism (Zen, in Japanese) made use of the "shock effect" of humorous and incongruous images to bring about enlightenment, much as Zhuangzi used humor to question rationality. The use of humorous and incongruous images for their shock value was borrowed by poets in the Song dynasty (960–1279) and later periods.

Humor in Periods of Unrest

Advances in printing and publishing contributed to the spread of humorous literature. Two periods of political unrest and technological change in later Chinese history produced a flood of humorous writing spanning the spectrum from escapist entertainment to harsh satire: the early seventeenth century, when the Ming dynasty was in decline, and the Republican period between the fall of the Qing dynasty (1912) and the founding of the People's Republic (1949). In the earlier period, humorous and erotic novels, such as *Jinpingmei* (Golden Lotus), and comic short stories, such as those collected by Feng Menglong (1574–1646), were immensely popular. During the 1920s and 1930s, China's greatest satirist, Lu Xun (1881–1936), criticized Chinese society and politics in essays and short stories published in some of the hundreds of newspapers and literary journals that appeared in those years. Lu Xun also promoted woodblock printing and satirical cartoons that the illiterate masses could understand. In this era, the writer Lin Yutang (1895–1976) introduced the English word "humor" into the Chinese language and argued that China needed more of it.

During the era of Mao Zedong (1949–1976), and particularly during the Cultural Revolution (1966–1976), sincere revolutionary fervor was held up by the Communist Party as the only proper attitude toward life. Humor did not entirely die out, but it was dangerous politically. In Taiwan, the Nationalist Party also clamped down on political expression, but apolitical humor was not discouraged.

Humor Themes

The themes of Chinese humor often resemble those in other parts of the world: stock characters such as the henpecked husband and the lusty widow abound in published joke books. Confucian and Buddhist institutions and thought are also popular objects of humor, especially in plays and opera plots from before the twentieth century. Residents of one part of China often make fun of those of another. However, this sort of regional humor and jokes about foreigners are not as prominent in China as humor involving ethnicity and nationality is in Europe and North America. The nature of the Chinese language, which has a relatively small number of different sounds, encourages puns and wordplay. These are particularly common in the performance humor called *xiangsheng*, which resembles vaudeville dialogue.

Humor Today

The decades of the 1980s and 1990s, during which ideological orthodoxy disintegrated in both the People's Republic of China and Taiwan and the use of the Internet mushroomed, may be the beginning of another great age of humor in Chinese history. A growing appetite for humor in the People's Republic of China (PRC) has led publishers to comb traditional literature and pull out the funny bits for hot-selling anthologies. Lin Yutang's writings from the 1920s and 1930s are enjoying new popularity, and, in both Taiwan and the PRC, the television sitcom has become a well-established form.

Kristin Stapleton

Further Reading

Ebrey, Patricia Buckley, ed. (1993) *Chinese Civilization: A Sourcebook.* 2d ed. New York: Free Press.

Harbsmeir, Christoph. (1989) "Humor in Ancient Chinese Philosophy." *Philosophy East and West* 39, 3: 289–310.

———. (1990). "*Confucius Ridens:* Humor in the *Analects.*" *Harvard Journal of Asiatic Studies* 50, 1: 131–161.

Hyers, Conrad. (1973) *Zen and the Comic Spirit.* Philadelphia: Westminster.

Kao, George, ed. (1974) *Chinese Wit and Humor.* New York: Sterling.

Kowallis, Jon. (1986) *Wit and Humor from Old Cathay.* Beijing: Panda.

Kupperman, Joel J. (1989) "Not in So Many Words: Chuang Tzu's Strategies of Communication." *Philosophy East and West* 39, 3: 311–317.

Lin Yutang. (1936) *The Little Critic.* Shanghai: Commercial Press.

Mair, Victor, trans. (1994) *Wandering on the Way: Early Taoist Tales and Parables of Chuang Tzu.* New York: Bantam.

Owen, Stephen, ed. and trans. (1996) *An Anthology of Chinese Literature: Beginnings to 1911.* New York: Norton.

Wells, Henry W. (1971) *Traditional Chinese Humor: A Study in Art and Literature.* Bloomington, IN: Indiana University Press.

HUN SEN (b. 1952), prime minister of Cambodia. Hun Sen is the prime minister of Cambodia and has been the dominant player on the Cambodian political stage for more than fifteen years. Born at Peam Koh Sna village in Kompong Cham Province on 4 April 1952, Hun Sen attended a local primary school before attending the Lycée Indra Devi in Phnom Penh (1965–1969). In 1970, he joined the Cambodian liberation forces under the leadership of the Communists and the patronage of deposed ruler Prince Norodom Sihanouk. In 1975, as Communists troops launched their final assault on Phnom Penh, Hun Sen was being treated in a field hospital and eventually lost his left eye. In the same year, he married Bun Rany, with whom he had three sons and three daughters (one of them adopted).

Hun Sen (L) meets General Secretary of the Communist Party of Vietnam Le Kha Phieu in Hanoi on 14 December 1998. (AFP/CORBIS)

Hun Sen rose through the ranks of the Khmer Rouge before eventually defecting to Vietnam. He was a leading figure in the Vietnamese-sponsored invasion that ousted the Khmer Rouge in 1979. At age twenty-seven he became the new regime's foreign minister and was appointed prime minister in 1985 at the age of thirty-three. Hun Sen was a leading figure in the negotiations that led to Cambodia's 1991 peace agreements and to the elections of 1993. After his party lost those elections, he refused to concede defeat and was appointed second prime minister. In July 1997, Hun Sen ousted First Prime Minister Ranariddh and eventually secured absolute power at the 1998 elections. A controversial figure, widely criticized for his record on human rights and his links with corrupt business persons, Hun Sen is often referred to as the "strongman" of Cambodian politics.

David M. Ayres

Further Reading

Brown, MacAlister, and Joseph Zasloff. (1998) *Cambodia Confounds the Peacemakers, 1979–1998.* Ithaca, NY: Cornell University Press.

Mehta, Harish, and Julie Mehta. (1999) *Hun Sen: Strongman of Cambodia.* Singapore: Graham Brash.

HUNAN (2001 pop. 63.1 million). Located in south central China, Hunan Province covers an area of 209,773 square kilometers and is bordered by Hubei Province to the north, Guangdong and Guanxi Provinces to the south, Kiangsi Province to the east, and Sichuan Province to the west. Hunan Province lies on the fertile Hunan plain, the richest agricultural land in China. The province's summers are hot and humid; the temperature there can reach close to 38°C. Heavy rains are also common during the summer months. Hunan's capital is Changsha, which has a population of 2 million. Other major cities in Hunan Province include Hengyang, Xiangtan, and Zhuzhou.

Hunan Province has a long history and can trace its origins to the Warring States period (475–221 BCE), when it was a part of the kingdom of Zhu. Later, the region around Changsha became the center of Zhu culture. Sometime between the seventh and tenth centuries, ethnic Han Chinese began migrating to Hunan, displacing the native Miao and Yao peoples. Successive invasions by the Mongols in the thirteenth century and the Manchus in the sixteenth century drove the Miao and Yao farther south and west as Han Chinese immigrated in large numbers.

Hunan Province has long been known for its agricultural and industrial output. It is a major rice-growing region, but it also produces large amounts of citrus fruit, shellfish, sugarcane, tobacco, and tung oil seed. Hunan Province also has large deposits of nonferrous metals, including lead, zinc, mercury, tungsten, and copper. Industrially, Hunan produces chemical fertilizers and locomotives as well as iron and steel.

Hunan has also influenced the course of modern Chinese politics. Zeng Guo-fen, who suppressed the Taiping Rebellion, was born in Hunan, as was Mao Zedong (1893–1976), chairman of the Chinese Communist Party and founder of the People's Republic of China.

Keith A. Leitich

Further Reading

Chen, Jerome. (1992) *The Highlander of Central China: A History, 1895–1937*. Armonk, NY: M. E. Sharpe.

Perdue, Peter C. (1987) *Exhausting the Earth: State and Peasant in Hunan, 1500–1850*. Cambridge, MA: Council on East Asia, Harvard University.

HUNDRED DAYS REFORM Defeat by Japan in the Sino-Japanese War (1894–1995) greatly affected the Qing dynasty (1644–1912) government of China and many young Chinese Confucian scholars. Some of these scholar-officials, particularly Kang Youwei (1858–1927) and Liang Qichao (1873–1929), called for dramatic changes in the structure of government, the examination system for entrance into government service, and the relationship of the government to the Chinese people, although they clothed these changes in traditional Confucian principles.

The young emperor, Guang Xu (1871–1908), was caught up in the fervor for reform and committed himself to carrying out a comprehensive reform program for approximately one hundred days, hence the phrase "Hundred Days Reform." From mid-June to mid-September 1898, the emperor issued some forty reform decrees.

The decrees called for education reform by replacing the centuries-old "eight-legged" essays with an exam more reflecting current affairs, establishing an Imperial University, and providing classes in foreign affairs and languages, economics, medicine, and the sciences. The decrees also sought changes in government, including eliminating the dual Manchu-Chinese system of control, eliminating some unneeded positions, and streamlining administration. Finally, the decrees called for government support for building railways, developing the economy, and improving the capital as well as for providing government protection of missionaries, simplifying legal codes, and preparing an annual budget. These measures were designed both to reform the government and to impress foreign powers in order to slow down the pace of foreign encroachments on Chinese sovereignty.

As one might expect, there was a backlash. The empress dowager, Cixi, allied with conservative elements in the Imperial City and across the nation and prepared a counterstroke. Rumors had floated around Beijing for days of a coup, and as the emperor slowly moved, the empress dowager and her allies moved faster. On 21 September 1898, she seized control of the emperor, announced that he was incapacitated, took over all reform documents, and seized control of the government. Many of the reformers were arrested and executed, but Kang and Liang managed to escape. The reforms were undone, and one outcome was the so-called Boxer Rebellion, which accelerated foreign encroachments on China.

Charles Dobbs

Further Reading

Cohen, Paul A., and John E. Schrecker, eds. (1976) *Reform in Nineteenth-Century China*. Cambridge, MA: Harvard University Press.

Kwong, Luke S. K. (1984) *A Mosaic of the Hundred Days.* Cambridge, MA: Harvard University Press.

HUNDRED FLOWERS CAMPAIGN In May 1956, Mao Zedong, the paramount leader of the People's Republic of China (PRC), announced that the Communist government would relax its strict control over freedom of thought and expression. Mao adopted the slogan of "Let a hundred flowers bloom together, let the hundred schools of thought contend" and invited intellectuals to voice criticism of party cadets and government policies. Mao intended to win over the alienated intellectuals by giving them a degree of intellectual freedom. More access to foreign publications, for example, was given to intellectuals who worked in schools, colleges, and universities, as these people were losing faith in the Chinese Communist Party (CCP) after the introduction of a Soviet-style education system to China starting from 1949, in which liberal arts education was discarded in favor of science and technology education.

The Hundred Flowers Campaign was not quick in taking off. On the one hand, there was resistance to criticism within the CCP. On the other hand, Chinese intellectuals were reluctant to criticize the government, fearing reprisal. It was only in the spring of 1957, after Mao's open reassurance, that members of democratic parties, writers, journalists, teachers, and professionals in China started to criticize communist rule, government policy, and party members openly. In extreme cases, wall posters appeared in public denouncing the whole communist system. Some even questioned the legitimacy of CCP rule over China. Mao and other leaders of the CCP were all shocked by the volume and intensity of the criticism.

By early July, just five weeks after the inauguration of the Hundred Flowers Campaign, a dramatic new campaign was launched by the CCP, shifting the target of criticism from the CCP to the intellectuals. Recent critics of the regime were severely criticized by party members, and about half to three-quarters of a million intellectuals were denounced or blacklisted. Some were arrested, and many were sent to the countryside to "rectify their thinking through labor." It was only in 1979, three years after the death of Mao, that Deng Xiaoping, the new leader of the CCP, restored a "decent name" to these denounced intellectuals.

Stephanie Chung

See also: **Chinese Communist Party; Deng Xiaoping; Mao Zedong**

Further Reading

Goldman, Merle. (1967) *Literary Dissent in Communist China.* Cambridge, MA: Harvard University Press.

MacFarquhar, Roderick. (1960) *The Hundred Flowers Campaign and the Chinese Intellectuals.* New York: Praeger.

HUNGRY GHOST FESTIVAL After Chinese New Year, the annual Hungry Ghost Festival *(Zhong Yuan)* is perhaps the next most popular celebration among the Chinese. Celebrated for thirty days beginning on the first day of the seventh moon of the Chinese lunar calendar (usually around August), the festival has roots in Chinese forms of social life, Taoist folk religion, and Buddhism. It is believed that during this period the gates of hell (purgatory or the underworld) are thrown wide open, and ghosts—euphemistically called "good brothers"—are free to roam the realm of the living once again.

The Feast of the Wandering Souls, more commonly known as the Hungry Ghost Festival, is an inauspicious time. Hungry ghosts may prey on the living out of anger and resentment. Weddings are not held in this month, and ghost stories of mishaps and ill fortune circulate to keep the living alert. Children are particularly vulnerable, and parents take care to prevent them from swimming in the open sea or camping in forests, for example.

To appease this legion of anonymous ghosts, offerings are made outside of Chinese homes at nearby road junctions, country lanes, and open spaces, but care is also taken not to invite them into the homes. Neighborhood groups and clan and trade associations have more elaborate celebrations lasting for a few days. Temporary sheds are built in open spaces to house a

A ritual specialist jumps over a fire at the Hungry Ghost Festival held by the Chinese community in Kuala Lumpur, Malaysia, in August 1999. (AFP/CORBIS)

number of deities. These deities are made of papier-mache and are burnt at the end of the festival. The chief of these deities—called Phor Tor Kong in Hokkien—is the keeper of purgatory, who keeps a watchful eye over the wandering ghosts. Sumptuous feasts are provided to fete both deities and ghosts. An assortment of meat dishes, rice, noodles, sweet cakes, fruits, wine, and other drinks, as well as joss sticks, paper money, and paper clothes, are laid out. Additionally, entertainment is provided in the form of traditional Chinese opera, live singing bands, and open-air film showings. Besides fulfilling ritual obligations, the Hungry Ghost Festival is occasionally used to raise funds and awareness to address concerns pertaining to the well-being of diaspora Chinese communities, particularly in areas like Chinese education, ethnicity, and culture.

Yeoh Seng-Guan

Further Reading

Debernadi, Jean. (1984) "The Hungry Ghost Festival: A Convergence of Religion and Politics in the Chinese Community of Penang, Malaysia." *Southeast Asia Journal of Social Science* 12, 1: 25–34.

Jordan, David K. (1972) *Gods, Ghosts, and Ancestors: The Folk Religion of a Taiwanese Village*. Berkeley and Los Angeles: University of California Press.

Tan, Sooi-Beng. (1988) *The Phor Tor Festival in Penang: Deities, Ghosts, and Chinese Ethnicity*. Clayton, Australia: Centre of Southeast Asian Studies, Monash University.

Teiser, Stephen. (1996) *The Ghost Festival in Medieval China*. Princeton, NJ: Princeton University Press.

Wong, C. S. (1967) *A Cycle of Chinese Festivals*. Singapore: Malaysia Publishing House.

HUNZA Deep in the mountains of the Hindu Kush in present-day northern Pakistan, high above sea level, lies a valley called Hunza. The Hunza valley is surrounded by the Karakoram Mountain Range, which extends from present-day India to Pakistan and into Jammu and Kashmir; its highest peak is K2 (8,611 meters), and sixty of its peaks in all tower around 6,700 meters. The Hunza River itself lies in Jammu and Kashmir, in the area controlled by Pakistan, and flows west and then south for 193 kilometers. Though most of the Hunza valley is located in Pakistan, it crosses the borders of today's Afghanistan and China. Karimabad, a grouping of six villages, is the principal populated area in this fertile valley.

The Hunza valley is dotted with glacial lakes and rivers that form in concurrence with glacial ice flows in the mountains. Due to these glacial flows, the Hunza valley is fertile and has sustained isolated populations of Hunza people, who speak a language unrelated to any other, throughout the centuries. As these glaciers melt, the glacial water (sometimes referred to as glacial milk due to its opaque white color from the minerals found in it) flows through the valley, and the people living in Hunza use it to irrigate their crops. The entire valley is well cultivated; every inch of arable land is put to use. Perhaps because of the mineral-rich water and fertile soil, the Hunza people are famous for their long lives, some living to be 120 years old.

Jennifer Nichols

Further Reading

Elphinstone, Mountstuart. ([1839] 1972) *An Account of the Kingdom of Caubul*. Reprint. Karachi, Pakistan, and New York: Oxford University Press.

HUSSEIN ONN (1922–1990), prime minister of Malaysia. Hussein Onn became the third prime minister of Malaysia (1976–1981) upon the sudden demise of Abdul Razak. His renowned strength of character and impeccable integrity saw him through various challenges. Son of Onn bin Ja'afar, founder of the United Malays National Organization (UMNO) party, Hussein spent his early years in the military and in World War II saw action in the Middle East. Following his discharge, he joined his father's struggle in UMNO; they both left UMNO in 1951. Hussein went to Britain to read law.

Urged by Abdul Razak, his brother-in-law, Hussein rejoined UMNO in 1968. He became minister of education (1971), deputy prime minister (1974), and prime minister. During his single-term premiership, Hussein faced severe political challenges, including pressure from right-wing elements within his own party (UMNO) over the "Harun case," divisions within the ruling coalition (which since 1971 was the Barisan Nasional [National Front], comprised of UMNO, two other major parties, and several minor parties), and a secessionist threat from the state of Sabah.

In the "Harun case," Harun bin Idris, a prominent and charismatic UMNO politician, was charged with corruption and criminal breach of trust and subsequently convicted in November 1977 to serve a two-year prison sentence. His appeal to the Privy Council was rejected; his appeal for pardon from the king of Malaysia was also turned down. The political repercussions were immense because Harun commanded mass Malay support not only from the youth but also from the "UMNO Old Guard." Hussein as president of UMNO and prime minister withstood the pressure from Harun's partisan supporters to at least arrange a pardon. Hussein stood his ground, and Harun served out his prison sentence.

In 1976, Hussein supported Berjaya (United People's Party of Sabah) in ousting Mustapha bin Datu Harun and his United Sabah National Organization (USNO), the ruling party in Sabah since 1967. Mustapha had been accused of having secessionist tendencies—namely, the separation of Sabah from Malaysia to join with three territories of the southern Philippines—Mindanao, Palawan, and Sulu—to form a new nation.

In December 1977, the Barisan Nasional expelled a component member, the Pan-Malayan Islamic Party (PAS), for its recalcitrant stand over the imposition of emergency rule in the state of Kelantan following the dismissal of PAS-appointed Mentri Besar.

Hussein hastened implementation of the New Economic Policy (NEP), emphasizing rural development to improve the economic situation of the Malays in relation to that of other ethnic groups. At the same time, more non-Malays benefited from civil service employment and land ownership. And more safeguards were afforded to foreign investments. Nonetheless, there were worrying signs of non-Malay dissatisfaction over the pro-Malay economic and education policies of the government.

Ooi Keat Gin

Further Reading

Means, Gordon P. (1991) *Malaysian Politics: The Second Generation.* Singapore: Oxford University Press.

Morais, J. Victor. (1981) *Hussein Onn: A Tryst with Destiny.* Singapore: Times Books International.

Snodgrass, Donald R. (1980) *Inequality and Economic Development in Malaysia.* Oxford: Oxford University Press.

HUSSEIN, SADDAM (b. 1937), president of Iraq since 1979. Saddam Hussein presides over one of the most repressive regimes in the Middle East. He was born near Takrit, a small town on the Tigris about one hundred miles from Baghdad. In 1955, attracted by Arab nationalism, he joined the fledgling Iraqi Ba'ath Party.

In July 1958, the Iraqi monarchy was overthrown and a republic installed. In October 1959, Saddam Hussein was involved in an unsuccessful attempt to assassinate the president, ʿAbd al-Karim Qasim. He fled to Egypt until Qasim's overthrow in February 1963.

Saddam Hussein at a ceremony honoring military officers in Baghdad on 4 January 2000. (AFP/CORBIS)

On his return, he headed the civilian wing of the Iraqi Baath and by 1969 had become Iraq's vice president. Through the 1970s he gradually consolidated his power.

The nationalization of the Iraqi Petroleum Company in 1972 gave the government—now equivalent to Saddam Hussein and his entourage—full control over the country's oil revenues. Saddam Hussein defeated the Kurdish opposition movement in 1975 and turned against the Communists. By the mid-1980s, most Iraqi intellectuals, and almost all Iraqi leftists, had been killed, imprisoned, or forced into exile.

In July 1979, Saddam Hussein took over the presidency and less than a year later he launched an invasion of the Islamic Republic of Iran. After initial successes, the Iraqis were driven back by Iran; the war continued for eight years, during which Iraq used chemical weapons against Iranian forces. In 1988, Saddam Hussein initiated a massive campaign against the Iraqi Kurds, known as *al-Anfal* (the spoils of war), during which at least 100,000 Kurds were captured and killed. During and after the Iran-Iraq War, a personality cult evolved around the "Great Leader."

In another bid for regional supremacy, Saddam Hussein invaded Kuwait in August 1990. By late February 1991, however, he had negotiated a cease-fire with the multinational forces under United Nations auspices and U.S. leadership, after weeks of aerial bombardment and five days of ground war, followed by rebellions in the Kurdish North and the Shiʿite

South. Iraqi troops retreated from Kuwait, but Hussein soon regained control in southern Iraq and Kurdistan.

U.N.-imposed sanctions after the Gulf War caused the people of Iraq great suffering but hardly affected its leaders. An oil-for-food agreement, which, if adopted earlier, might have alleviated much of the malnutrition and infant mortality the country experienced, was eventually accepted in 1996. Saddam Hussein's power base is fragile, but his monopoly of the means of coercion, the fragmentation of the opposition, the absence of serious rivals, and fear of the chaos that might follow his downfall have combined to keep him in supreme power for over two decades.

Peter Sluglett

Further Reading

Farouk-Sluglett, Marion, and Peter Sluglett. (2001) *Iraq since 1958: From Revolution to Dictatorship.* 3d ed. London: I. B. Tauris.

Makiya, Kanan (formerly Samir al-Khalil). (1998) *Republic of Fear: The Politics of Modern Iraq.* Rev. ed. Berkeley and Los Angeles: University of California Press.

Tripp, Charles. (2000) *A History of Iraq.* Cambridge, U.K.: Cambridge University Press.

HUYNH TAN PHAT (1913–1989), vice president of Vietnam. Huynh Tan Phat was born into a family of small landowners in 1913 in the province of Ben Tre, South Vietnam. After graduating from high school in My Tho, Phat attended the Superior School of Fine Arts in Hanoi, where he involved himself in anticolonial student organizations. Back in Saigon he opened his own architectural firm in 1940. Although a very successful architect, he devoted more of his time to political activities than to his profession. He played an important role in the August Revolution that brought independence to Vietnam in 1945. During the War with France (1946–1954) he was arrested many times by the French because he was responsible for the information and press services of the underground Vietnamese government. In 1962, he was elected to the position of vice chair of the National Liberation Front of South Vietnam, an organization that fought against the South Vietnam regime, assisted by the United States. In 1976, the National Assembly elected him vice president of the Socialist Republic of a reunited Vietnam. He died in 1989 at the age of seventy-six.

Truong Buu Lam

Further Reading

Huynh Van Tieng, et al. (1995) *Lam Dep Cuoc Doi. Huynh Tan Phat, con nguoi va su nghiep.* (To Make Life Beautiful: Huynh Tan Phat, the Man and His Achievements). Hanoi, Vietnam: Nha Xuat Ban Chinh tri Quoc Gia.

Pike, Douglas. (1966) *Viet Cong: The Organization and Technique of the National Liberation Front of South Vietnam.* Cambridge, MA: MIT Press.

HWANG SUN-WON (1915–2000), Korean fiction writer. Hwang was born near Pyongyang, Korea (now North Korea), and educated at Waseda University in Tokyo. He was barely in his twenties when he published two volumes of poetry. His first volume of stories appeared in 1940, and he subsequently concentrated on fiction, producing seven novels and more than a hundred stories.

In 1946 Hwang and his family moved from the Soviet-occupied northern sector of Korea to the American-occupied southern sector. He taught at Seoul High School in September of that year. Like millions of other Koreans, the Hwang family was displaced by the civil war of 1950–1953. From 1957 to 1993 Hwang taught at Kyung Hee University in Seoul.

Hwang is the author of some of the best-known stories of modern Korea, including "Pyol" (Stars, 1940), "Hak" (Cranes, 1953), and "Sonagi" (Shower, 1959), among others. He began publishing novels in the 1950s; his most important work in this genre includes *Namu tul pital e soda* (Trees on a Slope, 1960), about the effects of the civil war on three young soldiers; *Irwol* (The Sun and the Moon, 1962–1965), a portrait of an outcast man; and *Umjiginun song* (The Moving Fortress, 1968–1972), an ambitious effort to synthesize Western influence and native tradition in modern Korea.

The length of Hwang's literary career, spanning seven decades, is virtually unparalleled in Korean letters. But it is his craftsmanship that sets Hwang apart from his peers. His command of dialect, his facility with both rural and urban settings, his variety of narrative techniques, his vivid artistic imagination, his diverse constellation of characters, and his insights into human personality make Hwang at once a complete writer and one who is almost impossible to categorize.

Bruce Fulton

Further Reading

Holman, Martin, ed. (1989) *The Book Of Masks: Stories by Hwang Sun-won.* London: Readers International.

———. (1990) *Shadows of a Sound: Stories by Hwang Sun-won.* San Francisco: Mercury House.

Poitras, Edward W., trans. (1980) *The Stars and Other Korean Short Stories by Hwang Sun-won.* Hong Kong: Heinemann Educational Books.

HYDERABAD (2001 pop. 3.1 million). The capital of the Indian state of Andhra Pradesh, Hyderabad lies in the eastern part of the Deccan plateau in southern India on the banks of the Musi River. Established in 1591, the city served as the capital of the Qutb Shahi dynasty and of the independent state of Hyderabad. The Qutb Shahi ruler Mohammed Quli Qutb Shah (1580–1612) founded the city of Hyderabad, and under his patronage it became the leading center of Islamic art, literature, and scholarship in southern India. He constructed the royal and ceremonial structures, which became the focal point of the city. Notable among these is a large archway, the Charminar, which stands at the junction of the four major streets of the city. During the reign of his successor, Mohammed Qutb Shah (1612–1626), work was begun on the imposing Mecca Mosque, which could accommodate nearly ten thousand people.

Hyderabad lost its independence when the Mughal empire (1526–1857) extended its rule over the Deccan. Taking advantage of the political turmoil after the death of the Mughal emperor Aurangzeb in 1707, Asaf Jah, Nizam ul Mulk (1734–1748), the Mughal viceroy in the region, declared the independent state of Hyderabad. Toward the end of the eighteenth century, the state of Hyderabad became a protected ally of the British East India Company.

The Nizams of Hyderabad concentrated on developing the city as a center of Islamic learning. The Dairatul-Maarif-it Osmania was founded in 1888 to collect and translate into Urdu rare original Arabic manuscripts. Today the Salar Jung Museum houses a large collection of Persian, Arabic, and Urdu texts amassed by the Nizams. In 1918, the Osmania University was established by Nizam Mir Usman. It was the first Indian university to use an Indian language (Urdu) as the medium of instruction. A University College for women was founded in 1926.

After India gained independence in 1947, conferences were held with the rulers of the princely states to ensure their joining the Indian Union. In September 1948, the Nizam surrendered, and the state of Hyderabad became part of the Indian nation. In 1956, the states of the Indian Union were reorganized according to language groups, and the city of Hyderabad became the capital of the newly formed state of Andhra Pradesh. Today Hyderabad is a modern city boasting several industries. It is particularly famous for its film industry and as a center of computer science and information technology.

The Charminar, Hyderbad's best-known monument. It was built in 1591 to ward off an epidemic. (REUTERS NEWMEDIA INC./CORBIS)

Sanjukta Dasgupta

Further Reading

Luther, Narenda. (1995) *Hyderabad: Memoirs of a City.* Hyderabad, India: Orient Longman.

Naidu, Ratna. (1990) *Old Cities, New Predicaments: A Study of Hyderabad.* New Delhi: Sage.

HYOGO (2002 est. pop. 5.5 million). Hyogo Prefecture is situated in the western region of Japan's island of Honshu. Once mainly agricultural, it has been overtaken by industry in the south. It occupies an area of 8,382 square kilometers. Hyogo's main geographical features include a hilly north, central mountains and highlands, and coastal plains in the south. Awajishima, the largest island in the Inland Sea, forms a partial land bridge between Honshu and Shikoku. Hyogo is bordered by the Sea of Japan, Osaka Bay, and the Inland Sea and by Kyoto, Osaka, Okayama, and Tottori prefectures. The present prefecture was formed in 1876 from the old provinces of Harima, Tajima, and Awaji and incorporated parts of the former provinces of Settsu and Tamba as well.

The prefecture's capital is Kobe, situated on Osaka Bay. A cosmopolitan port of around two million residents, including seventy thousand foreigners, Kobe is second only to Yokohama in its volume of international shipping. Operating as a China trade port since the Nara period (710–794 CE), it was little more than a cluster of fishing villages until 1858, when the Tokugawa shogunate declared it an open port. Hyogo Prefecture is a modern industrial center, specializing in ships, railway cars, iron and steel, rubber, and textiles, as well as sake and the famous beer-fed Kobe beef. The city largely has recovered from the 1995 earthquake, which killed five thousand people and destroyed one hundred thousand structures. It is home to Kobe University, to museums displaying Chinese art and *namban* (western-style) works by Japanese artists, and to a unique inventory of nineteenth-century Japanese and Victorian architecture. Hyogo's other important cities are Nishinomiya, Amagasaki, and Himeji.

Archaeological remains near the city of Akashi indicate prehistoric habitation of Hyogo. The prefecture's strategic location made it a frequent battlefield during the twelfth-century war between the Taira and Minamoto warrior clans. In the Edo period (1600/03–1868) it was divided into small domains. Hyogo's rich cultural tradition includes Bunraku theater, which originated in the folk puppet theater of Awajishima, and the Himeji castle, the most spectacular of the nation's twelve remaining feudal fortresses. Scenic areas include the Inland Sea and the San'in Coast National Park.

E. L. S. Weber

Further Reading

"Hyogo Prefecture." (1993) In *Japan: An Illustrated Encyclopedia*. Tokyo: Kodansha.

Belarus
Ukraine
Moldova
Romania
Bulgaria
Greece
Black Sea
Istanbul
Ankara
Turkey
Georgia
Caucasus Mts.
T'bilisi
Armenia
Yerevan
Azerbaijan
Baku
Caspian Sea
Kazakhstan
Astana
Aral Sea
Syr Dar'ya
Amu Dar'ya
Kara-Kum
Lake Balkash
Almaty
Bishkek
Tian Sh
Kyrgyzstan
Tashkent
Fergana Valley
Uzbekistan
Turkmenistan
Ashgabat
Dushanbe
Tajikistan
Pamirs
Taklimakan Desert
Adana
Nicosia
Cyprus
Syria
Lebanon
Israel
Jordan
Tigris
Euphrates
Baghdad
Iraq
Zagros Mountains
Tehran
Iran
Kabul
Peshawar
Jammu and Kashmir
Islamabad
Afghanistan
Lahore
Himalaya
Indus River
Kuwait
Persian Gulf
Pakistan
New Delhi
Nepa
Kathma
Ganges River
Egypt
Saudi Arabia
Qatar
Karachi
Red Sea
United Arab Emirates
Oman
India
Arabian Sea
Mumbai
Eritrea
Yemen
Sudan
Djibouti
Somalia
Madras
Lakshadweep
Ethiopia
Sri Lanka
Colombo
Maldives
Male
N
Uganda
Kenya
Democratic Republic of the Congo
Rwanda
Burundi
0 500 1000 Miles
0 500 1000 Kilometers
Tanzania
Indian
Zambia
Mozambique
Madagascar
Zimbabwe
Mauritius
Port Louis
Réunion
60°E
R